Cassell's Chronology of
WORLD HISTORY

Cassell's Chronology of
WORLD HISTORY

Dates, Events and Ideas that Made History

HYWEL WILLIAMS

WEIDENFELD & NICOLSON

For Dewi Rhys Williams

First published in Great Britain in 2005
by Weidenfeld & Nicolson

10 9 8 7 6 5 4 3 2 1

A CIP catalogue record for this book is available from
the British Library.

ISBN 0-304-35730-8

Printed and bound in Finland by WS Bookwell

Weidenfeld & Nicolson
Wellington House
125 Strand
London WC2R 0BB

www.orionbooks.co.uk

Contents

Before his analytical work is completed, the historian, who began by noting movements in the landscape – commotions only on the surface of the countryside – may find that he is embarked on a geological examination of the scene. Where in the first place he had recorded only superficial motions taking place above ground, he may end by referring a great part of these to a subsidence occurring far below.

Sir Herbert Butterfield, *George III and the Historians* (1957)

Preface

The idea of a universal history that sets out to record and explain the most important features in the history of the world's civilizations – and so to link, compare and contrast those events and developments that occur at the same time in different places around the world – is an ancient as well as a modern one. It is a striking fact of world history itself that such works tend to be written at times of unusual dislocation, when the constellation of the world's great powers is changing and cultural forces are assuming a new and challenging form.

Those challenges are welcome to some world historians and unsettling to others, but they invariably supply the context to their work and help to explain their decisions about what does and does not matter in history. Herodotus (*c*.484–*c*.425 BC) conceived his history (450 BC) against the background of Athenian achievement and Persian threat – an early example of the clash of civilizations. His readiness to travel and to discover historical evidence drawn from beyond the confines of the Greek world shows his awareness of the need for a universal, rather than just a Greek, history. Polybius (*c*.200–*c*.118 BC) wrote his history, which covers the years 220 to 146 BC, because he was convinced that since the late 3rd century BC 'the affairs of Italy and Africa have been interlinked with those of Greece and Asia, all tending towards one end'. In the 1st century BC there was a crop of world histories, most notably that of the Greek author Strabo (*c*.64 BC–*c*.AD 23), which sought to take into account the new, world-transforming, Roman autocracy. The universal history written by the philosopher Ibn Khaldun (1332–1406) in Algeria between 1375 and 1379 – the *Muqaddimah* ('introduction') – is, on the other hand, deeply marked by the author's awareness of Islam's decline and its loss of social cohesion.

In the 17th century French classicism, with its conviction of cultural supremacy, gave a new impetus to the writing of universal history. The majestic *Discours sur l'histoire universelle* (1681) by the prelate Jacques-Bénigne Bossuet (1627–1704) has a fugue-like glory as it relates the varieties of historical experience to the dominion of a Christian providence that shapes the world. A more secular but equally confident synthesis, the *Essai sur les moeurs et l'esprit des nations* (1756) by Voltaire (1694–1778), gives a total explanation of history from the 9th to the 17th century from the point of view of a universal reason emerging in the world and purging it of superstition. These statements of world history were the fruits of self-confidence. But the English-speaking world's most ambitious universal history was the result of a deep pessimism. The vast learning and comparativist zeal dis-

played by Arnold Toynbee (1889–1975) in *A Study of History* (1934–61) was inspired by his conviction that the West was in decline, that its liberal elites were no longer regenerating themselves and that nemesis was lying in wait.

No world historian, therefore, can pretend to stand outside of the stream of time and be the uniquely authoritative observer and judge of history. A world history may be an exalted subject, but there is no one key that explains the whole of the past, and the present book inevitably has its own particular context. It is an early-21st-century work written by a European Welshman who regards all nations as regions. The immediate background to the writing of this book is the present world crisis in relations between the Middle East and the West. That particular episode is only the latest stage in what has been a dominant story of the 20th century – the revolt of the colonized against former imperial powers, the subsequent cultural rejection of the colonial legacy and the confusions, cruelties and asserted self-respect that follow in the wake of that rejection. These themes are evident in this book, but in doing them justice I have also tried to place these colonial collisions of modern history in the light of a much older story: the clash of cultures, a theme that is as ancient as humanity itself.

All historical writing is précis informed by personality. I have selected events, developments and ideas in the light of my own reading, research, thinking and experience. The 100 key thinkers in world history, whose core doctrines are summarized in the book, have been chosen because of their influence on contemporaries and on posterity. The definition of a 'thinker' has been correspondingly broad and includes soldiers, scientists, theologians, artists, historians, economists, poets and novelists as well as philosophers and politicians. They are not necessarily the profoundest of their kind, but they are, I believe, the ones who have been most important historically and whose ideas have survived their death.

What follows, therefore, is a chronology that is also a series of interpretations of the history of humanity in its civilized condition. The structure of the book illustrates the truth set out by Marc Bloch in *The Historian's Craft* (1949):

> Life is too short, and science too vast, to permit even the greatest genius a total experience of humanity. Some men will always specialize in the present, as others do in the Stone Age or in Egyptology. We simply ask both to bear in mind that historical research will tolerate no autarchy. Isolated, each will understand only by halves, even within his own field of study; for the only true history, which can advance only through mutual aid, is universal history.

Context, therefore, is everything. In order to understand the particular event we have to move beyond it and relate it to other events.

The dateable event is the basic unit of the study of history, and therefore dateable events are at the core of this book. But the event itself is composed of many different elements since it consists not just of what happened but also of what people imagined had happened or what they wanted to happen, their hopes and fears, evasions and dreams. History, consequently, is not just a selection of the available and surviving evidence. It is also an interpretation of how people in the past themselves interpreted and understood what happened to them as they lived out their lives in the world. This means that the event that the historian has to explain is a social fact and not an individual one: it is itself the sum total of many individuals interacting with, and reacting to, each other. Which is why history is related to, but different from, biography, whose narrative reflects the perspective of its subject.

What makes an event into a reliable 'fact' is, naturally enough, contestable. Writing this book has been for me an education in history's own version of the winnowing process, which discards – through chance and neglect – both the valuable evidence as well as the trivial record. There is also, of course, the sheer difficulty of establishing what actually happened in the light of conflicting testimonies offered by participants and observers who may be selfish, vicious, romantic, confused or just plain forgetful when it comes to truth. This is why history as a subject is perhaps the most demanding of all the human sciences. But there are at least two 'lessons' of history, and of historical writing, that seem pretty incontestable. First, there is the need to be humble about one's own judgements; second, there is the duty to be sceptical about the dogmatism of others. Views, beliefs and conclusions frequently change simply because the writing of history, rather like a human life itself, is a process of continuous revision. So far as my judgements in this book are concerned I have tried to achieve the utmost accuracy. The responsibility for any faults of expression, errors of fact and dubious interpretations rests on my shoulders alone.

I owe a great debt to my family and especially to my parents, Raymond and Granwen Williams, for their unstinting support in the course of writing this book. For both its conception and its completion I am grateful in particular to Rosie Anderson, Chris Bell, Georgina Capel, Anthony Cheetham and Richard Milbank, whose editorial vigilance and flair steered this work to its publication. In a longer perspective it is a pleasure to recall how the Master and Fellows of St John's College, Cambridge, encouraged my first steps in historical study. Other influences on this book, which I record with pleasure, include my past pupils at the University of Cambridge and at Rugby School who taught me to question my own assumptions; civil service colleagues from my time in Whitehall showed how it is harder to implement a policy than it is to formulate it, a truth sometimes ignored by the historian isolated in the study; Sir Peregrine Worsthorne, as editor of the *Sunday Telegraph*, first helped me to reach for a wider readership as a journalist; Alan Rusbridger, editor of the *Guardian*, and Seumas Milne, editor of that paper's comment and analysis pages, continue to be encouraging patrons of that ambition. At their best, both journalism and history are naturally subversive of any kind of orthodoxy. It is a privilege to be given the opportunity to attempt both.

I also wish to record a particular indebtedness to 11 books and their authors for a quality of writing that has inspired me. All share that combination of talents that is the mark of a classic historical work: a lucid analysis of the sources along with a compellingly artistic shaping of the material. Historical facts are modified and corrected, interpretations change and develop, but the following books are touched by a quality of greatness that sets them apart from the usual run of historical work, which is fated to be superseded by the latest research. All have, in their different ways, contributed to the thinking that lies behind my own book.

The *Annales* (115) of Tacitus (56–*c.*120) remains one of the best of all books about politics because it is so implacably sceptical about motives and so dispassionate in its irony about politicians. *The Roman Revolution* (1939) by Sir Ronald Syme (1903–89) also analysed the republic's fall and did so in a consciously Tacitean style. But, written with edge in the age of Mussolini and Hitler, Syme's work also shows how the present can help to illuminate the past and that the passing of some 1900 years had not altered the characteristic mentality of thuggery. Marc Bloch (1886–1944), killed as a member of the Resistance in occupied France, was a personally brave figure in a profession that is rarely called upon to suffer. His *Feudal Society* (Vol.1 1939, Vol.2 1940) is a continuing revelation in its picture of the network of social customs and beliefs that animated and gave coherence to an entire culture.

The Making of English Law: King Alfred to the Twelfth Century, Vol.1 *Legislation and its Limits* (1999) by Patrick Wormald (1947–2004) is a forensic masterpiece that explores the startling precocity of Anglo-Saxon civilization. Carolingian kinship supplies the European and continental milieu of 9th-century England, but Wormald proved that his country was, in another respect, unique. His book shows how the common law of England, far from being the sudden invention of Henry II's reign in the 12th century, developed during that of Alfred the Great three centuries earlier and was itself built on Bede's claim, in his early 8th-century history, that the English were a chosen people. In demonstrating the longevity and the depth of English institutional life and identity Wormald also helped to explain why his countrymen, 1100 years after Alfred, found it so difficult to adjust to any political authority located beyond England's borders. *A History of the Crusades* (1951–4) by Sir Steven Runciman (1903–2000) shows how analysis is not the enemy of narrative history but its complement. His graceful prose brings to life that first, lethal clash between East and West as well as communicating an elegiac understanding of the sorrows of the Hellenic world caught between.

The Civilization of the Renaissance in Italy (1860) by Jacob Burckhardt (1818–97) remains the best single work of cultural history ever written, as the author brings his cultivated, pessimistic and rather anti-democratic eye to bear on the movement that created our modern picture of humankind. *History of the Latin and Teutonic Nations from 1494 to 1514* (1824) by Leopold von Ranke (1795–1886) is an exhilarating early work by the man who went on to be the founding father of modern historical scholarship. It illustrates why and how the 'national principle', which explains the vitality of a nation, also invigorated the whole 19th-century approach to historical development. Almost a century on and the world is still living through the consequences of the international breakdown that occurred in the early 20th century. *The Eastern Front 1914–17* (1975) by Norman Stone (b.1941) disinters the sorrowful terrain of Armageddon in a compelling combination of political history and military strategy.

I first read *A History of Wales: From the Earliest Times to the Edwardian Conquest* (1911) by Sir J.E. Lloyd (1861–1947) during a west Wales childhood spent within sight of the medieval castle of Dinefwr, which is perched high above the winding majesty of the River Tywi and whose ruins were a mute yet eloquent witness to the fact of conquest. The continuities and hierarchies of a country town where the past shadowed the present so magnificently were in themselves a good historical education, for the surrounding scene was a daily illustration of the truth that all history is, initially, local and geographical. It is an affair of the square mile with its gossip and rumour, its solidarities and ancestors, its roots and confines. World history is but the accumulation of many such local histories.

Richard Cobb (1917–96) had a profound historical appreciation of this sense of place, of the locality that shapes individuals and events. He also brought a novelist's eye for the human to his study of French revolutionary history. All his works – but especially perhaps *The Police and the People: French Popular Protest 1789–1820* (1970) – are history as poetry, showing a rare compassion in their portrayal of lives lived on the margins of society. Cobb's crooks, thieves and vagrants, his poor and dispossessed, as well as his quietly struggling petit bourgeois just about hanging on to respectability, are all non-ideological beings condemned to live in the eye of an ideological storm. They are a reminder that history is impoverished when it concentrates on those psychotic types who are attracted to the exercise of power.

History is the study of humanity, and its finest practitioners have understood both the tragic and the heroic dimensions of life. Sometimes their work has been deepened as a result of encountering both of those qualities in their own lives and times. Henri Pirenne (1862–1935) started writing his unfinished *History of Europe* (1936) in February 1917 while he was detained by the German military authorities in Creuzburg, Thuringia. But the book's origins, and the reason for its urgent pace, lie in the course of lectures Pirenne had given in the summer of 1916 on the history of his own country to his fellow detainees at Holzminden, a camp for civilian prisoners of war. As he later recalled:

> The listeners were jammed together. Inside a suffocating heat was radiated from the tarred paper roof. Thousands of fleas were jumping all over the place, leaping in the sunlight like the drops of a very fine spray. Sometimes I fancied I could hear them, so profound was the silence of all these men, who listened while a fellow Belgian spoke to them of their native country, recalling all the catastrophes which it had suffered and overcome.

Pirenne shows how the critical mind can work its way through personal anguish and still make sense of history.

To all these authors, both living and dead, I am grateful for showing me the range, depth and possibilities of history and for helping me thereby in the writing of this book.

HYWEL WILLIAMS
Tangier–Paris–Abertawe–London, 2000–2005

NOTES FOR THE READER

Cassell's Chronology of World History consists of a sequence of 'year entries' starting in 135,000 BP and following the course of world history up to the end of 2004. Within each year entry historical events are listed under a sequence of regional and thematic sub-headings, these being:

Europe
Middle East and North Africa
Asia
The Americas
Sub-Saharan Africa
Australasia and Oceania
Economy and Society
Science and Technology
Arts and Humanities

These are largely self-explanatory, although there are, inevitably, some grey areas. Most of the events of Russian history, including Russia's imperial conquests in the Caucasus, will be found under the heading **Europe**. Russia's 19th-century territorial gains in Central and East Asia, however, will be found under **Asia**, as will events in the former Central Asian republics of the USSR following the latter's breakup in 1991. The heading **Middle East and North Africa** covers an area stretching from Morocco in the west to Iran's borders with Afghanistan in the east, and from Egypt's border with Sudan in the south to Turkey in the north.

The entries included under the headings **Economy and Society**, **Science and Technology**, and **Arts and Humanities** can, for reasons of space, be only representative of humanity's achievements in science, literature and the arts.

Under each regional or thematic sub-heading, events are listed in simple chronological order. Specific dates always precede less precise ones: thus **23 May** comes before **May**, and both of the latter precede those events that are simply assigned to the year in question rather than to a specific day or month within it, and which are introduced by a dash, thus:

21 Aug. In Bosnia-Herzegovina the Muslim-dominated city of Bihac falls to the Serbs.
Aug. Civil war breaks out in Chechnya between separatist and pro-Russian forces.
31 Dec. In Bosnia-Herzegovina the warring factions sign a four-month ceasefire agreement.
– In Britain the Trident nuclear weapon system comes into use with the Royal Navy.

Abbreviations

AD	Anno Domini (after Christ)
b.	born
BC	Before Christ
BP	Before Present (that is, a date representing the radiocarbon date rather than calendar years, when AD1950 is used as an anchor point for the 'present' date)
C	central
c.	*circa* (about)
d.	died
E	east/eastern
fl.	*floruit* (flourished)
Mt/Mts	Mount/Mountains
N	north/northern
r.	reigned
S	south/southern
W	west/western

Introduction: The Idea of Progress

Can history be turned into the story of progress? At a material, scientific and technological level the answer is obviously that it can. In the early 21st century millions of individuals can exercise choices that were once considered the prerogatives of gods. They can travel by air and even be taken into space. They influence governments and on a regular basis may also dispose of them if they so wish. Their daily diet may consist of rare delicacies gathered from all over the globe. And some of their diseases can be made to disappear with the easy digestion of a tablet.

But it was a different idea of progress that first became popular in the mid-19th century, and that now appears both brash in its confidence and naïve in its expectations. It was, certainly, founded on the fact of material advance: the sudden and greater ease of movement by railway and steamship, the beginnings of effective public sanitation and signs of a reduction in the incidence of disease. In the advanced and developed world of the West these victories seemed to signify and to secure a real moral progress. Nobody supposed that humanity was suddenly getting better at producing saints and geniuses, but there was a new confidence in the possibility of a well-ordered society whose populations would be increasingly literate and numerate – who could think rationally as well as have money in their pockets when they went to shop. The intellectual advances and interests that were once the sole preserve of a small educated or leisured elite had appeared to spread further and to be founded on deeper roots. Once the sceptical courtiers of the 18th century had sneered at superstition when they gathered in gossipy little groups. A century later the educated and concerned met in large public meetings where they debated the great issues of religion and science, franchise reform and freedom of trade. They bought books and read newspapers, they joined ethical societies and agitated within political parties.

The sensitivities of a post-colonial age, helped by the sociological awareness of class and culture, have eroded such confidence. It was once conventional to suppose that this 19th-century advance represented a culture in every way superior to that of the non-European, be it Bantu or Algonquin, Pitjantjara or Hindu. Ethically minded secularists and Christian missionaries shared a common belief in progress, at least in the European sense of that term. Such certainty has long since vanished.

There is, moreover, a further reason for scepticism. The history of the first half of the 20th century dissolved the connection between material or scientific progress and a better moral order. Technological advance was twice turned to the business of mass slaughter on the battlefield, and then to the genocide and ethnic cleansing that afflicted Europe during this period. Material progress was seen to mingle with moral regress.

Professional historiography has come up with two other difficulties in considering progress and finding it wanting. Historical knowledge has grown vastly in recent years, and this has deepened our understanding of the past. The idea of a grand narrative in any of the human sciences has fallen out of fashion. Christian providence, Freudian psychology, positivist science, Marxist class-consciousness, national autonomy, fascist will: these have all attempted to portray the big picture and sought to supply a narrative that gives shape and meaning to the human past. When it came to practical political implementation, some universal explanatory systems proved to be achievable only by repression and widespread death – and this was one reason for the general suspicion that a single unifying theory was impossible. The liberal idea of progress might not be a bloodthirsty creed, but as a plausible unifying explanation it was seen to share in the defects endemic to all such general theories. It was self-satisfied, and adopted a selective approach to the available evidence.

It now suits us to reject the quest for progress as a kind of intellectual unity. The belief in progress can seem a specious exercise in special pleading from those who are the historical winners as they shunt the historical losers aside. Being perhaps more sensitive than any previous generation to the rights of the defeated, we wish to protect them from so arrogant a treatment.

The second reason for the death of progress as an idea is internal to historical writing as a professional activity. At 19th-century universities, especially at Berlin and Göttingen, the idea of 'historicism' emerged. This meant that the historian, on disappearing into the archive, had to discard the prejudices of the present in order to understand the thought-patterns of people of the past. Anybody who really wants to understand how the world of the American South operated before the Civil War should be prepared to understand how slavery, even among intelligent and compassionate human beings, could still be seen as a natural fact of life. Only when this ability to think oneself into the mental assumptions of a bygone era had been achieved would it be possible to answer questions such as: Was there a necessary connection between the creative energies of Italian Renaissance artists and the murderous energies of the princes who were the patrons of such artists?

And yet the idea of progress has a long history itself. It had a sudden birth in Greece in the early 5th century BC and was a genuinely new historical departure. No idea of history as purposive disturbs the lists of Babylonian kings and their laws. Babylonian astrology, the core discipline of science in the ancient Near East, was designed to prove the repetition of world periods, a belief that precludes even the possibility of progress. Hinduism, a religion of repetitous ritual, ensured that the Indian mind would be stubbornly uninterested in history and in official record-keeping, let alone in any idea of progress.

The optimism of classical Greece was a sudden and unheralded miracle. It resulted from the defeats inflicted on the Persian empire in 490 BC and 480 BC – events that instilled intellectual self-confidence and democratic experimentation. But it was balanced by caution regarding the jealous gods, with their unpredictable capacity to wreck human prosperity. That caution is reflected in Thucydides' *History of the Peloponnesian War* – which is in part an illustration of the role played by freakish chance in human affairs. Progress here was a real advance, but it was impossible to rely on its continuance. The new idea took a knock – but not a fatal one – when the philosopher Plato began to describe human history as a series of human cycles.

The 18th-century *philosophes* also recognized the precarious nature of progress. This was why they spent so much time excoriating fanaticism and superstition. In *Candide* Voltaire satirized all those who think that present suffering can be assuaged by faith in the idea of an ultimate purpose. Historical progress did exactly the job required of it by the Enlightenment thinkers: it showed history as a series of episodic fits and starts. Their pages show that it is perfectly possible to believe in the reality of progress without also believing in its inevitability – and it is the inevitability of progress that has been the main object of attack by the historically minded critics. The *philosophes* also observed the obvious truth that customs vary around the world and through history. Voltaire, so often thought to be the apostle of an unchanging reason, thought that Islamic societies were 'so different from everything we are used to that they should show us how varied is the picture of the world'.

These philosophic historians measured human variety against the standard of fundamental human nature – those passions and affections that are a constant feature of the human condition. Their historical conclusions issued from a judgement shared by reader and author about what constituted luck, cruelty, treachery and loyalty. Without some kind of common understanding of what these terms mean it is difficult to see how history of any kind can be written.

It is in this restricted sense that progress is both a real, if episodic, feature of history as well as being something that is knowable to posterity. René Descartes once sneered that 'Historians of Rome know no more than Cicero's servant girl.' She, at least, had lived there and knew the smell and feel of it all. The historicist assertion of the great strangeness of the past is a necessary reminder that we tend to assume that present assumptions can be applied to it. But the same insistence on its strangeness can lead to the idea that the past is dead and so cannot be understood.

In fact, the existence of a common humanity gives us the possibility – in principle, at least – of understanding how past peoples lived, thought and acted. And the observation of progress that emerges in that picture is something a little more certain than a common illusion and a little less certain than a genetically programmed necessity. For both the writers of history and its readers it seems a necessary idea, if not an inevitable one.

1

The Ancient and Medieval Worlds

135,000 – 1449 BP

1. The Ancient and Medieval Worlds

If you were to take three apparently very different people – a Babylonian of the 2nd millennium BC, a French person in the 12th century AD and a Chinese subject of the Han dynasty in the 1st century BC – they would have found each other's languages incomprehensible. But any one of them would have recognized some of the features of the societies lived in by the other two.

All were societies in which ownership of land was the most important form of wealth, as well as the means by which prestige could be gained and aristocratic status maintained. All were hierarchical societies in which some were born to rule, some to fight, some to serve as priests or scholars, and yet others to work the land. Not one of these societies would have acknowledged notions of human rights or of equality. Most people died young – to live over the age of 40 was to be old. Although some people moved surprisingly long distances – wandering as nomads across the Asian steppes, for example, or, in medieval Europe, embarking on crusades or pilgrimages – life for most was narrow and circumscribed, and travel was laborious and dangerous. Literacy was for a very small elite. All of these similarities make any differences between these geographically and chronologically separated societies relatively trivial – certainly when one compares the lives of the members of these societies with those of a 21st-century office worker in Manhattan, London, Hong Kong or Mexico City.

The world's first cities were governed by rulers who claimed divine status. The idea of a sacred kingship is one of the great connecting themes of the period. Ideas of democracy, important to a limited extent in Greek cities and in Rome, were entirely atypical. The city-states of Mesopotamia were the first to move beyond the lineage- and kinship-based systems of tribes. Because loyalties could no longer be based solely on blood relations, there was a need to develop ideologies of power – structures of religion and politics that could bind people together in shared beliefs. And once that had begun, city-states became dynamic entities with a capacity to expand when the politics of the times and where the geographical context allowed them to do so.

The original city-states of Mesopotamia became absorbed into larger empires – first the Akkadian, followed, by the start of the 2nd millennium BC, by the Babylonian and the Assyrian. Monumental public art announced the beginning of a new phase in world history. Egypt was different. Here there was a unitary kingdom from around 3000 BC. From those origins Egypt expanded in the south to Nubia and then north into the Levant, thereby uniting the Mediterranean civilization with the African.

But in about 1200 BC this whole world collapsed before a wave of shattering invasions from the north. The Mycenean civilization that had emerged on the Greek mainland by 1600 BC was overthrown. Thracians and Phrygians destroyed the Hittite kingdom established on the Anatolian plain. Egypt kept the invaders out but was so devastated by their raids and the demands of war that its civilization was impoverished and its centralized state collapsed. It took hundreds of years for the region to adapt. Assyria and Babylon eventually recovered. The Greeks relearned the habit of living in cities. But Egyptian power never got over the crisis, one that proved to be far greater than the more familiar disaster that befell the early medieval period – the so-called Dark Ages – in Europe.

The fall of the original Indus valley civilization in India came somewhat earlier – by about 1800 BC – but had similar causes. Waves of invading Aryans swept down from the north in around 1500 BC to complete an economic decline. The arrival of this pastoral Indo-European people was just one part of a population movement that would affect much of Eurasia. The Aryans spoke a language that came from the same linguistic stock as nearly all modern European languages. Further east, China was now an evolved society, and by 1760 BC the Shang state had concentrated power around an urban centre.

The story of civilization in the Middle East, the Mediterranean world and India during the 1st millennium BC is one of the evolution of ever more organized governments. The Assyrian and Babylonian empires continued to dominate the Middle East, but the most significant newcomer was Persia. Its story began with the westward push of the Medes, an Iranian people from Central Asia who established the kingdom of Media southwest of the Caspian Sea. The Persians, another Iranian people, made the same move from the steppes. They established the initially minor kingdom of Persia to the west of Media, but then, under their king Cyrus, took over the Median empire. In 539 BC Persia conquered Babylon, creating an empire that merged cultures and civilizations in a potent mix. The city-states of Greece formed Persia's most significant opponent, halting its westward expansion in the 5th century BC and also establishing the Western view of Persia as a land of tyranny. But although the Greek cities shared a culture, they were proverbially quarrelsome and locked in more or less constant warfare. Very different was Carthage, the North African city that started as a Phoenician colony, but which by the 4th century BC had established its own independent and powerful trading empire in the western Mediterranean. Around the same time a strong centralized state was emerging in India. In China, however, the Zhou (Chou) kingdom was breaking up in anarchy.

Accounts of the emergence of civilized societies often concentrate on state formation, but the view from the Eurasian steppes provides a different perspective. Between 1000 BC and 500 BC the pastoralist tribes of the western steppes adopted a nomadic existence. That nomadic lifestyle would later be adopted by the peoples of the eastern steppes – the Turko-Mongolians. The roaming dynamism of these peoples on horseback would periodically break into the civilized world of settled farming communities with terrifying suddenness and appalling violence. Yet their influence was not wholly destructive. Their control over the steppes and the adjacent areas led to the establishment of transnational and intercontinental trade routes.

By 400 BC Central America was witnessing a transition from tribal societies, in which chieftains commanded loyalty, to sophisticated and organized states, as attested by the impressive remains of the Olmec, Maya and Zapotec civilizations. The world's most significant exception to the trend was the African continent south of Egypt, which at this time had only one state, the kingdom of Cush, centred on the city of Meroe. Bordering Egypt itself, Meroe was strongly influenced by that cultural dynamo. Elsewhere in Africa Bantu farmers were expanding from their base in the east and moving into the continent's central area. But this was simply a process of settlement and not one of state formation.

By 1 BC the Roman empire had grown from its republican city-state base to dominate the Mediterranean world and rule all the urban civilizations of Europe and North Africa. In the east the Han empire of the Chinese offered a similar structure in an Asiatic setting. These developments gave Eurasian civilization at its western and eastern limits a common quality.

From the 3rd century AD onwards Rome suffered incursions as Germanic tribes shifted westwards under pressure from the peoples of the steppes. The break-up of the Chinese empire of the Han into three states also occurred in the 3rd century, and for similar reasons, as the Huns pressed in from the north. The Gupta empire in the north of India proved to be the last large-scale political order to be sustained by forces native to the sub-continent and was crumbling by the late 5th century.

Europe lived through the collapse of Roman authority until Charlemagne revived the idea of empire in the 9th century. This, though, was a Europe divided between the Roman Church of the Latin West and the Orthodox Church of the Greek East. In the West there was a notable recovery of the economy and society from the 11th century onwards. In the East, where the old Roman empire had not collapsed but transformed itself into the Byzantine, there was a slow process of decline.

The new dominant empire of Eurasia was that of the Muslims. The expansion of the Arabs from their peninsula in the 7th and 8th centuries led to the end of the ancient Persian empire, and also to the dissolution of much of the Greek Christian world. In its place, Islam created a cultural and, at times, political unity that spread from Spain right across North Africa, through the eastern Mediterranean, into the Middle East and across the Indian Ocean. In China in the 1st millennium AD a great empire reasserted itself, under the successive dynasties of the Sui, Tang and Song (Sung), and, thanks to new irrigation schemes, China's vast land resources were now intensively cultivated. But in the 13th century China was again divided into different states, exposing it to attack

Some were born to rule, some to fight … yet others to work the land.

by the nomadic Mongols from the steppes. Under their leader, Genghis Khan, the Mongols were a far greater threat than any previous barbarian invader. Not just in China but also in Russia and in eastern Europe the Mongols destroyed patterns of settled life, forms of government and economic capacity. Further west, the Mamluk dynastic rulers of Egypt – a military caste of mostly Turkic origin – inflicted a first defeat on the Mongols in 1260. In the east, however, the Mongols had fundamentally weakened the social structures and their capacity to respond to new challenges. The resurgent Europe of the 15th century was able therefore not just to 'discover' a new world but also to start dominating the old one.

135,000 BP

SUB-SAHARAN AFRICA
- Date of the earliest fossils of anatomically modern humans, discovered at Omo in Ethiopia.

115,000 BP
- Beginning of the last glacial period of the Pleistocene Ice Age.

100,000 BP

SUB-SAHARAN AFRICA
- Anatomically modern humans begin to migrate out of Africa. Their migrations are made easier by low sea levels, the result of much of the world's water being locked in vast continental ice sheets.

90,000 BP

MIDDLE EAST AND NORTH AFRICA
- By now modern humans have reached the Middle East.

75,000 BP

ASIA
- Modern humans are living in China and SE Asia.

50,000 BP

ASIA
- Humans colonize Japan, which is connected to Korea by a 'land bridge'.

45,000 BP

MIDDLE EAST AND NORTH AFRICA
- Date of the earliest known musical instrument, a bone flute from N Africa.

40,000 BP

EUROPE
- Modern humans begin to colonize Europe where they gradually begin to displace the indigenous Neanderthals, a subspecies of modern humans.

AUSTRALASIA AND OCEANIA
- Around this time humans undertake the first maritime migrations, making the crossing from SE Asia to Australia and New Guinea (then a single island).

32,000–14,000 BP

EUROPE
- Period of cave art traditions in Europe.

31,000 BP

AUSTRALASIA AND OCEANIA
- Humans colonize Tasmania.

28,000 BP

EUROPE
- The Neanderthals become extinct in Spain, their last European stronghold.

18,000 BP
- The last glaciation reaches its height, then begins to recede. Sea levels are 130m (425 feet) below today's.

17,000 BP

EUROPE
- Cave paintings executed at Lascaux, France.

15,000 BP

THE AMERICAS
- About this time, or possibly earlier, humans begin to colonize N America after crossing the Bering Straits, a 'land bridge' between Siberia and Alaska.

14,000 BP

ASIA
- The Jomon hunter-gatherers of Japan make the earliest known pottery.

12,000 BP

MIDDLE EAST AND NORTH AFRICA
- Natufian hunter-gatherers in the Levant and Syria begin to harvest wild cereals.

11,000 BP

MIDDLE EAST AND NORTH AFRICA
- Hunter-gatherers in Syria begin to cultivate wild cereals. At around the same time, hunter-gatherers in the Zagros Mts (Iraq–Iran border) begin the intensive management of flocks of wild sheep and goats.

THE AMERICAS
- Humans have colonized Tierra del Fuego at the southern tip of S America.

10,000 BP (8000 BC)
- The end of the last glaciation is accompanied by a rapid rise in global sea levels.

8000 BC

MIDDLE EAST AND NORTH AFRICA
- Barley, einkorn and emmer wheat are cultivated from wild cereals in the Fertile Crescent, an area of the Middle East that embraces the Nile, Tigris and Euphrates river valleys and adjacent areas. Permanent farming villages begin to develop in the region.

7500 BC

MIDDLE EAST AND NORTH AFRICA
- Flax is used to manufacture textiles in the Middle East.

7000–6700 BC

MIDDLE EAST AND NORTH AFRICA
- Goats, sheep and pigs are domesticated in the Middle East.

6500 BC

MIDDLE EAST AND NORTH AFRICA
- Jericho, in the Jordan valley, is the first major city. It is walled for protection, has a population of some 2500 and is sustained by a perennial spring.

ASIA
- Rice cultivation begins in the Yangtze River valley in China.

6200 BC

SCIENCE AND TECHNOLOGY
- Earliest evidence of copper smelting, at Çatal Hüyük in Turkey.

6000 BC

MIDDLE EAST AND NORTH AFRICA
- Cattle are domesticated in the Middle East.
- Around the same time, irrigation is used for the first time, in the foothills of the Zagros Mts.

ECONOMY AND SOCIETY
- Farming begins in Egypt, the Indian subcontinent and S Europe.

5500 BC

ASIA
- Cotton is cultivated in the Indian subcontinent.

5200 BC

ASIA
- Earliest evidence for the domestication of chickens in the Yellow River valley, China.

4500 BC

ASIA
- The water buffalo is domesticated in SE China.

SCIENCE AND TECHNOLOGY
- The sail, the plough and the potter's wheel are invented in Mesopotamia.

4300 BC

EUROPE
- The first megalithic tombs are built in W Europe. Megalithic structures are those built from one or more large boulders set upright in the ground.

4300–3100 BC

MIDDLE EAST AND NORTH AFRICA
- Towns and cities, often centred on temple complexes, develop on the flood plains of Mesopotamia.

4000 BC

EUROPE
- Farming has spread to Britain and S Scandinavia.
- Horses are domesticated in what is now Ukraine.

3800 BC

SCIENCE AND TECHNOLOGY
- Bronze is invented in Mesopotamia. Copper is alloyed with arsenic (or, from c.3000 BC, tin) to make a hard alloy, which retains a sharp edge better than copper does.

c.3650 BC

SCIENCE AND TECHNOLOGY
- Wheeled vehicles are invented, probably in the Middle East: their use spreads rapidly to S Asia and Europe.

c.3500 BC

MIDDLE EAST AND NORTH AFRICA
- The appearance of the earliest writing system, based on pictographs, in Uruk in S Mesopotamia marks the emergence of the Sumerian civilization.
- The Sahara Desert begins to spread in N Africa as climate changes following the end of the last glaciation lead to a reduction in rainfall. The land, which had been green and fertile, turns to desert.

THE AMERICAS
- In the Andes the first pottery-using cultures have developed, while on the Pacific coast of S America permanent fishing villages have been established.

c.3400 BC

MIDDLE EAST AND NORTH AFRICA
- The hieroglyphic writing system begins to be developed in Egypt.

c.3200 BC

ASIA
- In the Longshan culture, the first hierarchical societies are found in China.

c.3100 BC

MIDDLE EAST AND NORTH AFRICA
- King Narmer of Upper Egypt achieves the unification of Egypt.

c.3000 BC

MIDDLE EAST AND NORTH AFRICA
- Sumerians develop a cuneiform script alphabet consisting of about 600 signs. They have already developed a written language, which uses picture-signs or pictographs.

ECONOMY AND SOCIETY
- Potatoes are being grown and alpacas and llamas are being domesticated in the Andes Mts.
- In the Middle East meat is cooked with herbs, and figs, grapes, honey and cucumbers are eaten.

SCIENCE AND TECHNOLOGY
- Copper smelting begins and the potter's wheel is introduced in China.
- Cotton fabric is being woven in the Indus valley.

2920 BC

MIDDLE EAST AND NORTH AFRICA
- King Menes founds the first of Egypt's historical dynasties.

SCIENCE AND TECHNOLOGY
- The Egyptians develop copper mines in Sinai.

2900 BC

MIDDLE EAST AND NORTH AFRICA
- The cuneiform script becomes formalized in Sumer and will remain unaltered for centuries.

c.2700 BC

ECONOMY AND SOCIETY
- Olive trees are now grown in Crete, which also exports olive oil.

SCIENCE AND TECHNOLOGY
- The Chinese develop the yang and yin theory and apply it to acupuncture and herbal medicine.

2630 BC

MIDDLE EAST AND NORTH AFRICA
- Djoser becomes king of Egypt. During his 20-year reign the first pyramid is built under the direction of Imhotep, the first architect whose name is known to history.

2600 BC

ASIA
- An urban civilization develops in the Indus valley. Its pictographic writing system has not been deciphered.

THE AMERICAS
- Along the Pacific coast of S America the monumental ceremonial centres of the Aspero tradition are being built.

ECONOMY AND SOCIETY
- Egyptians are developing the preservation of fish and poultry by sun-drying techniques.

2600–2500 BC

MIDDLE EAST AND NORTH AFRICA
- Rich burials with human sacrifice take place in the 'Royal Cemetery' at Ur in Sumeria.

2575 BC

MIDDLE EAST AND NORTH AFRICA
- The accession of Snefru to the throne marks the beginning of the Old Kingdom Period of Egyptian history. Snefru's reign sees Egypt conquering the Nubians and the Libyans. Snefru is commemorated in the two pyramids of Dahshur at Memphis.

2551 BC

MIDDLE EAST AND NORTH AFRICA
- Khufu (Cheops) becomes king of Egypt. He builds the first and largest of the Great Pyramids of Giza in which he is buried on his death in 2528 BC.

2520 BC

MIDDLE EAST AND NORTH AFRICA
- Khafre (Chephren), builder of the Great Sphinx and the second of the Great Pyramids of Giza, becomes king of Egypt.

2490 BC

MIDDLE EAST AND NORTH AFRICA
- Menkaure, builder of the third and smallest of the Great Pyramids of Giza, becomes king of Egypt.

c.2400 BC

ECONOMY AND SOCIETY
- Four-wheeled war wagons are used by armies in Mesopotamia, the first use of wheeled vehicles in warfare.

2350 BC

MIDDLE EAST AND NORTH AFRICA
- King Urukagina, king of Lagash in Sumer, promulgates the earliest known law code.

THE ROOTS OF CIVILIZATION:
River-valley Civilizations of Mesopotamia, the Indus and the Nile

Civilization as we know it was born in the very first cities. It was in cities that a settled and urban lifestyle emerged, with temples and palaces, organized streets and sewerage systems, granaries, warehouses and rubbish shoots. Surrounding the city were the fields and pastures that provided the surplus food and hence the wealth to support it. Urban societies also developed the hierarchies of power that made possible the distribution of this food and wealth. Cities gave birth to the first legal codes, political structures and religious systems, allowing large numbers of people to live close together in an orderly and peaceful way.

Cities developed in the course of the 3rd millennium BC in various parts of the world, though always in broad river valleys. The Nile, Indus and Tigris and Euphrates river systems became the basis for urban civilizations in the western Eurasian landmass, while the Yangtze and Yellow River performed a similar function in the east.

Farmers in Mesopotamia needed to work together to construct the first flood-control and irrigation schemes, and it was these that made city life possible. Irrigation was vital because there was no rainfall in early autumn when the newly planted crops needed water, and when spring arrived the flooding rivers threatened the crops. In Egypt collective action was also needed to store water from the annual inundation of the Nile for use in the dry season. In the Indus valley too there was a problem of flooding as the river system – fed by snowmelt from the Himalayas – flooded across the plain in summer. From about 3000 BC the waters were contained by extensive building programmes, and irrigation schemes grew out of these. By about 2300 BC civilization in the Indus valley was fully evolved. Mohenjo-daro in the south and Harappa in the north were the two major cities, and they provide the first examples of city streets built on a gridiron plan.

The Sumerians, the first Mesopotamian civilization, were based in the far south of what is now Iraq, and here they developed a number of city-states. Their greatest city was Uruk. Its Eanna Temple precinct was built in about 3500 BC, and by 3000 BC the population of Uruk was some 40,000. Like all such large Sumerian cities, Uruk was supported by a network of smaller towns and villages surrounding it. The temple and the palace were the two institutions basic to these Sumerian cities, for religion was fused with politics. The ruler governed in the name of the city's god, and it was the ruler who looked after the temples. He owned the estates of the temple, produce from which supported the temple staff – its priests, craftsmen and administrators.

Sumer is also the place where writing was invented, and each city had a 'tablet house' or writing school to train future officials. At first writing was in the form of pictographs, but later symbols with a phonetic value evolved. By about 2500 BC Sumerian influence had led to the establishment of important city-states in northern Mesopotamia.

Between 2300 and 2100 BC Sargon I, king of Akkad, and his successors established their rule over Sumer. For the first time in history we see the features of a true empire established across a vast landmass: military garrisons, provincial governorships and the domination of the language of the ruling group. It was also Akkadian civilization that first celebrated the idea of the divinity of a king. Naram-Sin, Sargon's grandson, called himself the 'god of Akkad'.

The difficulty of maintaining communications and control over so huge an empire led to the collapse of Akkad. The next power to emerge was an intermediate kind of organization. Like the old Sumerian city-states, Ur's power was based on the central city. Its influence spread beyond that of the Sumerian city-states, but it was not as ambitiously expansive as Akkad. The ruler Ur-Nammu established his power base in Ur in about 2112 BC – and then went on to conquer the cities of Sumer.

But the culture of the Mesopotamian south was in rapid decline by 2000 BC. By about 1900 BC crop yields had collapsed to about a third of those of the early 3rd millennium BC. The land could no longer support the city. Similar

Homo sapiens *had become a civilized, urban animal, and was to remain so.*

land-exhaustion caused the decay of the Indus valley civilization. In Egypt after c.2040 BC strong central government emerged after a period of disunity, but China continued to be a fragmented, chaotic region.

Some have looked for a global cause for this general decline in the early civilizations in the years after 2000 BC. Perhaps climate change played its part, but it is impossible to be certain. Although the individual cities and states collapsed, the idea of civilization remained. Within a few years new cities, cultures and states would begin to form. *Homo sapiens* had become a civilized, urban animal, and was to remain so.

2334 BC

MIDDLE EAST AND NORTH AFRICA
– Sargon I, ruler of the city of Akkad, conquers Mesopotamia: the Akkadian empire will dominate Mesopotamia for the next 150 years.

2300 BC

EUROPE
– The conventional beginning of the Bronze Age in Europe.

ASIA
– Rice is introduced from the Indus valley to N China and becomes the basis of a complex civilization. By the start of 2200 BC the Chinese have domesticated dogs, goats, pigs, oxen and sheep. They have also learned how to mill grain.

THE AMERICAS
– In Mesoamerica permanent farming villages and pottery are appearing.

c.2205 BC

ASIA
– The start of the legendary Xia (Hsia) dynasty, which will rule most of Chinese territory.

2193 BC

MIDDLE EAST AND NORTH AFRICA
– An invasion of Gutian tribes from the Zagros Mts leads to the collapse of the Akkadian empire.

2150 BC

MIDDLE EAST AND NORTH AFRICA
– After the Nile flood fails for several years in succession, Egypt suffers famine and popular unrest.

2134 BC

MIDDLE EAST AND NORTH AFRICA
– Central power collapses in Egypt, initiating the end of the Old Kingdom. The First Intermediate Period, a time of local power struggles, follows.

c.2112 BC

MIDDLE EAST AND NORTH AFRICA
– Ur-Nammu founds the 3rd dynasty of Ur in Sumer.

2100 BC

SCIENCE AND TECHNOLOGY
– The first ziggurats (monumental temple platforms) are built at Ur, Eridu, Uruk and Nippur in Sumer.

2040 BC

MIDDLE EAST AND NORTH AFRICA
– King Mentuhotep's restoration of centralized government in Egypt marks the beginning of the Middle Kingdom Period.

2004 BC

MIDDLE EAST AND NORTH AFRICA
– After Ur is sacked by the Elamites, the Sumerian civilization goes into decline.

c.2000 BC

EUROPE
– Construction of the main stage of the Stonehenge megalithic stone circle in S England is completed. Megalithic structures are composed of one or more large boulders set upright in the ground.
– The emergence of the Minoan palace civilization on Crete. The culture is based around large royal centres, 'palaces', in which specialist craftsmen work under a central control providing goods for a wide-ranging maritime trade network. The culture is named in the 19th century by British archaeologists in honour of Minos, a legendary king of Crete.

ECONOMY AND SOCIETY
– Merchants from the town of Phylakopi, on the Aegean island of Milos, are trading in the local volcanic glass, obsidian.
– Egyptians abandon abortive attempts to domesticate the gazelle, the antelope and the oryx.
– Watermelons are being grown in Africa, figs in Arabia, tea and bananas in India, apples in the Indus valley.

SCIENCE AND TECHNOLOGY
– Cretan sea power is sustained by ships carrying single square sails.
– The new power of Babylonia is developing decimal notation.

ARTS AND HUMANITIES
– *The Epic of Gilgamesh* is the first written myth. Written in Sumerian cuneiform, it recounts the story of a legendary king, Gilgamesh, and mentions a great flood from which mankind is rescued by the building of an ark.

Let me show you Gilgamesh, a man of joy and woe.

The Epic of Gilgamesh (2nd millennium BC)

1982 BC

MIDDLE EAST AND NORTH AFRICA
- Death of King Amenemhet (Ammenemes) II of Egypt; he is succeeded by his son Senusret I.

1878 BC

MIDDLE EAST AND NORTH AFRICA
- King Senusret (Sesostris) III succeeds his father Senusret II. His reign will last until 1842 BC, and he will turn Egypt into a genuinely great power based along the length of the Nile valley. He will also dig a canal through the first cataract of the Nile, allowing boats to penetrate further upriver. During his reign Egyptian forces invade Palestine and Syria in order to protect Egypt's trade routes.

1842 BC

MIDDLE EAST AND NORTH AFRICA
- Death of King Senusret III of Egypt. He is succeeded by Amenemhet III, who will reign for 45 years. Amenemhet III will develop mines in the Sinai area as well as encourage the first extensive network of Egyptian irrigation.

1813–1781 BC

MIDDLE EAST AND NORTH AFRICA
- Assyria emerges as a major power under King Shamshi-Adad I.

c.1800 BC

ASIA
- The Indus valley civilization goes into decline. The soil of the Indus valley becomes too saline to support extensive crop growth as a result of excessive irrigation. The great cities of Mohenjo-daro and Harappa collapse (c.1750 BC) as a consequence.

THE AMERICAS
- Along the Pacific coast of S America intensive irrigation agriculture begins, while throughout the region U-shaped ceremonial centres are being built.

ECONOMY AND SOCIETY
- By now prohibitions against eating pork have developed among some Middle Eastern peoples. These are mostly shepherding tribes who are fighting the farmers who keep pigs as domestic animals.

1797 BC

MIDDLE EAST AND NORTH AFRICA
- Death of King Amenemhet III of Egypt. His son Amenemhet IV will reign until 1787 BC as the last king of the 12th dynasty, known as the Theban dynasty. On his death the powers of Egyptian kingship decline.

1792 BC

MIDDLE EAST AND NORTH AFRICA
- Hammurabi, sixth king of the 1st dynasty of Babylon, conquers Mesopotamia and develops an extensive legal code as well as massive programmes of public works. He makes Babylon the capital of his empire.

1766 BC

ASIA
- Foundation of the first historical Chinese dynasty, the Shang, by King Tang, who overthrows the Xia (Hsia) dynasty and is revered as a humane ruler.

1750 BC

MIDDLE EAST AND NORTH AFRICA
- Death of King Hammurabi of Babylon.

1700 BC

EUROPE
- Knossos in Crete becomes the dominant centre of the Minoan civilization.

ECONOMY AND SOCIETY
- Abraham, first of the Hebrew patriarchs, has left Ur in Mesopotamia to found a new nation in Canaan (between Syria and Egypt). Jews, Christians and Muslims will acclaim his monotheism, and Abraham's son, Isaac, together with his grandson, Jacob, will propound Judaism.
- Rye is grown in the E Mediterranean and becomes the major bread grain for the Celts, Slavs and Teutons of the N, where the growing season is much shorter.
- Leavened or raised bread is invented in Egypt.

SCIENCE AND TECHNOLOGY
- The two-wheeled horse-drawn chariot is invented in the Middle East.

1640 BC

MIDDLE EAST AND NORTH AFRICA
- Hyksos tribesmen from Palestine and Syria invade and conquer Lower Egypt, marking the end of the Middle Kingdom and the beginning of the Second Intermediate Period, a time of local power struggles. The Hyksos introduce much new technology into Egypt, including the wheel and bronze.

1626 BC

EUROPE
- The Minoan civilization of Crete is seriously disrupted by the violent eruption of a volcano on the neighbouring Greek island of Thera (Santorini).

c.1600 BC

EUROPE

– Emergence of the Mycenaean civilization in Greece. Named after the chief city of Mycenae, this is a violent culture of heroes and warfare.

MIDDLE EAST AND NORTH AFRICA

– The Canaanites, a people of modern Lebanon and Israel, invent the first alphabet. It is a syllabic script which uses 28 letters.
– The cat is domesticated in Egypt.

ASIA

– The earliest forms of pictographic writing are developed in China.

1595 BC

MIDDLE EAST AND NORTH AFRICA

– The city of Babylon is sacked by the Hittite king Mursilis I, who will reign until c.1590 BC. The Hittites are an Indo-European people from what is now Turkey.

c.1557 BC

ASIA

– In China the Shang dynasty makes Zhengzhou its capital.

1550 BC

MIDDLE EAST AND NORTH AFRICA

– Ahmose (Ahmosis) becomes king of Egypt and founds the 18th dynasty. He drives the Hyksos out of Lower Egypt, reuniting the country, an event that marks the beginning of the New Kingdom Period.

1504 BC

MIDDLE EAST AND NORTH AFRICA

– Accession of Djehutymes (Thutmose or Tuthmosis) I as king of Egypt. His reign will see the ancient Egyptian kingdom reach its greatest extent following the conquest of Palestine, Syria and Upper and Lower Nubia.

c.1500 BC

ASIA

– Aryan nomads are emigrating from the Eurasian steppes and arriving in India.
– By now horse-drawn vehicles are being used by the Chinese. They are also weaving silk. China's Shang dynasty is based at Anyang on the Yellow (Huanghe) River.

SCIENCE AND TECHNOLOGY

– Egyptians are using geometry to obtain accurate measurements of field boundaries. This has become a necessity because the annual flooding of the Nile eliminates the dividing lines of properties.

1492 BC

MIDDLE EAST AND NORTH AFRICA

– Thutmose II, illegitimate son of Thutmose I, becomes king of Egypt and reigns along with his wife and half-sister Hatshepsut.

1479 BC

MIDDLE EAST AND NORTH AFRICA

– Egyptian king Thutmose II dies after a reign that has seen successful military campaigns against the Nubians and the Syrians. Hatshepsut assumes the title of king (1473 BC), despite her sex, and rules as regent for her infant nephew and stepson Thutmose III, son of Thutmose II.

c.1470 BC

MIDDLE EAST AND NORTH AFRICA

– Queen Hatshepsut of Egypt consolidates her reign by building two obelisks at Karnak. She has also built a great temple near Thebes on whose walls is portrayed an expedition to the land of Punt.

1458 BC

MIDDLE EAST AND NORTH AFRICA

– Egyptian king Thutmose III has now begun his personal rule following the death of his stepmother Hatshepsut. The title 'pharaoh' (meaning 'great house') becomes established usage during the reign. He builds walls around Hatshepsut's obelisks and tries to remove all memory of her reign.

c.1456 BC

MIDDLE EAST AND NORTH AFRICA

– Pharaoh Thutmose III defeats the rebel ruler of Kadesh in Syria at the battle of Megiddo.

c.1450 BC

EUROPE

– Crete is conquered by the Mycenaean Greeks, bringing the Minoan civilization to an end.

c.1440 BC

THE AMERICAS

– At Waywaka, Peru, the first known metalwork – including tools and ornaments of beaten gold – in the Andes is completed.

1425–1306 BC

IRON AGE BEGINS IN ASIA MINOR □ CHINESE INTRODUCE WAR CHARIOTS □ TUTANKHAMEN BURIED AT THEBES

1425 BC

MIDDLE EAST AND NORTH AFRICA
- Egyptian pharaoh Thutmose III dies. His son Amenhotep (Amenophis) II succeeds; he wages successful military campaigns in Judaea and on the Euphrates.

1401 BC

MIDDLE EAST AND NORTH AFRICA
- Pharaoh Amenhotep II dies and is succeeded by his son, Thutmose IV, who will marry a Mittanian princess and ally Egypt with Babylon and the Mittani. He will campaign in Phoenicia and Nubia and finish the construction of his grandfather Thutmose II's obelisk.

c.1400–1122 BC

ASIA
- In China the Shang dynasty moves its capital from Zhengzhou to Anyang. The royal burials there include human sacrifice.

c.1400 BC

ECONOMY AND SOCIETY
- In Mesoamerica the Olmec, probably the first developed civilization of the area, begin farming maize.

SCIENCE AND TECHNOLOGY
- The Iron Age begins in Asia Minor, where a reliable and economic method has been found for the industrial smelting of iron.

1391 BC

MIDDLE EAST AND NORTH AFRICA
- Pharaoh Thutmose IV dies and is succeeded by Amenhotep (Amenophis) III. During Amenhotep's reign Babylonia will recognize Egypt's supremacy. The pharaoh campaigns in Upper Nubia and develops Thebes as a metropolis with great temples and public monuments. Hypostyle halls (chambers filled with massive columns) are built at Karnak, and the Temple of Amun is erected in Luxor. Egypt becomes a land of wealth and luxury with a public policy of conspicuous state expenditure.

1353 BC

MIDDLE EAST AND NORTH AFRICA
- Pharaoh Amenhotep III dies and is succeeded by Amenhotep IV, who later takes the name Akhenaten and introduces monotheism to Egypt. The new religion worships the sun god (or solar disc) Aten. He moves the capital to Akhetaten (modern Tell el-Amarna), deserting Thebes. The pharaoh thus arouses the hostility of the powerful priests of Amun. His wife Nefertiti is a keen supporter of the religious revolution.

The Hittite king Suppululiumas trades on Egypt's weakness during the reign in order to build a great empire extending S from Anatolia to the borders of Lebanon.

c.1350 BC

ASIA
- The war chariot is introduced in China.

1333 BC

MIDDLE EAST AND NORTH AFRICA
- Akhenaten's son-in-law, the nine-year-old Tutankhamun, succeeds to the throne of Egypt. He leads the return to the religion of the priests of Amun and also moves Egypt's capital back to Thebes from the new city built by Akhenaten. After his death Tutankhamun is buried at Thebes along with a collection of precious decorative objects. These will excite great interest when discovered by archaeologists Howard Carter and the earl of Carnarvon in 1922.

1323 BC

MIDDLE EAST AND NORTH AFRICA
- The priest Ay, who was vizier and chief adviser to Tutankhamun, succeeds as pharoah of Egypt. Not of royal blood, he gains the throne by marrying Tutankhamun's widow Ankhesenamen.

1319 BC

MIDDLE EAST AND NORTH AFRICA
- In a military coup the soldier Horemheb seizes the throne of Egypt. He secures his claim to the throne by marrying the sister of Nefertiti (see 1353). He founds Egypt's 16th dynasty and reorganizes Egypt's religion on traditionalist lines according to the wishes of the priests of Amun.

1307 BC

MIDDLE EAST AND NORTH AFRICA
- Pharaoh Horemheb dies and is succeeded by Ramesses I, who establishes the 19th dynasty. He plans and begins work on the great hypostyle hall at Karnak.

1306 BC

MIDDLE EAST AND NORTH AFRICA
- Pharaoh Ramesses I dies and is succeeded by his son, Seti (Sethos) I. Seti defeats the Libyans W of the Nile delta and makes peace with the Hittites. He also completes the colonnaded hall at Karnak, which his father began, and builds a great sanctuary to the gods at Abydos.

1290 BC

MIDDLE EAST AND NORTH AFRICA
- Pharaoh Seti I dies and is succeeded by his son Ramesses II.

1285 BC

MIDDLE EAST AND NORTH AFRICA
- Pharaoh Ramesses II narrowly avoids defeat by the Hittites at the battle of Kadesh in Syria.

1270 BC

MIDDLE EAST AND NORTH AFRICA
- Ramesses II of Egypt marries a daughter of the Hittite king and promises permanent peace with the Hittites. The pharaoh will complete Seti's temple at Luxor, embellish the temples at Karnak and Luxor and build statues of himself at Thebes. He will also construct out of the rock a new temple at Abu Simbel in Nubia. It is thought by some modern historians that it is during his reign that the Israelites flee from slavery in Egypt, settling finally in Canaan (*c.*1200 BC).

Moses (13th century BC)

The writings of the Bible are the only near contemporary accounts of the life of Moses, but his achievements as a leader of his people and as the effective founder of the Jewish religion are undoubted.

At some stage in the course of the 13th century BC the people of Israel left Egypt, where they had been enslaved. The Book of Exodus in the Bible gives the name of Moses to the man who led their escape and subsequent journey through the desert of Sinai. The details of the worship of Yahweh, or Jehovah, evolved during that journey. This religion was monotheistic, excluding all other gods and cults, and its single God was an ethical being, a deity who kept promises. This idea of a covenant between the Jews and their God elevated law into a sacred element in Jewish theology. At Mount Sinai the people of Israel entered into a covenant with Yahweh, and the Ten Commandments were given to Moses.

The conquest of Palestine followed the Mosaic religious revolution. Just as Israel had covenanted with Yahweh, so the tribes, now settled in their new territory, were bound together by solemn agreements. This was a new kind of human society: one bound together less by race, ethnicity or geography than by collective memory and shared moral commitment. The idea of God's holiness and unity would drive the Jewish rejection of other gods, whose vain pretensions became a subject for scorn and jokes. In the ensuing three millennia that same sense of an austere and beautiful perfection would inspire Jewish intellectual and artistic life in both its religious and secular forms.

1224 BC

MIDDLE EAST AND NORTH AFRICA
- Ramesses II, pharaoh of Egypt, dies and is succeeded by his son Merneptah, who has to quell uprisings in Syria and Palestine. By 1232 BC a major Libyan invasion has been defeated. Following Merneptah's death (?1223 BC), a succession of relatively insignificant pharaohs reigns briefly during a period of 20 years of civil unrest that brings the 19th dynasty to an end. The last of these pharaohs is a woman, Tausat (Tawsert), the only queen of Egypt, besides Hatshepsut, to be buried in the Valley of the Kings.

1200 BC

MIDDLE EAST AND NORTH AFRICA
- Sethnakhte's brief reign as pharaoh establishes Egypt's 20th dynasty.

*c.*1200 BC

THE AMERICAS
- In Mesoamerica, an important Olmec ceremonial centre is built at Tres Zapotes (S Veracrux). Huge stone heads will be found there during excavations in the 1930s.

SCIENCE AND TECHNOLOGY
- The Egyptians have learned how to make fine linen from stalks of flax.

1187 BC

MIDDLE EAST AND NORTH AFRICA
- Ramesses III, son of Sethnakhte, becomes the second pharaoh of the 20th dynasty. During his 32-year reign he repels further Libyan invasions and inflicts a naval defeat on the invading Sea Peoples from the N.

1184 BC

EUROPE
- Traditional date for the sack of Troy, a city in NW Anatolia (modern Turkey), by the Mycenaean Greeks under Agamemnon, king of Mycenae.

1150 BC

ECONOMY AND SOCIETY
- Aristocratic Egyptians now use chairs.

SCIENCE AND TECHNOLOGY
- By now Egyptian medicine has split. The 'scientific' school introduces new ideas in treating diseases, but their expense confines the treatment only to the rich. The continuing popularity of the magical school, which expels demons, owes much to its cheapness.

1125 BC

MIDDLE EAST AND NORTH AFRICA
- Nebuchadnezzar I becomes king of Babylon.

1122 BC

ASIA
- King Wu of Zhou overthrows the Chinese emperor Di-xin, who in an excess of grief burns himself to death. The foundation of the Zhou (Chou) dynasty follows in 1111. The Zhou will rule China until *c*.256 BC.

c.1100 BC

MIDDLE EAST AND NORTH AFRICA
- Tiglath-Pileser I leads his forces from the Assyrian heartland in the upper Tigris–Euphrates valley to the shores of the Mediterranean having conquered the Hittites. They now confront the Phoenicians, a maritime people living along the coast of what is now Lebanon and Israel.

c.1070–*c*.725 BC

MIDDLE EAST AND NORTH AFRICA
- Following the end of Egypt's New Kingdom, the period of the 21st–23rd dynasties sees internal disorder and the loss of Egypt's Middle Eastern dominance.

c.1020 BC

MIDDLE EAST AND NORTH AFRICA
- The Hebrew leader Saul becomes the first king of Judaea.

c.1006 BC

MIDDLE EAST AND NORTH AFRICA
- Saul, king of Judaea, is killed in battle with the Philistines at Mt Gilboa. David succeeds and is supposed to reign as king of Hebron until *c*.1000 BC, when he occupies the Canaanite city of Jerusalem and is in his turn anointed king of Judaea by the prophet Samuel. His reign is recorded as lasting until *c*.965 BC and, according to the biblical account, sees the destruction of Philistine power and the defeat of the forces of the Moabites, the Ammonites and the Edomites, local peoples in what is now Israel.

c.1000 BC

THE AMERICAS
- The Maya begin to settle the Yucatán peninsula, while maize is introduced in the Andes.

SCIENCE AND TECHNOLOGY
- Iron Age technology, which first arrived in the Near and Middle East 400 years earlier, has now moved to the Hallstatt region of Europe (in modern Austria).

c.965 BC

MIDDLE EAST AND NORTH AFRICA
- Judaean king David dies and his son Solomon, the son of David's second wife Bathsheba, succeeds. (David had reputedly arranged the death of Bathsheba's first husband in order to marry her.) Solomon reigns until *c*.928 BC and makes strategic alliances with the ruling priests of Egypt as well as with Hiram, Phoenician king of Tyre. Solomon's rule sees the building of the Great Temple of Jerusalem to house the Ark of the Covenant, a wooden box containing holy relics. Solomon builds a new royal palace and city wall in Jerusalem, introducing taxation to finance his public building projects and forced labour to erect them.

945 BC

MIDDLE EAST AND NORTH AFRICA
- The Libyan Shoshenq I seizes the Egyptian throne and establishes the 22nd (Bubastite) dynasty, which will provide Egypt's rulers for 200 years. Shoshenq will take advantage of a growing political crisis in Judaea, following Solomon's death and the succession of his son Rehoboam (*c*.928 BC). Ten northern tribes split from the Judaean kingdom and then establish the kingdom of Israel with Jeroboam as their king. In 924 BC Shoshenq (known as Shishak in the Bible) invades Judaea and loots Jerusalem and other cities.

900 BC

EUROPE
- The Etruscans establish Italy's first cities in Tuscany. Their towns are built on hillside terraces and are enclosed by walls of timber.

883 BC

MIDDLE EAST AND NORTH AFRICA
- Assyria's ruler Ashurnasirpal II, son of Tukulti-Ninurta II, starts a 24-year reign, which will see the revival of the Assyrian empire and the defeat of Babylonia. He annexes Phoenicia (878 BC) and his power extends over the E Mediterranean. He rebuilds Calah (Kalhu, Iraq) and establishes it as his imperial capital. He is succeeded by his son, Shalmaneser III (858 BC).

c.850 BC

ARTS AND HUMANITIES
- The Greek epic poems the *Iliad* and the *Odyssey* are composed and attributed to 'Homer' (see p. 14). The work of either a single poet or a group of poets, the poems are transcribed from an earlier oral tradition.

Homer (9th–8th century BC)

The great epics poems, the *Iliad* and the *Odyssey*, mark the beginning of ancient Greek literature. Both are ascribed to a figure known as 'Homer', about whom virtually nothing is known, although by tradition he was blind, and the poems were probably compiled on the Aegean coast of Asia Minor around the early 8th century BC. Whether the figure of 'Homer' represents a group of poets or a single poet who wrote down an earlier oral tradition cannot be established; historical and linguistic details in the poems indicate that the stories go back to the Mycenaean age (*c.*1450–*c.*1200 BC). Both poems were certainly intended for oral performance.

The *Iliad* is set during the Trojan War, the legendary conflict in which the Greeks sought to avenge the abduction by Paris, a Trojan prince, of Helen, wife of Menelaus, king of Sparta; the poem focuses on the anger of the Greek hero Achilles and its tragic consequences. The *Odyssey* has a more spacious canvas; it is set in the aftermath of the war, and follows the wanderings of Odysseus (also known as Ulysses) on his way home to his Greek island kingdom of Ithaca. Both poems establish the importance of character in literature. Achilles is the archetype of the warrior who chooses danger and glory rather than obscurity, and who lives by the warrior code of honour and loyalty. Hector, his foe, accepts that before death comes he needs to do 'some big thing first, that men to come shall know of it'. Although emerging from an age of heroes and hero-worship, both poems have transcended their origins and have had an immense influence on Western culture, from Virgil's *Aeneid* (1st century BC) and Dante's *Divine Comedy* (14th century) to James Joyce's modernist masterpiece *Ulysses* (1922).

814 BC

MIDDLE EAST AND NORTH AFRICA
- Traditional date for the foundation of the N African city of Carthage by settlers from the Phoenician city of Tyre.

811 BC

MIDDLE EAST AND NORTH AFRICA
- Sham shi-Adad V of Assyria, son of Shalmaneser III, dies. He has quelled a rebellion with Babylonian aid but lost part of his empire. His son Adadnirari V succeeds, with the queen mother Semiramis ruling as regent for four years.

c.800 BC

THE AMERICAS
- In Mesoamerica the Zapotec civilization develops a hieroglyphic script.

ECONOMY AND SOCIETY
- The *Vedas*, Aryan religious epics, give rise to the veneration of the cow in India.

776 BC

EUROPE
- The first recorded Olympic Games are held at Olympia in Greece, although the associated religious aspects of the games pre-date this period. Only Greeks are allowed to take part in the games.

c.772 BC

ARTS AND HUMANITIES
- Work begins on building the temple of Artemis at Ephesus, a Greek city in what is now Turkey. The temple will later be recognized as one of the Seven Wonders of the World.

771 BC

ASIA
- Military forces from N China destroy the Zhou (Chou) dynasty's capital at Hao on the Wei River. In 770 BC the capital is moved to Luoyang near the Yellow (Huanghe) River. Royal authority, however, declines.

753 BC

EUROPE
- Officially adopted date of the foundation of the city of Rome on a hilltop by the brothers Romulus and Remus. The date becomes the basis of Roman chronology: AUC (*ab urbe condita*) or 'from the foundation of the city' being the prefix of recorded dates.

c.750 BC

EUROPE
- The Greek alphabet is developed.

744 BC

MIDDLE EAST AND NORTH AFRICA
- Tiglath-Pileser III succeeds to the Assyrian throne. In the next seven years he will conquer Syria, Palestine, Israel and Babylon.

724 BC

EUROPE
- At the 14th Olympiad a second race on foot is added and competitors now have to run twice around the stadium, a distance of about 1km (½ mile).

722 BC

MIDDLE EAST AND NORTH AFRICA
- Samaria, the capital of Israel, falls to the Assyrians after a three-

year siege. Shalmaneser V dies during the seige (722 BC) and is succeeded by his son Sargon II, who takes some 30,000 Israelite prisoners of the ten northern tribes, whom he reputedly deports to C Asia. These, the 'lost tribes of Israel', disappear from recorded history, though they later become the subject of much speculation.

712 BC

MIDDLE EAST AND NORTH AFRICA
– Egypt is invaded from the S: a Nubian dynasty (the 25th) will rule until 657 BC.

708 BC

EUROPE
– The Olympic Games begin to acquire a more familiar form with contests in jumping, wrestling, and javelin and discus throwing.

704 BC

MIDDLE EAST AND NORTH AFRICA
– Sennacherib becomes ruler of Assyria and develops Nineveh as a metropolis.

c.700 BC

EUROPE
– Because of population growth and limited food resources Greek colonists are now leaving Greek territory and settling in other Mediterranean lands.

ECONOMY AND SOCIETY
– The first metal coinage is introduced in the kingdom of Lydia (modern Turkey).

SCIENCE AND TECHNOLOGY
– In the Middle East aqueducts are being built to supply growing cities with water.

696 BC

EUROPE
– Boxing is added to the 23rd Olympic Games.

689 BC

MIDDLE EAST AND NORTH AFRICA
– Sennacherib, ruler of Assyria, destroys Babylon, which is then rebuilt on a magnificent scale.

660 BC

ASIA
– Legendary invasion of Japan's main island, Honshu, by Japan's supposed first emperor, Jimmu Tenno, who crosses from the island of Kyushu. The legend provides Japanese culture with a claim to antiquity.

c.659 BC

EUROPE
– Greek colonists from Megara establish a settlement at what will become Byzantium, later Constantinople and eventually Istanbul.

c.650 BC

ECONOMY AND SOCIETY
– Deforestation is occurring on a wide scale in Greece as wood is used for houses, ships and charcoal. Soil erosion and loss of fertile land are a consequence.

c.627 BC

MIDDLE EAST AND NORTH AFRICA
– King Ashurbanipal of Assyria, the last significant ruler of the Sargonid dynasty, dies after a 43-year reign. After his death the Assyrian empire decays within 20 years.

625 BC

ECONOMY AND SOCIETY
– The Greeks adopt metal coins. They bear the image of an ear of wheat since grain was the previous unit of exchange.

624 BC

EUROPE
– In Greece Corinth's ruler, the tyrant Periander, one of the 'Seven Wise Men of Greece', finances his government with gold jewellery seized from the wives of the nobility.

621 BC

EUROPE
– Draco, the first major lawmaker in the Greek city of Athens, promulgates a legal code that metes out savage offences for minor offences. The word 'draconian' will later be coined to describe any severe punishment.

620 BC

ECONOMY AND SOCIETY
– According to tradition, the Book of Deuteronomy is composed by Israelite writers. It claims to be the testament of Moses (see p. 12) to the Jews. It imposes dietary restrictions and allows meat to be eaten only from an animal that chews the cud and has a cloven hoof. Camels, rock badgers, hares, pigs and fish without fins and scales are all unclean and cannot be eaten.

612 BC

MIDDLE EAST AND NORTH AFRICA
– Nineveh is occupied by the Medes and the Babylonians. The Assyrian empire is destroyed.

609 BC

MIDDLE EAST AND NORTH AFRICA

– The Egyptian pharaoh Nekau (Necho) II starts work on a new canal linking the Red Sea with the Nile. It is uncompleted and a vast labour force, possibly more than 100,000 men, dies in the attempt. (In 520 BC Darius of Persia resumes work on Nekau's project.) Another of Nekau's enterprises is more successful as one fleet of his ships will circumnavigate Africa in a voyage that takes several years. The expedition halts each spring to plant crops, moving on after the autumn harvest.

605 BC

MIDDLE EAST AND NORTH AFRICA

– Nékau II, pharaoh of Egypt, is defeated by the new ruler of Babylon, Nebuchadnezzar II, at Carchemish in Syria.

c.600 BC

EUROPE

– Greek colonists found the city that will become Marseilles in what is now S France.

MIDDLE EAST AND NORTH AFRICA

– Babylon's famed luxury continues during this century. River-boats bring copper, silver, gold and vegetable oils to the city from fields N of the Tigris. Dyestuffs, glassware, textiles and precious stones are imported into the city. Public buildings are typically decorated by blue, yellow and white enamelled tiles. Water pumped from the Euphrates irrigates the Hanging Gardens. But disease also becomes a problem; plague spreads to Babylon occasionally because of the pollution of irrigated canals, which breed disease-carrying flies and mosquitoes.

THE AMERICAS

– The earliest Mayan temple-pyramids are built.

ECONOMY AND SOCIETY

– On the island of Lesbos, the Greek poet Sappho is the priestess of a religious cult dedicated to love. The association of her name with female homosexuality is a more recent one.

597 BC

MIDDLE EAST AND NORTH AFRICA

– Nebuchadnezzar II, the last great king of Babylon, invades Judah and returns to Babylon with Jewish prisoners of war. In 587 BC he occupies Jerusalem after a 16-month siege. He seizes the Jewish occupants and carries them off into the Babylonian exile or captivity, which will last until 538 BC. The Great Temple of Jerusalem is destroyed (586 BC). In 573 BC Nebuchadnezzar occupies Tyre after a 13-year siege. He will then invade Egypt (568 BC) before dying (562 BC).

594 BC

EUROPE

– Solon the lawmaker establishes the rule of the richest (timocracy) in Athens and embarks on constitutional reform, having regained Salamis from the Megarians in 556 BC. Solon's edict forbidding the export of agricultural produce from Athens leads to the excessive planting of olive trees. Their roots, which suck up moisture but do not hold the soil together, lead to further erosion of the Greek hillsides.

593 BC

MIDDLE EAST AND NORTH AFRICA

– Napata, capital of the kingdom of Cush, is sacked by the Egyptians. Subsequently, the S administrative centre of Meroe (in modern Sudan) becomes the Cushite capital and, with its surrounding area, develops into a major power and a centre of Egypto-Cushite culture.

Laozi (Lao-tzu) (6th century BC)

Laozi has had a profound effect on Chinese thought and society for millennia, and yet his life and character are shrouded in legend. It is said that the 'old philosopher' wanted to remain unknown, and the idea of a recluse who searches for inner peace became an important part of his appeal. Laozi is credited with the authorship of the *Daode Jing* (or *Tao-te Ching*), and is therefore traditionally seen as the founder of Daoism, which advocates *Dao* (the way) and its character-istic *De* (virtue) – though that work may in fact have been written by a group of scholars, possibly in the 3rd century BC.

Daoism first became influential during the social breakdown of the Warring States period (475–221 BC). Daoism and Confucianism share a common ancestry in the Chinese view of the natural created order, in which the hierarchical natural world is analogous to the order of the wider universe. The elevation in Daoism of the principle of order was to become the foundation of the later recovery at a social and metaphysical level, while Confucianism provided a more ethical and secular component. Daoism became an important element in Chinese cultural identity, for it appealed to both nobility and peasantry.

Like Buddhism, which it greatly influenced, Daoism preached the need to be free from selfish purpose, and its way was one of compassion and humility.

During the Han dynasty (206 BC–AD 220) Daoism evolved into a religion, and Laozi became Lord Lao, who reappeared on earth to instruct the rulers of the world throughout history. He was venerated as a saint. During the Tang dynasty (618–907) Laozi was worshipped as an imperial ancestor. Subsequently, Daoism shaped not only the culture of China but also that of Vietnam, Japan and Korea.

c.565 BC

EUROPE
- Greek general Peisistratus commands Athenian forces in the conquering of Salamis from the Megarians. He organizes Greece's first political party, the *diakrioi*, composed of the interest groups of small farmers, merchants and artisans.

ECONOMY AND SOCIETY
- Daoism (Taoism) is spreading from the state of Lu in China. (See Laozi, p. 16.)

c.562 BC

MIDDLE EAST AND NORTH AFRICA
- Nebuchadnezzar II of Babylon dies.

561 BC

EUROPE
- Greek general Peisistratus makes himself ruler of Athens, but is then expelled by Lycurgus and Megacles, from the noble family of the Alcmaeonids.

559 BC

EUROPE
- In Athens Megacles the Alcmaeonid transfers his support to the deposed ruler Peisistratus, who is then restored to power.

556 BC

EUROPE
- In Athens a renewed quarrel with Megacles the Alcmaeonid leads to Peisistratus being exiled again.

MIDDLE EAST AND NORTH AFRICA
- Nabonidus, last king of Babylon, starts his reign. He is driven from his throne in 539 BC by King Cyrus II of Persia.

c.553 BC

ECONOMY AND SOCIETY
- Persian prophet Zoroaster (Zarathustra) (see box) dies (he was born c.630 BC). Persian religious thought and culture are being moulded by his teachings.

550 BC

MIDDLE EAST AND NORTH AFRICA
- Cambyses I, king of Persia, dies and is succeeded by his son Cyrus II (the Great) who will create a new Persian empire that unites the Medes, the Persians and other peoples.

ECONOMY AND SOCIETY
- Croesus, king of Lydia in W Asia Minor, introduces the first metal coins of defined purity and weight.

Zoroaster (Zarathustra) (c.630–c.553 BC)

The Iranian religious reformer Zoroaster was born near modern-day Tehran, and later trained as a priest. He claimed to have received a vision from the god Ahura Mazda, the Wise Lord, and his new religious system placed Ahura Mazda at the heart of the previously polytheistic Iranian national religion. The figure who is reflected in the Zoroastrian scriptures (the *Aveda*) and hymns (*Gathas*) – many of which he may have written – is a serious religious thinker.

Zoroaster claimed that Ahura Mazda was the only god worthy of worship because he is the creator of heaven and earth as well as the source of moral order in the world. There are certain entities or beings who are subordinate to him but who, nonetheless, exemplify Ahura Mazda's properties: justice, truth, wholeness and immortality. These properties also include 'desirable dominion', which is anticipated as a kingdom yet to be realized.

Zoroaster, therefore, invented eschatology. But he also taught another novelty – the resurrection of the body. This idea may have influenced the Israelites during their wanderings and, through Judaism, was then incorporated into Christianity. Zoroaster also introduced an ideal of purity into religious worship. He reacted against the practice of sacrificing cattle and also against orgiastic excesses of drink and drugs in ritual celebration. But he did retain the ancient cult of fire as a symbol of purification.

In 588 BC Zoroaster is said to have converted Vishtapsa, ruler of the Central Asian kingdom of Chorasmia, and later, during the reign of Darius I (522–486 BC), Zoroastrianism became the state religion of Persia. It survives in parts of Iran among the Gabars, and among the Parsees (or Parsis) of India, who are descended from Zoroastrians who left Persia after the arrival of Islam.

---

549 BC

MIDDLE EAST AND NORTH AFRICA
- Armenia becomes a Persian satrapy (province) and will remain so until 317 BC.

546 BC

EUROPE
- Supported by Thessaly and Naxos, Peisistratus returns again to power in Athens. In a series of fundamental reforms he exiles his opponents and confiscates their lands, which are then used to benefit the poor, turning the *hectemoroi* (share-croppers) into landowners. Since the hereditary priesthoods are part of the power base of the Athenian nobility, he introduces the new religious cult of Dionysus as state policy to undermine their power.

INDIA AND HINDUISM:
The Invention of a Country

Hinduism, and by extension the concept of India, originated with the arrival of Aryan peoples in southern Asia some time around 1500 BC. Pastoral by origin and semi-nomadic by instinct, these Indo-Europeans were shepherds, smiths and farmers who had mastered the plough and knew how to cultivate crops. But they were also warriors and horsemen. They moved the base of Indian culture eastwards from the Indus valley towards the Ganges and entirely recast it, for the Aryans brought with them a structure that was both social and religious, which enabled a truly civic society to evolve. Their new imposed order would become synonymous with India itself. Shiva, India's oldest god, survived the arrival of the Aryans, but almost everything else changed.

Even before they arrived in India the Aryans probably had a priestly class and a warrior class. On Indian soil the two groups would be called the Brahmins and the Ksatriya, and it was their arts of religious interpretation and warfare that would help set the seal on the victory of the invaders, for the Aryans made India into a Hindu civilization, and in doing so they also gave the country something it did not have before – a literature. The holy scriptures of Hinduism, the Vedic Hymns, were written in Sanskrit some time in the 6th century BC, and it was the function of the Brahmins to interpret these and expound them. Dating from many centuries earlier, the *Rig Veda* (Praise of Knowledge) is a great oral collection, recording the migration and subsequent settlement of the Aryans.

Socially, the Aryans were organized in tribes and families: this was a patriarchal and hierarchical society and also one in which the fire of the hearth was sacred. Near the bottom of the Aryan structure were the farmers – or Vaisya – who often (against official doctrine) intermarried with the conquered race, the Dusas. But below these were the outcast majority – the people who then, as now, were responsible for the manual work: the casual workers, the itinerants, the beggars and the cleaners of streets. Caste was the Aryan idea that came to define India. It was accepted as a divinely ordained institution that gave coherence and order to an otherwise chaotic world.

Worshippers of all castes established their solidarity by engaging in religious rituals. The religion of the Hindus evolved into an undogmatic belief in a single power – an ultimate truth that was realized in many manifestations. Hinduism evolved a whole pantheon of gods, and its sheer variety meant that this was a religion that had something for everyone. Some of the key beliefs of Hinduism are contained in the 'Bhagavadgita' ('Song of the Lord'), part of the *Mahabharata* – the world's longest epic poem – which achieved its written form at the end of the 5th century BC. The 'Bhagavadgita' provides the classical summation of the doctrine of *karma* and rebirth, a belief associated with the idea of a universal spirit present in all living things. Hinduism also invented the idea of the wise man or guru who was not concerned with politics or even particularly with ethics. Gurus focused instead on the ultimate and mystical truth of being itself.

The claims of religion would have a greater hold on India than any particular political structure. The fundamental beliefs of Hinduism would both influence and outlast all the passing states and empires of the subcontinent. The fact that the Aryans were organized tribally made natural the development of a number of small states. In the hills of the northwest their governments were often a kind of loquacious democracy, with a chief or *raja* chairing the discussion. Down in the plains monarchies developed. And further to the south the tradition of the Hindu-influenced tribe remained strong. But everywhere there were villages where the villagers chose their own headmen and discussed their problems communally. Gandhi's 'India of a thousand villages' was founded on an ancient reality.

For centuries Indian history witnessed the rise and fall of a succession of empires, each of which expanded and attracted allies and client-states until it dominated part or all of the subcontinent, then collapsed into the earlier form of competing states. Notable among these were the Mauryan empire of the 4th and 3rd centuries BC, and that of the

It could be said that Hinduism … invented a country.

Guptas in the 4th and 5th centuries AD. Under the Guptas literary Sanskrit scaled new peaks in its retelling of the Hindu epics. This was also an age of progress in the fields of astronomy and mathematics – notable developments included the concept of zero and the use of the decimal system. The Gupta period, with its revival of Hinduism following a period of Buddhist hegemony, is sometimes regarded as the Classical Age of India, a period that witnessed the establishment of Hindu traditions in the art, architecture, literature and philosophy of India. It could be said that Hinduism had invented a country.

546 BC *continued*

MIDDLE EAST AND NORTH AFRICA

– Forces of the Persian king Cyrus II conquer the army of Croesus, king of Lydia, at Sardis. Croesus is spared by Cyrus, but Lydia becomes Persian controlled. In 539 BC Cyrus defeats Nabonidus, king of Babylon. When Belshazzar, son of Nabonidus, tries to fight back (538 BC) he is defeated. Cyrus destroys the city of Babylon and allows the Jews to return to Jerusalem, where they will rebuild Solomon's Great Temple. Cyrus is killed fighting a tribe to the E of the Caspian Sea in 529 BC. He leaves an empire that extends from the Caucasus to the Indian Ocean, and from the Indus to the Mediterranean. Cambyses II, his son, succeeds.

528 BC

ECONOMY AND SOCIETY

– Siddhartha Gautama (see box) finds enlightenment at Bodh Gaya, near Benares, India. An aristocrat who has renounced luxury and practised a five-year penance, Siddhartha will preach a new religion to be known as Buddhism. He will be called the Buddha (Enlightened One). His religion will spread from India to China and then Japan.

527 BC

EUROPE

– In Athens, after the death of the ruler Peisistratus, his sons Hippias and Hipparchus succeed him.

525 BC

MIDDLE EAST AND NORTH AFRICA

– Persian king Cambyses II defeats Egypt's ruler Psamtik (Psammetichus) III at Pelusium and so adds the Nile delta to the Persian empire. A vast Persian army, perhaps amounting to as many as 50,000, is lost in a sandstorm as it marches to occupy the desert oasis and sacred city of Amun. In 522 BC Cambyses II dies while attempting to return from Egypt to deal with the usurpation of his throne by Gaumata, a Magian priest. Gaumata is killed by Darius Hystaspis, Cyrus's son-in-law, who becomes Darius I, ruler of Persia (521 BC).

516 BC

ECONOMY AND SOCIETY

– Completion of the reconstruction of Jerusalem's Temple by the Jews.

*c.*515 BC

ARTS AND HUMANITIES

– Birth in Elea, S Italy, of Parmenides, who founds eleaticism, a leading pre-Socratic school of Greek philosophy. Parmenides and his followers are the first metaphysicians since they assert that the universe only appears to change. In spite of appearances, the universe is really solid throughout and immobile.

509 BC

EUROPE

– Rome becomes a republic. The Tarquin kings are expelled. The legendary foundation story describes the rape of aristocratic Lucretia by Tarquinius Sextus, son of the king Tarquinius Superbus. Before committing suicide, Lucretia tells her father and her husband Lucius Tarquinius Collatinus, the Roman general, of the rape. Her cousin Lucius Junius Brutus, at the head of a popular force, then expels the Tarquins. In Rome during this century the municipal drain known as the Cloaca Maxima has been built in order to drain the local marshy land in what will become the site of the Forum.

Siddhartha Gautama (the Buddha) (*c.*563–*c.*483 BC)
Prince Siddhartha Gautama was to become the founder of the Buddhist faith. He was the son of a provincial king in Kapilavastu, a small city-state in modern Nepal. Warfare was rife, and Gautama's home city was defeated by a neighbouring power and most of his family were massacred. These experiences of conflict lie behind his system of belief, which led him to be known as the Buddha or Enlightened One.

The Buddha spread his ideas as an itinerant preacher in the various Indian states, rejecting the orthodox beliefs of the Hindu religion. The Buddha himself had a scornful attitude towards Hinduism's Brahmin clergy and their ascetic practices. Purity, he said, did not derive simply from abstinence and the observation of dietary regulations. He was suspicious of clerical self-interest – which he saw especially in the Brahmins' support for war and capital punishment. The Hindu establishment's support of the caste system, he thought, had vicious consequences and gave a spurious religious authority to a secular system.

The Buddha urged renunciation of the world through contemplation. Spiritual freedom meant the renunciation of material possessions, and his followers also had to renounce all passion and ambition. Even the hope of immortality was a form of selfish ambition and a way of keeping the self imprisoned. Life was a state of unending pain: every sentient being experienced it for the simple reason that pain was the result of sentience. The goal of enlightenment was indifference to such pain. Detachment from the senses and their needs and desires was therefore the key. Nirvana was the Buddha's term for that detachment, which alone could bring freedom. He also founded a monastic order to give an institutional expression to his beliefs. Buddhism became a strongly missionary religion, spreading from India to China and then to Japan and large areas of Southeast Asia.

509–480 BC

ATHENIANS DEFEAT PERSIANS AT MARATHON □ SIDDHARTHA GAUTAMA, THE BUDDHA, DIES

– Cleisthenes, son of Megacles (see 561 BC), introduces a more democratic constitution at Athens. An attempt by leading noblemen to block the reforms by calling in a Spartan army is foiled by popular resistance.

c.500 BC

ASIA

– In India King Bimbisara has made Magadha the leading Hindu kingdom.
– Jin becomes the most powerful Chinese state.

THE AMERICAS

– State formation begins in the Oaxaca valley in Mesoamerica.

AUSTRALASIA AND OCEANIA

– Polynesian culture has begun to develop in Fiji, Samoa and Tonga.

ECONOMY AND SOCIETY

– By now Phoenician wealth and power are established features of Mediterranean life. The Phoenician galleys are the basis of the country's prosperity, bringing gold and ivory from Africa, silver from Spain, tin from Cornwall, gold, iron and lead from the Black Sea, and copper and grain from Cyprus. The economy and society are based on the slaves who are also imported to Phoenicia on a massive scale.

SCIENCE AND TECHNOLOGY

– Greek philosopher Heraclitus (Heracleitus) is teaching at Ephesus. His view – that all of nature and of humanity are in a state of perpetual flux, that everything is mutable – has profound ethical implications for Greek philosophy. He is later known as the 'weeping' philosopher.

ARTS AND HUMANITIES

Sun Tzu, *The Art of War*, military treatise.

490 BC

EUROPE

15 Sept. The Athenians defeat the Persians at the battle of Marathon. Miltiades leads 11,000 Greeks who defeat King Darius's army of 15,000 some 40km (25 miles) NE of Marathon. The event inaugurates a long-lived Athenian–Persian conflict and forms the background to the Athenian civilization that follows. The story of Pheidippides running from Athens to Sparta and then from Marathon to Athens to bring the news becomes part of Athenian mythology. In the 19th century the feat will lead to the popularity of 'marathon' races.

c.483 BC

ASIA

– The first state in Ceylon (Sri Lanka) is founded by King Vijaya.

ECONOMY AND SOCIETY

– Aged 84, Siddhartha Gautama, the Buddha (see p. 19), dies at Kusinagara, India, after eating too much pork, the consequence of abandoning the strict vegetarianism he had preached for most of his religious career.

480 BC

EUROPE

19 Aug. Persian king Xerxes, son of Darius, gains a victory at the battle of Thermopylae when 20,000 Persians defeat 300 Spartans and 700 Thebans under the Spartan leader Leonidas. Leonidas detains the Persians just long enough for the main Greek force to escape. Having broken through the pass at Thermopylae, which leads from Macedonia into the rest of Greece, the Persians occupy Attica and destroy Athens.

Confucius (c.551–479 BC)

The great Chinese philosopher Confucius (a latinized form of Kongfuzi or K'ung Fu-tzu) was born in present-day Shandong province. He became an administrator in his native Lu – one of the small states that emerged from the chaos of the collapsing Zhou (Chou) dynasty – and later became a peripatetic teacher of ethics, seeking a ruler who welcomed his belief that ethics was the key to order and prosperity.

Confucianism gave individuals a sense of duty and self-worth at a time when political and social structures had collapsed. The Chinese dissolution into regional states in the 5th century BC, while creating a general crisis of order, also created more career opportunities for able bureaucrats. This proved an important element in the rise of Confucianism, and by the 2nd century BC it had become the official philosophy of the Chinese imperial state. Confucianism emphasized the virtue of precisely defined rights and duties within a strongly hierarchical order – whether within the family or within the state.

Although a reformer, Confucius also maintained that he was doing nothing more than restoring the code of social conduct that had bound the early emperors. But Confucius's effect was novel: his idea of nobility relied on an individual being philosophically refined and educated rather than simply being of noble birth.

At the beginning of the 2nd century BC, Confucian scholars compiled five books, the Five Classics, that summed up the original teaching of the sage. By the end of the century qualification for an imperial administrative job came to depend on being able to write in the Confucian style and on proficiency in the interpretation of the Confucian philosophy.

20 THE ANCIENT AND MEDIEVAL WORLDS: 135,000 BP–1449

Revenge follows for the Greeks with the naval victory at Salamis (23 Sept.). Under the command of the Athenian general Themistocles, fewer than 400 Greek ships lure more than 1000 Persian ships into the restricted waters of the Bay of Salamis, where they are rammed and sunk.

479 BC

EUROPE
27 Aug. At the battle of Plataea the Greeks under the Spartan general Pausanius defeat the Persians led by Mardonius. The Persian invasion of Greece ends.

ECONOMY AND SOCIETY
– Death of Chinese philosopher and sage Confucius (K'ung Fu-tzu) (see p. 20). In 495 BC he had resigned as prime minister of Lu when its ruler abandoned himself to a life of luxury. For the next 12 years he travelled across China from state to state, teaching essentially secular principles of conduct based on the family and respect for tradition. His ethical system, recorded in the *Analects,* will remain fundamental to Chinese thought to the present day.

Sincerity is the end and beginning of things.

Confucius, *The Doctrine of the Mean* (c.500 BC)

c.475 BC

SCIENCE AND TECHNOLOGY
– Iron use spreads to China, some 1000 years after it was first introduced in the Middle East.

472 BC

ARTS AND HUMANITIES
– Greek playwright Aeschylus has already won his first prize for drama in the annual contest in honour of the god Dionysus in 484 BC. He now composes *Persae* (The Persians), the first in a series of plays that will transform tragedy and build on its religious roots, while developing it as a literary form of high gravity and intense beauty. But in 468 BC he will be outshone in the Athenian prize for drama by a rising new Greek playwright, Sophocles.

462–458 BC

EUROPE
– With nobleman and soldier Pericles as the dominant political figure, democratic institutions are completed in Athens.

Euripides (c.485–406 BC)
The Greek dramatist Euripides wrote 92 plays, of which 17 survive. His first stage success came in 441 BC, when he was 44. Like his near-contemporaries Sophocles and Aeschylus, he reworked the ancient Greek myths in the form of tragedy, but his attitude towards these myths – and towards Greek religious beliefs – was more sceptical. He depicts his protagonists as ordinary, vulnerable human beings rather than larger-than-life heroes, and gives them naturalistic dialogue. The fates that befall these characters are shown to derive almost entirely from their own psychological flaws, rather than the predictions of the oracle at Delphi or some family curse. Such conventional superstitions may be voiced by the chorus, but as Euripides developed artistically, the chorus became less and less significant in his plays. His characters correspondingly stand more and more centre stage, and embody the concerns of his own time, rather than the values of a long-past heroic age.

Euripides often uses his characters to illustrate extreme psychological conditions, and the weakness of reason. The *Bacchae*, for example, deals with an orgiastic nature religion and portrays the murder of Pentheus by a group of women, including his own mother. In *Medea*, the heroine, about to murder her own children, recognizes both the horror of what she is about to do and the compulsion that forces her to act: 'My passions are stronger than my counsels,' she declares. Euripides seems to be reflecting, in his concern with the dark and irrational side of human nature, and in his innovative depiction of neurosis and insanity, something of the loss of self-confidence in the Athens of the late 5th century BC, at the time of the long drawn out Peloponnesian War.

458 BC

EUROPE
– Lucius Quinctius Cincinnatus, a Roman general, is summoned from his farm to defend the city of Rome from the invading Aequians. Within 16 days, according to tradition, Cincinnatus is named dictator of Rome, summons his forces, defeats the Aequians, resigns the dictatorship and returns to his farm. The tale becomes one of the founding myths of Roman 'virtue'.

457–445 BC

EUROPE
– In Greece the First Peloponnesian War, between Athens and Sparta, leaves Sparta dominant in the Peloponnese.

457 BC

ARTS AND HUMANITIES
– Athenian statesman Pericles sets about his self-appointed task of making Athens pre-eminent in public architecture and the arts. Although Athens is effectively democratic, slaves constitute 25–35% of the *polis* or city-state's population.

456 BC

ARTS AND HUMANITIES

– Death of Greek playwright Aeschylus, author of the tragic trilogy the *Oresteia* (*Agamemnon*, *The Libation Bearers* and *The Eumenides*).

c.455 BC

SCIENCE AND TECHNOLOGY

– In Athens Greek philosopher Anaxagoras teaches a dualistic and atomistic theory of the world's structure. Anaxagoras maintains that atoms are the ultimate constituents of all objects and that these particles contain a mixture of qualities.

450 BC

ECONOMY AND SOCIETY

– The temple of Theseus, a legendary Athenian king, is built in Athens.

c.450 BC

EUROPE

– By now the Indo-European peoples known as the Celts have migrated from C Europe and crossed the English Channel.

ECONOMY AND SOCIETY

– By now in the Sayan Mts in C Asia, the reindeer is becoming domesticated.

447 BC

ARTS AND HUMANITIES

– Work begins on the Parthenon temple on the Acropolis at Athens.

c.446 BC

ARTS AND HUMANITIES

– The Greek lyric poet Pindar dies aged 80. His great Pindaric odes celebrate the athletic victories at Olympia.

c.440 BC

ARTS AND HUMANITIES

– *Antigone* by Greek playwright Sophocles describes how the heroine defies Creon, king of Thebes, by insisting on traditional burial rites for her brother. Although the observance of tradition supplies the motif, *Antigone* becomes a key statement about the individual's right to oppose a ruler's despotic authority in the name of conscience.

438 BC

ARTS AND HUMANITIES

– In Athens the Parthenon is completed and consecrated. This temple to Athena, goddess of Athens in her role as *parthenos* (virgin), is to be hailed by modern writers as the finest Doric temple of the ancient world, although the Greeks of the later Hellenistic period did not include it in their list of the Seven Wonders of the World.

c.435 BC

ARTS AND HUMANITIES

– Phidias, an Athenian sculptor, completes at Elis his gold and ivory statue of Zeus, which is installed at Olympia.

433 BC

EUROPE

– Pericles leads Athens into an alliance with Corcyra (Corfu), the enemy of Corinth. Corinth appeals for help to Sparta, whose food supply from Sicily is itself threatened by the alliance concluded between Athens and the states of Rhegium and Leontini. Aegina is heavily taxed by the Athenians and wants independence, while Megara's economy also suffers because of Pericles' economic sanctions: the two states support the Corinthian appeal to Sparta.

Herodotus (*c.*484–*c.*425 BC)

The Greek writer Herodotus, who established history as a discipline, was born in the Greek city of Halicarnassus in Asia Minor. His originality lay in his questioning and testing of historical sources in a systematic way. His *History* (in Greek *historie*, literally meaning 'enquiry') is the first great historical narrative, and seeks to explain why the Greeks and the Persians were at war in the early 5th century.

In trying to establish the origins of the Graeco-Persian War, Herodotus looked beyond the immediate disputes and searched for a long-term cause. He used evidence drawn from geography and myths, recorded the social customs and traditions of different societies, and looked at why different countries behaved as they did. In particular, he drew a sharp contrast between the city-state culture of the Greek world and the monarchical culture of the Middle East. Western suspicion of the Orient as the natural home of the secretive courtier and the cruel tyrant owes much to Herodotus.

Herodotus travelled widely in North Africa, Mesopotamia, Egypt, the Black Sea and the Crimea. He gathered information everywhere by questioning the locals and by listening attentively to their stories – tales that he found valuable historically because they summed up the popular folk consciousness. Herodotus' enquiries, a pioneering blend of anthropology and history, amounted to a whole new way of looking at human society. In particular, he introduced to historical thought the question of why some civilizations rise while others fall. It was not for nothing that Cicero called Herodotus 'the father of history'.

431 BC

EUROPE

– The Athenian empire enters the Second Peloponnesian War against Sparta, which lasts until 404 BC. Potidaea in Chalcidice makes the first move by revolting against Athenian dominance, and Athens blockades the rebels. Sparta declares war on Athens; Corfu declares war on Corinth. Spartan forces move into Attica and destroy the countryside around Athens. The war among the Greeks is fought between the democratic sea-power Athens and the militaristic kingdom of Sparta. But Sparta also uses a form of anti-imperialist language in the campaign against Athens. Athenian leader Pericles protects Athenian grain imports by building the Long Walls linking the city with its port, Piraeus.

ARTS AND HUMANITIES

– Greek dramatist Euripides (see p. 21) wins the Athenian dramatic competition. Sceptical of conventional views about the gods and unnerving in his descriptions of the irrational, Euripides has become a controversial and subversive figure in Athenian intellectual life. His *Medea* breaks new ground in its depiction of a savage act of retaliation when the wife of the unfaithful Jason kills her children and her husband's mistress.

430 BC

EUROPE

– In the Second Peloponnesian War (see 431 BC) Potidaea surrenders to Athens. But plague has broken out in Athens in the form of a scarlet fever, possibly originating from Ethiopia. The Spartans kill all Athenian captives lest they catch the disease.

SCIENCE AND TECHNOLOGY

– Greek philosopher Hippocrates teaches in plague-stricken Athens that disease is not a punishment from the gods but has rational origins. He experiments using dissection and vivisection on animals and learns to treat the body as a single organism. He is now seen as the father of modern medicine, and the Hippocratic oath for all doctors is named after him.

– Death of Empedocles, a Greek philosopher who has postulated that the world is composed of four elements: earth, air, fire and water.

c.430 BC

ARTS AND HUMANITIES

– Greek scholar Herodotus (see p. 22) is writing a *History* (or 'enquiry'), his view of the Graeco-Persian conflict of 490–479 BC. He mixes straightforward historical narrative with anthropology and geography in his descriptions of the E Mediterranean, writing with an originality that earns him the title of 'father of history'. In observing the fact of different customs and varieties of systems of belief, Herodotus also contributes to the Athenian philosophical debate about the relationship between objectivity and relativity.

c.430–c.420 BC

ARTS AND HUMANITIES

Sophocles, *The Maidens of Trachi*, tragedy.

429 BC

EUROPE

– In the Second Peloponnesian War (see 431 BC), Athenian general Phormion leads the Athenian navy to victory over Sparta at Chalcis and Naupactus. But in Athens itself as many as half of the population are dead of the plague, including the Athenian leader Pericles. Thucydides, the historian of the war, observes that the remainder of the population have lost fear and respect for the gods and so civil breakdown follows.

c.429–c.425 BC

ARTS AND HUMANITIES

Sophocles, *Oedipus Rex*, tragedy.

428 BC

EUROPE

June Mitylene, chief city of Lesbos, revolts against rule from Athens.

ARTS AND HUMANITIES

Euripides, *Hippolytus*, play showing the struggle in the soul between sexual desire and asceticism.

427 BC

EUROPE

July As the Second Peloponnesian War (see 431 BC) rages on, Mitylene surrenders and the Athenians exact a terrible revenge on the city's inhabitants. But Athenian ally Plataea surrenders (Aug.); the inhabitants are slaughtered by the Spartans and the city is destroyed.

426 BC

EUROPE

– The Second Peloponnesian War (see 431 BC) takes a new turn when democrats in Corfu rebel and the state switches allegiance from Sparta to Athens. The general Demosthenes and Cleon, politician, soldier, populist and demagogue, revive Athenian self-belief. Demosthenes wants Sicily, Boeotia and the whole of the Peloponnese to be part of an expanded Athens. His invasion of Boeotia fails, but by his great victories at Olpae and Idomene he crushes Peloponnesian and Ambraciot influence on the Ambraciot Gulf (now the Gulf of Larta).

c.426 BC

ARTS AND HUMANITIES

Euripides, *Andromache*, tragedy.

425 BC

EUROPE

– In the Second Peloponnesian War (see 431 BC) Athenian general Demosthenes traps the Spartan fleet at Navarino Bay. Athenian militarism dictates that the Spartan offer of peace talks is refused and that the Spartan ships should not be returned. Athenian statesman and general Cleon leads reinforcements, which overwhelm the trapped Spartans on the island of Sphacteria.

424 BC

EUROPE

– Brasidas, a Spartan general, leads an army through Boeotia and Thessaly to Chalcidice. The city of Amphipolis surrenders. The Athenian naval force led by Thucydides to resist Brasidas has only limited success, as a result of which Athenian general Cleon punishes Thucydides by exiling him for 20 years.

423 BC

EUROPE

April In the Second Peloponnesian War (see 431 BC) the truce of Laches is an attempt by Athens to stop Spartan general Brasidas' advance. But Brasidas advances on Athens with the aim of freeing the Spartan prisoners of war seized at Sphacteria.

ARTS AND HUMANITIES

Aristophanes, *The Clouds*, comedy.

422 BC

EUROPE

– As the Second Peloponnesian War (see 431 BC) drags on indecisively, Athenian and Spartan generals Cleon and Brasidas are killed in battle as they confront each other near Amphipolis.

421 BC

EUROPE

11 April The peace of Nicias is a brief pause in the Second Peloponnesian War (see 431 BC). Alcibiades, Pericles' nephew, builds up a new anti-Spartan alliance between Athens and the states of Argos, Elis and Mantineia. Meanwhile, the states of Corinth and Boeotia will not support the peace and maintain their support for Sparta.

ARTS AND HUMANITIES

Aristophanes, *The Peace*, comedy, reflecting the politics of the year of the peace of Nicias.

c.420–c.413 BC

ARTS AND HUMANITIES

Sophocles, *Electra*, tragedy.

419 BC

EUROPE

– In the Second Peloponnesian War (see 431 BC), King Agis of Sparta leads his forces against Argos and in the battle of Mantineia (Aug. 418 BC) wins a decisive victory. Alcibiades persuades the Athenians to follow a new strategy: the defeat and crushing of Syracuse in Sicily and of Carthage.

415 BC

EUROPE

22 May In the Second Peloponnesian War (see 431 BC), as the Athenian army prepares to sail for Sicily, the sacred Herms (phallic sculptures) in Athens are secretly mutilated. Alcibiades is accused of the crime and of violating the Eleusinian Mysteries, a secret religious ceremony. He arrives in Sicily but is then ordered back to face trial. He escapes to Sparta, is condemned to death in Athens in his absence and defects to the Spartans.

ARTS AND HUMANITIES

Euripedes, *The Trojan Women*, tragedy dealing with the massacre by the Athenians of the male population of Melos, a state that tried to remain neutral during the war.

414 BC

EUROPE

April Athenian forces advance on Syracuse, Sicily, but Lamachus, the Athenian commander, is killed and the fleet is defeated. Gylippus, the commander of the Spartans, arrives to help the Syracusans. The Athenians send a second force under the leadership of Demosthenes.

ARTS AND HUMANITIES

Aristophanes, *The Birds*, comedy.

413 BC

EUROPE

July Athenian general Demosthenes arrives at Syracuse but fails in a night attack to storm the Syracusan defences; his army suffers heavy losses, and he advises withdrawal from the siege. His fellow general Nicias delays the evacuation, and the Athenian fleet is destroyed by the Syracusans (Sept.). Demosthenes and Nicias are captured and executed. The Athenian survivors of the massacre are sent as slaves to the quarries of Syracuse, where most of them eventually die.

412 BC

EUROPE

– Exiled Athenian general Alcibiades (see 415 BC) wearies his Spartan hosts, quarrels with King Agis and departs. He is recalled to command the Athenian fleet after a revolution in Athens (411 BC). The oligarchs Antiphon, Peisander and Phrynichus mount a coup against the democratic institutions

(July), intending to negotiate with Sparta. But a counter-coup establishes the Constitution of the Five Thousand and the Second Peloponnesian War (see 431 BC) continues.

411 BC

ARTS AND HUMANITIES

Aristophanes, *Lysistrata*, comedy satirizing Athenian life, in which the women win their anti-war campaign by denying sexual relations to their husbands.

410 BC

EUROPE

Mar. Athenian general Alcibiades gains a decisive victory over the Spartan fleet and its Persian allies at Cyzicus in the Sea of Marmara.

ARTS AND HUMANITIES

Timotheus of Miletus, *Persae* (The Persians), tragedy, a 4th-century BC copy of which is the earliest surviving papyrus written in Greek.

409 BC

EUROPE

– Athenian general Alcibiades goes on to conquer Byzantium (later Constantinople and now Istanbul) for Athens, securing the land route for the grain supply to Athens from the Black (Euxine) Sea.

ARTS AND HUMANITIES

Sophocles, *Philoctetes*, tragedy, showing the continuing power of the Trojan wars as a parable for war-time Athens.

408 BC

EUROPE

16 June Alcibiades returns to Athens in triumph. Democratic institutions have been restored in the city. He is appointed general with autocratic powers and then returns to Samos to command the fleet. Lysander, the Spartan commander, aided by the Persians, starts to build up a great fleet at Ephesus.

407 BC

EUROPE

– Antiochus, Alcibiades' deputy, disobeys instructions by provoking the Spartans under Lysander, who then defeats the Athenian fleet at Notium. Alcibiades is relieved of command.

407–406 BC

ARTS AND HUMANITIES

– During this winter Greek playwright Euripides (see p. 21) dies at the age of 77. He has, however, finished *The Bacchae*, the last great Greek tragedy and one that shows the force of the savage and irrational in human affairs.

406 BC

EUROPE

– The Second Peloponnesian War (see 431 BC) continues to go awry for the Athenians, and after a further Spartan naval victory, Athenian general Alcibiades escapes to the Hellespont (Dardanelles), disgraced. The Athenians gain a naval victory at Arginusae. Sparta offers peace, which Athenian ruler Cleophon rejects. Lysander takes charge of a Spartan fleet in the Hellespont.

ARTS AND HUMANITIES

– Greek playwright Sophocles dies at the age of 90.

405 BC

EUROPE

– The Athenian fleet pursuing Lysander's Spartan fleet suffers a catastrophic defeat at Aegospotami in the Hellespont, effectively breaking Athenian naval power. Pausanius, the Spartan king, lays siege to Athens: Lysander's fleet blockades the port of Piraeus. Cleophon is tried and executed in 404 BC as a scapegoat for the disaster.

ARTS AND HUMANITIES

– The Erectheum, built in the Ionian style, is completed on the Acropolis of Athens. The female figures portrayed as holding up the roof with raised arms are called caryatids (because modelled on women from the town of Caryae) and become a much-imitated architectural device.

404 BC

EUROPE

25 April Under siege by Spartan forces, the Athenians have no choice but submission, which ends the Peloponnesian Wars. To the sound of triumphalist Spartan lutes, the city walls of Athens, emblems of Athenian pride and independence, are torn down and the Athenian empire is dissolved. But Spartan triumph proves short-lived. Their war has been subsidised by Persian gold, and when the Spartans and Persians go to war (400 BC) Persian subsidies are transferred to Athens and an increasingly powerful Thebes, which will emerge as the real winner of the Peloponnesian Wars.

401 BC

ARTS AND HUMANITIES

– Greek historian Thucydides dies at the age of 60, leaving behind his *History of the Peloponnesian War*, a classic of contemporary history, profound in its psychological grasp of the key actors and ground-breaking in its analysis of historical causation.

– Sophocles, *Oedipus at Colonus*, tragedy. The play wins a posthumous prize for its author when performed at the Festival of Dionysus.

THE CLASSICAL WORLD:
Polis and Republic in Greece and Rome

The culture of classical Greece, which reached its pinnacle in the 5th century BC, had a profound effect on Western civilization, an effect that has lasted to the present day. Concepts such as democracy, philosophy and history originated in Greece, along with styles of art and architecture that remain with us.

Agricultural land in Greece exists in small pockets divided by mountain ranges. As a result, the key Greek political institution was the *polis* or city-state – a city with its surrounding farmland. Each *polis* was proudly independent. Among the more important of the 70 or so *poleis* were the militaristic Sparta, the democratic Athens and the proverbially wealthy Corinth.

The defining event in Greek history was the victory, in the wars of 490 and 480 BC, of the Greeks over the vastly larger and wealthier Persian empire. Thereafter, with a new self-confidence, they poured money into building temples, markets and public buildings. It was these that established the symmetry of proportion and naturalistic style of sculpture that we now recognize as classical.

Aristotle, in summing up the Greeks' concept of themselves, wrote: 'The Hellenic people, situated between Europe and Asia, are likewise intermediate in character.' He believed the Greeks were uniquely equipped for freedom, and that even their language was happily attuned to express precise distinctions and abstract ideas. Politically, the Athenians drew the lesson from the Persian wars that Eastern kings were effete, while their own democratic institutions were morally and materially superior. Their democracy involved debate and openness, whether informally in the *agora* (marketplace) and the *gymnasium* (school) or formally in the assembly. It was an honour – not a constraint – for a citizen to be called to serve the *polis*. The victories won by Athens were the achievements of a citizen army and a citizen navy.

Those Greeks who chafed at Athenian arrogance found a champion in Sparta. The 27-year conflict between these states, the Peloponnesian War, ultimately sapped the strength of all Greece. Classical Greece ended in conquest by a kingdom on the northern fringes of the Greek world: Macedon. Under powerful Macedonian rulers like Alexander the Great, Greek culture would be spread far across the Mediterranean and Middle East. But the fountainhead of Greek thought – the proud and independent *polis* – died with the classical era.

Meanwhile, in about 510 BC, a modest city in central Italy threw off the rule of Etruscan kings and formed its own alternative type of government, a republic. The Roman state was dominated by war and law. Each year the citizens elected two consuls, who were the most senior officials of state with specific control over military affairs. Lesser officials adjudicated in legal conflicts or organized public works, religious festivals and other state duties. All Roman citizens had a vote in these elections, but they were divided into three classes on the basis of birth and wealth. The patricians were a small elite group of families who alone were eligible to stand for election to certain positions. The *equites* were those non-patricians wealthy enough to pay high taxes and devote their lives to the unpaid duties of state. The vast mass of citizens were plebeians, who had fewer rights but were still considerably more privileged than the peoples conquered by Rome. As in Athens, slavery was an unquestioned legal right and social fact.

By around 290 BC most of Italy was allied to or subject to Rome. A long drawn-out struggle with the greatest power of the western Mediterranean, the North African city of Carthage, followed. By 146 BC the Romans had defeated Carthage, and had conquered much of Greece and southern Gaul (France) to boot. These wars changed Rome dramatically. No longer just an agrarian state, it was the centre of a vast empire. Perversely, success brought ruin to many Roman citizens. Small peasant holdings were no longer viable, as cheap food imports and the output of large estates run by slaves dominated the markets. Increasingly, the mass of Roman citizens lived in Rome itself, and the fact that many were unemployed made them willing to sell their votes in return for food, money or entertainment. Before long, successful generals were using troops to bully their way into office.

Concepts such as democracy, philosophy and history originated in Greece.

Bloodshed became common in Roman politics, until Julius Caesar established a populist, reforming dictatorship. Caesar was murdered in 44 BC, and power was seized by his nephew Octavian. Octavian (Augustus) described himself as 'restoring the republic', giving power back to elected officials while ousting those who abused their positions. But he also used his own wealth and power to ensure that only his own candidates could win elections. In this way he instituted a dictatorship behind a façade of democracy. Augustus handed on to his successors a Rome that had became an empire, ruled by an emperor. Republican democracy had perished.

Socrates (c.469–399 BC)

The teaching of the Greek philosopher Socrates is known only through the writings of his admiring pupil Plato. He appears in the Platonic dialogues as the ironic inquisitor who exposes false assumptions and illusions through his critical analysis of his interlocutor's opinions.

At the age of 70 Socrates was sentenced to death for 'corrupting the youth and introducing strange gods'. His exposure of hypocrisy and dishonesty among the leading citizens of Athens had made him deeply unpopular, and he was a useful scape goat after the Athenian defeat in the Peloponnesian War. Socrates believed that his contemporaries pursued goals in life without knowing whether those goals were important or not, and at his trial said, 'The unexamined life is not worth living.' This attitude established the Western idea that the aim of philosophy is to question accepted views. While engaged in his diagnostic process, Socrates made the important claim that he, unlike others, at least knew that he did not know. This, he thought, put him several steps ahead of conventional opinion, which was not only lazy but also sometimes vicious. Socrates asserted that truth was both discoverable and objective. It was truth that supplied the measure of knowledge, and not the subjective attitudes of human beings.

Socrates' method laid the foundations of logic as a branch of philosophy, and his emphasis on ethics drew the focus of Greek philosophy away from its earlier speculations about the nature of the physical world. His influence on Western culture has been that of a rationalist, but he also had a mystical side, for he maintained that he was protected by a personal guardian spirit that spoke directly to him.

401–399 BC

MIDDLE EAST AND NORTH AFRICA

– At the battle of Cunaxa (fought N of Babylon in 401 BC) Persia's ruler Artaxerxes II defeats and kills his brother Cyrus the Younger, who has led a rebellion against him. Among the commanders of the Greek mercenaries in the rebel army is Xenophon, whose *Anabasis* describes how he led his 10,000 men back to the Black Sea.

c.400 BC

ASIA

– In China the Jin state has begun to disintegrate.

THE AMERICAS

– In Mesoamerica the Olmec civilization has begun to decline.

399 BC

EUROPE

– Greek philosopher Socrates (see box) is condemned to death by the nervous and intolerant Athenian authorities for allegedly corrupting Athenian youth with his questioning of conventional ideas. He drinks the poison hemlock.

396 BC

EUROPE

– The Romans take the first step on the road to empire, conquering the Etruscan city of Veii after a ten-year siege.

392 BC

ARTS AND HUMANITIES

Aristophanes, *Ecclesiazusae* (Parliament of Women), comedy.

Plato (c.429–347 BC)

The Greek philosopher Plato was a pupil of Socrates, and was in turn the teacher of Aristotle, the third great philosopher of ancient Greece. Central to Plato's philosophical approach is his concept of ideas (called Forms), immaterial but very real entities that embody the highest reality; objects in the real world are merely imperfect shadows of these Forms. Thus a table is but an imperfect copy of the idea of 'table-ness', while the supreme entity is the 'idea of the good'.

The execution of Socrates in 399 BC led Plato to the view that society would never be well governed until philosophers were rulers, or rulers were philosophers. He established the Academy (c.387 BC) in order to attempt to educate such a class of rulers. The literary form that Plato perfected, the dialogue, demonstrates how truth is arrived at through a process of dialectic. His masterpiece in this form, the *Republic*, is a blend of metaphysics, ethics and political thought achieved with a literary grace never since equalled in philosophy.

Plato hated democracy because it indulged conflicting views rather than pursuing objective truth. Rhetoric was for him the opposite of philosophy: he despised the sophists of Athens who, for a fee, taught aspiring democratic politicians how to construct arguments without regard for their truth. Plato was also disturbed by the power of art to arouse passionate emotions, so disrupting his goal of the contemplative, ordered and rational self. He famously, therefore, advocated the expulsion of the poets from society.

Debates arising from Plato's assertions have been at the core of much philosophy up to the present, and it has been said that Western philosophy since has been nothing more than a series of footnotes to Plato.

390 BC

EUROPE

– The Cisalpine Gauls, those Celts living S of the Alps, sack Rome. Brennus, leader of the Gauls, responds to Roman complaints about the severity of the peace terms by declaring *Vae victis* (Woe to the conquered).

c.387 BC

ARTS AND HUMANITIES

– Plato (see p. 27) establishes a school, known as the Academy, near Athens. It teaches philosophy and science in accordance with his own principles. In his *Republic* Plato advises the need for rule by philosopher-kings, as a reaction against the demagoguery of Athenian democratic politics. The idea of a platonic order of perfectly objective timeless truth, of which the earthly representatives are mere shadows, will have a deep influence on subsequent European thought, especially Christianity.

367 BC

SCIENCE AND TECHNOLOGY

– Greek philosopher Aristotle (see box) becomes a student at Plato's Academy in Athens.

364–321 BC

ASIA

– Under the Nanda dynasty, the Hindu kingdom of Magadha comes to dominate the Ganges plain in the N of the Indian subcontinent.

359 BC

EUROPE

– Philip II becomes king of Macedon and embarks on an expansionist programme.

356 BC

ARTS AND HUMANITIES

– A disturbed Greek named Herostratus burns down the temple of Artemis at Ephesus. It is later argued that the goddess had been absent from her temple at the time in order to attend the birth of Alexander the Great (see p. 29), king of Macedon, which occurred that same night. The temple will be rebuilt on a magnificent scale.

354 BC

ARTS AND HUMANITIES

– In Halicarnassus in Asia Minor a tomb is built for Mausolus, Persian satrap of Caria, and its splendour gains for it – and its patron – a new word: mausoleum.

c.350 BC

ASIA

– The militarized Qin state becomes dominant in China.

THE AMERICAS

– In Mesoamerica the earliest Maya city-states, including Tikal (Guatemala), begin to appear.

SCIENCE AND TECHNOLOGY

– The crossbow is invented in China.

Aristotle (384–322 BC)

The Greek philosopher Aristotle was born in Chalcidice, the son of a court physician of King Amyntas II of Macedon. As a young man Aristotle moved to Athens, where he was taught by Plato, before returning home to become tutor of the future Alexander the Great. He then returned to Athens, where he established his own school of philosophy, the Lyceum. The fragmentary nature of his surviving work – mostly based on lecture notes – made it open to later interpretation. Medieval thinkers tended to take his word as writ, so ignoring Aristotle's own emphasis on empirical investigation (which was also at odds with Plato's method).

Aristotle was interested in how human beings, institutions, societies and ways of thinking actually operate. He thought that each human activity and specialist area of knowledge was organized around a particular principle. His biological studies led him to an interest in evolution. Growth meant change from acorn to tree and from child to adult, but it was also the gradual unfolding of a quality that subsisted throughout the process, so that there was continuity as well as novelty. He was the first Western thinker to argue that there was a metaphorical as well as a literal truth. Unlike Plato, he accepted that different disciplines vary in precision and can exist side by side without impugning each other's authority.

Aristotle travelled widely in the eastern Aegean and throughout mainland Greece, and he was impressed by the variety of human tastes, manners and institutions he encountered. He was a great classifier, categorizing states according to their systems of values, dissecting plants and animals, and regarding history as a kind of comparative anthropology. He was also the first literary critic of the West, defining the distinctive effect of tragedy as a balance between pity and fear. Without his influence, logic, metaphysics, theology, history, political science, aesthetics, biology, zoology and botany would all have been very different.

343–341 BC

EUROPE

– In the First Samnite War Rome defeats the Samnites, a people of C Italy, winning control of Campania.

342 BC

SCIENCE AND TECHNOLOGY

– Greek philosopher Aristotle (see box) becomes tutor to the son of Philip II of Macedon, the future Alexander the Great.

340 BC

EUROPE

– Philip II of Macedon fails to capture Byzantium (later Constantinople and now Istanbul) because the sentries have seen his army advance by the light of the crescent moon. The Byzantines show their gratitude by adopting the crescent symbol of the goddess Hecate as their own iconographic symbol.

– Alarmed by the expansionist policies of Philip II of Macedon, the Athenians set up the Hellenic League as an anti-Macedonian alliance.

338 BC

EUROPE

2 Aug. At the battle of Chaeronea in W Boeotia the Athenians and the Thebans are defeated by Philip II of Macedon, ending Greek resistance to Macedonian domination. All the major Greek states except Sparta are forced to join the Macedonian-controlled Corinthian League. Philip II of Macedon prepares to invade Persia.

336 BC

EUROPE

– Philip II of Macedon is assassinated at a wedding feast, probably at the instigation of his wife Olympias. Their son succeeds as Alexander III of Macedon (see box), taking command of his father's anti-Persian expedition.

335 BC

SCIENCE AND TECHNOLOGY

– Aristotle (see p. 28) returns to Athens and opens the Lyceum (which contains a natural history museum, a library and a zoological garden) in a gymnasium dedicated to Apollo Lyceus, the god of shepherds. This is the setting for his scientific and philosophical work. In science he describes animal anatomy and evolution in a comparative system, which starts with the facts available and then builds up a general theory. The same spirit animates his accounts of political systems and ethics.

Alexander the Great (356–323 BC)

Alexander III of Macedon has been hailed as a military and cultural genius who revolutionized the Western world. He succeeded to the throne of Macedon on the assassination of his father Philip in 336 BC – an event in which he (or his mother) may have been complicit. He continued the imperial policy that had established Macedonian domination of Greece, and his campaign against Persia laid the foundations of an Asian–European empire that stretched from Greece to Egypt to the edge of the Eurasian steppes and as far as the Indus valley.

Cultural mingling followed in the wake of Alexander's armies. Greek-style cities were established, and Alexander encouraged his men to marry into the local population. As a consequence, Greek became the language of the ambitious local elites during his reign and for long afterwards. But Alexander also imported ideas of oriental autocracy into the Greek mainland. In 331 BC he imposed the cult of Alexander as god on all Greek cities.

Alexander considered his life to be a revival of the Homeric warrior tradition, and presented himself as the adopted son of Zeus-Ammon, a culturally mixed Graeco-Egyptian-Libyan deity. His ability to come up with inspired symbolic gestures was entirely Homeric. Thus in 330 BC, when Darius III, king of Persia, was killed while fleeing from Alexander's forces, Alexander halted his advance to bury the Persian king himself, making the point that henceforth his campaigns were personal affairs of honour rather than the traditional Greek war against the barbarian. Alexander, by then fat and drinking heavily, died of a fever in Babylon while leading his complaining men back to Macedon. They had refused to advance further. But he had created a myth that would inspire later empire-builders, from Augustus to Hitler.

334 BC

MIDDLE EAST AND NORTH AFRICA

– Alexander III (the Great) of Macedon crosses the Dardanelles to invade the Persian empire. He defeats the Persian army at the battle of Issus in Cilicia (Oct. 333 BC). Persian king Darius III, however, escapes.

332 BC

MIDDLE EAST AND NORTH AFRICA

– Alexander III (the Great) of Macedon conquers Egypt and founds the city of Alexandria on the coast.

331 BC

MIDDLE EAST AND NORTH AFRICA

1 Oct. In a massive victory, Alexander III's army defeats the Persians at the battle of Gaugamela (on the Tigris in Upper

Mesopotamia). Darius III escapes again, but is murdered by the satrap (provincial governor) Bessus (330 BC). Alexander sacks the Persian capital, Persepolis, looting it of its treasures.

c.330 BC

SCIENCE AND TECHNOLOGY
– Greek philosopher Democritus further develops the atomic theory of matter. He teaches a version of determinism, maintaining that nothing happens by chance. Change is a reconstitution of the component particles and atoms are unbreakable and non-divisible.

329 BC

ASIA
– Alexander III (the Great) of Macedon (see p. 29) conquers Samarkand, capital of Sogdiana, in C Asia.

326 BC

EUROPE
– A second war breaks out between Rome and the Samnites.

ASIA
– Alexander III (the Great) of Macedon invades N India. His army, tired of fighting, persuades him to go no further and not to invade the Ganges valley. Alexander appoints Nearchus as his admiral, and Indian shipwrights build some 800 ships to transport his troops. Indian pilots are used to guide the ships through the Persian Gulf to Babylonia (325).

325 BC

SCIENCE AND TECHNOLOGY
– Alexander III's admiral, Nearchus, produces the first written reference to sugar cane when he describes 'honey-producing' Indian reeds. The Sanskrit word *sarkara* is adapted into the Arabic *sukhar*.

324 BC

ARTS AND HUMANITIES
– Menander introduces the 'New Comedy' to the Greek theatre, giving it a new, naturalistic turn. Where Aristophanes had been satirical and scabrous, Menander concentrates on the day-to-day domesticity of Athenian life.

323 BC

MIDDLE EAST AND NORTH AFRICA
– Alexander III (the Great) of Macedon dies in Babylon at the age of 33. The War of the Diadochoi (Successors) follows. For the next 42 years his generals, Antigonus, Antipater, Seleucus, Ptolemy, Eumenes and Lysimachus, will contest his imperial legacy.

ARTS AND HUMANITIES
– Following the death of Alexander III, the general Ptolemy seizes power in Egypt.

321 BC

EUROPE
– The Samnites defeat the Romans at the battle of the Caudine Forks. Roman prisoners are forced to bow under a yoke to humiliate them.

ASIA
– In the Indian subcontinent the Hindu state of Maghada is taken over by Chandragupta Maurya, founding the Mauryan empire.

319 BC

MIDDLE EAST AND NORTH AFRICA
– Alexander III's general Antipater dies. He names as his successor the elderly general Polysperchon. But Antipater's son, Cassander, challenges the succession, and the dissolution of Alexander's conquests accelerates.

317 BC

MIDDLE EAST AND NORTH AFRICA
– During the confusion after Alexander III's death, Ardvates, the Persian satrap of Armenia, makes himself an independent king. Other, only nominally conquered, Persian satraps follow suit.

316 BC

EUROPE
– In Macedon Cassander overthrows Polysperchon and kills Olympias, Alexander III's mother. He marries Thessalonice, Alexander's half-sister, who becomes his co-ruler. Eumenes and Antigonus, Cassander's rivals and former generals of Alexander, fight in battle at Media. Antigonus wins and Eumenes, captured, is then killed.

315 BC

EUROPE
– Macedonian ruler Cassander establishes the Macedonian city of Thessalonica, named in honour of his wife, the daughter of Philip II.

314 BC

EUROPE
– Macedonian general Antigonus (known as Monophthalmus, or One-eyed), battling against Cassander for supremacy, promises freedom to the Greek cities as a tactical ploy to gain their support. He wins over the Aetolians, and Cassander marches against them.

312 BC

EUROPE
- The Roman politician Appius Claudius Caecus starts to build the Appian Way, connecting Rome and Capua (N of Naples).

MIDDLE EAST AND NORTH AFRICA
- In the crumbling empire of Alexander III (the Great) of Macedon Antigonus is defeated by Cassander's allies, Seleucus and Ptolemy, at the battle of Gaza. He is captured but released.
- Seleucus, another of Alexander III's generals, establishes the Seleucid empire, which will rule Syria and Babylonia until 64 BC. He calls himself Nicator (the Conqueror) and is bent on extending his empire to the Indus valley. Ptolemy, for his part, takes the name Soter (Saviour) and rules Egypt until 285 BC.

310 BC

EUROPE
- Macedonian ruler Cassander imprisons and then murders Roxana, widow of Alexander III, and her son Alexander IV. Any realistic hope of rebuilding Alexander's empire is now lost.

308 BC

EUROPE
- Ptolemy, ruler of Egypt, is defeated at sea, off the coast of Cyprus, by Demetrius Poliorcetes (the Besieger), son of Antigonus Monophthalmus, who then (307 BC) lays siege to Rhodes. Despite employing thousands of men and sophisticated siege towers, he is unsuccessful. In honour of the victory, the Rhodians wiu build a gigantic statue of their patron god, Helios the sun god; it becomes known as the Colossus of Rhodes.

304 BC

EUROPE
- The Second Samnite War (see 326 BC) ends in Roman victory. Rome makes further territorial gains in the Italian peninsula.

301 BC

MIDDLE EAST AND NORTH AFRICA
- The 81-year-old general Antigonus, who has ruled Anatolia since Alexander III's death, is defeated by Seleucus and Lysimachus at Ipsus in Phrygia. Antigonus, the only general aspiring to rebuild Alexander's empire, is killed, and Demetrius, his son, flees to Ephesus.

c.300 BC

ASIA
- Turko-Mongol peoples are now adopting horse-based nomadism.

SCIENCE AND TECHNOLOGY
- Coal technology is advancing in Greece. The philosopher Theophrastus, in his work *On Stones*, describes how coals found in Liguria and Elis are used by smiths to burn like charcoal.

- Greek mathematician Euclid compiles his *Elements*, a description of the principles of geometry.
- Indian sugar is introduced to the Middle East.

ARTS AND HUMANITIES
- Athenian philosopher Epicurus argues that the aim of morality is pleasure. Although it is used subsequently to justify self-indulgence, Epicurus's philosophic account of pleasure extols honour, prudence and justice.
- Greek philosopher Zeno of Citium (see p. 33) opens his Stoic school of philosophy.
- Ptolemy establishes the Museum (Mouseion) of Alexandria. One hundred professors are state-paid and work at the Museum, which houses a library. Like Alexander III, Ptolemy has studied under Aristotle (see p. 28).

298 BC

EUROPE
- A third war breaks out between Rome and the Samnites, who have formed a formidable coalition with the Etruscans, Umbrians and Gauls.

295 BC

EUROPE
- Rome decisively defeats the Samnites and their allies at the battle of Sentinum.

c.293 BC

ASIA
- Chandragupta, ruler of the Mauryan empire (see 321 BC), abdicates in favour of his son, Bindusara, who goes on to conquer S India by 268 BC.

290 BC

EUROPE
- Rome completes the conquest of the Samnites, ending the Third Samnite War (see 298 BC). Rome now controls virtually all of the Italian peninsula.

289 BC

ASIA
- The Chinese philosopher and ruler Mencius (Mengzi) dies. He has refined Confucianism, stressing the duty of rulers to protect the ruled and the innate goodness of humanity.

285 BC

MIDDLE EAST AND NORTH AFRICA
- Ptolemy Soter, ruler of Egypt, adopts his son Ptolemy II Philadelphus as co-ruler. Ptolemy II becomes sole ruler on his father's death in 282 BC.

BUREAUCRACY AND INTELLIGENCE:
The Rise of China

There have been a number of common themes throughout the 4000 years of Chinese history: the threat from the northern tribes, the assertion of central control interrupted by periods of division, the vitality of a peasantry readily given to rebellion. There has also been a characteristic dream of Chinese unity that is both practical and yet based on an ideal of harmony between humankind and the natural environment.

According to legend, the first dynasty of China was the Xia (Hsia), established by about 2000 BC. Irrigation of the valley of the Huanghe (Hwang-ho or Yellow River), whose middle reaches comprised the supposed Xia state, enabled large-scale cultivation to begin. By the time of the Shang dynasty in the latter half of the 2nd millennium BC, Chinese civilization was acquiring stability and distinctiveness, and from this period dates the invention of Chinese hieroglyphic writing, which was to be the key to later bureaucracy. With stability there came expansion. Pioneers reached and passed the Huaihe (Hwai-ho) in the south. In the east they settled in the Shandong (Shantung) area. And in the west they were travelling up the banks of the Wei.

With this success came also divisions, as local rulers quarrelled with an often distant central authority and with each other. In the succeeding Zhou (Chou) epoch this disunity was exacerbated as barbarians in the northwest and the Han tribesmen of the Yangtze valley – who were culturally half-Chinese – pressed hard on the settled principalities. In 771 BC the capital city of Hao was destroyed and the Zhou imperial family fled to Luoyang, which then became, in theory, the capital and centre of China for half a millennium, until 249 BC. In reality, China broke up into warring principalities. At the beginning of the 6th century BC the kingdom of Wu, formed to the south of the mouth of the Yangtze, irrupted on to the scene, becoming another powerful element in the general chaos of the epoch known as the Warring States period.

But during this turbulent time there were also developments that shaped the future of China. As Chinese culture drove south it came across land where rice could be grown, a crop that could support the growing population. A silk industry was established, which in time came to be not only a source of luxury goods but also a tool in politics and diplomacy, for gifts of silk helped to seal treaties. This, too, was the age of the philosopher Confucius (c.551–479 BC; see p. 20). China's most famous thinker came from the official class of scribes and administrators who now thronged the courts of the Chinese states. Confucius defined Chinese morality as a question of family loyalty and communal honour. The Chinese religion was a social one, and it had no separate priesthood. Its cults and rituals were aimed at preserving unity between the human and the natural world. In the midst of political anarchy the rulers who aspired to hegemony continued to claim their imperial title, 'Son of Heaven', emphasizing the emperor's unique task of maintaining and establishing harmony.

Harmony, for the rulers in question, meant the subjugation of the other states. In the years 230–223 BC King Zheng of Qin annexed all the other states in modern Honan, Shansi and Hopeh. Two years later the kingdom of Zhou was defeated. Zheng assumed the title of Shi Huangdi, 'First Emperor'. In the north – in order to protect his new empire from the invading nomads of the steppes – he built the earliest sections of China's Great Wall. And he crushed the power of local warlords by dividing China into 36 provinces governed directly by his own officials. Local patriotism and attachment to particular local allegiances were seen as a threat to the unitary state. And so Zheng engaged in massive transfers of the population of China, uprooting his subjects and resettling them. Another form of unity was also imposed, as imperial reforms in the Chinese script gave the country a common form of writing.

> *Chinese unity ... is ... based on an ideal of harmony between humankind and the natural environment.*

Shi Huangdi exemplifies both the dynamism and the regression that would bless and curse the future pattern of Chinese history. His successor Liu Bang inaugurated the Han dynasty (206 BC–AD 220) – a period of imperial stability that allowed Chinese culture and civilization to flourish. Under the Han the rulers collaborated with the scholars and encouraged Confucianism as the basis of the state. It was during this period that the imperial civil service was established, with recruitment via open and competitive examination. The Han dynasty presided over the first great unitary state in China. The principles of government that it established would prove to have an abiding significance for the Chinese through all the dynasties that lay ahead.

284 BC

MIDDLE EAST AND NORTH AFRICA
- Ardvates of Armenia dies, having established an independent dynasty.

281 BC

EUROPE
- Seleucus Nicator, ruler of Syria, invades Macedon but is deceived and murdered by Ptolemy Ceraunus (brother of Ptolemy II), who takes Macedon himself. Seleucus is succeeded by Antiochus I Soter.

MIDDLE EAST AND NORTH AFRICA
- Alexander III (the Great) of Macedon's former generals still fight over the remnants of his empire. Seleucus Nicator, ruler of Syria, defeats and kills Lysimachus at the battle of Corupedion and extends his rule over much of Asia Minor.

ARTS AND HUMANITIES
- Chares of Lindos finishes the Colossus of Rhodes, a bronze statue 35m (120 feet) high of the god Helios (see 308 BC).

280–275 BC

EUROPE
- King Pyrrhus of Epirus invades Italy, but, despite winning victories over the Romans, his losses are unsustainable and he is forced to withdraw.

279–278 BC

EUROPE
- The Celts overrun Thrace and go on to invade Anatolia.

275 BC

SCIENCE AND TECHNOLOGY
- At Alexandria in Egypt the Pharos lighthouse is completed. It is later recognized as one of the Seven Wonders of the World.
- The Library in the Museum of Alexandria is effectively the senior research university of the Greek-speaking world. Its professor of medicine, Herophilus of Chalcedon, conducts post-mortem investigations and his school of anatomy produces descriptions of the alimentary canal, eye, spleen, liver, genitalia and brain tissues. Erasistratus gives names to the heart valves and establishes the connection between arteries and veins; he also researches the lymphatic ducts and the mechanisms of the central nervous system.

272 BC

EUROPE
- With the conquest of Tarentum (in SE Italy) the Romans have unified the Italian peninsula.

MIDDLE EAST AND NORTH AFRICA
- Ptolemy II of Egypt defeats the Seleucid king Antiochus I in the First Syrian War and annexes Miletus, Phoenicia and W Cilicia.

c.270 BC

SCIENCE AND TECHNOLOGY
- Greek philosopher Aristarchos of Samos postulates a heliocentric universe (i.e., with the sun at its centre).

268–233 BC

ASIA
- The reign of the Mauryan king Ashoka, who converts to Buddhism (c.260 BC) and introduces the religion to Ceylon (c.250 BC). He also founds India's first hospitals, placing them under Buddhist, rather than Hindu Brahmin, supervision.

c.265 BC

SCIENCE AND TECHNOLOGY
- Greek inventor and mathematician Archimedes begins a long and productive career. Among other things, he observes that a body dropped in liquid will displace an amount of liquid equal to its own volume if it sinks, but to its own weight if it floats.

Zeno of Citium (c.335–c.263 BC)

Zeno was the founder of the philosophical school known as Stoicism. The school took its name from the fact that he taught in the *Stoa Poikile* or Painted Colonnade, which stood off a corner of the marketplace in Athens.

Like other ancient systems of thought, Zeno's philosophy taught the principles of right conduct that would lead to happiness. The Stoics thought that right conduct involved understanding the structure of the universe and the relationship of an individual to that universe. Stoicism became especially popular with the Romans, who liked the practical nature of its recommendations. Understanding that as an individual you were part of a greater order meant that the Stoic philosophy was often a counsel of noble resignation. Being 'philosophical' in this context meant displaying calm in the face of both good fortune and adversity.

In Zeno's ideal world, as outlined in his *Republic*, there would be no institutions and none of the gymnasia and temples of the traditional Greek city-state. His would be a society comprising groups of wise individuals brought together by the understanding that all individuals share a common humanity. Zeno is also believed to have favoured a community of wives whose favours would be shared by his wise men, and to have advocated sexual permissiveness. Stoicism was based on the belief that the whole world is ordered by a divine will. Goodness and happiness lie in conforming to that will. For Stoics, emotion was an acceptable part of a well-run life, but passion was seen as a mental aberration with ill effects.

According to tradition he makes this discovery while getting into a bath and is so excited that he shouts *eureka!* (I have it!) and runs naked down the street to reach his workshop to finalize the discovery. He also devises the screw for raising volumes of water.

264–241 BC

EUROPE

– The First Punic War is fought between Rome and the N African city of Carthage over competition for spheres of influence in Sicily. The Romans know the Carthaginians as Punians because their ancestors came from Phoenicia (see 814 BC). The Romans have to build a navy from virtually nothing but in 260 BC win their first naval battle, under Gaius Duilius Nepos, at Mylae, using quinqueremes based on Carthaginian designs. The Carthaginians are then gradually ground down, losing all of Sicily and leaving Rome as the dominant naval power in the W Mediterranean.

260 BC

ECONOMY AND SOCIETY

– The first gladiatorial contests are held in Rome.

c.256 BC

ASIA

– The last king of China's Zhou (Chou) dynasty is deposed.

246 BC

MIDDLE EAST AND NORTH AFRICA

– Ptolemy II, king of Egypt, dies and is succeeded by his son Ptolemy III (Euergetes).

245 BC

MIDDLE EAST AND NORTH AFRICA

– Ptolemy III of Egypt invades Syria, Babylon and Susa, but in 243 BC a domestic rebellion in Egypt forces him to return.

237 BC

EUROPE

– As the Carthaginians expand into Europe, seeking compensation for the loss of Sicily and Sardinia to Rome, statesman and general Hamilcar Barca leads the Carthaginian army into the Iberian peninsula. He builds up a base for further operations against Rome. In 228 BC Hamilcar dies in battle against the local Celtiberians; his son-in-law Hasdrubal takes command. But in 221 BC Hasdrubal is assassinated, and Hamilcar Barca's son, Hannibal, replaces him.

230–221 BC

ASIA

– King Zheng of Qin unites China, reigning as Shi Huangdi (First Emperor) and establishing the Qin (Chin) dynasty.

222 BC

EUROPE

– The Roman legions move into Mediolanum (Milan) on the strategically crucial plain of Lombardy in N Italy.

221 BC

MIDDLE EAST AND NORTH AFRICA

– Ptolemy III of Egypt dies and is succeeded by his son, Ptolemy IV, who rules with his wife and sister Arsinoe III.

220 BC

EUROPE

– The Flaminian Way linking Rome with Rimini (in N C Italy) is completed.

219 BC

MIDDLE EAST AND NORTH AFRICA

– Antiochus III of Syria starts the Fourth Syrian War by seizing the province of Coelo-Syria from Egypt. In 217 BC, however, Egyptian hoplites (heavy infantry) defeat the Syrian army at Raphia. Notwithstanding this reverse, in 211 BC Antiochus III moves into Armenia, removes its ruler Xerxes and divides the country into two satrapies (provinces).

218 BC

EUROPE

– The Second Punic War breaks out between Rome and Carthage. A Carthaginian army under the young aristocrat Hannibal (see 237 BC) attacks Rome's allies in Spain; it besieges and captures Sagunto. But given Roman naval superiority, Hannibal can carry the war to the Romans only by an immensely difficult land invasion of Italy. He crosses the Alps and defeats one Roman army at the Ticino River and then another at the Trebbia River.

217 BC

EUROPE

24 June The Carthaginians under Hannibal, supported by Gaulish troops, defeat a Roman army led by Gaius Flaminius at the battle of Lake Trasimene (near Perugia).

216 BC

EUROPE

2 Aug. At the battle of Cannae the Carthaginian commander Hannibal wins one of the greatest victories of the ancient world against a Roman army. He lures the Romans forwards, then launches flank attacks to surround them on both sides and to the rear. About 60,000 Romans are killed for the loss of fewer than 7000 Carthaginians. Hannibal's tactics in this battle become a classic of military science and continue to be studied at military academies into the 21st century. Hannibal devastates the fields, depriving Rome of local grain and forcing the city to import stocks of grain, but he lacks the troops to take the city. The Romans seek to avoid battle in Italy, while they invade the Iberian peninsula themselves (210–206 BC). In 207 BC the Carthaginian army led by Hannibal's younger brother Hasdrubal Barca is defeated by a Roman army under the command of the two consuls Claudius Nero and Livius Salinator; Hasdrubal is killed. The Romans then take the battle to N Africa and in 204 BC besiege Carthage itself.

215 BC

EUROPE
– King Philip V of Macedon attempts to support the Carthaginians against Rome but is prevented from landing on the Italian coast by a Roman fleet. Several Greek states side with the Romans (211 BC), and Philip is forced to accept the peace of Phoenice (205 BC).

214 BC

ASIA
– Mongol tribes threaten the territories ruled by the Chinese Qin dynasty; work begins on a defensive wall extending 4000km (2500 miles) along the border with Mongolia to the sea.

212 BC

ASIA
– The Chinese emperor Shi Huangdi burns dissidents' writings and orders some scholars to be burned alive. He wishes to rewrite history so that it begins with his rule. He exempts works on medicine, astrology and agriculture from his war on learning. In 210 BC he dies, having created a new structure of 36 provinces, built a new capital at Xian and introduced a uniform system of laws, weights and measurements; 8000 life-size figures of soldiers in terracotta are buried in his tomb (the so-called 'terracotta army').

209–202 BC

ASIA
– Civil war erupts in China: the Qin dynasty is overthrown and the Han dynasty assumes power (206 BC). It will rule for over four centuries until AD 220.

c.205 BC

ARTS AND HUMANITIES
Plautus, *Menaechmi*, comedy.

202 BC

MIDDLE EAST AND NORTH AFRICA
19 Oct. The Second Punic War (see 218 BC) between Rome and Carthage ends with the battle of Zama (N Africa). The Roman general Scipio Africanus defeats the joint army of Numidians and Carthaginians led by Hannibal (see 183 BC). Carthage yields and surrenders its overseas colonies to Rome; all but ten of Carthage's warships are destroyed. The Carthaginians must pay Rome an annual tribute for 50 years and must seek Rome's permission to wage war.

201 BC

EUROPE
– At the battle of Chios Philip V of Macedon is defeated by the allied powers of Rhodes and Pergamum, ending his ambitions in Greece.

200 BC

MIDDLE EAST AND NORTH AFRICA
– At the battle of Pannium, during the Fifth Syrian War, the Syrian army under Antiochus III defeats the Egyptians.

ARTS AND HUMANITIES
Plautus, *Stichus*, comedy.

c.200 BC

AUSTRALASIA AND OCEANIA
– Polynesians settle in Tahiti.

197 BC

EUROPE
– At the battle of Cynoscephalae a Roman army in Thessaly defeats Philip V of Macedon. Philip surrenders his Greek territories; his army is reduced to 5000 men and his navy to five ships. He must pay Rome a monthly tribute and cannot declare war without Rome's permission.

196 BC

EUROPE
– Syrian forces under Antiochus III invade Greece, but this brings him into collision with the Romans, who are also expanding into the region.

c.195 BC

ARTS AND HUMANITIES
Plautus, *Persa* (The Persian), comedy.

191 BC

EUROPE
– The Romans defeat the Syrians under Antiochus III at Thermopylae.
– Cisalpine Gaul, the area S of the Alps inhabited by Celtic tribes, becomes a province of the Roman empire.

190-162BC

190 BC

MIDDLE EAST AND NORTH AFRICA
– The Roman generals Lucius Cornelius Scipio (Scipio Asiaticus) and his brother Scipio Africanus (see 202 BC) cross the Hellespont in pursuit of the Syrian king Antiochus III and defeat him at the battle of Magnesia (NE of Smyrna). Antiochus surrenders all his territories up to the Taurus Mts. Antiochus' two Armenian satrapies make themselves independent: Armenia Major and Armenia Minor.

c.189 BC

ARTS AND HUMANITIES
Plautus, *The Two Bacchaiades*, comedy. *The Captives* follows in c.188 BC and *The Threepenny Day* in c.187 BC. He writes *Amphitryon* and *Truculentus* in c.186 BC.

c.185 BC

ASIA
– In India the last Mauryan king of Magadha, Brihadratha, is overthrown by his own general, Pushyamitra Shunga. Under the Shunga dynasty, Magadha remains a major power, but when the dynasty falls (73 BC) it quickly declines.

184 BC

ARTS AND HUMANITIES
– The Roman playwright Plautus dies.

c.183 BC

MIDDLE EAST AND NORTH AFRICA
– The Carthaginian commander Hannibal, who has aided Antiochus III's war on the Romans, tries to flee. According to one story he escapes to the court of Bithynia's ruler Prusias II, but, knowing that he is about to be betrayed to the Romans, he commits suicide to avoid being paraded through the streets of Rome in a triumphal procession before being executed.

179 BC

SCIENCE AND TECHNOLOGY
– The earliest dated stone arched bridge is built by the Romans: the Pons Aemilius spans the River Tiber in Rome.

171–168 BC

EUROPE
– The Third Macedonian War. Perseus, successor to his father Philip V of Macedon, holds off the Romans until 168 BC, when, at the battle of Pydna, he is defeated by Lucius Aemilius Paulus. Perseus is paraded through the streets of Rome and will spend the rest of his life in captivity. Roman dominance in Greece is secured.

170 BC

SCIENCE AND TECHNOLOGY
– Paved streets are laid in Rome.

167 BC

MIDDLE EAST AND NORTH AFRICA
– Antiochus IV (Epiphanes) of Syria outlaws Judaism, destroys the Great Temple at Jerusalem and attempts to Hellenize the Jews by forcing them to worship statues of Greek gods.
– Mattathias of Modin leads a Jewish rebellion in Syria and escapes to the mountains with his five sons.

166 BC

MIDDLE EAST AND NORTH AFRICA
– The Jewish rebel Mattathias of Modin dies, but his son Judas (or Judah) continues to fight, becoming known as Maccabeus (the Hammerer).

ARTS AND HUMANITIES
April *The Women of Andros*, a comedy by the Roman playwright Terence (Publius Terentius Afer) is performed at the Megaleusian Games in Rome.

165 BC

ARTS AND HUMANITIES
Terence, *The Mother-in-Law*, comedy.

164 BC

MIDDLE EAST AND NORTH AFRICA
– The Jewish rebel Judas Maccabeus and his brothers retake Jerusalem and expel the Syrians. They purify the Great Temple of the statues of foreign gods erected there by Antiochus IV of Syria (see 167 BC).

163 BC

MIDDLE EAST AND NORTH AFRICA
– The infant Antiochus V succeeds as ruler of Syria on the death of his father Antiochus IV. Lysias, the regent, abandons the state's anti-Semitic policy, but Judas Maccabeus continues the rebellion, seeking political independence.

ARTS AND HUMANITIES
Terence, *The Self-Avenger*, comedy.

162 BC

MIDDLE EAST AND NORTH AFRICA
– Demetrius I Soter overthrows his cousin Antiochus V as ruler of Syria.

161 BC

ARTS AND HUMANITIES

Terence, *The Eunuch* and *Phormio*, comedies.

160 BC

MIDDLE EAST AND NORTH AFRICA

– Judas Maccabeus is killed at the battle of Elasa; his brother Jonathan continues to fight and recovers much of Judaea's independence by the time of his death in 143 BC.

ARTS AND HUMANITIES

Terence, *The Brothers*, comedy.

c.159 BC

ARTS AND HUMANITIES

– The Roman playwright Terence dies.

153 BC

EUROPE

– January replaces March (the first month of a new consulate) as the first month of the year in the Roman Republican calendar.

150 BC

MIDDLE EAST AND NORTH AFRICA

– The Roman aristocrat and orator Marcus Porcius Cato (Cato the Elder) declares that Carthage must be destroyed. Having brokered a truce between Carthage and Numidia in 157 BC, Cato is angered by Carthage's renewed attack on Numidia. Cato promotes his campaign by ending every speech, letter and statement with the words *Delenda est Carthago* (Carthage must be destroyed), no matter what the subject under discussion.

– The Romans support the successful rebel Alexander Balas who, having killed Demetrius I Soter in battle, now rules Syria.

THE AMERICAS

– In Mesoamerica El Mirador (Guatemala) has become the largest centre of Mayan civilization.

ARTS AND HUMANITIES

– Around this time the Greek historian Polybius (see box) publishes the first part of his *History*, describing the rise of Rome.

149 BC

EUROPE

– The Roman statesman Cato the Elder dies. His seven-volume *Origines* (beginnings), now lost, traced the origins of Rome and other Italian cities.

MIDDLE EAST AND NORTH AFRICA

– The Third Punic War between Rome and Carthage begins. A Roman army invades N Africa and besieges Carthage.

146 BC

EUROPE

– After the Greek city of Corinth rebels unsuccessfully against Roman rule the senate orders the replacement of democracies with more easily controlled oligarchies in all of Rome's subject territories. The Achaean League is dissolved and Greece falls under the supervision of the governor of Macedon, itself a province of Rome.

MIDDLE EAST AND NORTH AFRICA

– The Third Punic War (see 149 BC) ends when Carthage falls. The Carthaginian commander surrenders to Scipio Aemilianus; Carthage is burned and its lands become part of the Roman province of 'Africa'.

145 BC

MIDDLE EAST AND NORTH AFRICA

– Alexander Balas, Rome's puppet Syrian ruler, is killed in battle near Antioch. His son rules as Antiochus VI under a regent until 142 BC, when the son of Demetrius I Soter, Demetrius II Nicator, becomes king.

Polybius (c.200–c.118 BC)

The historian Polybius was Greek, but it was Rome that was to be the dominating influence on his life and works.

As a young man, Polybius was taken to Rome as a hostage to ensure that the Greek cities kept to a treaty with Rome. In Rome he was wise enough to win the friendship and favour of the city's leading politicians and generals. He used these contacts to gather information for his 40-volume history of the rise of Rome to world power, beginning in 220 BC and ending in 146 BC. In his history he argued that Rome was deservedly a great power and that his Greek countrymen should work within a Roman-dominated world rather than fight against it. Polybius maintained that the stability of its constitution was the reason Rome was both a stable society and a dynamic force for cultural advance. Correspondingly, it was the Greek consti-tutional instability that explained why Greece had lost its former power. He also invented new ideas of chronology to relate what was happening at the same time in different parts of the civilized world.

In describing the final Roman defeat of the Carthaginians in 146 BC, Polybius was describing a war he had seen at first hand. This perhaps explains the mixed views he puts forward. He argued that the savagery meted out to the defeated Carthaginians was necessary – but that it was also treacherous and ugly.

This complexity was new in historical writing, as was his idea of historical inevitability. Polybius believed that it was important to understand the causes of events so that relevant contemporary policies could be formulated. He was, therefore, the first pro-ponent of the idea of history as a source of instructive examples.

143–103BC

143 BC

MIDDLE EAST AND NORTH AFRICA
- Tryphon, a Syrian, kills the Jewish rebel Jonathan Maccabeus whose elder brother Simon succeeds him as leader of the Jewish resistance; Simon drives the Syrians from the citadel at Jerusalem.

142 BC

MIDDLE EAST AND NORTH AFRICA
- The Jewish rebel Simon Maccabeus liberates Jerusalem; the recovered Judaean independence will last until 63 BC.

141 BC

MIDDLE EAST AND NORTH AFRICA
- Mithridates I, ruler of Parthia, defeats the Syrian forces and conquers Babylonia and Media.

140 BC

ASIA
- Wu Ti of the Han dynasty becomes emperor of China; his reign sees the first direct cultural interchange with Europe, with the first caravans from China transporting apricots and peaches there. Indirect trade through middlemen in C Asia has been going on for centuries.

139 BC

MIDDLE EAST AND NORTH AFRICA
- Demetrius II Nicator of Syria attempts to reconquer Babylonia, where Mithridates I of Parthia is now based, but is captured and imprisoned until 129 BC.

135 BC

EUROPE
- The First Slave War begins in Sicily, when the Syrian Eunus leads a revolt of slave workers in the vast Roman-owned agricultural estates and occupies Henna and Tauromenium.

134 BC

MIDDLE EAST AND NORTH AFRICA
- The Jewish rebel Simon Maccabeus, along with two of his sons, is murdered by his son-in-law, the governor of Jericho. His surviving son John Hyrcanus I succeeds; he rules Judaea until 104 BC and extends its boundaries to Samaria, Idumaea and E of the Jordan River.

133 BC

EUROPE
- The Roman reformer Tiberius Sempronius Gracchus is elected tribune with a policy of limiting the size of land-holdings. The threatened landowners revolt, and Gracchus is murdered.

132 BC

EUROPE
- The First Slave War (see 135 BC) ends when the Romans capture Eunus, the leader of the revolt, who had proclaimed himself King Antiochus. Eunus dies in prison.

129 BC

EUROPE
- The Roman social reformer Scipio Aemilianus dies in suspicious circumstances.

MIDDLE EAST AND NORTH AFRICA
- The former Greek kingdom of Pergamum (in W Anatolia) is renamed the Roman province of 'Asia'.

123 BC

EUROPE
- Roman tribune Gaius Sempronius Gracchus takes up his late brother Tiberius' land reform cause. He enacts a legislative programme forcing the government to provide a set measure of grain to Roman citizens at a price below the market rate. He is killed in 121 BC heading an armed insurrection.

110 BC

SCIENCE AND TECHNOLOGY
- In the area of Baia, near the future city of Naples, cultured oyster beds are developed.

105 BC

EUROPE
- The Cimbri and the Teutones, two Germanic tribes from Jutland, move across the Rhône and into the Alps; they defeat two Roman armies at Arausio on the Rhône. The tribes then split up to plunder separately.

104 BC

EUROPE
- The Second Slave War begins when Tryphon and Athenion lead the Sicilian slaves in another revolt against Rome.

MIDDLE EAST AND NORTH AFRICA
- Aristobulus I succeeds his father John Hyrcanus I, ruler of Israel (see 134 BC). He completes the reclamation of Galilee and forces Judaism on the people of Hurae.

103 BC

MIDDLE EAST AND NORTH AFRICA
- Aristobulus I of Israel dies and is succeeded by his brother Alexander Jannaeus.

102 BC

EUROPE

– The Roman consul Gaius Marius defeats the Teutones at the battle of Aix-en-Provence. Although Roman law decrees otherwise, Marius has been re-elected consul since 107 BC. Two consuls are elected by the Roman citizens each year to serve as the most senior civil and military officials in Rome, the consuls deciding how to share their powers. Gaius Marius was born in poverty and joined the army. He rose through the ranks to become a wealthy and successful commander before entering politics to champion the cause of the poorer citizens.

101 BC

EUROPE

– Gaius Marius becomes one of the great national Roman heroes (along with his colleague Quintus Lutatius Catulus) by his victory over a Germanic tribe, the Cimbri, at the battle of Campi Raudii near Vercellae (in NW Italy).

100 BC

EUROPE

– The plebeian tribunes Saturnius and Glauca call for cheap corn for the Roman poor. The tribunes are officials elected annually by the plebeians (non-aristocratic citizens of Rome) to ensure that laws are enforced fairly and without regard to wealth. They are outlawed by Roman aristocrats in the senate and murdered with the support of the general Gaius Marius.

99 BC

EUROPE

– The Second Slave War (see 104 BC) ends when the Roman consul Marcus Aquillius defeats the Scilian rebel slaves.

96 BC

MIDDLE EAST AND NORTH AFRICA

– The Seleucid king of Syria, Antiochus VIII, is murdered by his court favourite Heracleon and succeeded by his half-brother and co-ruler Antiochus IX.

95 BC

MIDDLE EAST AND NORTH AFRICA

– The king of Syria, Antiochus IX, is killed in battle by the son of Antiochus VIII (see 96 BC), who succeeds him as Seleucus VI.

94 BC

MIDDLE EAST AND NORTH AFRICA

– Tigranes II deposes King Artanes of Armenia Minor and reunites Armenia. He marries the daughter of Mithridates II (the Great), king of Parthia, and invades Cappadocia

(EC Anatolia), but is forced to withdraw by the Roman general Lucius Cornelius Sulla.

92 BC

MIDDLE EAST AND NORTH AFRICA

– King Mithridates II (the Great) of Parthia allies with Rome and prepares to invade Mesopotamia.

91 BC

EUROPE

– Rome's Italian allies rebel, beginning the Social War (from *socii*, allies). They demand a greater say in decision-making and a greater share in the spoils of Roman expansion. The rebels establish a republic of Italia, with a capital at Corfinium.

88 BC

MIDDLE EAST AND NORTH AFRICA

– King Mithridates II (the Great) of Parthia dies. His son-in-law, Tigranes II of Armenia, invades Parthia and overruns four Parthian vassal states.
– Mithridates VI Eupator, king of Pontus, starts the first of three wars against Rome; he is supreme in Cappadocia, Paphlagonia, Bithynia and the S and E coasts of the Black Sea.

87 BC

EUROPE

– Rome ends the Social War (see 91 BC) by granting its rebellious Italian allies full Roman citizenship.
– The aristocratic Roman general Lucius Cornelius Sulla marches on Rome, kills the popular leader Publius Sulpicius Rufus and departs for Asia as military governor.
– Lucius Cornelius Cinna becomes a powerful demagogue attacking the Roman aristocracy.

86 BC

EUROPE

– Roman general Lucius Cornelius Sulla defeats Mithridates VI Eupator, king of Pontus, and his allies at Chaeronea near Thebes in C Greece and occupies Athens.

84 BC

EUROPE

– Roman general Lucius Cornelius Sulla forces Mithridates VI Eupator, king of Pontus, to evacuate the territories he has occupied; Sulla sails for Brundisium (Brindisi), leaving behind two legions to maintain order in Greece.

MIDDLE EAST AND NORTH AFRICA

– The king of Syria, Antiochus XII, having captured Damascus, is killed on an expedition against the Nabataeans (in modern Jordan).

82 BC

EUROPE

Nov. At the battle of the Colline Gate the Roman general Lucius Cornelius Sulla defeats the rebellious Samnites and appoints himself dictator, an office infrequently used in ancient Rome. Its holder is given wide-ranging powers for a specific period of time to tackle crises of state. Sulla orders the execution of hundreds of his political enemies, thus introducing a new and more violent aspect to the turbulent internal politics of Rome.

80 BC

EUROPE

– The Roman dictator Sulla stops free grain distribution to the poorer citizens of Rome. He ceases to be dictator and, after a year as a consul, retires voluntarily from public life.

78 BC

EUROPE

– Lucius Cornelius Sulla dies, having achieved his goal: the establishment of an aristocratic political system.

– The anti-senatorial Roman politician Marcus Aemilius Lepidus raises a rebel army in Etruria but is defeated outside Rome by Quintus Lutatius Catulus (see 101 BC).

77 BC

EUROPE

– The Roman politician Marcus Aemilius Lepidus (see 78 BC) is forced to withdraw to the Hispanic provinces by Gnaeus Pompeius (Pompey), a former follower of the dictator Sulla.

c.75 BC

SCIENCE AND TECHNOLOGY

– Greek physician Asclepiades of Bithynia makes a distinction between acute and chronic disease and advances influential theories of diet and exercise.

73 BC

EUROPE

– The Third Slave War begins: Spartacus, a Thracian slave and gladiator, launches a slave revolt and uses Mt Vesuvius near Naples as the base for his campaign.

72 BC

EUROPE

– Spartacus' slave army defeats a force of Roman legions.

71 BC

EUROPE

– At the battle of Lucania the wealthy Roman politician Marcus

Licinius Crassus defeats the slave army led by Spartacus, who is killed (see 73 BC). Many of Spartacus' supporters are crucified. The general Pompey returns from Spain, destroys the remainder of the slave army and takes the credit for the victory by reaching Rome with the news first, thus making an enemy of Crassus.

MIDDLE EAST AND NORTH AFRICA

– King Mithridates VI Eupator (see 88 BC) is driven out of Pontus by the Roman legions under Lucius Licinius Lucullus; he flees to the court of Tigranes II of Armenia.

70 BC

EUROPE

– In Rome the wealthy politician Crassus and successful general Pompey temporarily bury their differences to break with the Roman aristocracy and use the support of the army to gain the consulship. The privileges of the tribunate, removed by the dictator Sulla, are restored.

– Crassus and Pompey resume free grain distribution to Rome's adult male citizens.

MIDDLE EAST AND NORTH AFRICA

– Tigranes II of Armenia, ruling over an empire extending from the Ararat valley in the N to Tyre on the Mediterranean coast in the S, plans a new capital at the head of the River Tigris, to be called Tigranocerta. He styles himself 'king of kings', the traditional title of the ancient Persian emperors.

69 BC

MIDDLE EAST AND NORTH AFRICA

– The Roman general Lucius Licinius Lucullus defeats Tigranes II of Armenia, who has taken Syria and is advancing on Pontus.

ECONOMY AND SOCIETY

– Lucullus sends the first cherry tree back to Europe from his campaign in Syria.

68 BC

MIDDLE EAST AND NORTH AFRICA

– The Roman troops in Armenia mutiny; the general Lucullus retreats S. Mithridates VI Eupator, king of Pontus (see 71 BC) starts to regain his territories.

67 BC

EUROPE

– The Roman general Quintus Caecilius Metellus defeats the Mediterranean pirates who have been disrupting Rome's grain supplies from Egypt and N Africa.

65 BC

MIDDLE EAST AND NORTH AFRICA

– The Roman general Pompey captures King Tigranes II of

Armenia and makes him a vassal of Rome. He also drives Mithridates VI Eupator, king of Pontus, back to the Black Sea; Mithridates flees to the Crimea.
- Pompey organizes Rome's Asian and Syrian territories into four new provinces and establishes Cappadocia, E Pontus, Galatia, Judaea and Lycia as vassal states.

ECONOMY AND SOCIETY
- Pompey introduces to Rome apricots from Armenia, peaches from Persia, plums from Damascus, quinces from Sidon and raspberries from Mt Ida, SE of Troy.

64 BC
EUROPE
- Lucius Sergius Catilina (Catiline), a former Roman governor of Africa, is defeated for the second time as a candidate for consul, this time by the orator and philosopher Marcus Tullius Cicero (see p. 42). Catiline leads a conspiracy against the state, which involves many leading citizens.

MIDDLE EAST AND NORTH AFRICA
- The last Seleucid king of Syria, Antiochus XIII, is killed by the Arab prince of Emesa.

63 BC
EUROPE
- The Roman consul Cicero denounces the conspirator Catiline. Catiline and his followers are arrested and put to death without appeal.
- Mithridates VI Eupator, king of Pontus, commits suicide in the Crimea after learning that his son has rebelled.

MIDDLE EAST AND NORTH AFRICA
- The Roman general Pompey captures the Temple of Jerusalem from Jewish rebels after a 3-month siege.

ARTS AND HUMANITIES
- Marcus Tullius Tiro, slave secretary of the Roman orator Marcus Tullius Cicero, invents shorthand.

c.62 BC
EUROPE
- The city of Florence is founded on the River Arno, Tuscany.

60 BC
EUROPE
- On his return from the governorship of the Hispanic provinces Roman politician Gaius Julius Caesar (100–44 BC) forms a triumvirate to rule Rome in alliance with Pompey and Crassus (see 70 BC). Caesar was born into an impoverished branch of one of Rome's most ancient and aristocratic families and entered politics in an effort to restore the family's fortunes. Caesar's political and military successes will result in his family

name in various forms (Kaiser, tsar) becoming a title signifying a supreme ruler.

59 BC
EUROPE
- The Roman triumvirate (see 60 BC) distributes lands in the Campania (S Italy) among Pompey's veterans and is strengthened by the marriage of Julius Caesar's daughter Julia to Pompey.
- Julius Caesar is granted Cisalpine Gaul and Illyria for a term of five years.

58 BC
EUROPE
- The Roman general Julius Caesar invades Gaul, beginning the Gallic Wars, and defeats the Helvetii tribe at Bibracte (modern Autun): he aims to build a power base to rival that of Pompey.
- In Rome the wealthy wastrel Appius Clodius Pulcher distributes free grain to the people in an attempt to gain the support of the voting public.

58–52 BC
ARTS AND HUMANITIES
Julius Caesar, *Commentarii de bello Gallico* (Gallic Wars), history.

57 BC
EUROPE
- Appius Claudius Pulcher (see 58 BC) is elected to the position of praetor, the Roman official who presides at important criminal trials.
- The Roman general Julius Caesar's forces defeat the Belgae tribe in NW Gaul.
- The Roman senate gives the general Pompey powers to organize grain distribution and supply.

56 BC
EUROPE
- The Roman general Julius Caesar defeats the Veneti tribe in Brittany and the Aquitani tribe in SW Gaul.
- Julius Caesar meets Crassus and Pompey in Luca (Lucca) to confront Roman opposition to the triumvirate, the informal alliance the three men have formed to dominate Roman politics.

ARTS AND HUMANITIES
- Gaius Valerius Catullus (c.84–c.54 BC) writes verse in Rome, including love poems, epigrams and epics.

55 BC
EUROPE
- In Rome Pompey and Crassus are elected consuls. Julius

Caesar's command in Gaul is extended for another five-year term by the senate, while Crassus is given command of Syria, and Pompey of the Hispanic provinces.
— Julius Caesar invades SE Britain, but his poorly prepared expedition is soon forced to withdraw.

54 BC

EUROPE

— Caesar invades Britain for a second time. Having extracted promises of tribute, he retreats to Gaul.
— Julia, Pompey's wife and Caesar's sister, dies: the triumvirate (see 60 BC) disintegrates.

MIDDLE EAST AND NORTH AFRICA

— The Roman politician Marcus Licinius Crassus plunders the Great Temple of Jerusalem.
— Crassus invades Parthia but is defeated and killed at Carrhae (modern Harran in Syria).

ARTS AND HUMANITIES

— By this date Roman poet Lucretius (Titus Lucretius Carus) has written *De rerum natura*, a poem dealing with ethical and scientific issues.

52 BC

EUROPE

— The Gaul Vercingetorix, chief of the Arverni (Averni) tribe and leader of Gallic resistance to Roman imperialism, surrenders to the Roman general Julius Caesar, who has laid seige to his stronghold at Alesia (C France). Vercingetorix will be exhibited in Rome in 46 BC in Julius Caesar's triumph before being executed.

51 BC

EUROPE

— Caesar completes the conquest of Gaul bringing the Gallic Wars (see 58 BC) to an end.

ARTS AND HUMANITIES

Cicero (see box), *De republica*, political philosophy.

49 BC

EUROPE

— With his power base secure, Caesar moves on Rome. He crosses the Rubicon, the river that marks the boundary between Gaul and Roman soil proper without giving up his army, thus breaking the law and defying the legal authority of the Roman senate. Caesar defeats Pompey, who supports the senate, at Pharsalus in S Thessaly (9 Aug. 48 BC), becoming the effective, but disputed, ruler of Rome. Pompey escapes to Egypt and is killed by King Ptolemy XIII at Pelusium (near Alexandria). Caesar follows Pompey to Alexandria but stays to assist Cleopatra, joint ruler of Egypt with her brother Ptolemy, in the power struggle that rages there.

47 BC

MIDDLE EAST AND NORTH AFRICA

— The Roman ruler Julius Caesar marches on Asia Minor and defeats the king of Pontus, Pharnaces II, at Zela.

46 BC

EUROPE

— The Roman ruler Julius Caesar returns to Italy to suppress the mutiny in Campania before travelling to N Africa to quell a

---

Cicero (106–43 BC)

The great Roman orator and writer Marcus Tullius Cicero belonged to an established and well-to-do family. In 63 BC he became a consul, the leading government post in Rome. He was a great advocate of Roman republican politics as a force for virtue, and was a fiercely outspoken opponent of its enemies.

Cicero delivered speeches to the senate, to the law courts and to the popular assemblies, and many of these became celebrated for their polished style and the power of their delivery, as well as for their content. His great treatise on the subject, *De oratore*, influenced subsequent political

style throughout Europe. Defending oratory from Plato's criticism, the work described how the ideal orator should be educated in science, philosophy and rhetoric.

Cicero established a conservative idea of the public man, and he thought deeply about the philosophical context of political life. *De republica* showed that philosophy could be written in Latin as well as in Greek. Works such as *De fato* and *De divinatione* show the social nature of Roman religion and its function as an upholder of civic virtue. But he could also turn his pen to more intimate subjects in works such as *De amicitia*.

The freedom of individuals and of society

could be maintained, he thought, only if everyone acted as 'slaves to the public interest', which had been the great feature of Rome in previous generations. This influential consensual myth-making was also a way of avoiding difficulties – such as the poverty and indebtedness of Roman citizens – and so, ironically, played its part in the fall of the republic that Cicero eulogized. Cicero's conservative view of the Roman constitution as an evolutionary growth that should not be tampered with by individual reformers also ultimately helped to bring about the end of the republic. He himself was killed by his political enemies.

rebellion of 14 legions at Thapsus. He returns to Rome with the Egyptian queen Cleopatra as his mistress and is made dictator for ten years. Caesar then sails for Spain to suppress a rebellion led by Pompey's sons (Nov.).

45 BC

EUROPE

17 Mar. The Roman dictator Julius Caesar defeats Pompey's sons at Munda in Spain. In Rome he adopts his great-nephew Gaius Octavius Julius Caesar (Octavian, later known as Augustus) as his son (Sept.).

ECONOMY AND SOCIETY

– Julius Caesar enforces the Julian calendar according to reforms proposed by Sosigenes of Alexandria; the calendar has 365.25 days and starts on 1 January.

44 BC

EUROPE

– Julius Caesar is made dictator for life in Rome but is assassinated at the senate by republican conspirators, who include two former governors of Gaul, Decimus Junius Brutus and Marcus Junius Brutus, and Gaius Cassius Longinus (15 Mar.). Marcus Junius Brutus has been very close to Caesar and is rumoured to be his illegitimate son. The involvement of the Brutus family in the plot has great political impact as the family had been instrumental in ousting the despotic king Tarquin the Proud (see 509 BC) and is generally regarded as a stabilizing influence in Roman politics.
– Marcus Antonius (Mark Antony), a Roman general and long-time supporter of Julius Caesar, persuades the Romans to expel Caesar's assassins.

MIDDLE EAST AND NORTH AFRICA

– Caesar's mistress Cleopatra returns to Egypt with her son by Caesar, Caesarion. She murders her brother (and husband) Ptolemy XIII Philopater.

ARTS AND HUMANITIES

Cicero, *Philippics*, oratory.

43 BC

EUROPE

7 Dec. The Roman orator and philosopher Marcus Tullius Cicero (see p. 42) is executed by order of Mark Antony. Caesar's adopted son Octavian is complicit.
– The Roman general Mark Antony is defeated while pursuing Decimus Brutus, one of the assassins of Julius Caesar, and is forced to withdraw W to Gaul.
– The Roman Senate elects Caesar's adopted son, his nephew Octavian consul. He forms a second triumvirate, an informal alliance of three politicians, with the generals Mark Antony and Marcus Lepidus.

42 BC

EUROPE

– The second triumvirate (see 43 BC) deifies Julius Caesar and erects a temple to him in the Roman Forum. Roman magistrates must swear to support the late Caesar's constitutional arrangements.
– The Roman generals Mark Antony and Octavian defeat Caesar's assassin Gaius Cassius Longinus at Philippi in Macedonia. Cassius commits suicide, thinking his ally Marcus Brutus has been defeated. In reality, Brutus gains a victory over Octavian, but he is finally defeated and commits suicide.

41 BC

EUROPE

– The second triumvirate (see 43 BC) confiscates farmland in the Campania, a wealthy district in S Italy, to distribute among the returning legionaries.

MIDDLE EAST AND NORTH AFRICA

– The Roman general Mark Antony meets Cleopatra of Egypt at Tarsus; seduced, he follows her to Egypt.

ARTS AND HUMANITIES

– Roman poet Virgil (Publius Vergilius Maro) (see p. 45) publishes his *Eclogues*, pastoral verses.

40 BC

EUROPE

– Fulvia, the wife of Mark Antony, and Lucius Antonius, his brother, wage war on Octavian, Julius Caesar's nephew and adopted son. They are defeated at Perusia (Perugia); Fulvia dies and Mark Antony marries Octavian's sister Octavia. Octavian takes Gaul from Lepidus, leaving him only Africa.

39 BC

EUROPE

– By the pact of Mycenaeum, the second triumvirate (see 43 BC) recognizes the Mediterranean pirate Sextus Pompey as ruler of Sicily, Sardinia, Corsica and the Peloponnese.
– The Roman general Octavian divorces his second wife and marries Livia, the widow of nobleman Tiberius Claudius Nero.

38 BC

EUROPE

– The Roman general Octavian gains victories on campaign in Iberia.

MIDDLE EAST AND NORTH AFRICA

– The Roman general Mark Antony returns to Egypt to be with his mistress Cleopatra. He thus abandons his wife, Octavia, sister of Octavian, the nephew and adopted son of deceased Roman dictator Julius Caesar.

38–20BC

OCTAVIAN DEFEATS MARK ANTONY'S FORCES □ CLEOPATRA COMMITS SUICIDE □ ROMAN EMPIRE FOUNDED

ARTS AND HUMANITIES
– About this time Agesander, Polydorus and Athenodorus create the sculpture *Laocoön*.

37 BC

EUROPE
– Herod I (the Great) is confirmed as king of Judaea, having been made king in 39 BC by Octavian, Mark Antony and the Roman senate.

36 BC

EUROPE
– Marcus Vipsanius Agrippa, Roman general and supporter of Octavian, defeats the pirate Sextus Pompey, who flees to Miletus, where he is killed.
– The Roman general Lepidus occupies Sicily, but his troops desert to Octavian, who imprisons Lepidus at Circeii.

MIDDLE EAST AND NORTH AFRICA
– The Roman general Mark Antony marries the Egyptian queen Cleopatra despite being already married to Octavian's sister Octavia. He attacks Parthia, but is driven back to Armenia, thus losing his reputation for military invincibility.

35 BC

ARTS AND HUMANITITES
– The first book of Horace's *Satires* appears at about this time and is followed by a second volume in 30 BC.

32 BC

EUROPE
– The Roman general Mark Antony divorces Octavia; her brother Octavian effects the official state cancellation of Antony's right to command Roman legions in the E provinces. The move marks the start of civil war between the two Roman leaders and their supporters.

31 BC

EUROPE
2 Sept. At the battle of Actium (off W Greece) the Roman general Octavian gains a great naval victory over his rival Mark Antony and the Egyptian queen Cleopatra; Cleopatra escapes to Egypt with her ships and Antony follows, but their army surrenders to Octavian.

30 BC

MIDDLE EAST AND NORTH AFRICA
30 Aug. The Roman general Mark Antony commits suicide after hearing a false report of Cleopatra's death; Cleopatra commits suicide, and her son Caesarion is murdered. Thereafter Egypt remains the personal property of Octavian, who rules as king of Egypt. The fabulous wealth this brings him allows him to distribute great patronage and power in Rome. His heirs and successors maintain their personal rule of Egypt outside the Roman government system.

SCIENCE AND TECHNOLOGY
– The sundial is widely used in China as a clock.

ARTS AND HUMANITIES
Virgil (see p. 45), *Georgics*, poems.

29 BC

MIDDLE EAST AND NORTH AFRICA
– The Roman general Octavian, now master of the Roman empire, employs Greek sailors to reopen the ancient trade routes between Egypt and India.

27 BC

EUROPE
23 Jan. The Roman ruler Octavian is granted the title Augustus Caesar by the Senate. Octavian himself takes the title Imperator Caesar Octavianus but later adopts Augustus Caesar as his usual title. Augustus realizes that it was the naked exploitation of power that led to discontent with the rule of his uncle, the dictator Julius Caesar, and so to his murder. He therefore announces that he is restoring the traditional democratic constitution of Rome and refuses any position in the government. However, he uses his great wealth (derived from ruling Egypt) and special powers of arrest and detention to bestow patronage and influence throughout the state system. He ensures that only his supporters are elected to office and thus exercises almost unlimited power indirectly. This system remains the basis of Roman government for centuries to come. Augustus is thus recognized as the first emperor of Rome, although that title will not actually be used for some generations.
– The Roman emperor Augustus increases the number of Roman citizens entitled to receive free grain from 150,000 to 200,000.

24 BC

MIDDLE EAST AND NORTH AFRICA
– The Roman emperor Augustus appoints the prefect of Egypt, Aeilius Gallus, to incorporate spice-rich S Arabia into the empire; the campaign fails.

21 BC

EUROPE
– The city of Regensburg in Germany is founded.

20 BC

MIDDLE EAST AND NORTH AFRICA
– Herod I (the Great) of Judaea, a convert to Judaism, rebuilds Jerusalem's Great Temple.

44 THE ANCIENT AND MEDIEVAL WORLDS: 135,000 BP–1449

Virgil (70–19 BC)

The Latin poet Virgil (Publius Vergilius Maro) was born in Mantua and lived through the years of civil war, the fall of the Roman republic and the rise of Octavian as the emperor Augustus. Virgil looked at Rome with the eyes of an outsider from the north, and his celebration of the Roman virtues and of the Roman mission to civilize the world owed much to that fact. The statesman Maecenas and Augustus himself both patronized Virgil, making him a rich man.

Virgil's first work was the *Eclogues*, a collection of ten pastoral poems which anticipate his major theme: that classical myth and fable can evoke implicitly the world of contemporary events. Politics continue to be central in his next work, the *Georgics*, which describe the everyday life of Italian agriculture, but their true point is to celebrate the ancient Roman virtues of piety, public-spiritedness and hard work.

In his greatest work, the 12-book *Aeneid*, Virgil made his subject the founding of Rome by the Trojan exile Aeneas, whom Augustus claimed as an ancestor. The poet makes powerful use of the pathos of defeat and the ambiguities of imperial success. Aeneas becomes a figure who stands for the emperor himself, who has embraced the awesome task of a divinely ordained restoration of Roman order. The eulogy is real, but the political lesson is harsh. In order to fulfil his destiny Aeneas has to abandon his lover Dido, the queen of Carthage. He also has to kill opponents whom, left to his own devices, he would rather spare.

Aesthetically, Virgil revived the classical tradition by introducing innovation and artistic advance. Politically, his mythic and poetic endorsement of power politics had a profound influence on the Roman imperial mentality.

19 BC

EUROPE

– The Pont du Gard aqueduct near Nîmes, S France, is completed by Roman engineers; it is 550m (600 yards) long and 50m (160 feet) high.

ARTS AND HUMANITIES

21 Sept. The Roman poet Virgil dies in Brundisium (see box).
– Horace writes three books of *Odes*. About this time a volume of *Epodes* (lyrical poems) and two volumes of *Epistles* also appear; a treatise, *Ars poetica*, is written later and possibly completed after his death.
Virgil, *Aeneid*, epic poem.

18 BC

ARTS AND HUMANITIES

– The Roman poet Ovid (Publius Ovidius Naso) publishes his *Amores*, 50 light and sophisticated love poems, written in elegiac metre.

17 BC

ARTS AND HUMANITIES

– The Roman poet Horace publishes his *Carmina saeculara*, an ode sung by the young at a festival of games.

15 BC

EUROPE

– The frontiers of Rome are extended to the upper Danube after a campaign against the Germanic tribes.

14 BC

EUROPE

– The Roman emperor Augustus founds the Gallic colony Augusta Vindelicorum (later known as Augsburg, now in S Germany).

8 BC

ARTS AND HUMANITIES

– The Roman poet Horace dies at his villa at Licenza, about 40km (25 miles) from Rome. Like Virgil, he had benefited from the patronage of Maccenas.

7 BC

MIDDLE EAST AND NORTH AFRICA

– Some time between 10 BC and 5 BC Jesus of Nazareth (see p. 47) is born in Bethlehem, near Jerusalem.

4 BC

MIDDLE EAST AND NORTH AFRICA

– King Herod I (the Great) of Judaea dies and is succeeded as ethnarch (ruler) by his son Archelaus.

1 BC/AD 1

ECONOMY AND SOCIETY

– The Christian chronology was invented by the monk Dionysius Exiguus 525 and was the by-product of the need to establish a date for Easter. Wrongly, Dionysius decided that 753 AUC (*ab urbe condita*, 'from the foundation of the city [Rome]') was the year of Christ's birth. But the Christian gospels claim that Christ was born under Herod the Great (see 20 BC) and, therefore, by 750 AUC at the latest. It took until the 11th century AD for the new chronology to be widely accepted in the Latin W at the expense of the chronology of the indiction, which numbered years from the accession of the emperor Constantine. Its adoption in Greek Christendom took a further four centuries.

AD 1

ARTS AND HUMANITIES
- Around this time, Ovid writes his collection of erotic poetry *Ars amatoria* (The Art of Love).

5

EUROPE
- Roman legions defeat the Lombard tribes settled on the lower Elbe River, in Germany.

6

EUROPE
- By this time as many as a third of the population of the city of Rome are receiving free grain.

7

ARTS AND HUMANITIES
Ovid, *Metamorphoses*, poetry.

8

EUROPE
- The Roman emperor Augustus exiles the poet Ovid to the Black Sea town of Tomis (modern Constanta, Romania), ostensibly because his poems have scandalized Roman society with their erotic frankness, but more probably on account of rumours of an affair between Ovid and the emperor's granddaughter Julia.

9

EUROPE
- Battle of the Teutoburg Forest: Germanic tribes under Arminius destroy three Roman legions led by Publius Quintilius Varus. Varus kills himself in shame and his head is sent to Augustus. The independence of the Germanic tribes is assured, with the Rhine forming the natural boundary with Roman territory (but see AD 16).

ASIA
- The emperor Wang Mang of the Xin dynasty usurps the throne of China, temporarily overthrowing the Han dynasty (see 209–202 BC). He frees slaves by manumission, nationalizes land, splits up the large estates and establishes state granaries.

14

EUROPE
- **19 Aug.** The Roman emperor Augustus dies after reigning for 41 years. His stepson Tiberius Claudius Nero (son of the empress Livia by her first marriage) succeeds as Emperor Tiberius.

16

EUROPE
- The death of Varus is avenged: Drusus, son of the Roman emperor Tiberius, defeats Arminius, breaks up his Germanic kingdom and recovers the eagles of the legions lost in the battle of the Teutoburg Forest (see AD 9). The German tribes remain free of Rome.

17

MIDDLE EAST AND NORTH AFRICA
- Cappadocia (E Turkey) and Commagene (N Syria) are united into a Roman province. The emperor Tiberius sends his nephew Germanicus to Armenia to supervise the installation of a new king.

ASIA
- The Chinese emperor Wang Mang imposes a tax on slaveholding (see AD 9). The government requires regional commissions to establish high, median and low price levels for commodities and to buy surplus goods at a loss. Merchants object.

19

MIDDLE EAST AND NORTH AFRICA
- Germanicus, nephew of the Roman emperor Tiberius, is poisoned in Syria. The legate Piso is charged with the murder and commits suicide.

23

EUROPE
- Drusus, son of the Roman emperor Tiberius, is poisoned by Lucius Aelius Sejanus, the equestrian (aspirational, non-noble class) government official who exercises strong personal influence over the emperor.

ASIA
- Emperor Wang Mang (see AD 17) is killed in a Chinese rebellion, having tried to use state power to control the economy and protect consumers.

25

EUROPE
- The Roman emperor Tiberius moves to Capri from an increasingly hostile Rome on the advice of the prefect Lucius Aelius Sejanus.

ASIA
- The E Han dynasty is established in China by Guang Wudi; the dynasty is an offshoot of the main imperial line, which was overthrown by Wang Mang in AD 9. The E Han dynasty will last until 220.

c.30

SCIENCE AND TECHNOLOGY

- Roman physician Aulus Cornelius Celsus publishes his *De res medicos* (On Medicine), an influential medical text.
- A Chinese illustration shows a water-powered bellows, which powers an iron furnace in which agricultural tools are produced.

31

EUROPE

- The Roman prefect Lucius Aelius Sejanus is executed for treason on the orders of the emperor Tiberius.

33

MIDDLE EAST AND NORTH AFRICA

- Probable date of the death of Jesus of Nazareth, known as Jesus Christ. He is condemned for sedition by the Roman procurator of Judaea, Pontius Pilate, and crucified (probably in April) on Golgotha, a hill near the Damascus Gate of Jerusalem (see box).

I am the Resurrection, and the Life.

Bible, St John's Gospel 11:25

37

EUROPE

16 Mar. The Roman emperor Tiberius dies and is succeeded by his nephew Gaius Caesar, nicknamed Caligula. The nickname means 'little boots' and is an affectionate term coined in his childhood from his habit of wearing miniature military uniform. Gaius hates the term and bans its use as soon as he becomes emperor. He will prove to be a mentally unstable tyrant.

40

ECONOMY AND SOCIETY

- The Greek merchant Hippalus discovers that the monsoon winds change direction twice a year (a fact already known by Arab travellers), the SW wind prevailing from April to Oct. and the NE from Oct. to April. He journeys from Egypt to India and back within one year.

41

EUROPE

- The Roman emperor Gaius (Caligula) is murdered by his

Jesus Christ (*c*.5 BC–*c*.AD 33)

The life of Jesus of Nazareth is known through the four Gospels that are attributed to his followers Matthew, Mark, Luke and John. These contain details such as his birth in Bethlehem, his baptism by John the Baptist, the 40 days spent in the desert as Jesus wrestled with temptation and his subsequent preaching ministry. But they offer no record of Jesus's life in terms of factual and biographical testimony – for the simple reason that this was not the intention of the New Testament writers. The Gospels offer only an impressionistic series of sketches of the Galilean prophet. Their true focus lies in the record of a communal faith and the development of a Jesus-movement, which only later became a Church.

Jesus was a rabbi who taught in the prophetic traditions of the Israelite experience and in the Judaic traditions of the Temple at Jerusalem. He added nothing original to the body of Jewish teaching and law, but he did emphasize the need for an interior and character-filled understanding of that law rather than its ritualized application. The Gospels record his strong identification with the poor and the outcast in the Roman province of Judaea, his compassion, and his role as a powerful scourge of the self-righteous.

The subsequent success of Christianity has been founded on two doctrines, which have a strong human appeal: God's incarnation in the world, and then the Crucifixion by that world of His son. The revelation of a vulnerable God – first as an infant and then as a man nailed to the cross like a common criminal – changed human history. Plato had observed that the history of the world is the victory of persuasion over force. But in the person of Christ that philosophical insight became embodied in the person who called himself the Son of Man.

---

guard and is succeeded by his uncle Claudius (Tiberius Claudius Drusus Nero Germanicus).

43

EUROPE

- The Roman emperor Claudius sends an expedition, under the general Aulus Plautius, to conquer Britain. He follows, arriving after most of the fighting is over but in time to accept the surrender of the British kings Caractacus and Togodumnus at Colchester, E England.

44

MIDDLE EAST AND NORTH AFRICA

- James, a follower (and probably the brother) of Christ, is executed on the orders of Herod Agrippa I, the Roman client king of Judaea and grandson of Herod the Great.
- King Herod Agrippa I dies.

St Paul (c.AD 1–67)

Paul was the first codifier of Christian beliefs and, in many ways, the founder of the Christian Church. He was a Jew, born with the name Saul in the Greek city of Tarsus in Asia Minor. He was also a Roman citizen. At first he supported the anti-Christian campaigns waged by the Jewish council, or Sanhedrin, based in Jerusalem. He was charged with the task of disciplining Christians among the Jewish community at Damascus, but while travelling there he had a vision of the risen Christ and was converted.

Paul then headed the Christian mission to convert the gentiles, the non-Jews of the Roman empire. It was Paul who established the idea that Christianity was a universal religion, not just a Jewish sect. He travelled to Syria, Cyprus, Macedonia, Greece and Asia Minor. On his return to Jerusalem in AD 58 the Roman authorities detained him after a series of riots by Jews outraged by his activities. Paul used his status as a Roman citizen to appeal to the emperor and was transferred to Rome, where he was put to death under Nero in 67.

Pauline theology, as expressed in his letters, is effectively a presentation of the teachings of Christ filtered through Paul's own temperament. The flesh and the spirit were always at war within his character, and Paul introduced into Christianity a fascination with sexual desire that is not evident in the original Gospels. Paul developed a complete theology of original sin. This theology was universal, for Paul believed that all humans behave fundamentally the same regardless of their politics, ethnicity or culture. This perspective made Graeco-Roman culture look parochial. After Paul, it seemed naively intellectual to accept the Greek philosophical claim that acting badly was just the result of wrong thinking.

46

EUROPE

– The apostle Paul of Tarsus (see box) travels on a missionary journey to Cyprus and Galatia (in modern Turkey). Paul has taken the original Jewish teachings of Christ and developed Christianity as a universal religion that is to be proclaimed to the gentiles as well as to the Jews. Having Hellenized his Jewish name Saul after his conversion on the road to Damascus, Paul devotes himself to spreading the message of Christ through preaching and writing. He had previously been a devout follower of orthodox Judaism.

48

EUROPE

– The Romans invade W Britain. Campaigns follow over a 30-year period as the Romans attempt to control the area.

SCIENCE AND TECHNOLOGY

– Roman engineers start to build a network of roads throughout Britain.

49

EUROPE

– The Roman emperor Claudius expels those Jewish Christians who question the legitimacy of imperial rule.

50

EUROPE

– The Romans found Londinium (London). It is built at the lowest point on the Thames at which Roman engineers can construct a bridge.
– The Roman emperor Claudius fortifies a Germanic settlement on the Rhine and names it Colonia Agrippinae (modern Cologne, Germany) after his niece and fourth wife, Agrippina, who was born there.

54

EUROPE

– The Roman emperor Claudius dies having eaten poisoned mushrooms, part of the empress Agrippina's plot to rule through her son Nero (Lucius Domitius Ahenobarbus).

55

SCIENCE AND TECHNOLOGY

– Greek physician Pedanius Dioscorides publishes *De materia medica* (On Medical Substances), a botanical text.

58

MIDDLE EAST AND NORTH AFRICA

– Christian missionary Paul of Tarsus (see 46) arrives in Jerusalem: the Roman authorities arrest him and send him for trial before the procurator of Judaea.

59

EUROPE

– The Roman emperor Nero orders the killing of his mother Agrippina on the urging of his adviser, the Stoic philosopher Lucius Annaeus Seneca (Seneca the Younger).

60

MIDDLE EAST AND NORTH AFRICA

– Festus, the Roman procurator of Judaea, conducts the trial of the Christian missionary Paul of Tarsus, who makes an appeal for benevolence to Caesar (since he is a Roman citizen). Paul is later allowed to live in Rome, at first under house arrest, but is later given the freedom to continue travelling.

61-70

61
EUROPE
– Boudicca (Boadicea), queen of the Iceni in E Anglia, leads the SE British tribes in a bloody and destructive rebellion against Roman rule, which is crushed by the Roman legions in the S. Roman authorities order their engineers to build a 2.4m (8 feet) thick wall around Londinium (London).

63
ARTS AND HUMANITIES
Seneca, *Epistolae morales*, Stoic philosophy.

64
EUROPE
18 July A huge fire destroys over half of the city of Rome. The emperor Nero is said to have watched the spectacle, reciting verses about the destruction of Troy. He blames the fire on the Christians, whom he subsequently persecutes. Nero's reconstruction plan for the city includes wide streets and large squares, whose cleanliness is invigilated by the *aediles* (magistrates in charge of municipal affairs). The *aediles* also control the food supply by supervising grain storage and ensuring the freshness of meat, fish and poultry.

MIDDLE EAST AND NORTH AFRICA
– The Great Temple at Jerusalem has now been rebuilt.

Babylon is fallen, is fallen, that great city.

Bible, Revelation 14:8 (late 1st century AD) – an early Christian longs for Rome to suffer the fate of Babylon

66
EUROPE
– The Roman satirical writer Gaius Petronius is accused of treason by the emperor Nero and ordered to commit suicide.

MIDDLE EAST AND NORTH AFRICA
– The First Jewish Revolt against what Jews perceive to be the sacrileges of the occupying Roman soldiers breaks out.

ARTS AND HUMANITIES
Petronius, *Satyricon*, satire on Roman manners.

67
EUROPE
– Around this date Christian missionary Paul of Tarsus (see 46) is executed on the Via Ostia outside Rome.

MIDDLE EAST AND NORTH AFRICA
– The Roman general Vespasian (Titus Flavius Sabinus Vespasianus) and his son Titus enter Galilee. All the Jews of Caesarea have been killed by the local gentiles. The Jewish military leader Flavius Josephus (Joseph ben Matthias) holds the besieged fortress of Jotapata, but eventually yields and is treated leniently by Vespasian. Josephus later goes to Rome with Titus, becomes a Roman citizen and writes *History of the Jewish War* and *Jewish Antiquities* (a history of the Jews from the Creation to AD 66).

68
EUROPE
– The emperor Nero is sentenced to death by the senate. The praetorian guard recognizes the general Servius Sulpicius Galba as emperor. Nero commits suicide (9 June), thereby ending the Julio-Claudian line of emperors.

69
EUROPE
– The Year of the Four Emperors: eight Roman legions on the Rhine refuse to accept Galba as emperor and declare the legate Aulus Vitellius their emperor. Galba is murdered (15 Jan.) by Nero's friend Marcus Salvius Otho, who is recognized as emperor by the senate.
– Two of Vitellius's loyal legions defeat Otho at the battle of Bedriacum near Cremona, N Italy (19 April). Vespasian, legate of Judaea, is proclaimed emperor by the prefect of Egypt (1 July). The Danubian legions support Vespasian and defeat Vitellius (Oct.) in the second battle of Bedriacum. The senate recognizes Vespasian as emperor. The emperor Vitellius dies in a street battle (20 Dec.).

MIDDLE EAST AND NORTH AFRICA
– The Roman emperor Vespasian besieges Jerusalem; John of Giscala, leader of the Zealots (the party of revolt among the Jews), is in charge of the resistance movement.

70
EUROPE
– The emperor Vespasian returns to Rome, leaving his son Titus in charge of the Jerusalem campaign. The emperor quells a rebellion in Gaul, renews the tax system and rebuilds the Capitol, which was burned in civil war fighting. But the city's grain supply is affected by bad weather, preventing grain ships from arriving at Rome's port, Ostia.

MIDDLE EAST AND NORTH AFRICA
7 Sept. Jerusalem falls. The Romans destroy most of the Temple, leaving only the Wailing Wall standing. Most of Judaea becomes an imperial domain, and a Roman legion is stationed in Jerusalem, which is ruled by a senatorial legate. The Romans abolish the Jewish high priesthood, and the tax previously

paid by the Jews to support the Temple is now diverted to the Roman treasury.

73

MIDDLE EAST AND NORTH AFRICA
– Rather than surrender to the Romans, about 1000 Jewish Zealots commit mass-suicide at Masada, near the Dead Sea, bringing the First Jewish Revolt (see 66) to an end.

76

ASIA
– Chinese armies defeat the Xiongnu nomads (probably the Huns) who have been raiding China for 200 years.

77

EUROPE
– The Roman general Gnaeus Julius Agricola arrives in Britain to continue the conquest. The city of Deva (modern Chester) is founded by the Romans.

79

EUROPE
23 June The Roman emperor Vespasian dies and is succeeded by his son Titus (Titus Flavius Vespasianus).
24 Aug. Mt Vesuvius erupts: the Roman cities of Pompeii and Herculaneum (S of Naples) are buried in lava, mud and ashes.

SCIENCE AND TECHNOLOGY
– Pliny the Elder publishes his *Historia Naturalis*, an encyclopedia of natural history. He dies of suffocation from poisonous fumes while staying with a friend near Vesuvius to investigate the eruption (24 Aug.).

80

EUROPE
– A three-month period of celebration in Rome marks the opening of the Colosseum amphitheatre; the games held there will become a powerful tool of imperial politics.

SCIENCE AND TECHNOLOGY
– An epidemic of anthrax breaks out in the Roman world, killing thousands of animals and humans.

ARTS AND HUMANITIES
– The Roman poet Martial (Marcus Valerius Martialis) publishes his *Book of Spectacles*, a commemoration of the dedication of the Colosseum.

81

EUROPE
– The Roman emperor Titus dies and is succeeded by his brother Domitian (Titus Flavius Domitianus).

– The Arch of Titus in Rome commemorates Titus' triumph at Jerusalem in 70.

83

EUROPE
– The Roman general Gnaeus Julius Agricola defeats the Caledonians at the battle of Mons Graupius, somewhere in N Britain. Roman forces reach their northernmost point of occupation in the British Isles.

> *They make a desert and call it peace.*
>
> Tacitus (56–*c*.120) on the native British view of the Romans

84

EUROPE
– The Roman emperor Domitian recalls Agricola from Britain to help meet the challenge from Germanic tribes on the Rhine and Danube.

c.90

ECONOMY AND SOCIETY
– An anonymous Greek sea captain writes *The Periplus of the Erythraean Sea*, a sailing manual for the Indian Ocean.
– The Romans break the Arab monopoly in the spice trade as their ships sail from Egypt to India.

95

ECONOMY AND SOCIETY
– Roman agriculture is in crisis: malaria affects the marshy Campania area, whose fertile soil supplies the city with fresh produce. The malaria outbreak spreads from the Campania to the city.

96

EUROPE
18 Sept. The Roman emperor Domitian is stabbed to death by a freed slave, the empress Domitia and courtiers having conspired against him. The senior senator Nerva (Marcus Cocceius Nerva) succeeds.

97

EUROPE
– The Roman emperor Nerva recalls the general Marcus Ulpius Trajanus from the Rhine and adopts him in the temple of Jupiter on the Capitol (Oct.).

98

EUROPE

25 Jan. The Roman emperor Nerva dies suddenly and his adopted son Marcus Ulpius Trajanus succeeds as the emperor Trajan.

ARTS AND HUMANITIES

- The Roman historian Publius Cornelius Tacitus publishes his *Germania* (Germany), an account of the German peoples of the Rhine.
- The Jewish historian Flavius Josephus (see 67) dies around this date.

105

SCIENCE AND TECHNOLOGY

- The Chinese eunuch Zailun (Tsai Lun) invents a new technique for paper production, using bark, hemp and rags rather than the traditional materials of bamboo and wood.

106

EUROPE

- Dacia (Romania) becomes a Roman province when the emperor Trajan defeats its king, Decebalus, in battle.

110

ASIA

- By now the silk trade is a major tool of Chinese diplomacy, with silk traded in C Asia in exchange for luxury items and also used as a gift to appease the barbarian tribes along the N frontier.

113

EUROPE

- Trajan's Column is erected inside the newly rebuilt Forum in Rome; it illustrates in remarkable detail the emperor's military success in the province of Dacia (see 106).

114

MIDDLE EAST AND NORTH AFRICA

- The Roman emperor Trajan annexes Armenia to the Roman empire.

115

MIDDLE EAST AND NORTH AFRICA

- Roman forces occupy Mesopotamia (part of the Parthian empire) as far as the River Tigris.

ARTS AND HUMANITIES

Tacitus, *Annales*, an influential history of the years 14–68.

116

MIDDLE EAST AND NORTH AFRICA

- The Roman emperor Trajan makes Assyria a Roman province and, crossing the Tigris, annexes the Parthian province of Adiabene. He then advances as far as the Persian Gulf.

117

MIDDLE EAST AND NORTH AFRICA

- Revolts break out in many parts of the Roman empire, including Mesopotamia and N Africa. The Roman emperor Trajan dies in Cilicia in Asia Minor (8 Aug.). His nearest relative, Publius Aelius Hadrianus (Hadrian), learns that he has been adopted by Trajan only a few days before news of the emperor's death reaches him. Hadrian withdraws from Armenia, Assyria and Adiabene.
- Jews in the Middle East, exultant at Trajan's death, rise and kill both Greeks and Romans in a series of massacres.

118

EUROPE

- The rebuilding of the Roman Forum, commissioned by the emperor Trajan, is completed.
- By now Rome's population exceeds one million.

120

ARTS AND HUMANITIES

- The Greek writer Plutarch, who has studied in Athens and taught in Rome, publishes his *Parallel Lives*, a biographical study comparing 23 pairs of eminent Greeks and Romans, from Theseus and Romulus down to his own times.
- The Pantheon, commissioned by the Roman emperor Hadrian, is completed in Rome.

121

ARTS AND HUMANITIES

- The Roman historian Gaius Suetonius Tranquillus (Suetonius) publishes *Lives of the Caesars*, a group biography of the 12 emperors to date beginning with Julius Caesar and ending with Domitian.

122

ARTS AND HUMANITIES

- Following the arrival of the emperor during the spring, the Romans start to build Hadrian's Wall, a frontier wall extending some 116km (72 miles) from Wallsend on the River Tyne to the Solway Firth. Completed in 126, it marks the N boundary of Roman Britain. Its 16 forts provide a defensive barrier against the N tribes, including the Picts.

126–161

Gaius (c.110–180)

The Roman jurist Gaius was the most influential of all Roman writers on law. His *Institutiones*, written in the middle of the 2nd century AD, survive almost intact.

Gaius shows the variety of the sources for the law, including the decrees of the emperors, senatorial decrees and the edicts of the magistrates, as well as the judgements of the jurists themselves. He also shows how Roman law was governed by status, with different legal rights and duties for men, women, slaves and children. About half of Gaius's judgements deal with inheritances

and legacies, illustrating the concerns of the propertied order that ran Rome. They were the basis of Justinian's *Institutes*.

The Roman law described by Gaius was an original and essential feature of Roman civilization, for the Greeks had no theory of jurisprudence (although they did have a variety of legal codes). The earliest Roman laws were kept in memorized form, but were written down early in Rome's history when the citizens demanded written evidence of the basis on which the judges decided guilt and punishment. Roman law

shows the evolution of law from its original theological context. At first law was the concern of the college of priests, but by the 1st century BC there were independent legal consultants, who advised on cases brought to them by individuals. Increasingly, such jurists also served in the imperial court.

As an element in the Napoleonic legal code (see 1804), Roman law has entered into the mainstream of the modern legal tradition in much of continental Europe. It is strongly marked by declaratory clarity and a rationalist working out of legal principles.

126

ARTS AND HUMANITIES
– The Roman satirist Decimus Junius Juvenalis (Juvenal) publishes his *Satires*, incisive attacks on Rome's public life and morals.

ECONOMY AND SOCIETY
– Plague in N Africa spreads to Italy. Italian agriculture is already in decline, however, as cheaper imports from N Africa and Egypt in pre-plague days have depressed wheat prices.

130

ARTS AND HUMANITIES
– The Roman emperor Hadrian completes the building of the temple of Olympian Zeus begun in Athens in 530 BC.

132

MIDDLE EAST AND NORTH AFRICA
– Simon bar-Kokhba and Rabbi Eleazer lead a Jewish rebellion in Jerusalem that consumes Judaea. The austere monotheism of the Jewish faith is offended by the building of a Roman shrine to Jupiter on the site of the old Temple.

135

MIDDLE EAST AND NORTH AFRICA
– After a ruthless campaign, Roman forces under the general Sextus Julius Severus retake Jerusalem and kill Simon bar-Kokhba. The emperor Hadrian orders the total destruction of Jerusalem; a new city, Aelia Capitolina, is built on the site and Judaea is renamed Syria Palestina.
– In one of the seminal events of Jewish history, the Roman emperor Hadrian bars the Jews from Jerusalem and enforces a diaspora (dispersion), which scatters them across the empire.

136

ARTS AND HUMANITIES
– Hadrian's Villa Adriana near Tivoli (NE of Rome) is completed.

138

EUROPE
10 July The Roman emperor Hadrian dies at Baiae after adopting Titus Aurelius Fulvus Boionius Arrius Antoninus as his heir. Antoninus asks the senate to bestow the honour of divinity on the dead Hadrian and it agrees. For this act of piety and gratitude the new emperor will be called Antoninus Pius.

139

EUROPE
– A mausoleum is built at Rome for Hadrian and his successors. After centuries of use, rebuilding and alteration it remains a dominant building in Rome as the Castel Sant'Angelo.

140

EUROPE
– The Antonine Wall is built to extend Rome's hold on N Britain. Built of turf on cobbled foundations, it extends for 60km (37 miles) from the Firth of Forth to the Firth of Clyde.

161

EUROPE
7 Mar. The Roman emperor Antoninus Pius dies after a landmark reign: the provinces are commercially rich, a liberal programme of public aid helps cities with urban problems, aqueducts and baths are now a common sight across the Roman world. The dying emperor has adopted Marcus Annius Verus, who now reigns as Marcus Aurelius.

167
EUROPE
- The emperor Marcus Aurelius defeats a large invasion of Roman territory by Germanic tribes, who have destroyed aqueducts and irrigation channels.

168
EUROPE
- The Roman emperor Marcus Aurelius and his co-emperor Lucius Verus defeat the Marcommani, a Germanic tribe from the Danubian basin who have been active in NW Italy.

169
EUROPE
- The Roman co-emperor Lucius Verus dies.
- Roman forces effectively annihilate the Marcomanni after they break the peace terms of the previous year.

174
EUROPE
- Roman legions defeat the Germanic Quadi tribe: the victory is commemorated by a great column in Rome as a glorious moment in the attainment of the Pax Romana (Roman peace).

175
MIDDLE EAST AND NORTH AFRICA
- The Roman legions in Asia (modern Turkey), thinking the emperor Marcus Aurelius to be dead, revolt under the leadership of Avidus Cassius, who proclaims himself emperor but is betrayed by his previously supportive officers and decapitated, his head being sent to Marcus Aurelius as a show of loyalty.

176
EUROPE
- The Roman emperor Marcus Aurelius and his son Commodus re-enter Rome and are awarded a triumph, a parade celebrating a victory in war, for their military successes over the Germanic tribes N of the Alps.

177
EUROPE
- The Roman emperor Marcus Aurelius begins to kill Christians on a systematic scale, believing their opposition to emperor-worship to be a threat to state security.

180
EUROPE
17 Mar. The Roman emperor and philosopher Marcus Aurelius dies and is succeeded by his son Lucius Aelius Aurelius Commodus, who will prove to be one of the most bloodthirsty despots in Roman imperial history.

SCIENCE AND TECHNOLOGY
- The Greek doctor Galen (Claudius Galenus) publishes his *Methodus medendo* (Method for Physicians), a medical textbook that will remain the ultimate medical authority until well into the European Middle Ages.

ARTS AND HUMANITIES
Marcus Aurelius, *Meditations*, Stoic philosophy.

183
EUROPE
- The Roman emperor Commodus narrowly escapes death at the hands of assassins employed by his sister Lucilla and a number of senators. In retaliation, he sentences many Romans to death on suspicion of conspiracy.

185
EUROPE
- The Roman emperor Commodus empties the state treasury with his spending on spectacular gladiatorial shows. To raise more money to pay for these state entertainments he confiscates private property.

189
EUROPE
- Plague hits Rome again. The disease, which is probably smallpox, kills as many as 2000 people a day.

ARTS AND HUMANITIES
- The triumphal column of Marcus Aurelius is completed in Rome.

It's certain because it is impossible.

Tertullian (*c*.160–220) on Christianity

190
EUROPE
- Quintus Septimius Florens Tertullianis (Tertullian) is converted to Christianity. As a churchman he will have a decisive practical influence in Church administration, while his writings will emphasize how persecution has actually helped the growth of Christianity.

192

EUROPE

31 Dec. The Roman emperor Commodus is murdered and the Antonine line that has been in power since 138 comes to an end. Having found their names on an imperial list for execution, the emperor's mistress Marcia, his chamberlain Eclectus and the prefect of the praetorian guard Laetus hire the celebrated wrestler Narcissus to strangle the emperor.

193

EUROPE

– Publius Helvius Pertinax is nominated by the Roman senate and reluctantly succeeds as emperor, but he is soon murdered (28 Mar.) by members of the praetorian guard. Rome's richest senator, Didius Julianus, succeeds, paying 300 million sesterces for the imperial purple.

– The Pannonian legate Lucius Septimius Severus offers his troops on the Danube huge bonuses if they march with him to Rome to challenge Didius Julianus. Entering the city (1 June), Septimius Severus has Didius Julianus killed in the palace baths and succeeds as emperor.

195

EUROPE

– The Roman emperor Septimius Severus sacks the Greek city of Byzantium (later Constantinople, now Istanbul) for supporting a pretender to the throne, reducing it to a village.

197

EUROPE

– Clodius Albinus, the Roman legate in Britain, leaves Britain for Gaul to rally the support of legions in Germany. He declares himself emperor but is defeated by Septimius Severus and (19 Feb.) is killed at Lugdunum (Lyons, France).

200

ASIA

– The Huns (see 80) invade Afghanistan.

– According to later tradition, the Japanese empress Jingu sends a fleet to invade Korea. On seeing the vast fleet, the Koreans capitulate and offer to pay tribute.

ARTS AND HUMANITIES

– The Palestinian scholar Judah ha-Kadosh compiles 39 tractates of the *Mishnah*, the foundations of Jewish Talmudic law.

204

MIDDLE EAST AND NORTH AFRICA

– An economic recession threatens the N African province of Leptis Magna (modern Libya). The Roman emperor Septimius

Severus intervenes to buy up local supplies of olive oil, a staple of the Roman diet, which he then distributes for free in Rome.

211

EUROPE

4 Feb. Septimius Severus dies at Eboracum (York, N England) and is succeeded by his eldest son Marcus Aurelius Antoninus, called Caracalla after the hooded tunic he introduces from Gaul.

212

EUROPE

– The Roman emperor Caracalla extends Roman citizenship to all free male inhabitants of the empire by imperial edict, with the exception of a few limited groups, including Egyptians, who are technically outside the Roman system of government because they are ruled personally by the emperor.

c.213

EUROPE

– The Baths of Caracalla are completed in Rome.

217

MIDDLE EAST AND NORTH AFRICA

8 April The Roman emperor Caracalla is murdered at Edessa by a group of senior army officers while he is preparing for the invasion of Parthia. He is succeeded by Marcus Opellius Macrinus, one of the murderers.

218

MIDDLE EAST AND NORTH AFRICA

8 June The Roman emperor Macrinus is killed in battle near Antioch and is succeeded by the 12-year-old Syrian Varius Avitus Bassianus (Septimius Severus' grand-nephew by marriage) who calls himself Heliogabalus (Elagabalus) after the Syrian sun god. His mother Julia Maesa is effectively in charge.

220

ASIA

– In China the Han dynasty is replaced by the period of the Three Kingdoms: that of the Wei in the N (220–264), the Wu in the S (222–280) and the Shu Han in the W (221–263). China will go through a period of territorial fragmentation until the advent of the Sui dynasty in 581.

222

EUROPE

11 Mar. The Roman emperor Heliogabalus is murdered by the praetorian guard and succeeded by his cousin and adopted son Marcus Aurelius Severus Alexander. The reign of Severus Alexander will be dominated by his mother Julia Mamaea.

224

MIDDLE EAST AND NORTH AFRICA

– The Parthian Arsacid dynasty that rules Persia is overthrown by Ardashir, the vassal king of Fars (S Iran), who defeats and kills King Artabanus V at Hormuz. Ardashir becomes the first king of the Sassanian dynasty (named after Ardashir's grandfather Sassan), which will rule Persia until 642.

225

ASIA

– Tea drinking is developing in popularity in China.

SCIENCE AND TECHNOLOGY

– Chinese alchemists under the Wu dynasty (see 220) mix sulphur and saltpetre in the correct proportions and at the correct temperature to make an early form of gunpowder.

234

EUROPE

– The Roman emperor Severus Alexander decrees that bread rather than grain be issued to the Roman poor.

235

EUROPE

Feb. The Roman emperor Severus Alexander buys peace from the Germanic Alemanni tribe who have invaded Gaul.
18 Mar. The Roman emperor Severus Alexander is murdered by his troops stationed on the Rhine, who declare the Thracian Gaius Julius Verus Maximinus emperor.

238

MIDDLE EAST AND NORTH AFRICA

– Roman citizens in Africa revolt against Maximinus and elect as emperor Antonius Gordianus Africanus, the 80-year-old proconsul for Africa. Gordianus reluctantly accepts, but supporters of Maximinus besiege him at Carthage. Gordianus' son, another Gordianus, is killed and Gordianus commits suicide on hearing the news. The Roman people proclaim Gordianus' grandson, Marcus Antonius Gordianus, emperor. The praetorian guard murder Maximinus, and Gordianus' grandson becomes sole emperor as Gordianus III (June).

244

MIDDLE EAST AND NORTH AFRICA

– At the battle of Resaena the Roman emperor Gordianus III defeats the Persians and drives them back across the Euphrates. Gordianus is murdered by soldiers under the Arabian Marcus Julius Philippus, an officer in the praetorian guard. Philippus (now known as Philip the Arab) is proclaimed emperor and concludes a peace with the Persians.

247

EUROPE

– The Roman emperor Philip the Arab holds a great exhibition of games to celebrate the 1000th anniversary of the foundation of Rome in 753 BC.

249

EUROPE

– The Roman commander Gaius Messius Quintus Trajanus (Decius) quells a revolt of the troops in his native Pannonia (modern Austria and Slovenia). His troops proclaim him emperor. Decius kills the emperor Philip the Arab (see 244) who is marching to meet him in battle at Verona.

250

EUROPE

– The Roman emperor Decius attempts a full-scale restoration of paganism, bringing back the persecution of Christians as a state policy.

SCIENCE AND TECHNOLOGY

– Around this time Greek mathematician Diophantus of Alexandria writes *Arithmetica,* an algebraic text.

251

EUROPE

– The Roman emperor Decius and his son are killed fighting the Goths, a Germanic tribe, in the Dobrudja (Romania). The general Gaius Vibius Trebonianus Gallus (Gallus) succeeds and makes peace with the Goths, bribing them not to return.

253

EUROPE

– Aemilianus, governor of Pannonia (modern Austria and Slovenia) and Moesia (modern Serbia and Bulgaria), is declared Roman emperor by troops on the Danube. Although he defeats Gallus, he dies soon afterwards. Publius Licinius Valerianus (Valerian), a supporter of Gallus, is proclaimed emperor as the troops' favourite.
– Plague returns to Rome, sweeping from Egypt throughout Europe.

260

EUROPE

– Rome is an empire in crisis, its frontiers attacked by, among others, Berbers, Franks, Goths, Palmyrans and Vandals. Disease kills tens of thousands of people. The denarius, a bronze coin of great antiquity, is almost worthless; trade is paralysed and barter returns; tradesmen and small farmers are ruined. Large landowners seize the opportunity to increase their estates.

MIDDLE EAST AND NORTH AFRICA
- The Persian king Shapur I invites the Roman emperor Valerian to a conference at Edessa (SE Turkey) and seizes him treacherously, keeping him prisoner in humiliating circumstances. Valerian's son Publius Licinius Egnatius Gallienus (Gallienus) succeeds as emperor.

MIDDLE EAST AND NORTH AFRICA
- Emperor Gallienus is complicit in the assassination of an ally of Rome, Prince Odenaethus of Palmyra (in modern Syria). Odenaethus is succeeded by his wife Septimia Zenobia, who will extend the Palmyran realm from the Nile to the Red Sea.

EUROPE
- The Roman emperor Gallienus is killed by his own soldiers in Mediolanum (Milan) while besieging the pretender Aureolus. Another pretender, Marcus Aurelius Claudius (Claudius II), kills Aureolus and becomes emperor.
- Claudius II repels a Gothic invasion of the Balkans and is awarded the title Gothicus.

MIDDLE EAST AND NORTH AFRICA
- Zenobia of Palmyra (see 267) conquers Egypt and so controls part of Rome's grain supply.

270

EUROPE
- The Roman emperor Claudius II dies from the plague. He is succeeded by his brother Quintillus, who fails to get military backing and commits suicide. Lucius Domitius Aurelianus (Aurelian), a member of Claudius II's inner circle, becomes emperor.

271

EUROPE
- The Roman emperor Aurelian expels the Germanic Alemanni tribe from Italy. He abandons trans-Danubian Dacia as a lost cause and settles its Roman inhabitants in a new area carved out of Moesia (see 253) and named Dacia. He builds new walls (the Aurelian Walls) to protect the city of Rome and earns the epithet *Restitutor Orbis* (World Restorer).

272

EUROPE
- In Lutetia (renamed Paris by the early 4th century after its original pre-Roman inhabitants, the Gallic tribe of the Parisii), three Christians are beheaded on the road leading to the temple of Mercury, which stands on a hill that will be renamed Montmartre (Martyrs' Mount).

MIDDLE EAST AND NORTH AFRICA
- The Roman emperor Aurelian lays siege to Palmyra (see 267) and captures both Queen Zenobia and her son Vaballathus. She is marched in chains of gold before the emperor's triumphal procession but the emperor spares her life.

273

EUROPE
- The Roman emperor Aurelian increases the daily ration of bread in Rome to nearly 680g (1½ pounds) each for those who qualify.

MIDDLE EAST AND NORTH AFRICA
- Threatened by a revolt in Palmyra (see 272), the Roman emperor Aurelian intervenes and puts down the rebellion.

274

EUROPE
- At the battle of Châlons the Roman emperor Aurelian quells a rebellion in Gaul and recovers Rome's authority.

275

EUROPE
- The Roman emperor Aurelian prepares to invade Persia but is murdered by senior officers and succeeded by the elderly senator Tacitus.

MIDDLE EAST AND NORTH AFRICA
- Around this date St Anthony begins a hermetic life of study and prayer in the Egyptian desert, marking the beginnings of Christian monasticism.

276

EUROPE
- The Roman emperor Tacitus is murdered by his troops despite his victories over the Goths and the Alans, who are invading Asia Minor. He is succeeded by his brother, Marcus Annius Florianus, who is then himself murdered. The Illyrian Marcus Aurelius Probus succeeds.

MIDDLE EAST AND NORTH AFRICA
- The Persian religious teacher Mani is executed, having fallen foul of traditionalist Zoroastrian priests (see 553 BC). He taught for 30 years at the court of the Persian king Shapur I and made extensive missionary journeys to China, India and Turkestan. His system, Manichaeism, will become an important Christian heresy: it combines elements of the Christian salvationist tradition along with a Zoroastrian emphasis on dualism.

280

ASIA
- The Western Jin ruler Wudi reunites China temporarily.

282

EUROPE

– The Roman emperor Probus drives the Germanic Franks and Alemanni out of Gaul, strengthens Rome's defensive positions on the Danube and pacifies Asia Minor. He is murdered by his troops and succeeded by Marcus Aurelius Carus, his praetorian prefect. Carus wages a successful campaign against the Persians.

283

MIDDLE EAST AND NORTH AFRICA

– The Roman emperor Carus dies in Mesopotamia (reputedly after being struck by lightning) and is succeeded by his son and co-emperor Marcus Aurelius Numerius Numerianus.

284

MIDDLE EAST AND NORTH AFRICA

– The Roman emperor Numerian is assassinated by the Illyrian general Gaius Aurelius Valerius Diocletianus Jovius (Diocletian), who succeeds him and is proclaimed emperor (29 Aug.) at Chalcedon in Bithynia. Diocletian bases himself at Nicomedia in Bithynia, while his colleague Marcus Aurelius Valerius Maximianus Herculius (Maximian) controls the W part of the Roman empire from Mediolanum (Milan). The idea that the empire needs to be divided administratively gains currency.

– The Coptic Church in Egypt is now using 29 Aug. as the first day of its calendar.

291

ASIA

– The 'Rebellion of the Eight Princes': China is divided once again.

301

MIDDLE EAST AND NORTH AFRICA

– At Nicomedia the Roman emperor Diocletian introduces state control of prices and services as a measure against the collapse of the currency. The edict is difficult to enforce against merchants and traders in the E, while in the W it is not enforced at all.

– Armenia becomes the first state to make Christianity an official state religion.

302

EUROPE

– Diocletian's public baths open in Rome and prove to be the most lavish state enterprise yet with their 3000 rooms.

303

EUROPE

24 Feb. The Roman emperor Diocletian embarks on a state-sponsored persecution of Christians.

305

EUROPE

1 May Diocletian and Maximian abdicate as co-rulers of the Roman empire and a period of civil war ensues. Diocletian retires to Salona and is succeeded by the Thracian Galerius Valerius Maximanus (Galerius), the adviser who persuaded him to adopt anti-Christian legislation. Galerius co-reigns with the Illyrian Flavius Valerius Constantius (Constantius I), who succeeds Maximian.

306

EUROPE

25 July The Roman co-emperor Constantius I dies near Eboracum (York, N England). Constantine I (the Great), illegitimate son of Constantius I, is proclaimed emperor in York by the legions, but confines his claim to Britain and Gaul. He is one of six claimants to the imperial title. The emperor Galerius elevates Flavius Valerius Severus (Severus) to the rank of co-emperor. Marcus Aurelius Valerius Maxentius (Maxentius), son of Maximian (see 284), rebels and the praetorian guard declare him emperor.

307

EUROPE

11 Nov. The Roman co-emperor Severus dies. Galerius replaces him with Valerius Licinianus Licinius (Licinius).

311

EUROPE

May The Roman emperor Galerius dies after the rebel Maxentius forces him out of Italy. The rebel emperor Constantine begins to march on Rome.

ASIA

– The Chinese city of Luoyang is destroyed by Xiongnu (Hsiung-nu), or Huns, invaders from the N. China will be divided into N and S areas ruled by separate dynasties until 589.

312

EUROPE

– At the battle of the Milvian Bridge, Rome, Constantine I defeats his rival Maxentius and becomes the sole ruler of the Roman empire in the W. Constantine claims to have been inspired by a vision of the Cross in the sky bearing the words *in hoc signo vinces* (by this sign you will conquer) and adopts the words as his personal motto.

313

EUROPE

– The Edict of Milan, issued jointly by Constantine I and Licinius, emperor in the E, grants religious toleration to Christians throughout the Roman empire.

314

EUROPE

8 Oct. At the battle of Cibalae the Roman emperor Constantine I defeats his co-emperor Licinius, who loses most of his Balkan territories. Constantine is angered by Licinius's increasingly anti-Christian policy.

315

ARTS AND HUMANITIES

– The Arch of Constantine is built in Rome.

320

MIDDLE EAST AND NORTH AFRICA

– By now forces loyal to the Aksumite rulers of N Ethiopia have conquered the Cushite kingdom of Meroe (see 590 BC).

ASIA

– Chandragupta I founds the Gupta dynasty, which will rule N and C India until the 6th century. During his reign Chandragupta will endow at Bihar (NE India) a place of worship for Chinese Buddhists.

321

EUROPE

– Sunday becomes the Sabbath in the Roman empire: the emperor Constantine I forbids work on this day.

323

EUROPE

3 July At the battle of Adrianople (modern Edirne in European Turkey), Flavius Julius Crispus, son of the Roman emperor Constantine I, defeats the co-emperor Licinius. Licinius sustains another defeat at the sea battle of Chrysopolis (Scutari) (18 Sept.).

324

EUROPE

– Constantine I defeats Licinius, the emperor in the E, becoming sole emperor. By 325 Licinius will have been put to death on Constantine's orders. He begins to build Rome up after the catastrophes of the 3rd century: peace returns along the frontiers, a new coinage is introduced, supported by the booty of confiscation, and taxation is simplified.

325

MIDDLE EAST AND NORTH AFRICA

– The Roman emperor Constantine I summons the Council of Nicaea (in N Turkey), the first general council of the Christian Church. It formulates the view that God and the Son are of the same 'substance', in opposition to Arius (see 336) who has said they are not, thus effectively denying the divinity of Christ. Arianism is condemned as heretical. The statement of faith that will become the Nicene Creed is formulated, though it will later be altered.

326

EUROPE

– Fausta, the wife of the Roman emperor Constantine I, persuades him to execute Flavius Julius Crispus, Constantine's son by his first wife. His heirs will be the three sons born by his union with Fausta.

330

EUROPE

11 May The Roman emperor Constantine I dedicates Constantinople (modern Istanbul) as his new Roman capital, formalizing the eastward shift of Roman power. The city, built over the previous six years, is settled on the site of the ancient Greek city of Byzantium.

335

MIDDLE EAST AND NORTH AFRICA

17 Sept. The Church of the Holy Sepulchre in Jerusalem is consecrated on the spot believed to have been that of the tomb of Christ on the hill of Golgotha.

336

EUROPE

– Arius, propounder of the Arian heresy, is tortured to death in Constantinople for promoting his views, which are contrary to the findings of the Council of Nicaea (see 325).

337

EUROPE

22 May The Roman emperor Constantine I dies and his sons Constans I, Constantine II and Constantius II succeed as co-emperors.

340

EUROPE

Mar. At Aquileia, N Italy, the Roman emperor Constans I defeats and kills his brother and co-emperor Constantine II.

341

MIDDLE EAST AND NORTH AFRICA

- Coptic Christianity, the oldest version of the faith (along with Armenian Christianity), is introduced to Ethiopia and will become the state religion.

350

EUROPE

- The Roman emperor Constans I is murdered in a coup led by the soldier Magnentius, who is supported in the W. But Constans' brother and co-emperor Constantius II defeats Magnentius at Mursa and pursues him into Gaul.

353

EUROPE

Aug. The usurping emperor Magnentius is finally defeated and commits suicide, leaving Constantius II as sole emperor.

355

EUROPE

- The Alemanni tribe crosses the Rhine into Roman Gaul.

356

EUROPE

19 Feb. The Roman emperor Constantius II issues a decree closing down all the pagan temples of the Roman empire.

357

EUROPE

28 April The Roman emperor Constantius II visits Rome for the first time.

25 Aug. Flavius Claudius Julianus (Julian), cousin of the Roman emperor Constantius II, defeats the Germanic Alemanni tribe at Strasburg and pushes them back beyond the Rhine.

360

EUROPE

- The Huns, a nomadic tribe of horse riders from Asia, move into E Europe.
- Picts cross Hadrian's Wall (see 122) and attack Roman forces stationed in N Britain.

361

EUROPE

3 Nov. The Roman emperor Constantius II dies near Tarsus, Cilicia (in modern Turkey), as he marches to confront his rival Julian, who has been declared emperor by his troops in Gaul. The popular will in Constantinople is that Julian should become emperor.

11 Nov. Julian (known as the Apostate) enters Rome and embarks on an 18-month reign during which he will try to reinstate paganism as the organized state religion.

363

MIDDLE EAST AND NORTH AFRICA

26 June The Roman emperor Julian is killed in battle by the Persians and is succeeded by Flavius Jovianus (Jovian), captain of the imperial bodyguard.

- The Roman emperor Jovian signs a humiliating treaty with the Persian shah Shapur II and yields the kingdom of Armenia. Jovian dies at Dadastana (Feb.) before trying to return to Constantinople and is succeeded by Valentinian, a Pannonian general, who appoints his own brother Valens as co-emperor. Valentinian I rules the W empire from Britain to NW Africa, while Valens rules the E empire from the River Danube to the Persian frontier.

372

EUROPE

- A new wave of Hun invasions overruns E Europe. The Huns defeat their rivals the Alans and the Heruls. They also destroy the Ostrogothic empire ruled by Ermanaric and for a period are successful in absorbing the Ostrogoths. They systematically rout the Visigoths settled on the River Dniester.

ASIA

- Buddhism is by now spreading from China into Korea.

375

EUROPE

17 Nov. The Roman emperor in the W, Valentinian I, dies of apoplexy on the Danubian frontier. As a ruler he mixed capricious cruelty with occasional philanthropy, founding schools and providing doctors for the poor of Constantinople. His four-year-old son succeeds as Valentinian II, but the real power is held by his half-brother based in Milan, the 17-year-old Flavius Gratianus (Gratian).

376

EUROPE

- The Germanic Visigoth tribe, seeking refuge from the Huns, are allowed by the Romans to settle in lower Moesia (modern Bulgaria).

378

EUROPE

9 Aug. At the battle of Adrianople (modern Edirne in European Turkey) the Visigoths, mounted on horseback, kill the Roman emperor in the E, Valens. Roman foot soldiers are routed by the new power of cavalry. The Roman emperor in the W, Gratian,

summons his general Flavius Theodosius to replace Valens as emperor in the E.
– At Argentaria (Horburg) the Roman emperor Gratian defeats the southernmost branch of the Germanic Alemanni tribe.

379

EUROPE

19 Jan. The Roman emperor Theodosius I assumes office in the E and accommodates the Germanic Visigoth tribe by settling them as military allies in the Balkans.

MIDDLE EAST AND NORTH AFRICA

– Shapur II, shah of Persia, dies. During his reign he has not only confronted and defeated the Romans and conquered Armenia but has also rebuilt Susa, founded Nishapur and managed a huge population transfer from W territories to Susiana (Khuzistan).

383

EUROPE

– The Roman emperor Gratian is deserted by the forces stationed at Lutetia (modern Paris). He flees to Lyons and is then handed over to a rebel general and assassinated (25 Aug.).
– An insurrection in Britain and Gaul is led by Magnus Clemens Maximus, who is now recognized as emperor by Gratian's younger brother Valentinian II and his co-emperor Theodosius I. He rules as co-emperor with recognition in Britain, Gaul and the Hispanic provinces.

388

EUROPE

– Maximus breaks the boundaries of his limited power and marches into Italy. The co-emperor Theodosius I defeats him at Aquileia, N Italy (28 July), and he is murdered. Valentinian II, still only 17, continues as co-emperor.

390

EUROPE

– Bishop Ambrose of Milan, a scholar-administrator of considerable powers, forces the Roman emperor in the E, Theodosius I, to perform public penance for his massacre of 7000 rebels in Thessalonica the previous year.

391

MIDDLE EAST AND NORTH AFRICA

– The great Library of Alexandria, Egypt, is destroyed by fire. The Roman emperor in the E, Theodosius I, has ordered that all non-Christian books be destroyed.

392

EUROPE

15 May The Roman emperor Valentinian II is murdered at Vienne in Gaul at the instigation of the Frankish general Arbogast, who sets up Eugenius, a grammarian and rhetorician, as emperor.

394

EUROPE

6 Sept. The Roman emperor Eugenius is killed by legions loyal to Theodosius I, the Roman emperor in the E: Arbogast, the Frankish general who supported him, flees and commits suicide.

395

EUROPE

17 Jan. Theodosius I dies in Milan, and the Roman empire splits definitively into E and W halves. The E Roman empire becomes known as the Byzantine empire. Arcadius, son of Theodosius I, will govern the E from Constantinople. Theodosius' other son Honorius will rule the W from Milan, but under the dominance of his military commander, Stilicho, a Vandal and Honorius' father-in-law.
– The area around Rome, the Campania, is by now a malaria-infested swamp, ruined mostly as a result of bad agricultural practices.

397

EUROPE

– The Roman commander Stilicho drives Alaric and the Visigoths out of Greece after a tenacious two-year campaign. Stilicho is himself of Germanic extraction.
– Ninian, the son of a British chieftain, starts to evangelize the S Picts. He establishes a church at Whithorn in Galloway and is consecrated a bishop.

ARTS AND HUMANITIES

– Around this date Augustine (see p. 62), bishop of Hippo in N Africa, writes his *Confessions*, an intimate, psychological autobiography.

What have Christians to do with kings?

A North African dissident view, 4th century AD

401
EUROPE
- The Visigoths, a Germanic tribe, penetrate the N Italian peninsula under Alaric, their king.

402
EUROPE
6 April At the battle of Pollentia the Roman commander Stilicho stops the southward march of the Visigoths.

403
EUROPE
- The Roman emperor Honorius leaves Milan for Ravenna (NE Italy), which he makes the capital of the W Roman empire (see also 476).

406
EUROPE
23 Aug. The Roman commander Stilicho defeats an invading Germanic army under Radagasius at Florence.
- Vandal forces under King Gunderic cross the Rhine. Together with their allies the Alans and the Sciri, they proceed along the Moselle valley and sack Rheims, Amiens, Arras and Tournai. They then march S to Aquitaine (SW France).

407
EUROPE
- The usurper Constantine III departs from Britain to pursue his bid for the imperial throne.

408
EUROPE
22 Aug. The Roman emperor Honorius is persuaded to order the murder of his commander Stilicho by the jealous chancellor Olympus.
- The Visigoths, led by Alaric, besiege Rome.
- Arcadius, the Byzantine emperor, dies and is succeeded by his seven-year-old son Theodosius II, who is dominated by his sister Pulcheria.

409
EUROPE
- The Visigoth leader Alaric reinvades Italy and besieges Rome for a second time. He sets up a pagan emperor whom he then deposes.
- The Vandals cross the Pyrenees into the Iberian peninsula.
- Revolt in Britain against Constantine III (see 407 and 411) marks the end of Roman rule in Britain.

410
EUROPE
25 Aug. The Visigoths under Alaric sack Rome after a third siege. Alaric dies shortly afterwards on his way to Sicily.

SCIENCE AND TECHNOLOGY
- The Huns introduce stirrups, which enable horses to be ridden more easily.

411
EUROPE
- The usurper Constantine III is defeated near Arles by the Roman general Constantius. Constantine is taken prisoner and killed at Ravenna.

412
EUROPE
- Alaric's brother Ataulf leads the Visigoth forces into Gaul.
- The Byzantine emperor, Theodosius II, allows his sister Pulcheria to reign as regent.

415
EUROPE
- The Visigoths invade the Iberian peninsula, taking territory from their fellow Germans, the Vandals.

MIDDLE EAST AND NORTH AFRICA
Mar. Cyril, Christian bishop of Alexandria, incites a city mob to tear the neo-Platonic philosopher Hypatia from her chariot, strip her naked and scrape her to death with oyster shells.

421
EUROPE
- Emperor Honorius makes his brother-in-law co-emperor as Constantius III. However, Constantius soon dies (Sept.).

MIDDLE EAST AND NORTH AFRICA
- The Byzantine emperor, Theodosius II, sends an army into Persia where King Varahran has been persecuting Christians.

422
EUROPE
- The walls of Rome's Colosseum crack during an earthquake.

MIDDLE EAST AND NORTH AFRICA
- The Byzantine emperor, Theodosius II, concludes peace with the Persians.

423
EUROPE
- The Ostrogoths settled S of the Danube by Theodosius II organize a huge farm strike. They are bought off with a farm loan.

425

EUROPE

– A plague stops the advance of the Huns on Constantinople.

c.426

ARTS AND HUMANITIES

Augustine of Hippo, *The City of God*, a philosophical and theological account of the historical process.

427

ASIA

– Changsu, king of Korea, moves his capital from the banks of the Yalu River to Pyongyang.

429

MIDDLE EAST AND NORTH AFRICA

– A mass Vandal force under King Gaiseric (Genseric) invades N Africa by crossing the Strait of Gibraltar from the Iberian peninsula.

430

EUROPE

– The British Christian misisonary Patrick travels from SW Britain to convert Ireland.

MIDDLE EAST AND NORTH AFRICA

– The Vandals lay siege to Hippo, N Africa.

ARTS AND HUMANITIES

28 Aug. Augustine of Hippo (see box) dies during the siege of his city by the Vandals.

431

MIDDLE EAST AND NORTH AFRICA

– Nestorius, patriarch of Constantinople, is deposed for heresy and banished to the Libyan desert by the Council of Ephesus for preaching that Christ had two natures: human and divine. The Council of Ephesus recognizes Mary as the Mother of God, and the cult of the Virgin begins to spread W from Constantinople.

433

EUROPE

– Attila becomes leader of the Huns. Known to later Christian writers as the 'scourge of God', he will attack both the E (441–443 and 447–449) and W (450–452) Roman empires to force increases in the tributes paid to him.

438

ECONOMY AND SOCIETY

– *Codex Theodosianus*, a summary of Roman law, is published.

439

MIDDLE EAST AND NORTH AFRICA

– Carthage falls to the Vandals under Gaiseric (Genseric), who makes the city his capital.

443

EUROPE

– The Alemanni tribe settle in Alsace.

St Augustine of Hippo (354–430)

Perhaps the greatest of the Latin Church fathers, Aurelius Augustinus was born and educated in Tagaste, a town in Roman Numidia (eastern Algeria). This peaceful, prosperous place was a culturally mixed area. The peasants were Berbers and Phoenicians who spoke Punic, while Greek-speakers lived in the seaports, and the ruling elite spoke Latin. Augustine's thought reflects this varied milieu. For the last 34 years of his life he was bishop of Hippo, a busy seaport, and his position's practical requirements also inform his writings.

Intellectually, Augustine shaped the debate between faith and reason, between grace and will, that dominated medieval thought. He was convinced that human nature is afflicted by a pervasive egoism, and he brought the characteristic intensity of North African Christianity to bear on his analysis of original sin. But he also made the love of God central to Christianity, and he had a profound influence on all subsequent Western mystics. A rare literary stylist, he made the direct expression of feeling an essential part of literature, and in his *Confessions* (397) he invented a new prose genre.

Augustine rejected the neo-Platonic idea that the application of reason could lead to the knowledge of God. The Christian God was not some Platonic first principle uncontaminated by time and place but a real being revealed in an event – the incarnation. From this conviction came the Augustinian idea that time was linear and not cyclical, since God's will moved history forward purposely.

Augustine's masterpiece, *The City of God*, describes the tension between human instinct and the divine impulse, and it emphasizes that human society is incapable of establishing true justice. The work expounds Augustine's invention – a Catholic and sacramental Church that leads to, but is not equivalent to, the heavenly city.

444

SCIENCE AND TECHNOLOGY
- The Chinese have by now invented the wheelbarrow.

446

ASIA
- The northern Wei persecute Chinese Buddhists in an attempt to reassert the secular Confucianism of the Han Chinese.

449

EUROPE
- Britain is being settled by Germanic Angles and Saxons, who will eventually merge to become the English. Vortigern, a leader of the native British, has yielded land to German mercenaries in order to gain assistance in his war against the Picts.

AUSTRALASIA AND OCEANIA
- According to later legend, the Polynesian chief Hawaii-Loa discovers the Hawaiian islands after sailing from Tahiti.

SCIENCE AND TECHNOLOGY
- Metal horseshoes spread in Europe, improving transport speeds and agriculture.

450

EUROPE
- Theodosius II, Byzantine emperor, dies and is succeeded by Marcian, the consort of Pulcheria (see 408).

451

EUROPE
- At the battle of the Catalaunian Plain (Châlons in NE France), the Roman commander Flavius Aetius, aided by the Visigoths, defeats the Huns under Attila (see 433).

452

ASIA
- Anko kills his half-brother, the Japanese crown prince, and becomes emperor on the death of his father Ingyo. He then kills his uncle Okusaka and marries Nakatarashi, Okusaka's widow.

453

EUROPE
- Attila, king of the Huns, dies. Roman troops, aided by their German allies, drive the remaining Huns out of Italy.

455

EUROPE
- Rome is sacked by the Vandals under Gaiseric (Genseric), now based in N Africa.

THE AMERICAS
- The great city of Chichén Itzá is founded on the Yucatán peninsula (in modern Mexico) by the Mayans.

456

ASIA
- The Japanese emperor Anko is murdered by his cousin Mayuwa, the son of Okusaka (see 452).

457

EUROPE
- The Byzantine emperor Marcian (see 450) dies and is succeeded by Leo I.

460

MIDDLE EAST AND NORTH AFRICA
- Severe famine spreads across the Persian empire.

466

EUROPE
- The Huns invade Dacia (modern Romania) but are repelled by the Byzantine emperor, Leo I.

467

MIDDLE EAST AND NORTH AFRICA
- The Byzantine emperor, Leo I, has his general Anthemius elected emperor of the W Roman empire. They jointly attack the Vandal empire in N Africa.

468

EUROPE
- The naval fleet commanded by Basiliscus, brother-in-law of the Byzantine emperor Leo I, is attacked and defeated by the Vandal king Gaiseric (Genseric).
- Leo I repels the Huns in Dacia (modern Romania).

471

EUROPE
- The Byzantine commander Basiliscus murders the Goth Aspar for his part in the failure of the imperial fleet against the Vandals in 468. The Goths advance on Constantinople, but Zeno, the emperor's son-in-law, assassinates the Goths' leader Ardaburius and neutralizes the threat.

472

EUROPE
- Ricimer, a Gemanic general in Roman service, kills the W Roman emperor Anthemius and replaces him with Olybrius. Ricimer dies (19 Aug.) and the Burgundian Gundobad assumes control of the W army. Olybrius also dies soon afterwards (2 Nov.).

473

EUROPE

– The Burgundian Gundobad nominates Glycerius as emperor, but Julius Nepos, backed by the Byzantine emperor Leo I, marches on Rome, ousts Glycerius and makes himself emperor (24 June). Nevertheless, Euric, king of the Visigoths, declares the independence of his Gallic territories.

474

EUROPE

– The Byzantine emperor, Leo I, dies and is succeeded by his 17-year-old son-in-law Zeno.

475

EUROPE

Jan. The Byzantine emperor, Zeno, is usurped by his wife's uncle Basiliscus, who becomes emperor. Zeno is forced to leave Constantinople.

– Orestes, the Roman commander, drives Julius Nepos out of Italy and makes his son, Romulus Augustulus, Roman emperor in the W.

476

EUROPE

28 Aug. At Ravenna, NE Italy (see 403), the W Roman empire founded by Augustus in 27 BC comes to a formal end when the Roman emperor Romulus Augustulus is deposed by the Germanic warrior Odoacer, who becomes king of Italy. Odoacer sends the imperial regalia to the Byzantine emperor Zeno with a message informing him that they are no longer needed.

Aug. Zeno re-enters Constantinople and is re-installed as emperor. Basiliscus is exiled.

480

EUROPE

– The Visigothic kingdom is now the predominant W European power: with its centre at Toulouse (S France), it extends from the Loire in the N to Gibraltar in the S and from the Bay of Biscay in the W to the Rhine in the E.

481

EUROPE

– Childeric I, king of the Salian Franks and son of Merovech, after whom the Merovingian dynasty is named, dies. He is succeeded by his son Clovis. Born a pagan, Clovis I will become tha first Christian ruler of the Frankish kingdom (see 496). Louis, derived from Clovis's name, will become the principal name of the future kings of France.

482

EUROPE

– The Byzantine emperor, Zeno, issues the *Henoticon*, a letter intended to reconcile differences between the Churches of Rome and Constantinople. He is unsuccessful and schism results.

486

EUROPE

– Clovis I (see 481) overthrows Syagrius, the last Roman governor in Gaul, taking control of much of N France.

488

EUROPE

– An army of Ostrogoths led by Theodoric invades Italy, urged on by the Byzantine emperor Zeno. The Ostrogoths besiege Ravenna in N Italy (490).

491

EUROPE

– The Byzantine emperor, Zeno, dies and is succeeded by Anastasius I, a palace courtier.

493

EUROPE

– Odoacer (see 476) surrenders Ravenna to the Ostrogoth Theodoric, who then murders him. Theodoric (the Great) goes on to rule Italy as an Ostrogothic kingdom.

495

ASIA

– The Wei dynasty in China moves its capital to Luoyang.

496

EUROPE

– Clovis I, king of the Franks (see 481), defeats the Alemanni near Strasburg. He is converted to Christianity by his wife Clotilda of Burgundy and by Rémy, bishop of Reims.

c.500

EUROPE

– The Marcommani from Bohemia invade Bavaria. Their own former territories in Bohemia are occupied by the Czechs.

– The Scotti, a people from N Ireland, begin to settle the W coasts of N Britain. The Scotti (or Scots) will gradually displace the native tribes inland. The royal dynasty of the Scots will later gain power over neighbouring peoples, including the Picts of the Highlands and Britons of the Lowlands to create what will become the kingdom of Scotland.

502

EUROPE

29 Mar. Gundobad, king of Burgundy, issues a legal code at Lyons making Romans and Burgundians subject to the same laws.
– The Bulgars, a Turkic people, invade Thrace.

MIDDLE EAST AND NORTH AFRICA

– The Persians fight the Byzantine army and sack the town of Amida in N Mesopotamia.

ASIA

– In China Hsiao Yen (Wu Ti) marches on Nanjing and forces the Qi dynasty to resign its powers. He founds the Liang dynasty.

507

EUROPE

– Clovis I, king of the Franks, allied with the Burgundian king Gundobad, kills King Alaric II and defeats the Visigoths at the battle of Vouillé (near Poitiers). All the Franks on the left bank of the Rhine are united. Clovis annexes the Visigothic kingdom of Toulouse (see 480), although the Visigoths remain in control of the Iberian peninsula.

508

EUROPE

– The Ostrogoths under Theodoric drive the Franks from Provence, regaining Septimania (Languedoc) from the Visigoths.
– Clovis I, king of the Franks, establishes Lutetia (Paris, see 272) as the new Frankish capital in order to be near the power base of his new territories.

510

EUROPE

– Theodoric (the Great), ruler of the Ostrogoths from his capital at Ravenna, NE Italy, appoints as consul his friend the Roman philosopher Anicius Manlius Severinus Boethius. The office of consul, formerly the highest position in the Roman government, is now little more than an honorific post.

511

EUROPE

11 Nov. Clovis I, king of the Franks, dies. The Merovingian dynasty is continued by his sons, Theodoric, Chlodomer, Childebert and Chlothar (Lothair), who, following the Frankish tradition of partible inheritance, divide the kingdom into four and rule from capitals at Metz, Orléans, Paris and Soissons respectively (see 558).

516

EUROPE

– Gundobad, king of Burgundy, dies and is succeeded by his son

Sigismund, who will convert his people from Arian (see 325) to Roman Christianity.

517

ASIA

– The Chinese emperor Hsiao Yen, a Buddhist convert, backs a mission to introduce Buddhism to C China.

518

EUROPE

– According to the 9th-century Welsh chronicler Nennius, it is around this date that the British leader Arthur defeats the Saxons at Mount Badon (an unidentified location). There is, in fact, no secure evidence that Arthur ever existed, but through such writers as Geoffrey of Monmouth (see 1137) and Sir Thomas Malory (15th century), he becomes the medieval model of the chivalrous warrior-king (see also 537).
– The Byzantine emperor, Anastasius I, dies and is succeeded by the Illyrian soldier Justinus, as Justin I, who is counselled by his nephew Flavius Petrus Sabbatius Justinianus (Justinian).

519

EUROPE

– The Christian Churches of E and W are reunited, thus ending the schism of 482.

522

EUROPE

– Boethius (see 510) is arrested on charges of having conspired against the Ostrogoth king Theodoric (the Great) and imprisoned at Pavia, Italy. He is alleged to have addressed letters to the Byzantine emperor, Justin I, but maintains his innocence.

524

EUROPE

– The Roman philosopher and statesman Boethius (see 510 and below) is executed without trial in Pavia, Italy.
– Sigismund, king of Burgundy (see 516), is killed by Chlodomer and succeeded by Godomar.

MIDDLE EAST AND NORTH AFRICA

– War breaks out again between Persia and the Byzantine empire. It will last for eight years (see 532).

ARTS AND HUMANITIES

– Boethius, *The Consolation of Philosphy*, neo-platonic philosophy. Boethius's description of the love of wisdom and of the Christian God as the highest human happiness will become immensely influential in the early Middle Ages, and he will be accepted by Christian thinkers as one of their great teachers.

525

MIDDLE EAST AND NORTH AFRICA
- Ethiopian forces conquer the Yemen.

SCIENCE AND TECHNOLOGY
- Dionysius Exiguus, a Roman theologian and mathematician (see also 1 BC/AD 1), introduces a system of dating for the Christian era, using the chronological notation *Anno domini* (AD), meaning 'year of our Lord', i.e., in the year after the Nativity.

ARTS AND HUMANITIES
- The Egyptian Cosmas Indicopleustes travels up the Nile and as far E as Ceylon (modern Sri Lanka). He becomes a monk and writes *Topographia Christiana* to demonstrate the truth of the biblical account of the world and its creation.

526

EUROPE
30 Aug. Theodoric (the Great), king of the Ostrogoths, dies and is succeeded by his ten-year-old grandson Athalaric, with his grandmother Amalasuntha as regent.

MIDDLE EAST AND NORTH AFRICA
- The Persians defeat a Byzantine army.
- An earthquake in Antioch (modern SE Turkey) kills as many as 250,000 people.

ARTS AND HUMANITIES
- The monumental tomb of Theodoric (the Great) is built at Ravenna.

527

EUROPE
- The Byzantine emperor, Justin I, appoints his nephew Justinian as co-emperor in Constantinople. Justin I dies (1 Aug.) and is succeeded by Justinian who declares his wife Theodora empress.

528

MIDDLE EAST AND NORTH AFRICA
- At the battle of Daras in N Mesopotamia, Belisarius, Justinian I's commander, defeats the Persian forces.

529

EUROPE
- Ratisbon (modern Regensburg) is made capital of Bavaria.
- St Benedict of Nursia founds the Benedictine order of monks at Monte Cassino near Naples, Italy. Benedict's *Regula monachorum* (Rule of Monks), written in *c.*540, prescribes the daily life of a monk. The rule is the effective start of W European monasticism.

- Justinian I orders the closure of the Academy at Athens, which had been founded by Plato *c.*387 BC, on the grounds that its activities are un-Christian. Many of the staff leave for Syria and Persia.

ECONOMY AND SOCIETY
Justinian I, *Codex Vitus*, compilation of all Roman imperial laws.

530

MIDDLE EAST AND NORTH AFRICA
- The Byzantine commander Belisarius defeats the Persians again (see 528) but is eventually defeated at Callinicium.

532

EUROPE
Jan. The Nike revolt destroys large areas of Constantinople. Belisarius, the emperor Justinian I's commander, helps with the restoration of order amid much bloodshed.
- The Franks overrun the kingdom of Burgundy.

MIDDLE EAST AND NORTH AFRICA
- Justinian I signs a peace with the Persian king Chosroes I in order to free his armies for military operations in the W.

533

MIDDLE EAST AND NORTH AFRICA
- The Byzantine commander Belisarius invades N Africa, defeats the Vandals and regains the territory as a province for the Byzantine empire. N Africa will remain Byzantine until the Muslim Arab conquests of the 7th century.

534

EUROPE
- Toledo in C Spain becomes the capital of the Visigothic kingdom, which now controls the Iberian peninsula.

535

EUROPE
- Belisarius invades Sicily and moves N to conquer the Ostrogothic kingdom of Italy.

536

EUROPE
9 Dec. Belisarius conquers the city of Rome after taking Naples; Byzantine forces are now dominant in the Italian peninsula at the expense of the Ostrogoths.
- Theodahad, king of the Ostrogoths and nephew of Theodoric, is assassinated. He is succeeded by Witigis.

SCIENCE AND TECHNOLOGY
- Volcanic dust from eruptions in Asia causes an extremely severe Mediterranean winter.

537

EUROPE
- The Ostrogothic king Witigis tries to recapture Rome but the city resists in a year-long siege.
- According to later accounts, Arthur, a leader of the Britons, is killed in the battle of Camlan (see also 518). Arthur is said to have halted the Anglo-Saxon invasions of Britain and established a post-Roman state in Britain. He is killed in a civil war that later destroys the state and opens the way to further invasions.

ARTS AND HUMANITIES
   27 Dec. The Church of Hagia Sophia (Holy Wisdom) is dedicated in Constantinople. Ordered by Justinian I, it has been built by Anthemius of Tralles and Isidore of Miletus in the shape of the Greek cross.

538

ASIA
- A Korean delegation that includes Buddhists is formally received at the Japanese court by the emperor Senka.

539

EUROPE
- Uraius, the nephew of King Witigis, starves Milan into submission and many thousands of Milanese are killed.

MIDDLE EAST AND NORTH AFRICA
- The Persian king Chosroes I declares war on the Byzantine empire.

ASIA
- The Japanese emperor Senka dies and is succeeded by his half-brother Kimmei.

540

EUROPE
- Ravenna falls to Belisarius, who also captures the Ostrogothic king Witigis. Belisarius appoints Hildebad client king of the Ostrogoths and returns to Constantinople, taking Witigis with him.

MIDDLE EAST AND NORTH AFRICA
- Persian forces invade Syria and take Antioch from the Byzantine empire.

ARTS AND HUMANITIES
- The Roman historian and statesman Cassiodorus, who has held government posts under Theodoric and Athalric, retires from public life and devotes himself to writing and religion. He founds the monastery of Vivarium in Calabria, Italy, which becomes a centre for the translation of Greek texts.

541

EUROPE
- Justinian I, the Byzantine emperor, falls ill and has to abandon plans to invade the British Isles and Gaul.
- The Ostrogothic king Hildebad is murdered and is succeeded by his nephew Totila, who rebels against Byzantine rule.
- The plague that started in Egypt and spread to Constantinople will ravage much of the Romano-Byzantine world for the next 50 years.

542

ARTS AND HUMANITIES
- About this date the British writer Gildas completes *De excidio et conquestu Britanniae* (The Ruin and Conquest of Britain), a religious tract that includes an anecdotal and polemical history of post-Roman Britain.

543

EUROPE
- Rome falls to Totila and his Ostrogothic forces but is soon retaken by the Byzantine commander Belisarius after Totila moves to Ravenna.

545

EUROPE
- The Byzantine emperor Justinian I tries to impose the Roman date of Easter on the people of Constantinople, who respond with strikes and demonstrations.

546

EUROPE
- Cassiodorus (see 540) founds another monastery at Beneventum, S Italy.

547

EUROPE
- King Ida succeeds to the throne of Bernicia, the northernmost of the Anglo-Saxon kingdoms in Britain.

ARTS AND HUMANITIES
- King Ida builds Bamburgh Castle, now in Northumberland, NE England.
- The Church of San Vitale is built in Ravenna, Italy, with mosaic portraits of the Byzantine emperor Justinian I and his wife Theodora.

548

EUROPE
   June The Byzantine empress Theodora dies.

549

MIDDLE EAST AND NORTH AFRICA
- The Persians take Petra (in modern Jordan), an outpost of the Byzantine empire, and occupy it for two years.

ARTS AND HUMANITIES
- The Church of San Apollinare is completed at Classe near Ravenna.

550

EUROPE
- The Ostrogoth king Totila recaptures Rome.
- The Byzantine emperor Justinian I sends the eunuch general Narses to Italy to crush the Ostrogothic rebellion.
- St Dewi (David, the future patron saint of Wales) preaches an ascetic form of Christianity in what is later to become Wales. He founds a monastery in the SW, which becomes the centre of Welsh Christianity.

ARTS AND HUMANITIES
- Mosaics illustrating the last supper are installed in the Church of San Apollinare at Classe, near Ravenna.
- Around this date the Greek historian Procopius completes *De bellis* (On the Wars), a history of the Persian, Vandal and Gothic wars.

Musaeus Grammaticus, *Hero and Leander*, poetry.

552

EUROPE
June The Byzantine general Narses leads his forces to victory over the Italian Ostrogoths and kills their leader Totila at Taginae.

ASIA
- The king of Paikche in Korea sends Buddhist sutras (sayings) and images to Japan. The leader of the Soga clan urges the emperor to accept the gifts, and imperial permission is granted to build a temple to house and worship the images.

SCIENCE AND TECHNOLOGY
- The Byzantine emperor Justinian I introduces silk production to Europe, sending emissaries to China who will smuggle silkworms out of the country. Justinian will establish an imperial monopoly for silk production.

553

EUROPE
- Narses recaptures Rome and Naples on behalf of the Byzantine empire.

ARTS AND HUMANITIES
Procopius, *Anecdota* (Secret History), a gossipy account of leading Byzantine figures of the age.

554

EUROPE
- The Byzantine general Narses is made exarch (prefect) of Italy and completes the reconquest of the Italian peninsula. Justinian I's Pragmatic Sanction restores Italian lands taken from the Ostrogoths to their original landowners.

557

ASIA
- The Chen dynasty assumes power in China.

558

EUROPE
- Chlothar I, king of Soissons, reunites the Frankish kingdom when he becomes king of all the Franks on the death of Childebert I, king of Paris.

559

EUROPE
- An army of Huns and Slavs arrives at the gates of Constantinople. The commander Belisarius comes out of retirement to repel them.

560

EUROPE
- Eormenric, king of Kent, dies and is succeeded by his son Ethelbert (see 597 and 616).
- St Deiniol founds the Abbey of Bangor in N Wales.

561

EUROPE
- Chlothar I, king of the Franks (see 558), dies and his kingdom is divided: his sons Sigibert, Guntram and Chilperic rule Austrasia (the Rhineland), Burgundy and Neustria (W France), respectively.

563

EUROPE
- St Columba (Colum), an Irish missionary, founds a monastery on the island of Iona, W Scotland, as a base for the conversion of the Picts.

565

EUROPE
14 Nov. Emperor Justinian I dies at the age of 83 after a 38-year reign – probably the greatest in the history of the Byzantine empire. His nephew succeeds as Justin II, pays Justinian's considerable debts and declares religious toleration.

568

EUROPE

- The Lombard king Alboin founds a kingdom covering N and C Italy. Pressed from behind by the nomadic Avars, the Germanic Lombards have crossed the Alps and overrun the region.

571

ASIA

- The Japanese emperor Kimmei dies. His son Bintas succeeds.

572

EUROPE

- With the fall of Pavia to his army, the Lombard king Alboin (see 568) now controls almost the whole Italian peninsula.

MIDDLE EAST AND NORTH AFRICA

- The Byzantine emperor Justin II initiates a new war with Persia; it will last until 591.

573

EUROPE

- At the urging of his wife Brunhilde, Sigibert of Austrasia (the Rhineland) declares war on his brother Chilperic I of Neustria (W France) as Chilperic has murdered his wife to marry Brunhilde's sister. Sigibert is supported by German allies on the right bank of the Rhine who then overrun Paris and Chartres.

575

EUROPE

- Sigibert of Austrasia pursues Chilperic I as far as Tournai and is killed. Sigibert's young son succeeds as Childebert II, with the queen mother Brunhilde as regent.
- In C Europe the Slovenes have by now migrated into the lands that will form modern Slovenia.

577

EUROPE

- At the battle of Deorham forces from the Saxon kingdom of Wessex under Cuthwine and Ceawlin defeat the native Welsh. This decisive battle gives the Saxons effective control of the richest lands of lowland Britain. By this time the Germanic invaders are known as the English, while the native Romano-Britons have adopted the name Cymry, meaning 'comrades' and are known to the English as Welsh, meaning 'outsiders'.

578

EUROPE

- The Byzantine emperor Justin II dies after periodic bouts of insanity. His general Tiberius, who has been co-emperor, now rules as Tiberius II Constantinus.

579

MIDDLE EAST AND NORTH AFRICA

- King Chosroes I of Persia dies after a 48-year reign that has seen Persia's boundaries extended from the Oxus (modern Amu Darya River in C Asia) to the Red Sea.

580

EUROPE

- The Lombards (see 568) drive the last of the Ostrogoths out of Italy and begin to Italianize their names and try to assimilate.

581

ASIA

- In China Yang Jian, duke of Sui and chief minister of the northern Zhou (Chou), kills the last of the Zhou along with some 58 royal relatives. He inaugurates the Sui dynasty and proclaims himself Emperor Wendi.

582

EUROPE

- The Byzantine emperor Tiberius II Constantinus dies and is succeeded by his son-in-law Mauricius Flavius Tiberius (Maurice).
- Thrace and Greece have by now been overwhelmed by Slav invasions.

ARTS AND HUMANITIES

Cassiodorus, *History of the Goths*, of which only a fragment survives.

584

EUROPE

- Chilperic I of Neustria (W France) is murdered. He is succeeded by his son, who makes himself king of all the Franks, ruling as Chlothar II. Brunhilde (see 575) remains in power in Austrasia.
- About this time the Anglo-Saxon kingdom of Mercia emerges in C England.

585

EUROPE

- Hermenegild, son of the Visigoth king Leovigild, leads a revolt against his father after converting to Western Christianity from his father's Arian faith (see 325). Leovigild kills his son and proceeds to conquer the entire Iberian peninsula.

ASIA

- The Japanese emperor Bintas dies and is succeeded by his brother Yomei.
- The king of Paikche in Korea sends more Buddhist missionaries to Japan, where the Soga clan has now adopted Buddhism as an aspect of its rivalry with the Mononobe clan.

586

ASIA

– The Japanese emperor Yomei and his grandfather Soga Iname back Buddhism, while the Mononobe clan reject it as conflicting with the native Japanese Shinto religion. Shinto adopts Buddhist images so that each *kami*, or god, in Shinto has a counterpart in Buddhism.

587

EUROPE

– The first Christian conversions among the Lombards are recorded.

ASIA

– The Japanese emperor Yomei dies and is succeeded by a nephew of his grandfather Soga Iname, who will rule as emperor Sushun. Soga family agents kill the anti-Buddhist Mononobe Moriyo.

– Japan's first Buddhist monastery is founded.

588

EUROPE

– The Lombards, led by their king Authari and his wife Theodolinda, are converted to Christianity.

MIDDLE EAST AND NORTH AFRICA

– Arab, Khazar and Turkish forces invade Persia but are repelled.

– The Persian king Hormizd is deposed and killed after being defeated in battle by the Byzantines, whose emperor, Maurice, helps Hormizd's son to recover the throne: he will reign as Chosroes II.

589

EUROPE

– The Visigoth king Leovigild (see 585) is succeeded by Recared.

MIDDLE EAST AND NORTH AFRICA

– The Persian army mounts a coup against Chosroes II, who escapes to Constantinople.

ASIA

– The Sui emperor Wendi (see 581) reunites the Chinese empire by his defeat of the Chen dynasty ruling at Jingang (later known as Nanjing). The Chen dynasty has ruled in S China since 557.

590

EUROPE

– Gregory I is the first monk to be elected pope. He re-establishes civil institutions in Rome, repairs the ruined aqueducts, reforms the law courts and reinstitutes free grain supplies to the populace.

– Pope Gregory I begins to lay down the principles of papal authority over and above secular rulers and leads a campaign of Italian opposition to Lombard rule.

– The Lombard king Authari dies and is succeeded by Agilulf, Thuringian ruler of Turin. He marries the widow of the late king Alboin's grandson and so secures his legitimate line of descent. He converts to Christianity.

591

EUROPE

– Lombard forces gain military successes across N Italy.

MIDDLE EAST AND NORTH AFRICA

– The Byzantine emperor Maurice restores the Persian king Chosroes II to his throne and receives territorial concessions in return.

592

EUROPE

– The Byzantine emperor Maurice sends troops against the Avars and the Slavs who are threatening the Balkans and Constantinople.

ASIA

– The Japanese emperor Sushun is murdered by agents of his uncle Soga Umako. Sushun is succeeded by the empress Suiko, widow of the late emperor Bintas.

593

ASIA

– Empress Suiko becomes the first Japanese ruler to receive official recognition from China. During her reign Buddhism will become the established Japanese religion and Japanese culture will assimilate its Chinese influences.

– The Japanese empress Suiko's grandson, Crown Prince Shotoku, becomes prime minister, and Soga Umako retains his powerful influence in affairs of state.

– In Japan Crown Prince Shotoku founds the great monastery of Shitenno-ji at Osaka. Work begins on building the monastery's Temple of the Four Heavenly Kings.

594

ASIA

– The Japanese empress Suiko converts to Buddhism.

597

EUROPE

– The Italian Christian monk Augustine arrives in Thanet, Kent, to convert the English of the British Isles, having been sent on the mission by Pope Gregory I. Augustine baptizes King Ethelbert of Kent and founds the Benedictine monastery of Christ Church, Canterbury.

598

EUROPE
- The Byzantine emperor Maurice makes peace with the Lombard king Agilulf and concedes N Italy to him.

SCIENCE AND TECHNOLOGY
- The Saxon coulter (a lightweight plough with a knife blade to cut vertically and a ploughshare that cuts horizontally at the root) revolutionizes European agriculture in the N and W by enabling heavy clay soil to be ploughed.

c.600

ARTS AND HUMANITIES
- The core of the works attributed to Aneirin and Taliesin, the earliest poets writing in Welsh, are composed.

601

SCIENCE AND TECHNOLOGY
- The *Vaghbata*, an Indian collection of medical prescriptions, is compiled.

602

EUROPE
- The legions fighting the Avars on the Danube proclaim the centurion Phocas Byzantine emperor. Phocas executes his predecessor Maurice at Chalcedon in Bithynia, after forcing Maurice to witness the murder of his five sons.
- The Italian monk Augustine establishes the see of Canterbury in England and is made its archbishop.

603

EUROPE
- The bishopric of Rochester, England, is founded.
- The first St Paul's Cathedral is built in London, England.

604

EUROPE
12 Mar. Pope Gregory I (the Great) dies (see 590).
- In N England the Anglo-Saxon kingdom of Northumbria is formed by the merger of the kingdoms of Bernicia and Deira.

ASIA
- The Sui emperor of China, Wendi (see 581), is killed by his son, the new emperor Yangdi. Wendi has established civil service examinations, reduced the power of the military aristocracy and attacked hereditary privilege. Yangdi establishes a new Chinese capital at Luoyang.
- The Japanese Crown Prince Shotoku issues a constitution, the *Shotoku Taishi*, requiring veneration of the Buddha, recognition of Buddhist priests and the observance of Buddhist laws.

605

MIDDLE EAST AND NORTH AFRICA
- Persia resumes its military campaign against the Byzantine empire. Chosroes II will regain control of Armenia and Syria.

SCIENCE AND TECHNOLOGY
- A grand canal is built linking the Chinese capital of Luoyang to the Long River and is later extended to Hangchow (610).

606

ASIA
- Harsha of Thanesar establishes a N Indian empire. A devout Buddhist, he belongs to an offshoot of the Gupta dynasty (see 320).

607

ASIA
- The Japanese empress Suiko sends the first official Japanese envoy to China's Sui court.

ARTS AND HUMANITIES
- The Horyu-ji Temple and the hospital at Nara in Japan, commissioned by Crown Prince Shotoku, are completed.

608

MIDDLE EAST AND NORTH AFRICA
- The Persian army crosses the Taurus Mts and marches into Asia Minor; the Byzantine army puts up little resistance.

609

ARTS AND HUMANITIES
- The Pantheon at Rome is consecrated to Christian use as the Church of Santa Maria Rotonda.

610

EUROPE
5 Oct. Heraclius, son of the Byzantine governor of Africa, attacks Constantinople. He overthrows the Byzantine emperor Phocas and establishes a new Heraclian dynasty.

MIDDLE EAST AND NORTH AFRICA
- Muhammad (see p. 73), a former camel-driver and merchant, begins to preach a new religion at Mecca, in Arabia. His religion, Islam, will be a monotheistic purification of the polytheistic nature-worship of his fellow Arabs.

611

MIDDLE EAST AND NORTH AFRICA
- Chosroes II attacks Antioch in a major expansion of the Persian empire.

612

EUROPE

- Arnulf, adviser to Chlothar II, king of the Franks, becomes bishop of Metz, E France.
- Gall, a disciple of St Columban, founds the monastery of St Gall (Sankt Gallen), in modern Switzerland.

ASIA

- Chinese troops cross the Yalu River and enter Korea. They attack Pyongyang, but their losses are catastrophic.
- Harsha of Thanesar (see 606) assumes the title 'Emperor of the Five Indies'.

613

EUROPE

- Chlothar II, king of the Franks, defeats and captures Brunhilde, the queen mother, who has claimed Burgundy and Austrasia, and has her dragged to death by wild horses. Chlothar II now reigns over a reunited Frankish kingdom.
- Ethelfrith, in command of the Northumbrians, defeats the Britons in battle near Chester, NW England.

MIDDLE EAST AND NORTH AFRICA

- The Prophet Muhammad (see p. 73) is by now teaching his new religion openly. The traditionalist leaders of Mecca persecute his followers.

614

EUROPE

- Chlothar II issues the *Edictum Chlothacharii* as a constitutional document detailing the rights of the Church, of the nobility and of the sovereign.

MIDDLE EAST AND NORTH AFRICA

- A Persian army sacks Damascus.

615

EUROPE

- St Columban dies, having founded a monastery in the Apennines (in Italy) in the last year of his life.

MIDDLE EAST AND NORTH AFRICA

- Jerusalem is sacked by the Persians and the supposed 'True Cross' on which Christ was crucified is seized as part of the loot.

616

EUROPE

- Ethelbert, king of Kent (see 597), dies.

618

ASIA

- The Chinese emperor Yangdi is murdered by a courtier, the

new emperor Gaozu. Having seized the city of Changsen, Gaozu establishes the Tang dynasty, which will rule until 907.

620

MIDDLE EAST AND NORTH AFRICA

- With the capture of the island of Rhodes, Chosroes II has now re-established the limits of the Persian empire set by Darius I in the 6th century BC.

621

ASIA

- The Chinese government establishes a state department for the manufacture of porcelain.

622

MIDDLE EAST AND NORTH AFRICA

16 July Opposition from the leaders of Mecca forces the Prophet Muhammad to flee N to the town of Medina, a journey that will be commemorated as the *hejira* (flight) in Islamic worship.
- At the battle of Issus the Byzantine emperor Heraclius defeats the Persian army occupying Asia Minor (modern Turkey).

625

EUROPE

- The Avars and the Persians both attack Constantinople, but the Byzantine emperor Heraclius withstands the attacks.

626

EUROPE

- King Edwin of Northumbria captures and fortifies Edinburgh and starts to convert his subjects to Christianity.

ASIA

- Soga Umako, the Japanese power-broker behind the emperors (see 592 and 593), dies.
- The Chinese emperor Gaozu (see 618) abdicates and is succeeded by his son Taizong.

627

MIDDLE EAST AND NORTH AFRICA

- The Byzantine emperor Heraclius invades Assyria and Mesopotamia. He gains a great victory at the battle of Nineveh (12 Dec.) and once again saves Constantinople from the Persians.
- The Prophet Muhammad's opponents march on Medina and slaughter hundreds of Jews.

ECONOMY AND SOCIETY

- Sugar is discovered by Byzantine soldiers on the capture of the Persian castle of Dastagerd. Sugar has now travelled from India to Constantinople.

628

EUROPE

– Chlothar II, king of the Franks (see 613), dies and is succeeded (629) by his son Dagobert I.

MIDDLE EAST AND NORTH AFRICA

– The army mutinies against King Chosroes II of Persia. He is murdered (3 April) by his son, who takes the throne as Kavadh II. The new king makes peace with the Byzantine empire and the so-called 'True Cross' is returned to Jerusalem (see 615).

– Mecca falls to the forces of the Prophet Muhammad (see box below).

ASIA

– The Japanese empress Suiko dies and is succeeded by Jomei, grandson of her late husband Bintas.

629

MIDDLE EAST AND NORTH AFRICA

– The Byzantine emperor Heraclius recovers Jerusalem from the Persians (see 615).

630

MIDDLE EAST AND NORTH AFRICA

– The Prophet Muhammad returns to Mecca bearing with him the Koran (Qur'an), which, he claims, has been directly revealed to him as the revelation of God.

ASIA

– The Tang emperors of China receive Japanese ambassadors at their court.

632

MIDDLE EAST AND NORTH AFRICA

– **7 June** The Prophet Muhammad dies. His followers choose Abu Bakr to succeed as ruler of Islam, giving him the title of caliph at his seat of power, Medina. Abu Bakr's military response to a request from Syrian Arabs for help against Byzantine oppression will begin the era of Islamic conquests.

– Muhammad's daughter Fatima dies. Her two sons, Hassan and Hussein, will establish the Fatimid dynasty, which will rule Egypt and N Africa from 909 to 1171.

633

EUROPE

– Cadwallon, king of Gwynedd, in alliance with Penda of Mercia, kills Edwin, king of Northumberland, in battle near Doncaster in N England, but is himself killed (634) in battle by Oswald, Edwin's successor. Cadwallon's death ends the project to revive the British (early Welsh) kingdoms of N England.

MIDDLE EAST AND NORTH AFRICA

– Islamic forces attack Persia.

634

MIDDLE EAST AND NORTH AFRICA

– **22 Aug.** Caliph, Abu Bakr, dies and is succeeded by Muhammad's adviser Omar. During Omar's reign, which will last until 644, a holy war will claim Syria, Persia and Egypt for Islam.

635

EUROPE

– The Byzantine emperor Heraclius makes an alliance with Kuvrat, king of the Bulgars, to break the power of the Avars.

Muhammad (*c.*570–632)

The Prophet Muhammad, founder of the Islamic religion, was born in Mecca, Arabia. His family were merchants from the Quraysh tribe. He married and became a merchant but, according to Islamic belief, spent much time alone searching for wisdom and enlightenment. Then, in a moment of divine disclosure, he received a revelation from God, which was communicated through an angel. The message was threefold: God, or Allah, was one; Allah would judge humanity; and Allah commanded daily religious observance, prayer, regular fasting and acts of practical charity. Those who followed these commands became known as Muslims and their religion as Islam, the Arabic term for submission.

When he began preaching, Muhammad was seen as a dangerous threat to the local gods. In 622 he was driven out of Mecca and fled to Medina in the north. This journey became known as the *hejira* ('flight') and it came to symbolize the start of the Islamic era. In Medina the Prophet acted as arbiter in disputes between local tribes. These are reflected in the Koran (Qur'an), the holy book of Islam, with its detailed prescriptions for social conduct, property rights and inheritance. From the beginning, therefore,

Islam has been equated with a specific form of political and social culture.

By 630 the Muslims were able to return to Mecca, leading to the custom of pilgrimage to Mecca as a part of Islamic observance. It was on his last visit to Mecca that Muhammad preached his ultimate message to his followers: 'Every Muslim is a Muslim's brother, and the Muslims are brethren.' The community of Islam survived his death, bound together by communal rituals and faith in Allah. Within a few short years the expanding power of the Arabs was to spread Islam across much of the Middle East.

MIDDLE EAST AND NORTH AFRICA
- Damascus and Gaza fall to Islamic forces.
- Basra is founded at the head of the Persian Gulf at the confluence of the rivers Tigris and the Euphrates. As a major trading centre, it will deal in goods from India, Persia, Arabia and Turkey.

ASIA
- The Indian emperor Harsha leads an invasion into Chalukya territory (the Deccan) but is repelled.

636

MIDDLE EAST AND NORTH AFRICA
15 Aug. At the battle of Yarmuk, E of the Sea of Galilee, Islamic forces under Khalid ibn al-Walid defeat the Byzantine army and establish control of Syria and Palestine.

637

MIDDLE EAST AND NORTH AFRICA
- Islamic armies defeat Persian forces at Qadisiya (S Iraq) and at Ualula. They then take Ctesiphon and then invade Mesopotamia.

638

MIDDLE EAST AND NORTH AFRICA
- Islamic forces capture Jerusalem (it will remain in Muslim hands until 1099). Another Islamic army spreads out through Mesopotamia and a third reaches C Persia. The Persians appeal for Chinese aid.

639

EUROPE
9 Jan. Dagobert I, king of the Franks (see 628), dies and is succeeded by his six-year-old son as Clovis II of Neustria and Burgundy. Henceforth, power in the Merovingian Frankish kingdom will reside increasingly with the royal administrators known as the 'mayors of the palace', the kings themselves becoming rulers in name only.

MIDDLE EAST AND NORTH AFRICA
- Islamic forces invade Armenia and Egypt.

640

MIDDLE EAST AND NORTH AFRICA
- A Byzantine army is defeated by Islamic Arabs at Heliopolis, Egypt.

ASIA
- The Tang emperor Taizong sends a Chinese mission to research techniques of sugar manufacture at Behar in the Ganges valley, India.

641

ASIA
- The Japanese emperor Jomei dies and is succeeded by Kogyoku, his widow.

642

EUROPE
- In Britain the Christian King Oswald of Northumbria is slain in battle by the pagan Penda of Mercia.

MIDDLE EAST AND NORTH AFRICA
- At the battle of Nehawand (Niharvand) Islamic forces gain a decisive victory over the Persians under King Yazdegerd III, ending the Sassanian dynasty that has ruled Persia for four centuries (see 224).
- Alexandria capitulates and the Islamic conquest of Egypt is now complete.

644

MIDDLE EAST AND NORTH AFRICA
4 Nov. The caliph Omar is assassinated at Medina and is succeeded by Othman.

SCIENCE AND TECHNOLOGY
- The earliest evidence for the use of windmills, in Persia.

645

MIDDLE EAST AND NORTH AFRICA
- Alexandria is recaptured by the Byzantines, but the Islamic governor of Egypt, Abd Allah ibn Sa'd, retakes the city and starts work on building an Arab fleet.

ASIA
- In a palace coup the Japanese empress Kogyoku is removed by the Fujiwara (Kamatari) clan. Kotoku is made emperor and Nakano Oe (Emperor Tenji) becomes both crown prince and prime minister, inaugurating the Taika period, an era of reform.

646

ASIA
- Japan's administration is centralized by a great reform edict, with the emperor presiding over a bureaucracy on the Chinese model, established in a permanent capital city.

648

MIDDLE EAST AND NORTH AFRICA
- Cyprus falls to Islamic forces from N Africa. Other Islamic forces invade Armenia.

THE RISE OF ISLAM:
An Arab Revolution

The message that came out of the Arabian desert in AD 610 was simple, and its simplicity contributed to its success: there is no God but Allah, and Muhammad is his prophet. There were only three fundamentals of the faith: the holy Koran (Qur'an), which was God's word as revealed to Muhammad by an angel; the *Sunna*, which were the traditions and sayings ascribed to the Prophet; and the *ijma* or common accord of the faithful as they worshipped and prayed.

When Muhammad told the people of Mecca that the worship of the local gods was idolatry, he was received initially with mockery and then with hatred, for he was undermining a profitable industry in a city that had become a major pilgrimage centre. Gradually, however, Muhammad converted the various Arab tribes to his faith. He initiated a religious war of expansion, pushed on by a drought that forced the Arab tribes to break out of the Arabian peninsula. When they did so, they found that the Byzantine and Persian empires were demoralized and burdened by heavy taxation.

After the Prophet's death in 632, Abu Bakr, his father-in-law, succeeded as caliph (successor). Omar, the next ruler of the faithful, conquered Syria and then Palestine: Damascus fell in 635, followed by Jerusalem in 638. The seizure of Ctesiphon in 637 led to the fall of Persia, and the submission of Egypt followed when the Byzantines abandoned Alexandria in 642. In the west Cyrene and Tripoli were captured, and the Arabs found themselves on the frontiers of Tunisia. A new empire had arrived.

Within one generation nomads turned into administrators and discovered a talent for building towns like Baghdad and Fostat (which later became Cairo). And, at least initially, these new missionaries did not enforce conversion by the sword. The occupation was a military one and no more, with laws, customs and the native religion being respected. In 644 Omar was assassinated; his cousin and successor, Othman, was not deeply religious, and Islam wavered. Ali, son-in-law of the Prophet, killed Othman in 656 and began a fresh round of religious invigoration and conquest.

The evolution of the Arabs of the desert into an imperial power involved one crucial change: the establishment of a dynasty. The man who did this was Muawiyah, the cousin of the murdered Othman. He had been governor of Damascus before becoming caliph, and, in a break with the desert traditions of the Arabs, he named his son as successor, so founding the Umayyad dynasty. Damascus became an imperial capital, and the dynasty minted coins and employed Greek and Syrian officials – some of whom were Christians. The years 700–715 marked the zenith of Umayyad power, with the conquest of Transoxania, the Indus valley and Spain. In 732 the Arabs reached Poitiers in modern France, a feat that marked their furthest penetration into the West.

Amid these triumphs there grew a chronic conflict within Islam itself. The followers of Ali, who had been murdered in 661, declared their dead leader the last legitimate caliph in the bloodline of the Prophet and refused to accept the authority of the new Islamic rulers. Their faith became the Shiite branch of Islam, while those who recognized the caliphs represented the more numerous Sunni tradition.

But despite the succession disputes, the Arab achievement defied expectation and dazed all observers. Less than a hundred years after the Prophet's death his followers held the Mediterranean from the Bosphorus to Egypt and from Palestine to Spain. Their unity was sustained by one religion – Islam – and by one Arabic language, since translation of the Koran was prohibited. And with cultural strength came also treasure – corn and gold, ivory and silk from the caravan routes of the Sahara and Turkestan, as well as along the trade routes of the East.

> *The message that came out of the Arabian desert in AD 610 was simple ...*

The earlier dynastic unity of the Umayyads would disappear. Under the Abbasid dynasty the Islamic power base moved to Baghdad – which in 762 became the capital. Court ceremonial followed Persian traditions and removed the religion of the court from its original austere simplicity. By the 10th century the caliphate had become politically unimportant, and the caliph was restricted to the role of spiritual head of the faithful. Actual government was now a matter for local rulers, and a number of independent states emerged. The Umayyad dynasty ruled in Spain, where they oversaw a great cultural flowering before being overwhelmed by the Christians. In Egypt the Fatimids (909–1171) ruled effectively before falling to the Kurdish leader Saladin (Sala-ad-Din), the founder of the Ayyubid dynasty. Saladin's defeat in 1187 of the Christian king of Jerusalem at the Horns of Hattin shook the Christian West. From that point onwards Islam entered a new period of sustained territorial expansion and economic prosperity, a period that would last for centuries.

651

MIDDLE EAST AND NORTH AFRICA

– The Persian king Yazdegerd III, last of the Sassanian dynasty, is killed by Islamic invaders.

653

EUROPE

– At Toledo, Spain, the Visigoth king Recesswinth draws up the *Liber ludicorium*, which establishes legal equality between Goths and Hispano-Romans without regard to racial or cultural differences.

MIDDLE EAST AND NORTH AFRICA

– Armenia is conquered by Islamic Arabs.

654

EUROPE

– Arabs seize and plunder Rhodes.

ASIA

– The Japanese emperor Kotoku dies and the deposed empress, Kogyoku, is restored to the imperial throne under the name Saimei.

655

EUROPE

– King Penda of Mercia is killed in battle by King Oswy of Northumbria.

MIDDLE EAST AND NORTH AFRICA

– The Byzantine fleet under the command of Emperor Constans II Pogonatus is defeated by an Arab fleet at the battle of the Mast off the Lycian coast (SW Turkey).

656

MIDDLE EAST AND NORTH AFRICA

17 June The caliph Othman is assassinated at Medina. He is succeeded by Muhammad's nephew and son-in-law Ali ibn Abi Talib, but the succession is disputed.

661

MIDDLE EAST AND NORTH AFRICA

24 Jan. The caliph Ali is assassinated in Mesopotamia by a former follower. He is succeeded by his relative Muawiyah, who moves the seat of government to Damascus and founds the Umayyad caliphate, which will rule the Islamic empire until 750. The supporters of the late caliph Ali and his son Hussein will be called Shiites, one of the two principal branches of Islam.

ASIA

– The Japanese empress Saimei dies and is succeeded by Tenji, son of the emperor Jomei.

663

EUROPE

– Emperor Constans II Pogonatus moves the court of Byzantium from Constantinople to Italy in an attempt to stop the Arab conquest of Sicily and to restore Rome as the centre of the empire. But the Lombards resist. Constans fails and no Byzantine emperor in future will visit Rome.

664

EUROPE

– At the Synod of Whitby in N England, the Church in the British Isles accepts the Roman date for the calculation of Easter and thus the authority of the Roman, rather than Celtic, Church.

ASIA

– Kabul falls to Arab forces invading what is now Afghanistan.

668

EUROPE

15 July The Byzantine emperor Constans II Pogonatus dies mysteriously in his bath at Syracuse during a mutiny and is succeeded by his sons Constantine IV Pogonatus, Heraclius and Tiberius, who he has named as co-emperors.
– The Byzantine court returns to Constantinople.

MIDDLE EAST AND NORTH AFRICA

– Arabs assert control over Anatolia (modern Turkey).

669

EUROPE

– Theodore of Tarsus becomes archbishop of Canterbury and introduces a Roman parochial system with a centralized episcopacy.

670

EUROPE

– Arab forces take Chalcedon on the Bosphorus and besiege Constantinople.

MIDDLE EAST AND NORTH AFRICA

– Arabs found Kairouan (Tunis) and consolidate their hold on N Africa.

671

ASIA

– The Japanese emperor Tenji dies and is succeeded by his son Kobun. But the late emperor's brother Ooama objects that Kobun's mother was a commoner and that the emperor should be entirely of the blood royal.

672

ASIA

– The Japanese emperor Kobun is deposed and commits suicide. His uncle Ooama, supported by the powerful Fujiwara clan, assumes power and takes the imperial name of Tenmu.

675

EUROPE

– Childeric II, king of both the E and W Frankish kingdoms (since 673), is killed while out hunting: civil war breaks out in his kingdom.

677

EUROPE

– The Arabs lift their blockade of Constantinople and conclude a 30-year peace with the Byzantine empire.

678

MIDDLE EAST AND NORTH AFRICA

– The caliph Muawiyah dies at Damascus and is succeeded by his son Yazid. But the Kufans in Iraq invite Hussein, son of the late caliph Ali, to succeed (see 661).

680

EUROPE

– Bulgar forces occupy the Byzantine territory between the Danube and the Balkan Mts; other Bulgars control Wallachia, Moldavia and Bessarabia.

MIDDLE EAST AND NORTH AFRICA

10 Oct. At the battle of Karbala (SW of Baghdad), the caliph Yazid defeats Hussein, who is deserted by the Iraqi Kufans and killed. Hussein's death is regarded as a martyrdom by his followers, the Shiites. The city built on the battle site will become the Shiites' holy city.

681

EUROPE

– Bulgar tribes led by Khan Asparukh cross the Danube from the E, subjugate the Slavs and establish a kingdom.

682

MIDDLE EAST AND NORTH AFRICA

– Arab forces led by Uqbah ibn Nafi overrun the N African coast, taking Tangiers.

685

EUROPE

21 May At the battle of Nechtansmere (fought in Scotland, N of the River Tay), the Picts defeat the Northumbrians. Thereafter English settlement is restricted to the area S of the Firth of Forth, which is defended by the border fortress of Edinburgh. From this time Northumbrian power goes into a decline.

– The Byzantine emperor Constantine IV Pogonatus dies and is succeeded by his son Justinian II.

686

EUROPE

– English pagan resistance to Christianity ends with the conversion of the kingdom of Sussex.

ASIA

– The Japanese emperor Tenmu dies and is succeeded by his wife (and niece), Empress Jito. She executes her late husband's son on false charges of treachery.

687

EUROPE

– The first doge of Venice is elected. A monopoly in salt and fishing and a strategic position at the head of the Adriatic has led to Venetian prosperity.

– At the battle of Tertry in W France Pepin II defeats the Neustrian king Theuderic and reunites the Frankish kingdom.

688

EUROPE

– In England Ine, king of Wessex, subdues Essex and part of Kent.

689

EUROPE

– The Byzantine emperor Justinian II defeats the Slavs in Thrace and transfers many of them to Anatolia (modern Turkey).

690

EUROPE

– In England Wihtred becomes king of Kent and starts a 35-year reign remarkable for the codification of laws.

691

MIDDLE EAST AND NORTH AFRICA

– The caliph Abd al-Malik completes the Dome of the Rock mosque, Jerusalem.

692

MIDDLE EAST AND NORTH AFRICA

– Arab forces defeat the Byzantine emperor Justinian II at the battle of Sevastopol in Cilicia.

695

EUROPE
- Army officers cut off the nose of Byzantine emperor Justinian II and exile him to the Crimea. One of these officers succeeds as the emperor Leontius.

ECONOMY AND SOCIETY
- Islamic coins are minted for the first time.

697

MIDDLE EAST AND NORTH AFRICA
- Arab forces attack Carthage for the first time.

ASIA
- The Japanese empress Jito abdicates and is succeeded by the grandson of Emperor Tenmu: he will reign as Emperor Momu.

698

EUROPE
- The Byzantine emperor Leontius (see 695) is deposed by Tiberius III Apsimar, a former commander of the navy, who will gain military victories over the Arabs.

MIDDLE EAST AND NORTH AFRICA
- Carthage, the last Byzantine base in Africa, falls to the Arabs.

ARTS AND HUMANITIES
- By this time *Beowulf*, the first known English epic, has been composed.

700

EUROPE
- Thuringia, Germany, becomes part of the Frankish empire.

THE AMERICAS
- The leading Mesoamerican city, Teotihuacán, is destroyed.

ARTS AND HUMANITIES
Dandin, *The Adventures of the Ten Princes*, Sanskrit poetry.

701

ASIA
- The emperor Momu codifies the political law of Japan and in so doing becomes sole ultimate owner of all Japanese territory.
- Arab and Persian sailors visit the Moluccas Islands, Indonesia, for the first time.

702

EUROPE
- Duke Hetan II builds the circular church at Marienberg, near Wurzburg.

MIDDLE EAST AND NORTH AFRICA
- The Umayyad Mosque is built in Damascus.

705

EUROPE
- The Byzantine emperor Justinian II, nicknamed 'Rhinotmetus' (with a split nose), regains his throne (see 695).

707

ASIA
- The Japanese emperor Momu dies and is succeeded by his aunt, the empress Gemmei.

709

ARTS AND HUMANITIES
- The bishop of Avranches, Aubert, builds the oratory later known as Mont Saint-Michel in Normandy, France.

710

ASIA
- The Japanese empress Gemmei establishes Nara as the first permanent capital of Japan.

ECONOMY AND SOCIETY
- Sugar is planted in Egypt.

711

EUROPE
- Moors (Arabs and Berbers) from N Africa invade the Iberian peninsula under the command of Tariq ibn Ziyad. At the battle of Wadi Bekka (July) they defeat the Visigoth king Roderick. After Cordoba falls, Tariq moves on to Seville.
- The Byzantine emperor Justinian II Rhinotmetus is defeated and killed by troops rebelling under the leadership of Bardanes in N Anatolia: the Heraclian dynasty ends. Bardanes is proclaimed emperor under the name Philippicus.

ECONOMY AND SOCIETY
- The Moorish invasion leads to the introduction of rice, saffron and sugar to the Iberian peninsula.

712

EUROPE
- Seville falls to the Moors.

ASIA
- Xuanzong becomes emperor of China and will make his court a centre of Chinese culture.
- Arab forces led by Abu Kasim al-Thagafi conquer Samarkand, a city on the Silk Route from China that becomes a major centre of Islamic art and scholarship.
- Muhammad ibn Kasim makes the first Islamic conquests in India when he invades the Indus valley and conquers Sind.

ARTS AND HUMANITIES
Ono Yasumara, *Kojiki*, first history of Japan.

713

EUROPE

– Arab forces defeat the Byzantines. The emperor Philippicus is deposed and is succeeded by the conspirator Anastasius II.

714

EUROPE

– Pepin II, Frankish mayor of the palace (see 639), dies. His (illegitimate) son Charles Martel will make himself undisputed ruler (as mayor of the palace) of the Frankish lands over the next three years.

715

EUROPE

– The Byzantine emperor Anastasius II is deposed in an army rising and is succeeded by Theodosius III.

ASIA

– The Japanese empress Gemmei abdicates and is succeeded by her daughter Genshu.

716

EUROPE

– In England Ethelbald succeeds to the throne of Mercia (see 757). He will significantly increase its power in a 41-year reign.
– Lisbon falls to the Moors.

ECONOMY AND SOCIETY

– By now spices imported to France are being used in cooking.

ARTS AND HUMANITIES

– The Chinese landscape painter Li Suxun dies.

717

EUROPE

– The Byzantine emperor Theodosius III is deposed and is succeeded by Leo III, who inaugurates the Isaurian dynasty, which will last until 802. Constantinople is again besieged by Arab forces, but Leo repels them.

MIDDLE EAST AND NORTH AFRICA

– Omar II (Omar ibn al-'Aziz) becomes caliph and exempts Muslims from taxation.

ARTS AND HUMANITIES

– Japanese artists working at Nara complete the sculpture *Buddha with the Gods of the Sun and the Moon.*

718

EUROPE

Sept. The Byzantine emperor Leo III leads the destruction of the Arab fleet at Constantinople with the new Byzantine secret weapon, a combustible mixture known as 'Greek fire', and temporarily ends Arab expansionism.
– Pelagius founds the N Spanish kingdom of the Asturias.

720

EUROPE

– The Moors cross the Pyrenees and capture Narbonne, S France. They also invade Sardinia.

724

ASIA

– The Japanese empress Genshu abdicates and is succeeded by her nephew Shomu.

725

ASIA

– The Parsees, who follow Zoroastrian teachings (see 553 BC), move to Sanjan on the Gujarat coast of India. Having fled Persia on the arrival of the Islamic Arabs, they have been welcomed by local Hindu rulers.

726

EUROPE

– The Byzantine emperor Leo III forbids the worship of icons as superstitious, initiating the iconoclastic movement, which will come to dominate imperial politics for decades to come. Greece rises in revolt against Byzantium and a fleet of ships commanded by an anti-emperor sets sail for Constantinople; it is destroyed by 'Greek fire' (see 718).

730

EUROPE

– The Alemanni in Germany are incorporated into the Frankish empire as a duchy.
– Pope Gregory II excommunicates the Byzantine emperor Leo III for his iconoclasm.

731

THE AMERICAS

– The Mayan empire in C America is now experiencing its greatest expansion in power and sophistication.

ARTS AND HUMANITIES

Bede, *Historia Ecclesiastica Gentis Anglorum* (Ecclesiastical History of the English People), first classic of English history.

732

EUROPE

11 Oct. At the battle of Tours the Franks under Charles Martel (see 714) resoundingly defeat the Moors. A 90,000-strong

Moorish army under the Yemenite Abd ar-Rahman has invaded S France, crossed the Pyrenees, burned Bordeaux and destroyed the basilica of St Hilary at Poitiers but is now forced to retreat to the Pyrenees. The battle marks the northernmost point of the Islamic advance.
- Bubonic plague hits Constantinople again (as in 541) and kills as many as 200,000 of the population.

MIDDLE EAST AND NORTH AFRICA
- The Berbers revolt against the Moors in N Africa.

735

EUROPE
- Charles Martel (see 714) conquers Burgundy.
- The archbishopric of York, N England, is founded, with Egbert as archbishop.

737

EUROPE
- Theodoric IV, Merovingian king of the Franks, dies: a six-year interregnum follows (but see 639).

739

EUROPE
- Pope Gregory III asks Charles Martel (see 714) to lead a coordinated campaign against the Lombards, Greeks and Arabs.
- The missionary Wynfrith (St Boniface) founds the bishoprics of Passau, Ratisbon and Salzburg in Germany.

741

EUROPE
22 Oct. Charles Martel (see 714) dies having divided his lands between his sons Carloman and Pepin (the Short). Carloman receives the E territories, Austrasia, Alemmania and Thuringia along with suzerainty over Bavaria. Pepin gets Neustria, Provence and Burgundy.
- The Byzantine emperor Leo III dies after a 24-year reign during which he has saved the Byzantine empire from Islamic conquest. He is succeeded by his son Constantine V Copronymus.

742

EUROPE
- The Byzantine emperor Constantine V Copronymus defeats his brother-in-law Artabasdus, who has led a two-year rebellion against him. Established in his authority, the emperor renews the iconoclastic campaign of his predecessor, Leo III.

743

EUROPE
- Childeric III, last Merovingian king of the Franks, succeeds to the throne left vacant by Theodoric IV in 737 (see 751).

744

EUROPE
- Swabia (SW Germany) becomes a part of the Frankish empire.
- The Lombard king Liutprand dies, thus ending Lombard domination of Italy. In his 32-year reign he has defeated the dukes of Spoleto and Beneventum and made Lombardy the greatest power in Italy.

745

MIDDLE EAST AND NORTH AFRICA
- The Byzantine emperor Constantine V Copronymus invades Syria.

746

EUROPE
- The Byzantine emperor Constantine V Copronymus retakes Cyprus from the Arabs.
- Constantinople is struck by a terrible plague, the worst since 732.

748

ARTS AND HUMANITIES
- The Todai Temple near Nara, a masterpiece of early Japanese architecture, is completed.

749

MIDDLE EAST AND NORTH AFRICA
- At the battle of the Zab (in modern Iraq) Caliph Marwin I, last ruler of the Islamic Umayyad dynasty, is defeated.

ASIA
- The Japanese emperor Shomu abdicates and is succeeded by his daughter Koken.

750

EUROPE
- The duke of Cantabria, Alfonso I, establishes the kingdom of Galicia, N Spain.

MIDDLE EAST AND NORTH AFRICA
- The Abbasid caliphate is inaugurated by Abu al-Abbas as-Saffah, a descendant of the Prophet's uncle al-Abbas, who captures Damascus and kills most of the Umayyads. The caliphate will rule most of the Islamic world for the next 350 years.

751

EUROPE
- Charles Martel's son Pepin (the Short) has himself crowned king of the Franks (as Pepin III) at Soissons by Boniface (see 739), who is now archbishop of Mainz. The ecclesiastical crowning, which is new to the Franks, gives his reign an added

sacerdotal authority. The deposed Childeric III, the last Merovingian king (whose rule has been largely ceremonial), retires to a monastery.

SCIENCE AND TECHNOLOGY

– The first paper mill in the Islamic world is established at Samarkand.

752

ARTS AND HUMANITIES

– A 17m (55 feet) high statue of the Buddha, *Rushanabutsu*, is completed at Nara, Japan.

754

EUROPE

Jan. King Pepin III of the Franks is crowned at St Denis, Paris, by Pope Stephen II, who has appealed to the Franks for help against the Lombards.

MIDDLE EAST AND NORTH AFRICA

– The caliph Abu al-Abbas is succeeded by his brother al-Mansur, during whose 21-year reign authority of the caliphate will be recognized everywhere in the Islamic world except Morocco and the Iberian peninsula. Al-Mansur's uncle Abdallah, governor of Syria, revolts and is crushed; he is murdered on his nephew's orders.

ASIA

– A Chinese census shows the urban nature of Chinese life: 79% of the population live N of the Changjian (Yangtse) River. Changan has a population of 2 million and 25 other cities have a population of more than half a million.

756

EUROPE

– Pepin III defeats the Lombard king Aistulf and Ravenna (an exarchate of the Byzantine empire) falls into his hands. Pepin gives this area and the Republic of Rome to Pope Stephen II. The so-called Donation of Pepin founds the Papal States and the temporal power of the papacy. By this act – and its legal confirmation – Pepin recognizes the right of the papacy to be viewed as the heir to the Roman empire in Italian territory.

MIDDLE EAST AND NORTH AFRICA

15 May Abd ar-Rahman I is proclaimed emir of Cordoba, which becomes the capital of Islamic Spain. A Syrian prince who travelled to the Iberian peninsula the previous year, he is the sole member of the Umayyad dynasty to have escaped the massacre of 750.

ASIA

– The Chinese emperor Xuanzong abdicates following the death of his daughter-in-law and favourite concubine, Yang Guifei.

The Mongol general An Lushan rebels, occupies the capital and declares himself emperor. But he will be assassinated (757) at Luoyang. Millions die during the unrest and millions more flee to the S. Military leaders establish themselves as provincial rulers all over the country.

757

EUROPE

– In England King Ethelbald of Mercia is murdered at Seckington by his bodyguard and is succeeded by his kinsman Offa, who will bring Mercia to the height of its power.

ARTS AND HUMANITIES

– The Arab writer Ibn al-Muqaffa, best known for his translation of the Persian fables of Bidpai, is tortured at Basra on the orders of the caliph al-Mansur. His limbs having been severed, he is thrown while still alive into a burning oven.

758

ASIA

– The Japanese empress Koken (see 749) abdicates and is succeeded by her cousin Junin.

759

EUROPE

– A Frankish army retakes Narbonne, which has been in Arab hands since 720. The Franks also gain control of Septimania (modern Languedoc).

ARTS AND HUMANITIES

– *Manyoshu*, an anthology of Japanese poetry, is written by the emperor, the nobility and commoners.

761

ASIA

– The Japanese priest Dokyo becomes a favourite at court and the object of the emperor Junin's jealousy after he cures the empress mother Koken of an illness (see 758).

762

MIDDLE EAST AND NORTH AFRICA

– The caliph al-Mansur moves the capital of the caliphate from Damascus to Baghdad, which is now extensively rebuilt.

764

ASIA

– Fujiwara Nakamoro leads a revolt against the empress mother Koken of Japan but is crushed and forced into exile. Koken reassumes the throne, taking the name Shotoku, and makes her favourite, Dokyo, the prime minister.

765

EUROPE

– The three-field crop rotation system is by now established. The system ensures that a given plot of land is productive two years out of every three instead of every other year.

766

MIDDLE EAST AND NORTH AFRICA

– Baghdad is almost completely rebuilt as a circular city, 2.4km (1½ miles) in diameter, with the caliph's palace at its centre.

768

EUROPE

24 Sept. Pepin III (the Short), king of the Franks, dies and is succeeded by his son Charles who, reigning until 814, will be known as Charles the Great or Charlemagne. Pepin's other son, Carloman, becomes king of Austrasia.

ARTS AND HUMANITIES

– The Kasuga Shrine at Nara, Japan, commissioned by the Fujiwara family, is completed.

770

ASIA

– The Japanese empress Koken (Shotoku) dies. Fujiwara Nakamaro intrigues to prevent the succession of Crown Prince Ochi and ensures that the 62-year-old grandson of the emperor Tenji, Konin, becomes emperor.

SCIENCE AND TECHNOLOGY

– Horseshoes are by now widespread in Europe; farm implements can, as a result, be pulled on stony ground.

771

EUROPE

4 Dec. Charlemagne becomes king of all the Franks on the death of his brother Carloman, king of Austrasia. He marries Hildegarde of Swabia, daughter of King Desiderius (client-king of Lombardy). The Carolingian dynasty of Frankish kings, descending from Pepin III (see 768) and lasting until 987, is named after Charlemagne.

772

EUROPE

– Charlemagne, king of Franks, starts his 13-year campaign against the Saxons.

773

EUROPE

– Desiderius, king of Lombardy (see 771), invades the Papal States. Responding to a request for help from the pope, Charlemagne attacks, defeats and banishes Desiderius and then has himself crowned king of Lombardy.

774

EUROPE

– Charlemagne becomes the first Frankish king to visit Rome and confirms the Donation of Pepin (see 756) while emphasizing that he remains sovereign over the papal lands. By now Charlemagne has repudiated his marriage (771) to Hildegarde of Swabia. He absorbs Lombardy into the Frankish empire and establishes his rule in Venetia, Istria, Dalmatia and Corsica.

775

EUROPE

– The Byzantine emperor Constantine V Copronymus dies after a 34-year reign in which he has suppressed monasticism, pursued a vigorous policy of iconoclasm, restored the aqueducts and revived commerce. He is succeeded by his son Leo the Khazar (Leo IV), who continues the anti-Arab and anti-Bulgar campaigns.

MIDDLE EAST AND NORTH AFRICA

– The caliph al-Mansur (see 762) dies and is succeeded by his son al-Mahdi.

777

EUROPE

– The Frankish king Charlemagne is victorious over the Saxons and invades Moorish Spain. He is stopped at Zaragoza (Saragossa) where he makes a heroic defence of his position.

778

EUROPE

15 Aug. At Roncesvalles in the Pyrenees Basque forces crush the rearguard of the army of Charlemagne, king of the Franks, and his nephew Roland is killed. The episode will pass into legend and form the basis of several poetic renderings in which the Basques become Islamic Moors and Roland's death is accorded heroic status. The most celebrated version of the tale is the 11th-century *La Chanson de Roland* (The Song of Roland) (see 1095).

780

EUROPE

– The Byzantine emperor Leo IV dies (see 775) and is succeeded by his ten-year-old son Constantine VI. Leo's wife Irene, a dominating figure in the previous reign, becomes regent and restores icon-worship.

– Charlemagne, king of the Franks, encourages the spread of three-field crop rotation (see 765).

781

ASIA

- The Japanese emperor Konin dies and is succeeded by his son Kammu, who is half-Korean.
- By now Nestorian Christians are active as missionaries in China, where they build monasteries.

782

EUROPE

- At Verden (Germany) Charlemagne, king of the Franks, executes some 4000 hostage Saxons and imposes Christianity on the remainder. He issues the *Capitulatio de partibus saxoniae*, which makes Saxony a province of the Frankish empire.
- In England Offa, king of Mercia (see 757), builds a huge dyke to define and protect the W boundary of his kingdom against the Welsh.

MIDDLE EAST AND NORTH AFRICA

- Arab forces advance to the Bosphorus but are bought off by Byzantine imperial agents.

783

EUROPE

- The Saxons, led by Widukind (Wittekind), rebel against Charlemagne's rule and massacre a Frankish army. Charlemagne retaliates by killing more Saxon hostages and relaunches his military campaign against them.
- The Byzantine commander Staurakios leads a successful campaign against the Slavs settled in Greece and Macedonia.

785

EUROPE

- Charlemagne, king of the Franks, and the Saxon leader Widukind are reconciled. Widukind is baptized as a Christian at Attigny.

MIDDLE EAST AND NORTH AFRICA

- The Abbasid caliph al-Mahdi dies (see 754). His son, al-Hadi, succeeds and reigns for one year.

ASIA

- Fujiwara Tanetsugu engineers the marriage of his grand-daughter to Heizei, the son of the Japanese emperor Kammu.

786

MIDDLE EAST AND NORTH AFRICA

24 Sept. The calpih al-Hadi dies and is succeeded as Abbasid caliph by his brother Harun al-Rashid. Harun's ten-year reign will establish Baghdad as a centre of Arab culture and will see the expansion of the caliphate's influence over SW Asia and N Africa. He will also establish diplomatic relations with China.

787

EUROPE

- Under Pope Hadrian I, the Christian Council of Nicaea rules against iconoclasm in the E, allowing religious icons to be venerated.

788

MIDDLE EAST AND NORTH AFRICA

- Morocco rebels against the Abbasid caliphate (see 786) and establishes a rival authority.

790

EUROPE

- Elements in the Byzantine army mutiny against the party of the regent Irene and her monastic supporters. The army places Constantine VI on the imperial throne.
- By now Irish monks have arrived in Iceland.

792

EUROPE

- The Byzantine emperor Constantine VI recalls his mother Irene and makes her co-ruler of Byzantium.

793

EUROPE

8 June The Vikings raid the coast of Northumbria, N England, sacking the monastery of Lindisfarne and killing the monks. The Vikings are pagan sea-borne raiders from Scandinavia. They later settle in large numbers in parts of Europe and adopt Christianity.

SCIENCE AND TECHNOLOGY

- A paper mill is established at Baghdad as the Arabs benefit from the Chinese technology.

794

ASIA

- Heian (modern Kyoto) becomes the permanent Japanese capital and will remain so until 1868. It will be the focus of power by the great families of Fujiwara, Minamoto and Taira.

795

EUROPE

- The Vikings make their first attack on the lands that will become Scotland. They also begin to raid Ireland. Viking kingdoms will be established in Dublin, Limerick and Waterford.

CASTLE AND CATHEDRAL:
Europe's Middle Ages and the Idea of a Christian Civilization

By the year 800 the peoples of Europe had entered into what is now called the Middle Ages. This was a period dominated by the idea of Christendom, an awareness of the religious and cultural unity of Christian Europe. The spirit of Christendom was to find solid expression in the mighty cathedrals that were erected throughout the continent.

The heart of Christendom was the Church, and for most of Europe that meant the Church of Rome, with the pope at its head. The Church was a force for stability and social order, having inherited from the Roman empire the idea of written law codes. Since clerics were often the only people who could read and write, they had a key role to play in interpreting and administering the law.

The pope and the Church he ruled believed that they had a divine right to preside over spiritual affairs and Church business wherever it took place. Clergy were subject to Church law irrespective of any secular law in the land in which they lived. This gave clerical administrators a useful independence, but could lead to friction with secular authorities. Corruption and luxury were temptations for the less spiritually minded among the clergy. It was to counter these temptations that a succession of reformist movements arose, usually centred on monasteries, where the ordered life attracted many genuinely interested in learning and spirituality.

The unifying role of the Church was played out against a background of disintegrating secular authority. The Frankish emperors had revived the old Roman title but were unable to revive the Roman state, and a new secular order, now known as feudalism, arose in response to military pressures. The basis of feudalism was land and military might. A king would grant lands to a noble in return for military service. In return the noble held the lands and enjoyed the rents and payments in kind they produced. The noble parcelled out these lands to lesser knights and retainers in return for military service to help him meet his own obligations.

As cathedrals demonstrated the wealth and universal nature of the Church, so castles were the solid embodiments of secular authority. Castles allowed nobles to retain a hold over their lands with relatively small numbers of men. They made it easy for the nobles to defy higher authority and each other. Nobles of all ranks squabbled over land as castles proliferated and the powers of higher authorities generally declined.

In some areas bishops and other churchmen were also landowners and castle-builders. This, in turn, led to disputes between the secular and religious authorities. The most important of these, the so-called investiture controversy (late 11th and early 12th centuries), began when the Holy Roman Emperors and the popes disagreed over who should appoint bishops. The emperor argued that as they were his feudal inferiors, he should. The pope countered that bishops were clerics, so they were papal appointments. After decades of conflict, a compromise was reached that was more favourable to pope than emperor.

In only a few areas did the authority of rulers survive or increase. The king of England ruled a relatively homogeneous people in a land largely secure from invasion. This allowed the formation in time of a coherent nation-state, among the earliest of such political experiments.

As Europe emerged into the medieval period by far the most important form of wealth was land. Crops grew on land, livestock was raised on land, and the sparse surpluses that the land produced were the only real wealth. Most secular rulers saw manufacturing and trade merely as opportunities for taxation, and only gradually did merchants win more liberal trade laws. Even so, the 13th and early 14th centuries saw a rise in prosperity the like of which Europe had not known since the Roman empire. From 1310, however, a series of poor summers led to bad harvests and to famine and economic decline. In 1347 the Black Death hit an already weakened population, and about one-third of the people of Europe perished.

This was a period dominated by the idea of Christendom …

For a few years it seemed as if social, religious and economic life was to be disrupted permanently, even destroyed. But the institutions of medieval Europe proved equal to the challenge. The Church provided social stability, while secular rulers imposed law and order. For agricultural workers, the shortage of labour meant that wages increased dramatically. The increasingly important merchant networks recovered. But feudalism had outlived its usefulness. Military technology and economics had both moved on.

By 1400 Europe was emerging from a long period dominated by castle and cathedral. The new era was to be dominated by towns, cities and trade routes. The joint-venture company was outwardly less impressive than stone walls, but it made possible long voyages to trade with distant lands. By 1450 the Middle Ages were history.

796

EUROPE

26 July In England Offa, king of Mercia, dies after a 39-year reign during which he has established Mercian dominance over all of England S of the Humber.

– Charlemagne's army attacks the Avars (pagan, horse-riding raiders from E Europe) on the lower Danube.

797

EUROPE

– The Byzantine empress Irene deposes her son Constantine VI with army support, has him blinded and becomes sole ruler of the Byzantine empire until 802.

800

EUROPE

25 Dec. Pope Leo III crowns Charlemagne, king of the Franks, as emperor of the Romans. The Byzantine empress Irene refuses to recognize him, maintaining that only the Byzantine emperors are the legitimate rulers of Rome.

– The Athanasian Creed is formulated: it provides the Church in W Europe with a precise theological definition of Christianity.

MIDDLE EAST AND NORTH AFRICA

– The Aghlabid dynasty of Kairouan establishes its rule in NW Africa.

ASIA

– By now Zen (or Cha'an sect) Buddhism is dominant in China.

THE AMERICAS

– The Mesoamerican 'long-count' calendar goes out of use, signalling the decline of the Maya civilization.

SCIENCE AND TECHNOLOGY

– Islamic astronomer al-Fazari dies.

– Al-Batriq, translator of Greek medical texts into Arabic, dies.

– Arab scholar Jabir ibn Hayyan invents a more effective still for the distillation of liquids.

ARTS AND HUMANITIES

– Alcuin of York, a scholar in the service of Charlemagne and a key figure in the Carolingian Renaissance of learning, works on a corrected version of the Bible. He also compiles his *Lives of the Saints* and a series of letters to Charlemagne.

– The Basilica of St Anastasia is completed in Rome.
Anonymous, *Widsith*, Anglo-Saxon poem.
Cynewulf, *The Dream of the Rood*, Anglo-Saxon poem.

801

EUROPE

– The emperor Charlemagne seizes Barcelona, Spain, from Islamic occupation.

802

EUROPE

Mar. At Aachen the emperor Charlemagne's lords swear allegiance to him.

– The Byzantine empress Irene is deposed by Nicephorus I.

ARTS AND HUMANITIES

– Oviedo Cathedral is founded in Spain.

803

EUROPE

– In England the archbishopric of Lichfield is abolished. Henceforth there will be two archbishoprics in Britain: York and Canterbury.

MIDDLE EAST AND NORTH AFRICA

– Harun al-Rashid, caliph of Baghdad, overthrows the Barmakids, the Persian administrators of the Abbasid empire.

804

EUROPE

– The emperor Charlemagne completes the conquest and conversion of the Saxons.

ARTS AND HUMANITIES

19 May The Christian scholar Alcuin of York dies (see 800).

805

EUROPE

– The Byzantine emperor Nicephorus I defeats the Slav forces attacking Patras.

ASIA

– Saicho introduces Tendai Buddhism to Japan after being inspired by his visit to China.

ARTS AND HUMANITIES

– The Persian grammarian Kisa'i dies.

806

EUROPE

– Charles, the son of the emperor Charlemagne, defeats the Wends (Slavs of the Elbe and Saale areas).

MIDDLE EAST AND NORTH AFRICA

– Harun al-Rashid's military successes in Cappadocia force the Byzantine emperor Nicephorus I to pay tribute to him.

ASIA

– The Japanese emperor Kammu dies.

– Kukai founds Shingon Buddhism (an esoteric strain of the faith) in Japan.

807

EUROPE
- The Byzantine emperor Nicephorus I's naval force restores Greek imperial rule in Venice and Dalmatia.

808

EUROPE
- Godfred, king of Denmark, fortifies his S frontier.

810

EUROPE
8 July Pepin, king of Italy (and second son of Charlemagne, king of the Franks), dies having failed to conquer Venice. The Venetians recognize Byzantine rule and begin to develop their city as a major political force.

ASIA
- A Bureau of Archives is established in Japan to draft imperial decrees.

811

EUROPE
- The Byzantine emperor Nicephorus I attacks Krum, the Bulgar khan, and raids his capital city Pliska. Nicephorus is killed in a battle against the Bulgars (26 July) and is succeeded by his dying son Stauracius. After a palace coup, Michael I is proclaimed emperor (2 Oct.) and Stauracius resigns, dying three months later.
- In C Europe a Frankish army defeats the Avars (see 796), who subsequently become Christian.

SCIENCE AND TECHNOLOGY
- In China a shortage of specie leads the Tang emperors to issue drafts, which then develop into paper currency.

812

EUROPE
- Michael I, Byzantine emperor, recognizes Charlemagne as emperor of the Romans. Charlemagne abandons his claim to Venice.

813

EUROPE
June At Versinicia near Adrianople the Bulgars defeat a Byzantine army. The Byzantine emperor Michael I is deposed (11 July) and is succeeded by Leo V.
11 Sept. The emperor Charlemagne gives the imperial crown to Louis, his only surviving son.

MIDDLE EAST AND NORTH AFRICA
25 Sept. Al-Ma'mun murders his brother, seizes Baghdad and so reunites the Abbasid empire.

ARTS AND HUMANITIES
- In Spain the tomb of St James the Apostle is claimed to have been discovered at Santiago de Compostela. It will become one of the major pilgrimage centres of medieval Europe.

814

EUROPE
28 Jan. The emperor Charlemagne dies. He is succeeded by his son Louis I (the Pious).
14 April Krum, the Bulgar khan, dies and is succeeded by Omortag, who makes peace with the Byzantine emperor Leo V.

815

EUROPE
Mar. The Byzantine emperor Leo V deposes the Patriarch Nicephorus and summons a synod, which follows the Byzantine iconoclastic policy of rejecting icon worship.
- In England King Egbert of Wessex conquers Cornwall.

MIDDLE EAST AND NORTH AFRICA
- Ma 'ruf al-Karkhi of Baghdad, the first holy man of Sufi mysticism, dies.

ARTS AND HUMANITIES
- Shojiroku Shinsen compiles genealogies for Japanese noble families.

816

EUROPE
25 May Pope Leo III dies.

ARTS AND HUMANITIES
- Kukai establishes the headquarters of the Shingon sect (see 806) at a monastery on Mt Koya, Japan.

817

EUROPE
July At Aachen the emperor Louis I (the Pious) appoints his son Lothair co-emperor, thus dividing the kingdom his father Charlemagne created. His other sons, Pepin and Louis the German, govern Aquitaine and Bavaria, respectively.
- Louis I (the Pious) orders all monasteries to follow the rule of St Benedict of Nursia (see 529).

ARTS AND HUMANITIES
- The Church of San Prassede, Rome, is completed.
- Lihe (Li Ho), leading poet of the Chinese Tang dynasty, dies.

819

MIDDLE EAST AND NORTH AFRICA
- Al-Ma'mun (see 813) establishes his authority in Baghdad by suppressing a revolt.

ARTS AND HUMANITIES
- The Chinese poet Liu Zongyuan (Liu Tsung-yuan) dies.

820

EUROPE

25 Dec. The Byzantine emperor Leo V is murdered and is succeeded by Michael II, who inaugurates the Amorian dynasty.

ARTS AND HUMANITIES
- An Islamic law school is founded at Medina.
- Al-Shafi'i, the founder of the Islamic Shafi'ite rite, dies.
- The Hindu philosopher Sankara dies.

821

EUROPE
- Coenwulf, king of Mercia, dies.

822

ARTS AND HUMANITIES
- The Persian grammarian Farra dies.

823

EUROPE
- Pope Paschal I crowns Lothair (see 817) as king of Italy.

ARTS AND HUMANITIES
- Al-Waqidi, the historian and biographer of the Prophet Muhammad, dies.
- The Arab poet al-Attabi dies.
- The Chinese poet and philosopher Hanyu (Han Yu) dies.

825

EUROPE
- King Egbert of Wessex defeats the Mercians and conquers Kent, Sussex and Essex. This transforms Wessex from a minor kingdom into the dominant kingdom of Anglo-Saxon England.
- The Byzantine emperor Michael II defeats the pretender Thomas the Slav.
- The Italian king Lothair I's *Constitutio Romana* defines the emperor's authority in the C Italian papal lands.

826

EUROPE
- The emperor Louis I (the Pious) recognizes Nomenoe as chief of the Bretons. The Celtic Bretons of Brittany will maintain a precarious independence from the empire, and later from France, for centuries.

827

ARTS AND HUMANITIES
- Al-Hajjaj translates *Almagest* (Ptolemy's original Greek work on astronomy) into Arabic.
- A mosque in Amr features the earliest pointed arch to be constructed in Egypt.

828

EUROPE
- Louis the German, son of the emperor Louis I (the Pious), repels a Bulgarian invasion of Pannonia (modern Austria).

ARTS AND HUMANITIES
- The Arab religious poet Abu al-Atahiyah dies.

829

EUROPE
- The Vikings raid Saxony.

ASIA
- Forces of the Thai state of Nanzhao (Nanchao) in S China invade Szechuan.

830

EUROPE

April Pepin and Louis the German rebel against their father Louis I (the Pious), who regains his authority in the autumn.

SCIENCE AND TECHNOLOGY
- Indian mathematician Mahaviri writes *Ganitasarasamgraha*, a Hindu mathematical treatise on calculation.

ARTS AND HUMANITIES
- The Kairouan Mosque is built.
- Al-Ma'mun founds the Bayt al-Hikmah, a library, teaching and translation centre in Baghdad.
- In Wales Nennius compiles the core of the collection of historic documents known as *Historia Brittonum* (History of the Britons). (See also 518.)

Einhard, *Life of Charlemagne*, biography.

831

EUROPE
- In S Italy Salerno is seized by Islamic forces.
- The Bulgars again attack the Byzantine empire.
- In N Germany the bishopric of Hamburg is founded.

ARTS AND HUMANITIES

Paschasius Radbertus, *De sacramento corporis et sanguinis Domini Nostri*, religious treatise maintaining the doctrine of transubstantiation.

832

EUROPE
- The sons of the emperor Louis I (the Pious) again rebel against his rule (see 830).

ASIA
- Forces of the Thai state of Nanzhao (Nanchao) destroy the kingdom of the Pyu, the earliest known inhabitants of Burma.
- The confederation of Turkic tribes in Manchuria known as the Uighurs dissolves.

833

EUROPE
1 Oct. The emperor Louis I (the Pious) is deposed by his sons.

MIDDLE EAST AND NORTH AFRICA
7 Aug. Caliph al-Ma'mun dies and is succeeded by his brother al-Mutasim. The army of the caliphate is now Turkish-dominated.

ASIA
- The Chinese emperor Wenzong (Wen Tsung) fails to regain power from the eunuchs who have become power brokers in the court and government.
- The Japanese emperor Junna abdicates and is succeeded by his nephew Nimnyo.

SCIENCE AND TECHNOLOGY
- Al-Mamun founds an observatory at Baghdad to promote geographical exploration.

ARTS AND HUMANITIES
- The first Romanesque-style Lombard church, San Vicenzo in Milan, is completed. It incorporates a vaulted basilica.

834

EUROPE
- Louis I (the Pious) is restored to the Frankish throne (see 833) as his sons fall out.
- Vikings raid Frisia (Holland) and N France. From now on they will raid France's Channel coasts annually.

MIDDLE EAST AND NORTH AFRICA
- The caliph al-Mutasim expels the gypsies (the Jalt) from Iraq.

835

EUROPE
- Vikings extend their raids to England. They will sack London in 836.

836

MIDDLE EAST AND NORTH AFRICA
- The Abbasid caliph al-Mutasim moves his capital from Baghdad to Samarra.

837

EUROPE
- An Arab force based in Sicily sacks Brindisi, E Italy.

SCIENCE AND TECHNOLOGY
- A carrier pigeon service is established to communicate information across the Arab-controlled territories.

838

EUROPE
- Arab raiders from N Africa sack Marseilles, S France.

839

EUROPE
- Egbert, king of Wessex, dies and is succeeded by Ethelwulf.

840

EUROPE
- Louis I (the Pious) dies and is succeeded as emperor by his son Lothair (see 817). Civil war between Louis's sons follows.

841

EUROPE
- Vikings found Dublin as a raiding base and slave market.
- Vikings raid Rouen, in Normandy, NW France.
- Arabs attack settlements on the Adriatic coast of Italy.

ASIA
- The Uighurs (see 832) are pushed by the Khirgiz out of their imperial lands and move into the Tarim Basin in China.

842

ASIA
- The king of Tibet's empire collapses after he tries to suppress Buddhism.
- Nestorian monasteries in China are closed after the Uighurs are defeated.

843

EUROPE
- The treaty of Verdun ends the civil wars in the Frankish lands (see 840) and divides the Carolingian empire, which becomes three kingdoms: a 'Middle Kingdom', stretching from the North Sea to N Italy, is ruled by Lothair; the E Frankish empire (which will become Germany), is ruled by Louis II (the German); and the W Frankish empire (which will become France), is ruled by Charles II (the Bald). Lothair retains the title of emperor, which he inherited from his father, Louis I (the Pious). The treaty marks the effective beginning of the Franco-German divide in European history.

- Kenneth MacAlpin, king of the Scots, is recognized as king of the Picts. The unification of the two kingdoms is later recognized as the foundation of the medieval kingdom of Scotland, although the lands ruled by Kenneth MacAlpin are smaller than the later kingdom.
- Arabs capture Messina, Sicily.

844

EUROPE

- Vikings attack S Spain.

845

EUROPE

Nov. Breton forces defeat the army of W Frankish emperor Charles II (the Bald) at Balon.
- Vikings attack Paris.

ASIA

- The Chinese government launches a campaign of persecution against Buddhists.

846

EUROPE

Aug. Arab pirates attack Rome.
- The W Frankish emperor Charles II (the Bald) recognizes Brittany's independence.

ARTS AND HUMANITIES

- Ibn Khurdadhbih produces a geographical description of the roads in Asia.

847

EUROPE

- The Arabs lose Benevento, S Italy, to Frankish forces led by Louis II.
- In order to raise an army the W Frankish emperor Charles II (the Bald) introduces a system under which every free man chooses a lord under whom he is to serve. This will later develop into the feudal system.

ARTS AND HUMANITIES

- Work begins on the mosque at Samarra (see 836).

849

ASIA

- Pagan becomes the capital of the Burmese kingdom.

ARTS AND HUMANITIES

- The writings of German theologian Gottschalk of Orbais are condemned as heretical because they are thought to advance the doctrine of predestination and therefore deny human free will. He will die after 18 years in prison.

850

EUROPE

April Louis II, son of the emperor Lothair, is crowned emperor and king of Italy in Rome.
- Vikings establish bases on the rivers Rhine, Somme, Seine, Loire and Garonne in France.
- Vikings seize Kiev; the occupation leads to the development of the Varangian empire of the Rus.

ASIA

- Jayavarman II, the ruler who has united the Khmers of Cambodia, dies.

SCIENCE AND TECHNOLOGY

- Al-Khwarizmi, the Arab mathematician, algebraist, astronomer and cartographer, dies.

851

EUROPE

- Ethelwulf, king of Wessex, defeats the Vikings.

ARTS AND HUMANITIES

- Arab writer Silsilat al-Tawarikh writes of the journeys of Sulaiman the Merchant, the origin of the later tales of Sinbad the Sailor.

Johannes Scotus Erigena, *De divina praedestinatione* (On Divine Predestination), an attack on the heretical theories of Gottschalk (see 849).

852

EUROPE

May Arabs based in Sicily occupy Calabria, S Italy.

ARTS AND HUMANITIES

- Frechulp of Lisieux, author of a *History of the World*, dies.

853

EUROPE

- Vikings settled in Ireland (see 795) submit to Olaf, son of the king of Norway, who makes Dublin his capital.
- Vikings burn Tours, W France.
- An Arab dynasty is established at Bari, S Italy.

854

EUROPE

- Vikings sack Blois and Orleans, France.

ARTS AND HUMANITIES

- Al-Tabari, the Islamic scholar whose *Kitab wa-al-Dawlah* uses the Bible to defend Islam, dies.

855-865

855

EUROPE

28 Sept. Emperor Lothair I dies, having partitioned his lands among his three sons. The emperor Louis II (see 850) retains Italy, Lothair receives the central area from Frisia to the Alps (called *Lotharii regnum*, Lothair's Kingdom, and subsequently Lotharingia or Lorraine), and Charles receives Provence, S France.

Nov. The Byzantine empress Theodora's adviser Theoctistus the Logothete is murdered. Theodora's son Michael III succeeds as emperor.

ARTS AND HUMANITIES

– Ahmad ibn Hanbal, founder of the Hanbalite sect and compiler of 30,000 Islamic traditions in his *Musnad*, dies.

856

EUROPE

28 Dec. Vikings burn Paris.

857

EUROPE

– The kingdom of Navarre, N Spain, is established.

ASIA

– The Fujiwara family formally establish their regency, which will govern Japan in the name of a succession of puppet emperors.

ARTS AND HUMANITIES

– Yuhanna ibn Masawayh, author of the first Arabic treatise on ophthalmology, dies.

858

EUROPE

– Kenneth MacAlpin, king of Scotland, dies and is succeeded by his brother Donald I.
– Pope Nicholas I declares that bishops are his delegates and not subject to secular rulers.

859

EUROPE

– Vikings raid Algeciras, S Spain.
– The Arabs complete their conquest of Sicily.
– Eulegius, the anti-Islamic polemicist and archbishop of Toledo, is executed by the Moors.

860

EUROPE

June Vikings from Rus (see 850) fail to seize control of Constantinople.

SCIENCE AND TECHNOLOGY

– The sons of Musa ibn Shakir, Muhammad, Ahmad and Hasan, compile *The Book of Artifices,* the earliest known guide to mechanics.

ARTS AND HUMANITIES

– Hincmar, archbishop of Reims, writes *De divortio Lotharii* (On the Divorce of Lothair), outlining the reasons for his opposition to the plan of King Lothair (son of the emperor Lothair, see 855) to divorce his wife. The book is an important advance in the Western Church's involvement in defining the rights and duties of rulers.
– The Sufi theologian Dhu al-Nun dies.

861

EUROPE

– King Lothair divorces his wife, Theutberga, and marries his mistress, Waldrada.

MIDDLE EAST AND NORTH AFRICA

11 Dec. The Abbasid caliph al-Mutawakkil is murdered by his Turkish bodyguard when he appoints his illegitimate son, al-Mutazz as his heir. He is succeeded by his son al-Munstansir.

862

EUROPE

– Constantine I becomes king of Scotland.
– The Byzantine emperor Michael III sends the brothers Cyril and Methodius to convert the Slavs. Cyril will invent an alphabet (Cyrillic) to translate the Bible and liturgy into Slavonic.

MIDDLE EAST AND NORTH AFRICA

– The Abbasid caliph al-Munstansir is murdered by his half-brother al-Mutazz, who succeeds him.

863

EUROPE

Aug. Pope Nicholas I decrees that Ignatius should be restored as patriarch of Constantinople and that Photius, whom he excommunicates, should be removed from that office. In Oct. Nicholas removes the archbishops of Cologne, Trier and Ravenna from office.

ARTS AND HUMANITIES

– The Byzantine logothete (chief minister) Bardas Caesar founds a secular university, run by Leo the Mathematician, in Constantinople.

865

EUROPE

3 Feb. St Anskar, the bishop of Hamburg who has led Christian missions to Denmark and Sweden, dies.

- A great Danish Viking army invades East Anglia.
- Ethelbert, king of Wessex, dies and is succeeded by his brother, Ethelred I.

ASIA
- Around this date the Khazars, who inhabit an area on the lower Volga, adopt Judaism as the state religion.

ARTS AND HUMANITIES
- Johannes Scotus Erigena, *De divisione naturae* (On the Division of Nature). The work is condemned as pantheistic.

866

EUROPE
21 April The logothete Bardas (see 863) is murdered by the Byzantine emperor Michael III.

Aug. Boris I of Bulgaria rebels against the Church establishment in Constantinople because of its refusal to allow a separate Bulgarian Church. He offers allegiance to Pope Nicholas I.

1 Nov. In England, the Vikings occupy York.

- Charles II (the Bald) of France pays tribute to the Vikings, whose raids are threatening his kingdom.

ARTS AND HUMANITIES
- The oldest surviving Arabic paper manuscript is created.

867

EUROPE
21 Mar. In England Aelle, king of Northumbria, is killed by the Vikings, who now establish their rule in Northumbria.

24 Sept. The Byzantine emperor Michael III is murdered. His successor Basil I founds the Macedonian dynasty.

- The Byzantine patriarch Photius attacks Pope Nicholas I in a Church council held at Constantinople. He condemns the inclusion by the Western Church of the *filioque* clause in the creed in order to describe the procession of the Holy Spirit.

MIDDLE EAST AND NORTH AFRICA
- Ephesus is seized by the Paulicians, a militant and heretical sect who have revived Manichaeism and enjoy widespread support in Armenia.

868

EUROPE
- The Byzantine army establishes supremacy in the Balkans.

MIDDLE EAST AND NORTH AFRICA
- Ahmad ibn Tulun of Egypt establishes a virtually automonous local dynasty.

869

EUROPE
14 Feb. St Cyril (see 862) dies.

9 Sept. Charles II (the Bald) is crowned king of Lorraine following the death of his nephew Lothair (see 855).

30 Oct. The radical German theologian Gottschalk of Orbais (see 849) dies.

MIDDLE EAST AND NORTH AFRICA
Sept. The black slaves employed in the Abbasid's saltpetre mines in Iraq revolt.

870

EUROPE
8 Aug. By the treaty of Mersen Louis II (the German) agrees with Charles II (the Bald) on the partition of the kingdom of their nephew Lothair (see 855). Later in the year Charles occupies Provence.

- Greek Orthodox Christian evangelist Methodius is jailed by German bishops while on his Moravian mission.

ARTS AND HUMANITIES
- Al-Bukhari, the author of *al-Sahih*, an account of Islamic theology and law, dies.

871

EUROPE
2 Feb. Louis II (the German) frees Bari from Arab occupation.

April In England Ethelred I, king of Wessex, dies of wounds sustained in battle with the Danes. His brother Alfred (the Great) succeeds him.

- Svatopulk, de facto ruler of Moravia (in the modern Czech Republic), expels the E Franks from his lands.

ARTS AND HUMANITIES
- Al-Hakam, author of a history of the Islamic conquest of Egypt, N Africa and Spain, dies.

872

MIDDLE EAST AND NORTH AFRICA
- The Byzantine emperor Basil I defeats the Paulicians (see 867) and forces their conversion to Orthodox Christianity.
- Yaqub bin Laith as-Saffar conquers Khurasan (Iran), which has been ruled by the Tahirid dynasty.

SCIENCE AND TECHNOLOGY
- Ahmad ibn Tulun (see 868) establishes Cairo's first hospital. Hospitals are now widespread in the Arab world.

873

SCIENCE AND TECHNOLOGY
- Hunayn ibn Ishaq al-Ibadi, who translated Galen, Aristotle and Euclid into Arabic, dies.

ARTS AND HUMANITIES
- The Arab neo-Platonist philosopher al-Kindi dies.

874

EUROPE

– In England the Danes expel Burgred, last king of Mercia.
– The Germans release the Orthodox Christian missionary Methodius. Peace is established between Louis II (the German) and Svatopulk of Moravia (see 871), who swears allegiance to the E Frankish king.
– The Moors of Toledo are defeated by Christian Spanish at the Orbedo. The victory marks the beginning of the *Reconquista*, the reconquest of Spain by the Christians from Islamic rulers and settlers from N Africa. The process will take centuries.

ASIA

– The Samanid dynasty of Transoxiana, C Asia, is founded. The capital Bukhara becomes the centre of a Persian literary renaissance.

875

EUROPE

12 Aug. Louis II, son of Lothair I (see 850), E Frankish emperor and king of Italy, dies. The Byzantine emperor Basil I susequently takes possession of Bari.
25 Dec. Pope John VIII crowns Charles II (the Bald) as emperor of the W.
– Catalonia in NE Spain, once part of the Carolingian empire, is now ruled by the increasingly independent counts of Barcelona.
– Methodius baptizes the Bohemian Prince Borivoj.

ARTS AND HUMANITIES

– The Persian poet Hanzala of Badghis dies.

876

EUROPE

28 Aug. Louis II (the German) dies. His lands are divided among his sons. Carloman rules Bavaria and the E March, while Louis the Younger rules Saxony and Franconia. Charles (the Fat) rules Alemannia as Charles III.
– At around this date the Viking kingdom of York is founded: it will last until 954.

ARTS AND HUMANITIES

– Work begins on the Ibn Tulun Mosque, Cairo.

877

EUROPE

7 May Charles II (the Bald) orders the payment of a tax to bribe the Vikings to leave the area of the Seine.
14 June Charles II (the Bald) recognizes the hereditability of fiefs. By his grants to vassals, Charles consolidates the feudal system, under which the king grants lands in return for military service.
6 Oct. Charles II (the Bald) dies. His son Louis II (the Stammerer) is crowned king of the French (8 Dec.).

– In England the Danes establish themselves in Mercia. Danish soldiers settle the 'five boroughs' of Lincoln, Stamford, Nottingham, Derby and Leicester.

MIDDLE EAST AND NORTH AFRICA

23 Oct. St Ignatius of Constantinople, Byzantine prelate who opposed imperial interference in Church affairs, dies.
– Ahmad ibn Tulun of Egypt (see 868) seizes Syria from the Abbasids.

SCIENCE AND TECHNOLOGY

– Al-Battani begins his astronomical work in al-Raqqah.

ARTS AND HUMANITIES

– Johannes Scotus Erigena dies.

878

EUROPE

May In England King Alfred (the Great) of Wessex defeats the Danes at Edington. Guthrum, the Danish leader, is baptized a Christian.
– In Wales Rhodri the Great (Rhodri Mawr), prince of Gwynedd, Powys and Seisyllwg, dies: his kingdom dissolves.
– Oleg, ruler of Novgorod, seizes Kiev.

MIDDLE EAST AND NORTH AFRICA

– Muhammad al-Muntazar, the 12th imam of the Ismail'ite sect of the Shiite branch of Islam, disappears. As the 'Hidden Imam' or al-Mahdi, his return is prophesied by his followers.

879

EUROPE

– Louis II (the Stammerer), king of France, dies and is succeeded by his sons Louis III and Carloman. Louis III defeats the Vikings on the Loire (30 Nov.).
– The Byzantine emperor Basil I publishes a revised edition of Roman law.

ASIA

– Chinese rebels sack Guangzhou (Canton). Thousands of foreign traders, mostly Arabs and Persians, are killed.
– Nepal becomes independent of Tibet.

ARTS AND HUMANITIES

– Work begins on the Cathedral of Santiago de Compostela, Spain.

880

EUROPE

March By the terms of the treaty of Ribemont, France is divided between Carloman (who receives Aquitaine and Burgundy) and his brother Louis III (who receives N France).
– The Byzantine emperor Basil I expels the Arabs from Calabria, S Italy.
– Pope John VIII allows the use of Slavonic in the liturgy.

ASIA
– Varagunavarman II of Pandya, S India, is defeated in his attempt to crush the Cholas.
– The Chinese peasant rebel leader Huang Zhao (Huang Chao) declares himself emperor of China.

881

EUROPE
12 Feb. Pope John VIII crowns Charles III (the Fat) (see 876) as emperor.
– Vikings sack Liège, Cologne, Bonn, Aachen and Trier.

ARTS AND HUMANITIES
Anonymous, *Ludwigslied* (The Song of Louis), German historical ballad in praise of Louis III's victory over the Vikings (see 879).

882

EUROPE
15 Dec. Pope John VIII is murdered. Marinus I succeeds him.
– Charles III (the Fat) becomes ruler of Saxony and Bavaria on the death of Louis III and so reunites Germany.
– The Vikings sack Reims, France.

883

MIDDLE EAST AND NORTH AFRICA
– The forces of al-Mutamid suppress the black slave rebellion in Iraq (see 869).

ASIA
– Avantivarman, king of Kashmir, promotes extensive irrigation schemes in his kingdom.
– Huang Zhao (Huang Chao) is defeated by the Shaduo, the Turkish force allied to the Chinese emperor.

> *The Turks are … concerned solely with raid and foray.*
>
> al-Jahiz (*c*.776–*c*.869)

884

EUROPE
12 Dec. Carloman dies. He is succeeded by Charles III (the Fat) on the invitation of the French nobility. Charles therefore reunites Charlemagne's empire.
– Burgos, capital of Castile, is founded.

ASIA
– Huang Zhao (Huang Chao), the usurper emperor of China, is killed by the Turkish Shaduo, who now claim control over N China.

885

EUROPE
Nov. Vikings lay siege to Paris, which is defended by Count Odo.
– Pope Stephen V bans the use of Slavonic in the liturgy and Svatopulk expels Methodius' followers from Moravia after Methodius' death (6 April).

MIDDLE EAST AND NORTH AFRICA
– Both the Byzantine emperor Basil I and the caliph al-Mutamid recognize Ashot I (the Great) as king of Armenia.

ARTS AND HUMANITIES
Anonymous, *La Vie de Sainte Eulalie* (Life of Saint Eulalia), the first surviving French poem.

886

EUROPE
29 Aug. The Byzantine emperor Basil I dies and is succeeded by Leo VI.
– King Alfred (the Great) of Wessex expels the Vikings from London and, by treaty, defines the area of the Danelaw, that part of England that has been settled by Vikings, mostly from Denmark, and that recognizes Danish rather than English laws.

ARTS AND HUMANITIES
Anonymous, *The Basilica*, a Greek version of Justinian's code of Roman law.

887

EUROPE
Sept. The doge of Venice, Pietro Candiano, is killed in battle against the Slavs. His predecessor, Giovanni Participazio II, is restored as doge.
– German nobles depose Charles III (the Fat) as emperor.

ARTS AND HUMANITIES
Anonymous, *Rikkokushi*, six Chinese histories of Japan from 791 to 887.

888

EUROPE
13 Jan. Charles III (the Fat) dies and his empire disintegrates. In Germany Arnulf of Carinthia is declared king; in Italy various rivals contest for the crown; while in Burgundy an independent kingdom is established. In France itself royal authority collapses. Count Odo, seen as the best man to keep the Vikings at bay, is elected king of France by powerful nobles.
April Pietro Tribuno becomes doge of Venice by a new method of popular election.
24 June Odo defeats the Vikings at Montfaucon, France.
– The Moorish emir of Spain, al-Mundhir, is poisoned and is succeeded by his brother Abd Allah.
– The Arabs advance into Provence, S France.

SCIENCE AND TECHNOLOGY

– Ibn Firnas, a Spanish Muslim, tries to fly using feathers.

889

EUROPE

Feb. Guy, duke of Spoleto, is crowned king of Italy.

THE AMERICAS

– Tikal, once the dominant Maya city, is abandoned. Chichén Itzá in Yucatán becomes the main Maya centre.

ARTS AND HUMANITIES

– The first terraced stone pyramid in Cambodia, the Bakong Temple, is built in Angkor.
– Ibn Qutaybah, compiler of a narrative of Arab history, dies.

890

EUROPE

– Ashot I (the Great), king of Armenia, dies and is succeeded by Sembat I.

MIDDLE EAST AND NORTH AFRICA

– The headquarters of the Qarmatian sect of Ismail'ites is established in Iraq.

ASIA

– Mihira Bhoja I, who founded an empire in N India, dies.

ARTS AND HUMANITIES

Anonymous, *The Story of the Bamboo Gatherer*, the earliest Japanese prose narrative.

891

EUROPE

1 Sept. The Vikings are defeated at Louvain, modern Belgium, and later (Oct.) in Brabant.

ARTS AND HUMANITIES

– The Byzantine patriarch Photius, whose *Library* describes otherwise unknown and lost works by classical Greek authors, dies.

892

EUROPE

– King Alfred (the Great) of Wessex fortifies towns in anticipation of the Viking army's arrival in England from France.

MIDDLE EAST AND NORTH AFRICA

15 Oct. The caliph al-Mutamid dies and is succeeded by his son al-Mutadid, who restores the capital to Baghdad.

ARTS AND HUMANITIES

– Between now and his death in 899 King Alfred (the Great) of Wessex translates into English Bede's *Historia Ecclesiastica Gentis Anglorum* (Ecclesiastical History of the English People), Boethius's *De consolatione philosophiae* (The Consolation of

Philosophy), St Augustine's *Soliloquies* and Orosius's universal history, *Historia adversus Paganos*.
– The Arab historian al-Baladhuri, whose *Futuh al-Buldan* has described the Arab conquests, dies.

893

EUROPE

28 Jan. Charles III (the Simple) is crowned king of France after a revolt against Odo's rule (see 888).
– At Zamora Alfonso III, king of Asturias, defeats a rebellion led by a pretender to the title of Mahdi.
– Vladimir, king of the Bulgars, is deposed by his brother Symeon.

894

ARTS AND HUMANITIES

Asser, *Life of King Alfred*, biography of Alfred (the Great), king of Wessex.

895

EUROPE

– Bohemia regains its independence from Moravia and accepts the supremacy of Arnulf, king of Germany (see 888).
– The Magyars, nomadic raiders from Asia who have settled in the area between the Danube and the Dnieper, attack Bulgaria. Symeon, the king of the Bulgars, incites the Pechenegs, nomads in E Europe, to invade Magyar land. The Magyars move on and settle in C Europe.

ARTS AND HUMANITIES

– Al-Dinawari, author of the Persian history *The Long Narratives*, dies.

896

EUROPE

– King Alfred defeats a new Viking invasion of England.
– Symeon, king of the Bulgars, defeats the Byzantine army: the Byzantine emperor Leo VI pays tribute to him.

897

EUROPE

– Odo (see 893) regains the French crown.

ASIA

– In S India Aparajitha, the last Pallava king, dies: his lands are annexed by the Cholas.

898

EUROPE

1 Jan. Odo, king of France, dies and is succeeded by Charles III (the Simple).
– The Magyars (see 895) raid the Veneto, N Italy.

899

EUROPE

Sept. The Magyars ravage N Italy.

26 Oct. King Alfred (the Great) of Wessex dies and is succeeded by his son Edward the Elder.

– Arnulf, king of Germany, dies and is succeeded by Louis III (the Child).

MIDDLE EAST AND NORTH AFRICA

– The Qarmatians establish an independent state in Bahrain. For the next 300 years they will raid neighbouring states and rulers.

900

EUROPE

– Around this time King Harold I (Fairhair) unifies Norway.

ASIA

– Muslim rule extends to Transoxiana in C Asia; the Samanid dynasty replaces the Saffarids.

THE AMERICAS

– The Toltec kingdom of Mexico is established with its capital at Tula.

901

EUROPE

– The Magyars ravage Carinthia (in modern Austria).

ARTS AND HUMANITIES

– Thabit ibn Qurra, Arab translator of classical Greek texts on astronomy and mathematics, dies.

902

EUROPE

1 Aug. Ibrahim II of Kairouan destroys Taormina, the sole remaining Greek settlement in Sicily.

ARTS AND HUMANITIES

– The Japanese poet Sugawara Michizane dies.

903

EUROPE

– The Vikings burn Tours, W France.

SCIENCE AND TECHNOLOGY

– Ibn Rustah, author of the Arab geography, *The Precious Bags of Travelling Provisions*, dies.

– Persian writer Ibn al-Faqih writes *The Book of Countries*, a geographical study.

ARTS AND HUMANITIES

– The first ambulatory with side chapels is built in Europe at St Martin, Tours.

904

EUROPE

31 July An Arab fleet sacks Thessalonica, Greece.

ARTS AND HUMANITIES

– The Church of St John Lateran, Rome, is completed.

905

MIDDLE EAST AND NORTH AFRICA

– The Tulunid dynasty (see 868) becomes extinct, and the caliph regains control of Syria and Egypt (see 877).

ARTS AND HUMANITIES

– Anonymous, *Kokinshu*, anthology of Japanese and Chinese poetry.

906

EUROPE

– The Magyars subjugate Moravia and then raid Saxony.

– Regino of Prum's collection of canon law contains the laws against witchcraft that will be used in future persecutions.

907

EUROPE

– Oleg of Russia destroys the outskirts of Constantinople.

ASIA

– In China the Tang dynasty's last emperor is murdered by the peasant leader Zhuwen (Chu Wen), who then declares himself emperor. He inaugurates the 'Period of the Five Dynasties and the Ten Kingdoms', a time of chaos and warfare that will last until 960. An independent emperor is proclaimed to rule the Khitan (or 'Cathay'), the territory of the semi-nomadic Mongol tribes of N China.

908

EUROPE

– The Magyars defeat the Bavarians and then raid Saxony and Thuringia.

909

MIDDLE EAST AND NORTH AFRICA

7 Dec. Sa'id ibn Hussein is proclaimed Ubayd Allah al-Mahdi ('the divinely guided one') in Tunis, N Africa. He creates an Ismailite (Shiite) caliphate in opposition to the caliphate of Baghdad and founds the Fatimid dynasty.

ARTS AND HUMANITIES

– The Abbey of Cluny is founded in modern Burgundy, E France. Cluny later becomes a seat of great learning and the centre for a major reformation of Christian monasticism.

910

EUROPE

5 Aug. Edward the Elder of Wessex defeats the Danes of Northumbria at Tettenhall, Staffordshire; Halfdan, king of York, is killed.

911

EUROPE

21 Jan. Louis III (the Child), last German ruler of the Carolingian line, dies.

– Charles III (the Simple) receives the homage of Rollo, a Viking leader, who becomes a Christian. The grant to Rollo of Rouen, Lisieux and Evreux is the origin of the duchy of Normandy. The raids on N France end as the Vikings begin to be assimilated.

– The Byzantine empire makes peace with the Russians at Kiev.

912

EUROPE

April–May Arab forces defeat the Byzantine navy in an engagement off Chios.

15 Oct. Abd Allah, emir of Spain, dies. He is succeeded by Abd ar-Rahman III, under whom the Umayyad emirate in Spain will reach the peak of its power and cultural achievement.

ARTS AND HUMANITIES

– Monks fleeing Muslim intolerance in S Spain introduce the Mozarabic architectural style to N Spain.

913

EUROPE

Aug. Bulgarian invaders reach Constantinople.

– Oleg of Russia dies and is succeeded by Prince Igor.

914

EUROPE

Oct. King Edward the Elder begins the conquest of the Danelaw, the Viking-controlled areas in England.

– Ordono II, king of Galicia, transfers his capital from Oviedo to Leon, N Spain.

915

EUROPE

– Byzantine and Italian forces destroy Arab bases in C Italy.

ASIA

– The Chola king Parantaka I conquers the Pandya kingdom, S India.

ARTS AND HUMANITIES

– Regino of Prum, author of the *World Chronicle*, dies.

917

EUROPE

Aug. The Bulgarian king Symeon invades Thrace, becomes the dominant figure in the Balkans and demands that he be recognized as Greek emperor.

– The Danish kingdom of East Anglia is destroyed by Edward the Elder of Wessex.

– The Magyars pillage S Germany, Alsace and Burgundy.

– The Shiite caliph Ubayd Allah (see 909) conquers Sicily.

918

EUROPE

– In England, Edward the Elder of Wessex now controls Mercia and the Danish areas of the Midlands.

919

EUROPE

May Henry the Fowler, duke of Saxony, is crowned King Henry I, first of the Saxon line of German kings.

– The Viking leader Ragnald becomes king of Northumbria while acknowledging the overall rule of Edward the Elder, king of Wessex.

920

EUROPE

17 Dec. Romanus I Lecapenus seizes power and becomes joint Byzantine emperor with Constantine VII.

922

MIDDLE EAST AND NORTH AFRICA

– Al-Hallaj is murdered by the Abbasid inquisition and becomes the first Sufi martyr.

923

EUROPE

Sept. Civil war breaks out in the kingdom of Leon, Spain, after the death of Ordono II (see 914).

– The Vikings raid Aquitaine and the Auvergne, S France.

ASIA

– In China the Later Tang dynasty is founded by the leader of the Shaduo.

ARTS AND HUMANITIES

– Al-Tabari, author of the *Annals of the Apostles and the Kings* as well as a compendium of world history, dies.

924

EUROPE

17 July King Edward the Elder dies and is succeeded as king of

Wessex by his son Athelstan, who will claim to be king of a united England.
- The civil war in the kingdom of Leon, Spain, ends.
- The Magyars mount fresh attacks on Italy and also invade Germany and S France.
- Abd ar-Rahman III sacks Pampeluna (modern Pamplona), the capital of Navarre.

925

EUROPE
- Henry I of Germany becomes king of Lorraine.
- The viscounts of Anjou take the title of count to demonstrate their independence from Norman rule.
- William Longsword succeeds his father Rollo (see 911) as duke of Normandy.

SCIENCE AND TECHNOLOGY
- Al-Razi, author of the medical textbook *al-Hawi*, dies.

926

EUROPE
- Tomislav, king of Croatia, defeats the Bulgar king Symeon.

927

EUROPE
27 May The Bulgar king Symeon dies and is succeeded by his son Peter, who signs a peace agreement with the Byzantine emperor that restores Byzantine control of Serbia.

ASIA
- The Japanese fiscal system collapses.

ARTS AND HUMANITIES
- The Abbey Church of Cluny (see 909), in Burgundy, is dedicated.

928

EUROPE
- Henry I of Germany attacks the Wends, a pagan people of E Europe, and also forces the duke of Bohemia to accept his overlordship.

MIDDLE EAST AND NORTH AFRICA
- The Ziyarid dynasty is established in Jurjan (modern Turkmenistan).

929

EUROPE
16 Jan. Abd ar-Rahman III, Umayyad emir of Spain, declares himself caliph to show his independence from Baghdad.
4 Sept. The Wends are defeated by Henry I of Germany and become Christian.

28 Sept. Prince Wenceslas of Bohemia is murdered by his brother Boleslav I, who proclaims his independence from Henry I of Germany.
7 Oct. Charles III (the Simple), king of France, dies.

930

EUROPE
- The Althing, a representative assembly, is established in Iceland.
- Eric Bloodaxe succeeds his father Harold I (Fairhair) as king of Norway.

MIDDLE EAST AND NORTH AFRICA
- Followers of the Shiite Qarmatian sect sack the holy city of Mecca and remove the sacred Black Stone.

ASIA
- The Fujiwara family become Japan's effective rulers as regents acting in the emperor's name.

931

MIDDLE EAST AND NORTH AFRICA
- Spanish muslims seize Ceuta (now in Morocco) from the Berbers.

932

EUROPE
- Toledo is captured by Abd ar-Rahman III (see 912), who now controls the whole of Muslim Spain.

ASIA
- Annam (Vietnam) rebels against Chinese rule.

ARTS AND HUMANITIES
- On the Chinese government's instructions, wooden blocks are used to print Confucian, Buddhist and Daoist texts.

933

EUROPE
Mar. Henry I of Germany defeats the Magyars near Merseburg, Germany.
- Provence, S France, is united with the kingdom of Burgundy.

ARTS AND HUMANITIES
- Ibn Duraid, the compiler of an Arabic dictionary written in Persian, *The Collection of a Language*, dies.

934

EUROPE
- Henry I of Germany makes peace with Denmark and establishes Schleswig as a frontier territory.
- The Fatimid Shiite caliph Ubayd Allah (see 909) raids Genoa, Corsica and Sardinia.

935-944

935

EUROPE
- Haakon I (the Good) overthrows his half-brother Eric Bloodaxe as king of Norway.

MIDDLE EAST AND NORTH AFRICA
- The Ikshidids are established as the ruling dynasty of Egypt.

ASIA
- Wangjian (Wang Chien) becomes emperor of N China and establishes the Later Tsin dynasty.
- The Silla dynasty of Korea becomes extinct. Wang Kon founds the Koryo dynasty, which gives its name to the reunited country (Korea).

ARTS AND HUMANITIES
- Al-Ash'ari of Baghdad, the founder of Muslim scholastic philosophy, dies.

936

EUROPE
- **2 July** Henry I of Germany dies and is succeeded by his son Otto I (the Great).
- Louis IV becomes king of France.
- Gorm the Old becomes king of Denmark, founding the Jelling dynasty (rules until 1046).

ASIA
- The Khitan, a people from C Asia, settle in N China and make Peking (now Beijing) their S capital.

ARTS AND HUMANITIES
- The construction of the Palace of al-Zahru in Cordoba, Spain, begins.

937

EUROPE
- At the battle of Brunanburh, King Athelstan of England defeats a coalition of Scots, Vikings and Strathclyde Welsh.
- The Magyars invade S France.
- The Bretons defeat the Vikings at St Brieuc.

MIDDLE EAST AND NORTH AFRICA
- Muhammad al-Ikshid of Egypt seizes Palestine and Syria.

ARTS AND HUMANITIES
Ekkehard of St Gall, *Waltharii Poesis*, Latin poetic version of the story of Waltharius and Hildegund.

938

EUROPE
- Otto I of Germany takes control of Burgundy and establishes his authority in Bavaria.

939

EUROPE
- **27 Oct.** King Athelstan of England dies and is succeeded by his brother Edmund I.
- Otto I of Germany puts down rebellions in Saxony and Thuringia and seizes Franconia.

ASIA
- Ngo Quyen defeats the Chinese forces and establishes an independent kingdom of N Vietnam (Dai-co-viet).

940

EUROPE
- King Edmund I of England agrees that Northumbria will be ruled by Olaf Guthfrithson, king of Dublin, who is now in control of York.
- Otto I of Germany enters France to receive the homage of the French nobility.
- The French king Louis IV grants the county of Reims to the local archbishop.
- The pioneering reformer Dunstan becomes abbot of Glastonbury.

941

MIDDLE EAST AND NORTH AFRICA
- The Byzantine general John Curcuas conquers Mesopotamia.

ARTS AND HUMANITIES
- St Odo, the abbot of Cluny and monastic reformer, dies.

942

EUROPE
- **Nov.** King Louis IV of France is reconciled to the German king Otto I.
- King Edmund I of England regains the Danelaw, that part of England settled by Vikings, S of the Humber.
- Pilgrim, bishop of Passau, embarks on a campaign to convert Hungary.

ARTS AND HUMANITIES
- Sa'id al-Fayyumi, Arab translator of the Old Testament, dies.
- Al-Jahshiyari, the compiler of the first version of *A Thousand and One Nights*, dies.

944

EUROPE
- **16 Dec.** The Byzantine emperor Romanus I is deposed by his sons.
- King Edmund of England expels the Viking kings from York.
- The French king Louis IV is captured by the Vikings and (945) surrenders the town of Laon in order to be released.

MIDDLE EAST AND NORTH AFRICA
- Sayf ad-Dawla, founder of the Hamdanid dynasty, consolidates his position in Aleppo and extends his rule over N Syria.

945

EUROPE
- **19 Sept.** Cabiz, a Muslim theologian, is executed for maintaining that Christ was superior to Muhammad.
- King Malcolm of Scotland takes over the Welsh kingdom of Strathclyde when the native dynasty dies out.
- Igor of Kiev makes peace with the Byzantine empire but is killed soon afterwards.

946

EUROPE
- **26 May** King Edmund I of England is murdered by a fugitive whom he is trying to apprehend and is succeeded by his brother Edred.

MIDDLE EAST AND NORTH AFRICA
- The Buwayhid dynasty, the Shiite rulers of W Persia, capture Baghdad, adopt the title of sultan and rule the caliphate from their capital in Shiraz.

ARTS AND HUMANITIES
- Liu Hsu, author of the official history of the Chinese Tang dynasty, dies.

947

ASIA
- The Khitan (see 936) destroy the Later Tsin dynasty and found the Liao dynasty, which will rule NE China and Manchuria until 1125 (independently of the Song (Sung) dynasty).

948

EUROPE
- King Edred of England expels Eric Bloodaxe, son of king Harold I (Fairhair) of Norway, from Northumbria.
- Otto I of Germany establishes bishoprics in NE Germany in order to promote the conversion of the Wends (see 929).
- The Fatimid Shiite caliph of Kairouan, N Africa, establishes a governor for Sicily.

949

EUROPE
- Hywel Dda (Hywel the Good), king of Deheubarth, Gwynedd, Powys and Seisyllwg, dies having compiled the earliest collection of Welsh law (the *Leges Walliae*). His federation of territories dissolves.

950

EUROPE
- Through the intervention of Otto I of Germany, Laon (see 944) is restored to the French king Louis IV. Otto compels Boleslav I of Bohemia to recognize his sovereignty.
- Gyula, a Magyar leader, is converted and baptized in Constantinople. He returns with the first Hungarian bishop.

SCIENCE AND TECHNOLOGY
- Al-Farabi, Islamic philosopher who also wrote a treatise on musical theory, *The Grand Book on Music*, dies.

ARTS AND HUMANITIES
- The *Greek Anthology*, which contains the work of over 300 classical Greek writers, is discovered in Heidelberg.

951

EUROPE
- The Magyars ravage Aquitaine, SW France.

MIDDLE EAST AND NORTH AFRICA
- The Qarmatians restore the Black Stone to Mecca (see 930).

ASIA
- The short-lived Houzhu (Hou-Chu) dynasty (951–960) is established in China.

952

EUROPE
- The deposed Norwegian king Eric Bloodaxe recovers York, England, (see 954).

954

EUROPE
- **10 Sept.** Louis IV of France dies and is succeeded by his son Lothair.
- Eric Bloodaxe, the Norwegian king of York, is killed. Edred seizes York and becomes king of all England.

955

EUROPE
- **10 Aug.** Otto I of Germany decisively defeats the Magyars at Lechfeld, near Augsburg, S Germany. Hereafter the Magyars end their raids and settle down in Hungary.
- **23 Nov.** King Edred of England dies and is succeeded by Eadwig, the son of Edred's brother and former king, Edmund I.

956

ASIA
- The Oghuz Turks, led by Seljuk, arrive in Transoxiana from Turkestan.

ARTS AND HUMANITIES
- The Arab historian al-Mas'udi, author of a historical and geographical encyclopedia, dies.

957

EUROPE
June The Byzantine general Nicephorus II Phocas advances into Syria, taking the city of Hadath.

958

EUROPE
- The Byzantine general John Tzimisces takes Somosata and continues the Byzantine advance into Syria.
- Gorm the Old is succeeded by Harold II (Bluetooth) as king of Denmark.

ARTS AND HUMANITIES
- Chartres Cathedral burns down; work begins on its rebuilding. Liutprand of Cremona, *Antapodosis*, a record of world events.

959

EUROPE
1 Oct. King Eadwig of England dies and is succeeded by his brother Edgar.
7 Nov. Byzantine emperor Constantine VII Porphyrogenitus dies.
- Otto I of Germany sends missionaries to Russia.

960

ASIA
- The Karakhnids of C Asia become the first Turkish tribes to convert to Islam.
- Zhao Kuangyin (Chao K'uangyin) founds the N Song (Sung) dynasty of Chinese emperors. The Song will reunite the old area of the Tang dynasty after a century of disintegration.

961

EUROPE
Mar. Byzantine forces recover Crete from the Arabs.
26 May Otto, son of Otto I (the Great), is crowned king of Lorraine. Both are acknowledged kings of Italy (Sept.) when they capture Pavia.
- Abd ar-Rahman III, ruler of Moorish Spain (see 929), dies and is succeeded by al-Hakkam II.

ARTS AND HUMANITIES
- The University of Cordoba, S Spain, is founded.

962

EUROPE
Feb. Otto I (the Great) is formally crowned Roman emperor by Pope John XII, marking the generally accepted foundation of the Holy Roman Empire (the Christian empire in the W conceived in imitation of the Roman empire).

ASIA
- The Turkish dynasty of the Ghaznavids is founded in Afghanistan.

963

EUROPE
16 Aug. Nicephorus II Phocas is crowned Byzantine emperor.
4 Dec. The emperor Otto I (the Great) deposes Pope John XII; Leo VIII is elected to succeed him.
- King Mieszko I of Poland acknowledges the imperial rule of Otto I.

965

EUROPE
Aug. Byzantine forces recapture Cyprus from the Arabs.
1 Oct. John XIII becomes pope.
- English forces invade the kingdom of Gwynedd (N Wales).
- Harold II (Bluetooth) is baptized and thus establishes Christianity in Denmark.

ASIA
- The Khazars (see 865) are destroyed by an army from Kiev.

966

EUROPE
- The emperor Otto I (the Great) creates the territory of the Palatinate of the Rhine.
- King Mieszko I of Poland converts to Christianity and a missionary bishop arrives to convert Poland.

967

EUROPE
22 Dec. Pope John XIII formally crowns Otto II, son of Otto I (the Great), co-emperor.

ARTS AND HUMANITIES
- In Germany Magdeburg Cathedral is founded.
- The Chinese painter Licheng (Li Ch'eng) dies.
- Al-Isfahani, author of the *Great Book of Songs*, an anthology of quotations from Arabic poetry, dies.

968

EUROPE
- The Byzantine emperor Nicephorus II Phocas rejects a diplomatic mission sent by the emperor Otto I (the Great).
- The first Polish bishop of Poznan is consecrated.
- Pope John XIII creates the archbishopric of Magdeburg to ensure that the conversion of the Slavs is not wholly under the influence of Otto I (the Great).

ASIA
- Dinh Bo Linh, ruler of Dai-co-viet (N Vietnam), declares himself emperor; his rule is recognized by the Song (Sung) emperors of China (see 960).

969

EUROPE
10 Dec. Nicephorus II Phocas is murdered and is succeeded as Byzantine emperor by John I Tzimisces.
- The Pechenegs, nomadic raiders from Asia, besiege Kiev but are defeated by Svyatoslav of Kiev, who also conquers E Bulgaria.

MIDDLE EAST AND NORTH AFRICA
6 July The Fatimid caliph al-Mu'izz conquers Egypt and builds his capital at Cairo. A Shiite empire develops.
28 Oct. The Byzantine army takes Antioch and later Aleppo, Syria.

970

EUROPE
- Svyatoslav of Kiev invades Thrace, but is defeated by the Byzantine general Bardas Sclerus.

ARTS AND HUMANITIES
- Around this time the earliest manuscript copy of *Beowulf*, the Anglo-Saxon verse epic, is recorded.

971

EUROPE
23 April The Byzantine emperor John I Tzimisces expels Svyatoslav of Kiev from Bulgaria and the Crimea.

ASIA
- In China the Song (Sung) emperor establishes control over Guangzhu (Canton).

972

EUROPE
14 April Otto II is married to Theophano, John I Tzimisces's niece, thus allying the W Roman empire and the Byzantine empire.
- Boris II, king of the Bulgars, abdicates and Bulgaria is annexed to the Byzantine empire.
- King Edgar summons a council of the English Church to organize the reform of the monasteries.

MIDDLE EAST AND NORTH AFRICA
- The Berber governor of NW Africa, Yusuf Bulukkin, establishes the dynasty of the Zirids as an independent power in E Algeria.

ARTS AND HUMANITIES
- The Azhar Mosque (which also includes a university) is established in Cairo.

973

EUROPE
7 May The emperor Otto I (the Great) dies and is succeeded by his son, Otto II.
11 May Edgar is crowned king of England at Bath.
- Responding to Boleslav II of Bohemia's request, the emperor Otto II detaches Bohemia from the diocese of Regensburg and establishes the bishopric of Prague.

974

EUROPE
- The emperor Otto II defeats Harold II (Bluetooth) of Denmark.

MIDDLE EAST AND NORTH AFRICA
- An army from Cordoba defeats and abolishes the Idrisid dynasty of Fez.

975

EUROPE
8 July Edgar, king of England, dies and is succeeded by his 12-year-old son Edward.
- The bishoprics of Prague and Olmuc in Bohemia and Moravia are founded.

MIDDLE EAST AND NORTH AFRICA
- The Byzantine emperor John I Tzimisces enters Heliopolis, conquers N Palestine and takes Caesarea.

ARTS AND HUMANITIES
- The Great Mosque at Cordoba is enlarged.
Abu Mansur Muwaffaq, *The Foundations of the True Properties of Remedies,* Persian description of medicinal drugs.

976

EUROPE
10 Jan. The Byzantine emperor John I Tzimisces dies and is succeeded by Basil II and Constantine VIII, the sons of Romanus II. A Bulgarian war of independence follows, led by Samuel. The Byzantine general Bardas Sclerus leads a separate rebellion later in the spring.
July Otto II's cousin Henry the Wrangler, duke of Bavaria, attempts to gain the German crown from Otto II and is deposed.

MIDDLE EAST AND NORTH AFRICA
1 Oct. Al-Hakkam II, caliph of Spain (see 961), dies and is succeeded by his son Hisham II. Between now and around 1002, however, the real power in the Spanish caliphate resides with his regent, the high official al-Mansur (Almanzor), who will win spectacular victories against the Christians (see 988 and 997).

ASIA

Nov. In China Zhao Kuangyin (Chao K'uangyin), the first Song (Sung) emperor (see 960), dies and is succeeded by his brother Taizong (Tai Tsung).

ARTS AND HUMANITIES

– Cordoba University, Spain, becomes the most important university in both Europe and the Islamic world.
Al-Khwarizmi, *Key of the Sciences*, classification of areas of knowledge.

977

ARTS AND HUMANITIES

– The Chinese painter Guo Zhongshu (Kuo Chung-shu) dies.
Lifang (Li Fang), *Taibing Youlan (T'ai-ping yu-lan)*, a Chinese encyclopedia.

978

EUROPE

18 Mar. Edward (the Martyr), king of England, is murdered on the instigation of his stepmother and is succeeded by his half-brother Ethelred II. Edward, who has favoured the Church, is later (1000) canonized and widely venerated in England. Ethelred is never really trusted by the nobles, who suspect him of having been involved in the killing of Edward. He becomes known to history as Ethelred the Unready (a mistranslation of the Anglo-Saxon *unraed*, meaning uncounselled).
19 June The rebel general Bardas Sclerus defeats the Byzantine imperial forces in Anatolia.
Oct. The emperor Otto II invades France after the French king Lothair invades Lorraine.
– Haakon (the Great), king of Norway, is defeated and killed by the Danes.

ARTS AND HUMANITIES

– Work begins on Mainz Cathedral in Germany.

979

EUROPE

24 Mar. Bardas Sclerus is defeated by the Byzantine army.
– King Lothair of France has his son Louis V crowned as co-regent and revives the kingdom of Aquitaine (SW France).
– The emperor Otto II fails to defeat King Mieszko of Poland; they make peace and Mieszko does homage.

980

EUROPE

– A new wave of Viking attacks on England begins.
– Malachy II, king of Tara, Ireland, defeats the Danish king of Dublin, Olaf Sihtricson.

ASIA

– Le Dai Hanh seizes the throne of Dai-co-Viet (N Vietnam).

982

EUROPE

13 July The emperor Otto II, who has invaded Italy, is defeated in Apulia by allied Arab and Byzantine forces.
– Eric the Red begins a Viking invasion of Iceland.

ARTS AND HUMANITIES

Yasuyori Tamba, *Ishino*, the earliest known Japanese work on medicine.

983

EUROPE

7 Dec. Otto III, under the guardianship of his Byzantine mother Theophano, succeeds his father Otto II as emperor following the latter's death. Rebellion led by Henry the Wrangler (see 976) breaks out in Germany.
– The Wends of E Europe revolt against German rule and revert to paganism.

MIDDLE EAST AND NORTH AFRICA

– Ahmad ibn Buwayh Asud ad-Dawla gains overall control of Persia and adopts the title *shahanshah* or king of kings, the ancient title of the emperors of Persia.
– The authority of the caliph of Egypt now extends over Palestine and S Syria.

ARTS AND HUMANITIES

– Japanese scholar Minamoto no Shitagu, compiler of a Sino-Japanese dictionary, dies.

984

ARTS AND HUMANITIES

– The earliest known astrolabe is made in Isfahan, Persia. The astrolabe enables sailors to determine their latitude.

985

EUROPE

– Henry the Wrangler (see 976) recovers the duchy of Bavaria.
– The Byzantine emperor Basil II puts down a palace rebellion and assumes sole rule.

987

EUROPE

21 May Louis V, king of France, dies without an heir and is succeeded by Hugh Capet, duke of the Franks (3 July), who founds the Capetian dynasty, which will rule France until 1328.
14 Sept. Bardas Phocas proclaims himself Byzantine emperor.
– Svein I (Forkbeard) deposes his father Harold II (Bluetooth) as king of Denmark.
– Samuel becomes king of Bulgaria.
– A treaty of seven years' peace is signed between Egypt and the Byzantine empire.

THE AMERICAS
- The Toltec Kukulcán conquers the Maya in Yucatán and makes Chichén Itzá (see 889) his capital.

988

EUROPE
19 May The English Church reformer St Dunstan dies.
- Byzantine imperial forces ally with Vladimir of Kiev to defeat Byzantine rebel Bardas Phocas. Henceforth the Byzantine emperors have a Viking warrior guard, termed the Varangians.
- Vladimir converts to Orthodox Christianity and is rewarded with the hand in marriage of Anna, sister of the emperor Basil II. Vladimir's conversion founds the Russian Orthodox Church.
- Al-Mansur (Almanzor), regent of Cordoba, Spain, overruns Leon and makes the king of Leon subject to Cordoban rule.

989

EUROPE
1 Oct. The Byzantine rebel Bardas Phocas surrenders.

991

EUROPE
15 June The empress Theophano, who has ruled Germany as regent on behalf of her son Otto III (see 983), dies.
Aug. At the battle of Maldon, in Essex, England, Olaf Tryggvason defeats Byrhtnoth, ealdorman (governor) of East Anglia. The Vikings are paid a large amount of silver to leave. The tax raised to fund the bribe is known as the Danegeld.
- The Byzantine emperor Basil II conquers Albania and asserts his rule in Bulgaria.

992

EUROPE
- Venice's independence is recognized by both the Byzantine and the Western (German) empires.
- King Mieszko I of Poland dies. His kingdom is divided among his sons, one of whom, Boleslav Khrobry, will reunite Poland.
- Bohemia's first Benedictine monastery is founded at Brevnov.

993

EUROPE
- Pope John XV canonizes Ulric, bishop of Augsburg: the first canonization by a pope. Earlier canonizations had been bestowed by local clergy. In future the popes will increasingly monopolize the right to declare a person to be a saint.

ARTS AND HUMANITIES
Anonymous, The Battle of Maldon, Anglo-Saxon verse epic (see 991).

994

EUROPE
10 May The Vikings invade Ynys Mon (Anglesey), N Wales.
14 Sept. The caliph of Egypt defeats a Byzantine army near Antioch.

SCIENCE AND TECHNOLOGY
- The obliquity of the ecliptic is calculated at Ray, Persia.
- Persian scholar Haly Abbas writes The Whole Medical Art, a medical encyclopedia.

995

EUROPE
April The Byzantine emperor Basil II raises the siege of Aleppo by the Egyptians.
Aug. Henry the Wrangler dies (see 985). His son Henry succeeds as duke of Bavaria (see also 1002).
- Olaf I Tryggvason succeeds as king of Norway.
- Olaf the Tax King unites Sweden and begins its conversion to Christianity.
- The Byzantine emperor Basil II gains his first military victory over the Bulgars.

ARTS AND HUMANITIES
- Al-Warraq, author of the Index of the Sciences, dies.

996

EUROPE
21 May Pope Gregory V crowns Otto III as emperor. Gregory is expelled by the citizens of Rome (Sept.).
24 Oct. Hugh Capet (see 987) is succeeded as king of France by his son Robert II (the Pious).

MIDDLE EAST AND NORTH AFRICA
- Al-Hakim becomes Fatimid caliph of Egypt. His reign is characterized by the persecution of both Christians and Jews.

997

EUROPE
- Geza (St Stephen) becomes duke of Hungary and is baptized by German churchman Adalbert.
- The king of Croatia, Stephen Drzislav, dies.
- Samuel proclaims himself king of the Bulgars.
- German churchman Adalbert is murdered while on a mission to convert the Prussians.

ASIA
- The Ilkhans (Ilek Khans) of Persia subjugate the Samanid dynasty of Transoxiana, C Asia.

ARTS AND HUMANITIES
- Santiago de Compostela, NW Spain, is destroyed by the Islamic general al-Mansur on his expedition to Galicia.

998-1005

998

EUROPE

Feb. Otto III restores Gregory V as pope (see 996). Otto restores the chanceries of Germany and Italy, thereby recreating the imperial ideal of a single government.

– The Byzantine emperor Basil II, challenged by Samuel's ambition to establish a Bulgarian empire in the Balkans, gives Dalmatia to Venice as a protectorate.

ARTS AND HUMANITIES

– Ethelward translates a version of *The Anglo-Saxon Chronicle*, a history of England, from English into Latin.

999

EUROPE

3/4 April The first French pope, Sylvester II (Gerbert of Aurillac), is elected.

1000

EUROPE

31 Mar. The emperor Otto III crowns Boleslav I king of Poland and recognizes Poland's ecclesiastical and territorial independence.

– King Svein I (Forkbeard) of Denmark conquers Norway.

– Christianity is established in Iceland.

ASIA

– The Dai-co-viet kingdom (N Vietnam), invades Champa (S Vietnam).

THE AMERICAS

– The Andean empires of Wari and Tiwanaku collapse because of prolonged drought.

ARTS AND HUMANITIES

– A school of law is established in Pavia, Italy.

– By now cathedral schools, including those in Paris, Chartres, Tours and Orleans, are established in N France.

Anonymous, *Utsubo Monogatari*, collection of Japanese prose tales.

Anonymous, *Verses on the Captivity of Boethius*, French poetry.

1001

EUROPE

Feb. The Romans revolt against the emperor Otto III's rule. Henry of Bavaria (see 995) helps him to restore order, but Otto leaves Rome.

ASIA

27 Nov. Mahmud of Ghazni (in modern Afghanistan) defeats Jaipal of the Punjab at Peshawar and occupies the Punjab, N India; Jaipal commits suicide.

1002

EUROPE

23 Jan. The emperor Otto III dies and is succeeded by his cousin Henry of Bavaria, son of Henry the Wrangler, duke of Bavaria (see 976 and 995), who becomes Henry II (the Saint).

15 Feb. Ardoin leads an Italian revolt against German rule and is crowned king of Italy.

July Boleslav I of Poland recognizes Henry II as emperor but subsequently goes to war against him, believing Henry responsible for an assassination attempt.

13 Nov. (St Brice's Day) Many leading men of Viking descent are massacred in England on the orders of King Ethelred II (the Unready), who doubts their loyalty.

– The Venetian navy defeats a Muslim fleet besieging the Greeks of Bari, S Italy.

1003

EUROPE

1 Oct. All the German princes accept Henry II's title of emperor.

– The Byzantine emperor Basil II defeats Samuel of the Bulgars near Skopje.

– Brian Boru becomes High King of Ireland.

– King Svein I (Forkbeard) of Denmark invades England in retaliation for the previous year's massacre of those of Viking descent living in England (see 1002).

THE AMERICAS

– Leif Ericsson becomes the first European to reach North America.

ARTS AND HUMANITIES

– Pope Sylvester II, who has written widely on the abacus, the astrolabe and Spanish-Arabic numerals, dies.

– Stephen Asolik writes a universal history in Armenian.

1004

EUROPE

14 May Ardoin (see 1002) leaves Italy; the emperor Henry II is crowned king.

– Stephen of Hungary conquers Transylvania.

1005

EUROPE

– The emperor Henry II invades Poland, but is defeated by Boleslav I.

ARTS AND HUMANITIES

– Al-Hakim (see 996) founds the Dar al-Hikmah (Hall of Wisdom), a theological college, in Cairo.

– The Abbey Church of St Germain-des-Prés is founded in Paris.

Al-Sufi, *Geography*, the earliest known illustrated Arabic manuscript.

1006

EUROPE

Sept. Baldwin IV of Flanders rebels against the emperor Henry II and Robert II of France.

1007

EUROPE

1 Nov. The emperor Henry II founds the bishopric of Bamberg in order to convert the Wends.

– Boleslav of Poland recovers the Polish lands W of the Oder on his German campaigns.

MIDDLE EAST AND NORTH AFRICA

– The Kakuyid dynasty of Isfahan, Persia, is founded.

1008

EUROPE

– King Bagrat III unites Georgia in the Caucasus.

1009

EUROPE

14 Mar. German missionary Bruno Boniface is martyred while attempting to convert the Baltic tribe of the Jadzwingas.

– Hisham II and Muhammad II, successive caliphs of Cordoba, are deposed and succeeded by Suleiman. By now Islamic Spain is in political turmoil.

MIDDLE EAST AND NORTH AFRICA

27 Sept. Caliph al-Hakim (see 996) orders the destruction of the Church of the Holy Sepulchre, Jerusalem.

ASIA

– Mahmud of Ghazni (see 1001) conquers the principality of Ghur (in modern Afghanistan); Muslims settle in NW India.

ARTS AND HUMANITIES

– Work begins on Paderborn Cathedral, Germany.

– Mainz Cathedral, Germany, burns down; work begins on rebuilding it.

– The Siva temple in Tanjore, India, is completed.

1010

EUROPE

– King Robert II proclaims a Peace of God in France. The Peace of God is a Church-sponsored truce, which ends family feuds and local power disputes. Imposed on certain specified days, it allows churchmen, women and other vulnerable persons to travel or conduct business without fear of being attacked.

– In Islamic Spain Hisham II is restored as caliph of Cordoba.

ASIA

– Ly Thai-to seizes the imperial throne of Dai-co-viet (N Vietnam) and founds the Ly dynasty.

ARTS AND HUMANITIES

– Aimoin of Fleury, author of the *Historia Francorum*, dies.
Murasaki Shikibu, *The Tale of Genji*, Japanese novel.

1011

ARTS AND HUMANITIES

– Chen Pengnian (Ch'en P'eng-nien) writes a revision of the *Qianyun* (*Ch'ien-yun*) of Lu Fayan (Lu Fa-yen), a 7th-century Chinese phonetic dictionary.

1012

EUROPE

19 April In England the archbishop of Canterbury, Alphege, is murdered by the Vikings, who leave English (i.e., Anglo-Saxon) territory after being bought off by a massive payment of silver.

20 April Suleiman is re-established as caliph in Cordoba.

24 May Boleslav I of Poland pays homage to the emperor Henry II and retains all his conquests except Bohemia.

– Prosecutions for heresy are initiated in Germany.

– St Romuald founds the hermit monk order of Camaldoli.

1013

EUROPE

– King Svein I (Forkbeard) of Denmark defeats the king of England, Ethelred II (the Unready), who flees to Normandy. Svein is accepted as king of England.

1014

EUROPE

3 Feb. Svein I (Forkbeard), king of Denmark, Norway and England dies. In Denmark he is succeeded by his son Harold and in England by his other son Cnut. Ethelred II (the Unready), however, returns from Normandy to displace Cnut who then leaves England.

14 Feb. Henry II (see 1002) is crowned Holy Roman Emperor by Pope Benedict VIII. Anti-German riots break out in Rome.

18 April Brian Boru, High King of Ireland, dies in battle against a Viking–Leinster alliance at Clontarf, near Dublin; the Vikings living in Ireland accept Irish rule.

29 July The Byzantine emperor Basil II captures and blinds most of the Bulgarian army. King Samuel dies of shock on hearing the news.

ASIA

– Rajaraja the Great, king of the Chola dynasty and ruler of S India and Ceylon (Sri Lanka), dies.

1015

EUROPE

Aug. The Danish king Cnut (see 1014) invades England to reclaim the throne.

- The Muslims of Spain conquer Sardinia.
- St Vladimir I, prince of Kiev, dies. His son Svyatopolk I murders two of his brothers, but Jaroslav, a third brother, seizes Novgorod.
- Benevento, S Italy, establishes a commune for local self-government.

ARTS AND HUMANITIES
- Work begins on Strasburg Cathedral, in modern E France.

1016
EUROPE

23 April Ethelred II (the Unready), king of England, dies and is succeeded by his son Edmund Ironside.

June Forces from Pisa and Genoa reconquer Sardinia (see 1015).

18 Oct. After he is defeated at Ashingdon, Edmund II (Ironside) agrees to share England with Cnut.

30 Nov. Edmund II (Ironside) dies and Cnut becomes king of all England.

- Olaf Haroldson re-establishes Norway's independence from Denmark.
- Normans invade and settle S Italy.

1017
EUROPE

Aug. The emperor Henry II unsuccessfully attacks Poland.

ARTS AND HUMANITIES
- Genshin, a Japanese monk whose *Essentials of Salvation* has popularized Buddhism, dies.

1018
EUROPE

30 Jan. Poland and Germany conclude the peace of Bautzen.

21 July Boleslav I defeats Jaroslav of Novgorod, who has seized Kiev. An anti-Polish uprising forces him to retire, but he retains Czerwien and Przemysl for Poland.

- King Harold of Denmark dies and is succeeded by his brother Cnut, king of England.
- Thietmar, bishop of Merseburg and author of the *Chronicon*, dies.
- At the council of Pavia Pope Benedict VIII declares clerical marriage and the taking of concubines by priests to be wrong.

ASIA
- Mahmud of Ghazni seizes Kanauj, the capital of Panchala, India (see also 1009).

1019
EUROPE

- The Byzantine emperor Basil II completes the conquest of Bulgaria.

ARTS AND HUMANITIES
- Work begins on the cathedrals at Basel and Trier.

1020
MIDDLE EAST AND NORTH AFRICA
- Gagik I of Armenia dies and his kingdom is divided.

SCIENCE AND TECHNOLOGY
- The Chinese invent a floating magnet, which acts as a crude compass to aid navigation.

ARTS AND HUMANITIES
- Firdausi, author of the Persian national epic *The Book of Kings*, dies.
- The cathedral at Chartres, France, is rebuilt.

1021
EUROPE

Dec. The Byzantine army attacks Benevento, S Italy (see 1015).
- The emperor Henry II embarks on his third expedition to Italy.
- The Byzantine emperor Basil II reasserts his control in Georgia.

MIDDLE EAST AND NORTH AFRICA

13 Feb. Al-Hakim, caliph of Egypt, is murdered and succeeded by his son al-Zahir.

1022
EUROPE

1 Aug. At the Synod of Pavia, Italy, the emperor Henry II attacks the idea of married priests. He also discusses Church reform with King Robert II of France (11 Aug.).

- The emperor Henry II halts the Byzantine advance in Italy by taking Capua and Troia.
- The burning of heretics becomes an established policy of Church and secular rulers alike; members of the Bogomils, a sect judged to be heretical, are burned in Orléans, France.

1023
MIDDLE EAST AND NORTH AFRICA
- An independent Mirdasid emirate is established in Aleppo, Syria; the city is lost to the Byzantine empire.

ARTS AND HUMANITIES
- English churchman Wulfstan, author of the *Homilies*, dies.

1024
EUROPE

13 July Henry II, Holy Roman Emperor and last of the Saxon dynasty (see 919), dies. He is succeeded (4 Sept.) by Conrad II of Franconia, first of the Salian dynasty.

Dec. Pope John X1X approves the crowning of Boleslav I as king of Poland.

ASIA
- In China, Song (Sung) rule is established in Szechwan.

1025

EUROPE
- **15 Dec.** The Byzantine emperor Basil II (known as the Bulgar-slayer) dies. His brother (and previous co-emperor) Constantine VIII succeeds.
- Boleslav I, king of Poland, dies; his kingdom collapses.
- The Byzantine emperor Constantine VIII allies with Cnut of England and Denmark.
- Muhammad III of Cordoba is murdered and is succeeded by a ruler of the Moroccan Hammudid dynasty, rivals of the Umayyads.

ASIA
- The Hindu holy city of Somnath is sacked by Mahmud of Ghazni.
- Rajendra I, king of the S Indian Chola dynasty, leads a naval force against Sumatra and Malaya, destroying the Malayan empire.

1026

EUROPE
- Kings Anund of Sweden, Olaf II Haraldson of Norway, and Cnut's own regent in Denmark, Ulf, defeat Cnut at sea in the battle of the Holy River.
- The emperor Conrad II is crowned king of Italy.

1027

EUROPE
- **26 Mar.** The emperor Conrad II (see 1024) is crowned Holy Roman Emperor by Pope John XIX.
- **July** Emperor Conrad II gives Bavaria to his son Henry.
- Hisham III of the Umayyad dynasty becomes caliph of Cordoba.

1028

EUROPE
- **14 April** Henry, son of the emperor Conrad II, is crowned king of the Germans.
- Cnut expels Olaf from Norway; Cnut now rules Norway as well as Denmark and England.
- Sancho III of Navarre unites Castile to his kingdom.
- Bratislav of Bohemia defeats the Hungarians and adds Moravia to his kingdom.
- The Byzantine emperor Constantine VIII dies and is succeeded by Romanus III.

ARTS AND HUMANITIES
- Fulbert who, with Hildegaire, presided over the expansion of the cathedral school at Chartres (see 1000), dies.

1029

MIDDLE EAST AND NORTH AFRICA
- Al-Musabbili, author of a history of Egypt, dies.

ASIA
- The Cholas (see 1025) are expelled from Ceylon (Sri Lanka), and Vikramabahu I becomes king.

1030

EUROPE
- Stephen of Hungary is defeated by Bratislav of Bohemia.

ASIA
- **21 April** Mahmud, the emir of Ghazni and founder of a Muslim empire in NW India (see 1001), dies.

SCIENCE AND TECHNOLOGY
- Movable wooden characters are now used in Chinese printing.

ARTS AND HUMANITIES
- The cathedrals at Coutances (Normandy) and Speyer (Germany) are built.
- The Chinese painter Fankuan (Fan K'uan) dies.
- Ibn Miskawayh, author of a universal history, dies.

1031

EUROPE
- **20 July** Robert II (the Pious), king of France, dies and is succeeded by his son Henry I.
- **30 Nov.** In Islamic Spain the inhabitants of Cordoba abolish the caliphate and depose Hisham III, the last Umayyad ruler. Across Andalusia numerous minor Moorish kingdoms are established.
- King Malcolm II of Scotland pays homage to Cnut, king of England.
- Stephen I of Hungary makes peace with the emperor Conrad II and restores Vienna to German rule. He also cedes Moravia to Oldrich of Bohemia.
- King Mieszco II of Poland is expelled by Russian and German forces and his brother Bezprym is installed as king. By the end of the year Bezprym is murdered and Mieszko is restored.

1032

EUROPE
- The Orseole dynasty's rule in Venice ends; the practice of the doge's election by popular assembly is restored.

1033

EUROPE
- King Mieszco II of Poland surrenders his title and does homage to the emperor Conrad II.
- The Pechenegs, a nomadic people of E Europe, raid extensively across the Balkans.

1034

EUROPE

15 Mar. King Mieszco II of Poland dies; paganism re-emerges.

11 April Byzantine emperor Romanus III dies and is succeeded by Michael IV, who marries Romanus' widow Zoe.

1035

EUROPE

2 July Robert, duke of Normandy, dies and is succeeded by his illegitimate son, William.

12 Nov. Cnut, king of Denmark, England and Norway, dies. His sons Harthacnut and Harold Harefoot succeed in Denmark and England respectively. A third son, Svein, inherits Norway, but is deposed after a revolt and Magnus I Olafsson is installed as king.

– The Christian kingdom of Aragon, NE Spain, is established.

ARTS AND HUMANITIES

– Some 10,000 paintings, books and manuscripts written in Chinese, Tibetan and other E languages are walled up for safety at Dunhuang (Tun-huang), in the Xixia (Hsi Hsia) kingdom.

1036

EUROPE

June Denmark cedes Schleswig to the emperor Conrad II on the marriage of Harthacnut's daughter Gunhilda (Kunigunde) to Conrad's son Henry of Bavaria, later Henry III (see 1027).

– Conrad defeats a rebellion by the Luitizians, a pagan tribe of Wends E of the Elbe.

– The first Cluniac house in Germany is dedicated at Paderborn.

1037

EUROPE

Mar. The emperor Conrad II arrests the archbishop of Milan, Aribert, for attempting to assert his rule over the Church in Lombardy. Aribert escapes; Conrad lays siege to Milan.

– Harold I (Harefoot) is recognized as king of England (see 1035).

– The Christian kingdom of Castile-Leon, N Spain, is founded.

MIDDLE EAST AND NORTH AFRICA

– Seljuk Turks, having emigrated from C Asia in the 10th century, are now established in Khurasan, NE Persia.

ARTS AND HUMANITIES

– Avicenna (Ibn Sina), the great Arab philosopher and physician, and author of the *Canon of Medicine,* which collates Greek and Arabic medical science, dies.

– Work begins on Rouen Cathedral, NW France.

– Mosaics are prepared for Kiev Cathedral.

– The Persian poet Farrukhi dies.

1038

EUROPE

15 Aug. St Stephen I, king of Hungary, dies and is succeeded by Peter the German.

– King Bratislav of Bohemia sacks Cracow and seizes Silesia.

ASIA

– Li Huanghao (Li Huang-hao) leads the Tibetan tribes of W China (the Tanguts of Xixia) in rebellion against the Song.

1039

EUROPE

4 June The emperor Conrad II dies and is succeeded by his son, Henry III (the Black).

– In Wales Gruffudd ap Llywelyn, prince of Gwynedd and Powys, defeats an English invading force.

– In France Guy-Geoffrey of Aquitaine conquers the duchy of Gascony.

– Casimir I, son of Mieszko II, attempts to reassert unitary royal rule in Poland.

ARTS AND HUMANITIES

– Ali al-Hasan, author of a treatise on optics, dies.

1040

EUROPE

Mar. Harthacnut, king of Denmark, succeeds his brother Harold I (Harefoot) as king of England.

14 Aug. Duncan I, king of Scotland, is murdered and succeeded by Macbeth.

– The six sons of Tancred de Hauteville, a Norman adventurer, seize Melfi in Apulia from the Byzantines and begin to develop a Norman power base in S Italy.

– Stephen Vojislav establishes the independence of Zeta (modern Montenegro) in the Balkans from Byzantine rule.

MIDDLE EAST AND NORTH AFRICA

Feb. The Seljuk Turks (see 1037) conquer the Ghaznavid territories in Persia and depose Mas'ud I of Ghazni.

SCIENCE AND TECHNOLOGY

– Ahmad al-Nasawi, whose use of Hindi numerals establishes fractions, square and cubic roots, dies.

1041

EUROPE

4 May Rebels from Lombardy defeat the Byzantine forces with Norman aid.

May The emperor Henry III forces Bratislav to surrender all his Polish conquests except Silesia (see 1038).

ASIA

– The Chinese army fights the Tibetan tribes.

1042

EUROPE

8 June Harthacnut, king of England, dies and is succeeded by his half-brother Edward the Confessor, who is also the son of former King Ethelred II (the Unready).

12 June The empress Zoe's third husband, Constantine IX Monomachus, becomes the Byzantine emperor.

– Magnus I Olafsson, king of Norway, conquers Denmark.

– A popular revolt in Milan expels the local nobility.

1043

EUROPE

3 April Edward the Confessor is crowned king of England.

– The emperor Henry III and king Samuel Aba of Hungary establish the frontier between Austrian and Hungarian territory.

1044

EUROPE

– In Poland an archiepiscopal see at Cracow is established by Aaron.

ASIA

– The king of the Cholas, Rajendra I, dies having conquered the Pegu kingdom in Burma and the Andaman Islands.

– In China the Song (Sung) emperor is forced to pay tribute to the Xixia (see 1038).

– Anirudda becomes the first recorded king of Pagan in Burma.

1045

EUROPE

1 May Pope Benedict IX resigns and sells the papacy to Gregory VI.

– Edward the Confessor, king of England, makes Harold, son of the powerful nobleman Godwin, earl of East Anglia.

MIDDLE EAST AND NORTH AFRICA

– The Seljuk Turks (see 1037) raid Armenia for the first time.

ARTS AND HUMANITIES

– The Byzantine emperor Constantine IX Monomachus reestablishes the University of Constantinople.

– In NW Russia Novgorod Cathedral burns down; it is rebuilt in stone.

1046

EUROPE

25 Oct. In a council at Pavia, Italy, the emperor Henry III denounces simony, the practice of buying or selling ecclesiastical positions. His policy goals are Church reform and a peaceful, German-dominated Italy.

20 Dec. Henry III holds a synod at Sutri (near Rome) and deposes Popes Benedict IX and Gregory VI; he installs the bishop of Bamberg as Pope Clement II.

25 Dec. Pope Clement II crowns Henry III emperor.

1047

EUROPE

Jan. Pope Clement II denounces simony.

8 Nov. Benedict IX is restored as pope after the death (9 Oct.) of Clement II.

– Duke William puts down internal rebellions in Normandy.

1048

EUROPE

– Duke William of Normandy forms an alliance with the emperor Henry III and attacks Geoffrey Martel of Anjou. Alençon and Maine fall to William.

– The Pechenegs (see 1033) wage war in the Balkans.

MIDDLE EAST AND NORTH AFRICA

– Seljuk Turks (see 1037) sack Erzurum (NE Turkey).

SCIENCE AND TECHNOLOGY

– Al-Biruni, author of the *Description of India*, a study of astronomy, astrology and mathematics, dies.

1049

EUROPE

Oct. Pope Leo IX convenes councils that issue decrees to reform the Church.

ARTS AND HUMANITIES

– Work begins on Bayeux Cathedral in Normandy.

1050

EUROPE

– King Casimir I of Poland recovers Silesia from Bohemia (see 1038).

MIDDLE EAST AND NORTH AFRICA

– Tughril Beg, the Seljuk Turkish leader, takes Isfahan, which will become the capital of his empire in Persia and Khurasan, and overthrows the Kakuyid dynasty.

ARTS AND HUMANITIES

– Work begins on Westminster Abbey, England.

Anonymous, *Konjaku Monogatari*, a compilation of Japanese short stories.

1051

EUROPE

Sept. Godwin, earl of Wessex, is exiled to Flanders after attempting a rebellion against Edward the Confessor, king of England.

– Cathars, members of a heretical Christian sect who regard the physical world as fundamentally evil, are executed at Goslar, Germany.

1052

EUROPE

15 Sept. Godwin returns to England; Edward the Confessor restores him as earl of Wessex.

– Duke William of Normandy visits Edward and is possibly recognized in private as the English king's heir.

1053

EUROPE

15 April Earl Godwin, earl of Wessex, dies and is succeeded by his son, Harold.

18 June In the battle of Civitate (S Italy), Normans led by Humphrey de Hauteville capture Pope Leo IX.

1054

EUROPE

Feb. The French king Henry I allies with Geoffrey Martel (see 1048) and invades Normandy. He is defeated by Duke William at Mortemer.

19 April Pope Leo IX dies.

27 July Earl Siward of Northumbria defeats the Scottish king Macbeth at Dunsinane and installs Malcolm Canmore, son of the murdered Duncan (see 1040), as ruler of S Scotland.

– Cerularius, patriarch of Constantinople, is excommunicated for refusing to meet Cardinal Humbert and other papal representatives. A schism between the Byzantine and the Western churches ensues.

– The emperor Henry III awards Silesia to Poland after its dispute with Bohemia (see 1038 and 1050).

MIDDLE EAST AND NORTH AFRICA

– The Seljuk Turkish leader Tughril Beg (see 1050) raids Byzantine Asia Minor.

1055

EUROPE

11 Jan. The Byzantine emperor Constantine IX Monomachus dies; he is succeeded by his sister-in-law, the empress Theodora.

7 Feb. Jaroslav I, Great Prince of Russia, dies, ending the golden age of Kiev. His lands are divided among his five sons and civil war follows.

– Gruffudd ap Llywelyn, prince of Gwynedd and Powys, conquers S Wales.

MIDDLE EAST AND NORTH AFRICA

18 Dec. Seljuk Turks take Baghdad and end the rule of the Bawayhid dynasty. Tughril Beg becomes sultan and supreme secular ruler over the territories conquered by the Seljuks.

1056

EUROPE

17 June Gruffudd ap Llywelyn, prince of Gwynedd and Powys, raids into England and kills the bishop of Hereford. But later in the year he acknowledges the supremacy of Edward the Confessor, king of England, who recognizes Gruffudd's control of Welsh territory.

21 Aug. The Byzantine empress Theodora, last of the Macedonian dynasty, dies and is succeeded by Michael VI Stratioticus (the Aged).

5 Oct. The emperor Henry III dies and is succeeded by his son Henry IV.

– The Paterines, a popular movement aiming for Church reform and purification, establish a commune in Milan, N Italy.

1057

EUROPE

16 Aug. King Macbeth of Scotland is killed by Malcolm Canmore and succeeded by his stepson Lulach.

31 Aug. The Byzantine emperor Michael VI Stratioticus abdicates in favour of the general Isaac Comnenus, acclaimed by the Byzantine army.

Aug. The Norman leader Robert Guiscard, son of Tancred de Hauteville (see 1040), becomes count of Apulia, S Italy.

MIDDLE EAST AND NORTH AFRICA

– The Seljuk Turks sack Malatiya, on the Asian frontier of the Byzantine empire.

ASIA

– In SE Asia Aniruddha of Pagan (see 1044) defeats the king of the Mons of Thaton and annexes the Irrawaddy delta.

1058

EUROPE

17 Mar. Macbeth's stepson Lulach is killed by Malcolm Canmore who becomes king of Scotland.

5 April The nobles in Rome elect Cardinal John Mincius as Pope Benedict X.

Aug. Duke William of Normandy defeats the invading forces of the French king Henry I and Geoffrey Martel of Anjou (see 1054).

28 Nov. Casimir I (the Restorer), who re-established Polish unity and refounded the Polish Church, dies.

1059

EUROPE

23 May Philip I, son of Henry I, is crowned king of France.

Aug. Pope Nicholas II invests Robert Guiscard (see 1057) as duke of Apulia and Calabria and as count of Sicily.

25 Dec. The Byzantine emperor Isaac Comnenus abdicates and is succeeded by Constantine X Ducas.

- The Milanese revert to ecclesiastical rule from Rome (see 1042).

1060

EUROPE
4 Aug. Henry I, king of France, dies. Baldwin, count of Flanders, is guardian to the king's teenage son, King Philip I.
- Bela I kills his brother Andrew I to become king of Hungary.

ARTS AND HUMANITIES
- In Germany Mainz Cathedral is rebuilt.
- The Nan Paya and the Manuha temples are built in Pagan, Burma.

1061

EUROPE
28 Oct. Cadalus, bishop of Parma, is crowned Pope Honorius II in the presence of the emperor Henry IV at Basel.
- Robert Guiscard begins the Norman conquest of Sicily and captures Messina.

ASIA
- The Cumans, a nomadic tribe, migrate into S Russia from Kazakhstan.

1062

EUROPE
27 Oct. Alexander II is declared the true pope in a synod of the Church (see also 1061).

ARTS AND HUMANITIES
- The Abbey Church of St Miniato, Florence, is completed.

1063

EUROPE
5 Aug. Gruffudd ap Llywelyn, prince of Gwynedd and Powys, is murdered by his followers while fleeing from Harold, earl of Wessex: Wales is once again divided.

MIDDLE EAST AND NORTH AFRICA
- The Seljuk sultan Tughril Beg dies (see 1055) and is succeeded by his nephew Alp Arslan.

ARTS AND HUMANITIES
- Work begins on the Church of St Mark's, Venice.

1064

EUROPE
- The *Usatges* of Raymond-Berengar of Catalonia become the first feudal code.

MIDDLE EAST AND NORTH AFRICA
- The Seljuk sultan Alp Arslan conquers C Armenia.

ARTS AND HUMANITIES
- Ali Ibn Hazm, the Spanish Muslim pioneer of comparative religion, dies.

1065

EUROPE
8 May In Spain Ramiro I of Aragon dies attacking the Moors.

ASIA
- The Seljuk sultan Alp Arslan conquers Transoxiana in C Asia, while other Seljuk Turks invade Syria.

ARTS AND HUMANITIES
28 Dec. In England, Westminster Abbey is consecrated.
- A theological college is founded in Baghdad; others follow in Damascus, Jerusalem, Cairo and Alexandria.

1066

EUROPE
5 Jan. Edward the Confessor, king of England, dies. A meeting of nobles and churchmen pass over the claims of his nephew Edgar, who is a child, and elect Edward's brother-in-law, the warrior Harold Godwinson, earl of Wessex, to be king (6 Jan.).
25 Sept. Harold III (Hardrada), king of Norway, invades Northumbria but is defeated and killed by Harold II, king of England, at the battle of Stamford Bridge, near York.
28 Sept. Duke William of Normandy lands at Pevensey, Sussex, to invade England (see also 1052). Harold II marches S to face him.
14 Oct. William defeats and kills Harold II at the battle of Hastings. Harold is the last Anglo-Saxon king of England.
25 Dec. Duke William is crowned William I in Westminster Abbey, London, to become first Norman king of England.

ARTS AND HUMANITIES
- The Abbey Church of Bec, in Normandy, is constructed.

1067

MIDDLE EAST AND NORTH AFRICA
- The Seljuk Turks sack Caesarea in Palestine and defeat the Byzantine armies at Sebastea.

1068

EUROPE
- William I, king of England, suppresses a Northumbrian revolt.

MIDDLE EAST AND NORTH AFRICA
- Yusuf Ibn Tashfin, founder of the Almoravid (Berber) kingdom in Morocco, establishes Marrakesh as his capital.

ASIA
- Ly Thanh-tong of Dai-co-viet (N Vietnam) defeats Rudravarman III of Champa (S Vietnam) and annexes the N provinces of his kingdom.

– In Japan the Camera system of government has evolved by this date: the ruling emperor is usually a minor and the retired emperors rule in competition with the regents (the Fujiwara).

1069

EUROPE

Sept. The Harrying of the North: William I, king of England, crushes further rebellions in Northumbria.

– Mutamid becomes king of Seville; he takes Cordoba and so makes his kingdom the most important Muslim state in Spain.

1070

EUROPE

15 Aug. King William I of England deposes the Englishman Stigand as archbishop of Canterbury and appoints the Norman Lanfranc as his replacement.

Aug. The emperor Henry IV deprives the treasonous Otto of Nordheim of his estates in Saxony and Bavaria.

ASIA

– Chola power in Ceylon (Sri Lanka) is destroyed by Vijayabahu.

SCIENCE AND TECHNOLOGY

– Aylmer, monk and astrologer from Malmesbury (W England) who attempted winged flight, dies.

ARTS AND HUMANITIES

– In England work begins on Canterbury Cathedral and Bury St Edmunds Abbey.

1071

EUROPE

April Bari in S Italy falls to the Norman Robert Guiscard (see 1059), who has now expelled the Byzantines from Sicily.

19 Aug. The Seljuk sultan Alp Arslan destroys the Byzantine army at Manzikert in E Anatolia (Asian Turkey). He captures the emperor Romanus IV Diogenes, who is released after paying tribute. The Seljuks have now completed the conquest of Armenia. Following the battle, Turks will take possession of much of Anatolia (which will henceforth be Turkish). Seljuks will go on to conquer most of Syria later in the year.

24 Oct. The Byzantine emperor Romanus IV is imprisoned and deposed. Michael VII Ducas succeeds and appeals in vain for aid from the W Christian kingdoms.

– King William I expels the English freedom fighter Hereward the Wake from the Isle of Ely, E England.

ARTS AND HUMANITIES

– The Abbey Church of Monte Cassino, Italy, is dedicated.

1072

EUROPE

10 Jan. The Norman Robert Guiscard captures Palermo, Sicily.

– At an English Church council in Winchester, the primacy of Canterbury over York is asserted.

MIDDLE EAST AND NORTH AFRICA

15 Dec. The sultan Alp Arslan is assassinated on campaign in Transoxiana. His son Malik Shah succeeds him.

ARTS AND HUMANITIES

22 Feb. St Peter Damian dies.

– *Pravda*, a collection of Russian laws, is collated.

– In England work begins on Lincoln Cathedral.

1073

EUROPE

22 April The Italian cardinal Hildebrand is elected pope and takes the name Gregory VII.

MIDDLE EAST AND NORTH AFRICA

– The Seljuk Turk Suleiman ibn Qutlamish starts the conquest of Byzantine territory in Anatolia (Asian Turkey).

ASIA

– Zhou Dunyi (Chou Tun-I), pioneer of the Confucian revival in China, dies.

ARTS AND HUMANITIES

– Work begins on the Abbey of St Augustine, Canterbury, S England.

1074

EUROPE

Mar. Pope Gregory VII excommunicates Robert Guiscard, duke of Apulia. In this year he also sends papal legates to reform the French Church and announces the excommunication of married priests.

– King William I of England puts down a rebellion in the duchy of Normandy.

MIDDLE EAST AND NORTH AFRICA

– Sultan Malik Shah captures Aleppo, Syria.

ARTS AND HUMANITIES

– Sultan Malik Shah builds an observatory at Ray, Syria.

1075

EUROPE

24–28 Feb. Pope Gregory VII suspends seven German bishops who oppose clerical celibacy and begins a dramatic contest between Church and state by opposing the practice whereby secular rulers invest bishops with their sees. In his *Dictatus papae* he outlines his view of his own powers. This conflict between pope and emperor, known as the investiture controversy, dominates European politics for years.

Nov. The Saxon nobles surrender to the emperor Henry IV, who imprisons them.

- King William I's nobles put down a revolt by three earls in England.
- Geza I is crowned king of Hungary with a crown sent by the Byzantine emperor Michael VII Ducas.

ARTS AND HUMANITIES
- The Cathedral of Santiago de Compostela, NW Spain, is built.

1076

EUROPE

24 Jan. Pope Gregory VII threatens Emperor Henry IV with excommunication. Henry summons his bishops to Worms where they renounce their allegiance to Gregory, who excommunicates Henry later in the year.

16 Oct. A conference of German princes loyal to the pope threatens to depose Henry.

25 Dec. Boleslav II is crowned king of Poland with a crown sent by Pope Gregory VII in recognition of his zeal in re-establishing Church order. (Boleslav supports Gregory's campaign against the emperor Henry IV.)

MIDDLE EAST AND NORTH AFRICA
- The Fatimids of Egypt recover Jerusalem from the Seljuks, but Atsiz ibn Abaq, the Seljuk commander who has also taken Damascus (1075), expels them.

SUB-SAHARAN AFRICA
- The Berbers destroy Ghana, capital of the empire of Ghana in W Sudan.

ARTS AND HUMANITIES
- A national university is established in Dai Viet (modern Vietnam).
- Ibn Haiyan, author of a history of Muslim Spain, dies.

1077

EUROPE

Jan. Emperor Henry IV submits to Pope Gregory VII at Canossa in N Italy and is absolved from excommunication.

13 Mar. Henry's German opponents claim that the throne is elective and choose Rudolf, duke of Swabia, as king.

25 April Geza I, king of Hungary, dies and is succeeded by his brother Ladislas I.

- Alfonso VI, king of Castile and Leon, takes the title 'Emperor of all Spain'.
- Robert Guiscard, the Norman duke of Apulia, occupies the Lombard principality of Salerno, S Italy.

MIDDLE EAST AND NORTH AFRICA
- Suleiman ibn Qutlamish establishes the Seljuk sultanate of Rum in Asia Minor, with a capital at Nicaea (Isnik in Turkey).

ASIA
- Aniruddha, first king of a united Burma and founder of the Pagan dynasty, dies.

1078

EUROPE

31 Mar. The Byzantine emperor Michael VII Ducas abdicates and is succeeded by the general Nicephorus III Botaneiates.

Nov. Pope Gregory VII publishes a decree condemning lay investiture to spiritual offices thereby reigniting the investiture controversy (see 1075). In this year he also orders all bishops to found cathedral schools.

1079

EUROPE

Jan. Robert Curthose, son of William I, king of England, defeats his father in battle in Normandy.

- Emperor Henry IV grants the duchy of Swabia to Frederick, count of Stauffen.

MIDDLE EAST AND NORTH AFRICA
- Atsiz ibn Abaq (see 1076) is murdered on the orders of Malik Shah's brother Tutush. Tutush seizes Atsiz's principality in Syria.

1080

EUROPE

7 Mar. Pope Gregory VII deposes Emperor Henry IV in favour of Rudolf of Swabia. Henry IV retaliates by declaring Gregory VII himself to be deposed as pope (25 June). Gregory allies himself (29 June) with Robert Guiscard, the Norman duke of Apulia, S Italy.

15 May Walcher, bishop of Durham and earl of Northumberland, is murdered. King William I asserts his control of N England and invades Scotland. He builds a castle at Newcastle upon Tyne.

ARTS AND HUMANITIES
- The Bayeux Tapestry, recording the Norman invasion of England, is commissioned.
- Cathedrals are built in Cracow and Gniezno (Poland) and York (N England).
- The Abbey of St Sernin, Toulouse, S France, is founded.

1081

EUROPE

April In Poland a rebellion forces Boleslav II into exile. Civil war ensues and royal authority dissolves.

17 June Robert Guiscard, Norman duke of Apulia, invades Byzantine territory on the E Adriatic: he besieges Durazzo and occupies Corfu.

- King William I establishes Marcher lordships in S Wales to guard his W borders or 'marches'.
- Alexius I Comnenus, nephew of Isaac I Comnenus, succeeds Nicephorus II Botaneiates as Byzantine emperor.

1082-90

1082

EUROPE

21 Feb. Robert Guiscard, Norman duke of Apulia, takes Durazzo (in modern Albania) (see 1081).

1083

EUROPE

3 June Emperor Henry IV captures the Church of St Peter, Rome. His negotiations with Pope Gregory VII collapse.

– The county of Maine revolts against William I, king of England and duke of Normandy.

– The Byzantines recover Durazzo from Robert Guiscard, Norman duke of Apulia (see 1082).

– The former king of Poland, Boleslav II (see 1081), dies.

ARTS AND HUMANITIES

– Marianus Scotus, author of the *Chronicon*, a world history, who also corrected the accepted date for Christ's birth, dies.

1084

EUROPE

21 Mar. Emperor Henry IV enters Rome, deposes Gregory VII and installs Clement III as antipope (24 Mar.). Clement crowns Henry as emperor (31 Mar.).

May Robert Guiscard's Norman forces sack Rome and expel the German forces of Emperor Henry IV from the city.

– St Bruno founds the hermitage at Chartreuse, marking the beginning of the Carthusian monastic order.

1085

EUROPE

25 May Pope Gregory VII dies at Salerno, S Italy.

25 May In Spain Alfonso VI of Castile and Leon takes Toledo and defeats the Muslim kings of Valencia.

17 July Robert Guiscard, Norman duke of Apulia, dies. His son Roger Borsa succeeds as duke of Apulia and withdraws the Normans from Byzantine territories. His brother Roger succeeds to the Norman territories in Sicily and Calabria.

25 Dec. King William I orders a survey of all England, which will be recorded in the *Domesday Book*.

– The emperor Henry IV extends the 'Peace of God' over the entire Holy Roman Empire.

MIDDLE EAST AND NORTH AFRICA

– The Seljuks seize Antioch from the Byzantines.

1086

EUROPE

23 Oct. The Almoravid ruler Yusuf ibn Tashfin (see 1068), summoned to Spain by Mu'tamid of Seville (see 1069), defeats Alfonso VI of Castile at Azagal.

MIDDLE EAST AND NORTH AFRICA

– Suleiman, sultan of Rum (see 1077), is defeated and killed by Tutush (see 1079) while trying to seize Aleppo, Syria. He is succeeded by his son Kilij Arslan.

1087

EUROPE

30 May The emperor Henry IV crowns his son Conrad king of Germany.

9 Sept. King William I (the Conqueror) of England dies. His son Robert Curthose succeeds to the Norman domains, but faces baronial rebellion. William II (Rufus), second son of William I, is crowned king of England (26 Sept.).

MIDDLE EAST AND NORTH AFRICA

– A system of military fiefs is introduced in the Seljuk empire.

SCIENCE AND TECHNOLOGY

– Constantine the African, translator of Arab medical works into Latin, dies.

ARTS AND HUMANITIES

– Work begins on a new St Paul's Cathedral, London.

1088

EUROPE

June King William II suppresses a revolt in England led by his uncle Odo of Bayeux, bishop of Rochester.

– Urban II becomes pope.

1089

EUROPE

Sept. Pope Urban II negotiates with the Byzantine emperor Alexius I Comnenus on the possibility of organizing a crusade against the Turks.

MIDDLE EAST AND NORTH AFRICA

– David III becomes joint ruler of Georgia with his father George II.

– The Fatamids of Egypt recover Ascalon, Tyre and Acre in Palestine from the Seljuks.

ARTS AND HUMANITIES

28 May Lanfranc, archbishop of Canterbury, dies.

– The Church of St Nicola, Bari, introduces the Romanesque architectural style to Italy.

1090

EUROPE

Nov. Yusuf ibn Tashfin returns to Spain from Africa, takes Granada and founds the Almoravid dynasty.

– Roger Guiscard, Norman duke of Apulia (see 1085), takes Malta from the Arabs.

MIDDLE EAST AND NORTH AFRICA

- Al-Hasan ibn al-Sabbah, founder of the Assassins, establishes himself in the castle of Alamut, Iraq. The Assassins, named from their supposed habit of eating hashish (cannabis), are members of an extremist sect of Islam who use the murder of political and theological opponents as a routine tool, thus giving their name to such acts.

1091

EUROPE

- Yusuf ibn Tashfin (see 1090) conquers and then unites the Muslim kingdoms of Andalusia.
- Roger Guiscard, Norman duke of Apulia, completes the conquest of Sicily from the Arabs.
- Ladislas I of Hungary conquers Croatia.

MIDDLE EAST AND NORTH AFRICA

- The sultan Malik Shah makes Baghdad the Seljuk capital.

1092

EUROPE

- At the council of Soissons, French cleric Johannes Roscellinus is condemned for his heretical views on the Trinity.

MIDDLE EAST AND NORTH AFRICA

Nov. Sultan Malik Shah dies. Torn by civil war, the Seljuk empire disintegrates.

1093

EUROPE

April Rhys ap Tewdwr, ruler of the independent kingdom of Deheubarth in SW Wales, is killed resisting the Norman invasion of Wales.
- Alfonso VI of Castile seizes Lisbon and Cintra.

ARTS AND HUMANITIES

- The first example of ribbed vaulting appears in Durham Cathedral, N England.

1094

EUROPE

- The Welsh expel the Normans from NW Wales.
- Rodrigo Díaz de Vivar (El Cid) captures Valencia and defends it against Islamic forces.
- Urban II regains possession of the Lateran Palace, Rome. The supporters of the antipope, Clement III (see 1084), are routed. The emperor Henry IV loses power in Italy.

MIDDLE EAST AND NORTH AFRICA

29 Dec. Al-Munstansir, caliph of Egypt, dies: his N African empire collapses.
- The Seljuk leader Tutush seizes Aleppo, Syria, from its native ruler.

ARTS AND HUMANITIES

Al-Bakri, *The Book of Roads and Kingdoms*, earliest geographical work by a Spanish Muslim.
Anselm, *Why God became Man*, theology.

1095

EUROPE

25 Feb. Anselm, archbishop of Canterbury (since 1093), quarrels with William II, king of England, on the issue of episcopal obedience to pope and king.
Mar. Pope Urban II appeals to the rulers of W Europe to rescue Constantinople, threatened by Islamic invasion.
27 Nov. Pope Urban II proclaims the First Crusade. Raymond IV, count of Toulouse, becomes the first ruler to join it (1 Dec.). Over the following generations there will be several crusades organized by Christians from Europe seeking to recapture from Islamic rule the sacred Christian sites of the Middle East.

ARTS AND HUMANITIES

Anonymous, *La Chanson de Roland* (see 778), earliest extant *chanson de geste*.

1096

EUROPE

May–June Crusaders travelling through the Rhineland (Germany) instigate local attacks on Jews.
1 Aug. A force of crusaders led by the holy man Peter the Hermit arrives in Constantinople.
- The Normans complete their conquest of S Wales.

ARTS AND HUMANITIES

- Work begins on Vézelay Abbey, E France.

1097

EUROPE

Jan. The crusaders riot in Constantinople.
Oct. Anselm (see 1095) leaves England and goes into exile.
Oct. The English prince Edgar the Atheling defeats the pretender to the Scottish throne, Donald Bane, and places Edgar, his own nephew and son of deceased King Malcolm Canmore, on the throne of Scotland.

MIDDLE EAST AND NORTH AFRICA

21 May The crusaders defeat Kilij Arslan, Seljuk sultan of Rum, outside Nicaea in Asia Minor and (19 June) take the city. They defeat Arslan again (1 July) and seize his capital Iconium (Aug.).
21 Oct. The crusaders begin their siege of Antioch, N Syria.

1098

EUROPE

Oct. At the council of Bari, S Italy, representatives of the Byzantine and Western Churches debate the procession of the Holy Spirit from the Trinity.

MIDDLE EAST AND NORTH AFRICA

3 June The crusaders take Antioch.

– The Fatimids recover Jerusalem from the Seljuk Turks.

1099

EUROPE

5 Jan. Henry, son of Henry IV, is elected emperor. Henry IV is reconciled with his German opponents.

– Spanish Christian hero and warrior Rodrigo Diaz de Vivar (El Cid) dies (see 1094). Islamic forces recover Valencia.

MIDDLE EAST AND NORTH AFRICA

15 July The crusaders take Jerusalem, ending the First Crusade.

22 July Godfrey of Bouillon, a crusader leader from Boulogne, N France, is elected Defender of the Holy Sepulchre in Jerusalem.

12 Aug. The crusaders defeat the Fatimids at Ascalon.

– The Order of the Knights of St John of Jerusalem (the Hospitallers) is founded.

1100

EUROPE

2 Aug. William II (Rufus), king of England, dies in suspicious circumstances in a hunting 'accident' in the New Forest and is succeeded by his brother, Henry I, who recalls the theologian Anselm (see 1097) after being crowned (5 Aug.).

– Constantine Bodin, king of Zeta (see 1040), dies: the Serbian state (which had included the conquered Bosnia) disintegrates.

MIDDLE EAST AND NORTH AFRICA

April The emirs of Ascalon, Caesarea and Acre submit to the king of Jerusalem, Godfrey of Bouillon.

18 July Godfrey of Bouillon, king of Jerusalem, dies and is succeeded by his brother, Baldwin I.

SCIENCE AND TECHNOLOGY

– Adelard of Bath translates the work of the ancient Greek mathematician Euclid into Latin from Arabic.

1101

EUROPE

22 June Duke Roger I Guiscard of Sicily dies; he is succeeded by his son Simon.

MIDDLE EAST AND NORTH AFRICA

May Baldwin I, French crusader king of Jerusalem, seizes Arsuf and Caesarea, on the coast of Palestine.

23 June Raymond of Toulouse takes Ankara with a new crusading army from Constantinople. Raymond's army will be destroyed by the Danishmend (Turkish) army at Mersivan in Anatolia (Aug.).

4 Sept. Baldwin I, king of Jerusalem, defeats the Fatimids at Ramleh.

1102

MIDDLE EAST AND NORTH AFRICA

17 May The Fatimids defeat Baldwin I, French crusader king of Jerusalem, but Baldwin will defeat the Fatimids at Jaffa 11 days later (28 May).

1103

EUROPE

27 April King Henry I of England exiles the theologian Anselm after they quarrel over Anselm's refusal to accept bishops consecrated by the king (see 1100).

– Duke Simon of Sicily (see 1101) dies and is succeeded by his brother Roger II.

1104

EUROPE

– Philip I, king of France, cedes to Pope Paschal II over the investiture principle (see 1075).

– The diocese of Lund in Sweden is detached from the arch-bishopric of Hamburg and the first Scandinavian archbishop is consecrated there.

MIDDLE EAST AND NORTH AFRICA

Jan. The Turkish civil war ends: the Seljuk sultan Barkiyaruq cedes Iraq and Syria to his brother Muhammad. Sanjar, the third brother, holds Khurasan (Iran).

May Baldwin I, French crusader king of Jerusalem, takes the port of Acre (modern Akko, Israel).

1105

EUROPE

Dec. The emperor Henry IV is captured by his son Henry, who forces him to abdicate (he dies in 1106) and succeeds him as Henry V.

MIDDLE EAST AND NORTH AFRICA

28 Feb. Raymond IV, count of Toulouse, dies while besieging Tripoli in Palestine.

27 Aug. Baldwin I, French crusader king of Jerusalem, defeats the Fatimids decisively in the third battle of Ramleh.

1106

EUROPE

28 Sept. King Henry I of England defeats and captures his brother Robert, duke of Normandy, at Tinchebrai, reuniting England and Normandy.

– Yusuf ibn Tashfin, the Almoravid emir of Morocco and Spain (see 1068 and 1090), dies and is succeeded by his son Ali.

ARTS AND HUMANITIES

– Parma Cathedral in Italy is dedicated.

1107

EUROPE
- King Henry I of England and the theologian Anselm are reconciled over the investiture issue (see 1075 and 1103).
- The civil war in Poland ends when Zbigniev recognizes the supremacy of his brother Boleslav III.

ARTS AND HUMANITIES
- In England the central tower of Winchester Cathedral collapses; rib vaulting is introduced with the reconstruction work.

1108

EUROPE
29–30 July Philip I, king of France, dies and is succeeded by his son Louis VI (the Fat).
- Coloman (Kálmán) of Hungary grants Croatia its independence.

SCIENCE AND TECHNOLOGY
- The first embankment to protect rice fields from floods is built on the Red River, N Vietnam.

1109

EUROPE
- The emperor Henry V invades Poland on behalf of the exiled Zbigniev; he is defeated, and Boleslav III murders his brother Zbigniev.
- Duke Svatopulk of Bohemia is murdered, sparking civil war in Bohemia.

MIDDLE EAST AND NORTH AFRICA
12 July Tripoli (in modern Lebanon) surrenders to Baldwin I, crusader king of Jerusalem.

ARTS AND HUMANITIES
21 April The theologian Anselm dies. He will be canonized in 1720.
- William of Champeaux founds a theological school in the Abbey of St Victor, Paris.

1110

EUROPE
Aug. The emperor Henry V starts an expedition against Italy.
- Basil, leader of the heretical Bulgarian sect of Bogomils, is burned to death on the instructions of the Byzantine emperor Alexius I Comnenus.

SCIENCE AND TECHNOLOGY
- In Italy *Anatomia Porci*, an account of pig dissection, is produced at the Salerno medical school.

ARTS AND HUMANITIES
- The nave of Tournai Cathedral (in modern Belgium) is built.

- The great temple of Anantapanna, Pagan (modern Burma), is constructed.
- Nestor of Kiev, author of *The Primary Chronicle*, the first Russian history, dies.

1111

EUROPE
4 Feb. The emperor Henry V captures Pope Paschal II and, by the treaty of Sutri, forces him to accede to his conditions for the settlement of the investiture controversy (see 1075). Pope Paschal II crowns Henry V as Holy Roman Emperor (13 April).
- In what is now Ukraine, Russian forces crush the Cumans (see 1061).

SCIENCE AND TECHNOLOGY
- The Persian Sufi theologian and mystic Al-Ghazzali (Algazel) dies.

ARTS AND HUMANITIES
Guibert of Nogent, *Gesta Dei per Francos* (The Deeds of God through the Franks), a history of the First Crusade.

1112

EUROPE
- Pope Paschal II reneges on his deal with the emperor Henry V on investiture (see 1111). Henry is excommunicated by the synod of Vienne (Sept.). The Church splits into papal and imperial factions.
- The count of Barcelona, Raymond-Berengar III, gains the county of Provence, S France.

ARTS AND HUMANITIES
- Sigbert of Gembloux, author of the *Chronographia*, a world history, dies.

1113

EUROPE
- The count of Barcelona, Raymond-Berengar III, allies with the Pisans of N Italy to expel the Arabs from the Balearic islands in the W Mediterranean.

ARTS AND HUMANITIES
- Bernard of Clairvaux enters the convent of Cîteaux, in Burgundy, E France. A French ascetic monk and prolific writer, Bernard will draw up the statutes of the Knights Templar (see 1119).
- Peter Abelard (see p. 119) founds a school in Paris teaching philosophy, rhetoric and theology.

1114

EUROPE
7 Jan. The Holy Roman Emperor Henry V marries Matilda, daughter of King Henry I of England.

1 Oct. Henry V is defeated by rebels in the Rhineland.

– In the Byzantine empire many of the dissident Christians known as Paulicians have by now converted to Orthodoxy.

– Coloman (Kálmán), king of Hungary who conquered Dalmatia and Herzogovina, dies.

ARTS AND HUMANITIES

– Benevento Cathedral, S Italy, is rebuilt.

1115

EUROPE

7 July Peter the Hermit, a leader of the First Crusade (see 1096), dies.

ASIA

– Aguda (A-ku-ta) leads the nomadic Jürchen, a Manchu people, in rebellion against the Khitans of Liao and declares himself to be emperor of China, first of the Jin (Chin) dynasty.

ECONOMY AND SOCIETY

– A Cistercian house is founded at Clairvaux, C France, with Bernard of Clairvaux (see 1113) as abbot.

– Ivo of Chartres, who formulated canon law, dies.

1117

EUROPE

– King Henry I of England campaigns in Normandy to suppress a French-assisted local rebellion.

– The sultan of Iconium, Malik Shah, dies and is succeeded by Ma'sud I.

ARTS AND HUMANITIES

– In Italy Parma Cathedral is rebuilt after an earthquake.

1118

EUROPE

24 Jan. John of Gaeta is elected Pope Gelasius II. The Holy Roman Emperor Henry V, however, installs Maurice Bourdin, archbishop of Braga, as Pope Gregory VIII (an antipope).

7 April Pope Gelasius excommunicates Emperor Henry V.

15 Aug. The Byzantine emperor Alexius I Commenus dies and is succeeded by his son John II Comnenus.

– In Wales Gruffudd ap Cynan, prince of Gwynedd, embarks on an expansionist campaign which, by 1137, will have seen the authority of the royal house of Aberffraw extended into mid- and SW Wales.

MIDDLE EAST AND NORTH AFRICA

2 April Baldwin I, crusader king of Jerusalem, dies and is succeeded by Baldwin II, count of Edessa in Syria.

– Sanjar of Khurasan succeeds Muhammad I as Seljuk sultan.

ARTS AND HUMANITIES

– In England Peterborough Cathedral is built.

1119

EUROPE

29 Jan. Pope Gelasius II dies and is succeeded by Calixtus II. Calixtus officially approves (23 Dec.) the Cistercian order (an offshoot of the Benedictines).

MIDDLE EAST AND NORTH AFRICA

28 June Ghazi, ruler of the Danishmend Turks, defeats a crusader army at Antioch, killing Roger of Salerno, prince of Antioch.

– The Order of the Knights Templar is founded in Jerusalem. Their rule will be approved by Pope Honorius II in 1128.

ASIA

– Ballala Sena, king of Bengal, reorganizes the Indian caste system.

1120

EUROPE

25 Nov. William Adelin (the Aetheling), son and heir of Henry I, king of England, is drowned in the wreck of the *White Ship* in the English Channel. According to tradition, after the tragedy Henry never smiles again.

– Alfonso I, king of Aragon, Spain, defeats Islamic forces at Cutanda and Daroca.

– St Norbert of Xanten founds the Premonstratensian Order (so called because the site of the order's first house was previously pointed out by Norbet).

ASIA

– In China the Song (Sung) ally with the Jürchen against the Khitans of Liao (see 1115).

ARTS AND HUMANITIES

– The Abbey of Vézelay, E France, is burned and then rebuilt.

1121

EUROPE

29 Sept. The Holy Roman Emperor Henry V makes peace with his German opponents.

– In council at Soissons, N France, the Church condemns the philosopher Peter Abelard (see p. 119) for heresy (see 1113).

MIDDLE EAST AND NORTH AFRICA

27 Nov. Muhammad ibn Tumart, leader of the Almohads of the Atlas Mts, is acclaimed as the Mahdi (one guided by God). He begins to conquer the Almoravid territories in NW Africa.

ARTS AND HUMANITIES

– William of Champeaux (see 1109), who developed the philosophical theory of realism, dies.

1122

EUROPE

23 Sept. In Germany the concordat of Worms ends the

investiture controversy between the pope and the Holy Roman Emperor (see 1075).

- Byzantine forces destroy the Pechenegs of what is now S Ukraine.
- Tiflis (Tbilisi), the last Islamic centre in the Caucasus, falls to David III, king of Georgia.

ASIA

- The Jürchen found the Jin (Chin) dynasty in N China and Manchuria on the collapse of the Liao empire (see 947). They will rule N China until 1234.

ARTS AND HUMANITIES

Peter Abelard, *Sic et non* (Yes and No), a work that expounds the dialectical method as a feature of Christian theology (see box). Ari the Wise, *Islendingabok* (Book of the Icelanders), a history of the Norse settlement of Iceland.

1123

EUROPE

18 Mar.–5 April The First Lateran Council meets as the first general council of the Church in W Europe: it condemns simony and married priests.

MIDDLE EAST AND NORTH AFRICA

18 April The Danishmend Turkish emir Balak of Khanzit captures King Baldwin II of Jerusalem and destroys his army. Balak occupies Aleppo, Syria (June).
29 May A crusader army defeats the Fatimids at Ibelin, Palestine.

ARTS AND HUMANITIES

- The priory and hospital of St Bartholomew, London, is founded.
- Umar al-Khayyam, author of the classic Persian verse collection, *The Rubaiyat*, dies.

1124

EUROPE

- Lothair, duke of Saxony, occupies the lands of the pagan Slavs W of the Oder.
- Otto, bishop of Bamberg, begins the mission to convert Pomerania (in modern Poland).

MIDDLE EAST AND NORTH AFRICA

June King Baldwin II of Jerusalem is released by Balak of Khanzit upon payment of ransom.
7 July The Fatimids surrender Tyre (in modern Lebanon) to Baldwin II.
- The founder of the Assassins (see 1090), al-Hasan ibn al-Sabbah, dies.

1125

EUROPE

23 May The Holy Roman Emperor Henry V, last of the Salian dynasty of emperors, dies without direct heir.
30 Aug. The pro-papal Welf (or Guelph) nobles prevent the succession of Frederick of Swabia to his uncle's (Henry V's) throne, and Lothair of Supplinburg, duke of Saxony, is elected instead. Open warfare breaks out between the Welfs and the Hohenstaufen family, known as Waiblings (or Ghibellines) from their castle at Waiblingen.
- David III, king of Georgia, dies having gained independence from Byzantium. He is succeeded by his son Demetrius I.

ASIA

- The Jürchen, founders of the Jin (Chin) dynasty (see 1122), occupy Beijing. The Song (Sung) emperor Huizong (Hui Tsung) abdicates in favour of his son Qinzong (Ch'in Tsung).

Peter Abelard (1079–1142)

The philosopher and theologian Peter Abelard was born near Nantes, Brittany, and enjoyed extraordinary success as a teacher – most notably in the cathedral school of Paris. Handsome, independent-minded and scornful of his superiors, Abelard fascinated all who attended his lectures. His celebrated love-affair with one of his pupils, Héloïse, whom he married in secret, ended with her entry into a convent and his castration on the orders of Fulbert, Héloïse's uncle. After this Abelard became a monk, and the story of the couple's doomed love entered into the literature of European romance.

Abelard was an early hero of free thought,

being condemned for heresy in 1121 and again in 1140. His great achievement was to interpret Aristotle clearly and relevantly for the medieval mind. He was skilful in logic and dialectics, and his treatise *Sic et non* (Yes and No) (1122) outlines the application of dialectical reasoning to Christian thought. He also gained fame for his rejection of the belief that general categories (or 'universals') had real existence as things in themselves. Church suspicion centred on his interpretation of the Trinity as a metaphor for power, wisdom and love – divine attributes rather than the images of divine beings that was the orthodox interpretation.

In ethics Abelard was interested not so much in consequences as in the motives that led people to their actions. The goodness of an action, he taught, lay with the intention and will of the doer rather than in its conformity to a rule. Revealingly, the alternative title to his book on ethics is *Know Thyself*. His work established Paris as the most important university in 12th-century Europe, for it was there that he developed and taught his conviction that theology could be a synthesis of all human knowledge. His ardent investigations echoed, intellectually, the chivalric impulses of the age.

ARTS AND HUMANITIES
- The nave of Cluny Abbey in Burgundy collapses and is rebuilt with flying buttresses.
- The mosque of al-Aqmar, Cairo, is built.
- Raymond, archbishop of Toledo, Spain, translates the texts of Aristotle that survive in Arabic into Latin.

1126

EUROPE
- Alfonso I, king of Aragon, Spain, defeats an Islamic (Almoravid) army at Arinsol, near Lucena.

ASIA
- The Jürchen occupy Kaifeng, the Northern Song (Sung) capital, and capture the emperor Qinzong (Ch'in Tsung); Korea and Xixia (see 1038) become vassals of the Jin (Chin) dynasty.

SCIENCE AND TECHNOLOGY
- Adelard of Bath translates al-Khwarizmi's astronomical tables into Latin.

ARTS AND HUMANITIES
- Bernard of Clairvaux, *On the Love of God*, theology.

1127

EUROPE
20 July William I, Norman duke of Apulia, dies and is succeeded by his cousin Roger II of Sicily.
18 Dec. The emperor-elect Lothair's Waibling opponents elect Conrad of Hohenstaufen as their claimant to the imperial throne.

MIDDLE EAST AND NORTH AFRICA
- Imad ad-Din Zangi becomes atabeg (governor) of Mosul, in modern Iraq. He founds the Zangid dynasty and leads an Islamic fightback against the crusaders.

ASIA
- Following the sack of the Northern Song (Sung) capital (see 1126), Gaozong (Kao Tsung), another son of Huizong (Hui Tsung) (see 1125), establishes the Southern Song (Sung) dynasty at Hangzhou (Hangchow).

1128

EUROPE
17 June The English king Henry I's daughter, Matilda, who is also the widow of the Holy Roman Emperor Henry V, marries Geoffrey Plantaganet of Anjou, W France. In England she is recognized as her father's heir.
29 June Conrad of Hohenstaufen is crowned king of Italy.
- Afonso Henriques, count of Portugal, defeats the army of his mother Teresa to become ruler of all Portugal.

ARTS AND HUMANITIES
- The first Cistercian house in England is founded at Waverley, Surrey.

1129

MIDDLE EAST AND NORTH AFRICA
17 Dec. The Almohad Mahdi, Muhammad ibn Tumart (see 1121), dies and is succeeded by Abd al-Mu'min.

1130

EUROPE
25 Dec. Roger II is crowned Norman king of Sicily. Roger is immensely successful both militarily and as a civil administrator. He will introduce the silk industry to Sicily (see 1147).
- A pipe roll (a rolled parchment record) of the English exchequer for 1129–30 becomes the first surviving example of an English administrative record.

MIDDLE EAST AND NORTH AFRICA
- The Danishmend Turks massacre the army of Bohemond II of Antioch, which was about to attack the Armenians.

ASIA
- Yelü Dashi (Yeh-lü Ta-shih), one of the surviving members of the Khitan branch of the Liao dynasty (see 1122), founds the Western Liao in E Turkestan, also known as the Kara-Khitai dynasty.

SCIENCE AND TECHNOLOGY
- The physician Beneventus Grassus writes *Practica oculorum*, a medical treatise on eye diseases.
- The breast strap harness for horses is introduced into Europe and enables the drawing of heavier loads.

ARTS AND HUMANITIES
25 Oct. Pope Innocent II dedicates the Abbey Church of Cluny.
- Baudry de Bourgeuil, author of works of literature describing journeys in N France and England, dies.
- English monk Eadmer, author of a life of his friend St Anselm and a history of England, dies.
Anonymous, *The Ancren Rewle*, Middle English guide for anchoresses (religious recluses).

1131

EUROPE
8 Sept. The English barons pledge allegiance to Matilda as King Henry I's heir (see 1128). Henry's only legitimate son, William, and many other young nobles from the English court were drowned in the wreck of the *White Ship* (see 1120).

MIDDLE EAST AND NORTH AFRICA
21 Aug. Baldwin II, king of Jerusalem, dies and is succeeded by Fulk of Anjou.

ARTS AND HUMANITIES
- Cefalu Cathedral, Sicily, is constructed.
- Tintern Abbey is founded in SE Wales.
Ain al-Qudat al-Hamadhani, *Apologia*, Sufi mysticism.

1132

ARTS AND HUMANITIES
- The Palatine Chapel is built in Palermo, Sicily.

1133

EUROPE
4 June Pope Innocent II crowns Lothair II Holy Roman Emperor after Lothair campaigns in Italy for Innocent's restoration to the papal office against the rival claims of Anacletus II.

ECONOMY AND SOCIETY
- St Bartholomew's Fair, London, is founded.

1134

EUROPE
17 July Alfonso I, king of Aragon, Spain, is defeated by the Moors at Fraga.
7 Sept. Alfonso I dies; Navarre recovers its independence.
- The Holy Roman Emperor Lothair II makes Albrecht the Bear head of the Nordmark (the N frontier province of the empire), marking the beginnings of the house of Brandenburg.

ARTS AND HUMANITIES
- In France work begins on the first Gothic tower, the N tower of Chartres Cathedral.
- In Sweden work begins on Uppsala Cathedral.

1135

EUROPE
Mar. Conrad of Hohenstaufen (see 1127) and Frederick of Swabia (see 1125) submit to the rule of the Holy Roman Emperor Lothair II.
1 Dec. King Henry I of England dies and is succeeded by his nephew Stephen of Blois, who is crowned king (26 Dec.). Henry had nominated his daughter, Matilda, as his heir, but Stephen, a grandson of William the Conquerer, seizes power.

SCIENCE AND TECHNOLOGY
- Al-Jurjani, author of a Persian compilation of all known medical science, dies.

ARTS AND HUMANITIES
- In N England, Fountains Abbey is built.

1136

EUROPE
Feb. King Stephen of England cedes Cumberland (in NW England) to King David I of Scotland.
15 Aug. The Holy Roman Emperor Lothair II invests Henry of Bavaria (Henry the Proud) as duke of Saxony; he becomes thereby Germany's leading prince. Lothair subsequently invades Apulia and Calabria, S Italy.

SCIENCE AND TECHNOLOGY
- Silver mines are developed in Freiburg, Germany, which becomes a major metallurgical centre.

ARTS AND HUMANITIES
- The *Constitutio Domus Regis*, an important source for English constitutional history, documents the nature of King Stephen's household.

1137

EUROPE
22 July Louis, son of King Louis VI (the Fat) of France, marries Eleanor of Aquitaine, ruler of Aquitaine in her own right and therefore rich and a valuable wife. She will lead her own troops on a crusade (1147–9). Her marriage to Louis will be annulled (1152), and she will make an eventful marriage to Henry II of England.
1 Aug. Louis VI (the Fat), king of France, dies and is succeeded by his son Louis VII (the Young).
4 Dec. The Holy Roman Emperor Lothair II dies while returning from Italy.
- In Wales Gruffudd ap Cynan, prince of Gwynedd, dies and is succeeded by his son Owain Fawr (Owain the Great).

ARTS AND HUMANITIES
- Work begins on the W front of the Church of St Denis, Paris.
- Geoffrey of Monmouth, *History of the Kings of Britain*, account of early British history and Arthurian source. Although later recognized as fictitious, the chronicles will remain influential.

1138

EUROPE
3 Mar. Conrad of Hohenstaufen is elected German king of the Romans (as Conrad III) and thus emperor-elect. He immediately breaks up the dynastic holding of the Welf Henry the Proud (see 1136), granting Bavaria to Leopold of Austria. The war between Welfs and Waiblings is renewed.
May In England Robert, earl of Gloucester, illegitimate son of Henry I and half-brother of Matilda, leads a rebellion against King Stephen. Matilda bases her claim to the throne on the wishes of her late father Henry I, while Stephen argues that if women may claim the succession then he has a stronger claim, being William the Conquerer's grandson via the female line.
- Boleslav III of Poland dies while attempting to invade Russia. His lands are divided among his sons; the eldest, Vladislav II, becomes first Grand Prince of Poland. Civil war breaks out.

1139

EUROPE
20 April The religious reformer Arnold of Brescia is condemned by the Second Lateran Council.
June King Stephen of England arrests the bishops of Salisbury and Lincoln.

30 Sept. The empress Matilda arrives in England to lead her followers against Stephen.

– Jaropolk II of Kiev dies: the Russian federation dissolves.

ARTS AND HUMANITIES

– The Jewish poet and critic Moses ben Ezra dies.

Gratian of Bologna, *Decretum*, codification of canon law.

1140

EUROPE

Dec. The German king Conrad III defeats Welf, the brother of Henry the Proud, who had opposed the granting of Bavaria to Leopold of Austria (see 1138).

– At the council of Sens, France, St Bernard insists on the condemnation of the philosopher Peter Abelard (see p. 119) for his emphasis on the role of reason in theology.

– The first Cistercian and Premonstratensian houses are founded in Poland.

SCIENCE AND TECHNOLOGY

– The St Gothard pass in Switzerland is opened for commercial routes.

ARTS AND HUMANITIES

– The W front of the Church of St Denis in Paris is completed, marking the beginning of Gothic architecture. Work begins on the chancel with its famous stained glass windows.

Anonymous, *The Song of the Cid*, Spanish national epic.

1141

EUROPE

2 Feb. Robert, earl of Gloucester (see 1138), defeats and captures King Stephen of England.

3 Mar. The empress Matilda is proclaimed queen of England.

ASIA

9 Sept. The Seljuk sultan Sanjar is defeated at Samarkand by the Kara-Khitai (see 1130), whose empire will extend from China to the Oxus (modern Amu Darya River in C Asia).

ARTS AND HUMANITIES

Ordericus Vitalis, *Historia Ecclesiastica*, an ecclesiastical history of England and Normandy.

1142

EUROPE

May The civil war in Germany ends. The German king Conrad III grants Saxony to Henry the Lion, the heir of Henry the Proud of Bavaria, his Welf opponent.

ARTS AND HUMANITIES

21 April The French philosopher and theologian Peter Abelard dies.

– The English historian William of Malmesbury dies.

1143

EUROPE

8 April The Byzantine emperor John II Commenus dies while marching to attack Antioch; he is succeeded by his son Manuel I Comnenus.

– The citizens of Rome rebel against Pope Innocent II and proclaim a republic.

– Count Adolf II of Holstein founds Lübeck, N Germany, as an outpost against the Slavs.

MIDDLE EAST AND NORTH AFRICA

– The Armenians led by Theodore II start a rebellion to recover their independence on the death of the Byzantine emperor John II Comnenus (see above).

ARTS AND HUMANITIES

– Robert of Chester and Herman the Dalmatian provide the first Latin translation of the Koran.

1144

SCIENCE AND TECHNOLOGY

– Robert of Chester translates the Arabic *Book of the Composition of Alchemy*.

1145

MIDDLE EAST AND NORTH AFRICA

1 Dec. Following the capture (23 Dec. 1144) of the crusaders' outpost at Edessa (SE Turkey) by a Turkish army, Pope Eugenius III proclaims the Second Crusade.

SCIENCE AND TECHNOLOGY

– The earliest autopsy is recorded in China.

ARTS AND HUMANITIES

– The Great Mosque is built in Mosul (Iraq) and the Friday Mosque in Isfahan (Iran).

– Mosaics are installed in the apse of Santa Maria in Trastevere, Rome.

Kim Pu-sik, *History of the Three Kingdoms*, a history of Korea.

1146

EUROPE

– Pope Eugenius III asks St Bernard of Clairvaux to preach the Second Crusade. St Bernard will become the major intellectual figure in justifying and advancing the crusading enterprise.

– Vladislav II tries and fails to reunite Poland.

MIDDLE EAST AND NORTH AFRICA

– King Roger II of Sicily seizes Tripoli in N Africa.

1147

EUROPE

26 June The Slavonic Wends of E Europe sack Lübeck, but the

Saxon nobles counterattack (29 June). By Sept., however, they have called off their campaign. On 31 July, the Wends defeat the Danes.

MIDDLE EAST AND NORTH AFRICA

April The Almohad Abd al-Mu'min (see 1129) captures Marrakesh and so completes his conquest of Morocco's Almoravid kingdom. He then crosses into Spain where the Almoravid kingdom has already disintegrated.

3 Nov. Joscelin II, the former crusader count of Edessa, is defeated by the Syrian atabeg (Seljuk regent) Nur ad-Din, son of Imad ad-Din Zangi, when he attempts to recapture the city.

ARTS AND HUMANITIES

- At Engelburg woodcuts are used to illustrate manuscripts for the first time.
- King Roger II of Sicily (see 1130) establishes a colony of Greek silk-weavers from Thebes and Corinth at Palermo.

1148

EUROPE

- Empress Matilda is forced to leave England after failing to defeat her cousin and rival Stephen of Blois.

MIDDLE EAST AND NORTH AFRICA

24 July The army of the Second Crusade lay seige to Damascus but retreats due to lack of water (28 July).

ARTS AND HUMANITIES

- Mosaics are installed in the apse of Cefalu Cathedral, Sicily.
- Anna Comnena, author of the *Alexiad*, an historical account of her father the Byzantine emperor Alexius I, dies.
Anonymous, *Landnamabok* (Book of the Settlements), Icelandic chronicle.

1149

EUROPE

- Abd al-Mu'min's conquest of the Muslim kingdoms of Spain (see 1147) is now complete.

MIDDLE EAST AND NORTH AFRICA

29 June Raymond of Poitiers, prince of Antioch, is defeated and killed by Nur ad-Din, son of Imad ad-Din Zangi and atabeg of Edessa. The Second Crusade ends.

ARTS AND HUMANITIES

- *Le Codi*, written in the Provencal language, is the earliest vernacular version of Roman Law.
- The Church of the Holy Sepulchre, Jerusalem, is dedicated.

1150

MIDDLE EAST AND NORTH AFRICA

April Nur-ad-Din, atabeg of Edessa (see 1147), defeats, blinds and imprisons his crusader rival Joscelin II of Edessa.

ASIA

- The Temple of Angkor Wat, the mausoleum of King Suryavarman II in modern Cambodia, is constructed.

SCIENCE AND TECHNOLOGY

Hindu mathematician Bhaskara writes *Siddhantasiromani*, a treatise on mathematics and astronomy.

ARTS AND HUMANITIES

- Work begins on the cathedrals of Angers (France), Aversa (Italy), Le Mans (France), Lisbon (Portugal), Noyon (France) and Pecs (Serbia).

1151

EUROPE

13 Jan. Suger, abbot of St Denis, Paris, and regent for Louis VII (see 1137), dies.

7 Sept. Geoffrey Plantagenet, count of Anjou and Maine and husband of Empress Matilda, dies and is succeeded by his son Henry (see 1152 and 1154).

- The Byzantine emperor Manuel I Comnenus attacks Hungary; the war will last until 1167.

MIDDLE EAST AND NORTH AFRICA

- King Baldwin III of Jerusalem resists the Syrian atabeg Nur ad-Din's attempts to take Damascus.

ASIA

- Alaad-Din Husayn, sultan of Ghur (Afghanistan), destroys Ghazni.

1152

EUROPE

15 Feb. Conrad III, German king of the Romans and emperor-elect, dies. His nephew, Frederick I Barbarossa, is elected to succeed him (4 Mar.).

21 Mar. The marriage of Eleanor of Aquitaine and the French king Louis VII is dissolved. Eleanor marries Henry of Anjou (16 May). The marriage brings a vast area of what is now France into the possession of the future king of England (see 1154).

- At the synod of Kells the Irish Church acknowledges papal supremacy and organizes the Church into four archbishoprics: Armagh, Dublin, Cashel and Tuam.

ARTS AND HUMANITIES

- In France the romanesque Amiens Cathedral is consecrated.
- Work begins on the 'old cathedral' in Salamanca, Spain.
- John of Salisbury, *Historia Pontificalis* (History of the Papacy), a history of W Europe from 1148 to 1152.

1153

EUROPE

Jan. The future Henry II, son of the empress Matilda, lands in England and takes up his mother's campaign for the throne.

By a treaty (7 Nov.), Henry recognizes Stephen as king while Stephen accepts Henry as his heir.

MIDDLE EAST AND NORTH AFRICA

– King Roger II of Sicily (see 1130) takes Bona in N Africa; his empire now extends from Tripoli to Tunis.

ASIA

– The Jin (Chin) emperors of N China (see 1122) move their capital from Manchuria to Beijing.

ARTS AND HUMANITIES

20 Aug. St Bernard, abbot of Clairvaux (see 1115), dies.

1154

EUROPE

26 Feb. Roger II, the Norman king of Sicily, dies and is succeeded by his son William I, against whom the Byzantines counter-attack.

25 Oct. King Stephen of England dies. He is succeeded by Henry II, the first Plantagenet king. Controlling large swathes of territory in N and SW France (see 1152), as well as England (these territories are sometimes known as the Angevin empire), Henry is now the most powerful ruler in W Europe.

Oct. The German king Frederick I Barbarossa starts his first Italian campaign.

4 Dec. Nicholas Breakspear, the only English pope, is elected Pope Hadrian IV.

SCIENCE AND TECHNOLOGY

– The Arab geographer al-Edrisi constructs a planisphere, commissioned by Roger II of Sicily. He also writes *Roger's Book*, a complete description of the world with maps.

ARTS AND HUMANITIES

– The last entry is made in the *Anglo-Saxon Chronicle*: begun in 880, it records events in England from 449 to 1154.

1155

EUROPE

Jan. King Henry II of England appoints Thomas Becket as his chancellor. Thomas, from a rich merchant family, is the first Englishman to hold high office since the Norman conquest (1066).

Mar. Pope Hadrian IV places the rebellious citizens of Rome under an interdict, which forces them to expel their leader Arnold of Brescia (see 1139); he is later captured and burned as a heretic.

17 April The German king Frederick I is crowned king of Lombardy in Pavia. He is crowned Holy Roman Emperor by Pope Hadrian IV (18 June). The Romans rise up and force Frederick to withdraw to Germany.

– Pope Hadrian IV grants Ireland to King Henry II of England.

– The Wars of the Pretenders break out in Norway and Sweden; they will last until 1230.

MIDDLE EAST AND NORTH AFRICA

– The Carmelite order of mendicant friars is established on Mount Carmel, in the kingdom of Jerusalem.

1156

EUROPE

June The Holy Roman Emperor Frederick I marries Beatrice, heiress of Upper Burgundy.

11 Sept. The Holy Roman Emperor Frederick I grants the duchy of Bavaria to Henry the Lion, duke of Saxony.

Sept. Hungary recognizes the overlordship of Byzantium.

– King Henry II of England defeats his brother Geoffrey's revolt in Anjou.

ASIA

– Vikramanka, ruler of the powerful Rashtrakuta kingdom in the Deccan (S India), dies; the kingdom collapses.

1157

EUROPE

Oct. The Holy Roman Emperor Frederick I takes complete control of Burgundy. He rejects the theory of papal supremacy.

– King Henry II of England forces King Malcolm IV of Scotland to surrender Northumberland, Cumberland and Westmorland (all in N England), occupied by the Scots since 1136.

MIDDLE EAST AND NORTH AFRICA

– Sanjar, the Seljuk sultan (see 1141), dies: the Seljuk empire in Persia begins to dissolve.

ECONOMY AND SOCIETY

– Henry the Lion (see 1156) founds the city of Munich, S Germany.

– The bank of Venice is established; Venice will become one of the great trading cities of the world.

– King Henry II of England grants protection to the Hanse merchants based in Cologne and the Baltic (see 1241).

1158

EUROPE

July The Holy Roman Emperor Frederick I starts his second Italian campaign and captures Brescia. Milan falls to his forces on 8 Sept.

– King Henry II of England campaigns in Wales and gains the overlordship of Gwynedd and of Deheubarth.

MIDDLE EAST AND NORTH AFRICA

April King Baldwin III of Jerusalem defeats the Syrian atabeg Nur ad-Din at Butaiha in the Jordan valley.

ARTS AND HUMANITIES

22 Sept. Otto of Freising, biographer of Frederick I, dies.

– The Holy Roman Emperor Frederick I grants a charter to Bologna University.

1159

EUROPE

July The cities of Lombardy in N Italy rebel against the Holy Roman Emperor Frederick I. William of Sicily leads a league of the papacy to ally Brescia, Milan and Piacenza against him.

1 Sept. Pope Hadrian IV dies. A majority of the cardinals elect Pope Alexander III (7 Sept.); a pro-Frederick minority elect Pope Victor IV (an antipope). Neither faction is able to hold control.

1160

EUROPE

24 Mar. Pope Alexander III excommunicates Frederick I.

- Henry the Lion, duke of Saxony, begins the conquest of Wendish territory E of the Elbe.

MIDDLE EAST AND NORTH AFRICA

Nov. The Syrian atabeg Nur-ad-Din captures the crusader Reynald of Antioch.

- King William of Sicily loses all his father's conquests in N Africa.

ASIA

- Taira Kiyomori, a Japanese *daimyo* (feudal lord), gains control of the central imperial government.

SCIENCE AND TECHNOLOGY

- The Arab philosopher Averroes (Ibn Rushd) (see p. 130) writes *The Generalities of Medicine*, a medical encyclopedia.

ARTS AND HUMANITIES

- Work begins on the Gothic cathedral at Leon, N Spain, which features the first polygonal apse.
- Jean Bodel's *Le Jeu de St Nicholas*, the first French miracle play, is performed at Arras, N France.

1161

EUROPE

16 April King William of Sicily crushes a Sicilian rebellion and marches into Apulia and Calabria, S Italy.

Sept. The Holy Roman Emperor Frederick I besieges Milan, N Italy.

ASIA

- The Jin (Chin) emperors of N China attempt to conquer the Southern Song (Sung) empire but are defeated at the battle of Zaishi.

1162

EUROPE

Mar. The Holy Roman Emperor Frederick I allies with Pisa and Genoa against Sicily. Milan surrenders to his troops and is sacked on his orders (26 Mar.).

3 June In England Thomas Becket is consecrated archbishop of Canterbury. From being a worldly adviser to King Henry II, he becomes an ascetic advocate of Church rights.

- King Henry II of England raises Danegeld (see 991) as a tax for the last time.

ARTS AND HUMANITIES

- In France work begins on Poitiers Cathedral.
- Henry Aristippus, the Italian translator of Plato's *Phaedo* and *Meno*, dies.

1163

EUROPE

May The Almohad caliph of Muslim Spain and NW Africa, Abd al-Mu'min (see 1129), dies. His son Abu Yusuf Ya'qub al-Mansur succeeds him.

1 Oct. The archbishop of Canterbury, Thomas Becket, refuses the English king Henry II's demand that the clergy be tried in secular courts.

Oct. The Holy Roman Emperor Frederick I returns to Lombardy, N Italy, but withdraws after opposition fomented by Pope Alexander III.

ARTS AND HUMANITIES

- Work begins on Notre Dame Cathedral, Paris.
- The choir of St Germain-des-Prés, Paris, is consecrated.

1164

EUROPE

Jan. With the Constitutions of Clarendon Henry II of England limits the secular power of the clergy.

20 April The antipope Victor IV (see 1159) dies.

2 Nov. The archbishop of Canterbury, Thomas Becket, is condemned for contempt of court and goes into exile in France.

MIDDLE EAST AND NORTH AFRICA

10 Aug. The Syrian atabeg Nur ad-Din defeats and captures the crusader Bohemond III of Antioch at Artah.

- Spanish Muslims recapture Cordoba and Almeria.

ARTS AND HUMANITIES

16 May Héloïse, Peter Abelard's muse, dies. She had become an abbess, he had become a monk, and their letters are the subject of legend (see also p. 119).

- Peter Lombard, theologian and bishop of Paris, dies.

Chrétien de Troyes, *Erec et Enide*, Arthurian poetic romance.

1165

EUROPE

- King Henry II of England fails to subjugate the princes of Gwynedd, NW Wales.

ASIA

- In China the Jin (Chin) dynasty and the Southern Song (Sung) dynasty make a lasting peace.

1166-71

1166

EUROPE

- The Holy Roman Emperor Frederick I begins his fourth Italian campaign.
- At the Assize of Clarendon the English king Henry II specifies measures to prosecute criminals, including the jury system. The legal reforms over which Henry presides will become the key elements in the evolution of the English system of common law and the development of legal rights based on precedent and case law.

ARTS AND HUMANITIES

- In Germany Bonn Minster is dedicated.

1167

EUROPE

27 April The Lombard League, formed to oppose the Holy Roman Emperor Frederick I, starts the reconstruction of Milan.

29 May Forces of the Holy Roman Emperor Frederick I defeat the Romans. Frederick besieges and then makes peace with Ancona (July).

24 July Frederick I forces his way into Rome and the papal forces surrender. Pope Alexander III flees and the antipope Paschal III is installed. In Aug., however, Frederick's army is destroyed by fever and he has to return to Germany.

10 Sept. Empress Matilda, daughter of Henry I of England and mother of Henry II, dies.

- A conference of Cathar heretics meets near Toulouse, S France.

MIDDLE EAST AND NORTH AFRICA

18 Mar. Syrians, temporarily allied with the Fatimid caliph of Egypt, defeat King Amalric of Jerusalem at Ashmunein (N Egypt).

ASIA

- Bijjala, usurper of the kingdom of Rashtrakuta, India (see 1156), mutilates two holy men pioneering the revival of the Siva cult. He is then murdered.

1168

EUROPE

Sept. The antipope Paschal III dies; his successor Calixtus III is recognized by Frederick I as pope.

- Henry the Lion, duke of Saxony, marries Matilda, daughter of King Henry II of England.

THE AMERICAS

- The Toltec empire is destroyed by tribes (including the Aztecs) invading from N Mexico.

1169

EUROPE

8 Mar. Andrew of Suzdal sacks Kiev and becomes the most powerful Russian prince.

May Anglo-Norman adventurers established in Wales are invited into Ireland by Dermot MacMurrough to help him recover the kingdom of Leinster. They pave the way for the domination of Ireland by Henry II (see 1171).

15 Aug. Henry VI, son of Frederick I, is elected king of the Romans.

- King Casimir II of Poland invades Russia.

MIDDLE EAST AND NORTH AFRICA

Jan. Shirkuh, deputy of the Syrian atabeg Nur ad-Din, establishes control in Egypt. He dies (23 Mar.), and his nephew Salah ad-Din (Saladin) becomes vizir of Egypt.

- Kilij Arslan II, Seljuk sultan of Rum, takes Ankara in his conquest of the Danishmend Turks of E Anatolia.

1170

EUROPE

14 June The son of King Henry II of England, Henry, is crowned king of England by Roger, archbishop of York, enraging the exiled Thomas Becket.

22 July Henry II and Becket are reconciled at Fréteval, W France.

23 Nov. In Wales Owain Fawr (the Great), prince of Gwynedd, dies.

29 Dec. In England Thomas Becket is murdered in Canterbury Cathedral by knights loyal to Henry II after Henry has famously asked if no one will rid him of this 'turbulent priest'. Far from ending the problem of Church–king relations, the martyrdom of Becket will become a notorious event, and the archbishop's personality, as well as the cause for which he died, will be celebrated at his shrine in Canterbury Cathedral.

- Peter Waldo, a merchant of Lyons, starts the popular religious movement of the Poor Men of Lyons, or Waldenses.

SCIENCE AND TECHNOLOGY

Roger of Salerno, *Practica chirurgiae*, the earliest European textbook on surgery.

1171

EUROPE

16 Oct. King Henry II of England lands in Ireland (see also 1169); the Irish kings submit to him.

MIDDLE EAST AND NORTH AFRICA

Jan. The Syrian atabeg Nur a-Din seizes Mosul and Nisibin.

13 Sept. The last Fatimid caliph of Egypt (see 969), al-Adid, dies. Egypt becomes nominally subject to the caliph of Baghdad and is effectively ruled by Saladin (see 1169).

1172

ARTS AND HUMANITIES
- Palermo Cathedral, Sicily, is built.

1173

EUROPE
- In England a family feud erupts over the allocation by Henry II of territories to his sons.
- Bela III is crowned king of Hungary following the death of Stephen III in 1172.
- Vladislav II, king of Bohemia, abdicates and is succeeded by his son Frederick: civil war ensues for over 20 years.

1174

EUROPE
12 July King Henry II of England does public penance at Canterbury for the murder of archbishop Thomas Becket (see 1170).
30 Sept. Henry II makes peace with his rebellious sons, Henry, Richard, Geoffrey and John.
29 Oct. The Holy Roman Emperor Frederick I, on his fifth Italian campaign, begins the siege of Alessandria, N Italy.

MIDDLE EAST AND NORTH AFRICA
15 May The Syrian atabeg Nur ad-Din dies. Saladin, ruling in Egypt (see 1171), declares independence and seizes Damascus.
- Kilij Arslan II, Seljuk sultan of Rum, rounds off his conquest of the Danishmend Turks of E Anatolia.

ARTS AND HUMANITIES
- Monreale Cathedral, N Sicily, is built.
- In England the choir of Canterbury Cathedral is rebuilt after a fire.

1175

EUROPE
13 April The Holy Roman Emperor Frederick I abandons the siege of Alessandria, N Italy.

MIDDLE EAST AND NORTH AFRICA
May The caliph of Baghdad recognizes Saladin (see 1171) as sultan of Egypt and Syria.

ASIA
- Muhammad of Ghur begins his invasion of India.
- Genku founds the Pure Land (Jodo) sect of Buddhism in Japan.

1176

EUROPE
29 May The Lombard League defeats Holy Roman Emperor Frederick I at Legano, NW of Milan.
Oct. Emperor Frederick I makes peace with Pope Alexander III and recognizes his legitimacy as pope.

ECONOMY AND SOCIETY
- King Henry II of England, at the Assize of Northampton, establishes the rules for the administration of criminal justice.

ARTS AND HUMANITIES
- The first recorded Eisteddfod, a festival of poetry, is held in Cardigan, Wales.
- Work begins on Saladin's Citadel, Cairo.

1177

MIDDLE EAST AND NORTH AFRICA
25 Nov. King Baldwin IV of Jerusalem defeats Saladin at Montgisard.

ASIA
- Jaya Indravarman IV of Champa (S Vietnam) sacks Angkor, Cambodia (see 1150); Jayavarman VII becomes the leader of Cambodian resistance.

1178

EUROPE
30 July The Holy Roman Emperor Frederick I is crowned king of Burgundy at Arles, S France.
11 Nov. The Saxons complain formally to Frederick about the rule of Duke Henry the Lion, ruler of Saxony (see 1142).

1179

EUROPE
5–19 Mar. At the Third Lateran Council (a general council of the Church held in St John Lateran, Rome), a crusade is declared against the Cathar (Albigensian) heretics of Toulouse (see 1167).
24 June Henry the Lion, duke of Saxony, is put under the ban of the empire when he refuses to appear before Frederick to answer charges of misgovernment.
1 Nov. Philip II is crowned king of France in Reims, some months before the death of his father Louis VII (see 1180).
- Yusuf, Almohad ruler of Morocco (see 1163), tries, and fails, to take Lisbon, Portugal, by a naval expedition.

ARTS AND HUMANITIES
17 Sept. The theologian, poet and composer St Hildegarde of Bingen dies.

1180

EUROPE
13 Jan. At a diet held in Würzburg, Bavaria, Henry the Lion, duke of Saxony, is sentenced to lose his Saxon fiefs. Frederick I also deprives Henry of Bavaria (16 Sept.).
18 Sept. King Louis VII of France dies and is succeeded by his son Philip II, later known as Augustus for his achievements in increasing the power of the French monarchy.

ASIA

- Minamoto Yoritomo rebels against Japan's Taira rulers beginning the Gempei War.

SCIENCE AND TECHNOLOGY

- Europe's first windmill is recorded in St Sauvère de Vicomte, Normandy.
- The stern-post rudder is used in Europe instead of an oar for steering purposes.

ARTS AND HUMANITIES

- The Collège des Dix-Huit, the first college of the University of Paris, is established by Josce of London.
- In Normandy work begins on Lisieux Cathedral.
André le Chapelain, *De arte honeste amandi*, account of courtly love.

1181

EUROPE

- Richard and Henry, sons of King Henry II of England, dispute over territory in Aquitaine.
- Henry the Lion, duke of Saxony, submits to the Holy Roman Emperor Frederick I and is banished to England for three years. He retains only Brunswick among his former lands.
- The Pomeranian princes of Stettin become vassals of Frederick's Holy Roman Empire.
- Henry II redefines the military duties of English male subjects.
- Bourges, C France, becomes the first known example of a town's franchise being confirmed by the king of France.

ECONOMY AND SOCIETY

- By now, plea rolls, which record court proceedings, are being kept systematically in England.

ARTS AND HUMANITIES

- In Germany Worms Cathedral is built.

1182

EUROPE

Sept. Andronicus I Comnenus seizes power in Constantinople, murdering his nephew, the Byzantine emperor Alexius II Comnenus.

MIDDLE EAST AND NORTH AFRICA

Oct. Saladin, the sultan of Egypt and Syria and fighter against the crusaders, takes Edessa and Nisibin.

ARTS AND HUMANITIES

- In England Glastonbury Cathedral is rebuilt after a fire.
- Mosaics are installed in Monreale Cathedral, Sicily.

1183

EUROPE

11 June King Henry II of England's eldest son and co-ruler

Henry (see 1170), dies. The rivalry between Henry II's remaining sons intensifies.
25 June The Holy Roman Emperor Frederick I makes peace with the Lombard League (see 1159).

MIDDLE EAST AND NORTH AFRICA

18 June Saladin, the sultan of Egypt and Syria, takes Aleppo, Syria, and (24 Aug.) makes Damascus his capital.

1184

EUROPE

May Yusuf, Almohad caliph and ruler of NW Africa and Muslim Spain (see 1179), invades Portugal. However he dies (10 Sept.) and the attack is abandoned.
29 Oct. The Holy Roman Emperor Frederick I's son, Henry VI, is engaged to Constance, heiress to the kingdom of Sicily.
4 Nov. Pope Lucius III proclaims the persecution of heretics, which develops into the Inquisition (see 1231).
- Henry II of England encourages his youngest (and favourite) son John to seize Aquitaine from his brother Richard.
- Cyprus revolts against Byzantine rule.

SCIENCE AND TECHNOLOGY

- Armenian physician Mekhitur of Her writes *Consolation in Cases of Fever*, a medical guide.

1185

EUROPE

12 Sept. The Byzantine emperor Andronicus I Comnenus is killed in a riot in Constantinople. Isaac II Angelus succeeds; he defeats and expels the Normans (who have invaded Thrace) at Mosynopolis.
Sept. Henry the Lion, duke of Saxony, returns to Germany after being banished for three years.
- Peter and Ivan Asen, Bulgarian brothers who control fortresses near Turnovo, start an anti-Byzantine revolt.

ASIA

25 April At the naval battle of Danoura, the Taira government of Japan is destroyed ending the Gempei War. Minamoto Yoritomo becomes the effective ruler of all Japan. He will adopt the title *Sei-i-tai Shogun* (general) in 1192, founding the shogunate government that lasts until 1868.

ARTS AND HUMANITIES

- In England Oxford University is by now established.
Anonymous, *The Campaign of Igor*, the earliest significant work of Russian history, describing Igor of Novgorod's campaign against the Cumans in 1185.
Gerald of Wales (Giraldus Cambrensis), *Expugnatio Hibernica* (The Campaign in Ireland), an account of the conquest of Ireland by Henry II.
Marie de France, *Lanval, Lai le Freine* and *Fables*, courtly tales. Much of her work is based on Celtic material.

1186

EUROPE

27 Jan. Henry VI, son of Holy Roman Emperor Frederick I, marries Constance of Sicily. At the triple coronation in Milan, Frederick is crowned as king of Burgundy, Henry as Caesar, and Constance becomes queen of the Germans. The marriage strains relations with Pope Urban III, who encourages archbishop Philip of Cologne to rebel against Frederick; the emperor returns to Germany from Italy. Henry VI suppresses revolts in the Romagna and Campagna.

Dec. A conference of German bishops declares for Frederick I and against Pope Urban III.

– Geoffrey, son of Henry II of England, dies while jousting. As Henry favours his youngest son John as his successor, Richard allies with Philip II of France against his father and brother.

– Peter and Ivan Asen establish Bulgarian independence.

MIDDLE EAST AND NORTH AFRICA

Aug. King Baldwin V of Jerusalem dies and is succeeded by his mother, Sibylla, the wife of Guy de Lusignan, whom she crowns as king of Jerusalem.

ASIA

– Muhammad of Ghur destroys the Ghaznavid kingdom of the Punjab and takes Lahore, in modern Pakistan.

1187

EUROPE

17 Dec. Pope Gregory VIII, who has preached a Third Crusade, dies and is succeeded by Clement III (19 Dec.).

– The Byzantine emperor Isaac II Angelus recognizes Bulgarian independence. Peter Asen is crowned as Tsar Peter, though the effective ruler is Ivan.

MIDDLE EAST AND NORTH AFRICA

3 July Saladin, the sultan of Egypt and Syria, destroys the army of the kingdom of Jerusalem at the Horns of Hattin in Palestine. The king, Guy de Lusignan, is captured.

3 Oct. Saladin takes Jerusalem, which is now in Muslim hands for the first time since 1099.

ARTS AND HUMANITIES

18 Feb. Gilbert Foliot, writer and bishop of London, dies.

– Gerard of Cremona, the translator into Latin of some 100 Greek and Arab works on various topics, dies.

Svend Aggesen, *The Chronicles of the Kings of Denmark*, the first Danish history.

1188

EUROPE

Jan. Henry II of England and Philip II of France, temporarily reconciled, agree to go on crusade. They impose 'Saladin Tithes' to finance their expedition.

27 Mar. The Holy Roman Emperor Frederick I exiles Henry the Lion, duke of Saxony.

– Hamburg, N Germany, becomes an Imperial Free City.

MIDDLE EAST AND NORTH AFRICA

– Kilij Arslan II, sultan of Rum, abdicates and his kingdom is divided among his 11 sons: the succession is disputed.

ARTS AND HUMANITIES

– Work begins on Wells Cathedral, England.

– A mosque intended to be the largest in the Muslim world is built at Rabat, modern Morocco.

– Gerald of Wales (Giraldus Cambrensis), *Cambriae descriptio* (Description of Wales).

1189

EUROPE

May The Holy Roman Emperor Frederick I leaves Regensburg, Germany, on the Third Crusade.

6 July King Henry II of England dies. His son Richard I is crowned king of England (3 Sept.).

Oct. Henry the Lion (see 1188) returns to Germany and recovers much of Saxony and Holstein.

18 Nov. William II, king of Sicily, dies, and his cousin Tancred, count of Lecce, seizes the throne.

12 Dec. King Richard I leaves England on crusade.

– The Byzantine emperor Isaac II Angelus forces Stephen Nemanja to give up his conquests in Serbia.

MIDDLE EAST AND NORTH AFRICA

4 Oct. Saladin fails to relieve the siege of Acre by the crusaders.

ASIA

– The Japanese ruler Minamoto Yoritomo (see 1185) destroys the Fujiwara of Kiraizumi. His control of Japan is now complete.

1190

EUROPE

Mar. 150 Jews are murdered in York.

4 July Kings Philip II of France and Richard I of England meet at Vézelay and embark on crusade.

– The Bulgarians under Peter and Ivan Asen defeat the attempt of Isaac II Angelus, the Byzantine emperor, to reassert Byzantine imperial authority.

MIDDLE EAST AND NORTH AFRICA

18 May The Holy Roman Emperor Frederick I advances into Konya, the capital of Rum, W Turkey.

10 June Frederick is drowned in the River Saleph (now Göksu), Cilicia. His son Henry VI succeeds. The survivors of the German contingent arrive in Antioch (21 June).

– The Knights of the Cross (later known as the Teutonic Knights, a military order of German knights intended for service on crusade) are founded in Palestine.

ASIA

– Ballala II, the Hoysala king, destroys the Chalukya empire of S India.
– Reformed Buddhism is introduced into Burma from Ceylon (Sri Lanka).

SCIENCE AND TECHNOLOGY

– By now coal is being mined in Liège (modern Belgium) for use in the forging of iron.

ARTS AND HUMANITIES

– In N France the W front of Laon Cathedral popularizes the Gothic style for W façades.

1191

EUROPE

15 April In Rome Pope Celestine III crowns Henry VI as Holy Roman Emperor. Henry marches S to put down a rebellion in his wife Constance's kingdom of Naples.

Aug. The empress Constance is captured in a revolt in Salerno. Because of fever in his army, Henry has to raise the siege of Naples. He returns to Germany.

MIDDLE EAST AND NORTH AFRICA

12 July Crusaders led by King Richard I of England and King Philip II of France, capture Acre on the Palestine coast and massacre its inhabitants Jewish and Muslim alike. Philip II returns to France, leaving Richard undisputed leader of the Third Crusade.

7 Sept. King Richard I and the crusaders defeat Saladin at Arsuf, S Palestine.

ASIA

– Eisai introduces the Rinzai sect of Zen Buddhism from China into Japan.

1192

EUROPE

Sept. Civil war breaks out in Germany when Albert of Brabant, the papal candidate, is elected bishop of Liège against the wishes of Holy Roman Emperor Henry VI.

11 Dec. King Richard I of England, on the way home from the crusades (see below), is captured near Vienna by Leopold, duke of Austria. Richard's brother John claims to be king of England and builds an alliance with Philip II of France who will seize Richard's domains in Normandy.

MIDDLE EAST AND NORTH AFRICA

5 April Guy de Lusignan is deposed as king of Jerusalem, and Conrad, marquis of Montferrat, is elected in his place. Guy receives Cyprus in compensation.

28 April Conrad is murdered by the Assassins (see 1090).

5 Aug. King Richard I of England defeats Saladin outside Jaffa but is unable to mount a counter-offensive on Jerusalem. The Third Crusade ends with Saladin's Ayyubid dynasty in control of Syria, Palestine and Egypt. Richard agrees a truce with Saladin that gives Christian pilgrims access to Jerusalem.

1193

EUROPE

29 June The Holy Roman Emperor Henry VI (to whom Duke Leopold of Austria has surrendered the English king Richard I) agrees to release Richard, who becomes his vassal.

MIDDLE EAST AND NORTH AFRICA

3 Mar. Saladin, the sultan of Egypt and Syria and traditionally renowned for his knightly courtesy, dies: his empire disintegrates.

– Rashid ad-Din, ruler of the Syrian branch of the Assassins

Averroes (1126–98)

Averroes was the Latinized name of Ibn Rushd, an Arab born in Cordoba in Spain, which was then under Islamic rule. His contribution to Western culture was to popularize and comment on the writings of Aristotle and on Plato's *Republic*.

Averroes was a polymath, expert as a judge, as a philosopher and as an astronomer. He was also personal physician to the caliph. He thought that Aristotle's teaching was 'the supreme truth, because his mind was the final expression of the human mind', and his commentary on Aristotle is one of the finest produced in the Middle Ages. His aim was to purge Aristotle

of those Platonic elements that later commentators had introduced into his writings. His rigorous approach to this task disposed of many of the pseudo-religious ideas attributed to Aristotle. He was thus one of the most important Arabic preservers of classical learning, through which it became known in the West.

In his own system of belief Averroes denied both free will and personal immortality. The human intellect, he thought, was stirred into activity when brought into contact with the external active intellect that ruled the world. But at death the human intellect simply passed away into the

universal intelligence. Averroes's distinctiveness lay in the fact that he wished to be both an Aristotelian and a Muslim, a follower of Greek philosophy and of the Prophet. He also recognized the futility of subordinating either reason to faith or faith to reason. He therefore represented the direct opposite of the synthesis of faith and reason achieved later by Thomas Aquinas. Because of Averroes's materialist version of Aristotle and because he implicated the philosopher in his own views, Aristotle's teaching became controversial, and the University of Paris tried to ban it, until a Christian synthesis redeemed Aristotle's reputation.

(see 1090), dies. The Alamut branch recovers control of the whole order.

1194

EUROPE

3 Feb. King Richard I starts to build up an anti-French coalition in the Rhineland and Low Countries after learning of a revolt against his rule in England led by his brother John and supported by King Philip II of France (see 1192).

12 Mar. Richard I returns to England and (28 Mar.) captures Nottingham Castle, ending his brother John's revolt.

17 April Richard is re-crowned king of England. He leaves England for the last time (12 May). He routs the French at Fréteval (3 July) and reclaims most of his lost French territory.

20 Nov. Holy Roman Emperor Henry VI, who has already conquered S Italy, takes Palermo and gains control of all of Sicily. He is crowned king of Naples and Sicily (25 Dec.).

ECONOMY AND SOCIETY

– In England Hubert Walter, Richard I's vice-regent in his absence, institutes the office of coroner to keep records of crown pleas. He also makes an enquiry into land tenure.

ARTS AND HUMANITIES

10 June Chartres Cathedral is burned; its rebuilding inaugurates the high Gothic style of architecture.

1195

EUROPE

2 April Holy Roman Emperor Henry VI proclaims a crusade at Bari.

8 April Isaac II Angelus, Byzantine emperor, is deposed (and blinded) by his elder brother, who becomes Alexius III Angelus (see 1203).

6 Aug. Henry the Lion, duke of Saxony, dies.

ECONOMY AND SOCIETY

15 July Date of the earliest 'final concord', a triplicate record of English land transfer with the measure of the 'foot' filed in the royal treasury.

1196

EUROPE

April The Holy Roman Emperor Henry VI proposes that the office of Holy Roman Emperor becomes hereditary rather than elective. Pope Celestine III rejects this idea (17 Nov.).

25 Dec. Henry's son Frederick II is elected king of the Romans.

– Stephen Nemanja (see 1189) abdicates after founding a Serbian state independent of Constantinople.

– Ivan Asen I of Bulgaria (see 1186) dies.

ASIA

– Choe Chong-hon, a Korean general, massacres his rivals and restores Korean unity.

ARTS AND HUMANITIES

– Ephraim of Bonn writes an account of the persecution of the Jews in Germany, France and England.

1197

EUROPE

28 Sept. Henry VI, Holy Roman Emperor, dies: civil war breaks out between Henry's brother, Philip of Swabia, and Otto IV, son of Henry the Lion, duke of Saxony.

– Peter Asen of Bulgaria dies and is succeeded by another brother, Kaloyan.

ECONOMY AND SOCIETY

– Common weights and measures are established in England.

ARTS AND HUMANITIES

– King Richard I of England builds Château Gaillard, a state-of-the-art castle on the banks of the River Seine, protecting Normandy from French invasion.

1198

EUROPE

8 Jan. Pope Celestine III dies and is succeeded by Innocent III, who proclaims the Fourth Crusade to recover Jerusalem.

17 May Frederick, infant son of Holy Roman Emperor Henry VI, is crowned king of Sicily.

ARTS AND HUMANITIES

12 Dec. Averroes (Ibn Rushd) (see p. 130) of Cordoba, philosopher and author of commentaries on Aristotle, dies.

1199

EUROPE

6 April Richard I (the Lionheart), king of England, is killed while besieging the Castle of Chalus in France. He has spent most of his life on military campaigns outside England. Having died childless, he is succeeded by his younger brother John (27 May).

– To fund the Fourth Crusade Pope Innocent III imposes the first direct papal taxation of the clergy.

MIDDLE EAST AND NORTH AFRICA

– The Almohad caliph, Abu Yusuf Ya'qub al-Mansur, dies and is succeeded by his son, Muhammad al-Nasir.

ASIA

– Minamoto Yoritomo, first shogun of Japan (see 1185), dies.

ARTS AND HUMANITIES

– The Qutb Minar Mosque is built in Old Delhi, India.

1200

EUROPE

22 May By the treaty of Le Goulet, King Philip II of France recognizes King John of England as the late Richard I's heir in his French possessions. John cedes Evreux and the Vexin (in Normandy) to Philip.

– Llwelyn, prince of Gwynedd, seizes Anglesey, N Wales.

– The lay orders of the Beguines and the Beghards are founded in Liège, modern Belgium. Beguines are a lay sisterhood whose members do holy work but take no vows and may leave and marry. The Beghards are a similar order for men.

THE AMERICAS

– Around this date the Inca state is founded by Manco Capac in the Cuzco valley, Peru.

ARTS AND HUMANITIES

– Rouen Cathedral in Normandy burns down and is rebuilt.

– In France work begins on Bourges and Soissons cathedrals and the towers of Notre Dame.

– Zhuze (Chu His), whose system of Neo-Confucian orthodoxy (Zhuzeism) systematized Confucianism, dies.

Anonymous, *Carmina Burana*, miscellany (in Latin) of love songs, drinking songs and religious verse.

Anonymous, *Njala, Laxdal, Eyrbyggja, Egla* and *Grettla*, Icelandic sagas.

Beroul, *Tristan*, French version of Arthurian legend.

Anonymous, *Das Nibelungenlied*, Old High German epic.

Layamon, *Brut*, a history of England from Brutus to Cadwalader, the first poem written in Middle English.

Walter Map, *De nugis curialium*, satirical collection. Map has travelled to Paris and Rome and has become archdeacon of Oxford (1197).

1201

EUROPE

April Venice agrees to transport the Fourth Crusade to the Middle East in return for half of all its conquests.

– Bishop Albert of Riga establishes the city, which is on the Baltic coast of Latvia, as a base for trade and for the Christian conversion of the Livs in Latvia.

– King John grants a charter to the English Jews.

1202

EUROPE

30 April King Philip II of France declares King John of England's English lands forfeit when John fails to appear in court to answer charges from the barons of Poitou, W France.

15 Nov. The crusaders take Zara (in modern Croatia) from the king of Hungary and transfer it to Venetian control. The crusaders agree to help the deposed Byzantine emperor Isaac II Angelus (see 1195), an ally of Venice, to recapture his throne.

ARTS AND HUMANITIES

30 Mar. Joachim of Fiore, mystic writer and author of *The Everlasting Gospel*, dies.

Jean Bodel, *Congé*, verse adieu to friends.

1203

EUROPE

April King John of England's French vassals desert him, allowing King Philip II of France to overrun the Loire valley.

17 July The crusaders enter Constantinople; the Byzantine emperor Alexius III Angelus flees (see 1195), and the crusaders restore Isaac II Angelus, whose son Alexius rules as regent.

1 Aug. The crusaders enforce the coronation of Alexius IV Angelus as Byzantine emperor.

ASIA

– Jayavarman VII of Cambodia conquers Champa (S Vietnam).

ARTS AND HUMANITIES

– In Italy Siena University is founded.

1204

EUROPE

Jan. Chaos in Constantinople. Anti-crusader rioters proclaim a nobleman, Nicholas Canabus, emperor. The restored Byzantine emperor, Isaac II Angelus, is murdered. Canabus is imprisoned and Isaac's son and regent Alexius IV Angelus himself is then murdered (8 Feb.). Alexius V Ducas Murtzuphlus becomes emperor.

1 April Eleanor of Aquitaine dies. She is the widow of Louis VII of France and of Henry II of England, and the mother of Richard I (the Lionheart) and of John of England.

12 April The crusaders sack Constantinople for three days; the Byzantine emperor Alexius V flees.

16 May Baldwin, count of Flanders, is crowned Latin emperor of Constantinople. In Oct. Baldwin and Venice partition the Byzantine empire. Venice gains the Adriatic coast, Rhodes and the Aegean islands. Other crusaders hold their territorial gains as fiefs of Baldwin. The Fourth Crusade, diverted from its aims by Venetian and Byzantine intrigue, comes to an end without achieving the goals of Innocent III (see 1198).

24 June Philip II captures Rouen to complete the conquest of Normandy from the Plantagenets.

8 Nov. Kaloyan is crowned king of Bulgaria by a papal legate after he agrees to accept the authority of the Catholic Church.

– King Imre of Hungary dies and is succeeded by his son Ladislas III.

– Pope Innocent III grants a charter to the Swordbrothers, a military order of Knights of Christ, which were founded by Bishop Albert of Riga (see 1201) in 1200 to further the conversion of the Livs.

MIDDLE EAST AND NORTH AFRICA

May Alexius Comnenus, grandson of Andronicus I, seizes Trebizond on the Turkish Black Sea coast and establishes a new and independent Byzantine empire there, becoming known as Grand Comnenus. The Greek state centred on Trebizond will last until 1461.

ARTS AND HUMANITIES

13 Dec. Moses ben Maimon, author of *The Guide to the Perplexed*, dies.

1205

EUROPE

Feb. King Kalojan of Bulgaria attacks Adrianople in the Latin empire of Constantinople.

Mar. The English barons refuse to fight for King John in France.

14 April Kaloyan defeats and captures the Latin emperor Baldwin I outside Constantinople.

1 June Enrico Dandolo, doge of Venice, dies and is succeeded by Pietro Ziano.

– Dominic, a Spanish friar, is sent on a mission by Pope Innocent III to correct the heretic Cathars (Albigensians) of Toulouse.

1206

EUROPE

20 Aug. Henry of Flanders is crowned Latin emperor of Constantinople after the death of his brother Baldwin I in captivity in Bulgaria.

Dec. The monks of Canterbury, persuaded by Pope Innocent III, elect his friend and fellow student in Paris, Stephen Langton, as archbishop of Canterbury. This does not please King John.

ASIA

15 Mar. Sultan Muhammad of Ghur is murdered and succeeded by Qutb ud-Din Aybak, his deputy in India, who founds the dynasty of Slave Kings of Delhi.

– The Mongol empire is established: the Mongol prince Temujin, who has united Mongolia, takes the title of Genghis Khan and is recognized as khan in an assembly of Mongols. He proclaims the *Great Yasa*, or code of laws, for all Mongols.

ARTS AND HUMANITIES

– In Japan Fujiwara Nagatsune writes the earliest known work on landscape gardening.

1207

ASIA

– The Japanese government persecutes the Pure Land sect of Buddhism.

1208

EUROPE

17 Nov. Pope Innocent III asks the nobles of N France to take military action (the so-called 'Albigensian Crusade') against the Cathars (Albigensians) in S France.

– In Wales Llywelyn, prince of Gwynedd, occupies Powys.

MIDDLE EAST AND NORTH AFRICA

– The Almohad caliph al-Nasir (see 1199) captures the last Almoravid possessions in N Africa.

ARTS AND HUMANITIES

Saxo Grammaticus, *Gesta Danorum*, a history of early Danish kings and the source for Shakespeare's *Hamlet* (Amleth).

1209

EUROPE

22 July In S France the town of Béziers is sacked and its inhabitants massacred by the anti-Cathar crusaders under Simon de Montfort the Elder (see 1208). They go on to take Carcassonne (15 Aug.).

4 Oct. Pope Innocent III crowns Otto IV Holy Roman Emperor.

Oct. The Welsh princes accept the overlordship of King John.

MIDDLE EAST AND NORTH AFRICA

– Thamar, queen of Georgia, fights the Turks and seizes Kars, NE Turkey.

ARTS AND HUMANITIES

– In England an exodus of scholars from Oxford leads to the foundation of Cambridge University.

1210

EUROPE

Nov. The Holy Roman Emperor Otto IV (see 1197) is excommunicated by Pope Innocent III after he occupies Apulia in S Italy. Otto's German subjects are thereby freed of allegiance to him: a German civil war breaks out.

– Valdemar of Denmark conquers Danzig (Gdansk), on the Baltic coast, and E Pomerania from the Slavonic Wends.

– Pope Innocent III allows the formation of the mendicant order of St Francis (see p. 137), dedicated to the care of the poor. The brotherhood of Franciscans repudiate all wealth.

ASIA

– Qutb ud-Din, sultan of Delhi (see 1206), dies and his territories are wracked by Hindu rebellions.

– The earliest Burmese legal codes are compiled.

ARTS AND HUMANITIES

Gottfried von Strassburg, *Tristan und Isolde*, German narrative poem.

1211

EUROPE

Sept. Rebellious German princes offer the crown to Frederick, king of Sicily (see 1198). He becomes Frederick II.

– King John of England campaigns in Wales against Llywelyn, prince of Gwynedd.

ASIA

– The Mongol emperor Genghis Khan (see 1206) conquers the Kara-Khitai empire in E Turkestan and invades China.

– Iltutmish, Qutb ud-Din's son-in-law, becomes sultan of Delhi and quells the Hindu rebellions.

1212

EUROPE

16 July Alfonso VIII of Castile and Sancho VII of Navarre crush the Almohads at Las Navas de Tolosa. This marks a decisive stage of the Reconquista, the recapture of Spain from the Moors by the Spanish Christian kingdoms.

26 Sept. Frederick II (see 1211) confirms Bohemia's status as an independent fief within the empire.

9 Dec. Frederick II is crowned king of the Romans.

– Thamar, queen of Georgia, dies and is succeeded by her son, George IV.

– The Venetians occupy Crete.

– The Children's Crusade is destroyed when the party of several thousand children from France, the Low Countries and Germany is wrecked off the coast of Sardinia and the survivors are captured by Arabs.

ARTS AND HUMANITIES

Wolfram von Eschenbach, *Parzival*, German Arthurian romance.

1213

EUROPE

13 May King John of England submits to Pope Innocent III, accepts Stephen Langton as archbishop of Canterbury and receives England as a papal fief. He agrees to pay tribute.

3 June John agrees to a truce with Llywelyn, king of Gwynedd.

12 July Frederick II, king of the Romans, recognizes the papacy's Italian possessions and renounces his attempt to assert control over the papacy in Germany.

12 Sept. Simon de Montfort the Elder's forces (see 1209) defeat Raymond of Toulouse, in whose lands in S France de Montfort is conducting a vigorous military campaign against the Cathar (Albigensian) heretics.

15 Nov. Knights representing the English shires are summoned by King John to a council held in Oxford.

ARTS AND HUMANITIES

– French nobleman and historian Geoffroi de Villehardouin, author of *On the Conquest of Constantinople*, dies. Geoffroi was one of the leaders of the Fourth Crusade (see 1204).

1214

EUROPE

27 July King Philip II of France decisively defeats King John's anti-Capetian alliance, including Emperor Otto IV (see 1210), at Bouvines. The battle strengthens the position of the king of the Romans, Frederick II (see 1211), against the emperor.

18 Sept. John makes a truce with Philip II at Chinon and acknowledges Capetian (French) territorial gains at the expense of the Angevin empire.

Oct. In Spain civil war breaks out in Castile after the death of Alfonso VIII.

– In Germany Frederick II grants the Palatinate of the Rhine to the Wittelsbach family.

MIDDLE EAST AND NORTH AFRICA

– Ala ad-Din Muhammad conquers most of Persia and Transoxiana.

ARTS AND HUMANITIES

– In England a constitution is drawn up to govern Oxford University.

1215

EUROPE

8 Jan. Simon de Montfort the Elder (see 1213) is elected lord of Languedoc in a council at Montpellier, S France, after his campaign against the Cathar (Albigensian) heretics.

17 May English barons in rebellion against King John occupy London.

19 June At Runnymede on the Thames in S England peace terms are agreed between King John and the barons in Magna Carta (published 24 June), which limits the king's powers. Magna Carta is, in effect, the first written constitution in European history and comes to be regarded as a fundamental statement of English liberties. The court of Common Pleas is established in Westminster.

25 July Frederick II is recrowned king of the Germans.

Sept. By a papal bull Innocent III annuls Magna Carta.

13 Oct. Civil war resumes in England.

11– 30 Nov. The Fourth Lateran Council (a general council of the Church held in St John Lateran, Rome) ends the Albigensian Crusade (see 1208) and approves the papal proposal for a Fifth Crusade in Palestine. Simon de Montfort is granted the county of Toulouse. The council enacts reform of dioceses, imposes the first papal tithe on the clergy and orders that Jews should wear distinctive clothes.

– The Polish Church in synod accepts clerical celibacy.

ASIA

– Genghis Khan (see 1206) takes Beijing. The Jin (Chin) dynasty retreats to Kaifeng as its capital.

SCIENCE AND TECHNOLOGY

– St Thomas's Hospital is founded in London.

1216

EUROPE

1 June Henry of Flanders, Latin emperor of Constantinople (see 1206), dies and is succeeded by Peter de Courtenay.

16 July Pope Innocent III dies and is succeeded (18 July) by Honorius III.

19 Oct. King John of England dies after losing his baggage train while crossing the Wash, E England. His infant son, Henry III, is crowned at Gloucester (28 Oct.).

12 Nov. King Henry's council reconfirms Magna Carta.

22 Dec. Honorius III recognizes the Dominicans (St Dominic's Order of Friars Preacher).
- King Ottokar I establishes primogeniture in Bohemia by crowning his son, Wenceslas, as king.
- Innocent III authorizes the foundation of the St Claire's Order of Poor Ladies (the Poor Claires) a sister-order of the Franciscans, founded by St Francis of Assisi (see 1210).

1217

EUROPE

23 Aug. The French fleet in support of Louis, King Philip II's son who is campaigning for King John of England's opponents, is destroyed by an English fleet off Sandwich. By the treaty of Kingston (12 Sept.) the English rebels accept Henry III's rule and Louis leaves.
25 Sept. Afonso II, king of Portugal, defeats the Muslims at Alcazar do Sol.
- Bishop Albert of Riga (see 1210) defeats the Estonians.
- Theodore Ducas, despot (Byzantine local ruler) of Epirus, captures the Latin emperor of Constantinople, Peter de Courtenay (see 1216); Peter's wife, Yolande, becomes regent in Constantinople.
- The Franciscans (see 1210) formulate a constitution to run their order.

MIDDLE EAST AND NORTH AFRICA

Nov. The Fifth Crusade (see 1215) leaves Europe for Egypt, led by King Andrew II of Hungary; Beisan in Palestine is sacked.

ARTS AND HUMANITIES

- English scholar Alexander Neckam writes *De naturis rerum* (On the Nature of Things), a scientific encyclopedia.

1218

EUROPE

Mar. King Henry III of England and King Llywelyn of Gwynedd agree peace terms.
19 May The Holy Roman Emperor Otto IV dies.
25 June Simon de Montfort the Elder is killed at the siege of Toulouse (see 1215), where Raymond VI has been restored as count after a popular rebellion.
- Pope Honorius III announces a new crusade against the Cathars (Albigensians) in S France.
- Ivan Asen II becomes king of Bulgaria; he will add Epirus, as well as parts of Albania and Macedonia, to his realm.

MIDDLE EAST AND NORTH AFRICA

May The Fifth Crusade arrives in Egypt and lays seige to the city of Damietta in the Nile Delta.

ASIA

- Jayavarman VII of Cambodia rebuilds the city of Angkor Thom, including the Temple of Bayon.

1219

MIDDLE EAST AND NORTH AFRICA

Nov. Damietta falls to the Fifth Crusade. The crusaders decide to advance on Cairo.

ASIA

- The Mongol emperor Genghis Khan invades the Khwarazm empire, which extends over Persia and Transoxiana, in C Asia.
- In the Shokyu War in Japan the retired emperor, Toba II, is defeated in his attempt to recover his throne. Hojo Yoshitoki becomes regent of the shogunate and effective ruler. The Yoritomo family loses all influence.

1220

EUROPE

26 April Frederick II gives rights of independence to the German bishops in an attempt to secure the election of his son Henry as king of the Romans.
17 May King Henry III of England is crowned at Westminster Abbey.
22 Nov. Pope Honorius III crowns Frederick II Holy Roman Emperor (see 1211).
- The first constitution of the Dominican order rejects ownership of property.

MIDDLE EAST AND NORTH AFRICA

Aug. In Egypt crusaders under Cardinal Pelagius are trapped by the Nile flood and cannot escape from the armies of the sultan al-Kamil. They begin to return to Europe (Sept.).

ASIA

Dec. Ala ad-Din Muhammad (see 1214) dies fleeing from Genghis Khan, who is conquering Transoxiana.
- The Khmers of Cambodia withdraw from Champa (S Vietnam).

SCIENCE AND TECHNOLOGY

- In France the medical school of Montpellier University is established.

ARTS AND HUMANITIES

- In Spain the University of Salamanca is founded.
- Notre Dame Cathedral, Paris, is completed.
- Work begins on the cathedrals of Salisbury (England) and Amiens (France).
- The Mongols destroy Ray, the centre of the Persian ceramic industry.

Jien, *Jottings of a Fool*, first critical work of Japanese historiography.

1221

EUROPE

6 Aug. St Dominic dies (see 1205). A priest of the Spanish diocese of Osma, Dominic founded the order of Friars

Preacher, which also became known as the Dominicans and whose members were specifically entrusted with the task of preaching Christian doctrine. Living a life that was both contemplative and active, Dominicans became vigorous and influential upholders of Christian orthodoxy.

Aug. The first Dominican friars arrive in England.

MIDDLE EAST AND NORTH AFRICA

Feb. George IV of Georgia is defeated by a Mongol army near Tiflis (Tbilisi).

Aug. In Egypt Cardinal Pelagius is forced to sue for peace and withdraw. In Sept. the sultan al-Kamil enters Damietta, and the Fifth Crusade ends in ignominy.

ASIA

Nov. Genghis Khan defeats Jajal ad-Din and his army in Afghanistan. Samarkand is sacked.

THE AMERICAS

– Hunac Ceel of the Maya Cocom dynasty expels the Toltec rulers of Chichén Itzá (see 987).

ARTS AND HUMANITIES

– In Spain the choir of Burgos Cathedral is built.

1222

EUROPE

– King Andrew II of Hungary grants a Golden Bull, which limits royal power and maintains the power of the nobles.

– King Ottokar I of Bohemia gives his nobles the right to sole jurisdiction over their tenants.

ASIA

31 May A Mongol army overruns the Russians and Cumans on the Kalka, near the sea of Azov.

– Genghis Khan seizes Herat and conquers Afghanistan.

ARTS AND HUMANITIES

– In Italy Padua University is established.

– Snorri Sturluson, *The Edda*, collection of Icelandic myths drawing on pagan poems. Snorri will be assassinated (1241) because of political activity against Haakon IV Haakonsson, king of Norway.

1223

EUROPE

14 July King Philip II of France dies, having greatly enlarged the Capetian domains. His son Louis VIII (the Lion) is crowned his successor (Aug.).

– George IV of Georgia dies and is succeeded by his sister Rusadan.

MIDDLE EAST AND NORTH AFRICA

– The Franciscan order is granted the privilege of guarding the Holy Sepulchre, Jerusalem.

ARTS AND HUMANITIES

– Vincent Kadlubeck, the first Polish historian, dies.

1224

EUROPE

Feb. Amauri de Montfort yields the county of Toulouse to King Louis VIII of France.

5 May Louis VIII of France declares war on King Henry III of England and seizes Poitou and N Gascony.

10 Sept. Franciscan friars arrive in England.

– Bishop Albert of Riga takes Yuriev from the Russians and Estonians.

MIDDLE EAST AND NORTH AFRICA

– The Almohad caliph Yusuf II dies: the Almohad empire in Morocco and Spain disintegrates further (see 1212).

ARTS AND HUMANITIES

5 June The Holy Roman Emperor Frederick II founds the University of Naples, S Italy.

1225

EUROPE

7 Nov. Archbishop Engelbert of Cologne, deputy in Germany of Holy Roman Emperor Frederick II, is murdered.

9 Nov. Frederick II marries Queen Yolande, heiress to the kingdom of Jerusalem, and so adds the Crusader States to his dominions. He has vowed to embark on crusade in Aug. 1227.

– King Henry III of England reaffirms Magna Carta.

MIDDLE EAST AND NORTH AFRICA

– Jalal ad-Din defeats the Mongols and liberates Persia. He also defeats the Georgians at Garnhi and then sacks Tiflis (Tbilisi).

ASIA

– Tran Thai-tong becomes emperor of Dai Viet (Vietnam) and founds the Tran dynasty, which will last until 1400.

SCIENCE AND TECHNOLOGY

– Qaisar ibn Abi al-Qasim makes a celestial globe.

ARTS AND HUMANITIES

– Work begins on Geneva Cathedral (Switzerland) and Beverley Minster (England).

– St Francis of Assisi (see p. 137), *The Canticle of Brother Sun*, religious writings. The work reveals Francis's highly original theology of nature and shows how for him the whole of the created order, and not just humankind, unfolds the power and love of the Christian God.

Graindor de Douay, *Chanson d'Antioche* and *Conquête de Jerusalem*, narrative poems inspired by the crusades.

Snorri Sturluson, *Heimskringla*, history of Norse and Icelandic kingship.

Daniil Zatochnik, *The Petition*, the earliest Russian satirical work.

St Francis of Assisi (1182–1226)

St Francis of Assisi, founder of the Franciscan order, was one of the great Christian reformers of the medieval world. He was born Giovanni Bernadone, the son of a rich merchant in the central Italian town of Assisi, and as a young man he led a luxurious and dissolute life. In 1206 he was converted to a new understanding of Christianity. He decided to follow a literal interpretation of the Gospels, to abandon all possessions and to become a beggar in order to follow Christ. His example became an inspiration, and from 1209 converts started to gather around him. He expected his followers to imitate Christ's example of engagement with the world rather than monastic withdrawal, leading to the development of a new kind of religious figure, the friar. Francis's rejection of property was extreme: he refused to allow his followers even to handle coins. The Franciscan order that grew out of this group transformed the religious life of medieval Europe, while its understanding of practical charity lives on in campaigns both religious and secular. In Assisi Francis ministered to the needs of the lepers, the social outcasts, showing that Christianity was a life lived, not just a set of doctrines.

Francis left behind another legacy. Orthodox Christian belief, before Francis, had been unanimous in its emphasis on mankind's dominion over nature. But Francis's emphasis on the sanctity of God's creation led to a far higher estimation of the worth of animal life.

1226

EUROPE

30 Jan. King Louis VIII of France leads a crusade against Count Raymond VII of Toulouse and the Cathars (Albigensians). He forces Languedoc into submission.

6 Mar. A second Lombard League of N Italian cities is formed against the Holy Roman Emperor Frederick II.

3 Oct. St Francis of Assisi dies (see box).

8 Nov. Louis VIII of France dies. His son Louis IX (St Louis) is crowned, but his mother, Blanche of Castile, will act as regent.

– Duke Conrad of Masovia grants Chelmno in Poland to the Order of the Teutonic Knights as an offensive base for the conversion and conquest of the Prussians.

ASIA

– Genghis Khan destroys the Xixia (Hsi Hsia) kingdom in N China.

1227

EUROPE

18 Mar. Pope Honorius III dies and is succeeded (19 Mar.) by Gregory IX.

22 July The German count of Schwerin defeats Valdemar of Denmark at Bornhoved.

15 Sept. The Almohad ruler Idris becomes Muslim ruler of Spain.

24 Sept. An epidemic at Brindisi, S Italy, delays the embarkation of the Sixth Crusade. Pope Gregory IX excommunicates the Holy Roman Emperor Frederick II as a result (see 1225).

– Bishop Albert of Riga defeats the Osilians, who are then converted to Christianity.

MIDDLE EAST AND NORTH AFRICA

11 Nov. Al-Mu 'azzam, sultan of Damascus, dies and al-Kamil, sultan of Egypt, seizes Jerusalem.

ASIA

25 Aug. Genghis Khan dies; his empire is divided between his sons into E Asia, Turkestan, Mongolia and Kazakhstan (including European Russia). They agree to cooperate with each other, and Ogodai is chosen as the senior ruler.

– Dogen introduces the Soto sect of Zen Buddhism into Japan.

ARTS AND HUMANITIES

– In Spain work begins on Toledo Cathedral.

1228

EUROPE

28 June Holy Roman Emperor Frederick II embarks on crusade, but Pope Gregory IX upholds his excommunication (see 1227).

9 July Stephen Langton, archbishop of Canterbury, dies. Langton was one of the signatories of Magna Carta (see 1215).

– Robert de Courtenay, emperor of Constantinople, dies and is succeeded by his son Baldwin II.

1229

EUROPE

11 April The Albigensian Crusade ends with the treaty of Paris; Raymond VII of Toulouse submits to King Louis IX of France.

– Bishop Albert of Riga dies.

MIDDLE EAST AND NORTH AFRICA

18 Feb. The Sixth Crusade ends: the Holy Roman Emperor Frederick II makes peace with the sultan of Egypt, al-Kamil, and Jerusalem is partitioned between Christians and Muslims. Frederick has himself crowned king of Jerusalem (17 Mar.)

– Al-Ashraf takes Damascus and acknowledges the supremacy of his brother al-Kamil (sultan of Egypt). The Ayyubid empire formerly ruled by Saladin is now reunited.

ASIA

8 Feb. The caliph of Baghdad recognizes the conqueror of the Indian Muslim states, Iltutmish (see 1211), as sultan of India.

– The Shan tribe of Ahom (SE Asia) founds the kingdom of Assam (N Vietnam).

ARTS AND HUMANITIES

– In France Toulouse University is founded.

Guido Fava of Bologna, *La Gemma Purpurea* (The Purple Jewel), an early example of Italian prose narrative.

1230

EUROPE

April By defeating Theodore Ducas of Epirus (see 1217), Ivan Asen II, king of Bulgaria, adds territories on the Danube, on the Adriatic and in Thessaly to the Bulgarian empire.

23 July The Holy Roman Emperor Frederick II, newly returned from the Sixth Crusade, makes temporary peace with the pope at San Germano, and renounces his claims to the Papal States.

– Muhmmad ibn Yusuf seizes Granada, S Spain, and establishes the Nasrid dynasty.

– Wenceslas I succeeds his father Ottokar I as king of Bohemia.

– The Teutonic Knights advance in their conquest of Prussia.

ASIA

– Sukhodaya becomes the first Siamese (Thai) state to separate from Cambodia.

SCIENCE AND TECHNOLOGY

– Iron production spreads in Westphalia and Swabia (both in Germany) and in Hungary.

– Qia Sidao (Chia Ssu-tao) writes *Cu zhi jing* (*T'su chih ching*), a treatise on crickets, cultivated by the Chinese for their chirping.

ARTS AND HUMANITIES

– In Italy work begins on Siena Cathedral.

1231

EUROPE

Feb. Pope Gregory IX establishes the Papal Inquisition for the detection and punishment of heretics (see 1184).

May Henry, king of the Romans, grants territorial sovereignty to the German princes and (26 May) takes the Swiss canton of Uri from the Habsburgs, gaining access to the St Gothard Pass.

Dec. King Henry III of England ends his Welsh campaign and makes peace with Prince Llywelyn of Gwynedd.

– In England Simon de Montfort the Younger, earl of Leicester (son of Simon de Montfort, who led the Albigensian Crusade, see 1209), is by now a favourite at the court of Henry III.

MIDDLE EAST AND NORTH AFRICA

15 Aug. Jalal ad-Din (see 1225) is murdered by the Mongol forces who control Persia.

ASIA

– The Mongols prepare to invade Korea.

ECONOMY AND SOCIETY

– The Holy Roman Emperor Frederick II produces a code book based on Roman law for the kingdom of Sicily. He also introduces W Europe's first gold coinage (the *augustales*) and prescribes that medical doctors be examined by the University of Salerno (Italy). Frederick's variety of scientific, literary and philosophical interests will reflect the milieu of his court in Sicily, at the heart of Mediterranean intercultural influences.

– Pope Gregory IX's bull *Parens scientiarum* exempts the University of Paris from control by the cathedral.

ARTS AND HUMANITIES

– St Denis, Paris, is the first building with windows in a triforium.

1232

EUROPE

29 July King Henry III of England dismisses his justiciar (chief justice minister) and regent Hubert de Burgh and replaces him with the Frenchmen Peter des Roches and Peter des Rievaux, thereby irritating his barons.

– Ivan Asen II, king of Bulgaria, breaks off relations with the papacy.

ARTS AND HUMANITIES

– The Musansirhya Mosque is built in Baghdad, Iraq.

– Samuel ben Tibbon, who translated the works of Maimonides from Arabic to Hebrew, dies.

1233

EUROPE

30 July Conrad of Marburg, a priest leading an attack on religious dissidents in Germany, is murdered.

Aug. Richard, earl of Pembroke, allies with Prince Llywelyn of Gwynedd to rebel against Henry III.

1234

EUROPE

7 April Sancho VII, the last Spanish king of Navarre, dies.

– Pope Gregory IX proclaims war on the city of Rome after a local revolt forces him into exile.

– In England the barons force the expulsion of Peter des Roches and Peter des Rievaux (see 1232).

– In France Louis IX attains his majority (see 1226).

ASIA

– The Mongols destroy the Jin (Chin) dynasty of N China and seize their capital at Kaifeng.

ARTS AND HUMANITIES

– The University of Baghdad, Iraq, is founded.

1235

EUROPE

15 July Frederick II marries his third wife Isabella, sister of Henry III of England.

July In a diet (princely convention) at Worms, Germany, Henry is deposed as king of the Romans after a revolt against his father, the Holy Roman Emperor Frederick II.

– James of Aragon, Spain, completes his conquest from the Moors of the Balearic islands in the W Mediterranean.

– Robert le Bougre is appointed Inquisitor for France.

– The Bohemian king Wenceslas I grants administrative privileges to the town of Prague.

1236

EUROPE

14 Jan. Henry III marries Eleanor of Provence.

Jan. In England the statute of Merton is enacted at Merton Abbey in Surrey. Stating the causes of baronial oppostion to the king, it is the earliest statute on record in England.

29 June Ferdinand III of Castile and Leon (N Spain) takes Muslim Cordoba.

July At a diet (princely convention) in Piacenza, Italy, the Holy Roman Emperor Frederick II proclaims his wish to recover all Italy for the Empire. Pope Gregory IX responds by claiming, on the basis of the Donation of Constantine (a counterfeit 8th-century document claiming to record the emperor Constantine's granting of temporal authority to the pope) that the papacy has supreme temporal power.

Nov. The Holy Roman Emperor Frederick II burns Vicenza, NE Italy, before returning to Germany.

– The Teutonic Knights conquer W Prussia and defeat the Pomeranians.

– A Mongol army under Batu, grandson of Genghis Khan, defeats the Bulgars of the Volga. Mongol forces also take Georgia.

1237

EUROPE

Feb. Conrad, son of the Holy Roman Emperor Frederick II, is elected king of the Romans.

25 Sept. The treaty of York fixes the Anglo-Scottish border. Alexander II of Scotland renounces Scottish claims to Northumberland, Westmorland and Cumberland, N England.

27 Nov. Holy Roman Emperor Frederick II defeats the Lombard League at Cortenuova, but resistance continues in N Italy.

21 Dec. The Mongol army led by Batu (see 1236) destroys the principality of Riazan, Russia.

– Frederick II grants Vienna, Austria, the status of an imperial city.

– The Swordbrothers of Livonia (see 1204) are now allied to the Teutonic Knights.

SCIENCE AND TECHNOLOGY

– Chinese physician Chen Zuming (Ch'en Tsu-ming) writes *Furen dachuan liangfang* (*Fu-jen ta-ch'uan liang-fang*), a treatise on women's diseases.

ARTS AND HUMANITIES

4 Dec. The historian and Benedictine monk Roger of Wendover dies. His chronicle from the creation to 1235 is later extended by Matthew Paris.

Anonymous, the *Sachsische Weltchronik*, Old High German world history.

Guillaume de Lorris, *Le Roman de la Rose*, an influential French allegorical poem about sexual love.

1238

EUROPE

7 Jan. In England Simon de Montfort (see 1231) marries Eleanor Plantagenet, sister of Henry III.

8 Feb. Mongol leader Batu seizes Vladimir (in W Russia) and destroys Moscow. He defeats the princes of N Russia (4 Mar.); Yuri, prince of Vladimir, is killed. But, after failing to take Novgorod, Batu retreats to his base in the Don basin.

– Henry I, king of Poland, dies and is succeeded by his son, Henry II.

– The order of the Carmelite Friars spreads from Palestine to Sicily and S France.

MIDDLE EAST AND NORTH AFRICA

8 Mar. Al-Kamil, sultan of Egypt and Damascus, dies: civil war in the Ayyubid dynasty follows.

1239

EUROPE

20 Mar. Pope Gregory IX renews the excommunication of the Holy Roman Emperor Frederick II. Frederick invades the Romagna and Tuscany (June).

17–18 June The future English king Edward I is born.

– The Russian prince Jaroslav pays tribute to the Golden Horde (the Mongol force in Russia).

– King Bela IV of Hungary allows the Cumans (see 1061), pagan nomads fleeing the Mongols, to settle between the rivers Danube and Theiss.

– The king of France, Louis IX, holds a *parlement*, or court of law, for the first recorded time.

MIDDLE EAST AND NORTH AFRICA

1 Sept. A crusader force arrives in Acre but the Egyptians defeat them at Gaza (13 Nov.).

7 Dec. An-Nasir of Kerak destroys Jerusalem's fortifications and expels the garrison

ARTS AND HUMANITIES

– In England the central tower of Lincoln Cathedral collapses.

1240

EUROPE

22 Feb. The Holy Roman Emperor Frederick II reaches Rome but then withdraws to Sicily in the face of Roman resistance. Pope Gregory IX urges German resistance to Frederick but is largely ignored.

11 April In Wales Llywelyn ab Iorwerth, prince of Gwynedd, dies.

15 July Alexander Nevski of Novgorod (a city-state in NW Russia) defeats the Swedes on the River Neva.

Aug. Frederick II seizes Ravenna, Italy.

16 Nov. St Edmund Rich, archbishop of Canterbury, dies.

6 Dec. The Mongol general Batu (see 1236) sacks Kiev and lays Galatia to waste.

22 Dec. The inhabitants of the Swiss cantons of Schwyz, Uri and Unterwalden become subject to Emperor Frederick II.

ASIA

– Around this time the first European contact with China is made. China itself becomes receptive to Persian culture and to Islam.

SUB-SAHARAN AFRICA

– The Mandingo chief Sundiata defeats Sumanguru, ruler of the Ghanaian empire, and founds the empire of Mali.

ARTS AND HUMANITIES

– Bartholomew Anglicus, English Franciscan monk and author of an encyclopedia of the physical sciences, dies.
– Jacques de Vitry, author of a history of the Holy Land, dies. Anonymous, *Der Pfaffe Amis*, Middle High German collection of stories.

1241

EUROPE

9 April A Mongol army led by Khaidu defeats the Poles, Silesians and Teutonic Knights at Liegnitz and ravages Silesia. After entering Hungary through Moravia, another Mongol army under Batu defeats the Hungarians (11 April) at Mohi; it ravages the Danube plain but is halted by the Croatians at Grobnok.
April Forces of the Holy Roman Emperor Frederick II take Benevento, S Italy, and Faenza, N Italy.

Hard, terrible and extraordinary.

Italian view of the German imperial threat in the 1240s

3 May Frederick II's ships capture bishops travelling to Rome for a general council of the Church.
June Ivan Asen II, king of Bulgaria, dies. Koloman (Kaliman), his infant son, succeeds.
21 Aug. Pope Gregory IX dies and is succeeded by Celestine IV, who himself dies on 10 Nov.
10 Sept. Archbishop Siegfried of Mainz, Frederick II's regent in Germany, leads a rebellion against him.
11 Dec. Ogodai, the Great Khan of the Mongols (see 1227), dies.
25 Dec. Batu, the Mongol leader, takes Budapest, Hungary.
– The association between the N German cities of Hamburg and Lübeck lays the foundations of the Hanseatic League (see 1157).
– The French king Louis IX builds Aigues-Mortes as a crusader base in the Camargue, S France. It is the first French royal port on the Mediterranean.

MIDDLE EAST AND NORTH AFRICA

– Kaykhusraw II, sultan of Rum, crushes a rebellion led by the dervishes.

ASIA

22 Dec. The Mongols take Lahore, N India.

1242

EUROPE

5 April Alexander Nevski defeats the Teutonic Knights in a battle on the frozen Lake Peipus, N Russia.
– In order to elect a new Great Khan, the Mongols return to their capital, Karakorum, and evacuate C Europe.
– Swietopulk of E Pomerania leads a revolt of Prussians against the Teutonic Knights.
– Henry, king of the Germans and son of the Holy Roman Emperor Frederick II, dies.

1243

EUROPE

7 April King Louis IX of France and King Henry III of England make peace in the treaty of Bordeaux.
25 June After 18 months without a pope (see 1241), Innocent IV is elected to the papacy.
– The Jews of Belitz, near Berlin, are massacred.

MIDDLE EAST AND NORTH AFRICA

26 June At Kose Dhah, Anatolia, the Mongols defeat Kaykhusraw II of Rum and his Byzantine allies.

ARTS AND HUMANITIES

– Sainte Chapelle, Paris, is built to house the Crown of Thorns, purchased by Louis IX from the Byzantine emperor and said to have been worn by Christ at the Crucifixion.

1244

EUROPE

20 Mar. The capture by a French force of the fortress of Montségur in Languedoc, marks the final defeat of the Cathars (Albigensians).
Nov. Bishops and barons in England refuse to pay a tax to King Henry III and propose reform of central government.
Dec. A papal court is established at Lyons, France, by Pope Innocent IV.

MIDDLE EAST AND NORTH AFRICA

23 Aug. Salih Ayyub of Egypt forces the Christian occupiers out of Jerusalem and sacks the city.
17 Oct. The Egyptians defeat a Christian army and its Muslim allies of Damascus near Gaza, Palestine.

ASIA

16 April Jajnagar, raja of Jaipur, NC India, defeats the Muslim governor of Bengal, NE India.

1245

EUROPE

17 July In the general Church council held at Lyons, France, Pope Innocent IV declares the Holy Roman Emperor Frederick II deposed. The German princes are released from their allegiance.

ASIA

– The Mongols take Multan in the Punjab, N India.

– Innocent IV sends an embassy to the court of the Great Khan at Karakorum; this leads to the establishment of Christian missions in China.

ARTS AND HUMANITIES

– In England work begins on rebuilding Westminster Abbey.

– English philosopher and scientist Roger Bacon writes a commentary on Aristotle's *Metaphysics*.

1246

EUROPE

Jan. Beatrice, heiress of Raymond-Berengar IV of Provence, marries Charles of Anjou, brother of King Louis IX of France.

25 Feb. In Wales Llywelyn ap Gruffudd becomes prince of Gwynedd.

Nov. Michael Asen I, king of Bulgaria, who has succeeded his brother Koloman I (see 1241), confirms the Byzantine conquests in his territories.

– Frederick II suppresses a Sicilian revolt and deports the remaining Muslim inhabitants to Lucera.

ASIA

10 June The Turkish nobility who run Muslim India (the Forty) depose Mas 'ud of Delhi in favour of Nasir ud-Din Mahmud.

Aug. Güyük is elected Great Khan of the Mongols.

ARTS AND HUMANITIES

– In Italy work begins on Santa Maria Novella, Florence.

1247

EUROPE

16 June The pro-papal enemies of the Holy Roman Emperor Frederick II take Parma, Italy.

– The Great Khan Güyük confirms the appointments of Alexander Nevski as prince of Kiev and his brother Andrew as Grand Duke of Vladimir (a principality in W Russia).

– King Louis IX of France appoints *enqueteurs* to travel around France and monitor administration.

1248

EUROPE

18 Feb. An army from Parma, N Italy, defeats the Holy Roman Emperor Frederick II.

Mar. Pope Innocent IV sends another embassy to the Mongol court (see 1245).

25 Aug. The French king Louis IX sails from Aigues-Mortes (see 1241), beginning the Seventh Crusade.

– The Genoese take Rhodes, in the E Mediterranean, from the Byzantines.

ASIA

April Güyük, Great Khan of the Mongols (see 1246), dies.

SCIENCE AND TECHNOLOGY

– Al-Baytar, Arabic author of a compilation of medical drugs and their botanical source, dies.

ARTS AND HUMANITIES

– In Italy Piacenza University is founded.

– Roderigo Jiménez de Rada, author of a history of Spain and of a world history, dies.

1249

EUROPE

– W Finland is conquered by the Swedes.

MIDDLE EAST AND NORTH AFRICA

5 June King Louis IX of France lands in Egypt from Cyprus with a crusader army and (6 June) enters Damietta, a town in the Nile delta.

ARTS AND HUMANITIES

– In England University College, the first college of Oxford University, is founded.

1250

EUROPE

13 Dec. Frederick II, the Holy Roman Emperor, dies and is succeeded as emperor by his son Conrad IV.

– The Gascons revolt against King Henry III of England's deputy in France, Simon de Montfort the Younger (see 1231 and 1238).

– The cortes (parliament) of Castile summons town representatives, a new development for European politics.

MIDDLE EAST AND NORTH AFRICA

8 Feb. King Louis IX of France defeats the Egyptians at Mansurah but is captured (6 April).

2 May The last Ayyubid sultan of Egypt, Turan Shah, is murdered by his Mamluk slave guards. They elect their commander Aybak regent, and he founds the Mamluk dynasty.

6 May Louis IX surrenders Damietta in Egypt as part of the price of his release and retreats to crusader-held Acre, in Palestine.

ARTS AND HUMANITIES

– The Dominicans establish the first school of oriental studies in Spain at Toledo.

– In France the N tower and the transepts of Notre Dame Cathedral, Paris, are built.

Anonymous, *King Horn*, the earliest English verse romance.

1251

EUROPE

7 Jan. In Italy Florence allows the pro-papal Welfs (Guelphs) (see 1125) to enter the city.

Mar. The Holy Roman Emperor Conrad IV suppresses uprisings in Sicily.

May Simon de Montfort the Younger (see 1238) suppresses a rebellion in Gascony.

July The pro-Imperial Waiblings (Ghibellines) are expelled from Sicily.

– Prince Ottokar of Bohemia (who is also duke of Austria) and King Bela IV of Hungary fight for control of Styria, modern Austria.

MIDDLE EAST AND NORTH AFRICA

2 Feb. The Mamluk sultan of Egypt, Aybak, defeats an-Nasir Yusuf, prince of Aleppo, at Abbasa, Egypt.

ASIA

1 July Möngke is elected Great Khan of the Mongols.

1252

EUROPE

8 Mar. The pro-papal Welf forces attempt to form a union of Lombard cities in N Italy. A league of opposing pro-Imperial Waibling forces led by Verona and Cremona is formed (31 Mar.).

June The Holy Roman Emperor Conrad IV rejects Pope Innocent IV's proposal that Sicily be separated from the empire.

– The Romans rebel against Pope Innocent IV.

– The Teutonic Knights establish the city of Memel in Lithuania as a base for their campaigns in NE Europe.

– Alexander I Nevski is appointed Grand Duke of Vladimir, in W Russia, after his brother Andrew is expelled by the Mongols.

– Pope Innocent IV issues a papal bull that allows torture in the cross-examination of heretics.

ECONOMY AND SOCIETY

– King Afonso III of Portugal tries to regulate prices and wages by royal decree.

– The gold florin is minted for the first time in Florence.

1253

EUROPE

April Simon de Montfort returns to England to place himself at the head of the baronial opposition to Henry III.

10 Oct. In Italy the Holy Roman Emperor Conrad IV suppresses the Sicilian rebellion and recaptures Naples.

Oct. Donato Brancaleone, Waibling leader of the Roman rebellion, forces Pope Innocent IV to return to Rome.

– King Wenceslas I of Bohemia dies and is succeeded by his son Ottokar II.

MIDDLE EAST AND NORTH AFRICA

April An-Nasir Yusuf cedes Palestine to Aybak, Mamluk sultan of Egypt (see 1251).

– Genghis Khan's grandson, Hülagü, begins his conquest of the Abbasid caliphate.

ASIA

– The French king Louis IX sends two friars to the Great Khan's court at Karakorum to seek an alliance against Syrian and Egyptian Muslims.

– Kublai Khan, a grandson of Genghis Khan, conquers the Thai kingdom of Nanzhao (Nanchao) in SW China (see also 1260 and 1261). The population migrates to Siam (Thailand).

SCIENCE AND TECHNOLOGY

9 Oct. Robert Grosseteste, bishop of Lincoln and author of works on astronomy and Aristotle, dies. Grosseteste reformed abuses of Church finance in England but met opposition from the pope when he refused to appoint the pope's nephew to a canonry.

1254

EUROPE

9 April Pope Innocent IV again excommunicates the Holy Roman Emperor Conrad IV.

26 April An assembly of knights refuses to grant King Henry III of England a tax.

21 May The Holy Roman Emperor Conrad IV dies. Succession to the imperial throne is disputed until 1273.

11 July Louis IX returns to France from the Seventh Crusade (see 1250).

13 July The Rhenish League, a confederation of trading cities, is established in the Rhineland, W Germany.

11 Oct. Pope Innocent IV becomes king of Sicily, but dies in Naples (7 Dec.).

2 Nov. In Italy Manfred, the illegitimate son of the late emperor Frederick II, starts an anti-papal revolt and seizes Lucera; he defeats the papal army near Foggia and gains the loyalty of Apulia (2 Dec.).

12 Dec. Alexander IV is elected pope in Naples.

– Llywelyn ap Gruffudd, prince of Gwynedd, becomes the sole ruler of Wales.

– The Teutonic Knights establish Königsberg (modern Kaliningrad), named after the Bohemian king, Ottokar, in recognition of his help in the conquest of W Prussia.

– William of Holland (the pro-papal king of the Romans) holds a diet (princely convention) at Worms, in which German cities are represented for the first time.

MIDDLE EAST AND NORTH AFRICA

24 April The French king Louis IX leaves Palestine; civil war breaks out among the nobles of Outremer (the Crusader States).

13 Sept. The king of Armenia, Hethoum, becomes a vassal of the Great Khan, Mongka.

ECONOMY AND SOCIETY
- In Portugal, the cortes (parliament) is attended for the first time by town representatives.
- King Alfonso X of Castile and Leon publishes a legal code.

1255

EUROPE
Nov. Pope Alexander IV returns to Rome.

ASIA
- Batu, khan of the Golden Horde Tatars (Mongols), dies and is succeeded by his son, Sartak.

ARTS AND HUMANITIES
- Jacob Bonacosa, a Jew of Padua, N Italy, translates the works of Averroes.
- In Spain Leon Cathedral is constructed.

1256

EUROPE
28 Jan. William of Holland, king of the Romans (see 1254), dies.

MIDDLE EAST AND NORTH AFRICA
Dec. A Mongol army led by Hülagü (Ilkhan of Persia) besieges and captures the Assassin stronghold at Alamut, NW Iran. The Assassin Grand Master, Kurshah, is murdered.

ASIA
- Sartak, khan of the Golden Horde (see 1255), dies and is succeeded by Ulagchi.

ARTS AND HUMANITIES
- Jacob Anatoli, Hebrew translator of the works of Averroes, dies.

1257

EUROPE
13 Jan. At the first recorded meeting of the college of seven Electors of the Holy Roman Empire, Richard, earl of Cornwall (son of King John and brother of Henry III of England), is elected king of the Romans; he is crowned at Aachen (17 May).
May Pope Alexander IV leaves Rome again when the Waibling leader, Donato Brancaleone (see 1253), regains power.
- The Rhenish League of W Germany (see 1254) dissolves.
- King Alfonso X of Castile expels the last Almohads from Spain. He is excommunicated by Pope Alexander IV for repudiating his wife and marrying Beatrix de Guzman.
- Michael Asen I, king of Bulgaria, dies and is succeeded by Koloman II, the last of the Asen line.

MIDDLE EAST AND NORTH AFRICA
10 April Aybak, sultan of Egypt (see 1253), is murdered on the orders of his wife, Shajar; his son Nur ad-Din Ali succeeds.

ASIA
Dec. The Mongols raid the Punjab, NW India.

- The Mongols sack Hanoi, modern N Vietnam, but are then forced out of Dai Viet.

ECONOMY AND SOCIETY
- Adam Marsh, founder of the Oxford Franciscans, dies.

1258

EUROPE
Mar. Llywelyn ap Gruffudd (see 1254) claims the title of prince of Wales.
2 May King Henry III of England accepts the demand of Simon de Montfort and his baronial supporters that the government be reformed with a committee of 22 barons including the king. The Provisions of Oxford establish baronial control of the government (11 June).
28 May Louis IX, king of France, and Henry III, king of England, agree a peace treaty.
- The Great Khan Möngke orders a census of all Mongol-controlled territory.
- Alexander Nevski suppresses riots in Novgorod, E of Moscow.
- Louis IX bans private warfare in France.

MIDDLE EAST AND NORTH AFRICA
11 Jan. The Mongols under Hülagü defeat the Caliph al-Musta'sim at Anbar and destroy Baghdad, Iraq (10 Feb.). They murder al-Musta'sim (20 Feb.).

ASIA
- Ulagchi, khan of the Golden Horde (see 1256), dies and is succeeded by Batu's brother Berke, a Muslim.
- The Mongols under Kublai Khan invade China.
- The Mongols murder the last Ch'oe ruler in Korea.

ARTS AND HUMANITIES
- Robert de Sorbon, chaplain to Louis IX of France, establishes a college in Paris for graduates (the Sorbonne).
- After the sack of Baghdad, Iraq, by the Mongols (Feb.) the al-Azhar Mosque, Cairo, becomes Islam's greatest university.
- In Austria the W front of Vienna Cathedral is built.

1259

EUROPE
1 Aug. King Henry III of England makes peace with Llywelyn ap Gruffudd, prince of Wales (see 1258).
4 Dec. Henry III of England renounces his claims to Normandy, Maine, Anjou (all in W France) and the other former Angevin territories. He does homage to the French king Louis IX for Gascony.
- The anti-papal rebel leader Donato Brancaleone dies (see 1257) and Rome returns to papal control.
- The Mongols and Russians devastate Poland, Lithuania and Galicia.
- Louis IX abolishes the judicial duel, a traditional legal means of settling disputes in much of medieval Europe.

- The Provisions of Westminster reform the legal system of England.

MIDDLE EAST AND NORTH AFRICA

Dec. Nur ad-Din Ali, sultan of Egypt (see 1257), is deposed. His successor is Sayf ad-Din Qutuz.

ASIA

11 Aug. The Mongol Great Khan, Möngke, dies.
Sept. The Mongols invade Syria.

ARTS AND HUMANITIES

- The English chronicler Matthew Paris dies.

1260

EUROPE

July The Lithuanians defeat the Teutonic Knights at Durben, Lithuania, weakening the hold of the Knights on Lithuania and neighbouring Courland (part of modern Latvia).

MIDDLE EAST AND NORTH AFRICA

Mar. The Mongols under Hülagü enter Damascus: they now occupy the whole of Syria and have destroyed the Ayyubid sultanate. Because of a succession dispute (in which Mongka's brothers, Kublai and Ariqboga, are separately elected Great Khan), Hülagü removes the bulk of his army from the area.
3 Sept. Mamluk forces led by Baybars I destroy the remaining Mongol forces at Ain Jalut in Palestine, saving Egypt from Mongol attack. The Mamluks occupy Syria, and Baybars murders Qutuz, sultan of Egypt (24 Oct.). The Mamluks are now the major power in the E Mediterranean.

ASIA

- Kublai Khan is elected Great Khan of the Mongols. His introduction of Mongol religious toleration, which allows Islam and Christianity to enter China, proves unpopular.

ARTS AND HUMANITIES

- The Italian jurist Accursius, author of a textbook on civil law, dies.
- Al-Juwaini writes a Persian history of Genghis Khan, the all-conquering Mongol leader.

1261

EUROPE

13 Mar. Genoa makes the treaty of Nymphaeum with the Byzantines: the Genoese undertake to recover Constantinople from the Latins (see 1204) in return for trading concessions in the Byzantine lands previously given to the Venetians.
12 June After the death of Pope Alexander IV (25 May), Henry III, king of England, publishes the papal bull absolving him from his oath to observe the agreement with his nobles in the Provisions of Westminster (see 1259). Henry then dismisses the baronial officials (led by Simon de Montfort) who wish the royal power to be modified by the principle of representation.

25 July Michael VIII Palaeologus, Byzantine ruler of Nicaea, recaptures Constantinople, ending the Latin empire of Constantinople (founded after the Fourth Crusade in 1204) and restoring the Byzantine empire.
29 Aug. Pope Urban IV (Jacques Pantaleon) is elected; he offers the crown of Sicily to Charles of Anjou, 7th son of Louis VIII of France (and brother of Louis IX), hoping to weaken the hold of the imperialists on S Italy.

MIDDLE EAST AND NORTH AFRICA

4 July Baybars I becomes sultan of Egypt.

ASIA

- Kublai Khan continues the Mongol conquest of China. Beijing is rebuilt as his summer capital; his winter one is in E Mongolia.

ARTS AND HUMANITIES

- Italian philosopher and theologian Thomas Aquinas (see box) translates the works of Aristotle and composes the ecstatic hymn, 'Lauda Sion' (Praise Zion).

1262

EUROPE

- Llywelyn ap Gruffudd, prince of Wales, raids England.

St Thomas Aquinas (1225–74)

The greatest scholar and theologian of the European Middle Ages, Thomas Aquinas was born near Aquino in southern Italy, the son of the local count. He was educated first at the monastery of Monte Cassino and then at the University of Naples. Aquinas joined the Dominican order in 1244 and was sent to study at the University of Paris, where he subsequently taught.

The *Summa theologica*, which Aquinas started in 1266, was unfinished at his death, but remains the greatest testament to the idea of a unity of all knowledge, both sacred and secular. Aquinas was inspired in this ambitious project by Aristotle, for he sought above all to reconcile Christian revelation with the teachings of the pagan philosopher. In particular, he believed it was possible to use the Aristotelian model of reason in order to support Christianity. His *Summa contra gentiles* (1261–4) was probably written with the needs of the Spanish Dominicans in mind, because it shows how to defend Christianity against the arguments of Jewish and Islamic philosophers. He does so not by using arguments drawn from Christian revelation, but by applying the logic of Aristotle.

Aquinas's powerful and subtle thought guaranteed him an immense influence, to the point that the official philosophy of the Roman Catholic Church became known as Thomism. The Catholic Church clung to Thomism after the Reformation, and as late as the 19th century the system remained a powerful force within Catholic Christianity.

MIDDLE EAST AND NORTH AFRICA

- The Egyptian sultan Baybars establishes a series of vassal caliphs among the Abbasid dynasty.

ASIA

- Berke, khan of the Golden Horde (see 1258), and Ilkhan Hülagü go to war, further ensuring the safety of Mamluk Egypt from Mongol attack.
- Ganapati, ruler of S India, dies and is succeeded by his daughter Rudramba.
- Shinran founds the Sinsu (or True) sect of Japanese Buddhism.

SCIENCE AND TECHNOLOGY

- In Spain King Alfonso X (the Wise) of Castile and Leon, a great patron of learning, commissions Judah Cohen and Isaac ben Sid of Toledo to compile the Alfonsine Tables, describing the movement of the planets.

ARTS AND HUMANITIES

Adam de la Halle, *Le Jeu de la feuillée* (The Game of the Whip), the first French farce.

1263

EUROPE

3 Oct. King Alexander III of Scotland defeats King Haakon IV Haakonsson of Norway at the battle of Largs, ending Haakon's attempt to overrun the Hebrides (islands off NW Scotland). Haakon has already annexed Iceland and Greenland. He dies (15 Dec.) having united Norway and the Orkneys (islands off N Scotland). His son, Magnus VI (the Lawmender), succeeds.

14 Nov. Alexander I Nevski, Grand Duke of Vladimir, dies. His brother Jaroslav III succeeds him.

- Mindovg (Mindaugas), apostate conqueror of Livonia and prince of Lithuania, dies. As a result, the Teutonic Knights regain their influence in Lithuania.
- The Venetians defeat the Genoans, the allies of the Byzantines (see 1261), in a naval battle off Settepozzi, Italy.

MIDDLE EAST AND NORTH AFRICA

4 April The Egyptian sultan Baybars I attacks Acre (now Akko in N Israel), beginning a major campaign to eliminate the crusader kingdom of Jerusalem, county of Tripoli and principality of Antioch.

ARTS AND HUMANITIES

- In Italy, Urban IV renews the papal prohibition on the study of Aristotle at the University of Padua.

1264

EUROPE

23 Jan. By the Mise of Amiens Louis IX of France, as arbitrator of the Provisions of Oxford (see 1258), decides in favour of Henry III and against Simon de Montfort and the barons. Civil war in England follows.

5 Feb. The papal legate to England, Guy Foulquoi, is elected Pope Clement IV on the death of Pope Urban IV.

Feb. In N Italy, a new Lombard League of anti-imperial cities is formed around Ferrara and Milan.

7 April King Henry III recaptures Northampton from the rebels; Simon de Montfort, leader of the rebel barons, defeats and captures Henry at Lewes, Sussex (14 May). Henry accepts a form of governmental control by de Montfort's party (28 June). Pope Clement IV excommunicates Henry's opponents (21 Oct.).

ARTS AND HUMANITIES

7 Jan. In England Walter de Merton founds Merton College, Oxford.

- Italian sculptor Nicola Pisano and his assistants, including his son Giovanni, complete the pulpit of Siena Cathedral.

1265

EUROPE

20 Jan. An English Parliament is held by the victorious Simon de Montfort and is attended for the first time by elected burgesses and knights of the shire.

28 June Charles of Anjou is invested as king of Sicily by Pope Clement IV and asked to lead a crusade against his imperialist rival Manfred.

4 Aug. Prince Edward (son of Henry III, and the future King Edward I) and Gilbert de Clare, earl of Gloucester (a former ally of de Montfort's), defeat Simon de Montfort at the battle of Evesham. Henry III is rescued and de Montfort is killed.

MIDDLE EAST AND NORTH AFRICA

- The Mamluks of Egypt, under Sultan Baybars I (see 1263), capture the cities of Arsuf and Caesarea from the crusader kingdom of Jerusalem.

ASIA

8 Feb. Hülagü, the Mongol Ilkhan of Persia, dies and is succeeded by his son Abaqa.

ARTS AND HUMANITIES

- Birth in Florence, Italy, of Dante Alighieri (see p. 155), future poet and prose-writer who will establish his local Tuscan dialect as the standard for literary Italian.

1266

EUROPE

26 Feb. Charles of Anjou, son of Louis VIII of France, defeats and kills Manfred of Sicily at the battle of Benevento. Charles becomes king of Sicily.

2 July By the treaty of Perth, King Magnus VI (the Lawmender) of Norway (see 1263) abandons his claim to the Hebrides and Isle of Man to King Alexander III of Scotland.

31 Oct. The Dictum of Kenilworth asserts the power of Henry III of England over the defeated barons (see 1265).

- Swietopulk, prince of Pomerania, dies.

MIDDLE EAST AND NORTH AFRICA

23 July The Mamluk sultan of Egypt, Baybars I, seizes the Templar fortress of Safed and overruns Galilee (modern N Israel).

24 Aug. A Mamluk army defeats the Armenians and ravages Cilicia (SE Turkey).

ASIA

18 Feb. Mahmud, sultan of Delhi, dies and is succeeded by his deputy, Balban.

– Berke, khan of the Golden Horde, ends his war with the Ilkhan of Persia and is succeeded by Mangu-Temir, who exempts the Russian clergy from paying taxes.

ARTS AND HUMANITIES

– English Franciscan scholar Roger Bacon writes his metaphysical work *Opus maius* (The Greater Work). Bacon has unconventional ideas that are ahead of his time, including concepts for flying machines, motor vehicles and circumnavigating the world.

Anonymous, *The Mirror of the Eastland*, Chinese historical chronicle of Japan.

1267

EUROPE

Aug. Sicily rises in rebellion against Charles of Anjou.

28 Sept. By the treaty of Montgomery, Henry III of England recognizes Llywelyn ap Gruffudd as prince of Wales and as his vassal.

– Charles of Anjou, king of Sicily, captures Corfu from the Byzantines.

1268

EUROPE

23 Aug. Conradin (or Conrad V), son of the late Emperor Conrad IV, attempts to recover his father's kingdom of Sicily and is defeated by Charles of Anjou, king of Sicily, at Tagliacozzo. Charles orders Conradin's execution (29 Oct.), thereby terminating the Hohenstaufen dynasty.

MIDDLE EAST AND NORTH AFRICA

7 Mar. The Egyptian sultan Baybars I seizes the crusader city of Jaffa (modern Tel Aviv in Israel) and destroys the crusader city of Antioch (21 May), massacring its inhabitants.

ASIA

– The Mongol commander Khaidu rebels and seizes the khanate of Chaghadai in Turkestan.

ARTS AND HUMANITIES

– English ecclesiastic Henry of Bracton, author of the first summary of English law, dies.

– In England Balliol College, Oxford, is founded.

1269

MIDDLE EAST AND NORTH AFRICA

– Almohad rule in N Africa and Spain (see 1121) is ended by Ya 'qub III, founder of the Marinid dynasty, who captures Marrakesh, Morocco.

ASIA

– Jatavarman Sundara, supreme ruler in S India and Ceylon, dies and is succeeded by Maravarman Kulasekhara.

– Mongol forces invade S China and besiege the twin cities of Xiangyang (Hsiang-yang).

ARTS AND HUMANITIES

13 Oct. In England, Henry III's Abbey Church at Westminster is dedicated.

– The Mongol scholar Phagspa invents a new alphabet for Kublai Khan.

1270

EUROPE

1 July King Louis IX sails from France, leading the Eighth Crusade. He lands at Carthage (18 July) and takes Tunis (25 July), both N Africa. He dies (25 Aug.) and is succeeded by his son Philip III. Louis IX's brother Charles of Anjou, the king of Sicily, who has suppressed the Sicilian revolt, becomes leader of his brother's crusade and makes peace with the emir of Tunis (1 Nov.).

23 Nov. A storm destroys the crusaders' fleet at Trapani, Sicily, preventing Charles of Anjou from setting out for Constantinople and the Holy Land.

– Prince Edward of England departs on crusade.

ASIA

– Hemadri, administrator of the Yadava kingdom in S India, produces a digest of Hindu law.

SUB-SAHARAN AFRICA

– Yekuno Amlak leads a succesful rebellion against the Zague kings of Abyssinia and founds the Solomonid dynasty.

1271

MIDDLE EAST AND NORTH AFRICA

8 April The Mamluk sultan Baybars I takes the powerful crusader castle of Krak des Chevaliers, overrunning most of the inland part of the county of Tripoli.

9 May Edward, Henry III of England's heir, arrives at Acre, where the crusaders are under siege by the Mamluks under Baybars I.

21 Aug. The counties of Poitou and Toulouse are absorbed into the French royal domains following the death of Alphonse of Poitiers, uncle of Philip III.

SCIENCE AND TECHNOLOGY

– Paper manufacture is introduced to Italy from Islamic Spain and Sicily.

– Silk manufacture is established in Bologna, N Italy.

Ramón Lull (c.1235–1315)

The Christian mystic Ramón Lull was born in Majorca, and in his youth was a courtier and a troubadour poet. In 1272, while climbing Mount Randa in Majorca, he had a visionary experience, as a result of which he claimed to have seen all of God's attributes penetrating the whole created order. He then started to describe these qualities of goodness, greatness and eternity in a systematic way. His great work was the *Ars magna* (Great Art), which he completed in 1308. This outlined a kind of conceptual computer, a way of training the memory so that the mind could remember truth, but also of investigating the world so that truth could be revealed.

Lull's mnemonic method involved memorizing Aristotelian categories and meditating on their importance. But the most important of these categories were the words used to describe God's qualities, which gave his art a theological basis and aligned it with Christian cosmology. The single word for the attribute of goodness or greatness, for example, could be signified by one letter. Lull's diagrams and illustrations of revolving wheels, squares and triangles showed how this single letter could recur in different forms throughout the whole creation, from God, through angels and men, down to the animal and vegetable orders.

There had been previous memory techniques, but Lullism was original because it suggested that the method could also reveal new things about the world through its system of correspondences and connections. The 'science' used diagrams and figures, but there were no images to stir the mind: Lullism was severely intellectualist in its provocation of the powers of memory.

ARTS AND HUMANITIES

– Catalan scholar Rámon Lull (see box) translates his encyclopedia of theology, the *Libre de Contemplacio en Deu* (Book of Contemplation of God), from Arabic into Catalan.

1272

EUROPE

16 Nov. Henry III of England dies and is succeeded by his crusading son as Edward I (see 1271).

MIDDLE EAST AND NORTH AFRICA

22 May A peace treaty is agreed between Baybars I and the crusader kingdom of Acre.

1273

EUROPE

1 Oct. Rudolf, count of Habsburg, is elected king of the Romans, against the wishes of King Ottokar II of Bohemia.

– The Teutonic Knights suppress rebellions in W Prussia.

– Rámon Lull (see 1271) starts his mission to convert the Muslims.

ARTS AND HUMANITIES

– The Alhambra Palace in Granada, S Spain, is founded.

– The Sufi poet and mystic ar-Rumi dies, and his followers establish the Dervish order of the Mevleviye.

1274

EUROPE

7 May Pope Gregory X presides over a general council of the Church at Lyons, France, aiming to end the schism with the Byzantine Church. The ambassadors of Emperor Michael VIII Palaeologus accept the pope's supremacy (6 July). The council also recognizes the Dominican, Franciscan, Carmelite and Augustinian friars but suppresses smaller orders.

19 Aug. Edward I, now returned from the crusades, is crowned king of England. He orders a commission into local government in England, recorded in the so-called Hundred Rolls (a 'hundred' is a unit of English local government).

24 Oct. Rudolf I becomes the first Habsburg emperor when he is crowned Holy Roman Emperor at Aachen.

26 Oct. Genoa allies with the pro-imperial forces in Lombardy, NW Italy.

ASIA

– Kublai Khan sends a fleet to invade Japan but his ships are scattered by a typhoon at Hakata Bay.

ARTS AND HUMANITIES

7 Mar. The Dominican priest and theologian St Thomas Aquinas (see p. 144) dies. He leaves behind him his *Summa theologica*, the most systematic and complete synthesis of knowledge achieved in Europe during the Christian Middle Ages and the foundation-stone for the future development of scholasticism.

14 July St Bonaventura (Giovanni de Fidanza), the Doctor Seraphicus (Seraphic Doctor), dies. Bonaventura rose quickly through the Franciscan order and became a bishop and cardinal; he died from the rigours of his ascetic life.

– In Florence Dante Alighieri (see p. 155) meets his love and muse, Beatrice.

1275

EUROPE

Aug. Pope Gregory X persuades King Alfonso X of Castile (see 1262) to give up his claim to the title of king of the Romans. Gregory gains German support in N Italy through Rudolf of Habsburg, now king of the Romans.

– In England King Edward I holds his first Parliament at Westminster; it is attended by peers and elected knights and burgesses.

ASIA

– Marco Polo, a young Venetian merchant travelling with his father and uncle, arrives at the court of Kublai Khan in China. He will enter the service of the emperor and remain in China until 1292.
– The Nestorian (E Christian) patriarch of Baghdad, Iraq, creates an archbishopric of Peking (Beijing).

ARTS AND HUMANITIES

– In Germany, the naves of the cathedrals of Strasbourg and Essen are built.
Rámon Lull, *Libre del orde de cavayleria* (Book of the Order of Chivalry), an account of chivalry, written in Catalan.

1276

EUROPE

10 Jan. Pope Gregory X dies. Two successor popes, Innocent V and Hadrian V, die in the same year; Pope John XXI is elected (8 Sept.).
25 Nov. Rudolf of Habsburg, king of the Romans, besieges Vienna, Austria; Bohemia revolts and King Ottokar surrenders all his lands (including Austria and Styria) except Bohemia and Moravia to Rudolf. Rudolf makes Vienna his capital, marking the beginning of the Habsburg dynasty, which will last until 1918.
– Stephen Uros I of Serbia is deposed by his son, Stephen Dragutin.
– Magnus VI (the Lawmender) establishes a common law for all Norway.

ASIA

– In China Kublai Khan takes Hangzhou (Hangchow), the capital of the Southern Song (Sung) dynasty.

ARTS AND HUMANITIES

– Rámon Lull (see p. 147) founds a college of friars to study Arabic at Miramar, Spain.
– The Italian love poet Guido Guinizelli, a strong influence on Dante, dies.

1277

EUROPE

20 May Pope John XXI dies and is succeeded (25 Nov.) by Nicholas III.
24 June The Welsh prince Llywelyn ap Gruffudd refuses to pay homage to Edward I of England; Edward mounts a Welsh campaign and Llywelyn submits to Edward by the treaty of Conwy (9 Nov.).
– The Inquisition in France condemns Siger of Brabant, a teacher at the University of Paris, for his advocacy of the Averroist doctrine (see p. 130) that reason is separate from Christian faith.

MIDDLE EAST AND NORTH AFRICA

April The Mamluk sultan Baybars I invades S Anatolia and defeats the Mongols, but the Ilkhan Abaqa restores Mongol

control over the sultanate of Rum. Baybars dies (10 July) and is succeeded as sultan of Egypt and Syria by his son, Baraka, who will rule until 1279.

ASIA

– The Mongol leader Khaidu rebels at Karakorum, C Asia; Kublai Khan dispatches an army to quell him.

1278

EUROPE

Jan. Charles of Anjou, king of Sicily is crowned king of Jerusalem. He surrenders the vicariate of Tuscany, Italy, to Pope Nicholas III.
28 Aug. Rudolf I, king of the Romans, defeats and kills King Ottokar II of Bohemia. Wenceslas II succeeds, and civil war breaks out in Bohemia.
– By now the *parlement*, France's senior law court, is meeting regularly in the royal palace in Paris.

1279

EUROPE

14 Feb. Rudolf I, king of the Romans, recognizes papal authority over the empire.
– Florence, Lucca, Siena and other C Italian cities form a pro-Welf (Guelf) Tuscan League, with a customs union and a jointly funded army.
– The Byzantines impose Ivan Asen III as the Bulgarian ruler.
– Pope Nicholas III issues a decree to solve Franciscan disputes over property ownership.
– By the statute of Mortmain, King Edward I of England forbids the alienation of feudal land in grants to the Church.

ASIA

– Balban of Delhi crushes a rebellion in Bengal, NE India.
– An invading Mongol army is repulsed in the Punjab, NW India.
– Kublai Khan completes the Mongol conquest of China with a great naval victory near Macao: this marks the end of the Southern Song (Sung) dynasty.
– In SE India Kulasekhara of Pandya defeats Rajendra III, the last Chola ruler.

1280

EUROPE

10 Feb. Margaret II, countess of Flanders, dies and is succeeded by her son Guy of Dampierre, who is supported by King Philip III of France. The event marks the beginning of major French influence in Flanders.
22 Aug. Pope Nicholas III dies. He was the first pope to make the Vatican his residence.
– Ivan Asen III of Bulgaria is deposed by George I Terter.
– Workers' riots break out among Flemish cloth-weavers.
– Magnus VI (the Lawmender), king of Norway, dies; the legal code he introduced in 1274 will remain in use for more than 400 years.

ASIA

- Mangu-Temir, khan of the Golden Horde, dies and is succeeded by his brother Tuda-Mangu, who ravages the Russian principality of Vladimir and replaces its ruler, Grand Duke Dmitri, with Dmitri's brother Andrew. Nogay becomes khan of the Nogay Horde, ruling between the Danube and the Dnieper.

SCIENCE AND TECHNOLOGY

- In Germany a spinning-wheel is recorded for the first time.

ARTS AND HUMANITIES

14 Nov. The German theologian and writer Albertus Magnus of Cologne dies. A follower of Aristotle and teacher of Thomas Aquinas, Albertus travelled in Italy, France and Germany; like others interested in science and mathematics in his day, he was credited with being a magician.

- Italian artist Cimabue, teacher of Giotto, paints *Madonna Enthroned with Angels*.

- Rustico di Filippo, the first Italian poet to write comic verse, dies.

1281

EUROPE

10 April After an interregnum of six months, the new pope, Martin IV, is elected (22 Feb.) He excommunicates the Byzantines and abandons the reconciliation of 1274 between the Eastern and Western Churches.

3 July By the treaty of Orvieto, the Venetians promise to help Charles of Anjou, king of Sicily restore the Latin kingdom of Jerusalem.

- Pope Martin declares that the Byzantine emperor Michael VIII Palaeologus should be deposed.

- Peter III (the Great), king of Aragon, Spain, unites with the Byzantine emperor Michael VIII Palaeologus against Charles of Anjou, king of Sicily.

MIDDLE EAST AND NORTH AFRICA

30 Oct. Qalawun, sultan of Egypt, defeats a combined force of Mongols, Armenians and Knights Hospitallers in battle at Homs, W Syria.

ASIA

- Kublai Khan's renewed attempt at conquering Japan by sea fails after a typhoon destroys his fleet: the Japanese call it *kamikaze* (Divine Wind).

ARTS AND HUMANITIES

- In France the N transept of Rouen Cathedral is built.

1282

EUROPE

30 Mar. In Sicily a major rebellion (the Sicilian Vespers) breaks out against the rule of Charles of Anjou, son of Louis VIII of France; the French garrison in Palermo is massacred. Charles loses control of the island, and the Sicilians offer the crown to Peter III of Aragon (son-in-law of Manfred, see 1254 and 1266), who lands in Sicily (18 June) and becomes King Peter I of Sicily. Pope Martin IV declares him deposed as king of Aragon (18 Nov.) and proclaims a crusade against him.

Aug. King Edward I of England starts another Welsh campaign; the Welsh prince Llywelyn ap Gruffudd is killed in battle near Builth (11 Dec.). Deprived of his leadership, Welsh resistance to English rule begins to collapse.

11 Dec. The Byzantine emperor Michael VIII Palaeologus dies and is succeeded by his son Andronicus II Palaeologus, who renounces the reconciliation with the Western (Roman) Church (see 1274).

27 Dec. Rudolf I, king of the Romans, invests his sons, Albert and Rudolf of Habsburg, with the duchies of Austria and Styria, respectively.

- Leszek the Black, Grand Prince of Poland, conquers the rival Jadzwinga dynasty then confronts the Mongols.

- Lübeck (N Germany), Riga and Visby (an island in the Baltic Sea) form an alliance to protect their Baltic trade.

- Stephen Uros II, joint king of Serbia, takes Skopje in Macedonia from Byzantium.

MIDDLE EAST AND NORTH AFRICA

1 April Abaqa, Ilkhan of Persia, dies and is succeeded by his brother Tekuder, who converts to Islam.

ASIA

- Nicheren, founder of the Nicheren or Lotus Sect of Japanese Buddhism, dies.

ARTS AND HUMANITIES

- Albi Cathedral is built in S France.

1283

EUROPE

3 Oct. Dafydd ap Gruffudd (brother and successor of Llywelyn, prince of Wales) is executed in Shrewsbury, Shropshire, as a traitor against King Edward I of England.

- Skurdo, the last native Prussian leader, goes into exile in Lithuania.

- A popular uprising in Novgorod deposes the Grand Duke Andrew (see 1280): the khan Nogay restores Andrew's brother Dmitri.

- The Privilegio General of Aragon, Spain (a union of towns), is recognized by Peter III.

- In England a parliament at Acton Burnell, Shropshire (reputedly the first to include commoners), passes a statute providing for the prompter recovery of debts and removing the staple (exclusive market rights for major exports) from Calais to certain towns in Britain.

ASIA

- A seaborne invasion of Champa (S Vietnam) by the Mongols is repulsed.

1284

EUROPE

Feb. Pope Martin IV offers King Philip III of France the crown of Aragon, Spain.

4 April In Spain King Alfonso X (the Wise) of Castile and Leon dies: civil war breaks out.

5 June The Genoese destroy an Angevin fleet in the Bay of Naples; the Genoese also destroy the fleet of Pisa, a rival Italian city-state (6 Aug.).

16 Aug. Philip, son of Philip III (the Bold) of France (see 1285), marries Joanna I of Navarre, whose territory comes under the rule of the kings of France.

– Edward I's Statute of Rhuddlan extends English government to Wales.

SCIENCE AND TECHNOLOGY

– Reading glasses are first used, in Venice.

ARTS AND HUMANITIES

– In England, Peterhouse, the first college of Cambridge University, is founded.

1285

EUROPE

7 Jan. Charles I of Anjou, king of Sicily, dies.

28 Jan. Pope Martin IV dies and is succeeded (2 April) by Pope Honorius IV.

7 July Dietrich Holzschuh, who has claimed to be Frederick II, is executed by burning at the order of Rudolf I; Rudolf's authority as king of the Romans is maintained.

5 Oct. King Philip III (the Bold) of France dies and is succeeded by his son Philip IV (the Fair).

2 Nov. Peter III of Aragon dies and is succeeded by his son Alfonso III in Aragon, and by another son, James, in Sicily.

– The Baltic towns of the Hanse extend their trading privileges.

SCIENCE AND TECHNOLOGY

– William of St Cloud observes the sun through a camera obscura.

ARTS AND HUMANITIES

Duccio di Buoninsegna, *Rucellai Madonna*, painting, in Florence.

1286

EUROPE

– By the writ *Cirumspecte Agates*, King Edward I of England defines the issues that can be tried only in ecclesiastical courts.

– Alexander III of Scotland dies in a riding accident. Margaret, Maid of Norway, only child of Alexander's daughter (who died in childbirth) and King Eric II of Norway, becomes Scotland's infant queen.

ASIA

– Kublai Khan's invading army is defeated in Annam (N Vietnam); he gives up his plans to invade Japan.

ARTS AND HUMANITIES

– William of Moerbeke, translator of Aristotle from Greek, dies.

1287

EUROPE

31 May The Genoese defeat the Venetian fleet off Acre, in the kingdom of Jerusalem.

23 June James, ruler of Sicily, repels an Angevin invasion. His brother Alfonso III (ruler of Aragon, Spain) allies with King Edward I of England (15 July).

– The Nestorian monk and Mongol envoy Rabban Sauma visits European courts.

ASIA

– The Mongols are massacred near Lahore as they try to advance into the Punjab, NW India.

– Kublai Khan's army, driven out of Dai Viet, invades Burma and destroys the kingdom of Pagan. A period of anarchy follows in Burma.

1288

EUROPE

Feb. The new pope, Nicholas IV, is visited by an ambassador from Ilkhan Arghun, who is trying to gain support for an anti-Mamluk crusade.

– Leszek III (the Black), Grand Prince of Poland, dies: Mongol raids on Polish territory diminish.

1289

EUROPE

29 May Pope Nicholas IV crowns Charles II, son of Charles I of Anjou (see 1285), as king of Sicily.

2 June Florence becomes the dominant power in C Italy when it defeats the city of Arezzo at the battle of Campaldino.

– Pope Nicholas grants the college of cardinals half of all papal revenue.

– Margaret, Maid of Norway, is betrothed to Prince Edward (the future Edward II of England).

SCIENCE AND TECHNOLOGY

– A printing block is made in Ravenna in NE Italy.

– The Chinese Grand Canal is completed, linking Beijing with the Yellow River.

1290

EUROPE

19 July The Cumans murder the Hungarian king Ladislas IV; a succession dispute develops between Ladislas's heir Andrew, Albert, the son of Rudolf I king of Germany, and Charles of Anjou, France (the papacy's candidate).

Sept. Margaret, Maid of Norway, infant queen of Scotland since 1286, dies at sea en route from Norway to the Orkneys.

18 Dec. Magnus I (Barn-Lock), king of Sweden and founder of Swedish feudalism, dies.

– Edward I of England's statute *Quo Warranto* establishes the accession of Richard I (1189) as the limit of legal memory.

– Edward I expels the Jews from England.

MIDDLE EAST AND NORTH AFRICA

10 Nov. Qalawun, Mamluk sultan of Egypt (see 1281), dies. He is succeeded by his son, al-Ashraf Khalil.

– About this date Osman, a Turkoman chieftain in W Anatolia, declares his independence of the Seljuk Turks and begins to expand his territory in what is now NW Turkey at the expense of the declining Byzantine empire. From these small beginnings will develop the Ottoman empire.

ASIA

13 June The last Slave King of India, Kaikubad, is murdered and succeeded by the founder of the Khalji dynasty, Jalal-ud-din Feroz (Feroz Shah I).

ARTS AND HUMANITIES

9 June In Italy Beatrice, the muse of poet Dante Alighieri, dies. In his *Divina commedia* Dante (see p. 155) transformed his memory of Beatrice into an allegory of divine love.

1291

EUROPE

18 June Alfonso III of Aragon dies, bequeathing his Spanish domains to his brother James (see 1285), who returns to Sicily.

15 July Rudolf I, king of the Germans, dies and is succeeded by Adolf of Nassau (elected 10 May 1292).

1 Aug. The Swiss Cantons of Schwyz, Uri and Unterwalden form an anti-Habsburg defensive league.

MIDDLE EAST AND NORTH AFRICA

6 April Mamluks led by Sultan al-Ashraf besiege and destroy Acre (18 May), the last major stronghold of the crusader kingdom of Jerusalem. They take Beirut (31 July), completing their conquest of the kingdom of Jerusalem.

– The Teutonic Knights move their headquarters from Acre to Venice.

ASIA

– Khan Nogay (see 1280) deposes Tele-Buga and installs Tokhta as khan of the Golden Horde.

ECONOMY AND SOCIETY

– Venetian glass manufacture is concentrated on the island of Murano, to prevent fires in Venice itself.

ARTS AND HUMANITIES

– At Charing Cross, London, and throughout England, nine crosses are erected to mark the progression of the funeral cortege of the wife of Edward I, Queen Eleanor of Castile, who died on 28 Nov.

– In England work begins on the nave of York Minster.

1292

EUROPE

17 Nov. King Edward I of England, as overlord of the Scottish nobles, grants the Scottish crown to John Balliol. In this year Edward also orders that English judges train the legal profession, thereby originating the Inns of Court in London.

ASIA

– Kublai Khan sends a naval force to conquer Java, Indonesia.

– Marco Polo (see 1275) leaves China and sets out for Java and Sumatra.

1293

EUROPE

– Florence, Italy, is divided by infighting between the Black and the White factions of the pro-papal Welf (Guelph) party.

MIDDLE EAST AND NORTH AFRICA

13 Dec. Al-Ashraf, Mamluk sultan of Egypt (see 1290), is murdered.

1294

EUROPE

Jan. King Edward I of England agrees to surrender castles in Gascony to the French after attacks by Gascons on French seamen; the French seize Gascony and war breaks out.

Sept. The Welsh revolt against English rule: Edward has to postpone his planned invasion of France.

– King Philip IV of France imprisons Guy of Dampierre, count of Flanders (see 1280), following moves toward a dynastic alliance between England and Flanders.

– The Genoese defeat the Venetians in a sea battle off the Cilician coast, S Turkey.

ASIA

– Ala-ud-Din of Delhi sacks Deogir, capital of a Hindu kingdom in the W Deccan, SW India.

– Kublai Khan, Great Khan and founder of the Yuan dynasty of China, dies. He is succeeded by his grandson, Temur Oljeitu.

ARTS AND HUMANITIES

Thomas of Erceldoune (Thomas the Rhymer), *Sir Tristrem*, narrative poem on the Arthurian theme.

1295

EUROPE

June Pope Boniface VIII arranges a peace treaty between King Philip IV of France, Charles II of Sicily (see 1289) and King James II of Aragon (see 1291). James gives Sicily to Charles.

5 July France and Scotland form an alliance (the origin of the 'Auld Alliance').

– Otto IV, count of Burgundy, cedes his territory (the Franche Comté) to the French king Philip IV.

- Edward I of England holds his second (Model) Parliament.
- Marco Polo (see 1292) returns to Venice.

ASIA

19 July Ala-ud-Din (see 1294) is proclaimed sultan of Delhi after murdering his uncle, Feroz Shah I (see 1290).
- Ghazan, Ilkhan of Persia, makes Islam the state religion and, as sultan, declares his independence of the Great Khan.

ARTS AND HUMANITIES

Anonymous, *The Harrowing of Hell*, earliest known English miracle play.

1296

EUROPE

15 Jan. The Sicilians elect as their king Frederick II of Aragon.
29 Feb. Pope Boniface VIII issues a bull forbidding kings from taxing clergy; it is later modified by a further bull.
30 Mar. King Edward I of England takes Berwick-upon-Tweed and defeats the Scots at Dunbar (27 April). The Scottish king John Balliol abdicates (10 July). Edward returns to England having removed from Scone the Stone of Destiny, on which kings of Scotland are crowned (Aug.).

ASIA

- Chiang Mai, the capital of the new kingdom of Lan Na (modern Thailand) is founded.

SCIENCE AND TECHNOLOGY

- Lanfranchi of Milan writes *Chirurgia magna* (Great Surgery), a surgical treatise.

ARTS AND HUMANITIES

- Master Honoré, among the first known French miniaturists, decorates a breviary for King Philip IV of France.
- In Italy Arnolfo di Cambio begins work on Florence Cathedral.

1297

EUROPE

30 Jan. King Edward I outlaws the English clergy after they refuse to pay taxes; they surrender and are pardoned.
24 Feb. At a Parliament held in Salisbury, the English peerage refuse to serve Edward I in a war in Gascony.
May William Wallace leads a national uprising in Scotland against Edward I's rule and is victorious at Stirling Bridge (11 Sept.).
July Under French pressure, Pope Boniface VIII further modifies his claim for clerical immunity from royal taxation (see 1296).
11 Aug. Pope Boniface VIII canonizes the French king Louis IX who died in 1270.
24 Aug. Edward I of England sails for France to lead an invasion by his Flemish allies under Count Guy of Flander (see 1294).
7 Oct. Edward signs a truce with France. His regent in England, his son Edward, reissues Magna Carta to pacify protests against his father's style of government (10 Oct.).

- Pope Boniface VIII organizes a crusade under Charles II of Naples, James II of Aragon and the Genoese against Frederick II of Sicily.
- The Genoese ravage Venetian-held Crete and kill Venetian merchants working in the Byzantine empire.

ASIA

- Ala-ud-Din, sultan of Delhi, conquers the Hindu kingdom of Gujarat, NW India.
- Sultan Malik al-Saleh becomes the first Muslim ruler of Samudra in N Sumatra, Indonesia.

ARTS AND HUMANITIES

Giovanni Pisano, the pulpit of St Andrea, Pistoia, sculpture.

1298

EUROPE

22 July Edward I, king of England, defeats the Scots under William Wallace at Falkirk. The victory is due in part to the effectiveness of the longbow, the new English weapon.
27 July Albert of Habsburg, son of Rudolf I (see 1291), is elected king of the Romans, having defeated and killed Adolf of Nassau in battle at Göllheim on 2 July.

ARTS AND HUMANITIES

- In England a fire destroys the monastic buildings attached to Westminster Abbey.
- The Palazzo Vecchio, Venice, is built.
- Marco Polo, *Travels to Tartary and China*, travel account. Marco had travelled the overland route from Italy to China with his merchant father and uncle (see 1275).

1299

EUROPE

8 Sept. The Genoese destroy the Venetian navy off the Dalmatian coast; the defeat leads to changes in Venetian domestic politics – membership to the Great Council is now restricted.

ASIA

- Ala-ud-Din, sultan of Delhi, repels a Mongol army.

SCIENCE AND TECHNOLOGY

- The spinning-wheel (see 1280) is now in widespread use in England for manufacturing woollen yarn.

ARTS AND HUMANITIES

- The Zayn ad-Din Mosque, Cairo, is built.
Giovanni Pisano, the ivory *Madonna* in Pisa Cathedral, sculpture.

1300

EUROPE

- King Wenceslas II of Bohemia takes Pomerania and Greater Poland and is crowned king of the reunited Polish territories.

MIDDLE EAST AND NORTH AFRICA

– By now the Ottoman Turks, driven W by the Mongols, have occupied W Anatolia, in modern Turkey (see 1290).

THE AMERICAS

– By about this date the Aztecs (see 1168) have settled in the valley of Mexico.

ARTS AND HUMANITIES

– Guido Cavalcanti, Florentine poet and friend of Dante, dies.
Dante Alighieri, *Vita nuova*, love poetry.
Giotto di Bondone, frescoes in San Francesco, Assisi.

1301

EUROPE

14 Jan. With the death of Andrew III, the Arpad dynasty of Hungary ends. Wenceslas III, son of King Wenceslas II of Bohemia and Poland (see 1300), is elected and crowned.

7 Feb. King Edward I of England appropriates the title Prince of Wales and bestows it on his son.

1 Nov. Charles, count of Valois (son of Philip III of France), is summoned to Italy by Pope Boniface VIII to restore peace between the Black (Neri) and White (Bianchi) factions of the Welf (Guelph) party in Florence. He enters Florence and allows the exiled Black faction to return to the city, banishes the Whites and agrees to take responsibility for the affairs of the Florentine republic.

Dec. Pope Boniface VIII issues papal bulls accusing King Philip IV of France of misgovernment.

ASIA

– Ala-ud-Din of Delhi departs from the previous Muslim tradition of religious toleration by introducing a ban on drinking alcohol and other anti-Hindu legislation.

SCIENCE AND TECHNOLOGY

– In his treatise on Persian pottery, Al-Kashani describes the Chinese method of glazing earthenware.

1302

EUROPE

27 Jan. The Black faction of the Welfs (Guelphs), now in power in Florence, Italy, persecutes its opponents (who include the poet Dante) and issues sentences of death or exile.

10 April The earliest recorded meeting of the Estates-General in France is summoned by King Philip IV to oppose Pope Boniface VIII.

18 May The Flemings revolt against French occupation. On 11 July the communal militias of Ghent, Ypres and Bruges defeat a French army at Courtrai (also known as the battle of the Spurs).

24 Sept. The forces of Charles of Valois, captain-general of the papal and Neapolitan army, are destroyed by malaria. Charles II of Naples and Frederick II of Sicily declare a truce, ending the War of the Sicilian Vespers (see 1282).

18 Nov. Pope Boniface VIII's most famous bull, *Unam sanctam*, asserts the superiority of the papacy's spiritual power over secular rulers.

SCIENCE AND TECHNOLOGY

– Bartolomeo de Varignana of Bologna carries out the first post mortem examination.

ARTS AND HUMANITIES

Giovanni Cimabue, *St John*, Pisa Cathedral, mosaic.
Giovanni Pisano, the pulpit of Pisa Cathedral, sculpture.

1303

EUROPE

May King Edward I of England starts his seventh Scottish campaign. By the treaty of Paris between Edward and Philip IV of France (20 May), Gascony, SW France, is restored to England.

24 June King Philip IV summons all European rulers to a council to hear accusations against Pope Boniface VIII.

Sept. Boniface VIII releases the French people from allegiance to Philip IV; he is arrested (7 Sept.) at Anagni by Italian forces loyal to Philip. A popular rebellion in Anagni releases Boniface (12 Sept.). He dies (11 Oct.) and is succeeded by Benedict XI.

MIDDLE EAST AND NORTH AFRICA

– The Egyptian Mamluks defeat the Mongols of Persia and recover Damascus, Syria, for an-Nasir.

ASIA

– Mongols besiege Delhi, N India, but are unable to take the city.

SCIENCE AND TECHNOLOGY

– Taddeo Alderotti, the founder of a medical school at Bologna, N Italy, dies.

1304

EUROPE

Mar. The Scottish Parliament submits to King Edward I of England.

10 June In Italy the extreme wing of the Black faction of the Welf (Guelph) party starts a fire that destroys the centre of Florence.

7 July Pope Benedict XI dies, but pro- and anti-French cardinals are unable to elect a successor until 5 June 1305, when Clement V becomes pope.

– A Hungarian revolt forces Wenceslas III (see 1301) to return to Bohemia. His father Wenceslas II (see 1300) is expelled from Poland.

– The Byzantines lose Chios, in the Aegean Sea, to the Genoese.

ASIA

– In China the Christian missionary John of Monte Corvino is reported to have baptized thousands of converts.

ARTS AND HUMANITIES

– The Cloth Hall, Ypres (Belgium), is completed.

1305-9

ROBERT BRUCE CROWNED KING OF SCOTLAND □ DANTE WRITES DIVINE COMEDY □ PAPACY MOVES TO FRANCE

1305

EUROPE

21 June Wenceslas II of Bohemia dies and is succeeded by his son Wenceslas III, who is murdered (4 Aug.), ending the Premyslid dynasty.

23 Aug. The Scottish patriot William Wallace is executed in London as a traitor.

Oct. Albert, king of the Romans, forces the Bohemians to elect his son, Rudolf of Habsburg, as their king.

– King Edward I of England's ordinance of Trailbaston empowers the king to appoint judicial commissions to try and punish crimes of disorder.

ARTS AND HUMANITIES

Moses de Leon, *The Zohar*, a collection of cabbalistic texts influential in Jewish thought.

1306

EUROPE

25 Mar. Robert Bruce, leader of a national rebellion, is crowned king of Scotland at Scone.

7 May In Italy the Bolognese revolt against the papacy.

26 June Robert Bruce is defeated at Methven: Scottish resistance to the English collapses.

Nov. The Knights Hospitallers (a military order formed during the crusades) capture Rhodes from the Byzantines (see 1308).

– King Philip IV expels the Jews from France.

ASIA

– Another Mongol invasion of India is halted on the Indus, NW India.

ARTS AND HUMANITIES

25 Dec. The hymnologist and religious poet Jacapone da Todi dies. Giotto di Bondone, frescoes in the Arena Chapel, Padua.

1307

EUROPE

7 July King Edward I of England dies leading an army to Scotland and is succeeded by his son Edward II, who withdraws from Scotland and makes his lover Piers Gaveston earl of Cornwall (6 Aug.). Robert Bruce re-establishes himself in Scotland and defeats his rival John Comyn, earl of Buchan, at Inverurie (25 Dec.).

July Rudolf of Habsburg, king of Bohemia, dies; Henry, duke of Carinthia, is elected as Henry VII (15 Aug.).

6 Oct. In Italy an attempted counter-coup by the Black faction of the Welfs (Guelphs, see 1301) against the reformed Florentine constitution fails.

MIDDLE EAST AND NORTH AFRICA

– The Mongols destroy the Seljuk sultanate and annex Rum, in C Turkey.

ASIA

– The Mongol emperor Temur dies.

– The Hindu king of Deogir, Ramachandra, pays tribute to Ala-ud-Din, the sultan of Delhi.

SCIENCE AND TECHNOLOGY

– Dietrich of Freiburg writes a treatise on optics, meteorology and the rainbow effect.

ARTS AND HUMANITIES

– Dante Alighieri begins work on his *Divina commedia* (Divine Comedy), comprising *Inferno*, *Purgatorio* and *Paradiso*. It is one of the most influential works of the European Middle Ages.

1308

EUROPE

25 Jan. King Edward II of England marries Isabella, daughter of King Philip IV of France. Edward is crowned (25 Feb.).

18 May The English barons force Edward II to banish his favourite, Piers Gaveston, earl of Cornwall.

15 Aug. The Knights Hospitallers make the island of Rhodes their headquarters.

12 Nov. The Teutonic Knights seize Danzig (Gdansk) and kill the inhabitants.

27 Nov. Henry VII (count of Luxembourg) is elected king of the Romans.

– The Hungarian nobles make Charles Robert of Anjou king of Hungary; he becomes Charles I.

– The Scottish king Robert I (Robert Bruce) takes Aberdeen, conquers Galloway and threatens N England.

ASIA

– Prataparudradeva, the Hindu king of Telingana, S India, pays tribute to Ala-ud-Din, sultan of Delhi.

ARTS AND HUMANITIES

– In Italy Perugia University is founded.

– The theologian and philosopher Duns Scotus dies.

Duccio di Buoninsegna, *Maestà*, painting for Siena Cathedral.

1309

EUROPE

27 Mar. Pope Clement V declares Venice to be no longer a Christian state because it supports Falco d'Este, the ruler of Ferrara, which Clement claims as a papal fief. Papal forces defeat the Venetians (Aug.).

– The Teutonic Knights gain complete control of E Pomerania, NE Germany; their headquarters move from Venice to Marienburg.

– Feuds among the Italian cardinals and their allies persuade Pope Clement V to move the papacy to Avignon, France. The papal court will not return to Rome until 1377.

ARTS AND HUMANITIES

Jean de Joinville, *Mémoires*, a hagiographical account of King Louis IX of France.

Dante Alighieri (1265–1321)

The Italian poet Dante Alighieri is one of the most important figures in Western literature. He was a native of Florence, then experiencing a great period of literary and artistic renewal, and his intellectual energy seems to have been sparked off by the political turbulence of the city – in which he served as an official for many years, until banished for life when a faction of citizens hostile to his allies took control. He left Florence in 1302 and died in exile in Ravenna, where between 1307 and 1321 he composed his great Christian epic,

the Commedia (commedia simply means 'play'), later known as Divina commedia or, in English, Divine Comedy.

Dante's work reflects the rise of European vernacular literature, a cause he advocated himself in De vulgari eloquentia (begun c.1304). Poetry would still be composed in Latin after Dante, but the authority and range of his Divine Comedy showed the way ahead. It also made Dante's Tuscan dialect into the standard form of literary Italian.

In the Divine Comedy Dante describes three aspects of the afterlife in the three

stages of the book: the circles of hell in Inferno, the mount of expiation in Purgatorio, and heaven in Paradiso. The poetry has the irresistible dynamism of a mind drawn towards God and enraptured by the fulfilment of that desire. The work is sustained and made possible by a belief in the fundamental affinity of the human mind with the divine order, and its capacity to be touched by the ultimate truth. Hence the desire for knowledge – which also, in Dante's allegory, becomes the journey of the Christian soul in search of salvation.

1310

EUROPE

15 June In Italy, Venice and the papacy make peace; the Council of Ten is instituted to rule in Venice.

30 Aug. Bohemia rises against Henry of Carinthia's rule (see 1307); Elizabeth, daughter of Wenceslas II (see 1300), marries John, son of the Emperor Henry VII (see 1308), who duly invests his son-in-law as king of Bohemia.

– Lyons, in Burgundy, is occupied by the forces of King Philip IV of France.

ASIA

– The sultan of Delhi, Ala-ud-Din, sends an army to plunder S India.

SCIENCE AND TECHNOLOGY

– In China silk and iron are produced by water-powered machines.

ARTS AND HUMANITIES

– Exceptional mosaics are created in the monastery of St Saviour in Chora in Constantinople.

– Construction of the Doges' Palace begins in Venice.

– The Italian poet Dante Alighieri (see box) writes prose commentaries on his shorter poems.

– Around this time the English song 'Sumer is Icumen in' is composed.

1311

EUROPE

6 Jan. Emperor Henry VII is crowned king of Lombardy in Milan; he approves the despotic regimes of Matteo Visconti in Milan and Can Grande della Scala in Verona. Florence moves to defend itself against Henry.

16 Aug. King Edward II of England accepts Parliament's

proposals for the reform of English government, which include the foundation of the Privy Seal Office.

– King Philip IV expels the Lombards from France.

SCIENCE AND TECHNOLOGY

– Pietro Vesconte produces the earliest known navigational maps of the Mediterranean.

ARTS AND HUMANITIES

– Chairs of Arabic are created in the universities at Paris, Louvain (Belgium) and Salamanca (Spain).

– Henry of Meissen founds the Meistersingers (troubadors) of Mainz.

1312

EUROPE

April Pope Clement V suppresses the Knights Templar. Founded to fight in the crusades (see 1119), the Templars came to be used to safeguard crusader finances and became a powerful military and financial organization throughout Europe.

29 June In Italy Henry VII is crowned Holy Roman Emperor in the Lateran Palace (St Peter's is occupied by Romans hostile to him). Henry abandons his campaign against Florence (31 Oct.).

ASIA

– Tokhta, khan of the Golden Horde, dies and is succeeded by Uzbeg, a Muslim who converts the Horde to Islam.

– Thihathura, leader of the Shan people, establishes his capital at Pinya, N Burma.

ARTS AND HUMANITIES

– Cecco Angiolieri, Italian author of a collection of songs and sonnets, dies.

Dante Alighieri, De Monarchia, description of divinely ordained world government.

1313

EUROPE

13 Jan. The Scots expel the English garrison from Perth.

13 June Pope Clement V declares Naples to be under papal protection.

24 Aug. The Holy Roman Emperor Henry VII dies leading an army against Naples.

– John Balliol, the former Scottish king, dies.

– The Scots recover control of the Isle of Man.

ASIA

– Tran Anh-tong, emperor of Annam (N Vietnam), occupies Champa (S Vietnam) and establishes the Cham royal dynasty as puppet rulers.

SCIENCE AND TECHNOLOGY

– Alessandro della Spina, Italian scientist credited with the invention of spectacles, dies.

– German Franciscan friar Berthold Schwarz invents gunpowder, independently of its earlier Chinese invention (see 225).

ARTS AND HUMANITIES

– Abu Haiyan writes the earliest known Turkish grammar.

1314

EUROPE

20 April Pope Clement V dies (see 1316).

24 June The Scottish king Robert I (Robert Bruce) defeats King Edward II of England at Bannockburn: the English withdraw from Scotland. Edward's poor generalship further lessens his popularity with his barons.

19 Oct. Frederick of Austria is elected king of the Romans, but rival nobles elect Ludwig of Bavaria (20 Oct.): civil war breaks out in the Holy Roman Empire.

30 Nov. King Philip IV of France dies and is succeeded by his son Louis X.

MIDDLE EAST AND NORTH AFRICA

– The Mamluks of Egypt establish a Muslim as king of N Sudan (Dongola).

SCIENCE AND TECHNOLOGY

– Chinese magistrate Wangzhen writes a book on agriculture and technology, and has it printed with wooden blocks. This is the first example of printing with movable type.

ARTS AND HUMANITIES

– In England the *Mappa Mundi*, a large and ornate symbolic world map, is prepared in Hereford.

– Haithon, king of Armenia, writes a history and geography of Asia.

Chandesvara, *The Jewel Mine of Politics*, Hindu treatise on the science of government.

Rashid ad-Din, *Jami altawarikh* (Histories), a Persian universal history.

1315

EUROPE

17 Mar. Ludwig of Bavaria recognizes the Swiss federation and grants charters to many provincial leagues.

Aug. King Louis X of France fails to renew his father Philip's abortive campaign against Flanders.

29 Aug. In Italy Uguccione, despot of Pisa, defeats the armies of Florence and Naples at Montecatini.

15 Nov. The Swiss defeat Duke Leopold of Austria at Morgarten.

– Bohemian nobles force John of Bohemia (John of Luxembourg) to expel his German advisers and employ Bohemian lords.

– In Italy Frederick of Trinacria claims the title of king of Sicily and so initiates war with Naples.

– The Estonian nobility forms a representative assembly, the Landtag of Pernau.

SCIENCE AND TECHNOLOGY

– In England John of Gaddesden describes a device for extracting teeth.

ARTS AND HUMANITIES

20 Sept. The Catalan scholar Rámon Lull (see p. 147) dies.

– Simone Martini, *Maestà*, painting for the Siena townhall. Martini is a leading painter of the Siennese school and will enjoy papal patronage at Avignon (1339–44).

1316

EUROPE

2 May In an attempt to stir the Irish into rebellion against English rule, Edward Bruce, brother of King Robert of Scotland, is crowned king of Ireland.

5 June King Louis X of France dies; his posthumous son John I, born on 15 Nov., lives only five days. Louis's brother Philip V proclaims himself king (19 Nov.).

7 Aug. After two years the cardinals elect a successor to Clement V (see 1314) when they choose John XXII (Jacques Duèse) as pope.

– In Italy Ghiberto da Correggio is expelled from Parma and a republic is established.

– In Liège, modern Belgium, the prince-bishop gives his subjects the right to control legislation.

MIDDLE EAST AND NORTH AFRICA

– Uljaytu, sultan of Persia, dies and is succeeded by his nephew Abu Sa 'id.

ASIA

– Ala-ud-Din, sultan of Delhi, India, dies and is succeeded by Qutb-ud-Din Mubarak.

ECONOMY AND SOCIETY

– Famine in W Europe causes widespread mortality; population levels decline rapidly.

SCIENCE AND TECHNOLOGY
- In Italy Mondino dei Luizzi introduces dissection techniques in his work at Bologna University.

ARTS AND HUMANITIES
Abu-l-Barakat, *Al-sullam al-Kabir*, a Coptic–Arabic vocabulary.

1317

EUROPE
Feb. The Scottish king Robert I (Robert Bruce) joins his brother Edward on campaign in Ireland (see 1316).
31 Mar. Pope John XXII claims imperial rights of government in Italy for the papacy.
15 Aug. The people of Ferrara, N Italy, elect the d'Este brothers as rulers after massacring the Neapolitan garrison.
- In Italy the despot Uguccione (see 1315) is expelled from Pisa and Lucca.

ASIA
- Mubarak of Delhi annexes the Hindu kingdom of Deogir.

ARTS AND HUMANITIES
- Byzantine frescoes are painted for Nagoricino Church, Serbia. Simone Martini, *St Louis of Toulouse*, painting.

1318

EUROPE
8 April The Scottish king Robert I (Robert Bruce) takes Berwick-upon-Tweed and raids Yorkshire, N England, to exact tribute (May).
19 July Duke Leopold of Austria makes peace with the Swiss Forest Cantons.
14 Oct. Edward Bruce, king of Ireland, is defeated and killed by the English army at Faughard, near Dundalk.
- George V succeeds as king of Georgia.
- Pope John XXII persecutes the Spiritual Franciscans (Fraticelli), an Italian branch of the order that pursues strictly the Franciscan ideal of Apostolic poverty; four members are burned at the stake as heretics.

ASIA
- Tran Minh-tong, emperor of Annam (Dai Viet), deposes Che Nang of Champa (S Vietnam); Che A-nan is appointed military governor.
- Pope John XXII creates ten suffragan bishoprics for Persia; Armenia, Persia and India are granted to the Dominicans as a mission field, while the Franciscans get China.

1319

EUROPE
26 June In Spain, a Castilian invasion of the Moorish kingdom of Granada fails.
20 Sept. King Edward II of England abandons his siege of Scottish-held Berwick-upon-Tweed, N England.

Sept. The king of Sweden, Birger Magnusson, escapes to Denmark; Magnus VII Eriksson, king of Norway, Birger's nephew (aged three), is elected king of Sweden as Magnus II.
- Grand Duke Michael of Vladimir, Russia, is executed after being deposed by Uzbeg (see 1312) and succeeded by Juri of Moscow.
- King Eric VI of Denmark dies and his attempt at controlling the Hanse ends. The Hanse, an association of Baltic merchants, expels the English and Scots and gains a monopoly of trade with Norway.

ARTS AND HUMANITIES
- In England the chapterhouse of Wells Cathedral is completed.

1320

EUROPE
26 April By the Declaration of Arbroath, the Scottish nobility affirm to the pope that they reject English rule and are loyal to Robert I (Robert Bruce).
- John of Bohemia (see 1315) abdicates to become a knight errant, a wandering freelance adventurer.

ASIA
14 April In India, Mubarak of Delhi is murdered by his favourite, Khusraw, who succeeds him but is himself murdered by Ghazi Malik (Ghiyas-ud-Din Tughluq), who succeeds in turn.

SCIENCE AND TECHNOLOGY
- Henry de Mondeville writes *Cyrurgia* (Surgery), the first textbook on surgery by a Frenchman.

ARTS AND HUMANITIES
- The tomb of Shah Rukn-i Alam is erected at Multan in the Punjab, modern Pakistan.
- The first German Late Gothic architecture appears in the Church of the Holy Cross, Schwäbisch Gmünd.
Simone Martini, polyptych at Pisa, painting.

1321

EUROPE
April In Italy Milanese forces capture Vercelli.
19 Aug. King Edward II of England is forced by Parliament to banish his favourite, Hugh Despenser, and also Despenser's son, Hugh the Younger. The Despensers helped the king in the administration of his financial and land management affairs. This gave them both the opportunity to frustrate the ambitions of the barons and also the chance to enrich themselves.

SCIENCE AND TECHNOLOGY
- The French Jewish mathematician and philosopher Levi ben Gerson publishes *The Work of the Computer*, a description of algebra and arithmetic.

ARTS AND HUMANITIES
14 Sept. The Italian poet Dante Alighieri dies (see p. 155).
- In England work begins on the Lady Chapel, Ely Cathedral.

1322

EUROPE

2–3 Jan. King Philip V (the Tall) of France dies and is succeeded by his brother Charles IV (the Fair), last of the Capetian dynasty.

5 Jan. In Italy Milanese forces seize Cremona.

28 Sept. Ludwig of Bavaria (see 1314) defeats and captures his rival, Frederick of Austria, at Mühldorf in Austria.

– Florence decides no longer to employ Robert of Naples as protector when his term of office expires.

ARTS AND HUMANITIES

– In England, the central tower of Ely Cathedral collapses.

– The Chinese painter Zhao Mengfu (Chao Meng-Fu) dies.

1323

EUROPE

11 June The papal legate Bertrand du Poujet, commanding a military campaign against the Waiblings (Ghibellines), besieges Milan but abandons the siege when Ludwig of Bavaria sends troops to aid the Milanese.

8 Oct. Pope John XXII claims the right to confirm imperial elections, and demands that Ludwig surrender the kingship of the Romans since Ludwig claims imperial authority in N Italy.

– The English Exchequer is reformed by the treasurer, Walter Stapledon, bishop of Exeter.

– Pope John XXII condemns the idea of apostolic poverty; the Spiritual Franciscans (Fraticellii) (see 1318) revolt in N Italy.

– Michael Sisman of Vidin founds the last Bulgarian dynasty.

ASIA

– Yet another Mongol invasion of India is defeated; Tughluq of Delhi defeats and annexes the Hindu kingdom of Telingana, S India.

ARTS AND HUMANITIES

– In S France, an academy for troubadours is founded at Toulouse; troubadours are lyric poets whose compositions, most often in the Provençal language, celebrate chivalry and courtly love.

Levi ben Gerson, commentaries on Averroes (see p. 130), philosophy.

1324

EUROPE

23 Mar. King Ludwig of Bavaria is excommunicated; he denounces the pope and denies papal authority in Germany (22 May).

– Charles I quells the noble opposition in Hungary; he gives up holding parliaments.

– The Mongols kill Andrew and Leo, princes of Ruthenia.

MIDDLE EAST AND NORTH AFRICA

6 April Ghazi Orkhan succeeds his father Osman I (see 1290) as ruler of the Ottoman Turks.

SCIENCE AND TECHNOLOGY

– The first cannon are made of forged iron at Metz, E France.

ARTS AND HUMANITIES

– Marsilio of Padua, *Defensor pacis*, theological treatise arguing against the power of the clergy and in favour of a secular state (see 1327).

– William of Ockham, Oxford Franciscan and philosopher, is summoned to the papal court at Avignon and imprisoned.

1325

EUROPE

2 Feb. Andronicus II Palaeologus and his grandson Andronicus III are crowned co-emperors to halt civil war in the Byzantine empire.

13 Mar. Frederick of Austria renounces his claim to be king of the Romans in favour of Ludwig of Bavaria (see 1314).

– Charles of Valois, duke of Anjou, dies. His son will become Philip VI of France in 1328, the first of the Valois kings.

ASIA

Feb.–Mar. In India, Tughluq, sultan of Delhi, is murdered and succeeded by his son, Muhammad II.

– In China rebellions break out against the Mongol rulers.

THE AMERICAS

– The Aztecs (see 1300) settle on a site that marks the origin of Tenochtitlán (Mexico City).

ARTS AND HUMANITIES

– The Indian poet and historian Amir Khusraw of Delhi dies.

– Arab traveller and geographer Ibn Battuta starts his travels. Over a 30-year period he will visit Arabia, Persia, Anatolia, Mesopotamia, Bokhara, India, China, Sumatra, S Spain and Timbuktu.

Giotto di Bondone, frescoes for the four chapels of Santa Croce, Florence, Italy.

1326

EUROPE

15 Oct. In England King Edward II's treasurer, Walter Stapledon, bishop of Exeter (see 1323), is murdered in a popular rebellion in London. King Edward flees to Gloucester, but is captured at Neath Abbey (16 Nov.). He is deposed by an alliance of his alienated wife Isabella, sister of the king of France, her lover Roger Mortimer and other discontented barons. His son Edward, aged 14, is proclaimed Keeper of the Realm.

– The Despensers, Edward II's favourites, both father (26 Oct.) and son (16 Nov.), are executed.

– Vladislav of Poland lays waste to the Mark of Brandenburg, NE Germany.

1327

EUROPE

20 Jan. King Edward II of England abdicates in favour of his son Edward III and is murdered at Berkeley Castle, Gloucestershire, W England (21 Sept.). Queen Isabella and her lover, Roger Mortimer, will rule the country during the minority of Edward III.

31 Mar. King Charles IV of France whose sister, Isabella, rules England, and King Edward III of England, aged 15, make peace; Gascony returns to English rule. Charles had seized all the English possessions in France (1326) during the final days of the doomed Edward II.

– Pope John XXII condemns Marsilio of Padua's *Defensor pacis* (see 1324). The excommunicated Marsilio flees to the protection of Ludwig of Bavaria.

ARTS AND HUMANITIES

– Francesco degli Stabili, poet, astrologer and author of *Acerba* (a verse collection), is murdered in Florence by the Inquisition.

– Death of Meister Eckhart (Johannes Eckhart), Dominican priest, writer, professor at the university of Cologne and the greatest of all German mystics.

1328

EUROPE

7 Jan. Ludwig of Bavaria, now crowned king of Lombardy, N Italy, enters Rome and is crowned emperor as Louis IV; the pope declares a crusade against him.

24 Jan. King Edward III of England, aged 16, marries Philippa, daughter of the anti-French count of Hainault and Holland.

1 Feb. King Charles IV of France dies; the Capetian dynasty ends. Charles' widow is pregnant and his cousin Philip of Valois becomes regent. When Charles's daughter is born, Philip is elected Philip VI, first king of the Valois dynasty.

17 Mar. Edward III recognizes Robert I (Robert Bruce) as king of Scotland, ending the Scottish War of Independence.

22 May The Holy Roman Emperor Louis IV (Ludwig of Bavaria) declares Pope John XXII deposed and elects the antipope Nicholas V. Louis and Nicholas leave Rome (4 Aug.).

24 May The Byzantine co-emperor Andronicus II Palaeologus is forced to abdicate. He is succeeded by his grandson, Andronicus III Palaeologus.

– Alexander II, Grand Duke of Vladimir, is deposed on Khan Uzbeg's orders by Ivan, son of Daniel, prince of Moscow; Alexander of Suzdal is appointed Grand Duke.

– John of Monte Corvino, archbishop of Beijing (see 1304), dies.

MIDDLE EAST AND NORTH AFRICA

– The Karaman Turks extend their control in the ilkhanate of Persia and occupy Konya, the former capital of Rum, C Turkey.

SCIENCE AND TECHNOLOGY

– By this date the production of mirrors and silks is well established in Venice.

ARTS AND HUMANITIES

– The English Franciscan William of Ockham escapes from Avignon (see 1324) and joins the Holy Roman Emperor Louis IV.

Heinrich Suso, *Buchlein der Wahrheit* (Little Book of Truth), German mystical writing.

1329

EUROPE

7 June Robert I (Robert Bruce), king of Scotland, dies and is succeeded by his five-year-old son, David II.

Dec. The Holy Roman Emperor Louis IV returns to Germany, ending his attempts to control Italy.

– Joanna II is crowned queen of Navarre, N Spain; the territory is separated from France (see 1284).

– The Byzantine emperor Andronicus III Palaeologus recovers the island of Chios, in the Aegean Sea, from the Genoese.

ASIA

– Muhammad of Delhi removes the inhabitants of Delhi to Daulatabad, W India. He tries to introduce fiduciary currency to India, with brass tokens denominating value in silver.

SCIENCE AND TECHNOLOGY

Chinese scholar Youlu (Lu Yu), *Mo shi* (*Mo Shih*), a history of ink manufacture in China.

ARTS AND HUMANITIES

– The Italian humanist scholar and playwright Albertino Mussato dies.

Levi ben Gerson, *The Wars of the Lord*, a study of Aristotelian philosophy.

1330

EUROPE

28 June Stephen Uros III, king of Serbia, defeats and kills the Bulgarian tsar Michael Sisman near Velbuzd, establishing Serbian rule in Macedonia.

25 July The antipope Nicholas V (see 1328) resigns.

4 Aug. The Habsburgs recognize the Holy Roman Emperor Louis IV (Aug.).

29 Nov. Roger Mortimer, earl of March (see 1326), is executed as a traitor to King Edward III. Fearing that his mother's lover Mortimer is plotting to prevent him from gaining full control as king, the 18-year-old Edward has secretly entered Nottingham Castle with some of his friends, crept along the corridors, felled two guards, seized Mortimer at swordpoint and taken him to London for trial. Queen Isabella loses power but is allowed to live in luxurious retirement.

– The Teutonic Knights occupy Riga, in the E Baltic.

SCIENCE AND TECHNOLOGY

– Italian scholar Pietro Bruno publishes *The Precious Pearl*, a defence of alchemy.

ARTS AND HUMANITIES

– The last datable Sanskrit inscription in Cambodia is produced, marking the end of Indian cultural influence there.

– In England, the spire of Salisbury Cathedral is completed.

Anonymous, *The Little Flowers of St Francis*, record of the spread of St Francis's popularity.

Hamdallah Mustawfi, *Ta'rik-i guzida*, Persian history of the world.

Ramon Muntaner, *Chronica*, Catalan history.

Odoric of Pordenone, *Description of the East*, travel account.

Andrea Pisano, bronze doors of the Baptistery, Florence, sculpture.

1331

EUROPE

17 Sept. King Vladislav I of Poland defeats the Teutonic Knights at Plowce.

MIDDLE EAST AND NORTH AFRICA

2 Mar. The Ottoman ruler Orkhan (see 1326) takes Nicaea from the Byzantines.

ASIA

– Emperor Godaigo of Japan attempts to rule in place of the shogunate; he is deposed by the Hojo regency.

– *The Great Standard of Administration*, the official Chinese encyclopedia describing the (mostly Mongol) institutions of Chinese government, is written.

ARTS AND HUMANITIES

– The Jewish-Italian poet Emanuel ben Solomon, who wrote as Manoello Giudeo, dies.

1332

EUROPE

July King Philip VI of France takes the cross for a crusade proposed by Pope John XXII.

24 Sept. Edward Balliol kills the earl of Mar, regent of Scotland (12 Aug.), and is crowned king of Scotland in opposition to the young David II. He is, however, defeated by the earl of Moray at Annan (12 Dec.) and flees to England.

– Alexander III, Grand Duke of Vladimir, dies and is succeeded by Ivan I Kalita of Moscow. As the seat of the Metropolitan Peter (head of the Russian Orthodox Church), Moscow is already Russia's ecclesiastical capital; it now begins to emerge as its leading civic centre.

SUB-SAHARAN AFRICA

– The negus (emperor) of Abyssinia (Ethiopia), Amda Seyon I, repels invasion attempts by the sultan of Ifat, a Muslim ruler in N Abyssinia.

SCIENCE AND TECHNOLOGY

– The technique for distilling liqueurs spreads from Italy to France.

ARTS AND HUMANITIES

Taddeo Gaddi, *The Life of the Virgin*, fresco, in Santa Croce, Florence.

1333

EUROPE

May The young king David II of Scotland flees to France as a guest of King Philip VI. His rival Edward Balliol recognizes King Edward III of England as his overlord (12 June) and cedes Berwick-upon-Tweed and eight counties of S Scotland to him. But (1339) a Scottish rebellion forces Balliol out of Scotland. David II will return to Scotland in 1341, and Edward Balliol will surrender his claim to the Scottish throne to Edward III of England in 1356.

19 July A Scots force attempting to relieve the seige of Berwick-upon-Tweed, is defeated by the army of Edward III of England at the battle of Halidon Hill. Berwick surrenders to Edward III's forces the following day. Edward has already seized the Isle of Man from the Scots (8 June.).

25 Aug. In Moorish S Spain Yusuf I succeeds his murdered brother, Muhammad IV, as king of Granada.

– The Byzantine emperor Andronicus III Palaeologus recovers N Thessaly.

ASIA

– The Japanese emperor Godaigo defeats the Hojo regency (see 1331); Japan's capital is moved from Kamakura back to Kyoto.

– In China, the Mongol dynasty of the Yuan is under threat after famine and Yellow River floods hit the country.

– Bubonic plague (the Black Death) breaks out in China.

ARTS AND HUMANITIES

– King Charles IV of Bohemia (Charles of Luxembourg) begins construction of Karlstein Palace in Prague.

1334

EUROPE

4 Dec. Pope John XXII dies. He is succeeded (20 Dec.) by Benedict XII (Jacques Fournier).

ARTS AND HUMANITIES

– Scholars based in Oxford try to establish a university in Stamford, Lincolnshire, E England.

– Work begins on the Papal Palace, Avignon, S France (see 1309).

Giotto, the campanile of Florence Cathedral, architecture.

1335

EUROPE

2 April On the death of Henry, duke of Carinthia, the Holy Roman Emperor Louis IV confers the duchy and the S Tyrol on the Habsburgs; his sons receive the N Tyrol (Aug.).

– King John of Bohemia, Charles I of Hungary and Casimir III of Poland meet in Buda, Hungary, to decide that the Teutonic

Knights should restore two cities to Poland but may retain Pomerania as vassals to Casimir. In return, Casimir recognizes Bohemian overlordship over Silesia and John renounces his claim to the Polish crown.

MIDDLE EAST AND NORTH AFRICA
- Abu Sa'id, sultan of Persia, dies; the Mongol ilkhanate disappears.

ASIA
- Hasan, governor of Madura in S India, declares himself independent of the Delhi sultanate.

SCIENCE AND TECHNOLOGY
May In England, the abbot of St Albans, Richard of Wallingford, writer on trigonometry, dies.

ARTS AND HUMANITIES
- An illustrated copy of the Persian epic, Firdausi's *Shah-nama*, is made at Tabriz.

1336

EUROPE
- The French rebel Robert of Artois shelters in England.
- English wool exports to Flanders are suspended.
- Pope Benedict XII cancels the planned crusade to the Holy Land (see 1332).
- Pope Benedict XII publishes new rules for the administration of the Benedictine and Cluniac monastic orders as part of his reform of the Catholic Church.

ASIA
18 April Following a Hindu rebellion against Muslim rule, Harihara I is crowned king of the Vijayanagar empire in S India.
- Emperor Godaigo of Japan (see 1333) is overthrown by the warlord Ashikaga Takauji, who installs a new emperor. Godaigo flees from Kyoto and sets up a rival court. Civil war breaks out between the N and S provinces.

ARTS AND HUMANITIES
Andrea Pisano, decoration of the bronze doors to the baptistery of Florence Cathedral with scenes from the life of John the Baptist.

1337

EUROPE
24 May King Philip VI of France confiscates Gascony: the Hundred Years War between France and England begins. The English king Edward III, supported by Flanders, claims Normandy, Maine and Anjou, denies the legitimacy of Philip VI's title to the crown of France, and claims the French crown through his mother Isabella, daughter of Philip IV.
28 Dec. The Flemings accept James van Artevelde as their leader in the national rebellion against the count of Flanders.

- The Friends of God, a group of lay people inspired by the writings of the mystic Meister Eckhart (see 1327), become a force in German religious life.

MIDDLE EAST AND NORTH AFRICA
- Nicomedia, previously under Byzantine control, falls to the Ottoman Turks led by Orkhan (see 1326). The Byzantines, however, regain control of Epirus (W Greece).

ASIA
- A Muslim army sent from Delhi, India, to conquer Tibet is destroyed in the Himalayas.

1338

EUROPE
16 July In Germany the imperial diet meeting at Frankfurt states that the Electors of the Holy Roman Empire may elect the emperor without consulting the pope.
16 July King Edward III of England lands in Antwerp and meets his ally Emperor Louis IV at Koblenz (5 Sept.). Louis appoints Edward imperial vicar.
Aug. Under the terms of the treaty of Koblenz, the Holy Roman Emperor Louis IV supports the English claim to the French crown.
- The French king Philip VI declares all English-held territories in France null and void; he besieges Guienne in SW France and his navy raids and burns Portsmouth, S England.

ARTS AND HUMANITIES
Nikolaus von Jeroschin, *The Prussian Chronicle*, history of N Germany.

1339

EUROPE
23 Sept. Simon Boccanegra is elected the first doge of Genoa.
- Venice defeats and annexes Treviso in N Italy.
- Casimir III of Poland fails to conquer Galicia in C Europe; the Galicians are protected by Uzbeg, khan of the Golden Horde (see 1312).
- The Byzantine emperor Andronicus III Palaeologus sends an embassy to the pope to negotiate a reunion between the Eastern and Western Churches.

ASIA
- W Bengal rebels against the sultanate of Delhi and becomes an independent state.

1340

EUROPE
25 Jan. King Edward III of England formally declares himself king of France in Ghent, Flanders, where his right to the title is upheld by the Flemings.
Mar. John of Gaunt, son of King Edward III of England and father of King Henry IV, is born.

24 June The English fleet defeats the French navy at the battle of Sluys, facilitating an English assault on N France.

24 Sept. A truce is declared in the Anglo-French war when the English war chest is exhausted.

30 Oct. King Alfonso XI of Castile defeats the Spanish and Moroccan Muslims at the battle of Rio Salado.

– Valdemar IV Atterdag succeeds to the throne of Denmark and re-establishes domestic stability.

– The Florentine banking house of Peruzzi charges the English crown 120% interest on its loans for the French war.

ASIA

– Famine is widespread in N India; the sultan of Delhi creates a department of agriculture.

SCIENCE AND TECHNOLOGY

– Iron blast furnaces in the Liège region (modern Belgium) become the first European producers of cast iron.

ARTS AND HUMANITIES

– Anonymous, *The Prick of Conscience*, English religious poem.

1341

EUROPE

15 Mar. The emperor Louis IV makes peace with the French and ends his English alliance (see 1338).

6 June The English are expelled from Edinburgh, Scotland; the Scottish king David II returns from France (see 1333).

15 June The Byzantine emperor Andronicus III Palaeologus dies. John Cantacuzenus, supported by the mystical *hesychast* movement, challenges the succession of the emperor's nine-year-old son John V and his regent mother Anna of Savoy.

11 Nov. Jeanne de Penthièvre, contesting the right of her half-brother John de Montfort to inherit the dukedom of Brittany, recognizes the English claim to the French throne.

– The French government introduces a salt tax (the *gabelle*) to help increase war revenue.

ASIA

– Uzbeg, khan of the Golden Horde (see 1312), dies and is succeeded by his son Tinibeg.

1342

EUROPE

31 Mar. Scottish forces capture Roxburgh; the English are decisively expelled from Scotland.

25 April Pope Benedict XII dies. He is succeeded (7 May) by Clement VI (Pierre Roger).

Aug. Ludwig of Brandenburg, son of the Holy Roman Emperor Louis IV, marries Margaret of Tyrol, adding the Tyrol and Carinthia to the imperial domain.

– The city of Thessalonika, N Greece, rises in support of John Cantacuzenus' rebellion against the Byzantine imperial line (see 1341).

– Charles I of Hungary dies and is succeeded by his son Ludwig I.

ASIA

– Tinibeg, khan of the Golden Horde, is deposed by his brother Janibeg.

ARTS AND HUMANITIES

Simone Martini, *Christ Reproved by His Parents*, painting.

1343

EUROPE

4 Jan. Andrea Dandolo is elected doge of Venice; he is a friend of Petrarch.

8 July Casimir III of Poland cedes his Pomeranian territories to the Teutonic Knights.

– The Byzantine rebel John Cantacuzenus conquers Thrace with Ottoman support.

– King Edward III of England repudiates his debts (see 1340); the Florentine banking house of Peruzzi, which had lent him money for his French wars, goes bankrupt.

SCIENCE AND TECHNOLOGY

– French Jewish mathematician and philosopher Levi ben Gerson completes *Concerning the Harmony of Numbers*, a mathematical treatise.

ARTS AND HUMANITIES

– The political philosopher Marsilio of Padua (see 1324) dies in Munich.

William of Ockham, *Dialogues*, a philosophical defence of secular government.

1344

EUROPE

– Mongol forces are defeated on the River Vistula by the Poles, and in Transylvania by the Hungarians.

We saw a vast town on the move.

Ibn Battuta (1304–68) describes the Mongol army in the Caucasus

– King Alfonso XI of Castile seizes Algeciras, S Spain, from Moorish control.

– The Florentine banking house of Bardi collapses when King Edward III of England repudiates his debts (see also 1343).

– The group of Baltic merchants and cities allied for trade purposes calls itself the Hanseatic League.

– Pope Clement VI makes the see of Prague an archbishopric; the province of Bohemia is separated from Mainz.

MIDDLE EAST AND NORTH AFRICA
– A crusading league captures the port of Smyrna (now Izmir, Turkey) from the Turks.

SCIENCE AND TECHNOLOGY
– Italian horologist Jacopo di Dondi invents the clock dial.
– French Jewish mathematician and philosopher Levi ben Gerson dies.

1345

EUROPE
24 July Street riots spread in Ghent, modern Belgium; the local ruler, James van Artevelde, is murdered.
– Hungarian forces occupy Croatia.
– In Italy popular protests against the ruling merchant oligarchy spread in Florence; the rebels are defeated and their leader, Ciuto Brandini, is executed.
– The Ponte Vecchio (later so named) across the River Arno is completed in Florence.

ARTS AND HUMANITIES
– Notre Dame Cathedral, Paris, is completed.

1346

EUROPE
16 April Stephen Dushan, king of Serbia, proclaims himself emperor of the Serbs, Greeks, Albanians and Bulgars at Skopje. He prepares for a campaign against Constantinople with the aim of supplanting Byzantine rule.
26 July The English sack Caen, Normandy.
26 Aug. At the battle of Crécy, English and Welsh longbowmen inflict huge losses upon the French, who are resoundingly defeated. King Philip VI of France escapes to Amiens but John I, king of Bohemia, and Louis, count of Flanders, are both killed on the French side.
4 Sept. King Edward III of England begins his siege of Calais, France.
4 Oct. Poitiers, C France, falls to the English.
17 Oct. King David II of Scotland invades N England but is defeated and captured at the battle of Neville's Cross, near Durham.
– The French Estates-General withholds any further war levies.
– Charles I succeeds his father John I as king of Bohemia (see above) and is crowned king of the Germans at Bonn; he opens hostilities against the Holy Roman Emperor Louis IV in S Germany, (Aug.).
– The Teutonic Knights conquer Estonia.
– The Black Death, a form of bubonic plague, breaks out in a Tatar army that is besieging the Genoese-held city of Caffa in the Crimea. Refugees from the city carry the disease to Europe.

ASIA
– Shah Mirza establishes an Islamic dynasty in Kashmir.

ARTS AND HUMANITIES
– Parts of the Hagia Sophia, Constantinople, collapse after an earthquake.
Francesco Petrarca (Petrarch), *De vita solitaria* (On the Solitary Life), poetry in medieval Latin.

1347

EUROPE
21 May The rebel John Cantacuzenus (see 1341 and 1343) is named co-emperor of Byzantium as John VI Cantacuzenus, with John V Palaeologus as his ward.
May Cola di Rienzi, a papal courtier and the leader of a popular revolution against the ruling Roman nobility, names himself tribune. He proclaims the authority of the Roman people over the Empire (July) and is installed as tribune (Aug.).
4 Aug. Calais falls to the English and its citizens are expelled; it will be an English possession for the next 211 years (see 1558).
28 Sept. The English and the French agree a truce.
11 Oct. The Holy Roman Emperor Louis IV is killed while hunting; his rival Charles of Luxembourg becomes ruler of the German territories. He will be crowned as Emperor Charles IV in 1355.
– In Florence the populace attack prominent banking families, whom they hold responsible for the Florentine crisis.
– Pope Clement VI commands that Cola di Rienzi (see above) be deposed as a criminal. Helped by Ludwig of Hungary, Rienzi defeats the Roman nobility in battle (20 Nov.), but he abdicates (Dec.) and flees Rome.
– The Black Death reaches Constantinople, Cyprus, Naples, Genoa and Marseilles.

SCIENCE AND TECHNOLOGY
– Jane I, countess of Provence, establishes an officially approved and medically examined house of prostitution at Avignon in an attempt to control the spread of venereal disease.

ARTS AND HUMANITIES
Bernardo Daddi, *Madonna and Child Enthroned with Angels*, painting.

1348

EUROPE
Jan. In Italy, Hungarian forces invade the kingdom of Naples and take Aversa (24 Jan.).
April The Black Death reaches Florence and subsequently France, Spain and England (July–Aug.).
– Charles IV of Bohemia, king of the Romans, establishes the 'new town' area of Prague, and unites Bohemia (the modern Czech Republic) with Moravia, Silesia and Upper Lusatia (7 April).

– Anti-Semitism spreads in Europe; the Jews are blamed for spreading the Black Death and persecuted. Pope Clement VI issues a bull declaring the Jews innocent but cannot prevent a mass migration of Jews to Poland and Russia.
– King Edward III of England founds the Order of the Garter.
– The Teutonic Knights defeat the forces of two Lithuanian princes, extending their control over Lithuania.

SCIENCE AND TECHNOLOGY
– The French surgeon Guy de Chaulliac writes a detailed account of the Black Death and recommends bloodletting.

No bells tolled because almost everyone expected death.

Agnolo di Tura describes the Black Death in Siena, 1348

ARTS AND HUMANITIES
– King Charles IV of Bohemia, king of the Romans, establishes the University of Prague, the Carolinum.
Al-Umari, *Voyages of the Eyes*, a guide to Islamic-ruled lands.
Giovanni Villani, *A New History*, an account of world history.

1349

EUROPE
– Polish forces occupy Galicia.
– Pope Clement VI issues a bull against the religious radicalism of the flagellants.
– King Philip VI of France buys the Dauphiné (modern SE France) and adds it to French national territory.
– The Black Death spreads to Scandinavia and C Europe.

MIDDLE EAST AND NORTH AFRICA
– Ilkhan Nushirwan, ruler of Persia, dies; Mongol dynastic rule ends. The domain is divided among the Sarbadarids in Khorasan, the Muzaffarids in Fars, Kirman and Kurdistan, and the Jalyars in Iraq and Azerbaijan.

ARTS AND HUMANITIES
10 April William of Ockham, the English Franciscan friar and founder of philosophical nominalism, dies.
29 Sept. The English mystic Richard Rolle dies.
Niccolo da Poggibonzi, *A Book about Foreign Lands*, geographical and cultural description of the Middle East.

1350

EUROPE
27 Mar. King Alfonso XI of Castile dies while besieging the Moorish fortress of Gibraltar. He is succeeded by his son Peter I (the Cruel).
July The Roman rebel tribune Cola di Rienzi (see 1347) appeals to King Charles IV of Bohemia, king of the Romans, to help him against the Roman nobility; Charles has him imprisoned.
22 Aug. King Philip VI of France dies and is succeeded by his son John II.
– King Ludwig I of Hungary, having invaded the kingdom of Naples (see 1348), withdraws when he cannot enforce his authority.

ECONOMY AND SOCIETY
– By this date a fall in population resulting from the Black Death has caused livestock prices to fall; wheat, however, rises in price because of the lack of labourers. Across Europe farmland is converted into pasture.

ARTS AND HUMANITIES
– The poet Dafydd ap Gwilym composes verse in the traditions of medieval Welsh poetry.
Jan van Ruysbroeck, *The Adornment of Spiritual Marriage*, theological work.
Guillaume de Machaut, *Mass for Our Lady*, sacred music.

1351

EUROPE
– Ludwig I of Hungary accepts the provisions of the Golden Bull of 1222; the constitutional rights of the Hungarian nobility are confirmed.
– The parliamentary Statute of Provisors denies the papacy the right to appoint candidates to posts in the English Church.
– In Italy war breaks out between the city-states of Florence and Milan as Milan expands into Florentine-controlled Tuscany.
– The Statute of Labourers forces English labourers to accept work and aims to fix wages at their 1346 levels (labour costs are soaring because of the high death toll of the Black Death; see 1350). Increasingly, English landowners enclose common land to increase pasturage.
– Zurich joins the Swiss Confederation.

ASIA
– A second Siamese kingdom (see 1230) is founded at Ayutthaya, near modern Bangkok.

ARTS AND HUMANITIES
– Italian poet Francesco Petrarca (Petrarch) arranges his *Sonnets to Laura* into two separate collections.
– In S France, Perpignan University is founded.

1352

EUROPE

6 Dec. Pope Clement VI dies and is succeeded by Etienne Aubert who becomes Pope Innocent VI (18 Dec.).

– The Roman rebel tribune Cola di Rienzi (see 1350) is tried by a court of cardinals at Avignon and sentenced to death; he is pardoned and released by Pope Innocent VI after Clement VI's death.

THE AMERICAS

– Acamapichtli becomes the first king of the Aztecs (see 1325).

Who could shake the foundation of heaven?

An Aztec poem (*c*.1400 AD)

ARTS AND HUMANITIES

– Antwerp Cathedral (in modern Belgium) is completed.

Barani Ziya-ud-Din, *The History of Firuz Shahi*, history of Islamic rule in India.

Ranulf Higden, *Polychronicon*, world history.

Francesco Petrarca (Petrarch), *To Italy*, nationalist ode.

1353

EUROPE

– Berne joins the Swiss Confederation.

– Milan annexes Genoa, which now declares war on Venice.

– The first Statute of Praemunire prevents subjects of the English crown appealing to foreign courts (including papal jurisdiction).

ASIA

– The Champa of S Vietnam campaign to regain the Hue provinces of Annam (N Vietnam).

ARTS AND HUMANITIES

Giovanni Boccaccio, *The Decameron*, classic collection of tales.

1354

EUROPE

2 Mar. Gallipoli is seized from the Byzantines by the Ottoman Turks.

April The Hundred Years War (see 1347) resumes between France and England.

Aug. Pope Innocent VI gives Cola di Rienzi (see 1352) the title of senator; Rienzi returns to Rome and is killed by rioters (8 Oct.).

– At the battle of Sapienza, Genoa destroys the Venetian fleet.

ARTS AND HUMANITIES

– In S Spain the Alhambra Palace, Granada, is completed.

Ibn Battuta, *Gifts to Observers Dealing with the Curiosities of Cities and Wonders of Journeys*, account of journeys in Africa, the Middle East and the Far East.

Kitabatake Chikafusa, *Record of the Legitimate Descent of Divine Emperors*, Japanese imperial genealogy.

1355

EUROPE

5 April King Charles IV of Bohemia, king of the Romans (see 1347), is crowned Holy Roman Emperor in Rome.

17 April The doge of Venice, Marino Faliero, is executed for plotting against the ruling Venetian nobility.

11 Nov. The Byzantine co-emperor John VI Cantacuzenus (see 1347) is deposed and retires to a monastery; he is succeeded by his ward John V Palaeologus.

– King John II of France organizes a campaign against Edward, Prince of Wales (the Black Prince), who is ravaging France. Opposition, lead by Etienne Marcel, forces John to consult the Estates-General (French representative bodies) before he can impose new taxes; he dismisses the Estates-General and debases the coinage.

– Matteo Visconti, ruler of Milan, is murdered by his brothers Bernabo and Galeazzo.

– Stephen Dushan IV, king of Serbia (see 1346), dies while attempting to capture Constantinople; his empire disintegrates.

ASIA

– The Chinese monk Zhu Yuanzhang (Chu Yuan-chang) leads a national revolt against Mongol rule; he gains control of the city of Chiang-ning (modern Nanjing).

ARTS AND HUMANITIES

– In Italy, the campanile of Florence Cathedral is completed.

– The Italian painter Bernardo Daddi dies.

Taddeo Gaddi, *Madonna and Child with Angels*, painting.

1356

EUROPE

20 Jan. King Edward III of England invades Scotland. Edward Balliol surrenders his claim to the Scottish throne to Edward III of England.

19 Sept. At the battle of Poitiers in C France Edward, Prince of Wales (the Black Prince) the English king's son, resoundingly defeats the French. King John II of France is taken to England as a prisoner.

– The Holy Roman Emperor Charles IV issues the Golden Bull to reform the structure of the empire.

– A parliamentary assembly of three estates is established in Brabant (modern Netherlands).

– War breaks out between Hungary and Venice.

ASIA

– The Koryo dynasty of Korea asserts Korean independence of Mongol rule, but the local vassal lords rebel against the native dynasty.

1357

EUROPE

23 Mar. England and France declare a truce.

– In France the Estates-General, led by Etienne Marcel, passes a Great Ordinance to scrutinize royal tax collection and expenditure. Marcel allies with Charles II (the Bad), king of Navarre; the Estates-General dissolves into different factions. The regent, the Dauphin Charles, flees Paris to organize opposition to the Estates-General.

ASIA

– Janibeg (see 1342), khan of the Golden Horde, is killed by his son Berdibeg, who succeeds him.

ARTS AND HUMANITIES

– The nave of Gloucester Abbey, W England, is completed in the English Perpendicular style.

– Anonymous, *Sir John Mandeville, Travels*, travel writing. 'John de Mandeville' is unknown, but may have been the French writer Jean d'Outremeuse. The tales recount travels to Turkey, Persia, Syria, Arabia, N Africa and India, but are probably largely fictional.

Bartolus of Sassoferrato, *Commentaries on the Code of Justinian*, legal philosophy.

1358

EUROPE

18 Feb. Venice cedes Istria and Dalmatia to Ludwig I of Hungary.

22 Feb. In France Etienne Marcel, leader of the Estates-General, murders the marshals of Champagne and Normandy.

27 Mar. The Dauphin Charles escapes from Paris.

May Rioters in Paris protest at the increased taxes needed for the war with England. A peasant revolt (the Jacquerie, a name deriving from a French nickname for a peasant) breaks out in the Beauvais, N France, but the rebels are crushed (June).

31 July Etienne Marcel is assassinated.

2 Aug. The Dauphin Charles returns to Paris, where he restores order.

– The artisan guild members in Bruges, modern Belgium, rebel against the city's government.

– The captive French king John II agrees to restore large areas of the Angevin lands to England; his son, the Dauphin Charles, rejects the agreement. The Angevin (Plantagenet) kings of England previously held extensive lands in SW France as feudal lords (see 1152 and 1154).

ASIA

– Takauji, the Ashikaga shogun of Japan, dies and is succeeded by Ashikaga Yoshiakira.

ARTS AND HUMANITIES

– Francesco Petrarca (Petrarch) completes his autobiographical work *My Secret*, which he began in 1342.

1359

EUROPE

24 Mar. Under the terms of the treaty of London, King John II of France cedes the former lands of the Angevin empire in SW France to the English crown; the French Estates-General rejects the treaty.

4 Dec. The English king Edward III besieges Rouen in NW France.

ASIA

– Berdibeg (see 1357), khan of the Golden Horde, is killed and succeeded by his brother Kulpa.

ARTS AND HUMANITIES

Jean Buridan, *Questions on the Eight Books of Physics*, commentary on Aristotle.

Nicephorus Gregoras, *Historia*, history of Byzantium.

1360

EUROPE

8 May With the treaty of Brétigny, France and England agree a truce; King Edward III gives up his claim to the French crown and the French regent, the Dauphin Charles, gives up Calais, Ponthieu and Guienne (see 1338). He agrees to pay his father John II's ransom but cannot raise it.

– The Hanseatic League, an association of trading cities on the Baltic and North seas, now includes Hamburg, Hanover, Bremen, Cologne, Groningen, Danzig and Dortmund.

MIDDLE EAST AND NORTH AFRICA

– Orkhan (see 1324), leader of the Ottoman Turks, dies and is succeeded by his son Murad I, who now controls W Anatolia and Thrace.

ASIA

– Feroz Shah II, sultan of Delhi, rebuilds the city of Jaunpur in Uttar Pradesh.

– The Mongol warrior Timur Lenk (Tamerlane), leader of the Turkish Jagatai tribe, who claims descent from Genghis Khan (see 1206), conquers Transoxiana, in C Asia.

ARTS AND HUMANITIES

– In Germany Freiburg Cathedral is completed.

Richard Fitzralph, *Poverty and Salvation*, Christian tract.

1361

EUROPE

– Valdemar IV of Denmark, alarmed at the rise of the Hanseatic League to a position of confederated economic and political power (see 1360), declares war on the league.

– Following the death of Philip I de Rouvres, duke of Burgundy, the duchy of Burgundy becomes part of the personal property of the French crown.

– Buda is named the capital of Hungary.

ASIA

– The Champa dynasty in the S of Vietnam continue to campaign against Annam (N Vietnam).

– Authority in the Khanate of the Golden Horde disintegrates as the succession is disputed following the murder of Khan Nevruz.

ARTS AND HUMANITIES

9 June The French composer and musical theorist Philippe de Vitry dies. De Vitry was a master of the style known as *ars nova*.

1362

EUROPE

12 Sept. Pope Innocent VI dies and is succeeded by Urban V (28 Sept.).

– Ludwig I of Hungary conquers N Bulgaria and extends Hungarian control over the Balkans.

1363

EUROPE

6 Sept. John II of France gives the duchy of Burgundy (see 1361) to his son Philip (the Bold).

30 Nov. The Swedish nobles force the abdication of Magnus II Eriksson. He is replaced by their puppet Albert of Mecklenburg, who becomes Albert II.

– Valdemar IV of Denmark forces the Hanseatic League (see 1361) to accept a peace treaty that reduces its privileges.

– Lithuanian forces defeat the Mongols and advance to the Black Sea.

– Simon Boccanegra (see 1339), the first doge of Genoa, dies.

ASIA

– In India the sultanate of Delhi regains control of Sind province (in modern Pakistan).

SCIENCE AND TECHNOLOGY

– French physician Guy de Chauliac publishes *Chirurgia magna* (Great Surgery), an account of new surgical techniques.

1364

EUROPE

8 April King John II of France, imprisoned in England, dies and is succeeded by his son Charles V.

– The island of Crete rebels against Byzantine rule.

ARTS AND HUMANITIES

– King Casimir III (the Great) founds the University of Krakow, Poland.

– The Papal Palace, Avignon, France (see 1334), is completed.

1365

EUROPE

12 Mar. King Charles V of France recognizes John de Montfort as duke of Brittany.

5 May The English Parliament suspends the payment of tribute money to the papacy.

ARTS AND HUMANITIES

– The Doges' Palace in Venice is completed (see 1310).

1366

EUROPE

3 Mar. The Irish parliament passes the Statute of Kilkenny, prohibiting English–Irish intermarriage.

5 Mar. In Spain Henry of Trastamare expels Peter I (the Cruel) and is crowned King Henry II of Castile.

– Amadeus of Savoy leads a crusade against the Ottoman Turks; he seizes control of Gallipoli.

ARTS AND HUMANITIES

– The Italian painter Taddeo Gaddi dies.

Francesco Petrarca (Petrarch), *Canzoniere*, Italian song collection.

1367

EUROPE

16 Oct. Pope Urban V returns the papacy to Rome (from Avignon, see 1309), though a majority of the cardinals oppose the move to a city that is largely in ruins. The papacy soon reverts to Avignon.

19 Nov. The Confederation of Cologne is formed to organize the common Hanseatic financial system and to undertake retaliatory action against the Danes (see 1363).

3 April Edward, Prince of Wales (the Black Prince), invades Castile in support of the exiled Peter I (the Cruel) (see 1366). Henry II of Castile is defeated at Nájera, but illness forces Edward to withdraw.

ARTS AND HUMANITIES

– King Ludwig I of Hungary founds Pec University.

– Around this date William Langland begins to write *The Vision of Piers Plowman*, one of the greatest Middle English allegorical poems.

1368

ASIA

– In China the rebel leader Zhu Yuanzhang (Chu Yuan-chang) expels the Mongol Yuan dynasty from Beijing; he adopts the name Hongwu (Hung Wu) and is proclaimed first emperor of the Ming dynasty, which will rule China until 1644.

– Tibet regains its independence.

– Ashikaga Yoshiakira, shogun of Japan, dies and is succeeded by Hosokawa Yonyaki.

ARTS AND HUMANITIES

– The Arab traveller Ibn Battuta (see 1354) dies.

1369

EUROPE

1 Jan. Gascony rebels against English rule.

21 May King Charles V of France formally declares war on England, thereby resuming hostilities in the Hundred Years War.

10 Oct. The Byzantine emperor John V Palaeologus visits Rome seeking papal aid to repel the Ottoman Turks from Byzantine territory.

– Hungarian forces try, but fail, to invade Venetian territory.

ASIA

– Timur Lenk (Tamerlane) (see 1360) establishes control over Samarkand in Turkestan.

– The Chinese subjugate the state of Koryo (Korea) after 13 years of rebellion (see 1356).

ARTS AND HUMANITIES

Geoffrey Chaucer, *The Book of the Duchess*, a dream-poem.

1370

EUROPE

17 Feb. At the battle of Rudau, the Teutonic Knights defeat the Lithuanians.

19 Sept. Edward, Prince of Wales (the Black Prince), sacks Limoges, W France.

5 Nov. Casimir III (the Great) of Poland dies; King Ludwig I of Hungary is elected his successor.

30 Dec. Pope Gregory XI succeeds Urban V.

– The Hanseatic League defeats the Danish army; the peace of Stralsund, which gives the Hanseatic League a monopoly in Baltic trade, concludes the war between Denmark and the league.

SCIENCE AND TECHNOLOGY

– Iron needles are produced in Nuremberg, Germany.

ARTS AND HUMANITIES

– In England Exeter Cathedral is completed.

Anonymous, *Pearl*, English religious poem.

Jean le Bel, *Chronicle*, a history of England, France, Germany and Flanders.

Leonardo Bruni, *Twelve Books of Histories of the Florentine People*, humanist account of Florentine history.

1371

EUROPE

22 Feb. King David II of Scotland (see 1329) dies and is succeeded by his cousin, the first Stuart king, Robert II.

26 Sept. At the battle of Chernomen, the Ottoman sultan Murad I defeats the rulers of the Byzantine empire, Bulgaria and Macedonia; they recognize his rule in the Balkans.

ASIA

– Both Japan and the Khmer dynasty of Cambodia send tribute missions to the Chinese Ming dynasty (see 1368).

1372

EUROPE

– King Charles V of France regains Poitou and Brittany from England and defeats the English at La Rochelle, reasserting French naval power.

SCIENCE AND TECHNOLOGY

– Arabic scholar al-Damiri compiles *The Lives of Animals*, a zoological encyclopedia of both real and mythical creatures.

1373

EUROPE

16 June England and Portugal become permanent allies under the treaty of London.

23 July St Bridget, founder of the Brigittine order and patron saint of Sweden, dies.

8 Aug. Brandenburg, NE Germany, becomes a possession of the Holy Roman Emperor Charles IV, who unites it with Bohemia.

8 Aug. John of Gaunt, duke of Lancaster, commander of the English army and fourth son of the English king Edward III, invades France. From Calais he will campaign as far as Champagne and Burgundy.

– Aragon and Portugal sign a peace treaty with Castile.

SCIENCE AND TECHNOLOGY

– Canals with locks are built in the Netherlands.

1374

EUROPE

– King Ludwig I of Hungary and Poland grants the Polish nobility a charter of its privileges.

– After a colourful career of deposition, military defeat, temporary triumph and imprisonment, Magnus II of Sweden dies in a shipwreck.

SCIENCE AND TECHNOLOGY

– The German scientific and political writer Conrad von Megenburg dies.

ARTS AND HUMANITIES

19 July The Italian poet Francesco Petrarcha (Petrarch) dies.

Julian of Norwich, *Revelations of Divine Love*, account of her religious visions.

1375

EUROPE

27 June By the treaty of Bruges, France and England agree a truce.

– Valdemar IV Atterdag, king of Denmark, who recovered most of Schleswig, dies.

– The Holy Roman Emperor Charles IV recognizes the diplomatic existence of the Hanseatic League (see 1370).

MIDDLE EAST AND NORTH AFRICA
– Mamluk forces besiege Sis, the capital of Armenia. Leo VI, king of Armenia, surrenders to the governor of Aleppo; he is imprisoned in Cairo.

1376
EUROPE
24 April The 'Good Parliament' meets in Westminster: it asks Edward III to protect English merchants by expelling foreign merchants and banning the export of grain and cloth. John of Gaunt, duke of Lancaster (see 1373), influences Parliament against the policy.
10 June Wenceslas, son of the Holy Roman Emperor Charles IV (see 1355), is elected king of the Romans.
– The English religious activist and writer John Wyclif campaigns against the papacy and develops a theology of grace.
– Edward, Prince of Wales (the Black Prince), eldest son of Edward III of England, dies.

1377
EUROPE
17 Jan. Pope Gregory XI, persuaded by the arguments of the Italian mystic, Catherine of Siena, returns the papacy to Rome from Avignon (see 1309).
21 June King Edward III of England dies and is succeeded by his grandson Richard II, son of Edward (the Black Prince), and a minor. Thomas, duke of Gloucester, and John of Gaunt, duke of Lancaster, administer the government.
– The English Parliament levies a poll tax to finance the war with France, to be paid by every adult.
– Pope Gregory issues a bull accusing the English religious activist John Wyclif of heresy; Wyclif is summoned to trial by the bishop of London but street riots in London force the ecclesiastical court's suspension.

ASIA
– The N Vietnamese forces of Dai Viet (Annam) attempt, but fail, to invade the S; the king of Champa in the S invades Dai Viet.

ARTS AND HUMANITIES
– The French composer Guillaume de Machaut, a master of *ars nova*, dies.

1378
EUROPE
26 Mar. Pope Gregory XI (a Frenchman) dies and is succeeded by Urban VI, an Italian (8 April). When Urban announces the reform of the college of cardinals, the non-Italian cardinals, supported by France, elect Pope Clement VII as a rival pope.

Clement establishes himself in Avignon (1379), which becomes a rival seat of Church power. The ensuing period of upheaval in the Western Church is known as the Great Schism.
19 Nov. The Holy Roman Emperor Charles IV dies and is succeeded by his son Wenceslas, who transfers Brandenburg, NE Germany, to his half-brother, Sigismund, margrave of Brandenburg.

1379
ARTS AND HUMANITIES
– In England William of Wykeham founds Winchester College.

1380
EUROPE
8 Sept. At the battle of Kulikovo the Russians under Dmitri Donskoi, prince of Moscow, defeat the Mongols.
16 Sept. King Charles V of France dies and is succeeded by his 12-year-old son Charles VI (the Well-Beloved). France will be ruled by his uncles as regents until 1388.

MIDDLE EAST AND NORTH AFRICA
– Mongol–Turkish forces led by Timur (see 1360) overrun Persia.

1381
EUROPE
– Venice is victorious in the War of the Chioggia with Genoa.
– The Peasants' Revolt: Wat Tyler leads an English rebellion against the 1351 Statute of Labourers and a reimposition of the 1377 poll tax. Artisans and labourers from the SE march on London, burn the home of John of Gaunt, duke of Lancaster and uncle of the king, and behead the archbishop of Canterbury. They petition King Richard II, demanding abolition of serfdom and the poll tax (14 June) but Wat Tyler is killed by William Walworth, the lord mayor, and the revolt ends.
– The English Parliament passes its first Navigation Act to defend shipping interests.

1382
EUROPE
10 Sept. Ludwig I (the Great), king of Hungary and Poland, dies and is succeeded by his daughter Maria of Anjou.
– The new archbishop of Canterbury, William Courtenay, attacks the Lollards, the followers of religious activist John Wyclif (see 1376 and 1377). Wyclif withdraws to Lutterworth in the English Midlands.
– In Italy, wool workers in Florence, led by Michaele di Lando, rebel against the ruling nobility but are suppressed.

ASIA
– By this date Hongwu, Ming emperor of China, has asserted his control over the whole of China and expelled the Mongols.

1383

EUROPE

22 Oct. Ferdinand I, king of Portugal, dies and is succeeded by his widow, Leonora; John I of Castile, married to Ferdinand's daughter Beatrix, also lays claim to the throne.

ARTS AND HUMANITIES

– The playwright Zeami Motokiyo establishes the classical formalism of Noh drama in Japanese theatre.

1384

EUROPE

31 Dec. The English religious activist and writer John Wyclif dies.

– Castilian forces invade Portugal; Lisbon is besieged.

– Louis de Male, last count of Flanders, dies; his territories are inherited by his son-in-law Philip the Bold of Burgundy (husband of Margaret, heiress of Flanders and Artois). These territorial gains herald the start of 100 years of Burgundian power and prestige.

1385

EUROPE

14 Aug. At the battle of Aljubarrota, the Portuguese with English support defeat the forces of John of Castile; King John I establishes the new Aviz dynasty in Portugal.

– King Richard II of England attempts to govern independently of Parliament in a system of personal rule.

– The Ottoman Turks take Sofia, Bulgaria.

ARTS AND HUMANITIES

– In Germany, Heidelberg University is founded.
Geoffrey Chaucer, *Troilus and Criseyde*, Middle English romance.

1386

EUROPE

2 Feb. Jagiello (Jogaila) of Lithuania, the last pagan ruler in Europe, converts to Christianity so that he can be accepted as King of Poland as Vladislav II.

9 May The treaty of Windsor establishes the terms of England's alliance with Portugal.

9 July The Swiss defeat an imperial force: the Swiss confederation demands increasing autonomy from imperial rule.

MIDDLE EAST AND NORTH AFRICA

– Timur (see 1360) completes his conquest of Persia.

1387

EUROPE

– Olaf II, king of Denmark, dies and is succeeded by his mother Margaret, the daughter of Valdemar IV of Denmark and widow of Haakon VI of Norway.

– Gian Galeazzo Visconti, ruler of Genoa, marries Isabelle of Valois.

ARTS AND HUMANITIES

– By now Geoffrey Chaucer has begun work on *The Canterbury Tales*, a collection of stories written in prose and verse, told in Middle English by a group of pilgrims on their way to the shrine of Thomas Becket at Canterbury.

1388

EUROPE

15 Aug. A Scottish army under the earl of Douglas defeats an English army under Henry Percy, duke of Northumberland, at Otterburn (Chevy Chase) in Northumberland.

– Venice signs a commercial treaty with the Ottoman Turks to protect its trading position in the E Mediterranean.

ARTS AND HUMANITIES

– The first English translation of the Bible, instigated by John Wyclif (see 1384), is completed.

1389

EUROPE

18 June The French and English sign a three-year truce in the Hundred Years War.

20 June Murad I, the Ottoman sultan, defeats the Serbs at the battle of Kosovo. The Serbian empire, a coalition of Serbs, Bosnians and Albanians, is absorbed, as vassal territories, within the Ottoman empire. Although the battle ends in their defeat, the Serbs will adopt the battle as the central event in the evolution of their national identity.

28 Aug. A captured Serb noble assassinates the Ottoman sultan Murad I, who is succeeded by his son Bayazid I.

– Margaret of Denmark defeats the Swedish forces under Albert II.

1390

EUROPE

13 May King Robert II of Scotland, the first Stuart king, dies and is succeeded by his son Robert III.

1391

EUROPE

June Anti-Semitism spreads in Spain: Jews are killed in Seville and throughout Andalucia (June); the ghetto in Barcelona is burned (4–5 Aug.).

– The Byzantine Emperor John V Palaeologus dies and is succeeded by his son Manuel II Palaeologus.

ASIA

18 June The Jagatai Turk leader Timur (see 1360) defeats Toqtamish, the khan of the Golden Horde on the Kondurcha River in the Volga region of what is now Russia.

1392

EUROPE
- From this date Charles VI of France becomes mentally ill. The dukes of Burgundy and Berry assume governmental control in the French Kingdom.

ASIA
- The S branch of the Japanese ruling dynasty yields its rights to the N branch; Japan is restored to administrative and centralized order, ending a long period of warfare.
- The murderous warlord Yi Song-gye proclaims himself king of Korea, the first ruler of the Yi dynasty.

1393

EUROPE
- Ottoman forces conquer Bulgaria.
- Holy Roman Emperor Wenceslas tortures and kills his opponent, the priest John of Nepomuk, who will become the patron saint of Bohemia.

MIDDLE EAST AND NORTH AFRICA
- Timur (see 1360) establishes control over large parts of Mesopotamia (modern Iraq).

1394

EUROPE
- Jobst, margrave of Moravia, captures and imprisons the Holy Roman Emperor Wenceslas.
- King Richard II of England travels to Ireland to enforce his rule over the Irish nobility.

1395

ASIA
15 April Timur (see 1391) inflicts another defeat on Toqtamish, khan of the Golden Horde, on the River Terek in the N Caucasus.

1396

EUROPE
25 Sept. The Ottoman Turks defeat a crusader campaign in the Balkans led by King Sigismund of Hungary and the French commander John of Nevers in battle near Nicopolis, Bulgaria. Although supported by a naval fleet composed of Venetian, Genoese and Hospitaller forces, the Christian allies prove no match for the Ottoman military machine.
Oct. A diplomatic meeting near Calais between Richard II of England and Charles VI of France improves relations between the two kingdoms.

ARTS AND HUMANITIES
Francesco Petrarca (Petrarch), *Africa*, an unfinished epic poem on Scipio Africanus (see 202 BC), published posthumously.

1397

EUROPE
17 June Margaret of Denmark's great-nephew Eric of Pomerania is crowned king of a united Scandinavia, although Margaret continues to be the effective ruler of the countries confederated under the terms of the Union of Kalmar.
- In Italy Milanese troops invade Tuscany and fight the Florentines.

1398

EUROPE
- King Richard II of England loses political control. He fills parliament with his own supporters, executes three leaders of the opposition and exiles Henry Bolingbroke, son of the duke of Lancaster, John of Gaunt, the king's uncle.

ASIA
- Timur advances towards N India; having asserted his control over Persia, Mesopotamia and Afghanistan, he crosses the Indus (24 Sept.) and sacks Delhi (17 Dec.).

1399

EUROPE
- The duke of Lancaster, John of Gaunt, the king's uncle, dies, and King Richard II confiscates his estates. Henry Bolingbroke, John of Gaunt's son, returns to England while Richard is in Ireland (July). Richard returns to England but is captured by Henry, who becomes Henry IV, the first Lancastrian king. Richard abdicates (29 Sept.).
- A minor Welsh noble, Owain Glyndwr, takes up arms in a land dispute against an English neighbour. His uprising will become a national rebellion, reducing the English hold on Wales to a few castles.

ASIA
9 Jan. Timur takes Meerut in N India, then pulls back to the Indus River (Mar.); the kingdom of Delhi is left devastated.

1400

EUROPE
14 Feb. Richard II, deposed king of England, dies at Pontefract Castle in Yorkshire, possibly the victim of an assassination.
21 Aug. Rupert III, the Elector Palatine of the Rhine, is elected king of the Germans (Holy Roman Emperor) in place of the deposed emperor, Wenceslas.
Sept. Owain Glyndwr (see 1399), leads a rebellion against English rule: King Henry IV of England leads an army into N Wales, but despite initial successes is unable to crush the Welsh uprising.

ARTS AND HUMANITIES
25 Oct. In London Geoffrey Chaucer, the major figure in the early history of modern English literature, dies leaving *The Canterbury Tales* incomplete (see 1387).

– French chronicler Jean Froissart completes his *Chroniques* (Chronicles), a history of Europe 1307–1400 that contains the best-known contemporary account of the Hundred Years War.

1401

MIDDLE EAST AND NORTH AFRICA

9 July The Persian city of Baghdad (in modern Iraq) falls to military forces led by Timur (see 1360); the inhabitants of the city are massacred.

1402

EUROPE

14 Sept. Henry Percy, first earl of Northumberland, and his eldest son, Henry 'Hotspur', halt a Scots raiding party at Homildon Hill, Northumberland, England.

MIDDLE EAST AND NORTH AFRICA

28 July Timur (see 1360) defeats the Ottoman army led by Sultan Bayezid I at the battle of Ankara (in modern Turkey). Bayezid is taken into captivity.

1403

EUROPE

21 July At the battle of Shrewsbury, Henry IV, king of England, defeats and kills Henry 'Hotspur', eldest son of Henry Percy, earl of Northumberland, who has joined forces with Welsh rebels led by Owain Glyndwr (see 1400).

MIDDLE EAST AND NORTH AFRICA

8 Mar. Bayezid I, sultan of the Ottoman Turks, dies in captivity in Akehir (in modern Turkey). A succession struggle ensues among his sons: Mehmed I will emerge, in 1413, as his father's successor.

ASIA

– Yongle (Yung-Lo), son of Hongwu (see 1368), becomes the new Ming emperor of China, having overthrown his nephew Jianwen (Chien-En), who disappeared; he is presumed to have fled disguised as a monk.

1404

EUROPE

27 April Philip (the Bold), duke of Burgundy (see 1384), dies and is succeeded by his son John (the Fearless).

14 June Welsh rebel Owain Glyndwr (see 1400), who now controls most of Wales, assumes the title prince of Wales and convenes a parliament in Machynlleth: he allies Wales with France (14 July).

1405

EUROPE

– The Venetian army, as part of its campaign against the Carrara

and Visconti dynasties of Padua and Milan, respectively, occupies the Italian cities of Padua, Verona, and Vicenza (all in N Italy between Venice and Milan).

– French forces arrive in Wales to give military assistance to Owain Glyndwr's rebellion but withdraw after an unsuccessful attack on the English city of Worcester.

ASIA

17 Feb. Timur dies suddenly at Otrar (near modern Shymkent in Kazakstan). Although, through his efforts, the Mongols now control Persia, Mesopotamia, Afghanistan and parts of India, Timur's power has been largely centred on his personal abilities: his empire will not survive his death.

1406

EUROPE

6 Nov. Pope Innocent VII dies. He is succeeded by Gregory XII (Angel Correr).

– Robert III, king of Scotland dies. His son, James I, is a prisoner of the English and will not be released until 1424.

1407

EUROPE

23 Nov. Followers of John the Fearless, duke of Burgundy (see 1404), kill Louis, duke of Orléans; France is plunged into civil war. The Armagnacs support the new duke of Orleans and urge the vigorous prosecution of the war with England, while the Burgundian faction opposes the war.

1408

EUROPE

– Jan Hus, Czech religious reformer who has been campaigning against ecclesiastical abuses in Bohemia (modern Czech Republic), is suspended from his priestly duties by Zbynèk Zajíc, archbishop of Prague. In 1409 Hus will be excommunicated but will continue his campaign of reform.

1409

EUROPE

5 June In Italy the Council of Pisa deposes Pope Gregory XII of Rome and the antipope Benedict XIII of Avignon (see 1378); the conclave elects Alexander V, the Greek Franciscan Pietro Philarghi, as pope (26 June).

12 Dec. A papal bull is issued by Alexander V ordering all books written by English religious reformer John Wyclif to be surrendered. Archbishop Zbynèk of Prague publicly burns Wyclif's writings.

ARTS AND HUMANITIES

Donatello (Donato di Niccolò), *David*, sculpture, the first of several versions.

1410

EUROPE

3 May In Italy Pope Alexander V dies suddenly and is succeeded (17 May) by the Neapolitan Baldassare Cossa, who will reign as Pope John XXIII.

18 May Holy Roman Emperor Rupert III of Wittelsbach (see 1400) dies and is succeeded by Sigismund of Luxembourg, brother of the deposed Wenceslas of Bohemia (20 Sept.).

15 July Combined Polish–Lithuanian armed forces defeat the Teutonic Knights at the battle of Tannenberg in E Prussia (now NE Poland).

– Welsh rebel Owain Glyndwr goes into hiding as the Welsh national rebellion collapses.

ARTS AND HUMANITIES

– *Geographika Hyphogesis* (Guide to Geography) by Ptolemy (Claudius Ptolomaeus), Alexandrian mathematician and geographer (*fl.* AD 127–145), is translated from Greek into Latin.

1411

EUROPE

1 Feb. The Teutonic Knights regain their supremacy under the terms of the peace of Torun (in modern Poland). Poland and Lithuania fail to gain any Baltic territories and the Knights have only to surrender part of Lithuania.

5 June The Serbs ally themselves with the Ottomans in order to attack Suleiman, ruler of the Ottoman Turks in Europe, at Edirne (in European Turkey): Suleiman is killed and the Ottomans are internally divided between those loyal to his brother Prince Musa and those who support his brother Mehmed: Mehmed will emerge as ruler (see 1413).

– The kingdoms of Portugal and Castile negotiate a peace treaty: internal security enables Portugal to develop as a great power.

1412

EUROPE

16 May In Italy Giovanni Maria Visconti, duke of Milan, is assassinated: he is succeeded by his brother Filippo.

27 Nov. Margaret of Denmark, daughter of King Valdemar IV of Denmark and de facto ruler of Scandinavia, dies in Flensburg (in modern Germany); her great-nephew (see 1397) continues to reign as Eric VII of Denmark and Norway and as Eric XIII of Sweden, though his autocratic style of government is beginning to cause dissension.

ARTS AND HUMANITIES

– In Italy the University of Turin is founded.

1413

EUROPE

20 Mar. In London the English king Henry IV dies and is succeeded by his son Henry V.

MIDDLE EAST AND NORTH AFRICA

7 July The Ottoman (Turkish) succession (see 1411) is resolved when Prince Mehmed defeats and kills his brother Prince Musa at Jamurlu in Serbia: internal conflict ends in the Ottoman empire.

ARTS AND HUMANITIES

– German theologian and mystic Thomas à Kempis is ordained at Agnietenberg monastery in the Netherlands; he is widely believed to have written the highly influential devotional text known as *Imitatio Christi* (The Imitation of Christ).

– In Scotland St Andrews University is founded.

1414

EUROPE

9 Jan. The English government suppresses a religious rebellion near London led by the Lollards, religious dissidents who followed the radical teachings of the English Church reformer John Wyclif (see 1382).

5 Nov. The Council of Constance (Konstanz, Germany) opens. Its aims are to reform the Church of abuses, to promote its unity and to prosecute heresy. Jan Hus (see 1408), the radical Czech religious reformer, is allowed to attend under safe conduct.

MIDDLE EAST AND NORTH AFRICA

– Mehmed I, sultan of the Ottoman Turks, reasserts imperial control in Anatolia.

1415

EUROPE

13 Aug. Henry V of England invades France.

5 May The Council of Constance formally condemns the teachings of radical English Church reformer John Wyclif. Later in the month (29 May) Pope John XXIII is deposed by delegates to the Council.

6 July Jan Hus, the Czech religious reformer (see 1408), is burned at the stake in Constance for refusing to recant his heretical teachings.

25 Oct. English and Welsh longbowmen play a crucial role in the defeat of the French by the English at the battle of Agincourt: the French nobility suffer heavy losses in the battle; Henry V of England orders the slaughter of the French prisoners of war.

Enough to kill, enough to capture, enough to run away.

Dafydd Gam, a Welsh squire, describes the French army to Henry V, 14 Oct. 1415

– Welsh leader and rebel against the English, Owain Glyndwr, refuses the offer of a pardon by Henry V: Glyndwr is believed to have died soon afterwards.

MIDDLE EAST AND NORTH AFRICA
– The Portuguese take Ceuta (in Morocco).

ARTS AND HUMANITIES
– Donatello, *St Mark and St George*, sculpture for Church of San Michele, Florence, Italy.

1416

EUROPE
– Henry V, king of England, taking advantage of the weakened condition of France (see 1415), embarks on a three-year campaign in Normandy.
– Venetian forces defeat the Ottoman army in the Dardanelles (NW Turkey): the Ottoman empire is forced to sue for peace.

1417

EUROPE
11 Nov. The Council of Constance, with the backing of the Emperor Sigismund (see 1410), formally ends the schism within the Western Church (see 1378): having deposed Pope John XXIII and Pope Benedict XIII, elected in Rome and Avignon, respectively, the Council elects Cardinal Oddo Colonna as (unopposed) Pope Martin V.

1418

EUROPE
31 Dec. Following a siege of nearly five months, Rouen, in Normandy (N France), falls to the English.

1419

EUROPE
10 Sept. John the Fearless, duke of Burgundy (see 1404), is murdered at Montereau in France: he is succeeded by his son, Philip the Good (25 Dec.). Duke Philip allies himself with the English against Charles, the dauphin of France.
– Portuguese explorers reach Madeira, one of a small cluster of islands in the North Atlantic.

SCIENCE AND TECHNOLOGY
– Prince Henry of Portugal (Henry the Navigator), son of King John I, establishes the first European school of navigation in Sagres, Portugal.

ARTS AND HUMANITIES
– Filippo Brunelleschi, façade of the Ospedale degli Innocenti in Florence, Italy. The clarity and new sense of spatial and planar awareness found in Brunelleschi's design make it arguably the earliest façade to reflect the ideals of the Italian Renaissance.

1420

EUROPE
21 May Henry V, king of England, and Charles VI, king of France, sign the treaty of Troyes: Charles names Henry as his heir to the French throne and recognizes Henry as the duke of Normandy; Henry marries Catherine, daughter of Charles VI (2 June).
1 Nov. Bohemian followers of the heretical religious reformer Jan Hus (see 1408 and 1415), known as Hussites, defeat an army assembled by the pope and led by Sigismund, Holy Roman Emperor and king of Bohemia and Hungary, near Prague in Bohemia; this is the first of four attempts by the papacy to suppress the Hussites.

ARTS AND HUMANITIES
– Jan van Eyck, early Netherlandish painter who, with his brother Hubert, has perfected the use of oil as a medium for pigments, is by now at work on his panel depicting the Crucifixion.

1421

EUROPE
26 May Mehmed I, sultan of the Ottoman (Turkish) empire, dies at Edirne (in European Turkey) and is succeeded by his son Murad II, who continues the Ottoman policy of expansion into the Balkans.
1 June Meeting in Bohemia, the Bohemian and Moravian estates establish their own form of government and reject rule by the Holy Roman Emperor.
28 Oct. Milan, N Italy, annexes Genoa, a port in NW Italy, and the Visconti dynasty begins in earnest to establish Milan's supremacy in N Italy.

ASIA
– The Chinese capital is moved from Nanjing to Beijing.

1422

EUROPE
June Constantinople is besieged by Ottoman (Turkish) forces led by the Ottoman sultan Murad II, but the Byzantine emperor John VIII Palaeologus rallies his forces and forces the Ottomans to withdraw.
31 Aug. Henry V, king of England, dies at Bois de Vincennes, near Paris, France: his son, only nine months old, succeeds him as Henry VI.
21 Oct. Charles VI, king of France, dies in Paris: under the terms of the treaty of Troyes (see 1420), his son Charles the dauphin has been disinherited, and Henry VI of England becomes king of France.
30 Oct. Charles the dauphin defies the treaty of Troyes and declares himself king of France as Charles VII. England resumes war with France. John, duke of Bedford and an uncle of Henry VI, king of England, rules France in the name of his infant nephew; a second uncle, Humphrey, duke of Gloucester, controls England.

1423

EUROPE

– Under threat from the Ottoman Turks, the Greek city of Thessalonica cedes itself to Venice in an attempt to maintain its freedom; the Ottomans will, nevertheless, take the city in 1430.

1424

EUROPE

21 May James I of Scotland is crowned at Scone in Perthshire, Scotland, after being held in captivity by the English for 18 years (see 1406).

17 Aug. At Verneuil in France, a combined French and Scottish force loyal to Charles VII, king of France, is defeated by John, duke of Bedford and regent in France on behalf of Henry VI, king of England.

ARTS AND HUMANITIES

Lorenzo Ghiberti, bronze reliefs for the second set of doors for the baptistery in Florence, N Italy.

1425

EUROPE

21 July Manuel II Palaeologus, Byzantine emperor, dies and is succeeded by his son John VIII Palaeologus.

MIDDLE EAST AND NORTH AFRICA

– A Portuguese expedition seizes the Canary Islands, off NW Africa, from the kingdom of Castile, NW Spain.

1426

EUROPE

2 Feb. Venice declares war on Milan, N Italy; during the three-year war that follows Venice will gain control of the N Italian cities of Verona, Vicenza, Brescia and Bergamo.

– John, duke of Bedford (see 1422), returns from France and allies himself with his brother Humphrey, duke of Gloucester, who has acted as regent in England while John was in France.

ARTS AND HUMANITIES

– A university is founded in Louvain (in modern Belgium).

1427

EUROPE

Mar. John, duke of Bedford, returns to France to resume the war against Charles VII, king of France over the English claim to the French throne as set out in the treaty of Troyes (see 1420).

– The uninhabited Azores Islands are discovered in the N Atlantic by the Portuguese navigator Diogo de Senill.

1428

ASIA

– Vietnam becomes independent of the Chinese Ming empire,

though its new emperor, Le Thaito, founder of the Le dynasty, submits to Chinese suzerainty.

ARTS AND HUMANITIES

– Masaccio (Tommaso di Giovanni di Simone Guidi), noted painter of the early Italian Renaissance, dies in Rome, Italy. Filippo Brunelleschi, the sacristy of the Church of San Lorenzo in Florence, Italy; the rest of the church is not completed until 1469.

1429

EUROPE

23 Feb. Inspired by heavenly visions to liberate France from English control, Joan of Arc, a teenage girl from Domrémy in Lorraine, meets with Charles VII, king of France, at Chinon in France: she attempts to convince him that she has been chosen by God to lead the French against the English and to secure the French throne for Charles VII. After a second meeting (April) the dauphin provides her with a small armed force, and (8 May) she liberates Orléans from the English.

17 July Charles VII is finally crowned king of France at Reims.

– John, duke of Bedford and uncle of Henry VI, king of England, is replaced as Henry's regent in France by Philip the Good, duke of Burgundy (see 1419).

1430

EUROPE

23 May Having failed to take Paris, Joan of Arc enters Compiègne in Picardy, N France; she is captured by England's Burgundian allies and handed over to the English who imprison her in Rouen: she is abandoned by Charles VII.

1431

EUROPE

30 May After complex political and diplomatic negotiations between England, Burgundy and France, Joan of Arc is convicted of heresy in an ecclesiastical court and is burned at the stake in Rouen: she will be canonized 500 years later (16 May 1920) and remains a national hero in France.

16 Dec. Henry VI, king of England, now nine years old, is formally crowned king of France in the cathedral of Notre Dame in Paris.

ARTS AND HUMANITIES

Paolo Uccello, mosaic scenes (now lost) for St Mark's Cathedral in Venice.

1432

EUROPE

– Gonçalo Velho Cabral, Portuguese explorer, founds a colony on the island of Santa Maria in the North Atlantic; this is the earliest settlement in the Azores Islands (see 1427). By the end of the 15th century the Azores have become an important Portuguese outpost.

ARTS AND HUMANITIES

Jan and Hubert van Eyck (see 1420), the *Ghent Altarpiece*, a polyptych depicting the adoration of the mystic lamb for the high altar of the Church of St Bavo in Ghent, Flanders (modern Belgium).

1433

EUROPE

14 Aug. John I, king of Portugal and founder of the Aviz dynasty, dies in Lisbon, Portugal, after a reign of 44 years: he is succeeded by his son Edward I.

30 Nov. In Prague (modern Czech Republic), the Compacts of Prague are drafted by delegates of the Council of Basle in order to end the Hussite wars (see 1420): all but the most radical Hussite reformers agree to submit to the authority of the Holy Roman Emperor in return for limited freedom of worship. The Hussite wars have marked the emergence of a distinctive Czech nationalism and of anti-German sentiment in Bohemia.

MIDDLE EAST AND NORTH AFRICA

– Gil Eanes, Portuguese explorer, becomes the first traveller to round Cape Bojador (now part of the W Sahara) S of the Canary Islands.

ECONOMY AND SOCIETY

– Nicholas of Cusa, a German theologian, writes *Concordantia Catholica* (Catholic Concord) in which he pleads for moderate religious toleration and argues that Church authority lies with the councils of the Church.

ARTS AND HUMANITIES

Jan van Eyck (see 1420), *Man in a Red Turban*, painting.

1434

EUROPE

30 May At the battle of Lipany (in modern Hungary) Andrew Prokop, a Bohemian religious dissident, leads an army of radical anti-papist Taborites against a force of Bohemian Catholics and moderate Hussites (known as Utraquists): Prokop and his followers are defeated and Prokop is killed.

5 Oct. The Florentine banker Cosimo de' Medici returns from exile to rule Florence, N Italy, for the next 30 years.

THE AMERICAS

– The Aztecs of Tenochtitlán form the Triple Alliance with the nearby cities of Texcoco and Tlacopán.

ECONOMY AND SOCIETY

– African slaves are now being exported from Africa to Portugal.

ARTS AND HUMANITIES

Jan van Eyck (see 1420), *The Arnolfini Wedding*, painting.

1435

EUROPE

5 Aug. King Alfonso V of Aragon, NE Spain, is captured by the Genoese near the island of Ponza off the W coast of Italy: he is released following a treaty of alliance between Aragon and Milan in which Alfonso's claim to the throne of Sicily is recognized.

21 Sept. Following the death in Rouen, Normandy on 15 Sept. of John, duke of Bedford, regent in France for his nephew, King Henry VI of England, Charles VII of France and Philip the Good, duke of Burgundy, sign the treaty of Arras recognizing Charles as king of France and ending Burgundy's alliance with England against France (see 1419).

ARTS AND HUMANITIES

Fra Filippo Lippi, *Adoration of the Child*, painting.
Rogier van der Weyden, *The Descent from the Cross*, painting.

1436

EUROPE

13 April The French king Charles VII recaptures Paris from the English. Harfleur is recaptured later in the year.

ARTS AND HUMANITIES

– The dome of the cathedral of Florence, N Italy, is completed; designed by Florentine architect and engineer Filippo Brunelleschi, the dome remains an outstanding example of early Italian Renaissance architecture.

1437

EUROPE

21 Feb. James I, king of Scotland, is stabbed and killed by Sir Robert Graham in Perth. James II, the king's five-year-old son, is crowned his successor: Scotland descends into civil war.

9 Dec. Sigismund, Holy Roman Emperor and king of Hungary and Bohemia (see 1410), dies in Znojmo, Bohemia, and is succeeded by Albrecht V, duke of Austria as king of the Germans: the Bohemians refuse to accept him as their king, though he is formally crowned as such.

MIDDLE EAST AND NORTH AFRICA

– Portuguese forces, led by Prince Henry the Navigator, are prevented by the Moors from taking the port of Tangiers in Morocco: the Moors gain further control over the Strait of Gibraltar by demanding the Moroccan port of Ceuta from the Portuguese (see 1415).

1438

EUROPE

18 Mar. Albert, duke of Austria and king of the Germans, is elected Holy Roman Emperor: he will reign as Albert II.

7 July Charles VII, king of France, advances the authority of the French crown by issuing the Pragmatic Sanction of Bourges, which limits papal authority over French bishops and gives the crown a say in Church appointments.

9 Sept. Edward, king of Portugal (see 1433), dies and his six-year-old son Afonso V succeeds him.

– A baronial rebellion forces Eric VII, king of Denmark, Norway and Sweden (see 1412), to flee Denmark: he moves to Gotland in Sweden, but is soon ousted as Sweden's ruler when Charles Knutson is appointed regent by the Swedish diet.

THE AMERICAS

– Pachacutec (Pachacuti Inca Yupanqui) begins the period of Inca imperial expansion in the Andes.

1439

EUROPE

27 Oct. Albert II, king of the Germans and of Hungary and Bohemia and elected, but uncrowned Holy Roman Emperor, dies in Neszmély, Hungary: he will be succeeded by his posthumous son Ladislas V (the Posthumus) (see 1440).

– Christopher III, nephew of Eric VII (see 1438), succeeds as king of Denmark: he will be elevated to the thrones of Sweden and Norway in 1441 and 1442, respectively.

– Murad II, sultan of the Ottoman Turks, annexes Serbia: his conquest of Serbia is completed only in 1459.

ARTS AND HUMANITIES

– Fra Angelico (Guido di Pietro), Italian painter, enters the monastery of San Marco in Florence, N Italy, where he will execute a number of mural paintings, which are seen as his most important early works.

1440

EUROPE

2 Feb. Frederick of Habsburg, duke of Styria, is elected Holy Roman Emperor; he will reign as Frederick III.

22 Feb. Ladislas V (the Posthumus), son of Holy Roman Emperor Albert II, is born in Komárom, Hungary (modern Komarno in Slovakia): though technically he inherits the kingdoms of Bohemia and Hungary from his father (see 1439), only the Bohemians accept him as their ruler. Emperor Frederick III, a cousin of the infant king, serves as his regent; Vladislav III, king of Poland, is offered the crown of Hungary by the Hungarian nobility and accepts it as Ulászló I.

7 July The French town of Harfleur, Normandy, is recaptured by English forces under the command of Sir John Talbot, 1st earl of Shrewsbury.

ARTS AND HUMANITIES

9 July Jan van Eyck, early Netherlandish painter (see 1420), dies in Bruges (in modern Belgium).

– In Venice, Italy, the Ca' d'Oro, one of the most richly decorated palaces in the late Gothic style, is completed.

– The Platonic Academy is founded in Florence, Italy.

– In England King Henry VI founds a school at Eton.

1441

EUROPE

10 Dec. The treaty of Cavriana (by which peace is settled between Milan, N Italy, and the NE Italian trading state of Venice), is engineered by Francesco Sforza, working for the Venetians but married to Bianca, the daughter and heiress of Filippo Maria Visconti, duke of Milan.

1442

EUROPE

28 April The future King Edward IV of England, son of Richard, duke of York, is born in Rouen in France.

12 June Alfonso V, king of Aragon, is crowned king of Naples (see 1435).

– The French occupy territories in Gascony previously held by the English, leaving only Bordeaux and Bayonne in English hands.

1443

EUROPE

10 Nov. Ottoman Turkish forces invading what is now Bulgaria are defeated by an army led by the Hungarian János Hunyadi, *voivode* (military viceroy) of Transylvania (then Hungary, now in modern Romania): Hunyadi will go on to take Sofia, Bulgaria's capital city.

12 Dec. With his decisive victory in the battle of Zlatica, Murad II, sultan of the Ottoman Turks, halts the advance of János Hunyadi and his army into Thrace, NE Greece.

– The Albanian leader Skanderbeg (George Kastrioti) initiates an Albanian revolt against the Ottoman Turks.

1444

EUROPE

12 June At Szeged (now in Hungary), the Ottoman Turkish Sultan Murad II declares a ten-year truce with the Bulgarians, Serbians, Hungarians and Transylvanians. Within three months, however, the Hungarians and Transylvanians break the terms of the treaty and the conflict resumes.

10 Nov. Murad II, sultan of the Ottoman Turks, leads the Ottoman army to victory at the battle of Varna in Bulgaria: he crosses the Bosphorus (the narrow strip of sea separating Turkey from Europe) and defeats a combined Hungarian–Wallachian force. King Vladislav III of Poland (Ulászló I of Hungary) (see 1440) is killed, but János Hunyadi, *voivode* (military viceroy) of Transylvania, escapes.

1445

EUROPE

– Charles VII, king of France, establishes the first French standing army.

– Margaret of Anjou, daughter of René of Anjou, is married to Henry VI of England. Because of Henry's instability, she will play an unusually active political role in English politics.

MIDDLE EAST AND NORTH AFRICA

– Dinis Dias, Portuguese explorer, rounds Cape Verde, the westernmost point of Africa.

ARTS AND HUMANITIES

– Florentine sculptor Luca della Robbia (Luca di Simone di Marco della Robbia) completes a lunette (panel) depicting the Resurrection of Christ over the door into the N sacristy of the cathedral in Florence, N Italy; this relief sculpture is believed to be the earliest work executed solely in polychrome enamelled terracotta.

1446

EUROPE

– Portuguese national laws are codified for the first time.
– The Ottoman Turks occupy Corinth in Greece.

Better the Turkish turban than the Latin tiara.

Grand Duke Loukas Notaras, c.1462,
sums up the Greek view of the Latin West

ARTS AND HUMANITIES

15 April Filippo Brunelleschi, Florentine architect and engineer responsible for some of the most important architectural monuments of the early Italian Renaissance, dies in Florence, Italy.

1447

EUROPE

25 June The Polish nobility elects the grand prince of Lithuania as king of Poland: King Casimir IV unites the two countries to create a vast central European polity.

13 Aug. Filippo Maria Visconti, duke of Milan and last of the Visconti dynasty, dies. Milan, N Italy, establishes the Ambrosian Republic. Francesco Sforza, son-in-law of the late duke (see 1441), comes forward as the republic's military leader: his claims are contested by several opposing factions, including those supporting King Alfonso V of Aragon and Naples (see 1435 and 1442), whom Filippo Maria had in fact nominated as his successor, and Charles, duke of Orléans.

1448

EUROPE

5 Jan. In Hälsingborg, Denmark (now Helsingborg, Sweden), the death of Christopher III of Bavaria, king of Denmark, Norway and Sweden (see 1439) temporarily dissolves the Union of Kalmar (see 1397). The Swedish nobility chooses a new king (20 June): Karl Knutsson, leader of an important Swedish noble family and former regent of Sweden under King Eric, will reign as King Charles VIII; the Danish nobility elects Count Christian of Oldenburg to the throne of Denmark and Norway: he becomes Christian I, king of Denmark (1448–81), Norway (1450–81) and Sweden (1457–64), though the Danish diet will retain its power.

2 Feb. Representatives of Pope Nicholas V agree the concordat of Vienna with Frederick, Elector of Brandenburg, and other German princes. The concordat gives the German princes extensive powers over the Church in Germany. The papacy backs the concordat as a way of curbing the growing conciliar movement that aims to reform the Church.

16 Mar. Charles VII of France renews the war with England by recapturing Le Mans in the province of Maine in W France.

17 Oct. At the battle of Kosovo in Serbia, Murad II, sultan of the Ottoman Turks, defeats János Hunyadi and his Hungarian forces (see 1443 and 1444): this is the last unified attempt by European Christians to repulse the Ottomans from the Balkans and to wrest Constantinople from Ottoman control.

31 Oct. John VIII Palaeologus, Byzantine emperor, dies childless: he will be succeeded by his brother Constantine XI Palaeologus (crowned emperor in Jan.1449). Constantine will be the last emperor of Byzantium.

1449

EUROPE

24 May Afonso V of Portugal declares war on his uncle and regent, Pedro, duke of Coimbra, who is killed at the battle of Alfarrobeira.

ASIA

27 Oct. Ulugh-Beg, prince of Turkestan, is assassinated by an Islamic fundamentalist at Samarkand in the Timurid empire (modern Uzbekistan).

– Forces from W Mongolia defeat and capture Zhengtong (Cheng-t'ung), Chinese emperor of the Ming dynasty: an interim emperor, Jingtai (Ching-t'ai), is chosen. Jingtai reigns until 1457, when Zhengtong returns to power: he will rule until 1464.

– Ashikaga Yoshimasa becomes shogun of Japan: though his reign marks the beginning of a period of great cultural flowering in Japan, his shogunate is fraught with conflict, particularly over his succession (see 1467).

2

The Early Modern World

2. The Early Modern World

The pandemic known as the Black Death struck Europe in the mid-14th century, having already ravaged much of Asia and North Africa. The Black Death was an economic and a social catastrophe for Europe. Even the countries that got off lightly lost some 10 per cent of their populations. In the worst affected areas as many as half the population died. Wages rose for those who survived because of the labour shortage, yet this in turn led to social dislocation and rebellion.

But what historians call the early modern period (lasting from the mid-15th to the late 18th century) saw, in Europe at least, an economic upturn, rising population levels and commercial prosperity. This trend was somewhat arrested by a critical period in the 17th century, a period of religious and economic crises that led to political and social conflict.

Even when the progress stalled, the European dominance of the rest of the world remained an arresting fact. The opening up of maritime trade routes to Asia and especially the 'discovery' of America – and its subsequent colonization and exploration by the Portuguese, Spanish, English, French and Dutch – shaped both American and European history. The discovery of the New World resulted in a series of trade wars, as the European powers fought each other over the spoils. The British won out in the North American colonies, largely at the expense of the French, and the losses incurred by France in North America in the course of the Seven Years' War (1756–63) mark that conflict as one of the most decisive of world history. It shaped the cultural as well as the political course of the 19th and 20th centuries. The world's dominant culture hereafter would be Anglophone and not Francophone.

On the European mainland the period saw the rise of sovereign and independent states that acknowledged no higher legal authority other than that of the treaties to which they subscribed in advance of their own self-interest. The Protestant Reformation helped to create not just the Protestant creed but also the modern Catholic one. The Reformation marked the end of the idea of a united Christendom, for different countries now followed different forms of Christianity and could not be contained within the same structure. Charles V (reigned 1519–56) was the last Holy Roman Emperor who tried to give real meaning to his title; later holders accepted that they controlled little more than the prestige of the title and their own family lands.

France emerged as the major European power of the 17th century, and pursued a relentless campaign against the Austrian Habsburgs. The weakened Austria was ill-placed to defend Europe on its eastern frontier against the Ottoman

Turks, who remained an important threat right up until the end of the 17th century. Within Europe, the 18th century saw the rise of Prussia as a major player, its power based on a highly effective military machine, served in turn by an efficient bureaucracy.

The Thirty Years' War (1618–48) was the key event of the 17th-century crisis. Fought out largely in the German-speaking lands of central Europe and engaged in by most of the European powers, it was the last major religious war between the Catholic and the Protestant states. It ended in mutual exhaustion and a recognition that religion on its own should no longer determine foreign policy. Trade soon replaced religion as the major source of conflict, causing commercially successful Protestant states to wage war against each other. The Anglo-Dutch rivalry, for example, was fought out in a series of wars on the high seas in the second half of the 17th century. By the end of the 17th century northern Europe was, by and large, Protestant and prosperous, while southern Europe was comparatively poorer and Catholic. Such generalizations mask changes in fortune and isolated contradictions, but the overall picture was clear.

The decline of Spain was a long drawn-out domestic European story, but Spain's colonial empire in Central and South America was essentially unaffected throughout these three centuries. There the story remained one of commercial gain achieved largely by the forced recruitment of Native Americans and the importation of slaves from Africa to work the plantations and silver mines. Brazil, ruled by Portugal, was the world's largest single colony, but its vast interior was only just beginning to be explored in the 18th century. The East Indies had been a Portuguese preserve from the late 15th century, but during the 17th century the Dutch took over the role of leading trading nation and colonial power in the region.

The Ottoman empire underwent a great expansion, taking in the Balkans, Hungary, the shores of the Black Sea, Syria, Egypt and Arabia. They also attacked Persia, but there the ruling Safavid dynasty proved to be one of the great survivors of the period. At the end of the 18th century, Safavid Persia remained a powerful regional state and was able to take advantage of the long Ottoman slide into decrepitude.

Although various Muslim dynasties had ruled parts of north India for centuries, it was during the 16th century that Islam had its greatest impact on the subcontinent, for it was at this time that the Muslim Mughals moved southwards from their original base in Afghanistan. They adapted their Islamic culture to the conditions they found in the Indian territories that they conquered and so created a glittering civilization. Their empire extended over most of India and was initially a highly tolerant one, capable of embracing the original Hindu culture of India. From the beginning of the 18th century the Mughals began to lose their hegemony in India as the Marathas – a Hindu people based in the southwest – grew in power. Around the same time, pressure began to be felt from European merchants as they sought to secure trading contracts and safe bases from which to conduct business. The first to arrive were the Portuguese, followed by the Dutch and French. But those who triumphed in the course of the 18th century were the British, whose commercial empire thereby gained its greatest prize.

The fall of China's Ming civilization in the mid-17th century was also a result of pressure from the north, as nomads from the steppes pressed in on China's boundaries. The early 15th century had seen some major maritime successes as the Ming navy spread Chinese influence as far as the East African coast. This had raised the prospect of Chinese civilization spreading in a westward flow of power and conquest, just as the western European powers were beginning to move east, but the Chinese withdrew to their own boundaries. The Ming dynasty collapsed at the hands of northern invaders – the Manchu – who established a new Chinese imperial dynasty in 1644. These developments in Asia had a major geopolitical consequence – and one that was to the commercial advantage of Europe. The Chinese had been forced to move their defensive bases from the south and to concentrate politically and militarily on the north and centre of China. This left Southeast Asia open to European trading incursions.

Japan was a successful and autonomous Asian power during this period. It showed how a self-confident Asiatic society could do limited trade with the outside world but also keep the foreigner at bay. Westernization would eventually prove to be the undoing of other traditional forms of Asian civilization, but Japan in the 16th and 17th centuries enjoyed one of its great cultural flowerings in poetry, painting and drama, and the 17th century in Japan was also an age of political stability and administrative effectiveness. On the Southeast Asian mainland there were other, if less dramatic, developments. The Burmese and the Thais established effective unitary governments based on their very separate ethnic identities, thus starting a long period of rivalry between the two. The original Vietnamese state

expanded to the south, establishing authority over the whole territory now known as Vietnam. However, in around 1602 the area divided into two states, Tongking in the north and Cochin-China in the south.

As the various regions of the world came in touch with each other, so what happened in one part of the world could have an impact on a country thousands of miles away. For example, the prosperity that the Asian spice trade brought to the Dutch fuelled not only their economic strength and their successful political rebellion against Spain, but was also at the root of Amsterdam's rise as Europe's greatest centre of banking and credit.

The world was becoming increasingly dominated by seaborne trade and maritime power. The great land empires of previous generations either collapsed or stagnated in the face of new economic and military realities. The emerging powers were countries that had access to the Atlantic. They could exploit the wealth of Asia by importing it along the sea

The countries of the Atlantic seaboard could now ... entertain the idea that they were the true inheritors of the Earth.

lanes around Africa. In so doing they could ignore the overland trade routes that had originally brought goods from Asia to Europe. And that economic fact had its political and military consequences. The Mediterranean, once at the heart of European wealth and power, became something of a backwater, while effective banking structures, reliable communications and limited government meant that the countries of the Atlantic seaboard could now indulge their expansionist ambitions and entertain the idea that they were the true inheritors of the Earth.

1450

EUROPE

26 Feb. Francesco Sforza, self-styled heir to Filippo Maria Visconti (see 1447), mounts a successful coup against the Ambrosian Republic of Milan, N Italy; he enters the city as its new duke.

15 April The French defeat the English at the battle of Formigny: all of Normandy is once again under French control.

3 May William de la Pole, duke of Suffolk and favourite of Henry VI, king of England, is beheaded near Dover in Kent: accused of selling Anjou and Maine to France, he is blamed by the English for the loss of the war with France.

6 June In England a rebellion breaks out in protest at war taxation; Jack Cade emerges as its leader. Cade commands an armed force recruited in Kent and Sussex, which defeats royal forces at Sevenoaks in Kent (18 June). The rebels enter London (3 July) but are forced back at London Bridge and then disperse. Cade himself is hunted down and killed (12 July).

ECONOMY AND SOCIETY

– Pope Nicholas V gives the Portuguese the right to reduce to slavery all those living south of Cape Bojador, including the coast of Guinea, W Africa.

ARTS AND HUMANITIES

– In Scotland, the university of Glasgow is founded.
Paolo Uccello, three versions of *The Battle of San Romano*, paintings.

1451

EUROPE

2 Feb. Murad II, sultan of the Ottoman (Turkish) empire (see 1421), dies in Edirne (in European Turkey). He is succeeded by his 19-year-old son Mehmed II.

1452

EUROPE

19 Mar. Frederick IV, king of Germany, is crowned Holy Roman Emperor by the pope and reigns as Frederick III.

– Mehmed II, sultan of the Ottoman Turks, moves towards the final destruction of Constantinople: he completes the construction of a fortification that will control the flow of supplies to the city.

ARTS AND HUMANITIES

– In Vinci, near Florence, N Italy, Leonardo da Vinci (see p. 194), Italian humanist, artist, architect and engineer, is born: his two most famous works, *The Last Supper* and the portrait of *Mona Lisa*, will become icons of W European culture.

1453

EUROPE

6 April The siege of Constantinople by the Ottoman Turks begins: the city walls are attacked by cannon (12 April) and, six weeks later, the walls are breached and the Ottoman forces enter the city (29 May). The Byzantine emperor, Constantine XI Palaeologus (see 1448), is killed while resisting. The Ottomans sack the city, which now becomes their capital: they are able to begin their advance into mainland Greece and Albania.

17 July At Castillon, near Bordeaux in France, the French kill Sir John Talbot, earl of Shrewsbury, leader of an English and Gascon expeditionary force that has landed in the Gironde, SW France: his army is routed.

July Henry VI, king of England, becomes mentally unstable: his cousin, Richard, duke of York (see 1442), who himself has strong claims to the English throne, acts as regent.

19 Oct. Bordeaux falls to the French, marking the end of the Hundred Years War: the English are ejected from all of their French territories with the exception of Calais, the nearest port to England on the channel coast (see 1558).

MIDDLE EAST AND NORTH AFRICA

– Uzun Hasan, founder of the Ak Koyunlu (White Sheep) Turkmen dynasty, comes to power in Persia: he will establish Turkmen power in Armenia, Kurdistan, Azerbaijan and Persia, areas W of Caspian Sea.

ECONOMY AND SOCIETY

– The fall of Constantinople stimulates the need for Western powers to discover new trade routes to the E as Muslim rulers begin to impose high tariffs.

ARTS AND HUMANITIES

– Greek scholars flee Constantinople: they bring their learning to cultural centres in W Europe, most notably to Florence in Italy.

1454

EUROPE

9 April Hostilities between Venice, Milan and Florence are ended by the peace of Lodi: Francesco Sforza is confirmed as the duke of Milan (see 1450).

18 April Venice signs a treaty with the Ottoman (Turkish) empire.

Dec. Henry VI, king of England, recovers his reason (see 1453) and dismisses Richard, duke of York as regent.

SCIENCE AND TECHNOLOGY

– Movable metal type is used for the first time by printers in Mainz, Germany.

1455

EUROPE

22 May Having been excluded from the royal council, Richard, duke of York and former regent of Henry VI, king of England, leads a force loyal to him against a royal army at St Albans in Hertfordshire. Richard defeats the royal army and wins control of England. The battle marks the start of the intermittent

English civil wars known as the Wars of the Roses, fought between the houses of York and Lancaster.

SUB-SAHARAN AFRICA

22 Mar. Alvise Ca' da Mosto, a Venetian in the service of the Portuguese, sets sail for Africa: he will discover the Cape Verde islands off the W coast of Africa and explore the Senegal and Gambia rivers.

ARTS AND HUMANITIES

18 Mar. Italian painter Fra Angelico (Guido di Pietro) dies in Rome, Italy.

1 Dec. Lorenzo Ghiberti, Florentine sculptor of the early Italian Renaissance, dies in Florence, Italy. His *Commentarii* (Commentaries), an autobiography left incomplete at his death, remain an important document for students of the history of early Renaissance art.

– In Mainz, Germany, the Forty-Two-Line Bible, known as the Gutenberg Bible, is completed by the German printer Johannes Gutenberg using movable type.

1456

EUROPE

7 July Joan of Arc (see 1431) is rehabilitated by a French ecclesiastical court.

14 July János Hunyadi, governor of Hungary and *voivode* (military viceroy) of Transylvania (see 1443 and 1444), defeats an Ottoman army besieging Belgrade in Serbia. Sultan Mehmed II is forced to return to Constantinople.

11 Aug. János Hunyadi dies suddenly in Belgrade, but has ensured the independence of Hungary from Ottoman rule.

– Vlad III Tepes becomes ruler of Wallachia (part of modern Romania). He will launch campaigns against the Ottoman Turks (1456–62 and 1476–7) in which thousands of Turks are slaughtered. Tepes, whose practice of impaling his victims earned him the nickname Vlad the Impaler, is thought to be the original of Count Dracula.

ARTS AND HUMANITIES

François Villon (originally François de Montcorbier), *Les Lais* (The Legacy), later known as *Le Petit Testament* (The Short Testament), poem; one of the most important literary works of 15th-century France, it will be published in 1489.

Leon Battista Alberti, new façade for the Church of Santa Maria Novella in Florence, Italy, architectural sculpture.

1457

EUROPE

June Charles VIII, king of Sweden, is deposed after he attempts to extend his royal powers: Christian I of Denmark is crowned king of Sweden in a coup led by the Swedish nobility.

23 Nov. Following the execution of Laszlo Hunyadi, the son of the Hungarian national hero János Hunyadi, for the murder of Ulrich von Cilli, *de facto* ruler of Hungary, King Ladislas V (the

Posthumus) (see 1440) of Hungary and Bohemia is forced to flee to Prague in Bohemia (Czech Republic), where he dies suddenly at the age of 17.

1458

EUROPE

24 Jan. Matthias I Corvinus, second son of the Hungarian national hero János Hunyadi, is elected king of Hungary by the Hungarian diet.

2 Mar. The Bohemian diet elects George Podebrady, leader of the moderate Hussite Utraquists, as king of Bohemia.

27 June Alfonso V of Aragon, Naples and Sicily dies in Naples: he is succeeded by his brother John II in Aragon and Sicily; Florentine support helps to secure the rule of his illegitimate son Ferdinand in Naples.

1459

EUROPE

– Matthias I Corvinus of Hungary challenges the legitimacy of the rule of George Podebrady in Bohemia on the grounds of his supposed heresy as a follower of the Czech religious reformer Jan Hus (see 1408).

ARTS AND HUMANITIES

Andrea Mantegna, *Saint Zeno* altarpiece, painting.

1460

EUROPE

10 July Henry VI, king of England, is taken prisoner by the Yorkists (who back the claims to the throne of Henry's cousin Richard, duke of York; see 1455) at the battle of Northampton: among the Yorkist leaders is Richard's son Edward, earl of March, who will later reign as Edward IV (see 1461).

3 Aug. James II, king of Scotland, is killed while besieging Roxburgh Castle in a display of support for the Lancastrian cause: his young son succeeds as James III.

30 Dec. Richard, duke of York, claims the English throne and marches on London but is killed in battle at Wakefield in Yorkshire by an army raised by Margaret of Anjou, wife of Henry VI (see 1445).

SCIENCE AND TECHNOLOGY

– Venice builds a weapons factory on the island of Arsenal, a word that will spread across Europe. The factory helps to develop Venice's naval power.

ARTS AND HUMANITIES

Rogier van der Weyden, *The Seven Sacraments*, painting.

1461

EUROPE

29 Mar. Edward, earl of March and son of Richard of York, avenges his father's death by defeating the Lancastrians (supporters of Henry VI) at Towton in Yorkshire: Henry VI, king of England, and many of his followers are forced to flee to Scotland. Edward, earl of March, proclaims himself king of England: he will reign as Edward IV.

22 July Charles VII of France dies and is succeeded by his rebel son Louis, who is crowned as Louis XI (15 Aug.). Louis embarks on a policy of increasing royal control at the expense of the nobility, the Church, and provincial and urban centres.

ASIA

– Trebizond (modern Trabzon in NE Turkey), the last independent Byzantine state on the Black Sea, falls to the Ottoman Turks.

ARTS AND HUMANITIES

François Villon, *Le Grand Testament* (The Great Testament), the story of his life as an outlaw.

1462

EUROPE

27 Mar. Vasily II (the Blind), grand duke of Moscow, dies in Moscow: his son Ivan III (the Great) succeeds him and will expand the core Muscovite territory to establish the foundations of the modern Russian state.

1463

EUROPE

3 Dec. Frederick III, Holy Roman Emperor, unites Upper and Lower Austria on the death of his brother Albert VI, grand duke of Austria.

6 Dec. Matthias I Corvinus, king of Hungary, takes Bosnia from the Ottoman Turks: he claims Bosnia, Serbia, Moldavia and Wallachia for Hungary.

– Following Ottoman interference with its eastern trade routes, Venice declares war on the Ottoman empire.

1464

EUROPE

1 Aug. In Careggi, near Florence, Italy, Cosimo de' Medici, Florentine statesman and banker, dies.

SUB-SAHARAN AFRICA

– Sonni Ali founds the Songhai empire of the W African sahel.

ECONOMY AND SOCIETY

– Louis XI, king of France, establishes a national postal service.

ARTS AND HUMANITIES

18 June Rogier van der Weyden, Flemish painter, dies in Brussels.

1465

EUROPE

July In England Yorkist supporters of Edward IV capture King Henry VI and imprison him in the Tower of London.

ARTS AND HUMANITIES

Piero della Francesca, portrait diptych of Federigo da Montefeltro, future duke of Urbino, and his wife, Battista Sforza.

1466

EUROPE

19 Oct. The second peace of Torun (in modern Poland) is signed (see 1411): the Teutonic Knights accept the authority of the Polish crown and Poland gains access to the Baltic.

23 Dec. George Podebrady, king of Bohemia (see 1458), is excommunicated as a Hussite by Pope Paul II: he is deposed from the Bohemian throne and the pope encourages a Hungarian crusade against him.

ARTS AND HUMANITIES

13 Dec. Donatello, a major sculptor of the early Italian Renaissance, dies in Florence.

1467

EUROPE

15 June Philip III the Good (see 1419), duke of Burgundy, dies in Bruges (in modern Belgium); his 48-year reign has seen the emergence of Burgundy as a major European power: his son Charles the Bold succeeds him and launches (Oct.) a successful military campaign against Liège (in modern Belgium) and then declares war on Louis XI of France.

ASIA

May Japan collapses internally with the outbreak of what will become a ten-year civil war between Ashikaga Yoshime, the chosen successor of the shogun Yoshimasa (see 1449), and the shogun's son Yoshihasa.

SUB-SAHARAN AFRICA

– Zara Yacob, emperor of Ethiopia, dies; during a 34-year reign he has defended the country's heritage of Coptic Christianity against the threat of Muslim invasion.

1468

EUROPE

17 Jan. Skanderbeg, ruler of Albania (see 1443), dies in Lezhë: the Ottoman Turks, taking advantage of the power vacuum, prepare to invade Albania.

3 July Charles the Bold, duke of Burgundy, marries Margaret, sister of Edward IV, king of England: the match forges a political and commercial alliance between Burgundy and England and unites them once more against France.

1469

EUROPE

19 Oct. Ferdinand, son and heir of John II of Aragon in NE Spain, and Isabella, sister of, and heir to, Henry IV of Castile in N Spain, marry: their union creates the alliance that will unify Spain and lay the foundations of Spanish military and cultural greatness.

2 Dec. Piero de' Medici dies: control of the Florentine bank passes to his sons Lorenzo and Giuliano.

ASIA

– Nanak, Indian guru and founder of Sikhism, is born in the Punjab, India.

SUB-SAHARAN AFRICA

– The Portuguese explorer Fernão Gomes is granted a trade monopoly for the W coast of Africa by Portugal; in return he promises to explore at least 480km (300 miles) of coastline per year.

ARTS AND HUMANITIES

9 Oct. Fra Filippo Lippi, Florentine painter, dies in Spoleto, Italy.

1470

EUROPE

May The Venetians lose the Aegean island of Euboea to the Turks in the continuing war between the Ottoman (Turkish) and the Venetian empires.

Dec. In a move to halt the growing influence of Charles the Bold, duke of Burgundy (see 1467), Louis XI, king of France, successfully invades Picardy (in modern NE France).

– Matthias I Corvinus, king of Hungary, is proclaimed king of Bohemia, but the deposed George Podebrady (see 1466) fights back, gaining Polish support by promising the throne's succession to the Polish royal house, and forces King Matthias to accept his settlement of the succession.

– In England Richard Neville (the Kingmaker), earl of Warwick and of Salisbury, cousin (and previous ally) of Edward IV, helps King Henry VI to regain the English throne. Edward's younger brother, George, duke of Clarence, previously an ally of Warwick, subsequently defects to support Edward IV, whose army then defeats the forces commanded by Warwick in a battle at Stamford, Lincolnshire.

SCIENCE AND TECHNOLOGY

– Nicolas Jensen establishes a printing and publishing business in Venice, NE Italy, and is the first to use exclusively Roman letters as opposed to Gothic ones.

ARTS AND HUMANITIES

– In England work is completed on the building of York Minster.

1471

EUROPE

22 Mar. George Podebrady, Hussite king of Bohemia, dies in Prague, Bohemia: under the terms he has agreed with the Polish crown (see 1470), Podebrady is succeeded by Ladislas, son of King Casimir IV of Poland. He reigns in Bohemia as Ladislas II but is effectively a cipher for the exercise of power

by the Czech nobility: the succession leads to a seven-year war with Hungary.

14 April In England Richard Neville, earl of Warwick and of Salisbury, is defeated and killed in battle at Barnet, Hertfordshire, while fighting against the army of Edward IV, who reclaims the throne of England.

21 May In the Tower of London, King Henry VI of England is executed on the orders of Edward IV.

– Ivan III, grand prince of Moscow (see 1462), forces the city-state of Novgorod in NW Russia to cut off its links with Lithuania and to accept Moscow's supremacy: Moscow thereby becomes a powerful European nation-state.

MIDDLE EAST AND NORTH AFRICA

– Portugal wages a military campaign against the kingdom of Fez in Morocco: the port of Tangier is occupied by the Portuguese.

SUB-SAHARAN AFRICA

– A trade in gold, led by Portugal, is developing on the newly named Gold Coast (modern Ghana).

1472

EUROPE

– The Orkney and the Shetland islands, previously ruled by Norway, are incorporated within the kingdom of Scotland.

– In the Kremlin in Moscow, Ivan III, grand prince of Moscow, marries Zoë Palaeologus, niece of the last emperor of Byzantium.

SUB-SAHARAN AFRICA

– Portuguese explorer Lopo Gonçalves crosses the equator.

ARTS AND HUMANITIES

25 April Leon Battista Alberti, Italian architect, designer and humanist, dies in Rome, Italy.

– A university is founded in Munich, S Germany.

1473

EUROPE

– Burgundian forces under Charles the Bold occupy Alsace and Lorraine, previously the centre of the Frankish empire under Charlemagne (see 800) and traditionally allied with the German states.

– The island of Cyprus accepts Venetian rule.

ASIA

– In Japan Ashikaga Yoshimasa abdicates as shogun (see 1467) and is succeeded by his son Yoshihasa: civil war continues.

ARTS AND HUMANITIES

– The Sistine Chapel is begun within the Vatican complex in Rome, Italy; it is commissioned by Pope Sixtus IV and built by the Italian architect Giovanni dei Dolci.

Leonardo da Vinci, *Annunciation*, painting.

Martin Schongauer, *The Virgin of the Rose Garden*, painting.

1474-8

1474

EUROPE

4 April The Union of Constance, a defensive alliance against the Burgundians, is agreed between Sigismund of Austria and the Swiss cantons.

11 Dec. Infanta Isabella succeeds to the throne of Castile and Leon in N Spain on the death in Madrid of her half-brother, King Henry IV (the Impotent): the succession is contested by Henry's daughter, Joan, wife of Afonso V of Portugal.

SCIENCE AND TECHNOLOGY

– The Genoese explorer and navigator Christopher Columbus (Cristoforo Columbo) proposes a sea route to Cathay (China) that involves sailing W from Europe.

ARTS AND HUMANITIES

– The main body of Antwerp Cathedral is completed; the spire will not be added until 1518.

– Guillaume Dufay, Flemish composer of secular songs as well as of sacred music, dies.

1475

EUROPE

Feb. War breaks out between Portugal and Castile, N Spain, over the legitimate succession to the Castilian throne: the Castilian nobility has recognized Isabella as joint ruler with her husband Ferdinand V, son and heir of John II of Aragon (see 1469), but the Portuguese, under King Afonso V, claim the throne in the name of Afonso's wife, Joan, daughter of the late Henry IV (the Impotent) of Castile (see 1474).

4 July Edward IV of England lands in Calais in Normandy in support of the Burgundians. Louis XI of France quickly arranges a peace deal with Edward: under the terms of the treaty of Picquigny (29 Aug.), England will receive annual compensation along with free and safe trade access, while France secures peace with England for seven years.

ARTS AND HUMANITIES

6 Mar. In Caprese, Italy, Michelangelo (di Ludovico Buonarroti Simoni) (see p. 197), Italian Renaissance painter, architect, sculptor and designer, is born.

– In Bruges (in modern Belgium) the English printer William Caxton writes and prints *The Recuyell of the Histories of Troye*; his translation of the French original is the first book to be printed in the English language.

– In England Winchester Cathedral is completed.

1476

EUROPE

31 Jan. Vlad III Tepes (the Impaler, see 1456), now married to the sister of Matthias I Corvinus, king of Hungary, returns to the throne of Wallachia (in modern Romania).

2 Mar. Following a successful campaign to conquer Lorraine,

E France, the Burgundians advance on the Swiss cantons: they are soundly defeated by the Swiss near Lake Neuchâtel at Grandson, Vaud (in modern Switzerland).

26 Dec. Galeazzo Maria Sforza, duke of Milan, is assassinated by Milanese nobles: his seven-year-old son, Gian Galeazzo, succeeds under the regency of the boy's mother, Bona of Savoy. (Savoy borders modern SW France and NW Italy.)

ARTS AND HUMANITIES

Oct. The English printer William Caxton establishes the first English printing press at Westminster, London.

Carlo Crivelli, *The Demidoff Altarpiece*, painting.

Andrea del Verrocchio, *David*, sculpture in bronze.

1477

EUROPE

5 Jan. The battle of Nancy in Lorraine, E France, ends in a military and political disaster for Burgundy. Swiss pikemen slaughter the Burgundian cavalry, and Charles the Bold is killed in battle and his body is abandoned to wolves. French forces are now able to invade Burgundy, the Franche-Comté and Artois.

18 Aug. Maximilian, son of the Holy Roman Emperor Frederick III, marries Mary, daughter of the late Charles the Bold, duke of Burgundy: through this marriage the Habsburgs add the Netherlands to their territorial domain.

– Vlad III Tepes (the Impaler), ruler of Wallachia (see 1456 and 1476), is ambushed and killed.

ASIA

17 Dec. Hostilities conclude formally in the decade-long civil war in Japan with the confirmation of Ashikaga Yoshimasa as shogun (see 1473). Despite the cessation of open conflict, what follows is a century of internal instability, which sees the steady diminution in the authority of the Japanese royal family.

ARTS AND HUMANITIES

– In England, King Edward IV bans the playing of cricket; it is seen as undermining the compulsory practice of archery, which is an important part of the English military machine. Edward's initiative fails.

– Universities are founded in Uppsala in Sweden, and in Tübingen in Swabia and Mainz in Hesse (both in modern Germany).

1478

EUROPE

18 Jan. Following a brief conflict, Ivan III (the Great), grand prince of Moscow subjugates the city-state of Novgorod (see 1471) and absorbs its territory into that ruled by Moscow.

26 April In Florence, N Italy, the Pazzi family, influential bankers and rivals of the Medici, organize, with the approval of Pope Sixtus IV, an attack on Lorenzo and Giuliano de' Medici while they attend mass in Florence Cathedral: Giuliano dies of his wounds but Lorenzo (the Magnificent) survives to impose savage reprisals on the entire Pazzi family.

Nov. A papal bull is issued by Sixtus IV to ratify the Spanish Inquisition, set up in 1477 by Isabella of Castile and her husband Ferdinand of Aragon; the Spanish Inquisition is charged with the duty of rooting out those Jews who, although having formally converted to Christianity, are widely believed to continue to practise their Jewish faith in secret.

ARTS AND HUMANITIES

Perugino (Pietro di Cristoforo Vannucci), *The Martyrdom of St Sebastian*, mural at the church in Cerqueto, near Perugia, Italy.

1479

EUROPE

19 Jan. John II of Aragon dies in Barcelona (Spain) and is succeeded by his son Ferdinand as Ferdinand II of Aragon, who is also, by virtue of his marriage to Isabella of Castile (see 1469), Ferdinand V of Castile and Leon.

25 Jan. Under the terms of the treaty of Constantinople, peace is established between Venice and the Ottoman (Turkish) empire: the Venetians lose the island of Euboea (in the Aegean Sea) and Scutari (in modern Albania), as well as other towns on the Albanian coast. Venice agrees to pay an annual tribute of 10,000 ducats in order to continue to trade in and around the Black Sea.

7 Aug. The French military advance into Burgundian territory (see 1477), is halted when Maximilian of Austria, husband of Mary of Burgundy, defeats Louis XI, king of France, in battle at Thérouanne in Artois.

4 Sept. In Spain Ferdinand V and Isabella I agree on a peace deal with Portugal (see 1475), which now acknowledges Spanish rule in the Canary Islands, off NW Africa: Portugal is granted its trade monopoly on the W coast of Africa.

7 Sept. In Milan, Italy, Ludovico Sforza (il Moro) launches a coup against the rule of his young nephew Duke Gian Galeazzo Sforza.

ECONOMY AND SOCIETY

– The destruction of the city of Arras (now in NE France) in the war between France and Burgundy means that Brussels (in modern Belgium) is now the undisputed European centre for the production of tapestry.

ARTS AND HUMANITIES

Hans Memling, *The Mystic Marriage of St Catherine*, painting.

1480

EUROPE

May The Ottoman Turks besiege the island of Rhodes in the Aegean: they are repulsed by the Knights Hospitallers (see 1308).

10 July René, count of Anjou, dies without issue: Louis XI of France annexes his territories, which include not only Anjou in NW France but also Maine in NW France and Provence in S France.

– Ivan III (the Great), grand prince of Moscow, stops the payment of tribute to the Golden Horde, ending over two centuries of Russian subjection to the Tatars (Mongols).

ARTS AND HUMANITIES

– In Brussels (in modern Belgium) work is completed on the Town Hall.
Hans Memling, *The Seven Joys of Mary*, painting.

1481

EUROPE

– In N Italy Ludovico Sforza has ousted Bona of Savoy (see 1476) from the regency of Milan, and has established his authority over that of his young nephew, Duke Gian Galeazzo Sforza.

MIDDLE EAST AND NORTH AFRICA

3 May While preparing to campaign in Anatolia, Mehmed II (the Conqueror), sultan of the Ottoman (Turkish) empire, dies in Hunkârçayiri, near Maltepe in Turkey: his two sons, Djem and Bayezid, dispute the succession to the Ottoman sultanate. By the end of the summer Bayazid II emerges as the victor.

1482

EUROPE

27 Mar. Mary of Burgundy, daughter of Charles the Bold, the late duke of Burgundy, dies in a hunting accident: her husband Maximilian of Austria (see 1477) claims the right to rule the Netherlands as regent for their infant son Philip, but the estates of Brabant and Flanders (modern Belgium and NE France) deny his right to do so.

2 May Venice declares war on Ferrara: the two-year war, which ends in the acquisition of the Ferrarese city of Rovigo in NE Italy, marks the last territorial expansion of Venice on the Italian mainland. The Venetian republic now stands at the apex of its wealth and power.

23 Dec. The Habsburgs and Louis XI of France agree on the terms of the peace of Arras: as a result Burgundy and Picardy are absorbed into France.

ECONOMY AND SOCIETY

– Portuguese explorers discover bananas growing on the W coast of Africa.

ARTS AND HUMANITIES

10 Feb. Death of Luca della Robbia (Luca di Simone di Marco della Robbia), Florentine sculptor who founded the della Robbia family workshop, which specialized in enamelled terracotta.

1483

EUROPE

9 April Edward IV of England dies in Westminster, London. His will names his son Edward V as his successor and his brother, Richard, duke of Gloucester, as regent.

June In England Parliament declares Edward's sons, Edward V and Richard, duke of York, to be the illegitimate offspring of an invalid marriage: Richard, duke of Gloucester, brother of King Edward IV, is declared king; he will reign as Richard III. Two months later (Aug.) Edward's sons disappear from their rooms in the Tower of London. It is suspected, but never proved, that the 'Princes in the Tower' were murdered by their uncle so that he could succeed to the throne as Richard III.

30 Aug. Louis XI of France dies in Plessis-lès-Tours and is succeeded by his sickly young son Charles VIII; Louis's daughter Anne of Beaujeu acts as regent.

ECONOMY AND SOCIETY

2 Aug. Pope Sixtus IV appoints the Dominican priest Tomás de Torquemada, known for his severe intolerance of Muslims and Jews, as the first grand inquisitor of Spain (see 1478).

ARTS AND HUMANITIES

Sandro Botticelli (Alessandro di Mariano Filipepi), *Venus and Mars* and *The Adoration of the Magi*, paintings.

Piero Pollaiuolo (Piero di Jacopo d'Antonio Benci), *The Coronation of the Virgin*, an altarpiece for the Church of San Agostino, San Gimignano, Tuscany.

1484

EUROPE

12 Aug. In Rome, Italy, Pope Sixtus IV dies leaving the building of the Sistine Chapel (see 1473) as his most lasting legacy; Sixtus IV has pursued a diplomatic policy that has tarnished the papacy's reputation, especially in Italy where he implicated himself in internal Florentine politics and played a role in the Venetian decision to attack Ferrara (see 1482).

– John II, king of Portugal, rejects a request by Genoese explorer and navigator Christopher Columbus (Cristoforo Columbo) for financial support for a westward voyage to the Indies.

5 Dec. The newly elected Pope Innocent VIII (the Roman Giovanni Battista Cibò) launches a general attack against witches when he issues his papal bull condemning witchcraft; his attack is especially directed towards German witches and sorcerers.

ASIA

– In Japan, the tea ceremony has now been introduced to Japanese society by the shogun Ashikaga Yoshimasa (see 1473).

1485

EUROPE

7 Aug. Henry Tudor, earl of Richmond, lands at Milford Haven, S Wales, with an army made up of Frenchmen supplied by Charles VIII of France and a few hundred English exiles. Henry marches through Wales, attracting recruits along the way, and enters England, reaching Shrewsbury on 18 Aug.

22 Aug. Henry Tudor, earl of Richmond, and the last living male who can trace royal descent from the House of Lancaster,

defeats Richard III at the battle of Bosworth (near Leicester, England). Henry thereby becomes Henry VII, first monarch of the Tudor dynasty, and ends the Wars of the Roses (see 1455). Richard III is killed in the battle and will later be vilified by Tudor propagandists.

30 Oct. Henry VII of England is crowned king.

– The Habsburgs mount various attempts to extend their territories in Europe: Maximilian of Austria, widower of Mary of Burgundy (see 1482), seizes control of the towns of Bruges and Ghent (both in modern Belgium); meanwhile, his father, Emperor Frederick III, is expelled from Vienna by Matthias I Corvinus of Hungary.

– Both the French and the English royal courts reject requests by Genoese explorer and navigator Christopher Columbus (Cristoforo Columbo) for financial help to mount an expedition to the Indies by a westward route.

ARTS AND HUMANITIES

– *Le Morte d'Arthur* (The Death of Arthur), written by Sir Thomas Malory in 1470, is printed for the first time by English printer William Caxton.

Sandro Botticelli (Alessandro di Mariano Filipepi), *Birth of Venus*, painting.

1486

EUROPE

16 Feb. On the abdication of his father, Emperor Frederick III, Maximilian of Austria is elected king of the Romans (effectively king of Germany and a title traditionally held by the Holy Roman Emperor), and he is crowned (9 April) at Aix-la-Chapelle (Aachen, Germany) as Maximilian I.

1 May Genoese explorer and navigator Christopher Columbus (Cristoforo Columbo) presents his plans for a voyage to the Indies to Ferdinand and Isabella of Spain: he wins their support.

ARTS AND HUMANITIES

– In Rome, Italy, *De Architectura* (On Architecture) by Vitruvius Pollio, a Roman architect of the 1st century BC, is printed for the first time; this text will prove fundamental to the development of Renaissance architectural theory.

1487

EUROPE

24 May In England the pretender Lambert Simnel claims to be the earl of Warwick, nephew of King Edward IV, and lays claim to the throne. Backed by supporters of the House of York, he is crowned Edward VI in Dublin Cathedral in Ireland. After landing in Lancashire, Simnel's army is easily crushed by Henry VII's forces at East Stoke, near Newark in Nottinghamshire (16 June).

– John II of Portugal sends the explorers Pero da Covilhã and Afonso Paiva on a journey across the Red Sea and the Arabian Sea to India and Ethiopia in search of spices.

1488

EUROPE

11 June James III of Scotland is defeated in battle near Stirling by rebellious Scottish nobles: he attempts to flee, but is killed by a cleric who supports the rebels. His son, James IV, succeeds to the Scottish throne.

SUB-SAHARAN AFRICA

Dec. Bartholomeu Dias, Portuguese explorer, returns to Portugal after sailing around the S tip of Africa, subsequently named the Cape of Good Hope.

ARTS AND HUMANITIES

7 Oct. Andrea del Verrocchio, Florentine painter and sculptor and teacher of Leonardo da Vinci, dies in Venice, NE Italy.
– In Munich, S Germany, the Frauenkirche is completed.

1489

EUROPE

14 Mar. Venice buys Cyprus from Catherine Cornaro, widowed queen of James II of Cyprus, the last ruler of the Lusignan dynasty.

ECONOMY AND SOCIETY

– An epidemic of typhus affects Aragon, NE Spain, when it is introduced by Spanish soldiers returning from Cyprus; this is the first European outbreak of the disease.

1490

EUROPE

6 April Matthias I Corvinus, king of Hungary, dies in Vienna and is succeeded by Ladislas II of Bohemia.
– A movement of radical reform sweeps through Florence, N Italy, led by the Dominican friar Girolamo Savonarola. He denounces Church abuses and the corruption of the city's rulers.

SUB-SAHARAN AFRICA

– Portuguese explorers arrive in the Congo: Nzinga Mbemba, the *manikongo* (ruler) of the Kongo kingdom, converts to Christianity.

ARTS AND HUMANITIES

Sandro Botticelli, *The Annunciation*, painting.

1491

EUROPE

7 Nov. Ladislas II, king of Bohemia and Hungary, and Maximilian I, king of the Romans (that is, of Germany), sign the treaty of Bratislava: Maximilian I acknowledges Ladislas II as king of Hungary and agrees to cease his attempts to capture Hungarian territory, while Ladislas II confirms the succession rights of the Habsburgs to the Hungarian throne should he die without an heir.

6 Dec. Charles VIII, king of France, marries Anne, duchess of Brittany, thereby adding Brittany, NW France, to the French royal domains. The annexation provokes England and will result in Henry VII of England declaring war on France.

ARTS AND HUMANITIES

2 Feb. German painter and printmaker Martin Schongauer dies in Breisach, Baden (in modern Germany).
– William Caxton, English printer and translator (see 1475 and 1476), dies in London.

1492

EUROPE

2 Jan. The conquest of Granada by Spanish forces extinguishes the last Moorish kingdom in Spain and consolidates the union of the Spanish monarchy under Ferdinand of Aragon and Isabella of Castile, each Catholic monarchs in their own right, but married to each other (see 1469).

31 Mar. Spanish Jews are given three months in which to accept Christianity or leave Spain; nearly 175,000 Jews are forced to flee.

9 April Death of Lorenzo de' Medici (the Magnificent), ruler of Florence from 1453; his son, Piero, will succeed him.

3 Aug. Italian navigator Christopher Columbus (Cristoforo Colombo), with financial backing from Queen Isabella of Spain, sails from Palos, SW Spain, in search of a W route to India.

10 Aug. Spanish churchman Roderigo Borgia is elected Pope Alexander VI. Urged on by his illegitimate son Cesare, Alexander will attempt to turn the papal office into a vehicle of power for the Borgia family.

2 Oct. Henry VII, first Tudor king of England, invades France after the French king, Charles VIII, accepts the claim to the English throne of Perkin Warbeck. A Fleming, Warbeck has convinced Charles that he is Richard, duke of York, the second son of Edward IV of England and one of the two young princes traditionally believed to have been murdered in the Tower of London (see 1483).

3 Nov. Peace of Etaples: Charles VIII of France expels the pretender to the English throne, Perkin Warbeck; in return for payment, England relinquishes all of its French territories except the port of Calais.
– Birth of William Tyndale, English religious reformer, who is responsible for the first translation into English of the New Testament.

THE AMERICAS

12 Oct. Christopher Columbus and his crew reach an island in the Bahamas (probably Watling's Island); he names it San Salvador and claims it for the kingdom of Spain.

SCIENCE AND TECHNOLOGY

– Leonardo da Vinci (see p. 194) working at the Sforza court in Milan, designs an early prototype of the helicopter.

ARTS AND HUMANITIES

20 April Birth in Arezzo, Tuscany, of Pietro Aretino, Italian playwright and poet.

– Bramante (Donato d'Angelo, 1444–1514), the most important Renaissance architect of his generation, begins work on the choir and cupola of Santa Maria delle Grazie in Milan. Carlo Crivelli, *Madonna of the Candle*, altarpiece.

1493

EUROPE

19 Jan. By the treaty of Barcelona, France cedes Roussillon and Cerdagne in S France to Spain following the French annexation of Brittany in 1491, which has alarmed England, Spain and the Holy Roman Empire; at the battle of Salins, Maximilian, king of the Romans (ruler of Germany), defeats a French force which had threatened to invade Germany.

4 Mar. Christopher Columbus returns to Lisbon in Portugal and announces that he has discovered 'the Indies'. Hostile contemporaries ask why Columbus went to Portugal first instead of reporting straight back to Spain, which was paying him.

3–4 May Pope Alexander VI publishes the bull *Inter Cetera*, dividing the New World between Spain and Portugal.

19 Aug. The claims of the Habsburgs to the throne of the Holy Roman Empire are confirmed as, on the death of Ferdinand III, his son Maximilian, king of the Romans (ruler of Germany), becomes Holy Roman Emperor elect.

25 Sept. Christopher Columbus departs on his second voyage to the 'Indies'.

THE AMERICAS

3 Nov. On his second voyage to the New World, Christopher Columbus sights Dominica in the West Indies. He will survey much of the Caribbean archipelago over the next three years, including Cuba, Puerto Rico, Antigua and Jamaica.

ECONOMY AND SOCIETY

– Syphilis appears in Europe for the first time; it arrives with sailors returning from the New World.

1494

EUROPE

25 Jan. Alfonso II succeeds to the throne of the kingdom of Naples and is recognized by Pope Alexander VI (see 1496); Charles VIII of France claims the throne by descent from the house of Anjou.

1 Sept. Charles VIII invades Italy to claim Naples.

12 Sept. Birth of Francis, nephew of the future Louis XII of France. The boy will grow up to become Francis I of France (see 1515), epitome of the versatile Renaissance prince.

8 Nov. French forces enter Lucca and (17 Nov.) Florence, where the Republicans, influenced by the religious and political radicalism of the Dominican friar Savonarola (see 1490), expel Piero de' Medici.

31 Dec. Charles VIII of France enters Rome; Pope Alexander VI flees to the Castel Sant'Angelo, a fortress in Rome.

MIDDLE EAST AND NORTH AFRICA

Nov. Birth of Suleiman I (the Magnificent), future sultan of the Ottoman Empire (see 1520).

THE AMERICAS

7 June Spain and Portugal agree on the division of the New World through the treaty of Tordesillas: Portugal gains all the lands E of a north–south line drawn 370 leagues W of Cape Verde and Spain is allocated the rest. Adventurers from other countries see no reason why they should be bound by this treaty.

ARTS AND HUMANITIES

11 Jan. Death of Domenico del Ghirlandaio (Domenico Bigordi), the last of the great painters of 15th-century Florence.

24 May Birth of the artist Jacopo (Carucci) da Pontormo, a leading proponent of Mannerism (a distinctively exaggerated style of the High Renaissance).

Aug. Birth of the painter Correggio (Antonio Allegri), a High Renaissance artist of the Parma School.

17 Nov. Death of Giovanni, Count Pico della Mirandola, Florentine neo-Platonist philosopher.

You shall ordain for yourself the limits of your nature.

Giovanni Pico della Mirandola expresses what he takes to be God's attitude towards humanity in his *Oration on the Dignity of Man* (1486)

– *The Scale of Perfection*, an English mystical text by the 14th-century monk Walter Hylton, is printed.

Sebastian Brandt, *Das Narrenschiff* (The Ship of Fools), a satire on the folly of humanity.

Jean Mauburnus, *Rosetum Exercitiarum Spiritualium*, the first systematic study of musical instruments.

Johann Reuchlin, *De Verbo Mirifico*, a study of cabbalistic magic.

1495

EUROPE

28 Jan. Charles VIII, king of France, leaves Rome and enters Naples (22 Feb.). Alfonso II, king of Naples, has fled to Sicily. His son, who will shortly follow his father to Sicily, rules briefly as Ferdinand II.

31 Mar. Pope Alexander VI forms the League of Venice, the members of which include the Holy Roman Empire, Spain,

Venice and Milan. Founded to protect Christian Europe from the powerful Ottoman empire, the League of Venice works initially to expel the French from Italy.

12 May Charles VIII of France is crowned king of Naples and (5 July) defeats the League of Venice at the battle of Fornovo near Parma.

July Ferdinand II of Naples begins the reconquest of his kingdom. Aided by Venetian and Spanish factions, Ferdinand and his troops meet with stiff resistance from the French; it will be several months before serious gains are made.

7 Aug. The diet (princely convention) of Worms, at which peace is proclaimed within the Holy Roman Empire. Private warfare is abolished, an Imperial Chamber and Court of Appeal established and an imperial tax introduced.

25 Oct. John II (the Perfect), king of Portugal from 1481, dies; he is succeeded by his cousin, Manuel d'Aviz, who will reign as Manuel I (the Fortunate) until 1521.

– Portugal expels the Jews.

ARTS AND HUMANITIES

– The Aldine Press, founded in Venice by Aldus Manutius (1494), begins its publication of Greek classics. Aristotle's complete works are published in five volumes (1495–8) and represent the first printed editions of ancient Greek philosophy. As they become widely available across Europe, the works of Aristotle and other classical Greek writers will begin to have a major influence on European thought.

– Leonardo da Vinci (see p. 194) begins painting *The Last Supper* in the Church of Santa Maria delle Grazie in Milan; Leonardo's experimental oil-based fresco technique means that his work will begin to deteriorate shortly after it is completed.

1496

EUROPE

5 Mar. Henry VII, king of England, authorizes Italian navigator Giovanni Caboto (John Cabot) and his son Sebastiano (Sebastian) to discover new lands.

Sept. James IV of Scotland invades Northumberland in support of Perkin Warbeck (see 1492), pretender to the English throne.

Sept. The Holy Roman Emperor Maximilian I (see 1493) leads an army to expel the French from Italy.

21 Oct. Philip the Handsome, duke of Burgundy and son of the Emperor Maximilian I, marries Joanna the Mad, the heiress to the Spanish crown.

ARTS AND HUMANITIES

– John Colet, English humanist, starts his Oxford lectures.

– The Scottish Parliament passes an act requiring householders to send their sons to school from the age of eight.

Johann Reuchlin, *Sergius*, play (in Latin), the earliest instance of comedy in the German theatre.

Richard Rolle, *The Abbaye of the Holy Ghost* and *The Travels of Sir John Mandeville*, a mythical tale of a pilgrimage to the Holy Land based on an anonymous 14th-century text.

1497

EUROPE

Mar. Lucretia Borgia, illegitimate daughter of Pope Alexander VI (see 1492), is divorced from Giovanni Sforza and is married to Alfonso d'Este, eldest son of Ercole, duke of Ferrara (1471–1505). This union helps to cement the pope's alliance with the kingdom of Naples through Alfonso's mother, Eleonora of Aragon, granddaughter of Alfonso I of Naples.

May In England heavy taxation to support the wars against Scotland and France provokes Cornish (W England) riots; an army of 15,000 leaves Taunton to attack London.

14 June Juan Borgia, duke of Gandía and illegitimate son of Pope Alexander VI, is murdered, probably by his brother Cesare; Cesare replaces Juan as his father's favourite and now directs papal politics.

Aug. Prince Arthur, eldest son and heir of Henry VII of England (until Arthur's early death on 2 April 1502) is promised in marriage to Catherine of Aragon, daughter of Ferdinand V and Isabella I of Spain. Catherine later marries Arthur's younger brother Henry, who will become Henry VIII of England (see 1509).

5 Oct. After the defeat of his rebel forces at Taunton, Somerset, Perkin Warbeck, the pretender to the English throne, flees and is captured at Beaulieu, Hampshire.

28 Oct. John of Denmark (r.1481–1513) defeats the Swedes and, entering Stockholm, revives the Scandinavian Union of Kalmar (see 1397).

THE AMERICAS

2 May John Cabot (see 1496) sails from Bristol and reaches the American coast at Cape Breton Island (24 June) before exploring Newfoundland. He believes he has discovered the land of the Great Khan (China).

SUB-SAHARAN AFRICA

9 July Portuguese navigator Vasco da Gama leaves Lisbon to sail to India; in December he rounds the Cape of Good Hope.

ARTS AND HUMANITIES

16 Feb. Birth of Philip Melanchthon, humanist scholar and Protestant reformer.

– The Italian artist Perugino starts work on his murals in the Collegio del Cambio, Perugia.

– Birth in Augsburg, Bavaria, of the German portrait painter Hans Holbein the Younger.

1498

EUROPE

7 April Louis, duke of Orléans, becomes Louis XII, king of France on the death of his cousin Charles VIII; the duchy of Orléans and county of Blois are united with the titles and territories of the French crown. Charles VIII is the last Valois king of the direct line, but the dynasty continues as Valois-Orléans (Louis XII) and Valois-Angoulême (Francis I) (see 1515).

22 May The Dominican friar Savonarola, *de facto* ruler of Florence after the expulsion of the Medici (see 8 Nov. 1494), is sentenced to death following his excommunication (June 1497) for seeking the deposition of Pope Alexander VI. Savonarola is executed by strangulation and burning (23 May) and becomes a martyr in the cause of anti-clerical republicanism in Florence.

14 July Louis XII of France confirms the peace of Etaples (see 1492), and strengthens the provisions against receiving and aiding English rebels who reject Tudor dynastic authority.

2 Aug. The treaty of Marcoussis, signed by Louis XII of France and Ferdinand of Spain, effectively dissolves the League of Venice (see 31 Mar. 1495) and a Franco-Spanish division of the kingdom of Naples is planned.

16 Sept. Death of Tomás de Torquemada, Spanish inquisitor.

– Death of John Cabot (see 2 May 1497).

ASIA

20 May Vasco da Gama arrives on the Malabar coast of W India, having rounded the Cape of Good Hope, explored the Mozambique coast and discovered the sea route to India.

THE AMERICAS

30 May Italian-born navigator Christopher Columbus leaves on his third voyage (see also 1492 and 1493), in the course of which he discovers Trinidad (31 July) and S America (1 Aug.) when he lands near the mouth of the Orinoco River.

ARTS AND HUMANITIES

– Desiderius Erasmus, the Dutch humanist, teaches at Oxford.

– Michelangelo (see p. 197), *Pietà*, sculpture; the best known of several, this was commissioned by Cardinal Jean de Bilhères Lagraulas for his burial chapel in St Peter's, Rome.

Albrecht Dürer (see p. 203), *The Apocalypse*, woodcuts.

1499

EUROPE

8 Jan. Louis XII of France retains the duchy of Brittany for the French crown by marrying Anne, duchess of Brittany, the widow of Charles VIII of France (see 6 Dec. 1491).

Feb. Florence joins the French alliance, which seeks the partition of Milan.

Mar. In Spain Cardinal Francisco Jiménez de Cisnéros tightens the repression of the Moors of Granada.

July War breaks out between the Ottoman Turks and Venice: the Turks raid Venetian territory in Albania and Dalmatia along the Adriatic coast.

12 Aug. The Ottomans defeat the Venetian fleet at Sapienza; shortly thereafter the Ottomans capture Lepanto (29 Aug.) and Vicenza (Sept.).

11 Sept. The French take Milan, the duke, Ludovico Sforza, having fled the city (2 Sept.).

22 Sept. The peace of Basle ends the Swabian War between Emperor Maximilian I and the Swiss League; the Swiss now gain their independence from imperial jurisdiction and taxation.

6 Oct. Entry of Louis XII of France into Milan.

23 Nov. Execution of Perkin Warbeck, pretender to the English throne (see 1492).

– War breaks out between the Swiss cantons and the Swabian League; the Swabian League, under Albert of Bavaria-Munich, is defeated at Dornach in Switzerland.

THE AMERICAS

May Spanish explorer Alonso de Ojeda and Italian-born navigator Amerigo Vespucci leave Spain for S America and discover the mouth of the River Amazon.

Sept. Spanish explorer Vicente Yanez Pinzon, who sailed with Columbus on his first voyage, leaves on a three-month voyage in the course of which he explores the Brazilian coast.

ARTS AND HUMANITIES

– The Aldine Press publishes Francesco Colonna's *Hypnerotomachia Poliphili*, an allegorical and architectural romance whose 172 woodcuts and floriated initials signal a high point in the techniques of Renaissance printing.

– Florentine painter Luca Signorelli continues the fresco cycle at Orvieto Cathedral begun by Fra Angelico in 1447. Initially commissioned to paint only the ceiling vaults, Signorelli is asked the following year (1500) to design and paint the walls as well. These murals will be among the first large-scale dramatic works of the Cinquecento.

– Death of Marsilio Ficino, Florentine Neo-Platonic scholar.

– Birth of Sir Thomas Elyot, English courtier and political theorist.

1500

EUROPE

5 Feb. Ludovico Sforza, duke of Milan, aided by German and Swiss mercenaries, recovers Milan from the French; two months later (8 April), the French army regains control and Ludovico is sent in captivity to France.

24 Feb. Joanna the Mad, daughter of Ferdinand and Isabella of Spain and wife of Philip the Handsome, archduke of Austria and duke of Burgundy, gives birth in Ghent to the future Holy Roman, Emperor Charles V.

10 April At the diet (princely convention) of Augsburg, Maximilian I, Holy Roman Emperor, concedes a representative supreme executive council for the empire as part of his overall plan for a strong imperial government with a standing army. Later (2 July) an edict of the diet implements a Council of Regency with representatives from the three colleges of Electors, princes and cities. Germany is divided into six 'circles' or administrative areas.

5 May Georges d'Amboise, cardinal of Rouen, becomes governor of Milan; the Italian states accede to France's occupation.

5 May Ferdinand II of Spain suppresses a Moorish revolt in Granada; this uprising follows the mass conversions to Catholicism forced on the Moors by Cardinal Cisnéros and his inquisitors.

1500-2

1 Oct. Cesare Borgia, son of Pope Alexander VI, campaigns in the Romagna in C Italy and, with French aid, takes Rimini and Pesaro on the Adriatic coast.

11 Nov. Louis XII of France and Ferdinand II of Spain sign a secret treaty for the conquest and partition of Naples: Spain is allocated Apulia and Calabria while France stands to gain Abruzzi, Terra di Luvoro, Naples and Gaeta.

THE AMERICAS

22 April Portuguese explorer Pedro Alvarez Cabral lands in Brazil, which he claims for Portugal and names Tierra de Vera Cruz. This causes shock in Spain, where it was not believed that Brazil extended so far east and that all the Americas were Spanish territory.

– Gaspar de Corte Real, Spanish navigator, explores the east coast of Greenland and Labrador.

SUB-SAHARAN AFRICA

10 Aug. Diego Diaz, Portuguese navigator, discovers Madagascar.

ARTS AND HUMANITIES

8 May Birth of Peter Martyr Vermigli, Florentine theologian and religious reformer.

1 Nov. Birth of Benvenuto Cellini, Italian sculptor and gold-smith. Cellini will work primarily in a style associated with the last phase of the High Renaissance; Cosimo I de' Medici, grand duke of Tuscany, will be among his most important patrons.

– Publication of first edition of *Till Eulenspiegel*, the oldest collection of German tales, in Lübeck, N Germany.

Hieronymus Bosch, *The Ship of Fools*, painting (see 1494).

Sandro Botticelli, *Mystic Nativity*, painting.

Erasmus (see box), *Adages*, compilation of Greek and Latin proverbs with extensive commentary.

1501

EUROPE

17 Jan. Cesare Borgia returns to Rome, the Papal States of C Italy having been brought under direct papal rule as a result of his campaign in the Romagna.

June The French enter Rome and assure the pope, Alexander VI, that they will not interfere with his expansionist policy. Alexander VI confirms the Franco-Spanish treaty governing the division of Naples and names Louis XII of France king of Naples. The French conquest of Naples begins in July.

July Ferdinand II of Spain declares the kingdom of Granada to be Christian; further repression of the Moors follows.

4 Aug. Louis d'Armagnac, duke of Nemours, is named viceroy of Naples by Louis XII of France.

7 Nov. Edmund de la Pole, earl of Suffolk, is denounced as a traitor by Henry VII of England after his attempt to raise forces abroad in pursuit of his Yorkist claim to the English throne.

– Ivan III (the Great) of Russia invades Polish Lithuania.

– The states of Basle and Schaffhausen become members of the Swiss Confederation.

Erasmus (1469–1536)

The Renaissance thinker Desiderius Erasmus was born in Rotterdam, but considered himself 'a citizen of the world, known to all and to all a stranger'. He represents in his life and writings the values of Christian humanism – tolerant, urbane and anti-dogmatic. The humanism Erasmus espoused was a reaction against late medieval scholarship, which had become stale and obsessed with detail. His immense scholarship contributed to the great revival of interest in the pre-Christian classics (which the new technology of printing was bringing to a wider audience), and his translation of the Greek New Testament showed up the flaws in the Vulgate, the official Latin translation approved by the Church. Indeed, he was a great critic of the abuses of the Church, although he maintained a neutral position regarding the conflict between Rome and the Lutheran reformers.

Erasmus's career was founded on a wide readership, a good courier service and rulers who rewarded him with cash when he dedicated his works to them (for his part, he aimed to educate princes in the ways of peace). This made possible a life of itinerant independence. He became a great friend of the English churchman Thomas More, and he developed a vision of a pan-European community of scholars sustaining each other by correspondence. It was while staying in England with More that he wrote *The Praise of Folly* (1511), which satirizes both church and society. Among his other works are the *Adages* (1500), a compilation of classical phrases and quotations that became an indispensable reference book for writers; and *De civilitate* (1530), which outlines the humanist view of decorum and good manners.

MIDDLE EAST AND NORTH AFRICA

– Ismail the Sufi, sheik of Ardabil, gains power in Persia through his victory at the battle of Shurnur. He founds the Shiite Safavid dynasty, which will rule Persia until 1736.

THE AMERICAS

May Amerigo Vespucci (see 1499) leaves Portugal to explore the S American coast.

ARTS AND HUMANITIES

– Earliest use of italic type at the Aldine Press, Venice.

– Florentine sculptor and painter Michelangelo (see p. 197) begins work on his statue *David*.

– The first book of music printed with movable type, the *Harmonice Musices Odhecaton*, is published in Venice.

1502

EUROPE

2 Mar. Holy Roman Emperor Maximilian I ends the consti-tutional experiment in the Holy Roman Empire; he dismisses

Leonardo da Vinci (1452–1519)

The Italian artist, inventor and scientist Leonardo da Vinci is often regarded as the greatest all-round genius there has ever been. He exemplifies the Renaissance ideal of the universal man who takes all areas of knowledge as his province and whose specialism is all humanity.

Leonardo trained as a painter under Verrocchio, who is said to have been so impressed by his pupil's skill that he gave up his own artistic career. In the 1480s Leonardo worked in Milan for Duke Ludovico Sforza in Milan, where he painted his famous fresco of *The Last Supper*. In this and some other paintings his technical experiments with his materials led the works to deteriorate badly. His subsequent career took him to Florence, Rome and France. It was in Florence that he painted the *Mona Lisa*, perhaps the best-known painting in the world. Because it is now so familiar, it is difficult to appreciate what a breakthrough it was in the art of portraiture, particularly in its depiction of inward character.

As an engineer and inventor, Leonardo came up with all kinds of devices, such as a parachute, a giant crossbow and a helicopter. However, as far as is known, no working examples of these were built.

Leonardo also studied the natural world, both for its own sake and as an aid to his painting. He looked at and drew such phenomena as water in motion, rocks and the weather and studied the effect of light and shade.

The anatomical drawings by Leonardo were revolutionary, in that they were based on the dissection of human, rather than animal, cadavers, and in their fusion of beauty with precision have never been surpassed. In such work as this, Leonardo's achievement was to transcend the division between the arts and sciences invented by later generations.

Berthold of Henneberg, arch-chancellor, from his post. From this point the executive council (see 1500) will diminish in importance.

2 April Arthur, prince of Wales, heir to the English throne of Henry VII, dies, leaving his younger brother, the future Henry VIII, as heir. Arthur also leaves Catherine of Aragon as his widow; subsequently she marries Henry VIII, and her failure to produce a male heir will lead to Henry's marital and religious difficulties.

19 June The treaty of Aachen is negotiated between England and the Holy Roman Empire; one result of this agreement will be to bar English refugees from Aachen in Germany.

July War breaks out between France and Spain after they quarrel over the details of the partition of Naples; Louis XII of France is assured of papal neutrality after he bribes Cesare Borgia, illegitimate son of Pope Alexander VI.

Dec. French troops support Cesare Borgia in the suppression of a revolt by the Orsini clan and Cesare's condottieri. Cesare Borgia takes Urbino (31 Dec.) and murders the chief plotters against him, Vitellozzo Vitelli and Oliverotti da Fermo.

– Peasants' rebellion in Speyer, Germany caused by increases in taxes.

THE AMERICAS

11 May The Italian-born navigator Christopher Columbus, ill and out of favour, leaves on his last voyage: he will explore Honduras and Panama.

ARTS AND HUMANITIES

– Publication of the first printed edition of *The Peloponnesian War* by Thucydides, the classical Greek historian.

– Ferdinand and Isabella of Spain commission Bramante to design the Tempietto in order to mark the spot in Rome where St Peter was crucified; once completed (after 1511) the Tempietto will introduce a fully developed High Renaissance style to Roman architecture.

Josquin des Près, first book of masses, sacred vocal music.

1503

EUROPE

8 Feb. Henry Tudor, the future King Henry VIII of England, is created Prince of Wales.

Mar. Venice signs a peace treaty with the Turks, ceding Lepanto and other holdings in the Peloponnese (S Greece), but retaining some Ionian islands.

23 June Henry Tudor, Prince of Wales, is engaged to Catherine of Aragon, widow of his elder brother Arthur (see 2 April 1502).

18 Aug. Pope Alexander VI, father of Cesare Borgia, dies.

22 Sept. The election of the Sienese Francesco Todeschini as Pope Pius III removes Cesare Borgia's power base: princes in the Romagna and other papal states deposed by Borgia rise against him and the Orsini family return to Rome.

Nov. Venice invades the Romagna.

29 Dec. The French are defeated by the Spanish at the Garigliano (a river in S Italy); this consolidates the Spanish conquest of Naples and Spanish control of S Italy.

– Poland surrenders the left bank of the River Dnieper to Russia.

MIDDLE EAST AND NORTH AFRICA

3 Sept. Ferdinand II of Spain sends an army to N Africa to fight the Moors; Mers-el-Kebir falls to Spain.

THE AMERICAS

20 Jan. Spain establishes the Casa Contratación (department of trade) to oversee American affairs.

– The Portuguese send the first African slaves to Brazil.

SCIENCE AND TECHNOLOGY

13 Dec. Birth in Saint-Rémy, France, of Nostradamus (Michel de Nôtredame), physician and astrologer.

– Spanish military engineer Pedro de Navarro is the first to use explosive mines, during the siege of Naples by the French.

ARTS AND HUMANITIES

– Leonardo da Vinci (see box p. 194) begins work on the painting *Mona Lisa*, believed by many to be of La Gioconda, wife of the banker Zanobi del Giocondo.

Thomas à Kempis, the first English edition of *Imitatio Christi*, devotional manual completed in 1427.

1504

EUROPE

25 Jan. The English Parliament passes statutes against retainers (paid military dependants) and liveries (dependants' uniforms) in order to stop private warfare and to place guilds and companies under state supervision.

31 Jan. France cedes Naples to Spain under the treaty of Lyons: Naples will remain under Spanish control until 1713.

23 April Holy Roman Emperor Maximilian I pronounces the ban of the empire on Rupert, son of the Elector Palatine, who has seized Landshut in S Germany following the death of his father-in-law, George, duke of Bavaria-Landshut.

22 Sept. The treaty of Blois is signed by Louis XII of France, Maximilian I of the Holy Roman Empire and his son, Philip the Handsome of Burgundy. Louis XII's daughter is to marry Philip's son Charles, the future Holy Roman Emperor Charles V. If Louis dies without a male heir, Charles is to inherit Milan, Blois and Brittany. By a secret treaty Louis is allowed to retain Milan and agrees to join Maximilian in an attack on Naples.

24 Nov. Isabella of Castile (see 1469 and 1474) dies. Joanna the Mad, wife of Philip the Handsome of Burgundy, is now heir to Castile.

– By the Constitution of Radom, the diet becomes the legislative organ of Poland.

ARTS AND HUMANITIES

11 Jan. Birth in Parma, Italy, of Parmigianino (Francesco Mazzola), Mannerist painter.

– The University of Santiago de Compostela in Spain is founded by papal bull.

– Raphael, *Marriage of the Virgin*, painting; this work will stand alongside Bramante's Tempietto (see 1502) as a classic of High Renaissance aesthetic style.

1505

EUROPE

April At the Diet of Cologne, the Holy Roman Emperor Maximilian I obtains support from the German princes for an expedition to Hungary in support of Ladislas II against rebellious Hungarian nobles. Maximilian also begins his reform of the empire according to a model of universal monarchy.

27 Oct. Death of Ivan III (the Great), grand duke of Russia (see 1462); he is succeeded by his son, who will reign as Vasily III until his death on 21 Nov. 1533.

Nov. Ferdinand II of Spain signs the treaty of Salamanca and undertakes to rule Castile jointly with his daughter, Joanna the Mad (see 1504), and her husband, Philip the Handsome of Burgundy.

SUB-SAHARAN AFRICA

– The Portuguese occupy the E African port of Kilwa (in modern Tanzania). This gives them a base on the long, dangerous voyage round Africa to India.

ECONOMY AND SOCIETY

17 July Martin Luther (see p. 201), German Church reformer, enters the Augustinian friary at Erfurt in Germany.

– English humanist John Colet is appointed dean of St Paul's, where he lectures on the Scriptures.

– Birth of John Knox, Scottish Church reformer.

ARTS AND HUMANITIES

– The Italian architect Bramante is commissioned by Pope Julius II to rebuild St Peter's in Rome; work begins on Bramante's Greek-cross design, but a succession of important architects (among them Michelangelo) will leave their marks on the completed building.

– Birth of Thomas Tallis, English composer.

– Giovanni Bellini, altarpiece for the Church of San Zaccaria in Venice; this work is perhaps the best-known example of the *sacra conversazione* (holy conversation) composition popular in Renaissance painting.

Jakob Wimpfeling, *Epitome Rerum Germanicarum*, the first history of Germany based on original sources.

1506

EUROPE

Mar. Holy Roman Emperor Maximilian I arranges the marriage of the infant princess Anne of Hungary to his grandson, Archduke Ferdinand, younger son of Philip the Handsome of Burgundy and Joanna the Mad; the alliance will guarantee the Habsburg succession to Hungary and Bohemia.

20 May Death in Valladolid, Spain, of Italian-born navigator Christopher Columbus.

May Louis XII of France breaks the betrothal between his daughter Princess Claude and the future Holy Roman Emperor Charles V (see 22 Sept. 1504), thus preventing the union of the French royal house and the Habsburg family. Instead he selects as a future son-in-law Francis of Angoulême, duke of Valois and Louis's heir presumptive.

19 Aug. King Alexander I of Poland dies; his brother, who will reign as Sigismund I, succeeds him (20 Oct.) but will not be crowned until 24 Jan. 1507.

Aug. Pope Julius II leaves Rome at the head of an army to subjugate Perugia in C Italy.

25 Sept. Death of Philip the Handsome at Burgos in Spain. His widow, Joanna, is unable to rule because of insanity. Castilian nobles nominate a council of regency under Cardinal Francisco Jiménes de Cisnéros.

– Niccolò Machiavelli (see p. 199), statesman and political reformer, forms the Florentine militia, the first Italian national army.

ECONOMY AND SOCIETY

7 April Birth near Sangesa, Navarre (in Spain), of Spanish churchman and Jesuit St Francis Xavier. Christianity will be introduced into India, SE Asia and Japan as a result of his missionary work.

ARTS AND HUMANITIES

13 Sept. Death of N Italian painter Andrea Mantegna.

– The *Laocoön* group, a Hellenistic work of the 1st century BC, is unearthed in Rome; the emotional intensity and contorted musculature of its figures will have a profound influence on Renaissance sculpture.

Johann Reuchlin, *Rudimenta Linguae Hebraicae*, a landmark in Hebrew scholarship.

1507

EUROPE

12 Mar. Death near Viana, Spain, of Cesare Borgia, soldier and illegitimate son of Pope Alexander VI.

25 Mar. Louis XII of France attacks Genoa with a Swiss army to restore order after the popular uprising of the year before; the city falls (28 Mar.) to Louis's troops. France will annex Genoa on 11 May.

April Within the Holy Roman Empire, the Diet of Constance restores the imperial chamber and places imperial taxation and armed levies on a permanent basis; the unity of the empire is recognized.

April The States-General of the Netherlands appoints Margaret of Austria as regent during the minority of her nephew, Archduke Charles, the future Charles V, Holy Roman Emperor.

June Meeting at Savona (Tuscany) between Emperor Maximilian I and King Louis XII of France; they agree to sell Pisa to Florence.

July Triumphal processions in Rome mark the military success of Pope Julius II in enlarging the Papal States. The pope now plans a league against Venice.

MIDDLE EAST AND NORTH AFRICA

– Alvise Ca'da Mosto, Venetian explorer, publishes *La prima navigazione per l'oceano alle terre de' negri della Bassa Ethiopia*, an account of his exploration of Gambia.

ARTS AND HUMANITIES

20 Feb. Death of Gentile Bellini, Venetian painter.

– In his *Cosmographie Introductio*, German cartographer Martin Waldseemüller proposes that the new world be called 'America'

since Amerigo Vespucci (see 1499) was the first explorer to conclude that he had discovered a new continent and not part of Asia.

– Henry VII of England appoints Polydore Vergil, Italian scholar, as Historiographer Royal (see 1534).

– Pope Julius II proclaims an indulgence in order to raise money to rebuild St Peter's in Rome.

1508

EUROPE

6 Feb. Holy Roman Emperor Maximilian I issues the proclamation of Trent; this states that he will no longer seek formal coronation by Pope Julius II but will accept (with Julius's consent) the title of emperor-elect.

6 June Maximilian is forced to sign a three-year truce with the Venetians after being defeated by them at Friulia, NE of Venice.

10 Dec. The League of Cambrai is formed by Louis XII, king of France, Emperor Maximilian I and Margaret of Austria, regent of the Netherlands and aunt of the future emperor Charles V (see April 1507); its aim is to conquer Venice.

– Birth in Piedrahita, Old Castile (Spain), of Fernando Alvarez de Toledo, duke of Alva; he will go on to serve as governor general of the Netherlands from 1567 to 1573 and to conquer Portugal (1580).

MIDDLE EAST AND NORTH AFRICA

– Pedro Navarro, count of Olivetto and naval mercenary, leads a Spanish expedition to N Africa and takes Peñon de la Gomera, an island off the Moroccan coast. For years pirates from N Africa have preyed on European shipping and coastal towns.

ECONOMY AND SOCIETY

– Emperor Maximilian I creates his banker Jakob Fugger of Augsburg a knight of the Holy Roman Empire.

– Guillaume Budé, French humanist, publishes his *Annotationes in Pandectas*, in which he criticizes the medieval interpretations of Roman law.

ARTS AND HUMANITIES

– Birth in Padua or Vicenza (Italy), of Andrea Palladio (Andrea di Pietro), Italian classical architect.

– Regular courses in Greek begin at the university of Paris under Italian scholar Girolamo Aleandro.

– *The Maying or Disport* by Geoffrey Chaucer is the first book to be printed in Scotland.

– Sienese architect and painter Baldassare Peruzzi is commissioned to build the Villa Farnesina, Rome. The interior of the villa will be decorated with frescoes by Peruzzi, Raphael and others.

– Michelangelo (see box p. 197) begins to paint the ceiling of the Sistine Chapel, Rome. The painter Raphael (Raffaello Santi) also enters the service of Pope Julius II.

– Giorgione, *The Tempest* and *The Pastoral Symphony*, paintings;

HENRY VIII CROWNED KING OF ENGLAND ☐ FRENCH DEFEAT VENETIANS AT BATTLE OF AGNADELLO.

1508-10

Michelangelo (1475–1564)

For many, Michelangelo Buonarroti was the greatest artist of the Italian Renaissance and a multi-talented genius – as well as being a sculptor and painter, he was also an architect and a poet.

Born in Caprese, a small town near Florence, Michelangelo was apprenticed to the painter Domenico Ghirlandaio, but left the studio at the age of 14 claiming that he had nothing else to learn. He attracted the patronage of the Medici ruler of Florence, Lorenzo the Magnificent, and was able to study ancient Roman statuary in the Medici collection. It was the commission in 1498 to produce a *pietà*, a devotional study of the Virgin holding the body of the dead Christ, that first made his name. Extracting two figures from a single block of marble, Michelangelo emphasized both the unity of his composition and the tension between the figures of a dead naked male and a live clothed female. His next commission was for a study of the biblical *David* (completed 1504), a statue that embodies the proud spirit of Florence.

Michelangelo's concern with dynamic form and expressive movement achieved full realization in his paintings for the ceiling of the Vatican's Sistine Chapel, which took him four years to complete, painting mostly alone and while lying on his back. This work shows humanist confidence and energy in its revival of classical forms, but it also features moving scenes of grief and sorrow drawn from the Book of Genesis in the Bible. In 1541 Michelangelo unveiled *The Last Judgement*, a fresco painted on the east wall of the Sistine Chapel. It displays a scene of glory and suffering that reflects the tragedy of religious conflict then unfolding across Europe.

Giorgione is credited with developing the arcadianism, eroticism and use of the rich palette of smoky hues that come to define the Venetian school of painting.

1509

EUROPE

18 Mar. Holy Roman Emperor Maximilian I confirms his daughter, Margaret of Austria, as regent in the Netherlands on behalf of her nephew, the future Charles V.

23 Mar. Pope Julius II joins the League of Cambrai (see 10 Dec. 1508).

1 April The League of Cambrai declares war on Venice.

22 April Henry VIII is crowned king of England following the death of his father, Henry VII, at Richmond, Surrey (21 April).

27 April Pope Julius II excommunicates the Venetian Republic.

14 May The French defeat the Venetians at the battle of Agnadello. The French acquire supremacy in N Italy; the pope annexes Faenza, Rimini and Ravenna while over-running the Romagna; Ferdinand II, king of Spain, takes Otranto and Brindisi; Emperor Maximilian I annexes Verona, Vicenza and Padua.

11 June In England King Henry VIII marries Catherine of Aragon (see 1502).

17 July The citizens of Padua rebel against imperial rule; Emperor Maximilian I lays siege to the city.

Sept. Fearing French power, the pope makes peace with Venice; in 1510 he will desert the League of Cambrai (see Feb. 1510).

12 Oct. Emperor Maximilian I, having failed to recapture Padua, leaves Italy for the Tyrol.

– An earthquake destroys Constantinople.

MIDDLE EAST AND NORTH AFRICA

May Spanish troops under Cardinal Ximenez take Oran (in modern Algeria) from the Moors.

ASIA

– Francisco d'Almeida, Portuguese viceroy of the Indies, defeats the Muslim princes of NW India. He then establishes Portuguese supremacy in the Indian Ocean by defeating the combined Indian and Egyptian fleets off Diu in Gujarat. This victory is important in establishing European sea trade with India and the East.

ECONOMY AND SOCIETY

10 July Birth in Noyon, Picardy, of Jean Cauvin (John Calvin) (see p. 213), French theologian and Church reformer.

ARTS AND HUMANITIES

29 June Death of Lady Margaret, countess of Richmond and Derby. Mother of King Henry VII of England, Lady Margaret was known for her patronage of the arts and education.

– Dutch humanist Desiderius Erasmus (see p. 193) visits England and lectures at Cambridge University (1509–11). Matthias Grünewald, the *Isenheim Altarpiece*, painting for a monastic hospital dedicated to St Anthony.

1510

EUROPE

Feb. Pope Julius II withdraws from the League of Cambrai (see 10 Dec. 1508) and (24 Feb.) lifts the excommunication of Venice; the republic restores the pope's ecclesiastical rights in Venice.

Mar. Pope Julius II declares war on the duchy of Ferrara, France's ally, and takes the city of Modena with 15,000 Swiss mercenaries (May); this marks the end of the League of Cambrai.

3 July Pope Julius II invests Ferdinand II, king of Spain, with the kingdom of Naples, thereby gaining the Holy Roman Emperor's support for the anti-French alliance.

Sept. Louis XII of France summons a synod of French bishops at Tours to condemn the pope's actions; the synod backs the king's anti-papal war and recommends the calling of a general council of the Catholic Church.

Oct. Swiss mercenaries desert the pope to avoid fighting against the French.

ASIA

Mar. The Portuguese acquire Goa on the W coast of India.

– The Uzbeks are defeated in battle by Shah Ismail I of Persia, first of the Safavid dynasty (see), near the city of Marv in Khorasan.

ARTS AND HUMANITIES

17 May Death in Florence of Italian painter Sandro Botticelli.

6 Oct. Birth in Norwich, Norfolk, of John Caius, English scientist, doctor and educationalist.

25 Oct. Death in Venice of Giorgione, Italian artist.

– John Colet (born 1467), humanist scholar and collaborator with Erasmus and Sir Thomas More, establishes St Paul's School in London.

– Sir Thomas More, English scholar and diplomat, translates into English the *Life* of the Italian humanist Giovanni Pico della Mirandola (see 1494).

Desiderius Erasmus (see p. 193), *Institutio Christiani Principis*, political theory discussing the education of a Christian prince.

1511

EUROPE

Feb. Pope Julius II, fighting in N Italy, fails to take Ferrara (see Mar. 1510) and loses Mirandola, having captured the city a month previously (Jan.).

May The French capture Bologna and expel the papal troops.

1 Sept. Churchmen who are opposed to Pope Julius II and his policies meet first in Florence and then in Milan.

5 Oct. Pope Julius II forms the Holy League, allying the papacy with Venice and Ferdinand II, king of Spain, in order to drive the French out of Italy.

13 Nov. England intervenes in European politics when King Henry VIII decides to join the Holy League.

17 Nov. England and Spain form an alliance in order to attack French cities in Navarre and Guienne, SW France.

– King Henry VIII reforms the English navy.

ASIA

– The Portuguese capture of Malacca on the Malaysian peninsula further extends their trading potential to the East.

THE AMERICAS

– Diego de Velázquez de Cuéllar and a group of Spanish settlers occupy Cuba; Baracoa, the first European settlement on Cuba, is established.

ECONOMY AND SOCIETY

– Martin Luther (see p. 201), German ecclesiastical reformer, is sent by his order (the Augustinians) to Rome.

– Vasily III, grand duke of Russia, appoints a patriarch of Moscow.

ARTS AND HUMANITIES

30 July Birth in Arrezzo in Tuscany (Italy), of Giorgio Vasari, art critic; a Mannerist painter and architect of some renown,

Vasari built the Uffizi Palace in Florence and also acquired posthumous fame for his biographies of famous Italian painters.

– The Dutch humanist Desiderius Erasmus is appointed professor of Greek at Cambridge University.

Erasmus, *Encomium Moriae* (In Praise of Folly), satire written in England in 1509.

1512

EUROPE

10 April Birth of James V, king of Scotland, father of Mary Queen of Scots (see 1542); his grandson, James VI, will become James I of England (see 1603).

April Holy Roman Emperor Maximilian I and the Swiss join the Holy League (see 5 Oct. 1511). The English burn villages on the Breton (French) coast. Gaston, count of Foix and leader of the French forces, is killed in the battle of Ravenna (11 April); the French win the battle, but Gaston's death arrests the French advance in Italy.

June The French withdraw from Milan.

July The Spanish under the duke of Alva invade Navarre (modern NE Spain); papal forces recover Bologna.

12 Aug. An English fleet under Sir Edward Howard destroys 25 French vessels in the harbour of Brest (NW France). At the congress of Mantua (N Italy) the Holy League agrees to restore Medici rule in Florence; the Swiss restore Milan to Duke Maximilian Sforza and acquire Lugano, Locarno and Ossola; Parma and Piacenza are conceded to the papacy.

Oct. The imperial diet (princely convention) meets in Cologne; the number of administrative 'circles' is increased, including an Aulic (pertaining to the personal council of the emperor) circle, which will be under the emperor's sole control. The Swabian League is renewed for another ten years; the duke of Württemberg, the Elector Palatine and the margrave of Baden form a rival union.

– Poland goes to war with Russia over sovereign control of White Russia (modern Belarus).

MIDDLE EAST AND NORTH AFRICA

April Bayazid II, the Ottoman sultan, abdicates in favour of his youngest son, Selim; after defeating his two brothers in the ensuing civil war, he will reign as Selim I. Bayazid II dies (25 April), shortly after abdicating.

THE AMERICAS

22 Feb. Death in Seville, Spain, of Amerigo Vespucci, the navigator after whom the Americas were named.

ECONOMY AND SOCIETY

3 May The Fifth Lateran Council (general council of the Western Church held in the Church of St John Lateran, Rome) convenes; the doctrine of the immortality of the soul is declared a dogma of the Church.

– Martin Luther, German Church reformer, is made professor of biblical studies at the University of Wittenberg in Germany.

ARTS AND HUMANITIES

Josquin des Près, second book of masses, sacred vocal music.

1513

EUROPE

20 Jan. Christian II becomes king of Denmark and Norway after the death of his father John I; he continues to claim Sweden for the Danish crown against Sten Sture the Younger.

21 Feb. Death of Pope Julius II; Giovanni de' Medici will be elected to succeed him as Pope Leo X (9 Mar.).

Mar. Louis XII of France renews the French alliance with Venice in order to regain Milan. The Holy Roman Emperor Maximilian I allies himself with the Holy League (see 1511).

5 April The treaty of Mechlin is signed; Emperor Maximilian I, Henry VIII of England, Ferdinand II of Spain and the pope unite for an invasion of France.

June In SW Germany peasants led by the revolutionary Joss Fritz rebel against Habsburg rule in the area around Freiburg in the Black Forest; the rebellion is put down and its leaders flee.

July James IV of Scotland declares war on England.

Aug. Henry VIII of England and Emperor Maximilian I defeat the French at the battle of the Spurs, near Thérouanne in the Netherlands.

9 Sept. The Scots are heavily defeated by an English army at the battle of Flodden, near Branxton, Northumberland (England). King James IV of Scotland is among the dead; he will be succeeded by his young son James V, whose mother, Margaret Tudor, sister of English king Henry VIII, will be named regent.

All political power is rooted in violence.

Francesco Guicciardini *History of Florence* (1538)

24 Sept. The city of Tournai, a French territory in the Netherlands (now in Belgium), surrenders to the English.

12 Oct. The English and imperial forces renew their anti-French alliance; Henry VIII of England leads his army into France (30 Oct.).

Dec. Louis XII of France is reconciled with the papacy.

ARTS AND HUMANITIES

– Italian diplomat and writer Niccolò Machiavelli (see box) begins writing his political treatise *Il principe* (The Prince), which will be published in 1532.

– Establishment of a Greek printing press in Rome.

– Florentine sculptor and painter Michelangelo (see p. 197) begins works on his sculpture *Moses,* which is intended as part of the tomb of Pope Julius II in St Peter's in Rome.

Niccolò Machiavelli (1469–1527)

Born in Florence, Machiavelli was from 1498 an administrator serving the city during its years as a republic. The return to power of the Medici family in 1512 brought this career to a close, and his subsequent years in retirement were spent in literary productivity. His most famous book, *The Prince*, was written in 1513, but was only published posthumously. In the last year of his life, when Florence was at war against the Holy Roman Empire, Machiavelli returned to government and was put in charge of repairing the city's defences.

Machiavelli's *The Prince* was admired for its realism by his contemporaries, who were able to read the book in manuscript while he was still alive. After its publication it rapidly gained a huge readership, which it has never lost. *The Prince* reflects the competitive brutality of Italian Renaissance politics and the diplomatically unstable alliances between and among the various Italian states. Machiavelli himself preferred republican government, but his advice to rulers is consciously made applicable to anyone seeking power. He is, therefore, the first political writer to make a distinction between his own beliefs and his analysis of the real world. *The Prince* examines specific actions and people, both historical and contemporary, and uses them as object lessons to make general points. The clever ruler, he writes, believes that the end of a stable society justifies the means of achieving it. Therefore the clever ruler prefers to be feared than to be loved. He knows how to deal with people, flattering their vanity while seeing through flatterers himself, and uses a reputation for generosity, justice and humanity to gain his ends. This is what constitutes the *virtu* of a prince – his ability to do his job.

– Pope Leo X opens a sculpture gallery in the Vatican in Rome.

Niccolò Machiavelli, *La mandragola* (The Mandrake Root), comedy.

1514

EUROPE

April Henry VIII of England and Ferdinand II of Spain declare a truce with Louis XII of France.

20 July A peasants' rebellion in Hungary, led by George Dózsa, is crushed by John Zápolya, ruler of Transylvania, near Temesvár in the Banat.

8 Sept. Polish–Lithuanian forces defeat the army of Vasily III of Moscow (see 1505) at Orszha (in modern Belarus).

9 Oct. The marriage between Louis XII of France and Mary Tudor, sister of Henry VIII of England, is announced; they had married earlier by proxy (18 Aug.).

– Publication of *Decretum Tripartium Juris* by Istvan (Stephen) Verboczy, which settles the Hungarian constitution by declaring that the king is independent of pope and emperor, and that serfdom is fixed: nobles' powers are strengthened.

MIDDLE EAST AND NORTH AFRICA

24 April Selim I, the Ottoman sultan, starts his march to Persia through the Turkish cities of Erzinjan and Erzerum.

23 Aug. Selim I defeats Shah Ismail of Persia (see 1501) at Chaldiran in Armenia and (7 Sept.) enters Ismail's capital city of Tabriz in Azerbaijan.

ECONOMY AND SOCIETY

15 Sept. Thomas Wolsey, a humbly-born adviser to King Henry VIII of England, becomes archbishop of York.

– The corporation of Trinity House is established in London to control pilotage and provide navigational systems for the River Thames.

ARTS AND HUMANITIES

– The collected works of Cardinal Nicolaus Cusanus (Nicholas of Cusa), 15th-century German theologian, are published in three volumes in Paris; Nicholas maintains that, although there are limits to human knowledge, God can be understood by intuition.

– *Septem Horae Canonicae*, the first book printed in Arabic type, is published in Fano, Italy.

– Work starts on the Complutensian Bible, financed and directed by Cardinal Francisco Jiménez de Cisnéros. Edited and printed at Alcala de Henares outside Madrid in Spain, this polyglot Bible is the high point of Spanish humanist scholarship with the texts of the Old Testament printed in Hebrew, Greek and Latin, while the New Testament is printed in Greek and Latin. It will be published in 1522.

1515

EUROPE

1 Jan. Francis, duke of Angoulême (see 1494), becomes Francis I of France on the death of his uncle, Louis XII, in Paris.

April The Anglo-French peace treaty originally negotiated between Henry VIII of England and Louis XII of France is renewed by Henry VIII and Francis I of France; they plan to attack Lombardy in N Italy.

July The Congress of Vienna meets to settle relations between the empire, Poland and Hungary: Mary, granddaughter of Emperor Maximilian I, is to marry Louis, son of King Ladislas II of Hungary (see 1516), while Maximilian's grandson Ferdinand is to marry Anne Jagiello, heiress of Bohemia and Hungary. These arrangements will allow the Habsburgs to gain Bohemia and Hungary on Louis's death.

10 Sept. Thomas Wolsey (see 15 Sept. 1514) is named cardinal and (24 Dec.) becomes lord chancellor of England.

13 Sept. Francis I of France defeats the Swiss and Venetian armies at Marignano and conquers the duchy of Milan in N Italy.

7 Nov. The treaty of Geneva is signed by the Swiss and the French: the Swiss retain their S conquests (the modern canton of Ticino) in return for recognizing French sovereignty over the duchy of Milan.

11 Dec. By the treaty of Bologna, Pope Leo X surrenders the N Italian cities of Parma and Piacenza to the French.

– Frederick III (the Wise), duke of Saxony, joins the union of the Elector Palatine, the duke of Württemberg and the margrave of Baden.

MIDDLE EAST AND NORTH AFRICA

– Selim I, the Ottoman sultan, conquers E Anatolia and Kurdistan.

ECONOMY AND SOCIETY

21 July Birth in Florence, Italy, of St Philip Neri, founder of the Oratorian Order. A priest and mystic, he will prove particularly influential during the Catholic Counter-Reformation.

– A decree of the Fifth Lateran Council, *De Impressione Librorum* (On the Printing of Books), forbids the publication of any work unless it has been examined by the relevant ecclesiastical authority.

ARTS AND HUMANITIES

– Antonio Allegri da Correggio, a Renaissance artist born in Parma in N Italy, begins work on his *Madonna of St Francis*. Little recognized by his contemporaries, Correggio comes to be seen as a stylistic innovator who develops many of the main features of the baroque style.

– Publication of *Epistolae obscurorum virorum* (Letters of Obscure Men), a collective satire that makes fun of the 'scholastics' who oppose the new humanist scholarship. Written in dog-Latin, it is influential in establishing the view that scholasticism in the universities and the Church is a reactionary force. A second volume will appear in 1517.

– The Italian painter Raphael completes his tapestry cartoons for the Sistine Chapel, Rome; he also paints a portrait of Badassare Castiglione, a noted courtier, and executes frescoes in the Stanza dell'Incendio in the Vatican, Rome.

– In England Hampton Court Palace is commissioned by Cardinal Wolsey (see 10 Sept. 1515).

– Birth in Kirby Wiske, near York, of Roger Ascham, English humanist and educationalist. Ascham will serve as tutor to the future Queen Elizabeth I.

1516

EUROPE

23 Jan. Archduke Charles of Austria, the future Emperor Charles V, becomes king of Spain on the death of Ferdinand II; he founds the Spanish branch of the Habsburg dynasty. Cardinal Francisco Jiménes de Cisnéros is appointed regent.

13 Mar. Death of King Ladislas II of Hungary and Bohemia; his son, Louis, aged ten, will reign as King Louis II.

13 Aug. By the terms of the treaty of Noyon, Francis I of France retains Milan and renounces the French claim to Naples; King Charles I of Spain, the future Holy Roman Emperor, agrees to marry Princess Louise of France, daughter of Francis I.

18 Aug. By the Concordat of Bologna, Francis I of France gains the right to appoint French bishops and abbots, though his nominations must have papal approval; appeals to Rome from France are restricted. This is a victory for the Gallican theory of the French Church's independence.

29 Nov. Francis I of France signs the treaty of Freiburg, agreeing to peace with the Swiss; this treaty will remain in force until 1789.

13 Dec. Holy Roman Emperor Maximilian I overturns his treaty arrangements with England and, by the treaty of Brussels, accepts the treaty of Noyon (see 13 Aug.). The empire's Italian claims are withdrawn in return for 200,000 ducats, and Verona is transferred to Venice.

MIDDLE EAST AND NORTH AFRICA

24 Aug. Selim I, the Ottoman sultan, having conquered N Mesopotamia, defeats the Mamluk sultan of Egypt, Kansu al-Guari, near Aleppo in Syria, and kills him. Selim I annexes Syria.

ARTS AND HUMANITIES

29 Nov. Death in Venice of the Venetian painter Giovanni Bellini.

– The original Latin text of Sir Thomas More's *Utopia* is printed in Louvain (in modern Belgium); the translation into English will not appear until 1551.

– Publication in Basle in Switzerland of the first Greek text of the New Testament; annotations by the Dutch humanist Desiderius Erasmus (see p. 193) accompany it.

– Death of Hieronymus Bosch, Flemish painter.

– Birth in Boston, Lincolnshire, of John Foxe, English Protestant controversialist and martyrologist.

– García de Resende, *Cancioneiro geral*, an anthology of Portuguese and Spanish poems; it will become a landmark in the evolution of Portuguese literary consciousness.

Ludovico Ariosto, *Orlando Furioso*, a chivalric epic and one of the most important works of Italian Renaissance literature.

Peter Martyr, *De Rebus Oceanicus et Novo Orbe* (Decades of the New World), the first discussion of the European discovery of the New World.

Josquin des Près, third book of masses, sacred vocal music.

Raphael, Villa Madama in Rome.

Titian (Tiziano Vecellio), *The Assumption*, painting in the Church of the Frari, in Venice.

1517

EUROPE

April Cardinal Wolsey, lord chancellor of England (see 10 Sept. 1515), begins secret peace negotiations with France.

1 May The Evil May Day riots in London: apprentices attack foreigners living in the city. Some 60 rioters are hanged.

31 Oct. The German Church reformer Martin Luther (see box) nails his 95 theses to the door of the Palace Church in Wittenberg, Saxony. He denounces the sale of indulgences (remission of sins purchased with money) by, among others, the German Dominican friar Johann Tetzel; the event marks the formal start of the German Reformation.

8 Nov. Death of Cardinal Jiménes de Cisnéros, recently appointed regent of Spain (see 23 Jan. 1516). Habsburg rule in Spain is now a reality, and Charles I, grandson of Holy Roman Emperor Maximilian I, makes a triumphal entry into Valladolid, C Spain.

MIDDLE EAST AND NORTH AFRICA

22 Jan. The Ottomans occupy Cairo after defeating the Mamluks.

17 July The sherif (chief magistrate) of Mecca accepts Ottoman suzerainty over Arabia.

ECONOMY AND SOCIETY

– Closure of the Fifth Lateran Council: Pope Leo X declares that all necessary Church reform has been accomplished.

– Coffee is introduced into Europe.

Martin Luther (1483–1546)

Martin Luther instigated the Reformation that split the medieval Church. Born in Saxony, the son of a miner, Luther became a monk and priest. He visited Rome in 1511 and was appalled by the worldly nature of the Church and its spiritual and moral laxity. In 1517 he famously pinned to the church door at Wittenberg his 95 theses on Church reform. They were soon printed and circulated throughout Germany. What started as a movement for reform ended with a complete break from Rome and the establishment of a Europe-wide Protestant movement.

Basic to Luther's theology was the idea of justification by faith, by which humanity could earn salvation not by good works, but by faith alone. He offered an austere vision of sinful beings alone before a God whose grace was free but who could not be manipulated. This was a direct attack on the papal practice of selling indulgences that promised remission of time in purgatory and forgiveness for sins. Luther's admired translation of the Latin Bible into German – so that everybody could understand it – confirmed Protestantism as a faith that rejected the idea of the priest as a mediator between God and the individual.

Luther was himself a socially conservative figure who was protected by the German princes and appalled by the extremism he had unleashed. He condemned the rebels in the German Peasants' War (1524–5), furious that his principles were being used to justify the rights of the peasantry. After his death, the spiritual independence he had asserted became one of the founding elements of modern European consciousness. His supposed refusal to recant at Augsburg (1518) – 'Here I stand; I can do no other' – is apocryphal, but it became a popular summation of individual moral commitment.

EUROPE'S DRAMA:
Renaissance and Reformation

The term 'Renaissance' (meaning 'rebirth') was first used by art historians in the 19th century, to denote the revival of interest in the classical tradition in the 15th and 16th centuries. The period of the European Renaissance was also marked by upheavals in religion and politics. When the Renaissance began in the early 15th century, Europe was a relatively poor area of the world that lagged behind China and the Near East in terms of economic prosperity and technology. After a period of turmoil, Europe was transformed into a rich, dynamic culture, a culture that looked outward to the rest of the world with considerable self-assurance.

At the start of the period, humanism, a cultural movement based on the study of ancient Greek and Roman literature and learning, ministered to the new European pride and popularized the myth of 'the Middle Ages' (a term invented at this time) as a time of unlettered barbarism. The core technique of this classical revival was a movement *ad fontes* (to the sources) – the desire to recover the original texts, purging them of monkish accretions. The scholars engaged in this task could gain employment outside the Church, for example as diplomats, court advisers or propagandists. Notable examples include Machiavelli and Erasmus.

In parallel to the humanism of the scholars, artists and architects were also looking back to classical models. The Gothic style of architecture gave way to new buildings inspired by Roman villas and Greek temples, with rounded arches, elegant pillars and sometimes massive domes. Painters and sculptors were not only employed by the Church but also found work with wealthy private clients, who were as likely to commission a scene from classical mythology as a religious picture. There was a new interest in the nude, symptomatic of the change of focus during the Renaissance, from God to man.

A political characteristic of the period is the tension between centralized royal authority and the traditional privileges and local power bases of the aristocracy. France in the early 17th century and England under the Tudors, for example, saw attempts to concentrate power in the person of the monarch. But the reactions to central royal power were often virulent: the rebellion of the Fronde in the 1640s dragged France back into the aristocratic anarchy of the previous century's wars of religion; and in the 17th century the attempts of the Stuart monarchs Charles I and James II to impose an absolute monarchy met with rebellions from aristocratic factions and parliamentary interest groups.

The rivalry between central and regional power was often exacerbated by divisions in the Church. The 16th-century German monk Martin Luther was one of many who saw a need for dramatic reform in the Roman Catholic Church in order to root out corruption and what they saw as dubious religious teachings. Luther's skill was in publicizing his demands for change and engaging the enthusiasm of rulers and laity in the movement. Although Luther had wanted to reform the Catholic Church, he ended up bringing about a definite split between Catholics and the reformers, now known as Protestants. Europe became divided by religion as well as by dynastic disputes, and religious wars broke out.

At the same time, Catholicism reinvented itself creatively through the Counter-Reformation. This movement energized the laity with its populist techniques: new feasts, saints and processionals crowded the church calendar. And the Catholic reform movement also streamlined church administration and gave birth to such well-disciplined organizations as the Jesuits, equipping it anew for the fight against Protestant heresy.

In the forefront of the fight against Protestantism was the Habsburg dynasty, which extended its power across Austria, the Holy Roman Empire, the Low Countries and Spain. The most powerful of the Habsburg monarchs was Charles V (Holy Roman Emperor 1519–56) and his son Philip II (king of Spain 1556–98). Their story was one of imperial over-ambition. While leading the Christian resistance to Ottoman expansion in the Mediterranean, they also attempted to expunge the Reformation in their lands in northern Europe. In 1567 Philip's largely Protestant subjects in the Netherlands began a long revolt against Spanish rule, a

Europe was transformed into a rich, dynamic culture.

revolt that merged with the much wider conflict of the Thirty Years' War (1618–48).

The Thirty Years' War was the defining struggle of the period. From the peace of Augsburg in 1555 until 1618 the central European and German-speaking states of Europe had been largely free from conflict, but an attempt to eradicate reformist teachings in Bohemia sparked off war. The ensuing struggle was latterly as much dynastic and political as religious, and involved many of the European powers. The impact of the war was horrendous, with some areas of Germany suffering a decline in population of up to 50 per cent. By the time peace came, the Holy Roman Empire had fallen apart, while France, Sweden and the United Provinces (the Netherlands) had all emerged as powers to be reckoned with in Europe.

1517 *continued*

SCIENCE AND TECHNOLOGY

- A Nuremberg gunsmith invents the wheel-lock musket.

ARTS AND HUMANITIES

- In England Richard Fox, bishop of Worcester, establishes Corpus Christi College, Oxford.
- Dutch humanist Desiderius Erasmus (see p. 193) helps to found the Collège de Trois Langues in Louvain in the duchy of Brabant, the Netherlands; the college will promote the study of Latin, Greek and Hebrew.
- Publication of *Propalladia*, a collection of seven plays by Bartolomé de Torres Naharro, the first Spanish playwright to write comedy.
- Birth in Hunsdon, Hertfordshire (England), of Henry Howard, earl of Surrey, poet and soldier.

Quentin Massys (or Metsys), *Erasmus*, painting.

Johann Reuchlin, *De Arte Cabbalistica*, a study of Jewish mysticism.

1518

EUROPE

2 Oct. Cardinal Wolsey, lord chancellor of England, achieves his diplomatic triumph: in the treaty of London it is agreed that all major European powers will unite to fight the Ottoman Turks. The treaty is signed by England, the papacy, France, the Holy Roman Empire and Spain.

12 Oct. At the diet of Augsburg in Germany, Church reformer Martin Luther (see p. 201), summoned by Cardinal Cajetan, professor of metaphysics at Padua, refuses to withdraw his 95 theses against the Church (see 1517).

MIDDLE EAST AND NORTH AFRICA

- Foundation of the Barbary states of Algiers and Tunis under Selim I, Ottoman sultan.

THE AMERICAS

- Charles I of Spain grants the Portuguese Lorens de Gominot the first licence (*asiento*) to import 4000 African slaves into the Spanish American colonies over the next eight years.

ECONOMY AND SOCIETY

- Birth in London of Sir Thomas Gresham, financier and founder of the Royal Exchange.

SCIENCE AND TECHNOLOGY

- The Portuguese establish a trading factory in Colombo, Ceylon (modern Sri Lanka).
- King Henry VIII founds the Royal College of Physicians in London at the behest of his private physician Thomas Linacre; the Royal College is the earliest licensing body for medical practitioners.
- German scholar Johannes Trithemius (John Tritheim) publishes his *Polygraphia* (Many Types of Writing), an early treatise on code systems.

Albrecht Dürer (1471–1528)

Albrecht Dürer was born and died in Nuremberg, Germany. His influence gave a north European character to the previously Italian-dominated Renaissance in the visual arts. His core achievement are his portraits, which illuminate an intensity of character, draw the spectator into the sitter's inner life, and introduce a new note of spontaneous emotionalism into the genre.

Works such as his treatises on geometry (1525) and on human proportion (1528) place Dürer within the Renaissance tradition of the intellectually inquisitive artist. He was original, however, in acting as his own publisher and in the scale on which he used trade fairs and agents to sell his prints. His wood-cuts and engravings flooded the European art market and, imported into Italy, changed artistic tastes. He benefited from his entrepreneurial instinct for the expanding market for art, and he was the first European artist of consequence to become rich through his own commercial flair.

Part of Dürer's influence was his interest in topography. Accustomed to a Bavarian landscape of steep and narrow valleys, he introduced the jagged edge of the wild landscape into European art. This differentiated him from the Italian landscape tradition, which had been dominated by a search for the calmly idealized. His belief that 'art is embedded in nature' is embodied in such works as his study of a hare.

Dürer was also interested in himself in an artistically original way. His most famous self-portrait shows him confidently draped in finery and ringlets. Dürer believed that an artist is defined by creative capacity, a quality he considered to be missing in the craftsmen of Nuremberg, whose artefacts were reproduced skilfully but repetitively. We owe to him, therefore, the idea that the exploration of personality provides art with its highest aim.

ARTS AND HUMANITIES

29 Sept. Birth of the Venetian Mannerist painter Tintoretto (Jacopo Robusti). A master of drama and moody atmosphere, Tintoretto paves the way for the fully developed baroque style of the 17th century.

- German scholar and ecclesiastical reformer Philip Melanchthon is appointed professor of Greek at Wittenberg University in Saxony (Germany).
- Completion of the Cathedral of Notre Dame in Antwerp, Flanders (modern Belgium).

Albrecht Dürer (see box), *Maximilian I*, painting.

Raphael, *Pope Leo X*, painting.

1519

EUROPE

12 Jan. Death of Maximilian I, Holy Roman Emperor (see 1486 and 1493): Charles I of Spain and Francis I of France prepare for the imperial contest to succeed him.

27 Jan. Martin Luther (see p. 201), the German Church reformer, agrees, in a private discussion with the papal chamberlain, Charles von Militz, to write a private letter of submission to the pope.

16 Feb. Birth in Châtillion-sur-Loing, France, of Gaspard II de Coligny, future Huguenot (French Protestant) leader.

31 Mar. Birth in Saint-Germain-en-Laye, France, of Henry II, king of France (see 1547).

13 April Birth in Florence, Italy, of Catherine de Medici, future wife of Henry II of France and mother of three French kings (Francis II, Charles IX and Henry III); an adroit politician, she will serve as regent of France (1560–74) and greatly influence the course of the French religious wars.

May Henry VIII of England decides that he will be a candidate for the imperial throne.

12 June Birth of Cosimo de' Medici (the Great), duke of Florence from 1537 and grand duke of Tuscany from 1569; he will die in 1574.

24 June Death of Lucretia Borgia, illegitimate daughter of Pope Alexander VI and wife of Giovanni Sforza and, later, Alfonso d'Este of Ferrara (see 1497).

26 June Martin Luther, the Church reformer, debates in public with the German Catholic theologian Johann Eck at Leipzig in Saxony. Luther will publish his disputations in Leipzig and goes further than before in questioning the authority of the pope and of general councils of the Church.

28 June Charles I of Spain, Sicily and Sardinia is elected Holy Roman Emperor; he will reign as Emperor Charles V. He is helped by the financial backing of the Fuggers of Augsburg, a rich and powerful family of bankers. The pope withdraws his opposition to Charles at a late stage in the contest, and the German princes wish to exclude Francis I of France. The stage is now set for a Habsburg–Valois conflict.

4 July Death of Johann Tetzel, a German Dominican whose selling of indulgences was criticized by Martin Luther (see 1517).

THE AMERICAS

20 Sept. Ferdinand Magellan, a Portuguese subject in the service of Spain, leaves on his expedition to S America. He will explore the Rio de la Plata estuary and sail around Cape Horn (1520). Magellan will be killed in the Philippines (27 April 1521), and the expedition, which completes the circumnavigation of the globe, will continue under the Basque Sebastien del Cano.

8 Nov. The Spanish conquistador Hernán Cortés enters Tenochtitlán, Mexico, and is received by Montezuma, the ruler of the Aztecs (see 1300).

ARTS AND HUMANITIES

2 May Death at Cloux, France, of Leonardo da Vinci (see p. 194), Italian artist, intellectual and inventor.

16 Sept. Death at Sheen, Surrey (England), of John Colet, English humanist theologian and founder of St Paul's School in London.

– Publication in Basel (modern Switzerland) of *Germania* by the Roman historian Tacitus; edited and annotated by the German scholar Bild aus Rheinau (Beatus Rhenanus), it will become an important text in the evolution of German national identity.

– In England St George's Chapel in Windsor Castle is completed; work on the chapel started in 1473.

Diego de Siloe, the Escalera Dorada (Gilded Stairs) in Burgos Cathedral, Spain.

1520

EUROPE

18 Jan. Christian II of Denmark and Norway defeats the Swedish army at Lake Malar in Sweden; the Swedish regent, Sten Sture the Younger, will die of his wounds (3 Feb.), thereby removing the main opposition to King Christian's reconquest of Sweden. Christian II will be crowned king of Sweden on 1 Nov.

May Emperor Charles V leaves Spain for N Europe and visits Henry VIII of England at Dover and Canterbury (26–31 May).

4–24 June Henry VIII of England and Francis I of France meet at the Field of the Cloth of Gold in Picardy, near Calais, France, a diplomatic encounter resulting in a treaty (6 June) that confirms the betrothal of their children, respectively Mary Tudor and the Dauphin Francis, and ends French involvement in Scottish affairs.

15 June Pope Leo X excommunicates the German Church reformer Martin Luther.

14 July The revolt of the Comuneros in Castile and Toledo in Spain: local nobles and gentry are forced to support the rebellion, which asserts the constitutional liberties of the regional towns and cities. A Holy League is formed at Avila to protest against the Habsburg abolition of ancient local rights.

13 Sept. Birth in Bourne, Lincolnshire (England), of William Cecil, Lord Burghley, politician and influential adviser to Queen Elizabeth I of England.

23 Oct. Charles I of Spain is crowned as Holy Roman Emperor Charles V in Aachen in Germany; he promises to live in Germany, to preserve the rights of the Estates and to restore the council of the regency.

8 Nov. In Sweden a bloody confrontation known as the Stockholm Bloodbath, in which King Christian II kills leading Swedish nobles and churchmen, precipitates a national revolt under the future Swedish leader Gustavus Vasa.

10 Dec. Martin Luther burns in public the papal bull *Exsurge*, which has excommunicated him. In his 'Address to the most Serene and Mighty Imperial Majesty and to the Christian Nobility of the German Nation' he urges the nationalization of the Church. He starts work on *The Babylonish Captivity of the Church*, which attacks all sacraments except baptism and the eucharist.

MIDDLE EAST AND NORTH AFRICA

21 Sept. Selim I, Ottoman sultan, dies and is succeeded (30 Sept.) by Suleiman I (the Magnificent). Under Suleiman the Ottomans will extend their political and cultural influence by expanding their empire further into Europe and the Middle East.

TURKIC POWER:
The Ottoman Challenge to the West

The Ottoman Turks created the most powerful military empire in the history of the Islamic world. Yet they had not been among the first Muslims, and had only been converted to Islam after emerging from the Eurasian steppes in the early Middle Ages.

By the year 1500 the Ottomans – that branch of the Turks ruled by the dynasty founded by the warrior Osman in the late 13th century – were one of the three main forces in the Islamic world. The Ottoman empire, centred on its capital in Istanbul (formerly Constantinople), comprised Anatolia (much of modern Turkey), most of the shores of the Black Sea, Greece and the Balkans. The Ottomans had gained their greatest victory with the capture of Constantinople in 1453, an event that marked the final end of the last vestiges of the ancient Roman empire. Just three generations later, in 1521, the Ottomans captured Belgrade, and victory at the battle of Mohács in 1526 gave them Hungary. These victories over Christian opponents were matched by persistent campaigning against the Safavid dynasty, Persia's Shiite Muslim rulers. That struggle ended in long-term deadlock but the decisive defeat of Mamluk Egypt opened the way to further Ottoman advance into Arabia and North Africa.

As important to Ottoman success as these military victories was the religious prestige that came in the 1510s when the sherif (chief magistrate) of Mecca recognized the sultan of the Ottomans as caliph – the spiritual successor to the Prophet Muhammad. Military power was now merged with sacred authority. The Ottoman empire was thus the last great expression of the universality of the Islamic ideal. It held together a vast diversity of regional centres within a single system of taxation and administration. It also transmitted the *sharia* (religious law), declared itself the guardian of the holy centres of Islam, and organized pilgrimages to these shrines. But although the Ottoman empire was thoroughly Islamic in concept, it was also a multi-religious and multi-ethnic empire. It contained within it Greeks, Serbs, Bulgarians, Romanians, Armenians, Turks, Arabs and others. The faiths of Jewish and Christian subjects were officially recognized.

By the mid-16th century the Ottomans had conquered Syria, Arabia, Mesopotamia, Egypt and most of North Africa. These advances brought to the Ottomans a vast amount of wealth. They now controlled the Mediterranean termini of overland caravan routes extending from sub-Saharan Africa in the southwest to China in the northeast.

The commodities of this trading network – gold, ivory, slaves, spices, silks and precious manufactured goods – were the objects of Western desire, and the resulting trading relationships blunted the edge of Western aggression: Venice and France were both, at times, allies of the Ottomans. While it sometimes suited both sides to enjoy peace, war was seldom far distant. The unbroken run of Ottoman military victories over Christendom ended at the siege of Malta in 1565, and was turned back six years later at the great Christian naval victory of Lepanto. But Ottoman power was not ended, and as late as 1683 the empire could raise an army of 140,000 men to lay siege to Vienna. The failed attempt to capture the Austrian capital proved to be the final thrust of the Turks against Christian Europe. Expansionist Russia scored a series of successes in its 1768–74 war against the Ottomans – a conflict that ended in the Russian occupation and annexation of the Crimea.

Ottoman military decline had at least some of its origins in economic changes. The overland trade routes that had given the Ottomans their great wealth became less important as Europeans developed their own maritime routes to Africa and Asia. This commercial shift took a long time, but the loss of trade was the single most important cause for the decline of the Ottoman empire. Economic difficulty led to political uncertainty. Soon it began to matter rather more than it had in the past that there was no longer a clear line of dynastic succession. Meanwhile, the local elites were growing stronger at the expense of the centre, as provincial governors became concerned with their own regional interests. By the later 18th century the Ottomans were losing power and prestige, and in the early 19th century the empire began to fall apart. It had become the 'sick man of Europe'.

> *The Ottoman empire was … the last great expression of the universality of the Islamic ideal.*

The Ottoman empire was finally dissolved after World War I, and the dynasty ejected. Its most lasting legacy has been the language of the Ottoman state's ruling administrative and warrior elite. Turkish, just one of the Turkic linguistic group, became a major world language and remains comprehensible to speakers of other languages encountered on a journey from Istanbul to Beijing.

1520 *continued*

ASIA

– Portuguese traders begin to settle in China.

SCIENCE AND TECHNOLOGY

– In Nuremberg in Germany, gunsmith Gaspard Kotter invents rifling in the barrels of firearms.

ARTS AND HUMANITIES

– Francis I, king of France, founds the Royal Library in his palace at Fontainebleau; he appoints French humanist scholar Guillaume Budé as librarian.
– The Italian painter, sculptor and architect Michelangelo (see p. 197) works on the Medici Chapel in the Church of San Lorenzo in Florence.
Raphael, the Pallazzo Pandolfini in Venice.

1521

EUROPE

Feb. Gustavus Vasa, Swedish revolutionary and later king of Sweden, leads a popular rebellion against Danish rule; Uppsala is surrendered to Vasa's troops.

26 Mar. Emperor Charles V convenes the first diet of Worms; the German reformer Martin Luther (see p. 201) is permitted to present his religious views in the face of strong opposition from the emperor and the pope. Luther refuses to recant (18 April) and an order is proclaimed (25 May) for the destruction within imperial territory of all of Luther's writings.

23 April Defeat of the popular Spanish Comuneros army (see 14 July 1520) by the nobility and their forces at Villalar in Spain; the Comuneros leaders are executed the following day (24 April).

28 April Emperor Charles V grants his brother, Archduke Ferdinand I of Austria, Habsburg possessions in Lower Austria, Carinthia, Styria and Carniola.

16 May The Edict of Worms imposes on Martin Luther the ban of the empire.

17 May In England, Edward Stafford, duke of Buckingham, is executed for treason; it is feared that he might attempt to claim the English throne.

28 May Emperor Charles V and Pope Leo X agree on a secret treaty to expel the French from Milan.

25 Sept. Emperor Charles V and Cardinal Wolsey, lord chancellor of England, agree in the secret treaty of Bruges that war will be declared on France in Mar. 1523.

25 Sept. Suleiman I, the Ottoman sultan (see 21 Sept. 1520), conquers Belgrade and marches into Hungary.

19 Nov. The imperial and papal armies under Prospero Colonna invade Milan, now held by the French; the Habsburg–Valois war will last until 1526.

1 Dec. Pope Leo X dies from malaria in Rome.

13 Dec. John III (the Pious) succeeds his father, Manuel I (the Fortunate), as king of Portugal.

ASIA

27 April Portuguese explorer Ferdinand Magellan is killed in a skirmish with chief Lap-Lapu, on the small coral island of Mactan in the Philippines.

THE AMERICAS

13 Sept. Spanish troops, under the conquistador Hernán Cortés (see 8 Nov. 1519), occupy Tenochtitlán, capital of the Aztecs, after an eight-week siege; Mexico is now under Spanish rule.

ECONOMY AND SOCIETY

– German theologian Philip Melanchthon publishes *Loci Communes* (Commonplaces), in which he begins to define Lutheran doctrine.
– Henry VIII publishes *Assertio Septem Sacramentorum* (The Assertion of the Seven Sacraments) against Martin Luther. On 11 Oct. Pope Leo X grants Henry the title *Fidei Defensor* (Defender of the Faith) as a reward (the title is still used by British monarchs).

SCIENCE AND TECHNOLOGY

– Silk manufacture is introduced in France.

ARTS AND HUMANITIES

April Michelangelo starts work on the tombs of Giuliano de' Medici and Lorenzo de' Medici in the Medici Chapel in San Lorenzo, Florence.

27 Aug. Death at Condé-sur-l'Escaut, France, of the Franco-Flemish composer Josquin des Près, whose synthesis of counterpoint and harmony is one of the high points of Renaissance vocal music.

1522

EUROPE

9 Jan. Adrian Florensz Dedal of Utrecht, regent (1516–17) and viceroy (1520–22) of Spain, is elected Pope Hadrian VI.

30 Jan. The powerful German port of Lübeck on the Baltic Sea joins forces with Gustavus Vasa, leader of the Swedish revolutionary movement (see Feb. 1521), who declares war on King Christian II of Denmark, Norway and Sweden.

27 April Spanish and imperial troops defeat the French and Swiss near Milan; the French retreat from Lombardy and Duke Francesco Maria Sforza is restored to the duchy of Milan.

30 May Imperial forces drive the French from Genoa.

May Henry VIII of England declares war on France and Scotland.

19 June Emperor Charles V visits England and signs the treaty of Windsor with Henry VIII; both rulers pledge to invade France in May 1524.

24 Aug. Gustavus Vasa is appointed administrator of Sweden and vows to free the whole of Sweden from Danish rule; later in the year (Nov.) the Danish nobility will also rebel against King Christian II.

Aug. The German city of Trier is besieged by imperial knights led by the Protestant reformer Franz von Sickingen and the poet Ulrich von Hutten; this campaign, known as the Knights' War,

1522-4

is part of a larger uprising against the episcopal sees and other spiritual powers of the empire.

Dec. Ottoman forces capture the island of Rhodes off the S coast of Turkey from the Knights Hospitallers (see 1308).

ASIA

– Jiajing (Chia ching) becomes emperor of Ming China.
– Portuguese ships reach Brunei, NW Borneo.

THE AMERICAS

15 Oct. Hernán Cortés (see 13 sept. 1521), Spanish conquistador, is appointed governor of New Spain (Mexico) by Emperor Charles V, who is also king of Spain.

– Pascual de Andagoya discovers Peru.
– Spanish troops under Pedro de Alvarado conquer Guatemala, C America.

ECONOMY AND SOCIETY

– Martin Luther (see p. 201) introduces eucharistic communion and a German liturgy for the Wittenberg laity; in Sept. his translation of the New Testament appears.
– In the Swiss city of Zürich, the radical Church reformer Ulrich Zwingli condemns both fasting and the celibacy of priests.

ARTS AND HUMANITIES

30 June Death in Bad Loebenzell, Germany, of the German humanist Johann Reuchlin.

– Birth of Margaret of Austria, daughter of Emperor Charles V and future wife of Ottavio Farnese, duke of Parma; Margaret, duchess of Parma, will be a lavish patron of painting, sculpture and architecture.
– The Polyglot Bible (see 1514) is published at the University of Alcala de Henares, Spain.

1523

EUROPE

Mar. Civil war in Denmark; Christian II, king of Denmark, Norway and Sweden, is deposed and his uncle becomes Frederick I of Denmark and Norway.

April In the English Parliament in London, Sir Thomas More is elected Speaker. A move to increase taxation to pay for the French wars is opposed.

April In Germany the Knights' War (see Aug. 1522) ends when the rebel stronghold at Landstuhl in the Rhineland is attacked by the armies of the archibishop of Trier and the landgrave of Hesse; the leader of the revolt, Franz von Sickingen, is killed. Ulrich von Hutten goes into exile and dies in Zürich (29 Aug.).

7 June Gustavus Vasa captures the Swedish capital Stockholm and is elected King Gustavus I Vasa of Sweden (see 1521 and 1522).

Aug. Venice joins the anti-French League.

14 Sept. Pope Hadrian VI (see 9 Jan. 1522) dies; Giulio de' Medici will be elected to succeed him as Pope Clement VII (19 Nov.). The illegitimate son of Giuliano de' Medici, Giulio was brought up in Florence at the court of his grandfather, Lorenzo the Magnificent.

ASIA

– Portuguese traders are expelled from China, where they have settled since 1520.

ECONOMY AND SOCIETY

– The first marine insurance policies are issued in Florence.

ARTS AND HUMANITIES

– Music for the keyboard is printed in Italy using for the first time right- and left-hand staves of five lines each and measures divided by bar lines.

Hans Holbein the Younger, *Erasmus*, painting.

Martin Luther, *Von Welticher Oberkeyt*, treatise discussing political obedience.

Hans Sachs, *Die Wittenbergische Nachtigall* (The Wittenberg Nightingale), poetic encomium of German religious reformer Martin Luther.

Titian, *Bacchus and Ariadne*, painting.

1524

EUROPE

Jan. Frederick of Saxony, Elector of the Holy Roman Empire, and Philip, landgrave of Hesse, the lay leaders of Lutheranism, demand a national synod to discuss Church reform. In the course of this year Silesia, Pomerania, Brandenberg-Culmbach, Brunswick-Lüneburg, Schleswig and Holstein embrace Lutheranism.

25 May Henry VIII, king of England, and Emperor Charles V form a new anti-French League in support of the rebel Charles, duke of Bourbon and constable of France; Duke Charles has fled from France after a dispute with King Francis I. By late summer Duke Charles will occupy Aix-en-Provence (8 Aug.) and lay siege to Marseilles (19 Aug.).

June Start of the Peasants' War in Germany; the peasants rebel against feudal services and enclosures. By Aug. the rebellion, led by revolutionary preacher Thomas Müntzer – who believes in a more radical Reformation and preaches that the poor are God's chosen people – will spread to Swabia, Franconia, Bavaria, the Tyrol, Carinthia, Thuringia and Alsace.

15 July Emperor Charles V prohibits the holding of a German ecclesiastical synod on Church reform.

26 Oct. The Spanish surrender Milan to the French.

Oct. German Protestant princes, led by Frederick III, Elector of Saxony, and Philip, landgrave of Hesse, meet at Ulm in Baden-Württemberg to plan a campaign against Emperor Charles V; they will meet again later in the year (Dec.) at Speyer, N of Karlsruhe in Germany.

– By the treaty of Malmö, King Frederick I of Denmark and Norway formally confirms the independence of Sweden under King Gustavus I Vasa, thereby ending the Union of Kalmar (the union of Denmark, Norway and Sweden negotiated in 1397).
– Ulrich Zwingli, the Swiss reformer (see 1522), establishes his power base in the Swiss city of Zürich; reformers Matthew Zell and Martin Bucer take control in Strasburg.

ASIA

24 Dec. Death in Cochin, India, of Vasco da Gama, Portuguese explorer who sailed around the Cape of Good Hope to reach Asia from Europe.

THE AMERICAS

Jan. Financed by Francis I of France, Giovanni da Verrazano, the Florentine navigator, explores the North Atlantic seaboard from Cape Fear to Newfoundland, discovering New York Bay and the Hudson River.

SCIENCE AND TECHNOLOGY

20 Oct. Death in London, England, of Thomas Linacre, English physician instrumental in the founding of the Royal College of Physicians (see 1518).

ARTS AND HUMANITIES

– Death in Isenheim, Alsace (modern France), of German painter Hans Holbein the Elder.

– Publication of second and final edition of *Colloquia familiaria* (Domestic Colloquies) by the Dutch humanist Desiderius Erasmus (see p. 193); the first edition appeared in 1516.

– In London the printer Wynkyn de Worde publishes *Oratio* (Oration) by the English scholar Robert Wakefield; this is the first English work to use italic type.

– The Florentine sculptor and painter Michelangelo (see p. 197) begins work on the Bibliotheca Laurenziana in Florence; commissioned by the Medici, the Laurentian Library is intended to house their magnificent collections.

Philippe de Commynes, *Mémoires*, history; outlining the reigns of Charles the Bold and Louis XI of France, it is the first French historical work not to be written as a chronicle.

Martin Luther, *Geistliche Lieder* (Holy Songs), hymnal.

1525

EUROPE

24 Feb. Emperor Charles V defeats the French and Swiss at the battle of Pavia, S of Milan; Francis I, king of France, is imprisoned in Spain. Charles now dominates Italy; he will regain Milan and Genoa in the course of the year.

20 Mar. Louise of Savoy, mother of Francis I and regent of France while King Francis is imprisoned in Spain, asks the *parlement* in Paris to proscribe Lutheran preaching; later this year Jacques le Sevres's translation of the New Testament will be burned.

10 April Formation of the new, Protestant, duchy of Prussia when Albert von Hohenzollern, grand master of the Order of Teutonic Knights, surrenders his lands to Sigismund I, king of Poland; Albert becomes duke under Polish suzerainty.

May Final suppression of the rebellion known as the Peasants' War in Germany (see June 1524) by various armies of regional nobility, notably the forces of the Swabian League under Philip of Hesse. Thomas Müntzer, the most radical of the rebel leaders, is executed (27 May) following a devastating defeat at Frankenhausen in Thuringia (15 May).

July German Catholic princes meet at Dessau, N of Leipzig, to discuss the establishment of a Catholic League to stop the spread of Protestantism.

14 Aug. England agrees on peace terms with France as Cardinal Thomas Wolsey, the English lord chancellor, seeks to recreate a balance of power within Europe.

THE AMERICAS

– Foundation of Santa Marta in New Granada, the first Spanish settlement in what will become Colombia.

ECONOMY AND SOCIETY

30 Dec. Death in Augsburg, Bavaria, of Jakob II Fugger, German banker and merchant.

SCIENCE AND TECHNOLOGY

– Hops are introduced to England from Artois (N France).

ARTS AND HUMANITIES

– The translation into English by Protestant reformer William Tyndale of the New Testament is published in Worms in Germany; this is the first translation of the New Testament into English.

– Birth of Pieter Bruegel the Elder, major Flemish painter, probably in Breda in Brabant (modern Netherlands).

– Birth in London of John Stow, English scholar and antiquary.

– Cardinal Thomas Wolsey, lord chancellor of England, endows Cardinal College in Oxford; the college will be refounded by King Henry VIII as Christ Church in 1546.

1526

EUROPE

14 Jan. Francis I, king of France, and Holy Roman Emperor Charles V conclude the treaty of Madrid. Francis I, still imprisoned in Spain (see 24 Feb. 1525), surrenders the duchy of Burgundy and his claims to Naples, Milan, Genoa, Flanders and Artois; in return he will be released from captivity (17 Mar.).

27 Feb. The League of Gotha, a group of German Protestant princes, is founded. John Frederick, Elector of Saxony, and Philip, landgrave of Hesse, are the founding members; later (2 May) they will be joined by the princes of Mecklenburg, Brunswick-Lüneburg, Anholt, Brandenburg-Ansbach and Mansfeld.

23 Mar. Emperor Charles V forbids religious innovation in imperial territories but also seeks to persuade Pope Clement VII to summon a general council of the Church.

23 May Pope Clement VII forms the League of Cognac to oppose Emperor Charles V by uniting France, Milan, Venice and Florence; this overturns the treaty of Madrid signed on 14 Jan.

29–30 Aug. Suleiman I, the Ottoman sultan, defeats the Hungarians at the battle of Mohács in Hungary; Louis II, king of Hungary and Bohemia, dies. Suleiman will shortly take the Hungarian city of Buda (10 Sept.). Hungary will remain under foreign control up until 1918.

23 Oct. Following the death of King Louis II of Hungary and Bohemia, Ferdinand I, archduke of Austria and brother of Emperor Charles V, is elected king of Bohemia.

10 Nov. John Zápolya, *voivode* (military viceroy) of Transylvania, is crowned king of Hungary by Hungarian nobles eager to avoid Habsburg domination.

ASIA

27 April The Mughal emperor Babur, a descendant of the Mongol conqueror Genghis Khan, defeats Ibrahim Lodi, the sultan of Delhi, at the battle of Panipat; in Nov. he will invade the Punjab. By his victory at Panipat, Babur establishes the Islamic Mughal dynasty, which will last until 1761 and will establish a vast Indian empire.

ARTS AND HUMANITIES

– German portrait painter Hans Holbein the Younger visits England.

1527

EUROPE

1 Jan. Habsburg administration of Austria is reorganized under Ferdinand I, archduke of Austria and newly elected king of Bohemia (see 23 Oct. 1526).

30 April At Westminster, an Anglo-French alliance is signed by Cardinal Thomas Wolsey, lord chancellor of England, and the French bishop of Tarbes.

6 May Rome is sacked by imperial forces; Italy again falls under the control of Holy Roman Emperor Charles V. Order is not restored in Rome until Feb. 1528.

16 May Florence once more becomes a republic; the Medici rulers, nephews of pope Clement VII, are exiled.

21 May Birth in Valladolid, Spain, of Philip II, son of Emperor Charles V and future king of Spain and Portugal, who will reign over Spain at its most powerful (see 1556).

24 June Religious reformation begins in Sweden. The Swedish diet accepts the demands laid down by King Gustavus I Vasa and places the Swedish Church and all of its property under royal control.

5 Nov. Ferdinand I of Austria and Bohemia, brother of Charles V, is recognized as king of Hungary by the diet meeting at Buda; Ferdinand will be formally recognized only in Dec.; the rival king, John Zápolya (see 10 Nov. 1526), will continue to claim the throne until 1528.

ASIA

16 Mar. The Mughal emperor Babur (see 27 April 1526) defeats a Hindu confederacy led by Rana Sangha, ruler of Udaipur, at Kanwanha near Agra in India.

ARTS AND HUMANITIES

21 June Death in Florence, Italy, of Niccolò Machiavelli (see p. 199), Italian statesman and political philosopher.

Niccolò Machiavelli, *Istorie fiorentine* (History of Florence).

1528

EUROPE

22 Jan. Henry VIII of England and Francis I of France declare war on Holy Roman Emperor Charles V; this will lead (Mar.) to a suspension of trade between England and the Netherlands, England's most important European trading partner.

June Economic problems in England resulting from the hostilities between England and the Habsburgs lead to widespread civil unrest in England; the government is forced to declare a truce with the empire.

28 Aug. The French army surrenders at Aversa in the kingdom of Naples and is expelled from Naples and Genoa.

ECOMONY AND SOCIETY

– Establishment in Italy of the Capuchin order, so called because of their distinctive four-pointed hood known as a *capuccio*. Founded by former members of the Franciscan order, the Capuchin order set out to return to the original strictures established by St Francis of Assisi before his death in 1226. The order will experience rapid, eventually worldwide, expansion.

SCIENCE AND TECHNOLOGY

– Paracelsus, Swiss alchemist and physician, publishes *Die Kleine Chirurgie* (The Small Book of Surgery), the first European surgical manual.

ARTS AND HUMANITIES

– Philip Melanchthon, humanist intellectual and Lutheran reformer, proposes pan-German educational reform.

Baldassare Castiglione, *Il libro del cortegiano* (The Book of the Courtier), a guide to courtly behaviour; a translation into English will appear in 1561.

Desiderius Erasmus (see p. 193), *Ciceronianus*, satire on scholarly followers of Cicero.

Ulrich von Hutten, *Arminius*, an allegorical dialogue describing the Reformation as a German national movement.

William Tyndale, *The Obedience of a Christian Man*, religious and political thought.

1529

EUROPE

April The minority of German Protestant princes attending the Second Diet of Speyer in Germany read a 'Protest' against the Catholic majority, who reverse the earlier Church reforms passed in 1526; the term 'Protestant' is born.

10 May Suleiman I, Ottoman sultan, leaves Constantinople to attack Austria. He is in league against the Habsburgs with John Zápolya, claimant to the Hungarian throne elected by anti-Habsburg factions within the Hungarian nobility (see 10 Nov. 1526).

26 June The treaty of Kappel ends the Swiss civil war between the Catholic Forest cantons and the Protestant Civic League. The Catholics agree to end their alliance with the Habsburgs, and both factions agree to allow limited freedom of conscience for individuals.

29 June The treaty of Barcelona is agreed: Holy Roman Emperor Charles V will be formally crowned by Pope Clement VII (see 24 Feb. 1530) and invested with the kingdom of Naples.

5 Aug. In the treaty of Cambrai, Francis I of France renounces all claims to Italian territory and Emperor Charles V renounces his claim to the duchy of Burgundy; Habsburg rule in Italy is confirmed. Henry VIII of England accedes to the treaty (27 Aug.).

21 Sept.–15 Oct. Ottoman forces under Suleiman I lay siege to Vienna.

26 Oct. In London Cardinal Thomas Wolsey falls from power. His fall is due to his failure to thwart Habsburg expansion and to obtain a divorce from Catherine of Aragon (who has failed to produce a healthy male heir) for King Henry VIII (see 1509). The humanist scholar and politician Thomas More is appointed lord chancellor of England.

4 Nov. The opening in England of the first session of the Reformation Parliament. Unsuccessful attempts are made, notably by the jurist Thomas Cromwell, to defend Cardinal Thomas Wolsey, and clerical abuses are attacked. The Parliament sits until 17 Dec.

SCIENCE AND TECHNOLOGY

– Emperor Charles V initiates the construction of the Imperial Canal of Aragon.

ARTS AND HUMANITIES

– In France, King Francis I founds the Collège de France as an institute of advanced study.

1530

EUROPE

24 Feb. At Bologna in N Italy Charles V, who has ruled as Holy Roman Emperor since 1519, is formally crowned Holy Roman Emperor by Pope Clement VII (see 29 June 1529).

25 June In Germany seven Protestant princes sign the Confession of Augsburg, a statement of Protestant beliefs prepared by Philip Melanchthon. The Confession is presented to Emperor Charles V, but some Protestants, particularly followers of the Swiss reformer, Ulrich Zwingli, object to the conciliatory tone of the document.

25 Aug. Birth at Kolomenskoye, near Moscow, of the future Ivan IV (the Terrible), grand prince of Moscow and tsar of Russia.

4 Nov. In England Cardinal Thomas Wolsey is arrested as a traitor after the discovery that he has corresponded secretly with Pope Clement VII; before he can be tried he dies, in Leicester, on 29 Nov.

31 Dec. At Schmalkaldin in Thuringia, Germany, Protestant princes, including the elector of Saxony and the landgrave of Hesse, form the Schmalkaldic League against Emperor Charles V.

– The English Parliament outlaws the procurement from Rome of licenses allowing clergy to hold more than one living.

– By a grant of Emperor Charles V, Malta becomes headquarters of the Knights Hospitallers (see 1308).

ASIA

26 Dec. Babur, first Mughal emperor of India (see 27 April 1526), dies in Agra, India. He is succeeded by his son Humayun, who will reign 1530–40 and 1555–6.

ECONOMY AND SOCIETY

24 May A list of heretical books is drawn up in London, and William Tyndale's translation of the Bible into English is burned.

SCIENCE AND TECHNOLOGY

– Gemma Frisius, Flemish cosmographer, claims that longitude can be discovered by means of time differences.

ARTS AND HUMANITIES

– Francis I of France creates the post of Imprimeur du Roi (Printer to the King) for typographers.

Correggio (Antonio Allegri), frescoes in the dome of Parma Cathedral; begun in 1526, the work depicts the Assumption of the Virgin.

1531

EUROPE

5 Jan. Holy Roman Emperor Charles V formally selects as his heir his brother, Ferdinand I, archduke of Austria and king of Bohemia; Ferdinand I is duly elected king of Germany and (31 Jan.) signs a truce with John Zápolya, *voivode* of Transylvania (see 1526), concerning their dispute over the Hungarian crown.

Jan. Emperor Charles V appoints his sister, Mary of Hungary, widow of Louis II of Hungary, as regent of the Netherlands.

11 Feb. The English King Henry VIII is recognized as supreme head of the Church of England; English clergy are forced to pay a fine to the king for the offence of recognizing Cardinal Wolsey's legatine authority. In the previous month (Jan.) Pope Clement VII forbade Henry VIII to remarry until his divorce from Catherine of Aragon has been officially sanctioned by Rome.

Sept. Civil war breaks out in Switzerland between Protestant Zürich, dominated by the reformer Ulrich Zwingli and his followers, and the Catholic Forest Cantons.

11 Oct. Death of Swiss Protestant reformer Ulrich Zwingli at the battle of Kappel in Switzerland. The following month will see the end of the second Swiss civil war with the inhabitants of each canton and district allowed by the new treaty of Kappel (23 Nov.) to worship as they choose.

ECONOMY AND SOCIETY

– Spanish theologian and physician Michael Servetus publishes *De Trinitatis Erroribus* (On the Errors of the Trinity), in which he denies the Trinity; this is the first statement of Unitarianism.

ARTS AND HUMANITIES

22 Jan. Death of Florentine painter Andrea del Sarto; perhaps best known for his *Madonna of the Harpies*, del Sarto is a major influence on the development of Mannerism.

– Emperor Charles V founds the University of Granada in Spain.

Sir Thomas Elyot, *The Boke Named the Governour*, a manual on education for statesmanship.

Beatus Rhenanus (Bild aus Rheinau), *Rerum Germanicarum Libri Tres* (Three Books on German Matters), the first German history.

Juan Luis Vivès, *De Tradendis Disciplinis* (On the Discipline of Teaching), educational theory, in which he urges the expansion of the curriculum to include cooking, building, clothes design, navigation and agriculture.

1532

EUROPE

26 April Suleiman I, the Ottoman sultan, invades Hungary.

15 May In England, a convocation of English clergy ratifies Thomas Cromwell's *Submission of the English Clergy*. King Henry VIII now controls all aspects of the English Church; the following day Thomas More, lord chancellor and keeper of the Great Seal, resigns in protest. More is replaced (20 May) as keeper of the Great Seal by Thomas Audley.

26 May Francis I of France coordinates an alliance between those German princes who oppose the election of Ferdinand I, archduke of Austria and king of Bohemia, as king of Germany. Fundamentally an anti-Habsburg movement, this alliance unites both Catholic and Protestant members of the German nobility.

7–8 Aug. Retreat from Hungary of Suleiman I who (Sept.) ravages Carinthia (in modern Austria) and Croatia.

22 Aug. Death in Canterbury of William Warham, archbishop of Canterbury and a major opponent of attempts by King Henry VIII to establish secular and royal authority over the English Church.

Sept. Holy Roman Emperor Charles V invades Italy.

THE AMERICAS

15 Nov. Francisco Pizarro, conquistador, leads a Spanish expedition from Panama for the conquest of Peru; his forces capture Atahualpa, emperor of the Incas (16 Nov.).

ECONOMY AND SOCIETY

– Jean Calvin (see p. 213), French Church reformer, urges a religious reformation in Paris.

SCIENCE AND TECHNOLOGY

– Birth in Plymouth, England, of Sir John Hawkins, explorer and naval commander. Largely responsible for the organization and training of the English navy, Hawkins is also believed to be the first Englishman to be involved in the slave trade.

– Portuguese settlers in Brazil introduce the cultivation of sugar cane.

ARTS AND HUMANITIES

– French writer, scientist and priest François Rabelais publishes the satirical allegory *Pantagruel*, in which he recommends a scientific curriculum.

– The first collected edition of Geoffrey Chaucer's works is published by the English printer William Thynne.

Robert Estienne, *Thesaurus Linguae Latinae* (Thesaurus of the Latin Language), the first Latin dictionary.

Niccolò Machiavelli (see p. 199), *Il principe* (The Prince), political treatise.

1533

EUROPE

25 Jan. King Henry VIII of England secretly marries his mistress Anne Boleyn.

30 Jan. In England, Protestant reformer Thomas Cranmer is consecrated archbishop of Canterbury.

10 April Thomas Cranmer, archbishop of Canterbury, declares the marriage between King Henry VIII of England and Catherine of Aragon void; Rome has not yet officially sanctioned the divorce. Later this year (11 July) Henry will be excommunicated for bigamy by Pope Clement VII.

10 April Death of Frederick I, king of Denmark and Norway. In Denmark a civil war, the Counts' War, ensues when the Danish diet, largely composed of Catholics, refuses to recognize the accession of Frederick's son Christian, stadtholder of Schleswig-Holstein, because of his Lutheranism; the diet supports the accession of the infant Hans, Frederick's younger son.

25 April Birth in Dillenburg, Nassau, of William I (the Silent), first stadtholder of the Netherlands.

22 June Peace treaty between Suleiman I, the Ottoman sultan (see 21 Sept. 1520), and Ferdinand I, archduke of Austria, king of Bohemia and ruler of Germany. Archduke Ferdinand retains the part of Hungary still in his control, while John Zápolya, *voivode* (military viceroy) of Transylvania and ally of Suleiman I (see 10 May 1529), remains king of the rest of the territory; both men pay tribute to the sultan.

7 Sept. Birth, to King Henry VIII of England and his wife, Anne Boleyn, in Greenwich, near London, of Princess Elizabeth, who will rule England as Queen Elizabeth I (see 17 Nov. 1558).

4 Dec. Following the death of his father, Vasily III (21 Nov.), the three-year-old Ivan IV (the Terrible) becomes grand prince of Moscow. Ivan's mother, Yelena Glynskaya, acts as regent. King Sigismund I (the Old) of Poland will shortly begin a war with Russia over the sovereignty of Lithuania.

– In France, Henry duke of Orléans, second son of Francis I and future Henry II of France, marries Catherine de' Medici (see 13 April 1519).

THE AMERICAS

26 July The Spanish conquistador Pizarro executes Atahualpa, the Inca emperor (see 15 Nov. 1532); Pizarro and his forces march on Cuzco (in modern Peru); in the course of this year the Spanish will also conquer the Yucatán (in modern Mexico) and colonize La Plata (in modern Argentina).

– John III, king of Portugal, creates hereditary captaincies in Brazil.

ECONOMY AND SOCIETY

- Spanish humanist and church reformer Juan de Valdéz and his followers in Naples urge doctrinal reform within the Catholic Church.
- Under the leadership of the German Melchior Hoffmann, Anabaptists, who practise adult baptism, are expelled from Germany after claiming that Strasburg will soon become the New Jerusalem.
- Protestantism becomes popular at the French court through the influence of Madame d'Etampes, mistress of King Francis I.
- St Philip Neri (Filippo de' Neri), Florentine religious reformer, arrives in Rome; known as the Apostle of Rome, Neri begins to set up informal prayer groups in an attempt to reinvigorate lay spirituality. His order, the Congregation of the Oratory, will be formally approved by Pope Gregory XIII in 1575.

ARTS AND HUMANITIES

6 July Death in Ferrara, Italy, of Italian poet Ludovico Ariosto, author of *Orlando Furioso* (1516).
- The earliest printed madrigals are published in Rome in Italy. Hans Holbein the Younger, *The Ambassadors*, painting.

1534

EUROPE

15 Jan. The Act of Succession officially recognizes the marriage of Henry VIII and Anne Boleyn (see 25 Jan. 1533) and requires members of both Houses of Parliament, all clergy and public officials to swear an oath acknowledging the legitimate future accession to the English throne of one of the children born of the king's new marriage.

9 Feb. The Anabaptists (see 1533) establish a proto-Communist state in Münster in Westphalia (Germany).

25 Sept. Death of Pope Clement VII; he is succeeded (13 Oct.) by the Italian Alessandro Farnese, who will reign as Pope Paul III.

3 Nov.–18 Dec. In England, during the seventh session of the Reformation Parliament, the Act of Supremacy is passed, which formally severs all ties with Rome and establishes King Henry VIII as supreme head of the English Church. The Reformation Parliament also passes a second Act of Succession, which makes the oath of loyalty statutory and ensures that Henry VIII's newly extended powers will pass to all future English sovereigns. The crown will now oversee ecclesiastical appointments and will receive one-tenth of all income from Church benefices.

THE AMERICAS

10 May Jacques Cartier, French navigator, sights the coast of Labrador (modern Canada).

ECONOMY AND SOCIETY

15 Aug. Spanish priest Ignatius Loyola (see box) founds the Order of the Society of Jesus (the Jesuits) in Paris.
- In England enclosure has led to a loss of arable land and farmers are forbidden by Parliament to own more than 2000 sheep.

St Ignatius of Loyola (1491–1556)

St Ignatius Loyola (originally Iñigo Lopez de Recalde) was the single most influential figure of the Catholic Counter-Reformation, the movement that revived the Roman Church in the second half of the 16th century and enabled it to respond to the Protestant challenge. He was born into the Spanish aristocracy and served as a soldier until he was severely wounded in battle. During his long convalescence, Loyola turned to Christ for solace and soon became devoted to an austere religious life.

After a pilgrimage to the Holy Land, he helped found the Society of Jesus (the Jesuits), a society dedicated to missionary work. Ignatius organized the Jesuits militaristically, with a general at their head. He saw the Catholic Christian struggle for minds and souls as a battle, and the Jesuits as soldiers whose aim was activity rather than contemplation. Thus the idea of the Church was reasserted to suit the needs of the modern world: while Protestantism became engaged in an individual search for inner salvation, Catholicism placed more emphasis on the communal celebration of the sacraments. It was the Jesuit approach that informed the Catholic Church for the remainder of the second millennium.

Ignatius's *Spiritual Exercises* (1548) is a manual in training for perfection. It was written for both the clergy and the laity, and turned prayer into a discipline. As educators and courtiers the Jesuits demonstrated a subtle understanding of power and argument, and showed how an intellectual elite can exercise a significant practical influence on the political domain.

ARTS AND HUMANITIES

- German Protestant reformer Martin Luther (see p. 201) publishes his translation of the Bible into German.
- Death of Italian painter Correggio (Antonio Allegri), best known for his *Jupiter and Io*, and his frescoes in the Cathedral and Church of San Giovanni Evangelista in Parma.
- Polydore Vergil (see 1507) completes a history of England, *Historia Anglica*.

François Rabelais, *Gargantua*, the second part of his satire *Pantagruel* (published in 1532).

1535

EUROPE

11 June A Danish–Swedish army led by King Christian III of Denmark and Norway defeats the troops and the naval force of the Hanseatic port of Lübeck; the era of Hanseatic naval power ends. Christian III is able to conquer the Island of Fyn and all of Zeeland except for Copenhagen.

22 June Execution of St John Fisher, bishop of Rochester, for refusing to swear an oath of loyalty to Henry VIII, king of England, in London. A humanist scholar, Fisher strongly opposed England's break from Rome. Two weeks later (6 June)

Sir Thomas More, former lord chancellor of England and keeper of the Great Seal, is executed on the same charge.

25 June The forces of Hesse invade Münster in Westphalia, which has been in the control of the Anabaptist sect (see 9 Feb. 1534). The Anabaptist leader Jan Boekelszoon (John of Leyden) is executed and Catholicism restored.

MIDDLE EAST AND NORTH AFRICA

July Holy Roman Emperor Charles V, aided by his Genoese admiral Andrea Doria, takes the city of Tunis from Khair ad-Din (Barbarossa), its Ottoman ruler. Barbarossa flees to Algiers, and Charles V extends the Spanish conquest of the N African coast.

THE AMERICAS

– Jacques Cartier, the French navigator, explores the sites that will become Quebec and Montreal.

ARTS AND HUMANITIES

– In England Thomas Cromwell, jurist and principal secretary to King Henry VIII, publishes injunctions that encourage humanist principles in secular learning and forbid the study of canon law at Cambridge.

Hans Holbein the Younger, *King Henry VIII of England*, painting.

1536

EUROPE

14 April In England the final session of the Reformation Parliament meets; royal assent is given for the dissolution of the 376 lesser monasteries. Wales is incorporated into England with all legal proceedings to be in the English language; English law replaces Welsh law governing succession to property.

19 May Execution of Anne Boleyn, second wife of Henry VIII of England and mother of Queen Elizabeth I (see 7 Sept. 1533), on charges of adultery and incest; she has produced no surviving male heir. Later this month (30 May) Henry VIII will marry Jane Seymour.

11 July The Ten Articles of the Church of England, approved by Convocation, are presented to the English Parliament.

25 July Holy Roman Emperor Charles V invades Provence in S France; the French army, led by the duke of Montmorency, lays waste to the land in order to hinder the Spanish advance. Despite these tactics, Charles V besieges Marseilles.

29 July The city of Copenhagen surrenders to Christian III, king of Denmark and Norway (see 11 June 1535); this establishes King Christian's authority over all of Denmark and Norway.

1 Oct. In Louth, Lincolnshire, England, the Pilgrimage of Grace begins; local people rise in protest against the Church reforms under Henry VIII, in particular the dissolution of local monasteries and new, heavier taxation. The rebels occupy the city of Lincoln. By 9 Oct. the uprising has spread to the East Riding in Yorkshire, and York is held by 16 Oct. By the end of the month (27 Oct.) the Pilgrimage of Grace has spread to Lancashire.

6 Oct. In Vilvorde, Flanders (Netherlands), William Tyndale, English scholar and Church reformer who produced the first

translation into English of the New Testament (see 1525), is burned at the stake.

30 Oct. Under pressure from the Lutheran king of Denmark and Norway, Christian III, the Danish Rigsråd (advisory council) agrees to abolish the episcopacy in Denmark and to confiscate all Danish lands held by the Church.

5 Dec. In England the Pilgrimage of Grace is abandoned when Thomas Howard, duke of Norfolk, offers pardons to the rebels in Doncaster, Yorkshire, and promises that their demands for the restoration of Catholicism and a separate parliament in York will be considered by the government.

ARTS AND HUMANITIES

12 July Death in Basle, Switzerland, of Desiderius Erasmus, Dutch humanist (see p. 193).

– Florentine painter, sculptor and architect Michelangelo (see p. 197) starts work on his fresco *The Last Judgement* on the altar wall of the Sistine Chapel in the Vatican in Rome.

– Florentine architect Jacopo Sansovino (Jacopo Tatti) begins work on the library of San Marco in Venice.

Jean Calvin (see box), *Institutio Christianae Religionis* (Institute of the Christian Religion), theological and political thought.

Jean Calvin (1509–64)

Born in Noyon, Picardy, Calvin was educated as a lawyer but was to find fame as a theologian and religious reformer. He established in Geneva a theocratic model of church–state government that became an inspiration to his followers throughout Europe. His theological masterpiece, *Institute of the Christian Religion* (1536), was a highly practical manual that became the founding text of the Calvinist churches. He ensured that the Protestant Reformation did not run out of steam either intellectually or politically, and was able to meet the challenge of a revived Catholic Church in the second half of the 16th century. He is the most completely systematic thinker to have been produced by Protestantism, with a remorselessly self-contained and logical style.

Calvin's God was a lawyer's delight, passionless and driven by contractual obligations. His most important attribute was power – the key to the Calvinist idea of predestination: God had pre-ordained some people to salvation and some to damnation, and having done so he could not break his own contract. Neither prayer nor action could change God's will. History, the Church and politics were therefore led by 'the elect' – those chosen by God to effect his will. This was an idea of immense psychological appeal: Calvin created an elite and gave it a purpose. Those who believed themselves to be chosen by God could organize, scheme, spy and fight with self-confidence because their success was pre-ordained. But the fact that Calvin's God was so inscrutable also meant that it was only at the end of time that the elect would know who they actually were. Calvinism continued after his death to be the most important and influential of all Protestant systems of belief.

1537

EUROPE

7 Jan. Assassination of Alessandro de' Medici, duke of Florence; he is succeeded by his cousin Cosimo I (the Great) de' Medici.

8 Jan. Francis I of France revives the French claim to Artois and Flanders; he agrees a joint attack with Suleiman I, the Ottoman sultan, against Holy Roman Emperor Charles V.

10 Feb. In England, after periodic uprisings by anti-Protestant rebels, Sir Francis Bigod, leader of the Pilgrimage of Grace (see 1536), is captured. In July a number of the movement's leaders, including William Thirsk, former abbot of Fountains, and Adam Sedbar, abbot of Jervaulx, will be executed.

2 Sept. Christian III, king of Denmark and Norway, issues a Lutheran ordinance for the Danish Church (see 30 Oct. 1536).

24 Oct. Death of Jane Seymour, the English queen and third wife of King Henry VIII, after the birth (12 Oct.), in London, of Prince Edward; he will become Edward VI (see 28 Jan. 1547).

ASIA

– The Portuguese obtain Macao, S China, as a trading settlement.

THE AMERICAS

23 June Death, on his return voyage to Spain, of Pedro de Mendoza, Spanish conquistador who founded Buenos Aires (modern Argentina) and Asunción on the Paraguay River, the first permanent settlement in the S American interior.

SCIENCE AND TECHNOLOGY

– In his *Nova Scientia* (The New Science), published in Venice, Italian mathematician Niccolò Tartaglia explains the trajectory of bullets.

ARTS AND HUMANITIES

– An edition, in four volumes, of the complete works of the Roman statesman Marcus Tullius Cicero (see p. 42) is published in Venice; the text, edited and annotated by Italian scholar Pietro Victorius, sets new standards for classical scholarship.

– The translation of the Bible into English by Cambridge scholar and Augustinian friar Miles Coverdale, which was first printed abroad in 1535, is published in England and is the first complete Bible printed in England. King Henry VIII orders that a copy be placed in every choir of every church to make the text accessible to all.

– Florentine architect Jacopo Sansovino (Jacopo Tatti, see also 1536) starts work in Venice on the Mint and the façade of the Doge's Palace.

Michelangelo, new design for the Campidoglio on the Capitoline Hill in Rome.

1538

EUROPE

24 Feb. The childlesss John Zápolya, *voivode* of Transylvania and ruler of that part of Hungary that is not under Habsburg control (see 22 June 1533), signs the treaty of Nagyvárad by which Ferdinand I, archduke of Austria, king of Bohemia and king of Germany, will inherit the whole of Hungary on Zapolyá's death.

10 June German Catholic princes form the League of Nuremberg in opposition to the Protestant Schmalkaldic League (see 31 Dec. 1530).

18 June Francis I of France and Holy Roman Emperor Charles V agree to a ten-year truce, the truce of Nice. At Aigues-Mortes in S France (14–16 July) the king and the emperor discuss how to fight Protestantism and defeat the Turks. Threatened by diplomatic isolation, Henry VIII of England opens negotiations with the German Protestant princes, now united as the Schmalkaldic League.

16 Dec. Francis I of France issues an edict authorizing the persecution of French Protestants.

– Ottoman naval leader Khair ad-Din (Barbarossa, see July 1535) seizes the duchy of Morea (the Greek Peloponnese) from Venice.

THE AMERICAS

– Establishment of Bogotá, Colombia, as a Spanish stronghold by Gonzalo Jiménez de Quesada, Spanish administrator of New Granada (modern Colombia); Bogotá had been the capital city of the Chibcha kingdom.

ECONOMY AND SOCIETY

– Widespread iconoclasm sweeps across S England; many images, statues and shrines are destroyed by Protestants, some of whom are answerable to Thomas Cromwell, chief minister to King Henry VIII.

1539

EUROPE

15 Feb. The Elector of Brandenburg, Joachim II, becomes a Protestant; with the accession this year of the Protestant Henry as duke of Saxony, all N German states become Protestant.

April The English Parliament passes the Six Articles of Religion, which enforce transubstantiation, communion in one kind, chastity and celibacy of clergy, private masses and confession. This conservative Act presages a return to Catholic orthodoxy.

4 Oct. The treaty is signed for the marriage of Henry VIII of England to Anne of Cleves, sister of William, duke of Cleves, Jülich, Berg and Guelders, as part of the English–German Protestant alliance.

THE AMERICAS

– Spanish explorer Hernando de Soto and his forces land in Florida (SE USA).

–Spain annexes Cuba.

ECONOMY AND SOCIETY

– In Amsterdam Dutch Protestant leader Hendrik Niclaes (Henry Nicholas) founds the Family of Love, a radical Protestant group.

– France organizes a public lottery.

ARTS AND HUMANITIES
- Damiano de Goes writes the first history of the Portuguese in India.

Philip Melanchthon, *De Officio Principum* (The Office of Princes), political work authorizing rulers to use force when faced with heresy.

1540

EUROPE
6 Jan. Henry VIII of England marries Anne of Cleves (see 4 Oct. 1539).

14 Feb. Holy Roman Emperor Charles V enters Ghent in Flanders to quell the city's revolt after it has offered its allegiance to Francis I of France.

18 June In England Thomas Cromwell, earl of Essex and chief minister to Henry VIII, is arrested for treason. The charge has its roots in the king's anger at Cromwell's proposing the marriage with Anne of Cleves, whom Henry describes as 'a Flanders mare'.

23 July Following the death of John Zápolya, the infant John Sigismund Zápolya succeeds as king of Hungary despite the treaty of Nagyvárad (see 24 Feb. 1538). Ferdinand I, Archduke of Austria, king of Bohemia and king of Germany, invades to claim the whole of Hungary.

28 July Execution in London of Thomas Cromwell for treason. On the same day Henry VIII marries Catherine Howard, his fifth wife; her uncle, Thomas Howard, duke of Norfolk and lord treasurer of England, replaces Cromwell as chief minister.

ASIA
- Expulsion of Humayun, son of Babur (see 1530) and second Mughal emperor of India, from India by an Afghan force led by Sher Shah Suri who becomes emperor of Delhi. Humayun flees to Persia and will not return to Delhi until 1555.

ARTS AND HUMANITIES
22 May Death, near Florence, Italy, of Francesco Guicciardini, Italian scholar, statesman and historian.

23 Aug. Death of Guillaume Budé (Budaeus), French classical scholar who helped to found the Collège de France in Paris.

24 Aug. Death in Casalmaggiore, Cremona, in Italy, of Francesco Parmigianino (Francesco Mazzola), Italian Mannerist painter.

1541

EUROPE
Mar. The duke of Montmorency, constable of France, is disgraced and retires into private life.

5 April At the diet of Regensburg (Ratisbon), the Holy Roman Emperor Charles V, a staunch Catholic, is forced to admit Protestants to the imperial chamber.

6 Aug. Suleiman I, the Ottoman sultan, captures Buda and annexes the C part of Hungary, which will remain in Turkish hands until 1686.

29 Dec. Despite the opposition of the Hungarian nobility, Isabella, widow of John Zápolya and mother of the infant King John Sigismund Zápolya (see 23 July 1540), cedes Hungary to Ferdinand I, archduke of Austria, king of Bohemia and king of Germany, by the treaty of Gyalu.

THE AMERICAS
12 Feb. Founding of Santiago (modern Chile) by Spanish soldier Pedro de Valdivia.

21 May Hernando de Soto, Spanish explorer, discovers the Mississippi River, near modern Memphis, Tennessee (USA), and crosses what will become Arkansas and Oklahoma.

26 June Death in Lima or Cuzco, Peru, of Spanish conquistador Francisco Pizarro, who secured Peru for the Spanish.

- The French Protestant François de Robeval is appointed first viceroy of Canada by Francis I of France.
- Spanish conquistador Francisco Vázquez de Coronado crosses what will become Texas, Oklahoma and E Kansas (USA).
- Spanish explorer Francisco de Orellana makes the first descent of the River Amazon.

SCIENCE AND TECHNOLOGY
24 Sept. Death in Salzburg, Austria, of Paracelsus, German scientist and physician.

- Gerardus Mercator, Flemish cartographer, invents a terrestrial globe.

ARTS AND HUMANITIES
- Birth of the artist El Greco (Domenikos Theotokopoulos) in Candia, now Herakleion, Crete. After periods in Venice and Rome, he will settle in Toledo, Spain, by 1577.

1542

EUROPE
13 Feb. Execution of Catherine Howard, queen of England and fifth wife of King Henry VIII (see 28 July 1540), on a charge of adultery, in London.

21 July Pope Paul III establishes the Inquisition in Rome in an attempt to halt the spread of Protestantism. The Inquisition has the power to investigate and prosecute anyone accused of heresy against Catholic orthodoxy.

July Hostilities deepen between France and the Holy Roman Empire. Francis I of France signs a treaty with King Gustavus I Vasa of Sweden to thwart Holy Roman Emperor Charles V in his attempt to place the Catholic Princess Dorothea, daughter of King Christian II, on the Danish throne.

14 Dec. On the death of her father, King James V, in Falklands, Fife, the new-born infant Mary Stuart (better known as Mary Queen of Scots, born 8 Dec.) succeeds to the throne of Scotland.

ASIA
May St Francis Xavier (Francisco Javier), Jesuit missionary, arrives in Goa on the W coast of India; he will introduce Christianity to the people of S India, SE Asia and Japan (see 1552).

– Portuguese traders arrive on the island of Tanegashima off the S tip of Japan.

ECONOMY AND SOCIETY

24 June Birth in Fontiveros, Spain, of St John of the Cross (Juan de la Cruz), reformer of the Carmelite order in Spain and the most important disciple of the Spanish mystic St Teresa of Avila (see 1562 and 1582).

4 Oct. Birth in Montepulciano, C Italy, of St Roberto Bellarmine, Italian cardinal; he will become a vigorous cotroversialist and an outspoken defender of Catholic orthodoxy.

SCIENCE AND TECHNOLOGY

– Flemish physician Andreas Vesalius publishes *De Humani Corporis Fabrica* (On the Fabric of the Human Body) in which he outlines new principles of anatomy.

1543

EUROPE

22 Jan. In Westminster, London, the English Parliament re-establishes the Council of Wales and the Marches; Wales is divided into 12 counties.

12 July Henry VIII, king of England, marries Catherine Parr; widow of Lord Latimer, she is his sixth and last wife.

SCIENCE AND TECHNOLOGY

24 May Death in Frauenberg, E Prussia (modern Frombork, Poland), of Nicolaus Copernicus, Polish astronomer who discovered the heliocentric movement of the planetary system (i.e., the movement of the planets around the Sun, rather than the Earth); his most important work, *De Revolutionibus Orbium Coelestium* (On the Revolutions of the Celestial Spheres), is published just before his death.

ARTS AND HUMANITIES

29 Nov. Death in London of German painter Hans Holbein the Younger.

– Birth in Lincoln of William Byrd, English composer.

– Work begins on the bronze *Diana of Fontainebleau* by Benvenuto Cellini, Italian Mannerist sculptor and goldsmith working at the court of Francis I of France.

– Thomas More, *The History of Richard the Third*; it will provide the inspiration for William Shakespeare's *King Richard III*.

1544

EUROPE

Feb. At the Fourth Diet of Speyer in the Rhineland Palatinate, German Protestant princes agree to finance Holy Roman Emperor Charles V for his campaigns against France and the Ottomans; in return, Charles V has promised to propose a council to reform the German Church.

1 May Renewed invasion of Hungary by the Ottomans (see 1541); Suleiman I divides the country into 12 *sanjaks* (administrative districts).

14 July Henry VIII of England crosses the English Channel to Calais to join forces with Emperor Charles V against Francis I of France in Picardy, NE France.

18 Sept. Francis I of France and Emperor Charles V sign the treaty of Crépy (Henry VIII of England is not consulted, despite being Charles's ally); both rulers agree to return all lands annexed since the truce of Nice (1538), with several exceptions: France and the Empire will ally themselves against Protestantism, and Charles of Orléans, second surviving son of Francis, will marry into the Habsburg dynasty.

19 Nov. Pope Paul III summons a general council of the Church to meet in Trent (Trento in modern N Italy) in 1545; this council, which will meet in various sessions until 1563, will define the aims of the Catholic Counter-Reformation.

SCIENCE AND TECHNOLOGY

– German scientist and mineralogist Agricola (Georg Bauer) publishes *De Ortu et Causis Subterraneis* (On Underground Origins and Causes), in which he expounds the principles of physical geology.

1545

EUROPE

24 Mar. At the diet of Worms in Germany, summoned by Pope Paul III, the German Protestant princes demand a national religious settlement for Germany independent of the general council of the Church. Holy Roman Emperor Charles V refuses.

12 April French forces massacre the Waldenses (Vaudois), a heretical group founded in the late 12th century and based on the principle of apostolic poverty; its members flee from S France and head for Switzerland.

8 July Birth at Valladolid in Spain of Don Carlos (Charles of Austria), prince of Asturias and son and heir of the future King Philip II of Spain.

27 Aug. Birth in Rome of Alessandro Farnese, duke of Parma, who, as regent of the Netherlands (1578–92), will maintain Spanish control over the Dutch.

9 Sept. Charles of Orléans, son of Francis I of France, dies, ending the hopes of a union between the French and Habsburg royal houses (see 18 Sept. 1544).

Nov. Ferdinand I, archduke of Austria and king of Bohemia and Germany, negotiates the truce of Adrianople with Suleiman I, the Ottoman sultan.

13 Dec. The Council of Trent (see 1544) convenes; it will meet periodically in Trent and Bologna until 1563.

Dec. The diet of the Protestant Schmalkaldic League of German princes (see 31 Dec. 1530) meets at Frankfurt in defiance of the Catholic Emperor Charles V.

ASIA

– King John III of Portugal appoints Portuguese navigator João de Castro as viceroy of Portuguese India.

– Humayun, exiled Mughal ruler of India (see 1540), conquers the province of Kandahar (modern Afghanistan).

SCIENCE AND TECHNOLOGY

- A botanical garden is established at the University of Padua in N Italy.
- Pioneering French surgeon Ambroise Paré describes how to treat gunshot wounds using modern surgical principles in his *La Méthode de traicter les playes* (The Method of Treating Wounds).

ECONOMY AND SOCIETY

- The Spanish begin to mine the rich deposits of silver in Potosí (in modern Bolivia); the arrival in Spain of so much extra silver will be one of the causes of European price inflation.

ARTS AND HUMANITIES

- Italian Mannerist sculptor and goldsmith Benvenuto Cellini publishes his autobiography, a work that remains an important text for art history.
- Death of John Taverner, English composer of sacred music.

1546

EUROPE

Feb. The Schmalkaldic League of German Protestant princes (see 31 Dec. 1530) prepares for civil war in Germany. Martin Luther (see p. 201), German Protestant reformer and theologian, dies in Eisleben, Saxony (18 Feb.), while attempting to negotiate an agreement to avoid conflict between the Catholic and Protestant factions.

> *Whatever your heart clings to – that is really your God.*

Martin Luther *Large Catechism* (1529)

7 June The treaty of Ardres ends England's war with France and Scotland; Henry VIII, king of England, will yield his territories gained in France; Francis I of France undertakes to pay out large pensions to Henry and his successors.

23 Dec. The German cities of Ulm, a key Protestant stronghold, and Frankfurt (29 Dec.) surrender to Holy Roman Emperor Charles V.

THE AMERICAS

- The Spanish found an archbishopric at Tenochtitlán (Mexico City) in Mexico.

ECONOMY AND SOCIETY

3 Aug. Etienne Dolet, French scholar and printer, is burned in Paris for publishing Protestant translations of the Bible.

SCIENCE AND TECHNOLOGY

14 Dec. Birth in Knudstrup, S Sweden (at this date under Danish rule), of Tycho Brahe, Danish astronomer.
- Gerardus Mercator, Flemish cartographer, claims that the earth has a magnetic pole.

ARTS AND HUMANITIES

26 Mar. Death in Carleton, Cambridgeshire, England, of Sir Thomas Elyot, English scholar.
- Under the patronage of King Francis I, reconstruction of the Louvre in Paris begins; the new complex has been designed by French architect Pierre Lescot.
- Michelangelo (see p. 197) is appointed chief architect of St Peter's in Rome, for which he designs its celebrated dome; he will continue the reconstruction of St Peter's begun by the architect Bramante (see 1505).

Michelangelo, the Palazzo Farnese in Rome.

1547

EUROPE

19 Jan. Execution in London of the poet Henry Howard, earl of Surrey and son of Thomas Howard, duke of Norfolk, for treason.

28 Jan. Death in London of King Henry VIII, the driving force behind England's break with the Roman Catholic Church and the father of three English monarchs; he is succeeded by his son, Edward VI, aged nine (see 1537).

Jan. The official opposition of the Council of Trent (see 1544) to the Protestant doctrine of justification by faith means that Holy Roman Emperor Charles V can never be reconciled with the German Protestant princes.

24 Feb. Birth in Regensburg, Bavaria, of Don John of Austria, natural son of Emperor Charles V (see 7 Oct. 1571).

31 Mar. On the death of his father, Francis I, at Rambouillet in France, Henry II, under the influence of Francis, duke of Guise, accedes to the French throne.

24 April Emperor Charles V defeats the Schmalkaldic League (see 31 Dec. 1530) at Mühlberg in Saxony; John Frederick, Elector of Saxony and an influential leader of the Protestant faction, is captured and (19 May) stripped of his possessions and condemned to death. Philip, landgrave of Hesse, the remaining Protestant leader, is captured on 20 June.

13 June Ferdinand I, archduke of Austria and king of Bohemia and Germany (see 24 Feb. 1538), agrees a five-year peace treaty with Suleiman I, the Ottoman sultan. For an annual tribute to Suleiman, Ferdinand is given rights over parts of W Hungary and permission to style himself king of Hungary.

1 Sept. At the diet of Augsburg in Bavaria in Germany, Emperor Charles V argues for the strengthening of the empire's executive capacity and for a theological compromise between Catholics and Protestants in order to maintain civil and religious order in Germany until a general council of the Church is convened to settle differences.

14 Sept. Birth in Amersfoort, Spanish Netherlands, of Johan van Oldenbarneveldt, who as a Dutch statesman will be actively involved in obtaining independence for the Netherlands.

Oct. Anti-Protestant policy tightens in France; in Paris La Chambre Ardente is created as a criminal court for the trial of heretics.

4 Nov. In England, the Act of Six Articles of Religion is repealed by Parliament (see April 1539); the English Reformation becomes more Protestant.

– Brittany is finally united with France.

ECONOMY AND SOCIETY

– The Inquisition is established in Lisbon, Portugal.

ARTS AND HUMANITIES

29 Sept. Birth in Alcalá de Henares, near Madrid, Spain, of Miguel de Cervantes Saavedra (see p. 241), author of *Don Quixote*.

– John Wilkinson, English scholar, publishes the first translation into English of Aristotle's *Ethics*.

– Italian scholar Peter Martyr (Pietro Martire Vermigli) lectures on the theology of the reformed Church at Oxford University.

– Edward Seymour, duke of Somerset, begins Somerset Place, in the Strand in London, England.

– The first book to be printed in the Welsh language, entitled *Yn y Ihyvyr hwnn* (In this Book), is published. It includes biblical passages and prayers.

– Birth, in Exeter, of Nicholas Hilliard, English portrait painter and miniaturist.

1548

EUROPE

1 April Sigismund II, grand duke of Lithuania, accedes to the throne of Poland on the death of his father, Sigismund I.

15 May In Germany a religious compromise between the Catholics and Protestants is attempted through the Augsburg Interim; clergy can marry; the laity may receive communion in both kinds; justification by faith is retained but modified; and all seven sacraments are kept.

July The 17 provinces of the Netherlands are absorbed into the Burgundian circle of the empire.

5 Sept. Death of Catherine Parr, sixth wife of King Henry VIII of England.

THE AMERICAS

9 April Gonzalo Pizarro, Spanish conquistador and leader of a movement for Peruvian independence, is defeated at the battle of Jaquijahuana by forces under Spanish general Pedro de la Gasca; Lima will now be the sole centre of Spanish administration in Peru.

SCIENCE AND TECHNOLOGY

– The Spanish mine silver in Zatecas (modern Mexico).

ARTS AND HUMANITIES

– The first theatre in Paris, the Hôtel de Bourgogne, is opened.

Tintoretto, *St Mark Freeing a Christian Slave*, one of a series of paintings on the life and death of St Mark.

Titian, *Charles V on Horseback*, painting.

1549

EUROPE

26 June The 17 provinces of the Netherlands are made independent of the Holy Roman Empire and form a circle of their own.

June Following the introduction of the Protestant Book of Common Prayer in England, Catholic peasants rebel in the West Country.

July In Norfolk, England, the Protestant Robert Kett leads an anti-enclosure revolt; a huge rebel camp is set up on Mousehold Heath in Norwich. John Dudley, earl of Warwick (later duke of Northumberland), will crush the rebellion (27 Aug.).

8 Aug. France declares war on England.

10 Oct. In England Edward Seymour, earl of Somerset, Lord Protector of England, falls from power; John Dudley, earl of Warwick, assumes the powers, but not the title, of lord protector.

5 Nov. Birth in Buhy, Normandy, of Philippe de Mornay, French diplomat and vigorous advocate of Protestant principle.

10 Nov. Death in Rome of Pope Paul III, the first pope of the Counter-Reformation.

– In Russia Ivan IV (the Terrible), grand prince of Moscow and tsar of Russia, summons the first Russian national assembly.

THE AMERICAS

– Under the patronage of King John III of Portugal, Thomé de Souza founds Bahia (modern Sao Salvador) as his administrative capital in Brazil.

SCIENCE AND TECHNOLOGY

– The first anatomical theatre is founded in Padua, Italy.

ARTS AND HUMANITIES

– Andrea Palladio (Andrea di Pietro), architect of the Venetian school, begins work on the Basilica (Palazzo della Ragione) in Vicenza, N Italy.

– Joachim du Bellay publishes *La Défense et illustration de la langue française* (The Defence and Illustration of the French Language), in which he defines the poetic theory of the Pléiade group of poets (based on the rejection of medievalism and the acceptance of models drawn from classical antiquity). *L'Olive* (The Olive), his poem written in the same year, demonstrates these principles.

1550

EUROPE

8 Feb. Election of Giovanni Maria Ciocchi del Monte, the Roman cardinal-bishop of Palestrina, as Pope Julius III.

24 Mar. The treaty of Boulogne is negotiated between France and England: in return for a substantial payment from France,

Bartolomé de Las Casas (1474–1566)

A Spanish missionary known as the Apostle of the Indians, Las Casas was born in Seville, southern Spain. He went to the Americas in 1502 and acquired indigenous Americans as slaves to work on his estate in Cuba. He was ordained in 1512 and two years later read a rebuke in the Old Testament Book of Ecclesiastes: 'He that sacrificeth of a thing wrongfully gotten, his offering is ridiculous, and the gifts of unjust men are not accepted.' It was a moment of dramatic revelation, showing him the injustice and tyranny of his own countrymen's treatment of the Native

American peoples. Las Casas gave up his own slaves, became a champion of the rights of the conquered Americans and launched an impassioned critique of 'the robbery, evil and injustice committed against them'.

Las Casas returned to Spain in 1515 to agitate for reforms, and wrote a history of Spanish rule in the Americas in order to publicize its evils. The great event of his life came in 1550, when Emperor Charles V ordered a debate in Valladolid on the justice or otherwise of the Spanish conquest and of the treatment of the indigenous Americans.

A council of 14 theologians heard evidence from Las Casas and his adversary, Juan de Sepulveda. The council failed to reach a conclusion, and Spanish conquests resumed in 1566.

Las Casas accepted the fact of human variety and declared that the truth of a religion should be demonstrated not by persecution of unbelievers but by their conversion. He himself converted thousands of Native Americans to Christianity and won for his converts protection from many abuses, though slavery and conquest continued largely unabated.

England will withdraw from the port of Boulogne earlier than agreed under the treaty of Ardres (see 7 June 1546) and will also abandon its gains in Scotland. This cessation of hostilities with England will allow Henry II of France to deploy his full military force against Holy Roman Emperor Charles V.

SCIENCE AND TECHNOLOGY

– Birth in Merchiston Castle, near Edinburgh, of John Napier, Scottish mathematician who will develop the theory of logarithms.

ARTS AND HUMANITIES

– Italian architect Andrea Palladio (Andrea di Pietro) begins work on the Villa Rotunda (Villa Capra), one of his finest buildings, in Vicenza, N Italy.

– The French poet Pierre de Ronsard publishes his *Odes*, Books I–IV; the second volume will appear in 1552.

Olaus Petri (Olaf Peterson), *Tobie Commedia*, the earliest Swedish drama.

Nicholas Udall, *Ralph Roister Doister*, the first English comic drama.

Giorgio Vasari, *Vite dei più eccellenti pittori, scultori e architetti* (Lives of the Most Excellent Painters, Sculptors and Architects); the earliest Italian art historical text, Vasari's *Lives* remains an important source.

1551

EUROPE

1 May The Council of Trent (see 1545) reopens in Trent, Tirol (Trento in N Italy); Protestant delegates are forbidden entry and the doctrine of transubstantiation is upheld.

17 Dec. Cardinal György Martinuzzi, *de facto* ruler of Transylvania, is assassinated by Giovanni Battista Castaldo, leader of the Habsburg forces in Transylvania; this occurs less than six months after Martinuzzi has signed a treaty

recognizing the rights of Archduke Ferdinand I of Austria to the Hungarian crown (19 July).

MIDDLE EAST AND NORTH AFRICA

14 Aug. Ottoman Turks capture the North African port of Tripoli (in modern Libya); Tripoli had been held by the Order of the Knights of St John (Knights Hospitallers), a Christian military order based in Malta (see 1530).

ECONOMY AND SOCIETY

– Taverns are licensed in England and Wales for the first time.

– Jesuit foundation of the Collegio Romano in Rome, Italy.

SCIENCE AND TECHNOLOGY

– Konrad von Gesner, Swiss scientist, publishes his *Historia Animalium* (History of Animals), which greatly advances the burgeoning study of zoology.

ARTS AND HUMANITIES

2 May Birth in London of William Camden, English historian and topographer.

– *Utopia*, written in 1516 by English scholar and statesman Thomas More (see 1535), is translated from Latin into English.

– Giovanni Pierluigi da Palestrina, Italian composer, is appointed musical director at St Peter's in Rome.

Titian, *St Jerome* and *Philip II of Spain*, paintings.

1552

EUROPE

15 Jan. The German Protestant princes and Henry II of France sign the treaty of Chambord: Henry II will receive three bishoprics in Lorraine (now a region in E France) in return for offering his financial support and military services to the Germans in support of their mutual conflict against Holy Roman Emperor Charles V. French forces will invade Lorraine on 13 Mar.

22 Jan. Execution of Edward Seymour, duke of Somerset (see 10 Oct. 1549), Lord Protector of England 1547–9, for treason.

4 April An army of German Protestants, led by Maurice, Elector of Saxony, and Albert Alcibiades II, margrave of Brandenburg, captures the prosperous Bavarian city of Augsburg.

10 April Henry II of France takes Metz in Lorraine; Protestant German forces under Maurice, Elector of Saxony, take Linz in Austria (18 April); the following day (19 April), Emperor Charles V escapes via the Brenner pass to Carinthia (in SE Austria).

April Ottoman forces under Ali Pasha, *beglerbeg* of Buda in Hungary, invade Transylvania and defeat the combined Hungarian and Habsburg armies at Szegedin in Hungary.

12 June Henry II of France retreats to Verdun, E of Metz, in Lorraine.

16 July–2 Aug. Negotiations are carried out between the Protestant Maurice, Elector of Saxony, and the Catholic Archduke Ferdinand I of Austria acting on behalf of the emperor. Lutherans are granted toleration within the Empire by the treaty of Passau (2 Aug.).

18 July Birth in Vienna of Rudolf II, future Holy Roman Emperor (1576–1612), son of Emperor Maximillian II and grandson of Emperor Ferdinand I of Austria, brother of Emperor Charles V.

ASIA

– Tsar Ivan IV (the Terrible) begins a Russian campaign against the Tatars and conquers Kazan and Astrakhan (in W Russia).

– In China the Jesuit missionary St Francis Xavier (see May 1542) dies of fever.

SCIENCE AND TECHNOLOGY

– Italian anatomist Bartolommeo Eustachio explains his discovery of the Eustachian tube and valve in his *Tabulae Anatomicae* (Anatomical Writings).

– English physician Dr John Caius publishes his analysis of the sweating sickness sweeping across England; it will become one of the earliest epidemiological studies.

ARTS AND HUMANITIES

14 Aug. Birth in Venice of Paolo Sarpi, Italian historian who was an early advocate of the separation of Church and state.

– In England, King Edward VI founds 35 grammar schools.
Pierre de Ronsard, second volume of *Odes* and first volume of *Amours*, poetry.

1553

EUROPE

1 Jan. Holy Roman Emperor Charles V retreats to Brussels (in modern Belgium); the Lorraine bishoprics of Metz, Toul and Verdun pass to the French crown.

Mar. In Germany Catholic and Protestant princes oppose the election of Philip of Spain, son of Emperor Charles V and the future King Philip II of Spain, as Holy Roman Emperor; they form the League of Heidelberg.

6 July In London King Edward VI of England dies of tuberculosis at the age of 16. The Protestant Lady Jane Grey, daughter of Henry, duke of Suffolk and granddaughter of Princess Mary, sister of King Henry VIII, is proclaimed queen of England by her father-in-law, John Dudley, the duke of Northumberland (10 July). The Catholic Princess Mary, the elder daughter of King Henry VIII and his first wife, Catherine of Aragon, and the heir apparent, gathers support for her claim to the throne.

14 July In England Lady Jane Grey is deposed; Princess Mary is proclaimed queen of England.

Aug. Under Queen Mary I of England, Roman Catholic bishops are restored to office.

14 Dec. Birth in Pau, Navarre, of Henry IV, who will be the first Bourbon king of France (r.1589–1610).

ASIA

– English explorers Hugh Willoughby and Richard Chancellor set out to discover a NE passage to China. Willoughby will die on the Kola peninsula in Russia; Chancellor reaches Archangel (modern Arkhangelsk) and travels S overland to Moscow.

ECONOMY AND SOCIETY

March In England the 42 Articles of the Church of England, stating the doctrinal principles of Anglicanism, are drawn up at a convocation of Anglican clergy.

– Spanish physician and theologian Michael Servetus denies the Trinity and the divinity of Jesus in his *Christianismi Restitutio* (The Restitution of Christianity). Jean Calvin, founder of Geneva's strict theocracy, has him burned at the stake for heresy (27 Oct.).

SCIENCE AND TECHNOLOGY

– Michael Servetus describes the pulmonary circulation of the blood.

ARTS AND HUMANITIES

9 April Death in Paris of François Rabelais, French poet and writer.

7 Oct. Birth in London of Edmund Spenser, English poet and author of *The Faerie Queene*.

16 Oct. Death of German painter Lucas Cranach the Elder.

14(?) Dec. Birth of Richard Hakluyt, English geographer.

– Paolo Veronese (Paolo Caliari), Italian Renaissance painter of the Venetian school, leaves Verona for Venice where he will remain until his death in 1588.

– A university is founded in Lima, Peru.

1554

EUROPE

25 Jan. In Rochester, Kent, Sir Thomas Wyatt organizes a rebellion against Queen Mary's proposed marriage to Philip of Spain, son of Emperor Charles V. Most factions of the rebellion are quickly crushed; to ensure that they pursue no further claims to the English throne, Lady Jane Grey, various of her relatives and others are beheaded in London (12 Feb.). Suspected of complicity in Wyatt's rebellion, Princess Elizabeth,

Queen Mary's half-sister and a Protestant with much popular support, is imprisoned in the Tower of London (18 Mar.).

25 July Queen Mary I of England marries Philip of Spain, heir to the Spanish throne.

Aug. Emperor Charles V allows his brother, Archduke Ferdinand I of Austria, king of Bohemia and Germany, to settle German religious divisions with a German diet (princely convention).

12 Nov. The English Parliament meets and re-establishes Catholicism in England.

THE AMERICAS

7 Oct. Birth in Hayes Barton, Devon, of Walter Ralegh, English explorer and adventurer.

- São Paulo, the first European settlement in inland Brazil, is founded by Portuguese Jesuits and their leader, Manoel de Nobrega.

ECONOMY AND SOCIETY

- The execution of Michael Servetus, Spanish theologian, in Geneva, Switzerland (see 1553) provokes Church reformer Sebastian Castellion (Sebastianus Castellio) to publish a tract entitled *De Hereticis* (Concerning Heretics) advocating religious toleration. Jean Calvin (see p. 213), French religious reformer, defends his decision to burn Servetus to death.

ARTS AND HUMANITIES

3 Oct. Birth in Beauchamp Court, Warwickshire, of English poet and author Fulke Greville, 1st Baron Brooke.

30 Nov. Birth in Penshurst, Kent, of Philip Sidney, English statesman and poet.

- Birth in Kent of John Lyly, English playwright and author.
Giovanni Palestrina, first book of masses, sacred vocal music.
Andrea Palladio (Andrea di Pietro), *L'Antichita di Roma* (The Antiquities of Rome), a guidebook to Roman antiquities that will remain the most important work on this subject until the late 18th century.

1555
EUROPE

9 April Following the death of Pope Julius III (23 Mar.), Marcello Cerveni, cardinal priest of Santa Croce and one of the co-presidents of the Council of Trent is elected pope; Pope Marcellus II will die in less than one month (1 May).

23 May Giampietro Carafa is elected Pope Paul IV.

25 Sept. The treaty of Augsburg allows Lutheran worship in German states (princedoms and free cities) where the rulers are Lutherans. Lutheran states will enjoy equal rights with Catholic ones; bishops and abbots who become Protestant, however, lose their positions. This 'ecclesiastical reservation' both maintains the Habsburg position and helps cause the Thirty Years War (1618–48). At the Diet of Augsburg Philip of Spain, son of Emperor Charles V, renounces his claim to the imperial crown in favour of his cousin Maximilian, son of Archduke Ferdinand I of Austria.

25 Oct. Emperor Charles V resigns the government of the Netherlands, Milan and Naples to his son Philip of Spain.

ASIA

- Humayun (see 1540) returns to India and reoccupies Delhi and Agra, but he will die within a year.

THE AMERICAS

- A French colony is established on the bay of Rio de Janeiro (modern Brazil).

ECONOMY AND SOCIETY

- The English Muscovy Company is established to trade with Russia.

ARTS AND HUMANITIES

- Zeno of Venice, Italian cartographer, publishes a map of the northern seas.
- Birth of Lancelot Andrewes, Anglican theologian, preacher and defender of the 'Catholic' nature of Anglican authority.
- Birth in Caen, Normandy, of François de Malherbe, French poet and literary critic.
Richard Eden, *Decades of the New World*, the first account in English of the discoveries in the New World.
Tintoretto, *St George and the Dragon*, painting.
Titian, *The Martyrdom of St Lawrence*, painting.

1556
EUROPE

16 Jan. Emperor Charles V resigns his rule over Spain to his son Philip, who will reign as Philip II of Spain; later this year (7 Sept.) Charles will resign the Holy Roman Empire to his brother, Archduke Ferdinand I of Austria, king of Bohemia and Germany. Pope Paul IV refuses to acknowledge Archduke Ferdinand as emperor and claims his own right to bestow the imperial title.

21 Mar. In Oxford, England, Thomas Cranmer, the first Protestant archbishop of Canterbury and influential adviser to King Henry VIII and King Edward VI, is burned at the stake as a heretic.

July Pope Paul IV persuades Henry II of France to resume the campaign against the Habsburgs in Italy by promising that Henry may place one of his sons on the throne of Naples.

17 Oct. Charles, former Holy Roman Emperor, leaves the Netherlands for Spain and withdraws to the monastery of San Yuste in Estremadura, Spain.

Dec. French forces under Francis, duke of Guise, invade Italy to secure the kingdom of Naples for the French crown.

ASIA

5 Nov. Akbar, Humayun's successor as Mughal emperor of India (see 1555), narrowly defeats the Afghans at Panipat, N of Delhi.

ECONOMY AND SOCIETY

31 July Death in Rome of Ignatius Loyola (see p. 212), founder of the Society of Jesus.

– The Jesuit mission is established in Prague in Bohemia (modern Czech Republic).

ARTS AND HUMANITIES

21 Oct. Death in Venice of the playwright Pietro Aretino, a major influence on the development of Italian prose.

Dec. Deaths of two important painters of the Italian Renaissance: Lorenzo Lotto, in Loreto, Italy, and Jacopo Pontormo, in Florence, Italy.

– Roland de Lassus, Franco-Flemish composer, becomes head choirmaster at the court of the duke of Bavaria in Munich, Germany.

1557

EUROPE

7 June England, now Spain's ally following the marriage between Queen Mary and Philip II of Spain, declares war on France.

11 July Death of John III, king of Portugal; his three-year-old grandson, Sebastian I, succeeds him.

10 Aug. The French are defeated by Spanish and English forces at St Quentin, France. Paris is now threatened; Francis, duke of Guise, and his troops are recalled from Italy to defend France.

Sept. With Rome under pressure from the advancing Spanish army, Pope Paul IV is forced into reconciliation with Philip II of Spain.

– Russians invade Livonia (S Estonia and N Latvia). Poland, Russia, Sweden and Denmark all claim the Baltic lands of the Order of Teutonic Knights (a German military order of Christian knights); the Swedes take Estonia, but the Russians are defeated and the Poles will rule Livonia until the Swedes occupy it in 1620.

ASIA

– Portuguese merchants settle permanently in Macao, S China.

ECONOMY AND SOCIETY

28 Feb. In London the first Anglo-Russian commercial treaty is signed.

– Pope Paul IV orders that the first *Index Librorum Prohibitorum* (Index of Prohibited Books) be undertaken; it is issued in 1559.

– Royal bankruptcies occur in Spain and France, partly because the American silver flooding into the European economy has encouraged them to run up huge debts to German, Dutch and Italian bankers.

SCIENCE AND TECHNOLOGY

– Welsh mathematician Robert Recorde publishes *The Whetstone of Wit*, the first work on algebra in English. He invents the equal sign and explains how to obtain square roots.

ARTS AND HUMANITIES

– The translation of Books 1 and 4 of Virgil's *Aeneid* by English poet and courtier Henry Howard, earl of Surrey (see 1547) is published posthumously; Howard is the first poet to use English blank verse (unrhymed iambic pentameters).

1558

EUROPE

7 Jan. The French, under Francis, duke of Guise, capture Calais from England. English disillusion with Queen Mary I's marriage to the Spanish King Philip II grows as the English forfeit their last holding on continental Europe.

14 Mar. Archduke Ferdinand I of Austria is elected Holy Roman Emperor; he will reign until 1564.

24 April Mary Queen of Scots marries the French dauphin (the future Francis II, see 10 July 1559).

21 Sept. Death of Charles V, former Holy Roman Emperor, in the monastery of San Yuste, Estremadura, Spain (see 17 Oct. 1556).

17 Nov. Death in London of Queen Mary I of England, daughter of King Henry VIII and his first wife, Catherine of Aragon; she is succeeded by her half-sister Elizabeth, daughter of Henry VIII and Anne Boleyn. On 20 Nov. Sir William Cecil is appointed principal secretary of state under Queen Elizabeth I; he will serve her in this capacity until his death in 1596.

ASIA

– Akbar, the Mughal emperor (see 1556), conquers Gwalior, Ajmer and Jaunpur in India.

SCIENCE AND TECHNOLOGY

– Jean Nicot, French ambassador to Spain, sends tobacco to Paris and the word 'nicotine' comes into use.

– The Portuguese introduce snuff to Europe.

ARTS AND HUMANITIES

21 Oct. Death in Agen, SW France, of Julius Caesar Scaliger, French physician and scholar.

John Knox, Scottish Protestant reformer, *First Blast of the Trumpet Against the Monstrous Regiment of Women*, pamphlet.

1559

EUROPE

1 Jan. Accession of Frederick II of Denmark and Norway on the death of his father, King Christian III of Denmark and Norway.

23 Jan. In England Parliament passes the Acts of Supremacy and Uniformity, legally underpinning Queen Elizabeth I's Protestant rule.

16 Feb. Pope Paul IV issues the papal bull *Cum Ex Apostolatus*: all heretical rulers are to be deposed. This justifies attempts by the Habsburgs and their supporters to threaten Protestant rulers.

2 April France, England and Spain sign the treaty of Cateau-Cambrésis: France is to return Calais to England in eight years if (Protestant) England shows no aggression towards (Catholic) Scotland; France restores Piedmont and Savoy to Duke Emmanuel Philibert of Savoy, governor of the Netherlands, while retaining the bishoprics of Metz, Toul and Verdun in Lorraine.

2 June Henry II of France issues the edict of Ecouen making printing without a licence a capital offence in France; this move is a further attempt to restrict French Protestants (Huguenots).

10 July Henry II of France dies in an accident during a tournament in Paris and is succeeded by his son, Francis II (during his brief reign he will be dominated by his mother, Catherine de Medici; see 1533); Francis, duke of Guise, and Charles, cardinal of Lorraine, convince their niece, the Catholic Mary Queen of Scots, wife of Francis II and great-granddaughter of Henry VII of England, to assume the title of queen of England.

Oct. Swedish forces take Estonia from Livonia (see 1557).

MIDDLE EAST AND NORTH AFRICA

May Selim, son of Suleiman I, the Ottoman sultan, defeats and murders his brother Bayazid in their fight over the succession to the sultanate.

ECONOMY AND SOCIETY

24 June In England the first Elizabethan Prayer Book is introduced.

ARTS AND HUMANITIES

Titian, *The Entombment of Christ* and *Diana and Calliste*, paintings.

1560

EUROPE

17 Mar. In France a Huguenot conspiracy is formed to rescue Francis II from the control of the Catholic Guise faction at the French court; in what becomes known as the Tumult of Amboise, the rebels attempt to storm the royal château at Amboise. They are defeated and summarily executed on the orders of Francis, 2nd duke of Guise. By April the religious dispute in France between Catholics and Protestants has reached such a pitch that armed conflict is rapidly becoming unavoidable.

April Francis II of France appoints Michel de L'Hôpital, constable of France, as chief minister. The edict of Romartin concedes that Protestant beliefs may not be treasonable and hints at an unofficial freedom of worship.

6 July The treaty of Edinburgh is signed by Scotland, England and France: both England and France agree to remove their armies from Scotland and to allow Scotland to run its own affairs. A Scottish Parliament is established in Edinburgh, and Mary Queen of Scots will abandon her claims to the English throne.

Aug. In Edinburgh the newly constituted Scottish Parliament establishes the Church of Scotland, which will adhere to Calvinism, and abolishes papal jurisdiction; Scottish Calvinist reformer John Knox is an important figure in the establishment of the new Church.

5 Dec. Francis II of France, son of Henry II of France and husband of Mary Queen of Scots, dies in Orléans in France; he is succeeded by his younger brother who will reign as Charles IX. Their mother, Catherine de Medici (see 10 July 1559), is named regent.

– Madrid is named capital of Spain.

ASIA

– Akbar, the Mughal emperor(see 1556), conquers the Rajput kingdoms of W India and Lower Bengal; a new capital is established at Agra.

ECONOMY AND SOCIETY

19 April Death of Philip Melanchthon, German humanist and Church reformer.

18 Oct. Birth in Oudewater, the Netherlands, of Jacobus Arminius (Jacob Harmensen), the Dutch theologian whose doctrine of Arminianism, countering the Calvinist doctrine of predestination, will be influential in 17th- and 18th-century England.

SCIENCE AND TECHNOLOGY

– Giambattista della Porta, Italian scientist, describes the camera obscura in his *Magica naturalis* (Natural Magic); della Porta also founds the first scientific society, the Academia Secretorum Natura, in Naples, Italy.

ARTS AND HUMANITIES

– Tintoretto (Jacopo Robusti), the Venetian painter, begins work on *The Descent from the Cross*.

– Italian architect Andrea Palladio (Andrea di Pietro) works on the refectory at San Giorgio Maggiore, Venice.

Pieter Bruegel the Elder, *Children's Games*, painting.

Pierre de Ronsard, *Les Discours* (The Discourses), a collection of poems about the religious wars in France.

Titian, *Venus with a Mirror*, painting.

Hsu Wei, *Jing P'Ing Mei* (The Plum in the Golden Vase), the first socially realistic Chinese novel.

1561

EUROPE

28 Jan. In France the persecution of Huguenots is suspended by the edict of Orléans.

28 Nov. The Order of the Teutonic Knights ceases to rule Livonia; in the union of Wilno (modern Vilnius) the last master of the Teutonic Knights, Gotthard Kettler, is made a secular duke and Livonia is ceded to Poland.

SCIENCE AND TECHNOLOGY

16 July German engineers start to mine for copper and lead in England.

– Gabriello Fallopio, Italian anatomist, publishes *Observationes Anatomicae* (Anatomical Observations), in which he describes for the first time the inner ear and the female reproductive system.

ARTS AND HUMANITIES

22 Jan. Birth in London of Sir Francis Bacon, philosopher and lord chancellor of England (1618–21).

May In London St Paul's Cathedral is damaged by fire.

– At Goa Portuguese monks introduce printing into India.

François Clouet, *Charles IX of France*, painting.

Julius Caesar Scaliger, *Poetices Libri Septem* (Seven Books of Poetry), a study of the literary theories of Aristotle.

1562

EUROPE

1 Mar. In France forces of Francis, 2nd duke of Guise (see 17 Mar. 1560), murder 1200 French Protestants in the massacre of Vassy, near Paris, and provoke the First War of Religion in France.

26 May Less than five months after swearing homage to Queen Elizabeth I of England (4 Jan.), Shane O'Neill, earl and captain of Tyrone, leads a war in Ireland against a rival clan, breaking the peace established under English rule.

20 Sept. Elizabeth I of England signs the treaty of Richmond with the Huguenot leader Louis de Bourbon, prince of Condé; English troops will occupy Le Havre (4 Oct.) and assist in the defence of Rouen and Dieppe.

22 Sept. Maximilian, son of Ferdinand I, succeeds his father as king of Bohemia; he is then elected king of Germany (20 Nov.).

19 Dec. In France Catholic forces under Francis, duke of Guise, narrowly defeat the Huguenots at the battle of Dreux, near Paris; the Protestant leader, Louis de Bourbon, prince of Condé, is captured. The Guise army marches towards Orléans.

THE AMERICAS

– A Huguenot colony is established at Charlesfort (modern Jacksonville, Florida, USA) by Frenchman Jean Ribault, who also claims Florida for France.

SUB-SAHARAN AFRICA

Oct. Sir John Hawkins, English seaman and slave trader, leaves Plymouth for Guinea in Africa where he begins a slave trade between Africa and the island of Hispaniola (modern Haiti and Dominican Republic).

ECONOMY AND SOCIETY

– In Spain the mystic Teresa of Avila founds an order of nuns.

ARTS AND HUMANITIES

12 Nov. Death in Zürich, Switzerland, of Peter Martyr Vermigli, Italian theologian and reformer.

1563

EUROPE

19 Mar. The treaty of Amboise ends the First War of Religion in France; Huguenots are allowed to worship in all those places where Protestantism was formerly established, except Paris.

May Ivan IV, grand prince of Moscow and tsar of Russia, conquers Polotsk in E Livonia from Poland.

27 July Uniting to expel the English, French troops regain Le Havre.

17 Aug. Charles IX of France, now 13 years old, is declared to be of age.

8 Sept. Maximilian II, king of Germany, is elected king of Hungary.

6 Dec. The Council of Trent ends (see 1545); the various sessions of the council have defined the doctrinal basis of the Counter-Reformation in the Catholic Church.

ECONOMY AND SOCIETY

– Plague in Europe spreads to England; 20,000 inhabitants of London will perish.

SCIENCE AND TECHNOLOGY

– Flemish cartographer Gerardus Mercator makes the first accurate survey and map of Lorraine.

ARTS AND HUMANITIES

– Ivan IV, tsar of Russia, orders the establishment of Russia's first printing press.

– Jesuits take over the administration of the university in Ingolstadt (S Germany); this marks the beginning of the Counter-Reformation in Bavaria.

– Spanish architects Juan de Herrera and Francisco Bautista begin work on the Escorial Palace, NW of Madrid, for Philip II of Spain.

– Birth in London of John Dowland, musician and composer.

John Foxe, *Actes and Monuments*, a lurid work of Protestant propaganda, describing persecutions under Queen Mary I. It becomes known as *Foxe's Book of Martyrs* and will exercise a considerable influence on English Protestantism.

Paolo Veronese (Paolo Caliari), *The Marriage of Cana*, painting.

1564

EUROPE

June Ivan IV, tsar of Russia, in the course of his struggle against the boyars (landowning nobles) has to withdraw from Moscow; he will return in 1565.

25 July On the death of Ferdinand I of Austria, his son Maximilian II succeeds as Holy Roman Emperor and as king in Austria, Bohemia and Hungary; other Habsburg lands pass to Emperor Ferdinand's younger sons, the archdukes Ferdinand and Charles.

18 Aug. Philip II of Spain orders the enforcement of the decrees of the Council of Trent (see 6 Dec. 1563) throughout his territories.

ECONOMY AND SOCIETY

25 May St Philip Neri (Filippo de' Neri), Florentine Church reformer, founds the Congregation of the Oratory in Rome.

27 May Death in Geneva, Switzerland, of Jean Calvin (see p. 213), French Protestant reformer.

SCIENCE AND TECHNOLOGY

15 Feb. Birth in Pisa, Italy, of Galileo Galilei (see p. 243), scientist, mathematician and astronomer.

ARTS AND HUMANITIES

6 Feb. Birth in Canterbury, Kent, of Christopher Marlowe, English dramatist and poet.

18 Feb. Death in Rome of Michelangelo Buonarroti (see p. 197), Florentine sculptor, painter and architect. His numerous unfinished works are sublime witnesses to the artist's search for perfection.

23 April Birth in Stratford-upon-Avon, Warwickshire, of William Shakespeare (see p. 236), English poet and dramatist.

– Italian artist Tintoretto starts work on his series of paintings for the Scuola di San Rocco in Venice.

– French architects Philibert de l'Orme and Jean Bullant begin work on the Palace of the Tuileries in Paris for Catherine de Medici (see 1533), the mother of the French kings Francis II, Charles IX and Henry III. The palace is built on the site of a tileworks (*tuilerie*).

1565

EUROPE

29 July In Edinburgh Mary Queen of Scots marries Henry Stuart, Lord Darnley. her second husband.

29 Sept. The Knights Hospitallers (Knights of St John) and Spanish troops led by García de Toledo, viceroy of Sicily, force the Ottomans to withdraw from Malta.

9 Dec. Pope Pius IV, Italian pope who oversaw the final session of the Council of Trent (see 1563), dies in Rome.

ECONOMY AND SOCIETY

– Sir John Hawkins, English navigator and slave trader, is the first Englishman to use tobacco.

SCIENCE AND TECHNOLOGY

– Pencils are made in England for the first time.

ARTS AND HUMANITIES

Thomas Norton and Thomas Sackville, Lord Buckhurst, *Gorboduc*, the earliest English tragedy in blank verse (see 1557).

Andrea Palladio, Church of San Giorgio Maggiore in Venice, architecture.

Pierre de Ronsard, *Elégies, mascarades et bergeries* (Elegies, Masquerades and Pastorals), poetry.

1566

EUROPE

7 Jan. Italian Dominican Michele (Antonio) Ghislieri is elected Pope Pius V.

9 Mar. David Rizzio, Italian secretary and adviser of Mary Queen of Scots, is assassinated in Mary's presence, on the orders of Mary's husband, Lord Darnley, in Holyrood House, Edinburgh.

5 April In the Netherlands the lesser nobility who oppose the imposition of strict Spanish Catholicism by its Habsburg rulers organize resistance and demand liberty of religious conscience and the withdrawal of the Spanish Inquisition. By late summer (10–8 Aug.) Protestant riots in the Netherlands will force the regent, Margaret of Parma, to acquiesce, and the Inquisition in the Netherlands will be disbanded.

19 June Birth in Edinburgh Castle of James VI, king of Scotland (later King James I of England), son of Mary Queen of Scots and her second husband, Lord Darnley; James's claim to the English throne is a strong one as both of his parents, as cousins

of Elizabeth I of England, are claimants to the English throne in their own right.

MIDDLE EAST AND NORTH AFRICA

5 Sept. Suleiman I (the Magnificent), Ottoman sultan, dies while on campaign in Hungary; he is succeeded by his son Selim II (the Drunkard). The increasingly powerful Janissaries, or Ottoman military and administrative elite, selected from Balkan Christian children, who were then raised as Muslims, become a hereditary caste.

ECONOMY AND SOCIETY

– English financier Thomas Gresham begins building work on what will become the Royal Exchange in London, England.

ARTS AND HUMANITIES

2 July Death in Salon, France, of Nostradamus (see 1503), French physician and astrologer.

1567

EUROPE

10 Feb. Henry Stuart Darnley, second husband of Mary Queen of Scots, is murdered (by means of an explosion) in Edinburgh.

15 May Mary Queen of Scots marries James Hepburn, earl of Bothwell, widely believed to have ordered the murder of Lord Darnley. Mary's and Bothwell's forces are defeated at Carberry Hill (June) by rebel nobles, and Mary is imprisoned on an island in Loch Leven.

24 July Mary Queen of Scots is forced to abdicate in favour of her infant son James. Mary's half-brother, James Stuart, earl of Moray, becomes regent.

8 Aug. Fernando, duke of Alva, arrives in the Netherlands as military governor with 10,000 Spanish and Italian troops. Alva establishes autocratic rule, underpinned by the Council of Troubles, popularly known as the Council of Blood (22 Aug.), and sets out to eradicate Protestantism in the Netherlands.

29 Sept. The Second War of Religion in France opens with the Protestant Conspiracy of Meaux, the aim of which is to capture Charles IX of France. The Huguenots fail to take the king or his mother, Catherine de Medici, who flee from Meaux to Paris; the Protestant leader Louis de Bourbon, prince of Condé, lays siege to the French capital.

6 Oct. With Margaret of Parma's resignation of the regency (see 5 April 1566), Ferdinand, duke of Alva, is in complete control of the Netherlands; Margaret will leave the Netherlands on 30 Dec.

Nov. A Protestant international force emerges as John Casimir of the Palatinate leads an army of German supporters to fight for the French Huguenots.

ECONOMY AND SOCIETY

21 Aug. Birth in Thoren-Glière, Savoy (modern France), of St Francis of Sales, Roman Catholic spiritual writer, director of souls and anti-Calvinist.

ARTS AND HUMANITIES

12 Feb. Birth in London of Thomas Campion, English writer, physician and Catholic martyr.

May Birth in Cremona of Claudio Monteverdi, Italian composer who will be a major influence on the development of opera.

Nov. Birth in London of Richard Burbage, English actor who was the first to play many of the most memorable roles in the plays of William Shakespeare (see p. 236).

1568

EUROPE

23 Mar. In France the treaty of Longjumeau ends the Second War of Religion. The rights accorded to the Huguenots in the treaty of Amboise (see 19 Mar. 1563) are confirmed.

2 May Mary Queen of Scots, having escaped from prison (see 15 May 1567), is defeated at Langside by rebel lords under Regent Moray (see 24 July 1567). Mary flees to England (16 May), where she will be imprisoned.

23 May The Eighty Years War between Spain and the Low Countries begins (it is popularly known as the Dutch Revolt). Count Louis of Nassau takes command of an army of Dutch rebels and German mercenaries; the Spanish, led by Count Aremberg, are defeated at Heiligerlee near Groningen in the Netherlands. Fernando, duke of Alva and governor of the Netherlands under the Habsburgs (see 8 Aug. 1567), confiscates the properties of William the Silent and other nobles who oppose Spanish rule (28 May).

23 July Don Carlos, prince of Asturias and, as the only son of Philip II, heir to the throne of Spain, dies in prison in Madrid. The feeble-minded Don Carlos was suspected of having plotted to kill his father.

30 Sept. Eric XIV of Sweden, declared insane by the army and nobility, is deposed, and his half-brother John III, duke of Finland, is proclaimed king of Sweden.

5 Oct. William the Silent, prince of Orange, leads an army into Brabant in the Spanish Netherlands; his troops include Dutch rebels, German mercenaries and sympathetic Huguenots. In Nov., however, he withdraws when the Spanish, under Ferdinand, duke of Alva, decline battle.

3 Dec. Spanish treasure ships with pay for Habsburg troops in the Netherlands are driven into Plymouth in S England by bad weather; Elizabeth I of England impounds the ships and commercial relations between England and Spain are suspended until 1574.

25 Dec. The Moriscos (Moors who have agreed to convert to Christianity) revolt in Spain; they desecrate churches in Granada.

ASIA

28 Dec. In Japan military leader Oda Nobunaga deposes the shogun (military ruler) in Kyoto and appoints Ashikaga Yoshiaki in his place. Oda Nobunaga gains new centralizing powers to quell rebellions.

ECONOMY AND SOCIETY

– English Catholic priest (later cardinal) William Allen establishes the English College at Douai in Picardy, NE France, to train Jesuit priests for the English mission.

1569

EUROPE

13 Mar. Henry, duke of Anjou, and his army of French Catholics and royalists defeat Huguenot forces at Jarnac; the leader of the French Protestants, Louis de Bourbon, prince of Condé, is killed. The Huguenots subsequently meet at Cognac in France to elect Henry de Bourbon, duke of Vendôme, as their leader and Admiral Gaspard de Coligny as their military commander (May).

Mar. Don John of Austria, half-brother of Philip II of Spain, is sent to quell the rebellion of the Moriscos in Granada.

1 July Under the Union of Lublin, Lithuania is united with Poland under the sovereignty of Sigismund II Augustus of Poland; there is to be a single state with a unified diet.

9 Nov. In England Thomas Percy, earl of Northumberland, and Charles Neville, earl of Westmorland, both Catholics, rebel against the Protestant regime and attempt to place the Catholic Mary Queen of Scots on the English throne; the Northern Earls, as they are known, meet with little success and by Dec. the rebellion is over.

SCIENCE AND TECHNOLOGY

– Tycho Brahe (see 1546), Danish astronomer, constructs a quadrant and a celestial globe at Augsburg in Bavaria.

– Flemish cartographer Gerardus Mercator produces a map of the world for navigational purposes.

1570

EUROPE

25 Feb. Pope Pius V issues the bull *Regnans in Excelsis*, excommunicating the Protestant Elizabeth I of England and declaring that her subjects owe her no allegiance; the bull provokes widespread anti-Catholicism in England.

14 April Under the Consensus of Sandomierz (in Poland), Lutherans, Calvinists and Moravians in Poland agree to unite against Catholic attempts to stamp out religious toleration and to hold joint synods as members of the Protestant communion.

April Birth in York, N England, of Guy Fawkes, later a conspirator in the Gunpowder Plot to blow up the English Parliament (see 1605).

8 Aug. The Third War of Religion in France ends with the signing of the treaty of St Germain-en-Laye. Huguenot gains include liberty of conscience, an amnesty and the towns of La Rochelle, Montauban, Cognac and La Charité as safe havens; the Huguenot military leader Admiral Gaspard de Coligny is now dominant at the French court.

13 Dec. Denmark recognizes the independence of Sweden by the treaty of Stettin, and Sweden abandons its claim to Norway.

ASIA

– The Japanese open the port of Nagasaki to overseas trade.

SCIENCE AND TECHNOLOGY

– The potato is introduced to Europe from S America.
– Abraham Ortelius of Antwerp, Flemish cartographer, publishes *Theatrum orbis terrarum* (Theatre of the Lands of the World), the first modern atlas.

ARTS AND HUMANITIES

Nicholas Hilliard, *Queen Elizabeth I of England*, painting.
Andrea Palladio, *Quattro libri dell'architettura* (Four Books on Architecture), an outline of his architectural principles.

1571

EUROPE

2 April–29 May In this session of the English Parliament an Act is passed that declares it treasonable to bring a papal bull into England; subscription to the 39 Articles of the Church of England, based on the 42 Articles of 1553, is enforced by statute on the clergy. Intolerance of Roman Catholicism has now been formally endorsed by the English government.

1 Aug. Ottoman forces take the port of Famagusta in Cyprus from the Venetians.

7 Oct. Don John of Austria, half-brother of King Philip II of Spain, leads naval forces from Spain, Venice and the Papal States to a decisive victory over the Turkish fleet at Lepanto off the island of Corfu (modern Greece). The Spanish writer Cervantes (see p. 241) loses his left hand in the battle.

SCIENCE AND TECHNOLOGY

27 Dec. Birth in Weil der Stadt, S Germany, of Johannes Kepler, German astronomer.

ARTS AND HUMANITIES

13 Feb. Death of Benvenuto Cellini, Florentine Mannerist sculptor and goldsmith.
– Birth of Italian painter Caravaggio (Michelangelo Merisi) in N Italy.

1572

EUROPE

1 April Dutch privateers (known as Sea Beggars) capture Brill in Holland; this small port becomes the first stronghold of the Dutch rebels in their struggle against the Spanish Habsburgs for independence.

1 May Pope Pius V dies in Rome; the Bolognese Ugo Boncampagni is elected his successor as Pope Gregory XIII (14 May).

2 June In England Thomas Howard, duke of Norfolk, is executed for his role in the papacy-backed Ridolfi plot (1571) to replace Elizabeth I with the Catholic Mary Queen of Scots.

June A new Ottoman fleet sets sail in a renewed effort to capture Cyprus from the Venetians.

7 July The Estates of Poland declare the monarchy to be elective

on the death of Sigismund II Augustus, last of the Jagiellon dynasty (6 July). Henry, duke of Anjou and heir to the French throne, is duly elected king of Poland (May 1573).

11 July English volunteers under the navigator Sir Humphrey Gilbert arrive in the Netherlands to fight the Spanish.

22–25 Aug. A plot hatched by the French queen mother, Catherine de Medici, and Henry, duke of Guise, to murder the Huguenot leader Admiral Gaspard de Coligny (see 8 Aug. 1570) fails. Catherine de Medici orders the liquidation of all leading Huguenots. In the ensuing Massacre of St Bartholomew's Day, Coligny and 3000 of his supporters are murdered in Paris; the mayhem spreads to the provinces, leading to the Fourth War of Religion in France. Those of moderate political opinion (the *politiques*) join the Huguenot camp.

– John the Terrible, *voivode* (military viceroy) of Moldavia, leads a campaign against the Ottomans who control his princedom; he is killed and his territory laid waste.

ARTS AND HUMANITIES

Jan. Birth in London of John Donne, English metaphysical poet.
11 June Birth in London of Ben Jonson, English dramatist.
– William Byrd, English composer, joins his fellow composer Thomas Tallis as organist of the Chapel Royal, the chapel of the English royal court.

1573

EUROPE

23 Feb. Sir John Perrot, English lord deputy of Ireland, defeats Irish rebels against the English crown.

7 Mar. The treaty of Constantinople ends the war between the Ottoman empire and Venice. Venice cedes Cyprus to the Ottomans and increases its annual tribute.

6 July The peace of Boulogne ends the Fourth War of Religion in France; the Huguenots are granted an amnesty but can only worship freely in the French cities of La Rochelle, Nîmes, Sancerre and Montauban.

7 Oct. Birth in Reading, Berkshire, of William Laud, a future anti-Puritan archbishop of Canterbury.

18 Dec. Fernando, duke of Alva, having failed to make headway against the Dutch rebels, asks to be relieved of his command and leaves Brussels (in modern Belgium); he is replaced as governor of the Netherlands by Don Luis de Requesens.

ECONOMY AND SOCIETY

– French jurist François Hotman publishes *Franco-Gallia*, in which he argues that kings can be deposed and should be elected.

ARTS AND HUMANITIES

– The Inquisition condemns the Italian painter Paolo Veronese (Paolo Caliari) for introducing 'vulgar' secular elements into his painting of the Last Supper. Veronese refuses to alter his composition, agreeing only to change the title of the work to *The Feast in the House of Levi*.

1574

EUROPE

23 Feb. The Fifth War of Religion breaks out in France.

30 May Death of Charles IX of France; his brother Henry, king of Poland and duke of Anjou, succeeds him as Henry III. Henry leaves Poland for France (18 June); the Polish Assembly subsequently deposes Henry from the Polish throne. On his way to France, Henry meets Emperor Maximilian II in Vienna; Maximilian urges a policy of religious toleration.

MIDDLE EAST AND NORTH AFRICA

July Ottoman forces take Tunis in N Africa from the Spanish; Tunis becomes an Ottoman vassal state with an elected governor.

SCIENCE AND TECHNOLOGY

– Jacob Verzellini, a Venetian living in London, uses soda ash extracted from seaweed instead of potash in glass manufacture; using this new ingredient, he is able to make clear crystal glass.

ARTS AND HUMANITIES

27 June Death of Giorgio Vasari, Florentine painter and art historian.

Tintoretto, *Paradise*, painting.

1575

EUROPE

8–15 Mar. Session of the English Parliament in the course of which English Puritans promote a more radical English reformation; Peter Wentworth, a Puritan member of Parliament, is imprisoned (12 Mar.) for attacking the queen's interference with parliamentary freedom of speech.

Mar. Elizabeth I of England agrees to prevent Dutch rebels from using English ports and English volunteers from serving under William the Silent, prince of Orange and leader of the Dutch independence movement. In return, Don Luis de Requesens (see 18 Dec. 1573), governor of the Netherlands, banishes all English political refugees from the Low Countries and allows English merchants to trade with Antwerp.

1 Sept. Philip II of Spain suspends all payments by the Spanish crown: Don Luis de Requesens is unable to pay his troops in the Netherlands.

15 Sept. In Germany John Casimir, son of the Elector Palatine, signs a treaty with the French Huguenots enabling a Calvinist army of 16,000 German and Swiss mercenaries to enter France; after some initial setbacks, the combined armies, led by John Casimir and Henry I de Bourbon, prince of Condé, begin their march across France.

17 Oct. King Rudolf of Hungary, son of Emperor Maximillian II, is elected king of Germany.

14 Nov. Elizabeth I of England refuses the offer of the sovereignty of the Netherlands made by the Protestant Dutch stadtholder, William the Silent, prince of Orange.

14 Dec. Stephen Báthory, prince of Transylvania, is elected king of Poland to replace the deposed king, now Henry III of France (see 30 May 1574).

ASIA

3 Mar. The Mughal emperor Akbar defeats the forces of Da'ud Khan, the Afghan ruler of Bengal, and conquers Bengal in E India.

SCIENCE AND TECHNOLOGY

– The first European imitation of Chinese porcelain is made in Florence in Italy.

ARTS AND HUMANITIES

17 May Matthew Parker, archbishop of Canterbury, dies in Lambeth, London, and leaves his collection of manuscripts to Corpus Christi College, Cambridge.

– English composers William Byrd and Thomas Tallis dedicate their *Cantiones Sacrae*, a selection of motets, to Queen Elizabeth I of England. The two composers are jointly granted a patent for the sole right to print music in England.

1576

EUROPE

Jan. The Huguenot and Calvinist armies, under Henry I de Bourbon, prince of Condé, and John Casimir of the Palatinate, march towards Vichy in France.

6 May France's Fifth War of Religion ends in a Huguenot advance: Protestants gain freedom of worship in all places except Paris and garrison eight strongholds. The terms of the peace of Monsieur provoke Henry of Lorraine, duke of Guise, to form an anti-Huguenot Catholic League.

12 Oct. Accession of Rudolf II, king of Hungary and Germany, as Holy Roman Emperor on the death of his father, Emperor Maximillian II. Under Emperor Rudolph's influence, particularly his patronage of the Jesuit Order, the Counter-Reformation develops rapidly in Austria.

4 Nov. The Spanish army mutinies and sacks Antwerp in the Netherlands. The Pacification of Ghent (8 Nov.) unites the 17 provinces of the Netherlands. The Dutch demand religious toleration, a representative assembly and the withdrawal of Spanish troops; the treaty is ratified by the States-General at Antwerp.

ECONOMY AND SOCIETY

– Jean Bodin, French political writer, publishes *Six livres de la république* (The Six Books of the Republic) in which he proposes a limited monarchy with property rights.

ARTS AND HUMANITIES

27 Aug. Death in Venice, Italy, of Titian (Tiziano Vecelli), Italian painter of the Venetian school.

– Warsaw University is founded in Poland.

– James Burbage, English theatre manager, builds a playhouse in Shoreditch, London.

Andrea Palladio, Church of Il Redentore in Venice.

Tomás Luis de Victoria, first book of canticles and masses, sacred vocal music.

1577

EUROPE

3 Jan. Henry III of France reneges on the peace of Monsieur; the Sixth War of Religion begins in France (Mar.) The treaty of Bergerac (17 Sept.) limits the concessions previously awarded to the Huguenots and allows freedom of worship only in those towns actually held by the French Protestants; this treaty ends the Sixth War of Religion.

12 Feb. Don John of Austria, the new Habsburg governor of the Netherlands, issues the Perpetual Edict. All Spanish troops are to leave within 20 days; all ancient liberties are to be restored to Dutch towns; the Dutch states are to pay the troops in the Netherlands the wages owed them. William the Silent, prince of Orange, refuses the terms.

23 Sept. William the Silent enters Brussels; the States-General depose Don John of Austria and, in defiance of the wishes of the Habsburg supporters, appoint William the Silent in his place (22 Oct.). Archduke Matthias, brother of Emperor Rudolph II, is appointed as the rival Habsburg governor of the Netherlands.

15 Nov. English adventurer Francis Drake leaves on his voyage around the world; he intends to attack Spanish colonies and shipping.

ARTS AND HUMANITIES

29 June Birth of Peter Paul Rubens, Flemish painter, in Siegen, Westphalia (in modern Germany).

– By this date the artist El Greco has settled in Toledo, C Spain.

1578

EUROPE

June The Swedish army defeats the Russians in the battle of Wenden in the Livonian War.

4 Aug. Sebastian I, king of Portugal, invades Morocco in N Africa and is defeated and killed at Alcázarquivir; his uncle, Cardinal Henry, becomes King Henry II of Portugal.

1 Oct. Don John of Austria, Habsburg governor of the Netherlands, dies from a fever in Bouges, near Namur (in modern Belgium); Alessandro Farnese, duke of Parma and nephew of Philip II of Spain, becomes governor of the Netherlands.

– John III of Sweden secretly converts to Catholicism; he quickly reconverts to Lutheranism.

ASIA

– Mohammed Khudabanda succeeds Ismail II as shah of Persia.

– Otomo Yoshishige, Japanese noble, converts to Christianity.

SCIENCE AND TECHNOLOGY

1 April Birth in Folkestone, Kent, of William Harvey, English anatomist who will study the circulatory system.

ARTS AND HUMANITIES

31 May Discovery of the Early Christian catacombs (underground tombs) in Rome.

John Lyly, *Euphues, or the Anatomy of Wit*, literary theory in which he establishes an elaborate literary style.

Pierre de Ronsard, *Sonnetes pour Hélène* (Sonnets for Hélène), poetry.

1579

EUROPE

25 Jan. The Netherlands divide; the Union of Utrecht is signed by the seven N provinces of the Netherlands, Holland, Zeeland, Utrecht, Gelderland, Friesland, Groningen and Overijssel, founding the Dutch Republic. By the Union of Arras (17 May) the S provinces of Maas and Lek are incorporated into the Spanish Habsburg empire.

ASIA

– Father Thomas Stephens, the first Englishman to live in India, settles in Goa.

THE AMERICAS

17 June Francis Drake, English explorer and adventurer, asserts English sovereignty over New Albion (modern California, USA).

ECONOMY AND SOCIETY

21 Nov. Death in London of Sir Thomas Gresham, English economist and founder of the Royal Exchange.

– The English College is founded in Rome, Italy, as a seminary for the training of English and Welsh priests.

ARTS AND HUMANITIES

St John of the Cross (Juan de la Cruz of Fontiveros), *The Dark Night of the Soul*, a classic of Spanish mysticism.

Andrea Palladio, the Olympian Theatre in Vicenza, N Italy, architecture.

Edmund Spenser, *The Shepheardes Calendar*, poetry.

1580

EUROPE

31 Jan. On the death of Henry II of Portugal, Philip II of Spain, one of several claimants to the Portuguese throne, recalls Fernando, duke of Alva, from the Netherlands to command an invasion of Portugal.

21 March Philip II of Spain and Murad III, the Ottoman sultan, agree to end their conflict over Mediterranean territories; each power will retain what territory it now holds.

April The Seventh War of Religion breaks out in France. Fighting is inconclusive; it is concluded with the treaty of Fleix (26 Nov.) which renews the treaty of Bergerac (see 1577).

7 July English Jesuits Robert Parsons and Edmund Campion land in England to begin the Jesuit mission for the reconversion of England to Roman Catholicism.

25 Aug. Spanish forces defeat the Portuguese at Alcántara and occupy Lisbon. Later this year (Oct.), Porto will also fall. The Spanish conquest of Portugal doubles Spain's overseas empire.

Sept. Italian and Spanish soldiers land in Ireland to aid Irish Catholic rebels in their fight against the Protestant English regime; this combined force is massacred by an army of English soldiers and Irish loyalists.

30 Nov. Francis Drake, English explorer and adventurer, returns to England.

ECONOMY AND SOCIETY

June England signs a commercial treaty with the Ottoman empire, securing trading rights similar to those already held by Venice and France.

– Robert Browne, English Protestant reformer, establishes the first congregation of Independents (Congregationalists) in Norwich, Norfolk.

ARTS AND HUMANITIES

10 June Death in Lisbon of Luis Vaz de Camões, Portuguese national poet.

Aug. Birth of John Webster, English playwright.

Aug. Death in Vicenza of Andrea Palladio (Andrea di Pietro), Italian architect of the Venetian school.

Jean Bodin, *De la démonomanie des sorciers* (On the Fiendishness of Sorcerers), tract against witchcraft.

Michel de Montaigne, *Essais* (Essays), an early example of the form, it is influential in the development of the essay as a literary genre.

Torquato Tasso, *Aminta*, pastoral drama.

1581

EUROPE

May Stephen I Báthory, king of Poland, invades Russia as part of the ongoing Livonian war (see 1557).

17 July Arrest, in Lyford, Berkshire, of the English Jesuit missionary Edmund Campion for treason; he is subsequently executed (1 Dec.).

26 July In the Netherlands, the publication of the Act of Abjuration, by which the N provinces of the Netherlands (see 25 Jan. 1579) renounce allegiance to Philip II of Spain.

ASIA

Aug. The Mughal emperor Akbar conquers Kabul, the capital of modern Afghanistan.

1 Sept. The Russian conquest of Siberia begins.

ECONOMY AND SOCIETY

24 April Birth in Pouy (modern St-Vincent-de-Paul), France, of St Vincent de Paul, French founder of the Congregation of the Mission.

SCIENCE AND TECHNOLOGY

– Italian scientist Galileo Galilei (see p. 243) discovers the principle of the pendulum.

– Robert Norman, English scientist, publishes his study of magnetism, *The Newe Attractive*.

ARTS AND HUMANITIES

Francisco Sanchez de las Brozas, *Quod Nihil Scitur* (What Cannot be Known), philosophy.

Torquato Tasso, *Gerusalemme Liberata* (Jerusalem Liberated), epic poetry.

1582

EUROPE

15 Jan. Peace is agreed between Ivan IV (the Terrible), tsar of Russia, and Stephen I Báthory, king of Poland, in the truce of Yam-Zapolski: Russia abandons Livonia and Estonia to Poland, thereby losing access to the Baltic Sea; Poland will withdraw from Velikiye Luki in Russia.

11 Dec. Death in Lisbon, Portugal, of Fernando Alvarez de Toledo, duke of Alva, Spanish military leader.

ASIA

21 June Oda Nobunaga, ruler of Japan, is killed by Akechi Mitsuhide at Kyoto; Akechi Mitsuhide is subsequently defeated and killed by the military leader Toyotomi Hideyoshi at Yamazaki (30 June).

ECONOMY AND SOCIETY

4 Oct. Death in Alba de Tormes, Spain, of St Teresa of Avila, Spanish Catholic nun and mystic (see 1562).

4 Oct. The Gregorian Calendar (named after Pope Gregory XIII), which advances the date by ten days and affirms 1 Jan. as the first day of the year, is adopted throughout Catholic Europe over the next 18 months. It is first introduced in the Papal States, Portugal and Spain; France adopts it on 10 Dec. and the Spanish Netherlands, Denmark and Norway follow (15 Dec.). Protestant countries continue to use the old dating system, the Julian calendar, until early in the 18th century.

ARTS AND HUMANITIES

28 Sept. Death of George Buchanan, Scottish humanist, whose Latin history of Scotland, *Rerum Scoticarum Historiae* (Histories of Scottish Matters), is published posthumously.

– Foundation of the University of Edinburgh in Scotland.

1583

EUROPE

15 Jan. Forces loyal to Francis, duke of Anjou, sack Antwerp as part of 'the French Fury', a frenzied attempt to assert power in the Spanish Netherlands; they fail to occupy Antwerp or Bruges.

Dec. In England Francis Throckmorton's plot for an invasion of England by forces under Henry, duke of Guise, to place the Catholic Mary Queen of Scots on the English throne is discovered by Francis Walsingham, English secretary of state and spymaster to Elizabeth I.

– Birth of John Pym, English parliamentarian.

ECONOMY AND SOCIETY

18 June In London William Gibbons becomes the first known person to take out a life insurance policy.

ARTS AND HUMANITIES

3 Mar. Birth in Eyton-on-Severn, Shropshire, of Edward, 1st Baron Herbert of Cherbury, English scholar, poet, courtier and soldier.

10 April Birth in Delft, in the Netherlands, of Hugo Grotius (see p. 251), Dutch juridical scholar.

25 Dec. Birth in Oxford of Orlando Gibbons, English composer.

Joseph Justus Scaliger, *Opus de Emendatione Temporum* (Work on the Correction of Time), history in which he provides a new chronology for the events of the ancient world.

1584

EUROPE

18 Mar. Death in Moscow of Ivan IV (the Terrible), tsar of Russia; he is succeeded by his son Fyodor I, last of the Rurik dynasty. Fyodor, weak in mind and unable to rule on his own, is dominated by Boris Godunov, brother of Fyodor's wife Irene.

17 June The Gregorian Calendar is adopted in the Catholic states of the Holy Roman Empire and the Catholic cantons of Switzerland.

10 July In England the Catholic plotter Francis Throckmorton (see Dec. 1583) is executed.

10 July William the Silent, prince of Orange, Calvinist leader of the movement for Dutch independence, is assassinated in his house in Delft by Balthazar Gérard, agent of Philip II of Spain; William's son, Maurice, prince of Nassau, succeeds his father as stadtholder of Holland and Zeeland.

23 Nov. The English Parliament meets and passes legislation to expel all Jesuits and seminary priests from England within 40 days.

ECONOMY AND SOCIETY

4 Nov. Death in Milan of St Carlo Borromeo, Italian cardinal and archbishop of Milan, whose reforming style has greatly influenced the spread of the Catholic Counter-Reformation.

ARTS AND HUMANITIES

– Sir Walter Mildmay establishes Emmanuel College, Cambridge, as a Puritan centre.

– The first book to be printed in Peru, a Roman Catholic catechism by Spanish missionary José de Acosta, is published in the Quichua language.

Giordano Bruno, *La Cena de le Ceneri* (The Ash Wednesday Supper), philosophy.

1585

EUROPE

7 July Henry III of France, lacking an obvious heir, signs the treaty of Nemours, yielding to the Catholic supporters of

The times we live in engender nothing but monsters.

Nicholas de Neufville, seigneur de Villeroy, reflects on French, and European, religious and civil wars, Feb. 1584

Henry, duke of Guise and revoking all toleration for the Huguenots; the so-called War of the Three Henries (Henry III of France, the Protestant Henry, king of Navarre, and the Catholic Henry, duke of Guise) for the French succession ensues.

7 Aug. Alessandro Farnese, duke of Parma and Habsburg governor of the Netherlands, sacks Antwerp in Flanders; exorbitant payments demanded by the victors result in Antwerp's decline as the centre of an international money market.

20 Aug. The treaty of Nonsuch, signed by England and the United Netherlands, pledges English troops to support the Dutch in their fight against the Catholic Habsburgs; England receives some Dutch territory as security. Robert Dudley, earl of Leicester and favourite of Elizabeth I, queen of England, arrives in the Netherlands to take command of the English troops (Dec.).

9 Sept. Birth in Richelieu, Poitou, of Cardinal Armand-Jean du Plessis, duc de Richelieu and chief minister of state under Louis XIII of France.

ASIA

– Akbar, the Mughal emperor, annexes modern Afghanistan.

THE AMERICAS

7 July An English expedition, funded by English explorer and courtier Sir Walter Ralegh and under the command of Richard Grenville and Ralph Lane, lands at Roanoke (in modern North Carolina, USA), with plans to establish an English colony there; conditions prove hard and the enterprise is abandoned. A second attempt, under Captain John White, will be made in 1587.

ECONOMY AND SOCIETY

28 Oct. Birth of Cornelius Jansen, Dutch Roman Catholic theologian, in Acquoi, near Leerdam in the Netherlands.

ARTS AND HUMANITIES

23 Nov. Death in Greenwich of Thomas Tallis, English composer and a master of counterpoint, best known for his 40-part motet *Spem in alium*.

27 Dec. Death of Pierre de Ronsard, French poet, in Saint-Cosme, near Tours in France.

Miguel de Cervantes (see p. 241), *Galatea*, pastoral romance.

1586-8

1586

EUROPE

4 Feb. Robert Dudley, earl of Leicester, accepts the title of governor and captain-general of the Netherlands; Elizabeth I of England forces him to resign the honour.

17 July Sir Francis Walsingham, secretary of state under Elizabeth I of England, uncovers the Babington plot to murder the queen. Anthony Babington and his co-conspirators are executed (20 Sept.). Mary Queen of Scots (see 2 May 1568), Catholic cousin of Elizabeth I, is implicated; she is tried for treason and sentenced to death (11 Oct.).

21 July English navigator Thomas Cavendish leaves Plymouth on his West-to-East voyage of global circumnavigation.

17 Oct. In the Netherlands the English courtier, poet and soldier Sir Philip Sidney dies after being fatally wounded in battle at Zutphen. He is mourned as a Protestant hero.

Nov. Establishment in Paris of a revolutionary Catholic government, the Council of the Sixteen; the new government will support the Catholic League, led by Henry, duke of Guise, in their fight against the Huguenots.

12 Dec. Death of Stephen I Báthory, king of Poland; his nephew, Sigismund III Vasa, is elected to succeed him.

ARTS AND HUMANITIES

– The Jesuit system of education is formulated in *Ratio atque Institutio Studiorum* (The Conduct and Institution of Studies) by Italian theologian Claudius Aquaviva.

William Camden, *Britannia*, the earliest topographical survey of England.

El Greco, *The Burial of Count Orgaz*, painting.

1587

EUROPE

8 Feb. Mary Queen of Scots, cousin of Elizabeth I of England and Catholic claimant to the English throne, is executed for treason in Fotheringhay Castle, near Northampton, England.

18 April John Foxe, English Puritan leader and martyrologist (see 1563), dies in London, England.

19 April Sir Francis Drake, English adventurer and navigator, sacks Cadiz in Spain and harasses Spanish ships along the Atlantic coast of Spain; Philip II of Spain is forced to postpone sending an Armada to England for another year.

Aug. Pope Sixtus V proclaims a Catholic crusade, the aim of which is the invasion of England and the deposition of the Protestant Elizabeth I of England.

ECONOMY AND SOCIETY

– Portuguese missionaries are banished from Spain.

SCIENCE AND TECHNOLOGY

– Italian architect and engineer, Antonio da Ponte, begins the construction of the Rialto Bridge over the Grand Canal in Venice.

1588

EUROPE

4 April Death of Frederick II of Denmark and Norway; he is succeeded by his son, Christian IV.

9 May Henry, duke of Guise, leader of the Catholic League, enters Paris and on the Day of the Barricades (12 May) establishes control of the city; King Henry III flees to Chartres (13 May).

11 July Henry III of France agrees to the demands of the duke of Guise. He summons the States-General to Blois where it is decreed that there will be no further toleration of the Huguenots within France and that the claims of the Protestant heir to the French throne, Henry of Navarre, will be set aside in favour of the Catholic Cardinal Charles de Bourbon. Guise becomes lieutenant-general of France.

21 July After the Spanish Armada is sighted off the coast of Cornwall, the English army, under Robert Dudley, earl of Leicester, is summoned to Tilbury, Essex.

29 July The Spanish Armada is defeated by the English fleet at the battle of Gravelines off the French coast. The Spaniards return to Spain by sailing N of Scotland, many ships being wrecked by storms.

16 Oct. Meeting at Blois, the States-General of France suggests the surrender of the French crown to the duke of Guise.

23 Dec. Henry, duke of Guise, is assassinated on the orders of Henry III, king of France; the duke's brother, Cardinal Louis, is assassinated the following day (24 Dec.). Charles, duke of Mayenne, brother of the two dead men, becomes the new leader of the Catholic League.

– Two tracts defending Presbyterianism and defaming English bishops are published in defiance of a Star Chamber decree; though the tracts are published under the name of Martin Marprelate, John Penry, who is suspected of their authorship, is arrested and is executed in 1593.

MIDDLE EAST AND NORTH AFRICA

Oct. Abbas I becomes shah of Persia.

SCIENCE AND TECHNOLOGY

– Thomas Hariott, English scientist, publishes his *Briefe and True Report of the New Found Land of Virginia*, in which he recommends tobacco for its supposed medicinal properties.

– Dr Timothy Bright, English physician, explains the principles of shorthand in *Characterie: The Arte of Shorte, Swifte and Secrete Writing*.

ARTS AND HUMANITIES

5 April Birth in Malmesbury, Wiltshire, of Thomas Hobbes (see p. 264), English political philosopher.

19 April Death in Venice of Paolo Veronese (Paolo Caliari), Italian painter of the Venetian school.

– Bishop William Morgan, Welsh scholar, translates the Bible into Welsh; his *Y Beibl Cyssegr-lan* (The Sacred Bible) lays the linguistic foundations of modern Welsh.

Cesare Baronius, *Annales Ecclesiastici a Christo nato ad annum 1198* (Ecclesiastical Annals from the Birth of Christ to the Year 1198), the first part of a history of the Catholic Church; this compilation is designed to refute a similar work, Protestant-inspired, entitled *The Magdeburg Centuries*.

Nicholas Hilliard, *Man Clasping a Hand* and *A Youth Leaning against a Tree among Roses*, paintings.

Michel de Montaigne, third volume of *Essais* (Essays).

1589

EUROPE

13 April From Plymouth, English naval commanders Sir Francis Drake and Sir John Norryes set sail with 150 ships and 18,000 men on their invasion of Portugal; having destroyed the Spanish port of La Coruña, they are repulsed at Lisbon, and the expedition ends in failure.

2 Aug. Henry III of France, the last of the Valois kings, is assassinated at Saint-Cloud, Paris. On his deathbed, Henry recognizes the Protestant Henry of Navarre as his successor as Henry IV, first of the Bourbon kings; Henry of Navarre establishes his headquarters at Tours (5 Aug.).

ECONOMY AND SOCIETY

– The metropolitan patriarch of Moscow claims his independence from the patriarchate of Constantinople; this marks the separation of the Russian and Greek Orthodox Churches.

ARTS AND HUMANITIES

William Byrd, *Songes of sundrie natures*, a collection of secular songs.

Richard Hakluyt, *The Principall Navigations, Traffiques and Discoveries of the English Nation*, geography.

1590

EUROPE

6 April Death in London of Sir Francis Walsingham, principal secretary to Elizabeth I of England.

14 May Henry IV of France defeats the army of the Catholic League at Ivry and marches on Paris.

5 Dec. Following the death in Rome of Pope Sixtus V (27 Aug.) and the very brief reign of Urban VII (15–27 Sept.), Cardinal Niccolò Sfondrati is elected as Pope Gregory XIV.

ASIA

– Shah Abbas I of Persia makes peace with the Ottomans; he is now free to begin his campaign against the Uzbeks who, under their leader Abdullah II, have advanced into Khorasan (in modern NE Iran and S Turkmenistan).

– Akbar, the Mughal emperor, conquers Orissa on the E coast of modern India.

SUB-SAHARAN AFRICA

– Ahmad al-Mansur, sultan of Morocco, annexes Timbuctu (in modern Mali) and the Upper Niger from the Songhai empire.

ARTS AND HUMANITIES

Giovanni de Bologna (Jean de Boulogne), *Mercury*, sculpture.

Nicholas Hilliard, *The Third Earl of Cumberland, Queen's Champion*, painting.

Isaac Oliver, *A Man Aged 27* and *A Girl Aged Five Holding a Red Carnation*, paintings.

Sir Philip Sidney, *Arcadia*, romance, published posthumously (see 17 Oct. 1586).

Edmund Spenser, the first three books of *The Faerie Queene*, poetry.

1591

EUROPE

15 May Dmitri, son of Ivan IV (the Terrible) of Russia and brother and heir of Tsar Fyodor I, is murdered, possibly by agents of Boris Godunov (see 1584); a false Dmitri will appear in Poland as a claimant to the throne in 1601.

Aug. Robert Devereux, earl of Essex, arrives in France with an English army to support the Protestant Henry IV of France, who is laying siege to Rouen.

Aug. The Spanish capture the English galleon *Revenge* off the Azores after an epic defence; Sir Richard Grenville, captain of the *Revenge*, is wounded in action and dies (31 Aug.).

21 Sept. French bishops meeting at Rouen accept the Protestant Henry IV as king of France, despite his excommunication by Pope Gregory XIV (1 Mar.).

25 Sept. The eight-year-old Christian II becomes Elector of Saxony on the death of his father, Christian I; his guardians, John George, Elector of Brandenburg, and the duke of Saxe-Weimar, crush Calvinism in the area and Saxony returns to Lutheranism.

29 Oct. Following the death of Pope Gregory XIV (16 Oct.), Cardinal Giovanni Antonio Fachinetti is elected to succeed him as Innocent IX; after only two months in office, Innocent IX dies (30 Dec.).

Oct. Philip II of Spain sends a Castilian army to Aragon to suppress popular support for Antonio Pérez, his former private secretary; Philip gains control of the law courts in the region.

ASIA

10 April James Lancaster, English merchant and seaman, leaves Plymouth on his first voyage to the East Indies.

ARTS AND HUMANITIES

8 Feb. Birth in Cento, outside of Ferrara, of Guercino (Giovanni Francesco Barbieri), Italian painter.

– Elizabeth I of England founds Trinity College in Dublin, Ireland.

Sir John Harington, English translation of *Orlando Furioso* by the Italian poet Ludovico Ariosto.

William Shakespeare (see p. 236), *King Richard III*, play.

Sir Philip Sidney, *Astrophel and Stella*, poetry, published posthumously (see 17 Oct. 1586).

COLONIAL COLLISIONS:
The European Push into Asia, the Americas and Africa

From the late 15th century onwards Europeans invaded, plundered, traded with and finally came to rule large areas of Asia, Africa and the Americas. Up until this time Europe had been mostly marginal to world history, but Europeans had an abundance of confidence – a belief in the superiority of their religion and culture that would enable a small portion of the western Eurasian landmass to impose its will on most of the rest of the world.

In 1453 Europe had suffered a major loss with the conquest by the Ottoman Turks of the ancient Christian city of Constantinople (modern Istanbul). But by the close of the 16th century, Europe saw the rest of the world not as a threat but as an opportunity. Commerce was the predominant cause for this shift in perspective. Initially, the sailors and explorers of Europe were principally traders rather than settlers: their numbers were small and they looked primarily for opportunities to make money by doing business in these distant lands.

In order to justify the conquest of cities and domination of kingdoms in the wider world, Europeans argued the superiority of Christian kingship and of Christian civilization to non-Christian societies and superstitions. But to begin with there was no consistent imperial ideology to justify the colonialist enterprise, and no sustained effort was made to emphasize ethical or religious improvements that might be imposed on other societies by Christian expansion. This would come later, in the 19th century, as administrators replaced traders and tried to bring rational bureaucratic order to institutions and systems that had grown haphazardly.

The European colonizers of the early modern period were divided along religious and national lines. The pioneering trade networks of the Portuguese and Spaniards were soon competing with Dutch, English and French rivals. These countries fought each other overseas as they did at home. From the 1590s the Dutch waged a steady and successful campaign against the Portuguese in Southeast Asia. In North America, however, the Dutch were no match for the French and English. The opening up of new trade routes to Asia and the Americas saw the rise of the Atlantic economy at the expense of the Mediterranean. The Italian banking system gave way to that of northern Europe, which had more sophisticated and more flexible credit mechanisms. The availability of credit enabled the seamen and merchant adventurers of Britain, the Netherlands, France and elsewhere to mount the expeditions that developed new Atlantic-based trade routes. The Mediterranean maritime powers simply could not compete.

Superior military technology and organization eased the Europeans' path to conquest. They may have been few in number, but their weapons were often superior – particularly their cannon-armed sailing ships, which few other powers could match. Sometimes, too, they were moving into a power vacuum. For example, in the 15th century China was forced to confront a growing challenge from the nomadic warriors of the northern steppes. As a consequence, it was losing interest in Southeast Asia and the Indian Ocean – regions which therefore became open to European exploitation. Elsewhere, highly centralized empires proved vulnerable to a targeted attack: the Incas of South America, for example, had an administration that insisted on all decisions being taken at the centre. When the Spanish adventurer Francisco Pizarro took the emperor Atahualpa prisoner, the Inca empire collapsed from the centre outwards.

In many cases European intervention worked to the advantage of some local powers at the expense of others – and intervention was therefore encouraged by those who benefited. The Portuguese trading settlements on the west coast of Africa weakened the Malian kingdom of Songhai, which had been the principal trading centre for the caravan routes across the Sahara. Consequently, Morocco and the neighbouring Hausa states attacked Songhai and established their dominance in the region.

There was no consistent imperial ideology to justify the colonialist enterprise.

Colonial expansion brought about not only the exchange of goods, but also the exchange of diseases. Europeans took smallpox and other infections to the Americas, killing up to half of some local populations, who had no immunity. Conversely, syphilis was taken back to Europe by returning voyagers. Once the initial pestilential exchanges were completed, both colonizer and colonized enjoyed steady rises in population. In most areas, however, it was the Europeans who had the technology and capital to exploit the local resources, while the indigenous peoples lacked both – and were often culturally averse to joining a European civilization that was coming to dominate the world. As the potential of these new lands became apparent, more and more Europeans emigrated to take advantage of the possibilities.

1592

EUROPE

15 Jan. Elizabeth I of England recalls Robert Devereux, earl of Essex, from his command in Rouen, France (see 1591).

30 Jan. Ippolito Aldobrandini is elected to succeed Pope Innocent IX; he will reign as Pope Clement VIII.

June Holy Roman Emperor Rudolf II makes peace with Poland by recognizing Sigismund III Vasa as king of Poland.

28 Aug. Birth in Brooksby, Leicestershire, of George Villiers, duke of Buckingham and favoured adviser of James I and Charles I of England.

3 Dec. Death in Arras in the Spanish Netherlands, of Alessandro Farnese, duke of Parma and Habsburg governor of the Netherlands.

– Fearing a Huguenot rebellion in the region, Henry IV of France annexes Périgord, C France.

– Plague breaks out in London, England.

ASIA

June Sir James Lancaster, English merchant and seaman, rounds the Malay peninsula.

– Toyotomi Hideyoshi, shogun of Japan, plans an invasion of China; Choson (modern Korea) refuses to allow the passage of Japanese troops and is consequently invaded.

SUB-SAHARAN AFRICA

– Portuguese settlers arrive in Mombasa (in modern Kenya).

SCIENCE AND TECHNOLOGY

22 Jan. Birth in Champtercier, Provence, of Pierre Gassendi, French scientist and philosopher.

– Italian scientist Galileo Galilei (see p. 243) analyses falling bodies and the raising of weights in his *Della scienza mechanica* (On the Science of Mechanics).

ARTS AND HUMANITIES

– The Vulgate translation of the Bible into Latin is issued with the approval of Pope Clement VIII.

– The ruins of the Roman city of Pompeii are discovered.

Tintoretto, *The Last Supper*, painting.

1593

EUROPE

March Sigismund III Vasa, king of Poland, tries to restore Roman Catholicism in Sweden and is successfully opposed by the Lutherans in a convention at Uppsala.

13 April Birth in London of Thomas Wentworth, earl of Strafford and adviser to Charles I of England.

29 May John Penry, Welsh Protestant and suspected author of the Martin Marprelate tracts (see 1588), is executed in England for denying the Royal Supremacy.

25 July Henry IV of France, formerly a staunch Protestant, becomes a Roman Catholic, thereby gaining the support of French Catholic nobles previously opposed to him.

SCIENCE AND TECHNOLOGY

– Italian scientist Giambattista della Porta publishes *De Refractione, Optices Parte* (On Refraction, the Division of Light) in which he describes binocular vision.

ARTS AND HUMANITIES

3 April Birth in Montgomery Castle, Wales, of George Herbert, a metaphysical poet.

30 May Death in a brawl in Deptford, near London, of English dramatist Christopher Marlowe.

9 Aug. Birth in Stafford of Izaak Walton, English author of *The Compleat Angler*.

– In London theatres are closed for most of 1593 because of an outbreak of the plague; they will reopen in May 1594.

William Shakespeare (see p. 236), *Venus and Adonis*, poem.

1594

EUROPE

27 Feb. Coronation of King Henry IV of France at Chartres in France.

22 Mar. Henry IV of France enters Paris. Gradually all of France will accept Henry's authority to rule; the Catholic League collapses. By the edict of St Germain-en-Laye, Henry grants freedom of worship to the Huguenots.

May Holy Roman Emperor Rudolf II meets the diet at Regensburg (in modern Germany); with the help of the Catholic German nobles, Rudolf secures finance for his war with the Ottomans in Hungary.

Aug. In W Ulster in Ireland, Hugh O'Neill, earl of Tyrone, allies himself with Hugh Roe O'Donnell, earl of Tyrconnell and lord of Fermanagh, in an uprising against the Protestant Elizabeth I of England; they appeal to the Catholic Philip II of Spain for aid.

9 Dec. Birth in Stockholm of Gustavus II Adolphus (Gustav Adolph), who will be king of Sweden (1611–32).

– Ottoman forces seize Raab (modern Györ, Hungary) from the Habsburgs.

ASIA

– The Mughal Emperor Akbar seizes Kandahar (in modern Afghanistan) from the Safavids of Persia.

ECONOMY AND SOCIETY

16 Oct. Death in Rome of William Allen, English Roman Catholic cardinal who oversaw the Douai–Reims translation of the Bible into English.

– Richard Hooker, English theologian, publishes the first four volumes of his *Of the Laws of Ecclesiastical Polity*, the first systematic defence of the historical and theological principles of the Elizabethan Church.

– The closure of the Lisbon spice market to Dutch and English merchants results in further Far Eastern voyages by these countries to break the Portuguese monopoly over the enormously lucrative spice trade.

ARTS AND HUMANITIES

2 Feb. Death in Rome of Giovanni Pierluigi da Palestrina, Italian composer of sacred polyphony.

31 May Death in Venice of Tintoretto (Jacopo Robusti), Italian painter.

14 June Death in Munich, Bavaria, of Roland de Lassus, Franco-Flemish composer.

June Birth in Villers, near Paris, of Nicolas Poussin, French painter.

– *Titus Andronicus* and *Romeo and Juliet*, plays by English dramatist William Shakespeare (see box), are first performed in London.

Christopher Marlowe, *Edward II*, play, published posthumously.

Thomas Morley, *Madrigals*, collection of songs for four voices.

1595

EUROPE

17 Jan. Philip II of Spain offers support to a Spanish claimant to the French throne; Henry IV of France declares war on Spain.

April Philip II of Spain promises aid for the Irish Catholic rebellion against the Protestant Elizabeth I of England (see 1594).

28 Aug. The English adventurers Francis Drake and John Hawkins leave Plymouth, Devon, on their last voyage to the Spanish Main. Their attempted raids on Spanish territories in the New World will end in failure; within six months a fever kills both Hawkins (12 Nov.) and Drake (28 Jan. 1596).

28 Oct. Sigismund Báthory, prince of Transylvania, and Michael the Brave, prince of Wallachia, defeat the Ottomans at Giurgiu (in modern Romania); Wallachia is no longer under Ottoman control.

THE AMERICAS

– Searching for the fabled city of El Dorado, the English explorer Sir Walter Ralegh travels 480km (300 miles) up the Orinoco River (in modern Venezuela).

ECONOMY AND SOCIETY

26 May Death in Rome of St Philip Neri, Italian priest and mystic.

ARTS AND HUMANITIES

2 Feb. Execution by hanging, in London, of Robert Southwell, Jesuit poet and English Catholic martyr.

25 April Death in Rome of Torquato Tasso, Italian poet.

Sir Philip Sidney, *The Defence of Poesie*, literary criticism, published posthumously.

Edmund Spenser, *Epithalamion*, an ode on marriage.

1596

EUROPE

24 Mar. Jean-Louis de Nogaret de La Valette, duke of Epernon, recognizes Henry IV as the legitimate king of France; Brittany and Savoy offer the only remaining opposition to the sovereignty of Henry.

30 June–4 July Lord Howard of Effingham and Robert Devereux, earl of Essex, lead an English expedition that sacks Cádiz in S Spain and attacks settlements along the Spanish coast.

23–26 Oct. Ottoman forces led by Sultan Mehmed III defeat Habsburg imperial forces at Hachova (modern Mezökeresztes, NE Hungary).

ECONOMY AND SOCIETY

– Threatened by bankruptcy, Spain is forced to devalue its currency.

ARTS AND HUMANITIES

Jan. Birth in Dinton, Wiltshire, of Henry Lawes, English composer.

31 Mar. Birth in La Haye, Touraine, of René Descartes (see p. 256), French philosopher and mathematician.

– Gresham College, endowed by the estate of English financier Thomas Gresham (d. 1579) is founded in London, England;

William Shakespeare (1564–1616)

Acclaimed by many as the greatest writer in the English language, Shakespeare was born in Stratford-upon-Avon, Warwickshire, and educated at the local grammar school. He became first an actor and then a prolific playwright, who ran his own theatre company in London before retiring to Warwickshire to live the life of a country gentleman.

Many of Shakespeare's 37 plays were published in his lifetime, but quite a number had to wait for the First Folio edition, published seven years after his death.

Shakespeare started as a writer mostly of history plays, drawing his inspiration from chronicles of the recent English past. He was an adroit judge of public taste and of the requirements of patronage: early works, such as *Richard III* were effective propaganda for the then reigning Tudor dynasty. Part of his subsequent appeal has been based on the English nationalism to which he gave a literary voice, but many of his works, notably the great tragedies such as *Hamlet* and *King Lear*, know no national boundaries. Shakespeare became a hero and source of

inspiration for later Romantic artists throughout Europe, including poets and composers, who saw in his heroes a quality of brooding and questioning introspection.

Linguistically, Shakespeare brought to the English language an eclecticism and variety never since equalled. He borrowed from books of proverbs and translations of foreign literature, but he also coined words and phrases with extraordinary fertility – coinages such as 'foul play', 'cold comfort' and 'thin air' with which our everyday speech is still littered.

a curriculum based on the seven liberal arts is offered to students.
- Blackfriars Theatre opens in London.

Edmund Spenser, *The Faerie Queene*, Books 4 and 5, poetry.

1597

EUROPE

25 Sept. In Brittany, NW France, Philippe-Emmanuel, duke of Mercoeur, recognizes the authority of Henry IV of France.

Nov. Because his army in the Spanish Netherlands is unable to defeat the combined forces of France and the United Provinces, Philip II of Spain opens peace negotiations with Henry IV of France.

- In England Parliament passes an Act permitting the exiling of convicted criminals to English colonies overseas as punishment.

ASIA

19 Mar. The Japanese resume their campaign in Choson (modern Korea).

- The Safavid Persian army defeats the Uzbeks, thereby preventing further Uzbek invasions of Khorasan (modern NE Iran and S Turkmenistan).

ARTS AND HUMANITIES

- *Henry IV*, Parts I and II, and *King John*, history plays by William Shakespeare, are performed for the first time in London.

Caravaggio (Michelangelo Merisi), *St Matthew*, painting.

John Dowland, *Book of Songs and Ayres*, music.

El Greco, *St Martin and the Beggar* and *The Resurrection of Christ*, paintings.

1598

EUROPE

7 Jan. Fyodor I, tsar of Russia, dies; Russian noble Boris Godunov, brother-in-law of Fyodor I, seizes the Russian throne. Six weeks later he is elected tsar of Russia by a national assembly (27 Feb.).

9 Feb. Elizabeth I of England dissolves Parliament; she has promised to reform monopolies and an Act has been passed to punish vagabonds and establish workhouses.

13 April In France the Edict of Nantes grants Huguenots freedom of worship where this has been exercised in the past two years; Huguenots are granted the same political rights as Catholics but are required to dissolve their provincial assemblies and reject alliances with foreign powers. The edict effectively ends the wars of religion in France.

May Philip II of Spain assigns the Spanish Netherlands to Archduke Albert of Austria and his daughter, the Infanta Isabella, who agree to marry; if they produce no heirs, the Spanish Netherlands will revert to the Spanish crown.

5 Aug. Death in London of William Cecil, Lord Burghley, chief adviser to Elizabeth I of England.

12 Aug. Pope Clement VIII seizes the duchy of Ferrara from Cesare d'Este, natural son of Alfonso II d'Este, duke of Ferrara (d. 27 Oct. 1597).

14 Aug. In Ireland the Catholic rebel Hugh O'Neill, earl of Tyrone, and his forces destroy an English army at Yellow Ford on the Blackwater River in Ulster.

13 Sept. Death of Philip II of Spain and Portugal in El Escorial, Spain; he is succeeded by his son, Philip III. The government is dominated by Francisco Gómez de Sandoval y Rojas, duke of Lerma and a favourite of the new king.

25 Sept. Duke Charles, regent of Sweden, defeats Sigismund III Vasa of Poland (Sigismund I of Sweden) at Stångebro, Sweden.

ASIA

- After the death, in Fushimi, of Japanese feudal ruler Toyotomi Hideyoshi, Tokugawa Ieyasu restores the shogunate in Japan.

SUB-SAHARAN AFRICA

- The Dutch found their first colony on the island of Mauritius in the Indian Ocean; they also send traders to settle in Guinea in W Africa.

SCIENCE AND TECHNOLOGY

- Tycho Brahe, Danish astronomer, describes his discoveries and instruments in *Astronomiae Instauratae Mechanica* (The Mechanics of a Restored Astronomy).

ARTS AND HUMANITIES

Jan. Birth in Paris of François Mansart, French baroque architect.

- Henry IV of France reforms the University of Paris; the new curriculum emphasizes the study of classics, the Bible and the natural sciences.

- In England the library at Oxford University is refounded by Sir Thomas Bodley.

- The poem *Hero and Leander*, left unfinished at his death by English dramatist Christopher Marlowe, is completed by English poet and translator George Chapman and published.

- Birth in Naples of Gianlorenzo Bernini, leading architect and sculptor of the Italian baroque school.

George Chapman, English translation of Homer's *Iliad*.

El Greco, *Cardinal Don Fernando Niño de Guevara* and *View of Toledo*, paintings.

Ben Jonson, *Every Man in his Humour*, comedy.

1599

EUROPE

27 Mar. In the hope that he will crush the Irish Catholic rebellions, Elizabeth I of England appoints Robert Devereux, earl of Essex, to the lord lieutenancy of Ireland.

25 April Birth in Huntingdon of Oliver Cromwell, leader of the parliamentary forces during the English Civil Wars (1642–51) and Lord Protector of England, Scotland and Ireland (1653–8).

July Spain's final attempt at an Armada against England is scattered by storms and ends in failure.

8 Sept. Robert Devereux, earl of Essex and lord lieutenant of Ireland, signs a truce with Irish rebel Hugh O'Neill, earl of Tyrone. Disobeying instructions from Elizabeth I of England, he leaves Ireland; he is arrested on his return to court (28 Sept.).

Oct. Michael the Brave, prince of Wallachia, deposes Andrew Báthory, the new prince of Transylvania, in Moldavia; Prince Michael assumes the Báthory titles.

Nov. Peace negotiations open in the Spanish Netherlands between Spain and the United Provinces of the Netherlands and between Spain and England; none of the parties can agree on terms, and the attempts to settle the various disputes are abandoned.

– In France Maximilien de Béthune, marquis de Rosny and the future duke of Sully, is appointed superintendent of finance; he reforms taxation, reduces the *taille*, encourages agriculture and industry, and begins the reform of the French road system.

ASIA

June Akbar, the Mughal emperor, personally leads a campaign of conquest in S India.

ARTS AND HUMANITIES

13 Jan. Death in London of Edmund Spenser, English poet and author of *The Faerie Queene.*

22 Mar. Birth in Antwerp (in modern Belgium) of Anthony Van Dyck, court painter to Charles I of England (see 1625).

6 June Birth in Seville of Diego y Velázquez, leading Spanish painter of the 17th century.

– *As You Like It, Julius Caesar, Much Ado about Nothing* and *King Henry V*, plays by William Shakespeare (see p. 236), are first performed in London.

– The Globe Theatre is built at Bankside in Southwark, London.

Juan de Mariana, *De Rege et Regis Institutione* (On the King and the Institution of Kingship), political theory in which he concludes that it is permissible to kill a tyrant.

Nicholas Hilliard, *Portrait of a Young Man*, painting.

1600

EUROPE

Jan. In Ireland the truce agreed in Sept. 1599 by Robert Devereux, earl of Essex, breaks down; Irish rebel Hugh O'Neill, earl of Tyrone, resumes hostilities against the English and invades Munster.

Feb. In the intermittent war between Poland and Sweden (see 1598), Duke Charles of Södermanland (later King Charles IX of Sweden) executes as traitors the main supporters of the pro-Polish party, led by his nephew King Sigismund III Vasa of Poland (Sigismund I of Sweden).

May Failure of the peace negotiations between England and Spain over the United Provinces of the Netherlands (see Nov. 1599).

5 Oct. Henry IV of France marries Marie de Medici.

ASIA

20 Oct. In Japan Tokugawa Ieyasu, leader of the ruling regency council, defeats his opponents of the Western Army at the battle of Sekigahara. Tokugawa hegemony is established and will endure until 1867.

31 Dec. Foundation by George Clifford, earl of Cumberland, of the English East India Company, whose organization numbers 216 merchants.

ECONOMY AND SOCIETY

2 Nov. Death in Kent, England, of Richard Hooker, Anglican theologian.

19 Nov. Birth of Charles I, king of England, Scotland and Ireland (r.1625–49), in Dunfermline Palace, Fife, Scotland. The sickly Charles is not heir presumptive as he has an older brother, Henry, who will die (1612) before he can inherit.

SCIENCE AND TECHNOLOGY

17 Feb. In Venice Giordano Bruno, the Italian philosopher, astronomer and mathematician, is burned at the stake for heresy.

ARTS AND HUMANITIES

– Birth of Claude de Lorraine, real name Claude Gellée, French painter of idealized landscapes.

Caravaggio, *Doubting Thomas, The Supper at Emmaus* and *The Crucifixion of Saint Peter*, paintings.

Ben Jonson, *Every Man out of His Humour*, play, an attack on the English dramatist Thomas Dekker.

William Shakespeare, *The Merchant of Venice* and *A Midsummer Night's Dream*, plays.

1601

EUROPE

7–8 Jan. Robert Devereux, the disgraced earl of Essex (see Sept. 1599), attempts a rebellion against Queen Elizabeth I's ministers in London; his attempt is crushed. Essex is executed for treason (25 Feb.).

15 July Archduke Albert of Austria, at the head of the Spanish Habsburg army of Flanders, begins the siege of the Dutch Republican enclave of Ostend, Flanders.

27 Sept. The future King Louis XIII (r.1610–43), is born at Fontainebleau, N France.

Sept. A Spanish expeditionary force lands at Kinsale, Co. Cork, Ireland, to assist the Irish rebels (see 1600).

27 Oct.–19 Dec. In England Elizabeth I's last Parliament meets and she again promises to reform monopolies. Her Golden Speech to Parliament (20 Nov.) gives an account of her reign.

24 Dec. English crown forces rout the Irish rebels at the battle of Kinsale.

– Polish acting commander-in-chief in Lithuania Jan Carol Chodkiewicz expels Swedish armies under Duke Charles of Södermanland (later King Charles IX of Sweden) from Riga, Livonia (now Latvia), then takes the city of Dorpat (now Tartu), Estonia.

– The False Dmitri, Grigory, a monk claiming to be the son of the former Russian tsar Ivan IV, appears in Moscow (see 1591); he is banished to Lithuania by Tsar Boris Godunov.

ASIA

1 Nov. In Japan Tokugawa Ieyasu, leader of the ruling regency council, takes Osaka Castle on the island of Honshu and makes Yedo (now Tokyo) his capital. He undertakes the redistribution of fiefs to prevent other *daimyo* (warlords) from threatening his hegemony.

– In N India the Mughal emperor, Akbar, annexes Khandesh.

SCIENCE AND TECHNOLOGY

24 Oct. Death in Prague, Bohemia, of Tycho Brahe, Danish astronomer (see 1546).

ARTS AND HUMANITIES

– William Shakespeare's *The Merry Wives of Windsor* (comedy, published 1602) and *Hamlet, Prince of Denmark* (tragedy, published 1603) are first performed in London.

Caravaggio, *Conversion of St Paul*, painting.

Pierre Charron, *De la sagesse*, philosophy; in it, Charron develops a system of stoic philosophy that requires no theological justification.

Bento Teixeira Pinto, *Prosopopeya*, poetry; the first Brazilian epic.

Lope de Vega, *El castigo del discreto* (The Wise Man's Punishment), comedy.

1602

EUROPE

2 Jan. The Spanish troops who landed in Ireland in Sept. 1601 are permitted to leave by English crown forces.

April Vigorous and successful Counter-Reformation policies are implemented in Austria, in the regions of Styria, Carinthia and Carniola. Holy Roman Emperor and king of Bohemia, Rudolf II, persecutes Protestants in Bohemia and Hungary.

– Birth in Pescina, Italy, of Giulio Raimondo Mazzarini, who, as Jules Mazarin, will succeed Richelieu as chief minister of France in 1642.

MIDDLE EAST AND NORTH AFRICA

– Persia and Turkey go to war.

ASIA

20 Mar. The United East India Company (i.e., the Dutch East India Company) is chartered by the States-General of Holland and has a trade monopoly between the Cape of Good Hope and the Straits of Magellan.

– Spanish traders arrive in E Japan.

SCIENCE AND TECHNOLOGY

– Tycho Brahe *Astronomiae Instauratae Progymnasmata* (Instruments for the Restored Astronomy), published posthumously, gives the plans of 777 fixed stars.

ARTS AND HUMANITIES

– The Bodleian Library opens in Oxford, England.
– Birth of the English composer William Lawes.
– William Shakespeare's *Troilus and Cressida* (published in 1609)

and *Twelfth Night, or What You Will* (published in 1623) are first performed in London.

Lope de Vega, *The Beauty of Angelica*, play, a sequel to Ariosto's *Orlando Furioso*.

1603

EUROPE

24 Mar. In England Elizabeth I dies and is succeeded by James VI of Scotland (son of Mary Queen of Scots) as James I of England and Ireland (crowned 25 July). James is the first Stuart king of England.

30 Mar. In Ireland the rebel earl of Tyrone is offered a pardon by the English crown; he submits to the English lord deputy of Ireland, Lord Mountjoy, at Mellifort: a general amnesty is pronounced.

17 July English seaman Sir Walter Ralegh is arrested on grounds of complicity in a plot for the dethronement of James I. He is found guilty of high treason (12 Nov.) but his death sentence is later commuted to imprisonment.

Sept. King Henry IV recalls the Jesuits to France.

Oct. An uprising breaks out in Transylvania against Emperor Rudolf II.

MIDDLE EAST AND NORTH AFRICA

22 Dec. Ahmed I succeeds his father, Mehmed III, as sultan of the Ottoman empire.

ASIA

– In Japan Tokugawa Ieyasu's dictatorship is confirmed when the emperor appoints him Edo Bakufu (military ruler).

ARTS AND HUMANITIES

– John Florio, an English lexicographer, translates Michel de Montaigne's *Essais* from French into English.
– Death of Pierre Charron, French philosopher.

Johannes Althusius, *Politica Methodice Digesta et Exemplis Sacris et Profani* (A Digest of Political Method), political theory advocating republican government, which influences much subsequent political thought, including that of John Locke (see 1632).

1604

EUROPE

19 Mar. The English Parliament convenes and initially opposes a proposal from James I for a union with Scotland (see 24 Mar, 1603).

No bishop, no king.

James I and VI, king of England and Scotland, speaking to Scottish Presbyterians in 1604

20 Mar. The Lutheran Duke Charles of Södermanland assumes the title of King Charles IX of Sweden.

Oct. The False Dmitri, claimant to the Russian throne, leads his army towards Moscow; he is defeated by Tsar Boris Godunov.

– Polish forces, under the acting commander-in-chief of Lithuania Jan Carol Chodkiewicz (see 1601), defeat Swedish forces in Estonia near Weissenstein.

MIDDLE EAST AND NORTH AFRICA

– Abbas I (the Great), shah of Persia takes Tabriz (NW Iran) from the Ottoman Turks.

ASIA

– Tomsk is founded as the capital of Siberia by the Cossacks, under the Stroganov dynasty; it protects the river crossings of the Ob and the Tom.

– The French East India Company is granted a charter.

ECONOMY AND SOCIETY

29 Feb. Death of John Whitgift; Richard Bancroft succeeds him as archbishop of Canterbury (10 Dec.).

SCIENCE AND TECHNOLOGY

– Maximilien de Béthune, duke of Sully and counsellor to the king of France, begins the construction of the Briare Canal, which links the Loire with the Seine.

– German astronomer Johannes Kepler discovers a new star, which he interprets as an omen. He also publishes his *Astronomiae Pars Optic* (Optical Part of Astronomy), a treatise on optics.

– Galileo Galilei (see p. 243), Italian scientist, discovers the law of falling bodies, which proves that gravity affects all objects with the same strength, regardless of their mass.

ARTS AND HUMANITIES

– Spanish dramatist Lope de Vega starts publication of his comedies in 27 volumes.

– In England Dr Reynolds, president of Corpus Christi College, Oxford, proposes the Authorized Version of the Bible (see 1611).

– William Shakespeare's (see p. 236) *Measure for Measure*, a tragicomedy, is first performed in London; it is published in 1623.

Roland de Lassus, *Magnum Opus Musicum*; a re-publication of most of his motets.

1605

EUROPE

5 Mar. Pope Clement VIII dies.

1 April Alexander de' Medici is elected Pope Leo XI, but dies (27 April). Camillo Borghese is elected Pope Paul V (16 May).

13 April Death of Russian tsar Boris Godunov: his son Fyodor II succeeds to the throne.

13 April The Protestant noble István Bocskay is elected prince of Transylvania by the diet (legislative assembly) of Szerenes.

10 June The False Dmitri enters Moscow, Russia. Tsar Fyodor II is assassinated by a noble faction. Dmitri is crowned (21 June).

5 Nov. In England the Gunpowder Plot, a Catholic conspiracy to murder James I and his ministers by blowing up the Palace of Westminster during the state opening of Parliament, is dicovered when Guy Fawkes, one of the plotters, is found and arrested in the cellars beneath Parliament. The other plotters, including Robert Catesby, flee, but are captured (8 Nov.) and brought to trial.

– The count of Auvergne and the duke of Bouillon lead a rebellion against Henry IV in S France.

ASIA

17 Oct. Akbar, Mughal emperor of India since 1556, dies in Agra, India. His son Jahangir succeeds him.

– Tokugawa Ieyasu retires as military ruler of Japan and is succeeded by his son Hidetada.

THE AMERICAS

– The Caribbean island of Barbados is claimed as an English colony.

AUSTRALASIA AND OCEANIA

– The Dutch seize Amboyna, Malaysia.

ECONOMY AND SOCIETY

13 Oct. In Geneva, Switzerland, Theodore Beza, the Protestant theologian who succeeded John Calvin as the leader of the Reformation in Geneva, dies.

SCIENCE AND TECHNOLOGY

19 Oct. Birth of Thomas Browne, English physician and essayist.

ARTS AND HUMANITIES

– William Shakespeare's *Othello, the Moor of Venice*, a tragedy, is first performed in London; it is published in 1622.

Sir Francis Bacon, *The Advancement of Learning*, the start of a project to build a scientific basis for knowledge (Part 2 is published in 1620).

Miguel de Cervantes, the first part of *El ingenioso hidalgo don Quixote de la Mancha*, known in English as *The Ingenious Knight Don Quixote de la Mancha* (second part published in 1615).

John Dowland, *Lachrymae, or Seaven Teares, in Seaven Passionate Pavans*, musical works for viol consort.

Tomás Luis de Victoria, *Officium defunctorum*, requiem known in English as the Office for the Dead or Requiem Mass.

1606

EUROPE

31 Jan. In England Guy Fawkes and his co-plotters (see 5 Nov. 1605) are executed by hanging, drawing and quartering.

April The Habsburg archdukes rebel against the Holy Roman Emperor Rudolf II and recognize his brother, the Archduke Matthias of Austria, as their leader.

17 May The False Dmitri, opposed by the boyars (nobles), is murdered in a Moscow uprising. His former supporter, Vasily Shuysky, usurps the throne and is proclaimed Tsar Vasily IV (19 May).

Miguel de Cervantes (1547–1616)

The Spanish writer Cervantes was born near Madrid into a family of minor gentry, who were probably converted Jews. This may explain their itinerant existence while Cervantes was growing up, and his own later difficulty in gaining regular employment at court.

Cervantes' own life was characterized by the sort of adventures and reversals of fortune that he would describe so vividly in the lives of his fictional characters. He fought and was gravely injured at the battle of Lepanto against the Turks (1571). In 1575, while sailing from Naples to Spain, he was captured by Barbary corsairs and sold into slavery in Algiers, where he remained for five years until his family could ransom him. He then tried his luck as a civil servant and searched for patronage at the royal court, but found it difficult to make a living. He was jailed twice for debt.

Cervantes wrote his classic novel, *Don Quixote*, in two parts. Part I was published in 1605, and Part II, a deeper work, in 1615. He achieved instant fame and success with this book, which easily eclipsed his other works. *Don Quixote* is, firstly, a parody of the chivalric romance, but its power also derives from Cervantes' profound understanding of Spain's world role, its ambitions, frustrations and defeats as well as the disturbing New World revealed by the American discoveries. His own experiences had taught him to look at life in a detached way, and in *Don Quixote* he turned that psychological aptitude into fiction. His book is, therefore, the first modern novel, and in it Cervantes showed the possibility and range of the novel as an exploration of reality.

---

23 June By the terms of the peace of Vienna between the Archduke Matthias and Hungary, István Bocskay is recognized as ruler of Transylvania (see 13 April 1605).

11 Nov. The prince of Transylvania, István Bocskay, facilitates the peace treaty at Zsitvatörök between the Turks (Ottoman sultan Ahmed I) and the Austrians (Holy Roman Emperor Rudolf II). The Habsburgs officially cede Transylvania to Bocskay, who governs under Turkish suzerainty and stops paying tribute to the Turks for the Habsburg part of Hungary.

18 Nov. The English Parliament opposes King James I's plans for a union with Scotland, arguing that the Scots would acquire a share of English trade as a result of the union of the two crowns.

29 Dec. István Bocskay of Transylvania, vassal of the Turks, dies in Kassa (now Kozice, in Slovakia).

THE AMERICAS

20 Dec. The London Virginia Company organizes three ships with 120 colonists, who leave for Virginia.

ECONOMY AND SOCIETY

– Episcopacy (church government by bishops) is restored in Scotland by the Scottish Parliament. Presbyterian ministers are banned.

– Pope Paul V places Venice under an interdict after the Council of Ten takes legal action against a priest.

ARTS AND HUMANITIES

6 June Birth in Rouen, France, of Pierre Corneille, French poet and classical dramatist.

15 July Birth in Leiden, United Netherlands, of Rembrandt van Rijn, Dutch painter.

– William Shakespeare's (see p. 236) *King Lear* (published in 1608) and *Macbeth* (published in 1623), both tragedies, are first performed in London.

Michael Drayton, *Poems Lyric and Pastoral*.

Joseph Justus Scaliger, *Thesaurus temporum* (Treasury of Time), a chronology of the ancient world.

1607

EUROPE

15 Mar. Duke Charles of Södermanland is crowned King Charles IX of Sweden, having held the title since 1604.

May Riots break out in the English Midlands against the enclosure of common land.

4 July James I, king of England, prorogues Parliament after its rejection of union with Scotland.

14 Sept. The so-called Flight of the Earls from Ireland: fearing arrest by the English crown, Hugh O'Neill, earl of Tyrone (see 1594) and Hugh Roe O'Donnell, earl of Tyrconnell, sail for Spain from Co. Donegal in NW Ireland. They will settle in Rome as papal pensioners.

19 Nov. King Philip III of Spain declares the Spanish crown bankrupt, thereby jeopardizing the Banco San Giorgio of Genoa.

ASIA

– The Nguyen dynasty of Dai Viet (now Vietnam) launches incursions into the Chinese provinces of Guangxi and Yunnan.

ECONOMY AND SOCIETY

14 May The Virginia Company of London, led by Captain John Smith, founds the first permanent English settlement in America in Jamestown, Virginia.

– The Bollandists, a congregation of Jesuits in Belgium, start work on a history of the Church following principles of critical historiography.

SCIENCE AND TECHNOLOGY

– Italian scientist Galileo Galilei (see p. 243) invents a thermometer.

ARTS AND HUMANITIES

Feb. The opera *La favola d'Orfeo* (The Legend of Orpheus) by Claudio Monteverdi, Italian composer, is first performed in Mantua, Italy. It is the earliest opera regularly performed today.

– William Shakespeare's *Timon of Athens*, a tragedy, is first performed in London; it is published in 1623.

William Byrd, *Gradualia, The Marian Masses*, sacred vocal music.

Ben Jonson, *Volpone, or The Fox*, comedy.

Cyril Tourneur, *The Revenger's Tragedy*, play.

1608-9

1608

EUROPE

April The False Dmitri defeats the Russian tsar, Vasily IV Shuysky, and marches on Moscow. Shuisky cedes Karelia (in the E of modern Finland) to Sweden in exchange for military aid.

25 June Emperor Rudolf II cedes Austria, Hungary and Moravia to his brother, Archduke Matthias of Austria, and promises him the succession to Bohemia in the treaty of Lieben.

– Gabriel Báthory, Calvinist prince, becomes ruler of Transylvania under the Turkish suzerainty of the Ottoman sultan, Ahmed I.

THE AMERICAS

July Samuel de Champlain founds a French fur-trading settlement at Quebec, Canada. The French ally with both Hurons and Algonquins against the Iroquois (all Native American peoples).

ECONOMY AND SOCIETY

6 Dec. Birth of George Monck, English general, duke of Albemarle and notable royalist during the English Civil Wars (1642–51).

SCIENCE AND TECHNOLOGY

– Italian scientist Galileo Galilei invents the microscope.

– Hans Lippershey, a Dutch optician, invents the refracting telescope. Galileo Galilei will hear of his invention and build his own telescope the following year.

ARTS AND HUMANITIES

9 Dec. Birth in London of John Milton (see p. 273), English poet, scholar and fervent republican.

– Italian composer Claudio Monteverdi's now lost opera *Arianna* is first performed in Mantua, Italy.

– William Shakespeare's (see p. 236) *Coriolanus*, a tragedy, is first performed in London; it is published in 1623.

– English poet and dramatist George Chapman's play *The Conspiracy and Tragedy of Charles, Duke of Byron, Marshal of France* is first performed, in London, but is soon banned at the request of the French ambassador.

Domenichino, *The Scourging of St Andrew*, fresco, in the Church of San Gregorio Magno in Rome.

El Greco, *Golgotha*, *View of Toledo*, and *Assumption of the Virgin Mary*, paintings.

Thomas Middleton, *A Mad World, My Masters*, satirical comedy.

1609

EUROPE

Feb. King Charles IX of Sweden, in the treaty of Teus, agrees to support Tsar Vasily IV Shuysky of Russia in opposing King Sigismund III Vasa of Poland, whose forces march towards Smolensk, in Russia. Sweden is to receive Karelia in exchange.

9 April Spain effectively recognizes the independence of the seven United Provinces of the Netherlands by signing a 12-year truce with Holland; the Emperor Rudolf II and Henry IV of France are the truce's guarantors.

17 June The United Provinces sign a 12-year alliance with England and France.

9 July The Holy Roman Emperor Rudolf II is forced by the Czech leader Karel, Elder of Zerotin, to grant a charter allowing freedom of religion in Bohemia.

Sept. In the aftermath of the earlier alliance between Russia and Sweden, King Sigismund III Vasa of Poland declares war on Tsar Vasily IV Shuysky of Russia. His son, Ladislas, lays claim to the Russian throne.

25 Nov. In Paris birth of Henrietta Maria, sister of Louis XIII of France and later queen consort of King Charles I of England. (d.1669).

MIDDLE EAST AND NORTH AFRICA

22 Sept. The duke of Lerma, chief minister of King Philip III of Spain, expels Moors and Moriscos from Spain. An estimated 300,000 become refugees to the Maghreb (N Africa) in the next five years.

THE AMERICAS

– Philip III of Spain gives complete control of the Indian missions to the Jesuits, who establish their first mission in Paraguay.

– Henry Hudson, English navigator, explores the Hudson River and Delaware Bay (S of modern New York).

ECONOMY AND SOCIETY

– The Dutch East India Company ships tea from China to Europe. It will reach Britain by 1615.

SCIENCE AND TECHNOLOGY

– Johannes Kepler, German astronomer, *De Motibus Stellae Martis* (On the Motion of the Star Mars), a treatise describing the movements of Mars.

ARTS AND HUMANITIES

21 Jan. Death of French scholar Joseph Justus Scaliger.

18 Feb. Birth of Edward Hyde, earl of Clarendon, English historian.

15 July Death in Rome of Annibale Carracci, Italian painter and engraver.

19 Oct. Death in Leiden, United Netherlands, of Jacobus Arminius, theologian and minister of the Dutch Reformed Church and father of the system of belief known as Arminianism, which opposes the Calvinist doctrine of predestination.

– William Shakespeare's *Pericles, Prince of Tyre*, a romantic drama, is published and first performed in London. His *Sonnets*, mostly written before 1600, are also published.

Orlando Gibbons, *Fantasies of Three Parts for Viols*; the first example of music in England printed with engraved plates.

Peter Paul Rubens, *The Artist and his Wife, Isabella Brant*, painting.

St Francis of Sales, *Introduction à la vie dévote* (Introduction to Devout Life), a Catholic devotional treatise.

Lope de Vega, *El arte nuevo de hacer comedias* (The New Art of Writing Plays), a treatise explaining his approach to theatre.

Galileo (1564–1642)

The Italian scientist Galileo Galilei, with his emphasis on the use of experimentation and mathematics in the investigation of the physical world, is regarded as the founder of modern physics. He undertook pioneering work on motion and gravity, but it is his astronomical discoveries for which he is most famous. Galileo made his first telescope in 1609, and his subsequent observations convinced him that the planets (including the Earth) moved around the Sun. This theory had been proposed by the Polish astronomer Nicolaus Copernicus in 1543, but he had had no means of testing the theory. Galileo published his findings in 1610, in his book *Sidereus nuncius* (The Starry Messenger).

Recognizing the possible hostility of the Church, Galileo tried to reconcile the conflict between the Sun-centred Copernican universe and biblical accounts by means of rhetoric. At first he won over the authorities, and in 1611 was congratulated by the pope on his discoveries.

But in 1613 Galileo published a new paper in which he stated quite overtly that Copernicus was correct. The resulting disputes led to the Church's formal denunciation of Copernican teaching in 1616. To escape imprisonment, Galileo promised not to publish anything to support the outlawed theory. After years of private study, he finally published the *Dialogue on the Two Chief World Systems* in

1632, demonstrating the truth of his discoveries. In 1633 he was summoned to Rome to be tried by the Inquisition. He was found guilty and obliged to abjure his Copernicanism, but he is said to have muttered as he did so, '*Eppur si muove*' ('and yet it [the Earth] moves'). Thereafter Galileo was allowed to live in his own house in Florence, but was forbidden from leaving the city or from publishing anything. But he continued his scientific researches and wrote two further books on gravitation and dynamics, which were published after his death. In November 1992 the Vatican finally publicly admitted that Galileo's view of the solar system was correct..

1610

EUROPE

12 Feb. Henry IV allies France with the German Union of Protestant States (formed 1608). He is now prepared to intervene in German domestic affairs, and the duke of Sully plans a European federation to secure peace and end Habsburg dynastic dominance.

14 May Henry IV is assassinated by François Ravaillac, a Catholic fanatic; he is succeeded by the nine-year-old Louis XIII. Marie de Medici, the queen mother, becomes regent, and her favourite, Concino Concini, displaces the duke of Sully.

23 May The House of Commons, lower house of the English Parliament, petitions James I against levying impositions.

19 July In Russia Tsar Vasily IV Shuysky is deposed after a defensive Swedish force, ally of the Russian tsar, is defeated by the invading Poles (see 1609). Vladislav, son of King Sigismund III Vasa of Poland, is offered the throne by the boyars (nobles).

19 Sept. After the death of his father, Frederick IV, leader of the German Protestant Union, Frederick V becomes Elector Palatine of the Rhine.

Oct. Sigismund III of Poland, jealous that his son Vladislav has been offered the Russian throne, marches on Moscow.

ASIA

– Conflict between the English and Dutch spreads in India.

THE AMERICAS

July Don Pedro de Peralta, Spanish governor of what is now New Mexico in the SW USA, founds the town of Santa Fe.

3 Aug. The English explorer Henry Hudson discovers Hudson Bay, N America.

ECONOMY AND SOCIETY

11 May Matteo Ricci, the Italian Jesuit missionary who introduced Christianity to China, dies there.

SCIENCE AND TECHNOLOGY

7 Jan. Italian scientist Galileo Galilei (see box) observes the satellites of Jupiter, the phases of Venus and the strange shape of Saturn through a powerful telescope of his own construction.

– Thomas Harriott, English astronomer, discovers sunspots at the same time as Dutch astronomer Johannes Fabricius, German priest Christoph Scheiner and Italian scientist Galileo Galilei.

ARTS AND HUMANITIES

4 July Birth of Paul Scarron, French poet and playwright.

18 July Death of Caravaggio, Italian painter, at Port'Ercole, Tuscany.

– William Shakespeare's *Cymbeline*, a tragedy, is first performed in London; it is published in 1623.

John Donne, *Pseudo-martyr*, prose work concluding that English Catholics should take the oath of allegiance to the crown.

Ben Jonson, *The Alchemist*, comedy.

Claudio Monteverdi, *Vespers*, sacred vocal music, dedicated to Pope Paul V.

Peter Paul Rubens, *Raising the Cross*, painting.

1611

EUROPE

Jan. James I of England starts negotiations for the marriage of Elizabeth, his daughter, to Frederick V, Elector Palatine of the Rhine.

24 Mar. Archduke Matthias of Austria, marching from Vienna with 10,000 men against the army of the Holy Roman Emperor Rudolf II, enters the Bohemian capital Prague.

25 Mar. In England Robert Carr, James I's favourite, is created Viscount Rochester.

4 April King Christian IV of Denmark declares war on Sweden (the War of Kalmar). Danish troops take the Swedish port of Kalmar, hoping to reconquer the country.

13 April A proclamation is issued that English settlers for the plantation of Ulster are to assemble in Dublin.

23 May Matthias is crowned king of Bohemia; his brother Rudolf II resigns the crown of Bohemia (11 Aug.).

30 Oct. Charles IX of Sweden dies. Queen Christina carries on the government in the interim until the Swedish estates elect Gustavus II Adolphus to the throne (Dec.). Aristocrat and diplomat Axel Oxenstierna is appointed chancellor.

27 Dec. The archdukes vow to ensure that the imperial crown will always remain in the House of Habsburg.

– Sir Thomas Sherley arrives in England as an ambassador on behalf of the shah of Persia, Abbas I, and arranges a commercial treaty.

– In England James I establishes the baronetage in order to raise money for the crown.

ASIA

– The first English settlement on the E coast of India at Masulipatam, Madras.

ARTS AND HUMANITIES

– William Shakespeare's (see p. 236) plays *The Tempest* and *The Winter's Tale* are first performed in London; both are published in 1623.

– The so-called Authorized Version of the Bible is published in England.

Orlando Gibbons, *This is the Record of John*, anthem.

Orlando Gibbons, William Byrd and John Bull, *Parthenia*, music for the virginals.

Ben Jonson, *Catiline, His Conspiracy*, tragedy.

Peter Paul Rubens, *Descent from the Cross*, painting.

Cyril Tourneur, *The Atheist's Tragedie, or The Honest Man's Revenge*, play.

1612

EUROPE

20 Jan. Archduke Matthias of Austria, king of Bohemia and Hungary, becomes Holy Roman Emperor after Rudolf II's death in Prague, Bohemia. Matthias is formally elected on 13 June.

24 May Death in Marlborough, Wiltshire, of Robert Cecil, earl of Salisbury, chief government minister of England. Robert Carr, Viscount Rochester, the king's favourite, takes over as secretary of state.

5 Nov. Death of Henry, a gifted and cultivated Prince of Wales and the eldest son of James I, king of England (known as the Hope of Protestantism).

– In Russia a patriotic alliance led by Kuzma Minin and Prince Pozharsky defeats the Poles, ending a period during which invasions by Sweden and Poland have threatened Russia's national survival.

THE AMERICAS

– The Dutch use Manhattan Island as a centre for the fur trade.

– Colonization of Bermuda starts from Virginia.

ECONOMY AND SOCIETY

11 April In England Bartholomew Legate of London and Edward Wightman of Lichfield are burned at the stake for religious heresy. They are the last such victims in English history.

– The first English Baptist church is founded at Pinner's Hall, London, by Thomas Helwys.

– Jakob Boehme, a German mystic, describes his mystical philosophy in his first book *Aurora, oder, Morgenröte im Aufgang* (Aurora, or the Coming of Dawn), which is condemned by the Lutherans.

SCIENCE AND TECHNOLOGY

Oct. Birth of Louis Le Vau, French baroque architect.

– Tobacco is first planted in Virginia.

– John Smith, English captain of the Virginia Company of London, produces the first detailed maps of the coast of N America from Penobscot Bay to Cape Hatteras.

ARTS AND HUMANITIES

8 Feb. Birth of Samuel Butler, English poet.

– The Accademia della Crusca publishes an Italian dictionary, the *Vocabolario*, which becomes the model for French and Spanish dictionaries.

– The tragedy *The White Devil,* by the English dramatist John Webster, is first performed in London (published in 1612).

Michael Drayton, the first part of *Poly-Olbion*, a description of British history and topography.

Orlando Gibbons, *First Set of Madrigals and Motets of Five Parts, Apt for Viols and Voices*, music.

El Greco, *Baptism of Christ*, painting.

1613

EUROPE

20 Jan. The peace of Knåred ends the Swedish–Danish war. Sweden gains Kalmar on Baltic coast.

14 Feb. Marriage of Elizabeth, daughter of James I, king of England, to Frederick V, Elector Palatine of the Rhine. The marriage will eventually lead to the Hanoverian succession to the English throne.

21 Feb. Michael Romanov, founder of the Romanov dynasty, is elected tsar of Russia by a representative assembly.

16 May The United Provinces, Netherlands, are allied with the Protestant Union of Germany.

13 Aug. Meeting of the German diet at Ratisbon. The Holy Roman Emperor Matthias asks for backing against the Ottoman Turks, and is supported by Catholic princes and opposed by Protestant ones.

Sept. Ottoman forces invade Hungary.

24 Oct. Calvinist Gabor Bethlen, with Ottoman protection, invades and becomes prince of Transylvania, replacing the Holy Roman Emperor Matthias's protégé Gabriel Báthory.

3 Nov. King James I makes Viscount Rochester (see 1611) earl of Somerset.

THE AMERICAS

- English colonists in Virginia destroy the French settlement at Port Royal, Nova Scotia and prevent French colonization of Maryland.
- French explorer Samuel de Champlain's journey advances up the Ottawa River.

ECONOMY AND SOCIETY

- Copper coins are first used in England.

SCIENCE AND TECHNOLOGY

- English goldsmith Hugh Myddelton finishes his 62km (39 miles) 'New River', which brings water into London.
- Italian scientist Galileo Galilei (see p. 243) uses his telescopic observations to champion the heliocentric (sun-centred) system first demonstrated by Polish astronomer Copernicus (see 1543).

ARTS AND HUMANITIES

- Claudio Monteverdi, the Italian composer, is appointed *maestro di capella* at St Mark's, Venice.
- William Shakespeare's (see p. 236) *Henry VIII, The Life of a King*, a history play, is first performed in London; it is published in 1623.
- English dramatist John Webster's *The Duchess of Malfi*, a tragedy, is first performed in London; it is published in 1623.
- Spanish theologian Francisco Suarez, in his *Defensio Catholicae Fidei contra Anglicanae Sectae Errores* (Defence of the Catholic Faith against the Mistakes of the English Sect), written at the prompting of Pope Paul V, argues that English subjects should not take the oath of allegiance, which he deems heretical.
- The Globe Theatre in Southwark, London, is destroyed by fire.
Guido Reni, Aurora frescoes in the Casino Rospigliosi, Rome.

1614

EUROPE

Jan. Gustavus II Adolphus of Sweden holds a diet (parliament), wins approval for his campaign against Russia and establishes a supreme court.

19 Feb. Henry II of Bourbon, 3rd prince of Condé, leads influential French nobles, such as the dukes of Nevers, Mayenne and Bouillon, to rebel against the queen mother, Marie de' Medici, and her Italian favourite Concino Concini (see 1610), whose failure to summon the Estates-General and to reform administrative shortcomings are unpopular.

15 May Condé's French rebellion comes to a successful end. Louis XIII promises to summon the Estates-General.

7 June James I, king of England, dissolves Parliament which has not passed a single Act. The king subsequently imprisons four members of the Commons who have opposed the crown.

Oct. The Estates-General meet in Paris for the last time before 1789; they attack the *taille* (tax) and the sale of offices.

THE AMERICAS

5 April In Virginia English planter John Rolfe marries Pocahontas, the daughter of Powhatan, a Native American chief. Rolfe also discovers how to cure tobacco so that it can be exported, thus starting the Virginia tobacco trade.

- The Dutch Estates-General grants the New Netherlands Fur Company a three-year monopoly of the N American fur trade.
- Cornelius Jacobsen Mey explores the Lower Delaware River.

SCIENCE AND TECHNOLOGY

- John Napier, Scottish mathematician, constructs his logarithmic tables, *Mirifici Logarithmorum Canonis Descriptio* (The Admirable Table of Logarithms).

ARTS AND HUMANITIES

7 April In Toledo, Spain, death of El Greco (Domenikos Theotokopoulos), Greek-born Spanish painter. In works such as *View of Toledo*, *The Burial of Count Orgaz* and *The Cleansing of the Temple* his expressionist style has blended Byzantine portraiture and Venetian brushwork with Spanish mysticism.

1 July In London death of Isaac Casaubon, renowned French classical scholar and Protestant theologian, who became an English citizen.

Sept. In Montmirail, France, birth of Jean-François-Paul de Gondi, cardinal of Retz. He will be one of the leaders of the Fronde rebellion (1648–53).

- Ben Jonson's comedy *Bartholomew Fair* is first performed in London; it will be published in 1631.
George Chapman, Books 1–12 of Homer's *Odyssey*, translation.
Sir Walter Ralegh, *The History of the World*, history, written during his captivity in the Tower of London.

1615

EUROPE

Mar. The dismissal of the Estates-General in France provokes Henry II of Bourbon, 3rd prince of Condé, to organize a second uprising (Aug.).

April Invasion of Lombardy by Charles Emmanuel, duke of Savoy, who is defeated by the Spanish viceroy, the marquis of Hinojosa.

6 May The Holy Roman Emperor Matthias, also king of Bohemia and Hungary, who is embracing a policy of religious toleration, recognizes the Protestant Gabor Bethlen (see 24 Oct. 1613) as prince of Transylvania in the peace of Tyrnau. In July the emperor signs a peace treaty with the Ottoman Turks.

9 Aug. Outbreak of civil war in France as the prince of Condé allies himself with the Huguenots, led by Henry, duke of Rohan, against the queen mother Marie de' Medici and the unpopular Concino Concini, marquis of Ancre, who is now marshal of France.

Sept. Henry, duke of Rohan, leads the Huguenots of Guienne and Languedoc, S France, in a rebellion against the corrupt and inefficient administration of Marie de Medici and Concino Concini.

9 Nov. The Bourbon and the Habsburg dynasties exchange brides at Burgos; as a result of the proxy marriages between Louis XIII and Anne of Austria (infanta of Spain), and between Philip of Asturias (heir to King Philip III of Spain) and Elizabeth of Bourbon (Louis XIII's sister), France agrees not to intervene in internal German Catholic policy.

ASIA

Jan. Sir Thomas Roe leaves England as the first English ambassador to the Mughal emperor Jahangir of India.

– The English fleet defeats the Portuguese off the coast of Bombay, W India.

– The Dutch seize the Moluccas, Indonesia, from the Portuguese.

SCIENCE AND TECHNOLOGY

– German astronomer Johannes Kepler's *Nova Stereometria Doliorum* (New Stereometry of Wine Barrels) discusses the capacity of casks, surface areas and conic sections.

ARTS AND HUMANITIES

– George Chapman, English poet and dramatist, finishes his translation of Homer's *Odyssey*.

Gianlorenzo Bernini, *The Goat Amalthea*, sculpture.

Salomon de Brosse, the Palais de Luxembourg, Paris.

William Camden, the first part of *Annales Rerum Anglicarum* (Chronicles of English Affairs), an account of the reign of Elizabeth I.

Miguel de Cervantes (see p. 241), Part II of *Don Quixote*, romance.

1616

EUROPE

3 Jan. Sir George Villiers, the new favourite of James I, king of England, is appointed Master of the Horse.

20 Mar. English explorer Sir Walter Ralegh is released from the Tower of London.

3 May The treaty of Loudun ends the French civil war: Henry II of Bourbon, 3rd prince of Condé, and his rebels are granted an amnesty but otherwise no concessions are made to the Huguenots. Italian Concino Concini remains marshal of France.

20 July In Rome death of Hugh O'Neill, 2nd earl of Tyrone, the Irish chieftain who lead an unsuccessful Catholic rebellion against English rule in Ireland (see 14 Sept. 1607).

July In England King James I starts to sell peerages.

1 Sept. In France the prince of Condé is arrested and imprisoned in the Bastille, Paris.

Oct. Catholic policies intensify in Bohemia.

20 Nov. In France the bishop of Luçon, Armand Jean du Plessis de Richelieu (Cardinal Richelieu from 1622), becomes minister of state for foreign affairs and war.

– The Native American Pocahontas (see 1614), who has travelled to England with her husband John Rolfe, is presented at the court of James I of England.

ASIA

1 June Tokugawa Ieyasu, who has been *de facto* Japanese military ruler or shogun since 1603, dies in Sumpu; his son Tokugawa Hidetada, official shogun since 1605, now rules alone.

– The Manchus (originally a nomadic people) invade China from the N.

SCIENCE AND TECHNOLOGY

18 Oct. Birth of Nicholas Culpeper, astrologer and author of a famous English herbal.

23 Nov. Death of Richard Hakluyt, English geographer.

– Italian scientist Galileo Galilei (see p. 243) is threatened by the Inquisition because he is teaching Copernicanism.

ARTS AND HUMANITIES

22 April Death in Madrid, Spain, of Miguel de Cervantes , author of *Don Quixote*.

23 April Death of William Shakespeare (see p. 236), English dramatist and poet, in his birthplace, Stratford-upon-Avon, Warwickshire.

– English architect Inigo Jones starts work on the Queen's House, Greenwich.

– Ben Jonson, *The Works of Benjamin Jonson*, plays; the first collected works of an English dramatist.

Peter Paul Rubens, *The Lion Hunt*, painting.

St Francis of Sales, *Traité de l'amour de Dieu* (Treatise on the Love of God), Catholic treatise spearheading the French Catholic spiritual revival.

1617

EUROPE

Jan. James I, king of England, makes his favourite George Villiers earl of Buckingham (see May 1623).

27 Feb. Peace is concluded between Russia and Sweden by the terms of the peace of Stolbovo. The Swedish king Gustavus II Adolphus surrenders his capture of Novgorod and obtains Karelia and Ingria; the Russia tsar, Michael I Romanov, surrenders his claim to Estonia and Livonia. Poland will remain at war with Sweden until 1618 (see 24 Dec. 1618).

7 Mar. English statesman Francis Bacon is appointed lord keeper and (7 Jan. 1618) lord chancellor.

21 Mar. The Native American Pocahontas (see 1616) dies off Gravesend, Kent, England, on her way back to Virginia.

24 April The marshal of France, Concino Concini, is murdered on the orders of Louis XIII, whose favourite, Charles d'Albret, duke of Luynes, now assumes the reins of government. Concini's champion, the queen mother Marie de Medici, is compelled to retire to Blois, SW of Paris, where she surrounds herself with opponents of the duke of Luynes, including Richelieu (see 20 Nov. 1616).

17 June James I and VI, king of England and Scotland, attends the Scottish Parliament; the Five Articles of Religion introducing Anglican notions of Church government into the Church of Scotland are approved.

29 June Crisis in C Europe: the Bohemian Estates recognize the emperor's cousin and heir, Archduke Ferdinand of Styria, as heir to the Bohemian throne. Ferdinand refuses the demand of the Bohemian Protestants (led by Count Heinrich von Thurm) that he should respect freedom of worship.

July In the United Provinces of the Netherlands, political and religious conflict intensifies between the Remonstrants (supporters of Arminianism, see 1560), supported by Johan van Oldenbarneveldt (advocate of the United Provinces) and Hugo Grotius (see p. 251), and the Counter-Remonstrants (strict Calvinists), who are championed by Maurice of Nassau, stadtholder of the United Provinces.

Sept. By the peace of Madrid, Venice and Austria agree to end the hostilities that broke out in 1616 as a result of the activities of Uskoks pirates in E Carniola and in Croatia.

Oct. The duke of Osuna plunders Venice with the help of the Spanish viceroy of Milan, Pedro de Toledo.

MIDDLE EAST AND NORTH-AFRICA

22 Dec. Ahmed I, Ottoman sultan since 1603, dies and is succeeded by Mustafa I.

THE AMERICAS

17 Mar. English explorer Sir Walter Ralegh leaves on his expedition to Guiana. He will reach the mouth of the River Orinoco on 31 Dec.

SCIENCE AND TECHNOLOGY

4 April Death of John Napier, Scottish mathematician (see 1614).

ARTS AND HUMANITIES

14 Oct. In Soest, Westphalia (Germany), birth of Peter Lely (original name Pieter Van der Faes), baroque portrait painter.

Dec. Birth in Seville, Spain, of Bartolomé Esteban Murillo, baroque Spanish painter, especially celebrated for his portraits with religious themes.

– Spanish theologian Francisco Suarez, in *De Legibus ac Deo Legislatore* (On Law and God the Lawgiver), denies the divine right of kings and allows the deposition of wicked rulers.

1618

EUROPE

23 May Count Heinrich von Thurn, leader of the anti-Habsburg Bohemian Protestants, leads a revolt against the Catholic policies of the Holy Roman Emperor's regents in Prague. The regents, Jaroslav Martinic and Vilém Slawata, escape after being thrown out of the window of the council room at Hradcany Castle, Prague (the Defenestration of Prague). The event marks the start of the Thirty Years War. Wenceslas William von Ruppa forms a provisional government in Prague.

June The Bohemian Protestant Union sends the military commander Count Ernst von Mansfeld to help Count Heinrich von Thurm's Bohemian rebels.

1 July Ferdinand of Styria is crowned king of Hungary.

23 Aug. Johan van Oldenbarneveldt, advocate of the United Provinces (see July 1617), is arrested for treason by order of Maurice of Nassau, prince of Orange, stadtholder of the United Provinces.

27 Aug. The general assembly of the Church of Scotland accepts episcopalianism with the approval of the Five Articles of Religion.

29 Oct. The English explorer Sir Walter Ralegh is executed on trumped-up charges on his return from Guiana (see 17 Mar. 1617). Ralegh has failed to find gold on the Orinoco River and has sacked a Spanish settlement in Guiana, angering Philip III of Spain, who demands that he be punished. James I has Ralegh beheaded on an old charge of treason (dating from 1603) for which he has already spent 13 years (1603–16) in the Tower of London.

Nov. Archduke Leopold becomes ruler of the Tyrol, Austria, on the death of his brother Archduke Maximilian.

24 Dec. Poland signs a two-year truce with Sweden (subsequently extended to 1621) and a 14-year truce with Turkey.

SUB-SAHARAN AFRICA

– The Dutch West African Company is founded.

ECONOMY AND SOCIETY

– In England Puritan objections are raised to King James I's *Book of Sports,* which allows the playing of popular sports.

ARTS AND HUMANITIES

– The English Privy Council suppresses John Selden's *The History of Tythes.*

– French architect Salomon de Brosse works on the Palais du Parlement, Rennes.

– Catherine de Vivonne, marquise de Rambouillet, starts a literary salon, bringing together writers and intellectuals at the Hotel Rambouillet, Paris.

Gianlorenzo Bernini, *Aeneas and Anchises,* sculpture.

1619

EUROPE

20 Mar. Death of the Holy Roman Emperor Matthias who, as king of Bohemia and Hungary, attempted a policy of religious toleration. His cousin the Archduke Ferdinand is elected to succeed him (28 Aug.). Ferdinand also assumes the crown of Bohemia and becomes Ferdinand II.

13 May In The Hague Johan van Oldenbarneveldt is executed; advocate of the United Provinces, he was found guilty of treason (20 Feb.). This increases the authority of Maurice of Nassau, prince of Orange. Hugo Grotius, jurist, is imprisoned because of his support for Oldenbarneveldt's position (see July 1617).

19 Aug. Deposition of Ferdinand II by the Bohemian diet, which

(26 Aug.) elects Frederick V, the Calvinist Elector Palatine, king of Bohemia.

Aug. Gabor Bethlen, Protestant prince of Transylvania, invades Hungary.

26 Sept. James I, king of England, refuses to support Frederick V, the Elector Palatine (his son-in-law), but promises to provide resistance in the event of the Palatinate being invaded.

28 Sept. Frederick V (the Winter King) accepts the Bohemian crown and is crowned (Nov.) in Prague.

Nov. Gabor Bethlen withdraws from Vienna.

ASIA

2 June The English and the Dutch sign a treaty regulating trade in the East. Disputes between the English and Dutch East India companies are to be resolved by a council in India and, if irresolvable, are to be referred to the English king and the States-General.

THE AMERICAS

30 July First American representative colonial assembly is held in Jamestown, Virginia, under George Yeardley, new governor of the colony.

– The first black Africans arrive in N America as servants on estates in Virginia.

ECONOMY AND SOCIETY

29 Aug. In Reims, France, birth of Jean-Baptiste Colbert, statesman who becomes controller general of finance under King Louis XIV.

17 Dec. Prince Rupert, future commander of royalist troops during the English Civil Wars, is born in Prague.

SCIENCE AND TECHNOLOGY

– In his lectures at St Bartholomew's Hospital, London, William Harvey, English physician, announces his discovery of the circulation of the blood.

ARTS AND HUMANITIES

6 Mar. In Paris birth of Savinien Cyrano de Bergerac, French satirist and dramatist.

13 Mar. In London death of Richard Burbage, English actor of Shakespearian tragic roles.

– French architect Salomon de Brosse finishes the Château de Blérancourt, in France.

– Inigo Jones, design for the Banqueting House, Whitehall, London; the building will be completed in 1622.

Francis Beaumont and John Fletcher, *A King and No King* and *The Maid's Tragedy*, tragedies.

Paolo Sarpi, *Istoria del Concilio Tridentino* (History of the Council of Trent).

1620

EUROPE

16 Feb. In Cölln, near Berlin, Germany, birth of Frederick William, future Great Elector of Brandenburg (r.1640–88).

May The dukes of Mayenne, Longueville and Vendôme lead a rebellion against King Louis XIII of France: they aim to overthrow his chief minister, the duke of Luynes (see 1617), and to restore Marie de Medici, the queen mother, to court.

19 June Catholic imperial forces, led by the Spanish viceroy of Milan, defeat the Protestant forces of the Swiss Grisons League, which are guarding the Valtellina Pass into Italy, in the Alps.

June Resumption of the Swedish–Polish war: Gustavus II Adolphus of Sweden occupies Livonia.

22 July English volunteers leave to serve the troops of the Elector Palatine in Bohemia.

25 July The Catholic leader Maximilian of Bavaria occupies Linz, Austria; Lower Austria submits to the Holy Roman Emperor, who can now attack Bohemia.

Aug. In France Richelieu negotiates peace between the crown and rebellious nobles.

Aug. Ambrogio Spinola, marquis of Los Balbases, a Genoese professional soldier, leads Spanish troops from the Netherlands into the Palatinate.

20 Sept. Defeat of the Poles by the Turks at Jassy, capital of Moldavia (now Iai, Romania).

8 Nov. The battle of the White Mountain, near Prague. Count Johan Tserclaes von Tilly, commanding the Catholic League, defeats the army of King Frederick V of Bohemia. Suppression of the Bohemian revolt and expulsion of Protestant clergy follows and Ferdinand II is restored to the Bohemian throne.

Dec. French Huguenots, fearful of persecution, hold an illegal assembly at La Rochelle on the W coast of France and decide on war.

THE AMERICAS

16 Sept. English Congregationalists (known in the 19th century as the Pilgrim Fathers), leave Plymouth, England, on the *Mayflower*, bound for N America. They land at Cape Cod, New England (now Provincetown, Massachusetts) on 21 Nov., and at New Plymouth, Massachusetts, on 26 Dec., where they establish the Plymouth Colony, with John Carver as governor.

SCIENCE AND TECHNOLOGY

– Dutch scientist Cornelius Drebbel devises a thermometer and builds a submarine, testing it beneath the River Thames in London.

– English statesman Sir Francis Bacon's *Instauratio Magna* (The Great Instauration) is an account of the scientific revolution, basing all knowledge and future progress on the application of experimental science.

ARTS AND HUMANITIES

1 Mar. Death of Thomas Campion, English poet, composer, musical and literary theorist, physician and medical practitioner.

31 Oct. In Wotton, Surrey, England, birth of John Evelyn, a country gentleman whose *Diary* will provide invaluable insights into the social, cultural, religious and political life of his age.

Gianlorenzo Bernini, *Neptune and Triton*, sculpture.

Diego Velázquez, *The Water-Seller*, painting.

1621

EUROPE

22 Jan. The Elector Palatine, Frederick V, is placed under the ban of the empire by the Holy Roman Emperor, Ferdinand II, who secretly transfers the Upper Palatinate and the Electorate to Maximilian of Bavaria.

28 Jan. Pope Paul V dies.

9 Feb. Italian clergyman Alessandro Ludovisi succeeds Paul V and becomes Pope Gregory XV, but dies in July 1623 in Rome.

Feb. The French Huguenot assembly at La Rochelle, W France, decides formally on rebellion against Louis XIII. It is led by Henry, duke of Rohan (the Huguenots' foremost general in the civil wars of the 1620s) and his younger brother, Benjamin of Rohan, seigneur de Soubise.

12 April King Louis XIII of France meets the rebel Huguenots at La Rochelle.

3 May English statesman Francis Bacon is impeached for corruption and imprisoned but is later pardoned by James I (Nov.).

3 June The Dutch West India Company is chartered.

Aug. The 12-year truce (agreed April 1609) between Spain and the United Provinces comes to an end; war resumes.

18 Nov. The English Parliament meets and the Commons petition King James to declare war on Spain in support of the Elector Palatine.

18 Dec. In England the House of Commons makes a Protestation denying the king's right to imprison MPs who have criticized his foreign policy. The king imprisons Sir Edward Coke (27 Dec.) for participating in the Protestation and (30 Dec.) tears from the Commons Journal the page recording the Protestation.

THE AMERICAS

– First settlement of Scottish emigrants in Acadia, which they will rename Nova Scotia in 1632 (now Canada).

ECONOMY AND SOCIETY

17 Sept. In Rome death of Italian cardinal and theologian Roberto Bellarmine, a staunch supporter of Catholic orthodoxy.

– The French Congregation of St Maur is founded under Benedictine Rule.

SCIENCE AND TECHNOLOGY

– In England Cornelius Vermuyden, Dutch engineer, is appointed by James I to drain the parkland around Windsor Castle.

ARTS AND HUMANITIES

31 Mar. Birth in Winestead, Yorkshire, England, of Andrew Marvell, metaphysical poet.

8 July Birth in Château-Thierry, France, of Jean de La Fontaine, French poet and author of the moralizing *Fables*.

22 July Birth in Wimborne St Giles, Dorset, England, of Anthony Ashley Cooper, earl of Shaftesbury, moral philosopher and politician in the government of King Charles II.

Gianlorenzo Bernini, *Rape of Proserpina*, sculpture.

Robert Burton, *The Anatomy of Melancholy*, medical and philosophical treatise on the types and causes of melancholia.

Anthony Van Dyck *Rest on the Flight to Egypt*, painting.

1622

EUROPE

7 Jan. In England John Pym, MP and parliamentary leader, is arrested for criticizing the crown's policies in Parliament.

8 Feb. James I of England dissolves the English Parliament.

June Catholic troops led by Count Tilly (see 8 Nov. 1620) win the battle of Hochst, the Palatinate is conquered and Frederick V is defeated.

Aug. Count Olivares, Gaspar de Guzman, nobleman from a political family, becomes Spain's chief minister.

18 Oct. By the treaty of Montpellier, the control by Huguenots of the towns of La Rochelle (W France) and Montauban (S France) is confirmed (having originally been guaranteed by the Edict of Nantes, see 15 April 1598).

ECONOMY AND SOCIETY

6 June Pope Gregory XV founds the Sacred Congregation for the Propagation of the Faith (known as Propaganda Fide) to propagate Catholicism and counteract Protestantism.

2 Aug. Journalists William Sheffard and Nathaniel Butter begin publishing *Newes from Most Parts of Christendom*, the first regular newspaper in English.

28 Dec. Death in Lyons, France, of St Francis of Sales, co-founder of the female religious order of the Visitation and author of the immensely influential classic of Counter-Reformation spirituality, *Introduction to the Devout Life* (1609).

– The papal chancery adopts 1 Jan. as the start of the New Year, replacing 25 Mar.

SCIENCE AND TECHNOLOGY

– English statesman and writer Francis Bacon publishes his *Natural and Experimental History*.

ARTS AND HUMANITIES

15 Jan. Birth of Molière (Jean-Baptiste Poquelin), French actor and playwright.

Michael Drayton, second part of *Poly-Olbion*, description of British history and topography.

Guido Reni, *Job*, painting.

Peter Paul Rubens, *The Medici Cycle*, 22 paintings commissioned for the Luxembourg Palace, Paris.

1623

EUROPE

25 Feb. Maximilian, duke of Bavaria, is granted the Upper Palatinate by the Holy Roman Emperor Ferdinand II. The empire's electoral college therefore now has a Catholic majority. The Bibliotheca Palatina is removed from Heidelberg to Rome.

May James I of England makes his favourite George Villiers duke of Buckingham (see Jan. 1617).

6 Aug. Matteo Barbarini is elected Pope Urban VIII.

30 Aug. Charles, Prince of Wales, and the duke of Buckingham leave Madrid following the breakdown of negotiations for the prince's marriage to the Infanta. James I of England breaks off the Spanish marriage treaty (Dec.) and war with Spain follows (Mar. 1624).

– Gustavus II Adolphus reforms the Swedish government.

– The United Provinces of the Netherlands agree a commercial treaty with Persia.

THE AMERICAS

– English colonies are settled in New Hampshire and Maine.

– David Thomas establishes the first English settlement in New Hampshire at Little Harbor, near Rye.

AUSTRALASIA AND OCEANA

Feb. English traders of the British East India Company at Amboyna, Indonesia, attempting to break into the Indonesian spice trade, are massacred by the Dutch.

ARTS AND HUMANITIES

19 June In Clermont-Ferrand, France, birth of Blaise Pascal (see p. 259), French mathematician and physicist, father of the theory of probability, the first digital calculator, the syringe and the hydraulic press.

4 July In Stondon Massey, Essex, England, death of the great English composer William Byrd, whose sacred and secular vocal music and music for virginals and viol consort exemplified the English polyphonic style. A Catholic, Byrd was prosecuted several times for recusancy (refusal of Roman Catholics to attend Church of England services).

11 Nov. In La Forêt-sur-Sèvre, France, death of Philippe de Mornay, diplomat and defender of the Huguenot cause during the French Wars of Religion (1562–98).

– English architect Inigo Jones starts work on the Queen's Chapel, St James's Palace, Westminster.

– The *First Folio* (first collected edition) of Shakespeare's plays, edited by actors Henry Condell and John Heminge, is published; it contains 36 plays (*Pericles* is not included).

Gianlorenzo Bernini, *David*, sculpture.

Tommaso Campanella, *La Citta de Sole* (The City of the Sun), philosophical description of a utopia.

François Mansart, Church of St Marie de la Visitation, Paris, architecture.

1624

EUROPE

31 Jan. Count Ernst von Mansfeld, a Roman Catholic mercenary fighting for the Protestant cause, leaves Dover with 12,000 men to support the Elector Palatine. The force lands in Holland but is prevented by James I of England from aiding the Dutch in the defence of Breda against the Spanish.

12 Feb. In England King James I's last Parliament convenes, in the course of which monopolies are declared illegal and supplies are voted to support an expeditionary force to help Frederick V recover the Palatinate.

10 Mar. England declares war on Spain.

Mar. Ernst von Mansfeld's force fails to recover the Palatinate.

13 Aug. Cardinal Richelieu is appointed first minister of France by Louis XIII.

12–22 Dec. An Anglo-French teaty is concluded. Charles, Prince of Wales, will marry Henrietta Maria, daughter of Henry IV and Marie de Medici.

ASIA

– Antonio de Andrade leaves the Jesuit mission at Agra, India, to start his exploration of the Himalaya and Tibet.

THE AMERICAS

24 June The Virginia Company of London is dissolved and Virginia becomes a colony of the English crown.

– The Dutch settle in New Amsterdam, Guiana.

– The Dutch West Indies Company defies the Portuguese by starting its operations in S America and W Africa.

ECONOMY AND SOCIETY

July Birth in Leicestershire, England, of George Fox, founder of the Society of Friends (Quakers).

SCIENCE AND TECHNOLOGY

– Henry Briggs, English mathematician and academic at Oxford, Cambridge and London, publishes his *Arithmetica Logarithmica*; it contains logarithms of 3000 numbers to 14 places.

– Pope Urban VIII, successor of Gregory XV, allows Italian scientist Galileo Galilei (see p. 243) to discuss the Copernican theory of the solar system in his lectures at Florence, Italy.

ARTS AND HUMANITIES

Gianlorenzo Bernini, design for the baldacchino (canopy) over the high altar in St Peter's in Rome; he also creates the sculpture *Apollo and Daphne*.

John Donne *Devotions upon Emergent Occasions*, prayers and meditations.

Frans Hals, *The Laughing Cavalier*, painting.

Edward, Lord Herbert of Cherbury, *De Veritate* (Concerning Truth), theology establishing the principles of English deism.

Nicolas Poussin, *The Rape of the Sabine Women*, painting.

1625

EUROPE

27 Mar. James I and VI, king of England and Scotland, dies and is succeeded by Charles I.

7 April Ferdinand II appoints the imperial commander Albrecht von Wallenstein general of the imperial forces and (13 June) a prince of the Holy Roman Empire.

13 June Charles I of England marries Henrietta Maria, sister of King Louis XIII of France, by proxy.

18 June Charles I's first Parliament meets. The Commons vote tonnage and poundage (taxes) for one year only instead of for the rest of the king's life: the king has to take out a forced loan.

18 June The Italian general Ambrogio di Spinola, leading a Spanish Catholic army, takes the town of Breda (United Provinces) after an 11-month siege.

9 Dec. England and the United Provinces agree by the terms of the treaty of The Hague to subsidize King Christian IV of Denmark and Norway in his anti-Habsburg campaign in Germany.

THE AMERICAS

– Sir William Courteen establishes the first English settlement in Barbados.

– The French occupy the Antilles (West Indies) and Cayenne (on the Atlantic coast of S America).

ECONOMY AND SOCIETY

– Vincent de Paul establishes the Order of the Sisters of Mercy in Paris.

– Bubonic plague sweeps London, killing over 40,000 people.

ARTS AND HUMANITIES

5 June Death at Canterbury, Kent, of Orlando Gibbons, English composer of sacred anthems, instrumental fantasias and madrigals (including *The Silver Swan*, 1612).

Sept. Death of John Webster, English dramatist.

Hugo Grotius (see box), *On the Law of War and Peace*, a discussion of international relations and law.

Inigo Jones, design for Covent Garden Church, London.

Nicolas Poussin, *Parnassus*, painting.

1626

EUROPE

6 Feb. The peace of La Rochelle, W France, is signed between the Huguenots and the French crown.

25 April The imperial commander-in-chief, Albrecht von Wallenstein, defeats Count Ernst von Mansfeld (see 1624) and his Protestant troops at the Bridge of Dessau on the River Elbe: he occupies Pomerania. Mansfeld's forces flee to Hungary, where they ally with Gabor Bethlen, prince of Transylvania (see 1613).

15 June In England Charles I, who refuses to dismiss his adviser, the duke of Buckingham, dissolves Parliament. The king resorts to another forced loan since no supplies are voted.

27 Aug. Count Tilly, who has joined forces with those of the imperial commander-in-chief, Albrecht von Wallenstein (14 Aug.) defeats Christian IV of Denmark at Lutter in the Harz Mts in N Germany. Christian abandons Brunswick and the Catholic League is dominant in N Germany.

Sept. Cardinal Richelieu, minister of state to King Louis XIII, abolishes the ancient offices of admiral and constable of France as he concentrates power in his own hands.

29 Nov. Count Ernst von Mansfeld dies at Rakovica, Bosnia.

Hugo Grotius (1583–1645)

The Dutch jurist and theologian Hugo Grotius (the latinized form of Huigh de Groot) was born in Delft, where his father was the burgomaster. His earliest interests were literary and historical, but his greatest achievement lies in his development of the idea of international law.

In 1604 Grotius was asked by the Dutch East India Company to justify its seizure of a Portuguese vessel. His treatise *On the Law of Prize and Booty* defended the seizure as an appropriate retaliation for the Portuguese deprivation of Dutch trading rights. Chapter 9 of that work was reprinted in 1609 as *The Free Sea*, and its defence of the freedom of the seas for all nations became an instant classic.

Grotius's masterly treatise *On the Law of War and Peace* (1625) was written while Grotius was in Paris, where he had fled from the religious upheavals in the Netherlands. The work proposed a new theory of international relations based on what he called natural law, which is ordained by God but is also based on the experience of human nature. States and their princes, he suggested, must recognize their mutual limits. Within their national boundaries their powers derive from their own laws, but beyond these boundaries is another law that they must also obey. The sensible course, he suggested, was to give up the theoretical unity of Christendom and to develop instead a legal framework within which independent states could work together. His aim was a system of agreements between nations – and, when these broke down, a system of rules to regulate the conduct of war. No such system was created in his time, but Grotius has been seen as the inspiration for the modern United Nations and for international agreements such as the Geneva Convention.

---

8 Dec. In Stockholm, Sweden, birth of Christina, who will become queen of Sweden in 1632.

THE AMERICAS

– The Dutch colony of New Netherlands settles New Amsterdam on Manhattan Island, N America.

– The French Company, formed to explore and develop the islands of America, is incorporated.

SUB-SAHARAN AFRICA

– The French settle on the Senegal River for the first time.

ECONOMY AND SOCIETY

– Vincent de Paul establishes the Congregation of Priests of the Mission at St Lazarus, Paris (known as the Lazarists).

– In France Louis XIII declares that anyone killing a rival in a duel will face execution.

ARTS AND HUMANITIES

5 Feb. Birth of Marie de Rabutin-Chantal, marquise de Sévigné, French writer.

28 Feb. Death of Cyril Tourneur, English dramatist.

12 Mar. In Easton Percy, Wiltshire, England, birth of John Aubrey, writer of biographies of his contemporaries.

9 April In London, death of Sir Francis Bacon, English statesman and writer, and lord chancellor of England (1618–21).

– George Sandys's version of Ovid, *Ovid's Metamorphosis Englished*, is the first translation of a classical work to be published in America.

1627

EUROPE

April Cardinal Richelieu, minister of state to King Louis XIII, forms a Franco-Spanish alliance.

2 June George Villiers, duke of Buckingham, sets sail from Portsmouth, England, to support the Huguenot defence of La Rochelle, W France, which is besieged by Cardinal Richelieu's forces (10 Aug.).

Sept. The Turks conclude a treaty with Holy Roman Emperor Ferdinand II, which reduces the influence of Gabor Bethlen, prince of Transylvania.

Oct. Count Tilly and Albrecht von Wallenstein (the imperial commander-in-chief) subdue Holstein, Schleswig and Jutland. King Christian IV of Denmark and Norway has to withdraw to Denmark.

ASIA

– Korea becomes a tributary state of China.

SCIENCE AND TECHNOLOGY

25 Jan. In Lismore, Ireland, birth of Robert Boyle, Anglo-Irish chemist and natural philosopher.

– Francis Bacon's posthumously published work *New Atlantis* proposes a national scientific and artistic museum.

ARTS AND HUMANITIES

4 July Death of English dramatist Thomas Middleton.

27 Sept. In Dijon, France, birth of Jacques-Bénigne Bossuet, French bishop, historian and theologian.

– German composer Heinrich Schütz's *Daphne*, the first German opera, is performed in Dresden.

1628

EUROPE

26 Jan. Albrecht von Wallenstein, imperial commander-in-chief, occupies the duchy of Mecklenburg. He assumes the title of admiral of the Baltic (21 April) and begins the siege of Stralsund (June). The city is defended by the Swedish–Danish treaty (of 29 April), which has brought Gustavus II Adolphus of Sweden into the war.

7 June In England King Charles I has to accept the Petition of Right, which declares arbitrary imprisonment, martial law, forced loans and the billeting of troops to be illegal.

11 June In England the House of Commons' Remonstrances attack Arminianism and ritualism in the Church of England

and demand that the king dismiss his favourite, the unpopular George Villiers, duke of Buckingham.

23 Aug. In Portsmouth, England, the duke of Buckingham is assassinated by John Felton, a Puritan fanatic.

23 Aug. Wallenstein is forced to lift the siege of Stralsund (German Baltic coast).

28 Oct. The French Huguenots in La Rochelle, W France, surrender to Cardinal Richelieu after a 14-month siege. The crown takes measures to curb the political independence of La Rochelle and other towns.

Dec. English politician Thomas Wentworth is appointed president of the Council of the North.

– Richelieu establishes French companies for the colonization of Canada and Senegal.

ASIA

Feb. Having killed all his male relatives to ensure his success, Shah Jahan becomes Mughal emperor of India.

– The Dutch seize the Spanish treasure fleet and occupy Java and Malucca (Indonesia).

THE AMERICAS

28 Sept. An English colony is established at Salem, Massachusetts, N America.

SCIENCE AND TECHNOLOGY

– William Harvey, English physician, publishes his discovery of the blood's circulation in *Exercitatio Anatomica de Motu Cordis et Sanguinis* (Anatomical Treatise on the Motion of the Heart and the Blood).

ARTS AND HUMANITIES

16 Oct. Death in Paris of François de Malherbe, French poet and precursor of French classicism.

Nov. Birth in Elstow, Bedfordshire, of John Bunyan, English Puritan preacher and writer, author of *Pilgrim's Progress* (1678).

Nov. Birth in London of Sir William Temple, diplomat and author.

René Descartes (see p. 256), *Règles pour la direction de l'esprit* (Rules for the Direction of the Mind), philosophy.

Nicolas Poussin, *Martyrdom of St Erasmus*, painting.

1629

EUROPE

20 Jan. In England Charles I's second Parliament convenes and attacks the king for levying tonnage and poundage (taxes) without parliamentary authority. The House of Commons passes resolutions against Archbishop William Laud's religious changes and the extra-parliamentary taxation (2 Mar.). Laud is a zealous church administrator who has won rapid ecclesiastical promotion. He was appointed (1622) confessor to the royal favourite, George Villiers. The Speaker is ordered by the king to dissolve the House but is held down in his chair while the Resolutions are read and passed. Charles I dissolves Parliament on the same day: it will not meet again until April 1640.

29 Mar. The Edict of Restitution of Church property in Germany provides for the restoration to the Catholic Church of all the property secularized since the peace of Augsburg in 1555. Albrecht von Wallenstein, the imperial commander-in-chief, and the Catholic League enforce the edict. Calvinist princes who were not party to the peace of Augsburg are unaffected.

22 May Christian IV of Denmark agrees by the peace of Lübeck that he will not intervene in imperial affairs.

16 June Wallenstein becomes duke of Mecklenburg.

28 June The peace of Alais ends the French Huguenot rebellion. The Huguenots, though granted freedom of worship, are forced to end their political activity. The civic administrations in Nîmes, Montauban and other cities are redrawn.

25 Sept. Sweden and Poland agree on the Truce of Altmark by which Sweden retains Livonia, Memel, Pillau, Braunsberg and Elbing. The truce is mediated by Cardinal Richelieu, minister of state to King Louis XIII, who tries to ally the Swedes with the Catholic League in Germany against the Habsburgs.

THE AMERICAS

– Richelieu establishes the Company of New France for the monopoly of Canadian trade.

ARTS AND HUMANITIES

– Italian artist Gianlorenzo Bernini is appointed chief architect of Saint Peter's, Rome, by Pope Urban VIII.

– King Charles I of England creates the Flemish artist, Peter Paul Rubens, a knight.

Lancelot Andrewes, *Sermons*. Andrewes, a bishop and scholar, was also one of the translators of the King James English version of the Bible (see 1611).

Thomas Hobbes, translation of Thucydides' *Peloponnesian War*.

Heinrich Schütz, *Symphoniae Sacrae*, music.

1630

EUROPE

29 May In London the future Charles II of England is born.

6 July Gustavus II Adolphus of Sweden, known as the Lion of the North, lands in Pomerania and leads his army into Germany.

July Meeting at Regensburg, Bavaria, the princes and Electors of Germany, encouraged by Cardinal Richelieu, minister of state to Louis XIII, king of France, demand that the Holy Roman Emperor dismiss Albrecht von Wallenstein, the imperial commander-in-chief. Ferdinand II complies (13 Aug.), and Count Tilly assumes command of his army.

10 Nov. In France the Day of Dupes, on which Richelieu unmasks the conspiracy against him of Marie de Medici. The queen mother is banished from Paris.

– The Hanseatic diet meets in Lübeck for the last time.

THE AMERICAS

– English Puritan governor John Winthrop arrives in Massachusetts with 1000 settlers to found Boston, and a town plan is drawn up (17 Sept.).

SCIENCE AND TECHNOLOGY

15 Nov. Death of Johannes Kepler, German astronomer and formulator of Kepler's laws of planetary motion.

– Over 650km (400 miles) of canals are built in the United Netherlands, providing the first regular public transport linking major towns and cities.

ARTS AND HUMANITIES

Anders Christensen, *Arrebo Hexaemeron*, a religious poem written in Alexandrines; it marks the start of a Danish literary revival.

Philippe de Champaigne, *Adoration of the Shepherds*, painting.

Pierre Corneille, *Clitandre*, tragi-comedy.

François de Malherbe, *Poetical Works*, published posthumously.

Peter Paul Rubens, *The Blessings of Peace*, painting.

Georges de la Tour, *Magdalene with the Lamp*, painting.

1631

EUROPE

23 Jan. Treaty of Bärwalde: France subsidizes Sweden for six years, to help free Germany from the control of Holy Roman Emperor Ferdinand II.

20 Feb. The German Protestant princes meet at Leipzig, Saxony, and decide to ally with Gustavus II Adolphus of Sweden.

3–13 April Gustavus II Adolphus seizes Frankfurt an der Oder.

20 May Count Tilly and his imperial troops sack Magdeburg; the town is destroyed.

30 May By the treaty of Fontainebleau between France and Maximilian of Bavaria, leader of the Catholic League, the league promises to support the king of France against his enemies, with the exception of the Holy Roman Emperor.

19 June Cardinal Richelieu masterminds the treaty of Cherasco to end the War of the Mantuan Succession. French and imperial forces leave Italy; the French candidate, Charles, duke of Nevers, is invested by Ferdinand II with the Duchy of Mantua. France obtains Pinerolo (in the Alps near Turin) and the duke is betrothed to Louis XIII's sister. France thus regains influence and territory in Italy.

19 June Tilly burns the city of Halle, near Leipzig in E Germany.

Aug. Tilly invades Saxony, E Germany.

17 Sept. Gustavus II Adolphus of Sweden, supported by the Saxons, defeats the Catholic forces of Count Tilly at the battle of Breitenfeld, near Leipzig.

Oct. Saxon troops invade Bohemia. Gustavus II Adolphus advances across Thuringia and Franconia towards the Rhine. The emperor asks Wallenstein to raise an army to oppose Saxony and Sweden.

15 Nov. Saxon forces seize Prague.

15(?) Nov. Würzburg, SE of Frankfurt, Germany, is taken by Gustavus II Adolphus who (Dec.) also occupies Mainz on the River Rhine.

THE AMERICAS

– The Dutch West India Company establishes a settlement on the Delaware River.

ARTS AND HUMANITIES

31 Mar. In London death of John Donne, English poet.

> *New philosophy calls all in doubt.*
>
> John Donne *An Anatomy of the World: the First Anniversary* (1611)

9 Aug. Birth of John Dryden, English poet, playwright and critic, and poet laureate.

10 Dec. Death of Hugh Myddelton, English goldsmith (see 1613).

23 Dec. In London, death of Michael Drayton, English poet.

Philip Massinger, *Believe As You List*, play.

Rembrandt van Rijn, *The Artist's Mother*, painting.

1632

EUROPE

13 April Holy Roman Emperor Ferdinand II reinstates Albrecht von Wallenstein as supreme imperial commander, with an army of 50,000 men, who are instructed to expel the Saxons from Bohemia.

14 April Gustavus II Adolphus of Sweden defeats Count Tilly's imperial army on the River Lech. Tilly is wounded and dies (30 April).

17 May Gustavus II Adolphus enters Munich; the Elector of Saxony enters Prague.

3 Sept. Gustavus II Adolphus attacks Wallenstein near Nuremberg but is repulsed. Wallenstein plunders Saxony.

6 Nov. Gustavus II Adolphus defeats Wallenstein at the battle of Lützen but is killed in action.

6 Nov. Queen Christina of Sweden appoints Axel Oxenstierna as chancellor and regent.

– John Selden, English historian and politician working for the Admiralty, explains England's claim to sovereignty of the sea in *Mare Clausum*.

THE AMERICAS

14 April Charles I, king of England, issues a charter for the government of Maryland. The governor can make laws and tax only with the consent of the adult male population.

ARTS AND HUMANITIES

29 Aug. In Wrington, Somerset, England, birth of John Locke, philosopher (see p. 285).

20 Oct. In East Knoyle, Wiltshire, England, birth of Christopher Wren, architect and geometrician.

31 Oct. In Delft, United Netherlands, birth of Jan Vermeer, painter.

23 Nov. Near Reims, France, birth of Jean Mabillon, monk and historian.

24 Nov. In Amsterdam, United Netherlands, birth of Baruch Spinoza, philosopher (see p. 275).

28 Nov. In Florence, Italy, birth of Jean-Baptiste Lully, who will be court composer to Louis XIV of France.

– The *Second Folio* of William Shakespeare's (see p. 236) plays is published.

Gianlorenzo Bernini, *Bust of Cardinal Scipio Borghese*, sculpture.

John Davies, *Antiquae Linguae Britannicae Dictionarium Duplex* (Welsh–Latin Dictionary).

John Donne, *Death's Duell*, his last sermon.

1633

EUROPE

23 April S German Protestants form the League of Heilbronn with Sweden and France against the imperial forces and the Catholic League.

May The French occupy the imperial duchy of Lorraine in E France.

18 June Charles I, king of England, is crowned king of Scotland. He orders the Scottish Parliament to prepare an Anglican-style liturgy.

June Imperial commander Albrecht von Wallenstein, in negotiation with the Elector of Saxony, proposes the repeal of the Edict of Restitution (Mar. 1629) as a means of securing peace. The emperor refuses the proposal.

6 Aug. English clergyman William Laud is elected archbishop of Canterbury and embarks on a 'High Church' policy of ritualism.

Aug. Wallenstein, now acting independently, opens negotiations with Count Axel Oxenstierna, regent of Sweden.

11 Oct. Wallenstein defeats the Swedish army at Steinau in Silesia.

14 Oct. The future James II, king of England, is born in London.

14 Nov. On the death of the Infanta Isabella in Brussels the Spanish Netherlands are governed directly from Spain. The States-General do not meet again until 1790.

Dec. Emperor Ferdinand II suspects Wallenstein of treachery and detaches his chief commanders from the general.

ASIA

– The English establish a trading post in Bengal, India.

THE AMERICAS

– The Dutch settle in Connecticut, N America.

SCIENCE AND TECHNOLOGY

20 Sept. Italian scientist and astronomer Galileo Galilei (see p. 243) is tried before the Inquisition at Rome: he is forced to retract his Copernican view of the universe and is placed under house arrest.

– Jacques le Mercier constructs the Palais Cardinal (now Palais-Royal), Paris.

Eppur si muove.

(But it does move.)

Galileo Galilei (1564–1642) – attributed to him
after he was forced to recant his belief that the
Earth moves around the sun

ARTS AND HUMANITIES

23 Feb. In London, birth of Samuel Pepys, known for his *Diary*,
which provides insights into London life during the 1660s.

3 Mar. Death of George Herbert, metaphysical poet, in Bemerton,
Wiltshire, England.

Abraham Cowley, *Poetical Blossoms*, poetry

John Donne, *Poems*, published posthumously.

John Ford, *'Tis Pity She's a Whore*, play.

George Herbert, *The Temple or Sacred Poems*, published
posthumously.

Christopher Marlowe, *The Jew of Malta*, play, published
posthumously.

1634

EUROPE

24 Jan. Imperial commander Albrecht von Wallenstein, who has
required a personal declaration of loyalty from his lieutenants
(the Pilsen Revers, 12 Jan.) is now declared a traitor by the
emperor.

7 May English lawyer and pamphleteer William Prynne, who
published the *Histrio-mastix* (1632), is sentenced by the court
of Star Chamber to a £5000 fine, life imprisonment and the
loss of both his ears in the pillory for publishing a work viewed
as an attack on Queen Henrietta Maria and King Charles I.

5–6 Sept. At the battle of Nördlingen the Swedes are defeated by
Austrian commander Matthias Gallas, leader of the imperial
forces; the Catholic cause revives in S Germany.

20 Oct. In England the first writs for Ship Money (a tax to
finance the Royal Navy) are issued in London and the port
towns. Charles I subsequently extends Ship Money to inland
towns, which contravenes traditional methods of raising
money for the navy.

Nov. In Germany Württemberg and Franconia are reconquered
from the Swedes by imperial forces.

– In his efforts to centralize French administration, Cardinal
Richelieu creates the office of intendant: as the crown's
representatives, the intendants weaken the powers of provincial
governors.

ARTS AND HUMANITIES

– The first Oberammergau Passion Play is performed in Bavaria.
The villagers vow to perform the play every ten years after an
outbreak of plague in 1633.

Pierre Corneille, *The Widow* and *The Maidservant*, comedies.

1635

EUROPE

30 April France and Sweden make an alliance with the treaty of
Compiègne: France pledges to wage war on Spain and make no
peace without Sweden's consent.

19 May The peace of Prague between the emperor and the
Elector of Saxony: the Holy Roman Empire is restored to its
condition before the Edict of Restitution (Mar. 1629) and the
Lutheran religion acquires privileged status. The Thirty Years
War is now a struggle between the Franco–Swedish alliance and
the House of Habsburg.

12 Sept. Sweden and Poland sign a 20-year truce.

27 Oct. Cardinal Richelieu arranges to buy the army of Bernhard
of Saxe-Weimar by paying a subsidy.

Nov. Thomas Wentworth, deputy of Ireland and from 1639
principal adviser to the king and 1st earl of Strafford, claims
Connaught (W Ireland) for Charles I. He invites settlers to
colonize the area.

THE AMERICAS

– Beginning of the extensive colonization of Connecticut; the
trading post of Windsor becomes home to religious refugees
from Dorchester, Massachusetts.

– Occupation of the Caribbean islands of Martinique and
Guadeloupe by the French.

– The Dutch seize Pernambuco (NE Brazil) from the Portuguese.

– N America's oldest secondary school, the English High and
Latin School, is founded in Boston, Massachusetts.

ARTS AND HUMANITIES

10 Feb. Founding of the Académie Française, Paris.

27 Aug. Death in Madrid of Lope Félix de Vega Carpio, prolific
Spanish dramatist.

– The tomb of the Merovingian king Childeric is discovered in
the Spanish Netherlands and leads to the development of
archaeology as a discipline.

Pedro Calderón de la Barca, *La vida es sueño* (Life is a Dream),
tragi-comedy.

Philippe de Champaigne, *Portrait of Richelieu*, painting.

Pierre Corneille, *Médée*, tragedy.

Rembrandt van Rijn, *Self-portrait with Saskia* and *Saskia in
Arcadian Costume*, paintings.

Peter Paul Rubens, ceiling of the Banqueting Hall, Whitehall, and
Infanta Isabella, paintings.

Anthony Van Dyck, *Charles I*, painting.

Diego Velázquez, *The Surrender of Breda*, painting.

1636

EUROPE

May Cardinal Ferdinand, infante of Spain, who commands troops
from Bavaria and Cologne, invades NE France. The prince of
Condé, governor of Burgundy, invades Franche-Comté.

4 Oct. Marshal Johan Banér leads Swedish forces to victory against imperial and Saxon troops at the battle of Wittstock. This success marks a revival of Swedish power in the Thirty Years War and restores Swedish influence in Germany.

22 Dec. Holy Roman Emperor, Ferdinand II, makes concessions to the imperial electors in order to secure the election of his son, the archduke Ferdinand, as king of Germany.

ASIA

23 May In an effort to expel the Portuguese from Ceylon (Sri Lanka), King Rajasinha II of Kandy reaches an agreement with the Dutch: the Dutch settle in Ceylon.

– Proclamation of the Qing (Ch'ing) dynasty of China by the Manchu at Mukden, Manchuria.

THE AMERICAS

June English-born colonist Roger Williams, banished from Massachusetts because he believed civil government could not govern the individual consciences of men, founds Providence, Rhode Island, as a colony enjoying complete religious freedom.

– The Dutch colonize Brooklyn (in modern New York) and settle by the shore of Gowanns Bay.

ARTS AND HUMANITIES

– Foundation of Harvard College, Cambridge, Massachusetts. Pierre Corneille, *Le Cid*, tragedy.

Anthony Van Dyck, *Charles I King of England on Horseback*, painting.

Diego Velázquez, *Prince Baltasar Carlos as a Hunter*, painting.

1637

EUROPE

15 Feb. Ferdinand II, who became Holy Roman Emperor in 1619, dies in Vienna. His son, Ferdinand III, becomes Holy Roman Emperor and will reign until 1657.

11 June By a majority of 10 out of 12, English judges asked for an adjudication by King Charles I decide that Ship Money is legal; John Hampden, a Member of Parliament, continues to refuse to pay.

30 June English lawyer and pamphleteer William Prynne (see 7 May 1654) is fined, sentenced to perpetual imprisonment and branded on the cheek with the letters SL (seditious libeller).

23 July Jenny Geddes starts a riot in St Giles's Cathedral, Edinburgh, by throwing a stool at the bishop's head in protest at his use of the new Laudian Prayer Book (see 18 June 1633).

THE AMERICAS

30 April Immigration from England to N America is restricted: propertied subjects can leave only if they take the oath of allegiance and are supplied with a certificate by the local justices of the peace.

SUB-SAHARAN AFRICA

Aug. Expulsion of the Portuguese from the Gold Coast (modern Ghana) by the Dutch.

– French traders establish a settlement at St Louis at the mouth of the Senegal River, W Africa.

ARTS AND HUMANITIES

6 Aug. Death in London of Ben Jonson, English dramatist and poet.

– Opening in Venice of the Teatro di San Cassiano, the first public opera house.

– English poet John Milton's *Comus, a Masque*, is performed at Ludlow Castle, Shropshire.

René Descartes (see box), *Discours de la méthode* (Discourse on Method), philosophy. He issues his *Geometry* as an appendix to the *Discours*. Other appendices state the law of refraction and analyse the rainbow.

René Descartes (1596–1650)

The philosopher, scientist and mathematician René Descartes was born in Touraine, France, and educated by the Jesuits. As a young man he joined the army of Prince Maurice of Nassau at Breda in the Netherlands. The experience of applying mathematics to military engineering stimulated him intellectually, and a vision experienced at Ulm on 10 November 1619 dazzled him with the possibility of a complete explanation of sciences previously thought to be distinct: arithmetic, geometry, music and astronomy as well as optics and mechanics. Among his important syntheses was the development of coordinate geometry, in which mathematical functions can be plotted on a graph.

Descartes' philosophical fame is based on his hypothesis of 'Cartesian dualism'– the idea that soul and body are entirely separate substances that can be understood separately but which are nonetheless conjoined while a human being is alive. However, humans are really mind, a thinking substance containing 'innate ideas' that is utterly different from body. It is mind that gives us real identity. Mind has to be known first, before any knowledge of the body is attainable. Descartes began by setting out to prove he himself existed. He got rid of everything that can possibly be doubted (such as evidence from the senses) in order to show what is logically indisputable. What he could not doubt was that he himself was thinking, and this resulted in his best-known adage: *Cogito ergo sum* – I think, therefore I am.

Cartesian clarity and rigour became a cultural style, influencing the literature, architecture, landscape design, military tactics and bureaucracy of 17th-century Europe. But the system's emphasis on the supremacy of rational deduction from first principles over empirical observation had a somewhat limiting effect on the development of the scientific method.

Anthony Van Dyck, *The Children of Charles I King of England*, painting.

1638

EUROPE

19 Feb. Charles I, king of England, issues a proclamation supporting the Scottish Prayer Book. A rebellion against the crown follows, with the assumption of power in Scotland by a group of representatives, the Tables. The Scottish National Covenant is signed by the clergy of Edinburgh (1 Mar.) and subsequently by the laity, as it is circulated throughout Scotland.

28 Feb. Death of Henry, duke of Rohan, French Protestant leader.

3 Mar. Renewal of the Franco-Swedish alliance for three years.

9 Sept. Charles I withdraws the Scottish liturgy and promises to call a Scottish Parliament as well as a general assembly.

16 Sept. Birth of the dauphin of France, the future Louis XIV, the first child of King Louis XIII of France and Anne of Austria.

28 Nov. The marquis of Hamilton dissolves in the king's name the Scottish general assembly, which (since 21 Nov.) has been meeting in Glasgow without Charles I's approval. It continues to sit and (20 Dec.) abolishes the episcopacy.

17 Dec. With the support of the French, Bernhard, duke of Saxe-Weimar, takes Breisach and secures the region of Alsace as his personal domain.

ECONOMY AND SOCIETY

6 May In Ypres, Spanish Netherlands (now Belgium), death of Cornelius Jansen, Roman Catholic reformer and founder of Jansenism.

Dec. Death of Père Joseph, Richelieu's secret agent.

SCIENCE AND TECHNOLOGY

– Italian scientist Galileo Galilei (see p. 243) experiments on gravity and publishes *Discorsi e dimostrazioni matematiche intorno a due nuove scienze attenenti alla meccanica* (Dialogues Concerning Two New Sciences).

ARTS AND HUMANITIES

– Italian baroque architect and sculptor Francesco Borromini starts work on San Carlo alle Quattro Fontane, Rome.
John Milton (see p. 273), *Lycidas*, elegy.
Nicolas Poussin, *Et in Arcadia Ego*, painting.

1639

EUROPE

Mar. Scottish Covenanters seize Edinburgh, Stirling and other major cities in Scotland. The First Bishops' War breaks out (24 May) between King Charles I and the Scots, as a result of the king's enforcement of Anglican observances on the Scottish Church, which wishes to abolish the episcopacy. Charles I gives in and signs the Pacification of Berwick (18 June), promising to defer to a Scottish Parliament and general assembly.

May Thomas Wentworth returns to London from Ireland (see Nov. 1635) and becomes Charles I's chief adviser.

18 July Bernhard, duke of Saxe-Weimar, dies of fever. His death prevents a crisis developing over the territory of Alsace.

Aug. The general assembly abolishes the episcopacy in Scotland.

21 Oct. Admiral Maarten Tromp, commanding the Dutch fleet, defeats a Spanish fleet that has taken refuge in the English Channel off Deal, Kent, S England, while on its way to Flanders.

30 Oct. The army formerly commanded by the late Bernhard of Saxe-Weimar (the Bernardine army) and now under the command of the duke of Longueville swears allegiance to France.

28 Dec. Longueville's forces cross the Rhine from the E and occupy the region of Alsace.

ARTS AND HUMANITIES

7 Feb. The Académie française starts work on the *Dictionary of the French Language*.

22 Mar. Death in London of Thomas Carew, royalist songwriter and poet.

21 May Death in Paris of Tommaso Campanella, Italian philosopher.

22 Dec. Birth in La Ferté-Milon, France, of Jean Racine, French dramatist and playwright, best known for his tragedies.
Pierre Corneille, *Cinna* and *Horace*, tragedies.
Peter Paul Rubens, *The Judgement of Paris*, painting.

1640

EUROPE

Mar. French forces complete the occupation of Alsace.

13 April–5 May In England the Short Parliament meets for the first time after Charles I's 11-year personal rule: it is dissolved when it refuses to vote money to the crown and criticizes the king's ecclesiastical policy.

12 May A revolt in Barcelona, Spain, spreads throughout Catalonia.

20 Aug. The Second Bishops' War starts as Scottish forces cross the River Tweed, enter England and (30 Aug.) enter Newcastle.

3 Nov. The Long Parliament (which will sit until 1653) is called and (11 Nov.) begins an attack on Thomas Wentworth, earl of Strafford, Charles I's chief adviser.

11 Nov. English parliamentarian John Pym denounces Thomas Wentworth, earl of Strafford, who is sent to the Tower of London (25 Nov.), accused of plotting to subvert the laws of England and Ireland.

1 Dec. Portugal rebels against Spanish rule and regains its independence under John IV of Braganza.

7 Dec. The House of Commons declares Ship Money to be illegal, presents the Root and Branch Petition to abolish episcopacy (11 Dec.), and impeaches Archbishop William Laud (18 Dec.).

Dec. Frederick William (the Great Elector) succeeds on the death of George William, Elector of Brandenburg.

MIDDLE EAST AND NORTH AFRICA

- Murad IV, Ottoman sultan, dies. He is succeeded by Ibrahim, the son of Ahmed I. Ibrahim will rule until 1648.

ASIA

- The British establish Fort St George in Bengal and a settlement that later becomes the city of Madras, India.

ARTS AND HUMANITIES

25 Jan. Death in Oxford, England, of Robert Burton, Anglican clergyman and writer.

30 May Death in Antwerp, Spanish Netherlands, of Sir Peter Paul Rubens, Flemish artist.

July Birth of Aphra Behn, novelist and England's first known female playwright.

Thomas Carew, *Poems*, published posthumously.

Pierre Corneille, *Polyeucte*, tragedy.

John Donne, *LXXX Sermons*, published posthumously.

Rembrandt van Rijn, *Self-portrait at the Age of 34*, painting.

Izaak Walton, *The Life of Donne*, biography.

1641

EUROPE

2 May In England the marriage takes place of Mary, daughter of King Charles I and Henrietta Maria, to William, son of the prince of Orange.

12 May Beheading on Tower Hill, London, of Thomas Wentworth, earl of Strafford, favoured adviser of King Charles I.

June Portugal allies with France and the United Provinces against Spain.

5 July The English Parliament abolishes the courts of Star Chamber and High Commission, accusing these institutions of extending King Charles I's prerogative powers during his personal rule.

21 Aug. France and Sweden extend their treaty of alliance. Sweden allies with Portugal.

23 Nov. The English Parliament approves the Grand Remonstrance against the king: it demands parliamentary approval for all appointments of ministers, the reduction of the temporal power of bishops and the referral of Church matters to a synod of Protestant divines. Domestic political reporting develops in England including (Nov.) the start of the regular publication, *Diurnall Occurences in Parliament*.

16 Dec. Italian-born French churchman and politician Jules Mazarin (see 1602) is elected a cardinal by Pope Urban VIII.

ASIA

Jan. After a five-month siege, the Portuguese settlement of Malacca (on the Malay peninsula) falls to the Dutch.

SCIENCE AND TECHNOLOGY

- Italian scientist Galileo Galilei (see p. 243) invents a clock with a pendulum and a pin-wheel escapement.

ARTS AND HUMANITIES

15 April Death in Naples, Italy, of Zampieri Domenichino, Italian baroque artist.

9 Dec. Death in London of Anthony Van Dyck, Flemish artist.

- John Evelyn, English author and diarist, begins to write his *Diary*.

John Barnard, *First Booke of Selected Church Musik*, collection of music, including 60 anthems by William Byrd; the publication is dedicated to King Charles I.

Pierre Corneille, *The Death of Pompey*, tragedy.

René Descartes (see p. 256), *Meditations on the First Philosophy*, philosophy.

Anthony Van Dyck, *Prince William of Orange*, painting.

Ben Jonson, *Timber or Discoveries*, a posthumous collection of Jonson's notebooks.

Nicolas Poussin, *Seven Sacraments* (first version) and *Bacchanalian Revels before a Term of Pan*, paintings.

1642

EUROPE

4 Jan. In England King Charles I attempts, and fails, to arrest five members of the House of Commons (John Pym, Denzil Holles, William Strode, John Hampden and Arthur Haslerig) for colluding with the Scots in an attempt to weaken his rule.

23 Feb. Queen Henrietta Maria, wife of King Charles I, seeking safety because of the deteriorating domestic situation, leaves England for Holland.

4 July The English Parliament forms a Committee of Public Safety to prepare for war.

22 Aug. The English Royal Standard is raised at Nottingham: the Civil Wars begin.

9 Sept. Robert Devereux, 3rd earl of Essex, leading the parliamentary army, leaves London for the Midlands.

12 Sept. In France Henry, marquis de Cinq Mars and favourite of King Louis XIII, is executed after chief minister Cardinal Richelieu discovers that he conspired with Spain in a plot to assassinate him.

23 Sept. In the English Civil Wars, Prince Rupert, nephew of King Charles I, defeats the parliamentarians under Essex at Powicke Bridge, Worcester.

23 Oct. Indecisive battle at Edgehill, Warwickshire, the first major battle of the English Civil Wars, between a parliamentarian army under Essex and the royalist army of King Charles I and Prince Rupert.

2 Nov. Defeat of the imperial army by the Swedes, under Marshal Lennart Torstenson, at the second battle of Breitenfeld, Saxony.

4 Dec. Death in Paris of Armand-Jean du Plessis, Cardinal Richelieu, chief minister (1624–42) to Louis XIII. Cardinal Jules Mazarin becomes chief minister.

5 Dec. English royalist forces occupy the town of Marlborough, Wiltshire.

13 Dec. English parliamentarian forces occupy the town of Winchester, Hampshire.

ASIA

– The final stage of the exclusion of the Portuguese from Japan (in progress since 1637) leaves the Dutch with a monopoly of foreign trade with Japan.

– Shah Abbas II accedes to the throne of Persia.

AUSTRALASIA AND OCEANIA

– Abel Janszoon Tasman, an explorer serving the Dutch East India Company, becomes the first European to see Van Dieman's Land and New Zealand. Initially named in honour of the governor-general of the Dutch East Indies, Van Dieman's Land will be renamed Tasmania in 1856.

SCIENCE AND TECHNOLOGY

8 Jan. In Arcetri, near Florence, Italy, death of Galileo Galilei (see p. 243), Italian mathematician, astronomer, and physicist.

– Italian scientist Evangelista Torricelli invents the barometer.

– French scientist and mathematician Blaise Pascal (see box) invents a machine for addition.

ARTS AND HUMANITIES

18 Aug. In Bologna, death of Guido Reni, Italian baroque artist.

25 Dec. In Woolsthorpe, Lincolnshire, birth of Isaac Newton (see p. 283), English physicist and mathematician.

Dec. In Paris birth of André Boulle, cabinetmaker and architect.

– Italian composer Claudio Monteverdi's opera *L'incoronazione di Poppea* (The Coronation of Poppaea) is performed in Venice. Monteverdi is official musician at St Mark's, Venice.

– English theatres are closed by government order.

Francesco Borromini, San Ivo della Sapienza, Rome.

Pierre Corneille, *Le Menteur* (The Liar) comedy.

Sir John Denham, 'Cooper's Hill', poem; the first example of a new genre in English verse, the pastoral descriptive poem.

Rembrandt van Rijn, *The Night Watch* (*Sortie of the Shooting Company of Captain Frans Banning Cocq*), painting.

1643

EUROPE

23 Jan. In the English Civil Wars the city of Leeds falls to the parliamentarians.

24 Jan. Gaspar de Guzman, Count Olivares, chief minister to King Philip IV of Spain, is removed from power following revolts in Catalonia and Portugal.

13 May In England Oliver Cromwell, leading the parliamentarian forces, defeats the royalists at Grantham, Lincolnshire.

14 May Louis XIII, king of France, dies in Saint-Germain-en-Laye near Paris; he is succeeded by the infant Louis XIV. Anne of Austria rules as queen mother and confirms Cardinal Jules Mazarin (Giulio Mazzarini) – to whom she is rumoured to be secretly married – as chief minister.

19 May The French defeat of Spanish forces at Rocroi, on the border of the Spanish Netherlands, marks the onset of Spanish military decline. Louis II, prince of Condé (known as the Great Condé), masterminds the French victory.

18 June John Hampden, English parliamentarian, dies in Thame, Oxfordshire, after being wounded in a skirmish at Chalgrove Field.

20 Sept. In England the royalists are defeated at Newbury, Berkshire.

25 Sept. The Assembly of Westminster (summoned by Parliament, 25 Sept.) adopts Presbyterianism by a Solemn League and Covenant between the Parliament of England and Wales and that of Scotland. A joint committee of the two kingdoms is later formed.

8 Dec. Death in London of John Pym, prominent MP and fierce opponent of King Charles I.

THE AMERICAS

May Connecticut, New Haven, and the Plymouth and

Blaise Pascal (1623–62)

A mathematician of genius, Pascal turned his formidable intellect to theology and philosophy. Born in Clermont-Ferrand, in central France, and brought up in Paris, Pascal acquired a reputation as a precocious mathematician and scientist. Between 1642 and 1644 he developed a calculating machine, and he also carried out original work in hydrodynamics and hydrostatics, investigated the vacuum, invented the syringe and established Pascal's law, which states that pressure in a fluid is equal throughout. His mathematical work became the basis of the modern probability theory. These

achievements alone would have made him a significant figure in the evolution of modern thought.

On 23 November 1654, however, Pascal experienced his 'night of fire' – a profound conversion that led to his entry into the Jansenist community at Port-Royal in January 1655. Pascal's *Lettres provinciales* (1656–7) consist of 18 religious letters attacking the Jesuits and their hypocrisy. It is a landmark in the history of French prose and of religious apologetics.

Pascal was a clever and rigorous controversialist with a talent for the cutting remark, but both his *Lettres provinciales*

and his *Pensées sur la religion* (Thoughts on Religion), which were published posthumously, submerged satire in a deeper spirituality. In these works Pascal put forward the idea that humanity is a mixture of the sublime and the abject. This sense of the inescapable contradictions of human nature was, he thought, absent in philosophy, and Christianity's understanding of this division in human nature was the sign of its truth. His sense of the paradoxical condition of humankind is Pascal's greatest legacy. Detached from his Christian conclusions, it survives in modern literary explorations of the absurd and the random.

Massachusetts Bay colonies combine to form the Confederation of New England.

SCIENCE AND TECHNOLOGY
- Parcel post is established in France.

ARTS AND HUMANITIES
1 Mar. In Rome, death of Girolamo Frescobaldi, Italian composer and virtuoso keyboard player, famous for his compositions for organ and harpsichord, which significantly advanced keyboard technique.

18 Sept. Birth of Gilbert Burnet, Scottish churchman and historian.

20 Sept. Death at the battle of Newbury, in the English Civil Wars, of Lucius Cary, 2nd Viscount Falkland, English royalist, religious writer and soldier.

29 Nov. Death of Claudio Monteverdi, Italian composer who made a major contribution to the development of the opera.

- Jesuit scholar John Bolland's edition of the *Acts of the Saints* (accounts of the lives of the Christian saints) establishes new standards of critical scholarship.

- The English royalist Sunday newspaper, *Mercurius Aulicus*, begins publication, as does its parliamentarian equivalent, *Mercurius Britannicus*.

Sir Thomas Browne, *Religio Medici* (Religion of a Doctor), essay.

Herman Conring, *De Origine Juris Germanici* (On the Origins of Germanic Laws), establishing the historical basis of German law.

John Milton, *The Doctrine and Discipline of Divorce*, religious tract.

1644

EUROPE
24 Jan. Parliamentarian commander Thomas Fairfax defeats the Irish royalists at the battle of Nantwich in Cheshire.

24 Jan. Scottish forces invade England.

24 Jan. Swedish forces invade Denmark, crossing the border into Jutland and establishing their control over the province.

2 July In England Thomas Fairfax, Oliver Cromwell and Edward Montagu, earl of Manchester, lead the parliamentarian army to victory against the royalists (led by Prince Rupert, nephew of King Charles I) at the battle of Marston Moor near York in Yorkshire.

14 July Queen Henrietta Maria of England flees to France.

3–5 Aug. The French occupy the Rhineland.

2 Sept. In the English Civil Wars the earl of Essex's army surrenders to Charles I at Lostwithiel, Cornwall.

17 Sept. The French take Mainz and, subsequently, Mannheim, Speyer, Worms and Oppenheim in the middle Rhine valley.

14 Oct. In London, birth of William Penn, English Quaker and founder of Pennsylvania.

22 Oct. In the English Civil Wars the city of Newcastle falls to a Scottish army under Alexander Leslie, 1st earl of Leven, in alliance with the English parliamentarians.

18 Dec. Queen Christina takes up the reins of government of Sweden.

- The English Parliament forbids the celebration of Christmas.
- In France peasant rebellions arise in the regions of Dauphiné, Languedoc, Normandy and Armagnac.
- The Spanish expel the French from the province of Aragon.

ASIA
- In China the Manchu Qing (Ch'ing) dynasty succeeds the Ming dynasty (which has ruled China since 1368).

SCIENCE AND TECHNOLOGY
- René Descartes (see p. 256), French philosopher and mathematician, publishes *Principles of Philosophy*, which expounds the laws of motion and the theory of vortices, bringing together philosophy and science.

ARTS AND HUMANITIES
Gianlorenzo Bernini, *Vision of St Teresa*, sculpture.

John Milton (see p. 273), *Areopagitica*, a political tract advocating an end to censorship of publications; his *Letter on Education* urges the reform of English education along the principles of Moravian educationalist J.A. Comenius.

Nicolas Poussin, *The Seven Sacraments* (second series), paintings.

Rembrandt van Rijn, *The Woman Taken in Adultery*, painting.

Samuel Rutherford, *The Law of Kings*, political tract maintaining that monarchs are elected and may therefore be deposed.

1645

EUROPE
10 Jan. In England, after being imprisoned since 1640 on a charge of treason, William Laud, archbishop of Canterbury and Charles I's unpopular religious counsellor, is beheaded on Tower Hill, London.

29 Jan. Peace negotiations begin to end the First English Civil War but fail (22 Feb.).

1 June Peace negotiations between the Holy Roman Empire and France (at Münster) and between the Holy Roman Empire and Sweden (at Osnabrück) begin and will eventually lead to the treaty of Westphalia (1648).

10 June In England Oliver Cromwell is reappointed Lieutenant-General of the New Model Army. He defeats the royalists at Naseby, Northamptonshire (14 June), and the city of Leicester falls to the parliamentarians (17 June). The royalists also lose Carlisle (28 June).

July After the death of his father, Michael I Romanov (tsar since 1613), Alexis I becomes tsar of Russia.

22 July In Toro, Spain, death of Gaspar de Guzman, count of Olivares and chief minister of Spain (1623–43).

3 Aug. French forces led by Marshal Turenne defeat the Bavarians at Nördlingen (near Allerheim, in Swabia, Germany) but then have to withdraw.

Aug. Swedish–Danish peace is agreed with the treaty of Brömsebro: the Danes lose the islands of Ösel and Gotland, E Baltic, and the Norwegian provinces of Jämtland and Härjedalen. Sweden becomes the foremost power in N Europe.

10 Sept. In the English Civil Wars Prince Rupert, nephew of King Charles I, surrenders Bristol, a key port in the W of England, to the parliamentarians.

13 Sept. James Graham, marquis of Montrose and leader of a royalist army of Highlanders and Irishmen, is defeated at Philiphaugh, Scotland, and flees to the Continent.

28 Sept. In England the royalists lose their stronghold in the town of Winchester.

– The Ottoman Turks try to invade Crete, prompting a Turkish–Venetian war.

THE AMERICAS

– Portuguese colonists in Brazil rebel against Dutch rule.
– Occupation of the island of St Helena, S Atlantic, by the Dutch.

SUB-SAHARAN AFRICA

– Capuchin monks travel up the River Congo in C Africa.

ECONOMY AND SOCIETY

– English political radical John Lilburne founds the Leveller movement (of those who would 'level all differences of position or rank amongst men') in Southwark, London.

SCIENCE AND TECHNOLOGY

– In Gresham College, London, and in Oxford, eminent scientists such as Boyle, Wilkins and Petty begin an association that will evolve into the Royal Society.

ARTS AND HUMANITIES

16 Aug. In Paris birth of Jean de la Bruyère, French satirist and moralist.

29 Aug. In Rostock, Germany, death of Hugo Grotius (see p. 251), Dutch jurist.

Edward, Lord Herbert of Cherbury publishes *De Causis Errorum* (The Causes of Error), philosophy.

– Italian-born Jean-Baptiste Lully (see 1632) is appointed violinist and kitchen boy at the French court.

John Milton (see p. 273), 'On the Morning of Christ's Nativity', 'L'Allegro' and 'Il Penseroso', poetry.

Heinrich Schütz, *Die sieben Worte Christi am Kreuz* (The Seven Words of Christ on the Cross), oratorio.

Edmund Waller, *Poems*.

1646

EUROPE

April Prague, Bohemia, falls to the Swedes under the leadership of Count von Königsmark.

5 May King Charles I of England surrenders to the Scots at Southwell, Nottinghamshire.

25 June The effective end of the First English Civil War comes with the fall of the traditionally royalist city of Oxford to the parliamentarian forces.

7 July The English Levellers advocate a more thorough revolution with the publication of the *Remonstrance of Many Thousands*, which urges abolition of the monarchy and the

House of Lords' veto on legislation, as well as asserting the sovereignty of the people.

30 July English parliamentary commissioners and Scots Covenanters at Newcastle upon Tyne present Charles I with the Newcastle Propositions: the king is to accept the Covenant, give up control of the armed forces for 20 years and agree to restrictions on Catholics. Charles proposes (17 Oct.) that he will give up control of the militia for ten years and will accept Presbyterianism for five years, as long as there is a controlled return to episcopacy. Negotiations fail.

30 July French troops led by Marshal Turenne and aided by the Swedes invade Bavaria. The Elector of Bavaria agrees to a truce (Sept.).

23 Dec. King Charles I is sold by the Scots to the English parliamentarians for the equivalent amount of their army's back-pay, £400,000.

24 Dec. After the failure of his negotiations with the Scots, King Charles I tries to escape to Europe, but fails.

THE AMERICAS

– English forces occupy the Bahamas.

ARTS AND HUMANITIES

– French schools use the textbooks on logic, grammar and mathematics produced by the Jansenist religious foundation of Port-Royal, Paris.

Sir Thomas Browne, *Pseudodoxia Epidemica or Enquiries into Received Tenets and Commonly Presumed Truths*, usually known as Browne's *Vulgar Errors*, philosophy.

Pierre Corneille, *Rodogune*, play.

Richard Crashaw, *Steps to the Temple*, poetry.

Bartolomé Esteban Murillo, *The Angel's Kitchen* and *The Miracle of St Diego*, paintings.

Rembrandt van Rijn, *The Adoration of the Shepherds*, painting.

James Shirley, *Poems*.

John Suckling, *Fragmenta Aurea* (Golden Fragments), a posthumous collection of poems.

Henry Vaughan, Welsh metaphysical poet, *Poems*.

1647

EUROPE

14 Mar. Death of Frederick Henry, the stadtholder of the United Netherlands; he is succeeded by his son, William II of Holland, prince of Orange.

18 May In England the House of Commons votes to disband the army: conflict develops between conservative parliamentarians and radical elements within the army.

4 June Cornet Joyce, under the orders of Oliver Cromwell, seizes King Charles I at Holdenby Hall, Northamptonshire; he takes him to Newmarket, Suffolk, as a prisoner of the New Model Army.

7 July Neapolitan patriot Tommaso Aniello (Masaniello) leads the Italian city of Naples to revolt against the Spanish: he is assassinated (16 July).

2 Aug. In England King Charles I rejects the 'Heads of the Proposals' in which the New Model Army demand biennial parliaments, religious toleration and parliamentary control over the army.

7 Aug. The New Model Army, led by Oliver Cromwell, enters London and takes control of Parliament.

8 Aug. English parliamentarian forces win a victory over the Irish at Dungan Hill.

1 Sept. The chief minister of France, Cardinal Mazarin, agrees terms with the duke of Modena for the invasion of Milan.

11 Nov. King Charles I escapes but is recaptured and imprisoned at Carisbrooke Castle, on the Isle of Wight (14 Nov.).

11 Nov. Rebellion breaks out again in Naples, Italy: Henry, duke of Guise, is elected duke of Naples.

24 Dec. The English Parliament presents King Charles I with further proposals, which he again rejects (28 Dec.). Charles now agrees with the Scots that he will impose Presbyterianism and abolish episcopacy in Scotland; the Scots, for their part, will control the militia, abolish the army, call a new Parliament and restore Charles I by force.

– The parliamentary commission to the University of Oxford results in the sacking of Anglican professors and heads of colleges.

– Rebellion breaks out in Moscow against Tsar Alexis I Mikhailovich (see 1645).

SUB-SAHARAN AFRICA

– Formation of the Swedish Africa Company.

SCIENCE AND TECHNOLOGY

– The lunar surface is charted for the first time in German astronomer Johannes Hevelius's *Selenographia* (Moon Map).

– Jean Pecquet, a French medical student, discovers the thoracic duct of the human body.

ARTS AND HUMANITIES

Oct. In England the Levellers draw up their manifesto, the *Agreement of the People*. Their agenda of decentralized government and legal rights for small property owners is popular among the army rank-and-file who are now represented on a democratically elected Army Council.

Abraham Cowley, *The Mistress or Several Copies of Love Verses*, a collection of poems.

Thomas Hobbes (see p. 264), *Elementa Philosophica de Cive* (Philosophical Elements Concerning Citizenship), philosophy.

Sir Peter Lely (originally Pieter Van der Faes from Westphalia but now settled in London), *The Young Children of Charles I*, *Charles I* and *The Duke of York*, paintings.

José Ribera, *St Paul the Hermit*, painting.

1648

EUROPE

30 Jan. Peace is agreed at Münster between Spain and the Netherlands ending the Eighty Years War (see 1568). The alliance between France and the United Netherlands is broken and the French chief minister Cardinal Mazarin's plan to gain the Spanish Netherlands is thwarted.

11 Feb. A Declaration by the English Parliament formally sets out King Charles I's misconduct.

21 Feb. Christian IV of Denmark and Norway dies and is succeeded by his son, Frederick III.

6 April Rebellion in Naples by Aniello (Masaniello) is put down by John Joseph of Austria and his forces.

1 May Royalist Scottish forces initiate the Second Civil War in England.

2 May The English and Welsh Parliament passes a Blasphemy Act.

20 May John II Casimir succeeds his brother King Vladislav IV Vasa of Poland.

May Zaporog and Dnieper Cossack forces, led by Bogdan Khmelnitsky, defeat the Polish noblemen who have been colonizing their lands. In the SE districts of Poland, Polish rule collapses.

June An anti-tax rebellion breaks out in Moscow.

17–20 Aug. English parliamentarian commander Oliver Cromwell and his New Model Army defeat the invading royalist Scottish forces at the battle of Preston, Lancashire.

26–27 Aug. A popular rebellion in Paris marks the beginning of the Fronde, a series of civil wars in France, which last until 1653 (during the minority of King Louis XIV) and which constitute, in part, a reaction against those policies begun under Cardinal Richelieu that were designed to diminish the influence of the nobility and increase the competence of central government.

27 Aug. Thomas Fairfax, the parliamentarian general, takes the town of Colchester, Essex, from its royalist governor Charles Lucas; this parliamentarian victory marks the end of the Second Civil War in Essex and SE England.

18 Sept. The English Parliament starts to negotiate with King Charles I under the terms of the treaty of Newport and (28 Sept.) Charles responds by offering concessions on the control of armed forces and Presbyterianism. Parliament rejects these concessions (2 Oct.).

24 Oct. The peace of Westphalia ends the Thirty Years War (see 1618). Sweden gains lands in Pomerania, access to the mouths of the rivers Elbe, Weser and Oder, an indemnity and the bishoprics of Bremen and Verden. France gains Alsace as well as Metz, Toul and Verdun. Brandenburg is compensated for the loss of parts of Pomerania by receiving Magdeburg, Halberstadt, Minden and Kammin. The independence of the Netherlands, the German princely states and the Swiss cantons is guaranteed. The status of the German ecclesiastical states is to be restored to what it was on 1 Jan. 1624. Emperor Ferdinand III recognizes the independence of the German states and their right to make treaties independent of him as long as their actions are not directed against the emperor. France and Sweden acquire the right to involve themselves in imperial affairs.

26 Nov. Pope Innocent X, angered by the recognition of

Calvinism in the peace of Westphalia, condemns it in the bull *Zelo domus Dei*.

6 Dec. English parliamentarian Col. Thomas Pride conducts a purge of the House of Commons, known as Pride's Purge. A number of Presbyterians are expelled and the remainder (an estimated 60 independent radical members) continue to sit as the Rump Parliament: they vote for Charles I to be tried (23 Dec.).

ECONOMY AND SOCIETY

– George Fox founds the Society of Friends (Quakers). Fox claims a divine revelation, which enables him to become a religious and mystical teacher.

SCIENCE AND TECHNOLOGY

– Belgian chemist J.B. van Helmont, in *Ortus Medicinae* (The Beginning of Medicine, published posthumously) coins the term 'gas' to describe carbon monoxide.
– German chemist J.R. Glauber obtains hydrochloric acid.

ARTS AND HUMANITIES

20 Aug. In London death of Edward, Lord Herbert of Cherbury, English philosopher and poet.
Claude de Lorraine (Claude Gelée), *Embarkation of the Queen of Sheba*, painting.
Robert Herrick, *Hesperides*, poetry.
José Ribera, *The Holy Family with St Catherine*, painting.

1649

EUROPE

15 Jan. The French court leaves Paris and the Fronde rebellion degenerates into a three-month war.
19 Jan. In the aftermath of the English Civil Wars, the trial of Charles I begins. Charles is beheaded in Whitehall (30 Jan.). The Prince of Wales, the future Charles II (see 1660), is in exile in The Hague.
11 Mar. In France the treaty of Rueil ends the first Fronde.
17 Mar. The English Rump Parliament abolishes monarchy (17 Mar.) and the House of Lords (19 Mar.).
15 May The Rump Parliament declares England a Commonwealth or free state.
18 Aug. The French court returns to Paris.
11 Sept. Oliver Cromwell sacks Drogheda and Wexford (11 Oct.) in Ireland. His troops massacre the Catholic garrisons for their refusal to surrender to parliamentarian forces.
15 Sept. In Oakham, England, birth of Titus Oates, instigator of the Popish Plot (see 1678).
Oct. The Diggers (or True Levellers) start their movement on St George's Hill, Surrey, and denounce the institution of private property.
Dec. Riots in Paris mark the beginning of the second Fronde.
– Lay patronage of ecclesiastical posts is abolished in Scotland.
– The privileges of English traders are abolished in Russia.
– The Holy Roman Empire establishes a standing army.

MIDDLE EAST AND NORTH AFRICA

Aug. Ibrahim, Ottoman sultan, who has been a weak ruler, is deposed and executed by the Janissaries. He is succeeded by Mehmed IV, his son.

ASIA

– The Persians capture Kandahar in Afghanistan.

THE AMERICAS

26 Mar. In Boston, Massachusetts, death of John Winthrop, English colonist and first governor of Massachusetts Bay Colony.
– Providence (later known as Annapolis, Maryland) is settled by Puritan exiles from Virginia; the Maryland Assembly passes an act granting toleration to all Christians who believe in the Trinity.

ECONOMY AND SOCIETY

– John Milton (see p. 273), English poet, defends Charles I's execution in *The Tenure of Kings and Magistrates*.
– John Gauden's *Eikon Basilike* defends monarchy as a principle and Charles I's conduct. Milton responds in his *Eikonoklastes*.

SCIENCE AND TECHNOLOGY

– Dutch physician Isbrand de Diemerbroek, in his *De Peste* (On the Plague), studies the plague.

ARTS AND HUMANITIES

21 Aug. In Loreto, Italy, death of Richard Crashaw, English religious poet.
4 Dec. In Hawthornden, near Edinburgh, Scotland, death of William Drummond of Hawthornden, Scottish poet.
John Donne, *Fifty Sermons*, published posthumously.
Richard Lovelace, *Lucasta*, poetry.

1650

EUROPE

18 Jan. In France the leaders of the Fronde (see Aug. 1648) including the princes of Condé and Longueville, are imprisoned; chief minister Cardinal Mazarin, however, forms an alliance with the former Fronde leaders.
2 Feb. Birth of Nell Gwyn, Welsh actress, orange seller and future royal mistress; she may, alternatively, have been born in 1642.
21 May In Edinburgh, Scotland, James Graham, 1st marquis of Montrose and Scottish royalist general, is executed.
26 May In Ashe, Devon, England, birth of John Churchill, later 1st duke of Marlborough and English general.
24 June Charles II, son of and heir to the late King Charles I, lands in England to claim his throne.
1 Aug. In England Oliver Cromwell and the Rump Parliament establish a Committee of Trade, creating a permanent economic council.
29 Sept. In France the second Fronde ends when peace terms are imposed on the SW city of Bordeaux.
Sept. Oliver Cromwell defeats the royalist Scots at Dunbar.

1650-1

4 Nov. In The Hague, United Netherlands, the future William III, stadtholder of the United Netherlands and king of England, is born.

THE AMERICAS

– The Dutch and the English agree on the frontiers of their N American colonies.

SCIENCE AND TECHNOLOGY

– German physicist Otto von Guericke invents the air pump and proves that air presses in all directions with equal force.

ARTS AND HUMANITIES

11 Feb. Death of French philosopher René Descartes (see p. 256), shortly after the publication of his *Traité des passions de l'âme* (Treatise on the Passions of the Soul).

Philippe de Champaigne, *Portrait of an Unknown Man*, painting.

Pierre Corneille, *Andromède* (Andromeda), tragi-comedy.

Bartolomé Murillo, *The Holy Family with the Little Bird*, painting.

Jeremy Taylor, *Rule and Exercises of Holy Living*, religious tract.

James Ussher, *Annales Veteris et Novi Testamenti*, history analysing the chronology of the Bible and concluding that the universe was created in 4004 BC.

Joost van den Vondel, *Manual of Dutch Poetry*.

1651

EUROPE

1 Jan. Charles II, son and heir of the late King Charles I, executed king of England and Scotland, is crowned king of Scotland at Scone.

6–7 Feb. In France chief minister Cardinal Jules Mazarin flees from Paris after the *parlement* votes to release the Fronde leaders.

Mar. Catholic and Protestant Leagues are formed in German territories in order to enforce the terms of the peace of Westphalia (see 24 Oct. 1648).

June The Cossacks make peace with the Russian Tsar Alexis I Mikhailovich.

3 Sept. In England Oliver Cromwell defeats Charles II at Worcester; Charles flees to France (17 Oct.).

7 Sept. Louis XIV, king of France, comes of age.

27 Oct. After a lengthy siege, the city of Limerick, Ireland, surrenders to the English parliamentarian army of Henry Ireton, Cromwell's son-in-law. Ireton dies in Limerick on 26 Nov.

Dec. With the support of an army of German mercenaries, former chief minister Cardinal Jules Mazarin returns to France, provoking renewed support for the cause of the Frondeurs and their leader, Louis II de Bourbon, prince of Condé.

ASIA

– Tokugawa Ietsuna, son of Tokugawa Iemitsu, becomes shogun of Japan and suppresses two rebellions in Edo province.

THE AMERICAS

– St Helena, a small island in the S Atlantic, is occupied by the English East India Company.

ECONOMY AND SOCIETY

– Closure of Cardinal Mazarin's Paris library and sale of its contents by order of the *parlement*.

SCIENCE AND TECHNOLOGY

– English physician William Harvey, in his *Exercitationes de Generatione Animalium* (Lectures Concerning the Generation of Living Creatures), establishes the principles of embryology.

ARTS AND HUMANITIES

5 July Death in London of architect Inigo Jones.

6 Aug. Birth of François de la Mothe-Fénelon, French archbishop, theologian and writer.

Richard Baxter, *The Saints' Everlasting Rest*, religious tract.

Gianlorenzo Bernini, portrait bust of Duke Francis I d'Este.

John Cleveland, *Poems*.

Sir William D'Avenant, *Gondibert*, chivalric epic.

John Donne, English poet, *Essays in Divinity*, theological essays, published posthumously.

Thomas Hobbes (see box), *Leviathan*, philosophy.

Paul Scarron, *Le Roman comique* (The Comic Novel).

Thomas Hobbes (1588–1679)

The English philosopher Thomas Hobbes reflects in his writings the breakdown of civil society and political authority during the English Civil Wars through which he lived. But he was also influenced by Galileo's application of mathematics to the understanding of the physical world, and came to the materialist conclusion that reality is reducible to matter in motion. From this conclusion, he sought to build a theory of nature, man and society.

His masterpiece is *Leviathan* (1651), a work that justifies absolute sovereignty as the only way to ensure security and peace within a society. Hobbes held that, in forming communities, human beings agree to hand over most of their 'natural' rights to a ruler, who is then bound to protect them against aggression. Even though human nature remains unchanged, the formation of such a society is a deliverance from the original 'state of nature', in which human lives were 'solitary, poor, nasty, brutish and short'. It was Hobbes who originated the idea of the social contract, the agreement to abide by rules that characterizes all societies. Hobbes believed that the only effective enforcer of those rules was a single ruler – a king. But Hobbes put limits on the king's power, and if he fails to ensure order and security, the people are justified in transferring their loyalty to a more effective ruler.

This authoritarian philosophy caused a sensation. During the 1640s, Parliamentarians saw Hobbes's theory as upholding absolute monarchy, while the Royalist supporters of Charles I, who believed in the divine right of kings to rule absolutely, were opposed to the secularism of Hobbes's position. Since Hobbes's day, both democrats and theocrats have raised similar objections.

Jeremy Taylor, *Rule and Exercises of Holy Dying*, religious tract.
David Teniers, *Village Feast*, painting.
Izaak Walton, *The Life of Wotton*, a biography of English poet and diplomat Henry Wotton.

1652

EUROPE

Feb. The English Rump Parliament passes an Act of Pardon and Oblivion to reconcile royalist opponents of its regime, with the exception of those found guilty of high treason.

Feb. The League of Hildesheim, between Sweden and N German Protestant states, is formed to maintain the peace terms of the peace of Westphalia (see 24 Oct. 1648).

29 Mar. Renowned military commander Marshal Henri de Turenne defeats rebel Frondeurs (see 1648) at Jargeau, France.

30 June–10 July The English government declares war on the United Netherlands, starting the First Anglo-Dutch War.

June A Fronde uprising in Paris leads to the establishment of a provisional Fronde government.

19 Aug. In France Cardinal Jules Mazarin retires into exile to facilitate Louis XIV's peace deal with the rebels and the offer of a general amnesty. Louis, a child king, has now come of age.

Sept. Dutch forces take Dunkirk in the Spanish Netherlands.

21 Oct. Louis XIV returns to Paris; the Frondeur leaders are exiled and Mazarin is recalled.

Oct. Barcelona, under French control, falls to John Joseph of Austria, viceroy of Naples, completing his reconquest of Catalonia for the Spanish Habsburgs.

30 Nov.–10 Dec. The Dutch fleet under Admiral Maarten Van Tromp defeats the English fleet off Dungeness, SE England.

– Louis II, prince of Condé and principal leader of the Fronde, signs alliances with Philip of Spain and the duke of Lorraine.

THE AMERICAS

– Maine is joined to the Massachusetts colony.

SUB-SAHARAN AFRICA

8 April The Dutch, under Jan van Riebeeck, found Cape Town, S Africa, as a post for the Netherlands East India Company.

ECONOMY AND SOCIETY

– Christopher Bowman opens the first London coffee house in St Michael's Alley, Cornhill.

ARTS AND HUMANITIES

Pierre Corneille, *Nicomède*, tragedy.
John Donne, *Paradoxes, Problems, Essays, Characters*, essays, published posthumously.
Rembrandt van Rijn, *Hendrickje Stoffels*, painting.
Henry Vaughan, *The Mount of Olives*, religious poem.
Roger Williams, *The Hireling Ministry None of Christ's*, political and religious tract.
Gerrard Winstanley, *The Law of Freedom in a Platform*, political theory advocating primitive communism and the abolition of buying and selling, and also advocating civil marriage.

1653

EUROPE

3 Feb. Cardinal Jules Mazarin returns to Paris after his exile.

18–28 Feb. The English fleet defeats the Dutch fleet off Portland, Dorset.

20 April Oliver Cromwell expels the Rump Parliament by force because it has debated the Bill for a New Representative against his orders; he then (29 April) establishes a council of ten members.

4 July The Barebones Parliament (named after a prominent MP, 'Praise God' Barebone), of 140 members, meets under Cromwell's supervision (until 12 Dec.).

3 Aug. In the SW French city of Bordeaux, a rebellion is crushed by the royalist army: the Fronde (see 1648) ends and a period of absolutist government begins.

5 Aug. A standing army is established in Brandenburg where the Great Elector Frederick William suppresses the diet of representatives.

16 Dec. The Barebones Parliament having resigned its powers (12 Dec.), the Instrument of Government establishes Oliver Cromwell as Lord Protector of England; he rules with only a small council of state.

– A peasants' revolt in favour of self-government breaks out in Berne, Switzerland.

ASIA

June The Dalai Lama of Tibet accepts Chinese sovereignty.

ECONOMY AND SOCIETY

– Prominent English Quaker James Nayler (1618–60) is persuaded by some of his female followers that he is a re-incarnation of Christ. The millenarian Fifth Monarchy men emerge as a sect.

ARTS AND HUMANITIES

12 Feb. In Fusignano, Italy, birth of Arcangelo Corelli, violinist and composer.

26 May In East Sutton, Kent, death of Sir Robert Filmer, English writer and champion of an absolutist concept of monarchy.

– Founding of Cheetham's Library, Manchester, England.

Francesco Borromini, St Agnese, Rome and St Andrea della Fratte, Rome.

Robert Filmer, *A Discourse Whether it be Lawful to Take Use for Money*, political philosophy written in response to R. Fenton's *Treatise of Usurie* (1612).

Peter Lely, *Portrait of Cromwell*, painting.

Matthew Locke, music for the masque *Cupid and Death* by James Shirley.

Jean-Baptiste Lully, music for Isaac de Benserade's ballet *La Nuit* (Night), in which Louis XIV plays the role of Le Roi Soleil (The Sun King).

Izaak Walton, *The Compleat Angler, or The Contemplative Man's Recreation*, philosophy.

1654-5

1654

EUROPE

5–15 April The treaty of Westminster ends the First Anglo-Dutch War. The Dutch agree to recognize the English Navigation Acts.

11–21 April Treaty of Commerce between England and Sweden.

12 April Oliver Cromwell, Lord Protector of England, establishes a union between Scotland and England, guaranteeing free trade and representation for the Scots in the Parliament at Westminster.

May The Ukrainian Cossacks accept Russian Tsar Alexis I Mikhailovich as their supreme leader, but keep their right to have an army and their own courts.

6 June Queen Christina of Sweden abdicates and is succeeded by Charles X.

7 June Louis XIV is crowned king of France at Rheims Cathedral.

28 Aug. In Stockholm Axel Oxenstierna, chancellor of Sweden since 1612, dies.

3 Sept. The first Parliament of the English Protectorate meets.

10 Sept. Alexis I Mikhailovich, tsar of Russia, takes Smolensk after the outbreak of war with Poland.

12 Sept. In England 100 republicans are expelled from the Westminster Parliament but are readmitted (15 Sept.).

THE AMERICAS

– The Dutch are driven out of Brazil by the Portuguese.

SUB-SAHARAN AFRICA

– Gambia, W Africa, becomes a colony of James, duke of Courland.

SCIENCE AND TECHNOLOGY

– French scientists and prominent mathematicians Blaise Pascal (see p. 259) and Pierre de Fermat establish the theory of probability.

– Francis Glisson discovers Glisson's Capsules, the fibrous sheath of the human liver.

ARTS AND HUMANITIES

Cyrano de Bergerac, *Le Pédant joué* (The Pedant Imitated), comedy.

Francesco Cavalli, *Serse*, opera. In 1660 it will be performed for the marriage celebrations of Louis XIV of France.

Johann Amos Comenius, *Orbis Sensualium Pictus* (The World in Pictures), the first picture book for children.

Pieter de Hooch, *Delft after the Explosion*, painting.

Peter Lely, *The Duet*, painting.

Molière (Jean-Baptiste Poquelin), *Le Dépit amoureux* (The Amorous Frustration), comedy.

Joost van den Vondel, *Lucifer*, tragedy.

1655

EUROPE

22 Jan. Lord Protector of England Oliver Cromwell dissolves the first Protectorate Parliament after its attempts to revise the Instrument of Government in order to reduce the size of the army and extend parliamentary power over the council of state.

11 –14 Mar. Penruddock's uprising occurs in Wiltshire, England; the small-scale royalist rebellion, led by Sir Joseph Wagstaff and John Penruddock, is easily defeated.

May The Catholic cantons of Switzerland reject plans by Zürich and Berne for a centralized Swiss state.

27 July Charles X, king of Sweden, invades Poland and starts the First Northern War; Frederick William, Great Elector of Brandenburg, invades Prussia to resist the Swedish advance.

9 Aug. England and Scotland are divided by Cromwell into 11 districts, each run by a major-general.

23 Aug. Charles X of Sweden defeats John II Casimir of Poland and takes Warsaw (30 Aug.) and Cracow (8 Oct.).

24 Nov. In England Oliver Cromwell forbids Anglican services.

Dec. Charles X of Sweden defeats the Great Elector's invasion of Prussia.

– Massacre of Protestants in the Vaudois, Switzerland.

– Jews are readmitted to England by Oliver Cromwell.

MIDDLE EAST AND NORTH AFRICA

28 April English admiral Robert Blake destroys a pirate fleet of the bey of Tunis and releases prisoners in Algiers, Algeria.

THE AMERICAS

– The Dutch annex New Sweden (now the region around Philadelphia) to their existing colony of New Netherlands (now the New York region).

SCIENCE AND TECHNOLOGY

John Wallis, English mathematian, one of the founders of the Royal Society, *Arithmetica Infinitorum* (The Arithmetic of Infinitesimals), a treatise on conic sections.

ARTS AND HUMANITIES

22 July Death in Paris of Savinien Cyrano de Bergerac, French satirist and dramatist.

– French scientist and mathematician Blaise Pascal retreats to Port-Royal, the community of Paris Jansenists.

Francesco Borromini, St Maria dei Sette Dolori, Rome.

William Drummond of Hawthornden, *A History of the Five Jameses*, history, dealing with the kings of Scotland from 1423 to 1524, published posthumously.

Sir Richard Fanshawe, translation into English from the Portuguese of the epic poem *The Lusiads* by Camões.

Thomas Hobbes (see p. 264), *De corpore* (On the Body), the first part of his *Elementorum Philosophiae* (Elements of Philosophy).

Jacob Jordaens, *The Presentation at the Temple*, painting.

Rembrandt van Rijn, *Woman Bathing in a Stream*, painting.

James Shirley, *The Gentleman of Venice*, tragi-comedy, and *The Politician*, tragedy.

Jeremy Taylor, *The Golden Grove, or A Manual of Daily Prayers*, religious tract.

Henry Vaughan, *Silex Scintillans* (The Glittering Flint), Parts 1 and 2, poetry.

1656

EUROPE

17 Jan. Treaty of Königsberg between Frederick William, Great Elector of Brandenburg, and Charles X of Sweden: Prussia becomes a Swedish fief.

24 Jan. The Protestant cantons of Zürich and Berne in Switzerland, are defeated by Catholic forces in the First Villmergen War.

Feb. After an attack by English forces on Jamaica and the formation of a Franco-English alliance, Spain declares war on England and later (April) signs a treaty with the exiled Charles II of England, who agrees to give up Jamaica in return for Spanish support for his restoration to the throne.

Mar. Swedish armies overrun Poland.

15–25 June Frederick William, Great Elector of Brandenburg, signs the treaty of Marienberg, promising military assistance to Sweden in the Northern War.

June Russia invades Sweden's Baltic territories.

29–31 July A Swedish–Brandenburg army defeats the Poles led by John II Casimir in Warsaw.

5–15 Sept. Treaty of Amity between England and France after Cardinal Jules Mazarin's negotiations with Spain fail: the treaty requires English participation in the French war against Spain in the Spanish Netherlands

9–19 Sept. English admiral Robert Blake captures a Spanish treasure fleet off Cadiz.

3 Nov. Russia and Poland sign the treaty of Vilna against Sweden. Poland promises to elect Tsar Alexis I Mikhailovich as King John II Casimir's successor, but never honours its undertaking.

20 Nov. Sweden cedes Prussia to Brandenburg under the treaty of Labiau.

– Afonso VI becomes king of Portugal on the death of John IV.

MIDDLE EAST AND NORTH AFRICA

– Mehmed Köprülü Pasa becomes grand vizier under Mehmed IV, Ottoman sultan.

ASIA

– The Dutch start to trade with China and seize Colombo, in Ceylon (Sri Lanka), from Portuguese control.

ECONOMY AND SOCIETY

Oct. Prominent English Quaker James Nayler and his followers enter Bristol in procession, imitating Christ's entry to Jerusalem, for which Nayler is arrested, imprisoned and severely punished.

SCIENCE AND TECHNOLOGY

29 Oct. Birth in England of Edmond Halley, astronomer.

– Dutch scientist Christiaan Huygens observes the satellites of Saturn.

ARTS AND HUMANITIES

Gianlorenzo Bernini, design for the piazza of St Peter's, Rome.
Abraham Cowley, *Poems*.

William D'Avenant, *The Siege of Rhodes*, opera with music by (among others) Matthew Locke and Henry Lawes; one of the first attempts at an English opera.

James Harrington, *Commonwealth of Oceana*, political philosophy, advocating republicanism, educational reform and public service by rotation.

Manasseh ben Israel, *Vindiciae Judaeorum*, political philosophy, defending the re-admission of Jews to England (see 1655).

André Le Nôtre, gardens of Vaux-le-Vicomte, France, landscape architecture.

Cardinal Pallavicino, *Istoria del Concilio di Trento* (History of the Council of Trent).

Blaise Pascal (see p. 259), *Lettres provinciales* (Provincial Letters), religious philosophy. A series of 18 anonymous pamphlets in support of Jansenist views, published 1656–7, they are placed on the Catholic Index of Prohibited Books by the Church.

Rembrandt van Rijn, *Titus Reading*, painting.

Diego Velázquez, *Las Meninas* (Maids of Honour), painting.

Jan Vermeer, *The Procuress*, painting.

1657

EUROPE

13–23 Mar. The treaty of Paris is signed between England and France as an anti-Spanish offensive.

31 Mar. The Humble Petition and Advice offers the title of king to the Lord Protector of England, Oliver Cromwell, who rejects it (3 April).

20–30 April English admiral Robert Blake defeats the Spanish fleet off Santa Cruz in Tenerife.

25 May In England a New Humble Petition and Advice creates a new House of Lords.

May Louis XIV, king of France, becomes a candidate for the title of Holy Roman Emperor.

26 June In England the Additional Petition and Advice increases the power of Parliament and Cromwell becomes Lord Protector for the second time.

17 Aug. Robert Blake, English naval commander, dies at sea off Plymouth, Devon, England.

19 Sept. Treaty of Wehlau: Poland renounces sovereignty claim over E Prussia in favour of Brandenburg, both German territories W of Poland.

6 Nov. Treaty of Bromberg: Brandenburg allies with Poland against Sweden and (10 Nov.) allies with Denmark.

– The Ottoman empire captures the islands of Tenedos and Lemnos from the Venetians.

THE AMERICAS

– The Dutch embark on war against the Portuguese in Brazil.

ECONOMY AND SOCIETY

– Drinking chocolate is first sold in London.

SCIENCE AND TECHNOLOGY

3 June Death in London of William Harvey, English physician.

ARTS AND HUMANITIES

20 Nov. In Middelburg, United Netherlands, death of Manasseh ben Israel (Manoel Dias Soeiro), founder of the modern Jewish community in England.

– Oliver Cromwell founds Durham College; it is dissolved after the Restoration (1660).

Richard Baxter, *A Call to the Unconverted*, religious tract.

Johann Amos Comenius, *Didactica*, a treatise on education.

Henry King, *Poems*.

Thomas Middleton, *Women Beware Women*, comedy, published posthumously.

Le Sieur Saunier, *L'Encyclopédie des beaux esprits* (Encyclopedia of Wit), the first reference book to use the word 'encyclopedia' in its title.

Willem van de Velde, *Dutch Men of War and Small Vessels in a Calm Sea*, painting.

1658

EUROPE

3 Feb. Oliver Cromwell, Lord Protector of England, dissolves Parliament after republican MPs present a petition for the re-establishment of a republic.

26 Feb.–8 Mar. The treaty of Roskilde ends the first Swedish–Danish war.

15–25 June The newly allied French and English army, under French marshal Henry de Turenne, defeats Spanish forces, who surrender Dunkirk to Britain.

15 Aug. The Rhenish League of German states is established under French protection after Louis XIV's failure to be elected Holy Roman Emperor. The second son of Ferdinand III becomes emperor as Leopold I.

3 Sept. In England death of Oliver Cromwell, who is succeeded as Lord Protector by his son, Richard.

Sept. Frederick William, Great Elector of Brandenburg, supports Denmark by blockading Charles X of Sweden.

MIDDLE EAST AND NORTH AFRICA

June Aurangzeb, the third son of Shah Jahan, imprisons his father after winning the battle of Samgarh for the Mughal empire. He is proclaimed emperor (31 July).

ASIA

– The Dutch take Jaffnapatam, the last settlement under Portuguese control in Ceylon (Sri Lanka).

ECONOMY AND SOCIETY

– The first banknote, devised by Palmstruck, is issued by the Swedish Riksbank.

– The Socinian sect, which denies the divinity of Christ, is expelled from Poland.

SCIENCE AND TECHNOLOGY

– Christiaan Huygens, Dutch physicist, invents the pendulum clock.

ARTS AND HUMANITIES

– Molière (Jean-Baptiste Poquelin), French playwright, forms the company of actors that becomes known subsequently (1680) as the Comédie Française.

– Death in England of Richard Lovelace, Cavalier poet.

Sir Thomas Browne, *Hydriotaphia or Urne-Buriall*, religious philosophy, considering mortality and including a discussion of cremation.

Thomas Hobbes (see p. 264), *De Homine* (On Man), political philosophy, the second part of his *Elementorum Philosophiae* (Elements of Philosophy).

Pieter de Hooch, *Courtyard of a House in Delft*, painting.

Georg Stiernhielm, *Hercules*, Swedish epic.

James Ussher, *Annals of the World*, history; a translation from the Latin of his *Annales*, published posthumously.

1659

EUROPE

7 May Restoration of the Rump Parliament in England (see 1653).

21–31 May The Dutch, French and English sign a treaty at The Hague forcing Sweden and Denmark to make peace.

25 May Richard Cromwell, son of Oliver Cromwell, resigns as Lord Protector of England and the Rump Parliament re-establishes the Commonwealth.

Aug. A royalist uprising in Cheshire is supressed by Maj.-Gen. Lambert, parliamentarian commander during the Civil War.

12 Oct. In England the army expels the Rump Parliament.

7 Nov. Peace of the Pyrenees between Spain and France: Spain renounces its claim to Alsace and cedes Roussillon and Cerdagne (in S France), Artois (in N France) and some fortresses in Flanders. Louis XIV will marry Philip IV's eldest daughter on condition that she renounces her claim to the Spanish throne.

16 Dec. In England, Gen. George Monck calls for a free Parliament, and the Long Parliament reconvenes (26 Dec.), excluding those expelled by Pride's Purge in 1648.

– James, brother of Charles II of England, enters into a secret marriage contract with Anne Hyde, a Catholic.

– Frederick William, Great Elector of Brandenburg, expels the Swedes from Pomerania and Prussia.

SCIENCE AND TECHNOLOGY

– Robert Boyle, Anglo-Irish scientist and philosopher, experiments on the common pressure of air in all directions.

ARTS AND HUMANITIES

– Birth in London of Henry Purcell, English baroque composer.

– The Preussische Staatsbibliothek (Prussian State Library) is founded in Berlin.

Pierre Corneille, *Oedipe* (Oedipus), tragedy.

Richard Lovelace, *Lucasta*, poetry, published posthumously.

Molière (Jean-Baptiste Poquelin), *Les Précieuses ridicules* (The Affected Young Women), comedy.

Diego Velázquez, *The Infante Philip Prosper* and *The Infanta Margarita Teresa*, paintings.

1660

EUROPE

1 Jan. Gen. George Monck crosses the River Tweed, leads his army S to London and declares for a free Parliament (16 Feb.).

23 Feb. On the death of Charles X, four-year-old Charles XI succeeds as king of Sweden.

16 Mar. The English Long Parliament (first elected in Nov. 1640 and restored in May 1659) dissolves itself.

4 April The exiled king of England and Scotland, Charles II, issues the Declaration of Breda, promising amnesty and religious toleration and paving the way for the Restoration of the monarchy.

25 April The Convention Parliament assembles and Charles II is officially proclaimed king of England (8 May).

3 May The peace of Oliva ends war between Poland, Sweden, Austria and Brandenburg. Sweden and Poland recognize Russia's sovereignty; John II Casimir of Poland renounces his claim to the Swedish throne.

28 May In Osnabrück, Hanover, the future George I, king of Great Britain and Ireland and Elector of Hanover, is born.

29 May Charles II enters London.

5 June In England birth of Sarah Jennings, duchess of Marlborough.

6 June Peace of Copenhagen ends the war between Sweden and Denmark; the Baltic is reopened to foreign warships.

Aug. Grosswarden, Transylvania, surrenders to the Turks. Holy Roman Emperor Leopold I subsequently agrees to send an army to stop the Turkish advance.

8–13 Oct. The Danish crown becomes hereditary after the *coup d'état* of Frederick III.

Oct. The English Parliament rejects the toleration to Nonconformists promised by Charles II in the Declaration of Breda.

– The Navy Discipline Act strengthens the Navigation Act in order to protect English trade from Dutch competition.

ECONOMY AND SOCIETY

27 Sept. Death in Pouy (now Saint-Vincent-de-Paul), France, of St Vincent de Paul, French founder of the Congregation of the Mission, a religious order that cares for the poor.

– Theatres are reopened in London.

ARTS AND HUMANITIES

1 Jan. In England Samuel Pepys begins his diary.

6 Aug. In Madrid, Spain, Diego Rodriguez de Silva y Velázquez, painter, dies.

16 Oct. Death of Paul Scarron, French poet and playwright.

– In England the Baptist John Bunyan is imprisoned in Bedford for unlicensed preaching (until 1672).

– Peter Lely, the British court painter, begins his series of paintings, the 'Windsor Beauties'.

– Frederick William, Great Elector of Brandenburg, begins the construction of Potsdam Palace, Prussia.

Francesco Borromini, design for the Collegio di Propaganda Fide, Rome.

Pierre Corneille, *La Toison d'or* (The Golden Fleece), tragedy.

John Dryden, 'Astraea Redux', poem that welcomes the return of Charles II as king of England.

James Howell, *Lexicon Tetraglotten* (Four-way Dictionary), an English–French–Italian–Spanish dictionary.

John Milton, *The Readie and Easy Way to Establish a Free Commonwealth*, political philosophy, advocating republicanism.

Molière (Jean-Baptiste Poquelin), *Sganarelle*, comedy.

Jan Vermeer, *Head of a Young Girl*, painting.

1661

EUROPE

7 Jan. First meeting of the English Council for Foreign Plantations.

9 Mar. In Vincennes, France, Cardinal Jules Mazarin dies; he has been first minister of France since 1642. Louis XIV starts his period of personal rule.

23 April Coronation of Charles II, king of England.

8 May Charles II's second Parliament, the Cavalier Parliament, meets.

21 June The peace of Kardis ends the Northern War between Russia and Sweden.

23 June–3 July Tangier, N Africa, and Bombay, India, are ceded to England as part of the dowry of Portuguese princess Catherine of Braganza on her marriage to Charles II (see 21 May 1662).

July The Prussian diet of Königsberg is dismissed after criticizing the Great Elector Frederick William.

6 Aug. Charles II of England mediates between the Dutch and the Portuguese; by treaty the Dutch retain Ceylon (Sri Lanka) and the Portuguese keep Brazil.

5 Sept. Nicholas Fouquet, French chief finance minister, is arrested and tried for treason; he is succeded by Jean-Baptiste Colbert.

20 Dec. In England the Corporation Act becomes law; all English and Welsh magistrates are to take Anglican communion and swear an oath of allegiance to the crown.

MIDDLE EAST AND NORTH AFRICA

Nov. Fazil Ahmed Köprülü Pasa, becomes grand vizier under Mehmed IV, Ottoman sultan.

THE AMERICAS

– John Eliot's translation of the Bible into the Algonquin language is the first complete Bible to be printed in the American colonies. The English-born Eliot emigrated to N America (1632) and became known as the Apostle to the Indians.

SCIENCE AND TECHNOLOGY

– John Graunt, English mathematician, publishes his *Natural and Political Observations on the Bills of Mortality*, providing statistical information for life insurance in England.

– Christiaan Huygens, Dutch physicist, invents the manometer for measuring the pressure of liquids or gases.

ARTS AND HUMANITIES

– Frederick William, Great Elector of Brandenburg, opens the Royal Library, Berlin.

- Founding of the Kongelige Bibliothek (Royal Library) in Denmark.
- Peter Lely is appointed court painter to Charles II of England.
- Charles II appoints Matthew Locke his court composer.
- Louis XIV of France establishes the Académie Royale de Danse.
- Lincoln's Inn Fields Theatre, London, is opened and is the first London playhouse to have a proscenium arch; it mounts the first production of *Hamlet* with scenery (28 Aug.).
- Birth in London of Daniel Defoe, English novelist.
- Birth of Nicholas Hawksmoor, English architect.

Louis Le Vau, designs for the Galerie d'Apollon, Louvre, and the Collège des Quatre Nations, Paris.

Rembrandt van Rijn, *Self-portrait as St Paul*, painting.

1662

EUROPE

8 Feb. Death in England of Elizabeth of Bohemia, the Winter Queen and aunt of Charles II, king of England.

Mar. In England legislation is introduced to the House of Commons to enforce a hearth tax at the rate of two shillings for each stove or fireplace.

19 May The Act of Uniformity ejects Presbyterians from the Church of England; the Licensing Act forbids the importation of non-Christian literature into England.

21 May Charles II of England marries the Portuguese princess Catherine of Braganza (see 1661).

June Afonso VI takes over the government of Portugal.

27 Oct. Charles II sells Dunkirk to France for £400,000.

- Under the Episcopal Ordination Act of Scotland, Presbyterian assemblies are forbidden and 400 ministers are ejected.

ASIA

- In China Kangxi, second emperor of the Qing (Manchu) dynasty, accedes to the throne at the age of eight. His personal rule will start when he is 15 and will last until 1722.
- Formosa is seized by the Chinese from the Dutch and becomes autonomous.

SCIENCE AND TECHNOLOGY

15 July In England the Royal Society receives its charter.

- Anglo-Irish scientist and philosopher Robert Boyle writes *The Sceptical Chemist*, proposing an early atomic theory of matter.

ARTS AND HUMANITIES

27 Jan. Birth of Richard Bentley, English clergyman and classical scholar.

19 Aug. Death in Paris of Blaise Pascal (see p. 259), French mathematician, physicist and philosopher.

- The final text of the Church of England's Book of Common Prayer is approved and enforced by the Act of Uniformity.
- In France Louis XIV begins to build the Palace of Versailles and appoints Charles Le Brun to be the principal painter and director of the Gobelins tapestries. André Le Nôtre designs the gardens and park.

- The earliest text of the Oberammergau Passion Play is produced.

Samuel Butler, *Hudibras,* Part 1, satire.

Thomas Fuller, *The Worthies of England*, history, published posthumously.

Molière (Jean-Baptiste Poquelin), *L'École des femmes* (School for Wives), comedy.

William Petty, *Treatise of Taxes and Constributions*, a work of political economy, arguing that the division of labour reduces production costs and approving the export of money.

1663

EUROPE

18 April The Turks declare war on Holy Roman Emperor Leopold I.

23 Dec. Permanent sessions of the German imperial diet are inaugurated at Ratisbon (modern Regensburg) after an intitial meeting (in Jan.) to discuss the Ottoman invasion of Hungary.

THE AMERICAS

24 Mar. Carolina is granted by the English crown to eight proprietors.

8 July Charles II grants a charter to Rhode Island, granting it the right to elect its own governor and to have religious toleration.

- France's controller of finances Jean-Baptiste Colbert makes the colony of New France a province with its capital at Quebec.

SUB-SAHARAN AFRICA

10 Jan. Charles II, king of England, grants a charter to the Royal Africa Company (see 1672).

ECONOMY AND SOCIETY

7 May In England the Theatre Royal, Drury Lane, is opened in London.

- First coinage of the gold guinea in England.
- Turnpike tolls are levied in England.
- Roger L'Estrange is appointed licenser of the English press.

SCIENCE AND TECHNOLOGY

- Anglo-Irish scientist and philosopher Robert Boyle writes *Concerning the Usefulness of Experimental Philosophy*.

ARTS AND HUMANITIES

- France's controller of finances, Jean-Baptiste Colbert, establishes the Académie des Inscriptions et Belles Lettres.

Gianlorenzo Bernini, design for the Scala Regia, Rome.

Francesco Borromini, design for the Church of St Andrea, Rome.

Samuel Butler, *Hudibras,* Part 2, satire.

Abraham Cowley, *Verses Upon Several Occasions*, poetry.

Gottfried Wilhelm Leibniz (see p. 295), *De Principio Individui* (On the Principle of the Individual), philosophy, defending the nominalist view (which argues that general terms are words, not descriptions of objects).

1664-5

1664

EUROPE

6 Mar. France allies with Frederick William, Great Elector of Brandenburg.

5 April In England the Triennial Act is passed: Parliament should meet at least once every three years.

May The English Conventicle Act, an anti-Nonconformist measure, prevents meetings of more than five people except in a private household.

1 Aug. Imperial forces defeat the Turks at St Gotthard-on-the-Raab. The treaty of Vasvar (10 Aug.) ends the war between the emperor and Turkey; the opposing armies withdraw from Transylvania.

– France's controller of finances Jean-Baptiste Colbert abolishes a range of internal tariffs.

THE AMERICAS

29 Aug. The British annex the Dutch colony of the New Netherlands (see 1624). The Dutch governor of New Amsterdam (Peter Stuyvesant) surrenders to English troops and the town is renamed New York.

15 Dec. Union of Connecticut and New Haven.

– Formation of the French Compagnie des Indes Occidentales to control French trade in Canada, W Africa, S America and the West Indies.

SUB-SAHARAN AFRICA

– The Dutch buy Swedish colonies on the Gold Coast (modern Ghana).

ECONOMY AND SOCIETY

– Armand Jean Le Bouthillier de Rancé establishes the austere Trappist order at La Trappe, Normandy. The order's rule includes manual work, vegetarianism and the maintenance of silence.

SCIENCE AND TECHNOLOGY

– English physician Thomas Willis publishes his study of the brain, *Anatome Cerebri Nervorumque Descriptio et Usus* (Use and Description of the Anatomy of the Brain and Nerves).

ARTS AND HUMANITIES

24 Jan. Birth of John Vanbrugh, English architect and playwright.

21 July Birth of Matthew Prior, English poet.

Jean de La Fontaine, Book 1 of the *Contes et nouvelles* (Tales and Short Stories), poetic accounts of folkloric French and Italian stories.

Molière (Jean-Baptiste Poquelin), *Le Tartuffe, ou l'imposteur* (Tartuffe, or the Impostor), comedy satirizing clerical hypocrisy.

Jean Racine, *La Thébaïde, ou les frères ennemis* (The Thebaid, or the Enemy Brothers), tragedy, produced by Molière. The austere beauty of Racine's classical tragedies will redefine French literary taste.

Jan Vermeer, *The Lace-maker*, painting.

Christopher Wren, design for the Sheldonian Theatre, Oxford.

1665

EUROPE

6 Feb. In London the future Queen Anne is born (see 1702).

22 Feb. Start of the Second Anglo-Dutch War.

6–17 June A combined Portuguese, French and British force defeats the Spanish at Montes Claros to secure Portugal's independence.

17 Sept. Death of Philip IV of Spain who is succeeded by his son Charles II.

Sept. Onset of the Great Plague (bubonic plague) in London.

9 Oct. The fifth session of the Charles II's Cavalier Parliament takes place in Oxford to escape disease-ridden London.

Oct. In England the Five Mile Act forbids any Nonconformist ministers who refuse to accept the Act of Uniformity from coming within 5 miles (8km) of their previous place of ministry.

THE AMERICAS

– English law and administration are introduced to New York.

– The first modern census takes place in Quebec, Canada.

– A native American, Caleb Cheeshateaumuck, graduates from Harvard.

ECONOMY AND SOCIETY

15 Feb. Pope Alexander VII orders the submission of the Jansenists, a sect within the Catholic Church that follows the teachings of Cornelius Jansen (see 1585).

SCIENCE AND TECHNOLOGY

– French astronomer Giovanni Cassini determines the rotations of Jupiter, Mars and Venus.

– Francis Grimaldi (Francesco Maria Grimaldi), Italian Jesuit professor of mathematics, describes his discovery of the diffraction of light in his *Physico Mathesis de Lumine* (The Physics and Mathematics of Light), published posthumously.

– Anglo-Irish scientist and philosopher Robert Boyle establishes his proof of the need for air if candles are to burn and animals are to live.

– Robert Hooke, an English experimental philosopher and architect, analyses the vesicular nature of cork, names the cavities of such substances as 'cells' and describes the microscope in his *Micrographia*. Hooke will help redesign London after the Great Fire (1666).

ARTS AND HUMANITIES

19 Nov. In Rome, Italy, French painter Nicolas Poussin dies.

– The first literary periodical, the *Journal des savants*, is published in Paris.

– Beginning of Claude Perrault's construction of the colonnade of the Louvre, Paris.

Edward, Lord Herbert of Cherbury, *Occasional Poems*, published posthumously. George Herbert, also a poet, was his brother.

Jean de La Fontaine, *Contes et nouvelles en vers* (Tales and Short Stories Put into Verse).

François, 6th duc de La Rochefoucauld, *Réflexions, ou sentences et maximes morales* (Reflections, or Axioms and Moral Maxims), philosophy.

Molière (Jean-Baptiste Poquelin), *Don Juan*, comedy.

Bartolomé Murillo, *The Rest on the Flight to Egypt*, painting.

Rembrandt van Rijn, *The Jewish Bride*, painting.

Jan Vermeer, *The Artist's Studio*, painting.

Izaak Walton, *The Life of Richard Hooker*, a biography of the English theologian.

1666

EUROPE

16–26 Jan. Following the terms of an earlier treaty, France helps the United Netherlands by declaring war against Britain. The French launch an offensive against Britain's only ally, the Holy Roman Empire, whose forces have invaded the E provinces of the United Netherlands. The United Netherlands allies with Frederick William, Great Elector of Brandenburg (16 Feb.).

May–Sept. In London, England, the Great Plague claims some 70,000 victims.

2–6 Sept. The Great Fire of London (starting from a bakery in Pudding Lane) destroys much of the city, including St Paul's Cathedral.

18 Nov. Scottish Covenanters loyal to Presbyterianism are beaten at the battle of Pentland Hills by royalist troops under Sir Thomas Dalziel, one of the few people ever to escape from the Tower of London. Dalziel joined Charles II in exile and fought for the Russians against the Tatars and the Turks (1655).

THE AMERICAS

April The French seize the Caribbean island of St Kitts from the English.

– Newark, New Jersey, is settled by Connecticut puritans.

ECONOMY AND SOCIETY

– The Bible is printed in Armenian.

SCIENCE AND TECHNOLOGY

– France's controller of finances Jean-Baptiste Colbert founds the Académie des Sciences, Paris.

– Gottfried Wilhelm Leibniz (see p. 295), German philosopher and mathematician, publishes his work on arithmetic, *De Arte Combinatoria* (On the Art of Combination), providing a theoretical model used in some modern-day computers.

– Isaac Newton (see p. 283), English scientist and mathematician, uses differential and integral calculus and measures the orbit of the moon.

ARTS AND HUMANITIES

26 June Richard Fanshawe, English diplomat, poet and translator, dies in Madrid, Spain, where he has been sent as an ambassador.

26 Aug. In Haarlem, United Netherlands, death of Frans Hals, portrait painter.

31 Aug. Queen Henrietta Maria, consort of King Charles I of England, daughter of Henry IV of France and sister of Louis XIII of France, dies.

– France's controller of finances Jean-Baptiste Colbert establishes the Gobelins Tapestry workshops in Paris.

Jakob Bidermann, *Ludi Theatrales Sacri* (Sacred Plays), collection of plays based on the *Spiritual Exercises* of St Ignatius Loyola (see p. 212), published posthumously.

Nicolas Boileau-Despréaux, *Contre les femmes* (Against Women), an anti-feminist satire.

John Bunyan, *Grace Abounding to the Chief of Sinners*, an autobiographical account of his spiritual journey.

Molière (Jean-Baptiste Poquelin), *Le Médecin malgré lui* (The Doctor Despite Himself) and *Le Misanthrope* (The Misanthropist), comedies.

Rembrandt van Rijn, *Portrait of Titus*, painting.

1667

EUROPE

20 Jan. End of the Thirteen Years War as Russia and Poland sign the treaty of Andrussovo; Poland cedes Smolensk and Kiev to Russia. Both countries agree to unite against the Ottoman Turkish threat.

21–31 Mar. Louis XIV and Charles II of England sign a secret treaty: England will not oppose a French invasion of the Spanish Netherlands if France does not assist the Dutch at sea.

24 May French troops invade the Spanish Netherlands and start the War of Devolution, which lasts until May 1668.

May The Turks lay siege to Candia, Crete.

12–13 June English naval disaster as the Dutch fleet raids the Chatham dockyard in the Thames estuary and seizes the *Royal Charles*, the royal barge.

21–31 July Peace of Breda between the United Netherlands, France and England: England gains Antigua, Montserrat, St Kitts, Cape Coast castle and the New Netherlands.

30 Aug. In England the earl of Clarendon resigns as lord chancellor, having been blamed for English failures in the Anglo-Dutch War. The new ministry (the Cabal) is composed of lords Clifford, Arlington, Buckingham, Ashley, and Lauderdale.

29 Nov. Clarendon is banished after his impeachment.

– Coup in Portugal: Peter, brother of King Afonso VI, banishes him to the Azores and becomes regent.

MIDDLE EAST AND NORTH AFRICA

– Shah Suleiman succeeds as shah of Persia.

SCIENCE AND TECHNOLOGY

– Founding of the National Observatory, Paris.

ARTS AND HUMANITIES

28 July Death of Abraham Cowley, English poet and philosopher, who fell out of favour with Oliver Cromwell but returned to England on the restoration of the monarchy.

13 Aug. Death of Jeremy Taylor, English religious writer, chaplain to Archbishop Laud and vice-chancellor of Dublin University.

30 Nov. In Dublin, Ireland, birth of Jonathan Swift, Irish author and satirist.

John Milton (1608–74)

The English poet John Milton was the son of a London businessman and was educated at St Paul's School in London and Christ's College, Cambridge. His was a fastidious and intellectual childhood, in the course of which he laid the foundations of the scholarship evident in his great epic poem, *Paradise Lost* (1667).

Milton is the most learned of English poets: not only Greek and Latin literature but also Hebrew and Italian find their echoes in his verse. But what gave him his literary range and depth of effect is the fact that he was stirred and radicalized by the great events of the English Civil Wars. In 1638 Milton travelled in France and Italy. When he returned to England he started a career as a vigorous polemicist. He attacked bishops, wrote in favour of divorce and attacked censorship in violent language. His essay *Areopagitica* (1644) is English prose's finest condemnation of censorship.

Milton's great work *Paradise Lost* was based on what he accepted as a literal truth: the invention of sin, the expulsion of Adam and Eve from Paradise, and all the woe that followed from this. It was also, of course, the ideal subject for a Puritan poet who thought that the Stuart Restoration demonstrated that the English had abandoned God. Milton's Christianity was an expression of his own integrity and his belief that neither individuals nor institutions have the right to coerce the views of others. Hence he objected in equal measure to the tyranny of the Stuart kings and the theocratic tendencies of the Presbyterians; however, his belief in tolerance did not extend to Roman Catholics.

– In his *Manufactures royales des meubles de la couronne*, France's controller of finances Jean-Baptiste Colbert extends state-sponsored production in the fine arts.

John Dryden, *Annus Mirabilis* (The Year of Wonder), memoirs, an account of 1666.

Gottfried Wilhelm Leibniz (see p. 295), *Nova Methodus Discendique Juris* (A New Method for Teaching Jurisprudence), political philosophy, describing the human relationship to divine law.

John Milton, *Paradise Lost*, Christian verse epic (see box).

Samuel Freiherr von Pufendorf, *De Statu Imperii Germanici ad Laelium Fratrem Dominum Trezolani Liber Unus* (The Present State of Germany), political philosophy and jurisprudence, attacking the rule of the Habsburgs and proposing a German Confederation of States with a federal army as well as the expulsion of the Jesuits.

Jean Racine, *Andromaque* (Andromache), tragedy.

1668

EUROPE

13–23 Jan. The Alliance of The Hague between the English and the Dutch: they agree on mutual military assistance and try to make peace between France and Spain. Louis XIV of France sees the Alliance as a betrayal by the Dutch of earlier Franco-Dutch agreements.

19 Jan. Louis XIV signs a treaty with the Holy Roman Emperor Leopold I for the future partition of the Spanish empire if Charles II of Spain dies without heirs. (Leopold and Charles both belong to the Habsburg dynasty.)

Feb. The French invade the imperial province of Franche-Comté (modern E France, bordering Switzerland and Germany).

2 May By the peace of Aix-la-Chapelle, which ends the War of Devolution (see 24 May 1667), France restores Franche-Comté but gains Lille, Tournai and other towns in Flanders from Spain.

19 Sept. John II (John Casimir), king of Poland, abdicates to become a priest.

ASIA

27 Mar. The English East India Company gains control of Bombay (W coast of India).

ECONOMY AND SOCIETY

– Foundation of Lund University, Sweden.

– Completion of the Oder–Spree Canal in E Germany.

SCIENCE AND TECHNOLOGY

– Isaac Newton (see p. 283), English scientist and mathematician, constructs the first reflecting telescope.

– English experimental philosopher and architect, Robert Hooke, *Discourse on Earthquakes*.

– Anthony van Leeuwenhoek, amateur Dutch scientist who originally ground lenses to inspect cloth fibres, provides the first accurate description of red blood corpuscles.

ARTS AND HUMANITIES

7 April Death of Sir William D'Avenant, English poet and dramatist.

23 June Birth of Giambattista Vico (see p. 300), Italian philosopher.

10 Nov. Birth of François Couperin, French composer and best-known member of a family of composers.

John Dryden, *An Essay of Dramatick Poesie*, criticism.

Jean de La Fontaine, *Fables choisies mises en vers* (Selected Fables Put into Verse).

Molière (Jean-Baptiste Poquelin), *Amphitryon*, comedy.

William Penn, *Sandy Foundations Shaken*, religious tract.

Jean Racine, *Les Plaideurs* (The Litigants), satirical comedy.

> *Honour, without money, is just a disease.*
>
> Jean Racine *Les Plaideurs* (1668) Act I, sc.I

1669

EUROPE

19 June Michael Wisniowiecki, a Lithuanian, is elected king of Poland, thereby frustrating attempts at French control of the country.

Sept. The Venetians surrender Crete to the Turks after a 21-year siege.

31 Dec. A secret treaty is signed between Frederick William, Great Elector of Brandenburg, and France. Brandenburg will support Louis XIV's claims in the Spanish Netherlands if France grants him land in the Rhine valley.

ASIA

– In India Mughal emperor Aurangzeb bans Hinduism.

– Bombay (W India) becomes part of the English East India Company's area of control.

– The first French trading stations are established in India.

– Abraham a Sancta Clara, the court preacher in Vienna, starts a religious revival.

THE AMERICAS

21 July English philosopher John Locke's (see p. 285) Constitution for Carolina is approved.

SCIENCE AND TECHNOLOGY

– Jan Swammerdam, Dutch naturalist, writes his *History of Insects*.

– Architect Sébastien le Prestre de Vauban's *La Conduite des sièges* describes his transformation of fortifcation techniques. A military engineer, de Vauban will invent the socket bayonet.

ARTS AND HUMANITIES

10 Mar. Death of John Denham, Irish poet.

31 May Last entry in the *Diary* of English diarist and admiralty official Samuel Pepys (see 1660).

4 Oct. Death in Amsterdam of Dutch painter Rembrandt van Rijn.

24 Oct. Death in London of William Prynne, English radical.

– Jean de Labadie, French Protestant theologian, refuses to sign the Confessio Belgica: he is sacked from his ministry and forms a Quietist congregation in Amsterdam.

– French architect Louis Le Vau begins the remodelling of Versailles.

– The Académie Royale des Opéras, the first home of the Paris opera, is founded.

Jacques-Bénigne Bossuet, *Oraison funèbre de la reine d'Angleterre* (Funeral Oration for the Queen of England), funeral oration on the death of Queen Henrietta Maria, wife of Charles I, which sets a new standard in French prose.

Hans Jakob Christoffel von Grimmelshausen, *Abenteuerlicher Simplicissimus* (Adventurous Simplicissimus), picaresque novel; a masterpiece of German baroque literature reflecting the German experience of the Thirty Years War (1618–30).

Jean Racine, *Britannicus*, tragedy.

1670

EUROPE

3 Jan. In London death of George Monck, duke of Albemarle and English royalist general during the English Civil Wars; he played an important part in the restoration of the Stuart monarchy (1660).

17 Feb. A defensive alliance is signed between France and Bavaria: Bavaria promises to support Louis XIV should there be an imperial election. In return, France grants the Elector a subsidy and marriage between his daughter and Louis XIV's son, Louis the dauphin of France.

April Hungarian nobles begin to conspire against the Habsburgs.

22 May–1 June The secret treaty of Dover between England and France: England receives subsidies, and Charles II will declare himself a Catholic and support Louis XIV's claim to the Spanish crown as well as French action in the United Netherlands.

May The United Provinces of the Netherlands appoint William of Orange their captain-general.

Aug. France occupies Lorraine in NE France, Charles duke of Lorraine having intrigued with the United Provinces.

21–31 Dec. The treaty of Boyne between France and England publicizes the treaty of Dover's provisions but omits the issue of Charles II of England's conversion to Catholicism.

– Christian V succeeds his father Frederick III as king of Denmark.

THE AMERICAS

– Charleston, Carolina, is founded.

– The Bahamas are granted to Carolina's proprietors.

ECONOMY AND SOCIETY

– Francois Michel le Tellier, marquis de Louvois, French politician and war minister, introduces uniforms to the French army.

ARTS AND HUMANITIES

10 Feb. Birth of William Congreve, English playwright and poet.

– Death of Louis Le Vau, French architect.

– John Blow, English composer, is appointed organist of Westminster Abbey.

– English poet John Dryden is appointed Historiographer Royal and Poet Laureate.

Pierre Corneille, *Tite et Bérénice* (Titus and Berenice), tragedy.

Peter Heylyn, *Aerius Redivivus*, a history of Presbyterianism.

Molière (Jean-Baptiste Poquelin), *Le Bourgeois Gentillhomme* (The Bourgeois Gentleman), comedy.

Blaise Pascal (see p. 259), *Pensées* (Thoughts), philosophical fragment and aphorisms, published posthumously.

Jean Racine, *Bérénice*, tragedy.

Baruch Spinoza (see p. 275), *Tractatus Theologico Politicus* (A Theological–Political Discourse), reflecting on the relationship between politics and religion.

Jan Vermeer, *The Pearl Necklace*, painting.

Izaak Walton, *The Life of George Herbert*, a biography of the English poet.

1671

EUROPE

21 April Birth of John Law, English financier.

22 April In England Charles II prorogues Parliament.

April Péter Zrínyi and other leaders of the Hungarian revolt against Habsburg rule (see April 1670) are executed.

June The Ottoman (Turkish) empire declares war on Poland.

Sept. The French military engineer Sébastien le Prestre de Vauban begins to build fortifications in the Netherlands.

12 Nov. Death in Nun Appleton, Yorkshire, England, of Thomas, Baron Fairfax, Cromwell's commander-in-chief of the parliamentary army during the English Civil Wars.

– The English crown resumes its control of the customs system.

– Death in England of Anne Hyde (see 1659), first wife of James, duke of York (the future James II of England), and mother of the future Mary II.

THE AMERICAS

Jan. The Welsh privateer Sir Henry Morgan destroys the Spanish colonial city of Panama, C America. Morgan will be knighted and made deputy governor of Jamaica in 1675.

SUB-SAHARAN AFRICA

– Founding of the French Senegal Company.

ECONOMY AND SOCIETY

– The Bible is printed in Arabic in Rome.

SCIENCE AND TECHNOLOGY

– German mathematician Gottfried Wilhelm Leibniz (see p. 295) develops an adding machine to aid multiplication.

ARTS AND HUMANITIES

Aphra Behn, *The Forced Marriage*, comedy.

Jacques-Bénigne Bossuet, *Exposition de la doctrine de l'église catholique sur les matières de controverse* (Exposition of the Doctrine of the Catholic Church on Controversial Issues), religious philosophy.

Lionel Bruant, design for the Hôtel des Invalides, Paris.

John Milton (see p. 273), *Paradise Regained*, epic sequel to *Paradise Lost* (1667), and *Samson Agonistes*, tragedy.

Christopher Wren, design for the Monument, London, to commemorate the Great Fire of 1666.

1672

EUROPE

2 Jan. A financial crisis hits the English Treasury; cash payments are suspended for 12 months. An economic council is formed with English philosopher John Locke (see p. 285) as its secretary.

15 Mar. The Declaration of Indulgence by Charles II of England extends toleration to Nonconformists and Roman Catholics (it will be withdrawn in 1673).

17 Mar. Britain declares war on the United Netherlands.

Baruch Spinoza (1632–77)

A Dutch Jew who worked as a lens-grinder, Spinoza turned to philosophy as a young man and regarded his trade as merely a way to afford food and lodgings.

Rejecting the idea that the Bible could be interpreted either literally or allegorically, he was expelled by the Amsterdam synagogue for heresy in 1656. In *A Theological–Political Discourse* (1670) he defended the idea of toleration in a liberal state; it was described by Christians as 'forged in hell by a renegade Jew and the Devil'. His principal work, *Ethics*, was published posthumously in 1677. In it he proposed that good and evil are relative, and that 'Virtue is nothing else but action in accordance with the laws of one's own nature.'

Spinoza was both a pantheist (seeing God in everything) and a determinist (denying the existence of free will). He rejected the idea that there was a clear division between the mental and the physical, and developed monism, the idea that the universe, and everything within it, forms a unity that can be explained as the working out of a single principle. He believed that the universe consists of a single substance, which he called *deus sive natura* (God or nature). He is the last philosopher to have produced a single metaphysical system explaining the nature of the world. Spinoza thought that happiness and freedom arrive when one grasps that the highest good consists of knowledge of the union between the mind and the whole of nature. Only such knowledge will free us from the tyranny of our emotions.

Spinoza's importance was twofold: he reached beyond the human-centred universe of his time to anticipate modern ideas of infinite space and humanity's tiny place within it, and he showed the possibility of causal explanation for human behaviour.

---

14 April France and Sweden agree on an anti-Dutch league. Frederick William, Great Elector of Brandenburg, allies with the Dutch (2 May).

15 June Sluices are opened in the sea defences in the United Netherlands to flood large areas and protect Amsterdam from the invading French army.

23 June An anti-French alliance is agreed between Frederick William, Great Elector of Brandenburg, and Emperor Leopold I, to defend the Holy Roman Empire.

4 July William of Orange is elected stadtholder of the United Netherlands and (8 July) becomes captain and admiral-general of the Union.

20 Aug. In the United Netherlands the De Witt brothers, leading republicans, are assassinated by a mob in The Hague as Jan de Witt goes to meet his brother Cornelius on his release from prison (where he has been serving a sentence for a false charge of conspiracy to poison William of Orange).

Dec. William of Orange is forced to abandon his siege of Charleroi and withdraw to Amsterdam.

ASIA

– The French occupy Pondicherry and the Coromandel Coast, S India.

THE AMERICAS

– French Jesuit missionary Jacques Marquette explores the area around what is now the city of Chicago.

SUB-SAHARAN AFRICA

– The English Royal Africa Company obtains a monopoly of the slave trade and subsequently builds forts in Acra and Sekondi (modern Ghana).

ECONOMY AND SOCIETY

– The synod of Jerusalem revives the Confession of Faith of the Greek Orthodox Church.
– French postal services are contracted out.

SCIENCE AND TECHNOLOGY

– Jan van der Heyden and his son make a flexible hose designed for fire fighting. A still life and landscape painter, van der Heyden made his money from his inventions, which also included street lighting.

ARTS AND HUMANITIES

Mar. In Dublin, Ireland, birth of Richard Steele, founder of the periodicals *The Tatler* and *The Spectator*.

1 May In Milston, Wiltshire, England, birth of Joseph Addison, essayist and dramatist.

Nicolas Antonio, *Bibliotheca Hispana Nova* (New Spanish Bibliography), a bibliography of Spanish books.

Claude Lorraine, *Aeneas at Delos*, painting.

Jean Racine, *Bajazet*, tragedy.

Christopher Wren, Church of St Stephen's Walbrook, London, architecture.

1673

EUROPE

Feb. The French *parlement*'s right to object to royal edicts is abrogated.

8 Mar. Charles II, king of England, withdraws the Declaration of Indulgence (15 Mar. 1672).

29 Mar. The Test Act, excluding Roman Catholics from public office in England, receives the royal assent.

10 April Frederick William, Great Elector of Brandenburg, makes a preliminary peace with France.

19 June Sir Thomas Osborne succeeds Lord Clifford as England's lord high treasurer and reforms public finance.

20 Aug. The United Netherlands sign treaties binding Spain, Holy Roman Emperor Leopold I and Charles, duke of Lorraine into a coalition against France.

10 Nov. Death of Michael, king of Poland.

11 Nov. Polish commander-in-chief John Sobieski defeats the Turks at Chocim (modern Khotin, Ukraine). The victory will help him win election as king of Poland in 1674.

12 Nov. William of Orange captures Bonn; Cologne and Munster sue for peace.

– In England James, duke of York, brother of Charles II, marries Mary of Modena (see 10 June 1688). As a Catholic, James has had to resign the office of Lord High Admiral in accordance with the Test Act (see above).

ASIA

– The French take Chandannagar, near Calcutta, NE India, and send an expedition to Ceylon (Sri Lanka).

THE AMERICAS

– French Jesuit Jacques Marquette and explorer Louis Joliet launch an expedition from the Mackinac Straits, along Lake Michigan and the Wisconsin River to the Mississippi River, reaching Arkansas on 17 July.

ARTS AND HUMANITIES

17 Feb. Death in Paris of Molière (real name Jean-Baptiste Poquelin), French comic dramatist.

15 Mar. Death in Rome, Italy, of Italian artist Salvator Rosa.

27 April First performance in Paris of Jean-Baptiste Lully's opera *Cadmus and Hermione*.

– English architect Christopher Wren is knighted.

– Danish composer Dietrich Buxtehude starts a series of evening concerts in Lübeck, N Germany.

Aphra Behn, *The Dutch Lover*, comedy.

John Dryden, *Marriage à la Mode* (Fashionable Marriage), comedy.

John Milton (see p. 273), *Poems upon Various Occasions*.

Molière (Jean-Baptiste Poquelin), *Le Malade imaginaire* (The Imaginary Invalid), comedy.

Jean Racine, *Mithridate*, tragedy.

1674

EUROPE

21 May John Sobieski (John III) is elected king of Poland.

June–Oct. French military engineer and siege strategist Sébastien Le Prestre de Vauban leads French armies to successes in Franche-Comté (E France), Flanders, NE France and W Germany.

Aug. French troops devastate the Palatinate, W Germany.

Nov. Marshal Henri de Turenne, French military commander, begins his advance across the Vosges Mountains from Lorraine to Belfort, E France.

– The States-General (Holland) declare the office of stadtholder to be hereditary in the House of Orange.

ASIA

– Sivaji, founder of the state of Maratha, W India, declares himself independent of the Mughal emperor of India, Aurangzeb, and concludes a treaty with Britain.

THE AMERICAS

9–19 Feb. Britain withdraws from the Dutch war; New York (New Amsterdam) is recognized as British.

SUB-SAHARAN AFRICA
– French Guinea (W Africa) is organized administratively.

SCIENCE AND TECHNOLOGY
Mar. In Basildon, Berkshire, England, birth of Jethro Tull, English agriculturalist whose innovative farming techniques revolutionized modern British agriculture.

ARTS AND HUMANITIES
19 Jan. First performance in Paris of Jean-Baptiste Lully's opera *Alceste, ou Le Triomphe d'Alcide*.

17 July In Southampton, Hampshire, England, Isaac Watts, English Nonconformist minister and poet, is born.

8 Nov. In Chalfont St Giles, Buckinghamshire, England, death of John Milton (see p. 273), English scholar, controversialist and author of the epic *Paradise Lost*.

9 Dec. In England the historian Edward Hyde, earl of Clarendon, dies.

– The Theatre Royal, Drury Lane, rebuilt after the Great Fire of London, reopens.

Nicolas Boileau-Despréaux, *L'Art poétique*, criticism.

Thomas Hobbes (see p. 264), translation of Homer's *Odyssey*.

Nicolas Malebranche, *De la recherche de la vérité* (On the Search for Truth), philosophy.

Bartolomé Murillo, *St Francis*, painting.

Jean Racine, *Iphigénie en Aulide* (Iphigenia at Aulis), tragedy.

1675

EUROPE
5 Jan. French marshal Henri de Turenne defeats Frederick William, Great Elector of Brandenburg, at Colmar, France.

12 Jan. The left bank of the Rhine is liberated from German control.

11 June France allies with Poland.

27 July Henri de Turenne, marshal of France (1643–68), is killed in battle at Sassbach, on the E bank of the Rhine.

22 Nov. Charles II prorogues the English Parliament for 12 months.

Dec. French military leader Louis II, prince of Condé, retires from military affairs.

ASIA
– In India Guru Gobind Singh organizes Sikh power on a political basis.

THE AMERICAS
9 Sept. The New England Confederation declares war on the Wampanoag Native American people. The war that follows is sometimes known as King Philip's War, after the name given by the colonists to the Wampanoag chief Metacomet.

SCIENCE AND TECHNOLOGY
Aug. In England the Greenwich Observatory is established on the S bank of the River Thames. John Flamsteed becomes the first astronomer royal.

– Anglo-Irish scientist and philosopher Robert Boyle invents the hydrometer to determine the density of liquids.

– German mathematician Gottfried Wilhelm Leibniz (see p. 295) develops the differential and integral calculus. The English scientist Isaac Newton (see p. 283), working independently of Leibniz, has made similar advances.

Isaac Newton, English scientist and mathematician, *Opticks*.

ARTS AND HUMANITIES
– Birth of Louis de Rouvroy, duc de Saint-Simon, French writer and courtier.

– In England, start of the publication of the Royal Society's *Philosophical Transactions*.

– In England the architect Sir Christopher Wren starts to rebuild St Paul's Cathedral, London (see 1666).

William Wycherley, *The Country Wife*, comedy.

1676

EUROPE
29 Jan. Fyodor III succeeds his father Alexis I Mikhailovich as tsar of Russia.

7–17 Feb. Secret alliance between Charles II of England and Louis XIV of France: neither is to help the other's enemy and Charles is to receive a French pension.

June A coup in Spain overthrows the queen mother, Mariana de Austria; the pro-French illegitimate son of Philip IV, John Joseph, takes over the government.

MIDDLE EAST AND NORTH AFRICA
3 Nov. The grand vizier of the Ottoman (Turkish) empire, Ahmed Köprülü, dies and is succeeded by his brother-in-law Kara Mustafa.

THE AMERICAS
3 Aug. Nathaniel Bacon, American colonial leader, publishes a reformist manifesto, *Declaration of the People of Virginia*. In Bacon's Rebellion, the governor of Virginia, William Berkeley, is forced to flee the colonial capital, Jamestown, but, following Bacon's sudden death, he puts down the rebellion using brutal methods.

SCIENCE AND TECHNOLOGY
– Isaac Newton, English mathematician, invents a way to solve algebraic equations with his binomial theorem.

ARTS AND HUMANITIES
– In England John Bunyan (see 1660) starts a second prison sentence (until 1677), during which he will start to write *The Pilgrim's Progress*.

John Dryden, *Aureng-Zebe*, tragedy in rhymed verse.

Sir George Etherege, *The Man of Mode*, comedy.

Roger Williams, *George Fox Digg'd Out of his Burrowes*, religious tract, arguing against Quaker teachings.

Sir Christopher Wren, design for Trinity College Library, Cambridge.

1677

EUROPE

16 Feb. In England the opposition politicians Anthony Ashley Cooper, earl of Shaftesbury, George Villiers, duke of Buckingham, Philip, Baron Wharton, and Lord Salisbury are arrested and imprisoned in the Tower of London for arguing that the present Parliament is illegal.

Feb. Charles II, king of England, declares that he has made an alliance with the Dutch and against the French.

Mar. Louis XIV, king of France, takes Valenciennes and St Omer in the Spanish Netherlands.

11 June The Swedes are defeated by a Dutch–Danish fleet.

4 Nov. William of Orange marries Mary, daughter of James, duke of York, brother and heir to Charles II of England (see 1671).

Dec. Frederick William, Great Elector of Brandenburg, takes Szczecin (modern Stettin in NW Poland) and pursues the Swedes to Riga.

Dec. King Christian V of Denmark is defeated by a Swedish force at Landskröna, breaking the Danish hold on Skania in Sweden.

THE AMERICAS

Mar. Massachussetts buys most of Maine from the heirs of Sir Ferdinando Gorges who founded two Plymouth companies in order to settle lands in New England.

– In Virginia Governor William Berkeley is removed from office for his brutal suppression of Bacon's Rebellion (see 1676). He dies the same year.

ARTS AND HUMANITIES

21 Feb. In The Hague, United Netherlands, death of Baruch Spinoza (see p. 275), Dutch philosopher.

– Death of the English composer Matthew Locke.

Johann Jacob Hofmann, *Lexicon Universale* (two volumes), the first treatment of knowledge in lexicon form in the arts and sciences.

Jean Racine, *Phèdre* (Phaedra), tragedy.

Baruch Spinoza, *Ethica ordine geometrico demonstrata* (Ethics Demonstrated According to the Geometrical Order), philosophy, published posthumously.

1678

EUROPE

9 Mar. Louis XIV of France captures Ghent and Ypres in the Spanish Netherlands.

10 Aug. Treaty of Nijmegen between France and the United Netherlands: the Dutch receive favourable commercial terms in place of Jean-Baptiste Colbert's tariffs and William of Orange, stadtholder of the United Provinces of the Netherlands, is restored to his estates in France, the Spanish Netherlands and the Franche-Comté.

13 Aug. In England rumours spread of a Catholic conspiracy known as the Popish Plot; it alleges that the pope has commanded the Jesuits to overthrow Charles II.

6 Sept. Anglican clergyman Titus Oates deposits before a London magistrate, Sir Edmund Berry Godfrey, his version of the Popish Plot.

17 Sept. Franco-Spanish treaty of Nijmegen: Spain cedes the Franche-Comté and a line of fortifications from the Marne to Dunkirk, while France gives back its conquests in the Netherlands and Catalonia.

30 Nov. In England, in a climate of hysteria fostered by Titus Oates's allegations of a Popish Plot, Roman Catholics are excluded from both Houses of Parliament.

– Emeric Tokoly becomes the leader of the Hungarian rebels against the Habsburgs.

– War breaks out between Russia and Sweden.

THE AMERICAS

– Frenchman René-Robert Cavelier, Sieur de La Salle, explores the Great Lakes of Canada.

SCIENCE AND TECHNOLOGY

– Thomas Thatcher, *A Brief Rule in Small Pocks or Measles*, the first medical publication in America.

ARTS AND HUMANITIES

4 Mar. In Venice, Italy, birth of Antonio Vivaldi, composer.

15 Aug. In London death of Andrew Marvell, English metaphysical poet.

1 Oct. Birth of Henry St John, Viscount Bolingbroke, author and political philosopher.

– The first German opera house opens in Hamburg.

John Bunyan, *Pilgrim's Progress*, Part 1, prose allegory.

Samuel Butler, *Hudibras*, Part 3, a satirical treatment of Puritan politics.

John Dryden, *All For Love*, tragedy.

Jules Hardouin-Mansart, design for the Marly Trianon, Versailles.

Jean de La Fontaine, *Fables choisies, mises en vers*, fables (a continuation of his collection).

Bartolomé Murillo, *The Virgin and the Christ Child Distributing Bread to Pilgrims*, painting.

1679

EUROPE

24 Jan. In England the Exclusion Crisis gathers pace: the Cavalier Parliament is dismissed by Charles II, king of England, because he fears it will exclude his brother James, duke of York, a Roman Catholic, from the succession.

4 Mar. James, duke of York, is banished to Antwerp in the Spanish Netherlands by his brother King Charles II in the hope that his removal will calm anti-Catholic feeling in England.

6 Mar. Charles II's third Parliament meets; its chief ministers are William Temple, Viscount Halifax (Savile), and the earls of Essex, Sunderland and Shaftesbury.

21 May The Exclusion Bill claims to exclude James, duke of York, from the line of succession to the throne of England because of his Catholicism. Charles II prorogues Parliament on 26 May and later dissolves it (12 July).

26 May The Habeas Corpus Amendment Act is passed in England: no one may be imprisoned for more than 24 hours without just cause being shown.

29 June Peace of St Germain-en-Laye between Sweden and Frederick William, Great Elector of Brandenburg, by which Brandenburg loses most of his conquests in Swedish Pomerania.

26 Sept. The treaty of Lund between Denmark and Sweden confirms the loss of Danish conquests.

7 Oct. Charles II's fourth Parliament meets but is immediately prorogued over the Exclusion Bill. Shaftesbury is dismissed, while William Temple, the earl of Essex and Viscount Halifax resign. They are replaced by a 'Tory' ministry dominated by Godolphin, Hyde and Sunderland. This marks the beginning of the use of the terms Whig and Tory to describe the two parties (the Whigs being those who wish to exclude James, duke of York, from the succession, the Tories being those who oppose the Exclusion Bill).

17 Dec. The queen mother, Mariana de Austria, regains power in Spain after the death of John Joseph; Habsburg influence is thereby re-established in Madrid.

THE AMERICAS

18 Sept. New Hampshire is created a separate province from Massachusetts.

ECONOMY AND SOCIETY

- France's controller of finances Jean-Baptiste Colbert requires that all French merchants be instructed in book-keeping and commercial law.
- Louis XIV, king of France, issues an edict against duelling.

SCIENCE AND TECHNOLOGY

- English astronomer Edmond Halley, *Stellarum Australium* (Catalogue of Southern Stars).
- Théophile Bonet, a Swiss physician, publishes *Sepulcretum*, presenting the results of over 3000 autopsies and thereby founding the study of morbid anatomy.
- German craftsman Johannes Kunkel develops the manufacture of glass at Potsdam, Germany.

ARTS AND HUMANITIES

5 Feb. In Amsterdam, United Netherlands, death of Joost van den Vondel, Dutch poet and dramatist.

4 Dec. At Hardwick Hall, Derbyshire, death of Thomas Hobbes (see p. 264), English philosopher and political theorist.

Gilbert Burnet, *History of the Reformation of the Church of England*, Vol. 1 (Vol. 2 is published in 1681). A Whig account of the English Reformation.

Charles Le Brun, interior decoration of the Galerie des Glaces, Versailles, painting.

Thomas D'Urfey, *Squire Oldsapp; or the Night-Adventurers, A Comedy*, play.

1680

EUROPE

21 Oct. In England Charles II finally allows his fourth Parliament to meet.

Oct. Charles XI of Sweden declares himself to be an absolute ruler.

4 Nov. The second Exclusion Bill bars Charles II's brother James, duke of York, a Roman Catholic, from the throne and declares it treason for him to re-enter England. The bill passes the House of Commons (11 Nov.) but is rejected by the House of Lords (15 Nov.).

ASIA

- Tokugawa Tsunayoshi becomes shogun (military ruler) of Japan.
- A French factory, or trading post, is founded in Siam (Thailand).

SUB-SAHARAN AFRICA

- First expedition to the Gold Coast of W Africa by Frederick William, Great Elector of Brandenburg.

SCIENCE AND TECHNOLOGY

- Anglo-Irish scientist and philosopher Robert Boyle obtains phosphorus by evaporating urine and distilling the residue with sand.

ARTS AND HUMANITIES

17 Mar. Death of François, duc de la Rochefoucauld, French writer.

26 July In Woodstock, Oxfordshire, England, death of John Wilmot, earl of Rochester, courtier, poet and writer of pornographic lyrics.

25 Sept. In London death of Samuel Butler, poet and satirist.

- English composer Henry Purcell is appointed organist of Westminster Abbey.
- First musical entertainments are held at Sadler's Wells, Islington, London.
- Italian Antonio Stradivari (Antonius Stradivarius) makes his earliest known cello.
- In France the Comédie Française, the French national theatre, is formed.
- Death of Sir Peter Lely, German-born English baroque portrait painter.

Robert Filmer, *Patriarcha or the Natural Power of Kings*, political philosophy, a defence of the divine right of kings (published posthumously).

Jules Hardouin-Mansart, design for the Chapel of Les Invalides, Paris.

César-Pierre Richelet, *Dictionnaire français* (French Dictionary).

Sir William Temple, *An Essay on Government* and *A Survey of the Constitution*, political philosophy.

Sir Christopher Wren, design for St Clement Dane's Church, London.

1681

EUROPE

11 Jan. Frederick William, Great Elector of Brandenburg, signs a defensive alliance with France.

18 Jan. In England Charles II's fourth Parliament is dissolved.

21–8 Mar. Charles II's fifth Parliament meets in Oxford but is dissolved when the Exclusion Bill is brought in.

30 Sept. French troops occupy the city of Strasburg (German–French border territory).

Sept. Renewal of the alliance between the United Netherlands and Sweden against Louis XIV of France: the treaty of Guarantee of The Hague upholds the land settlement of the treaties of Westphalia and Nijmegen and ultimately leads to the League of Augsburg (see 9 July 1686).

9 Nov. Holy Roman Emperor Leopold I confirms the political and religious freedoms granted to Hungary in 1606; Hungarian Protestants are granted religious toleration at the Diet of Oldenburg.

Nov. The French begin the siege of Luxembourg (ends 1682).

THE AMERICAS

– Tobago (off the NE coast S America) becomes a colony of the English aristocrat James, duke of Courland.

ECONOMY AND SOCIETY

– On the urging of Sir Stephen Fox (former paymaster general), Charles II, king of England, founds Chelsea Hospital to care for wounded and retired soldiers.

– Large numbers of Huguenots from N and W France begin to emigrate to England and the Netherlands.

SCIENCE AND TECHNOLOGY

– In France the Canal du Midi, devised by Baron Paul Riquet de Bonrepos, is completed. It joins the Bay of Biscay to the Mediterranean.

ARTS AND HUMANITIES

25 May Death of Pedro Calderón de la Barca, Spanish dramatist.

– First appearance of female professional dancers at the Paris Opera, in a production of Lully's ballet *The Triumph of Love*.

Gilbert Burnet, *History of the Reformation of the Church of England*, Vol. 2, history (see 1679).

Jacques-Bénigne Bossuet, *Discours sur l'histoire universelle* (Discourse on Universal History), describing secular history as the unfolding of divine and providential order.

John Dryden, *Absalom and Achitophel*, Part 1, satirical allegory.

Jean Mabillon, *De Re Diplomatica*, history; Mabillon establishes modern principles of critical historiography in this major study of medieval charters.

1682

EUROPE

Feb. Anthony Ashley Cooper, earl of Shaftesbury (see 1679), English politician, is released from the Tower of London.

Feb. Louis XIV, king of France, promises a pension to Maximillian II Emanuel, Elector of Bavaria.

Mar. The assembly of the French clergy approve Louis XIV's Declaration of Four Articles to establish the independence of the Gallican (French) Church; the pope's competence is limited to spiritual questions, and his views on questions of faith need the whole Church's approval; general councils of the Church are declared superior to the pope's authority.

17 June Birth of the future Charles XII of Sweden.

June Charles II's brother, James, duke of York, returns to England from exile in the United Netherlands.

5 July Death in Russia of Tsar Fyodor III Alekseyevich: Tsarina Sophia becomes regent on behalf of her infant brothers and joint rulers, Ivan and Peter.

29 Nov. In London death of Prince Rupert, commander of royalist troops during the English Civil Wars.

MIDDLE EAST AND NORTH AFRICA

Dec. The Turks proclaim Emeric Tokoly king of Hungary.

THE AMERICAS

9 April René-Robert Cavelier, Sieur de La Salle, claims Louisiana (a huge area of N America including the modern state of Louisiana plus Missouri, Arkansas, Iowa, Nebraska, North and South Dakota and Oklahoma) for France, having taken possession of the Mississippi Valley.

Oct. Pennsylvania adopts a constitution. The layout of the city of Philadelphia is planned.

SUB-SAHARAN AFRICA

– The Danes settle on the Gold Coast (modern Ghana).

SCIENCE AND TECHNOLOGY

– English astronomer Edmond Halley observes a comet that he will later calculate (1705) returns every 76 years.

– French philosopher Pierre Bayle, *Thoughts on the Comet of 1680*, criticizes superstitions about comets.

ARTS AND HUMANITIES

14 Mar. Death of Jacob van Ruysdael, Dutch painter.

3 April In Seville, Spain, death of Bartolomé Esteban Murillo, painter, after he falls from high scaffolding while painting an altarpiece.

19 Oct. In Norwich, England, death of Sir Thomas Browne, English physician and essayist.

23 Nov. In Rome, Italy, death of Claude Lorraine (Claude Gelée), French painter.

– Elias Ashmole, English antiquary and lawyer, founds the Ashmolean Museum, Oxford.

Arcangelo Corelli, *Concerti Grossi*, a landmark in the history of orchestral music.

John Dryden, *Religio Laici or a Layman's Faith*, religious reflections in verse, and *Absalom and Achitophel*, Part 2, a satirical allegory.

Sir Christopher Wren, design for Chelsea Hospital.

1683

EUROPE

21 Jan. Anthony Ashley Cooper, earl of Shaftesbury, English politician, who favoured the exclusion of James, duke of York, from the succession, dies in the United Netherlands, where he had fled to avoid a new trial for high treason.

Feb. The League of The Hague: Holy Roman Emperor Leopold I and Charles II of Spain join the Dutch–Swedish alliance against the French.

31 Mar. The Poles ally with the emperor against the Turks: King John III Sobieski of Poland promises Austria the assistance of 40,000 men should Austria be attacked.

Mar. Louis XIV of France demands a 30-year truce with the emperor and the German states.

12 June Discovery of the Rye House Plot (at Hoddesdon, Hertfordshire) to assassinate Charles II of England and his brother and heir, James, duke of York.

June The Ottoman (Turkish) imperial forces start the siege of Vienna, Austria.

6 Sept. Death in Paris of Jean-Baptiste Colbert, marquis de Seignelay, who was France's controller of finances (1665–83): Claude Le Peletier subsequently becomes France's chief finance minister.

12 Sept. John III of Poland and Charles of Lorraine raise the Turks' siege of Vienna. Kara Mustafa, the grand vizier, is executed (25 Dec).

4 Oct. The City of London forfeits its charter as the English crown tries to remove centres of Whig influence.

30 Oct. At Herrenhausen Palace, Hanover, Germany, the future George II, king of Great Britain, is born.

7 Dec. Execution of English Whig politician Algernon Sidney for plotting to assassinate King Charles II of England and his brother, James, duke of York, in the Rye House Plot.

25 Dec. James Scott, duke of Monmouth, illegimate son of Charles II, flees to the United Netherlands to escape arrests linked with the Rye House Plot.

Dec. Spain declares war on France.

MIDDLE EAST AND NORTH AFRICA

June Algiers, Algeria, succumbs to French bombardment.

ASIA

– Dutch traders are admitted at Canton, China.

– In China the Manchu (see 1644) conquer the island of Formosa (modern Taiwan). It will remain a Chinese possession until 1895.

THE AMERICAS

17 Oct. A charter of franchises and liberties is drawn up in New York.

SUB-SAHARAN AFRICA

– The Brandenburg (German) East African Company builds Grossfriedrichsburg on the Guinea coast of W Africa.

ARTS AND HUMANITIES

July Birth in England of Edward Young, writer.

25 Sept. In Dijon, France, birth of Jean-Philippe Rameau, composer and musical theorist.

15 Dec. In Winchester, Hampshire, England, death of Izaak Walton, writer.

– Charles II, king of England, appoints Henry Purcell court composer.

– The first St Cecilia's Day festival is held in London.

François Charpentier, *L'Excellence de la langue française*, grammatical and linguistic study.

Sir Christopher Wren, design for St James's Church, Piccadilly, London.

1684

EUROPE

12 Jan. After the death of Maria Theresa, his first wife, Louis XIV of France secretly marries Françoise d'Aubigné, marquise de Maintenon, known as Mme de Maintenon. In spite of previously having been Louis's mistress, Mme de Maintenon is pious and encourages dignified behaviour at court. She will exercise considerable political influence.

Feb. Frederick William, Great Elector of Brandenburg, offers a refuge to French Huguenots.

May In England the Charters of the City of London and of 65 other cities under Whig control are remodelled so the crown can veto the election of officers and of MPs.

15 Aug. The truce of Ratisbon (modern Regensburg) between France and the Holy Roman Emperor Leopold I; the French will retain their occupied positions in the Spanish Netherlands for 20 years.

Sept. The French bombard Genoa, Italy.

Nov. Jews are expelled from the city of Bordeaux, SW France.

MIDDLE EAST AND NORTH AFRICA

– The British withdraw from Tangier, Morocco.

ASIA

Dec. An embassy from Siam (Thailand) arrives at Versailles, France.

ECONOMY AND SOCIETY

– London streets are lit for the first time.

ARTS AND HUMANITIES

1 Oct. Death in Paris of Pierre Corneille, French dramatist.

10 Oct. Birth of Antoine Watteau, French painter.

– Takemoto Gidayu establishes a Japanese puppet play theatre, *Joruri*, in Tokyo.

– In Rotterdam the French philosopher Pierre Bayle establishes a literary review, *Nouvelles de la rébublique des lettres* (News from the Republic of Letters).

John Bunyan, *Pilgrim's Progress*, Part 2, prose allegory.

Sir Godfrey Kneller, *The Duchess of Portsmouth*, painting.

1685

EUROPE

6 Feb. Charles II, king of England, dies and is succeeded by his brother, the Roman Catholic James II.

20 May In London Titus Oates is convicted of perjury in his testimony about the Popish Plot, which he allegedly invented himself; he is flogged from Newgate to Aldgate and (22 May) from Newgate to Tyburn.

26 May Charles, Elector Palatine, dies and Louis XIV of France claims the Electorate for his sister-in-law, Elisabeth-Charlotte, duchess of Orléans.

11 June In England Monmouth's rebellion begins: James Scott, duke of Monmouth and illegitimate son of the late king Charles II, publishes a declaration accusing James II, his uncle, of usurping the throne.

6 July Monmouth is defeated at Sedgemoor, in Somerset, and beheaded (15 July).

Sept. Judge Jeffreys conducts his Bloody Assizes, sentencing many West Country rebels to death for partcipating in the Monmouth uprising. Some 320 people will be executed and hundreds more flogged, imprisoned or transported.

18 Oct. Louis XIV, king of France, revokes the Edict of Nantes (see 1598) and French Protestants (Huguenots) flee to Britain, the United Netherlands, Geneva and Brandenburg.

Un roi, une foi, une loi.

(One king, one faith, one law.)

Jacques-Bénigne Bossuet
(Louis XIV's court preacher)

ASIA

– The French send an embassy to Siam (Thailand).

ARTS AND HUMANITIES

23 Feb. Birth of the composer George Frideric Handel in Saxony, Germany.

12 Mar. Birth of George Berkeley, Irish Anglican bishop and philosopher.

21 Mar. Birth of Johann Sebastian Bach, German composer. His prolific compositions will attest to his universal musical genius.

26 Oct. Birth of Domenico Scarlatti, composer. Son of composer Alessandro Scarlatti, Domenico will also enjoy a successful musical career.

John Blow, *Venus and Adonis*, masque.

1686

EUROPE

June James II, king of England, Ireland and Scotland, introduces Roman Catholics into the Church and army.

9 July Formation of the anti-French League of Augsburg,

consisting of the Emperor, Spain, Brandenburg, Sweden, Saxony and the Palatinate (see Sept. 1681).

2 Sept. In Hungary Charles, duke of Lorraine, takes Buda from the Turks after Turkish occupation for 145 years (see 1541).

Oct. Russia declares war on the Ottoman (Turkish) empire and secures possession of Kiev by treaty with Poland.

11 Dec. Death of Louis II de Bourbon, prince of Condé, French noble and leader of the Fronde rebellion (see 1648).

ASIA

– In India the Mughal emperor Aurangzeb annexes the Muslim kingdom of Bijapur in an attempt to isolate the Hindu Maratha kingdom.

THE AMERICAS

May James II, king of England, Ireland and Scotland, remodels the N American colonies as the Federation of New England.

– The French settle in Arkansas.

SUB-SAHARAN AFRICA

– Louis XIV, king of France, annexes Madagascar.

SCIENCE AND TECHNOLOGY

14 May Birth of Gabriel Daniel Fahrenheit, in Danzig (now Gdansk, Poland), an instrument maker and physicist, who will devise the Fahrenheit thermometer.

ARTS AND HUMANITIES

15 Feb. First performance in Paris of Jean-Baptiste Lully's opera *Armide*.

– In France the Maison de St Cyr is founded near Versailles as a convent school by Louis XIV for Mme de Maintenon (see 1684), who directs it.

– The first Swedish theatre opens in Stockholm.

Pierre Bayle, *Commentaire philosophique sur les paroles de Jésus-Christ* (A Philosophical Commentary on the Words of Jesus Christ), philosophical and historical theology.

Chikamatsu Monzaemon, *Shusse Kagekiyo*, puppet play, produced in Tokyo.

1687

EUROPE

4 April James II, king of England, Ireland and Scotland, issues a Declaration of Indulgence for Liberty of Conscience, abolishing the penal laws and establishing freedom of worship for Roman Catholics and other dissenters.

12 Aug. Victory of an Austrian-Hungarian army under the duke of Lorraine and Louis William of Baden at the battle of Nagyharsány (Berg Hasan), near Mohács: for the first time in 150 years Hungary is free of Ottoman (Turkish) influence. The battle marks the end of Turkish expansion into Europe and is a key staging-post in the long decline of the Ottoman empire.

26 Sept. The Venetians take Corinth from the Ottoman Turks and besiege Athens, destroying the Parthenon and Propyleia with their bombardments; the Turks surrender the city (28 Sept.) and the Morea (Peloponnese) is subjugated.

11 Oct. The Hungarian diet of Pressburg renounces its right of resistance and recognizes the crown as the hereditary possession of the Habsburgs. As a result, Archduke Joseph, son of the Holy Roman Emperor Leopold I, is crowned king of Hungary (9 Dec.).

2 Nov. As a direct result of the Ottoman defeats by Austria (see above), Sultan Mehmed IV is deposed in a revolution in Constantinople and succeeded by Suleiman II, with Mustafa Köprülü as second vizier and later (1689) grand vizier (chief minister).

– James II, king of England, Ireland and Scotland, interferes with the appointment of lords-lieutenants for the English counties and also replaces Protestants in Oxford and Cambridge Universities with Roman Catholics.

– James II founds the Order of the Thistle (a Scottish order of knighthood).

THE AMERICAS

19 Mar. French explorer René-Robert Cavelier, Sieur de La Salle (see 1678), is murdered by his mutinous crew on the River Brazos (modern Texas).

– The French build Fort Niagara to prevent the British reaching the upper lakes of Canada.

Isaac Newton (1642–1727)

The discoveries of Isaac Newton have established him as one of the great original geniuses in the history of science and of mathematics. He was born in Lincolnshire, the son of an English farmer, and began his academic career at Trinity College, Cambridge. Fame and honours followed. However, as a man, Newton was awkward in character and could be vindictive and bitter. He famously became embroiled in a long and ugly debate with the German mathematician Gottfried Leibniz on the question of who had first invented the calculus. He also used his position as president of the Royal Society to put down rivals.

Newton's earliest experiments were with light and colour; by using a prism he showed that white light is actually made up of many colours. He later went on to propose his law of gravitation, which he demonstrated applied both to this world and to other heavenly bodies. This law, together with his three laws of motion, described the mechanics of the universe as it was then known. He set out his theories in his book *Philosophiae Naturalis Principia Mathematica* (1687), to international acclaim. Newton stressed the importance of the experimental method – a way of scientific thinking that used observation to establish how things behaved, rather than attempting to explain why they did so. This was counter to the current intellectual orthodoxy in Europe, which followed Descartes in emphasizing the importance of rational deduction from first principles (whatever the awkward facts indicated). The Newtonian revolution is at the root of the 18th-century Enlightenment, and itd descriptions of the universe held sway until the advent of Einstein's theories of relativity.

SUB-SAHARAN AFRICA

– Arguin, Guinea (W Africa) is established as a Brandenburg (German state) colony.

– French Huguenots, fleeing from religious persecution in France, settle at the Cape of Good Hope, South Africa.

SCIENCE AND TECHNOLOGY

– Isaac Newton (see box), English scientist and mathematician, *Philosophiae Naturalis Principia Mathematica* (Mathematical Principles of Natural Philosophy), the foundation statement of classical physics.

ARTS AND HUMANITIES

22 Mar. Death in Paris of Italian-born French composer Jean-Baptiste Lully.

21 Oct. Death of Edmund Waller, English poet and politician, exiled and heavily fined during the Cromwellian Interegnum, but allowed to return to England (1651).

16 Dec. Death of Sir William Petty, English political economist.

– Christian Thomasius' lectures on jurisprudence in Leipzig and Berlin are the first in Germany to be delivered in German and not in Latin.

Jacques-Bénigne Bossuet, *Oraison funèbre du grand Condé* (Funeral Oration on the Death of Louis II de Bourbon, prince of Condé).

1688

EUROPE

Feb. James II, king of England, Ireland and Scotland, recalls to England regiments that have been serving in the United Netherlands since 1678.

9 May In Potsdam, near Berlin, Germany, Frederick William, Great Elector of Brandenburg, dies; he is succeeded by Frederick III.

May Holy Roman Emperor Leopold I signs a treaty with Transylvania: Turkish suzerainty is removed and Transylvania becomes a province ruled by the king of Hungary.

10 June James Francis Edward Stuart, son of King James II and Mary of Modena (see 1673) is born; he will be known to history as the Old Pretender because of his claim to the thrones of England and Scotland. His son will be known as the Young Pretender.

30 June Seven Whigs, the Immortal Seven, Devonshire, Shrewsbury, Danby, Compton, Sidney, Lumley and Russell, invite the Dutch stadtholder William of Orange, grandson of Charles I of England and son-in-law of James II, to assume the English throne.

15 Aug. Birth of the future Frederick William I, king of Prussia.

6 Sept. The Turks lose Belgrade, Serbia, to the Emperor Leopold I; imperial forces subsequently occupy Bosnia, Serbia and Wallachia.

24 Sept. Louis XIV, king of France, declares war against the empire: the start of the Nine Years War (the War of the League of Augsburg; see 9 July 1686).

25 Sept. Louis XIV of France invades the Palatinate, causing German princes to unite against him.

30 Sept. The Dutch stadtholder William of Orange accepts the invitation from English Whigs and issues a manifesto calling for a free Parliament.

5 Nov. William of Orange lands at Torbay, SW England, with 12,000 men and enters the city of Exeter (9 Nov.).

Nov. The French occupy the Palatinate, destroying, among other cities, Heidelberg, Trier, Worms and Speyer.

19 Dec. William of Orange enters London.

25 Dec. James II escapes to France, having been deserted by his two daughters and almost everyone else. The English nobility embraces the Protestant William of Orange.

MIDDLE EAST AND NORTH AFRICA

– The French bombard Algiers, Algeria, and then negotiate a treaty with the bey (the city's ruler).

ASIA

– Revolution in Siam (Thailand) against French influence.

ECONOMY AND SOCIETY

– London underwriters begin to meet regularly in Lloyd's coffee house.

ARTS AND HUMANITIES

29 Jan. Birth in Stockholm, Sweden, of Emanuel Swedenborg, religious mystic and writer.

21 May Birth in London of Alexander Pope, English poet.

31 Aug. Death in London of John Bunyan, English puritan minister, preacher and writer.

Aphra Behn, *Oroonoko*, novel.

Jacques-Bénigne Bossuet, *Histoire des variations des églises protestantes*, historical work arguing that Protestantism's falsity is revealed in the fact of its internal variety, while Catholic truth is constant.

Jean de La Bruyère, *Caractères de Théophraste traduits du grec* (The Characters of Theophrastus), a collection of satirical sketches.

Charles Perrault, 'Le Siècle de Louis le Grand' (The Century of Louis the Great), a poem opening the literary Battle of the Ancients and Moderns in France.

George Savile, marquis of Halifax, moderate Whig politician, *The Character of a Trimmer*, political tract. His nickname derives from his efforts to steer a middle course between extremes.

1689

EUROPE

22 Jan. In England the Convention Parliament meets and declares that King James II has abdicated (28 Jan.), since his escape to the Continent leaves the throne vacant.

12 Feb. Declaration of Rights in England, by which it is illegal to make or suspend laws without parliamentary approval: the Dutch stadtholder William of Orange, grandson of Charles I,

and William's wife Mary, the daughter of the former King James II, are declared sovereigns for life (the Glorious Revolution). The Whig nobility has achieved its coup.

Feb. Following the systematic devastation of the Palatinate by the French, the German diet declares war on France.

12 Mar. James II, deposed king of England, Ireland and Scotland, arrives in Ireland (where he has numerous Catholic supporters) and holds a parliament in Dublin (May).

14 Mar. In Scotland the Convention Parliament meets in Edinburgh and proclaims William and Mary as sovereigns.

19 April In Rome, Italy, death of Christina, former queen of Sweden.

April Coronation of Dutch stadtholder William of Orange as King William III of Great Britain and Ireland and of his wife, Mary, as Queen Mary II.

2–12 May Britain and the United Netherlands join the League of Augsburg (see July 1686), which becomes the Grand Alliance against France.

24 May Toleration Act passed in England, exempting religious dissenters taking the oaths of allegiance and supremacy from penalties for non-attendance at church.

25 July Louis XIV of France declares war on England for joining the League of Augsburg.

21 Aug. Covenanter forces, supporters of the National Covenant (Protestants), defeat Scottish Jacobites, supporters of the deposed King James II, at Dunkeld.

Aug. After defeating the Turks, Louis William of Baden takes the town of Nissa and occupies Bulgaria.

11 Oct. Peter I (the Great) becomes tsar of Russia.

– Protestant uprising in the Cévennes, S France.

– Russia joins the war against the Ottoman (Turkish) empire.

THE AMERICAS

July Iroquois Native Americans massacre French settlers at Lachine, near Montreal.

– Natal, Brazil, becomes a Dutch colony.

– Louis XIV of France appoints Louis de Buade, comte de Frontenac, to be governor of Canada.

SCIENCE AND TECHNOLOGY

– The Dutch hold the first modern trade fair at Leyden.

ARTS AND HUMANITIES

18 Jan. Birth of Charles Louis de Secondat, baron de Montesquieu, French political philosopher.

16 April Death in London of Aphra Behn, the first female English dramatist and novelist to earn her living by writing.

18 April In London death of George, Baron Jeffreys of Wem, known as Judge Jeffreys, lord chancellor under King James II, noted for his severity after the Monmouth rebellion (1685).

Aug. Birth in England of Samuel Richardson, novelist and author of *Pamela* (see 1740).

Dec. First performance in London of Henry Purcell's opera *Dido and Aeneas*.

– The Advocates' Library is opened in Edinburgh.

John Locke (see box), *Two Treatises on Civil Government*, political philosophy, a justification of the constitutional revolution of 1688 in Britain.

Andrew Marvell, *Poems of Affairs of State*, poetry and letters, published posthumously.

Jean Racine, *Esther*, tragedy.

John Selden, *Table-Talk: Being the Discourses of John Selden*, short essays on political and religious subjects (published posthumously).

1690

EUROPE

16 Mar. Louis XIV, king of France, sends troops to Ireland to support the deposed King James II.

April Death of Apafi, prince of Transylvania. The Hungarian Estates recognize his son as prince, but the Ottoman Turks nominate Emeric Tokoly as his successor and send forces to enforce his claim.

1 July William III, king of Great Britain and Ireland, defeats the deposed King James II at the battle of the Boyne in E Ireland:

John Locke (1632–1704)

The English philosopher John Locke trained as a doctor and taught medical science at Christ Church, Oxford, but the political disgrace of his Whig patron, the earl of Shaftesbury, led to his exile from England in 1683. From then until 1689 he lived in the Netherlands, where he wrote his *Letter on Toleration* (1689), the first explicit defence of toleration as an ideal. From 1671 until its publication in 1690, Locke worked on his *Essay Concerning Human Understanding*, in which he maintained that experience was the only source of knowledge (a philosophical belief known as empiricism). He held that at birth the human mind is a blank sheet lacking any innate ideas, and that it uses reason to process information received via the senses, thereby producing understanding.

Locke's *Two Treatises on Civil Government*, published anonymously in 1689, were his response both to theorists of the divine right of kings and to Hobbesian absolutism (see p. 264). They also established Locke as a political thinker of international import, directly influencing the American Declaration of Independence (1776) and the Constitution of the United States (1787). Locke put forward the idea that governmental authority derives from the consent of the people – the social contract – and that any government may be justifiably overthrown if it infringes the natural rights of the individual and the will of the majority. It was this sanctioning of rebellion against 'unconstitutional' government that exerted a powerful influence on the American and French revolutions. Locke is thus the founding theorist of modern democracy, in which government is rooted in consent and legality.

James flees to France, his hopes of restoration to the English throne in tatters.

30 July Londonderry, in the N of Ireland, is relieved after a 150-day siege by the troops of James II.

6 Sept. William III, victorious, returns to England.

ASIA

24 Aug. Job Charnock, administrator of the English East India Company, founds Sutanati (modern Calcutta) as a trading post.

SCIENCE AND TECHNOLOGY

Denis Papin, French scientist, who lives and collaborates with others variously in Paris, London, Venice and Marburg, invents a pump with a piston raised by steam.

ARTS AND HUMANITIES

12 Feb. Death of Charles Le Brun, French architect.

– The Accademia dell'Arcadia is founded in Rome.

John Locke, *An Essay Concerning Human Understanding*, philosophy.

William Petty, *Political Arithmetic*, political economic theory, explaining the use of statistics.

1691

EUROPE

13 Jan. Death in London of George Fox, founder of the Society of Friends (Quakers).

18 Jan. King William III leaves England for the United Netherlands, where a congress of allies at The Hague meets to plan the defeat of France.

29 May Death of Cornelis Tromp, Dutch admiral.

19 Aug. Louis William of Baden defeats the Turks at Salem Kamen.

Oct. The capitulation of Limerick ends the Jacobite rebellion in Ireland; around 12,000 Irish people leave the country, many entering the service of King Louis XIV of France.

4 Dec. The Habsbugs are recognized as rulers of a reconquered Transylvania.

8 Dec. Death of Richard Baxter, English puritan and divine.

MIDDLE EAST AND NORTH AFRICA

June Ahmed II succeeds Suleiman II as sultan of the Ottoman (Turkish) empire.

SCIENCE AND TECHNOLOGY

30 Dec. Robert Boyle, Anglo-Irish scientist and philosopher, dies.

– German mathematician Gottfried Wilhelm Leibniz (see p. 295), *Protogaea* (The Primordial Earth) a study of geology.

ARTS AND HUMANITIES

June First performance in London of Henry Purcell's semi-opera *King Arthur*.

Claude Fleury, *Histoire ecclésiastique*, history, published in 20 volumes to 1720; it is the first complete history of the Christian Church on critical historical principles.

Leonardo de Figueroa, design for the Magdalene Church, Seville.

Jean Racine, *Athalie*, tragedy.

1692-4

1692

EUROPE

13 Feb. The Massacre of Glencoe, Scotland: following the refusal of the MacDonald clan to swear allegiance to King William III, clan members are slaughtered by their hereditary enemies the Campbells, in league with government forces.

Feb. The National Debt is established in England.

19–29 May The English defeat the French navy at La Hogue, thereby ending a proposed French invasion of England.

5 June Imperial troops under Louis William of Baden take Grosswardein from the Turks.

3 Aug. King William III is defeated at Steinkirke (Spanish Netherlands) by French forces under Francis Henry, duke of Luxembourg.

19 Dec. Duke Ernest Augustus of Hanover becomes the ninth Elector of the Holy Roman Empire following a treaty (Mar.) with the emperor.

ASIA

– Ijsbrand Iders explores the Gobi Desert, which stretches from Mongolia to China.

THE AMERICAS

– In Salem, Massachusetts, a series of witch trials take place, resulting in the execution of 19 people.

ECONOMY AND SOCIETY

– Queen Mary II of Great Britain and Ireland, ruling jointly with William III, founds Greenwich Hospital for wounded sailors and pensioners.

SCIENCE AND TECHNOLOGY

– The papers of English scientist and mathematician Isaac Newton (see p. 283) are accidentally burned.

ARTS AND HUMANITIES

April First performance in London of Henry Purcell's semi-opera *The Fairy Queen* (adapted from Shakespeare's *A Midsummer Night's Dream*).

18 May Death of Elias Ashmole, antiquarian and founder of the Ashmolean Museum at Oxford, England (see 1682).

18 May Birth of Joseph Butler, English theologian.

Edmund Gibson, edited edition of *The Anglo-Saxon Chronicle*, history.

1693

EUROPE

14 Mar. In England King William III vetoes bills to exclude 'placemen' (those with 'places' or offices of profit under the crown) from Parliament and introduces triennial parliaments.

April King Charles XI of Sweden declares himself an absolute monarch.

22 May The French again destroy the W German city of Heidelberg and go on to ravage the Rhineland.

Aug. King Louis XIV of France fails in his attempt to take the strategic imperial fortress of Liège: it will be his last appearance on the battlefield.

Dec. Louis XIV begins to negotiate for peace.

ASIA

– The Dutch take Pondicherry, S of Madras, India.

THE AMERICAS

Oct. A new charter is granted to the East India Company.

– The colony of Carolina is divided into North and South.

ECONOMY AND SOCIETY

– The Gallican (French) Church is reconciled with the papacy.

SCIENCE AND TECHNOLOGY

– English astronomer Edmond Halley compiles tables for calculating the distance from the sun.

ARTS AND HUMANITIES

Jean de La Fontaine, *Fables*, Vol. 3.

William Penn, *An Essay on the Present and Future Peace of Europe*, suggesting a European federation.

1694

EUROPE

25 April William Paterson is appointed first governor of the Bank of England, newly established by Parliament.

May King William III dismisses Tories from his ministry and introduces the prominent Whigs Charles Montagu, earl of Halifax, John, Baron Somers, Edward Russell, earl of Orford, and Thomas, marquis of Wharton. As a group they are referred to by historians as the 'Junto'.

3 Dec. In England the Triennial Bill becomes law: Parliament has to be elected every three years.

28 Dec. Queen Mary II, joint reigning English monarch with her husband William III, dies in London of smallpox.

ECONOMY AND SOCIETY

– Halle University (Germany) is founded.

ARTS AND HUMANITIES

26 Oct. Death of Samuel Pufendorf, German writer on jurisprudence.

21 Nov. Birth of François-Marie Arouet. As Voltaire (see p. 304), he will become a successful dramatist and be acclaimed as an essayist and propagandist for the 18th-century Enlightenment.

– Publication of the *Dictionnaire de l'académie française*, in two volumes.

– Louis XIV grants letters patent to the Académie des Jeux Floraux de Toulouse, founded by 14th-century troubadours and the most ancient academy in France.

– German-born English painter Godfrey Kneller begins painting his series of 'Hampton Court Beauties'.

Henry Purcell, *Te Deum in D*, sacred vocal music.

Sir Christopher Wren, design for Greenwich Hospital (see 1692).

1695

EUROPE

3 May In England an Act is passed attempting to prevent bribery in parliamentary elections.

9 May The Scottish Parliament meets to enquire into the massacre of Glencoe (see Feb. 1692).

June A Polish army defeats the Tatars at the gates of Lvov, in Poland.

1 Sept. King William III of Great Britain and Ireland takes Namur, Spanish Netherlands, from the French.

22 Nov. Tsar Peter I (the Great) returns to Moscow, Russia, after failing to take the Ottoman (Turkish) fortress of Azov on the River Don in S Russia.

— Birth of Henry Pelham, who will become a Whig politician and prime minister of Britain (1743–54).

MIDDLE EAST AND NORTH AFRICA

27 Jan. Ahmed II, Ottoman sultan, dies and is succeeded by Mustafa II.

ECONOMY AND SOCIETY

— Window tax is established in Britain.

— Berlin University is founded.

— A model school for pauper children is founded in Halle, Germany.

ARTS AND HUMANITIES

5 April Death in London of George Savile, marquis of Halifax, politician and writer (see 1688).

13 April Death in Paris of Jean de La Fontaine, French poet known for his *Fables*.

23 April Death in Llansantffraed, Breconshire, Wales, of Henry Vaughan, religious poet.

21 Nov. Death at the age of 36 of Henry Purcell, English composer. The greatest composer of English baroque, Purcell has written more than 500 works, including operas, incidental music for the theatre, church music and instrumental works.

— Birth in Lyons, France, of Louis-François Roubiliac, sculptor.

William Congreve, *Love for Love*, comedy.

John Locke (see p. 285), *The Reasonableness of Christianity*, philosophy.

Henry Purcell, incidental music for *The Indian Queen* and *The Tempest*.

1696

EUROPE

27 Feb. The Oath of Association is imposed on England and Wales to defend King William III and the Protestant settlement.

17 June In Wilanów, Poland, John III (John Sobieski), king of Poland, dies (see 2 June 1697).

29 July Tsar Peter I (the Great) of Russia takes Azov from the Turks, thereby finally securing access to the Sea of Azo (a gulf in the NE of the Black Sea).

July Louis XIV of France signs a peace treaty with Victor Amadeus II, duke of Savoy, who was hitherto part of the Grand Alliance against France; in exchange for his support, the duke regains Savoy, Nice, Susa, Casale and Pinerolo; his daughter is to be betrothed to Louis, duke of Burgundy, Louis XIV's grandson.

ASIA

Sept. Russia conquers the Kamchatka peninsula, in E Siberia.

— The English East India Company fortifies Sutanati (modern Calcutta), India, and renames it Fort William.

ECONOMY AND SOCIETY

— The English philosopher John Locke and the scientist and mathematician Isaac Newton (see p. 283) supervise the recoinage of British silver money.

— The English Board of Trade and Plantations is founded.

ARTS AND HUMANITIES

17 April Death of Marie de Rabutin-Chantal, marquise de Sévigné, famous for the informative, gossipy letters she wrote to her daughter over a period of 25 years, describing her impressions of the age of Louis XIV, king of France.

10 May Death at Versailles of Jean de La Bruyère, French satirist and moralist.

1697

EUROPE

21 Mar. Tsar Peter I (the Great) of Russia leaves for his visit to Prussia, the United Netherlands, England and Vienna (which lasts until Sept. 1698), which will inspire his Westernizing reforms of his homeland.

15 April After Charles XI's death, Charles XII succeeds as king of Sweden.

2 June Frederick Augustus I (the Strong), Elector of Saxony, converts to Roman Catholicism and is elected king of Poland as Augustus II (27 June).

10–20 Sept. End of the Nine Years War (War of the League of Augsburg; see 1688): by the treaty of Ryswick, France recognizes William III as king of Great Britain and Ireland and agrees to the chief garrisons in the Netherlands being manned by Dutch troops. By the peace of Ryswick (30 Sept.) between France and Austria, the right bank of the Rhine is restored to Austria and Lorraine is restored to its duke.

11 Sept. Austrian forces under Prince Eugène of Savoy defeat the Ottomans at Zenta, ending the Turkish campaign to recover Hungary.

ASIA

— China conquers W Mongolia.

ECONOMY AND SOCIETY

— The English writer Daniel Defoe recommends income tax and the establishment of benefit societies in his *An Essay upon Projects*.

1697–1700

PARTITION TREATY DIVIDES KINGDOM OF SPAIN □ BEGINNING OF GREAT NORTHERN WAR

ARTS AND HUMANITIES

18 Nov. Birth in London of William Hogarth, English satirical painter and engraver.

Pierre Bayle, *Dictionnaire historique et critique* (Historical and Critical Dictionary), two volumes, criticism.

John Blow, anthem for the opening of St Paul's Cathedral, London.

John Dryden, *Alexander's Feast* (second ode for St Cecilia's Day), poetry.

François de la Mothe-Fénelon, *Explications des maximes des saints sur la vie intérieure* (An Explanation of the Sayings of the Saints on the Inner Life), religious philosophy, condemned by Pope Innocent XII.

Sir John Vanbrugh, *The Provok'd Wife*, comedy.

1698

EUROPE

17 June The mercenary forces of Tsar Peter I (the Great) of Russia defeat the Streltzy (household troops) rebels in Moscow.

Sept.–Oct. Tsar Peter I executes the Streltzy rebels and imposes a tax on beards.

11 Oct. The poor health of Charles II, king of Spain, prompts King Louis XIV of France and King William III of Great Britain and Ireland to sign the First Partition treaty, to avoid war in Europe on the Spanish monarch's death. It divides the Spanish kingdom among three main claimants: Prince Joseph Ferdinand of Bavaria (grandson of the Holy Roman Emperor Leopold I) receives Spain, the Spanish Netherlands, Sardinia and Spanish America; Louis XIV's son, Louis the dauphin, gains Naples, Sicily and the Tuscan ports; Archduke Charles of Austria, second son of Emperor Leopold I, gets Milan.

23 Dec. On the death of Ernest I Augustus, Georg Ludwig (the future George I of Great Britain) succeeds as Elector of Hanover.

ASIA

– The French establish a legation in China.

THE AMERICAS

5 Sept. In Britain the New East India Company is granted a charter by King William III.

ECONOMY AND SOCIETY

– White's Chocolate House becomes the London headquarters of the Tory Party (see 1679).

– Dr Thomas Bray establishes the Society for Promoting Christian Knowledge.

SCIENCE AND TECHNOLOGY

– The first Eddystone lighthouse is built off the SW coast of England.

– British engineer Thomas Savery patents a pumping machine.

ARTS AND HUMANITIES

Jules Hardouin-Mansart, design for the Place Vendôme, Paris.

Andreas Schlüter, design for the Berlin Palace.

Sir Christopher Wren, design for the Painted Hall, Greenwich.

1699

EUROPE

26 Jan. The peace of Karlowitz is signed by Austria, Russia, Poland and Venice with the Ottoman (Turkish) empire. Hungary, Transylvania, Croatia and Slavonia (the E part of modern Croatia) are ceded to the Habsburgs; Poland gains the Ukraine and Russia retains its conquest of Azov.

1–11 June By the Second Partition treaty agreed between King Louis XIV of France and King William III of Great Britain and Ireland, the division of the Spanish kingdom established in 1698 is amended: Archduke Charles of Austria receives Spain, Spanish America and the Spanish Netherlands; Louis, the dauphin of France, gets Naples, Sicily and Lorraine; Charles, duke of Lorraine, receives Milan.

24 Aug. Denmark and Russia sign a convention for mutual defence. Denmark also allies (25 Sept.) with the empire and Poland against Sweden.

22 Nov. Partition of the Swedish empire by the treaty of Preobrazhenskoe, which is signed by Denmark, Russia, Saxony and Poland.

20 Dec. Tsar Peter I (the Great) of Russia announces that the new year will start on 1 Jan., replacing 1 Sept. in the traditional Russian calendar.

ECONOMY AND SOCIETY

– Gobind Singh, the tenth Sikh Guru, creates the Khalsa brotherhood.

ARTS AND HUMANITIES

21 April Death in Paris of Jean Racine, French poet and dramatist.

– Birth of Jean-Baptiste Chardin, French painter.

Richard Bentley, *Dissertation upon the Epistles of Phalaris*, a work of classical scholarship, which transforms textual criticism on a European scale.

François de la Mothe-Fénelon, *Les Aventures de Télémaque* (The Adventures of Telemachus), epic, suppressed in 1717 for its political content.

John Vanbrugh, design for Castle Howard, Yorkshire.

1700

EUROPE

May King Charles II of Spain and Holy Roman Emperor Leopold I reject the partition treaty meant to divide Spanish territory between France and Austria on the death of Charles II (see 1698 and 1699).

May Saxon troops under Augustus II, king of Poland, invade Swedish Livonia (modern Latvia and Estonia); they attack Riga, marking the beginning of the Great Northern War between King Charles XII of Sweden and the coalition of Hanover, Brandenburg, Denmark, Poland and Russia.

4 July Treaty of Constantinople: Russia and the Ottoman empire (Turkey) begin a 30-year truce; the Ottomans cede the Black Sea fortress of Azov (see 1695).

288 THE EARLY MODERN WORLD: 1450–1799

29 July William, duke of Gloucester, only survivor of 17 children borne by Princess Anne (sister of Mary II of England and future queen), dies at the age of 12. His death calls into question the future of the Protestant succession to the English throne (see 12 June 1701).

18 Aug. Charles XII of Sweden enforces the peace of Travendal on Denmark, which agrees to cease hostilities against Sweden.

3 Oct. Charles II of Spain appoints Philip of Anjou his heir. Charles dies on 1 Nov. Because Philip is grandson of Louis XIV of France and was brought up at Versailles, the appointment will precipitate the War of the Spanish Succession (1701–13). Philip, who reigns as Philip V, is the first of Spain's Bourbon kings.

16 Nov. Treaty between the Holy Roman Emperor and Frederick III, Elector of Brandenburg, who will support the Austrian Habsburgs in future imperial elections and supply troops for the anticipated war against France.

30 Nov. Swedish forces under King Charles XII defeat the Russian army of Tsar Peter I at Narva, near St Petersburg.

THE AMERICAS

– English-born jurist Samuel Sewall's *The Selling of Joseph* becomes the first American protest against slavery.

SUB-SAHARAN AFRICA

– The English Royal Africa Company loses its trade monopoly between the Gold Coast (modern Ghana) and Britain.

ECONOMY AND SOCIETY

– A reading room (subsequently the New York Society Library) is established in the City Hall, New York.

– German Protestants adopt the Gregorian calendar.

SCIENCE AND TECHNOLOGY

– Founding of the Prussian Academy of Sciences, with German mathematician Gottfried Wilhelm Leibniz (see p. 295) as president.

– English astronomer Edmond Halley compiles charts with lines of equal magnetic variation.

– English collector Sir John Cotton gives his grandfather's collection of books and manuscripts to the nation. It will be transferred to the British Museum in 1753.

ARTS AND HUMANITIES

1 May Death of John Dryden, English poet, playwright, critic and Poet Laureate.

11 Sept. Birth of James Thomson, Scottish poet.

William Congreve, *The Way of the World*, comedy.

1701

EUROPE

18 Jan. Frederick III, Elector of Brandenburg, is crowned Frederick I, king of Prussia.

Feb. Start of the War of the Spanish Succession; French troops occupy the S Spanish Netherlands, and Philip of Anjou (see 3 Oct. 1700) enters Madrid as Philip V of Spain.

12 June By the Act of Settlement, the Protestant succession to the English crown is secured in the House of Hanover and in the person of the Electress Sophia, Protestant princess of Hanover and grand-daughter of James I. This confirms the loss of any claim to the throne by the deposed King James II, also grandson of James I, and his heirs, and will give rise to the Jacobite rebellions of 1715 and 1745.

17 June In the Great Northern War Charles XII of Sweden invades Swedish Livonia (modern Latvia and Estonia), relieves Riga of Russian occupation and then invades Courland and Poland.

9 July Austrian military commander Prince Eugène of Savoy defeats the French at the battle of Carpi in Lombardy, N Italy.

27 Aug.–7 Sept. The Grand Alliance is formed between Britain, Holland and the Holy Roman Emperor against France.

6 Sept. James II, former king of England, Ireland and Scotland, dies. Louis XIV of France recognizes his son, James Edward Stuart (the Old Pretender), as James III. Louis's action is deigned to foment domestic discord in England and raises the prospect of French-supported Jacobite rebellions.

THE AMERICAS

– Antoine de la Mothe Cadillac founds a fort and trading settlement at Detroit in N America.

– Yale College, New Haven, Connecticut, is founded.

– As a result of the Bourbon accession to the Spanish throne, the French Guinea Company acquires a ten-year contract (*asiento*) to supply slaves to Spain's American colonies.

ECONOMY AND SOCIETY

– The Society for Propagating the Gospel in Foreign Parts is founded in London.

– Father Francisco Ximenez collects and translates the *Popul Vuh*, the sacred national book of the Quiche people of Guatemala.

SCIENCE AND TECHNOLOGY

– In England William III grants charters to weavers in Axminster (Devon) and Wilton (Wiltshire) to make carpets.

– English agriculturalist Jethro Tull invents a machine drill for sowing crops.

ARTS AND HUMANITIES

Daniel Defoe, *The Villainy of Stock-jobbers Debated*, a pamphlet on the expansion of the stock trade, and *The True-born Englishman*, a satire in defence of King William III.

Hyacinthe Rigaud, *Portrait of Louis XIV*, painting.

1702

EUROPE

1 Feb. Austrian forces under Prince Eugène of Savoy raid Cremona in the duchy of Milan, N Italy.

8–19 Mar. William III, king of Great Britain and Ireland, dies. He is succeeded by his sister-in-law, Anne (sister of Mary II), who will (unlike William) not be stadtholder in the United Netherlands.

24 Mar. The duke of Marlborough, John Churchill, becomes Captain-General of the British armed forces.

1702-4

23 April–4 May Britain, Holland and the Holy Roman Emperor declare war against France.

14 May In the Great Northern War Charles XII of Sweden takes Warsaw, Poland. He defeats the Poles at Klissow (19 July) and then takes Cracow.

12–23 Oct. John Churchill, duke of Marlborough, takes Liège.

– Rebellion of French Protestants (Camisards) in the Cévennes, SE France.

THE AMERICAS

16–27 Oct. The British plunder St Augustus in Florida in the war with Spain.

ECONOMY AND SOCIETY

2 Mar. In London a daily newspaper, *The Daily Courant*, appears for the first time.

ARTS AND HUMANITIES

– Abel Boyer, a Huguenot settled in England, compiles a French–English dictionary.

Daniel Defoe, *The Shortest Way with the Dissenters*, a satirical tract mimicking the views of English high churchmen, for which Defoe will be pilloried and imprisoned.

Cotton Mather, *Magnalia Christi Americana*, an ecclesiastical history of New England.

1703

EUROPE

21 April–2 May Portugal concludes a treaty with Britain and joins the Grand Alliance against France.

7–18 May John Churchill, duke of Marlborough, leads allied troops to occupy Cologne, and then takes the cities of Bonn, Limburg, Huy and Guelders. Eugène of Savoy campaigns at the same time in the Rhineland and S Germany. French forces retreat from both regions.

May In the Great Northern War Charles XII of Sweden defeats Russian Tsar Peter I (the Great) at Pultusk.

ECONOMY AND SOCIETY

17 June Birth of John Wesley (see p. 306), English religious reformer and founder of Methodism.

23 June Birth of Marie Leszczynska, future wife of Louis XV and queen of France.

16–27 Dec. By the terms of the commercial Methuen treaty (so-called because it was negotiated by a John Methuen) between Britain and Portugal, Britain imports Portuguese wines at a third less duty than French wines, while Portugal imports all its woollen goods from Britain. Port, a strong, sweet dark red wine, becomes popular in Britain from this date.

ARTS AND HUMANITIES

25 May Death in London of Samuel Pepys, admiralty official and diarist of London life in the 1660s.

– Ellis Wyn of Lasynys, *Gweledigaethau y Bardd Cwsc* (The Visions of the Sleeping Bard), a classic of Welsh prose.

1704

EUROPE

Jan. Augustus II (the Strong), king of Poland, is deposed as a result of Swedish military success in Poland.

18 May In Britain Robert Harley, a Tory and the future earl of Oxford, becomes secretary of state, responsible for N England and Scotland as well as for relations with the Protestant states of N Europe.

21 June Following a remarkable 400km (250 mile) march from Flanders to the Danube, and a rendezvous (10 June) between the duke of Marlborough's Anglo-Dutch contingent and the Austrian army of Prince Eugène of Savoy, the army of the Grand Alliance defeats a Franco-Bavarian army at Donauwörth, N of Augsburg, Bavaria.

7 July Stanislaw Leszczynski is crowned as Stanislaw I, king of Poland, at King Charles XII of Sweden's instigation, after the earlier deposition of former King Augustus II (Jan.).

24 July–4 Aug. A British fleet takes Gibraltar, the Spanish fortress guarding the entrance to the Mediterranean Sea.

2–13 Aug. John Churchill, duke of Marlborough, and Eugène of Savoy defeat the French and Bavarians at Blenheim in Bavaria. The battle severely dents the expansionist ambition of Louis XIV of France.

– The Test Act (see 1673) is introduced in Ireland.

THE AMERICAS

April The French, in alliance with the Native Americans, massacre the inhabitants of Deerfield, Connecticut Valley.

– *The Boston News-Letter* is the first American weekly newspaper.

SCIENCE AND TECHNOLOGY

– English physicist Isaac Newton (see p. 283) explains the emission theory of light in his *Optics*.

– John Harris edits the *Lexicon Technicum, or, a Universal English Dictionary of Arts and Sciences*, the first scientific encyclopedia.

– The Jesuits' *Dictionnaire de trévoux* provides a French and Latin dictionary of terms used in the sciences and arts.

ARTS AND HUMANITIES

12 April Death in Paris of Jacques-Bénigne Bossuet, French bishop and writer.

28 Oct. Death in Oates, Essex, of the philosopher John Locke (see p. 285).

– Italian musical instrument maker Bartolomeo Cristofori, famous for his harpsichords, builds the first pianoforte.

– English author Daniel Defoe starts a weekly newspaper, *The Review*.

– French orientalist Antoine Galland translates into French *The Arabian Nights Entertainment*, the first translation of the work into a Western language.

– The earliest German subscription library is opened in Berlin.

– German composer Johann Sebastian Bach writes his first cantata.

Thomas Archer, designs for the N front of Chatsworth House in Derbyshire, England.

Jonathan Swift, *A Tale of a Tub* and *The Battle of the Books*, satires on contemporary intellectual disputes.

1705

EUROPE

5 May Death in Vienna, Austria, of the Holy Roman Emperor Leopold I, who is succeeded by his son Joseph I.

7 July The Westernizing reforms of Peter I (the Great), tsar of Russia, spark a rebellion among the Astrakhan Tatars.

12 July Death in London of Titus Oates, the conspirator who alleged that there was a Popish Plot to kill King Charles II and place his Catholic brother James on the throne (see 1678).

4–15 Oct. A British fleet under Admiral Charles Mordaunt, earl of Peterborough, captures the Spanish city of Barcelona.

31 Dec. Death in Lisbon, Portugal, of Catherine of Braganza, Portuguese queen consort of King Charles II of England.

MIDDLE EAST AND NORTH AFRICA

– The Tunisian Husseinite dynasty, started by Hussein bin Ali, takes control of Tunis and rejects Ottoman (Turkish) rule.

SCIENCE AND TECHNOLOGY

– English astronomer Edmond Halley calculates that a comet seen in 1682 was the same as the comets previously seen in 1607, 1531 and earlier; he predicts, correctly, its return in 1758.

– The Berlin Royal Observatory is founded.

– English inventor Thomas Newcomen improves the steam engine by inventing a vacuum under the piston.

ARTS AND HUMANITIES

8 Jan. German-born composer George Frideric Handel produces his opera *Almira* in Hamburg.

– German composer Johann Sebastian Bach walks 320km (200 miles) to hear Dietrich Buxtehude, Danish organist and composer, direct the Abendmusiken at Lübeck, Germany.

Sir John Vanbrugh, design for Blenheim Palace, England; the palace is a gift from a grateful nation to the victorious general John Churchill, duke of Marlborough (see Aug. 1704).

1706

EUROPE

11–22 May British forces raise the French siege of Barcelona, Spain.

12–23 May English general John Churchill, duke of Marlborough, leads an Anglo-Dutch army to victory over the French troops of François de Neufville, duc de Villeroi, at Ramillies (Spanish Netherlands); the allied forces control the entire N and E of the territory.

June British and Portuguese forces enter Madrid, Spain.

Aug.–Oct. Louis XIV's first peace negotiations are rejected by the allies.

7 Sept. Prince Eugène of Savoy defeats the French at Turin; French troops subsequently leave Piedmont.

– Birth of Dick Turpin, English highwayman.

THE AMERICAS

17 Jan. Birth in Boston, Massachusetts, of Benjamin Franklin, American printer, publisher and inventor, who will help to draft the Declaration of Independence and the Constitution of the USA.

21 Aug.– 1 Sept. A French and Spanish attack on Charleston, South Carolina, is repulsed by British colonial forces.

SCIENCE AND TECHNOLOGY

– Christoph Semler founds a Realschule (scientific secondary school) at Halle, Germany, for the study of mathematics and applied science.

– Danish astronomer Ole Römer publishes his catalogue of astronomical observations.

ARTS AND HUMANITIES

27 Feb. Death of John Evelyn, English diarist.

28 Dec. Death in Rotterdam, United Netherlands, of Pierre Bayle, French scholar.

– *The Evening Post*, the first English evening newspaper, is issued in London.

– The German-born composer George Frideric Handel travels to Italy. The time he spends here will greatly influence his style of composition.

George Farquhar, *The Recruiting Officer*, comedy.

Hyacinthe Rigaud, *Self-portrait*, painting.

Sir John Vanbrugh, *The Mistake*, comedy.

1707

EUROPE

13 Mar. Holy Roman Emperor Joseph I occupies the Spanish kingdom of Naples (S Italy) and forces French troops to leave N Italy by the terms of the Convention of Milan.

1 May Union between England and Scotland as the kingdom of Great Britain; the Scottish Parliament is abolished and the Union Jack is adopted as a single flag for both countries. By the terms of the Act there is a single Parliament for England and Scotland, and the establishment of the Churches of England and Scotland remains in place.

11–22 Aug. A Perpetual Alliance is signed between Prussia and Sweden.

Oct. Queen Anne's second Parliament is revived as the first Parliament of Great Britain.

– French military engineer Sébastien le Prestre de Vauban publishes *Dîme royal* (Royal Tithe), in which he urges uniform taxation rates on land and income and attacks exemptions from taxation. Louis XIV orders the burning of the book.

ASIA

3 Mar. In India Aurangzeb, the Mughal emperor, dies and is succeeded by his son Bahadur Shah I; the Mughal empire begins to fall apart.

SCIENCE AND TECHNOLOGY

23 May Birth in Råshult, Småland, Sweden, of Carl von Linné

(Carolus Linnaeus), first botanist to develop the principles of taxonomy (the naming of species).

7 Sept. Birth in Montbard, France, of Georges-Louis Leclerc, comte de Buffon, naturalist.

ARTS AND HUMANITIES

25 Feb. Birth in Venice, Italy, of the dramatist Carlo Goldoni, the founder of Italian realistic comedy.

22 April Birth in Sharpham Park, Somerset, England, of Henry Fielding, who will contribute significantly to the development of the English novel.

9 May Death of Dietrich Buxtehude, Danish-born German organist and composer.

26 Dec. Death of Jean Mabillon, French scholar.

George Farquhar, *The Beaux' Stratagem*, comedy.

1708

EUROPE

13 Feb. English moderate Tory politician Robert Harley (later earl of Oxford) is dismissed as secretary of state and Robert Walpole, a Whig politician, is appointed secretary of state for war (25 Feb.).

23 Mar. The Catholic James Edward Stuart, the Old Pretender, son of the deposed James II, lands at the Firth of Forth, Scotland, but returns to Dunkirk after the French fleet supporting his attempt to seize the British throne is defeated by the British (27 Mar.).

30 June –11 July English general John Churchill, duke of Marlborough, and Prince Eugène of Savoy defeat the French at Oudenarde.

18 Aug. British forces occupy Minorca.

15 Nov. Birth in London of William Pitt (the Elder), earl of Chatham, future British prime minister.

– Russia is divided administratively into eight areas.

ASIA

29 Sept. Merger of the British East India Company and the New East India Company.

THE AMERICAS

– War breaks out in Brazil between the Portuguese administration and the Portuguese slave-raiding parties known as Paulistas; the war will end in government victory (1711).

SCIENCE AND TECHNOLOGY

– Jesuit missionaries complete the first accurate map of China.

– Dutch physician Herman Boerhaave's *Institutiones Medicae* (Medical Institutions) explains inflammation, obstruction and plethora in the human body.

ARTS AND HUMANITIES

1 Oct. Death of John Blow, English composer.

– The first Austrian theatre opens in Vienna.

– Death of Jules Hardouin-Mansart, French architect who completed the design of the Palace of Versailles.

1709

EUROPE

5 May Louis XIV of France rejects peace preliminaries proposed by Britain, the United Netherlands, Austria, Portugal and Savoy for ending the War of the Spanish Succession.

May German Protestants from the Palatinate begin a mass emigration to N America.

8 July Russian Tsar Peter I (the Great) defeats Charles XII of Sweden at the battle of Poltava, in S Russia.

19–30 July English general John Churchill, duke of Marlborough, and Prince Eugène of Savoy take Tournai (modern Belgium).

31 Aug.–11 Sept. The army of the Grand Alliance defeats the French at Malplaquet, N France. Heavy casualties lead the Tories to call Marlborough 'the Butcher'. Marlborough and Eugène go on to take the strategic town of Mons, in the Spanish Netherlands, from the French (9–20 Oct.).

– The first Russian prisoners are exiled to Siberia.

ASIA

– At Kandahar in Afghanistan, Afghans under the Ghilzan chieftain Mir Vais begin a revolt against the Safavid Persian dynasty that dominates the area.

– Tokugawa Ienobe becomes shogun in Japan.

ECONOMY AND SOCIETY

– Britain's first Copyright Act becomes law.

– Magnolias from Japan are introduced to England.

– The buildings of the French monastery of Port-Royal are destroyed and the remaining Jansenists (a Catholic sect) are expelled.

SCIENCE AND TECHNOLOGY

– In his *New Theory of Vision* Irish philosopher and churchman George Berkeley maintains that the eye only conveys sensations of colour and that perceptions of form are conveyed by touch.

– Iron master Abraham Darby conducts the first successful experiment for using coke to smelt iron in a blast-furnace at Coalbrookdale, Shropshire, England.

ARTS AND HUMANITIES

18 Sept. Birth in Lichfield, Staffordshire, England, of Samuel Johnson, essayist and lexicographer known for his *Dictionary of the English Language*.

– Composition of the song 'For He's a Jolly Good Fellow' after the English victory against the French at the battle of Malplaquet.

1710

EUROPE

27 Jan. The first Russian budget (treasury balance sheet) is published as part of Tsar Peter I's reforms.

15 Feb. Birth in Versailles, France, of Louis XV (great-grandson of Louis XIV), who will become king of France in 1715.

20 Mar. The trial opens in England of the political preacher Dr Henry Sacheverell (for preaching sermons criticizing the

Glorious Revolution and therefore seen as subversive by the Whig government): he is suspended from preaching for three years (23 Mar.).

8 Aug. Fall of Britain's Whig ministry: English moderate Tory politician Robert Harley (later earl of Oxford) and Henry St John (later Viscount Bolingbroke) form a Tory administration.

25 Nov. Queen Anne's fourth Parliament meets; it contains a majority of Tory members.

30 Nov.–10 Dec. British forces are defeated by the French at Brihuega, in Spain; the French defeat imperial forces at Villa Viciosa (10 Dec.).

– French churchman François de Salignac de la Mothe-Fénelon recommends the summoning of the Estates-General in France (representing the clergy, the nobility and the commons) as a measure of state reform.

THE AMERICAS

– War breaks out between the Portuguese and Brazilian natives, who are eventually defeated.

– The English South Sea Company, which mainly trades in slaves with S America, is founded.

AUSTRALASIA AND OCEANIA

– Mauritius, formerly a Dutch possession, becomes French.

SCIENCE AND TECHNOLOGY

– Prussian blue dye is invented.

ARTS AND HUMANITIES

4 Jan. Birth in Jesi, Italy, of Giovanni Battista Pergolesi, Italian composer.

– French philosopher Pierre Bayle's *Dictionnaire historique et critique* (Historical and Critical Dictionary), first published in 1697, is translated into English.

– George Frideric Handel, court composer to the Elector of Hanover (the future George I of England), visits London.

George Berkeley, *A Treatise Concerning the Principles of Human Knowledge*, philosophy.

Gottfried Wilhelm Leibniz (see p. 295) publishes *Théodicée* (Theodicy), philosophy, demonstrating that the existence of evil does not invalidate the creation of the world by a loving God.

Sir Christopher Wren, design for Marlborough House, London, England.

1711

EUROPE

19 Mar. War breaks out between Russia and the Ottoman empire (Turkey).

17 April Death of Emperor Joseph I; he is succeeded by his brother Charles III, king of Spain, as Holy Roman Emperor Charles VI.

1 May Peace of Szathmar, an agreement with Hungarian rebels by which Charles VI agrees to respect the Hungarian constitution.

1 Aug. Peter I (the Great), tsar of Russia, restores Azov (see 1695)

to the Ottomans and allows the return of King Charles XII to Sweden.

31 Dec. John Churchill, duke of Marlborough, is dismissed as commander-in-chief of British forces for voting against the peace preliminaries when they are placed before Parliament. He is replaced by James Butler, duke of Ormonde.

THE AMERICAS

22 Sept. The Brazilian city of Rio de Janeiro is captured by the French.

– The Tuscarora War breaks out in North Carolina; Native Americans kill settlers but will be defeated in 1712.

ARTS AND HUMANITIES

24 Feb. German-born composer George Frideric Handel's opera *Rinaldo* is first performed in London.

1 Mar. English journalists Joseph Addison and Richard Steele found *The Spectator*, aiming to bring literary and philosophical discussion into English coffee houses.

26 April Birth in Edinburgh of Scottish philosopher and economist David Hume (see p. 312).

– The Berlin Academy opens under German philosopher Gottfried Wilhelm Leibniz's presidency.

Alexander Pope, *Essay on Criticism*, poem.

1712

EUROPE

1–12 Jan. Opening of the Utrecht Congress, to end the War of the Spanish Succession.

17 Jan. British Whig politician Robert Walpole is imprisoned in the Tower of London for alleged corruption.

28 June Birth in Geneva, Swiss Confederation, of French philosopher and writer Jean-Jacques Rousseau (see p. 321).

12 July Death in Cheshunt, Hertfordshire, England, of Richard Cromwell, Lord Protector of England (1658–9) and son of Oliver Cromwell.

25 July Protestant Berne wins the battle of Villmergen between Catholic and Protestant Swiss cantons. The treaty of Arrau (11 Aug.) ends the Swiss War and guarantees the domination of Protestants over five Catholic cantons.

20 Dec. The Swedes defeat the Danes at Gadebusch (in Pomerania, N Germany), but the victory will not arrest Swedish decline in the Great Northern War.

ASIA

– A war of succession rages in India among the four sons of Mughal emperor Bahadur Shah.

ECONOMY AND SOCIETY

– Jane Wenham from Walkern, Hertfordshire, is the last person to be executed for witchcraft in England.

ARTS AND HUMANITIES

– Foundation of the Académie des Sciences, Belles Lettres et Arts in Bordeaux, France.

- German-born composer George Frideric Handel settles in London where he will write *Te Deum and Jubilate*, a musical celebration of the peace of Utrecht.
- Foundation of the Biblioteca National (National Library) in Madrid, Spain.
- Birth in Venice, Italy, of Francesco Guardi, Italian rococo landscape painter.

Thomas Archer, design for St Paul's Church, Deptford, England.
Gabriel Boffrand, design for the Hotel de Montmorency, Paris.
Alexander Pope, *The Rape of the Lock*, mock epic poem.
Jonathan Swift, *A Proposal for Correcting the English Language*, prose satire.

1713

EUROPE

25 Feb. Frederick William I succeeds his father Frederick I as king of Prussia.

25 Feb. As a result of diplomatic intrigues, Charles XII, king of Sweden, encamped in the Ottoman (Turkish) province of Moldavia since the Swedish defeat at Poltava (8 July 1709), is imprisoned by the Ottoman sultan Ahmed III.

16–27 Mar. By the peace of Utrecht (see below), Spain agrees to cede Gibraltar and Minorca to Britain and to grant the Royal Africa Company the *asiento* (see 1518), the right to export African slaves to Spain's American colonies.

31 Mar.– 11 April The peace of Utrecht: France dismantles its fortifications at Dunkirk, recognizes the Protestant succession in Britain and cedes Newfoundland, Acadia, Hudson Bay and the Caribbean island of St Kitts to Britain. Spain cedes the Spanish Netherlands to the Dutch; they are to be ceded to the Holy Roman Emperor once the Dutch have fortified seven border towns as a barrier against France. Britain recognizes the Bourbon Philip V as king of Spain; Spain and France are never to be united under one king. The duchy of Savoy is granted to Sicily. Overall, the treaty is a check to French power in Europe, and lays the foundations of Britain's imperial and commercial expansion.

ASIA

- Tokugawa Ietsugu, not yet of age, becomes shogun (military ruler) of Japan.

SCIENCE AND TECHNOLOGY

- A Board of Longitude is established in England.

ARTS AND HUMANITIES

14 Feb. Death in Naples, Italy, of Anthony Ashley Cooper, 3rd earl of Shaftesbury, English philosopher.

15 Oct. Birth in Langres, France, of Denis Diderot (see p. 315), philosopher and editor of the *Encyclopédie*.

24 Nov. Birth in Clonmel, Co. Tipperary, Ireland, of novelist Laurence Sterne.

- The Royal Spanish Academy is founded in Madrid.

Joseph Addison, *Cato*, verse tragedy.

Alexander Pope, *Windsor Forest*, poem celebrating the peace of Utrecht.
Abbé Charles de Saint-Pierre, *Projet pour la paix perpétuelle* (Project for Perpetual Peace), philosophy of international relations.

1714

EUROPE

27 July In England Queen Anne dismisses Robert Harley, earl of Oxford, from his post of lord high treasurer (he has effectively been her prime minister).

1 Aug. Death of Anne, queen of Great Britain and Ireland (see 29 July 1700); the Electress Sophia having died (28 May), George, Elector of Hanover, becomes George I of Great Britain and Ireland, thus continuing the Protestant succession, which excludes the Catholic James Edward Stuart, son of King James II (see 12 June 1701). He is the first of Britain's Hanoverian monarchs.

7 Sept. France signs the peace of Baden with the Holy Roman Empire and is allowed to keep the E region of Alsace and the city of Strasburg.

22 Nov. Charles XII of Sweden arrives in Stralsund after being released from Ottoman (Turkish) captivity.

MIDDLE EAST AND NORTH AFRICA

- The port of Tripoli (in modern Libya), ruled by Ahmad Bey, acquires independence from the Ottomans.

SCIENCE AND TECHNOLOGY

- French surgeon Dominique Anel invents a syringe for surgical treatments.

ARTS AND HUMANITIES.

8 Mar. Birth in Weimar, Saxe-Weimar, of Carl Philip Emanuel Bach, German composer and son of Johann Sebastian Bach.

2 July Birth in Erasbach, Bavaria, of Christoph Willibald Gluck, German composer.

- The Spanish Academy of Science is founded in Madrid.

James Gibbs, design for St Mary-le-Strand Church, London.
Gottfried Wilhelm Leibniz (see p. 295), *Monadologia* (Book on Monads), philosophy, explaining a theory of single units ('monads') as the ultimate structure of the universe.

1715

EUROPE

27 Mar. British Tory politician Henry St John, Lord Bolingbroke, fearing arrest by his Whig opponents for his part in the secret negotiations with France before the 1713 peace of Utrecht, flees to France. He becomes secretary of state to the Catholic prince, James Francis Edward Stuart (the Old Pretender), who claims the British throne as James III and whose supporters are known as Jacobites. Bolingbroke's action gives credence to the Whig propaganda that Tories are Jacobites.

April Formation of a grand anti-Swedish alliance, consisting of Prussia, Saxony, Poland, Hanover and Denmark.

10 June The British Parliament impeaches Bolingbroke.

9 July Moderate Tory politician Robert Harley, earl of Oxford, is imprisoned in the Tower of London by the Whig administration that has come to power under the new king, for his role in negotiations with France before the peace of Utrecht.

July Fear of Jacobite disorders leads the British Parliament to pass the Riot Act. The Habeas Corpus Act (see 1679) is suspended (12 July).

1 Sept. Death of Louis XIV, who is succeeded as king of France by his great-grandson Louis XV under the regency of his nephew, the duke of Orléans. This flouts Louis XIV's decree that power should be shared between Orléans and his illegitimate son, the duke of Maine.

6 Sept. The Jacobite rebellion known as the Fifteen starts at Braemar, Scotland, led by John Erskine, earl of Mar. The rebellion's aim is to restore the Catholic Old Pretender, James Edward Stuart, to the throne of Britain.

13–14 Nov. The Jacobites are defeated at the battle of Preston, Lancashire, NW England.

Gottfried Wilhelm Leibniz (1646–1716)

As a philosopher and mathematician, Leibniz aimed to combine Christian metaphysics with the rationalism of the Enlightenment. He was the last major philosopher to construct an entire theodicy justifying the ways of God and describing God's relationship to the created world.

Leibniz spent most of his career in Hanover as librarian to the duke of Brunswick-Luneburg. Despite the provincial obscurity of this post, Leibniz had a pan-European influence as a diplomat, and worked for the reunification of the Christian churches – something he saw as vital to the defence of Europe against the revived military and cultural threat of the Ottoman empire.

Leibniz is famous for regarding evil as a justifiable necessity. Since only God is perfect, the world he created cannot also be perfect. But that world is the least imperfect of all possible worlds, since it is not God's nature – as it were – to produce work that falls short of his best. So the world that we have is 'the best of all possible worlds'. His idea of the 'pre-established harmony' of the world is illustrated in his analogy of God as a clockmaker. Leibniz was impressed by the evidence of order in the universe and believed that such harmony could not be the result of chance. His God is the ultimate artificer who, having set up a mechanism, then withdraws from the scene.

Leibniz left more lasting legacies. He invented the calculus independently of Newton (the two quarrelled bitterly over who got there first), and in his *Monadologia* (1714) he portrayed a world composed of monads – ultimate constituents of matter grouped together to form complex entities. This imaginative intuition anticipated later discoveries about atoms and molecules.

---

22 Dec. James Francis Edward Stuart arrives at Peterhead, Scotland, to join the Jacobite rebels.

24 Dec. The Prussians take Stralsund in W Pomerania (a Swedish-held province in the Holy Roman Empire) from Sweden, and Charles XII of Sweden attacks Norway.

– The Ottoman Turks expel the Venetians from the Morea (Peloponnese, Greece).

THE AMERICAS

15 April A rebellion of the Yamassees and other Native American peoples breaks out in South Carolina. They are defeated and driven into Spanish-held Florida.

– Around this date significant numbers of German and Scots-Irish immigrants begin to settle in N America, often in areas previously ignored by settlers, such as Piedmont (modern Virginia).

ARTS AND HUMANITIES

7 Jan. Death in Cambrai, France, of French archbishop and liberal theologian François de la Mothe-Fénelon.

17 Mar. Death in London of Gilbert Burnet, Whig cleric and historian.

19 Mar. Death in London of Charles Montagu, earl of Halifax, writer and Whig statesman who established the Bank of England (see 1694).

30 Sept. Birth in Grenoble, France, of Etienne Bonnot de Condillac, empiricist philosopher.

Alain-René Lesage, *Histoire de Gil Blas de Santillane* (The Adventures of Gil Blas of Santillane), fiction, one of the first realistic novels.

Alexander Pope, verse translation of Homer's *Iliad*, Vol. 1.

Giovanni Battista Tiepolo, *The Sacrifice of Isaac*, fresco painting.

1716

EUROPE

10 Feb. James Francis Edward Stuart (the Old Pretender), who claims the British throne as James III, returns to France after the failed Jacobite rising (the Fifteen) and later dismisses Lord Bolingbroke as his secretary of state.

26 April The British Parliament passes the Septennial Act in the light of the Jacobite rebellion: parliamentary terms are extended from three to seven years (see 1694).

May Scottish banker John Law establishes a joint-stock Banque Générale in Paris; it will become the Banque Royale in 1718.

13 Oct. Austrian forces under Prince Eugène of Savoy defeat the Ottomans (Turks) at Peterwardein, Hungary.

13 Oct. Temesvar, last Ottoman possession in Hungary, falls to the Austrians.

24 Dec.– 4 Jan. 1717 By the terms of the Triple Alliance between Britain, France and the Netherlands, the French agree to support the British administration and crown in their resistance to Jacobitism. The British will support the duke of Orléans against Philip V of Spain.

ASIA

- Tokugawa Yoshimune becomes shogun of Japan.

ARTS AND HUMANITIES

1 Jan. Death in London of English playwright William Wycherley.

14 Nov. Death in Hanover, Germany, of German philosopher Gottfried Wilhelm Leibniz (see p. 295).

26 Dec. Birth in London of Thomas Gray, English poet best known for his *Elegy Written in a Country Church-Yard*.

- *Diario di Roma*, the first Italian newspaper, is published.
- Publication of the *Historical Register* in Britain, 'an impartial relation of all transactions, foreign and domestic'; it is published quarterly until 1738.

François Couperin, *L'Art de toucher le clavecin* (The Art of Playing the Harpsichord), musical theory. Born into a family of musicians, Couperin taught harpsichord to the children of Louis XIV.

Jean-Antoine Watteau, *La Leçon de l'amour*, painting.

1717

EUROPE

1 Jan. The Swedish ambassador in London, Count Karl von Gyllenborg, is arrested because of his involvement in a Spanish plot to help James Francis Edward Stuart (the Old Pretender) to invade England.

Feb. James Francis Edward Stuart is forced to leave France because of the Triple Alliance (France, Britain and the United Netherlands; see 1716) and takes refuge with the papacy.

17 May Birth in Vienna, Austria, of Maria Theresa of Austria, daughter of the Holy Roman Emperor Charles VI. Maria Theresa will be a renowned empress in her own right and also mother of Marie Antoinette (see 16 May 1770).

May Russian Tsar Peter I (the Great) visits Paris.

1 July The English Tory politician Robert Harley (earl of Oxford) is acquitted of conspiring with the French to bring the Catholic James Francis Edward Stuart (the Old Pretender) to the British throne (see 9 July 1715).

July Swedish ambassador Count Karl von Gyllenborg is released from arrest in Britain.

16 Aug. Austrian forces under Eugène of Savoy defeat the Ottomans (Turks) at Belgrade, Hungary, which they then occupy (17 Aug.).

- The Act of Grace releases Jacobite rebels in British prisons.
- James Stanhope, former British commander in Spain (1708–10) and current head of the Treasury and chancellor of the exchequer, enforces British Whig politician Robert Walpole's Sinking Fund to reduce the national debt by annual instalments.

ASIA

- W Mongolians capture the Tibetan city of Lhasa.
- Mir Mahmud succeeds Mir Abdullah in Kandahar, Afghanistan; the Abdalis of Herat rebel and establish a separate Afghan state.

THE AMERICAS

Jan. Governor Spotswood of Virginia makes a speech urging the settlement of areas surrounding Lake Erie.

Aug. Scottish banker John Law's Mississippi Company is given a monopoly of trade with Louisiana (see 1682).

ARTS AND HUMANITIES

19 Feb. Birth in Hereford, England, of David Garrick, actor, dramatist, theatrical producer and co-manager of the Drury Lane Theatre in London.

17 July George Frideric Handel's *Water Music*, a set of three suites for orchestra, is performed in a barge alongside George I's barge on the River Thames in London.

24 Sept. Birth in London of Horace Walpole, writer and historian.

Nov. Birth in Paris of Jean le Rond d'Alembert, philosopher and encyclopedist.

9 Dec. Birth in Stendal, Prussia, of Johann Joachim Winckelmann, art historian.

- In Germany Johann Sebastian Bach becomes Kapellmeister (court composer) to Prince Leopold of Anhalt-Cöthen.
- The pope sends the Italian scholar Joseph Simonius Assemani to search for sacred manuscripts believed to be in Egypt and Syria.

François de la Mothe-Fénelon, *Télémaque*, a version of Homer's *Odyssey*, Book 4, satirizing the court of Louis XIV.

Jean-Antoine Watteau, *Embarkation for the Isle of Cythera*, painting.

1718

EUROPE

June The Spanish army sails for Sicily, which it conquers by July.

7 July The tsarevich Alexis, eldest son and heir of Peter I (the Great), tsar of Russia, is murdered at his father's instigation.

21 July The peace of Passarowitz ends the war between Turkey and the Holy Roman Empire; the empire retains Belgrade (Hungary) and part of Serbia; Turkey keeps the Morea (Peloponnese, Greece), Venice keeps Corfu and its conquests in Dalmatia and Albania. The signatories agree to keep the peace for 25 years.

22 July–2 Aug. The Spanish seizure of Sicily leads to the anti-Spanish Quadruple Alliance between Britain, France, the Holy Roman Empire and Holland. The alliance's goals include the renunciation by the emperor and by Philip V, king of Spain, of claims to each other's territories and Spain's exchange of Sicily for Sardinia. War will be declared to secure Spain's agreement.

30 July Death in Buckinghamshire, England, of William Penn, English Quaker and founder of the American state of Pennsylvania.

31 July –11 Aug. British admiral Sir George Byng defeats the Spanish fleet off Cape Passaro, Sicily, after Philip V, king of Spain, rejects the terms of the Quadruple Alliance.

Nov. The king of Sicily surrenders his title at the command of the Quadruple Alliance and becomes king of Sardinia (see above).

11 Dec. Charles XII, king of Sweden, dies in an expedition against the Norwegian fortress of Fredrikshall; he is succeeded by his sister Ulrika Eleanora.

SCIENCE AND TECHNOLOGY

9 Sept. English industrialist Thomas Lombe obtains a patent for the introduction to England of a machine that will make thrown silk.

– English astronomer Edmond Halley discovers that certain stars have 'proper motions'.

– Etienne Geoffrey, an eminent French chemist, presents his tables of affinities (*Tables des rapports*) to the French Academy: it is the first systematic record of the chemical reactivity of elements.

ARTS AND HUMANITIES

George Frideric Handel, *Acis and Galatea*, masque.
Sir Godfrey Kneller, *Portrait of the Duke of Newcastle*, painting.
Jean-Antoine Watteau, *Fête champêtre*, painting.

1719

EUROPE

9 Jan. The conflict caused by the Spanish occupation of Sardinia and Sicily and by the framing of the Quadruple Alliance reaches crisis point: Philip, duke of Orléans and regent of France, declares war on Spain.

15 April Death in Saint-Cyr, France, of Françoise d'Aubigné, marquise de Maintenon, second wife of King Louis XIV.

28 April Whig politician and first lord of the Treasury, Charles Spencer (earl of Sunderland), fearing the creation of a large number of peers by the Tory ministry, introduces the British Peerage Bill to close the House of Lords: the measure is voted down by the House of Commons.

10 June Spanish invaders and their Jacobite supporters are defeated at Glenshiel, NW Scotland, and surrender (11 June). The main invasion fleet has been scattered by storms.

23 Sept. Liechtenstein becomes an independent principality of the Holy Roman Empire.

15 Dec. Following the French invasion occasioned by his policies, Cardinal Giulio Alberoni falls from favour in Spain and is exiled by King Philip V.

– The Holy Roman Emperor Charles VI expels the Spaniards from Sicily.

ECONOMY AND SOCIETY

– In Britain the South Sea Company, which has a monopoly of trade with S America, offers to assume half the British National Debt in exchange for further concessions (see Oct.–Dec. 1720).

SCIENCE AND TECHNOLOGY

– The French consul in Cairo, Egypt, sends the French Academy a description of the Egyptian method of manufacturing sal ammoniac (ammonium chloride).

ARTS AND HUMANITIES

17 June Death in London of Joseph Addison, English writer, politician and dramatist.

– English writer Daniel Defoe founds *The Daily Post*, which is published until 1746.

– Foundation of the *American Mercury* in Philadelphia and of the *Boston Gazette*.

Dimitrie Cantemir, *Tratat de Musica Turceasca*, the first book on Turkish music, published in Russia.

Daniel Defoe, *The Life and Strange Adventures of Robinson Crusoe, of York, Mariner, Written by Himself*, novel.

William Kent, decoration of the interior of Burlington House, London.

1720

EUROPE

1 Feb. Treaty of Stockholm between Prussia and Sweden: Prussia gains Pomerania, then a Swedish province in the Holy Roman Empire between the rivers Oder and Peene. In return, Prussia will help protect Sweden from Russian attack.

6–17 Feb. Peace treaty between Spain and the Quadruple Alliance; the Holy Roman Emperor gives up his claim to Spain and Philip V, king of Spain, renounces his claim to Italy. The emperor allows Charles, son of Philip and of Elizabeth Farnese, to succeed to the thrones of Parma, Piacenza and Tuscany. Savoy obtains Sardinia from the emperor in exchange for Sicily; the duke of Savoy becomes king of Sardinia.

3 July Treaty of Frederiksborg: Sweden recognizes Denmark's annexation of the duchy of Schleswig.

– Ulrika Eleanora, queen of Sweden (see 11 Dec. 1718), abdicates in favour of her husband, Frederick, landgrave of Hesse-Kassel, who becomes King Frederick I of Sweden.

THE AMERICAS

– Spain occupies Texas after fighting between Spain and France in Texas and Florida.

ECONOMY AND SOCIETY

21 May Scottish financier John Law's 'edict' states that there is too much money in circulation.

Oct.–Dec. The bursting of the 'South Sea Bubble' prompts a British financial and political crisis. The company's offer to take over the National Debt (see 1719) has led to financial speculation, leading to panic and then ruin for thousands of investors.

Dec. Scottish-born French subject and fraudster John Law flees from France after his schemes, including especially that of the Mississippi Company (see Aug. 1717), have led to national bankruptcy. He will die in poverty in Venice (1729).

SCIENCE AND TECHNOLOGY

– German physicist Gabriel Daniel Fahrenheit uses mercury in a thermometer.

– The French government establishes a group of technical government officials to oversee roads and bridges.

ARTS AND HUMANITIES

– The Royal Academy of Music is founded in London. George Frideric Handel composes and directs Italian operas under its auspices at the King's Theatre, Haymarket.

John Gay, *Collected Poems*, poetry.

George Frideric Handel, Harpsichord Suite No. 5 (the air and variations in the suite will later be nicknamed 'The Harmonious Blacksmith').

Nicholas Hawksmoor, design for St George's Church, Bloomsbury, London.

Thomas Hearne, *Robert of Gloucester's Chronicle*, history; the first scholarly edition of a medieval English text.

1721

EUROPE

9 Mar. In Britain John Aislabie, the former chancellor of the exchequer, is sent to the Tower of London for fraud because of his involvement in the South Sea Bubble.

3 April Robert Walpole, British Whig politician, becomes prime minister and chancellor of the exchequer. He transfers the South Sea Company's stock to the East India Company and the Bank of England.

15 April William Augustus, duke of Cumberland, third son of King George II and future military suppressor of Scottish Jacobite risings, is born.

10 Sept. Treaty of Rystad: Russia gains Sweden's Baltic provinces of Livonia, Estonia, Ingria and E Karelia but restores Finland.

2 Nov. Peter I (the Great), tsar of Russia, is proclaimed Emperor of All the Russias and is allowed to name his successor.

ASIA

– The Chinese suppress a rebellion in Formosa (modern Taiwan).

AUSTRALASIA AND OCEANIA

29 Dec. The French occupy Mauritius and rename it Ile de France.

SCIENCE AND TECHNOLOGY

– In Britain Lady Mary Wortley Montagu popularizes inoculation for smallpox and the Princess of Wales's inoculation makes it fashionable.

ARTS AND HUMANITIES

Mar. Birth of Tobias Smollett, Scottish satirical novelist.

8 July Death in London of Elihu Yale, Welsh educationalist.

18 July Death from tuberculosis in Nogent-sur-Marne, France, of the painter Jean-Antoine Watteau.

3 Aug. Death of Grinling Gibbons, English sculptor and wood carver of elegant decoration in palaces and great houses.

Johann Sebastian Bach, six *Brandenburg Concertos*, perhaps the greatest concerti of the musical high baroque.

Nathaniel Bailey, *A Universal Etymological English Dictionary*, the first English dictionary to use accentual marks, later used as the basis of his own dictionary by Samuel Johnson (see 1755).

Charles-Louis de Secondat, baron de Montesquieu, *Lettres persanes* (Persian Letters), a work of social satire, published anonymously.

1722

EUROPE

16 June Death in Windsor, England, of John Churchill, duke of Marlborough, military commander who defeated the French at Blenheim (1704).

30 June The Hungarian diet rejects the Pragmatic Sanction issued by the Holy Roman Emperor, Charles VI, in which he asserts the right of his daughter Maria Theresa to succeed him.

17 Oct. The Habeas Corpus Act (see 1679) is suspended in England after the discovery of a Jacobite plot by the bishop of Rochester to proclaim James Francis Edward Stuart (the Old Pretender) as King James III.

ASIA

8 Mar. Mir Mahmud of Afghanistan declares war on Persia and becomes shah on the defeat of Persia in Sept.

12 Sept. Russian forces seize the Persian strategic towns of Baku and Derbent on the Caspian Sea.

– Holy Roman Emperor Charles VI grants a charter for the formation of the Austrian East India Company to compete with the English and the Dutch for trade in the Indies, China and Africa.

ECONOMY AND SOCIETY

– The British Parliament decides that journalists should not report political debates.

SCIENCE AND TECHNOLOGY

– French scientist René-Antoine Ferchault de Réaumur describes how to make iron and analyses ferrous metals in his *L'Art de convertir le fer forgé en acier*.

ARTS AND HUMANITIES

Johann Sebastian Bach, *Das Wohltemperierte Clavier*, Part 1, 24 preludes and fugues for harpsichord.

Daniel Defoe, *A Journal of the Plague Year*, journalism, and *Moll Flanders*, novel.

James Gibbs, designs for the Senate House, Cambridge University and for St Martin-in-the-Fields Church, London.

Jean-Philippe Rameau, *Traité de l'harmonie* (Treatise on Harmony), musical theory.

1723

EUROPE

31 Mar. In the Swiss canton of Vaud, Jean-Abraham-Daniel Davel heads a rising against the rule of the Protestant canton of Berne; he is executed.

June British Tory politician and Jacobite conspirator Henry St John, Viscount Bolingbroke, is pardoned (see 1715); he returns from exile but is forbidden to sit in the House of Lords.

– King Frederick William I of Prussia establishes a General Directory of War, Finance and Domains, a department supervising military, police, economic and financial affairs.

SCIENCE AND TECHNOLOGY

– M.A. Capeller, a French chemist, publishes *Prodromus Crystallographie* (Introduction to Crystallography), the first account of crystallography.

ARTS AND HUMANITIES

25 Feb. Death in London of Sir Christopher Wren, astronomer and architect who has designed over 50 churches in London, including St Paul's Cathedral.

5 June Birth in Kirkcaldy, Fife, Scotland, of Adam Smith (see p. 330), economist.

20 June Birth in Logierait, Perthshire, Scotland, of Adam Ferguson, Scottish Enlightenment philosopher and historian.

7 Nov. Death in London of Godfrey Kneller, German-born English painter.

– Johann Sebastian Bach becomes Cantor (director of music) at St Thomas's in Leipzig, N Germany. Bach owes his appointment to the declining of the post by fellow composer Georg Philipp Telemann.

– Italian scholar Ludovico Antonio Muratori edits the first volumes of the *Rerum Italicarum Scriptores,* which will be published in 28 volumes up to 1751 and which consist of a vast collection of medieval chronicles, poems and letters.

– On the emperor's instruction, a *Gujin tushu jicheng* (Chinese Encyclopaedia) is published in China.

Johann Sebastian Bach, *Magnificat in E flat*, church music.

Gilbert Burnet, *History of My Own Time*, Vol. 1, memoirs, published posthumously.

Pietro Giannoni, *Storia civile del regno di Napoli* (Civil History of the Kingdom of Naples), constitutional history, establishing new standards in that discipline.

George Frideric Handel, *Ottone*, opera.

Nicholas Hawksmoor, design for Christ Church, Spitalfields, London.

Godfrey Kneller, *Portrait of Alexander Pope*, painting.

Pedro de Ribeira, design for the Toledo Bridge, Spain.

Voltaire (see p. 304), *La Ligue* (The League), also known as *La Henriade*, epic poem condemning religious extremism.

1724

EUROPE

14 Jan. Philip V, king of Spain, abdicates in order to retire to a monastery. His son becomes Luis I.

6 April In Britain the duke of Newcastle, Thomas Pelham-Holles, becomes secretary of state. His brother, Henry Pelham, becomes secretary of state for war.

21 May Death in London of Robert Harley, earl of Oxford, politician and leader of the Tories (1710–14).

5 June Death in Highgate, London, of Henry Sacheverell, English clergyman and political preacher (see 1710).

23 June Russia and Turkey agree on the treaty of Constantinople, directed against Persia, in which they recognize each other's conquests.

31 Aug. Luis I dies and Philip V returns as king of Spain.

ARTS AND HUMANITIES

Jonathan Swift, *Drapier's Letters*, political satire (published under the name 'M.B. Drapier') attacking the debasement of the Irish currency as an example of English hegemony over Ireland.

22 April In Königsberg, Prussia, birth of Immanuel Kant (see p. 334), philosopher.

24 Aug. In Liverpool, England, birth of George Stubbs, painter.

27 Dec. In London death of Thomas Guy, philanthropist who founded Guy's Hospital.

– George I, king of Great Britain and Ireland, founds professorships of modern history at Oxford and Cambridge universities.

– In England the Three Choirs Festival is founded for choirs in Hereford, Gloucester and Worcester.

Johann Sebastian Bach, *St John Passion*, church music.

François Couperin, *L'Apothéose de Lully* (The Apotheosis of Lully), chamber suites.

Daniel Defoe, *A Tour Through the Whole Island of Great Britain* (Vol. 1), travel book, the last volume of which is published in 1727.

James Gibbs, design for the Fellows' Building, King's College, Cambridge.

George Frideric Handel, *Giulio Cesare*, opera.

1725

EUROPE

8 Feb. In St Petersburg, Russia, Peter I (the Great), tsar of Russia dies and is succeeded by his widow, Catherine I, who is advised by Peter's collaborator, field marshal Prince Alexander Menshikov.

Feb. Louis XV, king of France, rejects the Spanish infanta who was to marry him. Spain becomes closer to the Holy Roman Emperor and Franco-Spanish relations deteriorate.

30 April The treaty of Vienna guarantees the Pragmatic Sanction (see 30 June 1722), leading to peace between the empire and Spain. By the supplementary treaty (1 May) Emperor Charles VI agrees to help Spain regain Gibraltar. A secret treaty (5 Nov.) provides for intermarriage between the imperial and the Spanish royal families and provides for a division of French territory in the event of war.

5 Sept. Louis XV marries Marie Leszczynski, daughter of King Stanislav I Leszczynski of Poland.

MIDDLE EAST AND NORTH AFRICA

– The Afghan Ashraf Shah succeeds Mir Mahmud as ruler of Persia (see 1722).

SUB-SAHARAN AFRICA

– Holland occupies the trading post of Grossfriedrichsburg (Fredericksburg) on the W African Gold Coast (modern Ghana) and renames it Fort Hollandia.

ECONOMY AND SOCIETY

- George I, king of Great Britain and Ireland, founds the Order of the Bath.
- Opening of Guy's Hospital, London, founded by English bookseller Thomas Guy.
- Holders of public office and witnesses in Pennsylvania, America, can take oaths without testifying to a belief in God.

SCIENCE AND TECHNOLOGY

- The St Petersburg Academy of Science is founded in Russia.

ARTS AND HUMANITIES

2 April In Venice, Italy, birth of Giovanni Casanova, ecclesiastic, soldier, spy, writer and libertine.

21 Aug. In Tournus, France, birth of Jean-Baptiste Greuze, painter of sentimental and moralizing genre subjects.

24 Oct. In Naples, S Italy, death of Alessandro Scarlatti, composer.

- The first full English text of *Sir John Mandeville's Travels* is published (authorship unknown).

Richard Burlington, design for the Villa at Chiswick House, Middlesex, England.

Antonio Canaletto, four *Views of Venice*, paintings, for Stefano Conti of Lucca.

Joseph Fux, *Gradus ad Parnassum* (Steps to Parnassus), essay on the theory of musical counterpoint.

Francis Hutcheson, *An Inquiry into the Original of Our Ideas of Beauty and Virtue*, moral and aesthetic philosophy.

Alexander Pope, translation of Homer's *Odyssey* and edited edition of *The Works of Shakespeare*.

Giambattista Vico (see box), *Scienza nuova intorno alla natura* (The New Science), philosophy, expounding a cyclical theory of historical change.

Antonio Vivaldi, *The Four Seasons*, concerti for violin and orchestra. Rediscovered in the 20th century, they will be among the most popular of all baroque concerti.

1726

EUROPE

11 June Cardinal André de Fleury becomes chief minister of Louis XV of France.

6 Aug. The Holy Roman Empire and Russia agree on an anti-Turkish military alliance.

17 Oct. Treaty of Wusterhausen: Prussia guarantees the Pragmatic Sanction (see 1722) and promises to help Austria in the event of war.

ECONOMY AND SOCIETY

27 Dec. St John of the Cross (see 1542) is canonized.

- Military roads are built in the Scottish Highlands by Gen. George Wade.

SCIENCE AND TECHNOLOGY

- John Harrison, an English clockmaker, invents the gridiron pendulum, whose length can remain constant in differing temperatures and which is, therefore, a more accurate device than any of its predecessors.

ARTS AND HUMANITIES

26 Mar. Death in London of John Vanbrugh, English dramatist and architect famed for designing Blenheim Palace in Oxfordshire (see 1705).

12 April Birth in Shrewsbury, England, of Charles Burney, musician and music historian.

May French writer Voltaire (see p. 304), accused of affronting a nobleman, is exiled from France and arrives in England, where he stays for three years. His sojourn will inspire Voltaire to write his *Lettres philosophiques sur les Anglais* (see 1733).

- Scottish painter and writer Allan Ramsay opens the first circulating library in Edinburgh.
- The Académie des Sciences, Belles Lettres et Arts is founded in Marseilles, France.
- French dancer Marie-Anne de Camargo, the first woman to perform an *entrechat quatre*, makes her debut at the Paris Opera.

Johann Lorenz von Mosheim, *Institutiones Historiae Ecclesiasticae*, applying critical principles to Church history.

Giambattista Vico (1668–1744)

The Italian historian and philosopher Giambattista Vico was born in Naples, where his father was a bookseller, and he spent almost all of his life in the city. He lived in obscurity as a teacher of rhetoric at the local university until he was appointed the royal historiographer at the local court in 1735. Handicapped as a result of a fall in childhood, Vico's life was one of poverty and constant humiliation at the hands of his clerical and royal patrons. But his book *The New Science* (1725) is a seminal work in the history of Western thought.

Vico rejected the Cartesian idea that scientific rationalism is the only measure of truth. He believed that the human sciences – such as history and the study of myth, ritual and language – were knowable through imagination, intuition and depth of feeling, because they are created by humans. In particular, history is a comprehensible science because the object studied is the sum total of actions made by human beings.

Vico held that the history of humanity comprised a cycle of phases: the original phase was brute barbarism; from this emerged the 'age of the gods', a theocratic era in which people are ruled by their fear of the supernatural; this was succeeded by an aristocratic age, the 'age of heroes', in which the patricians dominate the plebeians; via class conflict this age gives way to the 'age of men', an era of democracy and individualism; this age, however, may herald a reversion to the first phase, that of bestial chaos. Vico's work was little known until the 19th century, since when it has had a profound impact on the philosophy of history.

Jean-Philippe Rameau, *Nouveau système de musique théorique* (New System of the Theory of Music), treatise on music.

Jonathan Swift, *Gulliver's Travels: Travels into Several Remote Nations of the World*, prose satire.

James Thomson, *Winter*, poetry, the first part of his poetic sequence *The Seasons*.

Giovanni Battista Tiepolo, frescoes in the Bishop's Palace of Udine, Italy.

1727

EUROPE

Feb. Spain lays siege to the British fortress of Gibraltar: war ensues between Britain and Spain.

10 May In Paris birth of Anne-Robert-Jacques Turgot, French financial administrator under kings Louis XV and Louis XVI.

20–31 May At the Preliminaries of Paris, the Holy Roman Emperor Charles VI, in negotiation with Britain, France and Holland, agrees to suspend the trade of the Austrian East India Company for seven years.

29 May Peter II Alexeivich, grandson of Peter I (the Great), becomes tsar of Russia following the death of Catherine I.

11 June In Osnabrück, Hanover, death of George I, king of Great Britain and Ireland and Elector of Hanover; he is succeeded by his son as George II.

20 Sept. The ancient aristocratic Dolgoruky family, supporters of Tsar Peter II, engineer the removal of Prince Alexander Menshikov (Peter I's collaborator and leading minister; see 1725), from ministerial office and his exile in the Ukraine.

ECONOMY AND SOCIETY

– Curl's Case decides that in English law an obscene libel is a misdemeanour in common law and cannot be punished in an ecclesiastical court.

– The comte de Boulainvilliers researches the history of French local government in order to prove that the nobility should be given more power.

SCIENCE AND TECHNOLOGY

20 Mar. In London death of Isaac Newton (see p. 283), English physicist.

ARTS AND HUMANITIES

Feb. The German-born composer George Frideric Handel becomes a naturalized British subject. Later in the year he will compose four Coronation Anthems for the new king George II, including *Zadok the Priest*.

May In Sudbury, Suffolk, England, birth of Thomas Gainsborough, painter.

John Dyer, 'Grongar Hill', topographical poem.

William Kent, *Designs of Inigo Jones*, architectural study.

John Michael Rysbrack, *George I*, sculpture.

James Thomson, *Summer*, poetry, part of his poetic sequence *The Seasons*.

John Wood (the Elder), *Plans for Bath*, architecture.

1728

EUROPE

26 Feb. In Britain the publication of parliamentary debates is ruled to be a breach of privilege.

Mar. Spain raises the siege of the fortress of Gibraltar (started in 1727).

23 Dec. Holy Roman Emperor Charles VI and Frederick William I, king of Prussia, agree on the terms of the treaty of Berlin: Prussia's claim to the duchies of Berg and Ravenstein is recognized and Prussia guarantees the Pragmatic Sanction (see 1722).

SCIENCE AND TECHNOLOGY

3 Sept. In Birmingham, England, birth of Matthew Boulton, engineer.

28 Oct. In Marton-in-Cleveland, Yorkshire, England, birth of James Cook, explorer, naval captain and navigator.

– J.B. Labat's *Nouvelle Relation de l'Afrique occidentale* (New Account of West Africa) describes the coast of W Africa from Senegal to Sierra Leone.

– Fauchard's *Le Chirurgien dentiste, ou traité des dents* (The Dental Surgeon, or Treatise on the Teeth) advances dentistry.

ARTS AND HUMANITIES

Jan. John Gay's *The Beggar's Opera* (with Gay's book set to music by Johann Christoph Pepusch) is first performed in Lincoln's Inn Fields Theatre, London. It ridicules the contemporary fashion for Italian operas in London and is a huge popular success.

3 July Birth in Kirkcaldy, Fife, Scotland, of Robert Adam, architect.

15 Aug. Death in Paris of Marin Marais, French composer of music for the viol and virtuoso bass viol player.

10 Nov. In Co. Longford, W Ireland, birth of Oliver Goldsmith, poet and author.

Ephraim Chambers, *Cyclopedia, or Universal Dictionary of Arts and Sciences*, English encyclopedia.

Jean-Baptiste Chardin, *The Rain*, painting.

William Law, *A Serious Call to a Devout and Holy Life*, devotional treatise.

Alexander Pope, *The Dunciad*, Books 1–3, mock epic.

Jonathan Swift, *A Short View of the State of Ireland*, satire.

James Thomson, *Spring*, poetry, part of his poetic sequence *The Seasons*.

1729

EUROPE

21 Mar. Death in Venice, Italy, of John Law, Scottish financier (see 1671).

2 May In Szczecin, Prussia, Sophie Friederike Auguste von Anholt-Zerbst is born. She will become Catherine II (the Great), empress of Russia (1762–96).

29 Oct. –9 Nov. The treaty of Seville between Spain, France and Britain detaches Spain from its imperial alliance.

- Corsica, after a revolution, gains independence from Genoa but will remain technically dependent on the Italian state until 1768.
- Frederick Louis, Prince of Wales from 1729, son of George II, arrives in England.

ASIA
- Emperor Yongzhen (Yung Chen) forbids the smoking of opium in China.

THE AMERICAS
- James and Benjamin Franklin publish the *Pennsylvania Gazette*.
- North and South Carolina become colonies of Britain after their charter is forfeited as a result of misgovernment by the local estate proprietors.

SUB-SAHARAN AFRICA
11 Nov. Portugal loses the E African port of Mombasa to the Muscat Arabs.

SCIENCE AND TECHNOLOGY
- English scientist Stephen Gray discovers that some bodies conduct electricity and that others do not.
- English physicist Isaac Newton's *Principia Mathematica*, published in Latin, is translated into English by Robert Samber.

I don't feign hypotheses.

(Hypotheses non fingo.)

Isaac Newton *Principia Mathematica* (1713)

ARTS AND HUMANITIES
12 Jan. In Dublin, Ireland, birth of Edmund Burke, statesman and political writer.
19 Jan. Death in London of William Congreve, English playwright.
22 Jan. In Kamenz, Saxony, birth of Gotthold Ephraim Lessing, poet, critic and playwright.
1 Sept. Death in Carmarthen, Wales, of Richard Steele, essayist, journalist and founder of the periodicals *The Tatler* and *The Spectator*.
6 Sept. In Dessau, Anhalt, Germany, birth of Moses Mendelssohn, German Jewish philosopher.
- Dr Williams's Library is founded in London for the study of religion and philosophy.
- Henry Fielding's *The Author's Farce* is produced at the Haymarket Theatre, London along with a puppet show, *The Pleasures of the Town*, which features Mr Punch.
Johann Sebastian Bach, *St Matthew Passion*, oratorio.

Nicholas Hawksmoor, design for the quadrangle and hall of All Souls College, Oxford, and Castle Howard, Yorkshire, in England.
Richard Savage, 'The Wanderer', poem.
Jonathan Swift, *A Modest Proposal* (*for Preventing the Children of the Poor People from being a Burthen to the Parents*), satire, advocating ironically that the children of the poor in Ireland be eaten.
John Wood (the Elder), design for Queen's Square, Bath, England.

1730

EUROPE
11 Feb. Tsar Peter II of Russia dies. He is succeeded by Anna, daughter of Ivan V, half-brother of Peter I (the Great).
19 Mar. Birth of Charles Watson-Wentworth, marquis of Rockingham, future Whig prime minister of Great Britain (1765–6 and 1782).
15 May Resignation of Charles, 2nd Viscount Townshend as secretary of state (responsible for N England and Scotland as well as for relations with the Protestant states of N Europe), after a quarrel with Robert Walpole, British Whig prime minister. He retires to his farm (see below).
4 Aug. Frederick, crown prince of Prussia, who was enrolled in the Prussian army at the age of ten, is court-martialled for desertion and imprisoned by his father, King Frederick William I, as he attempts to escape to England.
30 Sept. King Victor Amadeus XI of Savoy abdicates and is succeeded by his son, Charles Emmanuel III.
- Louis XV, king of France, orders the Paris *parlement* not to interfere in politics after it has refused to accept the papal bull *Unigenitus Dei Filius*, published by Pope Clement XI on 8 Sept. 1713 and condemning the Jansenists, whose rigorous principles are increasingly perceived as a threat to the established order of the French Catholic Church.

MIDDLE EAST AND NORTH AFRICA
17 Sept. Ahmed III, Ottoman sultan, is deposed and succeeded by his nephew who becomes Mahmud I.

SCIENCE AND TECHNOLOGY
- Charles, 2nd Viscount Townshend invents a four-course system of crop rotation in Norfolk, England, growing clover and turnips. Although an eminent politician, he is known to his friends as 'Turnip' Townshend because of his agricultural researches.
- Zinc smelting is developed in England.

ARTS AND HUMANITIES
- In Seville, Spain, death of Leonardo de Figueroa, Spanish architect.
- Foundation of the *Daily Advertiser* in London; it is the first newspaper to depend on advertising for revenue.
William Hogarth, *Before and After*, painting.
William Kent, design for Holkham Hall, Norfolk, England.
Matthew Tindal, *Christianity as Old as the Creation*, religious philosophy, popularizing the idea of a non-miraculous Christianity.

1731-3

1731

EUROPE

10 Jan. The Italian Farnese line becomes extinct in the duchies Parma and Piacenza. When Don Carlos (son of Elizabeth Farnese and Philip V of Spain) succeeds, the Holy Roman Emperor, Charles VI, annexes the territories, while France and Britain refuse to assist Spain.

THE AMERICAS

– English trader Captain Robert Jenkins has his ear cut off by Spanish coastguards at Havana, Cuba, for trading in defiance of the Spanish monopoly. The incident will lead to the War of Jenkins's Ear (1739).

SCIENCE AND TECHNOLOGY

– French scientist René-Antoine de Réaumur invents an alcohol thermometer and a temperature scale setting water's freezing point at 0° and the boiling point at 80°.

ARTS AND HUMANITIES

26 April Death in London of Daniel Defoe, English writer.
– *The Gentleman's Magazine* is launched in London.
Johann Sebastian Bach, *Klavierübung*, Part 1, harpsichord music.
William Hogarth, *Harlot's Progress*, painting.

1732

EUROPE

7 July In order to strengthen the authority of the French crown, Louis XV exiles 139 members of the *parlement* of Paris; however, they are soon recalled (Dec.).

31 Oct. On the orders of Count Leopold von Firmian, archbishop of Salzburg, thousands of Salzburg Protestants are exiled; they settle in E Prussia, encouraged by Frederick William I, king of Prussia.

– The Italian state of Genoa regains some of the control over Corsica it had lost in 1729.

THE AMERICAS

11–22 Feb. In Westmoreland County, Virginia, birth of George Washington, first president of the USA (1789–97).

June James Oglethorpe is granted a charter to establish a colony in Georgia.

ECONOMY AND SOCIETY

– The Moravian Brethren, founded in Bohemia by Count Zinzendorf in 1722, start their Christian mission in the West Indies and in Greenland.

– Religious leader Johann Conrad Beissel founds the Ephrata Community (or Seventh-Day Baptists, known as Dunkards) in Germantown, Pennsylvania.

SCIENCE AND TECHNOLOGY

23 Dec. Birth in Preston, Lancashire, England, of Richard Arkwright, textile industrialist and inventor.

ARTS AND HUMANITIES

24 Jan. Birth in Paris of Pierre-Augustin Caron de Beaumarchais, French dramatist.

29 Feb. Death in Paris of André-Charles Boulle, furniture maker.

31 Mar. Birth in Rohrau, Austria, of Franz Joseph Haydn, composer.

5 April Birth in Grasse, France, of Jean-Honoré Fragonard, painter.

4 Dec. Death in London of John Gay, English poet and writer.

– Covent Garden Theatre is opened in London.

– Olof von Dalin founds the first Swedish satirical weekly, *Then Svanska Argus*.

Jean-Baptiste Chardin, *Kitchen Table with Shoulder of Mutton*, painting.

George Frideric Handel, *Esther*, the first English oratorio.

Handel has turned to English oratorio following the decline in popularity of Italian opera resulting from the success of John Gay's *The Beggar's Opera* (see 1728).

Francesco Scipione, marchese di Maffei, *Verona illustrata* (Verona Illustrated), a history of the city of Verona in four volumes.

Johann Heinrich Zedler, *Universal-Lexicon*, the first of 64 volumes (published up to 1750).

1733

EUROPE

1 Feb. In Warsaw, Poland, death of Augustus II (the Strong), king of Poland, Austria and Russia. His son, Frederick Augustus II, Elector of Saxony, becomes King Augustus III of Poland. Potocki, primate of Poland (and supporter of former King Stanislaw I Leszczynski), subsequently bars non-Catholics from election to the throne, and Prussia allows Stanislaw I Leszczynski, the popular deposed king of Poland, to ride through Prussia to Poland.

14 Aug. Start of the War of the Polish Succession: Russia and the Holy Roman Empire recognize the right of the Elector Augustus III of Saxony while France supports Stanislaw I. France declares war (10 Oct.) on the Holy Roman Emperor Charles VI.

7 Nov. France and Spain form an anti-British alliance by the treaty of Escurial and guarantee each other's possessions. The treaty declares the indivisible union of the two branches of the Habsburg family.

THE AMERICAS

June Denmark takes control of Santa Cruz, West Indies.

– James Oglethorpe founds Savannah, Georgia, last of the English colonies in N America, as a refuge for the persecuted and the indigent.

ECONOMY AND SOCIETY

– Latin is abolished as the written language of proceedings in English courts of law.

– Prussia introduces military conscription.

Voltaire (1694–1778)

Born as François-Marie Arouet, Voltaire invented his own name, and a similar rejection of established convention marked his whole career. His declared intention was to make all revealed religion, and especially Catholic Christianity, appear ridiculous. In a great range of writings he used satire, jokes and an exquisite literary style – most famously in the fable *Candide* (1759) – to subvert authority. He preached a positive message about toleration and individual rights and a negative one about organized religion, which he regarded as little better than superstition.

Voltaire's agenda of a secular state, divorce rights, the suppression of feudalism, proportional taxation and the abolition of torture was unattainable in the France of his time, but was widely influential. He was the most powerful opponent ever encountered by the *ancien régime*, the establishment of inherited privilege that dominated continental Europe in his day. He sensationalized individual cases of injustice and prejudice in order to highlight abuses of power.

Though he was a great believer in reason, Voltaire despised arid system-making and preferred the relaxed empiricism more usual among British thinkers. This is why he admired Newton and Locke at the expense of Descartes. His *Lettres philosophiques sur les Anglais* (1733) encouraged the French to be more like the English in politics and culture. Voltaire also argued that history was neither a mere chronicle of events nor the unfolding of divine design. *The Age of Louis XIV* (1751) and his *Essai sur les moeurs* (1756) proposed that what mattered in the long run was the cultural 'spirit of the age' rather than individual people or events.

SCIENCE AND TECHNOLOGY

13 Mar. Birth near Leeds, Yorkshire, England, of Joseph Priestley, scientist who will discover oxygen (see 1774).

26 May English inventor John Kay patents his flying shuttle, a loom shuttle that cuts the labour needed for a loom by one-third.

ARTS AND HUMANITIES

23 Jan. George Frideric Handel's opera *Orlando* is first performed in London.

28 Aug. Giovanni Battista Pergolesi's opera *La serva padrona* (The Servant as Mistress) is first performed in Naples. A prototype of the *opera buffa* (a type of humerous opera with characters from everyday life), it will lead to the *guerre des bouffons* (between supporters of French and Italian opera) when it is first performed in Paris.

12 Sept. Death in Paris of François Couperin, composer.

1 Oct. First performance in Paris of Jean-Philippe Rameau's opera *Hippolyte et Aricie* (Hippolytus and Aricia).

– The Serpentine, a curving lake in London's Hyde Park, is created.

– German composer Johann Sebastian Bach presents a shorter version of the Mass in B minor to the Elector of Saxony along with a petition for the position of court composer.

Alexander Pope, *Essay on Man*, poem.

Antoine-François Prévost, *Manon Lescaut*, novel, the seventh volume of his *Mémoires et aventures d'un homme de qualité* (Memoirs of a Man of Quality).

Voltaire (see box), *Lettres philosophiques sur les Anglais* (Philosophical Letters on the English), commentary whose observation of English political and social life is intended to reproach French government and administration.

1734

EUROPE

Mar. The Spanish army crosses the Neapolitan border, conquers Naples (May) and defeats (25 May) the imperial forces at the battle of Bitonto.

May The French occupy Lorraine (E France) and the Electorate of Treves.

30 June In the War of the Polish Succession, Russian troops take the Polish city of Danzig (Gdansk), besieged since Oct. 1733.

June Franco-Spanish troops defeat the Austrians at Parma, Italy.

2 July King Stanislaw I Leszczynski is expelled from Poland and flees to Prussia.

Oct. An attempt to reach peace in the War of the Polish Succession is made in Vienna, Austria: Stanislaw I renounces his claims to Poland and receives the duchy of Lorraine, which will revert to France on his death.

Oct. Peasant rebellions in Serbia and Hungary are suppressed.

28 Dec. In Balquhidder, Perthshire, Scotland, death of Rob Roy (Robert MacGregor), Scottish rebel.

ECONOMY AND SOCIETY

– The first American horse race is held at Charleston Neck, South Carolina.

SCIENCE AND TECHNOLOGY

– Birth, near Constance, Austria, of the physician Franz Anton Mesmer, an early experimenter with hypnotism.

ARTS AND HUMANITIES

– Mme de Lambert's *Avis d'une mère à sa fille* (Advice of a Mother to her Daughter) advocates the study of the classics and philosophy by women.

Johann Sebastian Bach, *Christmas Oratorio*.

Nicholas Hawksmoor, design for the W towers of Westminster Abbey, London.

William Kent, design for the Treasury (now the Old Treasury Buildings), Whitehall, London.

Charles-Louis de Montesquieu, *Considérations sur la cause de la grandeur des Romains et de leur décadence* (Thoughts on the Cause of the Greatness and the Decline of the Romans), history.

George Sale, translation of the Koran into English.

1735

EUROPE

Aug. The Russian army reaches the Rhine in the War of the Polish Succession: Cardinal André de Fleury, the chief minister of France, sues for peace.

3 Oct. Peace preliminaries in the War of the Polish Succession are held at Vienna (Austria): the Holy Roman Emperor receives Parma and Piacenza; Don Carlos (the Spanish heir) can succeed to the throne of Naples and Sicily, but that throne is not to be united with that of Spain; Stanislaw I Leszczynski renounces his claim to Poland and is to receive Lorraine when the grand duke of Tuscany dies (with Lorraine reverting to France on Stanislaw's death). France guarantees the Pragmatic Sanction (see 1722).

ASIA

– Qianlong (Ch'ien Lung) becomes emperor of China.

THE AMERICAS

30 Oct. Birth of John Adams, second president of the United States of America.

– English evangelicals Charles and John Wesley (see p. 306) make a missionary journey to Georgia, N America. They will return in 1738.

– Charles de la Condamine commands a French scientific expedition to explore the River Amazon.

SCIENCE AND TECHNOLOGY

– Swedish botanist Carolus Linnaeus, (originally Carl von Linné) publishes his *Systema Naturae* (System of Nature), a botanical treatise classifying plants by genus and species that remains in use today.

ARTS AND HUMANITIES

16 April First performance in London of George Frideric Handel's opera *Alcina*, which is based on an incident from the epic poems *Orlando Furioso* by Ludovico Ariosto.

5 Sept. In Leipzig, Germany, birth of Johann Christian Bach, youngest son of Johann Sebastian Bach and also a composer.

Samuel Johnson, translation of Father Jerome Lobo's *A Voyage to Abyssinia*, published anonymously.

– The Bible is translated into Lithuanian.

– English evangelist John Wesley starts to write his *Journals*, which he continues until 1790.

– William Hogarth completes *The Rake's Progress*, a cycle of eight paintings; Hogarth also campaigns for the passage of a Copyright Act securing the protection of painters' and engravers' interests.

Johann Sebastian Bach, *Klavierübung*, Part 3, harpsichord music.

Pierre Carlet de Chamblain de Marivaux, *Le Paysan parvenu* (The Fortunate Peasant), novel in several volumes.

Jean-Philippe Rameau, *Les Indes galantes* (The Courtly Indies), ballet.

1736

EUROPE

26 Jan. Stanislaw I Leszczynski abdicates as king of Poland.

17 April Baron Theodore of Neuhof, a German adventurer and military conspirator, is proclaimed king of Corsica after he promises to free the island from Genoese rule.

May Repeal of the English statutes against witchcraft (see 1712).

May Russia, with imperial support, attacks Turkey with the aim of recapturing the fortress of Azov on the Black Sea. The troops, supported by Charles VI, Holy Roman Emperor, move to the Crimea (July), triggering a declaration of war by the Ottoman empire (Turkey). Russia calls on the defence treaty of 1726 and asks Austria for support. The Russo-Turkish War lasts until 1739.

MIDDLE EAST AND NORTH AFRICA

Feb. Nadir Shah deposes the last king of the Safavid dynasty (which has ruled Persia since 1501) and becomes king of Persia.

THE AMERICAS

29 May In Studley, Virginia, birth of Patrick Henry, American politician, who will be known for his tirade 'give me liberty or give me death'.

ECONOMY AND SOCIETY

– Pope Clement XII condemns freemasonry.

– *The Gentlemen's Magazine* begins to print reports of British parliamentary proceedings and gives the first and last letters of speakers' names.

SCIENCE AND TECHNOLOGY

19 Jan. In Greenock, Renfrewshire, Scotland, birth of James Watt, engineer.

16 Sept. In The Hague, United Netherlands, death of Gabriel Daniel Fahrenheit, physicist who invented the alcohol and mercury thermometers.

– The Académie Française sponsors an expedition to Lapland directed by Swedish scientist Anders Celsius to measure the arc of the meridian.

– Glass in imitation of the Bohemian style is manufactured in Venice by Giuseppe Briati.

ARTS AND HUMANITIES

17 Mar. In Pozzuoli, Italy, death from tuberculosis of the composer Giovanni Battista Pergolesi at the age of 26.

25 Mar. In London death of British architect Nicholas Hawksmoor.

Johann Sebastian Bach, *Easter Oratorio*.

Joseph Butler, *Analogy of Religion Natural and Revealed*, religious treatise.

Gabriel Boffrand, design for the Pavillion for the Hôtel de Soubise, Paris.

William Hogarth, *The Good Samaritan*, painting.

Giovanni Battista Pergolesi, *Stabat Mater*, sacred vocal music.

John Wesley (1703–91)

The founder of Methodism never wanted to establish a separate Church, but the dynamism of the movement he founded could not be contained within the structures of the established Church of England. The Methodist Church became the most influential of all the English nonconformist churches, and the spread of the British empire gave it a global dimension. Methodism was so named because it called for greater discipline and regularity in the conduct of life. Wesley and his followers wished to create serious and energetic people focused on the truth that salvation in the next world depended on good conduct in the here and now. That vigour was part of the same process of renewal and inventiveness that was turning Britain into the world's first industrialized economy.

Tireless as an itinerant evangelist, Wesley saw that Christianity had to be re-presented to the urban and rural masses, and he did so in open-air, revivalist meetings. His social views were conservative and hierarchical, but the movement had a wide appeal, attracting converts among both the industrial working classes and the professional middle classes. Methodist devotion concentrated on the person of Christ, and the intensity of its appeal related it to the Romantic movement. Personal experience and conversion were what made a Methodist, and those qualities could be heard in the hymns of heart-struck assurance (many of them written by John's brother Charles Wesley, 1707–88), which were a distinctive feature of Methodist services.

The new religious energy, however, also introduced a new anxiety and concern about sexual conduct – forces that would become important aspects of the English national character. More generally, Methodism inculcated a powerful preoccupation with respectability, appearance, diligence and literalism. This latest chapter in the history of English Protestantism also amounted to a major reassertion of English individualism.

1737

EUROPE

4 May Death of the last of the Kettler line, rulers of the Polish fief of Courland. The successor, Duke Ernest Johann von Biron (the lover of Empress Anna of Russia), manoeuvres to promote Russian interests in Courland.

9 July Death of Gian Gastone de' Medici, grand duke of Tuscany and the last of the Medici line. As agreed in the treaty of 1735, Francis Stephen, duke of Lorraine, receives Tuscany and Stanislaw I Leszczynski (ex-king of Poland) acquires Lorraine.

20 Nov. In London Queen Caroline (Caroline of Brandenburg-Ansbach), consort of King George II and patroness of such writers as Alexander Pope and John Gay, dies. The queen has been George II's valued adviser on affairs of state and has acted as regent when he is abroad. George is grief-stricken at her death and famously says he will never marry again but only take mistresses.

– The Turkish army defeats the forces of Maria Theresa of Austria (daughter of Holy Roman Emperor Charles VI), who are fighting in aid of the Russians.

THE AMERICAS

April The American colonial official William Byrd lays out Richmond, Virginia (named after Richmond in London).

ECONOMY AND SOCIETY

– Canonization of St Vincent de Paul (see 1660) by Pope Clement XII.

– English evangelist John Wesley's (see box) *Psalms* and *Hymns* are published in Charleston, South Carolina.

– George II, king of Great Britain, founds Göttingen University, Germany, with Johann Lorenz von Mosheim as first chancellor.

– The Licensing Act restricts the number of theatres in London.

SCIENCE AND TECHNOLOGY

– French scientist René-Antoine de Réaumur publishes *Histoire des insectes* (History of Insects).

ARTS AND HUMANITIES

2 Mar. British writer and lexicographer Samuel Johnson and actor David Garrick leave Lichfield for London.

27 April Birth in Putney, England, of Edward Gibbon, historian.

11 Aug. Birth in London of Joseph Nollekens, sculptor.

24 Oct. First performance in Paris of Jean-Philippe Rameau's opera *Castor et Pollux*.

– Inauguration of the building of the Radcliffe Camera, Oxford, designed by English architect James Gibbs.

François Boucher, designs for *The Story of Psyche* for the Beauvais tapestry factory.

Jean-Baptiste Chardin, *The Draughtsman*, painting.

Louis-François Roubiliac, bust of the composer George Frideric Handel.

1738

EUROPE

26 Feb. The reformer Samuel von Cocceji becomes Prussia's minister of justice and modernizes Prussia's civil law.

28 Mar. In Britain a parliamentary debate on the affair of Jenkins's Ear (see 1731), during which the preserved ear is held up in the House of Commons, leads to calls for war with Spain (see Oct. 1739).

9 May Britain's Mediterranean fleet is reinforced. Ships are also sent to the West Indies and troops are dispatched to the colony of Georgia in N America following a border dispute with Spain.

27 May Turkish forces take Orsova from the Austrians; imperial troops withdraw to Belgrade, Hungary.

4 June Birth of the future George III, grandson of George II and son of Frederick Louis, prince of Wales; he will become king of Great Britain and Ireland in 1760.

21 June Death in Raynham, Norfolk, England, of Charles, Viscount Townshend, the Whig politician who initiated the League of Hanover, which allied Britain, France and Prussia against Austria and Spain; he was also noted for his agricultural research (see 1730).

10 Oct. The Swedish War party (the Hats) displace the peace party (or Caps) and an alliance is formed with France.

18 Nov. The treaty of Vienna, based on the 1735 preliminaries, ends the War of the Polish Succession (see 1733).

31 Dec. In London birth of Charles, marquis of Cornwallis, British military commander and colonial administrator.

ASIA

– Nadir Shah of Persia drives the Afghans out of Persia and goes on to conquer all of modern Afghanistan.

THE AMERICAS

– English evangelist George Whitefield joins John Wesley (see p. 306), founder of Methodism, in Georgia, N America, to lead the mission of the 'Great Awakening'.

ECONOMY AND SOCIETY

– Forced labour to repair and build roads, the *corvée*, is introduced in France by the controller-general, Philibert Orry.

– A papal bull against freemasonry, *In eminenti*, is issued by Pope Clement XII.

SCIENCE AND TECHNOLOGY

28 May Birth in Saintes, France, of Joseph Guillotin, French doctor and inventor of the guillotine.

15 Nov. In Hanover, Germany, birth of Frederick William Herschel, astronomer who will discover the planet Uranus.

– Swiss mathematician Daniel Bernoulli's *Hydrodynamica* (Hydrodynamics) analyses pressure and velocity in fluids.

ARTS AND HUMANITIES

10 Oct. Near Springfield, Massachusetts, N America, birth of Benjamin West, neoclassical painter.

– French historian Louis de Beaufort subjects the records of early Roman history to close criticism and decides that most of it is mythical.

– Rocco de Alcubierre starts the excavation of the Roman city of Herculaneum, buried by the eruption of Mount Vesuvius in AD 79.

– Foundation of the imperial Ballet School in St Petersburg.

Jean-Baptiste Chardin, *La Gouvernante*, painting.

Samuel Johnson, 'London', poem, imitating the Roman poet Juvenal's third satire.

Ludovico Antonio Muratori, *Antiquitates Italicae* (The Antiquities of Italy), historical scholarship, published in six volumes the last of which appears in 1742.

Louis-François Roubiliac, bust of Alexander Pope.

1739

EUROPE

3–14 Jan. The Convention of Pardo endeavours to resolve Anglo-Spanish conflict over the *asiento* (slave) trade and shipping, but Spain insists on the right to search British ships for smuggled goods. The recall of the English fleet from the Mediterranean follows but is then revoked.

7 April In Knavesmire, York, England, execution of Dick Turpin, English highwayman.

22 July Imperial forces are defeated by the Turks at Crocyka; Ottoman troops then advance to Belgrade. At the peace of Belgrade (18 Sept.) between the Holy Roman Empire and Turkey, Austria cedes Orsova, Belgrade and Serbia (territories it had gained by the earlier peace of Passarowitz, see 21 July 1718). By the treaty of Belgrade (23 Sept.) between Russia and Turkey, the tsar restores all Russian conquests except Azov, which is dismantled as a military garrison. Russia agrees not to keep ships in the Black Sea or the Sea of Azov.

8–19 Oct. England declares war on Spain, which has refused the Convention of Pardo (see above). The so-called War of Jenkins's Ear (see 1731 and 1738) will later merge into the War of Austrian Succession (see 1740).

ASIA

– Nadir Shah of Persia sacks the city of Delhi (NE India) and conquers the Punjab (in modern India and Pakistan).

THE AMERICAS

Nov. British admiral Edward Vernon takes Porto Bello (in modern Panama) from the Spanish.

ECONOMY AND SOCIETY

– Establishment of the Foundling Hospital, London, by the philanthropist Thomas Coram.

– Bishop August Gottlieb Spangenberg establishes the Moravian Church in America.

SCIENCE AND TECHNOLOGY

– Jean d'Alembert publishes his *Mémoire sur le calcul intégral* (Memoir on Integral Calculus).

ARTS AND HUMANITIES

16 Jan. First performance in London of George Frideric Handel's oratorio *Saul*.

4 April First performance in London of George Frideric Handel's oratorio *Israel in Egypt*, which he will subsequently revise.

19 Nov. First performance in Paris of Jean-Philippe Rameau's opera *Dardanus*.

Jean-Baptiste Chardin, *Saying Grace* and *The Maid Returning from Market*, paintings.

George Dance, design for the Mansion House, London.

David Hume (see p. 312), *A Treatise on Human Nature* (Books 1 and 2; Book 3 will be published in 1740), philosophy.

Jonathan Swift, *Verses on the Death of Dr Swift*, a mocking elegy to himself.

1740

EUROPE

31 May In Postdam, Prussia, Frederick William I, king of Prussia dies and is succeeded by his son, Frederick II (the Great).

20 Oct. In Vienna, Austria, Charles VI, Holy Roman Emperor, dies; he is the last Habsburg emperor. He is succeeded by his daughter Maria Theresa, who becomes archduchess of Austria. The succession is contested by the Elector of Bavaria, by Frederick Augustus II of Saxony and by Philip V, king of Spain. Britain and Holland support Maria Theresa.

28 Oct. Death of Empress Anna of Russia, daughter of Ivan V and niece of Peter I (the Great): her successor, Ivan VI, the grandson of her sister Catherine, is placed under the regency of Anna's favourite, Ernst Biron, duke of Courland. Commander-in-chief Count Burkhard Christoph von Münnich gains effective power as Russian first minister and banishes Biron to Siberia.

11 Nov. Count János Pálffy is appointed governor (palatine) of Hungary by Queen Maria Theresa.

16 Dec. In a bid to acquire global renown, Frederick II (the Great), king of Prussia, attacks Silesia, one of the richest Habsburg possessions, sparking the First Silesian War and the War of the Austrian Succession.

– George Anson, commander of a Pacific squadron of six vessels, leaves England on what will be an epic circumnavigation of the globe.

ASIA

– Nadir Shah of Persia annexes territory S of the Aral Sea, extending his influence in what is now Uzbekistan.

– Bengal, NE India (modern Bangladesh), acquires independence under Mughal Alivardi Khan.

ECONOMY AND SOCIETY

6 Feb. Pope Clement XII dies and is succeeded (17 Aug.) by Benedict XIV.

– Frederick II, king of Prussia, abolishes torture and introduces freedom of the press and freedom of worship in Prussia.

SCIENCE AND TECHNOLOGY

– British instrument maker Henry Hindley invents a machine for cutting the teeth of clock wheels.

– Invention of the Saxony blue dye extracted from indigo (made in Germany).

– Frederick II, king of Prussia, establishes the Berlin Academy of Science.

ARTS AND HUMANITIES

29 Oct. In Edinburgh, Scotland, birth of James Boswell, writer.

– Frederick II, king of Prussia, denounces cynical power politics in his *The Refutation of Machiavelli's Prince or Anti-Machiavel*.

– English composer Thomas Augustine Arne's masque *Alfred* is first performed; it contains the patriotic song 'Rule, Britannia!'
François Boucher, *Morning Toilette*, painting.

Antonio Canaletto (originally Giovanni Antonio Canal), *Return of the Bucintoro*, painting.
William Hogarth, *Captain Coram*, painting.
Samuel Richardson, *Pamela or Virtue Rewarded*, novel written in the form of letters. It is a popular sensation across Europe.
Louis de Rouvroy, duc de Saint-Simon, *Mémoires*, published in stages until 1752 and a classic, mordant account of life at the French court.

1741

EUROPE

3 Mar. Count Burkhard Christoph von Münnich, Russian first minister, is dismissed from office.

13 Mar. In Vienna, Austria, the future Holy Roman Emperor Joseph II is born; he is the son of Maria Theresa and Francis I.

10 April King Frederick II of Prussia is victorious against Maria Theresa's Austrian forces at Mollwitz; he conquers Silesia.

8 May By the terms of the treaty of Nymphenburg, France agrees to support Elector Charles Albert of Bavaria's claim to the imperial throne. Bavaria also gains by treaty (28 May) Spanish support to partition Habsburg territory. France and Prussia agree to partition the empire by the treaty of Breslau (5 June).

25 June Maria Theresa, archduchess of Austria, accepts the crown of Hungary.

15 Aug. French troops cross the Rhine and invade S Germany, Austria and Bohemia.

9 Oct. Frederick II (the Great), king of Prussia, and Maria Theresa, Habsburg ruler of Austria, agree in the secret treaty of Klein Schnellendorf that lower Silesia will be ceded to Prussia: Prussia subsequently breaks the treaty when Frederick II enters Neisse (1 Nov.) and agrees terms with Saxony and Bavaria for the partition of the empire.

26 Nov. French troops supported by Bavarian and Saxon forces occupy Prague.

Dec. After a bloodless coup, Elizabeth (daughter of former tsar Peter I) becomes empress of Russia, replacing Ivan VI and his mother, Anna Leopoldovna.

THE AMERICAS

– British forces attack Cuba but fail to capture it.

SCIENCE AND TECHNOLOGY

21 Feb. Death, near Hungerford, Berkshire, England, of agriculturalist Jethro Tull, whose seed drill and farming techniques formed the foundations of modern agriculture.

– Swedish botanist Carl von Linné (Carolus Linnaeus) starts the first botanical garden in Uppsala, Sweden.

ARTS AND HUMANITIES

22 Aug.–12 Sept. German-born English composer George Frideric Handel writes his oratorio *Messiah*.

11 Sept. In London birth of Arthur Young, whose writings on agriculture publicize the new farming practices associated with the Agricultural Revolution.

18 Oct. In Amiens, France, birth of Pierre Choderlos de Laclos, novelist and author of *Les Liaisons dangereuses* (Dangerous Liaisons).

19 Oct. English actor David Garrick makes his London debut as Richard III.

30 Oct. In Chur, Swiss Confederation, birth of Angelica Kauffmann, neoclassical painter.

– American statesman Benjamin Franklin founds *The General Magazine* in Philadelphia, Pennsylvania.

Johann Sebastian Bach, *Goldberg Variations,* for harpsichord, written for a pupil of Bach's allegedly at the request of a nobleman who required nightly performances of music to relieve his insomnia.

Caspar Wilhelm von Borck, translation of Shakespeare's *Julius Caesar*, the first printed German translation of a Shakespeare play.

François Boucher, *Autumn*, painting.

Henry Fielding, *Shamela*, a satire of Samuel Richardson's novel *Pamela* (see 1740).

Jean-Philippe Rameau, *Pièces de clavecin en concert*, chamber music for harpsichord, violin and viola da gamba.

Bartolomeo Rastrelli, design for the Summer Palace in St Petersburg, Russia.

Jacques-Germain Soufflot, design for the Hôtel-Dieu in Lyons, France.

1742

EUROPE

9 Jan. British Whig politician Robert Walpole is created earl of Orford but resigns his offices of first lord of the treasury and chancellor of the exchequer after 21 years in government (11 Jan.). Walpole is usually regarded as the first 'prime minister' of Britain.

24 Jan. Charles Albert, Elector of Bavaria, is elected as Holy Roman Emperor Charles VII.

April Frederick II of Prussia's military campaign in Moravia fails.

28 July The peace of Berlin between Maria Theresa of Austria and Frederick II (the Great), king of Prussia, ends the First Silesian War: Prussia gains Silesia and Glatz (modern Klodzko in SE Poland) but agrees to withdraw (with Poland) from the coalition against Maria Theresa.

7–18 Nov. Britain and Prussia form an alliance against France. Britain also secures the neutrality of Russia (11–22 Dec.) and the occupying French troops are forced to leave Prague (12 Dec.).

16 Dec. In Rostock, Mecklenburg (N Germany), birth of Gebhard Leberecht von Blücher, Prussian field marshal.

ASIA

– Joseph-François Dupleix becomes governor general of the French territories in India.

ECONOMY AND SOCIETY

– The first cotton factories are opened in Birmingham and Wolverhampton in the English Midlands.

SCIENCE AND TECHNOLOGY

14 Jan. In Greenwich, London, death of Edmond Halley, the English astronomer who first calculated the orbit of Halley's Comet.

– Swedish scientist Anders Celsius invents the centigrade or Celsius thermometer.

ARTS AND HUMANITIES

13 April George Frideric Handel's oratorio *Messiah* is performed for the first time in Dublin.

14 July In Cambridge, England, death of Richard Bentley, classical scholar.

François Boucher, *La Pêche chinoise*, a series of nine cartoons for the Beauvais tapestry factory.

Henry Fielding, *Joseph Andrews*, novel.

Edward Young, *Night Thoughts on Life, Death and Immortality*, a poetic meditation on the death of his wife.

1743

EUROPE

April Maria Theresa of Austria is crowned queen of Bohemia in Prague.

16–27 June George II, king of Great Britain and Ireland, defeats the French at Dettingen, in Bavaria. This is the last occasion when a British king leads his army into battle.

17 Aug. Peace of Abo ends the war between Russia and Sweden: the S part of Finland is ceded to Russia.

25 Oct. France and Spain resume their anti-British offensive by the Alliance of Fontainebleau and plan to seize the fortress of Gibraltar from British control.

MIDDLE EAST AND NORTH AFRICA

– War breaks out between the Ottoman empire (Turkey) and Persia.

THE AMERICAS

13 April In Shadwell, Virginia, birth of Thomas Jefferson (see p. 329), third president of the USA (1801–9).

ECONOMY AND SOCIETY

5–6 Jan. Welsh Calvinistic Methodists under George Whitefield's leadership form the first Methodist Association.

July Birth in Peterborough, England, of William Paley, an influential Anglican priest and theologian who will put forward the 'argument from design', an argument for the existence of God that contends that the universe is too complex not to have been designed by a supernatural power.

– American statesman Benjamin Franklin and others found the American Philosophical Society.

SCIENCE AND TECHNOLOGY

26 Aug. Birth in Paris of Antoine-Laurent Lavoisier, father of modern chemistry.

– French astronomer Joseph-Nicolas Delisle invents a method for observing the movements of Mercury and Venus.

ARTS AND HUMANITIES

23 May In London death of Thomas Archer, English baroque architect.

1 Aug. Death of Richard Savage, English writer. Savage's tumultuous and debt-ridden life becomes an early example in English letters of the romantic theme of the artist as a mis-understood outsider.

17 Sept. In Ribemont, France, birth of Marie-Jean Caritat, marquis de Condorcet, mathematician, philosopher and political radical.

George Frideric Handel, *Dettingen Te Deum*, oratorio celebrating George II's victory at Dettingen.

William Hogarth, *Marriage à la Mode*, narrative paintings.

Alexander Pope, *The Dunciad*, mock-epic poem (the final edition of Pope's lifetime).

1744

EUROPE

21 Feb. A Franco-Spanish fleet defeats the British fleet off Toulon, S France.

4–15 Mar. France declares war on Britain and later (26 April) on Maria Theresa's Austria.

5 May The union of Frankfurt: Frederick II (the Great), king of Prussia, Holy Roman Emperor Charles VII, the Elector Palatine and the landgrave of Hesse agree to force Maria Theresa of Austria to restore her conquests to Bavaria and restore the constitution of the Holy Roman Empire.

5 May Austrian troops invade Alsace, in NE France, but are then allowed to withdraw by the French (Aug.).

25 May Prussia acquires the principality East Friesland on the death of the territory's last prince, Charles Edward of Cirksena.

6 June France guarantees the union of Frankfurt.

15 Aug. Frederick II's invasion of Saxony starts the Second Silesian War. After Frederick takes Prague (16 Sept.) he is deserted by the French and driven back to Saxony by the Austrians.

28 Dec.– 8 Jan. 1745 Britain, Austria, Saxony–Poland and the United Netherlands unite against Prussia in the Quadruple Alliance.

ECONOMY AND SOCIETY

– Eruption of Mt Cotopaxi in the Spanish colony of Peru, S America.

SCIENCE AND TECHNOLOGY

– French philosopher and mathematician Jean le Rond d'Alembert publishes his *Traité de l'équilibre et du mouvement des fluides* (Treatise on Equilibrium and on Movement of Fluids).

– The first map produced by modern surveying methods is created by French cartographer César-François Cassini.

ARTS AND HUMANITIES

20 Jan. Death in Naples, Italy, of Giambattista Vico (see p. 300), philosopher of history and forerunner of modern anthropology.

30 May Death in Twickenham, near London, of English poet Alexander Pope.

25 Aug. In Mohrungen, East Prussia, birth of Johann Gottfried von Herder (see p. 337), German writer, philosopher and historian.

– N American statesman Benjamin Franklin prints and sells *Cicero's Cato Major* in Philadelphia.

Johann Sebastian Bach, *Das Wohltemperierte Clavier*, Book 2, 24 preludes and fugues for harpsichord.

Samuel Johnson, *Life of Richard Savage*, a pioneering study in literary biography (later included in Johnson's *Lives of the Poets*).

1745

EUROPE

20 Jan. In Munich, Bavaria, Charles VII, Holy Roman Emperor dies. His son, Maximilian Joseph of Bavaria, agrees to support the imperial candidature of Maria Theresa's husband, Grand Duke Francis.

18 Mar. In London Robert Walpole, earl of Orford, British Whig politician and prime minister, dies.

2–13 April Britain agrees to pay subsidies to Archduchess Maria Theresa of Austria.

22 April By the peace of Füssen, Maria Theresa of Austria restores her conquests to Bavaria; in turn, Maximilian Joseph, Elector of Bavaria, renounces his claim to the imperial throne.

30 April–11 May British forces, led by William Augustus, duke of Cumberland, are defeated by Marshal Maurice de Saxe's French forces at the battle of Fontenoy (in modern Belgium). The French proceed to conquer the Austrian Netherlands.

4 June Frederick II (the Great), king of Prussia, defeats the army of Maria Theresa, which is attempting to invade Silesia.

23 July Start of the Jacobite rising known as the Forty-Five: the Catholic prince Charles Edward Stuart (Bonnie Prince Charlie or the Young Pretender), son of James Edward Stuart (the Old Pretender), lands on Eriskay in the Hebrides, Scotland, to attempt to regain the Scottish and English thrones. British soldiers are brought back from the Low Countries to meet the threat (25 July).

15–26 Aug. George II, king of Great Britain and Ireland and Elector of Hanover, promises by the convention of Hanover to negotiate peace with the Prussians; he abandons support for Austria.

2 Sept. The Jacobites rout a British government army at Prestonpans, E of Edinburgh, Scotland.

9 Sept. Madame de Pompadour becomes Louis XV's acknowledged Maitresse-en-Titre (official mistress); she is installed as such in Versailles.

11 Sept. Jacobite forces enter Edinburgh, Scotland, in support of Bonnie Prince Charlie's attempts to recover the throne.

12 Sept. Francis Stephen, grand duke of Tuscany and the consort of Archduchess Maria Theresa of Austria, is elected Holy Roman Emperor (as Francis I), beginning the Lorraine–Tuscany line.

17 Sept. Bonnie Prince Charlie enters Edinburgh; he proclaims his father (the Old Pretender, see 1715) King James VIII of Scotland.

Sept. The Franco-Spanish army defeats the Austrians at Basignano, in the kingdom of Sardinia, Italy; Frederick II defeats the Austrians at Soor, N Bohemia.

Nov. Frederick II's Prussian forces defeat the Austrians at Hennersdorf in Moravia.

4 Dec. The Jacobites advance to Derby, C England, but have to retreat (6 Dec.). They gain a minor victory at Penrith, Cumbria (18 Dec.).

25 Dec. By the peace of Dresden, Prussia retains Silesia but recognizes Francis I as emperor.

THE AMERICAS

16 June The British take Cape Breton Island, Nova Scotia, from the French; they then take the fortress of Louisburg at the mouth of the St Lawrence River.

SCIENCE AND TECHNOLOGY

– The German scientist Ewald Georg von Kleist invents the Leyden jar, which collects and stores electricity.

ARTS AND HUMANITIES

10 Oct. In Dublin, Ireland, death of the Anglo-Irish writer and satirist Jonathan Swift.

– English novelist Henry Fielding edits *The True Patriot*, a pro-government publication.

– The song 'God Save the King' is first performed in the Drury Lane Theatre, London. Possibly written by the composer Henry Carey, it will become the British national anthem from 1822.

1746

EUROPE

16 Jan. Jacobite troops supporting Prince Charles Edward Stuart (Bonnie Prince Charlie) are victorious against the royal army at Falkirk, Scotland.

10 Feb. George II refuses to admit William Pitt (the Elder) into the cabinet as secretary for war; however, after the failure of attempts to form an administration, Pitt and his colleagues return to office and Pitt is made joint vice treasurer for Ireland.

20 Feb. The French marshal, Maurice de Saxe, occupies Brussels, Austrian Netherlands.

16 April The Jacobites are crushed at Culloden, Inverness-shire, Scotland: William Augustus, duke of Cumberland, is henceforth known by his enemies as the 'Butcher' for the brutality of his suppression both of the Jacobites and of Scottish clans suspected of Jacobite sympathies. Culloden is the last pitched battle fought on British soil.

6 May In Britain William Pitt (the Elder) becomes paymaster-general for the armed forces and Henry Fox becomes secretary for war.

2 June Archduchess Maria Theresa of Austria, pursuing the restoration of Silesia, allies with Russia against Prussia.

June In his drive against Austria, the French marshal, Maurice de Saxe, occupies the city of Antwerp, Austrian Netherlands.

20 Sept. With the help of Flora Macdonald, Bonnie Prince Charlie escapes to France after five months of wandering through the Highlands of Scotland.

11 Oct. The Italian republic of Genoa surrenders to Maria Theresa's forces. But the French under Maurice de Saxe defeat the Austrians at Raucoux (11 Oct.), and Maria Theresa loses the Austrian Netherlands.

Dec. Rebellion in Genoa against Maria Theresa's army.

– Prussia declares its legal independence from the jurisdiction of imperial courts.

ASIA

7 July In the colonial rivalry between England and France, worsened by the conflicts of the War of the Austrian Succession, the French fleet commanded by Bertrand de la Bourdonnais arrives at Pondicherry, SE India; later, Joseph, marquis of Dupleix, conquers Madras from the British (10–21 Sept.).

– Widespread persecution of Christians in China, under the regime of the Manchu emperor Qianlong (Ch'ien Lung).

THE AMERICAS

22 Oct. Foundation of the College of New Jersey (subsequently Princeton University), N America.

SCIENCE AND TECHNOLOGY

– In his *Disputationes Anatomicae Selectiones* (Selected Anatomical Disputes), Swiss botanist, poet and anatomist Albert von Haller advances the study of anatomy and describes the contraction of muscles.

– The first geological map of France is created by French naturalist and palaeontologist Jean-Etienne Guettard.

ARTS AND HUMANITIES

12 Jan. Birth in Zurich, Swiss Confederation, of Johann Heinrich Pestalozzi, educator who will advocate education for the poor.

30 Mar. In Fuendetodos, Spain, birth of Francisco José de Goya y Lucientes (see p. 360), painter.

28 Sept. Birth in London of William Jones, orientalist and philologist.

Antonio Canaletto, *View of Whitehall*, painting.

George Frideric Handel, *Judas Maccabaeus*, oratorio, composed in honour of the duke of Cumberland for his victory at Culloden (see above). It includes the chorus 'See the conquering hero comes'.

1747

EUROPE

4 May William IV of Orange-Nassau, the grand-nephew of William III, king of England, Ireland and Scotland, is elected chief magistrate (stadtholder) of the United Netherlands.

29 May Prussia and Sweden conclude the alliance of Stockholm, providing for mutual defence if either is attacked.

21 June–2 July British forces led by William Augustus, duke of Cumberland, are defeated by the French army led by Marshal Maurice de Saxe near Maastricht, United Netherlands.

June Britain allies with Russia but refuses to aid the Russian campaign against Sweden.

6 July French and Spanish troops break the British and Austrian blockade of the Italian republic of Genoa.

1 Aug. After the repression of the 1745 Jacobite rising (see 16 April 1746), the British Parliament bans the wearing of tartan on pain of imprisonment, in a series of laws devised to root out the cultural individuality of the Scottish Highlands.

10–21 Dec. Britain, the United Netherlands and Russia agree the Convention of St Petersburg: Russian troops are allowed to pass through Germany, and Britain subsidizes 30,000 men.

ASIA

– Nadir Shah, ruler of Persia, is murdered in Afghanistan and one of his generals, Ahmad Shah proclaims himself king; Afghanistan becomes independent of Persia.

SCIENCE AND TECHNOLOGY

– The world's first sexually transmitted disease clinic is opened at the London Lock Hospital in England.

– French philosopher and mathematician Jean le Rond d'Alembert publishes his *Réflexions sur la cause générale des vents* (Reflections on the General Cause of Winds).

– British engineer Benjamin Robins describes the physics of a spinning projectile to the Royal Society.

– British Astronomer Royal James Bradley investigates the rotation of the earth's axis.

ARTS AND HUMANITIES

– English writer and lexicographer Samuel Johnson begins his *Dictionary of the English Language*.

– The Biblioteca Nazionale is founded in Florence, Italy, in memory of Antonio Magliabecch, whose library of 30,000 volumes was bequeathed to the grand duke of Tuscany.

– The National Library of Warsaw, Poland, opens.

– English writer Horace Walpole, 4th earl of Orford (son of Robert Walpole, and a Whig MP in 1741–67), buys Strawberry Hill, a house near London that he will reconstruct in the 'Gothick' style.

Benjamin Franklin, *Plain Truth, or Serious Considerations on the Present State of the City of Philadelphia*, political tract.

Bartolomeo Rastrelli, reconstruction of the Peterhof Palace, St Petersburg, Russia.

Samuel Richardson, *Clarissa, or The History of a Young Lady*, a novel in the form of letters, published in seven volumes, 1747–8.

George Whitefield, *God's Dealings with George Whitefield*, spiritual autobiography.

1748

EUROPE

Feb. Russian troops pass through Bohemia and march towards the Rhine.

7–18 Oct. Conclusion of the peace of Aix-la-Chapelle, ending the War of the Austrian Succession: Francis I's position as Holy Roman Emperor and Frederick II of Prussia's conquest of Silesia are both recognized. The French evacuate the Austrian Netherlands, recognize George II as king of Great Britain and Ireland and transfer Madras, India, to British control in exchange for the town of Louisbourg, on Cape Breton Island, Nova Scotia. Don Philip of the Spanish Bourbon family acquires Parma and Piacenza in Italy. Spain accedes to the treaty (9–20 Oct.).

MIDDLE EAST AND NORTH AFRICA

– Rukh Shah (grandson of the late Nadir Shah, murdered in 1747) becomes ruler of Persia.

ASIA

6–17 Oct. The French raise the British siege of Pondicherry, SE India.

David Hume (1711–76)

The Scottish philosopher David Hume was born near Edinburgh and educated at that city's university and in France. He was a radical empiricist, holding that no knowledge is possible beyond experience. In *A Treatise of Human Nature* (1739–40) and *Philosophical Essays Concerning Human Understanding* (1748) he studied the way we think but came to doubt whether philosophers could discover the truth about anything. It was not his philosophical works, however, but his *History of Great Britain* (1754) that brought him fame in his own lifetime.

Hume divided consciousness into two components. Impressions came first, and ideas were based on those impressions. He therefore denied that human beings are born with innate ideas. They have two faculties that enable them to bring ideas together and to establish relationships between them. One is memory, the other is imagination. Hume detected seven ways in which ideas could be linked: resemblance, identity, space and time, quantity, quality, contrariety, and cause and effect.

Hume showed much scepticism about common assumptions, which he held to be no more than mental habits. He showed that the link of cause and effect cannot be proved logically, that it is impossible to establish that external objects exist when we are not around to look at them, and denied that there is some kind of continuous entity (the self) that holds all our experiences together. The idea that such a thing existed could be justified, according to Hume, only as a kind of operating principle to get us out of bed in the morning. Even mathematics and science, he thought, could not have objective validity. He was, however, the most humane of sceptics and was reconciled to the fact that most of humanity, including himself, carried on believing in all kinds of truths that could not be justified when scrutinized logically.

SCIENCE AND TECHNOLOGY

- Swiss mathematician Leonhard Euler publishes his *Analysis Infinitorum* (Analysis of Infinities), a pioneering introduction to pure mathematics.
- English benefactor Thomas Lowndes endows a chair of astronomy at Cambridge University, England.
- English physician John Fothergill's *Account of the Sore Throat, Attended with Ulcers*, describes diphtheria.
- British industrialist Daniel Bourn invents water-powered rollers, particularly for use in iron milling.

ARTS AND HUMANITIES

15 Feb. Birth in London of Jeremy Bentham, philosopher.

12 April Death in London of William Kent, architect also known for his gardens.

20 April Birth in Paris of Jacques-Louis David, painter.

27 Aug. Death in Richmond, Surrey, England, of James Thomson, Scottish poet known for his poetic sequence *The Seasons*.

25 Nov. Death in London of English poet and hymn-writer Isaac Watts.

- Archaeological excavations begin at Pompeii, Italy.

Thomas Gray, *Odes*.

David Hume (see p. 312), *Philosophical Essays Concerning Human Understanding* (a rewriting of Book I of the *Treatise*), philosophy, expounding an empiricist theory of knowledge.

Charles-Louis de Secondat, baron de Montesquieu, *De l'esprit des lois* (The Spirit of the Laws), political philosophy, which compares different legal systems in their historical context.

1749

EUROPE

11 May In Britain the Consolidation Act of the Royal Navy for the improvement of the senior service is passed.

14 May Maria Theresa, Archduchess of Austria, unites the Bohemian and the Austrian chanceries.

July The Spanish Bourbons' ambitions having been achieved in the Italian duchies, Ferdinand VI, king of Spain, ends the Family Compact with France.

ASIA

- Joseph, marquis de Dupleix, French governor general in India, gains control of the Carnatic (modern Karnataka in S India) in a war of succession in the Deccan and replaces the Indian ruler (the nawab) with his own nominee.

THE AMERICAS

- The British settlement of Halifax, Nova Scotia, is established and leads to boundary disputes with French colonists.

SCIENCE AND TECHNOLOGY

- Denis Diderot (see p. 315), French philosopher and encyclopedist, expounds his doctrine of materialism in *Lettre sur les aveugles à l'usage de ceux qui voient* (Letter on the Blind for the Use of the Sighted) and is imprisoned.

- Italian Giacobbo Rodriquez Pereire invents a sign language for the deaf and mute. He presents a pupil to the Paris Academy of Sciences as a demonstration of his system.

ARTS AND HUMANITIES

17 Mar. First performance of George Frideric Handel's oratorio *Solomon*, a musical paean to British Hanoverian kingship.

28 Aug. In Frankfurt am Main, Germany, birth of Johann Wolfgang von Goethe (see p. 359), universal genius: writer, poet, playwright, scientist, musician, philosopher and administrator.

17 Dec. In Aversa, kingdom of Naples, birth of Domenico Cimarosa, Italian composer of operas.

Gottfried Achenwall, *Staatsverfassung der Europaischen Reiche* (The Political Constitutions of European States), a political and statistical survey of Europe.

Johann Sebastian Bach, *Die Kunst der Fuge* (The Art of the Fugue), music that explores complex polyphonies, left unfinished at Bach's death.

Henry St John, Viscount Bolingbroke, *Idea of a Patriot King*, political philosophy.

Charles-Etienne Bonnet, abbé de Condillac, *Traité des systèmes* (Treatise on Systems), philosophy.

Henry Fielding, *The History of Tom Jones, a Foundling*, a landmark in the early history of the English novel.

Thomas Gainsborough, *Mr and Mrs Robert Andrews*, painting.

George Frideric Handel, *Music for the Royal Fireworks*, orchestral suite celebrating the peace of Aix-la-Chapelle (see 7–8 Oct. 1748).

Ewald Christian von Kleist, 'Der Frühling' (Spring), poem.

Tobias Smollett, translation from French of the novel *Histoire de Gil Blas de Santillane* by Lesage.

1750

EUROPE

24 Sept.–5 Oct. In a treaty with England, Spain gives up its monopoly in the trade in slaves between Spain, the Spanish empire and Africa in return for confirmation of other trade rights.

10 Oct.–10 Nov. England agrees to an alliance between the empire and Russia.

30 Nov. In Chambord, France, death of Maurice, comte de Saxe, victorious field marshal for the French against Austria during the War of the Austrian Succession (1740–8).

THE AMERICAS

- The indigenous Sioux people are defeated by the Chippewa at the battle of Kathio.

- Thomas Walker discovers a break in the geological formation of the Appalachians (between SW Virginia and SE Kentucky) and names it the Cumberland Gap.

- In line with mercantilist economic theories, the British Parliament passes the Iron Act, restricting the capacity of the American colonies to produce iron goods: they are allowed to produce pig iron, which will be exported to Britain to manufacture iron goods, but cannot produce their own iron products. However, the attempt fails and iron mills in America flout the provisions of the Act.

ECONOMY AND SOCIETY

– In England the Jockey Club is founded.

SCIENCE AND TECHNOLOGY

– Mathematician and astronomer Nicolas Louis de Lacaille leads a French expedition to the Cape of Good Hope to observe the stars of the S heavens and to determine the lunar and solar parallax.
– English physician John Canton proposes the manufacture of artificial magnets.
– English physicist William Watson provides the first description of platinum.
– Foundation in Sweden of the Stockholm Academy of Sciences and Observatory.

ARTS AND HUMANITIES

Literature

23 Jan. In Modena, Italy, death of the scholar and historian Ludovico Antonio Muratori.
20 Mar. English writer Samuel Johnson starts his periodical *The Rambler*.
– The Benedictines of Saint-Maur publish a *Dictionnaire de l'art de vérifier les dates des faits historiques* (Dictionary of the Art of Verifying Historical Dates and Facts), which provides a historically reliable chronology from the birth of Christ to 1750.
– An expurgated edition of John Cleland's *Fanny Hill, or the Memoirs of a Woman of Pleasure*, is published. Written in 1748–9, the novel sets the standard for English erotic fiction.
– Frederick II (the Great), king of Prussia, writes *Oeuvres du philosophe de Sanssouci* (Philosophical Works from Sanssouci). Sanssouci is the small, elegant palace Frederick has built near Berlin where he can retreat and where he will later be buried, surrounded by the graves of his dogs.
Ferdinando Galiani, *Trattato della moneta* (Treatise on Money), expounding the theory of mercantilism and flows of money.
Abbé Prévost, *Manuel lexique; ou dictionnaire portatif des mots français*, French dictionary.
Jean-Jacques Rousseau (see p. 321), *Discours sur les lettres, sur les arts et les sciences* (Discourse on the Sciences and the Arts), philosophy.

Visual Arts and Architecture

– Westminster Bridge, London, is opened.
Lancelot (Capability) Brown, Warwick Castle Gardens in Warwickshire, England.
François de Cuvilliés, the Residentztheater, Munich.
William Kent, design for the Horse Guards barracks for the cavalry stationed at Whitehall, London.

Music

28 July In Leipzig, Saxony, German composer Johann Sebastian Bach dies. A master of counterpoint, Bach has spent his last months totally blind following an unsuccessful operation.

– Johann Breitkopf uses movable type to print music for the first time, in Leipzig, Saxony.

1751

EUROPE

31 Mar. The Prince of Wales, Frederick Louis (father of the future George III), dies in strange circumstances at Leicester House, London. His death may have been caused by an abscess created by a blow on the head from a cricket ball.
20 April Jurist and Prussian chancellor Samuel von Cocceji compiles the *Juris Fridericiani* (Code of Frederick), which replaces Roman law in Prussia.
May The Portuguese statesman the marquès de Pombal limits the power of the Inquisition in Portugal and decrees that no *auto da fé* (sentencing and execution of heretics) can take place without the government's authorization.
22 Oct. William IV, stadtholder of the United Netherlands, dies and is succeeded by his son William V, who first reigns under the regency of his mother Anne, sister of King George II of Great Britain and Ireland.
12 Dec. In Battersea, London, death of Henry St John, Viscount Bolingbroke, Tory politician and historian and sometime Jacobite intriguer.

ASIA

31 Aug. In the first of his major military successes, English soldier and colonial administrator Robert Clive (Clive of India) defeats French governor general Joseph, marquis de Dupleix, and takes the Indian town of Arcot, capital of the Carnatic (modern Karnataka), in S India. Dupleix is also defeated by Clive at Arni.
– Following local unrest around the imperial residency at Lhasa, China invades Tibet and establishes control over the Dalai Lama.

THE AMERICAS

– The British settlement of Georgetown is founded on the Potomac River in Maryland. (Georgetown will be incorporated into Washington, D.C., in 1895.)

ECONOMY AND SOCIETY

29 Mar. Death of Thomas Coram, English philanthropist. He founded the Foundling Hospital in London.
Mar. Parliament passes an Act bringing Great Britain's calendar 11 days forward to bring it in line with the Gregorian calendar of continental Europe. 1 Jan. becomes the start of the New Year (see 1752).
– The École Supérieure de Guerre, a training school for officers, is established in Paris.

SCIENCE AND TECHNOLOGY

– Swedish botanist Carl von Linné (Carolus Linnaeus) publishes *Philosophia Botanica* (Botanical Philosophy).
– Swedish mineralogist Axel Cronstedt isolates nickel from niccolite.

- American scientist and statesman Benjamin Franklin experiments on electricity. His experiments in Philadelphia lead him to discover the electrical properties of lightning.

Time is money.

Benjamin Franklin; advice to a young tradesman (1748)

- The British lieutenant governor of New York, Cadwallader Colden, a noted botanist, writes *Principles of Action in Matter*, a study of physics.
- Foundation of the Göttingen Society of Sciences, Germany.
- French naturalist Pierre-Louis de Maupertuis shows, in his *Système de la nature* (System of Nature), how offspring have the characteristics of both parents.
- Robert Whytt, an English doctor, makes a distinction between voluntary and involuntary motions and goes on to develop his theory of reflex action.

ARTS AND HUMANITIES

Literature

April The first volume of the *Encyclopédie ou Dictionnaire raisonné des sciences, des arts et des métiers* (Encyclopedia, or Classified Dictionary of the Sciences, Arts and Trades) is published in Paris. Edited by Denis Diderot (see box), the project includes such figures as the philosopher Charles-Louis de Secondat, baron de Montesquieu, and the mathematician Jean le Rond d'Alembert among its contributors.

30 Oct. In Dublin, Ireland, birth of Richard Brinsley Sheridan, Irish-born playwright and Whig politician.

- Thomas Pelham-Holles, duke of Newcastle and chancellor of Cambridge University, endows the annual award of a medal for classical scholarship.
- American statesman, publisher and inventor Benjamin Franklin founds the Pennsylvania Academy (subsequently the University of Pennsylvania).

Henry Fielding, *Amelia*, novel.

Frederick II (the Great), king of Prussia, *Mémoires pour servir à l'histoire de la maison de Brandenbourg*, memoirs.

Thomas Gray, *Elegy Written in a Country Church-Yard*, poem.

David Hume (see p. 312), *Enquiry Concerning the Principles of Morals* (a rewriting of Book 3 of the *Treatise*), philosophy.

Tobias Smollett, *The Adventures of Peregrine Pickle*, novel in four volumes.

Visual Arts and Architecture

François Boucher, *La Toilette de Venus* (Venus at the Mirror), painting.

Jacques-Ange Gabriel, the royal chateau of Choisy; he now starts work on the École Militaire, Paris.

William Hogarth, *Gin Lane*, engraving.

Music

23 Jan. Birth in Rome of Muzio Clementi, pianist and composer.

1752

EUROPE

17 Mar. The British House of Lords passes a bill for the Scottish estates forfeited in the Jacobite rebellions (see 1715 and 1745) to be bestowed on the crown and their revenues used for the development of the Highlands.

14 June Treaty of Aranjuez: Spain and the Holy Roman Empire offer each other guarantees for their European possessions. The treaty is subsequently agreed to by Sardinia, Naples and Parma.

- The Paris *parlement* seizes the temporal possessions of the archbishop of Paris.

Denis Diderot (1713–84)

In 1745 Diderot, then a writer making a precarious living out of translations and pamphlets, was commissioned to produce a French version of Ephraim Chambers's *Universal Dictionary of Arts and Sciences* (see 1728). What he produced was an entirely different work. 'The portrait of the achievements of the human spirit in different subjects and at different times' that he announced on the eve of the 1751 publication of Volume I was to become known as the *Encyclopédie*. In 1759, by order of King Louis XV, publication of the *Encyclopédie* was suspended after Diderot included subversive political material. Nonetheless, he persisted in his work. He was rescued from bankruptcy by cash gifts from Catherine II, empress of Russia, and published the 28th volume in 1772. Other editors were responsible for the remaining 7 volumes.

Diderot adopted the insights of the Enlightenment into how life should be lived in 18th-century France and made them into universal truths for all humanity. He assembled a team of writers (including Voltaire and Jean-Jacques Rousseau) who shared his philosophy, and their collaboration resulted in a world-view that quickly became a widely held alternative to the contemporary established order.

It was Diderot who made the idea of the pursuit of happiness a central Enlightenment goal. Rejecting any division between matter and spirit, Diderot maintained that materialism was the only philosophy that could both explain the different aspects of nature and maintain their underlying unity. The *Encyclopédie* attracted a vast readership, and the views it espoused dramatically influenced political, social and philosophical thought in the 18th century and beyond, and helped to prepare the ground for both the French and the American revolutions.

ASIA

June French forces at Trichinopoly (modern Tiruchchirappalli), SE India, surrender to English soldier and colonial administrator Robert Clive.

– Afghan forces occupy Lahore (in modern Pakistan).

ECONOMY AND SOCIETY

14 Sept. The Act of Mar. 1751 takes effect: Britain goes over to the Gregorian calendar in use on the Continent, and to make up for the 11-day difference, the period 3–13 Sept. is omitted from the year. London rioters protest at the loss of 11 days of their lives, but mostly object to the real loss of 11 days' pay.

SCIENCE AND TECHNOLOGY

– N American scientist and statesman Benjamin Franklin invents a lightning rod, which deflects electricity and protects buildings.

– The Manchester Royal infirmary is founded in N England.

– French scientist René-Antoine de Réaumur experiments on the digestive system and shows that digestion is a chemical process.

– In America Benjamin Franklin helps to establish the Philadelphia Contributionship for the Insurance of Homes from Loss by Fire.

– The Liberty Bell, Philadelphia, is cast in a local foundry.

ARTS AND HUMANITIES

Literature

13 June In King's Lynn, Norfolk, England, birth of Fanny Burney, novelist and letter writer.

20 Nov. In Bristol, England, birth of Thomas Chatterton, poet-prodigy.

Christopher Smart, *Poems on Several Occasions*. His acadamic career ruined by a secret marriage, Smart lives by his writing until mental illness overtakes him (see 1756).

– The *Encyclopédie* (Encyclopedia) project (see 1751) is condemned by the French authorities for its robust philosophical scepticism, but attempts to suppress it are half-hearted.

– French educationalist and author Jean-Jacques Rousseau's (see p. 321) play *Le Devin de village* (The Village Soothsayer) is first performed, at Fontainebleau, in France.

Henry St John, Viscount Bolingbroke, *Letters on the Study and Uses of History* (two volumes), philosophy of history, published posthumously.

Visual Arts and Architecture

– Birth in London of John Nash, English architect who will develop Regent's Park in London.

François Boucher, chalk portraits of Madame de Pompadour.

Music

26 Feb. First performance in London of George Frideric Handel's oratorio *Jephtha*, composed during the onset of the composer's blindness.

Charles Avison, *Essay on Musical Expression*, a landmark in music criticism, publishing the views of professional musicians about fellow professionals.

Christoph Willibald Gluck, *La clemenza di Tito* (The Clemency of Titus), opera.

1753

EUROPE

11 Jan. Pope Benedict XIV agrees a concordat with Ferdinand VI, king of Spain, and allows the Spanish crown its rights to Church patronage and appointments.

8 Mar. In Britain George II gives royal assent to a tax on land at two shillings in the pound in England and Wales.

5 May Frederick II (the Great), king of Prussia, is informed of the secret articles (concerning mobilization of troops) of the Austro-Russian treaty of mutual defence. France informs Britain of its obligation, under the Franco-Prussian treaty of 1741, to aid Prussia in case of an attack.

7 July The British Parliament passes the Jewish Naturalization Act to end legal discrimination against Jews in Britain; the measure, meeting widespread opposition, is repealed in 1754.

– Louis XV of France supports the archbishop of Paris and exiles the Paris *parlement* in their conflict over ecclesiastical rights.

– The Marriage Act in Britain bans marriage by unlicensed ministers of religion and requires the calling of banns in Anglican churches.

ASIA

Dec. The French governor general in India, Joseph-François, marquis de Dupleix, negotiates at Madras with representatives of the British government but demands to be the recognized ruler of the Carnatic (modern Karnataka in S India).

THE AMERICAS

Aug. French troops advance from Canada and occupy the Ohio valley, establishing settlements, which they name Fort le Boeuf and Fort Presqu'Isle. The British lieutenant-governor of Virginia sends George Washington of the Virginia militia to issue them with an instruction to withdraw.

18 Sept. The British colonial governors in N America are instructed to secure the allegiance of the indigenous Iroquois people since war with France now seems inevitable.

SCIENCE AND TECHNOLOGY

– Swedish botanist Carl von Linné (Carolus Linnaeus) publishes *Species Planatarum* (The Species of Plants).

– Scottish naval surgeon James Lind's *Treatise on the Scurvy* describes how citrus fruit helps prevent the disease, which is common among British seamen.

ARTS AND HUMANITIES

– The Villa dei Papyri, along with several scrolls, is excavated at the city of Herculaneum, S Italy, which was buried by the eruption of Mount Vesuvius in AD 79. Excavations began in 1738.

Literature

11 Jan. The Irish-born antiquarian and physician Sir Hans Sloane dies in London and bequeaths his collection of books, manuscripts and artefacts to the nation, forming the basis of the British Museum.

14 Jan. In Oxford, England, death of George Berkeley, Anglican bishop, scientist and philosopher.

5 April The British government grants a foundation charter for a museum (the British Museum) to house the Sloane collection. Sir Robert Bruce Cotton's library is transferred to the British Museum Library.

David Hume (see p. 312), *Essays and Treatises on Several Subjects*, philosophy, published in four volumes (to 1756).

Georges-Louis Leclerc, comte de Buffon, *Discours sur le style* (Discourse on Style), lecture delivered on his election to the Académie Française.

Samuel Richardson, *Sir Charles Grandison*, novel in four volumes (to 1754).

Visual Arts and Architecture

François Boucher, the 'Lever du Sol' (Sunrise) and the 'Coucher du Sol' (Sunset), designs for Gobelins tapestries.

1754

EUROPE

6 Mar. In London death of Henry Pelham, who has been Whig prime minister since 1743; he is succeeded by his brother Thomas, duke of Newcastle.

23 Aug. In Versailles, France, the future Louis XVI, king of France, is born; he is the grandson of Louis XV, whom he will succeed in 1774.

– Birth in Paris of the French politician Charles-Maurice de Talleyrand.

ASIA

– As British power grows in India, the French governor general, Joseph-François, marquis de Dupleix, is recalled to France.

THE AMERICAS

19 June As the French threat to British N America grows, the Albany Convention meets and assembles representatives of New York, Maryland, Pennsylvania and the six colonies of New England along with the chiefs of the six tribes of the Iroquois Confederation (Cayuga, Mohawk, Oneida, Onondaga, Seneca and Tuscarora). Benjamin Franklin proposes, and the Convention accepts, the idea of a voluntary union of the 13 British colonies.

3 July The French defeat George Washington's expeditionary force in the Ohio valley (see Aug. 1753). They go on to build Fort Duquesne (the future Pittsburgh) at the head of the Ohio River; this will become the cause of a war between the British and the French in N America.

ECONOMY AND SOCIETY

– The Royal and Ancient Golf Club is founded in St Andrews, Fife, Scotland.

– King's College, New York, the future Columbia University, is founded.

– Christ Church, Philadelphia, is completed. Its 60m (200 foot) steeple makes it the tallest building to date in N America.

– French naturalist Pierre-Louis de Maupertuis outlines, for the first time, a detailed theory of evolution in his *Essai sur la formation des corps organisés* (Essay on the Formation of Organized Bodies).

ARTS AND HUMANITIES

Literature

– Scottish philosopher and historian David Hume publishes the first volume of his six-volume *History of Great Britain* (to 1762).

– Birth of the English editor Thomas Bowdler, whose expurgations of Shakespeare will give the word 'bowdlerize' to the English language.

Visual Arts and Architecture

– The Winter Palace, St Petersburg, Russia, designed by Bartolomeo Rastrelli, is completed.

– The Amalienborg Palace, Copenhagen, Denmark, designed by Nikolaj Eigtved, is completed.

François Boucher, *The Judgement of Paris*, painting.

William Hogarth, *The Election*, painting.

1755

EUROPE

19 Sept. The Anglo-Russian Convention of St Petersburg: Russia will supply troops to Britain for the defence of its German electorate of Hanover (threatened by French invasion), in return for annual subsidies.

17 Nov. In Versailles, France, Louis-Xavier-Stanislas is born. He is the grandson of Louis XV, the brother of Louis XVI and Charles X and will be king of France (in title only) from 1795.

20 Nov. William Pitt (the Elder) is dismissed as paymaster-general of Britain; Henry Bilson-Legge, chancellor of the exchequer, and George Grenville, treasurer for the navy, also leave the ministry in opposition to the payment of subsidies to Russia for the protection of the German electorate of Hanover.

ASIA

– Rangoon (modern Yangon) is founded as the Burmese capital by King Alaungpaya (Alompra or Aungzeya) of Burma (Myanmar), a client of the East India Company and an opponent of the French expansion in the region.

THE AMERICAS

20 Feb. Gen. Edward Braddock lands in Virginia at the head of two regiments in order to become commander-in-chief of the British forces in N America and to develop British strategy against the French threat.

16 June After being besieged by British forces led by Col. Robert Monckton, Fort Beauséjour on the Acadian peninsula (modern Nova Scotia) in French Canada surrenders. Some 6000 Acadians who refuse to swear allegiance to George II are dispatched S to Georgia and South Carolina. The property of the remaining 9000 Acadians is confiscated.

9 July French and Native American forces combine to defeat the British on the Monongahela River near Fort Duquesne: Gen. Braddock is mortally wounded.

8 Sept. French forces are defeated by British colonial forces at the battle of Lake George.

– William Shirley, governor of Massachusetts, leads an expedition to the Niagara. He gets as far as Oswego and leaves a garrison there.

ECONOMY AND SOCIETY

– Moscow University is founded in Russia.

– American scientist and statesman Benjamin Franklin's *Observations Concerning the Increase of Mankind* sets the tone for American confidence, predicting that the population of the colonies will double in 20 years' time: nature, he says, can be tamed, poverty is not inevitable, and limits on population growth can be lifted.

– Beginning of a 'mini Ice Age' lasting several decades; in one of the coldest winters on record, the Golden Horn around Constantinople in the Ottoman empire freezes over.

– An earthquake destroys Lisbon, Portugal: over 30,000 people die in the quake and tidal wave and great fire that ensue.

SCIENCE AND TECHNOLOGY

– Joseph Black, a Scottish chemist, shows that magnesium is different from lime and is a distinct substance.

– German philosopher Immanuel Kant (see p. 334), in his *Allgemeine Naturgeschichte und Theorie des Himmels* (Universal Natural History and Theory of the Heavens), explains his theory for the formation of the solar system from a primordial nebula and posits that our galaxy is just one of many in the universe.

ARTS AND HUMANITIES

Literature

10 Feb. Death in Paris of Charles-Louis de Secondat, baron de Montesquieu, political philosopher and writer.

– English writer Samuel Johnson's *Dictionary of the English Language* begins publication in instalments; it will be completed in 1773.

– The French Church condemns the *Encyclopédie* (Encyclopedia); mathematician Jean d'Alembert resigns his position as joint editor.

Jean-Jacques Rousseau (see p. 321), *Discours sur l'origine de l'inégalité parmi les hommes* (Discourse on the Origins of Inequality between Men) and *Discours sur l'économie politique* (Discourse on Political Economy), political philosophy.

Visual Arts and Architecture

Jean-Baptiste Greuze, *A Father Explaining the Bible to his Children*, painting.

Music

– Josef Haydn writes his first string quartet around this date.

1756

EUROPE

16 Jan. Treaty of Westminster between Britain and Prussia: King Frederick II (the Great), king of Prussia, guarantees the neutrality of Hanover, in order to defy French attempts to

seize the German provinces of King George II of Britain. In response, the French draw diplomatically closer to the Austrians.

1 May Treaty of Versailles between France and Austria: the Habsburg monarchy will be neutral in an Anglo-French war but France and Austria will aid each other if attacked by Prussia.

17 May Following the treaty of Versailles, which has created two power blocs in Europe (Austria, France, Russia, Sweden, and Saxony against Prussia, Britain and Portugal), Britain declares war on France: the Seven Years War begins on 9 June.

29 Aug. Frederick II (the Great), king of Prussia, invades the German Electorate of Saxony and subsequently takes Dresden, its capital. The United Netherlands and Sweden remain neutral.

ASIA

21 June Of the 146 British prisoners taken captive by the nawab of Bengal, only 23 are left alive on their release from the small guard-room, known as the 'Black Hole of Calcutta', in which they have been kept. The episode becomes an inflammatory element in British anti-Indian propaganda.

THE AMERICAS

– The College of New Jersey moves from Newark to its new buildings in Princeton.

ARTS AND HUMANITIES

Literature

– The English poet Christopher Smart is confined to an asylum.

Voltaire (see p. 304), *Essai sur les moeurs et l'esprit des nations* (Essay on the Customs and Spirit of Nations) and *Poème sur le désastre de Lisbonne* (Poem on the Disaster at Lisbon), on the earthquake of 1755 in Lisbon, Portugal.

Visual Arts and Architecture

Thomas Gainsborough, *The Artist's Daughter Chasing a Butterfly*, painting.

Music

27 Jan. In Salzburg, Austria, Wolfgang Amadeus Mozart, musical prodigy and genius, is born.

1757

EUROPE

17 Jan. The Habsburg monarchy declares war on Prussia after a Prussian army takes possession of the German Electorate of Saxony.

14 Mar. In Portsmouth, England, Admiral John Byng is shot on his own quarter-deck after being court-martialled for negligence. Byng had failed in an attack on a French fleet defending Minorca in 1756.

6 April William Augustus, duke of Cumberland, the captain-general of British land forces at home and in the field, refuses to take command of the army in Germany unless Whig politician William Pitt (the Elder) resigns from the government; he fears that Pitt will not grant the necessary military and financial support for the task: Pitt resigns.

1 May Second treaty of Versailles between France and the Holy Roman Empire against Prussia: Prussia will be partitioned, losing Silesia and the fortress of Glatz (modern Klodzko) to Austria. France will increase annual subsidies to Austria until then. In return, Austria gives Louis XV full sovereignty in some cities of the Austrian Netherlands.

6 May Having invaded Bohemia, Frederick II (the Great), king of Prussia, defeats Prince Charles of Lorraine, brother of Holy Roman Emperor Francis I, at Prague in Bohemia. Frederick's army is subsequently defeated at the battle of Kolin, E of Prague (18 June), and withdraws from Bohemia. Frederick recovers his position with a decisive victory over the French at the battle of Rossbach in Saxony (5 Nov.), before defeating the Austrians at the battle of Leuthen, near Breslau (now Wroclaw) in Poland (5 Dec.).

June William Pitt (the Elder) is recalled to form a coalition government with the duke of Newcastle.

9 Oct. In Versailles, France, the future Charles X, king of France, is born. The grandson of Louis XV, he will become king in 1824.

ASIA

28 Jan. Afghan forces seize Delhi and then annex the Punjab.

23 June The battle of Plassey establishes British dominance in India. Forces under Robert Clive of the East India Company, aided by a British naval squadron, defeat Suraja Dowla, the nawab of Bengal, retake Calcutta and seize the French settlement at Chandernagor. Clive installs Mir Jafar, a client nawab, as nominal ruler but is himself the effective ruler of Bengal, NE India.

SCIENCE AND TECHNOLOGY

– Scottish physician James Lind's *On the Most Efficient Means of Preserving the Health of Seamen* advocates ways of preventing typhus. Lind is a Scottish physician who has served in the Royal Navy.

– British navigation improves with the invention of the sextant by John Campbell.

ARTS AND HUMANITIES

Literature

David Hume (see p. 312), *Four Dissertations*, including the essay 'Natural History of Religion'.

Visual Arts and Architecture

– French court architect Jacques-Ange Gabriel completes his additions to the Louvre, Paris.

Jean-Baptiste Greuze, *The Fowler*, painting.

William Hogarth, *Portrait of Garrick and His Wife*, painting.

1758

EUROPE

1 Jan. The Russians take possession of E Prussia, left defenceless while the Prussian army is engaged against the Swedes in Prussian Pomerania.

11 April The London Convention: Britain will grant Prussia an annual subsidy of £670,000 and will keep an army in Germany.

23 June Having been driven back across the Rhine, the French army is defeated by the Prussians at the battle of Crefeld (Krefeld), a town in Gelderland-Moers, Germany.

25 Aug. Frederick II (the Great), king of Prussia, defeats the Russian force that has invaded Prussia. The Austrians defeat the Prussians at the battle of Hochkirch, but Frederick maintains his position against the Austrians in Silesia and Saxony.

30 Dec. Secret treaty of Paris: France will maintain troops in Germany and subsidize the Holy Roman Emperor until he regains the duchy of Silesia (now held by Prussia) and the fortress of Glatz (modern Klodzko).

THE AMERICAS

8 July James Abercrombie, British commander-in-chief in N America, is defeated by the French while trying to take Fort Ticonderoga on Lake George.

26 July British forces defeat the French and seize Louisburg, Nova Scotia. They then seize Fort Frontenac and Fort Duquesne, which is renamed Pittsburgh.

SUB-SAHARAN AFRICA

– British troops conquer Senegal in W Africa: it will remain under British rule until 1783.

ECONOMY AND SOCIETY

3 May Pope Benedict XIV dies in Rome and is succeeded (6 July) by Carlo della Torre Rezzonico who becomes Pope Clement XIII.

– Swedish theologian and religious visionary Emanuel Swedenborg, *The New Jerusalem*; the Church of the New Jerusalem is established by his followers.

– French physician and economist François Quesnay's *Tableau économique* maintains that agriculture is the only real source of national wealth. Quesnay is a member of a school of economists known as physiocrats, who believe in the inherent goodness of man.

ARTS AND HUMANITIES

Literature

David Hume (see p. 312), *An Enquiry Concerning Human Understanding*, the final version of his *Treatise of Human Nature* (first published 1739), philosophy.

Visual Arts and Architecture

François Boucher, *The Mill at Charenton*, painting.

Thomas Gainsborough, *The Artist's Daughter with a Cat*, painting.

1759

EUROPE

13 Jan. In Portugal the marquis of Tavora and his wife are executed for leading a revolution and plotting the demise of King Joseph I (the Reformer).

April The French defeat an allied army under Ferdinand, duke of Brunswick, at Bergen in N Germany. The French go on to occupy Minden, on the River Wieser, in July.

23 July The Prussians are heavily defeated by the Russians at the battle of Kay.

1 Aug. A combined British-Hanoverian force defeats the French at Minden, W of Hanover.

10 Aug. Ferdinand VI of Spain dies and is succeeded by his half-brother Charles III (Don Carlos de Borbón).

12 Aug. A combined Russian-Austrian army defeats Frederick II (the Great), king of Prussia, (whose army is defending Dresden) at Künersdorf (now in Poland). Dresden falls three weeks later.

20 Nov. The British navy defeat the French at Quiberon Bay, off Brittany, to complete an *annus mirabilis* of British victories.

ASIA

8 April Robert Clive, governor of the British East India Company's Bengal possessions, seizes Masulipatam and drives the French from the Deccan, S India.

THE AMERICAS

13 Sept. France loses its Canadian territories to the British: British general James Wolfe defeats the French field marshal Louis-Joseph, marquis de Montcalm, at the battle of the Plains of Abraham near Quebec. Both Wolfe and Montcalm are mortally wounded.

ECONOMY AND SOCIETY

– Arthur Guinness establishes a brewery in Dublin, Ireland.

– The Jesuits are expelled from Portugal.

SCIENCE AND TECHNOLOGY

– German anatomist Kaspar Friedrich Wolff's researches develop the modern study of anatomy and embryology.

– German physicist Franz Aepinus publishes his *Tentamen Theoriae Electriciatis et Magnetismi* (An Attempt at a Theory of Electricity and Magnetism), the first work to relate mathematical methods to electricity and magnetism.

– Foundation of the Bavarian Academy of Science.

ARTS AND HUMANITIES

Literature

Samuel Johnson, *The History of Rasselas, Prince of Abyssinia*, philosophical romance.

Voltaire (see p. 304), *Candide, ou L'Optimisme* (Candide, or Optimism), fiction satirizing the lazy optimism that claims that 'all is for the best in the best of all possible worlds'. Reflection on the Lisbon earthquake (see 1755) has led Voltaire to revise his earlier optimism about progress.

Visual Arts and Architecture

Joshua Reynolds, *The Seventh Earl of Lauderdale*, painting.

Music

20 April Death in London of George Frideric Handel, German-born English baroque composer. Handel, a prolific and versatile composer, and inventor of the English oratorio, has been blind since 1752.

William Boyce, 'Heart of Oak', a song with words by David Garrick that will be adopted by the Royal Navy.

1760

EUROPE

23 June The Prussian troops guarding the passes into Silesia at Landshut, Bavaria, are crushed by the Austrians under Baron Gideon Ernst von Laudon, who then take the fortress of Glatz (modern Klodzko).

15 Aug. Frederick II (the Great), king of Prussia, defeats the Austrian forces at Liegnitz, Silesia (present-day Legnica, Poland). The Russian army attacks and burns areas of Berlin, capital of Prussia, but then has to retreat as Frederick returns to the city.

25 Oct. In London George II, king of Great Britain and Ireland, dies. He is succeeded by his grandson as George III.

3 Nov. Frederick II (the Great), king of Prussia, defeats the Austrians at Torgau, on the River Elbe, Saxony; the Austrians evacuate the electorate of Saxony but keep a presence in its capital, Dresden, which Frederick now controls.

ASIA

Jan. In India, British general Sir Eyre Coote defeats the French at Wandiwash, breaking French power in the Deccan.

– Tokugawa Ieshige, shogun of Japan, abdicates and is succeeded by Tokugawa Ieharu, his son.

ECONOMY AND SOCIETY

– The Botanical Gardens open in Kew, London.

SCIENCE AND TECHNOLOGY

– English geologist John Michell posits that earthquakes are the result of friction between two layers of rock.

– French astronomer Charles Messier begins the first catalogue of nebulous stars.

– American scientist and statesman Benjamin Franklin writes *Some Account of the Success of Inoculation for the Smallpox in England and America*.

ARTS AND HUMANITIES

Literature

Denis Diderot (see p. 315), *La Religieuse* (The Nun), novel and critique of the Church (not published until 1790).

James Macpherson, *Fragments of Ancient Poetry Collected in the Highlands of Scotland*.

Laurence Sterne, *The Sermons of Mr Yorick* and *The Life and Opinions of Tristram Shandy, Gentleman*, fiction satirizing the conventions of the novel.

Visual Arts and Architecture

Chin Nung, *The Buddhist Monk Lo-han*, painting.

Thomas Gainsborough, *Mrs Philip Thicknesse*, painting.

1761

EUROPE

15 Aug. Family Compact (defensive alliance) between France and Spain: Spain will declare war on Britain if no Anglo-French peace is concluded by 1 May 1762.

Sept. William Pitt (the Elder), British Whig prime minister, fails to persuade his colleagues to declare war on Spain in response to its threats to support France.

5 Oct. Pitt resigns as prime minister. John Stuart, 3rd marquis of Bute, forms a Tory administration.

– Britain intervenes in Portugal to help repel an invasion by Spanish and French forces.

ASIA

– In India, British general Sir Eyre Coote takes Pondicherry from the French.

SCIENCE AND TECHNOLOGY

– The Bridgewater canal opens, linking Liverpool with Leeds: it is the first British canal of major economic importance.

– Joseph-Louis Lagrange, French mathematician, publishes his complete calculus.

– Italian physician Giovanni Morgagni publishes *De Sedibus et Causis Morborum per Anatomen Indagatis* (On the Seats and Causes of Diseases Investigated by Anatomy), one of the first books on pathological anatomy.

Jean-Jacques Rousseau (1712–78)

Rousseau was born in Geneva but left the city in 1728 to embark on a life-long itinerant existence. Irascible, contradictory and moody, he was the first modern intellectual, self-consciously alienated from society. He detested the patronage system, and his whole oeuvre can be seen as a cry against dependency, summed up in his famous maxim: 'Man is born free but everywhere is in chains.' He was also the first major thinker to make his own personality an important subject of investigation. In his posthumously published *Confessions* (1782) he invented a new kind of literary form, blending autobiography, fictional narrative and philosophical reflection.

Rousseau was convinced that human society, with its hierarchies, rules and orders, was deeply artificial – something that did not suit humanity's 'natural' state. He believed that a pure and therefore happy state of nature only existed in the behaviour of animals, children and 'the noble savage' of primitive societies, untouched by the decadence of modern civilization. This attitude set Rousseau at odds with the thinkers of the 18th-century Enlightenment, who approved of the evidence of progress they saw around them. Rousseau expressed these ideas in his novel *Emile* (1762), an account of the unspoiled nature of children, and in *The Social Contract* (1762), a work of political philosophy in which he champions the sovereignty of the people and advocates direct democracy, in which all issues are put to the popular vote. Rousseau's cultural 'primitivism' had a great influence on the Romantic movement, with its emphasis on individual feeling rather than rational social order, while his political philosophy influenced the growth of republicanism and mass democratic politics.

ART AND HUMANITIES

Literature

Jean-Jacques Rousseau (see box), *Julie ou la nouvelle Héloïse* (Julie, or the New Eloise), romantic novel.

Music

– Joseph Haydn completes his Symphonies Nos. 6–8. He is appointed vice-Kapellmeister to the court of Prince Esterházy at Eisenstadt and will remain in the service of Esterházy and his successor until 1790. This professional stability will give rise to a vast musical output.

1762

EUROPE

4 Jan. Britain declares war on Spain and on the Spanish Bourbon territories in Naples and Parma (Italy).

5 Jan. In St Petersburg, Russia, Elizabeth, tsarita of Russia, dies. She is succeeded by her deranged son, Peter III.

5 May Treaty of St Petersburg: Tsar Peter III makes peace with Prussia and returns Pomerania to Prussian rule. Sweden also withdraws from the anti-Prussian coalition.

May In Britain the earl of Bute (James Stuart) becomes first lord of the Treasury (prime minister) following the resignation of the duke of Newcastle.

22 May Treaty of Hamburg: Russia restores all conquests made during the Seven Years War and agrees to a military alliance with Prussia.

May Portugal refuses to close its ports to British ships, thereby provoking Spanish forces to invade Portugal in retaliation; their troops take the towns of Braganza and Almeida.

17 July A palace coup overthrows Tsar Peter III, who is murdered with the assent of his wife, Grand Duchess Catherine Alexeevna; she succeeds him as Catherine II (the Great).

12 Aug. In London the future George IV, king of Great Britain and Ireland, is born. He is the son of George III and Charlotte Sophia of Mecklenburg-Strelitz.

THE AMERICAS

17 Mar. The first St Patrick's day parade of Irish immigrants takes place in New York.

– British naval forces take the West Indies islands of Martinique, Grenada, St Lucia and St Vincent from France, and also Havana in Cuba from Spain. British forces also occupy the Spanish colony of Manila in the Pacific.

ECONOMY AND SOCIETY

3 Feb. English dandy Richard 'Beau' Nash dies in Bath, S England, having transformed masculine taste in dress and decorum.

– Catherine II, tsarita of Russia, replenishes her treasury by secularizing the property of the clergy, owners of over a third of the land in the country.

– The Equitable Life Assurance Society is established in London.

– Jean-Jacques Rousseau's *Émile, ou traité de l'éducation* (Emile, or A Treatise on Education) encourages 'child-centred learning'.

SCIENCE AND TECHNOLOGY

– The Swedish doctor Nils von Rosenstein advances the modern study of childcare with his *The Diseases of Children and their Remedies*.

ARTS AND HUMANITIES

Literature

– French educationalist and author Jean-Jacques Rousseau's (see p. 321) *The Social Contract* causes a controversy with its assertion that 'Man is born free but everywhere is in chains' and emphasizes the idea of a contract between the rulers and the ruled. Rousseau-esque ideas become part of the common political vocabulary among the opponents of the *ancien régime* in Europe.

William Falconer, 'The Shipwreck', poem.

David Hume (see p. 312), *History of England* (sixth and final volume of a work begun in 1754), history.

Visual Arts and Architecture

Johann Zoffany, *The Farmer's Return*, portrait of the English actor David Garrick in his role in the play.

Music

5 Oct. First performance in Vienna of Christoph Willibald Gluck's opera *Orfeo ed Euridice*.

– The six-year-old Wolfgang Amadeus Mozart plays for the Empress Maria Theresa in Vienna.

1763

EUROPE

10 Feb. Treaty of Paris: the Seven Years War ends with a decisive shift in the balance of power in Britain's favour. French territories in Canada are ceded to Britain along with Grenada in the West Indies and Senegal in Africa. France regains Pondicherry and Chandernagor in India and the islands of Guadeloupe and Martinique in the West Indies. In N America France cedes New Orleans and Louisiana (a vast territory including modern Louisiana, Missouri, Arkansas, Iowa, Nebraska, North and South Dakota and Oklahoma) to Spain.

April In Britain Lord Bute resigns as prime minister and is succeeded by George Grenville.

Nov. In Britain Parliament resolves that John Wilkes's newspaper *The North Briton* number 45 is a seditious libel (it has questioned the truthfulness of statements in the king's speech).

ASIA

– Mir Qasim, nawab of Bengal, is defeated at Patna by the forces of the British East India Company; he is deposed and replaced by a Company nominee.

THE AMERICAS

– The Mississippi now forms the legal boundary between the British colonies and the Louisiana territory that France has ceded to Spain (see above).

– By the treaty of Paris (see above) Spain cedes Florida to Britain but recovers all of Britain's Cuban conquests as well as the Philippines, but loses Minorca.

– Detroit and other British forts are besieged by a coalition of Native American peoples, including the Algonquins and the Iroquois, led by the Ottawa chief Pontiac. The French withdraw their support of the Ottawa, and the British retain their settlements.

ECONOMY AND SOCIETY

– English potter Josiah Wedgwood is now producing cream-coloured tableware for a mass domestic market.

SCIENCE AND TECHNOLOGY

– English astronomer Nevil Maskelyne's *The British Mariner's Guide* shows how measurement of the stars can be used to calculate longitude. The *Guide* becomes an important element in British maritime supremacy.

ARTS AND HUMANITIES

Literature

Frederick II (the Great), king of Prussia, *Histoire de la Guerre de Sept Ans* (History of the Seven Years War).

Catharine Macaulay, *History of England from the Accession of James I to that of the Brunswick Line* (eight volumes), history.

Voltaire (see p. 304), *Traité sur la tolérance* (Treatise on Tolerance), a passionate defence of toleration and denunciation of legal abuses.

Visual Arts and Architecture

– The Church of La Madeleine is completed in Paris.

– Completion of the first synagogue in N America, built at Newport, Rhode Island, and designed by the American architect Peter Harrison.

Jean-Baptiste Greuze, *The Paralytic Cared for by his Children*, painting.

Francesco Guardi, *The Election of the Doge of Venice*, painting.

George Romney, *The Death of Wolfe*, painting.

Music

– The young Mozart performs publicly in Munich, Augsburg, Mainz and Frankfurt.

1764

EUROPE

Jan. In Britain John Wilkes is expelled from the House of Commons (see 1763).

19 April The British parliament passes a Currency Act that forbids the British colonies to print paper money.

7 Sept. Stanislaw Augustus Poniatowski, the former lover of Catherine II (the Great), tsarita of Russia, is elected king of Poland; as Stanislaw II, he is the last independent king of Poland.

ASIA

22 Oct. Mir Qasim (deposed nawab of Bengal and nawab of Oudh) is defeated by the forces of the British East India Company at Buxar, in Bihar, E India: British control extends over the Indian provinces of Bengal and Bihar.

– Hyder Ali, a Muslim commander, seizes Mysore in S India and claims the territory's throne.

THE AMERICAS

24 May James Otis, a Boston lawyer, makes a speech denouncing 'taxation without representation'.

Aug. Protests in Boston against the British colonial policy spreads among the merchants, who now start to boycott British goods.

– French navigator Louis de Bougainville claims the Falkland Islands (Iles Malouines) in the S Atlantic for France.

AUSTRALASIA AND OCEANIA

– The island of La Réunion (Bourbon), in the Indian Ocean, becomes a French crown colony.

ECONOMY AND SOCIETY

26 Nov. The Jesuits are expelled from France.

SCIENCE AND TECHNOLOGY

– The French engraver and typographer Pierre-Simon Fournier writes a *Manuel typographique*, which classifies different kinds of typefaces.

ARTS AND HUMANITIES

Literature

– *On Crimes and Punishment* by Italian jurist Cesare, Marchese di Beccaria, becomes a Europe-wide publishing phenomenon. Its condemnation of capital punishment and rejection of torture as inhumane becomes an influential element in the Enlightenment.

Voltaire (see p. 304), *Dictionnaire philosophique* (Philosophical Dictionary).

Visual Arts and Architecture.

26 Oct. In London death of English satirical painter William Hogarth.

– Scottish architect Robert Adam designs his drawings of *The Ruins of the Palace of the Emperor Diocletian*. Adam's classical and historically based style of architecture becomes a predominant element in 18th-century English taste.

– The royal palace in Madrid is completed.

Music

12 Sept. Jean-Philippe Rameau, French musical theorist and composer of operas and music for the harpsichord, dies in Paris.

Wolfgang Amadeus Mozart, Sonata for Piano and Violin No. 1 and Symphonies Nos. 1–4.

1765

EUROPE

22 Mar. The British parliament passes a Stamp Act, which requires that newspapers, pamphlets, almanacs and legal documents produced in the American colonies should have revenue stamps placed upon them. This attempt at imposing taxation on the colonial province coincides with the start of an economic depression in the colonies.

15 May The British Parliament passes the Quartering Act, which obliges American colonists to provide supplies and accommodation in barracks for British troops stationed in the colonies.

16 July In Britain George Grenville resigns as prime minister and is replaced by the marquess of Rockingham.

13 Aug. Archduke Leopold, son of Holy Roman Emperor Francis I and of Maria Theresa, archduchess of Austria, begins his 25-year reign over the grand duchy of Tuscany (Italy).

18 Aug. In Innsbruck, Austria, Francis I, Holy Roman Emperor since 1745, dies; he is succeeded by the Habsburg heir Joseph II, son of Maria Theresa.

ASIA

May Robert Clive, governor of the British East India Company in Bengal, begins his administrative reforms in the provinces of Bengal and Bihar.

12 Aug. Mughal emperor Shah Alam II gives Robert Clive the right to collect revenue within Bengal.

THE AMERICAS

7–25 Oct. Representatives of 9 of the 13 American colonies meet and draw up a Declaration of Rights and Grievances in protest against the Stamp Act (see above).

ECONOMY AND SOCIETY

– The Parisian inn-keeper Boulanger defies the monopoly enjoyed by caterers in the sale of cooked meats. He sells his own, is sued and wins his case, thereby establishing the origins of the modern restaurant trade.

SCIENCE AND TECHNOLOGY

– James Watt of Glasgow invents the steam engine, whose condensor uses exhaust steam extracted from the cylinder of the engine.

– In France the rivers Loire and Rhone are linked by a canal.

ARTS AND HUMANITIES

Literature

Horace Walpole, *The Castle of Otranto*, fiction establishing the genre of the Gothic novel.

Visual Arts and Architecture

François Boucher, *Madame de Pompadour*, painting.

Jean-Honoré Fragonard, *The Swing*, painting.

Jean-Baptiste Greuze, *Young Girl Weeping over her Dead Bird*, painting.

Joseph Wright of Derby, *A Philosopher Giving a Lecture at the Orrery*, painting.

Music

– The Boston printer Thomas Fleet publishes *Mother Goose*, melodies including 'Baa Baa Black Sheep', 'Jack and Jill' and 'Little Miss Muffet'. His mother-in-law, Elisabeth Foster Goose, has combined traditional French tunes with the words of Charles Perrault in singing songs to Fleet's son.

Wolfgang Amadeus Mozart, Symphony No. 5.

1766

EUROPE

23 Feb. Stanislas I Leszczynski, former king of Poland, dies; Lorraine reverts to its allegiance to the French crown.

Feb. The British Parliament repeals the Stamp Act.

18 Mar. The British Parliament passes a Declaratory Act stating that the crown in Parliament has the authority to make laws that are enforceable in all British colonies.

Aug. The marquis of Rockingham, prime minister of Britain, dies. William Pitt, earl of Chatham, is appointed in his place.

MIDDLE EAST AND NORTH AFRICA

– Ali Bey takes power in Egypt and proclaims independence from the Ottoman empire.

ECONOMY AND SOCIETY

26 Feb. Catherine II (the Great), tsarita of Russia, grants freedom of worship in Russia.

– The Prater Park opens in Vienna as an amusement park for the local population; it is built on land donated to the city by the emperor Joseph II, who now rules with his mother Maria Theresa as co-regent.

– James Christie founds an art auction house in London.

– The first paved footpath is laid, in Westminster, London.

– French inventor Bourgeuis de Châteaublanc invents the first street lamp with a wick and reflector.

SCIENCE AND TECHNOLOGY

– In England construction work begins on a canal to join the River Trent with the Mersey: the effect will be to open a link between the North Sea and the Irish Sea.

ARTS AND HUMANITIES

Literature

Oliver Goldsmith, *The Vicar of Wakefield*, comic novel.

Visual Arts and Architecture

Johann Zoffany, *Queen Charlotte and the Two Eldest Princes*, painting.

Music

Joseph Haydn, *Grosse Orgelmesse* (Great Mass with Organ).
Wolfgang Amadeus Mozart, *Kyrie in F*.

1767

EUROPE

Dec. In Britain a new ministry under Augustus Henry Fitzroy, duke of Grafton, succeeds that of William Pitt, earl of Chatham.

ASIA

– Burmese troops invade Siam (modern Thailand). They destroy the kingdom of Ayuthia but fail to retain hold on the country.

THE AMERICAS

9 June The passing by the British Parliament of the Townshend Revenue Act causes another political protest in Boston. Tea, glass, paint, oil, lead and paper imported into the American colonies now have tax duties imposed on them: the towns-people of Boston bind themselves to an agreement not to import such goods.

– The North Carolina explorer Daniel Boone travels through the Cumberland Gap and reaches 'Kentuckee'.

ECONOMY AND SOCIETY

1 Mar. Charles III, king of Spain, expels the Jesuits from Spain, then from the Spanish Bourbon territories of Parma and Sicily in Italy.

SCIENCE AND TECHNOLOGY

– English clergyman and chemist Joseph Priestley's *The History and Present State of Electricity* explains the rings formed on metal surfaces by electrical discharges. He also pioneers the manufacture of carbonated water.

– American whaling ships make their first expedition to the Antarctic.

ARTS AND HUMANITIES

Literature

Laurence Sterne, *The Life and Opinions of Tristram Shandy, Gentleman* (final volume), novel.

Visual Arts and Architecture

– Completion of the Cathedral of St Andrew in St Petersburg, Russia, designed by the Italian architect Bartolomeo Francesco Rastrelli.

Gotthold Ephraim Lessing, *Minna von Barnhelm*, play.

Joseph Wright of Derby, *An Experiment on a Bird in an Air Pump*, painting.

Music

25 June Death of the prolific German baroque composer Georg Philipp Telemann. During his lifetime he has been the most celebrated German composer, with a higher reputation than J.S. Bach.

26 Dec. First performance in Vienna of Christoph Willibald Gluck's opera, *Alceste*; in the preface Gluck expounds his belief that opera is a form of drama, not just a musical entertainment.

1768

EUROPE

15 May France buys the island of Corsica from Genoa.

Oct. The Ottoman empire declares war on Russia: the occupation of Poland by Russia has disturbed the balance of power in C Europe and the Middle East.

– In retaliation for the expulsion of the Jesuits from Spain, Pope Clement XIII confiscates the Spanish Bourbon territory of Parma, Italy, prompting Ferdinand I, the Bourbon king of Naples, to invade the Papal States. France seizes the papal city of Avignon, S France.

THE AMERICAS

22 Sept. In America delegates from the towns of Massachusetts meet to compile a list of their grievances against the British crown. The British government reacts by sending two infantry regiments to the colony.

14 Oct. The treaty of Hard Labour confirms the cession of Cherokee lands in Virginia and Carolina to the British crown. The treaty of Fort Stanwix confirms the cession of Iroquois lands between the Ohio and the Tennessee rivers.

- Samuel Hearne embarks on his exploration by foot of the territory between Hudson Bay and the Arctic Ocean. His survey confirms that there is no Northwest Passage linking the Atlantic with the Pacific Ocean.
- Charlotte, North Carolina, is founded and named after King George III's consort, Charlotte Sophia of Mecklenburg-Strelitz.

AUSTRALASIA AND OCEANIA
25 May James Cook of the British navy sets sail in HMS *Endeavour* to establish an observatory in Tahiti.

ECONOMY AND SOCIETY
- Britain's first privately owned library opens to the public in Liverpool; others follow in Sheffield, Hull, Bristol and Birmingham.

SCIENCE AND TECHNOLOGY
- William Heberdeen, a London doctor, analyses angina pectoris.

ARTS AND HUMANITIES
Literature
Thomas Gray, *Poems*, poetry collection including *Elegy Written in a Country Church-Yard*.
Laurence Sterne, *A Sentimental Journey through France and Italy*, satire on the sentimentality of many contemporary novels. Sterne dies in London leaving only half of *A Sentimental Journey* published.
Ueda Akinari, *Ugetsu-monogatari* (Tales of the Rainy Moon), compilation of Chinese and Japanese short stories.
Visual Arts and Architecture
20 April In Venice, Italy, death of painter Antonio Canaletto.
Jacques-Ange Gabriel, design for Le Petit Trianon, Versailles.
Music
Joseph Haydn, Symphony No. 26 (*Lamentatione,* Lamentation).

1769
EUROPE
Feb. Austria occupies the Polish territories of Lemberg (modern Lviv, Ukraine) and most of Galicia and Lodomeria (in the W of modern Ukraine) in the Carpathian Mts; Emperor Joseph II and Frederick II (the Great), king of Prussia, agree on a partition of Poland.
Nov. Russian forces occupy Moldavia and Wallachia (modern Romania) and enter its capital, Bucharest, in the course of the Russo-Ottoman war.

ASIA
June Hyder Ali, sultan of Mysore, India (see 1764), persuades the East India Company in Madras to guarantee British military aid in the event of attacks on his territories.
- By now the East India Company is operating in N Borneo.
- Bengal (NE India) suffers from the worst famine yet recorded, with the death of some 10 million people.
- Nepal is unified after the Katmandu Valley is finally conquered by the Gurkhas.

THE AMERICAS
16 May Virginia's representatives convene in the House of Burgesses and reject the British Parliament's right to tax the American colonies. As in Massachusetts, the Virginians agree not to import any goods on which a duty has been imposed.
19 May The Virginia assembly is dissolved by the British government as a result of its protests against the transfer of colonial treason trials to Westminster, London.
- Spanish Franciscan missionaries and explorers are now colonizing California: San Francisco Bay is named, and San Diego is founded. The Spanish plant vines in California.
- New England Congregationalists establish Dartmouth College, New Hampshire.

AUSTRALASIA AND OCEANIA
- British explorer James Cook arrives in Tahiti, establishes an observatory and sails on to New Zealand.
- French navigator Louis de Bougainville attempts to reach New Holland (Australia) from the NW, but fails because of the Great Barrier Reef. He later completes the first French circum-navigation of the world.

ECONOMY AND SOCIETY
2 Feb. Pope Clement XIII dies in Rome and is succeeded (19 May) by Lorenzo Ganganelli, who becomes Pope Clement XIV.
- English publisher and biographer John Debrett publishes *Debrett's Peerage and Baronetage*.

SCIENCE AND TECHNOLOGY
- French engineer Nicolas-Joseph Cugnot produces a steam road carriage to carry four people at a speed of 3.6 kph (2¼ mph).
- Scottish engineer James Watt establishes, with English engineer Matthew Boulton, the Boulton and Watt Foundry in Birmingham in the English Midlands.
- English inventor Richard Arkwright patents a spinning frame that produces cotton so fine and durable that it can be used to weave fabric mechanically.

ARTS AND HUMANITIES
Literature
- English actor and playwright David Garrick organizes the first annual Shakespeare festival at Stratford-upon-Avon, England.
Sir William Blackstone, *Commentaries on the Laws of England* (four volumes).
Music
1 May First performance in Salzburg of Wolfgang Amadeus Mozart's opera buffa *La finta semplice* (The Feigned Simpleton).
Joseph Haydn, Symphony No. 48, (*Maria Theresa*).

1770
EUROPE
10 Feb. In Britain King George III's favourite, Frederick, Lord North, takes office as prime minister at the head of a new Tory government.

12 Feb. Adolph Frederick, king of Sweden, dies. His son and successor Gustav III will regain monarchical ascendancy over the riksdag (parliament) in the face of dangers from Prussia and Russia.

12 April The British Parliament repeals the Townshend Revenue Act (see 1767).

16 May Marie-Antoinette, daughter of Maria Theresa, archduchess of Austria, marries Louis, the French dauphin, at Versailles, France.

6 July The Russian navy defeats the Ottomans (Turks) at the battle of Chesme off the coast of Anatolia (Asian Turkey).

Sept. The Holy Roman Emperor Joseph II and Frederick II (the Great), king of Prussia, meet at Neustadt, Moravia, to discuss means of putting an end to the Russian expansion.

5 Dec. In Denmark the administration of Count Johann von Struensee, a former doctor and the virtual ruler of the country as lover of Queen Caroline Matilda, consort of the deranged King Christian VII, attempts to create an enlightened absolute monarchy, introduces freedom of the press and new attacks on aristocratic privilege.

– Russian Cossacks conquer the Crimean peninsula and extend the empire of Catherine II (the Great), tsarita of Russia.

ASIA

10 Feb. Maratha troops from the Deccan drive the Afghan invaders out of Delhi and install Shah Alam, the exiled Mughal emperor, as a pliant ruler.

– Burma finally accepts nominal Manchu suzerainty after several Manchu Chinese invasions since 1765.

THE AMERICAS

Jan. At the 'battle' of the Golden Hill, New York, British troops engage with American colonists for the first time. The Sons of Liberty erect poles, inscribed with anti-government slogans; a skirmish follows when British troops dismantle the pole in Golden Hill.

5 Mar. The Boston 'massacre' shows the gravity of the British problem in N America. When British troops fire on protestors the casualties are slight: three people are killed outright, two are mortally wounded and six are injured. The jury in the subsequent court case acquits the troops. But the incident has propaganda value for the colonial cause.

16 May At the battle of Alamance British troops defeat a rebellion of North Carolina farmers protesting against the imposition of British taxes.

AUSTRALASIA AND OCEANIA

– British navigator, naval surveyor and explorer James Cook, accompanied by naturalist Joseph Banks, arrives in Australia. The bay where he lands will be named Botany Bay.

ECONOMY AND SOCIETY

– The *London Evening Post* becomes the first English newspaper to print parliamentary reports.

– The *Massachusetts Spy* begins publication in Boston as a pro-colonial Whig newspaper.

SCIENCE AND TECHNOLOGY

– English weaver and carpenter James Hargreaves patents his spinning jenny, which will transform textile production first in Britain and then globally.

ARTS AND HUMANITIES

Literature

24 Aug. Thomas Chatterton commits suicide at the age of 17: the English poet has produced precocious pastiches of medieval English verse.

– The poet Christopher Smart dies insane.

Oliver Goldsmith, *The Deserted Village*, extended narrative poem lamenting change in rural England.

Paul Heinrich Dietrich, baron d'Holbach, *Système de la nature* (The System of Nature), philosophy denying any divine element in the ordering of the natural world.

Visual Arts and Architecture

30 May Death in Paris of François Boucher, painter, engraver, tapestry expert and designer.

Jean-Antoine Houdon, *Denis Diderot*, sculpture.

Benjamin West, *Penn's Treaty with the Indians* and *Death of General Wolfe*, paintings announcing the arrival of a distinctive American school of painting that blends narrative realism with classical composition.

Music

17 Dec. Birth in Bonn of German composer Ludwig van Beethoven (see p. 356).

26 Dec. First performance in Milan of Wolfgang Amadeus Mozart's opera seria *Mitridate, rè di Ponto* (Mithridates, King of Pontus).

1771

EUROPE

19 Jan. In a *coup d'état* Chancellor René de Maupeou abolishes the French *parlements* and replaces them with a system of courts under royal control, thus increasing monarchical power in the country.

22 Jan. Spain cedes the Falkland Islands to Britain to avert a threatened war.

6 July Austria reaches agreement with the Ottoman (Turkish) empire to force Russia to restore its conquests in the Crimea, after Russian troops occupy the khanate of the Crimea (an Ottoman client-state) in June.

ECONOMY AND SOCIETY

– Opening of Josiah Wedgwood's new pottery works in Etruria, Stoke-on-Trent, England.

SCIENCE AND TECHNOLOGY

– John Hunter, Scottish surgeon, publishes *The Natural History of the Human Teeth*.

ARTS AND HUMANITIES

Literature

17 Sept. Death of Scottish author Tobias Smollett, in Livorno,

Italy. A medical graduate, Smollett sailed as a surgeon's mate in an expedition against the Spanish and enjoyed a subsequent literary success in London.
– Publication in London of the first edition of the *Encyclopaedia Britannica*, the oldest English-language encyclopedia. Preliminary parts had begun appearing weekly in 1768.
Denis Diderot (see p. 315), *Le Fils naturel, ou les épreuves de la vertu* (The Natural Son, or The Proofs of Virtue), play.
Henry Mackenzie, *The Man of Feeling*, popular sentimental novel.
Tobias Smollett, *The Expedition of Humphry Clinker*, novel.

1772

EUROPE
16–17 Jan. Count Johann von Struensee (see 1770) is deposed by the Danish nobility. He is tried and beheaded. His administration is replaced by a reactionary aristocratic group led by Ove Høegh-Guldberg.
22 June In Britain Lord Mansfield, the lord chief justice, rules that an escaped slave becomes free as soon as he or she sets foot on English or Welsh soil.
5 Aug. Frederick II (the Great), king of Prussia, leads the First Partition of Poland: Russia annexes White Russia (modern Belarus) and the territory extending to the rivers Dvina and Dnieper; Austria takes Red Russia, Galicia and Lodomeria as well as part of Cracow; Prussia takes Polish Prussia except Danzig and Thorn.
19 Aug. In a coup for enlightened despotism, Gustav III, king of Sweden, removes the power of the riksdag to initiate legislation. In the course of his reign he will follow the enlightened path of lifting censorship, proclaiming religious tolerance, encouraging trade and abolishing torture.

ASIA
– Warren Hastings, administrator for the East India Company, becomes governor of Bengal and extends British control over Indian trade.
– Edo (modern Tokyo), the capital of Japan, is destroyed in a fire.

AUSTRALASIA AND OCEANIA
– English navigator, naval surveyor and explorer James Cook embarks on a second expedition to the Pacific.

SCIENCE AND TECHNOLOGY
– English clergyman and chemist Joseph Priestley coins the name 'rubber' to describe the new material that can remove pencil marks.
– English chemist Daniel Rutherford separates nitrogen from carbon dioxide.

ARTS AND HUMANITIES
Literature
– The French *Encyclopédie*'s final volume, edited by Denis Diderot, is published.
Gotthold Ephraim Lessing, *Emilia Galotti*, play.

Honoré-Gabriel Riqueti, comte de Mirabeau, *Essai sur le despotisme* (Essay on Despotism), political philosophy.
Visual Arts and Architecture
Claude-Nicolas Ledoux, the Hôtel de Montmorency, Paris.
Giorgio Massari, the Palazzo Grassi, Venice.
Antonio Rinaldi, the Marble Palace in St Petersburg, Russia.
Johann Zoffany, *The Members of the Royal Academy*, painting.
Music
26 Dec. First performance in Milan of Wolfgang Amadeus Mozart's opera *Lucio Silla*.
Joseph Haydn, Symphony No. 45 (*Farewell*).
Wolfgang Amadeus Mozart, Divertimenti for Strings in D major and B Flat.

1773

EUROPE
10 May Parliament passes a Tea Act, which reduces the amount of tax duty paid on tea imported into Britain: the aim is to help the East India Company, which has a surplus of tea in domestic storage, but the full duty is kept on tea shipped to the American colonies.
May The British Parliament passes a Regulating Act with the aim of asserting government control over the East India Company, now seen as a usurper of administrative order in India.
21 June Under pressure from France, Spain and Portugal, Pope Clement XIV dissolves the Jesuit order in his bull *Dominus ac Redemptor noster* (Our Lord and Redeemer).
– The Austrian emperor Joseph II expels the Jesuits from his territories.

MIDDLE EAST AND NORTH AFRICA
8 May Ali Bey, the ruler of Egypt, dies after being mortally wounded in a skirmish with Ottoman (Turkish) rebels. Muhammad Bey assumes power in his place and recognizes Ottoman suzerainty in the country.
25 Dec. Mustafa III, sultan of the Ottoman empire, dies and is succeeded by his brother Ab-dul-Hamid I.
– The Wahabbi, Islamic fundamentalist rulers of Arabia, annex Riyadh (Saudi Arabia).

THE AMERICAS
7 June Antigua, capital of the Spanish captain-generalcy of New Spain (now Guatemala), is destroyed in an earthquake; more than 58,000 people die. The capital moves to Guatemala City.
16 Dec. 342 chests of tea imported from London are thrown into Boston harbour in the so-called Boston Tea Party. The Tea Act (see 10 May above) has injured middlemen merchants since it permits the sale of tea directly to retailers.
– Cooperation between the American colonies is strengthened when Virginia's House of Burgesses establishes a committee whose job it is to promote links with the other colonies.
– American explorer Daniel Boone is forced to retreat from Kentucky when his expedition is attacked by Native Americans.

SCIENCE AND TECHNOLOGY

– Scottish surgeon John Hunter starts a series of medical lectures in London and popularizes the idea of the ligature (rather than amputation) as a means of treating aneurysm.

ARTS AND HUMANITIES

Literature
Oliver Goldsmith, *She Stoops to Conquer*, comedy.
Music
Wolfgang Amadeus Mozart, Symphonies Nos. 22–28.

1774

EUROPE

10 May In Versailles, France, Louis XV, king of France, dies. He is succeeded by his grandson Louis XVI.

16 July Russia and Turkey sign a treaty ending their war: the Ottoman empire regains Moldavia and Wallachia, the Crimea gains its independence, and Russia gains control of the N coast of the Black Sea.

24 Aug. Louis XVI recalls the disbanded *parlements* and appoints Anne-Robert Turgot, writer and reformer, as controller general of finance. Turgot attempts a policy of French economic reform that attacks unnatural restraint of trade. He abolishes the Six Guilds of Paris since the guilds have tried to limit the number of artisans who can be trained. He also reintroduces the free trade in grain (abolished in 1766). A hard winter, which freezes the rivers, means that grain is difficult to transport by barge and the price of bread increases as a result. The government is blamed for the inflation.

– In England Robert Clive, administrator responsible for the establishing British power in India, commits suicide in the aftermath of a parliamentary enquiry (1772–3) into charges of corruption (of which he has been acquitted).

– Joseph I (the Reformer), king of Portugal, becomes mentally ill: his wife, Maria Anna, acts as regent and reduces the powers of the country's effective ruler, the marquis of Pombal (Sebastião José de Carvalho e Mello), whose many modernizing works have included replanning Lisbon after the earthquake of 1755 and breaking the power of the Inquisition.

– The Jesuits are expelled from Poland.

THE AMERICAS

31 Mar. The Boston Port Bill is granted the royal assent. This, the Massachusetts Justice Act and the Massachusetts Government Act, the British government's response to the Boston Tea Party (see 16 Dec. 1773), are known as the Intolerable Acts.

22 April The British merchant ship *London* is boarded by protestors in Boston and the cargo of tea on board is thrown into the sea. Further such incidents follow in ports in Maine and Maryland.

26 May The governor of Virginia dissolves the Virginia House of Burgesses after it has declared its support for the Boston Tea Party. Meeting unofficially in a tavern, the burgesses call for an annual inter-colonial congress.

1 June Boston harbour is closed as a punitive act of retaliation by the British government, but the other colonies respond by sending overland the foods that Boston needs to survive.

22 June The British Parliament passes the Quebec Act, which extends the province S to the Ohio and W to the Mississippi. In doing so it ignores the territorial claims of the colonies of Massachusetts, Virginia and Connecticut.

5 Sept. The First Continental Congress, including representatives of all the colonies except Georgia, meets at Philadelphia. It proceeds to adopt a Declaration of Rights and Grievances, and under the terms of the association subsequently adopted it agrees to import nothing from Britain after 1 Dec. Nothing will be exported to Britain, Ireland or the British West Indies after 10 Sept. 1775 unless British policy is changed. All the colonies, with the exception of Georgia and New York, will agree to the association's terms.

10 Oct. The Shawnee Native American people are defeated by settlers at the battle of Point Pleasant.

– Connecticut and Rhode Island colonies stop any further slave imports.

– Fort Harrod in Kentucky, established by James Harrod, becomes the first European settlement in the British N American colonies W of the Allegheny Mts.

ECONOMY AND SOCIETY

22 Sept. Pope Clement XIV dies in Rome.

– Luke Hansard, a London printer, starts to print the debates held in Parliament.

– Ann Lee, an English religious visionary and a member of the Shaking Quaker sect, arrives in Albany, New York state, and establishes a community of followers. The Shaker doctrine of celibacy means that the sect will have a precarious existence.

SCIENCE AND TECHNOLOGY

– English clergyman and chemist Joseph Priestley discovers oxygen.

– Karl Wilhelm Scheele, a Swedish chemist, discovers chloride and manganese.

ARTS AND HUMANITIES

Literature
Philip Dormer Stanhope, 4th earl of Chesterfield, *Lord Chesterfield, Letters to His Son, a guide to good manners*, philosophy.

Benjamin Franklin, 'On the Rise and Progress of the Differences between Great Britain and Her American Colonies', a series of articles published in the *London Public Advertiser*.

Johann Wolfgang von Goethe (see p. 359), *Die Leiden des Jungen Werther* (The Sorrows of Young Werther), novella.

Thomas Jefferson (see p. 329), *Summary View of the Rights of Americans*, political pamphlet published in both London and Williamsburg, Virginia.

Music
19 April First performance in Paris of Christoph Willibald Gluck's opera *Iphigénie en Aulide*.

Joseph Haydn, Symphony No. 55 (*The Schoolmaster*).

1775

EUROPE

7 May The Ottoman (Turkish) empire cedes its former Moldavian province of Bukovina (in the NE Carpathian Mts), to Austria.

THE AMERICAS

16 April American silversmith and copperplate printer Paul Revere rides to Lexington, Virginia, to warn the rebel leaders Samuel Adams and John Hancock that British forces are about to arrest them. American colonialists at Concord, Massachusetts, who have collected weapons ready for a rebellion, are alerted as British troops advance on both towns.

18 April The American Revolution (War of Independence) begins with the battles of Lexington and of Concord. The British win both engagements.

April The Royal Navy begins an 11-month siege of Boston. When the news of the battles reaches New York the local authorities close the port and arms are distributed to the citizenry.

10 May The Green Mountain Boys, a militia led by Ethan Allen, achieve the first American success of the war. They capture Fort Ticonderoga in New York state.

10 May The Second Continental Congress meets in Philadelphia: it will choose American merchant and revolutionary politician John Hancock as its president.

17 June At the battle of Bunker Hill (Breed's Hill), Boston, Massachusetts, British forces under Gen. Thomas Gage, defeat American forces under William Prescott. The British lose 226 killed and 828 wounded, while the Americans suffer about 450 casualties.

17 June American landowner and soldier George Washington is appointed commander-in-chief of the Continental army and arrives in Cambridge, Massachusetts, to take up his command.

13 Oct. The Continental Congress establishes an American navy and authorizes the building of two ships.

– The first American society to work for the abolition of slavery is established in Pennsylvania.

ECONOMY AND SOCIETY

15 Feb. Giovanni Angelo Braschi is elected Pope Pius VI.

ARTS AND HUMANITIES

Literature

– Thomas Paine, exiled from England to America, writes politically radical articles in his *Pennsylvania Magazine*.

– The English actress Sarah Siddons makes her debut at the Drury Lane Theatre, London, as Portia in Shakespeare's *The Merchant of Venice*.

Samuel Johnson, *A Journey to the Western Islands of Scotland*, travel literature.

Richard Brinsley Sheridan, *The Rivals*, comedy.

Visual Arts and Architecture

Jean-Baptiste Chardin, *Self-portrait*, painting.

Jacques-Ange Gabriel, the Place de la Concorde, Paris.

John Wood (the Younger), the Royal Crescent, Bath.

Music

13 Jan. First performance in Munich of Wolfgang Amadeus Mozart's opera buffa *La finta giardiniera* (The Feigned Garden-Girl).

23 April First performance in Salzburg of Mozart's musical drama *Il re pastore*.

Edward Barnes, 'Yankee Doodle', song adopted by the American army.

Thomas Jefferson (1743–1826)

Thomas Jefferson, the American revolutionary and statesman, was a cultivated country squire and a product of the 18th-century Enlightenment who spoke of a need to 'preach a crusade against ignorance'. But the drama of his times pushed him towards a very practical assertion of his hostility towards 'the artificial aristocracy of birth and wealth as against the natural aristocracy of talent and virtue'.

Jefferson's principles and his pen inspired the two documents that have influenced perhaps the greatest number of individuals in the modern world: the American Declaration of Independence and the American Constitution's Bill of Rights.

Jefferson produced the final draft of the Declaration of 1776 and was responsible for its famous phrases expressing the belief that 'men are created equal' with 'inalienable rights', and that these rights include 'Life, Liberty and the pursuit of Happiness'. In 1787 representatives of the newly independent United States met in Philadelphia to draft a new constitution. Jefferson, then absent in Paris as the new republic's representative, insisted on the need for a written definition of rights, for even a de facto democracy could not rely on the presumption that certain freedoms existed. The first ten amendments to the US Constitution became the Bill of Rights. Some,

such as the right to bear arms, express the self-interest of men of property. Others transcend this squirearchical context and have become the legal norms of democratic societies, including the requirement that persons and properties should not be searched and seized without due legal cause. Yet others are of humanitarian importance, such as the rejection of cruel and unusual punishments.

Jefferson has become the legal guardian angel of American individualism, but the Civil War of the 1860s would test to destruction his reservation of powers to the individual states at the expense of the federal authority.

1776

EUROPE

April Treaty of Copenhagen between Russia and Denmark: Catherine II (the Great), tsarita of Russia, abandons her claim to the Danish duchy of Holstein-Gottorp.

12 May The victim of court intrigues, Anne-Robert Turgot, French controller general of finance (see 1774), is dismissed by Louis XVI; the French minister of the interior, Chrétien de Malesherbes, resigns the same day.

Oct. Swiss banker Jacques Necker is appointed French finance minister to replace Turgot.

– Russian military commander Grigori Potemkin, favourite and lover of Catherine II, consolidates Russia's S flank by building a fleet on the Black Sea.

– English inventor and politician David Hartley introduces the first motion into the House of Commons to outlaw slavery; the measure fails.

Adam Smith (1723–90)

The founding theorist of free-trade capitalism was born in Kirkcaldy in Fife, Scotland, and was educated at the University of Glasgow and Balliol College, Oxford. He returned to Glasgow first as a professor of logic and then as professor of moral philosophy, but it was Glaswegian commerce that provided Smith's real education.

Commerce was the inspiration for his view that goods should be allowed to move freely between states, without tariffs. Smith believed that free trade was not merely a question of making merchants rich. Competition was part of a wider freedom and prosperity, that of civil society itself. In his view, any kind of monopoly was an abuse of power that undermined competitive efficiency. His first book, *The Theory of Moral Sentiments* (1759), brought him fame and a position as tutor in the household of Charles Townshend Smith. This gave him both financial security and the time to write his most famous book, *The Wealth of Nations* (1776).

Smith saw wealth not as hoarded treasure but as potential. The wealth of nations did not depend on how much gold and silver they had, but on their productive capacity, the education of their people and their consequent potential to expand and grow. He thought that society had an innate propensity for development. Even when individuals might think they were labouring for their own benefit, a kind of cooperative logic made social sense of what they did, producing wealth and social virtue on a scale beyond their own capacity.

Smith's work was eclipsed by the doctrine of central control of the economy for much of the 20th century, but from the 1970s onwards he has returned to favour as the prophet of the free market.

THE AMERICAS

27 Feb. At the battle of Moore's Creek Bridge Scottish settlers loyal to the British crown are defeated by the rebels.

17 Mar. British troops are evacuated from Boston.

15 May The Virginia Convention instructs Richard Henry Lee, its delegate to the Continental Congress, to propose independence. Lee proposes that the colonies form a confederation and that the constitution be approved by each state. The Congress adopts Lee's resolutions.

4 July The US Declaration of Independence, drafted by Thomas Jefferson (see p. 329), is signed in Philadelphia. It affirms that 'all men are created equal' and that their 'unalienable rights' include 'Life, Liberty and the Pursuit of Happiness'. '[T]o secure these Rights, Governments are instituted among Men, deriving their just Powers from the Consent of the Governed.'

27 Aug. British forces led by Gen. Sir William Howe defeat the colonial forces at the battle of Long Island. By now the colonial army is weakened by an epidemic of smallpox. The British forces have developed immunity to the disease.

11 Sept. Howe starts peace negotiations in a meeting with American leaders John Adams and Benjamin Franklin. However, on learning of the signing of a Declaration of Independence, he suspends the negotiations.

15 Sept. Howe lands in Kips Bay and occupies New York City. American commander George Washington is forced to retreat to Harlem Heights, where he stops the British advance.

28 Oct. Howe's forces defeat Washington's army at the battle of White Plains.

20 Nov. The British take Fort Lee from the American forces and Washington has to retreat across New Jersey.

25 Dec. Washington crosses the Delaware River and gains a decisive victory at the battle of Trenton.

ECONOMY AND SOCIETY

– Adam Weishaupt forms the religious sect of the Illuminati in Ingolstadt (Bavaria), a German society of deists and republicans who reject any Church and strive to comprehend the divine through enlightened thinking.

SCIENCE AND TECHNOLOGY

– The St Leger horse race is inaugurated in Doncaster, England.

– David Bushnell, an American inventor, pioneers the submarine with his device the Connecticut Turtle.

– Swedish chemist Karl Wilhelm Scheele discovers uric acid in kidney stones.

ARTS AND HUMANITIES

Literature

25 Aug. In Edinburgh, Scotland, death of David Hume (see p. 312), philosopher, historian, economist and essayist.

– The Bolshoi Theatre, Moscow, is established.

– The Burgtheater opens in Vienna, Austria.

Edward Gibbon, *The History of the Decline and Fall of the Roman Empire* (Vol. 1 of eight), history, completed in 1788.

Friedrich Maximilian von Klinger, *Sturm und Drang* (Storm and

Stress), the play that gives its name to an early German Romantic movement that is concerned with the depiction of extravagant emotions.

Adam Smith (see p. 330), *Inquiry into the Nature and Causes of the Wealth of Nations*, economics. Smith's book emphasizes the importance of the consumer in the economic process, advocates free trade as the most efficient way of guaranteeing consumer satisfaction, and stresses the importance of governmental law as the context in which free-trade measures can be promoted.

Music
Wolfgang Amadeus Mozart, Serenade in D, *Serenata Notturna*.
Augustus Montague Toplady, 'Rock of Ages', hymn.

1777

EUROPE
5 Mar. Following the death of Joseph I (the Reformer), king of Portugal, Maria I sacks the chief minister, the marques de Pombal, who had transformed the country's finances and its educational policies, reformed the army and reduced the powers of both the nobility and the Church.

30 Dec. Maximilian III Joseph, Elector of Bavaria, dies and is succeeded by the Elector Palatine, Charles Theodore; the Holy Roman Emperor Joseph II claims Lower Bavaria.

– France and the Swiss cantons form an alliance as a safeguard against potential Austrian invasion.

THE AMERICAS
3 Jan. American commander George Washington's forces defeat the British at the battle of Princeton, New Jersey, and Gen. Benedict Arnold defeats the British in Ridgefield, Connecticut. Although Gen. John Burgoyne defeats the Americans in Hubbarton, Vermont, the American army regains the offensive and, under the command of Gen. Nicholas Herkimer, the colonialists defeat the British at the battle of Oriskany.

You cannot conquer America.

William Pitt, earl of Chatham, 20 Nov. 1777

16 Aug. The battle of Benington ends in an American victory, but Washington is defeated at the battle of Brandywine, Pennsylvania. The French marquis de Lafayette, who has left France to serve in the Continental army as a major-general, is wounded at Brandywine.

19 Sept. The first battle of Saratoga, fought between a British force under Burgoyne and an American force under Benedict Arnold, ends in stalemate.

4 Oct. Washington is defeated at the battle of Germantown (now a suburb of Philadelphia), sustaining heavy casualties.

7–17 Oct. The second battle of Saratoga, a pivotal battle of the war, shows the strength of the American position; the British commander Gen. John Burgoyne surrenders to Gen. Horatio Gates, a former British soldier who has emigrated to N America. Burgoyne withdraws to Boston.

15 Nov. Under the terms of the Articles of Confederation adopted by the Continental Congress in Pennsylvania, at least nine of the confederated states have to agree before any important measures are binding on all. Unanimous agreement is needed for any changes proposed to the original articles. The Congress has no power to tax or to regulate trade. The Congress will go on to confiscate the lands of those loyal to the British crown.

– Treaty of San Ildefonso between Spain and Portugal: Portugal lays colonial claims to vast areas in the Amazon and the Paraná plains (S America).

– Brazil's capital is transferred from Bahia to Rio de Janeiro.

ARTS AND HUMANITIES
Literature
Richard Brinsley Sheridan, *The School for Scandal*, comedy.
Music
23 Sept. First performance in Paris of Christophe Willibald Gluck's opera *Armide*.

1778

EUROPE
3 Jan. Charles Theodore, Elector Palatine, recognizes the claim of the Holy Roman Emperor Joseph II to Lower Bavaria (see 30 Dec. 1777), despite the efforts of Frederick II (the Great), king of Prussia, to persuade Charles Theodor to resist.

July King Frederick II starts the War of the Bavarian Succession against the Austria of Joseph II. The Elector Palatine, Bavaria's new ruler, has been persuaded to accept the legitimacy of the Austrian claim to Lower Bavaria and part of the Upper Palatinate. Austrian troops have therefore occupied Lower Bavaria. But Frederick II, fearful of the Austrian advance, persuades the Elector to renege on his recognition of the claim. He also persuades Saxony and Mecklenburg to join him in an anti-Austrian alliance.

ASIA
– In the course of the Anglo-Maratha War in India, East India Company administrator Warren Hastings, governor of Bengal, takes Chandernagore, Pondicherry and Mahe.

THE AMERICAS
6 Feb. The French government signs a treaty with the American colonies and recognizes their independence. The Congress ratifies the treaty.

28 June George Washington defeats the British at Monmouth, New Jersey. Washington has replaced Gen. Charles Lee who, in the heat of the battle, starts a retreat. Lee is court-martialled and then found guilty.

4 July Native Americans ally with pro-British forces to attack and kill settlers in Wyoming valley, Pennsylvania, and in Cherry Valley, New York.

29 Dec. Savannah, Georgia, falls to the colonial American forces.

AUSTRALASIA AND OCEANIA

Jan. English navigator, naval surveyor and explorer Captain James Cook is the first European to reach the Sandwich Islands (modern Hawaii, first populated by Polynesians led by Hawaii-Loa c.AD 450) and names them after the first lord of the admiralty, the 4th earl of Sandwich. Cook then explores the N Pacific coast of N America.

ECONOMY AND SOCIETY

– France begins state control of brothels: the registration and medical inspection of prostitutes become compulsory.

– The Viennese quack doctor Franz Anton Mesmer establishes himself in Paris. 'Mesmerism' will claim to effect cures by means of hypnosis and astrological 'science'. Before Mesmer is unveiled as a fraud, Mesmerism will be a success in Parisian society.

SCIENCE AND TECHNOLOGY

– English inventor Joseph Bramah, working at his factory in Pimlico, London, patents a valve and siphon flushing system that will be the technical basis of the modern lavatory.

ARTS AND HUMANITIES

Literature

30 May Voltaire (François-Marie Arouet) (see p. 304), French author, historian and philosopher, dies in Paris.

If God did not exist he would have to be invented.

Voltaire, 1 Nov. 1770

2 July Jean-Jacques Rousseau (see p. 321), French writer, philosopher and political theorist, dies in Ermenonville, France.

3 Aug. The Teatro alla Scala, Milan, opens.

Fanny Burney, *Evelina, or the history of a Young Lady's Entry into the World*, novel.

Music

Wolfgang Amadeus Mozart, Symphony No. 31 in D major (*Paris*).

1779

EUROPE

13 May The treaty of Teschen ends the war of the Bavarian Succession: it recognizes the sovereignty of Charles Theodore, Elector Palatine (see 1777), and allows Austria to retain only a small part of Lower Bavaria.

– Spain commences a seige of Gibraltar that will last until 1783.

THE AMERICAS

29 Jan. The British take Augusta, Georgia, but are then defeated by American forces at Fort Royal, South Carolina.

16 June Spain declares war on Britain. The outbreak of war follows negotiations in which Spain formally requested that Britain recognize the independence of the American colonies. Britain has rejected the request and asked that Spain end its aid to the American rebels. France agrees to help Spain recover Gibraltar (see above) and Florida.

19 July An American fleet of 19 ships leaves Boston, aiming to drive off British troops at the head of Penobscot Bay, Maine, where they are building a new fort. But the expedition ends in disaster as British reinforcements arrive from Halifax, Nova Scotia.

21 Sept. The Spanish governor of Louisiana territory (see 1763) has assembled a combined Franco-Hispanic-German-Acadian-Native American and American colonial force, which has travelled from New Orleans. At the battle of Baton Rouge he defeats the British with a surprise attack, and the engagement ends British control of the Mississippi basin.

23 Sept. Scottish-born John Paul Jones leads a Continental navy flotilla into battle with the *Serapis*, a Royal Navy frigate escorting Britain's Baltic trading fleet. The *Serapis* surrenders to the American ships.

Sept. Spanish troops begin to drive the British out of the ports of the Gulf of Florida. The French seize the islands of St Vincent and Grenada in the British West Indies.

20 Oct. The Continental Army has to abandon its 34-day siege of British forces in Savannah, Georgia.

Oct. The British evacuate Rhode Island.

– The Continental Army, led by Gen. John Sullivan, confronts and defeats the British loyalists (known as Tories), who are in alliance with the Iroquois people in the Genessee Valley, New York.

AUSTRALASIA AND OCEANIA

14 Feb. English navigator, naval surveyor and explorer Captain James Cook is killed by the indigenous people on the island of Hawaii in an argument about a stolen boat.

ECONOMY AND SOCIETY

– In England the Oaks horse race is run for the first time, at Epsom, Surrey.

SCIENCE AND TECHNOLOGY

– English inventor Samuel Crompton invents the spinning mule, which takes spinning a stage on from the spinning jenny.

– In his *Experiments on Vegetables* the Dutch scientist Jan Ingenhousz establishes the basic principles of photosynthesis.

– Italian biologist and naturalist Lazzaro Spallanzani demonstrates experimentally that sperm-carrying semen is necessary to ensure fertilization.

ARTS AND HUMANITIES

Literature

– English poets William Cowper and John Newton collaborate to produce *Olney Hymns*. Newton, curate of Olney, Buckinghamshire and a former slave-ship captain before his conversion, writes 'Amazing Grace' and 'Glorious Things of Thee Are Spoken'.

Johan Wolfgang von Goethe (see p. 359), *Iphigenie auf Tauris*, play.

David Hume (see p. 312), *Dialogues Concerning Natural Religion*, philosophy, published posthumously. Although the dialogues were written in the 1750s, their scepticism about conventional 'proofs' of God's existence made Hume wary of publication during his lifetime.

Richard Brinsley Sheridan, *The Critic*, comedy.

Visual Arts and Architecture

6 Dec. Death in Paris of the painter Jean-Baptiste Chardin.

Thomas Gainsborough, *Blue Boy*, painting (a homage to the Flemish painter Van Dyck).

Music

18 May First performance in Paris of Christoph Willibald Gluck's opera *Iphigénie en Tauride*.

Wolfgang Amadeus Mozart, Symphonies Nos. 32 and 33 and Mass in C (*Coronation Mass*).

1780

EUROPE

10 Mar. The League of Armed Neutrality: Russia attempts to prevent British ships from searching neutral vessels for contraband; the League later includes France, Spain, Austria, Prussia, Denmark and Sweden.

2–8 July London is consumed by the last major anti-Catholic riots in Britain, the Gordon Riots. Lord George Gordon leads a mob of demonstrators to Parliament in support of a petition to restore the punitive disabilities on British Roman Catholics, which were partially removed by an Act of Parliament.

20 Nov. Britain declares war on the United Netherlands to prevent it joining the League of Armed Neutrality created by Russia.

28 Nov. In Vienna, Austria, Maria Theresa, archduchess of Austria and wife of Holy Roman Emperor Francis I, dies. Her co-ruler son, Joseph II, now rules alone. He decides to abolish serfdom in Hungary and Bohemia.

ASIA

Sept. The Second Mysore War breaks out in India; Hyder Ali, ruler of Mysore, decides to support the Marathas and attacks the nawab of Arcot, a British client-prince. He also attacks the Carnatic coast (modern Karnataka in S India) where the British have been in control. Meanwhile, the Marathas attack Madras, the centre of operations for the East India Company; British troops force the Marathas to withdraw.

THE AMERICAS

12 May Charleston, South Carolina, falls to British forces led by Sir Henry Clinton.

10 July 6000 French troops, led by the comte de Rochambeau, land in Newport, Rhode Island, but are subsequently pinned down by a British blockade of their fleet.

16 Aug. British forces under Charles, Lord Cornwallis, score a major victory over the colonial forces at Camden, South Carolina.

7 Oct. The battle of King's Mountain shows that the British are losing the South: local North Carolina settlers defeat the loyalist militiamen.

– James Robinson establishes a settlement in Tennessee on the Cumberland River; it will later be named Nashville.

ECONOMY AND SOCIETY

– In England the Derby horse race is run for the first time, at Epsom, Surrey.

SCIENCE AND TECHNOLOGY

– Italian scientist Lazzaro Spallanzani becomes a pioneer of artificial insemination with his experiments on dogs.

ARTS AND HUMANITIES

– The American Academy of Arts and Sciences is founded in Boston.

Visual Arts and Architecture

Sir Joshua Reynolds *Mary Robinson as Perdita*, painting.

Music

– Sebastien Erard constructs the first modern pianoforte, in Paris.

– Sebastiano Carezo invents the bolero dance.

Joseph Haydn, Symphonies No. 53 (*L'Impérial*, Imperial), and No. 63 (*La Roxolane*).

Wolfgang Amadeus Mozart, Symphony No. 34.

1781

EUROPE

18 Mar. Anne-Robert Turgot, French economist and former controller general of finance, dies in Paris.

13 Oct. Following a campaign against the monasteries and the religious orders in his territories, Joseph II of Austria issues an edict of Toleration, giving greater religious freedom to Protestants and Greek Orthodox (and also increasing the freedom of the press). Some 700 monasteries have been closed during the past eight years, weakening the Austrian Catholic Church's links with Rome.

– Catherine II (the Great), tsarita of Russia, cedes the E half of the Balkans to Joseph II of Austria: her strategic aim is to ensure the expulsion from Europe of the Ottoman Turks.

ASIA

1 July Hyder Ali, the ruler of Mysore, is defeated by British forces at Porto Novo in the Carnatic (modern Karnataka), S India.

– Dutch colonial settlements on the W coast of Sumatra (Indonesia) are seized by the British.

THE AMERICAS

17 Jan. American forces defeat their British opponents at the battle of Cowpens, North Carolina.

3 Feb. The capital of the island of St Eustatius, Oranjestad in the

West Indies, is attacked by Britain's Admiral George Rodney: he seizes some 250 ships of different nationalities, all of which carry matériel and goods helpful to the American cause. Rodney is later deprived of his share of the loot following protests against his actions in the Westminster Parliament.

1 Mar. The Articles of Confederation and Perpetual Union are adopted by the colonies (see 15 Nov. 1777): New York and Virginia have ceded their claims to the W territories.

2 Mar. The United States in Congress (previously called the Continental Congress) assembles for the first time.

6 July Charles, Lord Cornwallis, defeats the French under the marquis de Lafayette at Jamestown Ford, Virginia, but is then forced to withdraw along the York River.

30 Aug. A French fleet sailing from the Caribbean arrives in Chesapeake Bay, Virginia, cutting off Cornwallis's troops. The Franco-American troops begin their siege of Cornwallis's position at Yorktown.

5 Sept. The French fleet in Chesapeake Bay, under François, comte de Grasse, defeats a British fleet from New York under Admiral Thomas Graves, which was attempting to relieve the British position at Yorktown.

19 Oct. The surrender of British commander Charles, Lord Cornwallis, at Yorktown marks the effective end of British rule in the American colonies and the victory of the American revolutionaries.

31 Dec. Congress establishes by charter the American republic's first incorporated bank, the Bank of North America.

– Tobago, St Eustatius, Demerara, St Kitts, Nevis and Monserrat (West Indies) fall to Franco-Spanish naval forces.

– Charles Lynch presides over illegal courts in Virginia and issues summary punishments (known popularly as Lynch's Law) in order to stop the disorder that has accompanied the end of the American Revolution. His name is subsequently applied to any hanging carried out without a proper trial of the accused.

– Spanish settlers in California establish and name the city of Los Angeles.

SCIENCE AND TECHNOLOGY

1 Jan. In England, the first iron bridge is opened at the subsequently named Ironbridge, Shropshire.

– William Herschel, a German astronomer now established in England, discovers and identifes Uranus, the first such planetary discovery since Babylonian observation.

ARTS AND HUMANITIES

Literature

Edward Gibbon, *History of the Decline and Fall of the Roman Empire*, Vols. 2 and 3, history.

Immanuel Kant (see box), *Critique of Pure Reason*, a work that establishes the conceptual basis and vocabulary of modern philosophy.

Visual Arts and Architecture

Henry Fuseli, *The Nightmare*, a vividly Gothic painting characteristic of early Romanticism.

Music

29 Jan. First performance in Munich of Wolfgang Amadeus Mozart's opera *Idomeneo, rè di Creta* (Idomoneo, King of Crete).

1782

EUROPE

5 Feb. Spain seizes the previously British-held island of Minorca in the Mediterranean.

27 Mar. In Britain, following the resignation of Lord North (19 Mar.), Charles Watson-Wentworth, 2nd marquess of Rockingham, forms a new Whig ministry and starts peace talks with the Americans. Thomas Grenville is sent to Paris to open negotiations with Benjamin Franklin, who is acting on behalf of the colonists.

Immanuel Kant (1724–1804)

Kant was born in Königsberg (then in East Prussia; now Kaliningrad in Russia), studied at the local university and became a professor of logic there. He saw himself as the 'critical' philosopher, for he tried to show the limits that philosophical enquiry had to observe if it was to be productive. His *Critique of Pure Reason* (1781) and the *Critique of Practical Reason* (1788) are the foundation stones of modern philosophy.

Kant shows that the categories of space and time determine the way our minds work. They also equip us to understand the world, for those categories are basic to the natural order as well as being the organizing principles of our minds, linking ourselves with the world we inhabit. This truth is what makes knowledge possible, but anything that lies beyond those categories cannot be described in any meaningful way. Kant's philosophy therefore abandons traditional metaphysics and closes down a whole tradition of Western thought.

Having been brought up a Lutheran, Kant retained a respect for religious sentiment but denied the possibility of knowing God through reason rather than through human experience. His practical impact has therefore been an agnostic one.

Kant was the first philosopher to produce a system that tries to underpin a theory of freedom regardless of race, creed or nationality. He regarded human beings as autonomous – which meant that they should not be treated as instrumental means to someone else's ends. His 'categorical imperative' demanded that we should only act in such a way that we wish the principle by which we act should become a universal law. This universalism makes Kant the founder of all modern theories of universal human rights.

17 May In Britain repeal of the Ireland Act of 1720 grants legislative independence to Ireland. The parliament led by Henry Grattan will, however, be elected only by Protestants.

1 July Rockingham dies and is succeeded by William Petty, earl of Shelburne, as prime minister (11 July). Petty, another Whig, is an advocate of free trade and of Catholic emancipation.

30 Nov. The preliminary treaty of Paris is agreed between Britain and the American colonies, marking the formal end of the American Revolution (see 1775).

− Serfdom is abolished in Austria.

ASIA

6 April Chao P'ya Chakri becomes King Rama I of Siam (Thailand), founding the Chakri dynasty. He makes Bangkok his capital and establishes effective rule over the country's provinces and nobles.

17 May The treaty of Salbai ends the British–Maratha War in India (fought since 1775).

7 Dec. Hyder Ali, sultan of Mysore, dies and is succeeded by his son Tipu Sultan. The Second Mysore War continues.

THE AMERICAS

12 April A British fleet commanded by Admiral Sir George Rodney defeats a French fleet in the battle of the Saints, off the coasts of Guadeloupe and Dominica in the West Indies; Rodney's victory averts the danger of a Franco-Hispanic convergence of naval forces in the Caribbean and a joint attack on Jamaica.

July The British evacuate Savannah, Georgia, and Charlestown, Massachusetts.

− The Virginia state legislature allows the manumission (freeing) of slaves.

− The two-year indigenous revolt in the Spanish viceroyalty of Peru is finally crushed by the Spanish. José Gabriel Condorcanqui assumes the name Túpac Amaru, claiming descent from the original Inca rulers, and attacks Cuzco and lays siege to La Paz. His army is defeated.

SCIENCE AND TECHNOLOGY

− Johann Goeze discovers a parasite (later named the hookworm) in a badger's intestine.

ARTS AND HUMANITIES

Literature

Fanny Burney, *Cecilia*, novel.

Pierre Choderlos de Laclos, *Les Liaisons dangereuses* (Dangerous Liaisons), epistolary (letter) novel.

Thomas Jefferson (see p. 329), *Notes on Virginia*, political philosophy.

Joseph Priestley, *A History of the Corruptions of Christianity*, religious philosophy.

Jean-Jacques Rousseau (see p. 321), *Confessions*, memoir popularizing the literary style of intimate disclosure, published posthumously.

Johann Christoph Friedrich von Schiller, *Die Räuber* (The Robbers), a revolutionary play.

Visual Arts and Architecture

George Romney, *Lady Hamilton as a Bacchante*, painting.

Music

16 July First performance in Vienna of Wolfgang Amadeus Mozart's opera *Die Entführung aus dem Serail* (The Abduction from the Seraglio).

Wolfgang Amadeus Mozart, Symphony No. 35 (*Haffner*).

1783

EUROPE

6 Feb. Spanish forces lift their siege of the British fortress of Gibraltar (see 1779).

24 Feb. The British Parliament votes to end the American war.

April In Britain a coalition ministry, consisting of the Whig duke of Portland (William Henry Cavendish Bentinck, titular prime minister), Lord North (Frederick North, 2nd earl of Guilford) and Charles James Fox, is formed. Fox, a Whig, has been the leading parliamentary supporter of the American cause (along with the Irishman Edmund Burke).

7 May British MP William Pitt (the Younger) proposes a scheme for parliamentary reform, which gains the support of foreign secretary Charles James Fox but not that of home secretary Lord North.

3 Sept. The British government signs the definitive treaty of Paris, which recognizes the independence of the 13 American colonies. The treaty also returns Florida to Spain (which also gains N America W of the Mississippi) and gives the Bahamas to Britain. France regains St Lucia, Tobago, Senegal and its East Indies colonies.

Dec. At the age of 24, William Pitt (the Younger) becomes prime minister of Britain. He is the second son of the former prime minister William Pitt (the Elder), earl of Chatham.

− Russian military commander Grigory Potemkin has now completed his conquest of the Crimea and expelled the Ottoman Turks from the region: Russia annexes the Crimea.

− Humanitarian and anti-slavery sentiment is growing in Britain: the Society of Friends (the Quakers) starts a campaign 'for the relief and liberation of the Negro slaves in the West Indies, and for the discouragement of the slave trade on the coast of Africa'.

ASIA

− Japan is struck by famine; by the end of 1784 more than 300,000 people will have died of starvation.

THE AMERICAS

25 Nov. The last British troops leave New York.

26 Nov. The US Congress meets in Annapolis, Maryland.

23 Dec. American leader George Washington resigns as commander-in-chief of the Continental Army.

− The former regular soldiers and officers of the Continental Army are granted rights to settle the lands W of the Appalachians. But the American economy, burdened by war debt, lurches into recession and inflation. Britain prohibits the import of most American produce.

SCIENCE AND TECHNOLOGY

5 June The French Montgolfier brothers, Joseph and Jacques, demonstrate their hot-air balloon's power of vertical ascent.

– In England Henry Cort invents the puddling furnace for purefying iron.

– The Spanish chemists Fausto and Juan José d'Elhuyar isolate an acid from wolframite and thereby produce metallic tungsten.

– Thomas Cawley shows that sugar is present in a patient's urine and so makes the first diagnosis of diabetes.

– Italian professor of anatomy Luigi Galvani builds an electric cell; his name leads to the coining of the English word 'galvanize', meaning to behave as if stimulated by electricity.

ARTS AND HUMANITIES

Literature

William Blake, *Poetical Sketches*, poetry.

George Crabbe, *The Village*, poem offering a realistic riposte to Oliver Goldsmith's *The Deserted Village* (see 1770).

Gotthold Ephraim Lessing, *Nathan the Wise*, play.

Noah Webster, *Grammatical Institute of the English Language*; Webster's work will standardize American spelling and is a linguistic and grammatical contribution to the new unity of the United States.

Visual Arts and Architecture

Jacques-Louis David, *The Grief of Andromache*, painting.

Thomas Gainsborough, *The Duchess of Devonshire*, painting.

Music

Wolfgang Amadeus Mozart, Symphony No. 36 (*Linz*).

1784

EUROPE

28 Feb. The 'Methodist' transformation of English Christianity and social ethics acquires a formal recognition with the signing by English evangelist John Wesley (see p. 306) of a document that provides for Methodist chapels to be established independent of the structures of the established Church of England. He starts to ordain ministers of religion.

4 July Holy Roman Emperor Joseph II of Austria repeals the constitution of Hungary in a bid to break the power of the local Hungarian nobility and create a unified Habsburg empire; Hungary loses its separate feudal law courts.

– Serfdom is abolished in Sweden by the chief minister, Andreas Bernstorm.

MIDDLE EAST AND NORTH AFRICA

6 Jan. The Ottoman Turks sign the treaty of Constantinople, which recognizes the Russian annexation of the Crimea.

ASIA

13 Aug. The India Act, drafted by prime minister William Pitt (the Younger), represents the British government's attempt to place its relationship with India on a new footing and forbids interference in indigenous affairs: the East India Company is given a new constitution and it directors are now answerable to a board that is appointed by the crown in Parliament.

– An American ship arrives for the first time in Canton (modern Guangzhou, S China); carrying a cargo of ginseng root, the *Empress of China* sails from New York and returns with bartered goods, including silk and tea.

THE AMERICAS

14 Jan. The US Congress at Annapolis ratifies the 1783 treaty of Paris; the American War of Independence is formally ended.

– The Acadians (French settlers) who have remained in Nova Scotia and New Brunswick since the Seven Years War are now removed by the British government to Maine and Louisiana.

ECONOMY AND SOCIETY

– Valentin Haily opens, in Paris, the first school for the blind.

SCIENCE AND TECHNOLOGY

– Swedish chemist Karl Wilhelm Scheele discovers that citric acid is present in some plants.

– French chemist Antoine-Laurent Lavoisier shows that matter is indestructible; the French chemist also gives new names to chemical substances.

– Experiments by English natural philosopher Henry Cavendish show the specific gravity of hydrogen and demonstrate that water is produced when hydrogen is mixed with oxygen.

– French mineralogist René-Just Haüy establishes the principles of the science of crystallography in his *Essai d'une theorie sur la structure des cristaux* (Attempt at a Theory of the Structure of Crystals).

– American statesman Benjamin Franklin, now serving as the US minister to France, invents bifocal spectacles.

ARTS AND HUMANITIES

Literature

30 July Death in Paris of Denis Diderot (see p. 315), French Enlightenment philosopher and encyclopedist.

13 Dec. In London, death of English writer Samuel Johnson, author of the *Dictionary of the English Language*.

We know *our will is free, and* there's *an end on't.*

Samuel Johnson, 16 Oct. 1769, *Life of Samuel Johnson*, Vol. 2
by James Boswell

Pierre-Augustin Caron de Beaumarchais, *Le Mariage de Figaro* (The Marriage of Figaro), play; its critique of aristocratic values seen from the point of view of a servant will later be seen as heralding the French revolutionary upheaval.

Johann Gottfried von Herder (see p. 337), *Outlines of a Philosophy of the History of Man*, philosophy.

Johann Gottfried Herder (1744–1803)

The German poet and critic Johann Gottfried Herder was born in East Prussia and studied theology at Königsberg (modern Kaliningrad in Russia) before becoming a teacher and a preacher at Riga Cathedral. He subsequently worked as an itinerant private tutor before settling in Weimar, in eastern Germany.

Herder's restless temperament is reflected in his work. As a theologian and as a literary and historical thinker, he transformed German and European thought. He espoused the unity of the human personality, the superficiality of an exclusively rationalist view of life, and the need to understand the vitality of the human relationship to nature. In elevating this organic view of human development, he provided much of the philosophical basis for Romanticism as a literary and intellectual movement.

Herder's study of folksongs broke new ground and showed their importance as historical documents illustrative of the spirit of a people. And in his studies of the Bible as literature, of Homer and of Shakespeare, he started a whole new school of thought that emphasized the vitality of a total human engagement with nature and the natural. His greatest work is his *Outlines of a Philosophy of the History of Man* (1784). Here he accepted the fact of progress in human affairs, but advanced his view that civilizations are cyclical – they are born, they grow and then they die according to an inner law of development. Like human beings, civilizations need to be understood by using intuition and empathy. By such insights, Herder rescued whole areas of experience previously dismissed as 'primitive', and advanced the recognition of human variety.

Visual Arts and Architecture

Jacques-Louis David, *The Oath of the Horatii*, painting.
Francisco de Goya (see p. 360), *Don Manuel de Zuniga*, painting.
Joshua Reynolds, *Mrs Siddons as the Tragic Muse*, painting.
Thomas Rowlandson, political caricatures.

Music

Wolfgang Amadeus Mozart, concertos for pianoforte and orchestra in E flat (No. 14), in B flat (No. 15), in D (No. 16), in G (No. 17), in B flat (No. 18) and in F (No. 19).

1785

EUROPE

23 July Frederick II (the Great), king of Prussia, forms the League of Princes to oppose Holy Roman Emperor Joseph II's Bavarian exchange scheme and preserve the status quo among German states.

15 Aug. In France cardinal de Rohan is arrested for his involvement in the affair of the diamond necklace, in which the comtesse de la Motte has intrigued with the queen, Marie-Antoinette, to get the cardinal to buy a necklace for the queen. The affair comes to symbolize the perceived frivolity of the French monarchy.

8 Nov. Territorial disputes in the Netherlands between Austria and the Dutch Republic are resolved by the terms of the treaty of Fontainebleau: Austria yields its claims to Maastricht and the mouth of the River Scheldt while being granted land in Brabant and Limburg.

ASIA

– Warren Hastings, the British governor general of India, is charged with maladminsitration and returns to Britain.

THE AMERICAS

– The US Congress decides that the dollar will be the new official currency of the United States and adopts the decimal system invented by Thomas Jefferson (see p. 329). The single currency will consolidate the USA's political union.

SCIENCE AND TECHNOLOGY

7 Jan. Jean-Pierre Blanchard, a French man, and John Jeffries, an American, make the first aerial crossing of the English Channel in a hot-air balloon.

– English physician William Withering introduces digitalis as a medical drug in his treatise *An Account of the Foxglove*.

– Antoine-Auguste Parmentier encourages the French government to promote potato cultivation.

ARTS AND HUMANITIES

Literature

James Boswell, *The Journal of a Tour to the Hebrides with Samuel Johnson*, travel literature.
Immanuel Kant (see p. 334), *Fundamental Principles of the Metaphysic of Morals*, philosophy.

Visual Arts and Architecture

– The Rezzonico Palace, Venice, is completed, work on its construction having begun in 1667.

Music

– Wolfgang Amadeus Mozart, concertos for pianoforte and orchestra in D minor (No. 20), in C (No. 21) and in E flat (No. 22).

1786

EUROPE

31 May The French cardinal de Rohan is acquitted in the affair of the diamond necklace, a scandal that rocks the French royal family (see 15 Aug. 1785). The comtesse de la Motte is found guilty and is imprisoned. However, she subsequently escapes to live abroad.

17 Aug. In Potsdam, near Berlin, Frederick II (the Great), king of Prussia, dies; he is succeeded by his nephew, Frederick William II.

– Catherine II (the Great), tsarita of Russia, establishes a safe zone, the Pale, within which Jews may settle: the Pale will extend over SW Russia and Poland.

THE SENSE OF THE NEW:
The Enlightenment and the French Revolution

The wars between Protestants and Catholics had exhausted Europe by 1648. The peace that followed marked the start of a period during which Europe's rulers concentrated on the extension of their own internal competence, although the need to protect their borders and the desire to extend them meant that wars would continue. The centuries-long struggle for dominance between sovereign rulers and dissident nobles was ending, and it was the centralizing sovereigns who won.

'Absolutism' prevailed across Europe, and the France of Louis XIV was the most spectacular example of absolutism in action. The French nobility were persuaded to give up their power in return for wealth and status. They now flocked to the royal court at the Palace of Versailles to lobby the king for position and sinecures, while the local courts and civic government dwindled in significance. The French elite established a government of ordered efficiency, while Louis XIV cultivated his image as 'the Sun King', declaring that '*L'état, c'est moi*' ('I am the state.')

Europe was also changing intellectually, as well as politically. The Scientific Revolution – beginning with Copernicus and culminating in the work of Newton – had pushed theology to the background, as experimental science gained in prestige. In the 18th century, inspired by the new empiricism, the thinkers of what became known as the Enlightenment – some of them encouraged by absolutist monarchs such as Frederick the Great of Prussia and the Holy Roman Emperor Joseph II – sought rational systems that would bring resolutions to the ills of society. Atheism remained a crime, but scepticism about God could express itself as Deism – with God relegated to the status of an ultimate but obscure source of being.

At the same time there emerged a greater curiosity about non-European forms of life and belief. In the works of Montesquieu and Voltaire this attitude revealed itself in a kind of relaxed relativism, which accepted that codes of conduct varied in different societies. And the fact that people disagreed, even within European culture, was no longer an excuse for persecution, for supposing that one person's truth had to crush another's. The modern European idea of toleration was gaining ground.

But the cultivated milieu of the sceptic at court did not last. The breakdown of order in France began as a financial crisis of government, but public opinion proved to be a newly combustible political element. The Bourbon kings in their isolated court were unable to control it. A volatile populace had watched France's prestige being undermined by military defeat at the hands of Britain and Prussia in the Seven Years' War, while economic decline, exacerbated by the loss of many of France's overseas colonies, brought unemployment and poverty for many.

In 1789 the financial crisis forced Louis XVI to summon the Estates-General of clergy, nobles and commoners to approve his tax-raising plans. But the commoners withdrew to form their own National Assembly and ignored the king's requests. Instead, inspired by Enlightenment thinking, the National Assembly abolished feudal and other privileges, while the Declaration of the Rights of Man signalled the start of a new world of citizens who had rights rather than subjects who owed duties. The threat of foreign invasion soon closed down France's first democracy, however, and the bloodshed of the Terror followed. The elegantly formulated theories of the Enlightenment were swept away.

Meanwhile, a new way of doing things was developing in the northwestern corner of Europe. In the Civil Wars and the 'Glorious Revolution', Britain had already rejected absolute monarchy. By 1707, when England and Scotland formally united, the country enjoyed a relatively stable form of government and its parliament represented the interests of the propertied. The British kings held their court in London, the economic heart of their kingdom, not at an isolated palace such as Versailles. This meant that government policy was increasingly supportive of merchants, manufacturers and innovators.

The most successful countries were those that could summon reserves of credit, and here Britain led the way with the institution of a national debt and the establishment of the

The Declaration of the Rights of Man signalled the start of a new world ...

Bank of England. Not only did such institutions encourage trade, they also provided the necessary financial infrastructure for industrialization. The Industrial Revolution was born in Britain and, during the wars against Revolutionary France, Britain used its increasing wealth to subsidize its continental allies with massive payments of gold.

Rationalist impulses united the age of Enlightenment with that of the Revolution. Subsequent European history would show the divergence between the continental tradition and the empiricism of the English in questions of government and business.

1786 *continued*

ASIA

11 Aug. Penang on the Malay Peninsula is established by the British East India Company as a trading port.

– Tokugawa Ieharu, shogun of Japan, dies. After a six-year regency he will be succeeded by his relative Tokugawa Ienari, who will rule until 1837. Military rule will collapse and governmental inefficiency increase during this period.

THE AMERICAS

– The state of Maryland allows Delaware to build a canal linking the Delaware River with Chesapeake Bay (Virginia).

ECONOMY AND SOCIETY

– Frenchmen Jacques Balmat and Michel-Gabriel Paccard become the first mountaineers to climb Mont Blanc in the French Alps.

ARTS AND HUMANITIES

Literature

4 Jan. Moses Mendelssohn, German philosopher and critic, dies in Berlin.

William Beckford, *Vathek*, an oriental Gothic fantasy.

Robert Burns, *Poems Chiefly in the Scottish Dialect*, poetry.

Visual Arts and Architecture

Sir William Chambers, Somerset House, London.

Sir Joshua Reynolds, *The Duchess of Devonshire and her Daughter*, painting.

Music

7 Feb. First performance in Schönbrunn Palace, Vienna, of Wolfgang Amadeus Mozart's opera *Der Schauspieldirektor* (The Impresario).

1 May First performance in Vienna of Wolfgang Amadeus Mozart's opera *Le nozze di Figaro* (The Marriage of Figaro); it is based on a play by Pierre-Augustin Caron de Beaumarchais (see 1784).

Wolfgang Amadeus Mozart, concertos for pianoforte and orchestra in A (No. 23), in C minor (No. 24) and in C (No. 25); Symphony No. 38 (*Prague*).

1787

EUROPE

Jan. Holy Roman Emperor Joseph II embarks on a series of political reforms in the Austrian Netherlands designed to centralize and rationalize government bureaucracy: riots ensue in the towns of Louvain and Brussels.

14 Aug. King Louis XVI banishes the *parlement* of Paris to the small town of Troyes, NE France, to curb its increasing opposition to royal policies. He recalls it in an attempt to bridge differences between the monarchy and its *parlements*.

– Catherine II (the Great), tsarina of Russia, continues her expansionist policy and embarks on a second war against the Ottoman Turks: her aim now is to incorporate Georgia within her territories.

– Britain embarks on a policy of transporting to Australia the surplus population of its overcrowded prisons.

– English politician and philanthropist William Wilberforce starts his campaign to abolish slavery in the British colonies.

– Struggling with its agricultural policy, the French government abolishes the requirement that grain sellers and producers have to take their grain to a market. Because they can now sell directly to consumers and export freely, the granaries are left without reserve supplies.

MIDDLE EAST AND NORTH AFRICA

10 Aug. In an attempt to regain the Crimea, the Ottoman (Turkish) empire declares war on Russia.

ASIA

11–18 May Food riots start at Osaka, Japan, and spread to the major Japanese urban centres. Rice warehouses and other shops are attacked.

THE AMERICAS

7 Dec. Delaware ratifies the US Constitution and so becomes the first state of the union. Pennsylvania and New Jersey follow with their state ratifications.

– A new Constitution is drawn up for the United States of America: the Constitutional Convention meeting in Philadelphia, chaired by George Washington, is charged with the task of establishing the balance of powers between the individual states and the central, federal government.

– The Convention proposes that a slave be counted as three-fifths of a free man when the states' slave populations are counted for the purposes of taxation and representation.

– Richard Allen, a freed black slave, establishes at Philadelphia the Free African Society.

ECONOMY AND SOCIETY

31 May A cricket match is played at Lord's cricket ground, London, for the first time.

– The Edict of Versailles grants a measure of religious toleration to Protestants in France. Many commercially active Protestants emigrated following the revocation (1685) of the Edict of Nantes, and the French economy has suffered as a result.

SCIENCE AND TECHNOLOGY

– US entrepreneur John Fitch launches his first steamboat on the Delaware River; James Rumsey demonstrates his steamboat on the Potomac River.

– British captain William Bligh sets sail for Tahiti on HMS *Bounty*. His aim is to obtain breadfruit plants, which can then be planted in the Caribbean islands in order to improve the food supply and the colonial economy.

ARTS AND HUMANITIES

Literature

Thomas Clarkson, *Essay on the Slavery and Commerce of the Human Species*, political philosophy.

Johann Christoph Friedrich von Schiller, *Don Carlos*, play.

Visual Arts and Architecture

Jacques-Louis David, *The Death of Socrates*, painting.

Johann Heinrich Wilhelm Tischbein, *Goethe in the Campagna*, painting.

Music

29 Oct. First performance in Prague of Wolfgang Amadeus Mozart's opera *Don Giovanni*.

15 Nov. The German composer Christoph Willibald Gluck dies in Vienna, Austria.

Wolfgang Amadeus Mozart, *Eine Kleine Nachtmusik* (A Little Night Music), serenade.

1788

EUROPE

20 Jan. The *parlement* of Paris, positioning itself as the defender of French legal and constitutional rights, presents a list of grievances to Louis XVI against the French government.

9 Feb. Holy Roman Emperor Joseph II declares war on the Ottoman (Turkish) Empire.

9 May In Britain Parliament passes a motion for the abolition of the slave trade.

June Gustav III, king of Sweden, invades Russian Finland and embarks on a two-year war that will fail to secure him the Finnish territory he seeks.

13 Aug. In an effort to preserve peace in Europe, the Triple Alliance is formed between Prussia, Britain and the Dutch Republic.

27 Aug. The financial crisis of the French state forces Louis XVI to recall Jacques Necker as his finance minister (see 1776). Louis summons the Estates-General to meet in May 1789, the first time the body has met since 1614.

Nov. Louis XVI of France summons the Assembly of Notables, including influential nobles, members of the clergy and magistrates.

10 Dec. In Britain, following George III's bout of mental illness, the House of Commons discusses the question of a regency.

14 Dec. Charles III, king of Spain, dies. As an enlightened ruler he has improved the system of roads and canals, encouraged trade development and supported the American cause. He is succeeded by his second son, Charles IV, who fails to develop his father's policies.

THE AMERICAS

21 June The Constitution of the USA comes into force after its ratification by New Hampshire. The state assemblies of Georgia, Connecticut, Massachusetts, Maryland and South Carolina have ratified the Constitution between Jan. and May. Of the remaining four states, Virginia and New York will ratify later this year, North Carolina in 1789 and Rhode Island in 1790.

13 Sept. The city of New York is proclaimed the federal capital of the USA.

– A settlement on the Ohio River is established: it will subsequently be named Cincinnati.

AUSTRALASIA AND OCEANIA

18 Jan. British prisoners arrive for the first time in Botany Bay, Australia. They are then moved to a new settlement to be called Sydney.

ECONOMY AND SOCIETY

1 Jan. *The Times* of London starts publication; English printer John Walter has published the *Daily Universal Register* since 1785 and has now changed its name.

– Following a poor harvest, French wheat and grain prices soar. Finance minister Necker is forced to suspend all grain exports, and he reinstates the requirement that all grain be sold in local markets.

– The Marylebone Cricket Club (MCC) is founded in London and draws up the rules of cricket.

– Holy Roman Emperor Joseph II orders all Austrian Jews to take official German surnames.

ARTS AND HUMANITIES

Literature

Johann Wolfgang von Goethe (see p. 359), *Egmont*, play.

Immanuel Kant (see p. 334), *Critique of Practical Reason* (*Kritik der practischen Vernunft*), philosophy.

John Lemprière, *Classical Dictionary*.

Mme de Staël (Anne Louise Necker), *Lettres sur le caractère et les écrits de Jean-Jacques Rousseau*, biography.

Music

Wolfgang Amadeus Mozart, concerto for pianoforte and orchestra in D (No. 26, *Coronation*), Symphony No. 39 in E flat, Symphony No. 40 in G minor, Symphony No. 41 in C (*Jupiter*).

1789

EUROPE

3 Feb. British prime minister William Pitt (the Younger) introduces the Regency Bill: the Prince of Wales becomes regent but with limited powers. George III soon recovers from his illness, however.

5 May The French Estates-General meets at Versailles.

6 May The French Third Estate, representing commoners, refuses to meet as a separate chamber in the Estates-General but demands representation alongside the First and Second Estates (the clergy and nobility).

17 June The Estates-General, as a representative assembly, is renamed the National Assembly. Meetings are suspended and the members retire to an adjoining tennis court where they take an oath not to split up until France is given a constitution. Members of the nobility and the clergy join the members of the Third Estate, and the National Assembly's debates are dominated by the democratic oratory of Count Honoré-Gabriel de Mirabeau, who strives to reconcile the new constitutionalism with the maintenance of the king's executive authority .

11 July The French finance minister Jacques Necker is dismissed in a royalist *coup d'état*, triggering public disturbances in Paris.

12 July In Paris the Bastille prison is attacked and falls (14 July), with only seven prisoners inside. The event marks the effective overthrow of the French monarchy and the start of the French Revolution. The tricolour flag is adopted as the French national emblem, and the marquis de Lafayette is named commander of the new National Guard.

C'est une révolte?
Non, Sire, c'est une révolution.

(Is it a revolt? No, Sire, it's a revolution.)

Louis XVI, king of France, and the duc de la Rochefoucauld-Liancourt on hearing, in Versailles, that the Bastille has fallen (12 July 1789)

15 July The Commune de Paris is formed, with French astronomer Jean Sylvain Bailly as mayor: it is responsible for municipal administration.

26 Aug. The French National Assembly adopts the Declaration of the Rights of Man and the Citizen: these rights include those of liberty, property, personal security and freedom of expression for all men. The Declaration also states that men have an equal right to resist oppression and the right to enjoy freedom from illegal arrest and imprisonment.

5–6 Oct. The Paris mob riots and a revolutionary band, composed mostly of women, marches to Versailles. The royal family are rescued by Lafayette and removed to Paris.

Oct. The Austrian Netherlands (modern Belgium) declare their independence from Vienna. Holy Roman Emperor Joseph II has proposed that the peasantry pay 12% of the value of their land in taxes to the state and 18% of the value to their feudal landlords.

MIDDLE EAST AND NORTH AFRICA

7 April Selim III succeeds his uncle Ab-dul-Hamid I as sultan of the Ottoman (Turkish) empire.

ASIA

– In an effort to reform the sex trade, the Japanese government bans mixed bathing and opens supervised brothels in the Yoshiwara area of Edo (now Tokyo).

THE AMERICAS

1 April The House of Representatives holds its first meeting. George Washington takes office at New York's Federal Hall as the first president of the United States.

– North Carolina becomes the 12th state of the union by ratifying the Constitution.

– The first US state university, the University of North Carolina, is founded at Chapel Hill. Georgetown University (in what is now Washington, D.C.) is founded as a Jesuit college by the archbishop of Baltimore, John Carroll.

ECONOMY AND SOCIETY

July The price of bread reaches 4.5 sous per pound in Paris, and more elsewhere. The National Assembly votes for duty-free grain imports to relieve the widespread hunger.

SCIENCE AND TECHNOLOGY

– In France Dr Joseph Ignace Guillotin proposes to the National Assembly that a beheading machine (originally called a Louisette after Dr Antoine Louis) be used to dispatch enemies of the revolution.

– French chemist Antoine-Laurent Lavoisier writes *Traité élémentaire de chimie* (Elementary Treatise on Chemistry), the first modern textbook on chemistry, which lists 23 elements (see 1794).

– The German chemist Martin Heinrich Klaproth discovers zinc.

– Pears soap is introduced by the London soap-maker Andrew Pears.

ARTS AND HUMANITIES

Literature

Jeremy Bentham, *An Introduction to the Principles of Morals*, philosophy developing the idea of 'the greatest happiness of the greatest number' as the basis of ethics.

William Blake, *Songs of Innocence*, poetry illustrated with his own etchings.

Visual Arts and Architecture

– The monument to St Geneviève in Paris, originally begun in 1757 and designed by Jacques-Germain Soufflot, is completed. It will be known as the Panthéon (named after the Pantheon in Rome).

1790

EUROPE

20 Feb. Holy Roman Emperor Joseph II dies in Vienna; he is succeeded by his brother Archduke Leopold, the grand duke of Tuscany, who becomes Holy Roman Emperor Leopold II.

12 July French Jews gain a grant of civil liberties.

14 July Fête de la Fédération: a rally held in the Champ de Mars, Paris, celebrates the first anniversary of the storming of the Bastille. Louis XVI accepts the new constitution drawn up by the National Assembly.

27 July Treaty of Reichenbach between Prussia, Russia, Britain and the Dutch Republic: Austria is allowed to reconquer the Austrian Netherlands, which have been in revolt since 1789.

– The French government issues *assignats* (paper money) to revive trade: they are issued on the basis of security against the confiscated property of nobles who have emigrated.

ASIA

4 July Britain forms an alliance with the nizam (ruler) of Hyderabad against Mysore; the Third Mysore War begins.

THE AMERICAS

10 April The US Congress establishes a patent office to protect the rights of inventors and to promote innovation.

17 April In Philadelphia, Pennsylvania, death of Benjamin Franklin, scientist and diplomat and one of the authors of the American Declaration of Independence and US Constitution.

– Alexander Hamilton, secretary for the treasury, chooses a new national capital for the USA on the banks of the Potomac. Congress passes an act providing for the design of the city (16 July); President Washington appoints the French-born architect Pierre Charles L'Enfant to be its designer. L'Enfant will listen to no one and his grandiose designs, although magnificent, outrun the money and everyone else's patience. Dismissed from the project, he will die penniless (1825), living on the charity of a friend, but Washington will eventually be completed according to L'Enfant's plans and will reflect the design of his native Versailles.

– Congress passes an Act that forbids the taking of lands from Native Americans without the prior approval of Congress. But many states continue with the practice.

ECONOMY AND SOCIETY

– The first carbonated beverage company is started at Geneva by Jacob Schweppe, who will later move to London.

SCIENCE AND TECHNOLOGY

– A committee is established by the Paris Academy of Sciences to institute a new and uniform system of weights and measures.

ARTS AND HUMANITIES

Literature

Immanuel Kant (see p. 334), *Critique of Judgement*, philosophy, dealing with aesthetics.

Music

26 Jan. First performance in Vienna of Wolfgang Amadeus Mozart's opera *Così fan tutte, ossia la scuola degli amanti* (Women Are All the Same, or The School for Lovers).

1791

EUROPE

29 Jan. In France revolutionary politician Honoré-Gabriel de Mirabeau is elected president of the National Assembly, but he dies (2 April) at the age of 42 and support for the French royal family wanes. Having attempted to flee to the NE frontier, Louis XVI is arrested and returned to Paris with his wife and children. The king accepts the new French constitution (14 Sept.).

21 June King Louis XVI again tries to flee France but is intercepted at Varennes and forcibly brought back to Paris.

6 July Holy Roman Emperor Leopold II issues the Padua Circular, calling on other countries to support Louis XVI against the revolutionary National Assembly.

27 Aug. Declaration of Pillnitz: the Habsburg empire and Prussia declare themselves ready to intervene in support of Louis XVI, but British prime minister William Pitt wishes to remain neutral in the French Revolution.

3 Sept. France becomes a constitutional monarchy on the passing of its new constitution by the National Assembly.

14 Oct. The Society of United Irishmen is founded by the Irish Protestant nationalist Wolfe Tone to work for Irish independence from the British state: it unites Roman Catholics and Protestants and aims for parliamentary reform.

Oct. After the dissolution of the National Assembly, the new Legislative Assembly convenes in Paris and urges war against the Habsburg monarchy, which it perceives as a threat.

Dec. Gustav III, king of Sweden, proposes to undertake a campaign against revolutionary France.

THE AMERICAS

10 June The British Parliament passes the Canada Act, which divides the country into a mainly English Upper Canada and a mainly French Lower Canada, with two elected assemblies.

15 Dec. The Bill of Rights becomes US law as Virginia ratifies the first ten amendments to the 1787 Constitution. The first guarantees freedom of religion, of speech and of the press along with the right of peaceable assembly. The second allows the right to keep and bear arms. The fifth establishes legal rights, including the right not to be compelled to be a witness against oneself in a legal case. The seventh guarantees trial by jury. The tenth reserves to the states themselves those powers not delegated to the United States by the Constitution.

– In Britain the House of Commons rejects William Wilberforce's motion to prevent further importation of slaves into the British West Indies.

– In Paris the National Assembly votes to grant blacks born of free parents the same voting rights as French citizens. But the white colonists of Saint Domingue (Haiti) refuse to obey and prepare to secede. The island's free blacks and mulattos revolt to obtain their rights. Similar revolts occur in Martinique and the British island of Dominica.

– The first Bank of the United States receives a 20-year charter from Congress, succeeding the Bank of North America (founded in 1781).

ECONOMY AND SOCIETY

5 Dec. The *Observer* starts publication in London as a weekly newspaper; it is notorious for its reporting of sensational trials.

– Camembert, a soft cheese, is invented by Mme Marie Fontaine Harel at Vimoutiers, Normandy, France.

SCIENCE AND TECHNOLOGY

– In Paris the committee of the Academy of Sciences has advised the National Assembly to establish a natural standard for the metre, making it one ten-millionth part of a quadrant of the earth's circumference. It also recommends that the gram be standardized as the weight of one cubic centimetre of water at a temperature of 4° centigrade.

– William Gregor discovers titanium in the mineral ilmenite and isolates it for the first time.

ARTS AND HUMANITIES

Literature

Thomas Paine, *The Rights of Man*, political philosophy.

Marquis de Sade, *Justine*, philosophy in the form of a fictiona-lized account of sexual cruelty.

Visual Arts and Architecture

– English furniture designer Thomas Sheraton introduces a more austere style of furniture than his predecessors Thomas Chippendale and George Hepplewhite.

Carl Gotthard Langhaus, the Brandenburg Gate, Berlin.

Music

1 Jan. The Austrian composer Joseph Haydn arrives in England. He will stay until mid-1782 and will be lionized.

6 Sept. First performance in Prague of Wolfgang Amadeus Mozart's opera, *La clemenza di Tito* (The Clemency of Titus).

30 Sept. First performance in Vienna of Mozart's opera *Die Zauberflöte* (The Magic Flute).

5 Dec. The composer Wolfgang Amadeus Mozart dies in Vienna, leaving his D minor *Requiem* Mass unfinished (it will later be completed by his pupil Franz Süssmayr).

Joseph Haydn, Symphonies Nos. 94 (*Surprise*) and 96 (*Miracle*).

1792

EUROPE

7 Feb. Austria and Prussia (who support Louis XVI)) ally against revolutionary France.

1 Mar. Holy Roman Emperor Leopold II dies in Vienna; he is succeeded by his son Francis II, who is also, as Francis I, the first emperor of Austria.

23 Mar. In France the Girondist party forms a government.

20 April France declares war on Austria.

8 July France declares war on Prussia.

10 Aug. In Paris the revolutionary Georges Danton inspires a mob to attack the Tuileries Palace, massacring the Swiss Guard. The Legislative Assembly suspends the king's authority. A new revolutionary Commune shares power in Paris with the Legislative Assembly. The marquis de Lafayette is declared a traitor (19 Aug.) and flees to Liège in the Austrian Netherlands, where he is captured by the Austrians.

12 Aug. The French royal family is imprisoned on the order of the Legislative Assembly.

19 Aug. The Legislative Assembly dissolves all religious orders and institutes civil marriage and divorce.

Aug. Prussian and Austrian troops under Charles William Ferdinand, duke of Brunswick, invade France. The Prussians will be comprehensively defeated by French revolutionary forces at Valmy, SW of Reims (20 Sept.).

21 Sept. The French National Convention (a body that replaces the Legislative Assembly) meets and votes to abolish the monarchy. It decrees perpetual banishment for French émigrés.

22 Sept. The National Convention in Paris proclaims France a republic; a revolutionary calendar is introduced.

19 Oct. French forces led by the comte de Custine pursue the retreating Prussians as far as Mainz and Frankfurt am Main. Another French army takes Brussels and occupies the Austrian Netherlands.

Nov. In France the radical Jacobin party under Georges Danton ousts the moderate Girondists.

5 Dec. The trial opens of King Louis XVI of France before the National Convention in Paris.

– The Girondin government in France issues more *assignats* (paper money), to finance the war; inflation increases.

– Thomas Paine, in a new edition of his 1791 pamphlet *The Rights of Man*, urges the overthrow of the British monarchy. He is indicted for treason and escapes to France, where he is made an honorary citizen of the Republic.

MIDDLE EAST AND NORTH AFRICA

– Bubonic plague in Egypt claims over three-quarters of a million lives.

ASIA

– In India Tipu Sultan of Mysore cedes half of his territory (modern Karnataka) to Britain.

ECONOMY AND SOCIETY

17 May The New York Stock Exchange starts to operate inform-ally (see 1825).

– Denmark becomes the first country to abolish slavery.

SCIENCE AND TECHNOLOGY

– Having observed that long-staple sea island cotton (unlike upland short-staple cotton) can easily be separated from its seeds, American Eli Whitney invents a cotton gin. The cylinder he produces means that a slave can clear 23kg (50 pounds) of 1 pound).

ARTS AND HUMANITIES

Literature

Mary Wollstonecraft, *A Vindication of the Rights of Woman*, a pioneering feminist tract.

Music

Joseph Haydn, Symphonies Nos. 97 and 98.

Claude-Joseph Rouget de Lisle, 'La Marseillaise', song that becomes the anthem of revolutionary France.

1793

EUROPE

21 Jan. In the Place de la Révolution (later renamed the Place de la Concorde) Louis XVI of France is executed by guillotine. He has been tried before the National Convention, which has voted for his execution by 683 to 38 votes.

23 Jan. Poland is partitioned for the second time: Prussia takes Danzig while Russia takes Lithuania and the W Ukraine.

1 Feb. The French Republic declares war on Britain, the United Provinces and Spain; it annexes the Austrian Netherlands (modern Belgium). Britain, Austria, Prussia, the Netherlands, Spain and Sardinia form the First Coalition against France (13 Feb.) For Britain this is the start of two decades of warfare against France, during which Britain will fund a number of anti-French coalitions.

6 April In France the revolutionary politicians Maximilien Robespierre (see box) and Georges Danton establish (and head) the Committee of Public Safety, which has dictatorial powers.

24 April The French radical Jean Paul Marat is acquitted after a trial instigated by the Girondins (moderate republicans). He will now join Robespierre and Danton in overthrowing the Girondins and presses for a radicalization of the revolution, but a noblewoman and Girondin sympathizer, Charlotte Corday, horrified by all the executions, stabs him to death in his bath (13 July), a scene to be recorded in Jacques-Louis David's famous portrait. Corday is brought before the revolutionary tribunal and guillotined four days later, aged 25.

July The final overthrow of the Girondins ushers in a period of mass persecution and suppression of their opponents by Robespierre's Jacobins: it is known as the Reign of Terror.

23 Aug. The French republic imposes a levy on all men capable of bearing arms.

28 Aug. The comte de Custine (see Oct. 1792) is executed on a charge of treason: the Prussian army has recovered Mainz, with the allies taking Condé and Valenciennes. The British lay siege to Toulon.

16 Oct. The French queen, Marie-Antoinette, is executed, as are 21 Girondist deputies (31 Oct.).

Oct. Lyons falls to republican forces after a two-month siege: the city is devastated and much of the population massacred.

Dec. With the defeat of the British at Toulon, Corsican-born Napoleon Bonaparte (see p. 357) emerges as a national figure. He is promoted to the rank of general of brigade.

– A royalist rebellion breaks out in the Vendée, W France, after the revolutionaries attempt to conscript peasants into the national army. The revolt is brutally dealt with by by generals Louis-Marie Turreau and François Westermann. Between 300,000 and 500,000 are killed. The Jacobin judge Jean-Baptiste Carrier orders the execution of 13,000 in Nantes. The rebel army is crushed at Savenay (23 Dec.).

THE AMERICAS

12 Feb. Congress passes the Fugitive Slave Act, making it illegal to harbour or help a runaway slave to freedom.

25 Feb. President George Washington (re-elected this year for a second term) convenes the first US cabinet meeting, which consists of the secretaries of state for treasury and war, the attorney general and the postmaster general.

22 April Despite pressure from New York lawyer and politician Alexander Hamilton to support the British and from Thomas Jefferson to support the French, President George Washington decides to issue a Proclamation of Neutrality in the war in Europe.

– Scottish explorer and fur trader Sir Alexander Mackenzie reaches the Pacific, becoming the first European to cross the N American continent.

– The moderate former bishop of Autun, Charles Talleyrand, arrives in the USA to escape the Terror.

ECONOMY AND SOCIETY

10 Nov. The French republic abolishes worship of the Christian God. Jacques-René Hébert promotes a cult of reason as a substitute.

– The French government fixes wages and introduces maximum prices to stop the catastrophic inflation that has followed the fall in the value of the *assignats* (paper money).

– Samuel Slater lays the foundations of the US cotton industry by recreating from memory the machines he used as a textile worker in England.

– France makes education compulsory for all children from the age of six.

Maximilien Robespierre (1758–94)

Maximilien Robespierre, the French revolutionary who invented state terrorism, was a provincial lawyer from Arras in Picardy who had turned to politics. Robespierre's power base was the Committee of Public Safety, which was charged with the task of safeguarding the new republic against royalist agents. His central message, derived from Rousseau, was that the 'general will' should prevail over the individual. He proclaimed himself to be the mere servant of that will, and the sole love he professed was for an abstract idea of 'humanity'.

Robespierre defined 'the people' as only those citizens who were politically engaged patriots. Acting in their name, he also decided on their behalf what was, and was not, politically virtuous. He used both law and terror to instil 'correct' belief, and he systematized the idea of a 'counter-revolution' whose adherents had to be killed in the name of the state. Dubbed 'the Incorruptible' on account of his personal austerity, Robespierre terrified both liberals and conservatives by showing how mass democracy could be manipulated to totalitarian ends.

The terror Robespierre invented was entirely different from the occasional and capricious savagery of despots. It was instead a bureaucratic arm of government – calculated, ideological and implacable. From April 1793 until July 1794 Robespierre and his supporters at the radical Jacobin club ruled France. His own eloquent rhetoric, as well as the genuine fears of a royalist return, ensured his dominance at the National Convention. He had an adroit understanding of how technology can aid ideology: the swift and efficient guillotine anticipates the gas-chamber. In the spring of 1794 he launched the Cult of the Supreme Being, an alternative religion full of mystical enthusiasm for its object of worship – revolutionary humanity. The initiative showed the depth of Robespierre's manipulative insight into the psychology of the new collectivism.

ARTS AND HUMANITIES
Literature
Thomas Paine, *The Age of Reason*, an attack on Christianity from a deist point of view.

Friedrich von Schiller, *Die Geschichte des dreissigjährigen Krieges* (The History of the Thirty Years War), history, which the great German poet and critic had begun in 1791.

Visual Arts and Architecture
Jacques-Louis David, *The Death of Marat*, painting.

Music
Joseph Haydn, symphony No. 99 in E flat.

1794

EUROPE
Mar. Tadeusz Kosciuszko, a veteran of the American Revolution, attempts a Polish uprising, but it is suppressed by Russian and Prussian forces.

April Maximilien Robespierre (see p. 344) ensures that his rivals (and former friends) Georges Danton and Camille Desmoulins are sentenced to death and guillotined.

8 June Robespierre presides over the festival of the cult of the Supreme Being (a new official religion based on the philosophy of Rousseau). He is elected president of the National Convention in this same month.

26 June French military forces drive the duke of Coburg from Belgium.

28 July A conspiracy led by Louis Fouché topples Robespierre from power, along with his associate Louis Saint-Just. Both are guillotined, and the Reign of Terror comes to an end.

25 Oct. Prussia withdraws from the war against France.

– France becomes the first country to free its slaves when the French Legislative Assembly votes to free slaves in the French colonies. Slaves in the French colony of Saint Domingue (Haiti) rise under the leadership of Pierre Toussaint L'Ouverture. There are 500,000 slaves on the island and some 40,000 whites. Producing two-thirds of the world's coffee and half of its sugar, the colony accounts for one-third of French commerce.

MIDDLE EAST AND NORTH AFRICA
– The rebellion of Agha Mohammad Khan establishes the Qajar dynasty, which will rule Persia until 1925. The death of Lutf Ali Khan ends the Zand dynasty, established in 1750.

SCIENCE AND TECHNOLOGY
– French chemist Antoine-Laurent Lavoisier becomes a victim of the revolutionary Terror when he is guillotined as a tax farmer.

– The Ecole Normale for the training of baccalaureate (school leaving certificate) teachers is established in Paris. The Ecole Polytechnique becomes the world's first technical college, specializing in applied science and mathematics.

– At Carmarthen, Wales, the ironmaster Philip Vaughan patents radial ball bearings for the axle bearings of carriages.

– A British naval squadron shows the truth of James Lind's theory on the prevention of scurvy. Having sailed from Britain for Madras with a plentiful supply of lemons, it arrives 23 weeks later with only one seaman suffering from scurvy.

ARTS AND HUMANITIES
Literature
William Blake, *Songs of Experience*, poetry.

Johann Gottlieb Fichte, *Foundation of the Whole Theory of Science*, philosophy replacing the God accepted by Immanuel Kant (see p. 334) with an 'absolute mind'.

Music
Feb. The Austrian composer Joseph Haydn visits London again. He has been commissioned to write six new symphonies for the impresario Johann Peter Salomon.

– The Welsh popular song 'Gwŷr Harlech' (Men of Harlech) is published in London and claimed to be a song composed during the 15th-century English siege of the Welsh castle in the Wars of the Roses.

Joseph Haydn, Symphonies Nos. 100 in G major (*Military*) and 101 in D major (*Clock*).

1795

EUROPE
19 Jan. French forces under Charles Pichegru occupy Amsterdam in the United Provinces of the Netherlands, capture the Dutch fleet at Texel and establish the Batavian Republic, which will last until 1806.

21 Feb. The National Convention formally separates Church and state in France.

1 April On 12 Germinal of the revolutionary calendar, inflation leads to bread riots in Paris.

5 April Peace of Basle between France and Prussia: France retains its conquests on the left bank of the Rhine (pending peace with the Holy Roman Empire) and Prussia receives territories on the right bank. Other German states, including Saxony and Hanover, also agree terms with France.

23 April In Britain Warren Hastings, after a seven-year trial, is acquitted by the House of Lords for misconduct while governor general of India (1773–85). He has been made a scapegoat for the offences of the East India Company.

28 Sept. Britain, Russia and Austria join in the Alliance of St Petersburg against France.

5 Oct. Parisian rioters are dispersed by successful French Gen. Napoleon Bonaparte's (see p. 357) 'whiff of grapeshot'. The National Convention dissolves (26 Oct.) and the Directory of Five (including Paul-François Barras, initially an admirer of Napoleon), assumes office and will rule France until 1799.

24 Oct. Poland is partitioned for the third time: Russia takes the remainder of Lithuania and the Ukraine; Prussia takes Warsaw; Austria receives the remainder of the region of Cracow. Poland has ceased to exist.

25 Nov. Stanislaw II Augustus Poniatowski of Poland abdicates after the third partition of his country.

Nov. In Britain, after an attack on King George III, prime minister

William Pitt (the Younger) passes the Treasonable Practices and Seditious Meetings bills, which prohibit meetings of more than 50 people without prior notice to a magistrate.

SCIENCE AND TECHNOLOGY
– Scottish geologist James Hutton's *Theory of the Earth* develops the modern theory of the formation of the earth's crust.

ARTS AND HUMANITIES
Literature
William Blake, *Songs of Innocence and Experience: Shewing the Two Contrary States of the Human Soul*, poetry.

Marquis de Condorcet, *Tableau historique du progrès de l'esprit humain* (Historical Account of the Progress of the Human Spirit), philosophy, published posthumously. He proposes the perfectibility of humankind and describes the progress achieved to date.

Visual Arts and Architecture
Francisco de Goya (see p. 360), *The Duchess of Alba*, painting.

Music
29 Mar. In Vienna Ludwig van Beethoven (see p. 356) performs as soloist in his own Piano Concerto No. 2 in B flat, marking his debut as a composer and virtuoso.

– The Paris Conservatoire de Musique is founded.

Joseph Haydn, symphonies Nos. 103 in E flat (*Drumroll*) and 104 in D (*London*).

1796

EUROPE
9 Mar. In a civil ceremony the victorious French general Napoleon Bonaparte (see p. 357) marries Josephine, widow of the vicomte de Beauharnais, who was guillotined in July 1794.

Mar. British prime minister William Pitt (the Younger) enters negotiations for peace with France.

13 April Napoleon Bonaparte takes command of the French campaign against the Austrians in Italy: he defeats an Austrian force at Millesimo (13 April) and the Piedmontese at Modovi (22 April). Savoy and Nice are ceded to France. Napoleon enters Milan (15 May) and sets up the Lombard republic, having conquered the whole of Lombardy as far as Mantua.

10 May The journalist François Babeuf, leader of a conspiracy to overthrow the Directory in France, is arrested. He will be executed in 1797.

17 Nov. In Tsarskoye Selo, near St Petersburg, Russia, Catherine II (the Great), tsarita of Russia, dies; she is succeeded by her son, who becomes Paul I.

15 Dec. A French invasion fleet intended for Ireland leaves Brest, but a storm disperses the fleet of 43 ships and 15,000 men.

– British forces seize Ceylon (Sri lanka) and gain control of the Dutch Spice Islands (modern Indonesia) except Java.

ASIA
– China's Manchu emperor, Qianlong, abdicates after a 60-year reign. He has established Chinese control over Tibet, invaded Burma and Nepal, and established trade with the USA at Canton.

THE AMERICAS
17 Sept. US president George Washington declares in his farewell address that: 'It is our true policy to steer clear of permanent alliance with any portion of the foreign world.' Lawyer John Adams is elected president after a closely fought contest with Thomas Jefferson (see p. 329), who becomes vice-president.

SUB-SAHARAN AFRICA
21 June Scottish explorer Mungo Park reaches the Niger and is the first European to travel in the W African interior.

ECONOMY AND SOCIETY
– Amelia Simmons writes *American Cookery*, the first cookbook to contain indigenous American recipes.

SCIENCE AND TECHNOLOGY
– French astronomer Pierre-Simon Laplace, in his *Exposition du système du monde* (Account of the System of the World), posits that the solar system has been formed from a cloud of gas.

– English country doctor Edward Jenner develops the use of vaccination against smallpox using cowpox fluid.

ARTS AND HUMANITIES
Literature
Fanny Burney, *Camilla, or, A Picture of Youth*, novel.

Mme de Staël, *De l'influence des passions* (On the Influence of the Emotions), literary and psychological theory, written on the Necker family estate at Coppet, Lake Geneva, where she has fled to escape from the French Revolution.

Richard Watson, *An Apology for Christianity*, religious philosophy written in reply to the sceptical arguments of Thomas Paine's *The Age of Reason* (published in 1793).

1797

EUROPE
4 Jan. Napoleon defeats the Austrians at the battle of Rivoli, on the River Adige in Italy.

2 Feb. Mantua in Italy falls to the French after a six-month siege. Romagna, Bologna and Ferrara are ceded to France in the treaty of Tolentino (19 Feb.), concluded with Pope Pius VI.

9 July The French proclaim a Cisalpine republic, which includes Milan, Modena, Ferrara, Bologna and Romagna, while the republic of Genoa becomes the French puppet state of the Ligurian republic.

4 Sept. Republicans gain control of the Council of Five Hundred in Paris. The Directory is purged of royalists.

17 Oct. Treaty of Campo Formio: Austria cedes the Austrian Netherlands to France and, under secret articles, also cedes the left bank of the Rhine. Austria gains Venice, including the city itself and Venetian territory up to the Adige.

16 Nov. Frederick William II, king of Prussia, dies after a reign that has seen Prussia having been forced to cede all territory W of the Rhine. He is succeeded by his son, who becomes Frederick William III.

MIDDLE EAST AND NORTH AFRICA

- Agha Mohammad Khan of Persia, is assassinated. His nephew, Fath Ali Shah, succeeds.

ECONOMY AND SOCIETY

- An earthquake in Cuzco, Peru, kills over 40,000 people.
- Britain issues its first £1 notes and copper pennies.
- Cuban cigar makers make 'cigarettes' using paper wrappers to make small cigars.
- James Keiller of Dundee, Scotland, produces and packs the world's first commercial marmalade.
- The city of Quito in New Granada (modern Ecuador) is destroyed by an earthquake, killing 41,000 people.

SCIENCE AND TECHNOLOGY

- German chemist Martin Klaproth discovers and identifies cerium, titanium and zirconium as separate elements.

ARTS AND HUMANITIES

Literature

François-René de Chateaubriand, *Essai sur les révolutions* (Essay on Revolutions), history comparing ancient and modern revolutions.

Johann Wolfgang von Goethe (see p. 359), *Hermann und Dorothea*, pastoral epic.

Immanuel Kant (see p. 334), *Die Metaphysik der Sitten* (The Metaphysics of Morals), philosophy.

Visual Art and Architecture

- English painter Joseph Wright of Derby dies.

Joseph Mallord William Turner, *Moonlight: A Study at Millbank*, painting.

Music

13 Mar. First performance in Paris of Luigi Cherubini's opera *Médée* (Medea), which has a libretto by François-Benoît Hoffman based on the tragedy by the 17th-century French dramatist Pierre Corneille.

Joseph Haydn, 'Gott erhalte den Kaiser' (God Save the Emperor), hymn sung for the first time on the emperor's birthday. It will become the Austrian national anthem.

1798

EUROPE

Jan. France's Council of Five Hundred meets in the semicircular assembly hall of Louise-Françoise de Bourbon (the illegitimate daughter of Louis XIV). Since the most conservative Council members sit on the right and the revolutionaries on the left, the terms 'left', 'right' and 'centre' gain their modern meanings.

11 Feb. French forces under Napoleon Bonaparte (see p. 357) occupy Rome, and he proclaims a Roman republic. Pope Pius VI refuses to surrender his temporal power and leaves for Valence, France (15 Feb.), where he will die in 1799.

29 Mar. Swiss revolutionaries proclaim the Helvetian republic, a staunch ally of the French model. Geneva is annexed by France (16 April).

23 May United Irishmen and Catholic Irish nationalists rebel against British rule. At the battle of Vinegar Hill (21 June) the United Irishmen are defeated. A French army sent to support them surrenders to a British force under Charles, 1st Marquis Cornwallis (15 Sept.).

29 Nov. Ferdinand IV, king of Naples (Ferdinand I, king of the Two Sicilies), declares war against France and occupies Rome. As a result, France declares war on the kingdom of Naples (4 Dec.).

MIDDLE EAST AND NORTH AFRICA

19 May Napoleon sails from Toulon for Egypt. His army, accompanied by a retinue of scholars, archaeologists, historians and linguists, arrives in Egypt (1 July) and captures Alexandria (2 July). The Egyptian Mamluk cavalry are defeated at the battle of the Pyramids near Cairo (21 July) and Cairo falls (22 July), giving Napoleon control of Egypt.

1 Aug. At the battle of the Nile, a British fleet under Admiral Horatio Nelson destroys the French fleet, isolating Napoleon's Egyptian army from its homeland.

THE AMERICAS

- The so-called Alien and Sedition Acts are passed by a Federalist-controlled US Congress, anxious to clip the wings of Democratic-Republican journalists. They consist of the Naturalization Act (18 June), which increases the qualification period for US citizenship; the Alien Act (25 June), which allows President Adams to expel alien 'subversives'; the Alien Enemies Act (6 July), which permits the president to imprison, during time of war, any enemy subject living in the USA; and the Sedition Act (14 July), which forbids anyone from 'aiding any insurrection, riot, unlawful assembly or combination'. This last Act effectively suppresses editorial criticism of the president. All the Acts, except the Alien Enemies Act, will be repealed by 1802.
- Vice-President Thomas Jefferson's (see p. 329) opposition to the Alien and Sedition Acts inspires the Kentucky (16 Nov.) and Virginia (24 Dec.) Resolutions, passed by the legislatures of these two states. The Resolutions are key expressions of states' rights, and assert that individual states are the ultimate guardians of the liberty of the individual, and that the state legislatures have the right to declare Acts of Congress illegal when the federal government has acted unconstitutionally.

SCIENCE AND TECHNOLOGY

- Eli Whitney heralds US mass production with his 'jigs', metal patterns that guide machine tools, allowing exact replicas of manufactured items. Whitney gets a US army contract to deliver 10,000 muskets made from interchangeable parts.
- English country doctor Edward Jenner (see 1796) describes vaccination as a safer form of protection against smallpox than earlier methods of inoculation (see 1721). To prevent a negative public reaction to the idea of inoculation with an animal disease he uses the Latin word for cow (*vacca*) in his *Inquiry into the Causes and Effects of the Variolae Vaccinae*. A grateful British Parliament rewards Jenner with grants, and in France Napoleon orders that a medal be struck in his honour.

- Paper mill worker Louis Robert develops a machine that can make paper from wood pulp in a continuous roll.
- The Bavarian printer Aloys Senefelder develops lithography (invented in 1796), in which ink is used in dampened areas of a greased printing base, from which impressions are then taken.
- In his *Essay on the Principles of Population* English clergyman Thomas Malthus advances the theory that population grows geometrically while food production grows arithmetically. Malthus argues for population control and attacks proposals to reform the Poor Laws as inevitably doomed.

ARTS AND HUMANITIES

Literature
Charles Brockden Brown, *Wieland or the Transformation*, American 'Gothic' novel.
Samuel Taylor Coleridge and William Wordsworth (see p. 353), *Lyrical Ballads*, a poetic collaboration whose blank verse rebels against the formality of 18th-century poetic style and diction. Wordsworth's 'Lines composed a few miles above Tintern Abbey' becomes a major statement of the revolution in poetry that starts from the conviction that nature is a religious force that educates mankind in larger feelings of sympathy.
Maria Edgeworth, *Practical Education*, educational theory illustrating the reasoning of childhood by recording the conversations of children with their parents.

Music
- First performance in Vienna of Joseph Haydn's oratorio *Die Schöpfung* (The Creation).
Ludwig van Beethoven (see p. 356), Piano Sonatas Nos. 5–7.

1799

EUROPE
9 Jan. British prime minister William Pitt's income tax bill is passed by Parliament. Introduced to finance the war against France, the tax is levied at 10% on incomes above £200 and at reduced rates on incomes from £60 to £199.
22 Aug. Napoleon Bonaparte (see p. 357) leaves his army in Egypt (see below) to take command of French forces in Europe; he lands in Fréjus, SE France (9 Oct.).
26 Sept. The Russian army is driven out of Zurich in the Helvetian republic by the French. Russia subsequently withdraws from the anti-French coalition.
19 Nov. Assisted by Talleyrand and Emmanuel-Joseph Sièyes, Napoleon becomes First Consul of France in a *coup d'état* (the coup of 19 Brumaire in the revolutionary calendar). The Constitution of the revolutionary Year VIII is endorsed overwhelmingly in a referendum (24 Dec.), and the Directory is replaced by Napoleon's one-man rule.

MIDDLE EAST AND NORTH AFRICA
Feb. French forces under Napoleon Bonaparte invade Syria after the Ottoman empire declares war on France. The French take Jaffa but are repelled at the Syrian coastal city of Acre (Akko), which is defended by Ottoman troops aided by British forces

under Sydney Smith. Following an outbreak of plague in his army, Napoleon retreats to Egypt.
25 July Napoleon (see p. 357) and Joachim Murat defeat the Turkish force landed at Aboukir Bay, Egypt, but French forces under Barthélemy Joubert are defeated at the battle of Novi in Italy (15 Aug.). Napoleon leaves for Europe (22 Aug.), leaving his army in Egypt under the command of Jean-Baptiste Kléber.

THE AMERICAS
14 Dec. In Mt Vernon, Virginia, death of George Washington, commander-in-chief during the American Revolution and first president of the USA (1789–97). His two presidential terms have witnessed the emergence of political parties in the USA.
- John Fries leads a rebellion of French-Americans in protest against a US tax levied in anticipation of a US declaration of war on France. Federal troops march into Philadelphia and Fries is sentenced to death, but is later pardoned by President Adams.

ECONOMY AND SOCIETY
29 Aug. In Valence, France, Pope Pius VI dies.
- Bubonic plague strikes in N Africa and kills 300,000 people.
- Scottish explorer Mungo Park's *Travels in the Interior of Africa* is published.
- The Royal Military Academy, Sandhurst, is founded for the education of British officers.

SCIENCE AND TECHNOLOGY
- Philippe Lebon pioneers methods for producing inflammable gas from wood, and thereby gas lighting.
- English chemist Sir Humphry Davy produces nitrous oxide ('laughing gas') and suggests its use as an anaesthetic.

ARTS AND HUMANITIES
- A French army engineering officer, Capt. Boucard, discovers at Rosetta a block of basalt chiselled with Greek characters, Egyptian hieroglyphs and Egyptian demotic. The so-called Rosetta Stone will be used as the key to deciphering hieroglyphic writing and with it the history of ancient Egypt.

Literature
18 May Death in Paris of Pierre-Augustin Caron de Beaumarchais, French dramatist.
- First performance in Paris of Friedrich von Schiller's great trilogy of historical dramas *Wallenstein's Lager* (Wallensteins Camp), *Die Piccolomini* and *Wallenstein's Tod* (The Death of Wallenstein). Schiller has written the plays in 1797 and 1798.

Visual Arts and Architecture
Jacques-Louis David, *Les Sabines* (The Rape of the Sabine Women), painting.
Francisco de Goya, *Los Caprichos*, etchings satirizing Spanish society and the Church, subsequently seized by the Inquisition.
James Hoban, the executive mansion at Washington, D.C.

Music
- Ludwig van Beethoven completes his Piano Sonata No. 8 in C minor (*Pathétique*).
Joseph Haydn, Mass No. 10 in B flat (*Theresienmesse*).

3

The Nineteenth-
Century World

3. The Nineteenth-Century World

Educated Europeans in the 19th century often described the period in which they were living as an age of progress. The reach of European political and economic power and its ability to influence and shape the rest of the world according to its wishes were certainly the dominant facts of the century. European imperialism, already a force for three centuries past, now reached its peak of development.

In 1830 French troops invaded Algeria to suppress piracy, and the French acquisition of African colonies came to be seen as compensation for the loss of the French empire in North America. Later in the century, after their unification, Germany and Italy attempted to found similar power bases in Africa, as did the kingdom of Belgium. All these European countries now joined the older established empires of the Portuguese, Dutch and British.

Technological advances gave a new power and range to European economic development. Railways, steamships and the telegraph made the world a smaller place, giving populations a greater mobility and enabling an enormous increase in trade. There were also great advances in manufacturing processes, and by the end of the century electricity was replacing steam as the main source of power. More and more people were leaving the countryside to live and work in the factories of the growing towns. Politically, Europe also saw the birth of dynamic new nation-states – Italy was unified in 1870 and Germany the following year. Nationalism – inspired by the Romantic movement of the early 19th century – was one of the key political doctrines of the age.

The developments acclaimed as progress by Europeans suited their particular viewpoint. Europeans dominated the rest of the world in the 19th century – either directly from Europe or indirectly through the United States of America, which was mostly populated by Europeans. European capital financed the building of the colonial infrastructure, including roads and railways along which goods could now be transported. The European diet improved as foodstuffs, such as grain from North America and beef from South America, produced cheap and nutritious meals for the European table. The demands of European trade shaped the economies and political fortunes of the colonial populations, often disrupting indigenous cultures and economic systems.

The early 19th century had seen the emergence in Africa of powerful indigenous states such as the Zulu in the south and the Samori empire and the Hausaland Islamic state in the west. But these developments were cut short by the subsequent encroachment of European power, first in its commercial form and then in its settled and colonial form.

The Berlin Conference of 15 European states in 1884 effectively partitioned the whole of Africa. The great powers had been engaged in a 'scramble for Africa' as they pursued their own competitive interests across the continent. In Berlin they met to adjudicate and agree on the consequences of that scramble and to allocate to each other 'spheres of influence'. The new borders – often straight lines that ran for hundreds of miles – rarely reflected the reality of the boundaries between different ethnic groups, so storing up problems for post-colonial Africa.

In 1877 Britain annexed the Transvaal in southern Africa, a previously independent Afrikaaner state run by immigrants of Dutch descent. Two years later the British sought to pre-empt a feared strike on their southern African territories by the Zulu empire. The first British invasion ended in ignominious defeat at the battle of Isandhlwana (1879), and the huge resources of the British empire had to be brought to bear to defeat the Zulu. Almost immediately, the British were faced with a new uprising, this time by the Afrikaaners. The Afrikaaners took back the Transvaal in the First Boer (or South African) War of 1880–1 and then lost both it and the adjacent republic of the Orange Free State to Britain in the Second Boer War of 1899–1902. British power now straddled Africa 'from the Cape to Cairo'. In Britain's most distant colonies, the aboriginal peoples of Australia and the Maori of New Zealand also lost control of their own lands.

In India by the end of the century the British empire had became a fully administrative institution rather than a primarily commercial endeavour. This transformation had come about as a result of the Indian Mutiny of 1857, when the Indian troops employed by the British East India Company rose in a violent revolt that was put down only with great difficulty and after much bloodshed. The British government decided that strategic control of India was henceforth too important to be left in the hands of the British East India Company, the commercial enterprise that had hitherto ruled it, and so sovereignty over Company-ruled territories was transferred to the British crown in 1858. Henceforth India was in the hands of the Indian Civil Service, which sought both to administer Britain's lands and to work cooperatively with the many independent states that remained in India.

In Latin America uprisings led to the collapse of the two European colonial powers in the region. Portugal ceded independence to Brazil in 1825, and by 1824 only Cuba and Puerto Rico remained of the vast Spanish territories in the New World. But the new regimes in Latin America remained thoroughly colonial in economic and social terms. European cultural hegemony in these Latin American countries in fact increased as immigration rates soared in the post-liberation years and European and US businesses settled in to run the region's economies. In 1823 the USA announced the Monroe Doctrine, under which it would resist all attempts by European powers to interfere in the American hemisphere.

The USA began the century as a relatively unimportant new entity but ended it as an economic giant. The purchase from France of the Louisiana territory in 1803 had doubled the country's size and made possible the expansion of new settlements and commercial power right across the continent, at the expense of the indigenous peoples. But this expansion also put strains on the unity of the country. Those who believed in the authority of the central government found it difficult to respect the powers of the individual states to organize their own internal policies. The crunch came over slavery, the basis of the economy in the Southern states but illegal in the Northern states. The North's victory in the Civil War of 1861–5 was a victory for a particular kind of society: that of urban-based industry, mass democracy and largely unregulated economic development.

Russia's assumed role as the champion of pan-Slav identity remained one of the great themes of European politics in the 19th century. The ideology of pan-Slavism began largely as a way of justifying tsarist control over a disparate group of peoples in the face of rising nationalism. It proved useful in the contest with the Ottoman empire for control of the Black Sea and neighbouring lands, but was more of an embarrassment when it led to hostility to the Austrian empire from the 1870s onwards. Russia saw itself as the standard-bearer of the Orthodox faith and was a consciously conservative society. Economically, however, Russia continued to modernize itself – albeit slowly – and this inevitably produced some social changes, such as the emancipation of the serfs. The exploitation of Siberia and Russia's push into central Asia showed that Europe's last fully functioning autocracy could still be intermittently effective.

The political successes of the more democratic Western European states were not just the result of adroit diplomacy. Their power derived to a great extent from scientific advances that had led in turn to new industrial technologies. And at a popular level too there was a widespread belief in science as the answer to human problems. Science was reducing disease, improving hygiene and extending life itself, but it was also a powerful solvent of old certainties – as in the case of Charles Darwin's theory of evolution. If there was faith in progress and a better future, there was also, especially from the mid-century onwards, a pervasive mood of religious doubt as well as fear of disorder from below.

From 1871 onwards Europe was a largely peaceful continent. A wave of heavy industrialization saw production of coal, steel and iron soar, as countries such as Germany and France began to catch up on Britain's earlier industrial revolution. But this period of international peace and growing prosperity was also a time of challenge to internal political order throughout the European continent. The emergent trade union movement organized industrial workers to protest against poor working and living conditions, while more extreme anarchist and syndicalist movements sought nothing less than the downfall of the established order. Frightened governments tried to alleviate the emerging discontent by passing social legislation, such as the introduction of national insurance and state pensions. Free primary education became the norm in western Europe by 1900, and was provided by governments that wanted to educate the population into respectability and orderliness as well as in literacy and numeracy. It had been a very good century for some, but by its end the foundations of order were beginning to look precarious both within and beyond the boundaries of the European nation-states.

If there was faith in progress and a better future, there was also ... a pervasive mood of religious doubt as well as fear of disorder from below.

1800

EUROPE

13 Feb. The Bank of France is established by First Consul Napoleon Bonaparte (see p. 357) to improve the administration of public finance. To avoid national bankruptcy he raises 5 million francs from French and Italian bankers, establishes a national lottery and reduces ministerial budgets.

14 Mar. Luigi Barnabà Chiaramonte is elected Pope Pius VII.

14 June Napoleon wins a narrow but decisive victory over the Austrians at the battle of Marengo in Lombardy, NW Italy, having advanced through the Great St Bernard Pass with over 40,000 men (May). France is now poised to reconquer the rest of Italy, and in Paris Napoleon's political and military authority is confirmed.

1 Aug. The royal assent is given by King George III to the Act of Union, passed in the British and Irish Parliaments in March. It will come into effect on 1 Jan. 1801. (British prime minister William Pitt has used bribery to persuade the Irish parliament (see 1782) to vote itself out of existence.)

3 Dec. French general Jean-Victor-Marie Moreau, commander of the Army of the Rhine, wins a decisive victory over the Austrians at Hohenlinden, S Germany, effectively ending the War of the Second Coalition and leading to the treaty of Lunéville (see Feb. 1801).

MIDDLE EAST AND NORTH AFRICA

24 Jan. Convention of El Arish (al-Arish), NE Sinai: General-in-chief Jean-Baptiste Kléber (left behind when Napoleon returned to France; see 22 Aug. 1799) and Ottoman representatives agree to a French withdrawal from Egypt under terms agreed by the British naval commander. The terms are, however, repudiated by a senior British officer, Admiral Lord Keith. Keith's action encourages French resistance, leading to further conflict.

20 Mar. French forces defeat the Ottomans at Heliopolis.

14 June Gen. Kléber is assassinated in Cairo.

THE AMERICAS

7 May Congress, the national legislature of the USA, passes the Division Act, which creates the Indiana Territory (later state) out of the Northwest Territory.

17 Nov. The US Congress meets for the first time in Washington, D.C., the new federal capital and centre of government removed from New York.

– The rebel slave leader 'General Gabriel', also known as Gabriel Prosser, prepares to attack Richmond and take control of the state of Virginia in the USA's first slave uprising. The uprising is thwarted by bad weather and the mobilization of the state militia.

– German naturalist and geographer Alexander von Humboldt explores the Orinoco River, which, with its tributaries, is one of the four main river systems of S America. He proves it is connected to the Amazon by the Casiquiare Channel.

– The settlement that will develop into the city of Ottawa (now capital of Canada) is founded in SE Ontario.

– Thomas Jefferson, a Democratic Republican, gains a narrow victory in the US presidential election. After he ties with the Federalist candidate, Aaron Burr, with 73 votes, the election is taken to the House of Representatives. After 35 ballots, the opposition to Burr of Alexander Hamilton, the Federalists' leader, makes Jefferson president (from March 1801). Burr becomes vice-president (1801–5). Hamilton's action earns him the bitter hatred of Burr (see 1804).

SCIENCE AND TECHNOLOGY

– Alessandro Volta, Italian physicist, invents the electric storage battery and gives his name to the unit of electrical potential, the volt.

– In Britain Richard Trevithick, Cornish pioneer in the important new field of steam engineering, builds an engine to be used to power a vehicle on the road.

– Sir William Herschel, German-British astronomer, discovers infrared rays. Invisible beyond the red light of the sun's spectrum, they are shown to be necessary for the radiation of heat.

ARTS AND HUMANITIES

– The Library of Congress, the world's largest national library, is established in Washington, D.C., as the main repository of published works in the USA.

Literature

– In Britain the *Lyrical Ballads* of 1798 by William Wordsworth (see p. 353) and Samuel Taylor Coleridge are republished in a new edition with a preface by Wordsworth that expands on his belief in poetry as an alternative source of knowledge.

– In Britain the poet and hymn-writer William Cowper dies.

Maria Edgeworth, *Castle Rackrent*, novel.

Friedrich von Schiller, *Maria Stuart*, play.

Visual Arts and Architecture

Jacques-Louis David, *Madame Récamier*, painting.

Thomas Girtin, *The White House at Chelsea*, painting; its naturalism and use of strong colour influences the development of the 19th-century watercolour style.

Music

– First performance in Vienna of Ludwig van Beethoven's Symphony No. 1 in C major and Piano Concerto No. 1 in C major.

1801

EUROPE

1 Jan. In Britain the Act of Union comes into force, creating the United Kingdom of Great Britain and Ireland. Ireland will remain part of the United Kingdom until 1922.

9 Feb. The treaty of Lunéville is signed, ending the phase of the war between France and Austria that followed the battle of Marengo (see 14 June 1800). France's expanded frontiers, incorporating the Rhine, Alps and Pyrenees, are officially recognized, and the Italian republic is created (see 1802).

14 Mar. Britain's youngest ever prime minister, William Pitt (aged 24 in 1783), resigns as prime minister after George III

William Wordsworth (1770–1850)

Wordsworth, regarded by some as the greatest poet of the English Romantic movement, was born in Cockermouth in England's Lake District, and the landscape of his childhood would become the spiritual inspiration of his poetic maturity.

Wordsworth was educated locally and at St John's College, Cambridge. In 1790 he visited France and became a supporter of the democratic principles of the Revolution. In the summer of 1798 he worked with his fellow poet Samuel Taylor Coleridge on their joint production, *Lyrical Ballads*, which was to become the manifesto of English Romanticism. In 1799 Wordsworth settled back in the Lake District, in the village of Grasmere. It was here that he set to work on his great poetic testament and central achievement, *The Prelude*, a posthumously published (and uncompleted) spiritual autobiography in blank verse. Wordsworth was appointed Poet Laureate in 1843, but his literary output declined in his later years.

Wordsworth changed the language of poetry by proving that poetry could be written in 'a selection of the real language of men' and by using characters who were often humble or anonymous. The effect was democratic, for he showed that spiritual grandeur was to be found in the most ordinary of circumstances. He also made nature into a kind of religion for those liberals who could no longer believe in Christianity. In this respect his work was part of a reaction against the rationalism of the 18th century. In his poetry the conventional distinctions between form and content, between thinking and feeling, break down and are merged into a celebration of the sublime. He made literature and the work of the imagination into something deeply moral, an education of the human heart and mind. In doing so he introduced into English literature a quality of deep seriousness.

refuses to grant Roman Catholic emancipation. He is succeeded by Henry Addington, later 1st Viscount Sidmouth.

23 Mar. Tsar Paul I of Russia is murdered by army officers in a *coup d'état* designed to end four years of deranged rule and an erratic foreign policy, which had fluctuated between support for, and opposition to, France. He is succeeded by his eldest son Alexander I, who will make peace with Britain and later join the coalition against Napoleon (1805).

2 April The Danish fleet is defeated by the British at the battle of Copenhagen, aimed at preventing Danish neutrality circumventing the blockade of France. British Rear-Admiral Horatio Nelson, who is blind in one eye, pretends not to see the signal to withdraw ordered by his superior officer Sir Hyde Parker, who is recalled. Nelson assumes command of the fleet in May and is created a viscount the following month.

– German banker Mayer Amschel Rothschild becomes financial adviser to the landgrave of Hesse-Cassel. As agent for the British crown, he will organize payments supporting the European opposition to Napoleon.

THE AMERICAS

4 Mar. In Washington, D.C., the new US capital, Thomas Jefferson is installed as the third president of the USA, succeeding the Federalist John Adams. He will hold office until 1809.

SUB-SAHARAN AFRICA

– Osei Bonsu becomes *asantehene*, king of the Asante (Ashanti) in what is today S Ghana, W Africa. He is an able ruler and aggressively extends the limits of the Asante empire, leading to conflict with British forces on the Gold Coast.

ECONOMY AND SOCIETY

– Censuses taken in 1800 and 1801 show that China has a population of 295 million, India 131 million, the Ottoman empire 31 million, Japan 15 million, France 27.4 million, the German states collectively 14.1 million, Britain 10.4 million, Ireland 5.2 million, Spain 10.5 million, Egypt 2.5 million and the USA 5.3 million. The world population is estimated to be 900 million. Guangzhou (Canton) in China is the world's largest city with more than 1.5 million people. Nanjing (Nanking), Hangzhou (Hangchow) and the Japanese capital Edo each has a population of 1.5 million. London is Europe's largest city with 864,000 inhabitants. Constantinople has 598,000, Paris 548,000, and Kyoto (Japan) 530,000. Isfahan (Persia), Lucknow (N India) and Madras (S India) have 300,000 each, Manchester (England) 75,000, and New York 60,500.

– The University of South Carolina is established in the USA; it is one of the earliest higher education institutions in the country.

SCIENCE AND TECHNOLOGY

– French silkweaver Joseph Jacquard develops the automatic Jacquard loom, enabling relatively unskilled weavers to produce intricately designed silk textiles. He is awarded a pension by Napoleon.

– Cornish engineer Richard Trevithick's steam road vehicle (see 1800) is completed and used for the first time to carry passengers.

– The metric system of measurement is adopted and made compulsory by France's National Convention; the rest of continental Europe follows, but Britain and the USA continue with the imperial system.

ARTS AND HUMANITIES

Literature

– In Germany the Romantic poet Novalis (Friedrich Leopold von Hardenberg) dies.

François-René, vicomte de Chateaubriand, *Atala*, a tragic romance set among the native Americans of Louisiana.

Johann Pestalozzi, *Wie Gertrud ihre Kinder lehrt* (How Gertrude Teaches her Children), work of educational theory arguing that a child's development is based on observation, which drives comprehension and intellectual development.

Visual Arts and Architecture
– Italian sculptor Antonio Canova starts work on his most ambitious and expressive sculpture, *Perseus with Medusa's Head*.

Jacques-Louis David, *Napoleon Crossing the Alps*, painting, one of a series glorifying Bonaparte's exploits.

Joseph Mallord William Turner, *Calais Pier*, painting.

Music
– The Italian Niccolò Paganini, considered to be technically one of the greatest violinists, takes virtuosity to new heights in a rapturously received concert tour.

– Joseph Haydn, Mass No. 9 in D minor (*Missa in angustiis*). It will become known as the Nelson Mass, though Haydn has written it without knowing of Nelson's victory at the battle of the Nile.

– First performance in Vienna of Joseph Haydn's oratorio *Die Jahreszeiten* (The Seasons).

Ludwig van Beethoven (see p. 356), *Die Geschöpfe des Prometheus* (The Creatures of Prometheus), music for ballet. He completes his Piano Sonata No. 14, later nicknamed *Moonlight* after a description used by the mid-century poet and musicologist Heinrich Rellstab.

1802

EUROPE
26 Jan. Following the Franco-Austrian treaty of Lunéville (see 9 Feb. 1801) the N Cisalpine republic, established by France in April 1797, is renamed the Italian republic, with Napoleon Bonaparte (see p. 357) as president. This French satellite state annexes Piedmont (21 Sept.) and then Parma and Piacenza (Oct.).

27 Mar. Treaty of Amiens between France, Britain, Spain and the United Provinces ends the War of the Second Coalition (1798–1801) and brings a short lull in European conflict. Spain gives up Trinidad to Britain, the Dutch cede Ceylon to Britain, and the British give up all recent conquests to France and its allies. Hostilities will resume, however, on 16 May 1803.

19 May Napoleon creates the Légion d'honneur, a new republican order of merit, which rewards civil and military service to the state.

2 Aug. Napoleon is named First Consul for life and granted the right to nominate his successor.

– Napoleon reintroduces slavery in the French colonies, and his brother-in-law, Charles Leclerc, is sent to Haiti in the Caribbean to suppress the local slave rebellion. Leclerc sends Toussaint L'Ouverture, hero of black emancipation (see 1794), to France, where he dies in prison.

– In Britain the Health and Morals of Apprentices Act forbids cotton mills from hiring pauper children under the age of nine. Their working day is limited to 12 hours and they are not allowed to work at night.

– Following the treaty of Amiens, the British Parliament repeals income tax, a main method of financing the war with France; it is reintroduced in 1803.

THE AMERICAS
– John Marshall becomes chief justice of the USA; his court will establish fundamental principles for interpreting the US Constitution.

– The US Military Academy is established at West Point, New York state.

ECONOMY AND SOCIETY
– The Swiss wax modeller Marie Tussaud, commissioned to make death masks of the famous during the Paris Terror of 1792–3, begins touring Britain with her life-size waxworks. Madame Tussaud's later becomes a permanent London attraction (1835).

SCIENCE AND TECHNOLOGY
– English chemist John Dalton provides a clarification of atomic theory with his table of atomic weights. He has also given his name to colour blindness (Daltonism).

– The astronomer William Herschel discovers that some stars revolve around other stars (binary pairs).

– Friedrich von Humboldt, a German naturalist, discovers the nitrogen potential of guano, the droppings of seabirds, in islands off the W coast of S America. Its high nitrate content makes it ideal for use in fertilizer and explosives, and Peru will export huge quantities to Europe.

– Italian scientist Gian Domenico Romagnosi observes that an electric current flowing through a wire will cause a magnetic needle to line up perpendicularly with the wire. He is the first person to link electricity and magnetism.

– The *Charlotte Dundas*, built by Scottish engineer William Symington, is launched on the Clyde (W Scotland) and becomes the world's first commercially viable steam vessel.

– Thomas Wedgwood, son of the famous English potter Josiah, produces the first photograph achieved by sensitizing a paper with moist silver nitrate.

ARTS AND HUMANITIES
Literature
François-René, vicomte de Chateaubriand, *Le Génie du christianisme* (The Genius of Christianity), work of Christian apologetics.

Walter Scott, *Minstrelsy of the Scottish Border*, a collection of Scottish ballads, his first major publication.

Visual Arts and Architecture
9 Nov. Thomas Girtin, influential British painter in watercolours, dies at the age of 27.

15 Nov. Death of George Romney, one of the foremost British painters of his day.

1803

EUROPE
16 May The war between France and Britain resumes; the French Army of England is mustered and an invasion fleet assembled in Boulogne is ready to cross the Channel.

– Irish patriot Robert Emmet leads a rebellion against British rule in Ireland and tries to seize the viceroy. He is captured (25 Aug.) and hanged (20 Sept.).

THE AMERICAS

14 Feb. In the case of Marbury vs. Madison, US chief justice John Marshall establishes that any act of the US Congress that conflicts with the Constitution is null and void.

30 April The USA dramatically doubles its territory with the Louisiana Purchase. Charles Maurice de Talleyrand, now France's foreign minister, needs money for France's war and sells its American territories to the USA for 80 million francs. The US border now extends as far W as the Rocky Mountains. President Thomas Jefferson, however, has made the purchase without consulting the Senate, and Massachusetts and New York threaten to secede from the Union.

ECONOMY AND SOCIETY

– Eli Whitney's cotton gin is now boosting demand, and as cotton becomes profitable South Carolina starts to import slaves again. Cotton now exceeds tobacco as the chief US export crop.

– Thomas Moore, a Maryland farmer, patents the first ice refrigerator. His icebox consists of one wooden box placed inside another with the space between insulated with ashes.

– Abortion becomes a statutory crime in Britain.

SCIENCE AND TECHNOLOGY

– French chemist Claude-Louis, comte de Berthollet, joins the late Antoine Lavoisier in developing the modern nomenclature for chemical elements pioneered in his *Essai de statique chimique*.

– In Scotland building work begins on the 96km (60 mile) long Caledonian Canal linking the Atlantic Ocean and North Sea. It is designed by Scottish engineer Thomas Telford, one of the foremost civil engineers of the day.

– Morphine is isolated and named after the Greek god of dreams by the German pharmacist Friedrich Sertürner.

– An anti-personnel explosive shell, developed by the artillery officer Henry Shrapnel, is adopted by the British army.

ARTS AND HUMANITIES

Visual Arts and Architecture

– In Ottoman-occupied Greece, Thomas Bruce, 7th earl of Elgin, seeing that they are in danger of destruction, starts to remove parts of the marble frieze from the Parthenon in Athens (see 438 BC). Over the following nine years they are shipped to London and are kept in the British Museum as the Elgin Marbles.

Music

Ludwig van Beethoven (see p. 356), Symphony No. 2 in D major and Piano Concerto No. 3 in C minor. His Violin Sonata in A major (*Kreutzer*) sets new standards of complexity in sonata form.

1804

EUROPE

20 Mar. The duc d'Enghien (the French émigré leader) is shot at Vincennes after being condemned without a trial for organizing a French royalist conspiracy against Napoleon Bonaparte.

21 Mar. The Code Civil des Français (later known as the Code Napoléon), drafted by jurist Boulay de la Meurthe, is promulgated and applied throughout France and its occupied territories. As a code of civil law it builds on the traditions of Roman law and affects inheritance, mortgages, contracts and rights of property. French law becomes the basis of European law. However, in regarding an accused person as guilty until proven innocent it departs from US and British law.

18 May The French Senate and Tribunate proclaim Napoleon (see p. 357) as emperor, and a national referendum confirms the decision by a vast majority.

2 Dec. Napoleon is consecrated in Paris by Pope Pius VII in a grandiose ceremony designed to recall the coronation of Charlemagne in AD 800.

– King Francis I of Austria, Hungary and Bohemia (and Holy Roman Emperor Francis II) takes the title emperor of Austria.

– Spain, allied to France, declares war on Britain.

– Although rust destroys the English wheat crop and the price of bread rises, the British Parliament will not reform the protectionist system that discourages the import of foreign grain. This benefits the landed class, who dominate government, at the expense of consumers and adds to the growing demand for free trade.

THE AMERICAS

25 Sept. By the 12th amendment to the Constitution, a separate electoral ballot is required for the offices of US president and vice-president.

– The W part of the island of Hispaniola in the Caribbean becomes the independent republic of Haiti following a successful slave revolt and the defeat of an army sent by Napoleon to suppress it (see 1802).

– The former treasury secretary and US statesman Alexander Hamilton is killed in a duel with his bitter rival, Vice-President Aaron Burr (see 1800), following an alleged insult. Indicted in New York and New Jersey, Burr flees to Philadelphia and then to the South.

– US explorers Meriwether Lewis and William Clark start their expedition (1804–6) to explore the territory of the Louisiana Purchase made by the USA. They begin the ascent of the Missouri River to determine whether there is a river system linking the Pacific with the Gulf of Mexico.

SCIENCE AND TECHNOLOGY

– Frederick Winsor exploits Philippe Lebon's invention (1799) and demonstrates gas lighting in London.

ARTS AND HUMANITIES

Literature

– William Blake's poem 'Jerusalem' appears in the preface to the poet's long mythological poem *Milton* (written and etched 1804–8).

Friedrich von Schiller, *Wilhelm Tell*, play, which becomes an important statement in support of Swiss liberty in the face of Austro-German political designs.

Ludwig van Beethoven (1770–1827)

The career of the German composer Ludwig van Beethoven spanned the transition from classicism to Romanticism in music. He was born in Bonn, the son of a musician in the service of the Elector of Cologne. He studied briefly with Joseph Haydn in Vienna, and remained there for the rest of his life. His first fame was as a virtuoso performer on the keyboard, but as soon as he started to publish his own work his genius as a composer was immediately acclaimed.

Beethoven's work is the supreme example of Romanticism's readiness to express immediate feeling and subjective states of mind. His Symphony No. 3, the *Eroica* (1804), is a landmark in the history of Western music because it changed the symphonic structure and made it more flexible. Symphony No. 9, Beethoven's last, broke the symphonic rules by including a choral finale. Beethoven lived through the French Revolutionary and Napoleonic Wars, and was initially drawn to the democratic cause. Both he and his music have come to be seen as expressing the dynamic individualism of a modern age in which every man is a hero.

Beethoven's personality was, in the Romantic tradition, a wilful one, but he showed that a new idea of the genius had arrived in Europe – one that was both scornful of social and artistic convention and inspired by the inner law of its own creativity. The force of his personality made self-expression a fundamental element in music. The slow movements of his symphonies and concertos gave music a new, meditative quality, and the dissonances and formal explorations of his last string quartets anticipate the 20th-century avant-garde.

Music

– Ludwig van Beethoven (see box), Symphony No. 3 in E flat (*Eroica*); it was originally entitled *Bonaparte,* but, having republican sympathies, Beethoven angrily retracted the dedication on learning that Napoleon was to become emperor of the French.

1805

EUROPE

30 Mar. Admiral Pierre de Villeneuve breaks the British naval blockade of Toulon with the aim of providing protection for the French flotilla centred on Boulogne during the projected invasion of England. Lacking confidence to enter the Channel, he allows British admiral Horatio Nelson to blockade his fleet in the harbour of Cadiz, S Spain.

11 April Treaty of St Petersburg: Britain and Russia agree to set up a European league to liberate the N German states and Italy, and to defend the Netherlands, Switzerland and Naples. Britain will finance Russia and other members of this Third Coalition against France. Austria and Sweden will join the Third Coalition on 9 Aug. Napoleon (see p. 357) will be supported in the ensuing War of the Grand Alliance (1805–7) by Spain, Baden, Bavaria and Württemberg, Hesse and Nassau.

26 May In a ceremony of feigned antiquity, Napoleon Bonaparte, First Consul for life (1802) and self-declared emperor of France (1804), crowns himself in Milan Cathedral with the iron crown of the kings of Lombardy. His stepson Eugène de Beauharnais is named viceroy.

He had to happen. Don't let us haggle over greatness.

Charles de Gaulle discussing Napoleon with André Malraux, 1969

27 Aug. Napoleon despairs of naval support for the invasion of England and orders his army to leave Boulogne (N France) for Germany. He forces an Austrian surrender at Ulm (20 Oct.) and occupies Vienna.

21 Oct. British admiral Horatio Nelson's fleet intercepts and defeats the combined French and Spanish fleet of French admiral Pierre de Villeneuve off Cape Trafalgar near Gibraltar, destroying French naval power. Nelson's battle order declares that 'England expects every man to do his duty', and in the midst of the conflict he is himself killed by a French sharpshooter.

2 Dec. At Austerlitz in Moravia (modern Czech Republic), Napoleon inflicts a crushing defeat on the combined Austrian and Russian armies, which helps persuade Prussia not to join the Third Coalition. By the treaty of Pressburg (26 Dec.), Austria cedes Piedmont, Parma and Piacenza (all N Italy) to France, and the Tyrol (W Austria) and Augsburg (S Germany) to Bavaria, which, along with Württemberg (S Germany), becomes a kingdom in its own right. Baden is made a grand duchy. By the treaty of Schönbrunn (15 Dec.) Prussia cedes Cleves, Neuchâtel and Ausbach, and accepts France's acquisitions of territory in Germany and Italy.

Dec. Napoleon issues a proclamation ejecting the Bourbons from the throne of the kingdom of Naples.

MIDDLE EAST AND NORTH AFRICA

– The Albanian Mehmet Ali intrigues against the Mamluk rulers of Egypt and, following a popular uprising, is confirmed as viceroy of Egypt by the Ottoman sultan Selim III.

THE AMERICAS

4 Mar. Thomas Jefferson begins his second term as US president.

Nov. The American transcontinental expedition led by explorers Meriwether Lewis and William Clark reaches the Pacific coast (see 1804).

– Part of the Indiana territory is subdivided to create the territory (later state) of Michigan, USA.

ECONOMY AND SOCIETY

- Prussia abolishes internal customs duties to liberalize and improve its economy.
- A novel citrus fruit, the tangerine, starts to be exported from Tangier in Morocco to Britain and the rest of Europe, where it becomes widely popular.

SCIENCE AND TECHNOLOGY

- American shipowner Frederic Tudor pioneers the export of ice in insulated ships from the USA to Cuba, the Caribbean and S American ports.

ARTS AND HUMANITIES

- Haileybury College in Hertfordshire, England, is founded to train agents for the East India Company.

Literature

- The poet William Wordsworth completes the first version of his long autobiographical poem *The Prelude*. After much alteration, it will be published posthumously in 1850.
Walter Scott, *The Lay of the Last Minstrel*, poem.

Music

20 Nov. First performance in Vienna of Ludwig van Beethoven's (see p. 356) only opera *Fidelio, oder Die eheliche Liebe* (Fidelio, or Married Love).

1806

EUROPE

10 Feb. In Britain, following the death of Pitt the Younger (who has died on 23 Jan. on hearing of Napoleon's (see box) victory at Austerlitz), the Ministry of all the Talents is formed, with Lord Grenville as premier and Charles James Fox as foreign secretary.

6 May Britain announces a blockade of the Atlantic coast of continental Europe as far N as the River Elbe: the ships of neutral nations can trade freely if they are not carrying goods to and from French or French-allied ports.

12 July After one thousand years the title of Holy Roman Emperor is dropped by the ruler of Austria at Napoleon's insistence: Francis II continues to reign as emperor of Austria. The Confederation of the Rhine (Bavaria, Württemberg, Mainz, Baden and eight minor principalities) is established, bringing most German states under French rule and making war between France and Prussia inevitable.

14 Oct. Napoleon's forces defeat the Prussian army at the battles of Jena and Auerstädt in Saxony; Napoleon occupies Berlin (27 Oct.) and announces (21 Nov.) a blockade of Britain and closure of all continental ports to British trade. This is known as the Continental System: British textile mills begin to shut down as US supplies of raw cotton dwindle.

- Napoleon embraces the dynastic principle: he places his elder brother Joseph on the throne of Naples (30 Mar.) and his younger brother Louis on the throne of the United Provinces (formerly the Batavian republic; see 1795) (5 June).

THE AMERICAS

3 Sept. The Lewis and Clark expedition (see 1804) returns to St Louis, Missouri. It takes its place as an important milestone in the history both of US pioneering and of US natural sciences.

- Francisco de Miranda, Venezuelan resistance leader, fails in a national rebellion against Spanish rule.

SUB-SAHARAN AFRICA

- In the war against France and its allies, British troops recapture Cape Town, Cape Colony, from the Dutch. It becomes a permanent part of the British empire and will be officially ceded to Britain (see 1814).

ECONOMY AND SOCIETY

- The French blockade cuts off Britain from the supplies of French and oriental silk used to make strong warp threads for

---

Napoleon Bonaparte (1769–1821)

France's first emperor was born in Corsica and attended the military academy at Autun. Here the young artillery officer absorbed two potent French traditions of thought and endeavour. The first was the conviction – prevalent since the 17th century – of the glory of establishing French predominance in Europe by military means. But it was the second tradition, that of the 18th-century Enlightenment, that convinced Bonaparte of his country's unique mission to civilize its enemies as well as to subjugate them.

In the 1790s Bonaparte showed his abilities as a general in a series of victories over the enemies of revolutionary France. His successes encouraged him to launch a coup on 9 November 1799 against the republican government. He instituted an autocratic regime, installed himself (in 1804) as the Emperor Napoleon I, and strengthened central government. But the new system, and Napoleon's own example, also encouraged the meritocratic ascent of the talented. His civil laws, the Code Napoléon, prescribed a system of individual rights and legal equality that has inspired many other legal systems. Napoleonic France, with its exemplary bureaucratic efficiency and administrative clarity, can be regarded as the first modern European state.

Napoleon's military successes helped to popularize a cult of the relentless will, and Napoleon's turbulent personality was attuned to the new Romantic movement and its taste for dynamically reinvented lives. His downfall was the force he had himself helped to create: the nationalism of the countries occupied by his armies. He died in exile, having been defeated by an alliance of European powers at Waterloo (1815), but Bonapartism, a powerful political mythology inspired by Napoleon's unique combination of formidable intellect and unscrupulous force, outlasted him. Bonaparte's life would inspire for generations the dreams of ambitious men born in ordinary circumstances – and the idea of a liberal dictator has proved enduringly alluring.

cotton looms, but Patrick Clark in Paisley, Scotland, has developed a substitute cotton thread, and commercial production now starts.

– The social reformer and enlightened industrialist Robert Owen closes his New Lanark mill near Glasgow because of the French disruption of British cotton imports but continues to pay his workers full wages.

– William Colgate opens a soap manufactory at New York, USA.

ARTS AND HUMANITIES
Literature

– Noah Webster, *The Compendious Dictionary of the English Language*, the first Webster's dictionary, is published in the USA. Friedrich Hölderlin, 'Patmos', German lyric poem.
Anne and Jane Taylor, *Original Poems for Infant Minds*, collection of verse for children, including 'Twinkle, Twinkle Little Star'.

Visual Arts and Architecture

10 July The British painter and engraver George Stubbs, famous for sporting pictures, particularly of horses, dies in London.

22 Aug. Jean-Honoré Fragonard, eminent French rococo painter before the Revolution, dies in poverty; the Revolution leaves no clients for his style of painting.

– English architect John Nash starts work on the redesign of central London under the patronage of the Prince Regent (whose mistress is Nash's wife, Mary Ann).

– In Paris work begins on the Arc de Triomphe, to commemorate Napoleon's victories of 1805–6. It will be completed in 1836.

1807

EUROPE

7 Jan. The British government prohibits the ships of neutral nations from trading with France; the Royal Navy blockades French ports.

7–8 Feb. Prussian and Russian forces fight the French at Eylau in E Prussia; the engagement ends indecisively.

18 Mar. Strategic concerns in the war with France lead to a British occupation of Alexandria (Egypt); failure to defeat the Ottoman forces of Mehmet Ali results in the British withdrawal six months later.

24 Mar. George III dissolves Parliament rather than grant civil rights to British Roman Catholics. The Whig Ministry of all the Talents falls, and the duke of Portland (a Whig) becomes the (largely nominal) premier of a fractious Tory administration.

26 May The French occupy Danzig (Gdansk, Poland) and (14 June) defeat the Russians at the battle of Friedland in E Prussia. Napoleon (see p. 357) goes on to occupy Königsberg (now Kaliningrad, Russia).

7–9 July Napoleon concludes the treaty of Tilsit with the Russian tsar Alexander I and the Prussian king Frederick William III on a raft in the Neman River, ending the War of the Third Coalition. Prussia cedes to Napoleon all lands between the Rhine and the Elbe and recognizes the sovereign rule of his brothers in their respective European countries. Napoleon

agrees to Alexander's mediation in negotiating a peace with Britain. Russia recognizes the Grand Duchy of Warsaw, restores Danzig as a free city and agrees to Napoleon's mediation in concluding peace with the Ottoman Turks.

Sept. Copenhagen is bombarded by the Royal Navy, the Danes having joined the Continental System and closed their ports to British shipping (see 1806). Denmark allies itself with France and, following the treaty of Tilsit, Russia declares war on Britain (7 Nov.).

29 Nov. The Portuguese royal family, the Braganzas, flee from Lisbon to Brazil. Portugal's refusal to join Napoleon's Continental System has led to an invasion of the country by a French army commanded by Andoche Junot, duc d'Abrantès.

– Prussia's prime minister Baron Heinrich vom und zum Stein emancipates the country's serfs, to take effect in 1810.

– In Britain, following a nationwide campaign by William Wilberforce and the abolitionist movement, Parliament passes a bill forbidding the trade in slaves throughout the empire.

MIDDLE EAST AND NORTH AFRICA

28 May In Constantinople, the reformist Ottoman sultan Selim III is deposed by his janissaries (elite bodyguard) in favour of Mustafa IV.

THE AMERICAS

19 Feb. The former US vice-president Aaron Burr (see 1804) is arrested and charged with treason. He is accused of having tried to establish a new independent country consisting of Mexico and parts of Louisiana; he is acquitted.

22 Dec. US president Thomas Jefferson signs an Embargo Act prohibiting maritime exports and preventing the importation of British goods that can be substituted by other countries or that can be produced domestically. Although designed to hit back at French and British war-time restrictions on US trade with enemy countries, the move badly affects the US economy.

ECONOMY AND SOCIETY

– The Gold Cup horse race is run over a 4km (2 mile) course for the first time at the Royal Ascot meet in Berkshire, England.

SCIENCE AND TECHNOLOGY

– British chemist Humphry Davy gives sodium and potassium their names in his work *On Some Chemical Agencies of Electricity*.

– German doctor Franz Joseph Gall spreads the popularity of phrenology in Paris, claiming that the shape of the skull determines human mental capacity and emotional condition.

ARTS AND HUMANITIES
Literature

Charles and Mary Lamb, *Tales from Shakespeare*, stories for children by the brother-and-sister writing team. Mary has killed their mother 11 years before in a fit of insanity and is now regularly confined in an asylum.
William Wordsworth (see p. 353), *Poems in Two Volumes*, poetry collection, including the poems 'Milton! Thou shouldst be

living at this hour', 'Upon Westminster Bridge', 'The World is too much with us', 'Ode to Duty' and 'Intimations of Immortality from Recollections of Early Childhood'.

Visual Arts and Architecture

Jacques-Louis David, *Coronation of Napoleon*, painting; one of a series produced since 1802 glorifying Napoleon's achievements.

Music

Ludwig van Beethoven (see p. 356), Symphony No. 4 in B flat major and Mass in C major.

1808

EUROPE

Jan. On the pretext of guarding the coast against the British, French emperor Napoleon Bonaparte (see p. 357) orders 70,000 troops into Spain and they occupy Figuera, San Sebastian, Pamplona and Barcelona. Joachim Murat, the general in command, occupies Madrid (26 Mar.), and King Charles IV abdicates. His son becomes Ferdinand VII (Mar.) but is forced to abdicate (May). Napoleon makes his brother Joseph king of Spain, inciting a popular revolt (2 May), which is the start of the Spanish War of Independence, also known as the Peninsular War (1808–14).

1 Mar. The mentally ill king of Denmark, Christian VII, dies and is succeeded by his son, Frederick VI, who has been regent since 1784 and is allied to Napoleon.

23 July The independent Spanish army defeats French general Pierre Dupont de l'Etang and his poorly equipped forces at Bailén, S Spain; a British army under Sir Arthur Wellesley (Irish-born son of the earl of Mornington and future duke of Wellington; see 1814) arrives (1 Aug.) in Portugal to support the Spanish rebels.

Aug. Joseph Bonaparte, the new king of Spain, is forced to leave Madrid because of mounting opposition. Joachim Murat

replaces him as king of Naples and enters the city (Sept.) as King Joachim-Napoleon. He seizes the island of Capri in the Bay of Naples from the British.

– Napoleon reasserts French control of Spain by sending an army of 150,000 men. He retakes Madrid (4 Dec.) and Joseph returns as king.

MIDDLE EAST AND NORTH AFRICA

– Bayrakdar Mustafa, pasha (lord) of Ruşçuk (now Ruse, Bulgaria), tries to restore the deposed Ottoman sultan Selim III (see 28 May 1807), who is immediately murdered on the orders of the usurper Mustafa IV. Bayrakdar places Mahmud II (the Reformer) on the throne, and Mahmud orders the execution of Mustafa IV.

THE AMERICAS

1 Jan. The US Congress bans the import of slaves, but the trade continues illegally.

SCIENCE AND TECHNOLOGY

– After years of experimentation Nicolas Appert, a French chef, devises a method of sealing perishable food in jars for longer life, which improves the provisioning of Napoleon's armies.

– British chemist Humphry Davy isolates barium, boron, calcium and strontium.

ARTS AND HUMANITIES

Literature

– English journalist Henry Crabb Robinson's dispatches from Spain on the Peninsular War for *The Times* newspaper of London make him the first war correspondent. Robinson was also one of the founders of University College, London, and the Athenaeum Club in London.

Johann Wolfgang von Goethe (see box), *Faust,* Part 1, verse-drama addressing the contemporary and Romantic themes of personal dissatisfaction, ambition and the quest for knowledge (see 1832).

Johann Wolfgang von Goethe (1749–1832)

The German poet, novelist, dramatist and scientist Goethe had a towering influence on the arts in Germany and has been hailed as the last European whose genius was truly universal. He made his name as a representative of the early German Romantics with his novel *The Sorrows of Young Werther* (1774), a picture of the outsider alienated from society. However, he later embraced the harmony of Classicism, exemplified in his masterpiece, the verse drama *Faust* (Part 1, 1808; Part 2, 1832). Goethe wrote poems, plays, novels and short stories, but he was also a practical scientist who specialized in biology, optics and mineralogy. In addition he

produced original work on economics, horticulture, landscape gardening and architecture. From 1776 to 1786 he was the chief administrator of the German duchy of Saxe-Weimar and from 1791 to 1817 a highly professional director of the Weimar theatre. His intellectual mastery over such diverse fields has rarely been equalled.

Even when he was at his most classical, concerned with a disciplined serenity in art, Goethe remained faithful to the idea that literature is confessional – the expression of a personality. He is central to the German idea that intellectual development shapes,

and is shaped by, the whole character. His achievement showed how Classicism and Romanticism in the arts can be two aspects of the same rich, complex personality. Goethe's life and work came to personify the very nature of enlightened German culture as well as a more general European desire to understand the inter-connectedness of human phenomena. His humanism rejected narrow either-or attitudes and showed how genius could reconcile and embrace opposites, which is why Napoleon, after meeting Goethe in Erfurt, exclaimed: '*Voilà un homme.*'

Francisco Goya (1746–1828)

The Spanish painter Francisco Goya had an enormous influence on European art in the 19th century. But at first he followed a fairly conventional path. He successively mastered the baroque style of Tiepolo and then the neoclassical style of Mengs, both of whom were active at the Spanish court where Goya himself served from 1775 onwards. In the later 1780s he began to develop a more individual, more realistic style of portraiture, influenced by both Rembrandt and Velázquez. His fame, however, rests on his later works, whose power may owe much to his deafness, which, from 1792 onwards, forced him to rely increasingly on his imagination.

Goya is the first painter to portray madness convincingly, as in his unflinchingly grotesque study *The Madhouse* (1794). In 1799 he gave full expression to his satirical talent when he published *Los caprichos* – a series of 80 etchings attacking political, social and religious corruption. He also became the first modern war artist: his series of etchings *The Disasters of War* (1810–20) horrifically illustrate the consequences of Napoleon's invasion and conquest of Spain, while in his landmark painting *The Third of May 1808: The Execution of the Defenders of Madrid* (1814) the sufferings of the Spanish rebels on the point of death are highlighted in a style that is both monumental and impressionistic. Such a penetrating study of human agony, the result of a flair for dramatic composition combined with a humanitarian sensibility, was new in European painting. From 1820 Goya was taken over by pessimism and despair, and from this last period emerged the so-called black paintings, enigmatic and disturbing works such as *Satan Devouring His Children*.

Visual Arts and Architecture

– Francisco Goya (see box), court painter to Charles IV, continues in the same role under Joseph Bonaparte (see 1808) but goes on to record the horrors of the Spanish War of Independence.

Caspar David Friedrich, *The Cross in the Mountains*, painting; a landscape controversially painted as an altarpiece.

Jean-Auguste-Dominique Ingres, *The Valpinçon Bather*, painting; the study of bathers will become one of his favourite subjects.

Music

Ludwig van Beethoven (see p. 356), Symphonies No. 5 in C minor and No. 6 in F major (*Pastoral*), Piano Concerto No. 4 in G major and Triple Concerto in C major.

1809

EUROPE

16 Jan. The beleaguered commander of British forces in Spain, Sir John Moore, defeats a French attack but is killed at the battle of La Coruña (Corunna) on the NW coast (see 1817). Sir Arthur Wellesley succeeds him as commander of British forces in the Iberian peninsula (see 1808).

13 Mar. The Swedish military depose the mentally ill King Gustav IV Adolph and declare a provisional government under the duke of Sudermania (10 May). He is proclaimed king and reigns as Charles XIII.

12 May Napoleon Bonaparte (see p. 357), emperor of France, now returned from Spain, advances against the Austrians and captures Vienna, but at the battle of Aspern (21–22 May) he experiences his first defeat. Archduke Charles fails to exploit the Austrian advantage, allowing Napoleon to regroup and defeat the Austrian forces at the battle of Wagram (5–6 July).

5 July Napoleon annexes the Papal States in C Italy and imprisons Pope Pius VII, who will remain in custody until 1814.

28 July An Anglo-Spanish army commanded by Sir Arthur Wellesley defeats the French at Talavera, SW of Madrid. The victory gains Wellesley the title of Viscount Wellington.

4 Aug. Klemens von Metternich becomes Austrian minister for state and foreign minister (8 Oct.), beginning a 40-year career in that post. Emperor Francis I will make him a prince of the Austrian empire in 1813.

9 Sept. George Canning, British foreign secretary, resigns, complaining about the poor conduct of the Peninsular War.

21 Sept. Robert Stewart, Viscount Castlereagh, minister of war, is affronted and challenges Canning to a duel in which the former foreign secretary is wounded.

4 Oct. Spencer Perceval, a Tory, succeeds the duke of Portland (see 24 Mar 1807) as British premier.

14 Dec. Napoleon divorces Josephine de Beauharnais (she has two children from a previous marriage but has remained childless while married to him).

ASIA

– The treaty of Amritsar fixes the British East India Company's border in NW India at the Sutlej River and checks the advance of the powerful Sikh confederacy.

THE AMERICAS

4 Mar. James Madison becomes fourth US president. Jefferson's former secretary of state, Madison has run as the Democratic–Republican candidate, defeating the Federalist Charles Pinckney (Jefferson having declined to run for a third term).

30 Sept. US general William Henry Harrison 'negotiates' the treaty of Fort Wayne and gains 1.2 million hectares (3 million acres) of land for the USA from the Native Americans of Indiana.

SCIENCE AND TECHNOLOGY

– In his *Philosophie zoologique* Jean-Baptiste Lamarck postulates his theory of the inheritance of acquired characteristics.

ARTS AND HUMANITIES

Literature

6 Dec. (St Nicholas' Day) Diedrich Knickerbocker (US writer Washington Irving) writes *A History of New York from the Beginning of the World to the End of the Dutch Dynasty* in which he refers to a St Nicholas figure bearing gifts who enters homes by way of the chimney.

– Johannn Wolfgang von Goethe (see p. 359), German scientist, writer, dramatist and court official, writes *Die Wahlverwandtschaften* (The Elective Affinities), finding in the theory of chemical attraction an analogy for human relationships.

Music

Ludwig van Beethoven (see p. 356), Piano Concerto No. 5 in E flat major (*Emperor*).

1810

EUROPE

11 Feb. Napoleon Bonaparte, emperor of France (see p. 357), is married by proxy to the Austrian archduchess Marie Louise, eldest daughter of Francis I, in a match brokered by Metternich.

9 July France annexes the United Provinces after the abdication and flight of Napoleon's brother Louis (king since 1806), after he refuses to join the Continental System.

21 Aug. Jean-Baptiste Bernadotte, a French soldier, is elected crown prince by the Swedish riksdag; he arrives in Sweden (20 Oct.) and takes control of government as regent, with the name Charles John, during the illness of Charles XIII (see 1818).

Oct. In Britain George III suffers a recurrence of his mental illness.

THE AMERICAS

25 May A provisional government of the Rio de la Plata (now Argentina and Uruguay) is established by Spanish colonists in S America loyal to King Ferdinand VII, now a French prisoner in Europe. Juntas are established in Caracas (modern Venezuela) and Santiago (modern Chile).

16 Sept. Creole priest Miguel Hidalgo y Costilla, the father of Mexican independence, begins an uprising against Spanish colonial rule; rebels capture Guanajuato and Guadalajara and other cities in C Mexico but are soon defeated by government forces (see 1811).

SCIENCE AND TECHNOLOGY

– German engineer Rudolph Ackermann invents differential gears, enabling carriages (and later motor vehicles) to turn sharp corners.

– German doctor Christian Friedrich Hahnemann pioneers homeopathic medicine in his *Organon der rationellen Heilkunst* (Organon of Rational Medicine).

– French chemist Nicolas-Louis Vauquelin identifies the active element in tobacco and calls it nicotine after Jean Nicot, the French ambassador to Portugal who sent tobacco seeds back to Paris in 1550.

– Sugar-beet factories are established at Passy, France, by Benjamin Delessert to bypass the British blockade of imports, which stops sugar getting to France.

ARTS AND HUMANITIES

Literature

– Madame de Staël's *De l'Allemagne* (Of Germany) is published and arouses a strong interest in German Romanticism among the French reading public.

Visual Arts and Architecture

15 Aug. France's victory at Austerlitz (1805) is commemorated by a great column erected in the Place Vendôme, Paris. It is surmounted by the figure of Napoleon represented as Caesar.

11 Nov. German-British portrait painter Johann Zoffany dies in Middlesex, England.

Jacques-Louis David, *Napoleon Distributing the Eagles*, painting.

Francisco Goya (see p. 360), *The Disasters of War*, start of a series of 65 etchings of the Peninsular War.

1811

EUROPE

5 Feb. In Britain Parliament passes the Regency Act, allowing the Prince of Wales to reign in place of his father, King George III, who is mentally ill (see Oct. 1810).

15 Mar. Austria declares itself bankrupt as a result of the war with France.

5 May In the Peninsular War British forces defeat the French at the battles of Fuentes d'Onoro, Portugal, and Albuera, near Badajoz, Spain (16 May).

– In Britain Luddite rioters, named after their most prominent leader Ned Ludd, destroy newly introduced textile machinery, which threatens to make handloom operators redundant. They will be finally suppressed in 1813.

MIDDLE EAST AND NORTH AFRICA

1 Mar. Mehmet Ali, the Ottoman viceroy, massacres Egypt's Mamluk leaders whom he has invited to a banquet; he now rules without opposition.

ASIA

– Britain captures the Dutch colony of Batavia (Java, now in Indonesia), occupied by the French. Sir Thomas Stamford Raffles, English administrator and oriental scholar, who accompanies the expedition, will govern Java until 1816.

THE AMERICAS

10 Jan. A slave revolt in New Orleans, Louisiana, USA, is savagely quelled; heads of executed slaves are displayed by the roadsides.

2 Feb. President James Madison demands that Britain stop harassing neutral US shipping in the war with France (see 1812).

7 July Venezuela declares its independence. The Spanish regency created by Napoleon is rejected by the Venezuelan junta, which now urges other Spanish colonies in S America to seize their own independence. Venezuelan-born Francisco de Miranda, who has served in the Spanish army in the Napoleonic wars, returns to Venezuela and becomes head of the armed forces. Simón Bolívar, who was born in Venezuela but has studied law in Madrid, returns with the mission sent to London to seek British support and joins the fighting against the Spanish forces of occupation (see 1812), becoming the main revolutionary leader.

31 July Mexican nationalist leader Miguel Hidalgo y Costilla, captured following his defeat at Calderón (17 Jan.) by forces of the viceroyalty of New Spain, is executed at Chihuahua.

14 Aug. Influenced by the Venezuelan example, Paraguay proclaims its independence. Spain also loses control of Banda Oriental, Uruguay; José Miguel Carrera overthrows a reactionary junta in Santiago, Chile; and Cartagena in Colombia declares its independence (11 Nov.).

7 Nov. The Shawnee people of Oklahoma (originally Ohio) are crushed by US forces at the battle of Tippecanoe.

SUB-SAHARAN AFRICA

– A Portuguese expedition completes the first crossing of the African continent.

ECONOMY AND SOCIETY

10 May Britain adopts paper currency as a way out of financial crisis in a society strongly influenced by the economic theories of Scottish economist Adam Smith and English economist David Ricardo. Bank notes are issued in proportion to the amount of coins and bullion in the vaults of the Bank of England.

– Napoleon Bonaparte, emperor of France, decrees that French orphanages should provide turntable devices in perimeter walls so that unwanted children can be left anonymously. The measure is intended to increase the number of children taken into the foundling hospitals that provide a steady supply of recruits for the Napoleonic army.

– Restaurants in Paris have become more numerous since the start of the French Revolution. Eating habits evolve further under the influence of the Russian ambassador to Paris, Prince Alexander Kurakin, who popularizes the serving of meals in a sequence of courses (*à la Russe*) instead of together on the dining table (see also 1852).

– The grid pattern layout of streets widely used in Spanish colonial towns is adopted for New York in a plan set out by the city's commissioners.

SCIENCE AND TECHNOLOGY

– Italian scientist Amedeo Avogadro posits the law that equal volumes of all gases at the same temperature and pressure will contain equal numbers of molecules.

– Scottish anatomist Charles Bell, in his *New Idea of the Anatomy of the Brain*, identifies sensory and motor nerves.

– French chemists Bernard Courtois and Pierre Dulong discover, respectively, iodine and nitrogen chloride.

– Krupp Gussstahlfabrik (Cast Steel works) is established by Friedrich Krupp at Essen, Germany, in a shed next to his house. He is encouraged by a reward offered by Napoleon to anyone who can match the British production of cast steel.

ARTS AND HUMANITIES
Literature

Jane Austen, *Sense and Sensibility*, novel extracting universal moral themes from the confines of English country house society.

Johann Wolfgang von Goethe, *Dichtung und Wahrheit* (Poetry and Truth), first part of his autobiography.

1812

EUROPE

Mar.–April In the Peninsular War Arthur Wellesley recaptures the Spanish city of Badajoz (in French hands since Feb. 1811).

8 May The Spanish cortes (parliament) promulgates a constitution based on universal male suffrage.

11 May British premier Spencer Perceval is assassinated by a disgruntled businessman in the House of Commons. Lord Liverpool becomes prime minister (he will remain in office until 1827).

June Napoleon Bonaparte (see p. 357), emperor of France, invades Russia. At the bloody battle of Borodino (7 Sept.) on the Moskva River both sides suffer heavy casualties and Russian field marshal Prince Mikhail Kutuzov withdraws to save his troops. Napoleon enters Moscow and much of the city is burned.

22 July Arthur Wellesley defeats the French under Marshal Marmont at Salamanca, NW of Madrid.

19 Oct. The French retreat from Moscow begins after Napoleon fails to force a peace treaty on the Russians. In Nov. Kutuzov defeats marshals Ney and Davout at Smolensk. The Grande Armée, which originally numbered more than 600,000, is continually subjected to attacks by Cossacks and Russian guerrillas as it retreats and will decrease to around 100,000 men by the time it finally crosses the Neman River into Lithuania.

– The Luddite riots (see 1811) spread to other parts of N England as wheat prices and the cost of bread soar.

THE AMERICAS

26 Mar. An earthquake strikes Venezuela. Francisco de Miranda, leader of the independence struggle, is made dictator, but he is captured by colonial forces and sent to Cadiz in Spain, where he will die a prisoner (1816).

14 April Louisiana becomes the 18th state of the USA.

18 June Annoyed by the interdiction of trade with France and by the impressment of American sailors into the Royal Navy, the USA goes to war with Britain. On 16 Aug. Fort Dearborn on Lake Michigan is sacked by the British. At sea there are a series of duels between frigates: the USS *Constitution* destroys HMS *Guerrière* (19 Aug.) and USS *United States* defeats HMS *Macedonian* (23 Oct.). The war (known as the War of 1812) stimulates manufacturing production in the USA.

– Gerrymander becomes a popular term for rigging electoral boundaries to secure party advantage after the Massachusetts legislature, under Governor Elbridge Gerry, redraws senatorial districts to ensure Republican dominance.

– Rising Chilean nationalist leader Bernardo O'Higgins (illegitimate son of Ambrosio O'Higgins, governor of Chile and viceroy of Peru) opposes José Miguel Carrera's revolutionary regime.

ECONOMY AND SOCIETY

– In France the first plain-clothes detective force, the Brigade de la Sûreté, is founded by François-Eugène Vidocq. Vidocq is suspected of committing many of the crimes he 'solves'.

SCIENCE AND TECHNOLOGY

22 Aug. Swiss explorer and archaeologist John Lewis Burckhardt rediscovers Petra in modern Jordan, ancient capital of the Nabataean Arabs.

– The world's first commercial vacuum bottling, or canning, factory is opened at Massy near Paris by Nicolas Appert, the French chef who discovered the preserving process (see 1808).

– Gas lighting starts to spread in London with the formation of the British National Light and Heat Company.

ARTS AND HUMANITIES

Literature

– German philologists Jakob and Wilhelm Grimm publish the first volume of their fairy tales (including the stories of Bluebeard, Goldilocks and Sleeping Beauty).

George Gordon, Lord Byron, *Childe Harold's Pilgrimage*, Part 1, poem, which will be completed in 1818. Byron establishes the Romantic 'Byronic' hero and identifies himself with the cause of Greek independence from the Ottoman empire.

1813

EUROPE

3 Feb. At Breslau Frederick William III of Prussia issues a national appeal for all Prussians to mobilize against the French. By the alliance of Kalisch (28 Feb.), the basis of the Fourth Coalition, Prussia and Russia embark on a military campaign against Napoleon (see p. 357), whose disastrous Russian campaign emboldens his enemies in Europe.

3 Mar. The Swedes ally themselves with Britain, which has promised not to oppose the union of Sweden with Norway in return for a Swedish army taking the field against Napoleon in Germany. Crown Prince Bernadotte of Sweden leads an army of 120,000 in the Leipzig campaign. Bernadotte's wife is an ex-mistress of Napoleon, and her sister Julie is married to Napoleon's brother Joseph.

Mar. In N Germany Russian troops occupy Hamburg: the duke of Mecklenburg withdraws from the French-supporting Confederation of the Rhine (see 12 July 1806).

2 May An allied army attacks Napoleon at Lützen (Gross-Gorschen) on the River Elbe in Prussia, but fails to defeat him. The emperor enters Dresden, capital of Saxony, which was occupied by Russian and Prussian forces in March.

20–21 May After a hard-fought battle near the Saxon town of Bautzen, Napoleon forces the allies back across the River Spree into Silesia.

15 June In a treaty signed at Reichenbach, S of Leipzig, Britain agrees to subsidize Prussia and Russia in the war against France.

21 June In the Peninsular War in Spain the British commander Arthur Wellesley triumphs over French marshal Jean-Baptiste Jourdan at the battle of Vitoria and advances with his army through N Spain. The French-appointed king of Spain, Joseph Bonaparte, has returned to Paris. British and Spanish forces go on to take Pamplona in Navarre (31 Oct.). Wellesley defeats

French marshal Nicolas Soult at Toulouse (10 Nov.) after crossing the French frontier.

12 Aug. Austria declares war on France and the Prussian general Friedrich von Bülow defeats a French army at Grossbeeren (23 Aug.), thereby saving Berlin from occupation.

26 Aug. Gen. Gebhard Leberecht von Blücher defeats French forces at the battle of Katzbach (Kaczawa), in Prussia.

26–27 Aug. Napoleon gains his last major victory on German territory in the battle of Dresden, against an allied army.

6 Sept. At the battle of Dennewitz Sweden's Crown Prince Bernadotte prevents French marshal Michel Ney taking Berlin.

16–19 Oct. Napoleon is overwhelmingly defeated in the battle of Leipzig (also known as battle of the Nations) by the coalition of Russians, Prussians, Austrians and Swedes. His Saxon and Württemberg troops desert, and the allies storm Leipzig, capturing the king of Saxony. The Confederation of the Rhine and the French satellite kingdom of Westphalia in NW Germany, ruled by Napoleon's brother Jérôme Bonaparte, both dissolve. The former rulers are subsequently restored in Hesse-Cassel, Brunswick, Hanover and Oldenburg.

11 Nov. Dresden surrenders to the allies, followed by the towns of Stettin (21 Nov.), Lübeck (5 Dec.) and Danzig (30 Dec.) on the Baltic coast.

15 Nov. The Dutch rebel and expel the ruling French officials. An allied army enters the United Provinces, and a Swedish army under Count Bernadotte invades Danish Holstein.

– Following a mass trial at York, the leaders of England's Luddite movement (see 1811) are hanged or transported to Australia.

THE AMERICAS

14 Sept. The Mexican National Congress declares the country's independence from Spain and appoints José María Morelos y Pavón as its leader.

5 Oct. US forces defeat a combined British and Shawnee force at the battle of the Thames in Ontario, SE Canada, reasserting American dominance on land in N America.

9 Nov. US general Andrew Jackson defeats the Creek people in the Mississippi territory at Talledega, ending the Creek War (1813–14); they are forced to surrender much of their territory.

– Simón Bolívar, Venezuelan-born rebel leader, retakes Caracas (Venezuela) from Spanish colonial forces.

ARTS AND HUMANITIES

Literature

Jane Austen, *Pride and Prejudice*, novel.

Percy Bysshe Shelley, *Queen Mab*, poem opposing conventional Christianity and secular tyranny.

Johann Wyss, *The Swiss Family Robinson*, novel recounting the adventures of a family shipwrecked on a desert island.

Music

6 Feb. First performance in Venice of Gioachino Rossini's opera *Tancredi*, which is based on Tasso's *Gerusalemme liberata*.

8 Mar. The Royal Philharmonic Orchestra, London, gives its first concert.

22 May First performance in Venice of Rossini's opera *L'Italiana in Algeri* (The Italian Girl in Algiers).

Ludwig van Beethoven (see p. 356), Symphony No. 7 in A major.

Franz Schubert, Symphony No. 1 in D major.

1814

EUROPE

14 Jan. By the terms of the treaty of Kiel France's ally Denmark cedes Norway to Sweden. Sweden's effective ruler Marshal Bernadotte is anxious to acquire Norway as compensation for Sweden's loss of Finland to Russia in the war of 1807–9. Norway, however, refuses to accept the legality of the treaty and declares its independence.

1 Feb. Prussian field marshal Gebhard von Blücher, with Austrian and Russian support, defeats Napoleon (see p. 357) at the battle of La Rothière in France. But Napoleon goes on to defeat the Prussians at Nangis and Montereau in N France and refuses an allied offer to restore the French frontier as it existed in 1792. However, Bordeaux in SW France falls (12 Mar.) to the British commander Arthur Wellesley, now 1st duke of Wellington; Napoleon is defeated at the battle of Arcis-sur-Aube (20–21 Mar.); the allies storm Montmartre (30 Mar.) and then enter Paris (31 Mar.). Napoleon, once master of Europe, abdicates (11 April) but is allowed to govern the 245 sq km (95 square mile) island of Elba in the Mediterranean. France restores the monarchy, and Louis XVIII, who has been titular monarch since 1795, now reigns, with Charles Talleyrand as foreign minister.

17 May Norway adopts a new liberal constitution and elects Christian VIII of Denmark as king. Marshal Bernadotte's forces invade Norway. In the ensuing negotiations Bernadotte accepts the Norwegian constitution on condition that he is elected king.

21 June The kingdom of the Netherlands is created by the union of the United Provinces, the Austrian Netherlands and Luxemburg under William of Orange-Nassau, who becomes William I, king of the Netherlands, in 1815.

1 Nov. The Congress of Vienna convenes to establish the details of a general European peace.

Nov. The Norwegian storting (parliament) ratifies the union of the crowns of Norway and Sweden.

– Ferdinand VII (see 1808) is restored to the Spanish throne.

– The Netherlands prohibits the slave trade.

– The restored king of Piedmont in NW Italy, Victor Emanuel I, establishes the carabinieri as an elite paramilitary police force.

THE AMERICAS

24–25 Aug. A British force routs US militiamen at the battle of Bladensburg, Maryland, and occupies Washington, D.C., burning most of the public buildings, including the official residence of the president. It is later restored by its architect James Hoban and painted to conceal the fire damage, becoming known as the White House. The Capitol, the assembly building, is also destroyed along with the Library of Congress, and

ex-president Thomas Jefferson offers his private library at cost price to form the nucleus of the new collection.

24 Dec. The treaty of Ghent ends the Anglo-American War (begun in 1812), although the battle of New Orleans will be fought two weeks later because troops have not received the news that the war has officially ended.

SUB-SAHARAN AFRICA

– Britain pays £20 million to the Netherlands and acquires Cape Colony, South Africa (see 1806).

ECONOMY AND SOCIETY

– A new French law prohibits abortion except when the mother's health is threatened.

– The company of E.I. du Pont de Nemours (the modern Du Pont multinational chemicals conglomerate) emerges from the war of 1812 commercially strengthened through the profitable sale of gunpowder to the US government.

– John Jacob Astor, fur trader and New York property investor, increases his fortune through loans to the US government.

– In N Scotland the duke of Sutherland begins his programme of Highland clearances, removing his tenants and destroying their homes and traditional way of life to make way for more profitable sheep farming. Some 10,000 people, one-third of the county of Sutherland's population, will be cleared by 1822.

SCIENCE AND TECHNOLOGY

– English engineer George Stephenson produces his first steam railway locomotive in Northumberland, N England. He applies Richard Trevithick's steam engine (see 1800) to a vehicle that operates on steel rails, replacing horses to haul coal wagons.

ARTS AND HUMANITIES

Literature

26 Jan. Edmund Kean performs Shylock in Shakespeare's *The Merchant of Venice* at Drury Lane Theatre, London, the beginning of a long career as Britain's greatest Shakespearean actor.

Jane Austen, *Mansfield Park*, novel.

Lord Byron, *The Corsair*, poem.

Walter Scott, *Waverley*, the first of a series of Scottish historical novels.

William Wordsworth, *The Excursion*, poem in nine books.

Visual Arts and Architecture

– Francisco Goya (see p. 360) paints scenes from the bloody French suppression of the Spanish uprising in Madrid (2–3 May 1808).

– The Dulwich Gallery opens in London: it is the first public picture gallery in Britain.

Théodore Géricault, *The Wounded Cuirassier*, painting.

Music

23 May Beethoven's opera *Fidelio* (see 1814) is performed with a new overture at Vienna's Kärntnertor Theatre. Beethoven's fellow composer Franz Schubert has allegedly sold his overcoat in order to be able to afford the price of a ticket.

14 Aug. First performance in La Scala, Milan, of Gioachino Rossini's opera *Il Turco in Italia* (The Turk in Italy).

– The national anthem of the USA, 'The Star-Spangled Banner' by Francis Scott Key, is composed and published in the local newspaper after he has witnessed the bombardment (14 Sept.) of Fort McHenry, Baltimore, by British ships.

Ludwig van Beethoven (see p. 356), Symphony No. 8 in F major.

1815

EUROPE

1 Mar. In a renewed bid for power Napoleon Bonaparte (see p. 357) escapes from Elba and lands at Cannes on the French Mediterranean coast. He gathers support and reaches Paris (20 Mar.) where he starts a new reign that will last 100 days. Louis XVIII, the recently restored king, flees to Ghent in Flanders.

23 Mar. A Corn Law is passed in Britain prohibiting imports of foreign corn into Britain when the average domestic price of wheat is less than 80 shillings a quarter (duty-free imports are legal, however, when the price of wheat is more than this).

16 June In the events leading up to the battle of Waterloo in Belgium, French marshal Michel Ney, who has gone over to Napoleon having been despatched to arrest him, defeats a detachment of the British army of Arthur Wellesley, duke of Wellington, at Quatre Bras. The action prevents Ney from sending reinforcements to Napoleon, who fights, and defeats, the Prussians at Ligny.

18 June At Waterloo (S of Brussels) the allied army, consisting of British and Dutch forces with German troops from Brunswick, Hanover and Nassau, confronts Napoleon. The arrival, late in the day, of Prussian reinforcements led by Field Marshal Gebhard von Blücher helps the British-led forces to defeat Napoleon, who abdicates (22 June). He is exiled to the British island of St Helena in the S Atlantic (17 Aug.), where he will die (1821).

– The Congress of Vienna closes (9 June) after redrawing the post-war map of Europe and its overseas territories: a German Confederation of 39 states is created; Britain gains Ceylon (Sri Lanka) and the Cape of Good Hope from the Netherlands (see 1814); Austria regains Lombardy and Venetia in N Italy; Prussia makes gains in Germany; Switzerland becomes an independent confederation of 22 cantons; the pope is restored to temporal power in Italy, as are royal and princely dynasties elsewhere in Europe. The Grand Duchy of Warsaw is now fully partitioned among Prussia, Russia and Austria. Poland will not regain its independence until 1918.

– The general European peace depresses British trade as the Continental markets are saturated with British goods. Unemployment is made worse by the arrival of demobilized troops. British income tax, used to finance the war, is now suspended and will be resumed only in 1842.

THE AMERICAS

8 Jan. At the battle of New Orleans in the S USA, a US army led by Gen. Andrew Jackson defeats a British expeditionary force under Gen. Edward Pakenham. Unknown to both sides, a peace treaty had already been signed (see 24 Dec. 1814).

20 May A US naval force under Commodore Stephen Decatur leaves New York for the coast of N Africa in response to attacks on American shipping. A treaty is signed (30 June) with the bey of Algiers followed by agreements with the rulers of Tunis and Tripoli, in which they promise not to exact ransom or tribute from US merchant shipping and to stop pirate attacks.

– Spanish troops land in Venezuela, S America, and defeat the rebellion in the province of New Granada; its leader Simón Bolívar flees to Jamaica.

SUB-SAHARAN AFRICA

– Zulu power in SE Africa is increasing: Shaka, son of Chief Senzangakona, reorganizes the army, now equipped with the deadly short, stabbing assegai (spear). His 12-year reign (from 1816) will see the army increase to a force of some 40,000 men.

ECONOMY AND SOCIETY

– Berlin Jews open a 'reformed' temple (on the model of the temple opened in Seesen in 1810) and abandon traditional Mosaic rules on eating and dress.

SCIENCE AND TECHNOLOGY

5 April Tambora volcano on the island of Sumbawa in the E Indies (modern Indonesia) erupts, killing 50,000 people; it sends huge amounts of volcanic ash into the atmosphere, temporarily altering climatic conditions worldwide.

– English chemist Sir Humphry Davy invents a safety lamp for miners, with a metal gauze surrounding the flame to prevent the ignition of inflammable gas in coal mines.

– Scottish surveyor John McAdam invents the 'macadamized' roadway, which uses different grades of broken stones to shed water and resist wear and tear.

ARTS AND HUMANITIES

Literature

– Johann Ludwig Uhland, *Gedichte* (Poems), later (1816) supplemented by *Vaterländische Gedichte* (Patriotic Poems); these become popular as nationalist folksongs in tandem with a growing sense of German identity.

Benjamin Constant, *Adolphe*, a novel of psychological analysis.

Walter Scott, *Guy Mannering*, historical novel.

Music

– The quadrille, a type of square dance popular in Napoleonic France, is performed in Britain for the first time.

– Franz Schubert, *Der Erlkönig* (The Erl King), song setting for the ballad 'Erlkönig' by Johann Wolfgang von Goethe, and Symphonies No. 2 in B flat and No. 3 in D.

1816

EUROPE

2 July The *Medusa*, flagship of a squadron of four French naval vessels carrying the new colonial governor to Senegal, founders off the coast of W Africa. A raft is built for 149 people who cannot get into the rescue boats: 89 are lost in the following two days and 12 more die in the third night. A body is saved from sharks and eaten by the survivors. Following an enquiry, the ship's navigator, a civilian friend of the governor, is not prosecuted but the captain is imprisoned for three years (see Visual Arts and Architecture, 1819).

5 Nov. Metternich presides over the opening of the diet (assembly) of the German Confederation in Frankfurt am Main.

– France's Caisse des Depots et Consignations is founded as a central investment bank; it is obliged to invest in the public interest.

– Prompted by economic recession, Luddism (see 1811) revives in Britain with riots and attacks on industrial machinery. A violent protest occurs in London (2 Dec.) and outbreaks will continue sporadically around the country until 1818.

ASIA

– Britain returns Java, captured in 1811 during the Napoleonic Wars, to the Netherlands.

THE AMERICAS

16 Jan. The Portuguese colony of Brazil is proclaimed an empire under the Portuguese prince regent John. He succeeds to the crown of Portugal as John VI on the death of his insane mother, Maria I (20 Mar.), but remains in Brazil (see 1820).

29 July Argentina declares itself independent of Spain as the United Provinces of the Río de la Plata.

2 Dec. The Philadelphia Savings Fund Society opens and is the first US savings bank to accept deposits.

– José Gaspar de Francia, known as El Supremo, starts a 24-year dictatorship in Paraguay and rules oppressively over the Guarani people who form the majority of the population.

– Congress imposes a 25% duty on all imports in an attempt to encourage the US economy to become self-sufficient.

ECONOMY AND SOCIETY

– The German philosopher Georg Wilhelm Friedrich Hegel (see p. 371) completes his *Wissenschaft der Logik* (Science of Logic). His ideas will dominate German and then European and American philosophy and influence the young Karl Marx (see p. 419) in developing his theory of materialistic determinism.

– The English arbiter of fashion George 'Beau' Brummell flees to France to escape creditors; he becomes British consul in Caen (1832–40) but dies insane and in poverty (1840).

SCIENCE AND TECHNOLOGY

– French inventor Joseph-Nicéphore Niepce invents the celeripede, a two-wheeled forerunner of the bicycle. It cannot be steered and is propelled by walking.

ARTS AND HUMANITIES

Literature

July Richard Brinsley Sheridan, Irish-born politician and playwright, dies in poverty in London.

Jane Austen, *Emma*, novel.

Samuel Taylor Coleridge, 'Kubla Khan', poem (originally written in 1797).

John Keats, 'On First Looking into Chapman's Homer', poem.

Music

20 Feb. First performance in Rome of Gioachino Rossini's opera *Il Barbiere de Siviglia* (The Barber of Seville); like *Le nozze di Figaro*, it is based on the play by Beaumarchais.

1817

EUROPE

Mar. In Britain Parliament passes the Coercion Acts, which suspend temporarily the right of habeas corpus (see 1679) and attempt to ban seditious meetings. Such reactionary policies encourage further radical dissent.

– The rebellion against the Ottoman Turks led by Prince Miloš Obrenovic (1815–17) results in Serbian self-government (later independence) and the founding of a dynasty that will rule Serbia until 1842 (and from 1858 until 1903) at the expense of the rival Karageorgevic family.

MIDDLE EAST AND NORTH AFRICA

– Ismailis, following a neo-progressive form of Islam, start to donate 12% of their income to the Aga Khan in recognition of his claim to be a direct descendant of the Prophet Muhammad.

THE AMERICAS

12 Feb. Chilean nationalist forces, in revolt since 1810, defeat the Spanish at the battle of Chacabuco, leading to the country's independence (1818). Gen. Bernardo O'Higgins becomes supreme dictator of Chile.

4 Mar. James Monroe becomes fifth US president, having defeated the last Federalist candidate for the presidency, William Harris Crawford.

4 July Work begins on the 580km (360 miles) Erie Canal, linking Lake Erie with the Hudson River and the Atlantic Ocean, accelerating the development of the US Midwest and New York.

10 Dec. Missouri becomes a US state.

– Native Americans in Ohio are forced to cede their remaining 1.6 million hectares (4 million acres) of land to the USA.

ECONOMY AND SOCIETY

– English political economist David Ricardo publishes *On the Principles of Political Economy and Taxation*, which advances a labour theory of value and a notion of comparative costs. Both reflect the decreasingly agricultural nature of Britain's new capitalist economy.

SCIENCE AND TECHNOLOGY

– Scottish civil engineer John Rennie completes Waterloo Bridge, London.

– Welsh inventor Richard Roberts invents a screw-cutting lathe and a machine for planing metal.

– James Parkinson, an English surgeon, describes the disorder of the central nervous system that now bears his name.

ARTS AND HUMANITIES

– The University of Michigan is founded at Ann Arbor, and Harvard Law School is founded at Cambridge, Massachusetts.

NATIONALISM AND CAPITALISM:
The Dynamic Order of the 19th Century

Nationalism was the great political movement of 19th-century Europe, overthrowing established concepts of state and government. Capitalism was no less powerful, establishing economic ideas and practices that remain dominant to this day.

This was the age in which science ceased to be a matter of amateur curiosity for gentlemen, and instead became the launching pad for new industrial technologies. Real benefits and advances were transforming the lives of people. Railways reduced travelling times within countries, creating a more mobile pool of labour, while steamships, replacing sailing ships, did the same for transcontinental voyages. Railways and steamships also allowed a faster dispersal of goods, and also therefore their more rapid consumption, as raw materials were imported to Europe and manufactured goods exported. All this led to an expansion of demand and economic growth; in particular, the need to create new markets for manufactured goods led the European powers into a rush for new colonies. The developing international economy was founded on the fact that monetary systems of the advanced capitalist states were based on a single Gold Standard, with each country's currency being convertible at demand into the gold reserves held by that country.

With economic and technological power at their command, Europeans transformed the rest of the world by moving there to live, to trade and, sometimes, to govern. There were more Europeans than ever before because of better diet, improved public health and hygiene. But this population increase imposed a strain on the limited resources of the European landmass and led to the emigration of millions to the Americas and the Antipodes. There was also a mass movement from the country to the towns. This in turn produced new tensions for Europe's traditional rulers as the needs and desires of the peasantry were replaced by those of an urban and industrial workforce.

Nationalism – the belief that all those sharing a common linguistic, cultural or ethnic identity should be allowed to live within the same nation-state – proved to be the most potent ideology in 19th-century Europe. Some peoples had long lived in nation-states – the English and the French, for example – but it was not until the 19th century that nationalism became a dynamic force for change. When Napoleon abolished the Holy Roman Empire in 1806 he did so in order to replace it with a patchwork of states easily dominated by France. This aroused powerful nationalist reactions in the countries subjected to French domination, from Portugal in the west to Russia in the east. After the fall of Napoleon, the victorious powers met at the Congress of Vienna, and sought to return to the earlier dispensation, under which the boundaries of nationalities were ignored, and cities, regions, states and empires were regarded as the personal inheritances of the ruling dynasty. The Austrian empire in particular – which took in a great range of nationalities, including Germans, Italians, Slavs and Hungarians – was underpinned. The 1820s saw a period of political repression as the restored rulers sought to quell nationalist feeling.

Slowly the desire of nations to govern themselves became stronger. The Ottoman Turks had been forced to give Serbia some self-government by 1817, and Greece gained its independence in 1832, after an 11-year rebellion. In 1848 a liberal revolution in France overthrew King Louis-Philippe and established a more democratic republic. This sparked off a wave of revolutions in central Europe. Hungary, Croatia and the Czech territories all rejected Austrian rule in favour of national self-government and new, democratic constitutions. Democratic revolutions also broke out in the various Italian states, where the revolutionaries aspired to a unified country. There was a similar aspiration in the many German states, where an assembly met in Frankfurt and proposed national unification.

Most of these reform-minded revolutions collapsed within months, sometimes after military action by the established rulers and sometimes through lack of mass support, but nationalism continued to grow as a political force. In 1859 the king of Piedmont carefully prepared the diplomatic ground for the unification of most of Italy under his own rule. By 1871 Germany was likewise united under the rule of its most powerful state, Prussia, as a result of diplomatic manoeuvres and three short wars – with Denmark, Austria and France.

By the close of the 19th century the division of Europe into nation-states was incomplete. Both the Ottoman and the Austro-Hungarian empires still contained a multitude of nationalities, very few of whom enjoyed any real form of self-government. As a result, there was increased nationalist agitation and political action. Indeed, it was the assassination of an Austrian prince by a Serbian nationalist that precipitated the Great War of 1914–18. The defeat of the multinational empires in that war gave rise to new or reborn nation-states in central and eastern Europe, such as Czechoslovakia, Yugoslavia, Hungary and Poland. But those nations that had made up the Russian empire were gradually reabsorbed into the new Soviet Union. It would not be until the later 20th century that the various nations of this last great empire would break free.

1817 *continued*

Literature

– English poet John Keats publishes his first book of poems.

Walter Scott, *Rob Roy*, historical novel.

Charles Wolfe, 'The Burial of Sir John Moore at Corunna', poem (see 16 Jan. 1809).

Visual Arts and Architecture

John Constable, *Flatford Mill*, painting.

Music

25 Jan. First performance in Rome of Gioachino Rossini's opera *La Cenerentola* (Cinderella).

1818

EUROPE

5 Feb. Following the death of Charles XIII of Sweden, the adopted crown prince and former French general Jean-Baptiste Bernadotte succeeds to the throne as Charles XIV John.

9 Oct. The allies announce that the army of occupation, resident in France since the defeat of Napoleon Bonaparte (see p. 357), will be withdrawn (by 30 Nov.) because of the payment of war indemnity.

ASIA

– In the course of a war against the Pindari robber bands (1817–18) the British East India Company defeats the Maratha confederation and annexes Maharashtra, W India.

THE AMERICAS

12 Feb. Chile proclaims its independence from Spain.

20 Oct. The 49th parallel (49° N latitude) is agreed as the US–Canadian border in a convention between Britain and the USA. This agreement is later extended to include the disputed Oregon territory in the W (1846).

3 Dec. Illinois becomes a state of the USA.

– The US Congress adopts the Stars and Stripes as the country's flag; it consists of 13 stripes plus one star for each state in the union.

SUB-SAHARAN AFRICA

– In sub-Saharan W Africa the Muslim rebel Cheikou Ahmadou ejects the Peul Diallo dynasty, which has ruled the area of the Niger River since the 15th century.

ECONOMY AND SOCIETY

– The 'tin can', a tin-plated steel container used to preserve food and drink, is introduced to the USA by its English inventor Peter Durand, who was granted a British patent in 1810.

– German doctor Johann Siegert discovers the flavouring agent angostura bitters, derived from the bark of the tree *Gallipea aspuria*, at Angostura (now Ciudad Bolívar), Venezuela.

SCIENCE AND TECHNOLOGY

– English physician James Blundell, using a syringe, performs the first successful blood transfusion at Guy's Hospital, London.

ARTS AND HUMANITIES

Literature

Jane Austen, *Northanger Abbey* and *Persuasion*, novels published posthumously, Jane Austen having died in 1817.

Lord Byron, *Childe Harold's Pilgrimage*, fourth canto, poem.

John Keats, *Endymion*, Romantic epic, including the sentiment that 'a thing of beauty is a joy forever'.

Giacomo Leopardi, *All'Italia* (To Italy) and *Sopra il monumento di Dante* (On the Monument to Dante), poems that inspire Italian Romanticism and nationalism.

Walter Scott, *The Heart of Midlothian*, historical novel.

Mary Shelley, *Frankenstein or The Modern Prometheus*, novel popularizing the idea of the scientist who can create life.

Percy Bysshe Shelley, 'Ozymandias', sonnet.

Visual Arts and Architecture

– The newly built Prado in Madrid becomes the Spanish Royal Museum, open to the public.

Music

Franz Xaver Gruber, tune for *Stille Nacht, Heilige Nacht* ('Silent Night, Holy Night') by Austrian poet Joseph Mohr; it becomes a popular Christmas carol.

Franz Schubert, Symphony No. 6 in C major.

1819

EUROPE

16 Aug. A demonstration takes place at St Peter's Fields, Manchester, in favour of British parliamentary reform and repeal of the protectionist Corn Laws (see 23 Mar. 1815), which keep food prices high. The radical speaker Henry Hunt is arrested and the meeting forcibly dispersed by the mounted Manchester Yeomanry: 11 are killed and about 400 hundred injured in what becomes known as the Peterloo massacre, a sardonic pun on the victory of Waterloo (1815). Worried by the threat of revolution, Parliament passes the reactionary Six Acts (Dec.), which include a newspaper stamp duty, a limit on the size of public meetings, provisions for quick trials and increased penalties for 'seditious libel'.

Aug. Prince Klemens von Metternich of Austria persuades Prussia's ruler Frederick William III to issue the repressive Carlsbad Decrees. A commission is established in Mainz (July) that censors publications, controls the German universities and investigates private societies.

ASIA

– Sir Thomas Stamford Raffles, English administrator and Oriental scholar, occupies Singapore and persuades the sultan of Johore to lease the territory to the British East India Company. It now becomes a check on Dutch power in the E Indies.

– The European and US whaling industry has now expanded into Japanese coastal waters.

THE AMERICAS

22 Feb. Spain cedes E Florida and all its territory E of the Mississippi to the USA.

7 Aug. Nationalist leader Simón Bolívar defeats a Spanish army and occupies Bogotá (10 Aug.) in the colony of New Granada. The Congress of Angostura proclaims the independence of Great Colombia, consisting of New Granada, Venezuela and Quito; Bolívar becomes president and effectively military dictator of the new republic.

14 Dec. Alabama becomes a US state.

– William Channing, a Congregationalist minister in Boston, USA, founds the Unitarian Church, whose creed denies the Trinity and affirms the unity of God.

– The first stretch of the Erie Canal is opened and connects Utica with Rome, New York, USA.

AUSTRALASIA AND OCEANIA

8 May Kamehameha, ruler of the Hawaii, dies. His son, also Kamehameha, rejects traditional religion and the system of taboos and welcomes the arrival of Christian missionaries (1820). The population has declined dramatically since the landing of Captain James Cook (1778) owing to the diseases introduced by European and American visitors.

– William Smith lands on the South Shetland Islands in the S Atlantic and claims them for Britain.

ECONOMY AND SOCIETY

– The University of Virginia in the USA is chartered at Charlottesville with ex-US president Thomas Jefferson's active support; he lives nearby.

– Swiss confectioner François-Louis Cailler introduces bars of eating chocolate made by machine at Vevey, Switzerland.

SCIENCE AND TECHNOLOGY

30 June The US ship *Savannah* arrives in Liverpool, NW England, completing the first transatlantic crossing by steam power in 26 days.

– French physician René Laënnec invents the stethoscope.

ARTS AND HUMANITIES

Literature

Lord Byron, *Mazeppa*, poem.

John Keats, 'Ode to a Nightingale', poem.

Arthur Schopenhauer, *Die Welt als Wille und Vorstellung* (The World as Will and Idea), philosophy, expounding a pessimism that will become fashionable.

Walter Scott, *Ivanhoe*, historical novel.

Visual Arts and Architecture

John Constable, *The White Horse*, painting; it becomes one of his most admired works.

Théodore Géricault, *The Raft of the Medusa*, painting, which turns a political cause célèbre into a study of secular martyrdom (see 1816).

Music

– Franz Schubert completes the 'Trout' Quintet in A major (so called because it includes variations on Schubert's song (1817) of that name).

– By now Ludwig van Beethoven is completely deaf.

1820

EUROPE

29 Jan. In Britain King George III dies and is succeeded by the Prince Regent, who becomes George IV, king of Great Britain and Ireland. His estranged consort, Princess Caroline of Brunswick, refuses to grant him a divorce and is refused admission to Westminster Abbey at the coronation (July). A parliamentary attempt to deprive her of her titles is dropped (10 Nov.) in the face of popular support for the queen.

13 Feb. The heir to the French throne, Charles-Ferdinand d'Artois, duc de Berry (a nephew of Louis XVIII), is assassinated; his son and heir, the comte de Chambord, is born after his death (29 Sept.).

23 Feb. In Britain the Cato Street conspiracy to murder Lord Liverpool's cabinet is discovered. Five of its leaders are tried and hanged.

7 Mar. In Spain a rebellion led by Colonel Rafael Riego forces Ferdinand VII to restore the liberal constitution of 1812.

7 July Ferdinand I promises a national constitution to the people of the kingdom of Naples, S Italy, after a rebellion organized by secret societies, including the Carbonari. He also abolishes the Inquisition (see 1184).

24 Aug. In Portugal a rebellion starts in Oporto and spreads to Lisbon as popular disaffection grows with the British-influenced regency council that rules Portugal in the absence of the king in Brazil (see 1816).

THE AMERICAS

3 Mar. Missouri, part of the Louisiana Purchase (1803) and a US territory where slavery is legal, is controversially accepted into the union as the 24th state. Maine (created from parts of the state of Massachusetts) enters the Union on the same day, as a free state.

6 Mar. The Missouri Compromise dictates that slavery be abolished in the rest of the territory of the Louisiana Purchase.

– James Monroe is re-elected president of the USA by a majority of one vote in the electoral college. He has formulated the neo-racist, progressivist view that a 'hunter or savage state requires a greater extent of territory to sustain it than is compatible with progress and just claims of civilized life'.

SUB-SAHARAN AFRICA

July A British settlement is founded at Grahamstown, on the E coast of S Africa. Previously Dutch-dominated, the region now has some 4000 British settlers.

– The W African state of Liberia is founded by the Washington Colonization Society as a homeland for African-American former slaves.

ECONOMY AND SOCIETY

– Concrete is produced in the USA for the first time and is used in the building of the Erie Canal.

– Platinum deposits are discovered in the Ural Mts by Russian prospectors.

1820-1

ARTS AND HUMANITIES

Literature

– William Blake, English religious visionary and political radical, publishes an edition of the biblical Book of Job with his own illustrations.

John Keats, 'The Eve of St Agnes', 'La Belle Dame Sans Merci' and 'Ode on a Grecian Urn', poems.

Alphonse de Lamartine, *Méditations poétiques* (Poetical Meditations), one of the masterpieces of French Romanticism.

Sir Walter Scott, *The Monastery* and *The Abbot*, novels that help feed a public appetite for 'gothick' mystery and myth. Scott's Tory royalism reflects the contemporary support for reactionary politics in Britain, and he is created a baronet by George IV.

Eugene Scribe, *L'Ours et le pacha* (The Bear and the Pasha), comedy. Scribe's vaudeville comedies become a celebrated feature of Paris entertainment.

Percy Bysshe Shelley, *Prometheus Unbound*, lyric drama, and 'Ode to the West Wind', poem.

Visual Arts and Architecture

– An armless Classical Greek statue of Aphrodite is discovered on the Aegean island of Melos and has an important influence on contemporary sculpture (widely known as the Venus de Milo).

1821

EUROPE

Feb. Rebellions against Ottoman (Turkish) rule begin in Wallachia (S Romania) and Greece where, in Morea (the Peloponnese), the Turkish population is slaughtered. In Constantinople (Istanbul) the patriarch of the Greek Orthodox Church is hanged and its Greek population massacred by a vengeful Ottoman government. The Greek nationalist leader Alexandros Ypsilantis invades Moldavia (NE Romania), but the Ottoman army defeats his forces at the battle of Dragasani near Bucharest (19 June). Other Greek forces take Tripolis in Morea (5 Oct.), killing some 10,000 Turks. Austria and Britain warn Russia not to interevene to help her co-religionists in Greece, where the War of Independence will last until 1831.

Mar. King Victor Emmanuel I of Piedmont-Sardinia is forced to abdicate after refusing to accept a constitution. It is introduced under the more liberal regent Charles Albert, but his supporters are defeated at the battle of Novara, NW Italy (8 April), by an Austrian–Sardinian army, which restores the main royal house of Savoy under King Charles Felix, Victor Emmanuel's brother.

5 May Former French emperor Napoleon Bonaparte (see p. 357) dies on St Helena in the S Atlantic.

THE AMERICAS

24 Feb. Mexico declares its independence from Spain and also demands freedom for the provinces of Texas and California.

3 Mar. In his judgement on Cohens vs. Virginia, US chief justice John Marshall (see 1802) rules that the power of the US Supreme Court is superior to that of any state court in matters relating to federal (national) rights.

4 Mar. James Monroe begins his second term as US president.

24 June S American liberator Simón Bolívar defeats a Spanish army at Carabobo (24 June), establishing the independence of Venezuela (24 June), where he is proclaimed president (30 Aug.). He extends the liberation struggle into Quito (Ecuador).

22 July Peru declares its independence under interim president Gen. José de San Martín, a long-time fighter for independence; he later resigns (1822), enabling Bolívar to become ruler. After all his efforts on behalf of Spanish America, José de San Martín will die in exile in Boulogne, France, in 1850.

14 Sept. Costa Rica, El Salvador, Guatemala and Honduras jointly declare their independence from Spain. Panama also breaks free (Dec.) and merges with the Republic of Great Colombia.

– The Anglo-Saxon population of Texas (still a Mexican territory) is boosted by the foundation of the city of Austin, later capital of the republic and future US state, by Stephen Fuller Austin.

ECONOMY AND SOCIETY

– The universities of Buenos Aires (Argentina), McGill (Montreal, Canada) and George Washington (Washington, D.C., USA) are founded. The English High School in Boston, Massachusetts, opens as the first non-fee-paying public high school in the USA, and the state (1827) will require one to be opened in every town.

– Poker, a new card game derived from the Persian game *as nas*, the English game brag and the French *poque*, is now being played by sailors in New Orleans, southern USA.

– In England the *Manchester Guardian*, founded by John Edward Taylor, starts publication as a weekly newspaper. It will become a daily newspaper in 1855.

SCIENCE AND TECHNOLOGY

– Michael Faraday, English physicist and chemist, demonstrates the power of electro-magnetic rotation as the basis of the electric motor. Faraday was the son of a blacksmith, apprenticed to a bookbinder. He became interested in science through reading the books he bound. Mainly self-taught through mixing with scientists, he becomes a renowned experimental physicist.

ARTS AND HUMANITIES

Literature

23 Feb. The English Romantic poet John Keats dies in Rome of consumption at the age of 25.

Thomas De Quincey, *Confessions of an English Opium Eater*, creative journal.

G.W.F. Hegel (see p. 371), *Grundlinien der Philosophie des Rechts* (Elements of the Philosophy of Right).

Sir Walter Scott, *Kenilworth*, historical novel.

Visual Arts and Architecture

John Constable, *The Haywain*, painting.

Music

4 Mar. The American patriotic song 'Hail to the Chief', by the Scottish composers James Sanderson and E. Rilley, is played for the first time at James Monroe's second inauguration as president of the USA (see 1820). The lines are adapted from Sir Walter Scott's poem *Lady of the Lake*.

Georg Wilhelm Friedrich Hegel (1770–1831)

The German philosopher Hegel, a professor at the University of Berlin, was the last and greatest of the Idealist thinkers, and in his 'absolute Idealism' reality and our idea of it become one and the same thing. Hegel's philosophy was based on history, which he saw as the progressive realization of the idea of freedom. Believing that mind and the external world are but two aspects of a unity that he called 'Spirit', he saw history as the unfolding of the ends and purposes of this Spirit. Hegel believed that in each age Spirit manifests itself in different ways, and made the historical process itself the dynamic that explains how human beings and societies evolve. One period builds upon its predecessor and is the precursor to the next. This notion of a triadic development he called the dialectic: thesis led to anti-thesis, and both these stages would then, in turn, be corrected and incorporated in a new synthesis, which in turn would be confronted by its opposite, resulting in a new synthesis, and so on. A political conservative, Hegel believed that the supreme historical synthesis had been achieved in the combination of the Kingdom of Prussia and the Lutheran Church.

Hegel was enormously influential in the 19th century. The writing of history was transformed by his emphasis on how each epoch, civilization and culture shares certain characteristics, so that the same climate of opinion influences all aspects of a society's life – its art, culture, religion and economic life. Perhaps most significantly, Hegel's idea of the dialectic was taken up by Karl Marx, who saw the dialectical process as driven by material factors rather than by Spirit, and who transformed the dialectic into a force for revolutionary change.

18 Nov. First performance in Berlin of Carl Maria von Weber's opera *Der Freischütz* (The Freeshooter). His Concert Piece for piano and orchestra in C minor is also premiered this year. Franz Schubert, Symphony No. 7 in E major.

1822

EUROPE

13 Jan. The Greek representative assembly proclaims the nation's independence from the Ottoman empire. The Ottoman navy (April) massacres most of the population of the Greek island of Chios, off the W coast of Turkey, and in a naval battle (19 June) the Greeks destroy an Ottoman fleet. A Turkish army invades Greece (July) and forces the new independent government to flee from the mainland to the islands.

12 Aug. Believing he is being blackmailed because of his homosexuality, British foreign secretary Lord Castlereagh commits suicide. The subsequently reconstituted ministry represents a shift from reactionary policies within the Tory Party. George Canning, who had once fought a duel with Castlereagh (see 1809), replaces him as foreign secretary.

Robert Peel becomes home secretary and will form the London police force (see 1829).
– The potato crop fails in W Ireland.

THE AMERICAS

25 June Following the country's independence from Spain, Agustín de Iturbide is crowned Emperor Agustín I of Mexico.

1 Dec. The Portuguese regent Dom Pedro proclaims the independence of Brazil and is crowned Emperor Pedro I. His father, King John VI, has been forced by political opposition to return to Portugal (1816), and Pedro now reacts against the conservative policies of his father's government.
– In the W Indies Haiti liberates Santo Domingo, the city and E province of Hispaniola (now the Dominican Republic) from Spanish rule and unites the whole island.

SUB-SAHARAN AFRICA

– In W Africa the First Ashanti War, between the Asante (Ashanti) state and British forces on the Gold Coast (S Ghana), breaks out.

ECONOMY AND SOCIETY

– In Britain the *Sunday Times* newspaper is founded in London.
– Greenwich Village in Manhattan, USA, develops as people flee from New York city to escape an outbreak of yellow fever.

SCIENCE AND TECHNOLOGY

30 April The *Aaron Manby* is launched at Rotherhithe. The first iron steamship, it carries passengers across the English Channel.
– French inventor Joseph Niepce makes the first permanent photograph by fixing an image on paper.
– Francis Place, an English social reformer, advocates contraception using a soft sponge in his pamphlet *To the Married of Both Sexes of the Working People*.
– British engineer George Stephenson, inventor of the locomotive, finishes the world's first iron railway bridge on the Stockton-to-Darlington line in NE England.
– English mathematician Charles Babbage (see p. 383) conceives the idea of the Difference Engine, an early form of computer designed to compile mathematical tables.

ARTS AND HUMANITIES

Literature

– French historian Jean-François Champollion deciphers the inscriptions on the Rosetta stone (now in the British Museum, London) (see 1799). For the first time it is possible to read Egyptian hieroglyphics. Champollion goes on to establish the modern discipline of Egyptology.

Visual Arts and Architecture

13 Oct. Italian sculptor Antonio Canova dies in Venice, N Italy.
– John Nash completes the remodelling of the Royal Pavilion in Brighton, using a mixture of Classical and Oriental styles.

Music

1 Dec. Hungarian piano prodigy Franz Liszt makes his professional debut in Vienna (his first public performance was given in 1820, when he was nine years old).
Franz Schubert, Symphony No. 8 (Unfinished) in B minor.

1823

EUROPE

6 April The French government sends troops to Spain to defeat the liberal revolution of 1820. The policy is the brainchild of foreign minister and man of letters François-René, vicomte de Chateaubriand (see 1801); although he is dismissed (6 June) his plan succeeds with the French victory at the battle of Trocadero (31 Aug.) and the army's entry into the liberal stronghold of Cadiz. King Ferdinand VII is restored to power and his repressive regime will last until his death (1833).

– Abolitionists William Wilberforce and Thomas Fowell Buxton establish the British and Foreign Anti-Slavery Society in London.

THE AMERICAS

1 July An assembly at Guatemala City declares the sovereignty of the Federation of Central America, but the union of Costa Rica, Guatemala, Honduras, Nicaragua and San Salvador will eventually dissolve (see 1840).

2 Dec. President James Monroe announces the Monroe Doctrine to Congress, an important basis of future US foreign policy. It opposes further European involvement in the W hemisphere, both N and S America and commits the USA to remaining free of any entanglement in European affairs.

ECONOMY AND SOCIETY

20 July Pope Pius VII dies. He is succeeded (28 Sept.) by Annibale Sermattei della Genga, who becomes Pope Leo XII.

– Drilling for oil begins near the Caspian seaport town of Baku in Azerbaijan (part of the Russian empire) establishing Russia's petroleum industry.

– Asiatic cholera arrives at Astrakhan near the Caspian Sea in S Russia.

– According to popular legend, William Webb Ellis picks up the ball during a game of football at Rugby School in the English Midlands and runs with it. This is traditionally regarded as the origin of rugby football, the rules of which will be first codified and published in 1846.

– Tea bushes are discovered in the Assam region of E India, and tea plantations develop using immigrant Chinese labourers. This marks the end of China's monopoly in the production of tea.

SCIENCE AND TECHNOLOGY

5 Oct. The pre-eminent British medical journal, *The Lancet*, begins publication in London. Its founder, Thomas Wakeley, is a medical radical who campaigns against nepotism, the adulteration of foods and the power of the Royal College of Surgeons.

– English chemist and physicist Michael Faraday produces liquid chlorine, and the gas can now be used for water purification.

– Charles Mackintosh, Scottish chemist, patents the raincoat that bears his name: a waterproof layer of rubber is bonded to cloth.

– Sir Francis Ronalds invents an electric telegraph system, which he offers to the British Admiralty, but they reject it. However, he will be appointed superintendent of the Meteorological Observatory at Kew, London, in 1843.

ARTS AND HUMANITIES

Literature

Lord Byron, the last part of *Don Juan*, satirical poem.

James Fenimore Cooper, *The Pioneers*, novel, the first of his popular 'frontier' novels.

Alexander Pushkin, first part of *Eugene Onegin*, a novel in verse (1823–31).

Music

3 Feb. First performance in Venice of Gioachino Rossini's opera *Semiramide*.

Henry Bishop, 'Home Sweet Home', popular song, with lyrics by the American playwright John Howard Payne.

Franz Schubert, music for the play *Rosamunde, Fürstin von Cypern* (Rosamunde, Princess of Cyprus).

1824

EUROPE

16 Sept. King Louis XVIII of France dies and is succeeded by his brother, who becomes Charles X, last Bourbon king of France.

Oct. In the War of Independence the Greek army heavily defeats the Ottoman Turks at Mytilene on the island of Lesbos.

ASIA

24 Feb. The British governor general of India, Lord Amherst, declares war on Burma, whose army has captured the island of Shahpuri in the Bay of Bengal, and the British seize Rangoon (11 May). The First Anglo-Burmese War will last until 1826.

THE AMERICAS

2 Mar. In the case of Gibbons vs. Ogden, the US Supreme Court decides against monopolistic practices. The New York state legislature's grant of a monopoly to the steamboat operator Thomas Gibbons is deemed illegal since it violates the interstate commerce clause in the US Constitution.

24 May President James Monroe signs a bill establishing the US Army Corps of Engineers, whose work will assist civilian navigation and transportation as well as military campaigns.

6 Aug. In S America Spanish colonial armies are defeated by nationalists under Simón Bolívar at the battle of Junin and under Antonio José de Sucre at Ayacucho in Peru (9 Dec.), ensuring the country's independence.

– Robert Owen (see 1806) buys the experimental settlement of Harmony in Indiana from its founders, the German Lutheran Rappites. The settlement, renamed New Harmony, becomes the first of the American socialist communes that Owen is also establishing in England, Ireland and Mexico.

SUB-SAHARAN AFRICA

21 Jan. The forces of the W African Asante (Ashanti) empire defeat the rival Fante and other opponents near Akantamansu (now S Ghana). They include a British contingent whose commander, Sir Charles Macarthy, governor-in-chief of the Gold Coast forts, is captured and decapitated. His skull is used as a ceremonial drinking cup.

ECONOMY AND SOCIETY

- John Cadbury, a Quaker, starts a tea and coffee shop in Birmingham, England, and establishes what will become an international business synonymous with chocolate production.
- The Glenlivet whisky distillery in the NE Highlands of Scotland becomes the first to be officially licensed by government.
- Paolo Agnese establishes the first Italian pasta factory at Imperia.
- The Royal Society for the Prevention of Cruelty to Animals (the RSPCA) is founded in London.

SCIENCE AND TECHNOLOGY

- Englishman Joseph Aspdin of Leeds patents Portland cement, which is impervious to water and will be used in building and engineering construction.
- French scientist Nicolas-Léonard-Sadi Carnot in his *Thoughts on the Motive Power of Fire* observes that in relation to steam power heat alone is not enough to provide locomotion; rather it relies on hot steam condensing in a cold cylinder. Carnot's observations will be expressed by Scottish physicist William Thomson, Lord Kelvin, as the second law of thermodynamics.
- William Prout, a London doctor, shows that hydrochloric acid is the chief agent in human digestion.

ARTS AND HUMANITIES

- The Cherokee scholar Sequoya borrows letters from the Roman alphabet to create a written language, making the Cherokee people of the SE USA the first literate Native N Americans.

Literature

19 April English poet Lord Byron dies of fever at Missolonghi (Mesolóngion), C Greece, while supporting troops fighting for Greek independence from Turkey.

Sir Walter Scott, *Redgauntlet* and *Quentin Durward*, historical novels.

Visual Arts and Architecture

Eugène Delacroix, *The Massacre at Chios,* painting (see 13 Jan. 1822).

Music

- Ludwig van Beethoven's (see p. 356) *Missa Solemnis* (Mass in D major) and Symphony No. 9 in D minor receive their first performances. The latter, known as the *Choral Symphony*, has as its finale a setting of Schiller's 'Ode to Joy' for four soloists, chorus and orchestra (in the late 20th century it will be adopted as the anthem of the European Union).

Felix Mendelssohn, Symphony No. 1 in C minor.

Franz Schubert, String Quartet No. 14 in D minor (*Death and the Maiden*), the second movement of which is based on Schubert's setting (1817) of a poem by Matthias Claudius.

1825

EUROPE

4 Jan. Ferdinand I, absolutist king of the Two Sicilies in S Italy, dies and is succeeded by his son Francesco I.

April By a law of indemnity the French state compensates the aristocracy for lands seized during the French Revolution.

16 July In Britain Parliament approves legislation granting workers the right to take joint action to campaign for better pay and working conditions, but the bill restricts the provisions so narrowly that it effectively denies the right to strike.

1 Dec. Tsar Alexander I of Russia dies after eating poisoned mushrooms; he is succeeded by his brother, Nicholas I. The Decembrist uprising (26 Dec.) of progressive army officers opposed to tsarist autocracy is easily suppressed.

- In the Greek War of Independence Ottoman forces renew the siege of Missolonghi (Mesolóngion), and fresh forces from Ottoman Egypt land in the Morea (Peloponnese).

THE AMERICAS

9 Feb. John Quincy Adams (eldest son of John Adams, the second president; see 1796) is elected sixth president of the USA.

12 Feb. The Creek people repudiate the treaty by which their leaders ceded their tribal territory in Georgia to the USA (see 1813).

6 Aug. Bolivia, formerly Upper Peru, proclaims its independence following a war of liberation from Spain. It is named after Simón Bolívar, who drafts the new constitution. Antonio José de Sucre (victor of the battle of Ayacuchom; see 1824) becomes first president (1826–8) but will have to resign because of strong conservative opposition to his reformist policies.

25 Aug. Uruguay, a province of S Brazil since 1814, proclaims its independence following a rebellion supported by Argentina (which hopes to annex Uruguay). Brazil later declares war on Argentina, but the continued existence of Uruguay is assured.

29 Aug. The Portuguese finally recognize Brazil's independence.

9 Oct. The first organized group of Norwegian emigrants to the USA arrives in New York. They are mostly Quakers escaping from an intolerant established Church.

26 Oct. The Erie Canal (see 1817) opens in New York state, USA. Freight can now be moved from the Midwest to the E coast in ten days. Growing trade gradually encourages settlement at Fort Dearborn, the future Chicago, NE Illinois.

SUB-SAHARAN AFRICA

- Alexander Laing, Scottish explorer, reaches the city of Timbuktu (in modern Mali), W Africa.

ECONOMY AND SOCIETY

- Sacrilege becomes a capital offence in France.
- French lawyer and gastronome Jean-Anthelme Brillat-Savarin writes *La Physiologie du goût* (The Physiology of Taste), a humorous study of eating customs.
- The New York Stock Exchange is formally opened.
- Amherst College in Massachusetts, USA, a liberal-arts college founded in 1821 for men and women, becomes a chartered institution.

SCIENCE AND TECHNOLOGY

27 Sept. The world's first steam locomotive passenger service begins between Stockton and Darlington in NE England.

– The first US patent for tin-plated cans is granted to Thomas Kensett.

ARTS AND HUMANITIES

Literature

– Thomas Babington Macaulay, British historian and future politician, writes an essay on the poet John Milton for the *Edinburgh Review*; it brings him instant fame.

Franz Grillparzer, *King Ottokar, His Rise and Fall*, tragedy.

William Hazlitt, *The Spirit of the Age*, a collection of essays.

Alessandro Manzoni, *I promessi sposi* (The Betrothed), novel.

Jacques-Nicolas-Augustin Thierry, *The History of the Conquest of England by the Normans*, history.

Visual Arts and Architecture

16 April British painter and art critic Henry Fuseli dies.

29 Dec. French painter Jacques-Louis David dies in Brussels.

– English architect John Nash begins reconstructing Buckingham House as Buckingham Palace; it will become the London home of the British sovereign from 1837 on Queen Victoria's accession.

John Constable, *The Leaping Horse*, painting.

Music

– Franz Schubert completes his Symphony No. 9 in C major (Great).

1826

EUROPE

10 Mar. John VI (the Merciful), king of Portugal, dies and is succeeded by his son, who becomes Peter IV. As Emperor Pedro I of Brazil, the new king declines to return from S America and grants a liberal representative constitution to Portugal before abdicating in favour of his infant daughter Maria da Glória (Queen Maria II) under the regency of her uncle Dom Miguel.

THE MIDDLE EAST AND NORTH AFRICA

May The Ottoman (Turkish) janissaries (the sultans' elite troops), revolt in Constantinople after Mahmud II orders them to be disbanded; in response, the city mob attacks the janissaries and massacres over 6000 of them.

– Persia invades the Transcaucasian territories of SW European Russia but is defeated at the battle of Ganja (Gyanzha or Gäncä), Azerbaijan, at the start of a three-year war between the two countries.

ASIA

24 Feb. The First Anglo-Burmese War (see 1824) ends with the treaty of Yandabu: Burma cedes the territories of Assam, Arakan and Tenasserim to Britain.

– Dost Mohammad seizes the capital Kabul and becomes the overall ruler (khan) of Afghanistan. He deftly maintains the country's independence from rival powers Britain and Russia.

THE AMERICAS

4 July Thomas Jefferson and John Adams, former presidents of the USA, die.

22 Aug. Trader and explorer Jedediah Smith begins his journey from Great Salt Lake (in modern Utah) and becomes the first US citizen to enter California from the E (see 27 May 1831).

SUB-SAHARAN AFRICA

7 Aug. In W Africa the British army destroys the main Asante (Ashanti) force near Accra (port capital of modern Ghana) in the war that began in 1822.

– A series of border wars breaks out as Cape Colony, the British territory centred on Cape Town, S Africa, extends its territory.

ECONOMY AND SOCIETY

– Munich University, Bavaria, is founded.

– English shopkeeper John Horniman sells the first tea for retail purposes in sealed packages.

SCIENCE AND TECHNOLOGY

– Antoine-Jérôme Balard, French chemist, discovers bromide.

– In Paris Louis Daguerre goes into partnership with Joseph-Nicéphore Niepce to perfect the photographic process that will result in the daguerrotype (1839).

– Bavarian printer Aloys Senefelder, who discovered the lithographic printing process in 1796, opens a printing workshop to exploit the technique.

– James Sharp of Northampton, England, invents the first practical gas stove, which he uses in his own home.

– Unter den Linden, the main thoroughfare of the Prussian capital, Berlin, is now lit by gas lamps.

– The Zoological Society of London establishes the zoological gardens in London's Regent's Park. The 'zoo' will later open to the public (27 April 1828).

ARTS AND HUMANITIES

Literature

John Burke, *Burke's Peerage*, an exhaustive dictionary of the British peerage and baronetage.

James Fenimore Cooper, *The Last of the Mohicans*, novel.

Sir Walter Scott, *Woodstock*, historical novel.

Visual Arts and Architecture

– The first part of *The Birds of America* (1827–38, 87 parts), illustrated by John James Audubon, is published in Britain.

Eugène Delacroix, *Greece in the Ruins of Missolonghi*, painting.

Music

12 April First performance at Covent Garden, London, of Carl Maria von Weber's opera *Oberon*; the composer dies of tuberculosis in London (5 June).

– Ludwig van Beethoven (see p. 356) completes his String Quartet No. 13 in B flat major (its final movement, a fugue, is later detached as a separate work, the *Grosse Fugue*).

– The 17-year-old Felix Mendelssohn composes the overture to *A Midsummer Night's Dream*.

1827

EUROPE

Feb. British prime minister Lord Liverpool resigns after suffering a stroke; former prime minister George Canning succeeds

(10 April) and forms a government but dies shortly afterwards (8 Aug.); Lord Goderich becomes the new Tory prime minister (31 Aug.).

5 June Ottoman (Turkish) forces enter Athens and capture the Acropolis from Greek nationalists; by the treaty of London (6 July) Britain, France and Russia decide to support the Greeks if the Turks do not agree to an armistice.

16 Aug. Sultan Mahmud II rejects the allies' demand for a truce, and at the battle of Navarino (20 Oct.) British, French and Russian forces defeat the Ottoman Turkish–Egyptian fleet off the coast of the Peloponnese.

ASIA

1 Oct. In their war over Transcaucasia Russian forces defeat the Persians and seize a large swathe of the N Armenian plateau.

THE AMERICAS

26 Jan. Offended by Simón Bolívar's dictatorial presidency, Peru withdraws from his plan for a pan-continental Great Colombia.

20 Feb. Brazil defeats Argentinian and Uruguayan forces at the battle of Ituziango.

– The settlement of Bytown, the future Canadian capital Ottawa, is founded in SE Ontario (named after British army engineer John By).

ECONOMY AND SOCIETY

Feb. New Orleans, southern USA, holds its first Mardi Gras (Shrove Tuesday) carnival celebrations.

16 Mar. The first Afro-American newspaper, the *Freeman's Journal*, is published in New York by its founder, the Rev. Samuel Cornish, who has also established the first Afro-American Presbyterian church. Slavery has been abolished in New York (4 July), and the newspaper campaigns against the institution of slavery elsewhere.

– Britain decides on a uniform standard for an acre of land, which now measures 1/640th of a square mile. Continental Europe will measure land in hectares, with one hectare equalling 2.47 acres. Originally in England an acre was the area of land a yoke of oxen could plough in one day.

– The *Evening Standard* newspaper begins publication in London.

– The University of Toronto is founded in Ontario, Canada.

SCIENCE AND TECHNOLOGY

– French hydraulic engineer Benoît Fourneyron develops the first waterwheel turbine, in which pressurized water flows from the hub to the rim.

– English astronomer Sir John Frederick William Herschel invents contact lenses.

– The German physicist Georg Ohm discovers the law that bears his name, which states that there is an inversely proportional relationship between the strength of an electric current and the resistance of a circuit.

– London's Hammersmith Bridge, the first bridge built of stone and metal, opens to traffic.

– A sailing ship sets a new record of 26 days for the transatlantic crossing from New Orleans, S USA to Liverpool, NW England.

– English chemist John Walker invents the lucifer, the first striking match.

– German chemist Friedrich Wöhler isolates metallic aluminium from clay.

ARTS AND HUMANITIES

Literature

Heinrich Heine, *Das Buch der Lieder* (The Book of Songs), poetry.

Visual Arts and Architecture

22 Aug. English draughtsman, social satirist and caricaturist Thomas Rowlandson dies.

– The new Paris Bourse (Exchange), designed in the style of Rome's Temple of Vespasian, is completed.

Eugène Delacroix, *The Death of Sardanapalus*, painting.

Music

26 Mar. German composer Ludwig van Beethoven (see p. 356) dies after catching a chill while returning to Vienna from Gneixendorf (near Krems) in an open chaise.

– Franz Schubert completes his song cycle *Die Winterreise* (Winter Journey).

1828

EUROPE

25 Jan. The duke of Wellington, former career soldier, renowned for defeating Napoleon, becomes British prime minister at the head of the Tory Party, whose reactionary attitudes revive. The Tories traditionally protect the landed and agrarian interest; although Wellington modifies the Corn Laws, ostensibly to give consumers relief from high food prices, this fails to trigger the large-scale grain imports that would reduce the cost of bread.

26 April Russia declares war on the Ottoman empire, ostensibly in support of Greek independence; troops cross the Danube (8 June) and capture Varna, E Bulgaria (12 Oct.) The Russian forces settle in for the winter.

4 July The Portuguese regent Dom Miguel proclaims himself king and abolishes the liberal constitution; his infant niece and legitimate ruler, Maria II (Maria da Glória; see 10 Mar. 1826), flees to England while Portugal collapses into civil war.

16 Nov. By the London Protocol, Britain, Russia and France recognize the independence of Greek Morea (the Peloponnese) and the Cyclades islands.

ASIA

22 Feb. The treaty of Turkmanchai ends the Russo-Persian War (see 1 Oct. 1827): Persia is forced to cede large amounts of territory, including parts of Armenia; Russia gains exclusive rights to keep a navy on the Caspian Sea.

28 Dec. More than 30,000 people die in an earthquake in Echigo province, C Honshu, Japan.

THE AMERICAS

19 May In the USA the protectionist Tariff of Abominations is signed by President John Quincy Adams, raising duties on imported goods to protect farmers in the W and manufacturers on the E coast. Although Congress passes a Reciprocity Act (24 May), charging lower duties on goods from countries that reciprocate, the measure provokes widespread opposition (see 1830).

27 Aug. Uruguay proclaims its independence after British diplomatic mediation resolves hostilities between rival Argentina and Brazil. Uruguay is established as a buffer state.

Nov. Andrew Jackson, frontiersman, revolutionary soldier (when aged 13) and Democratic Party politician, is elected seventh president of the USA with 171 votes in the electoral college.

– Britain and the USA agree to extend indefinitely their respective zones of occupation in the NW territories; their common border will be established at the 49th parallel (line of latitude) in 1846.

SUB-SAHARAN AFRICA

22 Sept. Shaka, king and founder of the Zulu nation (in modern Natal, S Africa; see 1815), is assassinated. Demented by grief following the death of his mother, he had ordered random mass executions, provoking his half-brothers Dingane and Mhlangana to kill him and usurp the throne.

– Radama I, king of the dominant Merina people of Madagascar, dies and is succeeded by his xenophobic queen Ranavalona I.

Adolphe Quételet (1796–1874)

The founder of the modern science of statistics was born in Ghent in what became Belgium, and educated at the local university. Quételet was a mathematical prodigy, becoming a professor at the age of 23. In 1828 he was appointed to run the new Brussels Royal Observatory, and, having time on his hands while the observatory was being built, he began to think about the application of mathematics to humanity and human behaviour. The result was the new science of statistics. Using probability, he showed that social behaviour could be seen to have patterns of mathematical regularity.

Quételet's first study, *Sur l'homme*, was of the physical dimensions of different human beings, such as their height, size, weight and age. He established thereby the physical type of 'the average man' as the type or standard characteristic of each nation. Quételet thought that differences from this standard followed certain laws of accidental causes. He also thought that this law of the average type and its related variables applied not just to physical dimensions but also to moral behaviour and intelligence. He went on to relate these facts to the information available on different kinds of criminal behaviour.

Quételet's new science of statistics was meant to represent the application to social life of the same mathematical principles that had ensured spectacular advances in the physical sciences. It became his life's work to show the principles and methods by which census data should be gathered. Today, political and public debates are dominated by statistics – something that we owe to Quételet's pioneering work.

He had encouraged European-style modernization, but she is hostile to both British and French influences.

ECONOMY AND SOCIETY

– University College, London, is founded on secular and non-denominational principles with the prominent help of radical Scots jurist and Whig politican Henry Brougham (later Lord Brougham).

SCIENCE AND TECHNOLOGY

4 July Work begins on the construction of the Baltimore and Ohio railroad, which is officially chartered as the first US railway to carry freight and passengers.

– Adolphe Quételet (see box), Belgian statistician and astronomer, is appointed first director of the Royal Observatory in Brussels.

– Karl von Baer, an Estonian naturalist, discovers the mammalian ovum and so founds embryology as a modern science.

– The Delaware and Hudson Canal connects New York with Port Jervis on the Delaware River, NE USA.

ARTS AND HUMANITIES

Literature

July *The Spectator*, a weekly magazine dealing with politics and the arts, begins publication in London.

Alexander Pushkin, *Boris Godunov*, historical drama in verse.

Sir Walter Scott, *The Fair Maid of Perth*, historical novel.

Noah Webster, *American Dictionary of the English Language*, a pioneering work of lexicography.

Visual Arts and Architecture

16 April Former Spanish court painter Francisco Goya (see p. 360) dies in Bordeaux, France.

9 July French classical sculptor Jean-Antoine Houdon dies in Paris.

– French painter Eugène Delacroix produces 19 lithographs to illustrate a new French edition of Goethe's drama *Faust*.

Music

20 Aug. First performance in Paris of Gioachino Rossini's opera *Le Comte Ory* (Count Ory).

19 Nov. Austrian composer Franz Schubert dies of syphilis in Vienna.

1829

EUROPE

22 Mar. The London Protocol, agreed by Britain, Russia and France, recognizes the independence of mainland Greece (see 16 Nov. 1828).

13 April In Britain Parliament passes the Catholic Emancipation Act. The new law allows Catholics the right to vote, to sit in Parliament and to hold public office (except for the posts of lord chancellor and lord lieutenant of Ireland). Catholics have to swear an oath denying the papacy any power to intervene in British domestic politics and to recognize the Protestant royal succession. Tory prime minister Arthur Wellesley, duke of Wellington, and home secretary, Sir Robert Peel, have to endure fierce opposition to the measure from within their own party.

11 June The German-born Russian commander Hans Karl von Diebitsch gains victory over Ottoman forces at the battle of Kulevcha; he crosses the Balkans to seize and occupy Adrianople (Edirne) in European Turkey. The Turks sue for peace, and the war is brought to an end with the treaty of Adrianople (24 Sept.): Russia gains territory to the E of the Black Sea, extends its influence in the Danubian provinces and forces the Ottoman government to recognize Greek autonomy.

29 Sept. British home secretary Robert Peel establishes London's Metropolitan Police, giving his name to its officers who are commonly known as 'bobbies' or 'peelers'.

30 Nov. At the London Conference the European powers decide on complete autonomy for Greece, but the frontier is moved back to the Gulf of Corinth; Ioánnes Kapodístrias becomes president with dictatorial powers.

THE AMERICAS

4 Mar. Andrew Jackson begins his first term as US president.

15 Sept. Mexico abolishes slavery, but its territory of Texas is exempted from the provisions of the act (2 Dec.).

8 Dec. Future dictator of Argentina Juan Manuel de Rosas (see 1835) is made governor of Buenos Aires, with the support of the Federalist Party. He has defeated the Unitarios (centralist) forces (April), which had overthrown Col. Manuel Dorrego in 1828.

– Venezuela secedes from Simón Bolívar's Great Colombia, the S American federation including Colombia and Ecuador.

ECONOMY AND SOCIETY

10 Feb. Pope Leo XII dies. He is succeeded (31 Mar.) by Francesco Saverio Castiglione, who becomes Pope Pius VIII.

Oct. Tremont House in Boston, Massachusetts, opens as one of the first hotels with private rooms each with its own key.

– In England the Oxford and Cambridge boat race is rowed for the first time.

– US showman Phineas Taylor Barnum discovers, exhibits and exploits two young male 'Siamese twins', Chang and Eng. They arrive in Boston and then sail for England (Oct.), where they become objects of public curiosity.

– Cholera breaks out again in Astrakhan on the Volga River, S Russia.

SCIENCE AND TECHNOLOGY

– On the basis of evidence supplied by his former partner in crime William Hare, Irish body-snatcher William Burke is hanged in Edinburgh for murder that he undertook with the aim of supplying cadavers to Dr Robert Knox for dissection. At the time bodies could not be provided legally for the purpose of medical research.

– French photographic pioneer Louis Daguerre, in partnership with chemist Joseph-Nicéphore Niepce (see 1826), discovers the light sensitivity of silver iodide.

– Public mass transport starts in London with the introduction of the horse-drawn omnibus.

– An English-built steam locomotive is used on the first French railway line, which connects Lyons with St Etienne.

– The steam locomotive 'Rocket', built by railway engineers George Stephenson and his son Robert, wins the Rainhill Trials in Liverpool, England. The competition, sponsored by the Liverpool and Manchester Railway, establishes 'Rocket' as the best engine available, largely owing to its innovative multiple fire-tube boiler, which provides improved power and economy.

– Frenchman Barthélemy Thimonnier invents the sewing machine; when they are introduced to workshops in Paris they are destroyed by rioters who fear the loss of tailoring jobs.

ARTS AND HUMANITIES
Literature

– German publisher Karl Baedeker publishes his first guidebook, to Koblenz in Prussia (now in the Rhineland-Palatinate).

Honoré de Balzac, *Les Chouans*, novel, the first in a vast sequence known as *La Comédie humaine* (The Human Comedy).

Edgar Allan Poe, *Al Aaraaf*, poetry.

Visual Arts and Architecture

23 Mar. In conversation, Goethe (see p. 359) describes architecture as 'frozen music' (*erstarrte Musik*).

Joseph Mallord William Turner, *Ulysses Deriding Polyphemus*, painting.

Music

Mar. Felix Mendelssohn conducts J.S. Bach's *St Matthew Passion* in Berlin, its first performance since Bach's death in 1750.

3 Aug. First performance in Paris of Gioachino Rossini's opera *Guillaume Tell* (William Tell), his last.

1830
EUROPE

26 June George IV, king of Great Britain and Ireland, dies and is succeeded by his brother as William IV. The Tories are dismissed in the general election, and in the new Whig administration Charles, Earl Grey, becomes prime minister with Viscount Palmerston as foreign secretary. Palmerston will earn notoriety for his aggressively robust foreign policy.

29 July In France the July Revolution deposes the increasingly repressive King Charles X, whose four ordinances (26 July) seek to establish governmental control of the press and change the electoral system. The journalist-historian Louis-Adolphe Thiers and other influential liberals frustrate the demands of radicals for a republican constitution and choose as ruler Louis-Philippe, eldest son of the Bourbon duc d'Orléans, known as Philippe-Egalité (7 Aug). The new king is hailed as the 'citizen king'.

Aug. Following the July Revolution in Paris, the Belgians revolt against the union with the Netherlands imposed at the end of the Napoleonic Wars; the Dutch are forced to evacuate Brussels (Sept.), and an independent Belgium is proclaimed (4 Oct.). An international conference (20 Dec.) supports the dissolution of the United Netherlands (see 19 April 1839).

Nov. In Warsaw a Polish rebellion against Russian rule breaks out. Polish revolutionaries declare a nostalgic and symbolic union with Lithuania as part of their rebellion.

MIDDLE EAST AND NORTH AFRICA

5 July France begins colonizing Algeria, seeking to suppress the activities of Algerian pirates. French forces occupy Algiers.

THE AMERICAS

6 April Joseph Smith, claiming a visitation from an angel called Moroni, founds the Church of the Latter-day Saints in Fayette, New York. His *Book of Mormon* claims that the Native Americans were originally Jews who left the Middle East in the 6th century BC and to whom Christ appeared after the Ascension. The practice of polygamy among Smith's followers makes the Mormon Church controversial.

13 May Ecuador secedes from the union of Great Colombia (following the example of Venezuela; see 1829), whose chief proponents die shortly afterwards: Antonio José de Sucre, first president of Bolivia (1826–8), is assassinated (4 June) and Simón Bolívar dies a disillusioned man in Colombia (17 Dec.).

28 May US president Andrew Jackson signs the Indian Removal Act, which authorizes the forced removal of all Native Americans to lands W of the Mississippi River.

15 Sept. The treaty of Dancing Rabbit Creek cedes Choctaw lands E of the Mississippi to the USA.

22 Sept. Venezuela becomes an independent sovereign state.

– Fort Dearborn, the future city of Chicago in the US Midwest, introduces a new town plan and is now attracting increased settlement.

– The Southern states of the USA are still strongly opposed to the Tariff of Abominations (see 19 May 1828) because of the protectionist taxes levied on foreign trade. The conflict grows to threaten the union of the USA as Southern states contest the right of the federal authorities to impose tariffs that suit E-coast manufacturers and the agricultural W but not the cotton-exporting South.

– Mexico acts to declare illegal any further colonization of its territory of Texas by the USA.

ECONOMY AND SOCIETY

30 Nov. Pope Pius VIII dies.

– In his book *Rural Rides*, English journalist and reformer William Cobbett criticizes the pauperization of the working class by industrialization. He develops the idea of an English arcadia populated by an independent-minded, radical and self-sufficient peasantry.

– Cholera spreads into European Russia from Astrakhan, killing one million in 1830 alone and many more elsewhere in Europe. Attempts at cholera control are frustrated by Russian Orthodox clerical obscurantism, which condemns doctors and government officials and claims that quarantine controls are the work of the Antichrist.

– The US Congress makes abortion a statutory crime.

– The world's population now numbers around one billion, a huge increase on the 750 million estimated for 1750.

SCIENCE AND TECHNOLOGY

28 Aug. Peter Cooper demonstrates 'Tom Thumb', the first US-built steam locomotive. With only one year's schooling, Cooper becomes a successful and rich inventor and manufacturer.

15 Sept. In Britain services begin on the Liverpool to Manchester railway line, the first to carry both passengers and freight. William Huskisson, former president of the board of trade, is killed by the 'Rocket'.

– Irishman Aeneas Coffee invents the continuous still that ensures a faster process of distillation in whisky and gin production.

– English scientist Joseph Lister improves the design of the microscope.

– Non-Euclidean geometry receives its pioneering statement of first principles in the work of the Russian mathematician Nikolai Lobachevski, *Principles of Geometry*.

ARTS AND HUMANITIES

Literature

– The first performance in Paris of Victor Hugo's play *Hernani* is followed by a riot in which theatrical traditionalists clash with Romantic supporters of Hugo.

Stendhal (Marie-Henri Beyle), *Le Rouge et le noir* (The Red and the Black), French novel of military and clerical life.

Alfred, Lord Tennyson, *Poems, Chiefly Lyrical*, poetry.

Visual Arts and Architecture

Eugène Delacroix, *Liberty on the Barricades*, painting completed following the July Revolution in Paris.

Music

11 Mar. First performance in Venice of Vincenzo Bellini's opera *I Capuleti ed i Montecchi* (The Capulets and the Montagues), based on Shakespeare's *Romeo and Juliet*.

Hector Berlioz, *Symphonie fantastique*, a milestone in French Romantic composition.

Frédéric Chopin, Concerto No. 1 in E minor for piano and orchestra and Concerto No. 2 in F minor for piano and orchestra.

1831

EUROPE

25 Jan. The Polish diet dethrones Nicholas I (Romanov king of Poland) and declares Polish independence.

3 Feb. Popular revolts begin in the N Italian states of Parma and Modena demanding national union, independence and a liberal constitution; revolution spreads to the Papal States (Mar.), where opposition gathers to the temporal rule of the newly elected Pope Gregory XVI; Austrian forces help to suppress the revolts.

26 May The Russian army defeats Polish nationalist forces at the battle of Ostrolenko (NE of Warsaw), ending the six-month insurrection against Russian domination of the country; the capital Warsaw is occupied (8 Sept.), and the leaders of the Polish revolution escape to a life of exile in Paris.

4 June Leopold, son of the German duke of Saxe-Coburg, is elected to the throne of newly independent Belgium as the country's first king; he becomes Leopold I. A Dutch army invades Belgium (2 Aug.) with the aim of restoring the United Netherlands but is expelled by French forces.

9 Oct. The president of the council of the provisional government of Greece, Count Ioánnis Kapodístrias, is assassinated; his brother takes his place.

29–31 Oct. In Britain a bill proposing the reform of Parliament, already passed by the Commons (Sept.), is rejected by the House of Lords. Riots in support of the measure take place in Bristol.

– Violent protests break out in predominantly Catholic Ireland against the enforcement of tithes, which support the established Protestant Church.

– In Britain the Union of Northumberland and Durham coal miners is founded to campaign for better working conditions.

ASIA

19 Nov. Opposition to Hindu rule in the NE Indian state of Bengal is manifested in an uprising led by Titu Mir, who is killed (19 Nov.) by government forces.

– The British extend their rule to include the state of Mysore in SW India, giving as their reason the disorder in the territory.

THE AMERICAS

7 April Pedro I, emperor of Brazil, abdicates and returns to Europe; he is succeeded by his son as Pedro II.

27 May US trader and frontier explorer Jedediah Smith (see 22 Aug. 1826) is killed by the Comanche people on the Cimarron River, W USA.

21 Aug. In the Southern US state of Virginia, slave Nat Turner, claiming divine guidance, kills his master and family in their sleep; the scale of his slave revolt grows and over the next two days some 60 whites are killed before the uprising is suppressed. Turner and 16 associates are hanged (11 Nov.).

27 Dec. Samuel Sharp leads a slave rebellion in Jamaica, British W Indies. Sugar estate owners are forced to draw up documents freeing their slaves, who also demand compensation before they return to work. Although no whites are killed, the British government hangs Sharp and many of his supporters.

– Stone-cutters in New York protest against the use of stone cut by prison workers in the construction of university buildings. The protest is the first demonstration of collective action by the New York labour force.

ECONOMY AND SOCIETY

2 Feb. Bartolomeo Alberto Cappellari is elected Pope Gregory XVI.

9 Mar. The French Foreign Legion of mercenary soldiers is created. It will serve in N Africa, the Middle East and Indo-China.

9 Aug. The Mohawk and Hudson Railway begins a service between Albany and Schenectady in New York state; it will later (1853) become the New York Central line.

– A new London Bridge across the River Thames, built by eminent civil engineers George Rennie and his son John, is opened.

– The Wesleyan University in Connecticut and the University of the City of New York (later New York University) are founded in the USA.

– The population of the USA is now 13 million, surpassing that of Britain by 800,000.

SCIENCE AND TECHNOLOGY

29 Aug. British physicist Michael Faraday discovers electromagnetic induction, the process underlying the operation of the electric generator. Although US scientist Joseph Henry discovers this independently of Faraday, his work is not published. Nevertheless, the unit of induction, the henry, is named after him and he will proceed to pioneer the development of electric telegraphy.

– English naturalist Charles Darwin (see box) leaves Britain on HMS *Beagle* as part of a scientific expedition to S American waters and the Galapagos Islands (see 1859).

Charles Darwin (1809–82)

The English naturalist Charles Darwin was not the first to formulate the idea that all living things have evolved, rather than having been divinely created. However, in propounding his theory of natural selection, he *was* the first to come up with a plausible explanation of how evolution happens.

Darwin was born and educated in Shrewsbury before training to be a doctor in Edinburgh. He abandoned medicine to study zoology at Cambridge and in 1831 was chosen to be the naturalist on board HMS *Beagle*, then embarking on a survey mission to South America. It was during this five-year voyage that Darwin first appreciated the vast range of life on Earth and the fact that ancient rocks contained a bewildering variety of fossils. He was attracted by evolutionary ideas while observing the finches of the Galapagos Islands, but he formulated the theory after reading Robert Malthus's *Essay on the Principle of Population* (1798). Malthus argued that population rates increase geometrically while the means of subsistence do so arithmetically. Regular famine was therefore a natural mechanism for stabilizing population rates. This view of nature's innate savagery affected the sensitive Darwin deeply. It also inspired him intellectually.

Darwin published his findings in his book *On the Origin of Species by Means of Natural Selection* (1859). The book caused a sensation because it denied the biblical account of creation in the Book of Genesis and suggested that species had evolved by adaptation to the environment: individuals who possessed a characteristic better adapted to their environment were more likely to survive, breed, and pass on this favourable characteristic to their offspring. Darwin contended that life had no purpose and no design, apart from its own survival, and that it had not been created by a divine mind. Darwin also argued that different species shared common ancestors, and demonstrated that men and monkeys are thus related – a revelation that transformed humanity's view of itself.

- US inventor Seth Boyden patents a method of making malleable cast iron.
- The British Association for the Advancement of Science is founded.
- The anaesthetic and solvent chloroform is invented independently by the German chemist Justus von Liebig and the US chemist Samuel Guthrie.

ARTS AND HUMANITIES
Literature
Benjamin Disraeli, *The Young Duke*, novel romanticizing English aristocratic paternalism as a means of appeasing class conflict.

Franz Grillparzer, *Des Meeres und der Liebe Wellen* (The Waves of Sea and Love, or alternatively Hero and Leander), play.

Victor Hugo, *Notre Dame de Paris* (The Hunchback of Notre Dame), novel, and *Les Feuilles d'automne* (Autumn Leaves), poetry.

Visual Arts and Architecture
- The Barbizon school of French painters, which includes Théodore Rousseau and Jean-François Millet, hold their first Paris exhibition. They take their name from a village near Fontainebleau, and their work emphasizes direct observation of nature.

John Constable, *Salisbury Cathedral from the Meadows*, painting.

Eugène Delacroix, *The 28th of July 1830*, painting depicting the revolution in Paris.

Music
21 Nov. First performance in Paris of Giacomo Meyerbeer's opera *Robert le Diable* (Robert the Devil), which establishes a new grand operatic style with dramatic scenic effects and virtuoso arias.

26 Dec. First performance in Milan of *Norma,* Vincenzo Bellini's operatic masterpiece of lyrical tragedy.

Frédéric Chopin, *Grande Polonaise brillante,* for piano and orchestra.

1832
EUROPE
2 Feb. The government of Piedmont (NW Italy) discovers plans for an uprising to take place in June. It is organized by liberal republican Giuseppe Mazzini and his Young Italy association, founded in 1831, working for the political unification of the Italian peninsula.

4 June In Britain the first and deeply controversial Reform Act passes the House of Lords after King William IV threatens to create new peers to vote the measure through. Rotten boroughs, which have only a small number of voters, and pocket boroughs, which are subject to individual patronage, are abolished; parliamentary seats are redistributed in order to represent the growing urban population. Equivalent measures are subsequently introduced for Scotland and Ireland.

28 June Austrian foreign minister Prince Klemens von Metternich engineers the adoption of the Six Articles by the German

Confederation. The rulers of each state or principality are now forced to reject any decision of their representative estates (assemblies) that would undermine their authority; and the estates can no longer use the right to withhold supplies of money as a way of forcing through constitutional change. These measures strengthen the constitutional movement, and at the Hambach Festival (27 May) a mass meeting of S German democrats demands a united German republic.

8 Aug. Independent Greece establishes a monarchy; Otto I, son of King Ludwig I of Bavaria, becomes king of Greece.

THE AMERICAS
3 Mar. The Supreme Court rules that the US government has exclusive control over Native Americans and their lands in all the states of the union.

There it is – Old Glory!

Captain William Driver salutes the new national flag of the United States, Dec. 1831

24 Mar. The American Creek people sign a treaty ceding their lands E of the Mississippi to the United States.

April Chief Black Hawk leads the Native American Sauk (or Sac) and Fox peoples back across the Mississippi to resettle lands alienated to the USA in 1804; a four-month war ends at Bad Axe River, Wisconsin, where they are defeated by the Illinois militia allied to the Sioux; the remaining Sauk and Fox agree to a peace treaty (21 Sept.) forcing them to remain W of the Mississippi. The Chickasaw people cede their lands E of the river to the USA (14 Oct.).

May The Democratic Party of the USA (formerly the Democratic Republican Party) holds its first national convention in Baltimore; President Andrew Jackson is renominated for a second term and will defeat the Republican candidate Henry Clay in the presidential election later in the year.

14 July Congress reduces some of the duties imposed in the 1828 Tariff of Abominations, but protectionism is retained as government policy; President Jackson criticizes (10 Dec.) South Carolina's Ordinance of Nullification (19 Nov.), which rejects the legislation.

ECONOMY AND SOCIETY
- US doctor Charles Knowlton publishes *The Fruits of Philosophy: or The Private Companion of Young Married People*. It explains and advises on birth control methods, and he cites Thomas Malthus, the English clergyman and economist who has argued that famine is a natural mechanism designed to stabilize population levels. The booklet outrages contemporary sensibilities, and Knowlton is prosecuted and imprisoned for

three months, although his work becomes a bestseller and initiates the widespread use of contraceptives.

SCIENCE AND TECHNOLOGY
- The 558km (347 mile) Göta Canal, S Sweden, connects the North Sea with the Baltic.
- Samuel Morse, US inventor, starts work on developing an electric telegraph system.

ARTS AND HUMANITIES
Literature
22 Mar. Poet, dramatist and scientist Johann Wolfgang von Goethe (see p. 359) dies at Weimar, E Germany, having completed Part 2 of his masterpiece *Faust*; it was started around 1771 and Part 1 was published in 1808.
- In Britain book jackets are used by publishers for the first time.

Frances Trollope, *Domestic Manners of the Americans*, a highly critical popular account of the new country, to which she first travelled in 1827.

Visual Arts and Architecture
- Honoré Daumier begins his career as a painter and caricaturist critical of the government and rule of King Louis-Philippe of France.

Eugène Delacroix, *A Moorish Couple on Their Terrace*, painting.

Music
12 May First performance in Milan of Gaetano Donizetti's opera *L'Elisir d'amore* (The Elixir of Love).

Felix Mendelssohn, Piano Concerto No. 1 in G minor, Overture in B minor, *The Hebrides* (*Fingal's Cave*, whose theme the composer is said to have invented while visiting the Hebridean island of Staffa in 1829), and Symphony No. 5 in D minor (*Reformation*).

1833

EUROPE
22 Mar. The states of Prussia, Bavaria, Württemberg and Hesse-Darmstadt form the *Zollverein*, a customs union that marks an important stage in the process of German unification.

May A coalition of French, British and Spanish forces help Queen Maria II of Portugal to defeat and expel her usurping uncle Dom Miguel (see 4 July 1828). Dom Pedro, former king of Portugal and emperor of Brazil, has returned to the country to assist his daughter; he will die in 1834, leaving the young Maria to rule alone. Her reign will last until 1853.

28 June In France the Primary Education Act gives the Roman Catholic Church the right to control most of the country's primary schools.

14 July John Keble, Fellow of Oriel College, Oxford, accuses the British of 'national apostasy' in a sermon preached at the university church of St Mary's. The Oxford Movement is launched as a campaign to restore the Established Church of England to its supposed Catholic and pre-Reformation roots in doctrine, liturgy and discipline.

29 July In Britain the politician, evangelist and philanthropist

William Wilberforce dies just as his lifelong campaign for the abolition of slavery reaches its culmination: the Emancipation Act is passed by the House of Commons (23 Aug.), granting liberty to all slaves in the British empire on 1 Aug. 1834, although under a system of bound apprenticeship, which will last until 1837; slaves under the age of six are freed immediately and slave owners receive £120 million in compensation.

29 Aug. In Britain the Factory Act forbids the employment of children under 9 years of age; children up to 13 years are not allowed to work more than 48 hours a week, and those aged between 13 and 18 a maximum of 69 hours a week. The Tories oppose the measure.

29 Sept. King Ferdinand VII, the last Bourbon king of Spain, dies and is succeeded by his two-year-old daughter Isabella II; the king's brother Don Carlos claims the throne and, supported by Basque, Catalan and conservative-clerical factions, threatens civil war.

MIDDLE EAST AND NORTH AFRICA
4 May The war begun in 1832 between the Ottoman empire and its autonomous (effectively independent) Egyptian province under Mehmet Ali ends with the treaty of Kutahya; Egypt is granted the lands of Syria and Turkish Cilicia.

8 July The defensive treaty of Unkiar-Skelessi between the Ottoman empire and Russia allows for the closure of the Dardanelles (the narrow entrance to the Black Sea) to all except Russian ships in times of war.

ASIA
- A famine that will last three years begins in Japan.

THE AMERICAS
1 Jan. The Islas Malvinas, off the SE coast of S America, are claimed by Britain as the Falkland Islands; a gunboat is sent to assert British rights against Argentina, which has claimed the islands since its independence from Spain, the former colonial power, in 1820.

1 Mar. The Senate passes the Compromise Tariff Act, ending the conflict between the Southern cotton-exporting states, which have objected to high protectionist tariffs, and the industrial N of the country; by 1842 no tariff is to be levied on goods greater than 20% of their value.

ECONOMY AND SOCIETY
- Durham University in N England is officially established.
- Oberlin Collegiate Institute (Oberlin College), Ohio, opens as the first coeducational institute of higher education in the USA and admits African-Americans on equal terms with whites.
- The cholera epidemic that has spread westwards from Russia and continental Europe arrives in Scotland; it will cross the Atlantic to New York by the summer.

SCIENCE AND TECHNOLOGY
- In Britain the passing of the Anatomy Act means that cadavers can be acquired legally for medical research and no longer need to be stolen.

- The first clipper ship, with its characteristic fine hull lines and large sail area, is built in Baltimore, USA, for the China trade.
- The English doctor Thomas Hodgkin describes the cancerous disease of the glands and spleen, Hodgkin's disease, that is named after him.
- Walter Hunt of New York invents a sewing machine that has an eye-pointed needle and double lock stitch.
- German doctor Friedrich Wilde invents the diaphragm contraceptive with a rubber cap.

ARTS AND HUMANITIES

Literature

Honoré de Balzac, *Eugénie Grandet*, novel.

Thomas Carlyle, *Sartor Resartus* (The Tailor Retailored), historical and philosophical essay. It is superficially a discussion of the history of clothing but is in fact a startlingly original account of how different beliefs vary historically.

Carl von Clausewitz, *Vom Kriege* (On War), a classic exposition of the relationship between war, politics and diplomacy, published posthumously (Clausewitz died of cholera in 1831).

Charles Lamb, *Last Essays of Elia* (essays contributed to the *London Magazine*).

John Henry Newman, 'Lead, Kindly Light', hymn written during a difficult sea crossing from Palermo to Marseilles.

George Sand (Amandine Dupin, Baronne Dudevant), *Lélia*, novel, which adds to her controversial reputation. Her first novel, *Indiana* (1832), had asserted the right of women to independent lives. Sand, separated from her husband, has embarked on a love affair with the poet Alfred de Musset.

Music

26 Dec. First performance in La Scala, Milan, of Gaetano Donizetti's opera *Lucrezia Borgia*.

Felix Mendelssohn, Symphony No. 4 in A major (*Italian*).

1834

EUROPE

6 Mar. Six agricultural labourers from Tolpuddle near Dorchester, England, led by George Loveless, are convicted of taking illegal oaths and organizing a trade union. They are sentenced to seven years' transportation to Tasmania, but the 'Tolpuddle Martyrs' will be returned home (1836) because of the public outrage at their sentence.

26 May Portugal's six-year-long civil war ends with the defeat of Dom Miguel (see 4 July 1828). Miguel retires to Italy.

7 July Civil war begins in Spain as Don Carlos (second son of Charles IV of Spain) claims the throne from his infant niece Queen Isabella II. She is supported by France and Britain, who form a Quadruple Alliance with Spain and Portugal to guarantee the constitutional monarchies of the two latter states.

9 July In Britain prime minister Lord Grey resigns and is succeeded by fellow Whig Lord Melbourne (16 July).

1 Aug. Slavery is formally abolished throughout the British empire (see 1833).

14 Aug. In Britain the new Poor Law limits charitable payments to paupers who are old and ill. The healthy poor are set to work in newly established workhouses.

16 Oct. The Houses of Parliament in London are destroyed in a fire; some spectators applaud. A programme of rebuilding begins.

10 Dec. Following the resignation of the Whig prime minister Lord Melbourne, Sir Robert Peel becomes Tory prime minister.

17 Dec. Sir Robert Peel issues the Tamworth Manifesto. It commits the Tory party to accepting the 1832 Reform Act.

- Giuseppe Mazzini expands his nationalistic Young Italy association (see 1832) as a continent-wide Young Europe group to include Young Germany and Young Poland among others. His headquarters are in London, where British liberal values are sympathetic to various European nationalist causes.
- The notorious Spanish Inquisition for the extirpation of religious heresy is formally abolished.

ASIA

6 May Sikhs led by Ranjit Singh attack the Muslim city of Peshawar in the Punjab, NW India.

THE AMERICAS

29 Jan. Workers riot and strike on the Chesapeake and Ohio Canal; for the first time in a US labour dispute the army is sent in.

4 July Tensions within US labour emerge as unskilled workers in New York break up an anti-slavery meeting; they fear that emancipated slaves will take their jobs. In Philadelphia pro-slavery groups attack black homes.

- The US Whig party emerges in opposition to the autocratic presidency of Andrew Jackson.

SUB-SAHARAN AFRICA

- Increasing Dutch settlement in the E of South Africa leads to war with the indigenous Xhosa people.

AUSTRALASIA AND OCEANIA

- Edward Henty and his brothers settle territory that will develop into the Australian colony of Victoria.

ECONOMY AND SOCIETY

23 Dec. English economist and writer on population trends Thomas Malthus, who advocated birth control measures, dies.

- Baring Brothers of London, merchant bankers, enter the Chinese trade and acquire two ships for the purpose.
- Chantilly racecourse is opened NE of Paris.

SCIENCE AND TECHNOLOGY

- By now Louis Braille's system of communication using embossed dots, which blind people can read by touch, is spreading in popularity. It was first published in 1829 in France.
- The two-wheeled hansom cab, designed and patented by British architect Joseph Hansom, is introduced to London and soon becomes the city's most popular form of transport.
- The US inventor Jacob Perkins, working in Britain, invents a compression machine, which will evolve into a method of gas refrigeration.

ARTS AND HUMANITIES

Literature

Honoré de Balzac, *Le Père Goriot*, novel.

Edward Bulwer-Lytton, *The Last Days of Pompeii*, novel that helps to engender a romantic British view of Roman civilization.

Franz Grillparzer, *Der Traum ein Leben* (A Dream is Life), tragedy.

Alfred de Musset, *Lorenzaccio*, play.

Visual Arts and Architecture

– The Glyptothek sculpture gallery in Munich is completed.

– William Wilkins starts to design the National Gallery, London; it will be opened in 1838.

Eugène Delacroix, *Algerian Women at Home*, painting influential in the emergence of a new European view of the Orient as a place of languorous sensuality.

Jean-Auguste-Dominique Ingres, *The Martyrdom of St Symphorian*, painting for the Cathedral of Autun, France.

Music

Hector Berlioz, *Harold in Italy*, orchestral work based on Lord Byron's poem *Childe Harold* (see 1812).

Frédéric Chopin, *Andante Spianato*, for piano and orchestra.

Robert Schumann, *Carnaval*, solo piano music.

Charles Babbage (1791–1871)

Babbage, an English mathematician and inventor, is the first individual to have thought of the possibility of a fully automatic digital computer. From 1828 until 1839 he was Lucasian professor of mathematics at Cambridge and played an important role in the public and scientific life of his time, helping to found the Royal Astronomical Society (1820) and the Royal Statistical Society (1834). Babbage had the typical early Victorian confidence in the ability of science to bring progress and order to human affairs. These convictions lay behind his role in helping to establish an effective, modern and nationwide postal system in Britain. He also used his mathematical knowledge and understanding of probability to compile the first accurate actuarial tables.

Babbage's idea of the computer was based on the possibility of a machine that could calculate mathematical tables by mechanical means. This original idea came to him in about 1813 and, shortly afterwards, he built a small calculator that could perform mathematical calculations up to eight decimal places. He then received a government grant to enable him to work on the development of a calculator with a capacity for operating at up to 20 decimal places. By the 1830s Babbage's ambitions had developed further: he now had plans for what he called the 'Analytical Engine', which could work out mathematical calculations according to instructions encoded on punched cards. It also had a memory unit in which to store numbers. Babbage's design was not completed or built in his own lifetime. It was finally built in 1991 on the basis of Babbage's notebooks, which were rediscovered in 1937.

1835

EUROPE

2 Mar. Francis I, emperor of Austria, dies and is succeeded by his son, Ferdinand I, who will be dominated by Metternich. Francis I was the last Holy Roman Emperor (the title having been dropped in 1806).

18 April In Britain William Lamb, Lord Melbourne, forms a new Whig ministry after the resignation of Sir Robert Peel as prime minister.

9 Sept. In Britain Parliament recognizes the population shift to industrial centres by passing the Municipal Corporations Act, which reforms local government in England.

ASIA

– Dost Mohammad Khan establishes the Barakzai dynasty, which will rule Afghanistan until 1929.

THE AMERICAS

– Juan Manuel de Rosas, governor of Buenos Aires, assumes dictatorial powers and extends his authority over the 12 provinces of Argentina (see 1829).

– The US government enforces the treaty of 1832, which removes the Seminole people from their home in Florida to lands W of the Mississippi; the Seminole, led by Osceola, begin a guerrilla war and, aided by runaway African-American slaves, kill (28 Dec.) some 100 US soldiers (see 21 Oct. 1837).

SUB-SAHARAN AFRICA

– In S Africa Boer (Dutch settlers) begin the Great Trek to the N and E of the Orange River to escape British rule.

AUSTRALASIA AND OCEANIA

– Melbourne, port and future capital of the colony of Victoria (1851), is founded in S Australia. It is named after the British prime minister of the day (see above).

ECONOMY AND SOCIETY

5 May Continental Europe's first passenger railway opens, linking Brussels and Mechelen in Belgium. It is followed by a railway link between St Etienne and Lyons in France (9 July) and between Nuremberg and Fürth in Bavaria (7 Dec.).

– The Agence Havas is established as the French national news agency (it will be renamed the Agence France-Presse in 1945).

SCIENCE AND TECHNOLOGY

– Theodor Schwann, a German scientist, extracts the enzyme pepsin from the stomach wall and identifies it as an element in animal digestion.

ARTS AND HUMANITIES

Literature

Hans Christian Andersen, *Eventyr, fortalte for børnl* (Tales Told for Children), a collection of fairy tales including 'The Emperor's New Clothes' and 'The Snow Queen'.

Georg Büchner, *Danton's Death*, play about the power struggle between Danton and Robespierre during the French Revolution.

Théophile Gautier, *Mademoiselle de Maupin*, novel expressing belief in 'art for art's sake' as a reaction against a materialistic and philistine society dominated by bourgeois class interests.

Alexis de Tocqueville, *De la démocratie en Amérique* (Democracy in America), a work of political philosophy written after the author had travelled through the USA in 1831.

Visual Arts and Architecture

26 June French painter Antoine Gros, former official painter to Napoleon Bonaparte, drowns himself in the River Seine.

– The Japanese *ukiyo-e* (colour print) painter Hokusai Katsushika completes his *36 Views of Mount Fuji*: the treatment is the latest reinterpretation of Japan's national symbol, combining both nationalistic and religious significance.

Joseph Mallord William Turner, *Burning of the Houses of Lords and Commons*, painting.

Music

24 Jan. First performance in Paris of Vincenzo Bellini's opera *I puritani*.

26 Sept. First performance in Naples of Gaetano Donizetti's opera *Lucia di Lammermoor*, which is based on Walter Scott's novel *The Bride of Lammermoor*.

1836

EUROPE

10 Aug. In Spain the Carlist civil war (see 7 July 1834) deepens with insurrections in Aragon, Catalonia and Madrid; Queen Maria Cristina, wife of the dead King Ferdinand VII and regent for her daughter Isabella, is forced to restore the liberal constitution of 1812 in order to muster support against the conservative claimant Don Carlos.

THE AMERICAS

26 Jan. Michigan becomes a US state.

6 Mar. In the war for Texan independence, the Franciscan mission and fort at the Alamo, San Antonio, falls to an army commanded by the president of Mexico, Antonio de Santa Ana; there are no survivors from the garrison of 180 Texans and US citizens. Santa Ana is subsequently defeated at the battle of San Jacinto (21 April) and taken prisoner. A new independent Republic of Texas is announced (17 Mar.), with the Rio Grande forming the border with Mexico.

26 May The US Congress decides it has no authority over the slavery laws of individual states in the union.

15 June Arkansas becomes a US state.

– Vice-President Martin Van Buren is elected eighth president of the USA to succeed Andrew Jackson.

SUB-SAHARAN AFRICA

– In S Africa Boer farmers (see 1835) enter Natal and the Transvaal.

AUSTRALASIA AND OCEANIA

– The port of Adelaide, capital of the colony of South Australia, is founded.

ECONOMY AND SOCIETY

21 July The first Canadian railway links Laprairie on the St Lawrence River with St John in Quebec, E Canada.

– Hamburg steak, a patty of ground beef, which will become the popular hamburger, appears on the menu of New York's Del Monico's restaurant.

– Thomas P. Hunt, a US clergyman, taps a deep American psychological vein with *The Book of Wealth*, in which it is proved from the Bible that it is the duty of every man to become rich.

SCIENCE AND TECHNOLOGY

– HMS *Beagle* returns to Britain from its scientific survey of S American waters (see 1831).

– US inventor Samuel Colt patents his six-shooter revolver (see 1831), which will be an important weapon in the wars to extend the American frontier.

– Alonzo Philips of Massachusetts, USA, patents a phosphorus match.

– Joseph Schneider and his brother Adolphe buy the Le Creusot ironworks near Dijon, C France, which they transform into the largest steel manufacturing and munitions plant in the world.

ARTS AND HUMANITIES

Literature

Georg Büchner, *Woyzeck*, play. It will provide the basis of Alban Berg's opera *Wozzeck* (see 1925).

Charles Dickens (see p. 385), *Sketches by Boz*, stories using the author's pen name as a court reporter.

Ralph Waldo Emerson, *Nature*, prose rhapsody and statement of transcendentalist principles.

Nikolai Gogol, *The Government Inspector*, play.

Frederick Maryatt, *Mr Midshipman Easy*, novel.

Alfred de Musset, *Les Confessions d'un enfant du siècle* (The Confessions of a Child of his Time), autobiographical poem.

Visual Arts and Architecture

– The Arc de Triomphe, ordered by Napoleon Bonaparte, is completed in the Place de l'Etoile, Paris (see 1806).

Jean-Baptiste-Camille Corot, *Diana Surprised by Actaeon*.

Joseph Mallord William Turner, *Juliet and her Nurse*, painting in an impressionistic manner that abandons the artistic convention of realistic representation.

Music

29 Feb. First performance in Paris of Giacomo Meyerbeer's opera *Les Huguénots* (The Huguenots), which is set in France in 1572 and is based on the events of the St Bartholomew's Day Massacre.

9 Dec. First performance at the Bolshoi Theatre, St Petersburg, of Mikhail Glinka's opera *A Life for the Tsar*; from 1917 it is usually known in Russia as *Ivan Susanin*.

Felix Mendelssohn, *St Paul*, oratorio.

1837

EUROPE

20 June In Britain King William IV dies and is succeeded by his niece, Victoria; in his other kingdom of Hanover Salic Law forbids female succession, so the duke of Cumberland, George II's eldest surviving grandson, becomes King Ernest Augustus. Queen Victoria adopts Buckingham Palace as her London residence; William IV has earlier tried to get rid of the palace by offering it to Parliament as its new home after the fire of 1834.

ASIA

– Tokugawa Ienari, Japan's reforming shogun, resigns after 45 years in the post and is succeeded by his son Ieyoshi. There is a growing desire for the return of the emperor to a position of authority in the state, which will happen with the Meiji restoration (see 1868). International pressure is growing for Japan to open its ports to foreign trade.

– Famine spreads in Japan and provokes public riots. The new shogun, Tokugawa Ieyoshi, refuses to release grain from government stores.

THE AMERICAS

3 Mar. President Andrew Jackson's last act in office as president of the USA is to recognize the independent Republic of Texas. The number of Supreme Court justices increases from seven to nine. Martin Van Buren takes office on 4 Mar.

Mar. The New Orleans cotton brokerage firm of Herman Briggs & Co. collapses and sets off a serious economic crisis in the USA resulting from the over-valuation of land, inadequate regulation of banks and excessive market speculation.

10 May New York banks suspend payments and during the course of the year hundreds of businesses will fail: unemployment and bankruptcy spread.

21 Oct. The Seminole War in Florida effectively ends when Osceola and other leaders of the Seminole people are perfidiously seized by the US army while under a flag of truce (see 1835); his followers are defeated (25 Dec.) by Col. Zachary Taylor (known as Old Rough and Ready). The Seminole will be exterminated over the next few years, and Osceola will die in prison (1838).

5 Dec. Reformers and French Canadians led by Louis Joseph Papineau and the speaker of the legislative assembly of Lower Canada, William Lyon Mackenzie, rebel against British rule. The insurgents declare a provisional government and attack Toronto, though unsuccessfully; Papineau escapes to Paris and Mackenzie to the USA, where he will be imprisoned (1838).

– Smallpox speeds the destruction of Native American civilization: the Arika, Hidatsa and the Mandan people are wiped out along the Missouri River in the USA.

ECONOMY AND SOCIETY

18 Sept. Tiffany and Co. opens in New York. It will develop into a world-famous jewellery store.

8 Nov. Mount Holyoke Female Seminary, Massachusetts, opens as the first US college for women.

– In his *Phi Beta Kappa Address* at Harvard Ralph Waldo Emerson defines American scholarship (and the USA itself) as a ceaseless quest for originality and for liberation from the burden of the past, especially in its European ancestry.

– German educationist Friedrich Fröbel opens the world's first kindergarten in Blankenburg, Thuringia.

– Probability theory and statistical analysis are given new inspiration by the French mathematician Siméon Poisson whose *Recherches sur la probabilité des jugements* (Researches on the Probability of Estimates) are based on the numbers of those who die in the French army as a result of being kicked by mules.

– Candle and soap manufacturer Procter and Gamble, the future industrial multinational, is established in Cincinnati, Ohio, USA.

SCIENCE AND TECHNOLOGY

20 July London's Euston Railway Station opens. It is entered by way of a great Doric arch.

– US inventor Samuel Morse is granted a US patent for his magnetic telegraph; his assistant Alfred Vail devises a Morse code, using dots and dashes to represent letters.

Charles Dickens (1812–70)

One of the greatest British novelists of the 19th century, Dickens was the son of a government clerk who was imprisoned for debt. He had little formal education, but started his writing career as a journalist contributing to popular magazines. It was *Pickwick Papers* that made his name when it was published in serial form in 1836 and 1837. His subsequent novels were sold in the same serialized form, which meant that they were cheap enough to be bought by the artisan class that supplied Dickens with his earliest and most enthusiastic readership. Dickens never lost his sense

of this audience, people who were often of modest means, struggling for financial independence and impatient of paternalistic government.

Dickens's novels helped to establish a view of the essential geniality and broad-minded humour of the English. To this extent they confirmed a view the English already had of themselves as a non-ideological race of rough-and-ready empiricists. But the more serious side of Dickens also revealed England's rapacious and hypocritical side. In *Oliver Twist* (1837–8), for example, he described the effects of the new Poor Law

(1834) and the living conditions endured in the workhouses. 'Dickensian' became a generalizing adjective to describe the dehumanizing living and working conditions common among the poor of his time. His novels also established a general view that the effects of the Industrial Revolution had been almost uniformly vicious. Dickens was no political philosopher, however, and although he highlighted abuses within the system, he believed society would improve not by some revolutionary transformation but by individuals experiencing a change of heart.

– Isaac Pitman invents the first scientific shorthand system.
– US inventors John and Hiram Pitts patent the first steam-powered agricultural threshing machine, which successfully separates the chaff from the grain.
– The world's first steam tram is developed on the New York and Harlem Railroad.

ARTS AND HUMANITIES

Literature

29 Jan. Alexander Pushkin is mortally wounded in a duel and dies. His fellow Romantic novelist, poet and army officer Mikhail Lermontov, is transferred to a regiment in the Caucasus because he writes a poem critical of the imperial court after the death of Russia's greatest poet.

– German archaeologist Georg Friedrich Grotefend inaugurates a new chapter in the development of Middle Eastern scholarship by deciphering Persian cuneiform inscriptions.

Thomas Carlyle, *History of the French Revolution*, historical study influenced by a heroic version of secular destiny and individual drive as the motor of history.

Charles Dickens (see p. 385), *The Posthumous Papers of the Pickwick Club*, novel, which has previously appeared in a periodical in 20 monthly parts.

Harriet Martineau, *Society in America*, sociology.

Alfred de Musset, *Les Nuits* (Nights), poem.

William H. Prescott, *History of the Reign of Ferdinand and Isabella the Catholic*, historical study by the first great US historian.

Visual Arts and Architecture

31 Mar. English painter John Constable dies.
– The Thames embankment is completed in London.

Music

– The composer Frédéric Chopin meets the novelist George Sand. They will live together from 1838 to 1847.

Hector Berlioz, *Grand' Messe des Morts*, requiem mass.

Felix Mendelssohn, Piano Concerto No. 2 in D minor.

1838

EUROPE

8 May In Britain William Lovett, a former cabinetmaker, publishes a 'people's charter', urging universal suffrage without any property qualification.

31 July In Britain Parliament passes legislation extending the Poor Law Amendment Act of 1834 to Ireland, exacerbating an already grave problem of public order.

18 Sept. Richard Cobden of Manchester, England, founds the Anti-Corn Law League to campaign for an end to British economic protectionism (see 1815), which helps established landowners at the expense of working people and consumers.

ASIA

12 Dec. Chinese authorities attempt to execute an opium dealer but are prevented by British and US traders, who have established opium as an important trading commodity; the issue will become a cause of war between Britain and China (see 1839).

– Fearful of Russian influence in the region, the British invade Afghanistan from India in the First Afghan War, which lasts until 1842; its ruler, Dost Mohammad Khan (see 1835), is deposed and imprisoned.

THE AMERICAS

17 May Pro-slavery activists in Philadelphia, USA, burn down Pennsylvania Hall; immigrants in particular fear that freed slaves will displace them from their jobs.

– The Cherokee people are evicted from their lands in Alabama, Georgia and Tennessee where gold is discovered; 7000 US troops escort 15,000 Cherokee W along the so-called Trail of Tears to Oklahoma at the cost of 4000 lives.

– An uprising by indigenous people in Guatemala precipitates the break up of the Federation of Central America (see 1823); Honduras secedes.

– The future cities of St Paul, Minnesota, and Kansas City are founded in the US Midwest.

SUB-SAHARAN AFRICA

16 Dec. In Natal a Zulu army, having previously massacred a band of Boer settlers, attacks a second wagon train of Boer settlers but is driven off with heavy losses estimated at around 3000. The event becomes known as the battle of Blood River.

ECONOMY AND SOCIETY

– Regent's Park in C London opens to the public.

SCIENCE AND TECHNOLOGY

23 April The *Great Western* and *Sirius*, the first steamships to cross the Atlantic, arrive in New York from Britain. Both have been designed by English engineer Isambard Kingdom Brunel who, as chief engineer of the Great Western Railway, has also been responsible for constructing the company's viaducts, tunnels and bridges.

– Jöns Berzelius, Swedish chemist, shows that iron enables blood to absorb oxygen.

– Dutch chemist Gerard Mulder coins the word protein, derived from Greek and meaning 'of the first importance'.

– Charles de la Tour, French scientist, shows that fermentation depends on yeast fungus.

– German botanist Matthias Schleiden is the first to recognize cells as the basic structure of all plant life, giving rise to the cell-theory of physiology.

ARTS AND HUMANITIES

Literature

Charles Dickens, *Oliver Twist*, novel designed to shock and influence public sentiment in its portrayal of Britain's harsh Poor Law.

Victor Hugo, *Ruy Blas*, play.

Karl Immermann, *Münchhausen*, novel in which he idealizes the virtues of the German peasantry.

Visual Arts and Architecture

Eugène Delacroix, *Medea*, painting.

Music
10 Sept. First performance in Paris of Hector Berlioz's opera *Benvenuto Cellini*.

1839

EUROPE
19 April Twenty-four Articles: peace is declared between the Netherlands and Belgium, which becomes wholly independent.
13 June Prince Miloš I Obrenovic abdicates as ruler of Serbia; his autocratic style has created widespread opposition and Russian influence has been used to secure his removal. He is succeeded by his son Milan, who soon dies and is succeeded in turn by his second son (9 July), who rules Serbia as Prince Michael III.
31 Aug. After a series of defeats suffered by Carlist forces since 1836, the civil war in Spain is brought to a close with the Convention of Vergara: the pretender to the throne Don Carlos (see 7 July 1834) emigrates to France. Queen Isabella II will reign until 1868.

MIDDLE EAST AND NORTH AFRICA
21 April Ottoman forces invade Egyptian-controlled Syria in the continuing dispute with the ruler of Egypt, Mehmet Ali; the Turks are defeated at the battle of Nezib (24 June) and their navy surrenders at Alexandria; the Ottoman sultan, Mahmud II, is murdered by poison (1 July).
– In Afghanistan the British place the unpopular Shah Shuja on the throne while popular agitation continues in Kabul and elsewhere in the country to secure the restoration of Dost Mohammad Khan (see 1838).

ASIA
Nov. Illegally imported opium stored in a warehouse in the port of Canton by British merchants is destroyed by Chinese government officials; this sparks the First Opium War between China and Britain, which will last until 1842.

> *Wherever the European has trod, death seems to pursue the aboriginal.*
>
> Charles Darwin, 12 Jan. 1836, recorded in his *Zoology of the Voyage of the Beagle* (1840)

THE AMERICAS
11 Feb. John Lambton, earl of Durham, produces a report advocating the union of Upper and Lower Canada and the granting of self-government. The British government accepts his recommendations.
– Driven from Missouri, the Mormon religious community now settles in Nauvoo, Illinois, USA (see 1830).

ECONOMY AND SOCIETY
– The Grand National steeplechase is run for the first time at Aintree near Liverpool in NW England.
– Henley Royal Regatta is held for the first time in SE England.
– In the USA the West Point army cadet Abner Doubleday devises the rules for American baseball.
– Indian Assam tea arrives in Britain, and black tea begins to gain in popularity over Chinese green tea.
– The University of Boston and the Virginia Military Institute, Lexington, Massachusetts, are founded in the USA.

SCIENCE AND TECHNOLOGY
– The first railway line on the Italian peninsula is opened in the S between Naples and Portici.
– By heating rubber and sulphur US inventor Charles Goodyear creates vulcanized rubber, which has a wide variety of commercial uses.
– Kirkpatrick MacMillan, a blacksmith of Dumfries, SW Scotland, invents the modern bicycle, including a pedal system and brake (see 1861).
– Swiss chemist Christian Schönbein discovers ozone.
– English pioneer of photography William Henry Fox Talbot claims to have produced photographs earlier than Louis Daguerre, using a camera obscura along with silver chloride and salt as fixing agents. He also discovers that by waxing the oiling paper opposite to the image he can obtain a negative, or reverse, image from which he can reproduce a perfect positive copy on sensitized paper.

ARTS AND HUMANITIES
Literature
– Louis Blanc, French socialist pioneer, statesman and historian, advances the principle 'to each according to his needs, from each according to his abilities' in his essay *L'Organisation du travail* (The Organization of Work). He also founds the *Revue du progrès*.
Charles Dickens (see p. 385), *Nicholas Nickleby*, novel satirizing British education as utilitarian, mean spirited and biased towards empiricism.
Stendhal (Marie-Henri Beyle) *La Chartreuse de Parme* (The Charterhouse of Parma), novel.
Visual Arts and Architecture
Edwin Landseer, *Dignity and Impudence*, painting.
Joseph Mallord William Turner, *The Fighting Téméraire*, painting.
Music
Hector Berlioz, *Romeo and Juliet*, dramatic symphony.
Frédéric Chopin, 24 Preludes, Op. 28.

1840

EUROPE
10 Feb. In Britain Queen Victoria marries her German cousin Albert, son of the duke of Saxe-Coburg-Gotha. She makes a patriotic point of wearing only items of British manufacture at her wedding in London.

1 May The world's first adhesive postage stamp goes on sale in Britain; it is known as the Penny Black and bears the profile of Queen Victoria. The stamp stimulates use of the postal service, and twice as many letters are posted in 1840 as were in 1839.

7 June King Frederick William III of Prussia dies and is succeeded by his son, who becomes Frederick William IV.

7 Oct. William I, king of the Netherlands, abdicates at the age of 68 to marry an unpopular Belgian Catholic, the countess d'Oultremont; he is succeeded by his son William II.

MIDDLE EAST AND NORTH AFRICA

15 July By the terms of the treaty of London, Britain, Austria, Prussia and Russia unite to support the Ottoman empire against the expansionist Egyptian ruler Mehmet Ali. With French support, Mehmet Ali rejects the treaty. After British troops under the command of Sir Charles Napier seize Beirut in Egyptian-held Lebanon (10 Oct.), King Louis-Philippe of France abandons Mehmet Ali, who agrees (3 Nov.) to settle for a position as hereditary ruler of Egypt.

ASIA

June Britain formally declares war on China over the opium trade and commercial rights; British ships bombard the island of Zhoushan at the entrance to Hanchow Bay, S of Shanghai.

THE AMERICAS

23 July In Britain Parliament passes the Union Act, which combines the separate colonies of Upper and Lower Canada and provides for responsible self-government.

– Rafael Carrera seizes power in Guatemala; his regime will last for 25 years and will be the dominant force in C America.

– José Gaspar Rodriguez de Francia dies after 24 years as dictator of Paraguay.

– The World Anti-Slavery Convention has opened in London, but the American movement has split over the issue of women's rights. Leading abolitionist William Lloyd Garrison of Boston, USA, refuses to attend the London convention because it excludes women.

AUSTRALASIA AND OCEANIA

6 Feb. By the treaty of Waitangi the leaders of the Maori people of New Zealand cede sovereignty to Britain in exchange for protection against land expropriation by settlers. Disputes over land rights lead to fighting between Maoris and settlers.

ECONOMY AND SOCIETY

– Anna, duchess of Bedford, has introduced tea drinking as an afternoon recreation in England.

– The growth in world population is checked with the return of a major cholera epidemic, which will haunt the globe for the next 20 years and kill millions.

– Grapefruit trees are introduced into the US state of Florida.

SCIENCE AND TECHNOLOGY

– The Baltimore College of Dental Surgery, the first dental college in the USA, is established.

– Charles Choss, Swiss chemist, shows that calcium is necessary for bone development.

– The wooden steamship *Britannia* makes its first voyage from Britain across the Atlantic to Halifax and Boston for the Royal Mail Steam Packet Company, established in 1839 by Samuel Cunard with the help of a British government subsidy.

– British naturalist Charles Darwin (see p. 379) writes *Zoology of the Voyage of the Beagle* (see 1831). Darwin continues to study how species develop.

– English physicist James Joule writes *On the Production of Heat by Voltaic Electricity*. Joule will formulate the first law of thermodynamics: energy can be converted from one form to another but it cannot be destroyed. The unit of energy will be called the joule.

ARTS AND HUMANITIES
Literature

– In his work *Qu'est-ce que la propriété?* (What is Property?') French political activist and social philosopher Pierre-Joseph Proudhon asserts that property is theft. Early, pre-Marxist (non-scientific) socialism is now a Europe-wide phenomenon.

Richard Henry Dana, *Two Years Before the Mast*, an account of his journey to California and back around Cape Horn.

Friedrich Hebbel, *Judith*, play.

Mikhail Lermontov, *A Hero of Our Time*, novel.

Edgar Allan Poe, *Tales of the Grotesque and Arabesque*, collection of stories, including such gothic tales as 'The Fall of the House of Usher'.

Music

– Viennese ballet dancer Fanny Eissler introduces the polka, a quick dance of C European origin, to the USA while on a national tour.

– Antoine-Joseph (known as Adolphe) Sax, a Belgian instrument maker, invents a brass saxophone.

Felix Mendelssohn, Symphony No. 2 in B flat (*Lobgesang*).

Robert Schumann, *Dichterliebe* (Poet's Love), song cycle based on the poetry of Heinrich Heine.

1841

EUROPE

23 Aug. William Lamb, Lord Melbourne, Whig prime minister, dies and is replaced by Sir Robert Peel at the head of a new Tory administration. He reintroduces income tax (at 7d per pound on incomes over £150 per annum) and lowers import duties on raw materials and foodstuffs; grain imports are encouraged and food prices fall.

– Edward, son of Queen Victoria and Prince Albert, and future Edward VII, is born at Buckingham Palace in London.

MIDDLE EAST AND NORTH AFRICA

12 July The Convention of the Straits agreed by the great powers underpins the survival of the Ottoman (Turkish) empire: the Bosphorus and Dardanelles, connecting the Black Sea and the Mediterranean, are closed to all warships in peace-time.

ASIA

20 Jan. By the terms of a preliminary deal to end the First Opium War the Chinese agree to hand over the barren island of Hong Kong to Britain. British naval forces land there (26 Jan.), but both sides subsequently abandon the deal and the war continues.

Dec. Shah Shuja, puppet ruler of Afghanistan, is assassinated as opposition mounts to the British occupation; imperial forces are compelled to withdraw to India by way of the Khyber Pass (see 6 Jan.1842).

– The sultan of Borneo appoints Sir James Brooke to be rajah of Sarawak (now in E Malaysia). As an officer of the East India Company army, Brooke helped the sultan's uncle Muda Hassim suppress a tribal rebellion (1838). He sets about reforming the government of Sarawak and will rule until his death in 1868.

THE AMERICAS

4 Mar. William Henry Harrison, a Whig, takes office as ninth US president. He dies on 4 April, becoming the first US president to die in office.

6 April John Tyler, Harrison's vice-president, becomes tenth US president following Harrison's death.

Nov. The first group of settlers travelling to the Pacific coast of the USA through the Montana territory arrive in Oregon.

– The president of Peru, Gen. Agustín Gamarra, has thrown off Bolivian domination of the country and invaded Bolivia itself; during the course of the campaign he dies (20 Nov.). Civil war continues in Peru.

– Carlos Antonio López becomes president of Paraguay and establishes a totalitarian regime that will last until his death in 1862.

AUSTRALASIA AND OCEANIA

– The expanding territory of New Zealand becomes a British crown colony.

ECONOMY AND SOCIETY

– George Ripley, a minister in the Unitarian Church, founds Brook Farm, Massachusetts, one of the most successful of US communes, in which members are issued with shares and are paid a dollar a day. All heat, housing, food and clothing are provided communally, and facilities also include elementary and secondary schools and a higher education college. Novelist and short-story writer Nathaniel Hawthorne is among the original members of the commune.

SCIENCE AND TECHNOLOGY

– James Baird, a Scottish doctor, discovers the powers of hypnosis.

– In Prussian Thuringia Johann Nikolaus Dreyse designs the world's first breech-loading military rifle, the needle gun. It will have a decisive role in the success of the Prussian army after 1848, when it replaces the muzzle-loading rifle.

ARTS AND HUMANITIES

Literature

April US writer Edgar Allan Poe establishes the genre of the detective story in 'The Murders in the Rue Morgue', published in *Graham's Magazine*.

17 July The London magazine *Punch*, ostensibly devoted to humour, starts publication.

27 July Russian poet and novelist Mikhail Lermontov is killed in a duel at Pyatigorsk, SW Russia. This is his second duel.

– The *New York Tribune* is founded as a daily paper.

Robert Browning, *Pippa Passes*, drama in verse and prose.

Thomas Carlyle, *Heroes and Hero Worship*, essays; Carlyle's extreme individualism leads to the view that the historical process is guided by the actions and thoughts of 'great men'.

Charles Dickens (see p. 385), *Barnaby Rudge* and *The Old Curiosity Shop*, novels.

Alfred de Musset, *Le Souvenir* (Memory), poem.

Ralph Waldo Emerson, 'Self-Reliance', an essay devoted to the importance of nonconformity, is included in the first volume of his collected works.

Ludwig Feuerbach, *The Essence of Christianity*, work of philosophy asserting that Christianity is a human myth of perfection.

August Heinrich Hoffmann, *Deutschland über Alles* (Germany above Everything), poem expressing a desire for the unity of the German peoples; sung to a Haydn tune (probably adapted from Telemann) as the 'Emperor's Hymn', the poem becomes the Austrian national anthem and will become the German national anthem in 1922.

Music

28 June First performance in Paris of the ballet *Giselle*, with music by French composer Adolphe-Charles Adam; the choreography is by Italian Gian Coralli and Frenchman Jules Joseph Perrot.

Robert Schumann, Symphony No. 1 in B flat minor (*Spring*).

1842

EUROPE

5 May A major fire breaks out in the N German city of Hamburg; it lasts three days and destroys more than 4000 homes.

– Edwin Chadwick, in a report for the English Poor Law Commissioners (see 1834), exposes the insanitary living conditions suffered by much of the working class.

– Ruling Prince Michael III (see 1839) leaves Serbia, forced out by opponents of his reforms; Alexander Karageorgevic is elected to succeed him.

– In Britain the Mines Act comes into effect and bans the employment of women and of children under the age of ten, a practice that has been common in coal mines.

ASIA

6 Jan. The Anglo-Indian army under Lord Auckland retreats from Kabul and is subsequently massacred in the Khyber Pass; only one man out of a force of 20,000 reaches Jellalabad (Jalalabad) on the NW frontier, though some prisoners are later released. The Afghan forces are commanded by Akbar Khan, whose father, Dost Mohammad Khan, regains his throne.

29 Aug. The treaty of Nanjing (Nanking) ends the First Opium War between Britain and China (see Nov. 1839). The Chinese are forced to make extensive concessions: Britain acquires

Hong Kong; Shanghai and Canton are among the designated 'treaty ports' where foreigners receive special trading privileges; China is prevented from imposing any trade tariff larger than 5%, and the opium traffic continues. The war is a decisive victory for European colonialism and capitalism.

THE AMERICAS

9 Aug. The Webster–Ashburton treaty between the USA and Britain fixes the US–Canadian frontier.

– The child labour law of Massachusetts, USA, limits the working hours of children to between 10 and 12 hours a day.

– The chief justice of Massachusetts establishes the legality of trade unions and the validity of a strike for a closed shop (exclusive union recognition).

– Manuel Oribe, exiled president of Uruguay, gains the support of Juan Manuel de Rosas, the dictator of Argentina, in an effort to regain office.

ECONOMY AND SOCIETY

May Publication of the *Illustrated London News* begins.

– Notre Dame University is founded in Indiana, USA.

SCIENCE AND TECHNOLOGY

– US doctor John Gorrie, of Florida, pioneers air conditioning. Ice from Maine is ordered to lower the temperature in the room of his sick wife, but it is lost in transit and Gorrie has to improvise; he sets up a vessel of ammonia on top of a step-ladder and, on letting it drip, discovers a cooling effect.

ARTS AND HUMANITIES

Literature

Robert Browning, *Dramatic Lyrics*, poetry including his sardonic masterpiece 'My Last Duchess'.

Nikolai Gogol, *Dead Souls*, novel.

Thomas Babington Macaulay, *Lays of Ancient Rome*, poems.

Alfred, Lord Tennyson, *Poems*, poetry including 'Morte d'Arthur'.

Visual Arts and Architecture

– The Church of La Madeleine, Paris, is completed.

Music

9 Mar. First performance in La Scala, Milan, of Giuseppe Verdi's opera *Nabucco* (Nebuchadnezzar).

20 Oct. First performance in Dresden of Richard Wagner's (see p. 421) tragic opera *Rienzi, the Last of the Tribunes*, about the establishment of a Roman republic in 1347.

9 Dec. First performance in St Petersburg of Mikhail Glinka's opera *Ruslan and Lyudmila*.

Felix Mendelssohn, Symphony No. 3 in A minor (*Scottish*).

1843

EUROPE

– In Britain Chartist radical Feargus O'Connor advocates a cooperative land association, which will attract surplus industrial labour back to the countryside. His hope is that manufacturers will then be forced to offer better wages to the remaining industrial workers.

ASIA

Feb. The Muslim emirs of Sind (modern SE Pakistan) refuse to capitulate to the East India Company; a British–Indian army under Gen. Sir Charles Napier begins an offensive that leads to the defeat of Sind forces at the battle of Hyderabad (Mar.) and the conquest of the country. Napier's punning one-word Latin dispatch back to India reads *Peccavi* (I have sinned).

– Infanticide (*mabiki*) is a common custom in Japan, where the second and third sons are killed off. Girls are spared as they can be sold to work as servants, prostitutes or geishas (entertainers).

SUB-SAHARAN AFRICA

4 May In S Africa Natal is declared a British colony during the war with Boer (Dutch-descended) settlers, who continue to move further inland in their quest for self-determination.

– The Gambia, on the Atlantic coast of W Africa, ceases to be administered from the more easterly territory of Sierra Leone and becomes an independent British crown colony.

AUSTRALASIA AND OCEANIA

28 Nov. Britain and France recognize the independence of the Hawaiian islands in the C Pacific.

– The five-year long Maori War begins in New Zealand with the massacre of white settlers at Wairau, South Island.

ECONOMY AND SOCIETY

– Cigarettes, paper-wrapped miniature cigars, produced in Cuba since the late 18th century, now become popular in France.

– The sport of skiing is by now established in Norway.

SCIENCE AND TECHNOLOGY

19 July The steamship *Great Britain*, designed by English engineer Isambard Kingdom Brunel, is launched at Bristol, W England, and becomes the first iron-hulled steamship to cross the Atlantic. She also has the added innovation of a screw propeller.

– Charles Thurber of Massachusetts, USA, patents a typewriter.

ARTS AND HUMANITIES

Literature

26 Aug. The newspaper *La Réforme* starts publication in Paris.

Sept. In London the *Economist* magazine begins publication.

– In London the *Sunday News of the World* begins publication and its circulation soon reaches 6 million copies a week, becoming the largest selling newspaper in the world.

– In his first major philosophical work *Enten–Eller* (Either–Or), the Danish philosopher Sören Kierkegaard develops the basic tenets of existentialism.

Charles Dickens (see p. 385), *A Christmas Carol*, novella.

Prosper Mérimée, 'Carmen', short story that will later be used as the basis of the opera by Georges Bizet (see 1875).

John Stuart Mill (see p. 395), *Logic*, philosophical treatise.

Eugène Sue, *Les Mystères de Paris*, novel.

Visual Arts

– A statue of British naval hero Admiral Horatio Viscount Nelson is placed on top of a classical column in London's newly built Trafalgar Square.

Joseph Mallord William Turner, *The Sun of Venice Going to Sea*, painting.

Music

2 Jan. First performance in Dresden of Richard Wagner's (see p. 421) opera *Der fliegende Holländer* (The Flying Dutchman).

6 Feb. New York's Bowery Theater is the setting for the first of the minstrel shows; the genre will become a prominent feature of US entertainment, both reflecting and reinforcing a stereotyped view of African-Americans in the S states.

29 June First performance in Paris of Gaetano Donizetti's opera *Don Pasquale*.

Oct. At a performance of Shakespeare's *A Midsummer Night's Dream* in Potsdam, Felix Mendelssohn's additional pieces of incidental music for the play are performed.

1844

EUROPE

8 Mar. Charles XIV John (formerly Jean Baptiste Jules Bernadotte, a marshal in Napoleon's army), king of Sweden and Norway, dies and is succeeded by his son Oscar I.

MIDDLE EAST AND NORTH AFRICA

Aug. French forces fight a territorial war in Morocco. The war ends by the treaty of Tangier (10 Sept.).

THE AMERICAS

– Santo Domingo on the Caribbean island of Hispaniola becomes independent of Haiti (also on Hispaniola) and is renamed the Dominican Republic.

– The security transportation firm Wells, Fargo and Co. begins an express service between Buffalo and Detroit, USA.

– US religious leader William Miller begins his preachings that will lay the foundation of the Seventh-Day Adventist Church (see 21 May 1863).

ECONOMY AND SOCIETY

– The first retail cooperative society, a business owned by its members, is founded in England. The Rochdale Society of Equitable Pioneers opens a shop selling items for cash only and at local prices, the profits of the enterprise being shared among its members on an annual basis.

– British gold reserves have declined and joint stock companies have issued paper money; the British Bank Charter Act helps to eliminate all notes except those issued by the Bank of England.

– The Young Men's Christian Association (YMCA), a charity that addresses the social, physical and religious well-being of young men and boys, is established in London by Sir George Williams.

SCIENCE AND TECHNOLOGY

24 May Samuel Morse transmits the first telegraph message, sent from the Capitol in Washington, D.C., to Baltimore, Maryland, and then returned.

– The new process of producing paper from wood pulp, developed by German scientist Gottlob Keller, is now dramatically reducing the price of newsprint.

– Dentist Horace Wells from Boston, USA, pioneers anaesthetics by administering nitrous oxide (laughing gas).

– Scottish publisher Robert Chambers writes *Vestiges of the Natural History of Creation,* whose evolutionary conclusions anticipate the work of Charles Darwin (see p. 379).

ARTS AND HUMANITIES

Literature

Charles Dickens (see p. 385), *Martin Chuzzlewit*, novel.

Benjamin Disraeli, *Coningsby*, novel.

Alexandre Dumas *père, The Three Musketeers*, novel.

Karl Marx (see p. 419), *Introduction to a Critique of the Hegelian Philosophy of the Right*, political philosophy in which he (sympathetically) describes religion as 'the opium of the people'.

Visual Arts and Architecture

Joseph Mallord William Turner, *Rain, Steam and Speed*, the first major work of art to feature a train.

Music

9 Mar. First performance in Venice of Giuseppe Verdi's opera *Ernani*, which is based on Victor Hugo's play *Hernani*.

Felix Mendelssohn, Violin Concerto in E minor.

1845

EUROPE

– Potato crops fail throughout Britain and Europe due to blight, a fungal disease (*Phytophthora infestans*); Ireland is particularly badly hit. The famine encourages the anti-Corn Law agitators, who want to allow cheap imports of grain into Britain.

MIDDLE EAST AND NORTH AFRICA

– Mirza Ali Mohammed of Shiraz in Persia founds the Islamic Babi sect (which gives rise to the Baha'i movement), although the majority Shia clerical establishment denounces him as a heretic (see 1850).

ASIA

11 Dec. In India a Sikh attack on British territory in Hindustan leads to the outbreak of the First Anglo-Sikh War.

THE AMERICAS

3 Mar. Florida becomes a US state.

4 Mar. James Polk, a Democrat, becomes 11th US president, defeating Henry Clay, a Whig.

28 Mar. Mexico breaks off diplomatic relations with the USA after the Senate ratifies the annexation of the Republic of Texas (see 6 Mar. 1836); it is incorporated into the union later in the year (29 Dec.). In the summer of 1845 a journalist, John L. O'Sullivan, justifying the US annexation of Texas, argues that the US has a 'manifest destiny to overspread the continent allotted by Providence for the free development of our yearly multiplying millions'. 'Manifest destiny' soon becomes the catchphrase of US expansionists.

– Gen. Ramón Castilla, who assumed power following the death of President Agustín Gamarra (see 1841), is elected president of Peru and ends the long-running civil war.

1845-6

– The US Congress establishes the first Tuesday following the first Monday in November as the day for electing presidents and vice-presidents.

– The Methodist Episcopal Church of America splits into N and S divisions when Bishop Andrewes of Georgia, S USA, refuses an order to give up either his slaves or his bishopric.

ECONOMY AND SOCIETY

9 Oct. In Britain the theologian John Henry Newman becomes a Roman Catholic.

– The US Naval Academy is founded at Annapolis, Maryland.

– The Queen's College in Belfast, in the N of Ireland (now Queen's University), is founded by the British government as a higher education institution for non-Anglicans.

SCIENCE AND TECHNOLOGY

28 Aug. The *Scientific American* begins publication as a newspaper.

– British Arctic explorer Sir John Franklin's expedition is lost while searching for the Northwest Passage (the sea route connecting the Atlantic and Pacific across the N of Canada).

– British archaeologist Austen Henry Layard starts his survey of the Mesopotamian city of Nineveh (near Mosul in modern Iraq), where he will unearth the palace of the Assyrian kings.

– The ship *Rainbow* is launched in New York as an improved and faster version of the clippers that now compete with the screw-propelled iron steamships for transatlantic trade.

– Scottish inventor Robert Thomson patents a pneumatic tyre.

ARTS AND HUMANITIES

Literature

Robert Browning, 'Home Thoughts from Abroad', poem.

Benjamin Disraeli, *Sybil or The Two Nations*, novel making a political statement about Britain's two nations, the rich and the poor, who are entirely ignorant of each other's views and lives. Disraeli's programme to create 'one nation' is founded on the appeal of the British monarchy and (later) the empire and will recast the Conservative Party, which he will soon lead, as a popular political force.

Alexandre Dumas *père*, *Le Comte de Monte Cristo*, novel.

Friedrich Engels, *The Condition of the Working Class in England*, describing the atrocious living conditions of the urban poor.

Music

19 Oct. First performance in Dresden of Richard Wagner's (see p. 421) opera *Tannhäuser*, which is based on elements of medieval German mythology transplanted to a new world of German national identity and pseudo-religiosity.

Robert Schumann, Piano Concerto in A minor.

1846

EUROPE

28 June Britain's Corn Laws are repealed and Benjamin Disraeli's faction within the Tory Party denounces prime minister Robert Peel for abandoning protectionism. Grain duties are reduced (and later abolished) and Britain enjoys a cheap food policy.

Irish farmers have benefited from the Corn Laws as suppliers of the British domestic market, but in the new economic situation agricultural landlords switch from wheat to cattle, and many tenants are thrown off the land to increase pasturage.

30 June Robert Peel resigns as British premier, having failed to get the Coercion Bill (intended to preserve public order in Ireland) through Parliament. Lord John Russell becomes prime minister of a Liberal government; Viscount Palmerston becomes foreign secretary. The Tories split over the repeal of the Corn Laws: the Peelites (including W.E. Gladstone) will eventually join the Liberals, while the protectionists under Disraeli will be the creators of the modern Conservative Party.

– The potato crop in Ireland fails again, and mass starvation afflicts the population, with as many as 500,000 dying of hunger between 1846 and 1851. The crisis propels a new wave of 1.5 million Irish emigrants to the USA, Canada, Australia and Britain.

ASIA

– Treaty of Lahore ends the First Anglo-Sikh War: Sikhs renounce their claims to the territories of the Sutlej River in NW India.

THE AMERICAS

13 Jan. The USA goes to war with Mexico having failed to buy the New Mexico territory; Gen. Zachary Taylor defeats the Mexicans at the battle of Palo Alto (8 May), and the Mexican forces are forced to withdraw across the Rio Grande. Settlers in the Sacramento valley, California, declare their independence of Mexico (14 June), and the US commander John Drake Sloat subsequently claims possession of California for the USA (7 July). US naval forces take San Francisco (9 July) and Los Angeles (13 Aug.). The Mexican army at Monterrey, NE Mexico, is defeated by Gen. Taylor, who then occupies Monterrey.

30 July The USA moves to a freer trade policy as a result of the Walker Tariff Act which passes Congress. It lowers import duties and increases the number of duty-free goods, encouraging a boom in US trade.

28 Dec. Iowa becomes a US state.

ECONOMY AND SOCIETY

21 Jan. The *London Daily News* starts publication (the novelist Charles Dickens is its editor).

1 June Pope Gregory XVI dies. He is succeeded (16 June) by Giovanni Maria Mastai-Ferretti, who becomes Pope Pius IX.

SCIENCE AND TECHNOLOGY

– Britain adopts a standard gauge for railway tracks.

– The war with Mexico leads to a demand for more firearms for the US army; Samuel Colt receives orders for his new revolvers, which he mass-produces at his factory in Hartford, Connecticut.

– In Britain William Cooke and J.L. Ricardo set up the Electric Telegraph Company with a telegraph network linking the major cities.

– In the USA Richard Hoe of New York patents a rotary lightning press, which can print 10,000 sheets an hour and will replace the common flatbed press.

- US dentist William Morton, of Boston, advances modern anaesthesiology by using sulphuric ether on himself and a patient. Ether will be called an anaesthetic and is immediately used to treat the wounded of the Mexican War.
- In Germany Carl Zeiss opens a factory making optical instruments at Jena, near Weimar.
- Elias Howe of Spencer, Massachusetts, takes out a patent for a sewing machine.

ARTS AND HUMANITIES

- The Smithsonian Institution to promote knowledge is founded in Washington, D.C., by the US Congress with a bequest from English chemist James Smithson, illegitimate son of the duke of Northumberland.

Literature

Sept. The English poets Robert Browning and Elizabeth Barrett marry and then elope to Italy.

Honoré de Balzac, *La Cousine Bette*, novel, part of Balzac's *La Comédie humaine* (see 1829).

Edward Lear, *A Book of Nonsense*, poetry.

Henry Wadsworth Longfellow, *The Belfry of Bruges and Other Poems*, including 'The Arrow and the Song'. By now Longfellow is one of the USA's most widely read poets.

Jules Michelet, *Le Peuple*, novel calling on the French people to return to the ideals of the French Revolution and to oppose the class divisions that disfigure the society ruled over by Louis-Philippe.

Visual Arts and Architecture

- Trinity Church, New York, is completed in the now popular Gothic Revival style.

Edwin Landseer, *The Stag at Bay*, painting.

Music

Hector Berlioz, *The Damnation of Faust*, dramatic cantata based on Gérard de Nerval's French translation (1828) of Goethe's *Faust*.

Felix Mendelssohn, *Elijah*, oratorio.

Robert Schumann, Symphony No. 2 in C.

1847

EUROPE

- Legislation in Britain limits the working hours of 13–18-year-olds to ten hours a day.

THE AMERICAS

9 Mar. In the continuing US war with Mexico Gen. Winfield Scott lands troops S of Veracruz on the Gulf of Mexico in a large-scale amphibious operation. After a series of US successes Scott captures Mexico City.

10 July The first Chinese immigrants to the USA arrive in New York and will establish the city's Chinatown. Large-scale Irish emigration to the USA is supplemented by a growing number of people from Holland.

- Some 15,000 Mormons (a religious group) arrive on the shores of the Great Salt Lake, Mexican territory that will be ceded to the USA and form part of the state of Utah (see 1848). Their leader, Brigham Young, organizes his independent 'State of Deseret' centred on the new Salt Lake City with himself as president.

SUB-SAHARAN AFRICA

26 July Liberia in W Africa, settled by freed US slaves since 1821, becomes the first colony to gain independence. It has been colonized by free slaves since 1821 and is now internationally recognized as an independent republic.

ECONOMY AND SOCIETY

1 July The first US adhesive postage stamps go on sale.

- The Russian founder of modern anarchism, Mikhail Bakunin, is expelled from Paris. He is later sentenced to death in Austria, transferred into the custody of the Russian government (1851) and then exiled to E Siberia (1855).
- The Communist League of London commissions Karl Marx (see p. 419) and Friedrich Engels to write *The Communist Manifesto*.
- François Cartier founds the Paris jewellery shop that will bear his name and develop into a leading international brand.
- In London the French-born chef Alexis Soyer writes *Charitable Cookery, or the Poor Man's Regenerator* and establishes a soup kitchen to serve the capital's poor.
- The first covered shopping arcade in Europe opens in Brussels, Belgium.
- Hanson Crockett Gregory of Maine, USA, produces the ring doughnut.

SCIENCE AND TECHNOLOGY

- In Britain James Young Simpson uses chloroform as an anaesthetic.
- Italian chemist Ascanio Sobrero develops the explosive liquid nitroglycerine.

ARTS AND HUMANITIES

Literature

10 June The *Chicago Tribune* newspaper begins publication.

- The new British Museum building opens in London and the institution moves from its old home in Montagu House. A circular reading room will be opened in 1857.

Anne Brontë, *Agnes Grey*, novel.

Charlotte Brontë, *Jane Eyre*, novel.

Emily Brontë, *Wuthering Heights*, novel.

Henry Wadsworth Longfellow, 'Evangeline', poem describing the expulsion of the French Acadian community from Nova Scotia, E Canada, in the mid-18th century.

Frederick Marryat, *Children of the New Forest*, popular children's novel.

George Dibdin Pitt, *The Fiend of Fleet Street*, play featuring the first appearance of the demon barber Sweeney Todd.

Music

14 Mar. First performance in Florence of Giuseppe Verdi's opera *Macbeth*.

4 Nov. The German composer Felix Mendelssohn dies in Leipzig.

1848

1848

EUROPE

20 Jan. King Christian VIII of Denmark dies; his son and successor, Frederick VII, refuses to recognize the unilateral declaration of independence of Schleswig-Holstein (18 Mar.), the Danish-ruled but largely German-populated duchies at the S end of the Jutland peninsula; when Prussia sends troops to support the new government of the combined duchies (2 May) war is declared.

24 Feb. In Paris revolution forces King Louis-Philippe of France to abdicate. The Second Republic is proclaimed, and Charles-Louis-Napoleon Bonaparte (nephew of Emperor Napoleon) is elected president (10 Dec.). The revolution in France acts as a catalyst for liberal and nationalist uprisings throughout Europe.

13 Mar. Prince Klemens von Metternich, architect of reactionary government in much of C Europe since 1809, is forced to resign as Austria's foreign minister and chancellor following a revolution in Vienna. He goes into temporary exile in London and Brighton. The emperor of Austria, Ferdinand I, escapes from Vienna to Innsbruck (17 May) and later abdicates (2 Dec.); his nephew Franz Josef I succeeds and will reign until 1916. Serfdom is abolished in Austria in response to the political crisis.

15 Mar. The Hungarian diet (parliament) adopts the March Laws, which allow for autonomy (virtual independence) from Austria; the emperor is forced to agree to them (31 Mar.) but prepares a military strategy to crush the Hungarian nationalist movement (see 5 Jan. 1849).

17 Mar. A five-day revolution begins in Milan, N Italy, against continuing Austrian rule; it provokes the Piedmontese, NW Italy, to declare a patriotic war on Austria (23 Mar.) as the beginning of a process to liberate and unify the Italian peninsula; they are defeated at the battle of Custozza (24 July) by Field Marshal Count Joseph Radetzky, confirming Austrian rule in Lombardy N of Piedmont, and leading to an armistice (see 23 Mar. 1849).

10 April A demonstration takes place at Kennington in London in support of the Chartist manifesto but government fears of a mass uprising prove wildly exaggerated. The government suspends the Habeas Corpus Act (see 1679) in Ireland, where food prices remain high after successive failures of the potato crop.

13 April Following a revolt (Jan.) against the Spanish Bourbons, Sicily is declared independent of Naples.

17 June A Czech revolt is suppressed in Prague by Austrian troops.

June Gen. Louis-Eugène Cavaignac, governor general of French Algeria, becomes minister of war; his brutal suppression of the workers' revolt in Paris leads to the deaths of thousands on the barricades (in the so-called 'June days').

12 Sept. Switzerland adopts a new federal constitution in response to a short civil war (the Sonderbund War, begun in Oct.1847) and the defeat of the Catholic cantons. They had refused to accept the authority of the anti-clerical and liberal national diet, and a federal system now allows all cantons a measure of self-government and share of power.

– Britain's Public Health Act establishes the country's first national sanitary regulations.

– Count Pellegrino Rossi, prime minister of the Papal States in C Italy, is assassinated; Pope Pius IX, who ascended the papal throne as a liberal (see 1846), flees Rome and escapes S to Gaeta in the kingdom of the Two Sicilies (see 9 Feb. 1849).

MIDDLE EAST AND NORTH AFRICA

13 Oct. Mohammed Shah of the Qajar dynasty dies. He has ruled Persia incompetently for the past 13 years and is succeeded by his son Nasir ud-Din.

ASIA

– The Second Anglo-Sikh War breaks out when Sikhs rebel against British supremacy in the Punjab.

THE AMERICAS

24 Jan. James Marshall discovers gold in California; the news first appears in print in the *New York Herald* (19 Aug.) and the California gold rush begins.

2 Feb. The US–Mexican War ends with the treaty of Guadelupe Hidalgo. Mexico loses a third of its territory, including California, to the USA and has to cede all land N of the Rio Grande.

28 Mar. Death of the German-born merchant John Jacob Astor, the richest man in the USA (see 1814).

29 May Wisconsin becomes a US state.

– Costa Rica in C America declares itself a republic.

– The failure of the liberal revolutions of 1848 impels many Germans to emigrate to the USA, notably to the N state of Wisconsin.

– Zachary Taylor, the candidate of the Whig Party, is elected 12th president of the USA.

– The first Women's Rights Convention opens in New York.

ECONOMY AND SOCIETY

– German political philosopher Karl Marx (see p. 419), having returned to Cologne following the revolution in Paris, founds the journal *Neue Rheinische Zeitung*, but he will be expelled from Prussia in 1849.

– The New York News Agency is founded, using the telegraph to supply information to newspapers. It becomes the Associated Press (AP) in 1848.

– Publication of *The Communist Manifesto* by Karl Marx and Friedrich Engels. The pamphlet sketches a materialist and progressive historical philosophy that predicts the inevitable collapse of capitalism.

SCIENCE AND TECHNOLOGY

– British chemist John Mitchell writes *A Treatise on the Falsification of Foods and the Chemical Means Employed to Detect Them*, a landmark in the field of consumer protection.

– Sir John Simon, the City of London's first medical officer, establishes a public health service. By highlighting the environmental conditions that cause the spread of disease, Simon helps to establish the science of epidemiology.

- Irish-born physicist and mathematician William Thomson, professor of natural philosophy at Glasgow University, proposes an absolute scale of temperatures.
- London's Waterloo Station is opened, named after the great battle at which the duke of Wellington defeated Napoleon Bonaparte in 1815.

ARTS AND HUMANITIES

Literature

- François-René, vicomte de Chateaubriand, French Romantic writer and politician, dies.

Anne Brontë, *The Tenant of Wildfell Hall*, novel.

Charles Dickens (see p. 385), *Dombey and Son*, novel.

Elizabeth Gaskell, *Mary Barton*, novel bringing a new note of social realism to English fiction.

Thomas Babington Macaulay, first two volumes of his *History of England*, bestselling work of Whig history.

John Stuart Mill (see box), *Principles of Political Economy*, a work of political and economic philosophy following the free trade principles of David Ricardo, developed in the light of Mill's experience working for the East India Company.

William Makepeace Thackeray, *Vanity Fair*, novel.

John Stuart Mill (1806–73)

The English thinker John Stuart Mill is regarded as the founder of modern liberalism. He wrote on economics in *Principles of Political Economy* (1848), championed equality between the sexes in *On the Subjection of Women* (1869). and, while sitting as a member of Parliament, introduced a bill to give women the vote. Philosophically, he developed the theory known as utilitarianism (established by Jeremy Bentham in the later 18th century), by which the aim of government and society was to achieve 'the greatest happiness of the greatest number'.

In his book *Utilitarianism* (1863) Mill reformulated the philosophy, arguing that the quantity of a pleasure was not enough – its quality needed to be considered as well. There were, he said, some people whose pleasures were genuinely more worthwhile than those of others. This introduced an inconsistency into classic utilitarianism, but it was an influential idea because the kind of people Mill privileged in these terms were his own type: high-minded and cultured liberals who would become politically and socially influential in his time and long afterwards. In *On Liberty* (1859) Mill had produced a classic defence of the interests of this group. Impressed by the dangers of a 'tyranny of the majority', Mill defended the needs of a 'learned class'. He acclaimed democracy but feared its consequence: an overwhelming but ignorant majority that would persecute a minority. What the masses needed was an authoritative intellectual guide. Mill's tone and arguments have shaped all subsequent liberal arguments in favour of toleration; however, they have also opened him to the charge of self-interested elitism.

Visual Arts and Architecture

- English artists John Everett Millais, Dante Gabriel Rossetti and William Holman Hunt establish the Pre-Raphaelite Brotherhood, whose neo-medieval style aims to revive English art.

Music

Johann Strauss I, *Radetzky March*, composed in honour of the Austrian field marshal, Count Joseph Radetzky.

1849

EUROPE

5 Jan. Austrian forces occupy Buda (and adjoining Pest), capital of newly autonomous Hungary in an attempt to crush the movement for independence and regain control. Meeting in the provincial town of Debreczen, the increasingly radical Hungarian diet responds by deposing the Austrian emperor as king of Hungary (13 April); nationalist leader Lajos Kossuth is made provisional governor of the country. Austrian forces, aided by Russian troops, invade Hungary (17 June) and defeat the Hungarian militia at the battle of Temesvár (9 Aug.). Kossuth flees to Turkey (11 Aug.), and his comrades surrender at Vilagos (13 Aug.). The Austrians take a bloody revenge: nine generals are hanged and four are shot. Russia and Austria demand the extradition of refugees from neighbouring countries.

9 Feb. A republic is proclaimed in Rome. Italian nationalist Giuseppe Garibaldi (see p. 408), who was forced to leave the city in 1836 because of his anti-Austrian agitation, returns from Uruguay (his characteristic red shirt has its origin in Uruguayan cloth) and leads an army in support of the Roman republic under Giuseppe Mazzini. Garibaldi's army of Redshirts is heavily outnumbered by a combined force of French, Spanish, Austrian, Neapolitan and Tuscan troops. Garibaldi attacks the French lines (3 June) but is soon forced to evacuate Rome (July). A chastened Pope Pius IX (see 17 Mar. 1848), regretting his earlier liberal beliefs, returns to Rome; the papacy becomes increasingly hostile to the principles of the French Revolution, modern democracy and its aggressive secularism, views that will condition its dealings with the rest of the world for the remainder of the century. Garibaldi escapes to the USA.

23 Mar. The forces of Piedmont are again mobilized following the end of the armistice with Austria (see 1848) but are defeated for a second time at Novara in Lombardy, N Italy, by the army led by Field Marshal Radetzky; Charles Albert, king of Piedmont–Sardinia, abdicates in favour of his son Victor Emmanuel II.

May Republican revolts take place in Dresden, Saxony, and in the German state of Baden, later suppressed by Prussian troops.

26 June In Britain Parliament repeals the Navigation Acts, protectionist legislation favouring the British merchant navy first enacted in the mid-17th century.

- Under the legislation of 1846 repealing the Corn Laws, duties on foods imported to Britain are reduced to nominal levels. From being a self-sufficient agrarian economy Britain is now becoming a net importer of food, which is financed by the country's growing manufacturing sector.

ASIA

– British forces under Gen. Hugh Gough defeat the Sikh armies at Jallianwalla (13 Jan.) and Gujarat (21 Feb.), and the Sikhs surrender at Rawalpindi (12 Mar.); Britain annexes the Punjab (29 Mar.), ending the Second Sikh War.

THE AMERICAS

5 Mar. Zachary Taylor takes office as 12th US president.

– Cholera wipes out the leadership of the Comanche people, originally from the area of Wyoming and W central USA, but the Comanche continue to resist the white settlement of their lands (see 1867).

ECONOMY AND SOCIETY

– An epidemic of cholera in Britain affects London particularly badly.

– Harrods, a London grocery store, starts to trade and will develop into a major commercial company and global brand.

– The Free Academy, later the City University of New York, opens.

SCIENCE AND TECHNOLOGY

– Inventor James Bogardus designs and builds the first prefabricated cast iron and glass building in New York; it rises to five storeys.

– Hat-maker Thomas Bowler of London develops the bowler hat.

– French physicist Armand Fizeau establishes the speed of light at 300,000km (186,300 miles) per second.

– US inventor Walter Hunt of New York patents the safety pin.

ARTS AND HUMANITIES

Literature

7 Oct. US poet and short-story writer Edgar Allan Poe dies.

– James Anthony Froude, an Oxford clergyman, breaks with the Anglican Church and the reformist Oxford Movement (see 1833) by writing his controversial novel *Nemesis of Faith* (1848). He abandons orthodox Christianity and leaves for London, where he will establish himself as a historian.

Friedrich Hebbel, *Herodes und Mariamne*, play.

Henry David Thoreau, 'Civil Disobedience', essay asserting the importance of individual conscience. The American Thoreau regards all government as a threat to the individual's moral being.

Visual Arts and Architecture

10 May The Japanese *ukiyo-e* painter Hokusai Katsushika dies.

– The Chain Bridge opens, linking the adjoining cities of Buda and Pest, Hungary.

– The remodelling of the Kremlin Palace, Moscow, is completed.

William Holman Hunt, *Rienzi*, painting.

Music

16 April First performance in Paris of Giacomo Meyerbeer's opera *Le Prophète* (The Prophet).

25 Sept. Johann Strauss I dies; his son Johann takes over his father's orchestra (11 Oct.).

17 Oct. Frédéric Chopin dies of tuberculosis in Paris.

8 Dec. First performance in Naples of Giuseppe Verdi's opera *Luisa Miller*.

Robert Schumann, *Manfred*, overture and incidental music based on a verse-drama by Byron (1817).

1850

EUROPE

15 Jan. A British fleet blockades the main Greek port of Piraeus near Athens to force the Greek government to compensate the Gibralter-born Jew Don Pacifico, a British subject whose house has been ransacked during an anti-Semitic demonstration (Dec. 1849); the Greek government accepts the British demand (26 April), and in a speech to Parliament (29 June) the foreign secretary Viscount Palmerston defends and vindicates his actions. The episode, which draws the ire of France and Russia (guarantors, like Britain, of Greek independence) inaugurates a new chapter in British imperialism. Palmerston claims that Britain is the heir to the Roman imperial notion of citizenship summed up in the boast *Civis Romanus sum*.

> *England, the country that turns whole nations into its proletarians.*
>
> Karl Marx, *Neue Rheinische Zeitung*, 1 Jan. 1848

31 May In a move against radical republican elements enjoying increased electoral success, the French government of Louis-Napoleon Bonaparte limits the popular franchise and (9 June) bans many clubs and public meetings.

– The Amalgamated Society of Engineers is founded in Britain, reflecting the growing power of trade unions. The new institutions representing workers use direct action and collective bargaining to increase wages and improve working conditions.

– Britain's Royal Navy reduces the daily ration of rum from one-quarter to one-eighth of a pint.

MIDDLE EAST AND NORTH AFRICA

9 July Mirza Ali Mohammed, founder of the Islamic Babi sect, is executed for heresy in Tabriz, Persia (see 1845). Mirza Husayn Ali takes over the leadership of the movement, declares himself the prophet foretold by Mirza Ali Mohammed and develops Babism into the Baha'i faith. He takes the title Baha-Allah (Glory of God), which gives Baha'ism its name.

ASIA

– The Taiping rebellion against Manchu rule starts in S China under the leadership of Hong Xiuquan; he calls himself Tin-wang (Heavenly Prince) and claims to be the younger brother of Jesus Christ. The movement, a potent mixture of religion and politics, will take 14 years to suppress.

HIERARCHIES IN COLLISION:
China and Japan in the 19th Century

Up until the mid-19th century neither China nor Japan had any need to worry about what might happen should they come into contact with technologically advanced peoples from beyond the seas. The threats faced by both societies had been from traditional enemies: unrest within their own societies, and, in the case of China, barbarians from the Eurasian interior. Contact with European and Middle Eastern societies had largely been limited to controlled trading enclaves. But in the 19th century, the conservative hierarchies of the Far East came face to face with the impatience and intolerance of Western modernity. Old certainties would disappear, but the new challenge would also open up new possibilities.

From 1644 to 1911 China was ruled by the Manchu (Qing) dynasty, a non-Chinese regime from the north that had quickly adopted Chinese culture, like all previous conquerors. The administration of China was strongly hierarchical, dominated by Manchu officials who oversaw a period of cultural brilliance, and ruled what was now the greatest settled empire in history. But there were problems. Between 1650 and 1840 the Chinese population quadrupled to 400 million, causing pressure on land and consequently much unrest. By the 19th century Confucianism had become a sterile orthodoxy that resisted change. Foreign traders were confined to Guangzhou (Canton) in the south and Kyakhta on the Russian border in the north: the Western industrial economy and its goods were kept at bay since China's age-old trading interest lay in exporting its own range of high-quality goods in return for European silver and gold. War with Britain came in 1840, and under the treaty of Nanjing (Nanking) of 1842 the British leased Hong Kong while the Chinese were forced to open Xiamen (Amoy), Shanghai and Ningbo (Ning-po) as well as Guangzhou to trade.

China's crisis had internal as well as external causes. The Taiping (T'ai P'ing) or Great Peace movement was a peasant rebellion that built on and integrated the traditional secret societies of the south. Starting in 1850, the movement spread to control large areas of China. Even with the support of Western forces, it was 1864 before the Chinese government was back in control. Between 20 and 30 million Chinese died during this turbulent period.

Gradually, by the 1890s, China succeeded in modernizing itself: there was massive investment in railways and telegraph companies, as well as in armaments. Shipyards and arsenals were developed, and gunboats built for a great new Chinese fleet. In 1895, however, China lost a war with Japan over their conflicting claims to Korea. Then came the uprising of the Society of Harmonious Fists, or Boxers, who laid siege to foreign embassies in Beijing (Peking). The movement was crushed by armies sent by the Western powers and Japan. The victors then imposed an enormous indemnity that essentially ruined the Chinese state. The final trigger for Manchu collapse came in 1911, when industrial unrest coincided with peasant uprisings and army mutinies. The subsequent declaration of a Chinese republic suggested that a potent mixture of nationalism, democracy and socialism would be the future for China in the 20th century.

After opening up in a limited way early to European trade in the 16th and 17th centuries, Japan then turned its back on the world. External contact was limited to trade with the Dutch and Chinese at the southern port of Nagasaki. Administratively, Japan moved towards an effective central government. The emperor – a remote and divine being – reigned, but real power rested with a hereditary military strongman bearing the title of shogun.

In 1853 a US naval expedition under Matthew Perry arrived in Edo Bay and enforced concessions to Western trade. Civil strife followed and led to a coup in 1868 that created the Meiji ('enlightened rule') restoration: the emperor replaced the shogun as the country's effective ruler, and initiated a process of economic and technological modernization. Japan started from a position of strength because its society in the mid-19th century was urbanized and its economy was already industrializing. What followed therefore was a dramatic development, not a dislocating revolution. Industrial

Conservative hierarchies of the Far East came face to face with the impatience and intolerance of Western modernity.

policy created a modern army and navy – both of which were strengthened by conscription.

Japan decided to intervene in Korea, which it regarded as being in its sphere of influence. This led to wars with China (1894–5) and Russia (1904–5) in which the Japanese won sweeping victories. Korea became a Japanese protectorate and, in 1910, a full colony. It was also the first time an Asian country had defeated a European state. At the dawn of the 20th century, Japan had shown the shape of the century to come. Modern technology had infused an ancient and restored hierarchy with a new – and militaristic – purpose.

1850 *continued*

THE AMERICAS

29 Jan. A bill is introduced to the US Congress requiring the state of Texas to give up its claim to New Mexico territory, ceded to the USA by Mexico in the treaty of Guadalupe Hidalgo (see 2 Feb. 1848), in return for the federal government taking over the Texas state debt.

9 July US president Zachary Taylor dies of gastroenteritis after eating iced cherries and milk at a 4th of July independence celebration; Vice-President Millard Fillmore succeeds as the 13th president.

9 Sept. California is admitted as the 31st state of the USA.

18 Sept. The Fugitive Slave Act passed by the US Congress tries to strengthen the laws against escaped slaves by substituting federal for state penalties but runs into popular opposition.

– Congress abolishes flogging in the US navy.

– Tenements are now being built on a massive scale in New York.

ECONOMY AND SOCIETY

18 Mar. The American Express Company based in New York is founded through the amalgamation of three firms active in express security transport; it will grow into a major multinational company providing travel-related and financial services.

– The private Pinkerton Detective Agency is established in the USA by Scottish-American detective Allan Pinkerton, formerly of the Chicago police force, initially specializing in crimes on the railway.

– The University of Sydney, Australia, is founded.

– The Singer sewing machine is invented by Isaac Singer of New York.

– Bavarian-American businessman Levi Strauss invents sturdy canvas trousers for the prospectors working in the California goldfields. As jeans they will eventually be made of blue denim and become an international fashion item.

– *Harper's Monthly* fashion magazine begins publication in New York.

– US impresario P.T. (Phineas Taylor) Barnum engages soprano Jenny Lind (the Swedish Nightingale) for a concert tour of the USA, paying her $1000 a night.

SCIENCE AND TECHNOLOGY

– Robert Bunsen of Heidelberg University in Germany invents the Bunsen burner, widely adopted in laboratories because its gas flame leaves no sooty deposit on test tubes.

– German physicist Rudolf Clausius formulates the second law of thermodynamics: heat can pass only from a warmer to a colder body, not from a colder to a warmer body. The principle will be fundamental to the development of refrigeration.

– Hermann von Helmholtz, professor of physiology at Königsberg, E Prussia (now Kaliningrad, Russia), invents the ophthalmoscope to examine the interior of the eye.

– In England salmon are disappearing from the River Thames in London because of the increasing level of pollution.

ARTS AND HUMANITIES

Literature

23 April The British poet William Wordsworth dies. Alfred, Lord Tennyson will succeed him as Poet Laureate.

Elizabeth Barrett Browning, *Sonnets from the Portuguese*, poetry.

François-René, vicomte de Chateaubriand, *Mémoires d'outre-tombe*, posthumously published autobiography of a defining figure of early French Romanticism.

Charles Dickens (see p. 385), *David Copperfield*, novel. (Dickens says of it: 'Of all my books, I like this the best.')

Nathaniel Hawthorne, *The Scarlet Letter*, novel commenting on the intolerance of New England puritanism.

Henry Wadsworth Longfellow, 'The Building of the Ship', narrative poem asserting that the advancement of humanity depends on the survival and development of the union of the USA.

Alfred, Lord Tennyson, 'In Memoriam', poem expressing religious doubt and personal love inspired by the death of his sister's fiancé Arthur Hallam.

William Makepeace Thackeray, *Pendennis*, novel.

Visual Arts and Architecture

Mathew Brady, *Gallery of Illustrious Americans*, photography, beginning the era of celebrity imagery.

Jean-Baptiste-Camille Corot, *Morning, the Dance of the Nymphs*, painting.

Gustave Courbet, *The Burial at Ornans*, painting in a new, naturalistic style. (Courbet's *The Stone Breakers*, also exhibited this year, will be destroyed in World War II.)

Sir John Everett Millais, *Christ in the House of His Parents*, painting.

Music

28 Aug. First performance in Weimar of Richard Wagner's (see p. 421) opera *Lohengrin*, including the famous Bridal Chorus (Wedding March).

Robert Schumann, Symphony No. 3 in E flat (*Rhenish*), and Concerto in A minor for cello and orchestra.

1851

EUROPE

1 May The world's first trade fair, the Great Exhibition, opens in London. Planned by Prince Albert, husband of Queen Victoria, it reflects British commercial self-confidence and economic recovery after the 'hungry forties'. The glass and iron-framed Crystal Palace built in Hyde Park to contain the exhibits is the world's largest single structure.

2 Dec. In France President Louis-Napoleon Bonaparte confirms the family's autocratic trait and France's occasional preference for a strong ruler by organizing a *coup d'état* to extend his term in office and end the Second Republic. Helped by his half-brother Charles, duc de Morny (a fictitious title), Louis-Napoleon orders troops to occupy Paris; parliamentary deputies are arrested and troops fire on the unarmed demonstrators in the massacre of the Boulevards.

ASIA

- King Rama III of Siam (Thailand) dies and is succeeded by his half-brother, who abandons life as a Buddhist monk to reign as Rama IV. The new king continues his predecessor's policy of opening up his country to Western influences: roads are improved, printing presses are introduced, and Siam gets its first currency. He also employs an English governess for his children.

THE AMERICAS

15 Feb. The question of runaway slaves regains prominence in the USA when a fugitive slave, Shadrach, is rescued from Boston jail by a group of black demonstrators; a similar event takes place in Syracuse, New York, later in the year (1 Oct.).

We are not a nation, so much as a world.

Herman Melville on the US in *Redburn: His First Voyage* (1849)

15 May The Erie Railroad now links New York with the Great Lakes in the US Midwest.
4 July The first lines for the Missouri Pacific Railroad, the first railway W of the Mississippi river, are laid at St Louis, E Missouri.
23 July Sioux leaders sign a treaty ceding lands in Iowa and Minnesota to the US federal government.
24 Dec. The Library of Congress in Washington, D.C.'s Capitol building is badly damaged by fire, destroying most of the books donated to the library by Thomas Jefferson in 1814. Congress orders the necessary renovation and rebuilding.
- US publisher Amelia Jenks Bloomer urges reform of women's clothing in her magazine *The Lily* and wears loose trousers (bloomers) under a short skirt, a garment she introduced at the Women's Rights Convention in New York in 1848.
- Maine becomes the first US state to vote for a law prohibiting the sale and consumption of alcohol.
- The Oneida utopian religious community of farmers and mechanics in New York (established in 1848) introduces equal rights for men and women.

AUSTRALASIA AND OCEANIA

- In Australia, Victoria becomes a separate colony from New South Wales.
- Prospector Edward Hargreaves discovers gold in New South Wales, Australia. Chinese immigration that accompanies the gold rush leads to the first white supremacist demands in Australia for legislation to exclude other racial groups.

ECONOMY AND SOCIETY

22 Aug. The US schooner *America* wins the One Hundred Guinea Cup in a race around the Isle of Wight, England, organized by the Royal Yacht Squadron. The cup is renamed the America's Cup, and US vessels will retain the trophy until 1983.
Sept. The *New York Times* begins publication.
- Duke University, North Carolina, S USA, is founded.
- Northwestern University is founded near Chicago in the US Midwest.
- Paul Julius Reuter of Kassel, Germany, starts a telegraphic news service and moves to London to exploit the possibilities presented by the new under-sea cable laid between Dover and Calais (see below). His continental cable service provides information about stock prices and will also develop to include general news.

SCIENCE AND TECHNOLOGY

25 Nov. Samuel Colt addresses the Institution of Civil Engineers in Britain and claims that the British army will never be able to defeat the Boers and indigenous Africans in S Africa unless armed with his Colt revolver. The time taken by soldiers to reload the muskets currently in use enables enemy forces to regroup and attack.
- Scott Archer, an English architect, develops a wet collodion process for developing photographs that will replace the calotype and the daguerreotype.
- Bax and Company in London's Regent Street makes a new rain-coat from a chemically treated wool fibre, which will be called Aquascutum, challenging the dominance of the mackintosh.
- An under-sea telegraph cable is laid across the English Channel between Dover in England and Calais in France.
- The Krupps steel mill at Essen in Germany casts a 1950kg (4300lb) steel ingot in one piece, the previous record being a 1090kg (2400lb) ingot cast in Sheffield, England.
- German physicist Heinrich Ruhmkorff invents the high-tension induction coil, now known as the Ruhmkorff coil, which develops into the alternating electric current (AC) transformer.
- Building on the work of James Joule (see 1840), Professor William Thomson of Glasgow University produces a general and complete statement of thermodynamic theory. This will be developed further by Heinrich Hertz, the German physicist who discovers radio waves (1887).
- James Young of Scotland patents a technique for producing paraffin by the dry distillation of coal.

ARTS AND HUMANITIES

Literature

Nathaniel Hawthorne, *The House of the Seven Gables*, novel.
Eugène Labiche, *Un Chapeau de paille d'Italie* (An Italian Straw Hat), comedy.
Herman Melville, *Moby-Dick, or, The Whale*, epic novel of whaling and the quest for self-understanding.
Lewis Henry Morgan, *The League of the Iroquois*, anthropological study of the Seneca tribe.

Visual Arts and Architecture

27 Jan. US ornithological illustrator John James Audubon dies in New York.

19 Dec. English artist Joseph Mallord William Turner dies in Chelsea, London.

Edwin Landseer, *Monarch of the Glen*, painting.

Emanuel Leutze, *Washington Crossing the Delaware*, painting.

Music

11 Mar. First production in Venice of Giuseppe Verdi's opera *Rigoletto*, based on Victor Hugo's drama *Le Roi s'amuse* (1832).

– Hungarian composer Franz Liszt starts work on the first 15 in his series of *Hungarian Rhapsodies* for piano, which will be completed in 1854.

Robert Schumann, Symphony No. 4 in D minor.

1852

EUROPE

27 Feb. Lord Derby (Edward Stanley) becomes British prime minister following the resignation of Lord John Russell (23 Feb.).

4 Nov. Count Camillo di Cavour becomes prime minister of Piedmont.

2 Dec. Louis-Napoleon proclaims the Second French Empire and will reign as Napoleon III until 1870. The royal family are exiled, and Napoleon uses the constitutional device of a national plebiscite (Nov.) to confirm the return to imperial rule.

20 Dec. In Britain Lord Derby's administration resigns after the defeat of the chancellor of the exchequer Benjamin Disraeli's budget. A Liberal–Peelite coalition takes office under Lord Aberdeen. W.E. Gladstone becomes chancellor of the exchequer.

ASIA

– Pagan Min, king of Burma, is deposed; the British occupy Rangoon at the start of the Second Burmese War.

– Despite laws against emigration, some 50,000 Chinese have now left for the USA. Most have travelled to the Californian goldfields and are helped by a Chinese Immigration Agency.

THE AMERICAS

3 Feb. The dictator of Argentina, Juan Manuel de Rosas, is defeated at the battle of Caseros by the rebel Justo de Urquiza, who is supported by Brazil and Uruguay. Argentina now gives up the attempt at assimilating Uruguay and also recognizes Paraguay's independence (17 July).

– In the US presidential election Franklin Pierce, the Democratic Party candidate, defeats the Whig nominee Winfield Scott. The US Whig party now begins to decline and is internally divided on the slavery question.

– The Know Nothing Party, a nativist political group opposed to further immigration to the USA (especially of Irish Catholics), is organized.

– Massachusetts becomes the first US state to make school attendance effectively compulsory.

– The US states of Massachusetts, Vermont and Louisiana adopt anti-alcohol prohibition laws.

SUB-SAHARAN AFRICA

17 Jan. In the Sand River Convention the British agree to the independence of the Transvaal, which will become a Boer republic (see 1856).

AUSTRALASIA AND OCEANIA

– New Zealand's new constitution creates six provinces each with a council elected by propertied individuals.

ECONOMY AND SOCIETY

– In Paris Aristide Boucicaut begins to transform Bon Marché into the world's first department store. Small profit margins on individual goods are offset by bulk sales.

– French emperor Napoleon III gives the Bois de Boulogne to the people and city of Paris. He also starts a programme of public works under the direction of Baron Georges Haussmann, town planner, financier and prefect of the Seine, who widens streets and opens boulevards. The maintenance of public order dictates that the new civic layout enables troops to fire in a straight line at any body of demonstrators. In the process, much of the old city of Paris is destroyed along with much of its political volatility.

– Service *à la Russe* (Russian style) is introduced into English dining, with dishes being served in a sequence of courses rather than simultaneously (see 1811).

– Wells, Fargo and Co. establish a New York branch to ensure parcel delivery between New York and California.

– Chateau-sur-Mer is built for William S. Wetmore at Newport, Rhode Island, USA, which is now developing as an area of extravagant homes for America's new class of super-rich.

SCIENCE AND TECHNOLOGY

– A canvas hose is invented by gold miner Anthony Chabot in California; it permits the development of hydraulic mining techniques in the Californian gold rush.

– Elisha Graves of New York invents the safety elevator, which will allow the development of high-rise buildings.

ARTS AND HUMANITIES

Literature

– Russian novelist Ivan Turgenev is exiled to his estates after praising controversial writer and dramatist Nikolai Gogol in an obituary written after Gogol's death (21 Feb.).

Alexandre Dumas *fils*, *La Dame aux camélias*, play based on the author's novel of the same name (1848).

Gustav Freytag, *Die Journalisten*, comedy.

Théophile Gautier, *Emaux et camées* (Enamels and Cameos), poetry.

Nathaniel Hawthorne, *The Blithedale Romance*, novel reflecting Hawthorne's time at Brook Farm (see 1841).

Peter Mark Roget, *Thesaurus of English Words and Phrases*, reference work, the first of many editions.

Harriet Beecher Stowe, *Uncle Tom's Cabin*, novel offering a sentimental view of African-Americans but also contributing to the white American rejection of slavery.

William Makepeace Thackeray, *The History of Henry Esmond*, novel.

Visual Arts and Achitecture
– In London the Houses of Parliament are completed in Gothic Revival style by Charles Barry with interiors by Augustus Pugin.
Sir John Everett Millais, *Ophelia*, painting.

Music
Franz Liszt, *Fantasia on Hungarian Melodies* (Hungarian Fantasia) for piano and orchestra.

1853

EUROPE

9 Jan. Emperor Napoleon III of France marries the Spanish countess Eugénie de Montijo in a ceremony at the Tuileries Palace, Paris.

19 April Russia, anxious to gain equal rights with France in the Christian 'holy places' of Palestine, claims rights of protection over the Christians of the Ottoman empire. Ottoman Turkey rejects a Russian ultimatum (21 May).

31 May Tsar Nicholas I of Russia orders the invasion of the Ottoman (Turkish) Danubian provinces W of the Black Sea in a bid to increase Russian influence over Turkey; the Ottoman empire declares war (23 Sept.) and (4 Oct.) issues an ultimatum for Russia to evacuate the provinces. The dispute will lead to the Crimean War (see 1854).

30 Nov. The Russian fleet destroys the Ottoman Turkish fleet off Sinope in the Black Sea.

– Brunswick, Hanover and Oldenburg join the Prussian-led *Zollverein* (customs union), and the tariff-free zone now includes all German states except Austria.

– Queen Maria II (Maria da Glória) of Portugal dies. She is succeeded by her son Peter V.

ASIA

8 July Commodore Matthew Perry of the US navy arrives in Edo (Tokyo) Bay, Japan, in charge of a flotilla of seven ships. On the instructions of President Millard Fillmore he demands a trade treaty and then departs (16 July), promising that he will return for a reply in the spring of 1854.

23 July The ruling Japanese shogun Tokugawa Ieyoshi dies; his brother Iesada succeeds and will be forced to open two Japanese ports to trade (1854) in order to end a civil war created by the demands of the US government.

8 Aug. A Russian naval fleet arrives at Nagasaki, Japan, applying pressure to open trade relations and settle boundary disputes.

7 Sept. Shanghai falls to rebel forces as the Taiping rebellion continues in S China (see 1850).

– The Second Anglo-Burmese War (see 1852) ends with Britain's annexation of Pegu (Lower Burma). Pagan Min, king of Burma, is deposed by his brother Mindon Min, founder of the new Burmese capital of Mandalay, who becomes king.

– India's first railway line opens and links Bombay with Thana in the NW. James John Berkley, the English engineer who has built the line, will go on to complete the Bombay–Calcutta–Madras–Nagpur line by 1856.

THE AMERICAS

4 Mar. Franklin Pierce, a Democrat, becomes 14th US president.

11 Oct. The first US clearing bank, the New York Clearing House, opens in Wall Street, clearing $2 million on its first day.

30 Dec. The Gadsden Purchase treaty allows the USA to annex a tract of Mexican land S of the Gila River (now part of New Mexico and Arizona). The territory is crucial in providing the best route for building a railway between Texas and California.

– The Massachusetts Constitution Convention in the USA receives a petition in support of women's suffrage.

– Samuel Maverick of Texas, USA, rounds up his stray cattle and gives his name to unbranded stock and, by extension, to anyone who is independently minded.

AUSTRALASIA AND OCEANIA

– Britain stops transporting its convicts to the Australian island of Tasmania.

ECONOMY AND SOCIETY

– The University of Melbourne, Australia, is founded.

– George Crum, the chef at Moon's Lake House, Saratoga Springs, New York, invents the potato chip.

– English financier Samuel Montagu founds a firm and a foreign exchange that will become the world's largest centre for gold trading. London is now set to become the central clearing house of the international money market.

– In Britain Parliament approves the construction of an underground railway between Farringdon Street and Bishop's Road in Paddington, London, establishing the first urban mass-transit subway or metro.

SCIENCE AND TECHNOLOGY

– British aviation pioneer Sir George Cayley develops the first manned glider, which flies 457m (500 yards).

– A railway line opens linking Vienna with Trieste (NE Italy). Achieved by tunnelling through the Alps, it is the world's first mountain railway.

– The world's largest tree (*Sequoiadendron giganteum*) is discovered in California. It is named the wellingtonia, or giant redwood or California big tree.

ARTS AND HUMANITIES

Literature
– British poet and critic Matthew Arnold publishes his collected poems, including 'The Scholar-Gypsy' and 'Sohrab and Rustum'.
Charlotte Brontë, *Villette*, novel.
Charles Dickens (see p. 385), *Bleak House*, novel.
Mrs Gaskell (Elizabeth Cleghorn), *Cranford*, novel.

Visual Arts and Architecture
– John Ruskin, *The Stones of Venice*, the most detailed study of Venetian architecture in English. It is a key statement of Ruskin's philosophy, which demonizes the Renaissance and praises the gothic style as the product of a united pan-European culture with a proper (pre-industrial) appreciation of work and worship.
William Holman Hunt, *The Awakening Conscience*, painting.

Music

19 Jan. First performance in Rome of Giuseppe Verdi's opera *Il trovatore* (The Troubadour).Verdi's opera *La traviata* (The Wayward One), based on *La Dame aux camélias* by Alexandre Dumas *fils* (see 1852), is first performed in Venice on 6 Mar. Camille Saint-Saëns, Symphony No. 1 in E flat major.

1854

EUROPE

6 Jan. The British and French fleets enter the Black Sea to prevent a Russian invasion of Turkey (see 30 Nov. 1853). Concerned to prevent any further Russian advance to the W, Britain and France enter an alliance with the Ottoman (Turkish) empire (12 Mar.) and declare war on Russia (28 Mar.) after it ignores an ultimatum to evacuate the Danubian provinces (see 31 May 1853). In the ensuing Crimean War allied troops besiege Sevastopol on the Crimean peninsula and defeat the Russians at the battles of the Alma (30 Sept.); of Balaclava (25 Oct.), which includes the cavalry charge of the Light Brigade led by James Thomas Brudenell, 7th earl of Cardigan; and of Inkerman (5 Nov.).

– In the Crimea an epidemic of typhus in the Russian army infects the British and French troops, spreads to Constantinople and is carried by shipping into the wider Russian and Turkish population. Florence Nightingale, superintendent of a London hospital for invalid women, travels to Scutari (opposite Constantinople) and transforms the barracks hospital. She introduces new methods of sanitation, which will reduce the death toll from cholera, typhus and dysentery.

MIDDLE EAST AND NORTH AFRICA

13 July Abbas I, khedive (Ottoman-appointed viceroy) of Egypt, is assassinated and is succeeded by his uncle Sa'id Pasha. He grants a concession (30 Nov.) to build a canal from Port Said to Suez to his friend the French diplomat Ferdinand de Lesseps.

ASIA

Feb. Commodore Perry returns to Japan with ten US naval ships in the pursuit of trading rights (see 8 July 1853); by the treaty of Kanagawa (31 Mar.) the USA is granted access to Japanese trade through the two ports of Hakodate and Shimoda.

– The shogun Tokugawa Iesada decides to build a modern Japanese defence force.

THE AMERICAS

30 May The Kansas–Nebraska Act of the US Congress repeals a previous ban on slavery in the N part of the Louisiana Purchase (the Missouri Compromise, see 1820) and allows a referendum on slavery in the territories of Kansas and Nebraska. A vicious guerilla war between pro- and anti-slavery elements follows in Kansas (1855–7).

6 July In the USA the Republican Party is founded in opposition to the Kansas–Nebraska Act. It consists of former Whigs and Democrats who are opposed to slavery. The name 'Republican' is adopted from the Democratic-Republican Party, which was established by Thomas Jefferson and which dropped the word in 1828.

SUB-SAHARAN AFRICA

17 Feb. By the Convention of Bloemfontein with the Boers, Britain withdraws from land N of the Orange River in S Africa; the Boers now develop the Orange Free State.

ECONOMY AND SOCIETY

8 Dec. The papal reaction against modern liberalism gathers pace with Pope Pius IX's declaration that the Immaculate Conception of the Virgin is an article of faith. The ruling is a landmark in the development of the idea of papal infallibility, which states that the pope's teaching is uniquely authoritative and binding when he speaks on matters of faith.

– University College, Dublin, is founded and made fully open to Catholic students.

– The *Age* newspaper starts publication in the Australian city of Melbourne, Victoria.

– French newspaper *Le Figaro* starts publication as a weekly (it will become a daily newspaper in 1866).

SCIENCE AND TECHNOLOGY

– The English mathematician George Boole revolutionizes logic in *An Investigation of the Laws of Thought on which are Founded the Mathematical Theories of Logic and Probabilities*.

ARTS AND HUMANITIES

Literature

– Jakob and Wilhelm Grimm start work on their historical dictionary of the German language *Deutsches Wörterbuch*.

Charles Dickens (see p. 385), *Hard Times*, novel. Lord Macaulay condemns it for its 'sullen socialism'.

Gérard de Nerval, *Les Chimères*, collection of 12 sonnets that prefigure symbolist poetry in their dense allusiveness.

Alfred, Lord Tennyson, 'The Charge of the Light Brigade', poem commemorating the heroism of the British cavalrymen at the battle of Balaclava (25 Oct.).

Henry David Thoreau, *Walden, or Life in the Woods*, autobiographical and anti-materialist account of two years spent living in a hut by Walden Pond, near Concord, Massachusetts.

Visual Arts and Architecture

William Holman Hunt, *The Light of the World*, painting. Jean-François Millet, *The Reapers*, painting.

Music

27 Feb. German composer Robert Schumann attempts suicide by jumping into the Rhine; he is rescued by fishermen and committed to an asylum.

Hector Berlioz, *L'Enfance du Christ,* oratorio.

1855

EUROPE

26 Jan. The Piedmontese prime minister Camillo di Cavour, anxious to enlist Franco-British support for the cause of Italian unity, sends troops to fight with the allies in the Crimean War.

5 Feb. In Britain Henry John Temple, Viscount Palmerston, becomes prime minister after the resignation of Lord Aberdeen (over criticism of his war policy).

Feb. John Bright, radical orator, urges the withdrawal of British troops from the siege of Sevastopol in the Crimea, where they are suffering great hardship.

2 Mar. In Russia Tsar Nicholas I dies and is succeeded by his son Alexander II.

May The Paris International Exhibition opens as a triumphal assertion of French technology; the French economy, however, will run into difficulties in the second half of the 19th century as the French population declines. Equal inheritance rights, introduced by Napoleon I, have increasingly divided up – and therefore impoverished – land-holdings, as a result of which French families are now limiting their numbers.

11 Sept. The Russian army withdraws from Sevastopol in the Crimea after a year-long siege.

ASIA

Feb. The Japanese shogun Tokugawa Iesada signs commercial treaties with Russia and (Nov.) with the Netherlands.

30 Mar. In the treaty of Peshawar the British ally themselves with the Afghans against Persia, a country seen to be under the influence of Russia, whose forces are advancing into C Asia. Britain counters Russia in the 'Great Game' in order to protect British power in India.

– Siam (Thailand) signs its first foreign treaty and grants Britain the right to establish consulates and to trade throughout the kingdom. Similar treaties will follow with France and the USA (1856).

THE AMERICAS

– The states of Delaware, Indiana, Iowa, Michigan, New Hampshire, New York and the Nebraska territory adopt prohibition laws.

SUB-SAHARAN AFRICA

– Scottish missionary and explorer David Livingstone, on an expedition into C Africa from Cape Town, discovers the great waterfalls on the Zambezi River; they will be called the Victoria Falls after the current British sovereign.

– Ras Kassa proclaims himself king of kings in Ethiopia and reigns as Emperor Tewoderos II with British military aid, which suppresses further rebellions against him. He has deposed Ras Ali and conquered the territories of Tigre, Shoa and Goijam.

AUSTRALASIA AND OCEANIA

– The state of Victoria, Australia, introduces legislation to limit Chinese immigration, which has risen dramatically following the discovery of gold in New South Wales. A poll tax of £10 is imposed on each Chinese immigrant.

ECONOMY AND SOCIETY

29 June In London the *Daily Telegraph* newspaper begins publication. The Stamp Act (a tax on newspapers) has been repealed by Parliament, and many newspapers move from weekly to daily publication. By 1870 the *Daily Telegraph* will be the biggest selling newspaper in the world, with a circulation of over 270,000.

– Elmira Female College, New York, is founded and becomes the first US institution to grant degrees to women.

– Pennsylvania and Michigan State universities are founded in the USA.

– Les Grands Magasins du Louvre opens in the rue de Rivoli, Paris, and follows in the path of the successful Bon Marché department store (see 1852).

– The first US kindergarten opens in Waterstown, Wisconsin, as a school for immigrant children.

– The Young Women's Christian Association (YWCA), counterpart of the YMCA (see 1844), is founded in London.

– The British firm Smith and Phillips introduces a domestic gas oven.

SCIENCE AND TECHNOLOGY

6 Mar. The Roebling suspension bridge across the Niagara Gorge, between New York state, USA, and Ontario, Canada, is now completed, and the train that now crosses it is the first to do so on a bridge sustained by wire cables.

– Herbert Spencer's *Principles of Psychology* applies the idea of evolution to social progress.

– Henri-Etienne Deville, a French chemist, develops a practical method for producing aluminium.

– David Hughes, a British-born US inventor, patents the teleprinter, the technology of which will be the basis of the telephone, the hearing aid and the microphone.

– New York doctor Abraham Gestner adapts the Greek word for wax (*keros*) to describe his invention, kerosene (known as paraffin in Britain), a fuel derived from raw petroleum.

– A.H. Hassall causes a sensation with *Food and its Adulterations* in which he reports that most beer, bread, butter, coffee, pepper and tea contains traces of arsenic, copper, lead or mercury.

– English chemist Alexander Parkes patents a form of celluloid.

– The Sault Ste Marie Ship Canal in Ontario, S Canada, opens, linking Lake Huron with Lake Superior; the Great Lakes now become a vast inland waterway accessible to heavy shipping. The growth of the US city of Chicago is also boosted with the easy access now provided to the iron ore deposits of N Michigan and Minnesota, and expansion is further helped by the dredging of the Chicago River.

– The US Congress authorizes the building of a telegraph line linking the Mississippi River with the Pacific coast.

ARTS AND HUMANITIES

Literature

John Bartlett, *Familiar Quotations*, reference work that will reappear in successive editions.

Robert Browning, *Men and Women*, collection of poems, including 'Love Among the Ruins' and 'Childe Roland to the Dark Tower Came'.

Mrs Gaskell (Elizabeth Cleghorn), *North and South*, novel.

Friedrich Hebbel, *Agnes Bernauer*, play.

Gottfried Keller, *Der grüne Heinrich* (Green Henry), novel.

Charles Kingsley, *Westward Ho!*, historical novel set in the time of the Spanish Armada and inspired by the contemporary mood of war-time patriotism in Britain.

Henry Wadsworth Longfellow, *Song of Hiawatha*, poem.

Anthony Trollope, *The Warden*, novel, the first of his series of 'Barsetshire' novels.

Walt Whitman, *Leaves of Grass*, poetry introducing a new confessional tone into US verse. The 12 poems include 'Song of Myself' and 'I Sing the Body Electric'.

Visual Arts and Architecture

Ford Madox Brown, *The Last of England*, painting.

Gustave Courbet, *Interior of the Studio*, painting, subtitled *A Real Allegory Summing up Seven Years of My Life*. Courbet's work has been rejected by the Paris Exhibition, and he organizes a display of his own works in a shed nearby.

Roger Fenton, wood engravings of his photographs depicting scenes from the Crimean War, published in the *Illustrated London News,* create a new dimension in news reporting.

1856

EUROPE

Jan. The Victoria Cross, Britain's highest military decoration, is introduced.

1 Feb. The Crimean War ends with Russia agreeing to a preliminary peace conference to be held in Vienna. By the treaty of Paris (30 Mar.) the Danubian principalities are guaranteed, the Black Sea and parts of Bessarabia (modern Moldova) are neutralized, and the great powers agree to respect the independence of the Ottoman (Turkish) empire. By the terms of the Hatt-i-Humayun edict, the Ottoman Sultan Abdul-Mejid guarantees the property and security of his Christian subjects. Christians are also allowed to buy exemption from military service, torture is abolished, prisons are reformed, and liberty of conscience is guaranteed.

ASIA

13 Feb. Britain annexes the N Indian province of Oudh, provoking further hostility to British rule in the subcontinent.

– The Persian army occupies the town of Herat in Afghanistan, leading to war with Britain.

– The Second Opium War begins as Britain and France seek new commercial concessions from China; allied troops seize the port of Guangzhou (Canton).

– To honour the arrival of the first US consul-general in Japan the first bovine calf ever to be killed in the country is ceremonially slaughtered. Its mother is also milked to produce the first cow's milk ever to be drunk by humans in Japan.

THE AMERICAS

21 May The town of Lawrence in Kansas is sacked by pro-slavery immigrants. They regard their actions as justified by the idea of 'popular sovereignty' advanced by US judge Stephen Douglas,

and they want to turn Kansas into a slave state (see 30 May 1854). Their supporters pack the legislature of Kansas, and pitched battles follow between members of the Free Soil movement and the upholders of slavery. Abolitionists attack and hack to death five advocates of slavery (24 May) as retaliation for the sacking of Lawrence.

May The USA recognizes the adventurer William Walker as ruler of the C American state of Nicaragua after he has sacked the capital Granada. A US citizen, Walker led an armed faction into the country (1855) at the invitation of local Nicaraguan revolutionaries. He now envisages a C American military empire based on slave labour in an agricultural economy.

– James Adams, governor of South Carolina, urges the repeal of the 1807 act forbidding the trade in slaves.

SUB-SAHARAN AFRICA

12 July In S Africa Britain makes Natal, previously part of Cape Province, a crown colony.

– The Boers establish the Republic of the Transvaal, with Pretoria as its capital named after Marthinus Wessels Pretorius, the new president.

– British explorers Richard Burton and John Hanning Speke set out on an expedition to find the source of the River Nile. They will reach Lake Tanganyika, and Speke will become the first European to see Lake Victoria.

ECONOMY AND SOCIETY

– The US sewing machine company Singer and Co. introduces hire-purchase as a way of encouraging sales and also offers a trade-in allowance for any old sewing machines; sales double within a year.

– Scots-American railway telegraph operator Andrew Carnegie makes his first investment in the USA, where he will become the pre-eminent industrialist and the country's richest man.

– English tailor Thomas Burberry develops a raincoat that will compete with Mackintosh and Aquascutum.

– Cigarettes become common in London after being popularized by British troops returning from the Crimean War; the habit of smoking is widespread among the Russians. Robert Gloag, a Crimean veteran, opens the first British cigarette factory.

– The *Frankfurter Allgemeine Zeitung* newspaper starts publication in Frankfurt am Main, Germany.

SCIENCE AND TECHNOLOGY

– British engineer Henry Bessemer patents his 'converter', transforming molten pig iron into steel. The Bessemer process lowers the price of steel and popularizes its use.

– German scientist Theodor Bilharz, working in Cairo, identifies the parasite that causes the disease of the kidney and liver now known as bilharzia. The disease affects 70% of rural Egyptians.

– Johann Fuhrott discovers human fossils in the Neander Tal valley in the German Rhineland; French surgeon Paul Broca maintains that the skull is different in structure from that of modern man.

– William Perkin, an English chemistry student, produces the world's first synthetic dye. It is derived from coal tar and is

mauve in colour. Previous dyes have been made largely from vegetable matter, mostly roots, bark or berries.
- The Wabash and Erie Canal opens and is the largest waterway built in the USA; it is the result of 24 years of building work, but it will close down completely by 1874 because of the impact of the railways.

ARTS AND HUMANITIES

Literature
- US playwrights get legal copyright protection for their works.
Richard Burton, *Personal Narrative of a Pilgrimage to Al-Medinah and Meccah*, a memoir of his 1853 travels in the Islamic world disguised as a Pathan.

Visual Arts and Architecture
- In England, the sovereign's London residence, Buckingham Palace, is enlarged by the addition of a great ballroom.
William Holman Hunt, *The Scapegoat*, painting.

Music
29 July German composer Robert Schumann dies insane near Bonn. His wife Clara will edit his complete works.
Franz Liszt, *Orpheus* and *Les Préludes*, symphonic poems, and Piano Concerto No. 1 in E flat (revised version).

1857

EUROPE
10 Oct. The nationalist Irish Republican Brotherhood, whose members are known as Fenians, is founded in New York with the aim of overthrowing British rule in Ireland.
- Italian nationalist Giuseppe Garibaldi (see p. 408), who returned to Italy from the USA in 1854, establishes the Italian National Association to continue the struggle for the political unification of the Italian peninsula.

ASIA
4 Mar. The Anglo-Persian War of 1856 is ended by the treaty of Paris, in which Persia recognizes the independence of Afghanistan.
10 May The Indian (or Sepoy) Mutiny begins. The Enfield rifle introduced to the British army in India is an adaptation of a design by Samuel Colt; the rifle fires cartridges coated with beef and pork fat, offending both Hindu sepoys for whom cows are sacred, and Muslims for whom pigs are unclean. A mutiny breaks out among the sepoys (more than 95% of the British army in India), which is encouraged by local rulers opposed to British authority. At Cawnpore (Kanpur) over 200 British women and children are killed (15 July); a force from the Punjab loyal to the East India Company rulers regains Delhi (20 Sept).

THE AMERICAS
4 Mar. James Buchanan, a Democrat, becomes 15th US president, having defeated John C. Frémont, the Republican party's first presidential nominee, and Millard Fillmore, the Whig candidate.
6 Mar. In the USA the Supreme Court undermines the Missouri Compromise of 1820. It rules that Dred Scott, a slave from Missouri who has sued for freedom from his owner, may not claim freedom on the grounds that he has lived with his owner in states where slavery has been outlawed by the Missouri Compromise. The Supreme Court also says that a black person may not bring a suit in a federal court and claims that Congress never had the authority to ban slavery in the US territories.
Mar. The US adventurer William Walker, who has become president of Nicaragua (see May 1856), seizes goods belonging to Cornelius Vanderbilt's Accessory Transit Company; Vanderbilt organizes other C American countries to eject Walker from office. Walker surrenders to a US navy officer to escape capture (1 May), returns to the USA but then (Nov.) returns to C America. He is captured by a British naval officer in 1860 and returned to Honduras where he is court-martialled and executed.
11 Sept. Native Americans, led by followers of the Mormon religion, attack and kill 100 emigrants who are travelling to California on a wagon train. The attack in Utah territory, some 480km (300 miles) S of Salt Lake City, is on the orders of Mormon leader Brigham Young, who has been removed from the office of president of the independent 'State of Deseret' (see 1847) by President Buchanan. The president sends armed forces to re-establish federal rule in the region.
- The collapse of the Ohio Life Insurance and Trust Company causes a major economic recession in the USA. Some 5000 firms collapse after a period of economic boom and over-speculation. The steamship *Central America* also sinks off the coast of South Carolina near Charleston; over 400 lives are lost as well as 3 tons of gold, which increases the financial panic.
- Hinton Rowan Helper, a North Carolina farmer, writes *The Impending Crisis of the South, and How to Meet It*; he sees slavery as the cause of shame, poverty and ignorance in the S USA and points out its unprofitability since slavery ties up capital that, if invested in advanced machinery, would increase productivity.

ECONOMY AND SOCIETY
- In India the universities of Bombay, Calcutta and Madras are established.
- The University of California is founded at Oakland.
- The world's first alimony payments are established in Britain under the Matrimonial Causes Act.
- Work begins on the construction of Central Park, New York, under the direction of the landscape architect Frederick Law Olmsted. The public works programme helps to produce jobs at a time of economic depression.
- The New York department store of E.G. Haughwort installs the first commercial passenger elevator in its five-storey building on Broadway.
- In a response to the US economic crisis, the *New York Tribune* sacks all but two of its foreign correspondents; one of the two kept on is Karl Marx (see p. 419).
- The US wine trade begins with the planting of varietal grape vines in California by the Hungarian count Agoston Haraszthy de Mokcsa (see 1861).

SCIENCE AND TECHNOLOGY

12 May The New York Infirmary for Women and Children, a hospital run entirely by women, opens.

– Louis Pasteur, French chemist, shows that the lactic fermentation that ruins milk is caused by a living organism.

ARTS AND HUMANITIES

Literature

Charles Baudelaire, *Les Fleurs du mal*, lyric poetry collection, one of the greatest in French literary history. Its author is fined for offences against public morals, and six of the poems are banned from future editions (the ban will not be lifted until May 1949).

Gustave Flaubert, *Madame Bovary*, novel; Flaubert is prosecuted for immorality as a result but is acquitted.

Thomas Hughes, *Tom Brown's Schooldays*, a fictionalized account of his time as a boy at Rugby School under headmaster Thomas Arnold.

Visual Arts and Architecture

– Joseph Paxton designs Mentmore Towers in Buckinghamshire, England, as a neo-Elizabethan fantasy for Mayer de Rothschild.

Music

12 Mar. First performance in Venice of Giuseppe Verdi's opera *Simone Boccanegra*, based on the life of Venice's first doge.

Franz Liszt, *Eine Faust-Symphonie* (A Faust Symphony), which is based on Goethe's poem, and *Dante* Symphony, which is based on the *Divina commedia*.

1858

EUROPE

14 Jan. An assassination attempt on Emperor Napoleon III of France fails. The authorities execute Felice Orsini and Joseph Pieri, aggrieved Italian nationalists who are responsible for bomb explosions that have killed 10 and injured 150.

25 Jan. Victoria, daughter of Queen Victoria of Great Britain, marries Prince Frederick William of Prussia (later Frederick III). The music played at the service, Felix Mendelssohn's Wedding March from *A Midsummer Night's Dream* (see 1826) and Richard Wagner's (see p. 421) Wedding March from *Lohengrin* (see 1850), begins a popular tradition.

26 Feb. In Britain Lord Derby becomes prime minister of a Conservative government.

10 July Emperor Napoleon III of France secretly meets Count Cavour, prime minister of Piedmont, and agrees to an alliance in a war against Austria. Both agree that a pretext will be needed to justify the action to European public opinion. Napoleon, having sounded out the Russians and secured their approval, signs a treaty with Cavour (10 Dec.).

23 Dec. In Serbia Alexander Karageorgevic is deposed and succeeded by Miloš Obrenovic, the ruler who was deposed in 1839.

– Tsar Alexander II of Russia begins the emancipation of the country's serfs.

– Frederick William IV, king of Prussia, is officially declared insane; his brother William becomes regent.

ASIA

26–29 June The treaties of Tianjin (Tientsin) end Anglo-French operations against China in the Second Opium War (see 1856); China is obliged to open more ports to Britain, France, Russia and the USA. Later in the year China legalizes the trade in opium. Hostilities will resume in 1860 when China refuses to ratify the treaties.

29 July Japan's government, seeing the fate of China, signs a commercial treaty with the USA and hopes it will protect Japan from Western intervention. Similar treaties follow with Russia (19 Aug.), Britain (26 Aug.) and France (27 Oct.) as well as the Netherlands (18 Aug.). Prime minister Ii Naosuke is the guiding force behind these developments. The shogun Tokugawa Iesada, politically weak and physically ailing, dies and Ii Naosuke arranges for Tokugawa Iemochi to succeed.

2 Aug. Following the Indian Mutiny, British crown authority is established in India, superseding the rule of the East India Company.

THE AMERICAS

12 May Minnesota becomes a state of the USA.

16 June Abraham Lincoln accepts nomination as the Republican candidate for Illinois in the US Senate and warns that that the country cannot survive with half its population in slavery. He fails to be elected.

ECONOMY AND SOCIETY

11 Feb. In Lourdes, France, schoolgirl Bernadette Soubirous claims to have seen the Virgin Mary, a vision that reappears 18 times until July. She is cured of her asthma, and a chapel is built at a site reportedly favoured by the Virgin. Miraculous cures are claimed by those who visit the site.

27 Oct. The New York department store of R.H. Macy opens for business, selling goods for cash only.

– In New York Central Park is opened to the public.

– Philip Morris, a London tobacco merchant, opens a cigarette factory using tobacco leaf from Turkey.

– Ferdinand Carre, a French inventor, produces the first mechanical refrigerator.

– Charles Worth, an English dressmaker, opens a Paris shop and establishes the first haute couture fashion house. Worth creates his own designs and sells them to customers rather than designing according to individual requirements.

– New York cabinetmaker George Pullman designs the first plush sleeping car for the Chicago and Alton railroad.

– Quinine tonic water is patented in London and will become known as Schweppes tonic water.

SCIENCE AND TECHNOLOGY

16 Aug. Britain's Queen Victoria and President Buchanan of the USA exchange messages using the first transatlantic cable.

– Henry Gray, a London doctor, writes his *Anatomy of the Human Body, Descriptive and Surgical*.

– Friedrich August Kekulé von Stradonitz demonstrates the composition of organic molecules as long chains of carbon atoms.

– Alfred Russel Wallace and Charles Darwin (see p. 379) deliver a paper to the Linnaean Society in London on the idea of 'the survival of the fittest' as the key to the struggle by species to survive.

ARTS AND HUMANITIES

Literature

William Morris, *The Defence of Guenevere and Other Poems*.

Adelaide Procter, *Legends and Lyrics*, poetry, including the poem 'The Lost Chord'.

Visual Arts and Architecture

– London's Chelsea Bridge is completed (it will be rebuilt in the 1930s).

– In Britain Big Ben, the clocktower at Westminster Palace, home of the Houses of Parliament, begins to strike the chimes. It is named after the chief commissioner of works at the palace, Sir Benjamin Hall.

William Frith, *Derby Day*, painting.

Music

21 Oct. First performance in Paris of Jacques Offenbach's opera *Orphée aux Enfers* (Orpheus in the Underworld), which introduces the music that will come to be associated with the high-kicking 'cancan' dance.

– Covent Garden opera house, London, designed by Sir Charles Barry, is completed.

Johannes Brahms, Serenade No. 1 in D.

Franz Liszt, *Hunnenschlacht* (Battle of the Huns), symphonic poem.

1859

EUROPE

1 Jan. French emperor Napoleon III warns the Austrian ambassador of possible military action against his country, and Piedmont calls up its reserve troops (9 Mar.). Piedmont rejects the Austrian ultimatum to demobilize (23 April), and Austria invades Piedmont (29 April), providing France with a pretext for its own military action in support of Piedmont. France declares war on Austria (12 May), and the Piedmontese defeat the Austrians at Palestro (30 May). Italian nationalist, liberal revolutions eject the hereditary rulers of Tuscany and Modena; Franco-Piedmontese forces advance into Lombardy, and their success at the battle of Magenta (4 June) forces the withdrawal of the Austrian army. (The bloodiness of the battle leads to the naming after it of brilliant crimson dye.)

22 May Ferdinand II, king of the Two Sicilies, dies and is succeeded by his 13-year-old son, who becomes Francesco II.

10 June In Britain prime minister Lord Derby resigns. Palmerston will subsequently become prime minister for a second time.

24 June The battle of Solferino, near Verona, the most bloody and evenly balanced of the war in N Italy, ends with a Franco-Piedmontese victory over the Austrians.

11 July The Austrian emperor Franz Josef and Napoleon III of France meet to agree peace terms at Villafranca. Napoleon III,

frightened by the revolutionary conditions he has helped to create in Italy, wishes to end the war, while Franz Josef is anxious to put down a rebellion in his Hungarian territories. All over Italy the princely dynasties are returned to their thrones.

– Lionel Rothschild becomes Britain's first Jewish MP following the withdrawal of a parliamentary oath of office that required members to swear 'on the true faith of a Christian'.

THE AMERICAS

14 Feb. Oregon becomes a US state.

16 Oct. Anti-slavery activist John Brown leads a raid by abolitionists on the US federal arsenal at Harper's Ferry, Virginia. The raid is a signal for a general slave rebellion, which seeks to establish a new state as a home for slave refugees. Federal troops defeat Brown (18 Oct.), who is convicted of treason and hanged at Charleston (2 Dec.). A popular song, however, will claim that 'his truth goes marching on'.

– The legislature of the state of Georgia forbids any person to free slaves by act of last will and testament. It also passes a law allowing free blacks to be sold into slavery if they are found guilty of vagrancy.

– Huge deposits of gold and silver are discovered on Mt Davidson in Washoe, Nevada. George Hearst, a prospector from Missouri, makes his fortune buying a half-interest in a mine from a prospector who has decided that it is worthless.

AUSTRALASIA AND OCEANIA

– Queensland, Australia, is detached from New South Wales and becomes a separate colony.

ECONOMY AND SOCIETY

30 June French tightrope walker Charles Blondin crosses the Niagara Falls between Canada and the USA.

12 Nov. Jules Léotard performs the first flying trapeze circus act at the Cirque Napoléon, Paris.

– The world's first polo club, the Cachar Polo Club, is founded in Assam, NE India, by British residents.

SCIENCE AND TECHNOLOGY

25 April Work begins on building the Suez Canal linking the Mediterranean and the Red Sea. Ferdinand de Lesseps has sold stocks to French investors to finance the project and 44% has been sold to the khedive of Egypt, Sa'id Pasha (see 13 July 1854).

28 Aug. Oil is discovered at Titusville, Pennsylvania, USA, and the well is soon producing 400 gallons a day. The first commercial production of petroleum means that the world has an important new source of fuel.

– In Britain the publication of Charles Darwin's *On the Origin of Species by Means of Natural Selection, or the Preservation of Favoured Species in the Struggle for Life* creates a growing public and religious controversy (see 1831). Darwin's work outlines the principle of natural selection as the means by which species adapt to their environment and are therefore able to survive. His theory of development and of natural evolution rejects the idea that the conscious purpose and will, either of individual human beings or of God, is the reason the natural world has developed as it has done (see p. 379).

– London doctor Alfred Garrod shows that Galen's widely believed 2nd-century theory was wrong: gout is not caused by too much drinking and eating but by an excess of uric acid in the tissues.

– Louis Pasteur, French chemist and microbiologist, disproves the chemical theory of fermentation and also the idea of spontaneous generation. He shows that although some micro-organisms exist in the air, others (anaerobic organisms) cannot.

– Gaston Plante, a French physicist, invents a practical electric storage battery.

– Cocaine is isolated from the coca leaves brought back from Peru by the Austrian explorer Karl von Scherzer. It will be used, eventually, as an anaesthetic.

ARTS AND HUMANITIES

Literature

Charles Dickens (see p. 385), *A Tale of Two Cities*, novel.

George Eliot (Mary Ann Evans), *Adam Bede*, novel.

Edward Fitzgerald, translation of the 12th-century Persian poem *The Rubáiyát of Omar Khayyám of Naishapur*.

George Meredith, *The Ordeal of Richard Feverel*, novel.

John Stuart Mill, *On Liberty*, philosophical defence of liberalism.

Frédéric Mistral, *Mirèio*, narrative poem. Mistral is a founder-member of the Félibrige, an association for the cultivation of Provençal language and literature.

Alfred, Lord Tennyson, *Idylls of the King*, the first 4 of 12 connected poems on the subject of the Arthurian myths, which encapsulate Victorian medievalism.

Visual Arts and Architecture

Jean-Auguste-Dominique Ingres, *Le Bain turc* (The Turkish Bath), painting.

Edouard Manet, *The Absinthe Drinker*, painting.

Jean-François Millet, *The Angelus*, painting.

James Abbott McNeill Whistler, *At the Piano*, painting.

Music

17 Feb. First performance in Rome of Giuseppe Verdi's opera *Un ballo in maschera* (A Masked Ball).

19 Mar. First performance in Paris of Charles-François Gounod's opera *Faust*, based on Goethe's poem.

– German piano manufacturer Heinrich Steinweg, who established a factory in New York in 1853, produces an improved grand piano and (from 1865) calls himself Steinway.

Johannes Brahms, Piano Concerto No. 1 in D minor.

Charles-François Gounod, *Méditation sur le prélude de Bach* for voice, violin and organ, counterpoint to J.S. Bach's prelude from *Das Wohltemperierte Clavier*, set to the words of 'Ave Maria'.

1860

EUROPE

23 Jan. Free trade between England and France is established by a treaty of reciprocity.

Mar. In Italy plebiscites in Tuscany, Modena, Parma, Emilia and Romagna declare for union with the kingdom of Piedmont. Plebiscites in Naples and Sicily (Oct.) and Umbria (Nov.) have similar outcomes.

5 May Italian nationalist Giuseppe Garibaldi (see box) and some 1000 red-shirted followers sail for Marsala in Sicily: their aim is to create a united Italy under Victor Emmanuel II of Piedmont by force of arms. They land in Sicily (11 May) and, having joined forces with local rebels, defeat the Neapolitan forces at Calatafimi (15 May), seize Palermo (6 June), cross the Straits of Messina (22 Aug.) and occupy Naples (7 Sept.).

12 Aug. King Danilo I of Montenegro in the Balkans is assassinated. His successor, his nephew Nicholas I, will reign until 1918.

27 Sept. Prince Miloš Obrenovic of Serbia dies. He is succeeded by his son Michael III Obrenovic, who will try to democratize the Serbian constitution and seek to develop a role for Serbia as the leader of the Balkan states.

Giuseppe Garibaldi (1807–82)

The Italian patriot Giuseppe Garibaldi – the most charismatic figure in the struggle for the unification of Italy – was the most influential nationalist leader of 19th-century Europe. He had a genius for guerrilla warfare as well as an understanding of political symbolism. Diplomatic alliances among the European powers created the conditions for Italian unification, but it was Garibaldi who inspired a generation of Italians to overturn centuries of political fragmentation.

Having fought unsuccessfully against Austrian control of Venetia (northeast Italy) in 1848 and again in 1859, Garibaldi achieved fame with his great campaign of 1860. Arriving in Sicily with a band of 1000 red-shirted men, he assumed control of the rebellion against the king of Naples. His nationalist uprising spread from Sicily to the mainland, and his forces went on to conquer most of southern Italy. Garibaldi then yielded territorial control to the king of Piedmont, whose sovereignty extended over northern Italy. Venetia came under Italian rule after the Italians helped Prussia in its 1866 war against Austria. However, Rome was still in the hands of the pope, and a French garrison thwarted Garibaldi's dream of making the city the capital of a united Italy. Final victory came in 1870 when the Franco-Prussian War forced the withdrawal of the French from Rome, and the Italian national army marched in.

Garibaldi was not only a nationalist, but also an anti-clerical radical. However, his schemes for land redistribution had to be abandoned in the face of the political realities of post-unification Italy. He distrusted the new Italian parliament, his own preference being for a liberal dictatorship. But his elevation of the cause of unification over personal ambition made him a secular saint for 19th-century liberals and nationalists.

ASIA

12 Aug. The Second Opium War (see 1856) resumes; British forces deploy the first breech-loading rifled artillery seen in China. British and French forces take the port of Tianjin (Tientsin) in the NE (25 Aug.); they defeat Chinese forces and occupy the capital Beijing (12 Oct.), burning the imperial Summer Palace in retaliation for the Chinese seizure of the British diplomat Harry Parkes. The Chinese capitulate and sign the Beijing convention (14 Nov.) ratifying the treaties of Tianjin (1858).

– The port of Valdivostok on the Sea of Japan, close to the border of Korea, is founded by Russian explorers.

THE AMERICAS

16 Feb. The SS *Karrinmaru*, the first Japanese-built ship to reach the USA, arrives in San Francisco with a delegation that travels to Washington, D.C.

6 Nov. The Republican candidate Abraham Lincoln, who opposes the further extension of slavery, is elected 16th president of the USA; South Carolina adopts an Ordinance of Secession in protest against his election (20 Dec.).

20 Dec. In the USA South Carolina secedes from the Union.

SUB-SAHARAN AFRICA

– German influence is spreading in C Africa. German traders are now operating from Cameroon on the Equatorial coast of W Africa. Karl Klaus von der Decken is exploring E Africa, where he plans a German colony.

AUSTRALASIA AND OCEANIA

– The first N–S expedition across Australia leaves Melbourne. It is led by Irish-born explorer Robert Burke, who will die on the southward return journey (1861).

ECONOMY AND SOCIETY

17 April The first world heavyweight boxing championship, held at Farnborough in S England, ends in chaos: the British challenger Tom Sayers cannot use his right arm, while the US champion John C. Heenan is blinded by his own blood.

11 June The *Evening Standard* newspaper appears for the first time in London.

– The Melbourne Cup horse race is held for the first time, in Melbourne, Australia.

– Prestwick in SW Scotland hosts the first British Open golf tournament.

– The Pony Express service for mail delivery starts in the USA and operates between Montana and California.

SCIENCE AND TECHNOLOGY

– In Britain Parliament passes legislation against food adulteration following the death of those who have eaten green blancmange coloured with arsenite of copper.

– The Henry rifle, the first effective lever-action rifle, is patented by the US gunsmith Tyler Henry.

– Etienne Lancereaux diagnoses diabetes as a pancreatic disorder.

– US industrialist and philanthropist John Davison Rockefeller invests in the petroleum business now developing in Titusville, Pennsylvania, USA.

– The English inventor Frederick Walton coins the word linoleum to describe his new floor covering.

ARTS AND HUMANITIES

Literature

Jakob Burckhardt, *The Civilization of the Renaissance in Italy*, seminal work of cultural history.

Wilkie Collins, *The Woman in White*, mystery novel that is an important staging-post in the development of the detective novel.

George Eliot (Mary Ann Evans), *The Mill on the Floss*, novel.

Visual Arts

Edouard Manet, *The Guitarist*, painting.

Music

Johannes Brahms, Serenade No. 2 in A major.

1861

EUROPE

2 Jan. Debilitated by two years of insanity, Frederick William IV, king of Prussia, dies. His brother and regent, William I, succeeds and will reign until 1888.

17 Mar. Following the war with Austria and Giuseppe Garibaldi's (see p. 408) campaign in the S, a united kingdom of Italy is created. The new Italian parliament is established, with representatives from Lombardy, Piedmont, Parma, Modena, Lucca, Romagna, Tuscany and the Two Sicilies; Victor Emmanuel II of Piedmont's house of Savoy is king. Nice and Savoy have been ceded to France (1860) as compensation for assistance in the war of unification; the French retain control of Rome, which will join the united Italy in 1870 and become the country's capital; Austria will retain the province of Venetia until it is incorporated into the Italian state in 1866.

6 June Camillo Cavour, architect of the new Italian state, dies.

14 Dec. In Britain Queen Victoria's consort, Prince Albert, dies of typhoid fever. He has been a vigorous patron of the arts and sciences and promoter of public works in Britain, but his German origins and interference in political issues have made him an unpopular figure in public life. Overwhelmed by grief, the queen goes into an extended period of mourning. Her reclusiveness encourages a rise in republican sentiment.

– The emancipation of the Russian serfs, begun in 1858, is now completed. Alexander II's reforms allocate land to the serfs, which they can buy on the basis of annual payments spread over 49 years. Russian collectivism has deep roots, however, and the title to the redistributed land is given to village communities and not to individuals. The new peasants have the right to buy only half of the total amount of land they used to work as serfs, and the land is redistributed every 10–12 years in order to assure equality of holding. Russian agriculture remains backward: wooden ploughs are still used, crops are harvested with sickles or scythes, and the grain is threshed with hand flails.

AN AMERICAN CIVILIZATION:
Unity, Power and Race in the New World

When French, Dutch and English settlers arrived on the northeastern seaboard of North America in the 17th century they came not for short-term, quick results but to invest time and money in the exploitation of the area's potential agrarian wealth. By the mid-18th century British and French colonies were established. After the Seven Years' War, Britain gained all of French Canada, while Spain took the French Louisiana territories west of the Mississippi.

The developing culture of New England was rooted in English Puritanism. The English settlers had emigrated to escape persecution at the hands of the Anglican Church and the English crown, and the desire for religious freedom would motivate many later immigrants to the USA in the 19th and 20th centuries. Others would be seeking to escape peasant poverty and European overpopulation, while many Jews would flee to America to escape tsarist pogroms in Russia. Many of these immigrants would bring with them the collectivist traditions of peasant-based societies, which blended with the original pioneer concept of hardy individualism sustained by introspective, biblical Protestantism.

It was trade that drove the 13 original colonies away from Britain. In keeping with the mercantilist theory of the time, the British viewed the colonies as a source of raw materials and a market for manufactured goods, discouraging all other forms of trade or commerce. The colonies wanted to define their own role and especially resented taxation imposed from Britain. The war between the colonies and Britain – which broke out in 1775 – proved to be a form of French revenge for the loss of their North American territories, for it was French naval assistance that proved the decisive element in forcing the British to surrender in 1781. The United States of America was born out of those colonies that broke away, and Canada from those that remained loyal. In 1867 the Canadian colonies joined to form their own federal government in the shape of the Dominion of Canada.

Meanwhile, the US government was determined to extend westward. In 1803 the vast Louisiana territory was bought from France, which had re-acquired it from Spain, and in 1867 Alaska was bought from Russia. The fact that these lands were occupied by indigenous peoples was viewed as a mere practical difficulty, to be overcome with guns, treaties and purchase – a process that was effectively complete by 1890.

As the territorial limits of the USA moved west in the 19th century, the northeastern states became a growing industrial power. Railroads crisscrossed the country and

eased the transport of goods while also establishing links between the states, and the population now began to acquire its own identity as Americans with their own civilization rather than as emigrants from the Old World. Meanwhile, further waves of immigrants flooded into the new industrial cities. The resulting turbulence showed both the good and the bad side of a country where government was limited and where workers and employers were left to solve their own disputes without legal rights or obligations.

But while the northeast epitomized industrial capitalism, the Southern states remained an agrarian economy. Cotton from the South supplied a global market, and its large-scale plantations were worked by slave labour. The civil war that consumed the USA from 1861 to 1865 pitted these Southern states against the industrialized North. One root cause of the war was economic, but another was the tragic unfolding of a constitutional principle. The original Declaration of Independence of 1776 and the Articles of Federation adopted by Congress in 1777 made it clear that the 'United States' was a federation, with substantial rights reserved to the individual states. The powers of Congress were powers delegated to it from the states. But the emergence of the USA as a military and economic power made Congress (the

The tragedy of the American Civil War was that it pitted one idea of right, that of the individual ... against ... that of the states.

Senate and the House of Representatives) ever more dominant. In asserting their right to secede from the Union the southern Confederate states were declaring their right to exercise the self-government they thought they had merely loaned to the Union. Some European liberals sympathized with their cause, though they also applauded the fact that the eventual victory of the Union led to the abolition of slavery – an institution that had become associated with the cause of the South. The tragedy of the American Civil War was that it pitted one idea of right, that of the individual human being, against another, that of the states. Both principles had played their role in the forging of the American idea.

Once the war was over, the former slaves became US citizens. But racial prejudice both in the North and the South would continue to disfigure American life. It would be another century before American legislators passed the civil rights legislation that began to correct an historic injustice.

1861 continued

MIDDLE EAST AND NORTH AFRICA

25 June Abdul-Mejid, sultan of the Ottoman empire, dies. The reforms of his reign include the suppression of slavery. He is succeeded by his brother Abdul-Aziz, who embarks on a reign characterized by recklessness and waste.

ASIA

25 Feb. A French force relieves the blockade of Saigon in Indo-China. Almost 1000 French and Spanish troops have been besieged by forces from Annam led by Gen. Nguyen Tri Phuong. The French, now in command of the immediate area around Saigon, extend their influence to gain control of Cochinchina (S Vietnam).

THE AMERICAS

29 Jan. Kansas becomes the 34th US state.

1 Feb. Mississippi, Florida, Alabama, Georgia, Louisiana and Texas secede from the Union.

8 Feb. Delegates from Alabama, Florida, Georgia, Louisiana, Mississippi and South Carolina meet at Montgomery, Alabama, to approve a provisional constitution creating the Confederate States of America (CSA). Delegates from Texas, Arkansas, North Carolina, Tennessee and Virginia will quickly approve the constitution also. The states of Missouri and Kentucky will have dual status as US and CSA states.

9 Feb. Jefferson Davis is elected provisional president of the Confederacy (he will be confirmed by election in Oct.).

3 Mar. Last day in office of President James Buchanan, the only life-long bachelor to have occupied the White House.

4 Mar. In his inaugural address as US president Abraham Lincoln declares that: 'This country, with its institutions, belongs to the people who inhabit it.' The private detective Allan Pinkerton has reported a plot to kill Lincoln on his journey to Washington for the inauguration.

12 April The American Civil War (1861–5) begins when Fort Sumter in Charleston Harbor, South Carolina, is attacked and captured by a force under Gen. Pierre Gustave Toutant Beauregard, the commander of the Confederate army.

20 May Richmond, Virginia, becomes capital of the Confederacy.

21 July In the first major battle of the civil war, Confederate forces gain an inconclusive victory at the first battle of Bull Run, at Manassas Junction, NE Virginia. For his resistance of the initial Northern attack, Confederate general Thomas Jackson earns the nickname 'Stonewall'.

5 Aug. Money to pay the Union army and navy is raised by the introduction of income tax by the US Congress: 3% is levied on incomes above $800 a year.

10 Aug. A Confederate army wins the battle of Wilson's Creek, Montana, but in the same month Union forces seize Confederate forts on the North Carolina coast.

21 Oct. A Union army is defeated in the battle of Ball's Bluff on the Potomac River. Lincoln appoints Gen. George McClellan commander-in-chief of the Union forces. McClellan appoints Allan Pinkerton to head a new department of counter-espionage.

8 Nov. The British steamship *Trent* is stopped, and Union forces remove two former US senators, James M. Mason and John Slidell, now Confederate commissioners travelling to Britain and France. The incident damages British–US relations.

30 Dec. US banks suspend payments in gold.

– Apache raids on the US army and settlements in Arizona intensify. The prospect of the white invaders being ejected by Native Americans becomes a real possibility in the state.

– The Central Pacific Railroad is established to provide a trans-continental rail link.

ECONOMY AND SOCIETY

– Count Agoston Haraszthy de Mokcsa receives a commission from the California state legislature to bring various types of European grapevines to the state. The introduction of some 300 varieties transforms the Californian wine trade, which will develop into a world producer.

– Cyrus Hall McCormick's mechanical reaper (invented in 1831) is responsible for a rapid increase in agricultural productivity, which is an element in the success of the Union army in the American Civil War. The conflict has resulted in a shortage of farm hands as well as labourers (workers building the new railways are mostly recruited from China where the Taiping rebellion has caused massive disruption), but McCormick's invention means that America can still export some 50 million bushels of wheat from Chicago to Europe, where there is a serious drought. McCormick's reaper also represents a good investment, since he offers it for sale over a six-month period after a single downpayment.

– Henri Nestlé of Switzerland develops his financial interest in the chemical firm at Vevey run by Christopher Guillaume Keppel and becomes the owner after Keppel's retirement. Under the name of Nestlé it will develop into a multinational food company.

– The tinned food of Gilbert C. Van Camp of Indianapolis sustains Union troops in the civil war. Pork and beans form part of the staple army diet after Van Camp gains an army contract and will become a favourite US food.

– The official newspaper of the Vatican, *L'Osservatore Romano*, starts publication.

SCIENCE AND TECHNOLOGY

8 April Elisha G. Otis, inventor and patentee of the steam-powered elevator, dies. The elevator makes a fortune for the Otis Elevator Company and transforms the urban landscapes of the developed world.

– Supplied with saltpetre from Britain, Henry du Pont's Delaware factory in the USA produces gunpowder for the Union army and thereby profits from the American Civil War.

– US engineer Richard Gatling invents the Gatling gun, which can fire several hundreds rounds a minute. It gives the advantage to the Union side in the civil war.

– French inventor Pierre Michaux introduces his velocipede, a further development of the modern bicycle created by Kirkpatrick MacMillan in 1839. It is the first to possess cranks and pedals attached to the front wheels.

– Massachusetts Institute of Technology (MIT) is founded in the USA.

– A paper by French chemist Louis Pasteur, 'Mémoire sur les corpuscles organisés qui existent dans l'atmosphère', demonstrates the germ theory of disease and shows the falsity of the idea of spontaneous generation.

– Both Karl Wilhelm Siemens from Lower Saxony (known as Charles William Siemens after moving to England in 1844) and French engineer Pierre-Emile Martin have developed, independently of each other, a new open-hearth method of steel production. Using a gas-fired furnace, their technique burns less coal than the existing Bessemer process (see 1856) and leads to a rise in steel production.

– Tinned food becomes cheaper to produce when canner Isaac Solomon of Baltimore, USA, applies British chemist Sir Humphry Davy's discovery that the temperature of boiling water can increase to over 240°C (464°F) if calcium chloride is added. As a result the time spent processing a can of food is reduced from 6 hours to 30 minutes.

– Despite the opposition of Native Americans and the Confederate states, the Western Union telegraph line opens linking San Francisco and New York.

ARTS AND HUMANITIES

Literature

Isabella Beeton (Mrs Beeton), *Book of Household Management*, bestselling Victorian recipe book.

Charles Dickens (see p. 385), *Great Expectations*, novel.

George Eliot (Mary Ann Evans), *Silas Marner*, novel.

Thomas Babington Macaulay, *History of England*, fifth and final volume of his bestselling work of Whig history (see 1848).

Francis Palgrave, *The Golden Treasury of Best Songs and Lyrical Poems in the English Language*, anthology.

Charles Reade, *The Cloister and the Hearth*, novel.

Mrs Henry Wood, *East Lynne*, melodramatic novel.

Visual Arts and Architecture

– French artist Gustave Doré works on woodcut engravings to illustrate Dante's *Inferno*.

Music

Franz Liszt, Mephisto Waltz No. 1 and Piano Concerto No. 2 in A major.

William Henry Monk, 'Abide with Me', hymn.

Bedřich Smetana, *Wallenstein's Camp*, symphonic poem after Schiller.

1862

EUROPE

2 Feb. Monaco on the Mediterranean Riviera sells the towns of Menton and Roquebrune to France.

22 Sept. Otto von Bismarck becomes minister-president of Prussia.

– The American Civil War forces the closure of cotton mills in Lancashire, centre of the British textile industry and the major world producer, which have been cut off from their main source of raw cotton in the S USA. Britain, however, is officially opposed to slavery and depends on grain from the Northern Union states. It therefore decides not to recognize the breakaway Confederate states.

– The German-born king Otto I of Greece is deposed following a military revolt; he is rescued by a British warship and returns to Bavaria.

ASIA

20 Aug. US mercenary Frederick Townsend Ward leads imperial Chinese forces to victory over the Taiping rebels (see 1850) at Tzeki near Shanghai but is later killed in action (20 Sept.).

THE AMERICAS

Feb. In the American Civil War the Union army led by Gen. Ulysses S. Grant secures its first major successes against the Southern states, capturing Fort Henry and Fort Donelson in W Tennessee.

27 Mar. Confederate hopes of breaking through Union territory to the SW are dashed at the battle of Glorieta Pass in Santa Fe county, New Mexico.

6–7 April The battle of Shiloh on the Tennessee River ends inconclusively, with both sides claiming victory after sustaining heavy casualties.

16 April Congress abolishes slavery in the capital district of Columbia and then in the rest of the USA (19 June).

5 May French troops are defeated by a Mexican army at the battle of Puebla, S central Mexico. Encouraged by the Empress Eugénie, Emperor Napoleon III of France has intervened in Mexican internal politics on the side of the deposed former president Miguel Miramón. He hopes to create a French vassal empire in Mexico.

20 May The US Congress passes the Homestead Act, which declares that any US citizen may have, free of charge, 65 hectares (160 acres) of land on the W frontier providing it is improved and retained for five years. The land, however, is so arid and unproductive that most settlers find it hard to prosper. The Act nevertheless boosts US immigration, and almost 500,000 homesteaders will apply for, and one-third will actually receive, land in the next 20 years. Congress also grants some 40 million hectares (100 million acres) of land to the railroad companies linking the Mississippi with the Gulf and Pacific coasts.

31 May Federal troops sustain heavy losses at the battle of Fair Oaks and in the Seven Days' Battle (25 June–1 July) in an attempt to capture Richmond, Virginia; this results in their withdrawal from the peninsula between the James and York rivers extending towards the city.

17 Aug. A Sioux uprising begins in the N US state of Minnesota under the leadership of Little Crow.

22 Aug. President Lincoln writes: 'My paramount object in this struggle is to save the Union and is not either to save or to destroy slavery. If I could save the Union without freeing any slave I would do it; and if I could do it by freeing all the slaves, I would do it.' He makes emancipation a defining issue of the war, however, and his Emancipation Proclamation (22 Sept.) states that the slaves of the Confederate territories will become free on 1 Jan. 1863.

29–30 Aug. A Union army under Gen. John Pope is defeated by Confederate general 'Stonewall' Jackson (see 21 July 1861) in the second battle of Bull Run.

10 Sept. In Paraguay, central S America, dictator Carlos Antonio López dies. He is succeeded by his crazed son, Francisco Solano López.

17 Sept. The American Civil War battle of Antietam in Maryland ends indecisively, but the Confederate attempt, under Gen. Robert E. Lee, to take the fight into Union territory is frustrated. Female camp followers of Gen. Joseph Hooker's Massachusetts division of the Union army earn the nickname 'hookers'.

Nov. A body of former slaves, the 1st Regiment of South Carolina Volunteers, is formed in Boston for service in the Union army.

13 Dec. Ambrose Everett Burnside, who has replaced George Brinton McClellan as general in charge of the Union army, is defeated by Gen. Robert E. Lee at the battle of Fredericksburg, Virginia.

– Congress prohibits the distillation of alcohol without a licence but illegal whiskey production is widespread. The US navy abolishes, but later has to revive, the daily rum ration.

SUB-SAHARAN AFRICA

– English explorer John Hanning Speke confirms that the source of the River Nile is the lake he has named Victoria in equatorial E Africa. Speke will accidentally shoot himself while out partridge shooting in England in 1864.

ECONOMY AND SOCIETY

– The first Monte Carlo gambling casino opens in Monaco.

ARTS AND HUMANITIES

Literature

– Nihilism, a radical rejection of belief in any human institution or code of conduct, is introduced to European literature and politics by Russian writer Ivan Turgenev in his novel *Fathers and Sons*.

Victor Hugo, *Les Misérables*, novel.

Visual Arts and Architecture

– Alexander Turney Stewart has commissioned James Bogardus, the pioneer of skyscraper construction based on cast-iron load-bearing columns, to design his department store, later A.T. Stewart & Co., in New York's 10th Street. When complete it will be the world's tallest building.

Music

9 Aug. First performance in Baden-Baden of Hector Berlioz's opera *Béatrice et Bénédict*, which is based on Shakespeare's comedy *Much Ado About Nothing*.

10 Nov. First performance in St Petersburg of Giuseppe Verdi's opera *La forza del destino* (The Force of Destiny).

– 'The Battle Hymn of the Republic' is published in the USA by Julia Ward Howe, who has written the lyrics to the tune 'John Brown's Body'. With her husband, Samuel Gridley Howe, she publishes the Boston abolitionist periodical *The Commonwealth*, whose campaigning aims also include prison reform and the abolition of imprisonment for debt.

– Austrian botanist Ludwig Ritter von Köchel produces a list of authenticated compositions by Austrian composer Wolfgang Amadeus Mozart. His publication, the *Chronologisch-thematisches Verzeichnis* (Chronological-thematic Catalogue), is a masterpiece of modern musicology, which gives each work a 'Köchel number' identifying genuine compositions while also recording lost and doubtful works.

1863

EUROPE

22 Jan. A nationalist revolt breaks out in Poland. A Russo-Prussian alliance is set up to suppress it (8 Feb.).

15 Nov. Frederick VII, king of Denmark, dies and is succeeded by his cousin Christian IX, who will reign until 1906. Denmark is attempting to bring the region of Schleswig (which has a German minority) under Danish law, and to exclude the region of Holstein (which is largely German). When Christian IX signs a new Danish constitution uniting Schleswig and Denmark (18 Nov.), Austria and Prussia protest.

– Britain and France sign free-trade treaties with Belgium.

– The Greek parliament votes to invite Britain's Prince Alfred to be king of Greece, but the British government vetoes the idea. Instead, a Danish prince is chosen, ruling as George I (30 Mar.).

– At a meeting held in the Palais de l'Athénée in Geneva, Switzerland, the founding principles of the International Red Cross, originated by the Swiss philanthropist Henri Dunant, are established.

MIDDLE EAST AND NORTH AFRICA

– Sa'id Pasha, khedive of Egypt, dies and is succeeded by his nephew Ismail Pasha. Although the new ruler emphasizes the need for Western-style reform of the government he is soon in debt because of his extravagance.

THE AMERICAS

1 Jan. The Emancipation Proclamation by President Lincoln comes into effect, freeing some 4 million US slaves in the North. The proclamation will become universal with the defeat of the Confederate states in the civil war in 1865.

25 Jan. Lincoln replaces Ambrose Burnside with Gen. Joseph Hooker as commander-in-chief of the Federal army, which is defeated (1–4 May) at Chancellorsville, Virginia, by Confederate forces under Gen. Thomas 'Stonewall' Jackson, a key figure in Southern strategy, who is wounded by one of his own men and dies of pneumonia (10 May).

7 June Following military successes, French forces occupy

Mexico City; a group of French-sponsored Mexicans proclaims a Mexican empire (July) under the patronage of Napoleon III and offers the imperial throne to the Austrian archduke Maximilian, brother of the emperor Franz Josef.

20 June In the USA West Virginia, which seceded from the state of Virginia at the start of the civil war in 1861, is admitted to the Union as the 35th state. Its constitution calls for the abolition of slavery.

28 June Gen. Hooker is replaced as commander-in-chief of the Federal army by Gen. George Gordon Meade, who wins the battle of Gettysburg, Pennsylvania (1–3 July), an important victory that decisively alters the course of the war; the Confederate advance into the North is frustrated and the Southerners are routed.

11 July Conscription to the Union army begins under legislation passed by Congress (3 Mar.); draft riots follow in New York, with gangs attacking and killing blacks, tearing up railroad tracks and burning buildings.

21 Aug. Confederate guerillas led by pro-slavery outlaw William C. Quantrill (including Jesse James) burn Lawrence, Kansas, reducing the town to ashes.

19–20 Sept. Confederates under Gen. Braxton Bragg win the battle of Chickamauga in N Georgia, but Bragg fails to exploit his victory; two months later the Union army will decisively win the battle of Chattanooga (23–25 Nov.) and nullify the Confederate advantage.

3 Oct. President Lincoln proclaims the first annual US national Thanksgiving Day; the last Thursday in November is set aside to commemorate the feast given by the Pilgrim Fathers in 1621 for their benefactors among the Native American Wampanoag people.

19 Nov. Lincoln's oratory at the dedication of the national cemetery at Gettysburg develops the myth of democratic purpose: Lincoln memorializes the fallen and attributes to the Founding Fathers of the American republic the aim of establishing 'government of the people, by the people, and for the people'.

– President Lincoln authorizes a bill passed in 1862 by Congress guaranteeing the builders of the Central Pacific and the Union Pacific lines generous subsidies for construction work, ranging from $16,000 per mile for track laid across the plains to $48,000 per mile for track laid through the mountains.

– The Ruby Valley treaty signed with the Shoshone, Washoe and other Native Americans in Nevada grants them 9.3 million hectares (23 million acres) of mostly arid desert land. They cede to the federal authorities the right to allow railroads to be built across their territories.

ECONOMY AND SOCIETY

10 Jan. The London Underground, the world's first underground railway system, opens.

21 May The Seventh-Day Adventist Church is officially organized in the USA.

– The Football Association is established in London and draws up the rules for the game known in some countries as 'soccer'.

SCIENCE AND TECHNOLOGY

– Cotton textile production starts in Japan, which will become the world's largest exporter of cotton goods by the 1930s.

– The US Congress creates a National Academy of Sciences to advise the government on scientific issues.

– Belgian chemists Ernest and Alfred Solvay pioneer an improved method for producing soda at their plant near Charleroi.

– The commercial firm Source Perrier start to bottle the sparkling water emerging from a spring near Nîmes, S France.

ARTS AND HUMANITIES

Literature

– The first instalment appears of Russian writer Leo Tolstoy's *War and Peace*. Tolstoy (see p. 430) has liberated the serfs he employs on his country estate Yasnaya Polyana. His novel, a description of the impact on Russia of Napoleon's invasion of 1812, is an account of the historical forces at work in society and the relationship between impersonal forces and individual character.

– The Virginia City newspaper reporter Samuel Langhorne Clemens has adopted the nom de plume 'Mark Twain', the cry of the Mississippi riverboat men when sounding a two-fathom (3.66m/12 feet) depth of water.

George Eliot (Mary Ann Evans), *Romola*, novel.

Charles Kingsley, *The Water-Babies*, children's story. It becomes a favourite of Queen Victoria, who reads it to her children.

John Stuart Mill (see p. 395), *Utilitarianism*, work of ethics.

Henry Wadsworth Longfellow, *Tales of a Wayside Inn*, verse collection, including 'Paul Revere's Ride'.

Visual Arts and Architecture

13 Aug. French painter Eugène Delacroix dies.

2 Dec. The dome of the Capitol building at Washington, D.C., is capped.

– Japanese art spreads in popularity in Paris after US artist James Abbott McNeill Whistler promotes *ukiyo-e* prints.

– The Winged Victory of Samothrace, a classical statue discovered in excavations on the Greek island in the NE Aegean, is exhibited at the Louvre, Paris. It will influence contemporary taste and techniques in sculpture.

Edouard Manet, *Déjeuner sur l'herbe* (Luncheon on the Grass), painting portraying a naked woman lunching with two fully-clothed men. The jury of the 1863 Paris Salon is scandalized.

Music

30 Sept. First performance in Paris of Georges Bizet's opera *Les Pêcheurs de perles* (The Pearl Fishers).

4 Nov. First performance in Paris of Acts 3–5 of Hector Berlioz's opera, *Les Troyens* (The Trojans).

Anton Bruckner, Symphony in F minor.

1864

EUROPE

30 Oct. The peace of Vienna concludes the German–Danish war over Schleswig-Holstein (see 1863). Schleswig is ceded to Prussia and Holstein to Austria.

- Representatives of 26 nations sign the Geneva Convention, which affirms the neutrality of the Red Cross, establishes rules governing the humane treatment of the captured and wounded in time of war and prohibits methods of warfare that lead to unnecessary suffering.
- In France Napoleon III yields to public pressure and re-establishes the right to strike.
- A major Polish rebellion against Russian rule (see 22 Jan. 1863) spreads to adjoining Lithuania and White Russia (Belorussia). Russian forces intervene to re-establish their dominance in the region, and Polish autonomy is abolished. The Russian language is made a compulsory subject of study in Polish schools.

ASIA

19–21 July In China imperial forces led by Zen Guofan and the British general Charles George Gordon end the Taiping rebellion (see 1850) with the capture of Nanjing; the city is sacked over the course of three days, leading to the deaths of some 100,000 people.

1 Oct. A cyclone kills over 70,000 people in Calcutta, NE India, and destroys the city.

THE AMERICAS

10 Mar. Gen. Ulysses S. Grant is placed in command of all Union forces in the American Civil War; Gen. Robert E. Lee's Confederates defeat Union forces at the battle of Cold Harbor near Richmond, Virginia (1–3 June), but Union forces under Gen. William Tecumseh Sherman are victorious at Kenesaw Mountain (27 June) and Atlanta (22 July) in Georgia. Sherman exploits these victories by leading his 60,000-strong army on an eastward 'march to the sea' through Georgia (from 16 Nov.). Confederate forces are badly defeated at the battle of Franklin (30 Nov.) and at Nashville in Tennessee and elsewhere (mid-Dec.); Sherman occupies the city of Savannah, Georgia (22 Dec.). Northern forces exploit their adoption of the new and deadly Gatling guns.

10 April Archduke Maximilian of Austria accepts the imperial throne of Mexico offered in 1863 and reaches Mexico City (12 June).

31 Aug. Francisco Solano López, dictator of Paraguay, delivers an ultimatum to Brazil demanding its non-intervention in Uruguayan affairs; Brazil, however, invades Uruguay (Oct.) which seizes a Brazilian ship laden with arms (12 Nov.).

31 Oct. Nevada becomes the 36th US state.

Nov. The Cheyenne people rebel and are joined by Apache, Arapaho, Comanche and Kiowa warriors; many are killed by US forces commanded by John Chivington at Sand Creek, Colorado.

Nov. Gen. William T. Sherman's victory at Atlanta helps President Lincoln's re-election with 55% of the popular vote, winning 212 electoral college votes against the Democratic Party candidate George B. McClellan who musters only 21. 'War Democrats' have supported Lincoln, who is the candidate of the Republican unionists.

Dec. The US prison camp in Fort Sumner, New Mexico, houses more than 8000 Navajo people, marched there under the command of frontiersman Kit Carson; hundreds die of neglect and disease. Carson will be relieved of his command (1866).

ECONOMY AND SOCIETY

- Fish and chips becomes a popular dish in Britain. Now that ice is available in large quantities to trawlers, fish catches can be kept fresh during the extended periods at sea and on the long journeys back to port.
- English cricketer W(illiam) G(ilbert) Grace plays his first county cricket match at the age of 16.

SCIENCE AND TECHNOLOGY

- Charing Cross railway terminus opens in London.

ARTS AND HUMANITIES

Literature

Robert Browning, *Dramatis Personae*, collection of poems.

Fyodor Dostoyevsky (see p. 434), *Notes from Underground*, novella.

Edmond and Jules de Goncourt, *Germinie Lacerteux*, novel.

Anthony Trollope, *Can You Forgive Her?*, novel, the first of his Palliser series of political novels.

Jules Verne, *Voyage au centre de la terre* (Journey to the Centre of the Earth), novel.

Visual Arts and Architecture

- Photographer Mathew B. Brady of New York travels through the Southern states recording the devastation of the civil war.

Music

17 Dec. First performance in Paris of the operetta *La Belle Hélène* (Fair Helen) by Jacques Offenbach (Jakob Eberst).

Anton Bruckner, Symphony No. 0 in D minor (rev. 1869) and Mass in D minor.

Edvard Grieg, 'Ich Liebe Dich' (I Love You), song with lyrics by Hans Christian Andersen.

1865

EUROPE

14 Aug. The convention of Gastein regulates the occupation of Schleswig and Holstein.

18 Oct. British prime minister Lord Palmerston (Henry John Temple, 3rd Viscount Palmerston) dies and is succeeded by Lord John Russell.

10 Dec. Leopold I dies and is succeeded as king of the Belgians by his son Leopold II, during whose reign (lasting until 1909) Belgium will emerge as a colonial power in the Congo, Equatorial Africa.

THE AMERICAS

17 Feb. Union forces occupy Columbia, state capital of South Carolina, followed by the major port of Charleston (18 Feb.). Gen. Ulysses S. Grant takes Richmond, Virginia (3 April) and accepts the final surrender of Confederate forces under Gen. Robert E. Lee at Appomattox Courthouse (9 April).

3 Mar. The Colorado River Reservation in California and Arizona, W USA, is established by an Act of Congress now authorized by President Lincoln. It includes territory in the Mojave desert.

14 April President Lincoln is assassinated while watching *Our American Cousin* at Ford's Theatre, Washington, D.C. The actor John Wilkes Booth enters the presidential box, shoots Lincoln in the head and escapes, but he is later caught in Virginia (26 April) and dies either by suicide or at the hands of his captors. Vice-President Andrew Johnson succeeds as 17th president.

1 May By a treaty signed at Buenos Aires, Argentina, Brazil and Uruguay form an alliance opposed to Paraguay, which has seized an Argentinian river port (April).

May The white supremacist secret society the Ku Klux Klan (KKK) is formed in Pulaski, Tennessee. As a 'circle' (the Greek for which is *kuklos*), its members try to recapture the military fraternity of the war years, adopting elaborate rituals such as the burning of crosses at night-time meetings. The Klan tries to reassert white, Democratic Party control of Southern institutions.

10 Nov. Henry Wirz, Confederate commandant of the prison camp at Andersonville, Georgia, is hanged for 'murder, in violation of the laws and customs of war'. Although some 31,000 Union prisoners have died in Confederate camps, 26,000 Confederates have died in Union prisons.

...*boys, it is all hell.*

General Tecumseh Sherman describes war in his address to the Convention of the Grand Army of the USA, 11 Aug. 1880

18 Dec. The 13th amendment to the US Constitution is ratified and prohibits slavery or any other denial of liberty outside the due process of law.

- Officials from the Northern USA move into the South to take part in the work of post-war reconstruction. They are contemptuously named 'carpetbaggers' by the Southerners, a name apparently derived from their characteristic travelling bags made of carpet. Many of the incomers pack out the Southern legislatures and are assisted by collaborating Southerners nicknamed 'scalawags' (or 'scallywags').

SUB-SAHARAN AFRICA

- In S Africa the expansionist Boers of the Orange Free State declare war on the Basuto people.

ECONOMY AND SOCIETY

Sept. Cholera sweeps Paris, with some 200 dying daily (including French chemist Louis Pasteur's infant daughter, Camille).

- In Britain the religious campaigner William Booth establishes a Christian Mission in Whitechapel, E London, which leads to the foundation (in 1878) of the Christian charitable organization named the Salvation Army.

- Parliament passes the British Locomotives on Highways Act

(Red Flag Act), which, for the purposes of safety, requires that steam-powered carriages be preceded by men on foot waving red flags. The legislation has been supported by the stagecoach companies, who are worried by the success of steam.

- Cornell University is established in Ithaca, New York.

- In Philadelphia, USA, hatter John Batterson Stetson creates the Stetson ten-gallon hat.

- Edward Whymper leads a team of British mountaineers on the first ascent of the Matterhorn in S Switzerland, four of whom die on the descent.

SCIENCE AND TECHNOLOGY

- Tin cans are now made of thinner steel, and this leads to the introduction of the can opener.

- In Glasgow, Scotland, surgeon Joseph Lister develops the use of carbolic acid as an antiseptic in treating compound fractures.

- The Austrian botanist and Augustinian monk Gregor Mendel has been studying the genetics of garden peas. Now, in a paper read to the Brno Society for the Study of Natural Science, he explains that 'in any given pair of contrasting traits one trait is dominant and the other is recessive'. He also states that the first generation to issue from mixed parentage will all be hybrids, while in the second generation only half will be hybrids, one-quarter will reflect the true character of one parent and the other quarter will reflect the second parent's true trait. Mendel's fundamental units will later be called genes.

ARTS AND HUMANITIES

Literature

Lewis Carroll (Charles Lutwidge Dodgson), *Alice's Adventures in Wonderland*, fantasy illustrated by *Punch* cartoonist John Tenniel.

Charles Dickens (see p. 385), *Our Mutual Friend*, novel.

Algernon Charles Swinburne, *Atalanta in Calydon,* an attempt at an English-language poetic drama in classical form, including choruses.

Walt Whitman, *Drum-Taps*, collection of poetry.

Visual Arts and Architecture

- Edouard Manet's painting *Olympia* is accepted for the 1865 Paris Salon. The public is shocked by its portrayal of a nude clearly modelled by a prostitute.

Music

28 April First performance in Paris of Giacomo Meyerbeer's unfinished opera *L'Africaine* (The African Woman). This first performance is posthumous, Meyerbeer having died in 1864.

10 June First performance in Munich of Richard Wagner's (see p. 421) opera *Tristan und Isolde*.

Antonín Dvořák, Symphonies Nos. 1 in C minor (*The Bells of Zlonice*) and 2 in B flat.

Nikolai Rimsky-Korsakov, Symphony No. 1 in E flat minor.

1866

EUROPE

June The Austro-Prussian War (also known as the Seven Weeks War) breaks out. Prussia occupies Holstein after Austria calls on the diet (parliament) of the German Confederation to decide on the future of Schleswig and Holstein. When Austria responds by asking the diet to mobilize troops against Prussia, Prussia leaves the Confederation (14 June). Prussia invades Saxony, Hanover and Hesse-Kassel (16 June), occupying them within a week.

20 June In support of Prussia, Italy declares war on Austria, but Italian forces are defeated at Custozza in N Italy.

3 July Austrian Habsburg forces are defeated at the battle of Sadowa (Königgrätz) in Bohemia by the Prussian army under Count Helmuth von Moltke. The Austrians are disadvantaged by the use of muzzle-loading guns, which need to be reloaded standing up; the Prussians' breech-loading needle guns can be loaded lying down, making the soldiers less vulnerable in battle.

6 July In Britain Lord Derby forms a Conservative government following the resignation of Lord John Russell over the defeat of his Reform Bill.

26 July Preliminary peace treaty of Nikolsburg between Austria and Prussia.

23 Aug. The peace of Prague ends the Austro-Prussian War: the German Confederation, established in 1815 and led by Austria, is annulled; Schleswig and Holstein become Prussian, and Prussia absorbs Hanover, Hesse-Kassel, Frankfurt and Nassau; Austria is excluded from territory N of the River Main.

3 Oct. The treaty of Vienna ends the war between Italy and Austria. Austria cedes Lombardy and Venetia to Italy but retains Istria and Dalmatia, together with Ragusa (Dubrovnik).

24 Oct. Prince Carol of Hohenzollern-Sigmaringen is recognized as king of Romania by the Ottoman sultan. The Austrian prince has been invited to accept the throne by both liberal and conservative factions within Romania. The country will not gain its full independence until 1878, but Carol will reign until 1914.

ASIA

Aug. Tokugawa Yoshinobu becomes the last shogun of Japan and reigns briefly following the death of Iemochi, whose guardian he had been.

THE AMERICAS

12 Feb. The USA demands that French troops be removed from Mexico. Maximilian's position as emperor of Mexico is becoming untenable domestically and internationally (he is also archduke of Austria and younger brother of Emperor Franz Josef I and son-in-law of Leopold I of the Belgians).

3 April In its judgement on the case of *ex parte* Milligan the US Supreme Court sets limits to martial law and to the suspension of civilian law in war-time.

9 April The Civil Rights Act passed by Congress endows all former slaves with the rights of US citizenship. The Act invalidates the Dred Scott ruling of 1857.

30 July Race riots break out in New Orleans following an attempt to allow blacks the right to vote in Louisiana elections.

20 Aug. American labour gains a formal role with the formation of the National Labor Union at a meeting of the National Labor Congress in Baltimore, Maryland.

ECONOMY AND SOCIETY

– The US economy, after the inflation of the civil war period, lurches into depression.

– The Plum Street Temple in Cincinnati, Ohio, is built for the city's Jewish community, which, under the Rabbi Isaac Mayer Wise, is developing a distinct liberal and reformist Judaism.

– The Western Union Telegraph Company absorbs two smaller firms and becomes the first of the great industrial monopolies of the USA. The development poses a problem for American capitalism and its ethos of choice.

– The Syrian Protestant College, later renamed the American University, is founded in Beirut, Lebanon.

– Cholera remains an international health problem: London and Bristol in England record serious outbreaks, and some 50,000 are killed by the disease in New York City.

– Pioneering English travel agent Thomas Cook, having begun Cook's Tours and offered trips to Europe (1855), now arranges his first organized tours to the USA.

SCIENCE AND TECHNOLOGY

– The French army adopts the chassepot rifle (named after its inventor Antoine Chassepot), which is technically superior to the Prussians' breech-loading needle gun.

– Alfred Nobel, a Swedish engineer, develops nitroglycerine, discovered by the Italian chemist Ascanio Sobrero in 1847. He modifies the explosive substance to create a safe blasting powder called dynamite.

– The Cologne engineer Nikolaus Otto patents a primitive internal combustion engine.

– The first US oil pipeline now connects Pithole, Pennsylvania, with a railway line 8km (5 miles) away.

– Emil von Skoda, a Bohemian engineer, develops a machine plant at Pilsen that will become an important manufacturer of armaments.

ARTS AND HUMANITIES

Literature

– The first volume of the *Grand dictionnaire universel du XIXème siècle* (1866–76), edited by Pierre Larousse, is published in Paris. It is the first of the famous Larousse dictionaries and encyclopedias.

Fyodor Dostoyevsky (see p. 434), *Crime and Punishment* and *The Gambler*, novels.

George Eliot (Mary Ann Evans), *Felix Holt, The Radical*, novel.

John Henry Newman, *The Dream of Gerontius*, poem.

Algernon Charles Swinburne, *Poems and Ballads,* collected poetry (it is attacked by critics as 'unclean, morbid and sensual').

Visual Arts and Architecture

– English craftsman and socialist William Morris invents the Morris chair, with a sliding back.

Music

30 Mar. First performance in Prague of Bedřich Smetana's opera *Prodaná nevěsta* (The Bartered Bride).

12 Sept. *The Black Crook,* written by Charles M. Barras, is performed at Niblo's Garden, New York. It is the first major Broadway musical.

Anton Bruckner, Symphony No. 1 in C minor and Mass in E minor.

Pyotr Tchaikovsky, Symphony No. 1 in G minor (*Winter Daydreams*).

1867

EUROPE

17 Feb. The Hungarian diet (parliament) is opened. The Hungarian politician Ferencz Deák has engineered a constitutional settlement (the *Ausgleich*, or compromise) whereby Hungary acquires self-government within a Dual Monarchy of Austria-Hungary. The emperor of Austria (Franz Josef) also becomes king of Hungary (he is crowned on 8 June). Austria-Hungary operates unified foreign and war policies, but a separate Hungarian ministry (headed until 1871 by Count Andrássy) is responsible for the internal affairs of Hungary, Transylvania and Croatia-Slavonia. The vast Austro-Hungarian empire embraces not only modern Austria and Hungary but also the territories that will become the modern Czech Republic and Slovakia, together with parts of modern Poland, Ukraine, Romania, Croatia and Italy.

16 April The North German Confederation is formed under the leadership of Prussia.

15 Aug. In Britain the Second Reform Act extends the vote: borough elections are now open to all householders who pay the poor rates and also to lodgers who have been in their lodgings for more than a year and pay £10 a year or more in rent; county elections are open to owners of land with a rentable value of at least £5 a year and to tenants who pay at least £12 a year. Prime minister Lord Derby regards the Act (mainly Disraeli's work) as 'a leap in the dark'.

Sinn Féin.

(Ourselves alone.)

The mid-19th-century Irish nationalist slogan subsequently adopted as the name of a political party

Dec. Fenians (Irish nationalists) try to blow up Clerkenwell jail in London, killing 12 people.

– The German customs union, the *Zollverein* (see 1833), expands to include Baden, Bavaria, Hohenzollern and Württemberg.

ASIA

3 Feb. The Japanese emperor Komei dies. Following his death, the idea of restoring the imperial throne gains in popularity.

9 Nov. Mutsuhito Meiji becomes Japanese emperor, and leads a movement that aims to restore the rights of the emperor over the shogun (military leader).

THE AMERICAS

1 Mar. Nebraska becomes the 37th US state.

29 Mar. The British North America Act unites the separate provinces of Ontario, Quebec, New Brunswick and Nova Scotia in the Dominion of Canada. Ottawa will become its capital.

15 May Emperor Maximilian of Mexico surrenders to local opposition forces led by Benito Juárez. He is condemned to death by court martial and executed by firing squad (19 June), the victim of French emperor Napoleon III's costly and futile vision of a Latin American empire.

– The USA purchases Alaska from Russia for $7,200,000.

– The Comanche people agree to settle on reservation land in the Oklahoma territory of the USA (see 1849).

– The New York State legislature votes to establish a free school system.

ECONOMY AND SOCIETY

– Atlanta University in Georgia, USA, is founded.

– Congregationalists establish Howard University for Negroes near Washington, D.C., and propose admission for all, regardless of age, sex or previous level of educational achievement.

– In Britain John Chambers has founded an amateur boxing club with the support of John Sholto Douglas, 8th marquess of Queensberry, and now draws up the rules that will govern the sport (the Queensberry Rules).

– The first volume of *Das Kapital* by German political theorist Karl Marx (see p. 419) is published and exerts a powerful influence on modern thought and political affairs. Marx argues that capitalism is an unstable social and economic system and calls for revolutionary agitation on the part of the working classes.

– The newspaper that will later become *La Stampa* starts publication in Turin, N Italy, as *Gazetta Piemontese*.

– A railway line is opened linking Innsbruck in Austria with Bolzano in Italy through a tunnel built under the Brenner pass.

SCIENCE AND TECHNOLOGY

– Emperor Napoleon III urges the French chemist Hippolyte Mège-Mouriés to start the development of synthetic butter, which will lead to the introduction of margarine (1869).

– The French scientist Georges Leclanché invents the first effective dry cell battery.

ARTS AND HUMANITIES

Literature

Matthew Arnold, 'Dover Beach', poem.

Walter Bagehot, *The English Constitution*. Bagehot popularizes the idea that the British Constitution is an informal and evolutionary entity owing everything to precedent and little to fixed planning.

Henrik Ibsen, *Peer Gynt*, play.

Anthony Trollope, *The Last Chronicle of Barset*, novel.

Emile Zola, *Thérèse Raquin*, naturalistic novel.

Visual Arts and Architecture

14 Jan. French painter Jean-Auguste-Dominique Ingres dies in Paris at the age of 86.

Karl Marx (1818–83)

The German social, political and economic theorist Karl Marx was to become the inspiration of 20th-century communism. He was born in Trier and studied philosophy, law and classical literature at the universities of Bonn and Berlin. With the socialist Friedrich Engels he drafted *The Communist Manifesto* (1848). After the failure of the democratic revolution in Germany in 1848 Marx became an exile in Britain. His principal work is *Das Kapital*, the first volume of which was published in 1867 with volumes 2 and 3 published posthumously in 1885 and 1895.

Marx took an understanding of historical development and Hegel's idea of the dialectic (see p.371) to develop a materialist philosophy of history. Basic to Marx's philosophy is the idea of conflict: for Marx the essence of history was the struggle between classes. He believed that the major determinant of people's thoughts and actions was the social class to which they belonged, and he defined social class in terms of economic roles.

Marx saw bourgeois capitalism, which had itself superseded aristocratic feudalism, as a system that was doomed to self-destruct because of its own contradictions. Capital grows and expands – but the more it is concentrated in the hands of the few the closer the system comes to breakdown. Liberals who seek to alleviate the suffering of the poor therefore miss the point. The eyes of the proletarians need, instead, to be opened to the fact of their suffering – and the ensuing revolution will sweep away the capitalist system. The proletarians will then establish a dictatorship to protect this revolution, but eventually the state itself will wither away, as mankind recovers from its divided consciousness and is healed.

Marx's detection of the self-interest that lies behind dominant ideologies has made him into the most necessary of modern political thinkers – and his critical insights are as relevant to the 'Marxist' governments which have claimed him as their inspiration as they are to his more obvious enemies.

– The Galleria Vittoria Emanuele in Milan, a glass-roofed arcade designed by Giuseppe Mengoni, is completed.
– French landscape painter Théodore Rousseau dies.
Edouard Manet, *Execution of Maximilian*, painting.

Music

11 Mar. First performance in Paris of Giuseppe Verdi's opera *Don Carlos*, which is based on Schiller's drama.

27 April First performance in Paris of Charles Gounod's opera *Roméo et Juliette*.

Modest Musorgsky, *A Night on the Bare Mountain*, orchestral work.

Johann Strauss II, *An der schönen blauen Donau* (The Blue Danube), concert waltz.

1868

EUROPE

29 Feb. In Britain a Conservative government is elected with Benjamin Disraeli as prime minister; in the November general election, however, the Liberal Party returns to government and William Ewart Gladstone, a former Tory, becomes prime minister.

23 April The reactionary prime minister of Spain, Ramón Maria Narváez, duke of Valencia, dies. The liberal military stage a coup against Queen Isabella II (17 Sept.), and Admiral Juan Batista Topete y Carballo proclaims the end of absolutist rule in Spain (18 Sept.). The queen flees to France (29 Sept.), and Marshal Juan Prim forms a provisional government (5 Oct.). Universal suffrage and a free press are established and the Order of the Society of Jesus (the Jesuits) is abolished in Spain.

10 June King Michael III Obrenovic of Serbia is assassinated by followers of the rival Karageorgevic dynasty near Belgrade. He is succeeded by his cousin Milan IV.

ASIA

3 Jan. The Tokugawa shogunate, which has ruled Japan since 1603, is abolished and the Meiji dynasty is restored under Emperor Mutsuhito. The new emperor signs an oath (6 April) requiring him to be guided by an elected assembly. The imperial family moves into the Kyuju Palace (formerly the citadel of the shoguns) in the centre of Tokyo (as the Japanese capital is renamed).

28 July The Burlingame treaty signed between China and the USA in Washington, D.C., defines mutual rights of immigration and emigration. It is named after the former US representative to China, Anson Burlingame, who is appointed by the Chinese government to head a delegation to Europe and the USA in order to negotiate treaties on China's behalf.

– Sir James Brooke, British rajah of Sarawak (NW Borneo), dies and is succeeded by his nephew, Charles.

– Rama IV, king of Siam (Thailand), dies; the new king, Rama V (Somdeth Phra Paraminda Maha), establishes personal rule and abolishes slavery and feudalism, introduces the telegraph and educational reforms and opens the country's first railway.

– The Russians occupy Samarkand in Uzbekistan, C Asia.

THE AMERICAS

18 Feb. In the USA President Andrew Johnson dismisses secretary of war Edwin M. Stanton and contravenes a law requiring the Senate's approval for the dismissal of certain elected officials. Radical elements in the Republican Party oppose Johnson's protection of white supremacists in the South. The House of Representatives votes (21 Feb.) to impeach the president, accusing him of 'high crimes and misdemeanours'. The trial begins before the Senate (30 Mar.), but enough Democrats ally with the Republicans to prevent the impeachment, which fails by a single vote to gain the necessary two-thirds majority.

The Republican Party disowns Johnson and nominates the civil war hero Ulysses S. Grant for the presidency; Grant wins the national election with 53% of the vote (Nov.).

18 July The 14th amendment to the US Constitution becomes law. It specifies that 'all persons born or naturalized in the United States … are citizens of the United States' and that 'no State shall make or enforce any law which shall abridge the privileges or immunities of citizens of the United States'. The US Congress has made ratification of the amendment by Southern states a condition of re-admission to the Union.

12 Aug. The US army forces the Navajo leaders to sign a treaty confining them to reservations spread across Arizona, New Mexico and Utah, which are mostly in desert and semi-desert areas.

Aug. A series of earthquakes devastates Ecuador and Peru, killing over 25,000 people.

31 Dec. The forces of the anti-Paraguayan coalition (Argentina, Brazil and Uruguay) occupy Asunción in Paraguay (see 1865). After four years of war some two-thirds of the adult population of Paraguay are either dead or living as refugees. The dictator President Francisco Solano López remains at large.

– Cuba declares war on Spain, whose colonial regime has failed to reform the country's institutions and still permits slavery.

– An eight-hour day is introduced for US government workers.

SUB-SAHARAN AFRICA

10 April In the Abyssinian campaign, military action is taken by Britain following the mistreatment of British missionaries and traders. Tewoderos II, emperor of Ethiopia, is defeated at the battle of Arogee by an Anglo-Indian force under Gen. Sir Robert Napier. Tewoderos commits suicide before the expeditionary force reaches the capital at Magdala (13 April) and frees the imprisoned British captives. The Ethiopian state disintegrates following Napier's withdrawal.

– Basutoland (Lesotho) in S Africa is annexed by Britain; the Sotho have been defeated by the forces of the Orange Free State, which now protests at the British annexation.

ECONOMY AND SOCIETY

– The game of badminton is invented at the duke of Beaufort's Gloucestershire estate of that name.

– The All England Croquet Club is founded in Wimbledon, SW London, and holds its first championship matches, but lawn tennis will overtake the game in popularity.

– In Japan Iwasaki Yataro, a prominent supporter of the imperial Meiji restoration and the process of Westernization, starts to build up the Mitsubishi industrial conglomerate.

– Tabasco sauce is created by Edward McIlhenny on Avery Island off the Louisiana coast, S USA.

– The plant louse phylloxera spreads to Europe from the USA via imported vines and devastates European vineyards.

– James Walter Thompson starts to sell advertising space in groups of magazines rather than in individual publications and starts the US advertising empire of J. Walter Thompson.

SCIENCE AND TECHNOLOGY

– French archaeologist Edouard Lartet is the first to discover the remains of human skeletons from the Upper Palaeolithic period (c.35,000–10,000 years ago). They are given the name Cro-Magnon man after the rock shelter where they are found near Périgueux in the Dordogne, SW France.

– US inventor Christopher Sholes constructs a typewriter with keys set in the (QWERTY) order that will become universal; it will be sold as the Remington typewriter (see 1874).

– In the railway industry George Westinghouse, an American inventor, has developed an air-brake that can set the brakes simultaneously throughout the whole train by means of a steam-driven air pump.

ARTS AND HUMANITIES

Literature

18 Oct. *La Prensa*, which becomes the highest circulation newspaper in S America, starts publication in Buenos Aires.

Wilkie Collins, *The Moonstone*, novel. It features Sergeant Cuff, one of the first detectives in English literature.

Music

21 June First performance in Munich of Richard Wagner's (see p. 421) opera *Die Meistersinger von Nürnberg* (The Mastersingers of Nuremberg).

Johannes Brahms, *Ein Deutsches Requiem* (A German Requiem).

Anton Bruckner, Mass in F minor.

Edvard Grieg, Piano Concerto in A minor.

Nikolai Rimsky-Korsakov, Symphony No. 2 (*Antar*).

1869

EUROPE

6 Feb. Greece agrees to withdraw its forces from the Mediterranean island of Crete following the Ottoman (Turkish) empire's ultimatum of 1868. The inhabitants of Crete have been in revolt against Turkish rule since 1866, demanding union with Greece.

MIDDLE EAST AND NORTH AFRICA

17 Nov. The Suez Canal opens to ships sailing between the Mediterranean and the Gulf of Suez.

ASIA

Mar. The *daimyo* or lords of the four most powerful Japanese clans, the Satsuma, Choshu, Tosa and Hizen, surrender their territories to the new Japanese emperor; they are immediately created provincial governors of their former territories.

THE AMERICAS

Mar. Ulysses S. Grant becomes 18th US president.

10 May The Union Pacific and Central Pacific railroads (starting respectively from the E and W seaboards of the USA) converge in Utah. Travelling time between New York and San Francisco now falls to just eight days. The first transcontinental US transport route has been made possible by government loans and subsidies, as well as Chinese and Irish labour.

13 July Riots break out in San Francisco against Chinese workers.

Richard Wagner (1813–83)

The German composer Richard Wagner achieved early recognition with his operas *Rienzi* (1842) and *The Flying Dutchman* (1843). His success freed him from the need to please patrons and allowed him to develop his idea of the 'total work of art' (*Gesamtkunstwerk*) to which various arts contribute. The result of this artistic philosophy was Wagner's own four-part cycle of 'music dramas', *The Ring of the Nibelung*, in which the conventions of opera are almost entirely abandoned. Wagner's most important musical innovation was the leitmotiv, a short musical theme representing an abstract idea or a character. The recurrence of these leitmotivs lends a unity to the vast achievement of *The Ring*. In this epic theatrical work, based loosely on pagan German legends, Wagner achieved his goal of an authentically German and contemporary aesthetic.

Wagner was the dominant cultural figure of 19th-century Germany – and it was Wagner who responded most powerfully to the creation of the new Reich of 1871. He came to regard his work as the highest aesthetic expression of the German nationalism of the age. *The Ring*'s central message is that the pursuit of power demands the sacrifice of love, and it lays a powerful curse on what it sees as the wretchedness of modern materialism. It also undeniably exalts an ideal of strength and mastery achieved by the power of the imagination – something that was particularly to appeal to Wagner's later Nazi admirers.

24 Sept. The first 'Black Friday' on Wall Street ruins many investors. Speculators have tried to corner the market in gold and by increasing its price have destroyed New York banks and businesses. The US government is forced to intervene and to sell its gold reserves to lower the price.

Sept. The anti-alcohol National Prohibition Party is established in Chicago, Illinois, USA.

– The National Woman Suffrage Association is established by Susan Brownell Anthony and Elizabeth Cady Stanton. It will campaign for a constitutional amendment giving all American women the right to vote.

– The publisher of the *New York Herald* newspaper, James Gordon Bennett, commissions the Welsh-born Henry Morton Stanley to mount an expedition to search for Scottish missionary David Livingstone, whose whereabouts in Africa are unknown and whose fate is causing concern.

– Louis Riel, leader of Manitoba's *métis* or mixed French-Canadian and indigenous races, leads the Red River rebellion against the Canadian government. He captures Winnipeg and establishes a provisional government aimed at protecting his people's traditional land rights.

– Uriah Stephens establishes the Noble Order of the Knights of Labor, a secret American trade union organization.

– Alexander Turney Stewart, a New York department store

millionaire, starts Garden City, Long Island, a community designed for those living on moderate incomes.

– Cornelius Vanderbilt gains a monopoly in rail transport between New York City and Buffalo.

– Wyoming territory grants women the vote, the first US territory to do so.

ECONOMY AND SOCIETY

8 Dec. The First Vatican Council is convened by Pope Pius IX. It is the first universal council of the Catholic Church since the Council of Trent (1545–63). The council will proclaim the dogma of papal infallibility in the bull *Pastor aeternus* (see 1870).

– In Britain the Contagious Diseases Act allows the police to arrest female prostitutes.

– In the USA a cannery is opened in Camden, New Jersey, by Joseph Campbell and Abraham Anderson, which leads to the establishment of the Campbell Soup Company.

– Coffee rust spreads from the Indian Ocean island of Ceylon (Sri Lanka) to the rest of E and SE Asia and throughout the Pacific region. The industry is temporarily destroyed, and tea cultivation spreads because of the inflation in coffee prices.

– In the USA Henry John Heinz and L.C. Noble start a food processing and retailing company, selling processed horseradish in clear glass bottles. Competitors sell horseradish in green bottles to disguise the fact that their product contains turnip filler.

– The Kirin brewery, the first in Japan, is established in Yokohama by the American entrepreneur William Copeland.

– Hippolyte Mège-Mouriés produces margarine commercially. It is patented as 'butterine' in Britain.

– Girton College, the first Cambridge University college for women, is founded.

– The first public elementary school in Japan opens at Kyoto.

SCIENCE AND TECHNOLOGY

4 Nov. The weekly scientific journal *Nature* starts publication in London; British biologist Thomas Henry Huxley writes an essay popularizing the idea of scientific advance.

– The Norwegian doctor Gerhard Henrik Armauer Hansen discovers the leprosy bacillus. Leprosy is named Hansen's disease.

– Daily weather bulletins are introduced by the US astronomer and meteorologist Abbe Cleveland.

– German naturalist Ernst Haeckel coins the word 'ecology' and advocates environmental balance. He popularizes Charles Darwin's theory of evolution in Germany.

– US Baptist missionary Jonathan Scobie, working in Yokohama, Japan, invents the rickshaw to transport his invalid wife.

ARTS AND HUMANITIES

Literature

– US illustrator Thomas Nast starts his series of caricatures in the New York magazine *Harper's Weekly* caricaturing the group surrounding the state senator William 'Boss' Tweed (the Tweed Ring) who are defrauding the city treasury.

Louisa May Alcott, *Little Women*, novel.

R(ichard) D(odderidge) Blackmore, *Lorna Doone*, novel.

Robert Browning, *The Ring and the Book*, long poem in blank verse. Its critical and commercial success establishes Browning's reputation.

Fyodor Dostoyevsky (see p. 434), *The Idiot*, novel.

Gustave Flaubert, *L'Education sentimentale* (A Sentimental Education), novel.

Anthony Trollope, *Phineas Finn*, novel, second in the 'Palliser' series.

Music

8 Mar. The composer Hector Berlioz dies in Paris.

22 Sept. First performance in Munich of Richard Wagner's (see p. 421) opera *Das Rheingold* (The Rhine Gold), the one-act prologue to his opera cycle *Der Ring des Nibelungen* (The Ring of the Nibelung).

– Vienna's Staatsoper (national opera company) opens.

1870

EUROPE

25 June Queen Isabella II of Spain abdicates; Prussian minister-president Otto von Bismarck puts forward Prince Leopold of the ruling Hohenzollern dynasty of Prussia as a candidate for the Spanish throne. Leopold accepts the offer.

2 July The French learn of Prince Leopold's acceptance of the offer of the Spanish throne and are determined to prevent it for strategic reasons. Following French representations to King William I, head of the Prussian royal house of Hohenzollern, Leopold's acceptance is withdrawn (12 July), but Napoleon III's demand that no Hohenzollern prince will assume the Spanish throne in future is resisted. This is made clear to the French ambassador at Ems spa in the Prussian Rhineland, where William is staying for a rest cure, and an account of the meeting is sent by telegram to the Prussian minister-president Otto von Bismarck (13 July). Before making it public, Bismarck alters the wording of the Ems telegram, turning it into an inflammatory document with the aim of provoking war with France.

19 July France declares war on Prussia, thereby starting the Franco-Prussian War of 1870–1.

Aug. In the Franco-Prussian War French armies sustain heavy defeats by Prussia at Weissenberg, Bavaria (4 Aug.), Wörth and Spicheren, Alsace (6 Aug.), and at Gravelotte and St Privat, near Metz, Lorraine (18 Aug.). Thereafter, the advancing Prussians besiege the 170,000-strong French Army of the Rhine (under Marshal Bazaine) in the fortress town of Metz, which will hold out until 27 Oct.

1 Sept. The French 1st Army Corps under Marshal MacMahon, endeavouring to relieve Metz from the W, is trapped and defeated in the decisive battle of the Franco-Prussian War at Sedan, close to the Belgian border (2 Sept.). Napoleon III surrenders and is taken prisoner (along with 100,000 French soldiers), a French republic is proclaimed (4 Sept.) and the Prussian army begins a 135-day siege of Paris (19 Sept.). Parisians will eat cats and dogs to avoid starvation and will even consume Castor and Pollux, the elephants at the Paris

Zoo. The French Second Empire has collapsed in the ruins of Napoleon's foreign policy.

20 Sept. Italian troops enter Rome following the withdrawal of French troops (who have been garrisoned in the city of Rome for its defence) to fight the battle of Sedan. The unification of Italy, initially helped by Napoleon III's diplomatic ambitions, is now completed amid his personal and political ruination.

8 Oct. Radical republican politician Léon-Michel Gambetta escapes from Paris by balloon to organize French provincial resistance to the Prussians and to sustain popular opposition to the imperial regime of Napoleon III.

16 Nov. The duke of Aosta, son of King Victor Emmanuel of Italy, is elected king of Spain and will reign as Amadeo I.

– In Britain William Edward Forster's Education Act encourages elementary education by increasing public money and allowing local education boards to build new schools.

– In Ireland Isaac Butt forms the Home Rule Association, the aim of which is a devolutionary settlement and the repeal of the 1801 Act of Union between Britain and Ireland.

ASIA

21 June An anti-Western mob in Tianjin, E China, attacks a Catholic orphanage and kills more than 20 foreigners, including French and Belgian nuns.

Sept. Westernization gathers pace in Japan: the emperor orders his subjects to adopt surnames.

THE AMERICAS

1 Mar. President Francisco Solano López of Paraguay is killed in his country's six-year war with its neighbours, which is ended by treaty (20 June). Having lost around 100,000 dead and over 600,000 wounded, Paraguay is reduced to a population of some 30,000 men and 200,000 women. Brazil, Argentina and Uruguay seize large tracts of the country.

30 Mar. Hamilton Fish, US secretary of state, proclaims the ratification of the 15th amendment to the US Constitution extending citizenship to all born in the USA regardless of race or colour.

15 July Canada creates the province of Manitoba in the Midwest.

24 July The first railway car to travel from the Pacific Coast reaches New York City on the new transcontinental line.

– In the USA Thomas Nast creates the donkey symbol as an emblem to represent the Democratic Party. He will later create the elephant as a symbol for the Republicans (1874).

– Hiram Rhoades Revels of Mississippi becomes the first black US senator, and J.H. Rainey of South Carolina is the first black congressman.

– Women get the vote in Utah territory, W USA.

ECONOMY AND SOCIETY

18 July The First Vatican Council votes in favour of the idea that the pope is 'infallible' when he speaks *ex cathedra* on issues of faith and morals. The vote reflects the Catholic Church's feelings of vulnerability in the face of radical nationalism and liberalism (see 20 Sept. above), which seem to threaten its very existence.

- The 182-year-old insurance agency Lloyds of London is incorporated and its 'names', belonging to various syndicates, accept unlimited liability for the insurance underwritten by each syndicate. It appeals to many public figures enticed by the prospect of an easy return on investment but who lack commercial experience.
- Heinrich Schliemann starts to excavate the site of ancient Troy in W Turkey. Schliemann, who has acquired US citizenship and has amassed a fortune from supplying military equipment in the Crimean War, will go on to discover the city of Priam described by Homer. At Mycenae in the Greek Argolid he will uncover golden treasures of Homeric civilization.
- St Pancras Station opens in London.

SCIENCE AND TECHNOLOGY

- The banana trade develops between Jamaica in the Caribbean and N American ports.
- Russian chemist Dmitri Ivanovich Mendeleyev organizes the periodic table of elements and arranges them according to atomic weight in *The Principles of Chemistry*.
- Deoxyribonucleic acid (DNA) is discovered at Tübingen in Germany by the Swiss chemist Johann Friedrich Miescher but is not yet understood to be the conveyor of genetic material.

ARTS AND HUMANITIES

Literature

9 June English writer Charles Dickens (see p. 385) dies, leaving the unfinished novel *The Mystery of Edwin Drood*.

Lewis Carroll (Charles Lutwidge Dodgson), *The Hunting of the Snark*, poem.

Benjamin Disraeli, *Lothair*, novel. The first edition sells out in two days.

James Anthony Froude, *History of England from the Fall of Cardinal Wolsey to the Defeat of the Spanish Armada* (12 vols, 1856–7), ground-breaking work of history based on archival research.

Jules Verne, *Vingt mille lieues sous les mers* (Twenty Thousand Leagues Under the Sea), novel.

Visual Arts and Architecture

- Sandringham House in Norfolk, E England, is completed for Queen Victoria as a private royal residence.

1871

EUROPE

18 Jan. The German Second Reich (empire) is proclaimed in the Hall of Mirrors in the Palace of Versailles, SW of Paris. The united German empire is the successor to the Holy Roman Empire dissolved by Napoleon Bonaparte in 1806. King William I of Prussia becomes German Kaiser (emperor) and Otto von Bismarck his chancellor. Bismarck's diplomacy has created a unified German state by bringing together Prussia, Bavaria, Saxony and Württemberg together with five grand duchies, 13 duchies and principalities and the free cities of Hamburg, Bremen and Lübeck.

28 Jan. Paris capitulates to German troops after a long siege. An armistice with Germany is signed. A preliminary peace is signed at Versailles (26 Feb.).

16 Feb. The veteran French politician Louis-Adolphe Thiers is elected president of the Third Republic; meeting in Bordeaux, SW France, the French National Assembly declares Napoleon III formally deposed (1 Mar.), and he retires to England where he will die in 1873.

26 Mar. A left-wing central committee emerges in Paris calling itself the Commune; socialist government in France becomes a practical possibility and is seen as a threat to the established European political order. The Communards, humiliated by the National Assembly's capitulation to German forces, seize and execute Gen. Lecomte and Gen. Thomas, who are in command of French government troops and who are also attempting to disarm the citizenry. The Commune is crushed by the French army in the so-called *semaine sanglante* or 'bloody week' (21–28 May) when some 20,000–30,000 Parisians are killed on the barricades. The Tuileries Palace and part of the Louvre are gutted by fire.

10 May By the peace of Frankfurt France cedes Alsace and part of Lorraine to Germany and has to pay an indemnity of 5 billion francs. German troops are to stay on French soil until the sum is paid.

4 Dec. Germany adopts the Gold Standard for its currency valuation.

- In the *Kulturkampf* (Conflict of Beliefs, 1871–87) the new German state embarks on a trial of strength with the Catholic Church in the wake of the Vatican Council's decrees (see 18 July 1870). The new German state is a model of the secular national-ism, which the Church opposes, and Bismarck is determined to quash any idea that the first loyalty of Catholics is to the pope and the Vatican. A programme of official persecution of Catholics begins in Germany.
- In Britain Parliament abolishes the sale of army commissions.
- Germany turns to protectionism and raises tariff barriers to encourage Germany to be independent of France in its food supplies. Despite these measures German wheat will continue to fall in price and the crisis in agriculture will cause social distress and lead to German emigration to the USA. Under free trade American grain is so cheap that British grain cannot compete.

ASIA

29 June The Japanese currency is reformed and is now based on the yen (29 Aug.). An imperial decree changes Japan's administration and replaces feudal fiefs with Western-style prefectures. New taxation laws are introduced (8 Oct.) based on the equal treatment of Japanese subjects. State education will become universal and compulsory, although fee-based. With the arrival of metal type and printing presses a Japanese daily newspaper begins publication.

- British residents in Burma establish the Rangoon Oil Company, which will later become the Burmah Oil Company.
- Submarine telegraph cables are laid from Vladivostok in the

Russian Far East to Shanghai, Hong Kong and Singapore via Nagasaki in Japan.

THE AMERICAS

3 Mar. In the USA the Indian Appropriation Act stops the practice of making treaties with the leaders of Native American peoples, who are thereby recognized as independent powers. Instead, Native Americans become wards of the federal government.

20 July British Columbia joins the Dominion of Canada.

8–14 Oct. The worst fire in American history to date starts in Chicago, Illinois, and spreads as a forest fire to Michigan and Wisconsin.

– The Costa Rican president Tomás Guardia commissions Henry Meiggs to build the national railway line from Port Limón on the Caribbean coast to the capital, San José. Meiggs's nephew, Minor Cooper Keith, will finish the project in 1890.

– The US National Rifle Association is founded. It has the initial aim of promoting the safe use of guns (since so many civil war soldiers were ill trained), but it will become a powerful lobby defending gun ownership.

– Brigham Young, leader of the Mormons and married to 27 women, is arrested in Salt Lake City on charges of polygamy. The practice of polygamy will delay Utah's admission to the Union until 1896.

SUB-SAHARAN AFRICA

Oct. American newspaperman Henry Morton Stanley discovers the Scottish missionary and explorer David Livingstone at Ujiji on Lake Tanganyika, E Africa. Livingstone and Stanley thereafter establish that the lake is not the source of the Nile. Stanley fails to persuade Livingstone to leave Africa with him.

– In S Africa Britain absorbs Basutoland into Cape Colony and also annexes the Kimberley diamond mines.

ECONOMY AND SOCIETY

– John Pierpont Morgan becomes a partner in Drexel, Morgan and Company in Philadelphia and New York, which he will reorganize as the banking house J.P. Morgan in 1895.

– The town, later city, of Birmingham is founded in Alabama, S USA.

– Dodge City, Kansas, is founded and grows rapidly into a major US centre for the trade in buffalo hides and tongues.

– The University of Arkansas is founded in the USA.

– The growing popularity of American poker is further boosted by news that Queen Victoria is being taught the principles of the card game by the American ambassador to the Court of St James's in London, Robert Cumming Schenck.

SCIENCE AND TECHNOLOGY

– English naturalist Charles Darwin's (see p. 379) *The Descent of Man and Selection in Relation to Sex* claims that man is descended from an ape-like ancestor. Paradoxically, progressivist science seems to reveal an inhuman basis to humanity's advance and to question the nature of human progress .

– The gelatine emulsions pioneered by the British inventor

Richard Leach Maddox reduce the exposure time needed for a photograph from 15 seconds to a fraction of a second.

– French chemist Hippolyte Mège-Mouriés sells the rights to manufacture margarine to Jan and Anton Jürgens who open a factory at Oss in the Netherlands.

– The German army adopts the superior Mauser model of breech-loading rifle.

ARTS AND HUMANITIES

Literature
Fyodor Dostoyevsky (see p. 434), *The Possessed*, novel.
Thomas Hardy, *Desperate Remedies*, his first published novel.

Music
Mar. The Royal Albert Hall of Arts and Sciences opens in London as a multi-purpose venue, but it becomes particularly associated with musical concerts. The hall is named after Prince Albert, late consort of Queen Victoria.

24 Dec. First performance in Cairo of Giuseppe Verdi's opera *Aida*. Commissioned by the khedive of Egypt, the opera is not written to mark the opening of the Suez Canal nor to celebrate the opening of Cairo Opera House.

– The British composer Arthur Seymour Sullivan composes the music for the hymn 'Onward Christian Soldiers', written by the folksong collector Sabine Baring-Gould.

1872

EUROPE

26 April Don Carlos, duke of Madrid, is proclaimed king of Spain by conservative supporters of the Carlist branch of the royal line (see 1833). A second Carlist civil war breaks out in Spain. Don Carlos enters Navarre, N Spain (May), from France, but his forces are repulsed by the ruling king Amadeo I (see 16 Nov. 1870).

14 May German chancellor Otto von Bismarck intensifies the clash with the Catholic Church in the *Kulturkampf* (see 1871) with a law expelling the Jesuits from Germany (25 June).

7 Sept. An informal understanding between the emperors of Germany and Austria-Hungary is established at a meeting in Berlin. Russia will be drawn into the agreement in 1873.

– In Britain the Adulteration of Food, Drink and Drugs Act makes the adulteration of consumables a serious offence. A Licensing Act limits the hours during which alcoholic drinks may be sold. Brewers and publicans are defended by the Conservative Party, which opposes the Liberal government's legislation.

ASIA

8 Feb. The British viceroy of India, Richard Southwell Bourke, earl of Mayo, is stabbed to death by an Afghan prisoner at a penal colony on the Andaman Islands in the Indian Ocean.

Aug. The Japanese government decrees universal and compulsory education.

14 Oct. Japan's first railway opens, linking Tokyo with Yokohama in C Honshu. It has been built by British engineers.

– Japan introduces compulsory national service.

THE AMERICAS

5 Nov. US President Ulysses S. Grant is re-elected despite his corrupt administration; Democrats and those Republicans who have not benefited from the post-civil war 'reconstruction' of the Southern states support journalist Horace Greeley, Grant's Liberal Republican opponent.

Nov. The *Mary Celeste* sets sail from New York harbour with a 10-man crew heading for Genoa, N Italy. On 5 Dec. the ship is discovered W of Gibraltar, intact but with nobody on board.

– Equal pay for equal work is guaranteed for federal employees by an act of the US Congress.

– The US Congress abolishes the federal tax introduced during the civil war.

SUB-SAHARAN AFRICA

– Takla Giyorgis II, emperor of Ethiopia, is succeeded by Yohannes IV, ruler of Tigre province (see 1868).

AUSTRALASIA AND OCEANIA

23 Nov. In Australia a telegraph line connects Adelaide in the S with Port Darwin on the N coast. This line is then extended to connect with lines through Asia to Europe.

ECONOMY AND SOCIETY

1 Mar. An Act of Congress creates the Yellowstone National Park in Wyoming, W USA.

16 Mar. Wanderers (a team of former public schoolboys) defeat the Royal Engineers in the first FA Cup final, played at the Kennington Oval in London.

June Jesse Jame's gang robs its first passenger train in Iowa, USA.

– Charles Taze Russell founds the Jehovah's Witnesses in the USA.

– Giovanni Battista Pirelli opens a shop in Milan; it becomes the global tyre manufacturer Pirelli and Company.

– Thomas Adams of New York produces a liquorice-flavoured chewing gum. He adds liquorice flavouring to the chicle gum, which is chewed by Native Americans.

– Beef eating is popularized in Japan by Emperor Mutsuhito, but most Japanese are still repelled by the idea of eating animal fat.

SCIENCE AND TECHNOLOGY

– The Belgian electrician Zénobe Théophile Gramme invents the industrial dynamo.

– John Wesley Hyatt of New York obtains a patent that allows him to embark on the commercial production of celluloid.

– German Egyptologist and novelist Georg Moritz Ebers discovers a papyrus (the Ebers papyrus) at Thebes, former capital of Upper Egypt, which describes ancient medical techniques.

ARTS AND HUMANITIES

Literature

21 Jan. Austrian playwright Franz Grillparzer dies.

Dec. At a meeting of British archaeologists the Assyriologist George Smith announces that he has deciphered a cuneiform tablet that contains the Babylonian epic poem relating to King Gilgamesh. It describes a great flood of the 3rd millennium BC, which is thought to confirm the biblical story of Noah.

– Sarah Bernhardt acts in *Ruy Blas* in her premiere with the Comédie Française in Paris.

Samuel Butler, *Erewhon*, satire of a utopia where there is no machinery. 'Erewhon' is 'nowhere' spelled (roughly) backwards.

Lewis Carroll, *Through the Looking Glass*, fantasy, the sequel to *Alice's Adventures in Wonderland* (1865).

George Eliot (Mary Ann Evans), *Middlemarch*, novel.

Thomas Hardy, *Under the Greenwood Tree*, novel.

Visual Arts and Architecture

– Depictions of London's slums by the French painter and illustrator Gustave Doré appear in the book *London: A Pilgrimage*.

– American photographer Eadweard Muybridge (originally Edward James Muggeridge from England) produces a sequence of photographs showing that the four feet of a running horse all leave the ground at the same time.

James Abbott McNeill Whistler, *Arrangement in Grey and Black No. 1: Portrait of the Painter's Mother*, painting.

Music

Anton Bruckner, Symphony No. 2 in C minor.

Pyotr Tchaikovsky, Symphony No. 2 in C minor (*Little Russian*).

1873

EUROPE

9 Jan. Napoleon III, former emperor of France, dies in exile in England.

11 Feb. King Amadeo I of Spain abdicates during the chaos of the second Carlist war. The First Spanish Republic is proclaimed (16 Feb.) by a majority vote in the Spanish cortes, and Emilio Castelar y Ripoli becomes president. The war continues.

24 May In France President Louis-Adolphe Thiers resigns after losing the support of the National Assembly. Representatives elect the reactionary autocrat Marie-Edmé-Patrice-Maurice MacMahon as his successor by an overwhelming majority.

16 Sept. The German army that has remained in France to ensure French payment of reparations after the Franco-Prussian War leaves France.

– Germany adopts the mark as its unit of currency.

– Swedish industrialists Robert and Ludwig Nobel, brothers of explosives inventor Alfred, build a refinery in Russia's Baku oil fields in Transcaucasia (now Azerbaijan). The area will become the world's leading petroleum producer.

ASIA

– Crop failure in Bengal, NE India, leads to widespread famine.

THE AMERICAS

5 Feb. The Bonanza Vein, containing the biggest silver reserves discovered since the Comstock Lode of 1859, is found in the Panamint Range in SE California, USA.

12 Feb. The Fourth Coinage Act stops the coinage of silver dollars and makes gold the sole monetary standard of the USA.

4 Mar. Ulysses S. Grant begins his second term as US president. Schuyler Colfax, Grant's vice-president during his first term, has been heavily implicated in the Crédit Mobilier financial scandal and has not been renominated. Henry Wilson becomes vice-president.

30 Aug. In Canada the Northwest Mounted Police is established, initially to stop trading in alcohol and arms among Native Americans of the Canadian Northwest Territories. They will later become the Royal Canadian Mounted Police.

– Both British and German agriculture and trade are now experiencing the full weight of American economic competition, but the US economy remains subject to cyclical shocks. When the Wall Street banking firm Jay Cooke and Company collapses (18 Sept.) prices fall heavily on the stock exchange (19 Sept.), which closes for ten days. In the 'Panic of 1873' some 5000 firms become bankrupt by the end of the year, leading to large-scale unemployment and to the opening of soup kitchens.

– During the US economic crisis Henry Clay Frick acquires, at small cost, most of the coal- and coke-producing reserves around Connellsville in Pennsylvania (which supply the steel-manufacturing industry of Pittsburgh).

– Belgian missionary Joseph De Veuster (Father Damien) arrives on the Hawaiian island of Molokai to care for lepers. He will die of the disease (now called Hansen's disease; see 1869) in 1889.

SUB-SAHARAN AFRICA

April War breaks out between Britain and the Ashanti (Asante) people in W Africa (modern Ghana): Britain attempts to suppress the local slave trade of King Kofi Kari-Kari.

May Scottish explorer David Livingstone dies at Chitambo (modern Zambia).

5 June Acting under pressure from the British government, which is itself responding to public opinion, Sultan Barghash closes the slave markets of Zanzibar.

SCIENCE AND TECHNOLOGY

1 Aug. US engineer Andrew Smith Hallidie's system of an 'endless-wire rope way' (patented in 1871) is realized with the introduction of the first cable streetcar in San Francisco.

– William Budd, a British doctor, demonstrates the contagious nature of typhoid fever.

– Scottish chemist Sir James Dewar invents the Dewar thermos bottle, which evolves into the thermos flask.

– The perfume industry in Grasse, S France, pioneers a new technique of extracting the essence of scent from flowers; volatile fluids dissolve the essential ingredients from flower roots, which are then isolated as they evaporate.

– Othmar Zeidler of Strasburg creates dichlorodiphenyl-trichlorothane (DDT). He does not know that it can be used as a pesticide.

ARTS AND HUMANITIES

Literature

10 July The French poet Paul Verlaine shoots and wounds his lover, the poet Arthur Rimbaud, in a Brussels hotel room.

Walter Pater, *Studies in the History of the Renaissance*, work of art history (Oscar Wilde will call it 'the holy writ of beauty').

Arthur Rimbaud (see p. 440), *Une Saison en enfer* (A Season in Hell); poetry and prose.

Mark Twain, *The Gilded Age*, political satire co-written with Charles Dudley Warner. The title will henceforth be used to stigmatize the post-Civil War period in the USA as an age of complacent materialism.

Jules Verne, *Le Tour du monde en quatre-vingts jours* (Around the World in 80 Days), novel describing the travels of Phileas Fogg.

Visual Arts and Architecture

Paul Cézanne, *The House of the Hanged Man*, painting.

Music

13 Jan. First performance in St Petersburg of Nikolai Rimsky-Korsakov's opera *The Maid of Pskov*, also known as *Ivan the Terrible*. His Symphony No. 3 in C is premiered later in the year.

Johannes Brahms, Variations on a Theme by Haydn (the *St Anthony Variations*), orchestral work.

Anton Bruckner, Symphony No. 3 in D minor.

Antonín Dvořák, Symphony No. 3 in E flat.

1874

EUROPE

17 Feb. In Britain W.E. Gladstone's first government is voted out of office; Benjamin Disraeli forms his second administration (21 Feb.). It is the first time since 1841 that a Conservative government has been elected with a clear majority.

15 Sept. The Prince of Wales visits France in the first visit to that country by a member of the British royal family since before the Revolution.

29 Dec. The exiled Alfonso, son of Isabella II, attending the military academy at Sandhurst in England, is proclaimed king of Spain (as Alfonso XII).

– A major agricultural depression affects Britain, attended by a wave of strikes among agricultural labourers and mass emigration from the countryside to the mill towns.

ASIA

April Japanese troops invade the Chinese island of Taiwan and assert claims to Okinawa in the Ryukyu Islands, E China Sea. The Japanese withdraw (Oct.) after China agrees to pay an indemnity for the death of 54 Okinawan seamen killed by the Chinese after being shipwrecked in 1871.

THE AMERICAS

– The Greenback political party, first organized in the Midwest, claims that shortage of money is the cause of the crash of 1873 and demands the issue of more dollar notes (greenbacks) to increase the amount of money in circulation. They also demand control of the large corporations that now dominate the US economy as well as reform of a corrupt political system.

SUB-SAHARAN AFRICA

– In W Africa the Ashanti War (see April 1873) ends with the entry of British troops, commanded by Sir Garnet Wolseley, into the Ashanti capital of Kumasi, which is sacked (4 Feb.).

AUSTRALASIA AND OCEANIA

– Britain annexes the Melanesian island group of Fiji in the SW Pacific.

ECONOMY AND SOCIETY

April Barnum's Hippodrome opens in New York. It will later be renamed Madison Square Gardens.

14 May Harvard and McGill universities play a football game in Montreal that is a precursor of American football (a modified version of rugby football).

– Levi Strauss (see 1850) produce the first blue jeans with copper rivets.

SCIENCE AND TECHNOLOGY

– Sophia Jex-Blake, British physician, founds the London School of Medicine for Women.

– The first typewriter is introduced for sale by E. Remington and Sons Fire Arms Company, USA, using the patent of Christopher Sholes (see 1868).

ARTS AND HUMANITIES

Literature

Thomas Hardy, *Far from the Madding Crowd*, novel.

Paul Verlaine, *Romances sans paroles* (Songs without Words), poetry.

Visual Arts and Architecture

– A group of painters rejected by the official Paris Salon establish their own exhibition. The group, which becomes known as the Impressionists, includes Paul Cézanne, Edgar Degas, Edouard Manet, Claude Monet, Camille Pissarro, Pierre-Auguste Renoir and Alfred Sisley and takes its name from a painting by Monet, *Impression: Sunrise* (painted in 1872). The name soon loses its pejorative connotation as a label for the school of artists who will transform European and world art.

Music

8 Feb. First performance in St Petersburg of the complete version of Modest Musorgsky's opera *Boris Godunov*. Musorgsky completes *Pictures from an Exhibition*, a solo piano suite, this year.

5 April First performance in Vienna of Johann Strauss II's operetta *Die Fledermaus* (The Bat).

Anton Bruckner, Symphony No. 4 in E flat (*Romantic*).

Antonín Dvořák, Symphony No. 4 in D minor.

Camille Saint-Saëns, *Danse macabre*, symphonic poem.

Giuseppe Verdi, *Requiem*, composed in memory of the poet, novelist and nationalist leader Alessandro Manzoni, who died on 22 May 1873.

1875

EUROPE

16 July The new French constitution is ratified and provides for a Chamber of Deputies and a Senate together with a president serving a seven-year term. Marie-Edmé-Patrice-Maurice de MacMahon continues as president.

– In the Balkans Bosnia and Herzegovina rebel against Ottoman (Turkish) rule, and the sultan Abdul-Aziz is forced to agree to administrative reforms.

MIDDLE EAST AND NORTH AFRICA

27 Nov. The Suez Canal comes under British control: prime minister Benjamin Disraeli has arranged a loan from the Rothschild bank enabling the British government to buy the controlling shares from the Egyptian khedive Ismail Pasha. Disraeli guarantees the British government itself as security for the £4 million loan in a diplomatic and fiscal coup that creates an international storm.

ASIA

Jan. Mu Zung, emperor of China (head of the Tonghzi dynasty), dies at the age of 19. The dowager empress Cixi, previously co-regent, adopts her nephew Zaitian, who at the age of four ascends the throne (25 Feb.) as the first Guangxu emperor.

THE AMERICAS

1 Mar. An act of the US Congress guarantees blacks equal rights in public places and allows them to serve on juries.

16 May Earthquakes in Colombia and Venezuela claim more than 15,000 lives.

– The resistance of the Comanche people to white ranchers in the Texan prairies comes to an end.

AUSTRALASIA AND OCEANIA

– In the SW Pacific the king of Fiji returns from a visit to New South Wales, Australia, with measles; the ensuing epidemic kills over a quarter of Fiji's population.

ECONOMY AND SOCIETY

May The Kentucky Derby horse race is held for the first time, at Louisville, Kentucky.

2 Aug. The first roller-skating rink opens in Belgravia, London.

24–25 Aug. English sailor and professional swimmer Capt. Matthew Webb becomes the first man to swim across the English Channel from Dover to Calais, completing the feat in 21 hours 45 minutes.

2 Oct. The Palace Hotel opens in San Francisco, California. The United States Hotel, Saratoga Springs, New York state, and the Palmer House Hotel in Chicago, Illinois, also open this year. They represent a new taste for luxury hotels and ostentatious opulence.

– Mary Baker Eddy publishes *Science and Health* in which she claims that the Bible has helped her to recover physically after a fall. Her system of faith healing will become influential as Christian Science. *Key to the Scriptures* will be published in 1883.

– Milk chocolate is created at Vevey in Switzerland by Henri Nestlé.

– The first canned baked beans are produced by the B & M brand for fishermen in Portland, Maine, USA.

SCIENCE AND TECHNOLOGY

– Scottish-American inventor Alexander Graham Bell discovers the principle of the electric telephone.

– Liverpool Street Station, London, is completed.

ARTS AND HUMANITIES

Visual Arts and Architecture

20 Jan. French painter Jean-François Millet dies at Barbizon, France.

22 Feb. French landscape painter Camille Corot dies.

– *Hermes Carrying the Boy Dionysus*, sculpted by Praxiteles of Athens in the 4th century BC, is discovered at Olympia, S Greece.

– The victory of the Germanic tribal leader Arminius over the Roman legions at the battle of Teutoburg Forest in Lower Saxony in AD 9 is commemorated on the site by the unveiling of a vast monument.

– The Paris Opera House, designed by Charles Garnier in flamboyant Beaux-Arts style, is completed.

Claude Monet, *Boating at Argenteuil*, painting.

Music

3 Mar. First performance in Paris of Georges Bizet's opera *Carmen*.

25 Mar. First performance in London of Arthur Sullivan's light opera *Trial by Jury*, to a libretto by W.S. Gilbert.

Antonín Dvořák, Symphony No. 5 in F major.

Pyotr Tchaikovsky, Piano Concerto No. 1 in B flat minor and Symphony No. 3 in D major (*Polish*).

1876

EUROPE

Jan. In Germany the Reichsbank is founded and will become the key institution in German economic management.

March A nationalist uprising takes place in Bulgaria; Ottoman Turkish forces slaughter thousands before the rebellion is fully suppressed.

April In Britain the Royal Titles Bill makes Queen Victoria empress of India. The idea comes from her prime minister Benjamin Disraeli. The queen repays the compliment by creating him earl of Beaconsfield.

Lady Amberley ought to get a good whipping.

Queen Victoria's view of an active feminist – writing to Theodore Martin, March 1870

30 June In the Balkans Serbia declares war on its overlord, Ottoman Turkey, and is joined by Montenegro (2 July); the Serbs will be defeated at Alecsinac in the E of the country (1 Sept.).

6 Sept. British Liberal Party leader William Ewart Gladstone's pamphlet *The Bulgarian Horrors and the Question of the East* is an important contribution to European politics and the issue of nationalist revolts against Turkey. Gladstone also seeks to capitalize on British domestic outrage at the events in the Ottoman (Turkish) empire as his party fights its way back to power.

– In Britain the Merchant Shipping Act prevents the overloading of ships to overcome insurance fraud and prevent loss of life. It follows the campaign led by social reformer and MP Samuel Plimsoll and requires owners to mark the sides of their ships with a visible loadline which becomes known as the Plimsoll line.

– The Russian anarchist Mikhail Bakunin organizes a secret revolutionary society, Land and Liberty.

MIDDLE EAST AND NORTH AFRICA

29 May Abdul-Aziz, sultan of the Ottoman (Turkish) empire, is deposed and dies four days later, probably by suicide. His nephew, Murad V, reigns for only three months and is declared insane and also deposed (31 Aug.). He is succeeded as sultan by his brother, Abdul Hamid II, who will occupy the throne until 1909.

23 Dec. The liberal-minded Ottoman grand vizier (prime minister) Midhat Pasha declares a new Turkish constitution providing for a parliamentary form of government along with freedom of the press and freedom of conscience; it is ignored by the new sultan.

– The Ethiopians are defeated in the war with Egypt that began in 1875.

ASIA

26 Feb. Japan recognizes Korea as independent of China in a treaty that designates three Korean ports open to Korean–Japanese trade.

– Drought affects the wheat fields of Shanxi province in NE China and the Deccan plateau in N India. In one of the great famines of the modern world almost 10 million people will die in N China and 5 million in India over the next three years.

THE AMERICAS

May Porfirio José de la Cruz Díaz leads an unsuccessful rebellion against the rule of President Sebastián Lerdo de Tejada of Mexico and flees to the USA; he returns (Nov.), defeats the government army at Tecoac and assumes power, setting the country on a new course that encourages economic development, public work projects and political stability.

25 June At the battle of the Little Bighorn, Sioux–Cheyenne forces led by Sitting Bull and Crazy Horse annihilate a 264-man detachment of the US 7th Cavalry led by Lt. Col. George Armstrong Custer.

1 Aug. Colorado becomes the 38th US state.

2 Aug. James Butler 'Wild Bill' Hickok, a US marshal, is murdered during a poker game in a saloon in Deadwood, Dakota territory.

Nov. The US presidential election ends in a dispute over 20 contested votes in the electoral college, enough to give either the Democratic candidate, Samuel Jones Tilden, or the Republican, Rutherford Birchard Hayes, the winning number (see 29 Jan. 1877).

– Apache leader Goyathlay, known to Americans as Geronimo, resists the confinement of his people on reservations and begins a ten-year campaign against white settlers in the SW USA.

ECONOMY AND SOCIETY

2 Feb. The US national baseball league is founded.

– A bequest from Johns Hopkins founds the university that bears his name in Baltimore, Maryland, USA.

– Russian revolutionary Mikhail Bakunin dies in exile in Berne, Switzerland. As the leading European anarchist of his time, Bakunin's influence will continue long after his death.

– The International Association for the Exploration and Civilization of Africa is established with Leopold II, king of the Belgians, as its patron; he will use it to exploit the riches of the Congo basin, Equatorial W Africa.

– The Scottish-Irish grocer Thomas Johnstone Lipton establishes his first shop in Glasgow, the start of an international chain of stores and related businesses that make him a millionaire by the age of 29.

– The *Corriere della sera* is established in Milan and will become Italy's major national daily newspaper.

SCIENCE AND TECHNOLOGY

3 Mar. In the USA Alexander Graham Bell is granted a patent for the telephone he has invented. The Western Union telegraph company retains Thomas Alva Edison to improve on Bell's invention.

– Compagnie Internationale des Wagons-Lits et des Grandes Express Européens is established to bring sleeping cars from America and operate them on European railways.

– US doctor John Kellogg starts to run the Western Health Reform Institute in Michigan, USA, and develops a range of dried cereals as healthy vegetarian foods.

ARTS AND HUMANITIES

Literature

– Melvil Dewey, librarian of Amherst College, Massachusetts, establishes the Dewey decimal system of cataloguing library books.

– Henrik Ibsen's play *Peer Gynt* (1867) receives its first performance with incidental music composed by his Norwegian compatriot Edvard Grieg.

George Eliot (Mary Ann Evans), *Daniel Deronda*, novel.

Henry James, *Roderick Hudson*, novel.

Stéphane Mallarmé, *L'Après-midi d'un faune* (The Afternoon of a Faun), poetry.

Mark Twain (Samuel Langhorne Clemens), *The Adventures of Tom Sawyer*, novel.

Visual Arts and Architecture

– Central Park in New York, opened in 1858, is completed.

Pierre-Auguste Renoir, *Au moulin de la galette*, painting.

Music

8 April First performance at La Scala, Milan, of Amilcare Ponchielli's opera *La Gioconda* (The Joyful Girl).

13 Aug. German composer Richard Wagner's (see p. 421) Festspielhaus in Bayreuth, Bavaria, hosts the first complete performance of his cycle of operas, *Der Ring des Nibelungen* (The Ring of the Nibelung). The Bayreuth festival begins with

performances of *Das Rheingold* (The Rhine Gold, 1869), *Die Walküre* (The Valkyrie, 1870), *Siegfried* (1872) and *Die Götterdämmerung* (The Twilight of the Gods, 1876). The performance is part of the politics of the new German national identity and is attended by the Kaiser as well as by the philosopher Friedrich Nietzsche (see p. 437), who at this time remains a supporter and theorist of Wagner's aesthetic.

7 Nov. First performance in Prague of Bedřich Smetana's opera *Hubička* (The Kiss).

Johannes Brahms, Symphony No. 1 in C minor.

Anton Bruckner, Symphony No. 5 in B flat major.

César Franck, *Les Eolides*, symphonic poem based on a poem by Leconte de Lisle.

1877

EUROPE

20 Jan. At the Constantinople conference the great powers are unable to bring about a Russian–Turkish accord.

24 April Russia declares war on Turkey in support of European Slavs suffering under Ottoman (Turkish) rule. Britain threatens war with Russia (21 July) if Constantinople is occupied. When the N Bulgarian city of Pleven is occupied by the Russians after a lengthy siege (10 Dec.) Turkey appeals to the European powers to mediate.

16 May In France President MacMahon forces the resignation of the prime minister, Jules Simon, in the crisis of *seize Mai*. He regards Simon as half-hearted in his opposition to the anti-clericalism that is now politically powerful in France's Third Republic. There are increasing fears of a return to the tradition of autocratic militarist rule, but French republicanism reasserts itself.

– Charles Bradlaugh and Annie Besant are put on trial in London because they have republished Charles Knowlton's tract *The Fruits of Philosophy* (1832), which advocates contraception. They are acquitted, and the ban on distributing information on contraception ends. The trial is a landmark in the history of freedom of speech in Britain.

– The Italian government makes state education compulsory from the ages of six to nine, but the law is widely disregarded.

MIDDLE EAST AND NORTH AFRICA

– The liberal Ottoman grand vizier Midhat Pasha is dismissed by sultan Abdul Hamid II.

ASIA

1 Jan. In a formal durbar (state reception) held in Delhi, N India, Queen Victoria is proclaimed (in her absence) empress of India as princely rulers gather to pay homage.

Jan. The Satsuma rebellion begins in Japan: samurai warriors, denied their pensions and forbidden their traditional right to wear two swords, react against the modernizing rule of the Meiji emperor. The new post-feudal order shows its strength when the modern national army crushes the reactionaries (Sept.).

THE AMERICAS

29 Jan. An electoral commission, consisting of eight Republicans and seven Democrats, is appointed to decide the result of the US presidential election (see Nov. 1876).

2 Mar. The US Congress awards the 20 disputed electoral college votes in the presidential election to Republican Rutherford B. Hayes, who thereby defeats Democrat contender Samuel Jones Tilden and becomes 19th US president (4 Mar.).

2 May Porfirio Díaz (see May 1876) becomes president of Mexico. He will rule the country with a dictatorial grip for most of the period up to 1911.

21 June Eleven members of the Molly Maguires, a secret Irish–American coalminers' organization, are hanged after ten years of criminal activity in Pennsylvania mining towns. (The organization has been infiltrated by agents of the Pinkerton detective agency.)

July Anti-Chinese riots start in San Francisco, California, and continue for several months.

Oct. The Nez Perce people in the NW of the USA surrender following a federal campaign to remove them from their lands.

– The Argentinian meat trade develops as the first cargo of beef leaves the country bound for France in a refrigerated ship.

– John D. Rockefeller's firm Standard Oil shows the power gained by monopolies and cartels in the US economy as it struggles with a major depression. Rockefeller signs a contract with the Pennsylvania railroad, which gives his company lower freight rates, allowing him to buy up his rivals in the oil industry.

SUB-SAHARAN AFRICA

12 April Britain annexes the South African Republic established by the Afrikaners, violating the 1852 Sand River Convention, which recognized the independence of the Transvaal. The British are trying to bring the Boers under imperial control.

AUSTRALASIA AND OCEANIA

20 Aug. Arthur Kennedy, governor of Queensland in Australia, authorizes a dramatic reduction in the number of Chinese immigrants allowed into the state.

ECONOMY AND SOCIETY

15–19 Mar. In the first cricket test match, Australia defeats England by 45 runs in Melbourne, Australia.

9–19 July The first Lawn Tennis Championships are played at Wimbledon, SW London, organized by the All England Croquet Club (see 1868).

6 Dec. The *Washington Post* newspaper is founded and runs a campaign against the newly elected US president Rutherford Hayes as an illegitimately appointed politician (see above).

SCIENCE AND TECHNOLOGY

29 Nov. US inventor Thomas Alva Edison demonstrates a phonograph or speaking machine, which records sounds on grooved metal cylinders. He patents the machine on 6 Dec.

– Louis-Paul Cailletet, French physicist, is working on the liquefaction of oxygen and nitrogen.

– Wilhelm Pfeffer, German botanist, outlines the theory of osmosis.

ARTS AND HUMANITIES

Literature

Gustave Flaubert, *Trois Contes* (Three Tales).

Henry James, *The American*, novel.

Anna Sewell, *Black Beauty: The Autobiography of a Horse*, novel that becomes a children's classic.

Count Leo Tolstoy (see box), *Anna Karenina*, novel.

Visual Arts and Architecture

31 Dec. French painter Gustave Courbet dies in exile in Vevey, Switzerland.

Edouard Manet, *Nana*, painting.

Music

4 Mar. First performance in Moscow of Pyotr Tchaikovsky's ballet *Swan Lake*.

2 Dec. First performance in Weimar, Germany, of Camille Saint-Saëns's opera *Samson et Dalila*.

Johannes Brahms, Symphony No. 2 in D major.

Count Leo Tolstoy (1828–1910)

Perhaps the greatest of Russian writers, Tolstoy was born on his family's estate of Yasnaya Polyana in central Russia. After seeing active service in the Crimean War, he settled in the early 1860s on his estate, combining work as a landlord with work on his two most celebrated novels *War and Peace* (1864–9) and *Anna Karenina* (1873–7). *Anna Karenina* is the tragic story of an adulteress, while *War and Peace* has a more epic sweep, examining the lives of three families of aristocrats at the time of Napoleon's invasion of Russia. Against this broad canvas, Tolstoy portrays particular characters with an eye for those details that reveal a greater truth. *War and Peace* is a historical novel that addresses the meaning of history itself, and in which the author combines both his faith and his scepticism: at one point Prince Andrei Bolkonsky, wounded at the battle of Austerlitz, wonders whether or not to pray, and concludes that 'Nothing is certain except the nothingess of everything I can conceive, and the majesty of something I cannot understand.'

After the publication of *Anna Karenina* Tolstoy scorned the claims of art and became preoccupied with ethical and moral questions. He rejected the Russian state and Orthodox Church as false authorities, denounced private property and raged against sexual desire. He even turned against his own earlier writings, declaring them worthless. Adopting a form of Christian anarchism, he rejected the idea that conversion could come through divine revelation and emphasized instead that it could only be the result of a self-examination that then led to political and social change. He attempted to put his teachings into practice, and in his own life time became a figure of great moral authority.

1878

EUROPE

9 Jan. The first king of unified Italy, Victor Emmanuel II, dies and is succeeded by his son as Umberto I.

9 Jan. The Turks are losing the Russo-Turkish War and request an armistice. Russian forces capture the strategic city of Adrianople (modern Edirne) in European Turkey, NW of Constantinople (20 Jan.). An armistice is agreed (31 Jan.) and by the treaty of San Stefano (5 Mar.) Romania, Montenegro and Serbia are granted independence; reforms are promised in the Ottoman (Turkish) administration of Bosnia and Herzegovina; and Bulgarian autonomy is guaranteed. The peace treaty is rejected by Britain, Germany, Austria and Italy. Britain agrees to support the Ottomans against further Russian attack in a secret treaty (4 June) and is allowed to occupy the strategic E Mediterranean island of Cyprus as a secure base of operations.

23 Jan. A trial of Russian revolutionaries ends with the acquittal of most of the accused, but many are re-arrested and sent to Siberian prison camps. Vera Zasulich has shot and wounded Gen. Trepov, the chief of police in St Petersburg (Jan.); the jury decides that this is a legitimate form of political protest and she goes into exile, joining the circle of Karl Marx. Political terrorism becomes a strategy of opposition to tsarist autocracy.

June–July The Congress of Berlin meets and the European powers carve up the Ottoman empire following its defeat by Russia; the German chancellor Bismarck and British prime minister Benjamin Disraeli are the chief arbiters. The independence of Romania, Serbia and Montenegro is confirmed; Bulgaria is divided into three parts: an autonomous Bulgaria N of the Balkans, an Ottoman province of Eastern Rumelia to the S (under a Christian governor) and Macedonia to the SW; Austria is allowed to occupy Bosnia and Herzegovina; Russia gains territory in Bessarabia and the Caucasus; and Britain gains Cyprus. This classic exercise in *ancien régime* diplomacy, dividing national communities to suit the purposes of established great powers, enrages the pan-Slavic movement, including Russia.

– The N Adriatic city of Trieste and the S Tyrol, parts of Austria, now become the focus of Italian nationalists who want to incorporate them into the united Italian kingdom.

In Europe we were hangers-on … but in Asia we are masters.

Fyodor Dostoyevsky's view of Russia's destiny in *Geok Teppe* (1881)

ASIA

– The Second Anglo-Afghan War begins over the pro-Russian sentiment evident at the emir's court in Kabul and the emir's refusal to receive a British representative there.

THE AMERICAS

28 Feb. The US Congress makes the silver dollar legal tender and reduces the number of dollar notes in circulation (31 May).

– Bolivia and Chile come close to war after Bolivia increases the export tax on nitrates being mined by the Chilean Nitrate Company. Nitrates have become essential to the global trade in armaments and as fertilizer.

ECONOMY AND SOCIETY

7 Feb. Pope Pius IX dies. He is succeeded by Gioacchino Vincenzo Pecci, who becomes Pope Leo XIII (20 Feb.).

12 Dec. The *St Louis Dispatch* newspaper begins publication; it is bought shortly afterwards by the Hungarian-American Joseph Pulitzer, who merges the paper with the *St Louis Post* to create the *Post-Dispatch*, the start of his newspaper empire.

– The world's first birth-control clinic is opened in Amsterdam by the Dutch suffragette Aletta Jacobs.

– In Britain the evangelical William Booth develops the Christian Mission (see 1865) into the Salvation Army, which will spread throughout the world.

SCIENCE AND TECHNOLOGY

15 Oct. Thomas Alva Edison establishes the Edison Electric Light Company in the USA.

– The Procter and Gamble Company in Cincinnati, USA, have created a hard, white soap. It will be named Ivory Soap (1882).

– In the USA the Remington Arms Company improves the Remington typewriter (see 1868) by adding a shift-key system that employs upper and lower case lettering on the same bar.

ARTS AND HUMANITIES

Literature

Theodor Fontane, *Vor dem Sturm* (Before the Storm), novel.
Thomas Hardy, *The Return of the Native*, novel.
Henry James, *The Europeans*, novel.

Visual Arts and Architecture

– An Egyptian obelisk (Cleopatra's Needle), originally built at Heliopolis in Egypt in the 15th century BC, is taken to England and erected on London's Victoria Embankment. A second obelisk from the same source will be erected in New York's Central Park in 1881.

– Louis Comfort Tiffany, son of the jeweller Charles Louis Tiffany, starts a factory in New York that becomes celebrated for the production of coloured glass items in the Art Nouveau style.

Edgar Degas, *Rehearsal on the Stage*, painting.
Pierre-Auguste Renoir, *Madame Charpentier and her Children*, painting.

Music

25 May First performance in London of Arthur Sullivan's operetta *HMS Pinafore*, to a libretto by W.S. Gilbert.
Johannes Brahms, Violin Concerto in D major.
Antonín Dvořák, *Slavonic Dances*, piano duet.
Pyotr Tchaikovsky, Symphony No. 4 in F minor.

1879

EUROPE

5 Jan. French republicans gain seats in the elections for the Senate but the parliamentary majority, including President MacMahon, remains predominantly royalist in its sympathies. With the decline of royalist support, however, his position becomes untenable, and he resigns (30 Jan.), to be succeeded as president by the conservative republican François-Paul-Jules Grévy.

7 Oct. Bismarck signs an Austro-German alliance promising mutual support in the event of either country being attacked by Russia. The treaty is periodically reviewed but will continue until 1918.

24 Nov.–9 Dec. In his famous Midlothian campaign (to win the Edinburghshire parliamentary seat) the Liberal statesman William Ewart Gladstone makes a series of speeches attacking the imperial and domestic policies of Disraeli's Conservative government.

28 Dec. In E Scotland the Firth of Tay railway bridge collapses as a train is crossing it, causing some 300 deaths.

– Michael Davitt founds the Irish Land League, a peasants' rights organization that fights against tenant evictions.

– Germany's agriculture is in a grave state and its industry has remained depressed since 1873, causing the government to adopt protectionist policies.

– In Russia the People's Will, a terrorist organization, is founded.

– Ireland's staple potato crop fails again.

MIDDLE EAST AND NORTH AFRICA

25 June After a rule marked by waste and extravagance, Ismail Pasha, khedive of Egypt, is deposed by the suzerain authority of the Ottoman (Turkish) sultan with the support of the European powers. He is replaced by Tewfiq Pasha.

ASIA

Feb. After the death of Shir Ali, emir of Afghanistan, his son Mohammed Yakub is forced by the British to accept the treaty of Gandamak (26 May), which brings to an end the Second Anglo-Afghan War (see 1878). The treaty allows Britain to occupy the Khyber Pass, close to the border with NW India; in return the British pay an annual subvention to the emir. The Afghans rebel (3 Sept.) and massacre the British legation at Kabul. British troops take Kabul (12 Oct.), and Yakub is forced to abdicate (19 Oct.), being succeeded by his cousin Abdul-Rahman, whose diplomacy balances Russian and British influence.

– India's harvest fails and much of the crop is eaten by starving rats.

THE AMERICAS

14 Feb. The War of the Pacific begins as Bolivia clashes with Chile over control of the Bolivian nitrate-producing territories; Chilean troops occupy Bolivia's coastal province.

6 Nov. Canadians observe their first Thanksgiving Day, which will later be moved to a Monday in October (1931).

– In the USA African-American cowboys begin to appear, especially in Kansas. This is partly a reflection of the growing limitations placed on the rights of former slaves in the states of the old Confederacy, which is encouraging many African-Americans to leave for more liberal states.

– The city of New York has now expanded within 12 months from 67th Street to 129th Street.

– The US agricultural economy booms because of widespread crop failures in Europe.

SUB-SAHARAN AFRICA

Jan. In S Africa British troops under Frederic Thesiger, Lord Chelmsford, are ordered to advance and defeat Cetewayo's Zulu forces, which are menacing the Transvaal (annexed by Britain in 1877). The Zulus make a surprise attack at Isandhlwana (22 Jan.), destroying one column of the British expeditionary force of 1600 men, but at Rorke's Drift an outpost of 140 soldiers under Lt. John Chard and Lt. Gomville Bromhead holds off more than 4000 Zulu warriors. After the arrival of 10,000 reinforcements (using the devastating breech-loading rifle) under Gen. Sir Garnet Wolseley the Zulus are defeated and King Cetewayo is captured at Ulundi (28 Aug.). Zululand is divided into 13 separate chiefdoms, which will all eventually be incorporated into Natal.

ECONOMY AND SOCIETY

– Trading in futures begins on the Chicago Board of Trade: crops of wheat are bought and sold for delivery at specified future dates, protecting producers from fluctuating prices.

– In his seminal work *Progress and Poverty* the American economist Henry George highlights the growing gap between the American poor and the American rich. George claims that land ownership is a form of monopoly and should therefore be taxed, whereas industry should be freed from taxes.

– Radcliffe College is founded with classes specifically for women at Cambridge, Massachusetts, USA.

– Mary Baker Eddy, US founder of the Christian Scientists, organizes in Boston the first Church of Christ, Scientist.

– Le Train Bleu starts its career as a luxury sleeper express service between Calais and Rome via Nice in the S of France.

– Low-price shopping develops in the USA following the success of the store opened by Frank Winfield Woolworth where all goods cost 5 cents.

– Milk bottles are now used to deliver milk in Brooklyn, New York.

SCIENCE AND TECHNOLOGY

21 Oct. Thomas Alva Edison invents an incandescent vacuum electric light bulb in the USA, and Sir Joseph Swan demonstrates his carbon filament light bulb in Newcastle upon Tyne, NE England (5 Feb.). Investors rush to put money into the Edison Electric Light Company as the prospect of cheap electricity becomes a possibility.

– In France bacteriologist Louis Pasteur finds that chickens infected with weakened cholera bacteria become immune to the usual form of the disease. Vaccines will develop from his discovery.

– German doctor Albert Neisser discovers the bacterium *Neisseria gonorrhoea,* which transmits the venereal disease gonorrhoea.

– The idea of conditioned reflexes gains in popularity following the experiments conducted on dogs by the Russian physiologist Ivan Pavlov. Pavlov shows that dogs salivate in the expectation of food. Pavlov's work will influence behavourial theory.

– The multiple telephone switchboard invented by Leroy B. Firman increases the number of US telephone subscribers, which jumps from 50,000 in 1880 to 250,000 in ten years.

– The last of the great bison herds of the S USA is exterminated by hunters at Buffalo Springs, Texas.

ARTS AND HUMANITIES

Literature

George Washington Cable, *Old Creole Days,* collection of stories reflecting the Creole society of Louisiana in the S USA.

Kate Greenaway, *Under the Window,* collection of rhymes with pictures for children.

Henrik Ibsen, *Et Dukkehjem* (A Doll's House), play.

Henry James, *Daisy Miller,* novel.

George Meredith, *The Egoist,* novel.

Visual Arts and Architecture

11 Feb. French painter and caricaturist Honoré Daumier dies.

– The New York architectural practice of McKim, Mead and White is established and goes on to design the Century, Harvard and University Clubs in Manhattan.

– The Cathedral of St Stephen in Limoges, C France, is finished after 603 years' work.

– St Patrick's Cathedral, New York, designed in the Gothic Revival style, is completed.

Music

29 Mar. First performance in Moscow of Pyotr Tchaikovsky's opera *Eugene Onegin,* which is based on Alexander Pushkin's verse novel of the same name (1823).

30 Dec. First performance in Paignton, Devon, England, of Arthur Sullivan's operetta *The Pirates of Penzance, or The Slave of Duty,* to a libretto by W.S. Gilbert.

Bedřich Smetana, *Má vlast* (My Fatherland), cycle of symphonic poems.

1880

EUROPE

8 Mar. The Conservatives lose the British general election: Benjamin Disraeli resigns as prime minister (18 April), and the Liberal William Ewart Gladstone becomes prime minister for a second time.

13 Sept. In Britain Parliament passes the Employers' Liability Act giving compensation to workers who have been injured at work.

– Tenant farmers refuse to harvest crops on Lord Erne's estates in Co. Mayo, Ireland, when Lord Erne's land agent, former British soldier Charles Cunningham Boycott, refuses to accept rents at lower levels fixed by tenants. This new campaign, involving the social and economic excommunication of landowners and their

agents, is organized by the Irish National Land League led by Charles Stewart Parnell as a protest against the iniquities of landlordism. Boycott is one of the first victims, and the word 'boycott' enters the English language.

MIDDLE EAST AND NORTH AFRICA

3 July Following Spanish aggression in N Africa, Morocco's independence is universally recognized by the terms of the Madrid convention.

THE AMERICAS

2 Nov. In the US presidential election the Republican candidate James A. Garfield defeats the Democratic challenger Winfield S. Hancock.

17 Nov. China and America agree on a Chinese Exclusion treaty giving the USA the right to refuse entry to Chinese immigrant workers to help limit their number (see 1882).

– The USA now has 100 millionaires; in 1840 there were fewer than 20.

SUB-SAHARAN AFRICA

30 Dec. Stephanus Johannes Paulus Kruger, nicknamed Oom Paul (Uncle Paul), proclaims the renewed independence of the Transvaal Boer Republic, annexed to Cape Colony by Britain in 1877.

– The Italian-French explorer and colonial administrator Pierre de Brazza establishes French Equatorial Africa as a protectorate and founds Brazzaville (now capital of the Republic of the Congo).

– In S Africa the Britons Cecil Rhodes and Alfred Beit found the De Beers Mining Corporation, which will eventually gain a monopoly in the S African diamond industry.

AUSTRALASIA AND OCEANIA

11 Nov. Ned (Edward) Kelly, Australian criminal, is hanged at Melbourne, Victoria. He has robbed banks in Victoria and New South Wales and, wearing his trademark body armour, fought police killing three constables.

– The Tahiti archipelago in French Polynesia, S Pacific, is annexed by France.

ECONOMY AND SOCIETY

– Rev. John Hartley wins the Wimbledon lawn tennis championships for the second time.

– Table tennis is invented by the Englishman James Gibb.

– The University of Southern California is founded in Los Angeles.

– Owens College is reorganized and becomes the University of Manchester, NW England.

– The world's first ice hockey club is formed at McGill University, Montreal, Canada.

SCIENCE AND TECHNOLOGY

15 Jan. The first British telephone directory is issued by the London Telephone Company. It contains 255 names.

3 June Alexander Graham Bell transmits the first wireless telephone message.

- The German scientists Karl Eberth and Robert Koch, working independently, discover the bacillus that causes typhoid fever. Koch also discovers a vaccine against anthrax.
- In the USA Thomas Alva Edison obtains a patent for his incandescent electric light bulb.
- French doctor Charles Laveran, working in Algeria, attributes malaria to a blood parasite.

ARTS AND HUMANITIES

Literature

8 May The French novelist Gustave Flaubert dies.

Henry Brooks Adams, *Democracy: An American Novel*.

Fyodor Dostoyevsky (see box), *The Brothers Karamazov*, novel.

Guy de Maupassant, *Boule de suif* (Ball of Fat), short story set in the Franco-Prussian War.

Mark Twain, *A Tramp Abroad*, travel sketches.

Lewis Wallace, *Ben-Hur, A Tale of the Christ*, historical novel.

Emile Zola, *Nana*, novel. It is part of Zola's ambitious cycle of *Rougon-Macquart* novels, which the novelist described as the 'natural and social history of a family under the Second Empire'.

Visual Arts and Architecture

4 Mar. The *New York Daily Graphic* becomes the first newspaper to incorporate a photographic reproduction.

Fyodor Dostoyevsky (1821–81)

The Russian writer Fyodor Dostoyevsky was born in Moscow, and was orphaned as a boy after the death of his mother and the murder of his father by rebellious peasants on the family estates. Dostoyevsky achieved early literary success, but in 1849 he was arrested and sent to Siberia for six years for taking part in an anti-government plot. After his release he left Russia to travel in England, France, Germany and Italy, and became convinced that Russia's spiritual greatness was founded on the fact that it was a Slavic civilization distinct from Western Europe. His novels *Crime and Punishment* (1866) and *The Brothers Karamazov* (1880) are imbued with this belief. They also exemplify two other great Russian literary themes: the inability of the law to capture the essence of the human soul, and the special grace that is accorded the sinner who rebels against God and then repents.

Dostoyevsky's novels reflect the Russian Tsarist state of his time, an era of violent terrorist attacks that led Dostoyevsky to comment, 'Everything is abnormal in our society.' As a writer he was drawn towards the portrayal of extreme moral positions, the pursuit of absolutes, and reckless adventurism heedless of consequences. The anti-hero, a figure who delights in rejecting social norms and who defines himself in terms of his opposition to society, is a Dostoyevskian archetype. Dostoyevsky was the first major literary artist to react against European liberalism on the grounds of its supposed shallowness. In asserting that civilization itself had become a form of corruption, Dostoyevsky contributed to a continent-wide unease in the late 19th century.

- After 634 years of work Cologne Cathedral in W Germany is completed. The twin spires, 157m (515 feet) high, will be the tallest structures in the world until 1889.

Arnold Böcklin, *Island of the Dead*, painting.

Music

24 June The national anthem 'Oh, Canada' is sung for the first time. The music is by Calixa Lavallée, the words (in French) are by Adolphe Routhier. Robert Weir will write the English lyrics in 1908.

Johannes Brahms, *Akademische Fest-Ouvertüre* (Academic Festival Overture) and *Tragische Ouvertüre* (Tragic Overture).

Antonín Dvořák, Symphony No. 6 in D major.

Pyotr Tchaikovsky, Piano Concerto No. 2 in G, Serenade in C major for strings and orchestra and *1812* Overture.

1881

EUROPE

13 Mar. Alexander II, tsar of Russia since 1855, is assassinated in St Petersburg. Sophia Perovskaya, head of a group of nihilistic revolutionaries, has organized the bomb attack. Alexander's son succeeds as Alexander III and makes Jews the scapegoats for his father's death. A series of pogroms (massacres) follows, which will cause millions of Russian Jews to emigrate.

19 April The British statesman Lord Beaconsfield (Benjamin Disraeli) dies. Robert Cecil, Lord Salisbury, becomes Conservative leader in the British House of Lords.

18 June The *Dreikaiserbund* (Three Emperors' League) is signed. Initiated by Bismarck, it is an informal agreement between Germany, Austria-Hungary and Russia.

28 June Following independence from Turkey, Serbia enters a secret alliance with the Austro-Hungarian empire.

16 Aug. The British prime minister W.E. Gladstone's reforming Irish Land Act sets up a tribunal to look at excessive rents.

13 Oct. Charles Stewart Parnell, Irish patriot and head of the Home Rule movement, is imprisoned by the British government for land agitation and the 'boycott' campaign against unpopular and absentee landlords (see 1880). Glamorized by his incarceration, Parnell becomes even more effective in appealing to tenant farmers to withhold their rents.

MIDDLE EAST AND NORTH AFRICA

12 May Tunisia becomes a French protectorate.

9 Sept. In Egypt the war minister Arabi Pasha leads a nationalist rebellion.

ASIA

- Political parties are founded in rapidly modernizing Japan.

THE AMERICAS

4 Mar. James A. Garfield takes office as 20th US president.

May William H. Bonney, the 21-year-old US outlaw known as Billy the Kid, escapes while on a murder charge. He is shot dead in New Mexico (15 July) by sheriff Pat Garrett. In death the New York-born Bonney becomes an American anti-hero, and to satisfy popular interest *The True Life of Billy the Kid* is written a few weeks after his death.

2 July President James Garfield of the USA is fatally wounded at Washington, D.C., railway station by an unsuccessful candidate for a government job, Charles J. Guiteau. Garfield dies (19 Sept.) and is succeeded by Vice-President Chester Alan Arthur (20 Sept.), who becomes 21st US president.

SUB-SAHARAN AFRICA

28 Jan. Following their unilateral declaration of independence (1880), Afrikaners in the Transvaal defeat British forces at Laing's Nek and Majuba Hill (27 Feb.) in the First South African (Boer) War. The treaty of Pretoria (5 April) grants self-government to the South African Republic of the Transvaal, which remains subject to British suzerainty.

ECONOMY AND SOCIETY

– Joseph Wharton, owner of a Philadelphia USA nickel mine, endows the Wharton School of Finance and Commerce at the University of Pennsylvania.

– The *London Evening News* starts publication.

– London's Savoy Theatre opens and becomes the first public building in the capital to have electric lighting.

– The first US lawn tennis championships are held at Newport, Rhode Island.

SCIENCE AND TECHNOLOGY

11 Oct. The American inventor David Henderson Houston patents photographic roll film.

– The steamship *Servia* of the British Cunard company enters service as the first ocean liner built of steel.

– Prussian-born US physicist Albert Abraham Michelson experiments on the speed of light and paves the way for Einstein's theory of relativity.

– US army doctor George Sternberg identifies the bacterium that causes pneumonia.

– In Venice, NE Italy, the motorized vaporetto begins largely to replace the traditional man-powered gondola.

ARTS AND HUMANITIES

Literature

Gustave Flaubert, *Bouvard et Pécuchet*, unfinished novel, published posthumously.

Anatole France, *Le Crime de Sylvestre Bonnard* (The Crime of Sylvestre Bonnard), novel.

Joel Chandler Harris, *Uncle Remus, his Songs and Sayings*, fiction. First in the 'Uncle Remus' series, which develops in literary form the black dialect the author hears on the Georgia plantations.

Henry James, *Portrait of a Lady* and *Washington Square*, novels.

Guy de Maupassant, *La Maison Tellier* (The Tellier House), short stories.

Johanna Spyri, *Heidi*, children's novel.

Visual Arts and Architecture

Claude Monet, *Sunshine and Snow*, painting.

Pierre-Auguste Renoir, *Luncheon of the Boating Party*, painting.

Music

10 Feb. First performance in Paris of Jacques Offenbach's opera *Les Contes d'Hoffmann* (The Tales of Hoffmann).

25 April First performance in London of Arthur Sullivan's operetta *Patience, or Bunthorne's Bride* to a libretto by W.S. Gilbert.

– In the USA the Boston Symphony Orchestra is founded.

– Actress and noted beauty Lillie Langtry, known as the Jersey Lily, makes her London stage debut.

Johannes Brahms, Piano Concerto No. 2 in B flat major.

Max Bruch, *Kol Nidrei* (All Vows), for cello and orchestra.

Anton Bruckner, Symphony No. 6 in A major.

Franz Liszt, Mephisto Waltz No. 2, orchestral work that he also transcribes for piano.

1882

EUROPE

2 May Irish politician Charles Stewart Parnell is released from prison in Dublin having agreed, together with his colleagues, to end the 'boycott' campaign (see 1880). By the Kilmainham treaty Parnell agrees to work to reduce unrest in Ireland in return for British government concessions on rent arrears owed by Irish tenants.

No man has a right to fix a boundary to the march of a nation.

Charles Stewart Parnell, 21 Jan. 1885

6 May Lord Frederick Cavendish, recently appointed chief secretary for Ireland, and his senior civil servant, Thomas Burke, are murdered by Fenians in Phoenix Park, Dublin.

20 May Germany, Austria and Italy form the Triple Alliance, pledging mutual support in the event of a French attack on any of its members during the next five years.

– In Britain Richard Marsden Pankhurst's campaign results in the Married Women's Property Act, allowing women to retain rights to their own property in marriage. His widow Emmeline will take up the cause of female suffrage after his death.

MIDDLE EAST AND NORTH AFRICA

11 July British concern about the strategic Suez Canal following anti-European riots in Egypt leads to the bombardment of Alexandria, on the Mediterranean coast, by ships of the Royal Navy, and British troops land at Ismailia in the canal area. The rebel nationalist Egyptian army under Arabi Pasha is defeated at the battle of Tel el-Kebir (13 Sept.); the British occupy Cairo (15 Sept.), ending the joint Anglo-French arrangements for the administration of Egypt (9 Nov.), established following the country's bankruptcy in 1876.

ASIA

25 April French forces seeking the colonial control of Indochina occupy Hanoi in Tonkin (now N Vietnam); widespread rebellion follows.

THE AMERICAS

3 April In the USA the outlaw Jesse James, who has been on the run since 1876, is shot by his cousin Robert Ford, who seeks the reward for his killing.

5 Sept. New York holds its first Labor Day parade.

– Federal Trust law is now exploited by American corporations to avoid state law, allowing John Davison Rockefeller to incorporate the Standard Oil Trust, which brings over 95% of the US petroleum industry under his control.

– The US Congress passes the first law restricting immigration; convicts and paupers are excluded, and a head tax is imposed on immigrants. The Chinese Exclusion Act excludes Chinese labourers for the next ten years.

SUB-SAHARAN AFRICA

May France establishes a protectorate in NW Madagascar and blockades the island to enforce its claim.

– Paul Kruger becomes president of the South African Republic of the Transvaal.

– The International Association of the Congo is created, an organization whose aim is the economic exploitation of the region.

– Italy seizes the port of Assab on the coast of N Ethiopia, the focus of the future colony of Eritrea (1890).

ECONOMY AND SOCIETY

2 Sept. Following the English cricket team's defeat by Australia at the Oval (29 Aug.), a notice lamenting the 'death' of English cricket appears in the *Sporting Times,* suggesting that the body be cremated and taken to Australia. When the English cricket team tours Australia in 1882–3 it is duly presented with an urn containing the ashes of a set of stumps. The contest for the 'Ashes' becomes the most hotly contested fixture in international cricket.

SCIENCE AND TECHNOLOGY

12 Jan. Street lights are introduced to new areas of London and are now generated by the Edison Electric Light Company. The Electric Light Act passed by Parliament requires local authorities to take over the privately run power companies after 21 years; the return on their investment is threatened, and the growth of power companies stalls. The Edison Illuminating Company starts to light New York offices (4 Sept.).

20 May The first railway through the Alps has been constructed via the St Gotthard tunnel, connecting Switzerland and Italy.

– Josef Breuer, Viennese doctor, uses hypnosis to cure hysteria. He also uses memory of past episodes to relieve present distress and becomes, with his friend Sigmund Freud (see p. 459), to whom he describes his experiments, a pioneer of psychoanalysis.

– German bacteriologist Robert Koch discovers the tuberculosis bacillus and shows that the disease is communicable.

ARTS AND HUMANITIES

Literature

Jan. Irish writer and wit Oscar Wilde arrives in New York for a US lecture tour.

– Henrik Ibsen's *Gengangere* (Ghosts) is performed for the first time in Oslo, Norway. Its frank exploration of the effects of inherited syphilis on a family will cause outrage.

Carlo Lorenzini (Carlo Collodi), *Le avventure di Pinocchio: Storia di un burattino* (The Adventures of Pinocchio: The Story of a Puppet), children's story.

Victorien Sardou, *Fédora,* play, a vehicle for French actress Sarah Bernhardt, who also popularizes the type of hat.

Visual Arts and Architecture

10 April British poet and Pre-Raphaelite painter Dante Gabriel Rossetti dies, a victim of addiction to the sleep-inducing drug chloral hydrate.

Paul Cézanne, *Self-portrait*, painting.

Edouard Manet, *Bar at the Folies-Bergère*, painting.

Music

26 July First performance at Bayreuth of Richard Wagner's (see p. 421) sacred festival drama *Parsifal.*

25 Nov. First performance at the Savoy Theatre, London, of Arthur Sullivan's opera *Iolanthe, or the Peer and the Peri* to a libretto by W.S. Gilbert.

1883

EUROPE

May In Germany a Sickness Insurance Law is passed: workers pay two-thirds of the insurance scheme and employers one-third.

MIDDLE EAST AND NORTH AFRICA

8 June By the terms of the treaty of Marsa with the bey of Tunis, the French gain control of Tunisia.

– Islamic nationalist Muhammad Ahmed ibn sa-Sayyid Abdallah of Dongola, Nilotic Sudan, declares himself to be the Mahdi (Arabic: divinely guided one) and leads a campaign against Anglo-Egyptian control of the Sudan. An Egyptian army under the British general William Hicks is defeated at the battle of El Obeid (5 Nov.); the Mahdi now controls the Sudanese province of Kordofan.

– Sir Evelyn Baring is appointed consul general at Cairo and effectively becomes the ruler of Egypt, now an informal protectorate of Britain, until his retirement in 1907.

ASIA

25 Aug. In Indochina the treaty of Hué establishes Tonkin, Annam and Cochinchina as French protectorates; China rejects the treaty.

27 Aug. Mt Krakatoa in the Sunda Strait between Java and Sumatra (now part of Indonesia) erupts in the greatest volcanic explosion since that of Santorini in the E Mediterranean in 1470 BC. More than 150 Indonesian villages are destroyed, and some 35,000 lives are lost.

THE AMERICAS

16 Jan. In the USA the Civil Service Reform Act establishes competitive examinations and aims to end corruption in job allocation within the federal government.

20 Oct. The treaty of Ancón ends hostilities between Chile and Peru in the War of the Pacific (see 1879); Chile is victorious and gains control of the Peruvian provinces of Tacna and Arica.

– The Southern Immigration Association is founded to encourage white Americans to migrate to the poorer states of the South, which are still recovering from the depredations of the American Civil War.

ECONOMY AND SOCIETY

14 Mar. The German philosopher, economist and social theorist Karl Marx (see p. 419) dies.

26 Mar. The most lavish party in US history, a fancy-dress ball, is held at the mock-Gothic mansion of William Kissam Vanderbilt on the corner of 5th Avenue and 53rd Street, New York.

– Russian Marxist philosopher, journalist and historian Georgi Valentinovich Plekhanov, working in Switzerland, founds the League of Struggle for the Emancipation of Labour and applies a Marxist analysis to Russia's economic and political condition.

– Gold Flake cigarettes are sold in London for the first time.

– César Ritz is appointed to run the Grand Hotel, Monte Carlo, and hires Auguste Escoffier as chef.

SCIENCE AND TECHNOLOGY

24 May In the USA the Brooklyn Bridge, designed by John Augustus Roebling, opens in New York City. It spans the East River between Brooklyn and Manhattan Island.

8 Sept. In the USA the Northern Pacific Railroad is completed.

4 Oct. The Orient Express train begins operations; it leaves Paris bound for Constantinople, but because the lines do not connect all the way, it ends at Bucharest, Romania, from where passengers complete the journey by ferry, another train and ship (see 1889).

– Work begins on the construction of the Panama Canal in Central America, connecting the Atlantic and Pacific Oceans.

ARTS AND HUMANITIES

Literature

– The explorer and linguist Sir Richard Burton translates the Indian classic of erotology the *Kama Sutra*.

– Friedrich Nietzsche (see box) publishes the first part of *Also Sprach Zarathustra* (Thus Spake Zarathustra), in which he delineates the concept of the *Übermensch* (superman).

Henrik Ibsen, *En Folkefiende* (An Enemy of the People), play.

Robert Louis Stevenson, *Treasure Island*, children's story.

Mark Twain (Samuel Langhorne Clemens), *Life on the Mississippi*, autobiography.

Visual Arts and Architecture

23 Jan. French artist and illustrator Gustave Doré dies.

30 April French painter Edouard Manet dies.

Music

14 April First performance in Paris of Delibes's opera *Lakmé*.

22 Oct. The New York Metropolitan Opera House opens.

Johannes Brahms, Symphony No. 3 in F major.

Anton Bruckner, Symphony No. 7 in E major.

Franz Liszt, Mephisto Waltz No. 3.

1884

EUROPE

June The new German Accident Insurance Law is introduced, paid for entirely by employers. It covers most wage earners. As in the case of the Sickness Insurance Law (see May 1883), German chancellor Otto von Bismarck is extending the state's

---

Friedrich Nietzsche (1844–1900)

The German thinker Friedrich Nietzsche did not write conventional philosophy, but offered a variety of radical and influential critiques of Western civilization in a range of genres.

Nietzsche's first and greatest complete work, *The Birth of Tragedy* (1872), identified the heart of tragedy in psychological terms. His early writings sought out the connections between modern European thought and its classical roots in a series of urgent and passionate essays. He resigned his chair of philology at Basle University in 1879 because of ill health, and in 1889 suffered a mental breakdown from which he never recovered.

In his later philosophy Nietzsche identified two key aspects of what he saw as the spiritual crisis in contemporary Europe: the fact that 'God is dead' and that humanity had yet to face up to that truth. The Christian belief in heaven was, he believed, intolerably egalitarian in offering consolation to so many. Nietzsche had a nostalgia for what he took to be an aristocratic code of conduct, transferred to the level of spirit and mind. His identification of the 'will to power' as the basis of all human achievement was profound. Personal and sexual relations, the rise of nations and societies, the acquisition and creation of knowledge – all show this urgent push of the will to impose itself on the world and make it knowable. For Nietzsche's ideal of mastery was fundamentally an aesthetic one: only through art could existence be justified. And the role of the *Übermensch* or 'superman' (a concept later twisted by the Nazis) was to effect this radical 'transvaluation of values' – a complete overthrow of the conventional distinction between the objective and the subjective.

competence into the area of welfare. Bismarck's aim is to consolidate support for the German Reich among the working class.
- In Britain the third Reform Act becomes law, extending the franchise to male agricultural workers. Five million Britons now have the vote.

MIDDLE EAST AND NORTH AFRICA
- The British governor of the Sudan, Gen. Charles Gordon, is given full powers by the khedive of Egypt to mount a rescue expedition to relieve Egyptian garrisons besieged there by Mahdist forces (see 1883). His requests for additional troops are refused by the British government, which had advised him not to accept the mission. Having come to the aid of the garrison in Khartoum, Gordon is trapped in the city by the Mahdi (12 Mar.).

ASIA
26 Oct. China rejects the idea of a French protectorate in Indochina (see 25 Aug. 1883) and declares war on France in the dispute over control of the region. French forces proceed to attack Taiwan.

THE AMERICAS
4 April By the treaty of Valparaiso Chile gains the disputed Bolivian province of Atacama, rich in nitrates. Bolivia thereby loses its access to the sea.

5 July The US Congress passes a second Chinese Exclusion Act, further restricting the immigration of Chinese labourers. Around half of California's agricultural labourers are now Chinese.

- Stephen Grover Cleveland becomes the first Democratic candidate to win the US presidency since 1856. The Republicans have described the Democrats as the party of 'Rum, Romanism and Rebellion'. The attack solidifies the New York Catholic vote in support of the Democrats in an association that will be deep and long lasting, as ethnic loyalties in the USA acquire a party political dimension.

SUB-SAHARAN AFRICA
24 April German insistence on a colonial role in Africa grows as Bismarck proclaims Namibia (SW Africa) a German colony and telegraphs Cape Town to that effect. A protectorate over the coast of Togoland (W Africa) is also declared (5 July) by the German consul at Tunis, N Africa, and over the Cameroon coast (also W Africa) a few days later.

15 Nov. Delegates from 14 nations attend a Berlin conference on the future of Africa and agree to campaign for the suppression of slavery (see Feb. 1885).

ECONOMY AND SOCIETY
- Toynbee Hall, the first university settlement founded to encourage the privileged student body to undertake social work among the poor, is established in London's East End.
- The Gaelic Athletic Association (GAA) is founded in Ireland, a key moment in Ireland's cultural and nationalist awakening.
- In Britain the Fabian Society is founded by a group of writers

and intellectuals, notably George Bernard Shaw, Beatrice Webb and her husband Sidney, devoted to progressive thought and long-term social change in Britain.
- The newspaper *Le Matin* begins publication in Paris.

SCIENCE AND TECHNOLOGY
- William Stewart Halsted, a New York doctor, develops local anaesthetic by administering cocaine. He becomes addicted to the drug, which is derived from the leaves of the South American shrub *Erythroxylon coca*.
- German inventor Paul Nipkow anticipates the technology of television with his invention of a rotating scanning device.
- German bacteriologist Friedrich August Johannes Löffler, working in Berlin, isolates the diphtheria bacillus.
- The British engineer Charles Parsons builds the first practical high-speed steam turbine.
- In the US Hiram Stevens Maxim invents a water-cooled, recoil-operated machine-gun that can fire up to 600 rounds a minute.

ARTS AND HUMANITIES
Literature
- The first volume of the *Oxford English Dictionary*, edited by James Murray, is published. The final volume will not appear until 1928.
Joris-Karl Huysmans, *A rebours* (Against Nature), novel, a seminal text of fin-de-siècle decadence, much admired by Oscar Wilde.
Charles-Marie-René Leconte de Lisle, *Poèmes tragiques* (Tragic Poems).
Mark Twain, *The Adventures of Huckleberry Finn*, novel, sequel to *The Adventures of Tom Sawyer* (1876).
Visual Arts and Architecture
5 Aug. The building of the Statue of Liberty begins on Bedloe's Island in New York Harbour.
Georges Seurat, *Une Baignade, Asnières* (Bather at Asnières), painting.
Music
19 Jan. First performance in Paris of Jules Massenet's opera *Manon*.
César Franck, *Les Djinns*, for piano and orchestra, and *Prélude, choral et fugue*, for piano.

1885

EUROPE
9 June In Britain William Ewart Gladstone's Liberal administration, criticized over the fall of Khartoum (see below) and mounting violence in Ireland, is defeated over a budget that seeks to raise taxes on beer and spirits. It is succeeded by a Conservative government, led by Robert Cecil, Lord Salisbury (25 June).
July The *Pall Mall Gazette* publishes a sensational exposé, researched and written by its campaigning editor William Thomas Stead and entitled 'A Modern Babylon', revealing the extent of female prostitution in London. The report leads to the rushed legislation of the Criminal Law Amendment Act (7 Aug.) and raises the age of consent from 13 to 16. Clause XI,

introduced by the radical MP Henry Labouchère, outlaws 'any act of gross indecency' between males.

23 Nov. In the British general election the Liberals win 335 seats to the Conservatives' 249, but Parnell's Irish Party holds the balance of power with 86 seats, and Lord Salisbury remains prime minister.

24 Nov. King Alfonso XII of Spain dies and his mother, María Cristina, becomes regent.

MIDDLE EAST AND NORTH AFRICA

26 Jan. In the Sudan forces led by the Mahdi capture Khartoum, and Gen. Gordon and his Egyptian garrison are killed; the British relief expedition arrives too late to save them (28 Jan.).

21 June The Mahdi dies and is succeeded by his son Abdullah el-Tasshi. His Dervishes continue to extend their control of the former Anglo-Egyptian Sudan, except the Red Sea fortresses (see 1896).

ASIA

9 June By the terms of the treaty of Tianjin (Tientsin) ending the Franco-Chinese War, France recognizes a fixed and inviolable S Chinese frontier and China agrees to France's protectorate over Tonkin, Indochina.

Oct. The Third Anglo-Burmese War begins after King Thibaw, son of Mindon Min, confiscates and refuses to restore the property of the Bombay-Burma trading company. Thibaw, last king of Burma, is exiled to India, where he will die in 1916.

– In India the Indian National Congress, which will lead to the movement to end British rule, is founded.

THE AMERICAS

4 Mar. Grover Cleveland takes office as the 22nd US president.

Mar. In a dispute over land rights, Louis Riel leads a rebellion of the Métis (mixed-race white and indigenous Americans) in the W territories of Canada against the central government. They establish their own government and fight Dominion troops sent to suppress them. Riel is eventually captured, charged with treason and hanged (16 Nov.).

SUB-SAHARAN AFRICA

6 Jan. Italian forces, with British support, consolidate their position around Massawa in Eritrea on the Red Sea coast and expand into the highlands of Abyssinia.

25 Jan. Germany annexes Tanganyika and Zanzibar in E Africa.

Feb. The Berlin conference on Africa ends with the main European powers agreeing to spheres of influence as a prelude to the imperial carve-up of the continent, known as the Scramble for Africa. In Equatorial W Africa a boundary is established between the N French Congo and the S Congo Free State, where concessionaires are granted much of the territory, but the central part is recognized as the private possession of Leopold II, king of the Belgians, who becomes its sovereign.

– British protectorates are established in N Bechuanaland (now Botswana), in S Africa (3 Mar.) and in the Niger River area of W Africa (5 June).

ECONOMY AND SOCIETY

– Bryn Mawr College for Women opens in Pennsylvania, USA.

– Stanford University in California is founded by the railway magnate Leland Stanford.

– In the USA the first self-service restaurant, the Exchange Buffet, opens in New York.

– George Parker founds the games company Parker Brothers in Salem, Massachusetts, USA.

SCIENCE AND TECHNOLOGY

6 July French chemist and microbiologist Louis Pasteur administers the world's first anti-rabies vaccine to Joseph Meister, a schoolboy who has been bitten by a rabid dog.

– A petrol-driven motor vehicle developed by Karl-Friedrich Benz operates at a speed of 14kph (9mph) in a demonstration at Mannheim, W Germany.

– The Winchester Repeating Arms Company in the USA begins manufacturing the Browning single-shot rifle invented by John Moses Browning, a Utah gunsmith.

– Francis Galton, an English geneticist, produces an identification system based on fingerprints. In *Hereditary Genius* (1869) he has already shown that no two sets of fingerprints are exactly alike.

– British manufacturer William Lever introduces Sunlight soap.

– In France G. Juzan develops a bicycle with two wheels of equal size, a feature also adopted for the 'Rover' safety bicycle built this same year by the British inventor John Starley.

ARTS AND HUMANITIES

Literature

– Irish writer and wit Oscar Wilde becomes a regular contributor to the *Pall Mall Gazette*, London.

– Russian geographer and geologist Prince Pyotr Kropotkin, imprisoned for anarchism in France, writes *Paroles d'un révolté* (Memoirs of a Revolutionary).

Henry Rider Haggard, *King Solomon's Mines*, adventure novel.

Henrik Ibsen, *Vildanden* (The Wild Duck), play.

Guy de Maupassant, *Bel-Ami*, novel.

George Meredith, *Diana of the Crossways*, novel.

Walter Pater, *Marius the Epicurean*, historical novel.

Emile Zola, *Germinal*, novel.

Visual Arts and Architecture

– In Chicago, USA, the Home Insurance Building is completed. Designed by William Le Baron Jenney, it is one of the first successful iron-framed buildings, and is generally regarded as the world's first skyscraper.

Music

14 Mar. First performance in the Savoy Theatre, London, of Arthur Sullivan's operetta *The Mikado, or The Town of Titipu* to a libretto by W.S. Gilbert. It is inspired by the current vogue for Japanese arts.

May–June The Boston Pops Orchestra is formed from the players of the Boston Symphony Orchestra and gives the first in a series of concerts of light classical music.

24 Oct. First performance in Vienna of Johann Strauss II's operetta *Der Zigeunerbaron* (The Gypsy Baron).

Johannes Brahms, Symphony No. 4 in E minor.

Antonín Dvořák, Symphony No. 7 in D minor.

César Franck, Symphonic Variations for piano and orchestra.

Franz Liszt, Mephisto Waltz No. 4.

Pyotr Tchaikovsky, *Manfred* Symphony.

1886

EUROPE

4 Jan. In France Gen. Georges-Ernest-Jean-Marie Boulanger is appointed minister of war. The right-wing Boulanger has ambitions to overthrow the French Third Republic. His anti-German speeches will come close to provoking war with Germany.

27 Jan. In Britain Lord Salisbury's first Conservative adminis-tration ends. William Ewart Gladstone forms his third ministry (12 Feb.).

Feb. In Britain the ambitious Liberal politician Sir Charles Dilke appears as a co-respondent in a scandalous divorce case. His career is ruined.

8 April The British prime minister W.E. Gladstone introduces the contentious Irish Home Rule Bill. It provides for an Irish parliament but control of the army and navy, as well as trade affairs, remains with Parliament at Westminster. Joseph Chamberlain resigns from the Liberal cabinet and leads a grouping of Liberal unionists.

8 June In Britain the Liberal government's Irish Home Rule Bill is defeated when 95 Liberal unionists side with the Conservative opposition. The Conservatives win the resulting general election (24 July). A second Salisbury administration is formed, which will last until 1892; it includes his nephew Arthur James Balfour as chief secretary for Ireland.

All the world over I will back the masses against the classes.

W.E. Gladstone, 28 June 1886

– In Spain Alfonso XIII, son of Alfonso XII, born the year after his father's death, becomes king of Spain.

ASIA

1 Jan. The Third Anglo-Burmese War (see 1885) ends. Britain annexes Upper Burma.

24 July China recognizes the incorporation of Burma into Britain's Indian empire, but the traditional decennial Burmese tribute to the Chinese emperor continues.

Arthur Rimbaud (1854–91)

The French poet Arthur Rimbaud was born in Charleville in the Ardennes, the son of an army officer and a farmer's daughter. He displayed a precocious brilliance in languages at the local school, and by the time he was 15 he had discovered his poetic voice. The early verse in his six-year literary career expressed a rebellious frustration against small-town life and its conventions, a capacity for blasphemy, and a gift for the transcendental lyric that is unsurpassed. Rimbaud became the poetic inspiration for the Symbolist school of French and European literature, and helped to liberate poetry from the constraints of metrical form.

As a teenage genius, Rimbaud also inspired a later cult of the adolescent outsider. He declared that he was a seer or *voyant* – gifted in his ability to see through the veil of creation. This persona entailed a good deal of arrogance, considerable quantities of drink and drugs, and a notable degree of sexual conceit. His homosexual affair with the older poet Paul Verlaine, his literary patron, was punctuated by bouts of depression on both sides. But even after Verlaine tried to shoot him in 1873 Rimbaud still entrusted the older man with the manuscript of his series of 40 prose poems, *Les Illuminations*, when he left France in 1875.

By then he had given up on poetry. He joined and then deserted the Dutch army in the East Indies, worked in the Yemen and then became an explorer and arms dealer in Ethiopia. He returned, ill, to France in 1891, had his right leg amputated in Marseilles, and died in hospital.

THE AMERICAS

1 May In the USA Chicago police fire into a crowd of protesting strikers, killing four and wounding many others. At a further gathering in Haymarket Square (4 May) the police kill some 20 protestors in apparent retaliation for the death of seven policemen in a bomb explosion. The Haymarket massacre establishes May Day as an important commemorative date in US working-class politics. Over 600,000 US workers will strike in 1886 campaigning for an eight-hour day.

4 Sept. The capture of the Apache chief Goyathlay (Geronimo) ends ten years of fighting on the Mexican border. It is the last of the major wars between white settlers and Native Americans.

28 Oct. The Statue of Liberty is dedicated in New York Harbour. It has been designed by the French sculptor Frédéric-Auguste Bartholdi and is the gift of the French people.

8 Dec. In Columbo, Ohio, Samuel Gompers founds the American Federation of Labor (AFL), an alliance of 13 craft unions.

SUB-SAHARAN AFRICA

Sept. Johannesburg is founded and laid out in the S African province of Transvaal following the discovery of gold in the Witwatersrand. To exploit its mineral wealth, British entre-preneur Cecil Rhodes establishes Consolidated Gold Fields Ltd, through which he extends his fortune.

ECONOMY AND SOCIETY
- The food shop Fauchon opens in Paris as a luxurious *épicerie*.
- Raffles Hotel opens in Singapore.

SCIENCE AND TECHNOLOGY
- German engineer Gottlieb Daimler completes work on developing his internal combustion engine.
- Charles Hall, US chemist, pioneers the commercial production of aluminium.
- The first electrolytic magnesium plant opens in Hameln, N Germany.
- In the USA John S. Pemberton has invented a headache and hangover cure made from coca shrub leaves and kola nuts which he begins to sell at Jacob's Pharmacy, Atlanta.

ARTS AND HUMANITIES
Literature
- The second volume of *Das Kapital* by German political theorist Karl Marx (see p. 419) is published posthumously.

Frances Hodgson Burnett, *Little Lord Fauntleroy*, children's novel.

Marie Corelli (Mary Mackay), *A Romance of Two Worlds*, the first of a string of bestselling melodramatic novels. Corelli is rumoured to be Queen Victoria's favourite novelist.

Thomas Hardy, *The Mayor of Casterbridge*, novel.

Henry James, *The Bostonians*, novel.

Friedrich Nietzsche, *Jenseits von Gut und Böse* (Beyond Good and Evil), philosophy.

Arthur Rimbaud (see p. 440), *Les Illuminations*, prose poems. Although published only now, by Rimbaud's former lover Paul Verlaine, the poems date from the early 1870s, when Rimbaud was a teenager.

Robert Louis Stevenson, *The Strange Case of Dr Jekyll and Mr Hyde* and *Kidnapped*, novels.

Count Leo Tolstoy (see p. 430), *The Death of Ivan Ilyich*, novella.

Visual Arts and Architecture
- French artist Georges Seurat has developed a pointillist style of painting using a myriad of small dots rather than brush strokes. His *Un Dimanche d'été à l'Ile de la Grande Jatte* (Sunday Afternoon on the Island of La Grande Jatte) is exhibited at the eighth and last exhibition of French Impressionists' works held in Paris.

Sir John Everett Millais, *Bubbles*, painting that will be used as an advertisement by the Pears soap company.

Auguste Rodin, *Le Baiser* (The Kiss), sculpture.

Henri Rousseau, *Carnaval du soir* (Evening Carnival), painting.

Music
31 July Death in Bayreuth of the Hungarian pianist and composer Franz Liszt.

Camille Saint-Saëns, Symphony No. 3 in C minor (with organ).

1887

EUROPE
11 Jan. German chancellor Otto von Bismarck advocates a larger German army. Franco-German tensions will increase during the year.

20 Feb. The Triple Alliance between Germany, Austria and Italy (see 1882) is renewed for a further five-year period.

18 May In France the right-wing general Georges Boulanger is excluded from a new administration formed by Maurice Rouvier. As war minister Boulanger has led a bellicose nationalist campaign for revenge (*revanche*) on Germany.

18 June Russia, having refused to renew the Three Emperors' League of 18 June 1881 with Germany and Austria-Hungary, signs a secret treaty with Germany.

21 June In Britain Queen Victoria celebrates her Golden Jubilee.

2 Dec. President François-Paul-Jules Grévy of France is forced to resign after revelations implicating his son-in-law in the sale of Légion d'honneur medals. He is succeeded by Marie-François Sadi Carnot. The scandal boosts the popularity of the nationalist Boulanger.

- Bulgaria elects Prince Ferdinand of Saxe-Coburg of Germany as king.

MIDDLE EAST AND NORTH AFRICA
22 May By the terms of the Drummond-Wolff convention Britain agrees to withdraw from Egypt within three years but retains the right to reoccupy Egypt if warranted by conditions of instability. Tewfiq Pasha, khedive of Egypt, refuses to ratify the convention.

ASIA
- The peninsula of Macao near Hong Kong is ceded to Portugal by the Chinese government.
- The Yellow (or Huang He) River flowing through C China bursts its banks, causing extensive crop failure and leading to a famine that kills about one million people.

THE AMERICAS
23 May The Canadian Pacific Railway reaches Vancouver on the W coast. It is the first single company transcontinental railway in N America.

- In the USA the Florida state legislature passes a law segregating blacks from whites in railway carriages.

SUB-SAHARAN AFRICA
21 June Intent on blocking the Transvaal Boers' putative link to the sea, Britain annexes Zululand, S Africa.

ECONOMY AND SOCIETY
- Polish philologist Lazarus Ludwig Zamenhof invents Esperanto, a universal language designed to further global understanding and peace.
- Louis Keller, golf promoter, publishes the first US social register.
- Around this date the British tobacco company W.D. & H.O. Wills introduces cigarette cards.

SCIENCE AND TECHNOLOGY
Jan. Large-scale electricity generation is introduced to Japan by the Tokyo Electric Light Company.

2 Mar. In the USA Anne Mansfield Sullivan of the Perkins Institute starts to work with Helen Keller, who lost her sight and hearing when only 19 months old. She teaches her to use her fingers to identify words spelled out on raised cardboard.

4 Mar. The German company Daimler introduces its first motor-car for sale.

– US physicist Thomas Alva Edison invents the first motor-driven phonograph, which plays wax recordings.

ARTS AND HUMANITIES

Literature

Arthur Conan Doyle, *A Study in Scarlet*, novel introducing his fictional detective Sherlock Holmes.

Sir Henry Rider Haggard, *She* and *Allan Quatermain*, novels.

Thomas Hardy, *The Woodlanders*, novel.

Henrik Ibsen, *Rosmersholm*, play.

Stéphane Mallarmé, *Poésies* (Poems), collection of lyrics, sonnets and elegies.

August Strindberg, *Fadren* (The Father), play.

Visual Arts and Architecture

Vincent Van Gogh, *Moulin de La Galette*, painting.

Music

4 Dec. First performance in Naples of Giuseppe Verdi's opera *Otello*, based on Shakespeare's tragedy *Othello, the Moor of Venice*.

Johannes Brahms, Double Concerto in A minor.

Anton Bruckner, Symphony No. 8 in C minor.

Gabriel Fauré, *Requiem*.

1888

EUROPE

6 Feb. In a speech to the Reichstag, German chancellor Otto von Bismarck states: 'We Germans fear God and nothing else in the world.' As a calculated threat to European rivals France and Russia, he discloses the terms of the Triple Alliance (promising mutual support in war to Austro-Hungary and Italy).

9 Mar. Emperor William I of Germany dies; he is succeeded by his son Frederick III who dies of throat cancer (15 June). He is succeeded by William II (Kaiser Wilhelm), son of Frederick III and Victoria, daughter of Queen Victoria of Britain. William II will reign until 1918, the last of the German king-emperors.

15 April Having retired from the army, Georges Boulanger is elected to the French chamber of deputies. He campaigns to overthrow the Third Republic and to install himself as dictator.

ASIA

17 Mar. Britain establishes a protectorate over Sarawak and over N Borneo (12 May).

THE AMERICAS

13 May Brazil's slaves finally achieve emancipation. The children of slaves were freed in 1871 and an 1885 law freed slaves who were over 60 years of age. Now all slaves are freed and without any compensation for their owners.

1 Oct. Still preoccupied with the issue of race and immigration, the US Congress passes a new Chinese Exclusion Act, outlawing the return of Chinese workers who have left the USA.

6 Nov. The Republican candidate Benjamin Harrison wins the US presidential election, defeating the Democratic incumbent Grover Cleveland.

SUB-SAHARAN AFRICA

30 Oct. In S Africa Lobengula, the Matabele king, signs a treaty giving entrepreneur-imperialist Cecil Rhodes mining rights in Matabeleland and Mashonaland (modern Zimbabwe). He has accepted a British protectorate.

ECONOMY AND SOCIETY

Oct. In the USA the *National Geographic* magazine starts publication in Washington, D.C.

– The *Financial Times* newspaper starts publication in London.

– 'Jack the Ripper' brutally murders five London prostitutes. His identity will never be conclusively established.

SCIENCE AND TECHNOLOGY

– George Eastman of New York invents the Kodak box camera. It enables amateur photographers to take acceptable photographs.

– Hungarian immigrant David Gestetner introduces the typewriter stencil in London.

– Theophilus Van Kannel of Philadelphia, USA, develops the first revolving door.

– In Britain John Boyd Dunlop patents the pneumatic bicycle tyre.

ARTS AND HUMANITIES

Literature

– Richard Burton publishes the final volume of his translation from the original Persian of *The Arabian Nights* (the first had appeared in 1885). Scheherazade, who entertains her husband with a new story each night in order not to be put to death, enters Western literature.

Edward Bellamy, *Looking Backward 2000–1887*, Utopian romance.

Henry James, *The Aspern Papers*, novella.

Rudyard Kipling, *Plain Tales from the Hills*, short stories.

Arthur Wing Pinero, *Sweet Lavender*, comic play.

Oscar Wilde, *The Happy Prince*, collection of children's fairy stories.

Visual Arts and Architecture

– The combined State, War and Navy Department building, designed by Alfred B. Mullett, is completed opposite the White House in Washington, D.C.

– The Washington Monument, 170m (555 feet) high, is opened to the public in Washington, D.C.

James Ensor, *The Entry of Christ into Brussels*, painting.

Auguste Rodin, *Le Penseur* (The Thinker), sculpture.

Henri de Toulouse-Lautrec, *Place Clichy*, painting.

Vincent Van Gogh, *Sunflowers*, *Arena at Arles* and *Night Café*, paintings.

Music

7 May First performance in Paris of Edouard Lalo's opera *Le Roi d'Ys* (The King of Ys).

3 Oct. First performance at the Savoy Theatre, London, of Arthur

Sullivan's operetta *The Yeoman of the Guard, or The Merryman and his Maid* to a libretto by W.S. Gilbert.
– The song 'L'Internationale', which will become the anthem of global communism and working-class solidarity, is published. The words, by Eugène Pettier, were written during the Paris Commune of 1871, and the music is by Belgian woodcarver Pierre Degeyter.
César Franck, Symphony in D minor.
Gustav Mahler, Symphony No. 1 in D major.
Erik Satie, *Gymnopédies*, for piano.
Pyotr Tchaikovsky, Symphony No. 5 in E minor.
Hugo Wolf, *Mörike Lieder*, song settings of poetry by Eduard Mörike. Among some 300 song settings Wolf also sets poems by Eichendorff and Goethe.

1889

EUROPE
30 Jan. Crown Prince Archduke Rudolf of Austria-Hungary and his mistress Baroness Marie Vetsera are found dead at his hunting lodge at Mayerling near Vienna. It is assumed that Rudolf has shot her before killing himself. Emperor Franz Josef's nephew, Franz Ferdinand, is now heir to the throne of Austria-Hungary.
6 Mar. King Milan IV Obrenovic (see 10 June 1868) of Serbia abdicates and is succeeded by his 13-year-old son Alexander.
1 April Georges Boulanger, threatening a *coup d'état* in Paris where he has widespread support, flees France for Brussels and then London after a warrant is issued for his arrest. He is tried by a court in absentia and condemned for treason.
15 Aug.–16 Sept. A month-long docker's strike takes place in London. It becomes one of the key events of British labour history and deepens workers' class-consciousness.

ASIA
11 Feb. The written Japanese constitution is agreed between the emperor and the prime minister, Kuroda Kiyotaka; it specifies that imperial ordinances have to be approved by the new bicameral diet (assembly).

THE AMERICAS
4 Mar. Benjamin Harrison becomes 23rd US president.
2 Oct. The first conference of American states is held in Washington, D.C. All Latin American countries (except the Dominican Republic) are represented, and a Pan-American Union is established, but plans for trade reciprocity and arbitration procedures to settle conflicts are rejected.
2 Nov. North and South Dakota become the 39th and 40th states of the USA. Montana becomes the 41st state on 8 Nov., and Washington the 42nd on 11 Nov.
15 Nov. Emperor Pedro II of Brazil is deposed by the army; a republic is proclaimed, and Gen. Manuel Deodoro da Fonseca becomes the new ruler (see 1891).
– Latin American coffee production begins a period of prosperity because of the failure of the coffee crop in Ceylon after a devastating attack of rust.

SUB-SAHARAN AFRICA
10 Jan. The Ivory Coast in W Africa becomes a French protectorate.
12 Mar. Yohannes IV, emperor of Ethiopia, is killed fighting the Muslim Sudanese followers of the Mahdi at Metemma. He is succeeded by the Italian-backed Menelik of Shoa, who triumphs over Ras Mangasha, the son and heir of Yohannes.
5 Aug. An Anglo-French agreement settles the borders of the Gold Coast (now Ghana) and Ivory Coast, Senegal and Gambia.
– In S Africa administration of the area N of the Transvaal and W of Mozambique is effectively contracted out by the imperial government to the chartered British South Africa Company run by Cecil Rhodes.

ECONOMY AND SOCIETY
8 July The *Wall Street Journal* starts publication. It has evolved out of the daily financial summaries provided by Dow Jones and Company (established 1882), which issues an industrial average recognized as the standard measure of stock market performance.
6 Aug. The Savoy Hotel opens in London under the management of César Ritz.
– In London the Cleveland Street scandal reveals that a group of English aristocrats have been using a gay brothel staffed by post office messenger boys.
– The Compagnie Universelle du Canal Inter-Océanique, the firm responsible for building the Panama Canal, becomes bankrupt owing to mismanagement, corruption and poor financial controls. In France responsibility is popularly attributed to Jews holding office in the company (see 1894).
– A two-year global epidemic of influenza begins and affects over a third of the world's population.
– American inventor Isaac Singer starts to sell electric sewing machines made by his company.

SCIENCE AND TECHNOLOGY
1 June The first through-train from Paris to Constantinople, the Orient Express, leaves the Gare de l'Est for the capital of the Ottoman empire (see 1883).
– Frederick Augustus Abel and James Dewar, English and Scottish chemists respectively, patent the explosive cordite.
– The Forth railway bridge spanning the Firth of Forth, N of Edinburgh, Scotland, is completed.

ARTS AND HUMANITIES
Literature
– The play *Fröken Julie* (Miss Julie), by August Strindberg, is first performed in Copenhagen, Denmark.
– The play *Vor Sonnenaufgang* (Before Dawn), by the German playwright Gerhart Hauptmann, is first performed in Berlin.
Henrik Ibsen, *Fruen fra Haven* (The Lady from the Sea), play.
Jerome K. Jerome, *Three Men in a Boat*, comic novel.
Rudyard Kipling, 'The Ballad of East and West', poem.
Maurice Maeterlinck, *Serres chaudes* (Hot House Blooms), collection of poems.

Robert Louis Stevenson, *The Master of Ballantrae*, novel.

Mark Twain (Samuel Langhorne Clemens), *A Connecticut Yankee in King Arthur's Court*, novel.

Visual Arts and Architecture

6 May The Paris Exhibition opens with the newly erected Eiffel Tower, designed by engineer Alexandre-Gustave Eiffel, as its centrepiece. One of the three lifts designed to ascend the 300m (984 feet) high tower is built by the Otis Company of New York.

27 Sept. New York's first skyscraper, designed by Bradford Lee Gilbert, is completed on Broadway.

– The Tacoma building in Chicago is completed. Designed by William Holabird, it is the first building with a framework made entirely of steel (rather than simply having steel supports).

Vincent Van Gogh, *Wheatfield with Cypresses*, *Starry Night* and *Self-portrait with Bandaged Ear*, paintings.

Music

7 Dec. First performance at the Savoy Theatre, London, of Arthur Sullivan's operetta *The Gondoliers, or The King of Barataria*, to a libretto by W.S. Gilbert.

– The English organist Robert Hope-Jones applies electricity to the organ. He eventually emigrates to the USA and sells his patent to the Rudolph Würlitzer Company of New York.

– Yamaha Torakasi founds the Japanese Musical Instrument Manufacturing Company having already introduced the first Japanese organ (1885) and the Yamaha piano (1887).

Antonín Dvořák, Symphony No. 8 in G major.

1890

EUROPE

20 Mar. Kaiser Wilhelm forces the resignation of Otto von Bismarck as chancellor of Germany after disagreements over policy. Leo von Caprivi becomes imperial chancellor.

18 June The German–Russian treaty of June 1887 is allowed to lapse.

17 Nov. The Irish nationalist politician Charles Stewart Parnell is cited as co-respondent in a divorce suit brought by William Henry O'Shea, whose wife Katharine has been Parnell's mistress since 1880. Parnell is destroyed by the scandal and resigns as an MP and as Irish nationalist leader (12 Dec.).

23 Nov. King William III of the Netherlands dies and is succeeded by his ten-year-old daughter Wilhelmina who will rule from 1898 as Queen Wilhelmina I. The Grand Duchy of Luxembourg is separated from the Netherlands because no woman can succeed to the ducal title.

ASIA

11 July Democratic elections are held in Japan but the suffrage is restricted to males over 25 years of age who pay at least 15 yen a year in taxes. The first Japanese diet sits (29 Nov.).

THE AMERICAS

2 July The US Congress passes the Sherman Anti-Trust Act, which aims to restrict the ability of major companies to establish monopolies and restrict competition.

3 July Idaho becomes the 43rd US state.

10 July Wyoming becomes the 44th US state.

1 Oct. US import duties rise to record levels following the passage through Congress of the protectionist McKinley Tariff Act.

1 Nov. The US state of Mississippi introduces measures, including a poll tax and literacy tests, designed to restrict the suffrage to whites.

15 Dec. In the USA the Sioux chief Sitting Bull is shot dead by police on a reservation in South Dakota.

29 Dec. At the massacre of Wounded Knee some 150 Sioux are shot when US soldiers attempt to disarm Sioux followers of the Ghost Dance cult. The US government's opening of the former Sioux lands in South Dakota to white settlement has led to what will be the last major act of resistance by Native Americans.

– Kansas farmers, afflicted by drought and bank debt, embrace the anticapitalist Populist movement that develops out of farmers' protests against economic hardship.

SUB-SAHARAN AFRICA

1 July Germany and Britain resolve their disputes by a formal agreement in which Germany gives up its claim to Uganda in E Africa and gains the North Sea island of Heligoland, while Zanzibar (also in E Africa) is recognized as a British protectorate.

17 July Cecil Rhodes becomes prime minister of Cape Colony, S Africa.

12 Sept. The settlement of Salisbury is founded in Mashonaland; when the territory is renamed Rhodesia in 1893 it will become the capital of the new colony.

28 Oct. The German East Africa Company cedes all its powers and possessions to the German government.

SCIENCE AND TECHNOLOGY

– In London the underground railway is converted to electricity and the coke-burning locomotives used since 1863 are withdrawn.

– Herman Hollerith, a US engineer and statistician, pioneers punch-card processing with the invention of a system of recording US census statistics by punching holes in sheets of paper (see also 1896).

– New York state introduces the electric chair for capital punishment as a supposedly humane alternative to hanging.

ARTS AND HUMANITIES

Literature

– In Britain the writer and designer William Morris founds the Kelmscott Press in Hammersmith, London.

– Lavinia Dickinson organizes the publication of her late sister's poems under the title *The Poems of Emily Dickinson*. Emily, who died in 1886, had lived a secluded life at Amherst, Massachusetts, USA.

Sir Arthur Conan Doyle, *The Sign of Four*, the second Sherlock Holmes novel.

Sir James Frazer, *The Golden Bough*, the first volume of a pioneering anthropological survey.

Knut Hamsun, *Sult* (Hunger), novel.

Alfred Thayer Mahan, *The Influence of Sea Power upon History, 1660–1783*, first volume of an influential work of history that predicts the defeat of the German navy in World War I.

William Butler Yeats, 'The Lake Isle of Innisfree', poem.

Visual Arts and Architecture

27 July The Dutch painter Vincent Van Gogh shoots himself at Auvers-sur Oise, France. He dies two days later (29 July).

Claude Monet, *Poplars*, painting.

Odilon Redon, *Les Fleurs du mal*, lithographs inspired by the poetry of Charles Baudelaire (see 1857).

Henri de Toulouse-Lautrec, *Dance at the Moulin Rouge*, painting.

Vincent Van Gogh, *Wheatfield with Crows*, *Portrait of Dr Gachet* and *Road with Cypress and Star*, paintings.

Music

15 Jan. First performance in St Petersburg of Pyotr Tchaikovsky's ballet *Sleeping Beauty*. His opera *The Queen of Spades* (based on a story by Alexander Pushkin) is premiered in St Petersburg on 19 Dec.

17 May First performance in Rome of Pietro Mascagni's opera *Cavalleria rusticana* (Rustic Chivalry).

4 Nov. First performance of Russian composer Alexander Borodin's opera *Prince Igor* takes place posthumously in St Petersburg; he died in 1887.

6 Dec. First (complete but posthumous) performance in Karlsruhe of Hector Berlioz's opera *Les Troyens* (The Trojans); the work will not be performed in its original French until 1960.

1891

EUROPE

6 May The Triple Alliance (see 20 May 1882) of Germany, Austria-Hungary and Italy is renewed for 12 years.

1 June German factory workers are given the right to form committees that will negotiate with employers on contracts of employment.

30 Sept. The French nationalist Georges Boulanger commits suicide in Brussels.

6 Oct. The disgraced Irish nationalist leader Charles Stewart Parnell dies, just four months after his marriage to Katharine O'Shea (see 17 Nov. 1890).

10 Oct. The first old-age pension plan comes into operation in Germany following the introduction of Otto von Bismarck's Old Age Insurance Act (1889). Workers and employers are compelled to pay equal amounts, with the pension payable at the age of 70 after a minimum 30 years of contributions.

- In the city of Vladivostok work begins on the building of the Trans-Siberian Railway linking Moscow with the Pacific coast.

- The Russian harvest fails and mass starvation follows.

MIDDLE EAST AND NORTH AFRICA

- At a meeting in Geneva, Switzerland, the Young Turk Movement is formed with the aim of reintroducing the constitution of 1876 in the Ottoman empire.

THE AMERICAS

Nov. Manuel Deodoro da Fonseca, the elected president of Brazil, is ousted from office following a revolt against his dictatorial rule (see 1889). The equally dictatorial rule of his successor Floriano Peixoto will lead to further rebellions.

- Following the failure of the Russian harvest, many Ukrainians migrate to the prairie lands of Canada.

SUB-SAHARAN AFRICA

15 April The Union Minière de Haut Katanga is established after Robert Williams, representing Cecil Rhodes, and Leopold II, king of the Belgians, negotiate an agreement allowing Rhodes to mine for copper in the Katanga territory of Belgian Congo.

- Leander Starr Jameson becomes administrator of the territories owned by the British South African Company.

AUSTRALASIA AND OCEANIA

Jan. Queen Liliuokalani becomes queen of Hawaii and confronts a league of white sugar planters, who form an Annexation Club to overthrow her.

ECONOMY AND SOCIETY

15 May In Italy the encyclical *Rerum Novarum* is issued by Pope Leo XIII. With its statement of the rights of workers and the duties of employers, it is a landmark in social thought.

- The University of Chicago is founded, largely funded by John D. Rockefeller.

- The first advertising agency is established in New York by George Batten.

- In the USA Asa Chandler, an Atlanta pharmacist, buys the rights to Coca-Cola and will market it as a soft, rather than medicinal, drink.

- While working at the YMCA training school in Springfield, Massachusetts, USA, the Canadian James Naismith invents basketball.

SCIENCE AND TECHNOLOGY

- A telephone link is established between London and Paris.

- The first electric oven for domestic use is sold in St Paul's, Minnesota, USA.

ARTS AND HUMANITIES

Literature

July The *Strand* magazine begins regular publication of Scottish writer Sir Arthur Conan Doyle's Sherlock Holmes detective stories with 'A Scandal in Bohemia'.

28 Sept. Hermann Melville dies in New York. He has completed the novel *Billy Budd*, but it will not be published until 1924. It will provide the basis of the opera *Billy Budd*, which will be written in 1951 by Benjamin Britten.

- Henrik Ibsen's play *Hedda Gabler* is first performed inMunich, Germany.

George Gissing, *New Grub Street*, novel.

Thomas Hardy, *Tess of the d'Urbervilles*, novel.

William Morris, *News From Nowhere*, utopian socialist fantasy.

Oscar Wilde, *The Picture of Dorian Gray*, novel.

Visual Arts and Architecture

20 Mar. The French Post-Impressionist artist Georges Seurat dies at the age of 31.

– The Wainwright Building in St Louis, Missouri, is completed. An unbroken vertical line from top to bottom, it will influence future skyscraper design. The architect, Louis Henry Sullivan, is assisted by his apprentice Frank Lloyd Wright.

– French painter Henri de Toulouse-Lautrec completes the first of his music hall posters. Lautrec was the son of first cousins and suffered from congenital dwarfism.

Edward Burne-Jones, *The Star of Bethlehem*, painting.

Paul Gauguin, *Two Tahitian Women on a Beach*, painting.

Claude Monet, *Haystacks*, painting.

Music

5 May Carnegie Hall opens in New York.

– The Chicago Symphony Orchestra is founded.

Sergei Rachmaninov, Piano Concerto No. 1 in F sharp minor.

1892

EUROPE

13 Aug. Following the British general election the Conservative administration of Lord Salisbury falls, and William Ewart Gladstone forms his fourth government (18 Aug.). The Liberals' period in office (1892–5) is but a short hiatus in a lengthy period of Conservative rule in Britain (1886–1906).

10 Nov. In France the Panama Canal scandal becomes public. The Canal's designer Ferdinand de Lesseps and others are charged with corruption and incompetence.

MIDDLE EAST AND NORTH AFRICA

– Tewfik Pasha, khedive of Egypt, dies. His reign has witnessed the Mahdi's seizure of Egyptian Sudan and the creation of a theocratic state, and the British establishment of a protectorate over Egypt itself. His son Abbas II succeeds and will reconquer the Sudan.

THE AMERICAS

5 May The Geary Chinese Exclusion Act is passed by the US Congress and extends the exclusion laws to prohibit Chinese immigration for another ten years.

Sept. A cholera epidemic begins in the USA.

12 Oct. A pledge of allegiance is introduced for US schoolchildren stating (in its eventual form): 'I pledge allegiance to the flag of the United States, and to the Republic for which it stands, one nation, indivisible, with liberty and justice for all.'

8 Nov. In the USA Democratic Party voters, opposing the protectionist McKinley Tariff Act introduced by Republican president Benjamin Harrison, defeat his re-election attempt. The Democratic Party's Grover Cleveland returns to office as US president.

– Catholic missionaries in New York start a campaign against the *padrone* system, which condemns many Italian immigrants to work as servants for those who assist their passage to the USA.

– The Populist Party gets more than a million votes in the US presidential election as farmers protest at the railroad companies' prices and policies and at their impoverishment by debt and mortgages.

– The New York immigration reception centre moves from Castle Gardens to Ellis Island.

SUB-SAHARAN AFRICA

May A rebellion of Arab slave-owners starts in the Belgian Congo; it is finally defeated by Belgian forces led by Baron François Dhanis (22 Nov.).

– Following the deposition of Behanzin, king of Dahomey (modern Benin), its people rebel against French rule.

AUSTRALASIA AND OCEANIA

– A nationwide strike in Australia is ended by the military.

ECONOMY AND SOCIETY

– English businessman Marcus Samuel breaks the sales monopoly of the US oil company Standard Oil in the Far East by sending his tankers through the Suez Canal to Singapore, Bangkok and other ports. His company will become known as Shell Oil, the Anglo-Dutch combine and one of the world's largest corporate entities.

– In the USA J.P. Morgan engineers a merger of the Edison and two other electrical companies to create the General Electric Company.

– Salesman William Wrigley Jr of Chicago, USA, starts to sell chewing gum.

– Italy raises the marriageable age for girls to 12.

– Players Navy Cut cigarettes are first sold in London.

SCIENCE AND TECHNOLOGY

– N.V. Philips Gloeilampenfabrieken begins to produce incandescent electric lamps in Eindhoven, the Netherlands.

ARTS AND HUMANITIES

Literature

Sir Arthur Conan Doyle, *The Adventures of Sherlock Holmes*, collection of detective stories.

George and Weedon Grossmith, *The Diary of a Nobody*, fictional diary of the petit-bourgeois clerk Charles Pooter.

Rudyard Kipling, *Barrack-Room Ballads* (including 'If', 'Gunga Din' and 'The Road to Mandalay'), poems.

Brandon Thomas, *Charley's Aunt*, play.

Oscar Wilde, *Lady Windermere's Fan*, play.

Visual Arts and Architecture

– Work begins on the construction of the Episcopal Cathedral of St John the Divine, New York, planned to be the world's largest cathedral and initially designed by George Lewis Heins and Christopher Grant La Farge.

– Marble House in Newport, Rhode Island, USA, is completed for William K. Vanderbilt to the designs of Richard Morris Hunt. It is based on the Grand and Petit Trianon, royal residences at the Palace of Versailles near Paris, France.

Paul Cézanne, *The Cardplayers*, painting.

Paul Gauguin, *The Spirit of the Dead Watching*, painting.

Music
16 Feb. First performance in Vienna of Jules Massenet's opera *Werther*, based on Goethe's novel *Die Leiden des jungen Werthers* (1774).

21 May First performance in Milan of Ruggiero Leoncavallo's opera *Pagliacci* (Clowns). It will come to be frequently performed as a double bill with Mascagni's *Cavalleria rusticana* (see 17 May 1890), the two operas being popularly referred to as 'Cav and Pag'.

18 Dec. First performance in St Petersburg of Pyotr Tchaikovsky's ballet *The Nutcracker*, which is based on a tale by E.T.A. Hoffmann.

Antonín Dvořák, *Carnival* Overture.

1893

EUROPE
13 Jan. Britain's Independent Labour Party is founded in Bradford by a group of socialists led by the socialist MP Keir Hardie.

8 Sept. In Britain W.E. Gladstone's second Irish Home Rule Bill is rejected by the House of Lords.

ASIA
— Laos in SE Asia becomes a French protectorate. France is now intent on establishing an Indochinese empire and its full military control of Laos will be secured within three years.

THE AMERICAS
5 May Prices drop dramatically on Wall Street and the market crashes. Some 600 banks will close and over 70 railroad companies will be placed in receivership by the end of June 1893. The resulting depression will last for four years.

16 Sept. About 2.4 million hectares (6 million acres) of N Oklahoma territory in the USA, formerly the property of the Cherokee people, are declared open to white settlement.

31 Oct. Congress repeals the Sherman Silver Purchase Act of 1890 and the USA returns to the Gold Standard; silver prices collapse.

— French Guiana, S America, is declared a French colony.

— In the USA Kelly's Industrial Army, a force of 1500 unemployed workers led by Charles Kelly, protests about the poor economic conditions suffered by working people by marching to the US Congress in Washington from California.

— The American Railway Union is founded in the USA by Eugene Debs.

SUB-SAHARAN AFRICA
10 Mar. The Ivory Coast in W Africa is formally declared a French colony.

10 May The British S African colony of Natal becomes self-governing.

23 Oct. Forces under Leander Starr Jameson of the British South Africa Company suppress a revolt by the Matabele people (now S and W Zimbabwe). Jameson's troops use machine-guns against the tribesmen. Lobengula, king of the Matabele, abandons his capital of Bulawayo (11 Nov.) and will die in exile in 1894.

13 Nov. The Boer Republic of the Transvaal in S Africa annexes the African state of Swaziland.

17 Nov. In W Africa Dahomey (now Benin) becomes a French protectorate.

AUSTRALASIA AND OCEANIA
17 Jan. Queen Liliukoalani of Hawaii abdicates. Islanders, with the connivance of the resident US minister, declare a republic after US marines land in support of American interests; Hawaii becomes a US protectorate (1 Feb.), but President Grover Cleveland revokes its protectorate status on 13 April.

— New Zealand becomes the first country to extend the suffrage to women.

ECONOMY AND SOCIETY
— In *The Division of Labour* the sociologist Emile Durkheim (see p. 448) puts forward the idea that society is an organism whose parts are interdependent.

SCIENCE AND TECHNOLOGY
11 July The first cultured pearl is produced by Mikimoto Kokichi on his pearl farm in Japan and leads to the development of a major industry.

6 Aug. In Greece, the Corinth ship canal linking the Gulf of Corinth and the Gulf of Athens is opened.

— The Norwegian explorer Fridtjof Nansen explores the polar Arctic and travels further N than any explorer to date.

— The first open-heart surgery is performed in Chicago, USA, by Daniel Hale Williams.

ARTS AND HUMANITIES
Literature
31 July The Gaelic League is founded in Ireland with the purpose of renewing the Irish language.

July Addressing the American Historical Association in Chicago on the theme of 'The Significance of the Frontier in American History', the historian Frederick Jackson Turner declares that the age of the frontier is now drawing to a close.

Gerhart Hauptmann, *Die Weber* (The Weavers), play.

José María de Heredia, *Les Trophées* (The Trophies), poetry.

Henrik Ibsen, *Bygmester Solness* (The Master Builder), play.

Maurice Maeterlinck, *Pelléas et Mélisande*, play.

Arthur Wing Pinero, *The Second Mrs Tanqueray*, play.

Oscar Wilde, *A Woman of No Importance*, play.

W.B. Yeats, *The Celtic Twilight*, collection of stories. The title will come to be used as an ironic description of the Irish literary revival.

Visual Arts and Architecture
— The Eros fountain, an improbable memorial to the philanthropist and British factory reformer Anthony Ashley Cooper, 7th earl of Shaftesbury, is opened in Piccadilly Circus, London.

Edvard Munch, *The Scream* and *The Voice*, paintings.

Music
1 Feb. First performance in Turin of Giacomo Puccini's opera *Manon Lescaut*.

9 Feb. First performance at La Scala, Milan, of Giuseppe Verdi's opera *Falstaff*, based on Shakespeare's *The Merry Wives of Windsor* and *King Henry IV* Parts 1 and 2.

9 Feb. The first staged musical striptease is performed at the Bal des Quatre Arts, Paris.

29 Dec. First performance in Weimar, Germany, of Engelbert Humperdinck's opera *Hänsel und Gretel*.

Antonín Dvořák, Symphony No. 9 in E minor (*From the New World*).

Mildred Hill, 'Happy Birthday to You', song.

Pyotr Tchaikovsky, Symphony No. 6 in B minor (*Pathétique*).

1894

EUROPE

5 Mar. In Britain the 84-year-old William Ewart Gladstone resigns as prime minister and his fourth and final ministry comes to an end, split by his support for Irish Home Rule. The Liberal Unionist Archibald Philip Primrose, earl of Rosebery, is Queen Victoria's choice as his successor.

20 Mar. Lajos Kossuth, Hungarian nationalist and leader of the 1848 revolution, dies in exile in Turin, Italy. His son Ferenc returns to Budapest to lead the party campaigning for Hungarian independence from Austria.

24 June President Marie-François-Sadi Carnot of France is assassinated in Lyons by an Italian anarchist, Santo Caserio. He is succeeded by Jean Casimir-Périer.

15 Oct. In France Capt. Alfred Dreyfus, a Jewish army officer, is arrested on a charge of spying for Germany.

26 Oct. Prince Chlodwig Hohenlohe succeeds Leo von Caprivi as imperial German Chancellor.

1 Nov. Tsar Alexander III of Russia dies and is succeeded by his son, Nicholas II, the last of the Romanov dynasty, who marries Princess Alexandra of Hesse-Darmstadt, Germany (26 Nov.). She is a granddaughter of Queen Victoria of Britain.

22 Dec. Anti-Semitism reaches a new peak in France with the conviction of Capt. Alfred Dreyfus, falsely accused of passing military intelligence to the Germans. Dreyfus is imprisoned on Devil's Island, French Guiana. The case will become a cause célèbre as French liberals campaign for his release. Anti-Semitism has been a feature of French public life since Jewish stockholders were blamed for the collapse of the Panama Canal company in 1889, an event regarded as a national humiliation.

– The German Reichstag moves into its new building in Berlin.

– In Britain the London Building Act limits new buildings to a height of 46m (150 feet).

ASIA

– Japan and China send troops to Korea in a clash over trade and influence in the peninsula. The Japanese sink the British ship *Kowshing*, which has been chartered to carry Chinese troops (25 July). Japan forces Korea to declare war on China (27 July) and follows suit shortly afterwards (1 Aug.). Britain agitates for a coalition of European powers and for the USA to intervene.

– In China Sun Zhong Shan (Sun Yat-sen) founds the Guomindang (nationalist party).

– The Dutch East Indies (now Indonesia) rebel against colonial rule. The revolt is suppressed but will break out again in 1896.

THE AMERICAS

May–June The Pullman strike brings the US railway network to a standstill. The strike is called by the American Railway Union in protest against the sacking of workers.

28 June The US Congress makes Labor Day, the Monday after the first Sunday in September, a public holiday.

4 July In Chicago, Illinois, violent clashes take place between striking railway workers and federal troops despatched by President Grover Cleveland to enforce a federal court injunction against the American Railway Union.

28 Aug. The Wilson–Gorman Tariff Act reduces US tariffs by 20%, but the basic features of the protectionist McKinley Act (1890) remain in place.

– The first railway across the S American Andes opens.

Emile Durkheim (1858–1917)

Emile Durkheim was effectively the inventor of sociology. Born in Lorraine, he came from a family with a long rabbinical tradition. This background shaped his sociology, which is dominated by the idea that society preserves itself through collective laws. He held a chair in sociology at the University of Bordeaux and then at the Sorbonne in Paris.

For Durkheim society is the sum of a mesh of customs and traditions that regulate the individual will. These customs and traditions are Durkheim's famous 'social facts' and are the subject matter of sociology. He was especially struck by the power of the 'conscious collective', the set of beliefs and duties that hold a society together. The division of labour in industrialized societies had produced a greater variety of occupations than those in previous societies. But a new kind of collective had emerged, in which there was a powerful interdependence between different social agents. This contradicted the established view that the division of labour had had a uniformly dehumanizing effect. In a similar way, Durkheim sought to challenge the view that crime is just a form of social wickedness. Society relies on visible sanctions, so crime has a social role since it gives society an opportunity to reinforce such sanctions. Both these theses illustrate the 'functionalism' of Durkheim's sociology, outlined in his *Division of Labour in Society* (1893) and *The Rules of Sociological Method* (1894). In his equally original study *Suicide* (1897) he argued that modern societies create a sense of rootlessness ('anomie') resulting from a lack of social cohesion. Durkheim's analysis of society as the true initial entity that explains the individual's satisfactions, desires and discontents seemed custom-made for the 20th century, when political and social history would be dominated by the collectivity.

- White American racism acquires a new focus with the campaign of the Immigration Restriction League, formed in Boston, to introduce literacy tests with the aim of excluding Asians, Latin Americans and Slavs.

SUB-SAHARAN AFRICA

15 Mar. France and Germany agree on the boundary between the Cameroons (a German protectorate since 1885) and the French Congo in Equatorial W Africa.

12 May In the continuing Scramble for Africa Britain and Belgium agree to territorial spheres of influence, which alarms both France and Germany. Britain is granted a lease on a corridor of land between Lake Tanganyika and Lake Albert Edward; in return Belgium is given a lease on lands W of the Upper Nile and N of the Congo–Nile link. Germany forces Britain to give up the corridor, which had been intended to realize the dream of a British territorial link between Cape Town and Cairo, while the French force the Belgians to cede their option on the northernmost part of their lease.

22 June Dahomey on the W African Bight of Benin becomes a French colony.

- Major gold reserves are discovered in Witwatersrand in the Boer Republic of the Transvaal, S Africa.

ECONOMY AND SOCIETY

- Radcliffe College for Women opens in Cambridge, Massachusetts, USA.
- Journalist Theodor Herzl of Vienna, covering the trial of French Jewish soldier Alfred Dreyfus in Paris, is inspired to write the founding text of political Zionism: *The Jewish State: An Attempt at a Modern Solution of the Jewish Question.*
- Michael Marks and Thomas Spencer start a department store in Manchester, NW England, which establishes the future international retail chain.
- At the Savoy Hotel in London the French chef Auguste Escoffier creates the dessert *Pêche Melba* (Peach Melba) in honour of the Australian soprano Nellie Melba.
- The US confectioner Milton Hershey creates the Hershey milk chocolate bar.

SCIENCE AND TECHNOLOGY

- In Britain Tower Bridge opens, spanning the River Thames near the Tower of London. It is designed by Sir Horace Jones and Sir John Wolfe-Barry, and the cantilever spans can be raised to allow ships to enter and leave the Pool of London.
- In NW England the 55km (35 mile) Manchester Ship Canal opens, linking Manchester with the Mersey estuary and its international markets.
- The bacillus *Pasteurella pestis*, which caused the Black Death (bubonic plague), is discovered by the Swiss and Japanese scientists A.E.J. Yersin and Kitazato Shibasaburo in Berlin.
- Eugéne Dubois, a Dutch palaeontologist, announces that he has discovered the fossils of an early humanoid living on Java, in Indonesia. The fossil remains of *Pithecanthropus erectus* are datable from 700,000 BC in the Upper Pleistocene era.

ARTS AND HUMANITIES

Literature

3 Dec. Scottish writer Robert Louis Stevenson dies in Samoa, S Pacific.

- Irish-born English newspaper entrepreneur Alfred Charles William Harmsworth buys and restructures the *London Evening News.*

Sir Arthur Conan Doyle, *The Memoirs of Sherlock Holmes*, detective stories.

George du Maurier, *Trilby*, novel.

Anthony Hope, *The Prisoner of Zenda*, adventure novel.

Rudyard Kipling, *The Jungle Book*, children's stories.

George Bernard Shaw, *Arms and the Man*, play.

Visual Arts and Architecture

- In Britain the Aesthetic Movement produces its showcase publication, *The Yellow Book*, a collection of essays by the movement's authors illustrated by Aubrey Beardsley.
- US glassmaker and interior decorator Louis Comfort Tiffany contributes to the Art Nouveau style by developing a technique for colouring molten glass.
- The US–Lithuanian critic and art dealer Bernard Berenson publishes *The Venetian Painters of the Renaissance*. He establishes new techniques for dating and authenticating works of art.

Edgar Degas, *Femme à sa toilette* (Woman at her Toilet), painting.

Claude Monet, *Rouen Cathedral*, painting.

Edvard Munch, *Anxiety*, painting.

Music

Anton Bruckner, Symphony No. 9 in D minor.

Claude Debussy, *Prélude à 'L'Après-midi d'un faune'* (Prelude to 'The Afternoon of a Faun'), tone poem.

Gustav Mahler, Symphony No. 2 in C minor (*Resurrection*).

1895

EUROPE

13 Jan. President Jean Casimir-Périer of France resigns and is succeeded by François-Félix Faure (17 Jan.).

April Vladimir Ilyich Ulyanov (who will later adopt the surname Lenin) (see p. 480) meets, and is influenced by, Russian journalist and historian Georgi Valentinovich Plekhanov, regarded as the father of Russian Marxism, in Geneva. He also travels to Zurich, Paris and Berlin before returning home where he is arrested for organizing strikes and writing dissident tracts (Dec.). Lenin's elder brother has already been executed (1887) by the tsarist state for plotting against the autocratic rule of Tsar Alexander III.

25 June In Britain, after the fall of the earl of Rosebery's Liberal government, Lord Salisbury becomes prime minister of a government composed of Conservatives and Liberal Unionists. Joseph Chamberlain becomes colonial secretary.

MIDDLE EAST AND NORTH AFRICA

1 Oct. In Constantinople Muslim Turks massacre Christian Armenians. In reponse Russia makes plans to take the city.

ASIA

17 April The treaty of Shimonoseki ends the Sino-Japanese War (see 1894). China is forced to recognize the independence of Korea and to cede Formosa (Taiwan) to Japan. China also agrees to pay a large indemnity and to open four extra ports to foreign trade. France gains commercial access to China's S provinces.

THE AMERICAS

24 Feb. A Cuban revolt against Spanish colonial rule begins.

SUB-SAHARAN AFRICA

Mar. Italian forces march into Ethiopia, aiming to expand Italy's possessions in NE Africa.

11 June In S Africa, Britain attempts to block the Boer Republic of the Transvaal gaining a corridor to the Indian Ocean by annexing Togoland. However, a new transport link is created with the opening of the Delagoa Bay Railway linking Johannesburg and Pretoria with the coast of Portuguese Mozambique (8 July).

Nov. Bechuanaland is annexed to Cape Colony.

29 Dec. Leander Starr Jameson, an associate of Cecil Rhodes, leads the Jameson raid from Bechuanaland into the independent Boer Transvaal with the aim of inciting a rebellion of *Uitlanders* (non-Boer whites) against the government of Paul Kruger (see also 1 Jan. 1896).

– The territory administered by the British South Africa Company S of the Zambezi River is named Rhodesia after Cecil Rhodes.

ECONOMY AND SOCIETY

– The London School of Economics is founded.

– The pioneering National Trust is created to conserve the British countryside and will develop as an organization also conserving the built heritage.

– The first American pizzeria opens in New York.

– In Huddersfield, N England, 22 northern rugby clubs break away from the Rugby Football Union to found the Northern Rugby Union (later to become the Rugby Football League).

SCIENCE AND TECHNOLOGY

8 Nov. Wilhelm Röntgen, professor of physics at Würzburg in Germany, discovers the X-ray.

– In Germany the Kiel Canal, linking the Baltic and North Seas, is opened.

– Belgian scientist Emile Van Ermengem discovers the botulism bacterium.

– Sigmund Freud (see p. 459), Austrian founder of psychoanalysis, collaborates with Josef Breuer in writing *Studien über Hysterie* (Studies in Hysteria) and postulates the sexual origin of mental disturbance.

ARTS AND HUMANITIES

Literature

14 Feb. *The Importance of Being Earnest* by Oscar Wilde is performed at St James's Theatre, London. Since 'earnest' is London society slang for 'homosexual', Wilde's comedy of assumed, double and covert identities is a provocative gesture by a homosexual writer.

April Oscar Wilde brings an action for libel against the marquess of Queensberry, who accuses him of homosexuality. The case collapses and Wilde is subsequently prosecuted at the Old Bailey in London. In the course of the trial Wilde is humiliated as one who has, in his own words, 'feasted with panthers' (had sex with London male prostitutes). He is sentenced to two years' hard labour (May). The conviction marks the start of a new era of state repression of homosexuals.

Joseph Conrad, *Almayer's Folly*, novel.

Stephen Crane, *The Red Badge of Courage*, novel.

Thomas Hardy, *Jude the Obscure*, novel.

Arthur Rimbaud, 'Le Bateau ivre' (The Drunken Boat), poem. Written in 1871 when Rimbaud was 16, it is now published by Rimbaud's former lover Paul Verlaine.

H.G. Wells, *The Time Machine*, novel.

Oscar Wilde, *An Ideal Husband*, play.

Visual Arts and Architecture

– The Venice Biennale opens, the first international exhibition of contemporary art.

Auguste Rodin, *Les Bourgeois de Calais* (The Burghers of Calais), sculpture.

Music

– In Britain Henry Wood conducts the first of the annual Promenade Concerts (or 'Proms') at the Queen's Hall, London.

Sergei Rachmaninov, Symphony No. 1 in D minor.

Richard Strauss, *Till Eulenspiegels lustige Streiche* (Till Eulenspiegel's Merry Pranks), tone poem.

Film

22 Mar. In Paris the brothers Louis and Auguste Lumière stage the first public screening of a motion picture using film projection at a rate of 16 frames per second. The film has been captured using a cine camera, the *cinématographe*.

20 May The first commercial showing of a film on screen takes place in New York with a 4-minute film of a boxing match.

1896

EUROPE

2 Feb. A Greek-inspired anti-Ottoman rebellion breaks out on the island of Crete in the E Mediterranean.

19 Feb. Bulgaria is recognized as a sovereign power by Russia following the conversion to Orthodox Christianity of Crown Prince Boris, son of Ferdinand I of Bulgaria. Formally, however, Bulgaria remains part of the Ottoman (Turkish) Empire.

24 Sept. Former Liberal prime minister W.E. Gladstone urges British action against Turkey following the Armenian massacres (see below).

– Anglo-German relations are in crisis following the sending of the Kruger telegram (see below).

MIDDLE EAST AND NORTH AFRICA

1 May The Shah of Persia, Nasir ud-Din, is assassinated and succeeded by his son Muzaffar ud-Din. Persia is increasingly under the influence of neighbouring Russia.

26 Aug. Christian Armenian nationalists attack the Ottoman Bank in Constantinople; the Turkish government responds with a campaign against Armenians, killing some 3000 and provoking an international outcry.

– Gen. Horatio Herbert Kitchener commands a joint British and Egyptian force to reclaim the Sudan from the control of the Khalifa (see 1885). The expedition's aim is to protect the Nile region from a French advance.

ASIA

– Over 20,000 people are killed in an earthquake in Japan.

THE AMERICAS

4 Jan. Utah becomes the 45th US state.

18 May In the case of Plessy vs. Ferguson the US Supreme Court rules that racially segregated railway carriages are legal on the basis of 'separate but equal' provision of public facilities.

11 July William Jennings Bryan wins the Democratic Party nomination for the US presidency. He is also supported by the Populist Party. However, a rise in wheat prices before election day (3 Nov.) loses Bryan some of his rural supporters and William McKinley wins the presidency for the Republicans.

17 Aug. Gold is discovered in Klondike near the Alaskan border in NW Canada and leads to a new gold rush.

SUB-SAHARAN AFRICA

1 Jan. Boer forces in the Transvaal repulse the Jameson raid at Krugersdorp (see 29 Dec. 1895) and Jameson himself surrenders (2 Jan.). The German Kaiser sends President Paul Kruger of the South African Republic a telegram of congratulations (3 Jan.). Jameson is turned over to the British authorities in S Africa, tried and convicted in England but given a light sentence. Cecil Rhodes resigns as premier of Cape Colony (6 Jan.), and a parliamentary committee in Cape Town finds him guilty of involvement in the Jameson raid.

18 Jan. The British occupy the Ashanti capital Kumasi, W Africa, in the course of the Fourth Ashanti (Asante) War.

1 Mar. Italian forces are defeated by the Ethiopians under King Menelik II at Adowa. The treaty of Addis Ababa ends the Italian protectorate over Abyssinia (26 Oct.).

6 June Major Jean-Baptiste Marchand, the explorer of the Niger River from sea to source, embarks on an expedition to assert French claims to S Sudan.

18 Aug. Madagascar is formally declared a French colony.

Oct. Britain suppresses a Matabele uprising in S Rhodesia.

ECONOMY AND SOCIETY

– In the USA, the College of New Jersey changes its name to Princeton University.

– The first modern Olympiad opens in Athens. Pierre de Fredi, baron de Coubertin, has campaigned for the restoration of the games with the support of Greek nationalists. The games were banned by the Romans in AD 194, and the Greeks have held minor games in 1859, 1870, 1875 and 1889.

– British journalist and newspaper magnate Alfred Harmsworth founds the *Daily Mail* newspaper, selling at one halfpenny.

SCIENCE AND TECHNOLOGY

– German scientist E. Baumann discovers iodine in the human thyroid gland.

– French physicist Antoine-Henri Becquerel discovers radioactivity in uranium.

– The US statistician Herman Hollerith (see 1890) forms the Tabulating Machine Company. It will later change its name to International Business Machines (IBM).

– Continental Europe's first underground railway opens in the Hungarian capital Budapest.

– Leyland Motors is founded in Lancashire, NW England.

– The world's first permanent wireless installation is established by the Marconi Wireless Telegraph Company on the Isle of Wight, S England.

ARTS AND HUMANITIES

Literature

Anton Chekhov, *The Seagull*, play.

Rubén Dario (Félix Rubén García Sarmiento), *Prosas profanas*, poetry.

Rémy de Gourmont, *Le Livre des masques* (The Book of Masks), a series of impressionistic sketches of Symbolist writers.

A.E. Housman, *A Shropshire Lad*, poetry.

Alfred Jarry, *Ubu Roi* (King Ubu), play, a forerunner of the 20th century 'theatre of the absurd'.

Oscar Wilde, *Salomé*, play.

Visual Arts and Architecture

– The Tate Gallery opens in London, endowed by the Liverpool sugar magnate Sir Henry Tate.

Music

1 Feb. First performance in Turin of Giacomo Puccini's opera *La Bohème* (The Bohemian Girl).

28 Mar. First performance at La Scala, Milan, of Umberto Giordano's opera *Andrea Chénier*.

11 Oct. Austrian composer Anton Bruckner dies in Vienna.

– The Manaus opera house opens some 1125km (700 miles) up the Amazon in N Brazil, financed by profits from the rubber trade.

James M. Black and Katharine E. Purvis, 'When the Saints Go Marching In', song.

Vincent d'Indy, *Istar*, symphonic variations.

Gustav Mahler, Symphony No. 3 in D minor.

Richard Strauss, *Also Sprach Zarathustra* (Thus Spake Zarathustra), tone poem based on Nietzsche's prose poem of the same name.

1897

EUROPE

6 Feb. The Cretan revolt against Turkey resumes and Crete proclaims union with Greece. Greek troops are sent in support, and the Turks declare war on Greece in retaliation (7 April). The Greeks are forced to withdraw, and, following intervention by the major European powers, an armistice is declared (19 May).

15 June Alfred von Tirpitz becomes German navy minister.

20 June In Britain Queen Victoria celebrates her Diamond Jubilee.

16 Dec. The peace of Constantinople ends the Greco-Turkish war.

MIDDLE EAST AND NORTH AFRICA

31 Aug. The first Zionist congress is held in Basle, Switzerland, and Hungarian-born Theodor Herzl outlines his plan for a Jewish settlement in Palestine. He will also offer to buy up the Ottoman national debt in return for Jewish rights in Palestine.

ASIA

28 Mar. The Japanese yen is tied to the Gold Standard.

14 Nov. German forces occupy Qingdao (Tsing-tao) in China following the murder of several German missionaries. In the wake of the German intervention, the other European powers agitate for territorial and trade concessions in China.

13 Dec. In response to Germany's seizure of Qingdao in China, Russia occupies Port Arthur in Manchuria.

THE AMERICAS

4 Mar. William McKinley takes office as 25th US president.

– As demand outreaches supply in Europe's wheat market the US Chicago speculator, Joseph Leiter, corners the market in wheat futures.

– Spain's liberal government offers autonomy to Cuba, but the island's nationalist movement wants complete independence and rejects the offer.

SUB-SAHARAN AFRICA

Feb. The Belgian army defeats the Dervishes of the Sudan and occupies Loda and Wadelai, but the Balelas rise (Sept.) against the Belgian occupiers in the Upper Congo, and the ensuing conflict lasts until 1900.

6 April Zanzibar, a British protectorate since 1890, abolishes slavery.

10 July The French force commanded by Jean-Baptiste Marchand (see 6 June 1896) occupies Fashoda in SE Sudan.

23 July France and Germany agree on the boundary between Dahomey and Togoland in W Africa.

ECONOMY AND SOCIETY

– Moss Bros. of London, founded by Moses Moss in 1860, develops its formal-wear hire business.

– The Waldorf-Astoria Hotel, New York, opens as the world's most luxurious hotel.

– A Ferris wheel, 64m (210 feet) high, is installed at the Prater Park, Vienna.

SCIENCE AND TECHNOLOGY

– The English physicist Joseph Thomson discovers the electron. Thomson takes forward the idea of atomic structure first suggested by English chemist John Dalton (1803) and then tabulated by Russian chemist Dmitri Mendeleyev (1870). He shows that each element has a different atomic weight and a different atomic number, which is the equivalent of the number of electrons revolving around the nuclei of the element's atoms.

– In Britain the soap manufacturer William Lever launches Lifebuoy soap.

ARTS AND HUMANITIES

Literature

– The new US Library of Congress is completed in Washington, D.C.

– The Theatre du Grand Guignol opens in Paris and will become celebrated for its horror plays.

Joseph Conrad, *The Nigger of the 'Narcissus'*, novel.

Stefan George, *Das Jahre der Seele* (The Year of the Soul), collected poems.

André Gide, *Les Nourritures terrestres* (The Fruits of the Earth), a hymn to life's pleasures in prose and verse.

Henrik Ibsen, *John Gabriel Borkman*, play.

Henry James, *The Spoils of Poynton* and *What Maisie Knew*, novellas.

Rudyard Kipling, *Captains Courageous*, novel, and 'Recessional', poem.

William Somerset Maugham, *Liza of Lambeth*, novel.

Charles Péguy, 'Jeanne d'Arc', poem.

Edmond Rostand, *Cyrano de Bergerac*, play.

George Bernard Shaw, *The Devil's Disciple*, play.

Bram (Abraham) Stoker, *Dracula*, novel.

H.G. Wells, *The Invisible Man*, novel.

Visual Arts and Architecture

– The Art Nouveau Gallery opens in Paris with an exhibition of the works of Edvard Munch. The gallery lends its name to the style of Art Nouveau (new art).

Paul Gauguin, *Where do we come from? What are we? Where are we going?*, painting.

Edvard Munch, *Frieze of Life*, painting.

Camille Pissarro, *Boulevard des Italiennes*, painting.

Music

3 April The German composer Johannes Brahms dies in Vienna.

Paul Dukas, *L'Apprenti Sorcier* (The Sorcerer's Apprentice), orchestral scherzo.

John Philip Sousa, 'The Stars and Stripes Forever', march.

1898

EUROPE

11 Jan. In France Major Count Walzin Esterházy is acquitted of the forgery of the key document in the Dreyfus case (see 22 Dec. 1894).

13 Jan. French writer Emile Zola's open letter to the French government, 'J'Accuse', prompted by the Dreyfus case, is published in *L'Aurore*. Zola protests that Dreyfus is the victim of an anti-Semitic plot. The article leads to Zola being imprisoned (23 Feb.).

28 Mar. Alfred von Tirpitz (see 15 June 1897) introduces the first German Navy Bill, initiating the expansion of German naval power to compete with Britain.

10 Sept. The Austrian empress Elizabeth is stabbed and killed by an Italian anarchist, Luigi Luccheni, at Geneva.

ASIA

25 April Russia and Japan agree not to interfere in Korean internal affairs by the terms of the Nishi-Rosen protocol, but the Japanese are permitted to develop their economic interests in the country.

21 Sept. In China the reactionary dowager empress Cixi (Tzu Hsi) seizes power and reverses the reforming policies of her nephew, Emperor Guangxu.

– The Huang He (or Yellow) River in Shandong province, China, bursts its banks killing many and flooding a huge area.

– An outbreak of bubonic plague in China and India develops into a ten-year epidemic, which kills about 3 million people.

THE AMERICAS

15 Feb. A Spanish–American War (lasting 112 days) is triggered by the sinking of the US battleship *Maine* in Havana harbour, Cuba, with the loss of 260 crewmen. The *New York Journal*, owned by William Randolph Hearst, has already aggravated the situation by publishing a stolen letter (9 Feb.), written by the Spanish ambassador to the USA, insulting President William McKinley. The US Republican administration wishes to end Spanish rule over Cuba and exploits these events to pursue a policy of imperial expansion; Theodore Roosevelt, assistant secretary of the navy, instructs (25 Feb.) the US fleet's Far Eastern squadron to prepare for an attack on the Spanish fleet in the Philippines, and the US army mobilizes (9 Mar.). Spain is conciliatory and attributes the loss of the *Maine* to an internal explosion, but the US Navy's enquiry concludes that the cause was external aggression (21 Mar.). The European powers call for a peaceful solution to the conflict, but McKinley is bent on war. The US Congress recognizes Cuban independence (19 April), and McKinley persists with demands that Spain de-colonize the island while promising that the USA has no plans to annex Cuba. Preparations for war proceed, and by the terms of the Volunteer Army Act (22 April) the Rough Riders (a volunteer cavalry contingent) are created and now organized by Theodore Roosevelt, who resigns as assistant secretary of the navy and becomes their colonel.

24 April Spain declares war, followed the next day by the USA. At the battle of Manila in the Philippines (1 May) the US navy sinks the ten ships of the Spanish squadron; other forces invade Guantánamo Bay (10 June) and Santiago in Cuba, where Roosevelt plays a leading role.

15 June At a public meeting in Boston an anti-imperialist league is formed to oppose the anticipated US annexation of the Philippines.

June The US Congress approves the US annexation of Hawaii. The islands are transferred to the USA on 12 Aug.

7 July President McKinley signs the resolution of Congress annexing the Hawaiian islands.

25 July US forces invade the Spanish island of Puerto Rico in the Caribbean.

12 Aug. Spain grants Cuba its independence.

10 Dec. The treaty of Paris ends the Spanish–American War: Spain withdraws from Cuba and cedes Puerto Rico to the USA. Spain also relinquishes the Philippines for $20 million. The treaty marks the end of Spain's remaining S American empire and the emergence of the USA as a major Pacific power.

– In the S USA the Louisiana state legislature restricts voting to those blacks whose forebears were eligible to vote in 1867, which amounts to a withdrawal of the franchise from black Americans in Louisiana. Race riots and lynchings follow across the S states.

SUB-SAHARAN AFRICA

2 Sept. Gen. Horatio Kitchener's British–Egyptian army defeats the forces of the khalifate at the battle of Omdurman in the Sudan, killing more than 10,000 Dervishes; Khartoum is retaken.

19 Sept. Gen. Horatio Kitchener reaches Fashoda on the Nile in SE Sudan where he confronts a French expedition which, under Jean-Baptiste Marchand, has marched from Brazzaville in the French Congo to the Sudan. Marchand claims the area W of the Nile for France but the British, concerned to maintain their mastery of the region, assert Egypt's claim to the Sudan; the French are forced to withdraw from Fashoda (3 Nov.).

ECONOMY AND SOCIETY

– Northeastern University, Boston, USA, is founded.

– The luxury Claridge's Hotel opens in London.

– The Paris Ritz opens with Auguste Escoffier as the chef.

– In the USA John Harvey and W.K. Kellogg introduce cornflakes.

SCIENCE AND TECHNOLOGY

– The German pharmaceutical firm Friedrich Bayer and Company of Munich introduce heroin, derived from opium, as a cough treatment.

– Marie Curie, French physicist, and her husband, Pierre, isolate radium.

ARTS AND HUMANITIES

Literature

Henry James, *The Turn of the Screw*, short story.

Arthur Wing Pinero, *Trelawney of the 'Wells'*, play.

Italo Svevo, *Senilità* (As a Man Grows Older), novel.

H.G. Wells, *The War of the Worlds*, science fiction novel.

Oscar Wilde, *The Ballad of Reading Gaol*, poem.

Visual Arts and Architecture

16 Mar. English artist Aubrey Beardsley dies of tuberculosis in Menton, France.

18 April French painter Gustave Moreau dies.

17 June English artist Sir Edward Burne-Jones dies.

– Work begins on the construction of the new Glasgow School of Art buildings designed by Charles Rennie Mackintosh following an architectural competition.

– Russian actor and theatre director Konstantin Stanislavsky founds the Moscow Arts Theatre; his 'method' of reproducing feeling on stage by empathetic means will revolutionize European acting techniques.

Music

Charles Ives, Symphony No. 1 in D minor.

1899

1899

EUROPE

16 Feb. President Félix Faure, who has opposed a new trial for French Jewish soldier Capt. Alfred Dreyfus (see Jan. 1898), dies. He is succeeded by Emile Loubet; a retrial is ordered (3 June).

9 Sept. At his retrial in Rennes Dreyfus's conviction is confirmed, although heavily qualified, and he is pardoned (19 Sept.). The Dreyfus affair leads to the founding of the militant right-wing nationalist movement Action Française, backed by the newspaper of the same name edited by Léon Daudet. Charles Maurras, the movement's founder, uses French history and literature to martial the forces of royalism, Catholicism and traditionalism that have been defeated and shaken by the Dreyfus affair.

– The Russian population is gradually expanding E into Siberia. The long process of Russian colonization of the region rapidly increases with the building of the Trans-Siberian Railway.

ASIA

– The USA proposes that the main Western countries represented in China should have areas of special interest in designated commercial zones. The European powers agree to the proposals.

THE AMERICAS

4 Feb. Having obtained the Philippines at the end of the Spanish–American War (see 10 Dec. 1898), the USA seeks to retain them as an imperial possession against the wishes of local nationalists. US soldiers, in an act of calculated aggression, open fire on irregular Filipino forces in Manila, and the three and a half year-long war that follows demonstrates the USA's intention to retain its new dominance in the Pacific.

10 April Theodore Roosevelt, now governor of New York, declares in a Chicago speech: 'I wish to preach, not the doctrine of ignoble ease, but the doctrine of the strenuous life.' The new American imperialism leads to a domestic debate about whether the principles of the republic allow such expansion.

SUB-SAHARAN AFRICA

21 Mar. An Anglo-French convention resolves the Fashoda Incident (see 19 Sept. 1898).

5 June In S Africa the Bloemfontein conference ends with Britain and the Boers failing to reach agreement on the extension of the franchise to non-Boer whites (*Uitlanders*) in the Transvaal.

9 Oct. The Transvaal president Paul Kruger sends an ultimatum demanding that Britain stop sending troops to S Africa. The Boers suspect the impending British annexation of Transvaal and its gold mines.

12 Oct. The second South African War, or Boer War, breaks out between Britain and the Boers of the Transvaal and the Orange Free State. Boer forces invade Natal and Cape Colony, laying siege to Mafeking (13 Oct.), Kimberley (15 Oct.) and Ladysmith (2 Nov.).

15 Dec. At the end of the 'black week' for British forces in S Africa, a British force under Gen. Sir Redvers Buller is defeated by the Boers at Colenso, Natal.

ECONOMY AND SOCIETY

Mar. Louis and Marcel Renault found the French vehicle manufacturer Renault Frères.

1 July The Italian vehicle manufacturer Fabbrica Italiana Automobili di Torino (FIAT) is founded by Giovanni Agnelli.

– The Nippon Electric Company (NEC) is founded. It will become Japan's dominant company in manufacturing electrical goods.

– Rosa Luxemburg, the Polish-born Marxist writer and revolutionary now living in Berlin, rejects the idea of a gradual evolution from capitalism to communism. Faith in liberal intent, she says, will not overcome the dominant force of factory-capitalism; change can only come by international revolution.

– The US philosopher John Dewey expounds his theory of education in *School and Society*.

– The US sociologist Thorstein Veblen criticizes 'conspicuous consumption of valuable goods' in his study *The Theory of the Leisure Class*.

– The end of the 19th century sees the start of a global cholera pandemic, which will last until the early 1920s.

SCIENCE AND TECHNOLOGY

– German chemist Felix Hoffmann and pharmacologist Heinrich Dreser develop aspirin in powdered form.

ARTS AND HUMANITIES

Literature

Anton Chekhov, *Uncle Vanya*, play.

E.W. Hornung, *The Amateur Cracksman*, novel, the first in a series featuring the gentleman-burglar Raffles.

Rudyard Kipling, 'The White Man's Burden', poem, and *Stalky and Co.*, tales of schoolboy life.

E. Nesbit, *The Story of the Treasure-Seekers*, novel for children.

Leo Tolstoy, *Resurrection*, novel.

Visual Arts and Architecture

29 Jan. French artist Alfred Sisley dies.

– Claude Monet paints *Water Lilies*, the first in a series of such paintings.

– Scottish architect Charles Rennie Mackintosh's new Glasgow School of Art building opens.

Paul Gauguin, *Two Tahitian Women*, painting.

Edouard Vuillard, *Paysages et intérieurs* (Landscapes and Interiors), lithographs.

Music

– African-American composer and pianist Scott Joplin's ragtime compositions for piano begin to appear in published form.

Isaac Albéniz, *Catalonia*, orchestral rhapsody.

Sir Edward Elgar, *Enigma Variations*, orchestral work, and *Sea Pictures*, song cycle for mezzo-soprano, chorus and orchestra.

Maurice Ravel, *Pavane pour une infante défunte* (Pavane for a Dead Princess), piano piece.

Arnold Schoenberg, *Verklärte Nacht* (Transfigured Night), string sextet.

Jean Sibelius, Symphony No. 1 in E minor and *Finlandia*, tone poem, which expresses Finnish nationalist feeling.

4

The Modern World

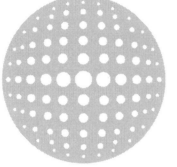

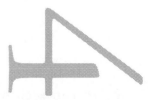

1900–2004

4. The Modern World

The history of the 20th century illustrates the effectiveness of the modern bureaucratic state. Both world wars showed the capacity of governments to mobilize armies and to equip their military machines. War also demonstrated the state's ability to mobilize the civilian workforce and to exploit industrial capacity to serve a national purpose. Technology extended government influence both in war and in peace. Radio, films and television were used by both democratic and autocratic regimes to communicate their propaganda. As horse and steam power were overtaken by the petrol engine, and the age of the telegraph yielded to that of the internet, it became easier for governments to amass information and to make their wishes become reality.

The 20th century's ideological systems also seemed to confirm the authority of government. Democratic states turned towards systems of welfare provision, partly as a means of ensuring social solidarity. David Lloyd George's introduction of social-security benefits into Britain prior to World War I anticipated the full-scale welfare state that was an essential ingredient of the 1945 settlement in western Europe. In the 1930s, fascism appeared to be the dynamic new ideological element in European politics. In Spain it built on Catholic conservatism; in Italy it used the rhetoric of empire and national pride; and in Germany it developed a racist and heavily militaristic character. Soviet communism placed its faith in the ideal of collectivism. In practical terms it used military force to occupy and enforce its ideals on the unenthusiastic populations of the Baltic states, Poland, Hungary, Romania, Bulgaria and Czechoslovakia.

But the effectiveness of government sometimes sowed the seeds of its own decline, as governments overreached themselves. The Soviet attempt to maintain an Asian empire while repressing its European satellites and organizing a centrally planned economy proved too much for the state apparatus to achieve. The fact that the Soviet Union survived for so long is testimony both to the power of the original ideas on which it was founded and the repression that enforced those ideas.

After the fall of Soviet communism in 1989–90, free-market principles helped to reconstruct the economies of those eastern European countries that could build on a pre-communist history of democratic civil institutions and capitalist drive. But Russia, which had never enjoyed either to any great extent, found it difficult to adapt. The fall of the Berlin Wall in 1989 led to the democratization of central and eastern Europe. But it also showed the power of another idea – that of a global capitalism, a phenomenon in which capital and goods flow freely between countries. Global capitalism

had initially been pioneered in Europe in the late 19th century, but by the end of the 20th century it was equated with the dynamism of the US economy.

The welfare states of democratic societies also ran into increasing difficulties from the 1970s onwards. Economic problems led to government cut-backs, and encouraged a more widespread critique of what government should and should not do. This led to the policy of privatization, as government-owned businesses and industries were sold off to the private sector.

The first half of the 20th century showed the potentially harmful effects of competitively pursued nation-state politics. Some thought this lesson was an obvious one to be drawn from World War I. But the Paris Peace Conference was dominated by the agenda of the US president Woodrow Wilson. Wilson believed in an international order founded on the collective security of nation-states and operating under an international organization (the League of Nations). Where it was thought necessary, the treaty invented or yoked together nations into states, as in the cases of Czechoslovakia and Yugoslavia. For Wilson the key to the post-1918 order was the collapse of the multinational dynastic empires of Russia, Germany, Austria-Hungary and the Ottoman Turks. But what emerged from the Wilson-inspired League of Nations was an arrangement which, to some, seemed to be an extension of empire. A system of mandates was established in the Middle East, by which the established European powers of Britain and France governed large areas of the former Ottoman empire as protectorates and prepared these territories for self-government. By these means, Britain's empire actually reached its greatest territorial expansion in the 1920s.

The weaknesses of European democracy in the interwar period were partly the result of a power vacuum. The USSR had withdrawn within its own borders to consolidate the communist revolution of 1917, pursuing a policy of 'socialism in one country'. The USA had embarked on a policy of isolation and had disengaged from European politics. It was left to Britain and France to try to limit German and Italian expansionism. The fact that both countries were also struggling to maintain global empires meant that their diplomacy could not focus consistently on the developing European crisis that would result in World War II.

The 20th century witnessed the persistent growth in influence of US culture and business on the rest of the world. But, although the USA sought to end the hegemony of the European empires, there was also a domestic aversion to foreign entanglement. The USA entered World War I late in

1917, and then only in response to German attacks on its merchant shipping. Similarly, the USA went to war in 1941 only after it was directly attacked, this time by Japan. The USA has generally been content to enjoy its commercial prosperity and cultural self-confidence in peace. It has only embarked on foreign adventures when it has perceived a threat to its own security or wealth.

A global catastrophe in two world wars encouraged the conclusion that a new international order was needed. The League of Nations failed in this role during the 1930s, but the United Nations was more successful from the 1950s onward. The ending of apartheid in South Africa (1994), for example, was largely a success for UN diplomacy and sanctions. The wars in Bosnia (1991–5) and in Iraq (2003–), however, were a failure for the UN, which found itself bypassed in both instances. The UN operated at a global level, but there were also regional groupings that bound states together. These included economic organizations such as the European Economic Community (later the European Union) and military alliances such as the North Atlantic Treaty Organization (Nato).

The mid-20th century witnessed the decolonization of Africa, southern Asia and other areas of European imperial rule. Sometimes decolonization was well-intentioned but ill thought-out, as in the partition of India in 1947. Sometimes it was the product of a violent national rebellion, as in the Algerian revolt against France (1954–62). Sometimes the liberated country descended into civil war, as happened in the Congo (1960–5) and Nigeria (1967–70). The initial outcome was rarely an orderly democracy – India being a notable exception.

China was the 20th century's superpower in waiting, and it went against Western expectations. First it married Marxist communism to the needs of a peasant and agrarian economy, while adding a dash of Confucian authoritarianism into the mixture. Then, after the death of Mao, China proved the possibility of uniting capitalism with a totalitarian state machine – thereby disproving the Western belief that political liberty and economic freedom were completely interdependent.

For most of the second half of the 20th century, the Middle East was a cockpit of turmoil and warfare. The creation in 1948 of Israel as a homeland for those European Jews who had survived the Holocaust led to frustration and resentment among the Arabs who were asked to make way

for the new state. Several wars followed, the conflicts being made all the more important on a global scale by the vast oil reserves of the region. In the last 20 years of the 20th century the region was transformed by the political radicalism of fundamentalist Islam, which became increasingly anti-Western in rhetoric and increasingly violent in its methods. The USA was the major object of attack. US power was demonized by an Islamic movement that saw all the internal social, political and economic problems of the Middle East as the consequence of US intrigue in pursuit of oil or in support of Israel. In 1979 the shah of Iran, an autocratic ruler friendly to the USA, was toppled in an Islamic revolution. The coming to power of the Taliban in Afghanistan seemed to consolidate the position of radical Islamist regimes in the area.

But when one group of Islamic extremists backed up their anti-American rhetoric with large-scale terrorist attacks from 2001 onwards the situation changed. No longer were the USA and other countries prepared to view radical Islam as merely a matter for the Muslim countries. Now the growing radicalism was seen as a direct threat to the prosperity, culture and peace of the West. The USA declared a 'war on terror' and set its formidable military and economic powers in motion. First to fall was the Taliban government of Afghanistan, as

The effectiveness of government sometimes sowed the seeds of its own decline.

American planes destroyed their grip on power and allowed other Afghan groups to take control. Next was Iraq, where the regime was overthrown in a lightning military campaign in 2003. In this war on terror, the USA has sought allies where it can, but has been impatient with the niceties of internationalism. Arguing that the international institutions designed to help relations between states are inadequate in a trans-global struggle against stateless terror organizations, the USA has ignored those who have protested against its actions. At the beginning of the 21st century, therefore, it was uncertain whether effective international order could be anything other than a synonym for US power.

1900

EUROPE

29 Jan. After three years of exile in Siberia, the Russian revolutionary Vladimir Ilyich Ulyanov (Lenin) (see p. 480) is released. He emigrates to Switzerland (16 July) and becomes the editor of the revolutionary newspaper *Iskra* (The Spark).

27 Feb. At a meeting of socialist organizations and trades unionists in London (including the Fabian Society and the Independent Labour Party, see 13 Jan. 1893), the Labour Representation Committee is formed. It will be renamed the Labour Party in 1906.

29 July In Italy anarchists assassinate King Umberto I at Monza. He is succeeded by his son, Victor Emmanuel III.

10 Oct. In Germany Chlodwig von Hohenlohe resigns as chancellor and is replaced by his foreign minister, the nationalist Prince von Bülow (17 Oct.).

16 Oct. In the so-called 'Khaki' election in Britain, the Conservatives, benefiting from British successes in the Boer War (and from continuing splits in the Liberal opposition), are re-elected. Lord Salisbury, who remains premier, is the last British prime minister to sit in the unelected House of Lords.

ASIA

20 Mar. The US, British, German, Russian, Italian and Japanese governments agree to an 'open door' policy in China: none will seek exclusive spheres of influence that could lead to partition. But within China anti-Western sentiment has already erupted into armed attacks on foreigners led by the Yi He Zhuan (I Ho Ch'uan), or Righteous Harmonious Fists, known in the West as the Boxers.

20 June As the Boxer rebellion gains momentum in China, the German envoy in Beijing is murdered and the foreign legations in Beijing are besieged for eight weeks. The dowager empress Cixi (Tzu Hsi) encourages the wave of xenophobia, which spreads throughout the country, and orders Chinese forces to support the Boxers. An international expeditionary force relieves the besieged legations (14 Aug.), but more than 200 foreigners are murdered in various parts of China. Russia responds to hostile fire across the Amur River by driving thousands of Chinese to their deaths in the river. In the autumn the Russians seize S Manchuria (4 Sept.).

THE AMERICAS

6 Mar. In the USA bubonic plague takes hold in San Francisco's Chinatown and begins to spread throughout the city.

14 Mar. The US government joins the Gold Standard, pinning the value of the dollar to gold.

Aug. A series of earthquakes in Ecuador and Peru kill thousands.

6 Nov. In the US presidential election the Republican incumbent William McKinley is re-elected over the Democratic candidate William Jennings Bryan.

SUB-SAHARAN AFRICA

10 Jan. In the Anglo-Boer War Gen. Frederick Roberts arrives in

South Africa to replace Sir Redvers Buller as commander-in-chief of the British forces, with Horatio Kitchener as his chief of staff and eventual successor (Nov.). British forces begin to reverse early humiliations, and despite defeat at Spion Kop (25 Jan.), Kimberley is relieved (15 Feb.), and Roberts forces the surrender of the Boer leader Piet Cronje (27 Feb.). The British relieve Ladysmith (28 Feb.) and then take the Orange Free State capital, Bloemfontein (13 Mar.). Mafeking is relieved after a 215-day siege (17 May), and the British take the Transvaal cities of Johannesburg (31 May) and Pretoria (5 June). Britain annexes the Orange Free State and the Transvaal (which now become the Orange River Colony and the Transvaal Colony, respectively). Boer leader Paul Kruger travels to Germany to plead for support, but Kaiser Wilhelm II refuses to see him (6 Oct.). A bitter guerrilla war develops as die-hard Boers are determined to fight until the end. Kitchener places some 120,000 Boer women and children in 'concentration camps' to stop them providing supplies and shelter to the fighting men. Some 20,000 will die of malnutrition and disease by the end of the war (31 May 1902).

ECONOMY AND SOCIETY

May–Oct. The 2nd Olympic Games are held in Paris.

14 June The first international championship motor race is run from Paris to Lyons, with the prize a cup donated by the New York publisher and playboy James Gordon Bennett.

Aug. The USA defeats Britain in the inaugural Davis Cup, an international challenge cup for men's lawn tennis, donated by Dwight Filley Davis.

− In Britain a university is founded in Birmingham, an industrial centre.

− Erich Weiss, a Hungarian-born US escape artist, adopts the name Houdini and begins a four-year European tour.

− André and Edouard Michelin, French tyre producers, commission the *Guide Michelin*, a guide to European hotels and restaurants.

− By this date there are more than 1.3 million telephones in use in the USA.

SCIENCE AND TECHNOLOGY

Jan. Britain's first petrol-fuelled omnibuses go into service in Norfolk.

2 July German aeronaut Ferdinand von Zeppelin launches the first rigid airship at Friedrichshafen on Lake Constance.

19 July The Paris Métro (underground railway) opens.

− French manufacturers Marcel and Louis Renault pioneer the glass-fronted, two-passenger motorcar.

− The first stage of the Trans-Siberian Railway opens between Moscow and Irkutsk in S Siberia.

− In the USA the Chicago Sanitary and Ship Canal connects the Great Lakes with the Mississippi and the Gulf of Mexico.

− In Germany the physicist Max Planck elaborates quantum theory, which will revolutionize understanding of atomic and subatomic processes.

− The US Navy becomes the first naval force to buy a submarine.

Sigmund Freud (1856–1939)

The Austrian psychiatrist Sigmund Freud was the founder of psychoanalysis. His ambition was to create a scientific psychology that explained the human mind in much the same way that the laws of physics and chemistry explain the phenomena of the physical world. Mental events, Freud believed, were determined by identifiable causes. Human beings, therefore, were not as free as they thought they were.

Freud's early clinical work involved cases of hysteria and sexual neurosis, and studying such cases led him to the claim that repressed emotions betrayed themselves by physical expressions. He experimented with 'free association', encouraging his patients to say whatever came into their heads. By these means Freud sought to revive the repressed traumas that determined their behaviour so that these could be confronted and resolved. Freud went on to study dreams, and his book *The Interpretation of Dreams* (1900) made three startling claims: that dreams express the fulfilment of desires we have suppressed; that human beings subconsciously desire sex with the parent of the opposite sex and to kill the parent of the same sex; and that children have sexual feelings. Subsequently Freud proposed that the human mind has three aspects: the id (instinct), the ego (conscious reason, which keeps the id under control) and the super-ego (self-criticism and self-judgement).

Freud's ideas about the unconscious and repression became part of everyday thought and speech in the 20th century – for example, in the common phrase 'Freudian slip'. His ideas opened up for discussion areas of human life – especially relating to sex – previously kept hidden. Freud's work led criminologists, educators and legislators to a more compassionate view of 'deviant' behaviour, and also had a profound influence on many creative artists in the 20th century.

- Austrian botanist Gregor Mendel's genetic laws, propounded in 1865, are confirmed and published by, among others, Hugo de Vries of the University of Amsterdam.
- Scottish-born US industrialist Andrew Carnegie endows the Carnegie Institute of Technology, Pittsburgh, USA.
- Austrian psychoanalyst Sigmund Freud (see box) publishes *Die Traumdeutung* (The Interpretation of Dreams). He applies psychoanalysis to the analysis of dreams as the revelation of unconscious desire.
- British archaeologist Arthur Evans discovers the Bronze Age site of the palace of Knossos, Crete. He has also discovered a pre-Phoenician script.

ARTS AND HUMANITIES

Literature

- British journalist Cyril Arthur Pearson founds the *Daily Express* newspaper.

L(yman) Frank Baum, *The Wizard of Oz*, children's novel.

Anton Chekhov, *Uncle Vanya*, play.

Sidonie-Gabrielle Colette, *Claudine à l'école* (Claudine at School), novel.

Joseph Conrad, *Lord Jim*, novel.

Gabriele D'Annunzio, *Il fuoco* (The Flame of Life), novel influenced by his fascination with Italian actress Eleanora Duse.

Theodore Dreiser, *Sister Carrie*, novel.

H(erbert) G(eorge) Wells, *Love and Mr Lewisham*, novel.

Visual Arts and Architecture

Paul Cézanne, *Still Life with Onions*, painting.

Gustav Klimt, *Philosophy*, mural for the University of Vienna.

Pablo Picasso (see p. 467), *Le Moulin de La Galette*, painting.

Pierre-Auguste Renoir, *Nude in the Sun*, painting.

John Singer Sargent, *The Wyndham Sisters*, painting.

Music

14 Jan. First performance in Rome of Giacomo Puccini's opera *Tosca*, based on the conflict in Rome in the 1790s between liberals and monarchists.

2 Feb. First performance in Paris of Gustave Charpentier's opera *Louise*.

15 Oct. In the USA Boston's Symphony Hall opens and the Philadelphia Orchestra gives its first concert (16 Nov.).

Samuel Coleridge-Taylor, *Hiawatha's Wedding Feast*, cantata based on the poem by Henry Wadsworth Longfellow.

Sir Edward Elgar, *The Dream of Gerontius*, oratorio based on a dramatic monologue by Cardinal Newman.

Gustav Mahler, Symphony No. 4 in G minor.

1901

EUROPE

22 Jan. In Britain Queen Victoria dies and is succeeded by her 60-year-old son, Edward VII, who becomes the first ruler of the House of Saxe-Coburg-Gotha.

22 July In Britain the House of Lords rules on the Taff Vale case (in which the Taff Vale Railway Company sued the Amalgamated Society of Railway Servants for damages); the society is fined £23,000 and the case establishes that a trade union can be held liable for damages caused by its members during a strike.

- By now Ludwig Nobel (brother of Alfred, the inventor of dynamite) and the Rothschilds (a banking and oil family) have developed the Baku oil fields in the Russian Caucasus (modern Azerbaijan), which produce most of the world's oil output. The USA, however, produces two-thirds of the world's total exported petroleum.

MIDDLE EAST AND NORTH AFRICA

- The Shah of Persia sells a 60-year concession for oil exploration in most of the country to New Zealand financier William Knox D'Arcy; D'Arcy will sell his concession to the Burmah Oil Co. in 1908, which will then form the Anglo-Persian Oil Co.

ASIA

7 Sept. The peace of Beijing ends the Boxer rebellion; China is forced to pay indemnities to the Western powers.

Sept. Filipino guerrillas massacre a US garrison on the island of Samar. US Gen. Jacob F. Smith's retaliation is so brutal that he is court-martialled. The rebellion will not be suppressed until 1906.

– George Curzon, viceroy of India, creates the North-West Frontier Province, separating Afghanistan from the Punjab.

THE AMERICAS

4 Mar. William McKinley starts his second term as US president.

12 June The provisons of the new Cuban constitution make it a virtual US protectorate.

6 Sept. US president McKinley is shot by Polish-American anarchist Leon Czolgosz. He dies of his wounds (14 Sept.) and Vice-President Theodore Roosevelt succeeds as the 26th president.

17 Oct. President Roosevelt entertains African-American leader Booker T. Washington at the White House, causing outrage in the Southern states of the USA.

18 Nov. The USA and Britain sign the Hay–Pauncefote treaty, agreeing that the USA will build and control a canal through the Panama isthmus.

– In the USA Alabama's new state constitution includes laws and clauses to disenfranchise African-Americans.

SUB-SAHARAN AFRICA

Oct. In S Africa British forces repel an attempted Boer invasion of Cape Colony.

26 Dec. In E Africa the Uganda Railway is completed: it links Mombasa with Lake Victoria.

AUSTRALASIA AND OCEANIA

1 Jan. The Commonwealth of Australia comes into being, incorporating New South Wales, Queensland, South Australia, Victoria, Tasmania, the Northern Territory and Western Australia.

ECONOMY AND SOCIETY

10 Jan. Oil is discovered in Texas.

Feb. The US financier J.P. Morgan acquires Andrew Carnegie's assets and creates the US Steel Corporation.

– The Imperial Tobacco Company of Great Britain and Ireland is created by Sir William Henry Wills.

– Chicago chemist Satori Kato invents instant coffee.

SCIENCE AND TECHNOLOGY

12 Dec. The Italian physicist Guglielmo Marconi transmits the first transatlantic wireless signals.

– Mass production of Oldsmobile automobiles begins in Detroit, Michigan, in the USA.

– German physicist W.C. Röntgen wins the first Nobel Physics prize for discovering the X-ray.

– Japanese-American scientist Takamine Jokichi and US chemist John Jacob Abel isolate adrenaline; eventually, it will be obtained more cheaply from the glands of cattle.

ARTS AND HUMANITIES

– The prizes endowed by Alfred Nobel are awarded for the first time.

Literature

Anton Chekhov, *Three Sisters*, play.

Rudyard Kipling, *Kim*, novel.

Thomas Mann, *Buddenbrooks*, novel.

Frank Wedekind, *Der Marquis von Keith* (The Marquis of Keith), drama.

Visual Arts and Architecture

– US architects Babb, Cook and Willard finish Andrew Carnegie's Fifth Avenue mansion in New York.

Paul Gauguin, *The Gold in their Bodies*, painting.

Gustav Klimt, *Medicine*, mural.

Edvard Munch, *Girls on the Bridge*, painting.

Henri de Toulouse-Lautrec, *Femme retroussant sa chemise* (Woman Rolling up her Shirt), painting.

Music

27 Jan. The Italian composer Giuseppe Verdi dies.

Anton Bruckner, Symphony No. 6 in A major (first complete performance).

Sir Edward Elgar, *Pomp and Circumstance*, march in D major.

George Enescu, *Romanian Rhapsodies*, orchestral works.

Sergei Rachmaninov, Piano Concerto No. 2 in C minor.

Alexander Scriabin, Symphony No. 2 in C minor.

1902

EUROPE

28 June The Triple Alliance (1882) of Germany, Austria-Hungary and Italy is renewed for another six years.

30 June–11 Aug. A colonial conference in London supports the principle of 'imperial preference', whereby Britain and its colonies set preferential tariffs for each other's products.

11 July In Britain Lord Salisbury (Robert Cecil, 3rd marquis of Salisbury) retires as prime minister and is succeeded by his nephew Arthur James Balfour.

– In Britain the Balfour Education Act abolishes the separately elected school boards set up in 1870 and replaces them with local education authorities answerable to local councils.

– Some 30,000 Russian students demonstrate against the tsarist regime's attempts to control their organizations. The head of the secret police is murdered (15 April) and riots follow.

MIDDLE EAST AND NORTH AFRICA

10 Dec. In Egypt the Aswan Dam on the River Nile is formally opened.

– In Arabia Abdul-Aziz ibn Saud, emir of the Wahabi, seizes Riyadh, capital of the Nejd, which is controlled by a rival tribe. This is an important step towards the creation of the future kingdom of Saudi Arabia in 1932.

ASIA

20 Jan. An Anglo-Japanese alliance recognizes Japan's legitimate commercial interests in Korea. A conflict with a third party means that either ally will remain neutral or, if the conflict spreads, support the other militarily. The treaty is a dent in Lord Salisbury's doctrine of Britain's 'splendid isolation'.

8 April Russia and China sign a convention by the terms of which Russian troops will be gradually withdrawn from Manchuria (see 13 Dec. 1897).

THE AMERICAS

8 May Mt Pelée, Martinique, erupts and continues to do so (20 May–30 Aug.): some 50,000 people are killed.

12 May A five-month miners' strike starts in the USA. It is the greatest single conflict so far in the history of labour relations in the USA. The strikers gain pay increases but fail to gain official recognition from employers of the United Mine Workers Union.

20 May Cuba's independence from Spain becomes effective; US troops leave the island.

9 Dec. British and German naval forces seize the Venezuelan navy after Venezuela refuses to comply with claims for compensation arising from the Venezuelan revolution of 1899. The Italian navy starts a blockade of the ports of Venezuela (19 Dec.). Venezuelan dictator Cipriano Castro is eventually forced to agree to arbitration by a commission of the Hague Tribunal (Feb. 1903).

– President Roosevelt institutes anti-trust proceedings against US corporations. John D. Rockefeller now controls some 90% of US oil-refining capacity, while J.P. Morgan's US Steel Corporation controls two-thirds of US steel-making capacity.

SUB-SAHARAN AFRICA

31 May The treaty of Vereeniging ends the Anglo-Boer War. The Boers accept British sovereignty in S Africa but are granted self-government in the Transvaal and the Orange River Colony.

6 Oct. In Rhodesia (modern Zimbabwe) the rail link between Salisbury (now Harare) and Bulawayo is completed.

ECONOMY AND SOCIETY

26 Mar. English-born S African statesman Cecil Rhodes dies. His will endows the Rhodes scholarships at Oxford University for young men from the USA, Germany and the British colonies.

– J.A. Hobson publishes *Imperialism*, a study of the economic interests that are assisted by colonialism.

– Mr and Mrs Morris Michtom of New York invent the 'teddy' bear, named after US president Theodore Roosevelt.

ARTS AND HUMANITIES

Literature

17 Jan. In Britain the *Times Literary Supplement* starts publication.

– US psychologist William James publishes *Varieties of Religious Experience*, extending the methodology of psychology to the understanding of religion.

J(ames) M(atthew) Barrie, *The Admirable Crichton*, play.

Arnold Bennett, *Anna of the Five Towns*, novel.

Sir Arthur Conan Doyle, *The Hound of the Baskervilles*, novel.

Joseph Conrad, *Heart of Darkness*, novella.

André Gide, *L'Immoraliste* (The Immoralist), novel.

Maxim Gorky, *The Lower Depths*, play.

Henry James, *The Wings of the Dove*, novel.

Rudyard Kipling, *Just So Stories*, short stories for children.

Walter de la Mare, *Songs of Childhood*, poetry for children.

John Masefield, *Salt Water Ballads*, poetry about the sea.

Beatrix Potter, *The Tale of Peter Rabbit*, illustrated children's story.

George Bernard Shaw, *Mrs Warren's Profession*, play. Its theme, organized prostitution, is deemed shocking and the police close it after one performance.

W.B. Yeats (with Lady Gregory), *Cathleen ni Houlihan*, play.

Visual Arts and Architecture

– French artist Paul Cézanne completes his last painting of Mont Sainte-Victoire, a mountain in Provence that has been his favourite subject as a painter since the 1880s.

– The Ritz Hotel (London) and Algonquin Hotel (New York) open.

Claude Monet, *Waterloo Bridge*, painting.

John Singer Sargent, *Lord Ribblesdale* and *The Duchess of Portland*, portraits.

Music

18 Mar. Italian singer Enrico Caruso makes his first phonograph recordings at the Hotel di Milano, Milan.

30 April First performance in Paris of Claude Debussy's opera *Pélléas et Mélisande*, based on a play by Maurice Maeterlinck.

Edward Elgar, *Coronation Ode*. Its finale is adapted from Elgar's *Pomp and Circumstance* March No.1, with words by A.C. Benson beginning 'Land of Hope and Glory'.

Charles Ives, Symphony No. 2.

Gustav Mahler, Symphony No. 5 in C sharp minor.

Jean Sibelius, Symphony No. 2 in D.

1903

EUROPE

13 April In Berlin, Germany, the Baghdad railway company is founded (a concession for the building of a railway from Berlin to the Persian Gulf was granted in 1899).

May In Britain the colonial secretary Joseph Chamberlain proposes the levying of tariffs to protect British industry and agriculture.

10 June Alexander Obrenovic, king of Serbia, is assassinated. Peter I, son of Alexander Karageorgevic, succeeds him.

14 Aug. In Britain the Irish Land Purchase Act is passed, facilitating the purchase of former estate lands by Irish tenants.

3 Oct. Emmeline Pankhurst founds the Women's Social and Political Union to work for women's suffrage in Britain. Its members will come to be known as suffragettes.

17 Nov. At the London conference of the Russian Social Democratic Party, Lenin (see p. 480) splits the party into two factions, the Bolsheviks and the Mensheviks. The former, Lenin's followers, are determined to be a tightly knit, secret organization of professional revolutionaries. The latter want to build a wide-based political party.

– Anglo-French relations improve following Edward VII's visit to Paris (May).

– Anti-Jewish pogroms take place in Russia, starting in Dec. and continuing into 1905.

ASIA

Jan. As emperor of India, Edward VII of Britain holds a magnificent coronation durbar (state reception) to celebrate his accession.

12 Aug. Despite the Sino-Russian agreement of 8 April 1902, Russian troops have yet to leave Manchuria. Japan protests to Russia.

THE AMERICAS

22 Jan. The Hay–Herrán treaty between the USA and Colombia grants the USA a 99-year lease on a canal zone across the isthmus of Panama. Congress ratifies the treaty (17 Mar.), but the Colombian senate rejects it (12 Aug.). President Roosevelt responds by despatching US marines to Panama to foment a rebellion in the proposed canal zone (31 Aug.), while the US cruiser *Nashville* prevents Colombian forces from entering the area. The Republic of Panama declares itself independent of Colombia (3 Nov.), and its independence is swiftly recognized by the USA (6 Nov.), which signs the Hay–Bunau–Varilla treaty with the new republic (19 Dec.). By the terms of this treaty the canal zone passes to the USA in perpetuity in return for $10 million and additional annual payments.

April The US Supreme Court upholds the Alabama constitution denying African-Americans the vote (see 1901).

SUB-SAHARAN AFRICA

Feb. In Britain a report by the British consul Roger Casement is published that reveals the brutal treatment by white traders of African and Indian workers in the Belgian Congo.

Mar. N Nigeria is occupied by the British.

ECONOMY AND SOCIETY

16 June The Ford Motor Company is incorporated in Detroit, Michigan, in the USA.

1–19 July The Tour de France cycling race is run for the first time.

20 July Pope Leo XIII dies. He is succeeded by Giuseppe Sarto, who becomes Pope Pius X (4 Aug.).

– In Britain Letchworth in Hertfordshire (hitherto a village) becomes the first 'garden city'.

– In Britain Alfred Harmsworth (the future Viscount Northcliffe) launches the *Daily Mirror* as a newspaper for the 'new woman'.

SCIENCE AND TECHNOLOGY

17 Dec. American aviation pioneers Orville and Wilbur Wright make the first successful aeroplane flights at Kitty Hawk, North Carolina, USA.

19 Dec. The Williamsburg Bridge opens, providing another link between Brooklyn and New York.

– In the Ruhr district of W Germany the Krupp family firm establishes metal-working industries.

ARTS AND HUMANITIES

Literature

– The Prix Goncourt is awarded for the first time to *Force ennemie* by John-Antoine Nau as the prize for the best French novel of the year.

Samuel Butler, *The Way of All Flesh*, novel (published posthumously after Butler's death in 1902).

Robert Erskine Childers, *The Riddle of the Sands*, espionage novel describing a German plot against England.

Henry James, *The Ambassadors*, novel.

Jack London (John Griffith), *The Call of the Wild*, novel.

J.M. Synge, *In the Shadow of the Glen*, play.

Kate Wiggin, *Rebecca of Sunnybrook Farm*, children's novel.

Visual Arts and Architecture

18 May French artist Paul Gauguin dies in the Marquesas Islands.

17 July American-born artist James McNeill Whistler dies.

13 Nov. French impressionist painter Camille Pissarro dies.

– Westminster Roman Catholic Cathedral in London is completed to a neo-Byzantine design by J.F. Bentley.

Music

20 Jan. First performance of *The Wizard of Oz*, a musical based on L. Frank Baum's novel (1900) at the Majestic Theater, New York, USA.

Béla Bartók, *Kossuth*, symphony.

Arnold Schoenberg (see p. 511), *Pelleas und Melisande*, symphonic poem.

1904

EUROPE

8 April The Entente Cordiale, resolving outstanding Anglo-French colonial differences over Egypt and Morocco, is concluded by France and Britain. Not yet a military alliance, the Entente nonetheless heightens German fears of encirclement.

28 July Vyacheslav Plehve, Russia's minister of the interior, is assassinated. Under his repressive regime the police have failed to control mobs responsible for anti-Jewish pogroms. The tsarist regime forbids political assemblies but appears to condone persecution of Russia's Jews.

21 Oct. In the Dogger Bank Incident, the Russian Baltic fleet, bound for the Far East (see below and Jan. 1905), sinks a British trawler in the North Sea in the mistaken belief that it is a Japanese torpedo boat.

ASIA

8 Feb. The Russo-Japanese War begins, fought over the issues of Russian influence in Manchuria and Japanese interests in Korea. The Japanese navy launches a surprise attack on Port Arthur (now Lüshun, China), a Russian-held treaty port in Manchuria (see 13 Dec. 1897).

10 Feb. Japan declares war on Russia. By the end of May Port Arthur will be cut off from Russian land forces in Manchuria.

25 Aug.–4 Sept. In the Russo-Japanese War, the massive battle of Liaoyang, SW of Mukden (modern Shenyang), ends inconclusively.

THE AMERICAS

8 Nov. US president Theodore Roosevelt defeats the Democratic candidate Alton B. Parker in the presidential election.

SUB-SAHARAN AFRICA

12 Jan. In South West Africa the Herero people rebel against German colonial rule. Their uprising is ruthlessly quelled (Aug.).

ECONOMY AND SOCIETY

21 May The Fédération Internationale de Football Association (FIFA), a global governing body for association football, is founded in Paris, France.

Nov. St Louis, Missouri, USA, hosts the 3rd Olympic Games.

SCIENCE AND TECHNOLOGY

21 Oct. The first section of the New York subway opens.

– The Trans-Siberian Railway opens. Begun in 1891, it links Moscow with Vladivostok and will open up Siberia to economic exploitation.

– Thomas Sullivan of New York invents the tea bag.

– US archaeologist Edward Thompson excavates the Toltec city of Chichén Itzá, in the Yucatán region of Mexico.

Max Weber (1864–1920)

The life and thought of the German sociologist Max Weber were shaped by the politics and administrative structure of the new German Reich established in 1871. He was educated at the University of Heidelberg, where he studied law and economics as well as economic history. His combination of interests led him to sociology, a subject he supplied with a whole range of comparative evidence, plus a supposedly value-free methodology.

Ancient agriculture and medieval trade were Weber's first subjects. From these he derived an interest in how religious thought might shape economic behaviour. His most famous work is *The Protestant Ethic and the Spirit of Capitalism* (1904–5), which proposed a connection between Calvinism and the development of capitalism in the 16th century. Previous thinkers had supposed that the development owed more to Judaism. Translated into English in 1930, the book enjoyed a great vogue.

Weber also studied the modern German state, its ability to organize and administer, and he became the first person to discuss the nature of modern bureaucracy and the rise of 'managerialism'. Modern government, he thought, was so different in scope, when compared with earlier kinds of government, that it was really a different kind of organization. In it the rule of administrators had replaced that of priests. But while one kind of authority had yielded to another, some features of the earlier society survived.

Weber, like Marx, thought class was fundamental. He believed class conflict would continue as an expression of bargaining power, because that was the way modern government and economics necessarily worked. He argued that socialism led not to freedom but to ever greater bureaucracy. Weber's thought and approach went on to dominate 20th-century sociology.

ARTS AND HUMANITIES

Literature

2 July Russian playwright Anton Chekhov dies.

27 Dec. The Abbey Theatre opens in Dublin, Ireland.

J(ames) M(atthew) Barrie, *Peter Pan, or The Boy Who Would Not Grow Up*, play.

Anton Chekhov, *The Cherry Orchard*, play.

Joseph Conrad, *Nostromo*, novel.

Henry James, *The Golden Bowl*, novel.

Jack London (John Griffith), *The Sea Wolf*, novel.

Luigi Pirandello, *Il fu Mattia Pascal* (The Late Mattia Pascal), novel.

Frederick Rolfe (Baron Corvo), *Hadrian the Seventh*, novel.

J.M. Synge, *Riders to the Sea*, play.

Frank Wedekind, *Die Büchse der Pandora* (Pandora's Box), play.

Visual Arts and Architecture

– Picasso (see p. 467) arrives in Paris and starts his 'pink period'.

Music

21 Jan. First performance in Brno of Leoš Janáček's opera *Jenufa*.

17 Feb. First performance at La Scala, Milan, of Giacomo Puccini's opera *Madama Butterfly*.

– Gustav Mahler completes his *Kindertotenlieder* ('Songs of the Death of Children'), a cycle of five songs with orchestral accompaniment (begun in 1901).

– In Russia Mikhail Fokine begins his revolution in choreography at the imperial ballet, St Petersburg, by emphasizing dance as a portrayal of character.

Sir Edward Elgar, *In the South*, overture.

1905

EUROPE

22 Jan. Bloody Sunday in St Petersburg, Russia. Troops open fire on demonstrators, killing more than 100. This, coupled with the national humiliation of defeat by Japan (see below), provokes a series of revolutionary outbursts. The tsar's uncle, Grand Duke Sergei, is assassinated (4 Feb.). At Odessa Russian sailors mutiny on the armoured cruiser *Potemkin* (June). Tsar Nicholas II is forced to grant a constitution, establish a parliament (duma) with legislative powers and grant civil rights (30 Oct.).

13 Aug. A national referendum endorses the decision (7 June) of Norway's parliament to end the 91-year-old union with Sweden. A treaty of separation is signed (26 Oct.) and Denmark's Prince Charles is elected king of Norway reigning as King Haakon VII.

16 Nov. Count Sergei Witte, a reformer, is appointed Russian prime minister.

4 Dec. In Britain the Conservatives, split on the issue of free trade and imperial protectionism, lose office; Sir Henry Campbell-Bannerman forms a Liberal government.

– In Ireland Sinn Féin, a radical nationalist party, is founded by Arthur Griffith.

– In the N of Ireland the Ulster Unionist Council is formed.

MIDDLE EAST AND NORTH AFRICA

31 Mar. A visit to Tangier in Morocco by Emperor William II of Germany triggers the first Moroccan Crisis. Germany objects to

French expansion in Morocco and also wishes to break up the Anglo-French Entente Cordiale of 1904.

ASIA

2 Jan. In the Russo-Japanese War the Russians surrender Port Arthur to the Japanese.

9 Mar. Japanese forces capture the strategically important Manchurian city of Mukden (Shenyang).

27–29 May The Russian Baltic fleet, having sailed round the world, is destroyed in a few hours in the straits of Tsushima (between Korea and Japan).

5 Sept. Following efforts by US president Theodore Roosevelt, the treaty of Portsmouth (New Hampshire, USA) ends the Russo-Japanese War. Russia and Japan agree to evacuate Manchuria. Russia has to evacuate the southern half of Sakhalin island and is forced to recognize the legitimacy of Japan's Korean interests. Russia also transfers to Japan the lease of the Liaodong peninsula.

– China decides to boycott US goods because US immigration laws discriminate against Chinese immigrants.

– China's government abolishes the Confucian examination system for the civil service, adopting Western-style education.

– The Indian National Congress launches its first major campaign opposing British rule.

THE AMERICAS

4 Mar. Theodore Roosevelt starts his first full term as US president.

25 July US business interests begin work on the construction of the Panama Canal.

– The Asiatic Exclusion League is founded in the W USA to try to ban Japanese immigration.

ECONOMY AND SOCIETY

5 May The *Chicago Defender*, the first major African-American newspaper, starts publication.

– The German sociologist Max Weber (see p. 463) publishes *The Protestant Ethic and the Spirit of Capitalism*.

– The first major epidemic of poliomyelitis breaks out in Sweden.

– American self-made millionaire Andrew Carnegie endows the Carnegie Foundation for the Advancement of Teaching.

SCIENCE AND TECHNOLOGY

– British engineer and designer Herbert Austin introduces the Austin motorcar.

– In the USA the Wright brothers patent their flying machine, which can now fly a circle of 39km (24.5 miles) in 38 minutes.

– German physicist Albert Einstein (see box) publishes his paper on the special theory of relativity. It leads to the mass-energy equation ($E=mc^2$) showing that particles of matter can produce vast amounts of energy, a crucial step in the development of nuclear weapons.

L'élan vital.

(The vital spring.)

Henri Bergson, *L'Evolution Créatrice* (1907)

ARTS AND HUMANITIES

Literature

E(dward) M(organ) Forster, *Where Angels Fear to Tread*, novel.

Heinrich Mann, *Professor Unrat*, novel; it will be made into a film as *The Blue Angel* (1930).

Rainer Maria Rilke, *Das Stunden-Buch* (The Book of Hours), poetry collection.

George Santayana, *The Life of Reason* (first of five volumes), philosophy.

George Bernard Shaw, *Major Barbara* and *Man and Superman*, plays.

August Strindberg, *Dödsdansen* (The Dance of Death), play.

H(erbert) G(eorge) Wells, *Kipps*, novel.

Edith Wharton, *The House of Mirth*, novel.

Albert Einstein (1879–1955)

The great physicist Albert Einstein was brought up in Germany, where he had a famously unsuccessful school career. From 1901 he was employed by the Swiss patent office, and in 1905 he published a series of theoretical papers that were to revolutionize physics. Among these was the proposal that light, as well as being a wave phenomenon, was also made up of particles (now known as photons). But the most famous of the 1905 papers was the special theory of relativity, which shows that – contrary to the picture of the universe provided by Isaac

Newton – neither time nor motion are absolute, but rather relative to the observer, and that only the speed of light is constant. He also showed the equivalence of mass and energy, which are linked by the formula $E = mc^2$ (where E is energy, m is mass and c is the speed of light).

In 1914 Einstein moved back to Germany to take up an academic post. In 1916 he published his general theory of relativity, which demonstrated that gravitation is not a force, as Newton had stated, but rather a distortion in the space-time continuum

caused by the presence of mass. When experiments were carried out during the solar eclipse of 1919 that proved Einstein's theory, his reputation became global, and he was awarded the Nobel prize for physics in 1921. Einstein, a Jew, moved to the USA in 1933, and in 1939 he urged President Roosevelt to begin work on an atomic bomb, for fear that Nazi Germany would make one first. For the rest of his life Einstein campaigned for nuclear disarmament, although, ironically, it was his formula $E = mc^2$ that had made nuclear weapons possible.

Visual Arts and Architecture

– Les Fauves (including Maurice de Vlaminck, Henri Matisse and André Derain) exhibit their paintings at the Salon d'Automne, Paris, showing a new freedom in the use of colour.

Henri Matisse, *Luxe, calme et volupté* (Luxury, Calm and Voluptuousness), painting. The title comes from the refrain of the poem *L'Invitation au voyage* by Charles Baudelaire.

Pablo Picasso (see p. 467), *The Absinthe Drinker*, *Seated Harlequin with Red Background* and *At the Lapin Agile*, paintings.

Music

9 Dec. First performance in Dresden of Richard Strauss's opera *Salomé*, which is based on Oscar Wilde's play (1896).

30 Dec. First performance in Vienna of Franz Lehár's operetta *Die lustige Witwe* (The Merry Widow).

Claude Debussy, *La Mer* (The Sea), tone poem.

Sir Edward Elgar, *Introduction and Allegro* in G minor for strings.

Gustav Mahler, Symphonies Nos. 6 in A and 7 in B minor.

Alexander Scriabin, *The Divine Poem*, Symphony No. 3 in C minor.

1906

EUROPE

12 Jan. In Britain the Liberal Party under Sir Henry Campbell-Bannerman wins a huge majority in the general election and embarks on a programme of social reform. The Labour Party (formerly the Labour Representation Committee) wins 29 seats.

10 Feb. HMS *Dreadnought* is launched by the Royal Navy. With its ten 12-inch guns it is by far the most powerful battleship afloat. By the third German Navy Bill the German government increases the tonnage of its battleships (5 June).

24 May Nicholas II grants a broad franchise in Russia but will not free political prisoners. The duma (parliament) is dissolved when it proves uncooperative with the government (21 July).

6 June Pyotr Stolypin becomes Russian prime minister, Count Witte having been dismissed in May. Stolypin begins to reform the traditional communal system of land ownership. Peasants can now receive their own share of the land and work it privately.

12 July French courts clear Alfred Dreyfus of charges of treason in an attempt to end the scandal associated with his conviction (1894). Dreyfus is rehabilitated, restored to his rank and awarded the Légion d'honneur (22 July).

– Sir Edward Grey, British foreign secretary, states privately to the French government that Britain has a moral obligation to support France in the event of a German attack.

– The Liberal government in Britain, reacting to Labour Party pressure, introduces free school meals.

– In Britain the Trade Disputes Act overturns the Taff Vale judgement of 1901.

– King Christian IX of Denmark dies and is succeeded by his son Frederick VIII.

MIDDLE EAST AND NORTH AFRICA

16 Jan. The European powers meet at Algeciras in S Spain to resolve the Franco-German Moroccan Crisis.

8 April At the Algeciras Conference France and Spain are given joint control of Morocco under a Swiss inspector. Franco-British cooperation at the conference has left Germany isolated.

– Muzaffar ud-Din, shah of Persia, is forced to grant a constitution.

ASIA

– The All India Muslim League is formed. It opposes the Indian National Congress's aims of an independent India, fearing Hindu domination. Initially it supports British rule but will eventually (1940) demand a separate Muslim state.

THE AMERICAS

18 April An earthquake tremor hits San Francisco at 5:13 a.m. The three-day fire that follows destroys most of the city and kills 2500 people.

14 Aug. Race riot in Brownsville, Texas. 160 African-American soldiers will receive dishonourable discharges over the affair (Nov.).

– The American Jewish Committee is founded to protect Jewish rights.

– President Theodore Roosevelt receives the Nobel Peace Prize for helping negotiations ending the Russo-Japanese War (1904–5). Roosevelt also becomes the first sitting US president to travel abroad when he visits Panama (Nov.).

SUB-SAHARAN AFRICA

4 July Ethiopia, although declared independent, is divided into British, French and Italian zones of influence.

6 Dec. In S Africa Britain grants self-government to the Transvaal and Orange River colonies.

ECONOMY AND SOCIETY

– The *Daily Mail* invents the word 'suffragettes' to describe Emmeline Pankhurst, her daughters, Christabel and Sylvia, and their supporters who are campaigning for votes for women in Britain.

– The president of Princeton University, Woodrow Wilson, says that the motorcar, 'a picture of the arrogance of wealth', is helping to spread socialism in the USA.

– A special interim Olympic Games are held in Athens to mark the tenth anniversary of the modern Games.

– The German-born hairdresser Karl Nessler introduces the permanent wave in Britain.

SCIENCE AND TECHNOLOGY

– German chemist August von Wassermann and, independently, Hungarian chemist Lazlo Detre invent the Wassermann blood test for the detection of syphilis.

ARTS AND HUMANITIES

Literature

Henry Watson Fowler and Francis George Fowler, *The King's English*, guide to good and bad use of English.

John Galsworthy, *The Man of Property*, novel, the first of the *Forsyte Saga* novels.

Carl Gustav Jung (1875–1961)

The son of a Protestant pastor, the pioneer psychotherapist Carl Gustav Jung was born in Kesswil, Switzerland, and studied medicine at the University of Basle. In 1905 he became a lecturer in psychiatry at the University of Zurich and then developed a private practice. He introduced the noun 'complex' into psychiatry and showing how a hesitant response to certain words revealed an inner preoccupation. He also introduced the terms 'introvert' and 'extrovert' to describe two fundamental human types: the extrovert is interested in the outside world, while the introvert is preoccupied with the workings of his own mind.

Jung started off as a colleague of Freud, but the two fell out after Jung published *Psychology of the Unconscious* in 1912, in which he developed the idea of a 'collective unconscious' that was common to all humanity and that lay behind all personal experiences. Jung rejected Freud's emphasis on the central role of sex, and held that the unconscious was not just a repository for personal unhappy memories and traumas. He maintained rather that all of us are born with the unconscious already present in our minds. Its myth-bearing capacity links us with our ancestors and restores meaning to a fractured existence. Jung's idea of an 'archetype' which personifies the essence of certain human traits – and which he detected in myths and fairy stories – was powerfully suggestive. Certain human types, he thought, were drawn to certain archetypes. These ideas have influenced modern advertising, whose subliminal power and imagery link a product with a targeted buyer.

Joel Chandler Harris, *Uncle Remus and Brer Rabbit*, tales.

Jack London (John Griffith), *White Fang*, novel.

Robert Musil, *Die Verwirrungen des Zöglings Törless* (Young Törless), novel.

George Bernard Shaw, *The Doctor's Dilemma*, play.

Upton Sinclair, *The Jungle*, novel exposing the horrific working conditions in Chicago's meat-packing industry. Its publication leads to a US government investigation into Chicago's slaughterhouses.

Visual Arts and Architecture

22 Oct. French Post-Impressionist painter Paul Cézanne dies. Cézanne's later work influences the emergence of a new radical artistic movement that will be known as Cubism.

Max Beckmann, *Young Men by the Sea*, painting.

André Derain, *The Pool of London*, painting.

Raoul Dufy, *Street Decked out with Flags at Le Havre*, painting.

Pablo Picasso (see p. 467), *Portrait of Gertrude Stein*, *The Flower Vendors* and *Boy Leading a Horse*, paintings.

Music

11 Nov. First performance in Leipzig of Dame Ethel Smyth's opera *The Wreckers*.

1907

EUROPE

Mar. In Russia the second duma (parliament) meets and is dismissed when it refuses to cooperate with the government. A third duma, elected on a narrower franchise (Nov.), will prove more amenable.

14 June In Norway women gain the right to vote.

7 July The Triple Alliance of Germany, Austria-Hungary and Italy is renewed for another six years.

12 Dec. The Bolshevik Vladimir Ilyich Lenin (see p. 480) flees Russia for a second time and will not return until 1917.

– Following Britain's agreement with Russia on zones of influence in Asia (see below), the Entente Cordiale (8 April 1904) is now the Triple Entente. This will become a formal military alliance in 1911.

– A great-power peace conference is held in The Hague, the Netherlands (June–Oct.). The resulting Hague Convention provides for the humane treatment of prisoners of war and outlaws the use of poisons as weapons of war.

MIDDLE EAST AND NORTH AFRICA

19 Aug. Russia recognizes diplomatically Britain's dominant position in the Persian Gulf, and the two powers agree spheres of influence in C Asia. An Anglo-Russian Entente follows (31 Aug.), further heightening German fears of encirclement.

Aug. The conservative prime minister of Persia, Atabegi-Azam, is assassinated and is succeeded by the liberal Nasir ul-Muk.

– Muzaffar ud-Din, shah of Persia, dies and is succeeded by his son, Mohammed Ali.

ASIA

10 June France and Japan sign a treaty guaranteeing equal trading rights for both in China and recognizing the legitimacy of Japan's special interests in parts of Manchuria, the Chinese province of Fukien and Mongolia.

19 July Ko-jong, emperor of Korea, abdicates: the Japanese, already in occupation of Korea, now officially make Korea a Japanese protectorate (25 July).

– An outbreak of bubonic plague kills more than one million people in India.

THE AMERICAS

20 Feb. In the USA the Immigration Act is passed by Congress, making immigration more difficult. It excludes those thought to be socially undesirable and raises the tax payable on arrival to $4 a head.

13 Mar. The New York stock exchange collapses. President Roosevelt (20 Aug.) attacks 'malefactors of great wealth' and Woodrow Wilson of Princeton University says that the problem with the US economy is the financiers, not the big corporations. A run on banks follows (Oct.) as depositors remove their money. To relieve the crisis, the financier and philanthropist J.P. Morgan lends the money needed to prevent the closure of the New York stock exchange.

14 Mar. President Roosevelt issues an executive order restricting Japanese immigration to the USA.

16 Nov. Oklahoma becomes the 46th state of the USA.

– President Roosevelt allows United States Steel to buy the Tennessee Coal, Iron and Railroad Co. Anti-trust activists criticize the move, which, however, leads to a return of economic confidence and stock market recovery.

AUSTRALASIA AND OCEANIA

– New Zealand gains dominion status within the British empire.

ECONOMY AND SOCIETY

– In Britain Lord Baden-Powell, a hero of the Boer War, establishes the Boy Scout movement.

SCIENCE AND TECHNOLOGY

Sept. The Cunard line's SS *Lusitania* makes its debut voyage as the world's largest liner. The Cunard line's SS *Mauretania*, which is also launched, is only slightly smaller.

– In the USA the Hurley Machine Corporation launches the first electric washing-machine. The first portable vacuum-cleaner also goes on sale.

– Swiss psychiatrist Carl Gustav Jung (see p. 466) publishes *Psychology of Dementia Praecox*. Jung meets Freud in Vienna and the two men begin a seven-year collaboration.

ARTS AND HUMANITIES

Literature

26 June J.M. Synge's *The Playboy of the Western World* is first performed at the Abbey Theatre, Dublin, Ireland. Its perceived slurs on the morality of the Irish peasantry, together with the frankness of some of its language, outrage nationalist Ireland and leads to a week of riots.

Joseph Conrad, *The Secret Agent*, novel reflecting the new wave of anarchism sweeping through Western society.

E(dward) M(organ) Forster, *The Longest Journey*, novel.

Stefan George, *Der siebente Ring* (The Seventh Ring), poetry collection.

Edmund Gosse, *Father and Son*, autobiography.

William James, *Pragmatism: A New Name for Old Ways of Thinking*, philosophy.

Visual Arts and Architecture

– The French artist Georges Braque meets the Spanish artist Pablo Picasso (see box). The two men will work closely together over the next few years, creating the style of painting that will come to be known as Cubism (see 1908), which depicts surfaces and figures by means of shapes of a geometrical and cubelike character. They are influenced by the work of Paul Cézanne (see 1906), a memorial exhibition of whose work is held this year, and by African sculpture.

– Pablo Picasso completes the painting *Les Desmoiselles d'Avignon*, which heralds the arrival of Cubism. The painting will become an icon of modernism, but will not be exhibited in public until 1937.

– The Hotel Adlon opens in Berlin. It will attract the wealthy and famous, and will be destroyed in 1945 but rebuilt in replica at the end of the century.

André Derain, *The Bathers*, painting.

Henri Matisse, *Blue Nude*, painting.

Music

18 July Florenz Ziegfeld's revue *Follies of 1907* is staged in New York. Ziegfeld's show girls introduce a new vogue for the slim figure as a model for female fashion.

22 Dec. Russian ballerina Anna Pavlova dances in the production of *Le Cygne* (The Dying Swan), choreographed by Russian Mikhail Fokine at the Mariinsky Theatre, St Petersburg.

Frederick Delius, *Brigg Fair*, orchestral work.

Gustav Mahler, Symphony No. 8 in E flat major.

Maurice Ravel, *Rapsodie espagnole*, orchestral work.

Jean Sibelius, Symphony No. 3 in C major.

Pablo Picasso (1881–1973)

The Spanish artist Pablo Picasso was born in Malaga and trained as an artist in Barcelona. In 1904 he settled in Paris, where he quickly acquired celebrity status as the leader of the artistic avant-garde. Throughout his career, and with enormous energy, he continually tried out new styles and new ways of seeing the world.

In 1907, with his monumental painting *Les Demoiselles d'Avignon*, Picasso launched a new school of art, Cubism. In this great work, Picasso breaks with conventional perspective, which he considered a constraint on Western art. He blamed the Renaissance for the obsession with perspective, which he saw as responsible for a general loss of artistic vitality in Europe. Perception, he thought, should be multi-dimensional in art as it is in life. The *Demoiselles* was anti-Renaissance in other ways too. The five women show a primitive and very un-classical vigour, and reflect Picasso's appreciation of the primal energy of African art. European art, he thought, had become parochial and needed to be revived from the outside.

Picasso used archetypal symbols of love and sex, pain and suffering in a way that was both ancient and modern, both universal and particular. Picasso's *Guernica* (1937), arguably his greatest painting, was a response to the bombing of the Basque city of that name by the fascists during the Spanish Civil War. The work embodies both Picasso's horror at the barbarities of war, and his ultimate faith in humanity. Picasso maintained his political commitment, and left Spain for good after the victory in the Civil War of the fascist General Franco. But his work never lost its characteristically Spanish concern with suffering, tragedy and death.

1908

EUROPE

1 Feb. Charles I of Portugal is assassinated and succeeded by his son Manuel II, who ends the dictatorial rule of the prime minister João Franco. In 1910 the monarchy will be overthrown and Manuel II will flee to Britain, where he will die.

6 April In Britain Henry Campbell-Bannerman resigns as prime minister and dies (22 April). Herbert Asquith succeeds him (8 April), with David Lloyd George as chancellor of the exchequer.

14 June In Germany the fourth Navy Bill authorizes further naval expansion.

5 Oct. The Bulgarian government, nominally under Turkish suzerainty since 1878, though effectively independent, formally declares its independence and Prince Ferdinand becomes tsar.

6 Oct. The Austrian government formally annexes Bosnia and Herzegovina, which Austria has administered for the Ottomans since 1878. Slav sentiment in Russia and Serbia is outraged. The German government supports Austria's action. France and Britain object.

7 Oct. The Greek majority in the Turkish province of Crete declares its union with Greece.

27 Oct. Anglo-German relations deteriorate further after the *Daily Telegraph* publishes comments by Emperor William II that the German people are hostile to Britain.

– British Parliament votes for a means-tested non-contributory pension of 5d per week for a minority of people over 70.

MIDDLE EAST AND NORTH AFRICA

6 Jan. Mulay Hafid rebels against his brother Abdul-Aziz IV, sultan of Morocco, and defeats him at Marrakesh (23 Aug.). Germany recognizes the rebel as sultan (3 Sept.). Franco-German relations again deteriorate, but the new sultan, reigning as Abdul-Hafiz, announces that he will respect French and Spanish interests in Morocco as his brother did.

26 May The world's largest reservoir of oil to date is discovered in Persia. The British government buys the concession granted to William Knox D'Arcy of New Zealand by the shah of Persia (see 1901) and establishes the Anglo-Persian Oil Company (1909).

23 June The shah of Persia, Mohammed Ali, stages a Russian-backed coup. The national assembly is closed and martial law is imposed. He is, however, soon deposed.

July Following a revolt by reformist Young Turk nationalists in Macedonia (6 July), the Ottoman sultan Abdul Hamid II restores the constitution of 1876 (24 July). When the Turkish parliament opens (17 Dec.) the Young Turks are in the majority.

10 Nov. The khedive of Egypt appoints Boutros Ghali, a Coptic Christian, as Egypt's first native prime minister. Muslim riots follow.

ASIA

14 Nov. The Chinese emperor Guangxu dies. Cixi, dowager empress of China since 1862, dies the following day (15 Nov.).

She has opposed constitutional reform, and demands for change in China become harder to resist after her death.

THE AMERICAS

Nov. William Jennings Bryan runs for the third, and last, time as Democratic candidate for the presidency of the USA. He is defeated by William Howard Taft, who has been at the heart of the development of the new US imperial policy as governor of the Philippines, Roosevelt's secretary of war, suppressor of the Cuban rebellion and organizer of the construction of the Panama Canal.

– The US Bureau of Investigation is established. It will become the Federal Bureau of Investigation (FBI) in 1935.

SUB-SAHARAN AFRICA

18 Oct. The Belgian government annexes the Congo, which was previously personally ruled by the Belgian king Leopold II, whose brutal exploitation of its people caused an international scandal.

– A diamond is discovered in German South West Africa (now Namibia), and Consolidated Diamond Mines of South West Africa, a De Beers subsidiary, will exploit the find on being granted a licence by the German government.

ECONOMY AND SOCIETY

20 April The 59-year-old W.G. Grace plays his last first-class cricket match.

April–Oct. The 4th Olympic Games are held in London.

28 Dec. Messina, Sicily, is hit by a violent earthquake, which kills some 75,000 people.

– Two-sided phonograph record discs are now available from the Columbia Phonograph Co.

SCIENCE AND TECHNOLOGY

12 Aug. In the USA the Model T Ford motorcar is introduced.

16 Sept. US motor company General Motors is created.

21 Dec. US aviator Wilbur Wright wins the Michelin Cup for flying 124km (77 miles) in 2 hours 20 minutes.

– Chilean nitrates have previously been a necessity for manufacturing explosives and nitrogen fertilizer, but the invention of the Haber process for synthesizing ammonia, by German physical chemists Fritz Haber and W.H. Nernst, bypasses that need. Ammonia is now reducible to nitric acid for explosives, or sodium nitrate, or sulfate of ammonia, for fertilizers.

– German physicist Hans Geiger and New Zealand-born physicist Ernest Rutherford (later 1st Baron Rutherford of Nelson) develop the Geiger counter, which can detect radiation.

– In Japan the scientist Kikunae Ikeda isolates the taste enhancer monosodium glutamate (MSG) from seaweed.

ARTS AND HUMANITIES

Literature

W.H. Davies, *Autobiography of a Super Tramp*, an account of his experiences of homelessness.

E(dward) M(organ) Forster, *A Room with a View*, novel.

Kenneth Grahame, *The Wind in the Willows*, children's novel.

Maurice Maeterlinck, *L'Oiseau bleu* (The Blue Bird), play.

L.M. Montgomery, *Anne of Green Gables*, novel; the first in her series of books about the Canadian countryside.

Rainer Maria Rilke, *Neue Gedichte* (New Poems), poetry collection.

August Strindberg, *Spöksonaten* (The Ghost Sonata), play.

Visual Arts and Architecture

– The French art critic Louis Vauxcelles introduces the term 'cubism' to describe the style of painting of Georges Braque and Pablo Picasso (see 1907).

Pierre Bonnard, *Nude against the Light*, painting.

Constantin Brancusi, *The Kiss*, sculpture in a self-consciously primitivist style.

Wassily Kandinsky, *Murneau*, painting.

Gustav Klimt, *The Kiss*, painting.

Henri Matisse, *Harmony in Red*, painting.

Claude Monet, *The Doge's Palace, San Giorgio Maggiore* and *The Grand Canal*, paintings, part of a series of studies of Venice.

Music

Isaac Albéniz, *Iberia*, piano suite.

Claude Debussy, *Children's Corner*, collection of six piano pieces.

Frederick Delius, *In a Summer Garden*, orchestral work.

Sir Edward Elgar, Symphony No. 1 in A flat major.

Charles Ives, *The Unanswered Question*, for trumpet, four flutes and strings.

Sergei Rachmaninov, Symphony No. 2 in E minor.

Alexander Scriabin, *The Poem of Ecstasy*, orchestral work.

Harry Williams and Jack Judge, 'It's a Long Way to Tipperary', song.

1909

EUROPE

26 Feb. The Turks reluctantly recognize the Austrian annexation of Bosnia-Herzegovina, as do the European powers (9 April) (see 1908).

13 April The Turks recognize Bulgarian independence, as do the governments of Germany, Austria and Italy (27 April).

29 April In his 'People's Budget', the British chancellor of the exchequer David Lloyd George introduces taxation measures to finance Britain's growing welfare state. He proposes estate taxation and a 6d in the pound supertax on incomes above £5000 a year.

14 July In Germany Berhard von Bülow resigns as chancellor and is replaced by Theobald von Bethmann-Hollweg.

30 Nov. In Britain the Conservative-dominated House of Lords rejects Lloyd George's budget by 350 votes to 75, provoking a constitutional crisis over the powers of the unelected chamber.

17 Dec. Leopold II, king of the Belgians, dies and is succeeded by his son Albert I.

MIDDLE EAST AND NORTH AFRICA

1 Feb. Kamil Pasha, grand vizier of the Ottoman empire, is deposed by Young Turk nationalists and replaced by Hussein Hilmi Pasha.

13 April Rebel elements of the Turkish army mount a counter-revolution against the Young Turks. The rebels occupy Constantinople, but the city is recaptured by the Turkish army (19 April).

27 April Ottoman sultan Abdul Hamid II, who sympathizes with the counter-revolutionaries, is deposed by the Young Turks. The Young Turk-dominated parliament replaces him with his brother Mahmud V.

12 July In Persia the Bakhtiari tribal chief Ali Kuli Khan, reacting to the brutal conduct of Russian troops who have invaded his tribal lands in N Persia, captures Tehran and deposes the reactionary Russian-sponsored shah of Persia, Mohammed Ali Shah (16 July). Khan replaces the shah with his 12-year-old son Ahmad Mirza Shah.

ASIA

25 Nov. The former Japanese resident-general in Korea, Prince Hirobumi Ito, is assassinated by a Korean nationalist in Manchuria.

– In British-ruled India the Morley–Minto reforms increase the Indian representation in local government. The reforms are too limited to satisfy nationalists.

THE AMERICAS

4 Mar. William Howard Taft is inaugurated as 27th US president.

June The National Association for the Advancement of Colored People (NAACP) is formed in New York.

16 Dec. After encouraging a revolt against the Nicaraguan dictator José Santos Zelaya, who was rumoured to be considering allowing the Japanese to build a rival to the Panama Canal, the US government decides to intervene militarily in Nicaragua. Zelaya is replaced by José Madriz, but civil war continues until 1912, when a further intervention secures the rule of the more compliant Adolfo Diaz.

SUB-SAHARAN AFRICA

– The book *Labour in Portuguese West Africa* by British chocolate manufacturer and social reformer William Cadbury exposes the degrading working conditions and the slavery that persist in São Tomé and Principe. He persuades Quaker-owned cocoa and chocolate firms Fry and Rowntree to boycott cocoa from the two islands, eventually ending their role in the cocoa trade.

ECONOMY AND SOCIETY

– US businessman Gordon Selfridge opens Selfridge's department store in London.

– The first kibbutz opens at Degania Aleph in Palestine.

SCIENCE AND TECHNOLOGY

6 April The US explorer Robert Peary reaches the North Pole. Posterity, however, will cast doubt on Peary's claim to have reached the Pole on this or any other day.

25 July French aviator Louis Blériot flies his monoplane from Calais to Dover in 37 minutes. It is the first flight across an open sea.

31 Dec. The Manhattan Bridge opens. It is the third such bridge linking Manhattan with Brooklyn, New York.

– In the USA the chemist Leo H. Baekeland invents Bakelite, the first synthetic polymer. It is hard, indissoluble and inexpensive, and will be used to make objects as diverse as billiard balls and electrical insulators.

ARTS AND HUMANITIES

Literature

– American businessman Condé Nast buys *Vogue*, and turns it into an elegant fashion magazine.

André Gide, *La Porte étroite* (Strait is the Gate), novel.

H(erbert) G(eorge) Wells, *Tono-Bungay*, novel.

Israel Zangwill, *The Melting Pot*, play; the title introduces the phrase, which gains currency as the description of the merging together of peoples in the USA.

Visual Arts and Architecture

– Italian poet Filippo Tommaso Marinetti issues the First Futurist Manifesto. With its emphasis on speed and clarity and the rejection of the past in the name of the machine age, it sets the tone for modernism in the arts. Marinetti also advocates the abandonment of grammar and syntax.

– In Chicago the Robie House by Frank Lloyd Wright is completed.

– The Victoria and Albert Museum opens in London.

Georges Braque, *Violin and Palette,* painting.

Wassily Kandinsky, *Mountain*, painting.

Music

25 Jan. First performance in Dresden of Richard Strauss's opera *Elektra*.

18 May Russian composer Nikolai Rimsky-Korsakov's score provides the music for the ballet *Prince Igor*, which is performed at the Théâtre du Châtelet, Paris; Sergei Diaghilev is the choreographer.

4 Dec. First performance in Munich of Ermanno Wolf-Ferrari's opera *Il segreto di Susanna* (Susanna's Secret): her secret is that she smokes cigarettes.

Gustav Mahler, *Das Lied von der Erde* (The Song of the Earth), song-symphony.

Sergei Rachmaninov, Piano Concerto No. 3 in D minor, and *Ostrov myortvich* (The Island of the Dead), symphonic poem.

Arnold Schoenberg (see p. 511), *Fünf Orchesterstücke* (Five Pieces for Orchestra).

1910

EUROPE

1 Feb. In Britain the first Labour Exchanges for the unemployed are opened.

15 Feb. In Britain a general election is held on the vexed questions of Lloyd George's 'People's Budget' (see 29 April 1909), the power of the House of Lords and Home Rule for Ireland. The Liberals win with a reduced majority.

29 April In Britain the finance bill implementing the 'People's Budget' becomes law.

6 May In Britain King Edward VII dies and is succeeded by his son George V.

May The British House of Commons resolves to deprive the House of Lords of the right to veto finance bills.

28 Aug. Montenegro becomes an independent kingdom under Nicholas I.

4 Oct. A revolution overthrows the Portuguese royal house and a republic is proclaimed. King Manuel II flees to Britain.

18 Oct. Elentherios Venizelos becomes prime minister of Greece.

Nov. In Wales civil unrest breaks out in Tonypandy in the Rhondda Valley consisting of a wave of strikes in the mining industry. Home Secretary Winston Churchill (see p. 523) sends 300 extra police from London to quell the disturbances.

12 Dec. In the second British general election of the year, H.H. Asquith's Liberal Party wins again with a slightly increased majority.

MIDDLE EAST AND NORTH AFRICA

20 Feb. An Islamic nationalist assassinates the Egyptian prime minister, Boutros Ghali (see 10 Nov. 1908).

ASIA

22 Aug. Japan formally annexes Korea and renames the country Chosen.

THE AMERICAS

– A peasant revolution breaks out in Mexico, threatening the rule of President Porfirio Díaz. Francisco Madero seeks to overturn Mexico's inequitable system of landholding, which is dominated by wealthy landowners, usually of Spanish ancestry, who own vast estates: his radical aim is to break up the estates and forcibly redistribute land to the poor.

SUB-SAHARAN AFRICA

15 Jan. The French Congo is renamed French Equatorial Africa and is then divided into Gabon, Middle Congo and Ubanghi-Shari.

31 May Cape Colony, Natal, Transvaal and Orange Free State form the Union of South Africa, which becomes a self-governing dominion of the British empire (1 July).

15 Sept. Louis Botha, an Afrikaner (Boer), becomes prime minister of the Union of South Africa.

ECONOMY AND SOCIETY

– Dr Crippen, a US physician, murders and dissects his second wife in London. He is captured on board the SS *Montrose* as he tries to flee to Canada with his mistress. It is the first case in which radio has been used to catch a criminal. Crippen is later hanged.

– The Parisian craze for imitation sable leads to a Chinese hunt for Manchurian marmots. The marmots are suffering from bubonic plague, which is then transmitted to China's human population. More than 50,000 people will be killed in Manchuria and China (1910–12). Over the next decade the disease will kill some 1.5 million people in China and India.

– In Britain Lord Baden-Powell and his sister Agnes found the Girl Guides.

– In rugby union the Five Nations championship is held for the first time (France joining England, Scotland, Wales and Ireland).

SCIENCE AND TECHNOLOGY

- In France Marie Curie and A. Debierne isolate radium. Marie Curie also publishes her *Treatise on Radiography*.
- The philosophers Bertrand Russell and A.N. Whitehead publish the first volume of their *Principia Mathematica* (Principles of Mathematics).

ARTS AND HUMANITIES

Literature

21 April The US novelist Mark Twain dies.

10 Nov. The Russian novelist Count Leo Tolstoy dies.

Arnold Bennett, *Clayhanger*, novel; the first of his series describing life in industrial Staffordshire.

John Buchan, *Prester John*, novel.

Paul Claudel, *Cinq grandes odes* (Five Great Odes), lyrical and religious verse.

E(dward) M(organ) Forster, *Howards End*, novel.

H(erbert) G(eorge) Wells, *The History of Mr Polly*, novel.

Visual Arts and Architecture

- In Britain the art critic Roger Fry organizes a major exhibition of Post-Impressionist paintings at the Grafton Galleries, London.
- Antoni Gaudí, architect and Spanish mystic, finishes the Casa Milà, an apartment block in Barcelona.
- Wassily Kandinsky starts to develop his non-representational paintings, the first such examples in the history of Western art.

Umberto Boccioni, *The City Rises*, painting.

Georges Braque, *Violin and Pitcher*, painting.

Robert Delaunay, *The Eiffel Tower*, painting that brings a cubist perspective to a now-familiar subject.

Henri Matisse, *The Dance*, painting.

Pablo Picasso, *Portrait of Ambrose Vollard*, painting.

Music

4 June The Ballet Russe production of *Sheherazade* to Nikolai Rimsky-Korsakov's music and choreographed by Mikhail Fokine opens at the Théatre National de l'Opéra, Paris.

25 June First performance in Paris of the ballet *The Firebird*, to the music of Igor Stravinsky and choreographed by Mikhail Fokine.

10 Dec. First performance in New York of Giacomo Puccini's opera *La fanciulla del West* (The Girl of the Golden West).

26 Dec. The London Palladium opens as a theatre specializing in revues and vaudeville.

Béla Bartók, *Ket kep* (Two Pictures), orchestral work.

Gustav Mahler, Symphony No. 10 in F sharp major.

Ralph Vaughan Williams, *Fantasia on a Theme by Thomas Tallis*, orchestral work based on a psalm tune of 1567 by Thomas Tallis.

Film

- French motion picture pioneers Charles and Emile Pathé establish the newsreel company *Pathé-Gazette* and set up units to produce film newsreel across Europe, Japan and the USA.

1911

EUROPE

May The Black Hand terrorist group is founded in Belgrade, aiming to build a greater Serbian nation.

10 Aug. In Britain the Parliament Act become law, ending a constitutional crisis stretching back to 1909. The House of Lords abandons nearly all of its power to veto bills passed by the House of Commons. Henceforth it can only delay legislation. The British House of Commons votes to pay MPs a salary (£400 per year) for the first time.

22 Aug. In Britain, during an anti-German spy scare, Parliament passes an Official Secrets Act, making it a criminal act to publish classified information without permission.

14 Sept. Pyotr Stolypin, prime minister of Russia, is assassinated by a revolutionary. His reformist drive to revitalize Russia's institutions and build a class of prosperous peasants has, however, already ended in the face of Nicholas II's opposition.

8 Nov. In Britain A.J. Balfour resigns as Conservative Party leader and is succeeded by Andrew Bonar Law.

Dec. In Britain Parliament passes the legislation necessary for a National Insurance programme providing for the payment of sickness and unemployment benefit.

- Famine again causes mass starvation in Russia.

MIDDLE EAST AND NORTH AFRICA

1 July The German gunboat *Panther* arrives in Agadir to protect German commercial interests in Morocco. Its arrival raises Anglo-French fears about German expansionism, triggering a second international crisis over Morocco (see 1906).

29 Sept. Italy, seeking to acquire Libya, declares war on the Ottoman empire; Italian troops land at Tripoli (5 Oct.). Aircraft are used in warfare for the first time when Italian planes bomb an oasis near Tripoli (1 Nov.).

4 Nov. Germany agrees to recognize French rights in Morocco in return for the cession of territory in the French Congo, thereby ending the Agadir crisis.

5 Nov. Italy annexes Libya from the Ottoman empire. This display of Turkish weakness will encourage the Balkan states to seek to eliminate Turkey from the region (see 1912).

ASIA

Sept. In China floods cause more than 100,000 deaths.

11 Oct. Revolution against the Manchu breaks out in C China. The revolutionaries proclaim a Chinese republic (26 Oct.).

16 Nov. In China prime minister Yuan Shikai (Yüan Shih-k'ai) forms a cabinet.

29 Dec. A revolutionary assembly meeting at Nanjing elects Guomindang leader Sun Zhong Shan (Sun Yat-sen) president of the United Provinces of China.

THE AMERICAS

25 Mar. In New York a fire at the Triangle Shirtwaist Co. kills 146 people. The company's owners have flouted government safety regulations.

15 May Anti-trust action by the US Supreme Court breaks up John D. Rockefeller's Standard Oil Company.

25 May Porfirio Díaz resigns as president of Mexico following a peasant revolution (see 1910).

6 Nov. Francisco Madero becomes Mexican president.

– Samuel Zemurray, a Bessarabian-American, supplies Gen. Manuel Bonilla with money and mercenaries to overthrow the government of Honduras. Zemurray thereby gains concessions as a banana exporter from Honduras, which becomes known as a 'banana republic'.

Erst kommt das Fressen, dann kommt die Morale.

(Food first, morality afterwards.)

Bertolt Brecht, *Die Dreigroschenoper*
(*The Threepenny Opera*) (1928)

ECONOMY AND SOCIETY

– American economist Irving Fisher invents 'monetarism' in his book *The Purchasing Power of Money*. Fisher claims that prices rise relative to the supply of money and to the speed of its circulation.

– Joseph Schumpeter, an economics professor at the University of Graz, Austria, writes *Theory of Economic Development*. Translated into English (1934), the book will become a key economic text.

– Hiram Bingham, an American adventurer, discovers the lost Inca city of Macchu Pichu in the Peruvian Andes.

SCIENCE AND TECHNOLOGY

14 Dec. Roald Amundsen, a Norwegian explorer, leads his team to the South Pole a month ahead of Capt. Scott (see 18 Jan. 1912).

– In Britain the New Zealand-born physicist Ernest Rutherford puts forward the concept of the nuclear atom, consisting of a tightly packed positively charged nucleus surrounded by electrons.

– Italian electrical engineer Camillo Olivetti founds the Olivetti Co., at Ivrea, Piedmont. The company will become a major manufacturer of typewriters.

– Polish-born biochemist Casimir Funk of the Lister Institute coins the word 'vitamine' to describe the co-enzymes needed to make enzymes effective.

ARTS AND HUMANITIES

Literature

– Henry Watson Fowler and Frank George Fowler publish the first edition of the *Concise Oxford Dictionary*.

Max Beerbohm, *Zuleika Dobson*, novel; a satire of Oxford life.

Rupert Brooke, *Poems*.

Frances Hodgson Burnett, *The Secret Garden*, children's novel.

G(ilbert) K(eith) Chesterton, *The Innocence of Father Brown*, collection of detective stories.

Joseph Conrad, *Under Western Eyes*, novel.

Hugo von Hofmannsthal, *Jedermann* (Everyman), play.

Rudyard Kipling, 'The Female of the Species', poem; he concludes that the subject of his title is 'more deadly than the male'.

Saki (H.H. Munro) *The Chronicles of Clovis*, short stories.

Visual Arts and Architecture

– In Munich Wassily Kandinsky, August Macke and Franz Marc found the *Blaue Reiter* (Blue Rider) group of artists.

– German architect Walter Gropius creates a new kind of building for the Fagus factory, Alfeld, Germany; its skeleton is made of steel and its walls are made of glass.

– US architect Frank Lloyd Wright completes his building Taliesin East in Spring Green, Wisconsin, and in its name pays tribute to his Welsh-American lineage.

– Leonardo da Vinci's *Mona Lisa* is stolen from the Louvre in Paris. It will be recovered in 1913.

Georges Braque, *The Portuguese*, painting using stencilled letters.

Marc Chagall, *The Village and I*, painting.

Henri Matisse, *The Red Studio* and *The Blue Window*, paintings.

Pablo Picasso, *The Accordionist*, painting.

Maurice Utrillo, *Church at Châtillon*, painting.

Music

26 Jan. First performance in Dresden of Richard Strauss's opera *Der Rosenkavalier* (The Knight of the Rose). Hugo von Hofmannsthal supplies the libretto for Strauss's work, in which he turns towards 18th-century Mozartian pastiche and away from the modernism of his previous works.

18 May Death in Vienna of Austrian composer Gustav Mahler.

13 June Russian ballet dancer Vaslav Nijinsky dances the title role in *Petrushka* at the Théatre du Châtelet, Paris. Igor Stravinsky's score shows the composer adopting bitonality and syncopation.

Sir Edward Elgar, Symphony No. 2 in E flat major.

Charles Ives, Symphony No. 3 (*The Camp Meeting*).

Maurice Ravel, *Valses nobles et sentimentales*, work for solo piano that Ravel will orchestrate in 1912.

Alexander Scriabin, *Prometheus, the Poem of Fire*, orchestral work blending musical with visual effects.

Jean Sibelius, Symphony No. 4 in A minor.

Igor Stravinsky, *Firebird Suite*, based on his ballet of 1910.

1912

EUROPE

14 Jan. In France Raymond Poincaré forms a new government.

11 April British prime minister Herbert Asquith introduces a Third Irish Home Rule Bill. It arouses bitter opposition from Irish Protestants, especially in Ulster.

4 May Italy occupies the Ottoman-ruled Dodecanese Islands.

29 June Near-universal suffrage is adopted in Italy.

14 Aug. Bulgaria demands that Turkey grant autonomy to Macedonia. Bulgaria's action is a pretext for war with the Ottoman empire.

28 Sept. In the N of Ireland Unionist opponents of Irish Home Rule, now led by the lawyer Sir Edward Carson, sign a 'Solemn League and Covenant' pledging them to resist Home Rule.

8 Oct. The First Balkan War breaks out: the Balkan League (Montenegro, Serbia, Greece and Bulgaria), encouraged by Turkish weakness against Italy in North Africa (see 1911) attack the Ottoman empire, intending to divide its territory in Europe. The Bulgarians advance on Constantinople, but Russia intervenes saying it will not tolerate a Bulgarian presence in Constantinople, and the Bulgarians fail in their final onslaught. Serb forces defeat the Turks at Monastir, Macedonia (15–18 Nov.), and advance to the Adriatic. Austria-Hungary, however, opposes the idea of a Serbian foothold on the Adriatic, declaring its support for an independent Albania.

18 Oct. The treaty of Lausanne ends the one-year war between Italy and the Ottoman empire. The Turks, distracted by the Balkan conflict, agree to surrender Tripoli in Libya to Italy in exchange for the restoration of the Dodecanese Islands.

3 Dec. An armistice is declared between Turkey, Bulgaria, Serbia and Montenegro in the First Balkan War. Greece abstains. All the Balkan League members have gained considerable territory but little holds them together apart from ambition for territorial expansion, and none is satisfied with its conquests. Bulgaria seems destined to become the most powerful Balkan nation, but is temporarily weakened. Both Russia and Austria-Hungary are alarmed at the upheaval in the region. The potential for further conflict is high.

– The Royal Flying Corps (RFC), forerunner of the RAF, is created in Britain.

ASIA

12 Feb. The last Manchu emperor of China, Puyi (P'u-i), abdicates. Under provisional president Sun Zhong Shan (Sun Yat-sen), founder of the Guomindang (nationalist party), China becomes a republic.

30 July Japan's emperor Mutsuhito dies and is succeeded by his son Yoshihito.

THE AMERICAS

6 Jan. New Mexico becomes the 47th US state.

14 Jan. Arizona becomes the 48th US state.

15 April The British luxury liner SS *Titanic*, on its maiden voyage, collides with an iceberg off Newfoundland and sinks in 2½ hours. Only 711 of the 2224 people on board survive.

22 June Former US president Theodore Roosevelt abandons the Republicans and founds a Progressive Republican party.

5 Nov. The governor of New Jersey, Woodrow Wilson, wins the US presidency as the Democratic candidate, defeating Theodore Roosevelt and the incumbent president William Howard Taft.

– US President Taft despatches forces to protect US commercial interests from political unrest in C America and the Caribbean on three occasions this year: Honduras (Feb.), Cuba (June) and Nicaragua (Aug.). US marines will remain in Nicaragua until 1933.

ECONOMY AND SOCIETY

May–June The 5th Olympic Games are held in Stockholm, Sweden.

– Maria Montessori describes her teaching success in *The Montessori Method* and begins a teachers' training movement.

– *Pravda* (Truth) starts publication as the newspaper of Russian communism.

SCIENCE AND TECHNOLOGY

18 Jan. The British explorer Capt. Robert Falcon Scott arrives at the South Pole a month after his Norwegian rival Amundsen (see 14 Dec. 1911). Scott and four members of his team die of starvation and exposure on the return journey (Mar.) and their bodies are discovered in Nov. The events of Scott's expedition will be popularly represented as epic tragedy.

– By now palaeontologists have discovered in Sussex, England, the whole skull of Piltdown Man, whom they believe to be the 'missing link' between man and the apes. Piltdown Man will be revealed as a hoax in 1953, his jaw being that of an orang-utan.

– The international Radio-telegraph Conference adopts the Morse code signal SOS, three dots, three dashes and three dots, as the universal distress signal. Its use will be discontinued in 1997.

– Following the example of most other European countries, Britain's telephone network is nationalized.

ARTS AND HUMANITIES

Literature

Paul Claudel, *L'Annonce faite à Marie* (Tidings Brought to Mary), play.

Arthur Conan Doyle, *The Lost World*, novel.

Theodore Dreiser, *The Financier*, novel.

Amy Lowell, *A Dome of Many-Colored Glass*, poetry collection.

Thomas Mann, *Der Tod in Venedig* (Death in Venice), novella.

Romain Rolland, *Jean-Christophe*, last novel of a 10-volume sequence (*roman fleuve*).

Saki (H.H. Munro), *The Unbearable Bassington*, novel.

Rabindranath Tagore, *Gitanjali: Song Offering*, free-verse recreations of the author's Bengali poems.

Visual Arts and Architecture

– Jacob Epstein sculpts the tomb of Oscar Wilde for the Père Lachaise cemetery, Paris.

Giorgio de Chirico, *Melancholy*, painting.

Marcel Duchamp, *Nude Descending a Staircase, No. 2*, painting.

Juan Gris (José Victoriano Gonzalez), *Hommage à Picasso*, painting.

Amedeo Modigliani, *Head*, sculpture.

Pablo Picasso (see p. 467), *The Violin*, painting, and *Still Life with Chair Caning*, collage.

Music

8 June Russian ballet dancer Vaslav Nijinsky dances the role of Daphnis in *Daphnis et Chloé* performed to Maurice Ravel's music and choreographed by Fokine, at the Théâtre du Châtelet, Paris.

– First performance in Stuttgart, Germany, of Richard Strauss's opera *Ariadne auf Naxos* (Ariadne on Naxos). The libretto is by Hugo von Hofmannsthal.

William Handy, 'Memphis Blues', song; building on the musical tradition of black spirituals, Handy creates a characteristic melancholic 'blues' sound.

Arnold Schoenberg (see p. 511), *Pierrot lunaire* (Moonstruck Pierrot), for voice and chamber ensemble.

Film

- The French film *Queen Elizabeth*, starring Sarah Bernhardt, is the first feature-length motion picture to be seen in the USA.
- In the USA Mack Sennett founds the Keystone production company to make slapstick silent films.

1913

EUROPE

6 Jan. The London peace conference between Turkey and the Balkan states is suspended over the Turks' refusal to cede Adrianople, Crete and the Aegean Islands.

Jan. In Britain the Third Irish Home Rule Bill passes the House of Commons but is rejected by the Lords. In the N of Ireland the Protestant Ulster Volunteer Force (UVF) is founded by Sir Edward Carson to resist Irish Home Rule.

17 Jan. Raymond Poincaré becomes French president. Aristide Briand succeeds him as French premier (21 Jan.).

3 Feb. Bulgaria restarts hostilities in the First Balkan War.

18 Mar. King George I of Greece is assassinated in Salonika.

3 April British suffragette Emmeline Pankhurst is convicted of arson and imprisoned. The House of Commons rejects a women's franchise bill in May.

30 May The treaty of London ends the First Balkan War. The Serbs are outraged that the creation (at Austria-Hungary's insistence) of an independent Albania deprives them of access to the sea. Both Serbs and Greeks are jealous of Bulgarian territorial gains. They plot, with the Turks, to launch a surprise attack on Bulgaria. However, the Bulgarians, aware of their peril, gamble on a surprise attack of their own on the Greeks and Serbs (29 June). The Second Balkan War is brief (32 days). Bulgaria is defeated by a combination of Greeks, Serbs, Turks and Romanians. The treaty of Bucharest (10 Aug.) ends the war. The Turks retain Adrianople (Edirne in European Turkey) and Bulgaria loses territory to Serbia, Greece and Romania. As a result of the Balkan Wars, Russia decides that Serbia is vital to its survival, as it can ensure no other nation will capture the Dardanelles (an eventuality that would seriously damage the Russian economy). Austria-Hungary, however, now sees the rising power of Serbia as a threat. Any new confrontation in the region has the potential to develop rapidly into general warfare.

4 June British suffragette Emily Wilding Davison is killed when she runs in front of the king's horse at the Epsom Derby.

25 Nov. The Irish Volunteers are formed in S Ireland, in response to the formation in Jan. 1913 of the Ulster Volunteer Force by Protestants in the N of Ireland (Jan.).

ASIA

3 Sept. The Chinese base of Nanjing falls to Yuan Shikai (Yüan Shih-k'ai), who is elected Chinese president (6 Oct.).

Nov. President Yuan Shikai outlaws the Guomindang (nationalist party) of Sun Zhong Shan (Sun Yat-sen).

THE AMERICAS

18 Feb. In Mexico a coup topples President Francisco Madero and installs Victoriano Huerta, who proves to be brutal, despotic and incompetent. Madero is murdered (23 Feb.). Civil war follows.

4 Mar. Woodrow Wilson is inaugurated as 28th US president.

8 April Direct elections to the Senate of the USA are introduced by the 17th amendment to the US Constitution.

8 May Congress approves the Underwood–Simmons Tariff Act, which reduces import duties by 30%. America's wall of tariffs has been breached for the first time since the Civil War, but domestic industries are hard hit.

Nov. In Mexico Francisco ('Pancho') Villa and Venustiano Carranza lead a rebellion against President Huerta, whose government is also opposed by the USA.

SUB-SAHARAN AFRICA

25 Nov. The followers of London-trained lawyer Mohandas Gandhi (see p. 476) demonstrate when their leader is jailed after leading protests against racist laws in South Africa. The Natal police fire at the demonstrators.

- Albert Schweitzer, an Alsatian Protestant missionary, founds Lambaréné Hospital in French Equatorial Africa.

ECONOMY AND SOCIETY

- Henry Ford introduces the assembly-line method of production in the Ford Motor Company.
- French dress designer Gabrielle (Coco) Chanel revolutionizes female fashion at her boutique in Deauville, France, with a new simplicity and elegance of line.
- American historian Charles Beard claims in his *Economic Interpretation of the Constitution* that the propertied prejudices of the authors of the American constitution have led to economic inequalities in American society.

SCIENCE AND TECHNOLOGY

- The Manchester-based Danish physicist Niels Bohr proposes a model of atomic structure (the Bohr model).

ARTS AND HUMANITIES

Literature

- First performance in Vienna of George Bernard Shaw's play *Pygmalion*.

Alain-Fournier (Henri-Alban Fournier), *Le Grand Meaulnes* (The Lost Domain), semi-autobiographical fantasy.

Guillaume Apollinaire, *Alcools* (Alcohols), avant-garde poetry collection.

Robert Frost, *A Boy's Will*, poetry collection.

D(avid) H(erbert) Lawrence, *Sons and Lovers*, novel.

Osip Mandelstam, *Kamen* (Stone), poetry collection.

Marcel Proust, *Du côté de chez Swann* (Swann's Way), the first volume of his extended partly autobiographical novel *A la recherche du temps perdu* (Remembrance of Things Past), a satirical comedy of life in the Parisian aristocracy.

Miguel de Unamuno, *Del sentimiento trágico de la vida* (The Tragic Sense of Life), philosophy.

Visual Arts and Architecture

– Grand Central Station is completed in New York.

– A major exhibition of Post-Impressionist and Cubist art in New York (the so-called Armory Show) introduces modern European art to the USA.

Marcel Duchamp, *Bicycle Wheel*, the first 'ready-made'.

Ernst Ludwig Kirchner, *Berlin Street Scene*, painting.

Pablo Picasso (see p. 467), *Man with a Guitar*, painting.

Music

4 Mar. First performance in Monte Carlo of Gabriel Fauré's opera *Pénélope*.

13 June First performance in Paris of Sergei Diaghilev's Ballets Russes of *Le Sacre du printemps* (The Rite of Spring), a ballet with music by Igor Stravinsky and choreography by Vaslav Nijinsky. The dissonance of the music allied to the sexuality of the dancing causes a riot but the work opens a new chapter in the history of Western art and music.

– Between now and 1915 the term 'jazz' begins to be used for a type of African-American music, first developed in New Orleans and reaching Chicago by 1914. It is characterized by syncopation and the noisy use of percussion instruments together with trombone, trumpet and saxophone.

Frederick Delius, *On Hearing the First Cuckoo in Spring*, orchestral work.

Arnold Schoenberg (see p. 511), *Gurrelieder*, work for soloists, chorus and orchestra.

Anton Webern, *Six Pieces for Orchestra*.

Ralph Vaughan Williams, Symphony No. 2, *A London Symphony*.

Film

– English-born music-hall actor Charlie Chaplin signs a contract in New York to make films with Mack Sennett.

– The Fox and Universal film companies are formed in the USA.

1914

EUROPE

20 Mar. The Curragh mutiny in Ireland: 57 British officers say they would resign if ordered to enforce Home Rule in Ulster.

25 May In Britain the Third Irish Home Rule Bill passes the House of Commons, but the House of Lords votes for Ulster to be permanently excluded from Home Rule (July). A bill will later suspend Home Rule for the duration of World War I (18 Sept.).

28 June In Sarajevo, Bosnia-Herzegovina, Gavrilo Princip, a Serb extremist, assassinates the archduke Franz Ferdinand, heir to the throne of Austria-Hungary. Princip and his co-conspirators have been armed by the Serbian Black Hand organization (see 1911). The assassination sets in train the events that lead to the outbreak of World War I. The government of Austria-Hungary decides that it can no longer tolerate the Serbian threat and declares war on Serbia (28 July). The Russians decide they cannot allow the destruction of Serbia and mobilize as a warning to Austria-Hungary. The German empire is obliged to support

Austria-Hungary but is aware that war with Russia will probably lead to conflict with France. Germany's strategic Schlieffen Plan (devised in 1905) requires Germany to defeat France rapidly before turning to face Russia (thereby avoiding the need to fight on two fronts). The plan can work only if it starts the moment Russia begins its very slow mobilization. Thus Germany declares war on Russia (1 Aug.) and then on France (3 Aug.). Germany invades Belgium, a hitherto neutral country (4 Aug.) and the British, bound by the 1840 treaty of London to protect Belgium, declare war on Germany on the same day. Alliance systems and perceived self-interest ensure the war spreads rapidly: Montenegro declares war on Austria-Hungary (5 Aug.) and Serbia declares war on Germany (6 Aug.). Austria-Hungary declares war on Russia (6 Aug.) and Montenegro on Germany (8 Aug.). Finally, both France and Britain declare war on Austria-Hungary (10 and 12 Aug.).

7 Aug. The first soldiers of the British Expeditionary Force (BEF) land in France.

8 Aug. The Defence of the Realm Act (DORA) is passed in Britain, giving the government wide-ranging emergency powers.

14 Aug.–25 Aug. The battle of the Frontiers: the immediate French hope is to regain Alsace-Lorraine, lost to Germany in 1871, but the French forces that invade Lorraine are heavily defeated. French losses are on an unforeseen, tragic scale: 250,000 French soldiers lose their lives, for no gain.

20 Aug. German troops enter Brussels, but Belgian resistance is stronger than expected, and the rigid timetable of the Schlieffen Plan begins to break down.

23 Aug. The German 1st Army under Gen. Alexander von Kluck meets the BEF at Mons, S Belgium. The BEF and Belgian troops retreat S in the face of the German advance (24 Aug.–5 Sept.).

26–30 Aug. The battle of Tannenberg ends in humiliating defeat for two Russian armies that have invaded East Prussia. Gen. Ludendorff and Gen. von Hindenburg take some 100,000 Russian prisoners.

1 Sept. In Russia the name of the city of St Petersburg is changed to Petrograd as a patriotic gesture.

2 Sept. The French government moves to Bordeaux as German armies march on Paris.

5–12 Sept. The first battle of the Marne: as the commander of the German 1st Army, Gen. Alexander von Kluck, tries to rescue the collapsing timetable of the Schlieffen Plan by swinging E instead of W of Paris, he opens a gap between his troops and the German 2nd Army; Franco-British forces attack and the German advance is halted. All the German armies W of Verdun are forced to retreat to stronger defensive positions.

Sept. In the S part of the Eastern Front the Russians push the Austro-Hungarians back into Galicia, necessitating German reinforcements.

Sept.–Oct. On the Western Front the two sides try to outflank each other, moving N towards the English Channel in the 'race to the sea'. During the battle of Aisne (15–18 Sept.) the first trenches are dug on the Western Front.

Mahatma Gandhi (1869–1948)

Mohandas Karamshand Gandhi, known as Mahatma ('Great Soul') Gandhi, was the spiritual leader of Indian independence. He studied as a lawyer in London, and his ethical and spiritual convictions were a fusion of traditional Hinduism and Western liberal progressivism. He was a pacifist, although he supported the war effort of the British Empire both in 1914 and, initially, in 1939.

After qualifying as a lawyer, Gandhi practised in South Africa. While working to end discrimination against Indians there he developed the Hindu tactic of *dharna*, squatting in front of a house or office in order to draw attention to a grievance. From this there grew the *Satyagraha* (holding on to truth) movement that used passive resistance as a way of fighting South Africa's racial laws. *Ahimsa* (non-violence) would be Gandhi's core belief.

Returning to India in 1914, Gandhi joined the Indian National Congress and rose rapidly to become its leader by 1919. He at once issued a call for non-cooperation with those British laws he held to be unjust. In 1942, during World War II, he launched the 'Quit India Movement'. But Gandhi wanted India to change, not just to become independent. He embraced the cause of the Untouchables, the lowest of all Hindu castes whom he termed the 'Children of God'. He himself performed menial work traditionally allocated to the Untouchables, and he persuaded many high-caste Hindus to do the same. He was assassinated by a Hindu fundamentalist, Nathuram Godse, on 30 January 1948. The partition of India into Hindu and Muslim states had resulted in religious war rather than the tolerance he advocated, but Gandhi had made modern, independent India a reality.

11 Oct. The Germans take Ghent and then (15 Oct.) Ostend, Belgium. The Channel ports are now within their sight.

29 Oct. The Turkish navy bombards the Russian Black Sea ports of Sevastopol and Odessa. The Russians accordingly declare war on the Turks (2 Nov.) and the British and French follow suit (5 Nov.). On the same day the British annex Ottoman Cyprus, which has been occupied by Britain since 1878.

30 Oct.–24 Nov. German forces attempt to break the Allied line in the first battle of Ypres. The battle ends any possibility of swift German success. It is the start of a four-year period of trench warfare on the Western Front, as lines of defensive trenchworks stretch from the Swiss frontier to the English Channel.

2 Dec. Austro-Hungarian forces take Belgrade, but the Serbs retake the city (15 Dec.).

5–17 Dec. Austro-Hungarian forces attempt, but fail, to penetrate Russian lines outside Kraków in S Poland. The Russians inflict heavy losses.

24 Dec. On the Western Front many opposing troops enjoy an unauthorized Christmas truce, leaving their trenches and fraternizing with their enemies. Commanders on both sides are horrified, seeing this as a breakdown in fighting spirit.

MIDDLE EAST AND NORTH AFRICA

1 Oct. Turkey closes the Dardanelles.

– In order to protect its wartime oil supplies, Britain takes a controlling interest in the Anglo-Persian Oil Co.

ASIA

23 Aug. Japan declares war on Germany and on Austria-Hungary (25 Aug.).

– Mohandas Gandhi (see box) returns to India where he supports Britain's war effort even as he criticizes its government of India. He is, however, also developing his ideas of *satyagraha* (truth force) or passive resistance. He celebrates his return to India by staging a public fast.

THE AMERICAS

15 Jun. Cunard's passenger liner SS *Aquitania* arrives in New York on its maiden voyage. The vessel will soon be serving as a troopship.

28 June American suffragettes march on the Capitol, Washington, D.C.

15 July In Mexico Venustiano Carranza forces the resignation of President Huerta. Civil war follows between the forces of Carranza and those of his former subordinate, Francisco ('Pancho') Villa, who sets up a revolutionary government in the N of Mexico.

4 Aug. President Wilson declares US neutrality in the war between Austria-Hungary and Serbia. He will maintain that policy throughout the subsequent declarations of war made by European states.

15 Aug. The Panama Canal opens.

1 Nov. In the battle of Coronel the German Pacific squadron under Rear Adm. Graf Maximilian von Spee sinks the British cruisers *Good Hope* and *Monmouth* off the coast of Chile. It is Britain's first naval defeat in over a century, and battlecruisers are sent to exact revenge. At the battle of the Falkland Islands (8 Dec.) von Spee goes down with his flagship, the heavy cruiser *Scharnhorst*, and his squadron is destroyed.

SUB-SAHARAN AFRICA

1 Jan. Britain amalgamates N and S Nigeria as one colony.

26 Aug. German forces in Togoland surrender to Anglo-French forces: the German colony is divided between France and Britain.

Oct. The Boers of S Africa mount a pro-German rebellion, which is rapidly suppressed.

ECONOMY AND SOCIETY

20 Aug. Pope Pius X dies; he will be canonized on 29 May 1954.

3 Sept. Giacomo della Chiesa is elected as Pope Benedict XV.

– Mary Phelps Jacob of New York patents her invention, the elasticated brassière.

– American feminist Margaret Sanger introduces the term 'birth control' in her magazine *The Woman Rebel*. She is harassed by the authorities for advocating contraception but maintains her campaign to change both laws and attitudes.

ARTS AND HUMANITIES

Literature

5 Sept. French writer and poet Charles Péguy is killed at the battle of the Marne.

– The 28-year-old French writer Alain-Fournier (Henri-Alban Fournier) is killed in action near Verdun, France.

– In Britain the *Times Literary Supplement* is published for the first time as a separate periodical.

Robert Frost, *North of Boston*, poetry collection.

André Gide, *Les Caves du Vatican* (The Vatican Cellars), anti-clerical satire.

James Joyce, *Dubliners*, a collection of short stories, and *A Portrait of the Artist as a Young Man*, novel.

Edgar Rice Burroughs, *Tarzan of the Apes*, novel in which he develops the theme of a contrast between noble savagery and enfeebled culture.

Visual Arts and Architecture

– In Britain the first publication of *Blast*, a literary and artistic magazine edited by Percy Wyndham Lewis, pioneer of the Vorticist movement, marks the arrival of Modernism in Britain.

Georges Braque, *Glass, Bottle and Newspaper*, painting.

Giorgio de Chirico, *The Enigma of a Day*, painting.

Jacob Epstein, *The Rock Drill*, sculpture.

Music

David Ivor Davies (Ivor Novello), 'Keep the Home Fires Burning', song.

Ralph Vaughan Williams, *The Lark Ascending*, for violin and orchestra (revised in 1920).

1915

EUROPE

13 Jan. An earthquake in Avezzano, E of Rome, Italy, kills some 30,000 people.

18 Feb. Germany starts a U-boat (submarine) blockade of Britain in response to the Royal Navy's blockade of German ports.

10–13 Mar. On the Western Front British and Indian troops make small gains in the inconclusive battle of Neuve Chapelle.

22 April–27 May The second battle of Ypres: the Germans use poison gas for the first time.

26 April By the secret treaty of London Britain and France promise Italy territory and reparations from Austria-Hungary and Germany at the end of the war in return for joining the Allies.

7 May At 2.10 p.m. SS *Lusitania*, a Cunard Line passenger liner, is sunk off the coast of Ireland by a German U-boat. The ship was carrying a consignment of military ammunition, but among about 1200 people killed are 128 US citizens. The episode inflames anti-German sentiment in the USA.

15 May In Britain the First Sea Lord Sir John Fisher resigns in protest at the failure of the Dardanelles campaign in Turkey.

22 May In the worst rail crash in British history 227 people are killed and 246 injured in a collision involving a troop train at Gretna junction, near Carlisle.

23 May Italy declares war on Austria-Hungary. The Italians hope to consolidate their national territories by acquiring Austro-Hungarian-occupied territory in NE Italy, including the Alto Adige.

26 May In Britain H.H. Asquith forms a coalition government. David Lloyd George becomes minister of munitions.

23 June In the first battle of the Isonzo on Italy's border with Austria-Hungary Italian forces attack Austrian-held bridgeheads on the River Isonzo. Further battles will be fought here until 1917 on what becomes a static front.

4 Aug. British nurse Edith Cavell is arrested by the German authorities in Brussels. She is convicted on charges of helping Allied prisoners of war to escape and is executed (12 Oct.).

7 Aug. Warsaw falls to German forces. By the end of September the Russians have lost most of their Polish territories, Lithuania and Courland.

25 Sept. Gen. Philippe Pétain launches a new French military offensive in Champagne. British forces attack German lines at Loos in Pas-de-Calais. Meagre gains are made in a costly offensive that lasts until Nov. The British lose 60,000 casualties.

5 Oct. Allied troops land at Salonika (Thessaloníki) in Greece to aid Serbia.

7 Oct. Austria-Hungary invades Serbia and takes Belgrade (9 Oct.).

13 Nov. In Britain Winston Churchill (see p. 523) resigns as First Lord of the Admiralty over the failure of the Dardanelles campaign (see below).

19 Dec. Douglas Haig replaces Sir John French as commander-in-chief of British forces on the Western Front.

MIDDLE EAST AND NORTH AFRICA

19 Feb. British and French warships bombard the Dardanelles, Turkey, hoping to take Istanbul and open supply routes to Russia through the Bosphorus and the Black Sea. But three British warships are sunk in the Straits (18 Mar.), and the attempt is abandoned. Turkey strengthens its defences in the area.

24 April The Armenian holocaust begins; the Turkish government accuses the Armenian people of being pro-Russian and starts to deport them, killing those who resist. Some 1.75 million Armenians are deported, and over half a million are killed.

25 April Allied land forces invade the Gallipoli Peninsula, Turkey. They hope to succeed where the Royal Navy failed (19 Feb.), but all surprise is long lost, planning is inadequate, and Turkish resistance is far stronger than expected. Australian and New Zealand troops land in the wrong place (subsequently called ANZAC Cove). British and French troops at Cape Helles suffer terrible casualties. Trench warfare similar to that fought on the Western Front develops.

6 Aug. The British try to break the deadlock with landings at Suvla Bay on the Gallipoli Peninsula, but the same mistakes lead to an identical outcome.

Sept. A British force under Maj.-Gen. Sir Charles Townshend advances from Kut al-Amara, Mesopotamia (now Iraq), towards Baghdad. It is victorious at Ctesiphon (22 Nov.), but falls back in exhaustion to Kut al-Amara, where it is besieged by the Turks (7 Dec.).

18 Dec. British troops start to withdraw from the Gallipoli Peninsula. Winston Churchill (see p. 523) and Sir John Fisher (see above) are blamed for the failure of the campaign.

ASIA

18 Jan. The Japanese government presents a series of 21 demands to China: the Japanese want to take over German rights in Shandong, to extend Japanese leases in S Manchuria to 99 years and to force China not to lease or cede any part of its coast to a foreign power. When the Japanese back these demands with an ultimatum (7 May), the Chinese government is forced to concede on most points (23 May).

THE AMERICAS

13 May Following the sinking of the *Lusitania*, the US government sends a formal protest to Berlin.

8 June The antiwar US secretary of state William Jennings Bryan resigns in protest at President Wilson's belligerence towards Germany following the *Lusitania* sinking. He is replaced by Robert Lansing.

– In the USA the Ku Klux Klan is revived by William J. Simmons, who obtains a legal charter for his organization from the state of Georgia. The white supremacist body will attract a membership of 100,000 in the S states within six years. It will use violent tactics against not only African-Americans but also Jews and Catholics as it strives to secure the election of sympathetic politicians.

ECONOMY AND SOCIETY

– In Britain the National Institution of Women's Institutes is founded.

– Absinthe (a liqueur distilled from wine and wormwood) is outlawed in France since it can cause blindness.

SCIENCE AND TECHNOLOGY

– In the USA, the one millionth Ford motorcar is produced.

– The Japanese chemists Katsusaburo Yamagiwa and Koichi Ichikawa become the first scientists to experiment on animals. They demonstrate that coal tar is carcinogenic by painting it on rabbits' ears.

ARTS AND HUMANITIES

Literature

23 April English poet Rupert Brooke dies of blood poisoning and is buried on the Aegean island of Skyros. His five 'War Sonnets' (including 'The Soldier') have already been published, and his collection *1914 and Other Poems* appears after his death.

John Buchan, *The Thirty-Nine Steps*, spy novel.

Franz Kafka, 'Die Verwandlung' (Metamorphosis), short story.

D(avid) H(erbert) Lawrence, *The Rainbow*, novel.

Ford Madox Ford, *The Good Soldier*, novel.

W(illiam) Somerset Maugham, *Of Human Bondage*, novel.

Visual Arts and Architecture

– The anarchic and iconoclastic modern art movement known as Dada is founded in Zurich, Switzerland. Dadaism, which arises from indignation and despair at the catastrophe of World

War I, also develops in New York at around this time, where it is associated with such artists as Marcel Duchamp and Man Ray.

Marcel Duchamp, *The Bride Stripped Bare by Her Bachelors, Even*, construction on glass. It is one of the most esoteric works of artistic Modernism.

Marc Chagall, *Above the Town*, painting.

Pablo Picasso (see p. 467), *Harlequin*, painting.

Music

– Charles Ives completes his *Concord Sonata* for piano, with solos for viola and flute.

Manuel de Falla, *Nights in the Gardens of Spain*, work for piano and orchestra.

Felix and George Powell, 'Pack up Your Troubles in Your Old Kit Bag', song.

Jean Sibelius, Symphony No. 5 in E flat major.

Film

D(avid) W(ark) Griffith, *Birth of a Nation*, film inaugurating many techniques of cinematography, such as flashback and close-up, but causing controversy because of its open support of the Ku Klux Klan.

1916

EUROPE

21 Feb.–18 Dec. The battle of Verdun is fought on the Western Front. The German strategy is to break the French army by attacking an objective (the Verdun fortress system), which they know the French will defend to the last, and by killing French troops in vast numbers. In fact, losses on both sides are comparable, each losing about 400,000 men.

9 Mar. Germany and Austria-Hungary declare war on Portugal, which has been helping Britain invade German colonies in Africa.

24 April The Easter Rising against British rule in Ireland begins. Leaders of the Irish Republican Brotherhood, including Patrick Pearse, had intended a nationwide rebellion, but a series of accidents ensures that this does not happen. The rising in Dublin is crushed by the British after fierce street fighting, and 15 rebel leaders are convicted of treason and executed, thereby becoming important figures in the martyrology of Irish nationalism. The executions turn many Irish decisively against British rule.

31 May–1 June At the naval battle of Jutland, fought in the North Sea, the Germans inflict heavier losses on the British than they suffer, but gain no strategic advantage. The German High Seas Fleet returns to port and stays there, its morale deteriorating.

5 June Lord Horatio Kitchener, British war minister, is drowned off the Orkney Islands when HMS *Hampshire* is sunk by a mine. Lloyd George will replace him (6 July).

June–Aug. In the S part of the Eastern Front a Russian offensive led by Gen. Alexey Brusilov, launched to relieve pressure on the Italians who are buckling under an Austrian offensive in the Trentino area of the S Tyrol, pushes Austro-Hungarian forces back towards the Carpathians. German forces are withdrawn from other fronts to bolster the line. The Brusilov offensive devastates the Austro-Hungarian army but costs the

Russian army one million casualties, fuelling revolutionary discontent at home.

1 July–18 Nov. The battle of the Somme is fought on the Western Front. The Somme offensive, planned by Marshal Joseph Joffre and Field Marshal Douglas Haig, aims to smash the German hold on N France. 1 July becomes the worst day in British military history with 57,470 casualties, including 19,240 killed, 35,493 wounded, 2152 missing and 585 taken prisoner. The Germans sustain some 8000 casualties on the same day. During the 140-day offensive the Allied powers as a whole lose some 794,000 men and the Central Powers 538,888. The Allies succeed in driving the Germans back only 11km (7 miles).

3 Aug. In Britain Sir Roger Casement is executed for his role in the Irish rising.

27 Aug. Romania declares war on Austria-Hungary and launches an offensive in Transylvania.

28 Aug. Italy declares war on Germany.

30 Aug. Turkey declares war on Russia.

1 Sept. Bulgaria declares war on Romania.

15 Sept. The tank, invented by British soldier and inventor Ernest Swinton, is deployed for the first time during the battle of the Somme but proves mainly ineffective.

13 Oct. Britain experiences its worst air raids by Zeppelin airships.

16 Nov. The Polish general Józef Pilsudski gains recognition of an independent Poland from the Central Powers. Pilsudski has commanded a Polish force that has fought for Germany on the Eastern Front.

21 Nov. Franz Josef, emperor of Austria-Hungary, dies after a 68-year reign. He is succeeded by his grandson, who will rule (until 1918) as Charles I.

28 Nov. The German air force makes its first aeroplane raids on London.

1 Dec. A combined Austrian–German army defeats the Romanian army near Bucharest, which the Germans will occupy from 6 Dec. to Nov. 1918.

4 Dec. In Britain the Liberal government presided over by Herbert Asquith resigns and a coalition government is formed. The new prime minister is David Lloyd George who assumes control of imperial war strategy as the head of the war cabinet.

12 Dec. The Central Powers make a peace offer to the Allies. It is rejected (30 Dec.).

31 Dec. Russian faith healer Grigori Rasputin is murdered in St Petersburg in a conspiracy organized by Russian noblemen concerned at his influence over the tsar and tsarina.

– Because of war-time fuel shortages, Britain's Parliament passes a Summer Time Act, which brings clocks forward by one hour. The aim is to increase productivity on the basis of the increased amount of light in the summer months.

– In Britain compulsory military service is introduced for single men (27 Jan.) and married men (25 May).

MIDDLE EAST AND NORTH AFRICA

8 Jan. Britain completes the withdrawal of its forces from Gallipoli (see 18 Dec. 1915).

29 April Following a lengthy siege, the British surrender Kut al-Amara to the Turks (see Sept. 1915). Many British troops will die in captivity.

9 May Britain and France sign a secret treaty, the Sykes–Picot treaty, designed to divide the Middle East between the two powers after the war.

5 June Arab tribes begin their revolt against the rule of the Ottoman Turks by attacking the garrison at Medina. Faisal, son of Hussein ibn Ali, the grand sharif of Mecca, has persuaded his father to switch allegiance from the Central Powers to the Allies. The British archaeologist and soldier T(homas) E(dward) Lawrence has also urged the change of loyalty.

29 Oct. Hussein ibn Ali is proclaimed king of the Arabs and founds the Hashemite dynasty, which will rule the new independent kingdom of Hejaz until 1924.

ASIA

22 Mar. The Chinese president Yuan Shikai dies.

THE AMERICAS

9 Mar. 'Pancho' Villa, Mexican bandit and revolutionary, raids Columbus, New Mexico, as a reprisal against the USA for supporting his rival, Venustiano Carranza. The US army invades Mexico to hunt Villa down (15 Mar.).

May US marines land in the Dominican Republic to restore civil order; the occupation will last until 1924.

29 Aug. The US Congress passes a Naval Appropriations Act to finance a three-year programme of naval expansion.

7 Nov. Woodrow Wilson is re-elected president of the USA, defeating the Republican challenger Charles Evans Hughes by just 23 votes in the electoral college.

– A mass epidemic of poliomyelitis afflicts the USA. Some 6000 people die and many more are crippled.

– Jeanette Rankin of Montana becomes the first woman to be elected a member of the US House of Representatives.

ECONOMY AND SOCIETY

– American feminist Margaret Sanger establishes the first birth control clinic outside the Netherlands in Brooklyn, New York. The clinic is raided by police and Sanger briefly imprisoned.

– Russian political activist Vladimir Ilyich Ulyanov (Lenin) (see p. 480) publishes 'Imperialism, the Highest Stage of Capitalism', a revolutionary pamphlet.

– The 6th Olympic Games, scheduled to take place in Berlin, are cancelled because of the war.

SCIENCE AND TECHNOLOGY

– The German physicist Albert Einstein publishes *The Foundation of the General Theory of Relativity*.

– Treatment of war wounds encourages the development of plastic surgery.

– English scientist Edward A. Sharpey-Schafer coins the word 'insulin' to describe the hormones produced by the human pancreas.

Lenin (1870–1924)

Vladimir Ilyich Ulyanov, the communist revolutionary later known as Lenin, was born into a middle-class family at Simbirsk, central Russia. After studying to become a lawyer, he was imprisoned for urging the overthrow of the tsar. In 1900 he fled to Switzerland, where he formulated his ideas on communism and revolution.

Lenin believed a revolution would succeed only if power could be concentrated in the hands of workers' revolutionary councils, or soviets. At a conference in London in 1903 the Russian Social Democratic Party divided between the Bolsheviks (majority) who agreed with Lenin that the party should have room only for the dedicated revolutionary activist, and the Mensheviks (minority) who argued that the party should be a broad-based coalition.

Lenin was also the first theorist of economic globalism. He saw imperialism as a product of the search of capital for new markets. This meant, he believed, that the socialist revolutions of advanced capitalist societies, the bourgeois revolutions of early capitalist ones and nationalist struggles in colonized areas were all interlinked.

In the years that followed the 1903 conference, Lenin converted the party into a professional revolutionary organization that knew how to plot and prepare. His writings outlined the socio-economic conditions that would make revolution possible. He considered capitalism to be progressing rapidly in Russia. The revolution, he thought, would be first bourgeois and then proletarian. In March (February old style) 1917, the tsarist autocracy fell, to be replaced by a bourgeois democracy. Lenin hurried back to Russia and in November (October old style) led the Bolshevik coup that began the communist revolution. This was followed by a civil war, but by 1921 Russia was firmly in the control of the soviets. Lenin became the leader of the new Soviet Union (established 1922), and initiated the state terror that came to characterize the Soviet system.

– America psychologist Lewis Terman of Stanford University coins the term Intelligence Quotient (IQ) in his book *The Measurement of Intelligence*.

– Mechanical windscreen wipers are introduced in the USA.

– Mechanical home refrigerators become available in the USA.

ARTS AND HUMANITIES

Literature

28 Feb. The US novelist Henry James dies.

Harold Brighouse, *Hobson's Choice*, play.

John Buchan, *Greenmantle*, novel.

Robert Frost, *Mountain Interval*, poetry collection.

Ferdinand de Saussure, *Cours de linguistique générale* (Course in General Linguistics), posthumously published lecture notes that will come to be seen as the basis of structural linguistics and, more broadly, of the concept of structuralism in anthropology and literary theory.

Giuseppe Ungaretti, *Il porto sepolto* (The Buried Harbour), an early example of hermeticist poetry.

Visual Arts and Architecture

– Britain commissions the first official war artists.

Mark Gertler, *The Merry-Go-Round*, painting.

Georg Grosz, *Metropolis*, painting.

Henri Matisse, *Piano Lesson*, painting.

C.W.R. Nevinson, *Troops Resting*, painting.

Music

– The British composer Gustav Holst completes his orchestral suite *The Planets*, but it will not be performed until 1920.

Ernest Bloch, *Israel*, symphony.

Charle Ives, Symphony No. 4.

Hubert Parry, *Jerusalem*, choral setting of the poem by William Blake (1804).

Film

D(avid) W(ark) Griffith, *Intolerance*, film, starring Lillian Gish.

1917

EUROPE

1 Feb. Germany announces a policy of unrestricted submarine warfare.

2 Feb. In Britain bread rationing is introduced.

8–14 Mar. The February Revolution in Russia (23 Feb.–1 Mar. by the old style Julian calendar, which is still used in Russia): Russian garrison troops mutiny (10 Mar.) after two days of riots and strikes in Petrograd (St Petersburg). The duma (parliament) sets up a provisional government under Prince Georgi Lvov (14 Mar.). There are widespread demands for immediate peace and land reform. The provisional government, however, reassures the Allies that it will continue to remain in the war.

15 Mar. The Russian tsar Nicholas II abdicates, ending the rule of the Romanov dynasty (see 1613).

16 Mar. On the Western Front German troops strategically retreat to the Hindenburg Line (set up as a fortified line of defence by Field Marshal Paul von Hindenburg, the German supreme commander).

9 April–4 May The battle of Arras is fought on the Western Front: Canadian troops capture Vimy Ridge NE of Arras (9–14 April).

16 April The Russian Bolshevik leader Lenin (see box) arrives in Petrograd (St Petersburg). The Germans have helped him to travel home from exile in Switzerland by a circuitous route.

16 April–9 May On the Western Front a French advance under Gen. Robert Nivelle, aiming to capture the strategically important Chemin des Dames, ends in failure. Mutinies break out in the French army (17 and 29 April). Nivelle is relieved of his command and Gen. Philippe Pétain, the hero of Verdun (see 1916), is appointed chief of general staff to restore order (15 May). Leave and pay are improved, but 55 ringleaders of the mutiny are executed.

10 May After heavy losses of Allied shipping, the British Admiralty starts to convoy merchant ships.

7–14 June The British attack Messines Ridge in SE Belgium in preparation for a major new offensive.

14 June The first US troops arrive in France, following US entry into the war on 6 April (see below).

19 June George V of Britain drops all his German titles (derived from Queen Victoria's marriage to Prince Albert of Saxe-Coburg Gotha) and adopts the dynastic name of Windsor.

June London suffers its first air raids by German 'Gotha' bombers.

21 July Alexander Kerensky, formerly minister for war, heads a new provisional government in Russia, replacing the government of Prince Lvov.

31 July–10 Nov. During the third battle of Ypres in Belgium (also known as the battle of Passchendaele), Commonwealth troops sustain some 400,000 casualties. Much of the battle is fought in appalling weather conditions and only minimal gains are made.

9 Sept. Alexandre Ribot, the French prime minister, resigns. The former war minister, Paul Painlevé, heads a new French cabinet (12 Sept.). But Painlevé himself soon resigns and is replaced by Georges Clemenceau (16 Nov.). The veteran French socialist galvanizes the previously fading French war effort.

15 Oct. Dutch dancer Mata Hari (Margarethe Gertruda MacLeod), is executed by the French, having been convicted of spying for the Germans.

24 Oct.–10 Nov. The battle of Caporetto is fought on the Italian Front. Aiming to reach the Tagliamento River, Austro-Hungarian and German forces drive the Italians back 112km (70 miles). During the two-month campaign, some 300,000 Italian troops are taken prisoner and the same number deserts, but the Italians rally and stop the onslaught near Venice (7 Nov.).

6 Nov. The Bolshevik October Revolution starts in Petrograd (St Petersburg) (24 Oct. by the Julian calendar). By continuing the war and ignoring clamours for land reform, Kerensky's provisional government has lost the support of the people. Lenin's Bolsheviks offer immediate peace and land reform; their forces occupy key positions (including the Winter Palace), overthrowing the provisional government almost unopposed.

7 Nov. Following a walkout by other socialists, including the more moderate Mensheviks, a Bolshevik government, called the Council of People's Commissars, is formed under Lenin. Leon Trotsky (Lev Davidovich Bronstein) becomes commissar for foreign affairs, while a Georgian, Iosif Vissarionovich Dzhugashvili (Joseph Stalin), becomes commissar for national minorities.

20 Nov.–7 Dec. The battle of Cambrai is fought on the Western Front. 300 British tanks are involved in what is the first great tank battle in history. The initial British breakthrough, however, is nullified by a German counterattack (30 Nov.).

26 Nov. The new Bolshevik government in Russia offers an armistice to Germany and Austria-Hungary.

5 Dec. Russia and Germany sign an armistice.

6 Dec. Finland declares itself independent of Russia.

12 Dec. In Modane, France, in what is the worst train crash in history to date, 543 are killed when a troop train derails.

20 Dec. In Russia Felix Dzerzhinsky founds the All-Russian Extraordinary Commission for the Suppression of Counter-Revolution and Sabotage. The organization, known as the Cheka, will later assume successive acronyms: the GPU, the OGPU, the NKVD and the KGB. It becomes a powerful intelligence arm of the Soviet state.

MIDDLE EAST AND NORTH AFRICA

11 Mar. British troops occupy Baghdad in Mesopotamia.

July Arab forces led by T(homas) E(dward) Lawrence take Aqaba in NW Arabia. Lawrence also disrupts the Turkish communications link at a crucial point by blowing up the Hejaz railway.

29 June Edmund Allenby takes command of British forces in Palestine.

2 Nov. The British foreign secretary Arthur Balfour issues the Balfour Declaration, which states that the British government favours 'the establishment in Palestine of a national home for the Jewish people … it being clearly understood that nothing shall be done which may prejudice the civil and religious rights of existing non-Jewish communities in Palestine'.

7 Nov. The British take Gaza and go on to capture Jaffa (17 Nov.) and Jerusalem from the Turks (9 Dec.).

THE AMERICAS

17 Jan. British intelligence intercepts a message from the German foreign minister Arthur Zimmerman to the German ambassador in Washington. The note declares that Germany is about to start unrestricted submarine warfare, regardless of its effect on the USA. If the USA does declare war, says the note, Germany will offer Mexico an alliance to help it recover its former territories in Texas, Arizona and New Mexico.

31 Jan. The German government notifies the US government that unrestricted submarine warfare will start the next day. The US government breaks off diplomatic relations with Germany following the sinking of the US liner *Housatonic* by a German U-boat off Sicily (3 Feb.). The governments of Brazil and Peru follow the USA's lead, and the Chinese break off relations with Germany (14 Mar.).

1 Mar. The Zimmerman telegram (17 Jan.) is published in the USA. It causes outrage, but many Americans suspect a British ploy to entangle the USA in the war. Zimmerman himself confirms its authenticity (3 Mar.).

2 Mar. Congress makes Puerto Rico a US territory. Some 18,000 Puerto Ricans are drafted into the US army.

31 Mar. The US Senate ratifies a treaty making the Danish West Indies (including the Virgin Islands) US territory. Denmark relinquishes control on receipt of $25 million from the USA.

6 April The USA declares war on Germany. Gen. John Pershing, recalled from the pursuit of 'Pancho' Villa in Mexico (see Mar. 1916), leads the American Expeditionary Force.

2 July Vicious race riots break out in East St Louis, Illinois, sparked by the employment of African-Americans in a factory holding a government contract. It leaves thousands homeless, hundreds injured and 48 dead.

9 July President Wilson places the export of US food, fuel, iron and steel under government control. He sends US warships to convoy merchant ships heading for Britain and to join the blockade of Germany.

25 Oct. President Wilson endorses female suffrage. Some 20,000 campaigners parade in New York (27 Oct.). New York adopts a constitutional amendment giving women the vote (6 Nov.).

6 Dec. Two ships loaded with explosives for the Allied war effort, the Belgian *Imo* and the French *Mont Blanc*, collide off Halifax, Nova Scotia. The resulting explosion destroys the entire city.

7 Dec. The USA declares war on Austria-Hungary.

17 Dec. In a wartime extension of power, the US federal government takes over the railroads.

SUB-SAHARAN AFRICA

Oct. German troops led by Lt. Col. Paul von Lettow-Vorbeck invade Portuguese East Africa (modern Mozambique) from Tanganyika (modern Tanzania).

– The South African magnate Ernest Oppenheimer, supported by American financier J.P. Morgan, founds the Anglo-American Corporation of South Africa. It will grow to dominate control of the world's diamond reserves.

ECONOMY AND SOCIETY

– Russia is in the grip of a typhus epidemic which, over the next four years, will kill some 3 million people.

– The British Medical Council reports that half of the children in Britain's industrial towns are suffering from rickets.

SCIENCE AND TECHNOLOGY

– In the USA Clarence Birdseye introduces rapid freezing as a method of preserving food.

ARTS AND HUMANITIES

Literature

– The British poet Edward Thomas is killed at Arras on the Western Front. His collections *Poems* (Oct. 1917) and *Last Poems* (1918) are published posthumously.

– In the USA the Pulitzer prizes are awarded for the first time.

Lawrence Binyon, 'For the Fallen', poem.

Norman Douglas, *South Wind*, novel.

T(homas) S(tearns) Eliot, *Prufrock and Other Observations*, poetry, including 'The Love Song of J. Alfred Prufrock'.

Eugene O'Neill, *The Long Voyage Home*, play.

Paul Valéry, *La Jeune Parque* (The Young Fate), long poem.

P(elham) G(reville) Wodehouse, *The Man with Two Left Feet*, humorous short stories in which the characters Bertie Wooster and Jeeves first appear.

W.B. Yeats, *The Wild Swans at Coole*, poetry collection.

Visual Arts and Architecture

27 Sept. French artist Edgar Degas dies.

17 Nov. French sculptor Auguste Rodin dies.

– The French writer Guillaume Apollinaire coins the word 'surrealist' to describe Picasso's designs for the ballet *Parade*.

– Dutch artist Piet Mondrian founds, with Theo van Doesburg, the journal *De Stijl* (The Style). In his own work Mondrian develops a style of extreme formalism and abstraction based on horizontal and vertical lines.

Giorgio de Chirico, *Disquieting Muses*, painting.

Marcel Duchamp, *Fountain*, a 'ready-made' consisting of a urinal signed with the pseudonym R. Mutt.

L.S. Lowry, *Coming from the Mill*, painting.

Music

18 May The ballet *Parade* is performed by Diaghilev's Ballets Russes at the Théâtre du Châtelet, Paris, to music by French composer Erik Satie; the choreography is by Russian choreographer Léonide Massine and the costumes and scenery by Spanish artist Pablo Picasso (see p. 467).

– Jazz musicians including the cornet player Joe 'King' Oliver move to Chicago following the closure of the red light district in New Orleans (where jazz flourished). Louis Armstrong replaces Oliver in Kid Ory's Band and will himself move to Chicago and join Oliver's Creole Jazz Band (in 1922).

– The Original Dixieland Jazz Band moves to New York from New Orleans.

George M(ichael) Cohan, 'Over There', song for the American Expeditionary Force now embarked for the European war.

Ottorino Respighi, *The Fountains of Rome*, symphonic poem.

Maurice Ravel, *Le Tombeau de Couperin* (The Tomb of Couperin), suite for piano, dedicated to friends of the composer who died in World War I.

1918

EUROPE

1 Jan. In Britain sugar rationing is introduced, and rationing is extended to meat, butter and margarine (Feb.).

Feb. The British Labour Party adopts a constitution that includes 'Clause Four', which states the aspiration towards 'common ownership of the means of production'.

3 Mar. Russia and the Central Powers (Germany and Austria-Hungary) sign the treaty of Brest-Litovsk (in modern Belarus). Russia withdraws from the war. The Bolsheviks had hoped for an immediate revolution in Germany and the rest of Europe, but the German armies have driven back a disintegrating Russian army. In the end, the Bolsheviks have to accept ruinous terms, losing Russian and the Baltic provinces to the Central Powers, and accepting the independence of Finland and Ukraine. Moscow becomes the capital of Russia on the same day.

6 Mar. The Bolshevik party changes its name to the Russian Communist Party.

21 Mar.–5 April In their last major offensive (the German Spring Offensive or Ludendorff Offensive), German forces, led by elite *Stürmabteilung* (storm trooper) units and reinforced with units freed from the Eastern Front, quickly drive back Allied forces on the Western Front. A remarkable victory seems within their grasp. But they must win quickly, before huge US forces arrive in Europe, and they are unable to keep up their initial momentum. The Allied lines stabilize, and by July they will be ready to launch their own offensives against a now exhausted and dispirited German army.

1 April In Britain the Royal Air Force is founded, replacing the Royal Flying Corps.

8–10 April A Congress of Oppressed Nationalities, the subject peoples of the Habsburg empire (including Poles, Czechs, Slovaks, Romanians, Serbs, Croats and Slovenes), is held in Rome.

9 April British prime minister David Lloyd George introduces a bill extending military conscription to Ireland, provoking a storm of nationalist protest. The extension of conscription will later be dropped (20 June), along with the plan for Irish Home Rule.

21 April Baron Manfred von Richthofen, the Red Baron, the German pilot who has achieved the most 'kills' of Allied aircraft, is shot down and killed.

7 May Romania and the Central Powers (Germany and Austria-Hungary) sign the peace of Bucharest, by which Romania is permitted to annex Bessarabia.

May Carl von Mannerheim's White Finnish forces decisively defeat the Finnish Communists. Mannerheim will head an independent Finnish republic whose sovereignty will be recognized by Soviet Russia in 1919.

June American forces start their first independent action at Belleau Wood, France.

15–17 July On the Western Front, the Allies check the German advance in the second battle of the Marne.

16 July The Romanov family (the Russian tsar, the tsarina, their four daughters and son) are shot on Bolshevik orders at Ekaterinburg, Siberia (now Sverdlovsk). As Russia descends into civil war, the Bolsheviks will show themselves to be ruthless and pragmatic.

8 Aug. The 'Black Day of the German Army', according to Gen. Erich Ludendorff: at the battle of Amiens a massive British offensive, led by tanks, breaks the German line, inflicting 20,000 German casualties and takes 30,000 prisoners. The Germans fall back to the Hindenburg Line.

Aug. British forces land at Archangel, Murmansk and Vladivostok to support counter-revolutionary White forces in the Russian Civil War. French and US forces will also intervene, but the Allied actions will do little more than rally popular support to the Bolshevik cause.

12 Sept. Gen. John Pershing's US troops attack at St Mihiel, winning a remarkable victory.

28 Sept. British forces attack the Hindenburg Line, deemed the strongest defensive system in Europe: they break through in just six days.

29 Sept. Gen. Erich Ludendorff informs Kaiser Wilhelm II that the war is lost and that an armistice must be sought.

4 Oct. Ferdinand I of Bulgaria abdicates after the defeat of Bulgarian forces in Macedonia and the signing of an armistice between Bulgaria and the Allies (30 Sept.). He is succeeded by his son, Boris III.

14 Oct. The Czechoslovak National Council in Paris organizes a provisional government. Tomáš Masaryk is president and Eduard Beneš is foreign minister. The new country's independence is proclaimed (28 Oct.).

24 Oct.–2 Nov. Following the battle of Vittorio Veneto, fought on the Italian Front, the Austro-Hungarian army collapses.

28 Oct. Ordered to put to sea for a last attack on the Royal Navy, the German fleet mutinies at Kiel in N Germany. The mutiny becomes a revolution which spreads to Bremen, Lübeck and other parts of NW Germany.

31 Oct. Revolution breaks out in Hungary.

3 Nov. A Polish republic is proclaimed. Gen. Józef Pilsudski, a prisoner of the Germans since 1917 when he was accused of helping the Allied war effort, is released. He will become president of Poland (see 17 Jan. 1919).

7 Nov. A socialist revolution breaks out in Munich, Germany.

9 Nov. Kaiser Wilhelm II of Germany abdicates ending the rule of the Hohenzollern dynasty. A German republic is proclaimed (9 Nov.) with Friedrich Ebert as chancellor. The Kaiser goes into exile in the Netherlands.

11 Nov. An armistice is signed in a railway carriage at Compiègne, near Paris, between the defeated Germany and the victorious Allies. The armistice comes into force from 11 a.m. The war has resulted in the deaths of 1.8 million Germans, 1.7 million Russians, 1.4 million French, 1.2 million Austrians and Hungarians, 900,000 British imperial subjects, 460,000 Italians, 325,000 Turks and 115,000 Americans. In addition, some 20 million more have been wounded.

12 Nov. Charles I, emperor of Austria since 1916, renounces any role in the future government of Austria and of Hungary. Austria declares itself a republic. After some six-and-a-half centuries, the political power of the Habsburg dynasty in C Europe is ended.

13 Nov. In Russia the Bolsheviks annul the treaty of Brest-Litovsk (see 3 Mar. 1918).

16 Nov. Hungary proclaims itself an independent republic.

4 Dec. The kingdom of Serbs, Croats and Slovenes is proclaimed under the rule of Prince Alexander Karageorgevic, the future Alexander I of Yugoslavia.

14 Dec. In a hurried British general election, David Lloyd George's war-time coalition wins by a landslide. The coalition is dominated by Conservatives, and the Liberals are irrevocably split. Labour wins 63 seats, marking its breakthrough as a national party.

– In Britain the Representation of the People Act extends the suffrage to all women over the age of 30 and to all men over the age of 21. Female emancipation has been advanced by the role of women in the war effort and by their work in factories while men are away at the front.

A CONTINENT DIVIDED:

Europe from Armageddon to Reconstruction, 1914–89

From the outbreak of World War I (1914) until the fall of the Berlin Wall (1989), Europe was a divided continent. In 1914 Europe's monarchies were still largely in place and its aristocracies retained much political influence. But World War I, like the second global conflict that was to follow it, had deep political consequences. It brought the end of Habsburg, Romanov and Ottoman rule, creating new, and initially democratic, nation-states out of their former empires in Europe. The treaty of Versailles (1919) and the League of Nations sanctioned the principle of national self-determination.

Germany's fear of encirclement had been the single greatest cause of World War I, and its anxiety about its identity had encouraged the militarist tone of Wilhelmine politics. The same militarism re-emerged, in an even more vicious form, within the Nazi movement that hijacked Germany's postwar democracy. Fascism was a Europe-wide phenomenon. It fed off economic insecurity and everywhere encouraged a nostalgia for the militaristic comradeship of soldiers in the Great War. In its German form, fascism added an explicit racism that ultimately led to the deaths of some 6 million Jews. Moreover, the peace settlement at Versailles had created lasting resentment among those states – such as Germany and Italy – that felt unjustly treated by its provisions.

Soviet Marxism was the other great ideology of the 20th century, brought to power in Russia by the collapse of the tsarist regime in 1917. It preached universal comradeship, but was driven by the need to protect the achievements of the Russian Revolution against the real and perceived enemies that surrounded the USSR. These threats, together with an ideological commitment to centralized economic planning, turned Soviet Marxism into a totalitarian system, a system that enforced complete subservience to the state.

World War II (1939–45) saw the European democracies almost destroyed by Nazi Germany and Fascist Italy, until Hitler made the fatal error of attacking the USSR in June 1941. This, together with the intervention of the USA later that year, marked the turning of the tide. The Western democracies and Stalin's USSR became unlikely allies until the Axis was defeated. In the process, almost the whole of Europe was economically and politically devastated.

Out of the chaos of World War II there emerged a stronger recognition that international order required international institutions. The desire for collective security had led to the establishment of the United Nations (UN) by the Allies during the war, and under the UN umbrella various other organizations such as the World Bank were established with the aim of avoiding the financial crises that had helped fascism to flourish. Within Europe, the desire to avoid another European war led six countries, including the old enemies France and Germany, to sink their differences in the mutual economic interdependency enshrined in the European Economic Community (later the much-expanded European Union). But the EEC was also, initially, an exclusively Western European affair, and the reflection of a new division in Europe.

From 1945 to 1989, during the period of the Cold War, Europe was divided between the democratic West, allied to the USA in NATO, and the communist Warsaw Pact countries in the east, under the control of a new, Soviet, empire. The whole of the period 1914–89 can be viewed as a protracted European civil war, punctuated by the fragile truce of 1918–39. This civil war was fuelled by ideology, both in its fascist/anti-fascist phase in mid-century and in its communist/democratic phase thereafter.

The demands of total war had led to large-scale government intervention in economic life on both the Axis and Allied sides. Such interventions remained an important element in the economic and political stability of Europe after 1945, helping to create a period of economic expansion that

> *… 1914–89 can be viewed as a protracted European civil war, punctuated by the fragile truce of 1918–39.*

only ended with the oil-price crisis of the 1970s. The resulting strain on Western European economies led to a series of fiscal crises as governments recognized the end of the period of large-scale planning. At the same time, economic pressures grew on the Soviet economy, until it finally collapsed in the late 1980s, taking with it the USSR and the Warsaw Pact. The former Soviet satellite states in Europe decided that their future peace, security and prosperity lay with membership of the European Union.

The citizens of the victorious Allied states in 1945 had been through experiences that broke down the old barriers of class and privilege. By 1989 Western Europeans were more equal, more educated and more prosperous than at any time in their history. It was the force of their example and the appeal of their way of life that encouraged their fellow Europeans in the east as they swept aside the Iron Curtain.

1918 *continued*

MIDDLE EAST AND NORTH AFRICA

1 Oct. British and Arab forces capture Damascus in Syria. By now Turkish forces in Palestine are close to defeat.

30 Oct. The Allies sign an armistice with Turkey.

THE AMERICAS

8 Jan. US president Woodrow Wilson outlines to Congress his 'Fourteen Points for a Just Peace'. The new Russian Bolshevik government has made public the secret Allied agreements to divide Germany after the war, and Wilson's call for 'open covenants openly arrived at' is meant to counter the propaganda advantage gained by the Bolsheviks. Wilson urges self-determination for the European peoples on the basis of their national allegiances and proposes a League of Nations to enforce the new world order he envisages. His European allies have not been consulted and there are points, such as self-determination for peoples under Turkish rule, that they will not support.

1 Oct. The US Senate rejects the Woman Suffrage Amendment, which has passed the House of Representatives.

5 Oct. German chancellor Prince Max of Baden approaches President Wilson, seeking an armistice based on the Fourteen Points.

– Congress follows the British and German example and votes for Summer Time Legislation. The US farming lobby objects to the loss of early morning light, and the law is repealed (1919).

ECONOMY AND SOCIETY

Dec. 1918–1919 Some 21.64 million people are killed in the Spanish flu epidemic which, starting in China, spreads through Asia, Europe and the Americas. It will last until the spring of 1919.

– Britain's national debt stands at a record £8 billion, while the income tax rate has spiralled to 30% from the 15% of 1915.

– Inflation seizes hold of the German economy.

– Typhus continues to be the major threat to life in Galicia, Ukraine and the Black Sea area.

SCIENCE AND TECHNOLOGY

– Money is voted by the Dutch parliament to drain the Zuider Zee and create 800,000 additional acres of dry land.

ARTS AND HUMANITIES

Literature

7 April Isaac Rosenberg, English poet and painter, is killed in action in France.

4 Nov. English poet Wilfred Owen is killed in action in France.

9 Nov. French poet Guillaume Apollinaire (Wilhelm Apollinaris de Kostrowitzki) dies of wounds sustained (Mar. 1916) in action in France.

– The poems of Gerard Manley Hopkins are published posthumously, Hopkins having died in 1889.

Wyndham Lewis, *Tarr*, novel.

Heinrich Mann, *Der Untertan* (The Man of Straw), novel.

Lytton Strachey, *Eminent Victorians*, history establishing a post-war vogue for anti-establishment satire.

Booth Tarkington, *The Magnificent Ambersons*, novel.

Visual Arts and Architecture

2 Nov. Austrian artist Gustav Klimt dies in Vienna.

– David Low, the New Zealand cartoonist, joins the *London Star* newspaper; his political satires of the British governing class will become celebrated.

André Derain, *Still Life: Dead Game*, painting.

Paul Klee, *Gartenplan*, painting.

Amedeo Modigliani, *Portrait of Léopold Zborowski*.

Paul Nash, *We are Making a New World*, painting.

Music

25 Mar. The French composer Claude Debussy dies.

24 May First performance in Budapest of Béla Bartók's opera *A kékszakállú herceg vára* (Duke Bluebeard's Castle).

14 Dec. First performance in New York of Giacomo Puccini's *Il trittico* (The Triptych), consisting of *Il tabarro* (The Cloak), *Suor Angelica* (Sister Angelica) and *Gianni Schicchi*.

– The Original Dixieland Jazz Band tours Europe and spreads appreciation of American jazz in the Old World.

Arthur Honegger, *Le Dit des jeux du monde* (The Tale of the World at Play), orchestral work.

Sergei Prokofiev, Symphony No. 1 (*Classical*).

Film

– In the USA Warner Brothers Pictures is incorporated by Harry, Albert, Jack and Sam Warner.

– Louis B(urt) Mayer incorporates Louis B. Mayer Pictures.

1919

EUROPE

5 Jan. In Berlin the Spartacist revolt breaks out as German Marxists attempt to copy the Bolshevik seizure of power in Russia (1917). Right-wing *Freikorps* militias suppress the revolt and murder Spartacist leaders Karl Liebknecht and Rosa Luxemburg (15 Jan.). The threat of communist revolution inclines many Germans towards parties of the extreme right.

11 Jan. Romania annexes Transylvania from Hungary.

17 Jan. Józef Pilsudski becomes president of Poland (see 3 Nov. 1918).

18 Jan. The Paris Peace Conference opens, chaired by French prime minister Georges Clemenceau. The Conference will create a League of Nations following President Wilson's Fourteen Points (8 Jan. 1918). Settling the terms of the peace treaty with Germany will prove far more difficult.

21 Jan. In Dublin, Ireland, Sinn Féin members who have been elected to the British Parliament in the general election of Dec. 1918 but who refuse to take up their seats, meet and proclaim an independent Irish Republic and establish their own parliament (the Dáil). On the same day two policemen are ambushed and killed in a Republican attack in Co. Tipperary, an event usually regarded as the start of the Irish War of Independence (or Anglo-Irish War).

3–9 Feb. In Russia's civil war Gen. Anton Denikin, commander of one of the White Russian armies, defeats the Bolshevik Red Army in the Caucasus. The Red Army, however, makes gains elsewhere: it captures Kiev (3 Feb.), and invades Estonia (14 Feb.) and enters the Crimea (8 April).

6 Feb. The German national assembly meets, away from the revolutionary upheavals in Berlin, at Weimar, a town noted for its humanism and learning rather than the militarism that has brought Germany to its knees.

2 Mar. The Third International (Comintern) is founded in Moscow to organize worldwide communist revolution. But in the event it serves the needs of Bolshevik Russia rather than the cause of an international proletarian revolution.

21 Mar. A communist uprising led by Hungarian political leader Béla Kun ejects the Hungarian government, but by imposing a 'red terror' it alienates the people.

23 Mar. In Italy Benito Mussolini founds the Fasci d'Italiani di Combattimento (the Italian Fascist movement).

1 April In Ireland the Dáil (see 21 Jan.) elects Eamon de Valéra (who has recently escaped from Lincoln prison in England, where he has been imprisoned along with other Sinn Féin members on grounds of involvement in a non-existent 'German plot') as its president.

4 April A Bavarian Soviet Republic is proclaimed in Munich. Like the Spartacist revolt, it is suppressed within a month by *Freikorps* units. Bavaria will become a refuge for extreme right-wing nationalist groups bent on bringing down the Weimar regime.

The world must be made safe for democracy.

President Woodrow Wilson, 2 April, 1917

28 April German delegates arrive at the Paris peace conference. The Allies present their peace terms (see 28 June) on 7 May, but give the German delegation no opportunity to negotiate.

April Polish forces take advantage of the upheaval of the Russian Civil War and invade Lithuania and Ukraine.

21 June The German High Seas Fleet is scuttled at Scapa Flow, a British naval base in the Orkney Islands.

28 June The treaty of Versailles is signed between the Allies and Germany in the Hall of Mirrors in the Palace of Versailles. A controversial 'war guilt' clause forces Germany to accept sole responsibility for the outbreak of war in 1914. Germany returns Alsace-Lorraine to France. The Rhineland is to be demilitarized and occupied for 15 years. Other German territories go to Belgium and Poland, while the German colonies are to be administered under League of Nations' mandates. Strict limits are placed on Germany's military power. Reparations are imposed, but the figure is yet to be set. The Germans have been

given no chance to negotiate the terms, which cause horror in Germany, where the 'dictat' is universally denounced. The politicians responsible for signing the treaty will be denounced as 'November criminals' who have betrayed Germany. But differences will also emerge between the Allies. The USA will reject the treaty (1920) and turn to isolationism. The British will see the treaty as unjust and seek to rectify it, appeasing German grievances. The French, however, will seek to enforce every clause rigidly. There is, in short, no agreement on how to keep the peace in the future.

31 July The German assembly declares the 'Weimar constitution' (see 6 Feb.). With the Social Democratic politician Friedrich Ebert as its first president, the Weimar Republic embarks on its attempt to create a liberal democratic Germany, but it is already tainted by association with military defeat, Communist revolt and the humiliation of the treaty of Versailles. The Weimar constitution, which comes into force on 11 Aug., contains what many historians will come to regard as a fatal flaw: the provisions of Article 48 allow the president of the Republic to rule by decree in an emergency.

4 Aug. Romanian forces occupy Budapest. Béla Kun flees to Vienna.

20 Aug. In Ireland the Irish Volunteers become the standing army of the Irish Republic (the Irish Republican Army, or IRA). The IRA has embarked on a campaign of guerrilla attacks on members of the Royal Irish Constabulary (RIC) and other crown forces, who are seen as imposing what Irish republicans regard as Britain's illegal rule in Ireland.

10 Sept. The treaty of Saint-Germain forces the Austrians to recognize the independence of Czechoslovakia, Hungary, Poland and Yugoslavia. Austria, too, has to pay substantial reparations. There is widespread scepticism that this truncated state can even survive, but it is forbidden to unite with Germany.

12 Sept. The British declare the Irish Dáil (see 21 Jan.) a dangerous association. Sinn Féin and the IRA are outlawed (15 Oct.).

Sept. Adolf Hitler (see p. 509), an Austrian-born former soldier and failed artist, joins the German Workers' Party in Munich, Bavaria.

Oct. In the Russian Civil War White gains continue to be quickly cancelled out by Bolshevik ones. The Whites take Orel, SW of Moscow (13 Oct.), only to see it retaken by the Red Army. The Whites are too divided and the support offered by the Allied powers is too half-hearted to defeat an increasingly formidable Red Army. By the end of Oct. the Allies have withdrawn completely from N Russia.

14 Nov. The Romanians withdraw from Hungary. Hungary becomes once again a monarchy in theory, but the Allies will not tolerate the return of the Habsburg Charles I. It is, therefore, ruled by a regent (from 1920 Admiral Miklós Horthy). Those associated with the regime of Béla Kun fall victim to a 'white terror'.

15 Nov. In the Russian Civil War the Red Army takes Omsk and later Kharkov (13 Dec.).

27 Nov. The treaty of Neuilly forces the Bulgarians to recognize the sovereign independence of Yugoslavia and to pay $445

1919

million in reparations. The treaty also allows the ethnic transfer of 46,000 Bulgarian Greeks for 120,000 Greek Bulgarians.

29 Nov. In Britain Lady Nancy Astor becomes the first woman member of parliament to take her seat.

MIDDLE EAST AND NORTH AFRICA

15 May In pursuit of Greek premier Eleuthérios Venizélos's territorial ambitions, Greek forces occupy Greek-speaking Smyrna (modern Izmir) on Turkey's Aegean coast (with Allied military support).

July At a congress in Erzerum, Turkish nationalists under Mustafa Kemal (later known as Kemal Atatürk) decide to resist Allied plans for the dismemberment of Turkey. By the end of 1919 Atatürk's nationalists control much of the Anatolian interior, and have set up Ankara as a rival capital to Istanbul.

ASIA

Feb. The pro-British ruler of Afghanistan, Habibullah Khan, is murdered. His son, Amanullah Khan, who succeeds him, seeks to assert Afghanistan's independence. His forces invade India (May–Aug.), leading to the Third Anglo-Afghan War (May).

13 April British army troops commanded by Brig. Reginald Dyer fire on unarmed demonstrators in Amritsar, N India, after an attack on a female missionary. An estimated 379 are killed and 1200 injured in what becomes known as the 'Amritsar massacre'. It inflames popular opinion both in India and in Britain against British rule in the subcontinent. A British commission of inquiry censures Dyer who resigns from the army.

30 April The Paris Peace Conference transfers the Shandong Peninsula in China from Germany to Japan. The Chinese delegates abandon the conference.

8 Aug. The treaty of Rawalpindi (then in British India, now in Pakistan) ends the Third Anglo-Afghan War and concedes independence to Afghanistan.

THE AMERICAS

16 Jan. The 18th amendment to the Constitution becomes effective, prohibiting the sale of alcoholic drink anywhere in the USA. It will be widely violated and will fuel organized crime. It will be repealed in 1933.

Feb. US Republican senator Henry Cabot Lodge begins to campaign against US membership of the League of Nations. US isolationists feel that the obligations of League membership threaten US sovereignty.

20 June By a joint resolution of Congress a 19th amendment to the Constitution is adopted giving women the vote.

19 July Race riots break out in Washington, D.C., as white soldiers and sailors attack African-Americans. Chicago, which has seen large-scale migration of African-Americans from the S states during the war, experiences similar riots (27 July). Six US cities in all are affected.

2 Oct. President Wilson, touring the USA to whip up support for US entry into League of Nations, suffers a stroke.

19 Nov. The US Senate rejects the treaty of Versailles (and with it US entry into the League of Nations) by 53 votes to 38.

SUB-SAHARAN AFRICA

May The Paris Peace Conference gives German East Africa to Britain as a mandated territory. German South West Africa is assigned to South Africa. France receives the former German possessions of Togo and Cameroon in W Africa.

ECONOMY AND SOCIETY

11 Nov. The two-minute silence in memory of the dead of World War I is observed in Britain for the first time.

– British economist John Maynard Keynes (see p. 517), who has been representing the British treasury at the Paris Peace Conference, resigns in order to write a protest at the scale of the reparations imposed on Germany, *The Economic Consequences of the Peace*. He regards the punitive measures as politically unwise and as having a destabilizing impact on world economy.

– Widespread famine in E Europe as a result of a poor harvest and manpower shortages boosts the US economy; the price of wheat increases to $3.50 a bushel because of the increased demand.

– The Orient Express becomes the Simplon–Orient Express and, by using the Simplon tunnel to cross the Alps, avoids passing through German and Austrian territory.

– In Britain the Canadian-born Lord Beaverbrook buys the London *Daily Express* newspaper.

SCIENCE AND TECHNOLOGY

14–15 June British aviators John William Alcock and Arthur Whitten Brown become the first to fly across the Atlantic non-stop (from Newfoundland to W Ireland). They share a £10,000 prize awarded by the *Daily Mail* and both are knighted.

– French engineer and industrialist André Citroën introduces the Citroën motorcar. British engineer Walter Bentley introduces the Bentley motorcar.

ARTS AND HUMANITIES
Literature

10 Sept. The Avus autobahn is opened in Berlin, Germany.

– The Swiss Protestant theologian Karl Barth effects a theological revolution with *Der Römerbrief* (The Epistle to the Romans). His commentary undercuts many of the optimistic equations between divine intent and liberal humanism that have under-pinned German Protestant theology since the 19th century.

Johan Huizinga, *The Waning of the Middle Ages*, history.

W(illiam) Somerset Maugham, *The Moon and Sixpence*, novel.

H(enry) L(ouis) Mencken, *The American Language: A Study of the Differences between English as Written and Spoken by the English and the Americans*. The journalist's scholarly work is a major step in the evolution of a distinctive American culture.

Marcel Proust, *A l'ombre des jeunes filles en fleurs* (Within a Budding Grove), the second volume of his novel *A la recherche du temps perdu* (see 1913).

John Reed, *Ten Days that Shook the World*, study of the Bolshevik revolution; Reed, a US journalist and socialist, is indicted for sedition and escapes to Russia where he dies (1920).

Siegfried Sassoon, *War Poems*, poetry collection.

P(elham) G(reville) Wodehouse, *My Man Jeeves*, novel.

Visual Arts and Architecture

3 Dec. French painter Pierre-Auguste Renoir dies.

– German architect Walter Gropius founds the Bauhaus in Weimar. The centre is a new school of design whose modernism reflects the spirit of the new German Republic.

– Kurt Schwitters invents *Merz*, his nonsense word for his own personal vision of Dada (see 1915). He applies the term to the elaborate constructions of bits and pieces he picks up from dustbins and gutters.

Amedeo Modigliani, *The Blue Nude* and *Portrait of Jeanne Hébuterne*, paintings.

Music

10 Oct. First production in Vienna of Richard Strauss's opera *Die Frau ohne Schatten* (The Woman without a Shadow).

– First performance in London, by Diaghilev's Ballets Russes, of Manuel de Falla's ballet *El sombrero de tres picos* (The Three-Cornered Hat).

Edward Elgar, Cello Concerto in E minor.

Darius Milhaud, *Le Boeuf sur le toit* (The Ox on the Roof), ballet.

Film

– United Artists is founded by US film director D(avid) W(ark) Griffith and actors Charlie Chaplin, Mary Pickford and Douglas Fairbanks.

Robert Wiene, *The Cabinet of Dr Caligari*, film starring Conrad Veidt; prime example of Expressionism in the German cinema.

1920

EUROPE

5 Jan. Polish and Latvian forces take Dvinsk (now Daugavpils in Lithuania) from the Bolsheviks.

8 Jan. In the Russian Civil War Admiral Alexander Kolchak, nominally the leader of the Whites (since Nov. 1918), is defeated at Krasnoyarsk and withdraws across Siberia to Irkutsk, where his Czech allies hand him over to the Bolsheviks. He is summarily executed (7 Feb.).

17 Jan. In the French presidential elections, Paul Deschanel defeats Georges Clemenceau. The French reject Clemenceau because the treaty of Versailles is widely regarded as too lenient.

Jan. The treaty of Versailles (see 28 June 1919) is ratified and the League of Nations comes into being. The Paris Peace Conference ends.

8 Feb. In the Russian Civil War the Red Army takes the Ukranian Black Sea port of Odessa.

26 Feb. By the terms of the treaty of Versailles, France takes over the Saarland, which it will administer until 1935.

12–17 Mar. In Germany the Kapp Putsch attempts to overthrow the Weimar regime. Wolfgang Kapp and the right-wing *Freikorps* militias seize Berlin and the German government flees. The rebels declare Kapp chancellor, but, opposed by the civil service, faced by a general strike and lacking foreign recognition, the putsch soon collapses.

25 Mar. Reinforcements for the Royal Irish Constabulary (RIC), recruited from former members of the British army, arrive in Ireland to bolster crown forces in the Anglo-Irish War. The newcomers are soon dubbed the Black and Tans for their hybrid uniforms. Further reinforcements, composed of former British army officers, form the Auxiliary Division of the RIC (later known as Auxies) on 27 July. The deployment by the British of the Black and Tans and Auxiliaries leads to a vicious cycle of atrocity and counter-atrocity in the Anglo-Irish War, culminating in the events of 21 Nov. (see below).

28 Mar. In the Russian Civil War Novorossiisk on the Black Sea falls to the Red Army.

April Polish forces led by Józef Pilsudski begin an anti-Russian offensive in the Ukraine, taking Kiev on 7 May. The Red Army drives the Poles out on 11 June.

4 June By the treaty of Trianon between the Allies and Hungary, Hungary loses some three-quarters of its land. E Hungary is ceded to Austria; Slovakia to the new state of Czechoslovakia, Croatia to the new state of Yugoslavia. The Banat of Temesvar is divided between Yugoslavia and Romania. Romania also receives part of the great Hungarian plain and Transylvania.

6 June In elections to the German Reichstag (parliament), right-wing parties make significant gains from 'Weimar coalition' parties of the centre and left.

27 July The Red Army enters Poland and advances on Warsaw.

14 Aug. The new states of Czechoslovakia amd Yugoslavia form an alliance for mutual security. They are joined by Romania on 17 Aug. The alliance comes to be known as the Little Entente.

15–16 Aug. In the so-called 'Miracle on the Vistula' Polish forces (with French help) rout the Red Army in the battle of Warsaw. Poland and Russia sign a peace treaty at Tartu in Estonia on 12 Oct. The westward march of Bolshevism has been checked (for the time being).

16 Sept. The French president Paul Deschanel resigns because of ill-health. Alexandre Millerand, the prime minister, is elected to replace him (23 Sept.).

25 Oct. King Alexander of Greece dies of blood poisoning, after being bitten by a pet monkey. He is succeeded by his father, Constantine, who was deposed in 1917 (19 Dec.).

1 Nov. In the Russian Civil War Baron Peter Wrangel's White army, which had controlled S Russia, is driven back into the Crimea by the Red Army. Wrangel loses Sevastopol (14 Nov.) and leads his troops out of Russian territory to Constantinople. The Russian Civil War ends (16 Nov.). Russia is now in the grip of a terrible drought, and famine will claim millions of lives in a disaster exacerbated by Bolshevik policies.

12 Nov. Italy and Yugoslavia settle their differences in the treaty of Rapallo. Italy receives Istria, while Dalmatia goes to Yugoslavia. Fiume (modern Rijeka in Croatia) becomes a free city.

15 Nov. The League of Nations meets in Geneva for the first time. The League is weakened from the outset by the USA not being a member (the US Senate having finally rejected the Versailles treaty and League membership on 19 Mar.).

15 Nov. Danzig (modern Gdansk) becomes a free city under League of Nations supervision.

21 Nov. Ireland's first Bloody Sunday: Republicans organized by Michael Collins kill 14 British agents in Dublin. In retaliation RIC Auxiliaries (see 25 Mar.) kill 13 people at a Gaelic football match at Croke Park.

23 Dec. In Britain Parliament passes the Government of Ireland Act, which creates separate parliaments for Northern Ireland and Southern Ireland; each territory is expected to continue to elect its representatives to the Westminster Parliament.

− Having failed to conquer the Baltic states the Bolsheviks concede their independence.

MIDDLE EAST AND NORTH AFRICA

23 April In Turkey Mustafa Kemal (Kemal Atatürk) is elected president of a new Turkish assembly in Ankara.

25 April Former Ottoman Turkish-ruled territories in the Middle East are assigned by the Supreme Allied Council as League of Nations mandates to Britain and France: Britain receives Palestine and Mesopotamia (modern Iraq); while France receives Greater Syria (modern Syria and Lebanon).

25 July French forces occupy Damascus in Syria. Faisal, the Arab prince who assisted the Allies in their wartime Palestinian campaign and who had been Syria's nominal ruler, is expelled. He will be made king of Iraq by the British in 1921 in compensation. The French will divide Syria into sub-units (see below).

10 Aug. The treaty of Sèvres is signed between the Allies and Turkey. The Turks have to recognize the kingdom of Hejaz, provide an independent state for the Kurds, accept a French mandate for Syria and a British mandate for Mesopotamia and Palestine, the incorporation of Rhodes and the Dodecanese islands into Italy, and the incorporation of E Thrace, Smyrna and the remaining Aegean islands into Greece. After Kemal Atatürk's revolution it will be replaced by the treaty of Lausanne (1923), which secures better terms for Turkey.

20 Aug. In their mandate of Syria the French create Greater Lebanon (including Beirut, Sidon, Tyre, Tripoli and the Bekaa valley). It is the predecessor of the modern state of Lebanon.

THE AMERICAS

20 May Venustiano Carranza, president of Mexico, is killed by an assassin employed by his former ally, Alvaro Obregón, who opposes Carranza's increasingly reactionary policies. Obregón seizes Mexico City and is elected president (31 Aug.).

26 Aug. The 19th amendment to the US Consitution is ratified, granting women the vote.

2 Nov. In the US presidential election the Republican Warren Harding defeats Democrat James M. Cox and his prospective vice-president, Franklin Delano Roosevelt.

Dec. A six-month strike, called by the Amalgamated Clothing Workers of America, begins in protest at sweatshops. When the strike is defeated (June 1921) manufacturers continue with a 44-hour working week while workers have to accept a 15% wage cut and accept a 15% increase in productivity.

− The American Civil Liberties Union (ACLU) is founded; agents of the FBI infiltrate what is deemed a left-wing organization.

− The first conference of the Universal Negro Improvement Association is held in Liberty Hall, Harlem, New York. Delegates from 25 countries attend. Marcus Garvey, the Association's leader, outlines a plan for African-Americans to return to Africa and build a model Black nation.

AUSTRALASIA AND OCEANIA

Nov. The Queensland and Northern Territories Air Service (QANTAS) begins service in Australia.

ECONOMY AND SOCIETY

April–Sept. The 7th Olympic Games are held in Antwerp, Belgium.

− Britain introduces unemployment insurance for all workers except domestic servants and farm workers.

− French population levels, which have been falling consistently since the late 19th century, have suffered a further catastrophe in World War I. As a counter-measure, the French government makes abortion, and the dissemination of birth-control information, illegal. 'Back-street' abortions soar.

− Polish-born hairdresser Antoine de Paris (Antek Cierpilowski) invents the shingle bob haircut for women: it will dominate 1920s fashion.

SCIENCE AND TECHNOLOGY

2 Nov. The world's first radio broadcasting service, the Pennsylvania-based KDKA, goes on air to report the results of the US presidential election.

− In the USA John Thompson invents the submachine gun ('Tommy gun'). It will be the weapon of choice of Chicago gangsters.

ARTS AND HUMANITIES

Literature

− George Bernard Shaw's play *Heartbreak House* is first performed in New York.

Agatha Christie, *The Mysterious Affair at Styles*, her first detective story, introducing the Belgian detective Hercule Poirot.

Colette, *Chéri*, novel.

John Galsworthy, *In Chancery*, second novel of the *Forsyte Saga* series.

Ernst Jünger, *In Stahlgewittern* (The Storm of Steel), German war narrative based on the author's experience of World War I.

Sinclair Lewis, *Main Street*, novel.

Wilfred Owen, *Poems*, collected and edited by Siegfried Sassoon.

Ernst Toller, *Masse-Menschen* (Masses and Men), play.

Edith Wharton, *The Age of Innocence*, novel.

Visual Arts and Architecture

Max Beckmann, *Carnival*, painting.

Marcel Duchamp, *LHOOQ*, letters inscribed beneath a reproduction of the *Mona Lisa* on whose upper lip has been drawn a moustache, on the cover of a Dada manifesto.

Max Ernst, *Here Everything is Still Floating*, painting.

Amedeo Modigliani, *Reclining Nude*, painting; Modigliano dies after completing the painting (25 Jan.).

Music

– Gustav Holst's orchestral suite *The Planets* receives its first full public performance (see 1916).
Igor Stravinsky, *Pulcinella*, ballet.

Film

Fred Niblo, *The Mark of Zorro*, starring Douglas Fairbanks.
Paul Wegener, *The Golem*, film showing the influence of Expressionism on German cinema.

1921

EUROPE

23 Feb. Mutiny breaks out in the Russian navy at Kronstadt; it is brutally crushed by the Bolsheviks (7–8 Mar.).

8 Mar. French troops occupy the Ruhr Valley towns of Düsseldorf and Duisburg after Germany fails to make an inital reparations payment.

17 Mar. In Russia Lenin introduces the New Economic Policy (NEP), allowing some private ownership of industries. The USA rejects a Soviet request for normalization of trade relations (25 Mar.).

18 Mar. The Soviet–Polish treaty of Riga fixes the Soviet–Polish border.

27 April The Reparations Commission, established under the treaty of Versailles, decrees that Germany must pay a total of £6.6 billion ($33 billion) in 42 annual instalments. The German Reichstag (parliament) accepts an Allied ultimatum for the payment of reparations (11 May).

11 July A truce is declared in the Anglo-Irish War. Exploratory meetings between the British government and the Irish republicans are held to try to find a settlement (14–21 July), but no progress is made.

July Unemployment in Britain reaches its post-war peak of 2.5 million. Dropping afterwards to 1.2 million, it remains at that level until 1930 when it takes off again. As a result, the Labour Party's vote rises steadily until 1931.

16 Aug. Peter I of the kingdom of the Serbs, Croats and Slovenes (Yugoslavia from 1931), dies and is succeeded by his son Alexander I.

11 Oct.–6 Dec. An Anglo-Irish conference is held in London between republican delegates chosen by the Irish Dáil (parliament) and the British government. The Irish delegation includes Arthur Griffith and Michael Collins, but not Eamon de Valéra, the Dáil president and president of Sinn Féin.

6 Dec. The Anglo-Irish treaty is signed in London. It creates an Irish Free State with dominion status within the British Commonwealth, which stipulates an oath of allegiance to the British sovereign by Irish MPs. The treaty makes permanent the Government of Ireland Act of 23 Dec. 1920 which established the mainly Protestant statelet of Northern Ireland. Ireland is thus partitioned into the 26-county Irish Free State (Southern Ireland) and the 6-county Northern Ireland, which remains part of the United Kingdom. British and Irish negotiators agree that the final frontier between the two will be settled by a boundary commission. Irish republicans assume that this will so reduce Northern Ireland as to render it unviable, but in the event the border will remain as it is (see 3 Dec. 1925). The Anglo-Irish treaty so outrages many Irish republicans that it will lead to civil war (see 1922–3), and the partitioning of the country will lead to political conflict and intermittent terrorism in Ireland for the rest of the century.

– Economic crisis in Germany. A state of emergency is declared (Aug.–Dec.).

– In Russia famine claims some 3 million lives. Herbert Hoover, US secretary of commerce, organizes an American Relief Administration to raise aid. The Russian Famine Relief Act, which is passed by the US Congress (22 Dec.), organizes supplies to be sent to Russia. Bolsheviks have to accept the humiliation of allowing the Americans to organize relief within Russia themselves. The Russians employed by the Americans will be viewed with deep suspicion, and many will die in subsequent purges.

MIDDLE EAST AND NORTH AFRICA

Jan. Greek forces invade Anatolia: the Greek–Turkish War begins.

20 Feb. Reza Shah Pahlavi, a cavalry officer, expels Russian military personnel from Persia and assumes control of the country. Russia cedes joint command of the Caspian Sea to Persia. Pahlavi intends to rebuild a country near disintegration and dominated by foreign powers, notably Russia and Britain. In 1925 he will depose the shah, Ahmad Shah, and take the throne.

16 Mar. Russia and Turkey sign a treaty recognizing each other's borders.

23 Jun. Faisal, former king of Syria, arrives at Basra following a referendum administered by the British that approves his installation as king of Iraq. He thereby establishes the Hashemite dynasty, which will last until 1958.

21 July The Spanish army is defeated at the battle of Annual in Morocco, by a Moroccan force led by Abd al-Krim of the Rif. The defeat leads to a political crisis in Spain, which has already been destabilized by the assassination of the prime minister Eduardo Iradier (8 Mar.). The resulting inquiry reveals a degree of incompetence and corruption that reflects badly on the king, Alfonso XIII. He will encourage Gen. Miguel Primo de Rivera to launch a coup in September 1923, which will ultimately (1931) bring down the monarchy and launch Spain on the path to civil war (1936–9).

ASIA

4 Nov. Takashi Hara, prime minister of Japan, is assassinated by a nationalist fanatic, after he attempts to reduce the power of the military.

21 Nov. Afghanistan is recognized as an independent state.

– The Chinese Communist Party holds its first national congress in Shanghai.

THE AMERICAS

4 Mar. Warren Harding is inaugurated as 29th US president.

25 Aug. The USA signs a separate peace treaty with Germany.

Aug. Former US secretary of the navy and presidential aspirant

Franklin D. Roosevelt is afflicted by poliomyelitis and disabled for life.

12 Nov. The Washington international peace conference on naval disarmament and the Far East opens.

– The US government returns to protectionism, with high tariffs on agricultural imports to help the domestic economic crisis.

ECONOMY AND SOCIETY

5 May French dress designer Coco Chanel introduces Chanel No. 5, a scent that will become a leading brand.

– The US evangelist Frank Buchman founds the Oxford Group. It will be relaunched as Moral Rearmament in 1938.

SCIENCE AND TECHNOLOGY

10 Dec. Albert Einstein wins the Nobel prize for physics.

ARTS AND HUMANITIES

Literature

Anna Akhmatova, *Anno Domini MCMXXI*, poetry collection.
John Galsworthy, *To Let*, third novel of the *Forsyte Saga*.
Aldous Huxley, *Crome Yellow*, novel.
D(avid) H(erbert) Lawrence, *Women in Love*, novel.
Luigi Pirandello, *Sei personaggi in cerca d'autore* (Six Characters in Search of an Author), play.
George Bernard Shaw, *Back to Methuselah*, play.

Visual Arts and Architecture

Georges Braque, *Still Life with Guitar*, painting.
Max Ernst, *The Elephant Celebes*, painting.
Henri Matisse, *Odalisque in Red Trousers*, painting.
Piet Mondrian, *Composition with Red, Yellow and Blue*, painting.
Pablo Picasso (see p. 467), *Three Musicians*, painting.

Music

23 Nov. First performance in Brno of Leoš Janáček's opera *Káta Kabanová*.

– First performance of Sergei Prokofiev's comic opera *The Love for Three Oranges*, based on a comedy (1761) by Carlo Gozzi.

Arthur Honegger, *Le Roi David*, symphonic psalm for chorus and orchestra.

Film

Charlie Chaplin, *The Kid*, starring Charlie Chaplin.
Fritz Lang, *Destiny* and *Spies*.
Fred Niblo, *The Sheikh* and *The Four Horsemen of the Apocalypse*, starring Rudolph Valentino.

1922

EUROPE

7 Jan. In Ireland the Dáil (parliament) ratifies the Anglo-Irish treaty (see 6 Dec. 1921) by 64 votes to 57 following an emotionally charged debate. Eamon de Valéra, who opposes the treaty, resigns as president of the Dáil (9 Jan.) and is replaced by Arthur Griffith. A provisional Irish Free State government is formed (15 Jan.). De Valéra organizes republican opposition to this new government. The bitter split that opens up between supporters and opponents of the treaty will soon lead to civil war.

15 Feb. The permanent International Court of Justice opens at The Hague, its judges selected by the League of Nations. It will settle international disputes if both sides agree to accept its ruling.

31 Mar. The Reparations Commission agrees to allow Germany to pay war reparations in raw materials.

16 April By the terms of the treaty of Rapallo, Germany recognizes Bolshevik Russia. In a secret agreement, Germany is able to build and test weapons it is forbidden to possess according to the treaty of Versailles. Russia will share the technology.

15 May Following a ruling by the League of Nations, Germany unwillingly cedes Upper Silesia to Poland; few Germans accept that the loss is permanent.

24 June The German foreign minister, Walter Rathenau, is assassinated by nationalist extremists. They are outraged by his dealings with Russia at Rapallo (16 April).

28 June In Dublin, Ireland, Irish Free State forces commanded by Michael Collins bombard the Four Courts, which have been held by anti-treaty republicans since 13 April. This event marks the start of the Irish Civil War proper. A small-scale guerrilla war with relatively low casualties, it engenders much bitterness and cruelty nonetheless.

12 Aug. In Ireland Arthur Griffith, president of the Dáil, dies suddenly. Michael Collins becomes the new head of the Irish government, but he is ambushed and killed by anti-treaty IRA members in the W of Ireland (22 Aug.). W.T. Cosgrave succeeds Collins as chairman of the provisional government in the Irish Free State (25 Aug.). Huge crowds attend Collins's funeral in Dublin (28 Aug.).

Aug. The German stock market crashes and the mark falls from 162 to the dollar to over 7000 to the dollar.

27 Sept. King Constantine of Greece abdicates.

19 Oct. In Britain David Lloyd George resigns as prime minister. The Conservatives have withdrawn from his coalition government in protest at the Chanak crisis, which has brought Britain close to war with Turkey. A Conservative government is formed by Andrew Bonar Law (23 Oct.). In a general election held on 15 Nov. the Conservatives triumph and the Liberals are eclipsed by Labour, which is now the second biggest UK political party.

28 Oct. In Italy Benito Mussolini, a former journalist, leads his bands of *fascisti* in a 'March on Rome'. Mussolini's Fasci di Combattimento (fighting squads) are organized as an anti-communist, procapitalist, political force. They aim to intimidate the government into surrendering power. King Victor Emmanuel III refuses to grant his government emergency powers and instead invites Mussolini to form a government (31 Oct.).

– an old bitch gone in the teeth.

Ezra Pound, 'Hugh Selwyn Mauberley' (1920);
an American view of residual European civilization

24 Nov. In the Irish Civil War, the novelist and Irish patriot Erskine Childers is executed for illegal possession of a revolver.

6 Dec. The Irish Free State is officially proclaimed. The parliament of Northern Ireland votes to remain part of the UK (7 Dec.).

Dec. In Russia Lenin suffers his second stroke of the year.

– The Transport and General Workers' Union is formed in Britain, with Ernest Bevin as its first general secretary.

MIDDLE EAST AND NORTH AFRICA

15 Mar. The kingdom of Egypt is proclaimed. Ahmed Fuad, the sultan, becomes king on the end of the British protectorate. The Sudan remains under joint British–Egyptian sovereignty.

Aug. Turkish nationalists under Mustafa Kemal (Kemal Atatürk) begin a counterattack aginst the overstretched Greeks.

10 Sept. Turkish forces take Smyrna from the Greeks. Much of the city is burned and many of its Greek inhabitants are massacred. The defeated Greek forces return to Europe.

13 Oct. An armistice ends the Greek–Turkish War.

1 Nov. In Turkey the sultanate is declared to be abolished and a republic is proclaimed. Mehmed VI, the last sultan, flees Constantinople on a British gunboat (17 Nov.). Kemal Atatürk has accepted that the Dardanelles remain under an international commission in return for Adrianople and E Thrace reverting to Turkey.

ASIA

4 Feb. Shandong province is returned to China by Japan.

– China sinks deeper into civil war and anarchy, as warlords seize and plunder their own realms.

THE AMERICAS

6 Feb. The Washington Conference closes. The nine participating countries, including the USA, Britain, France, Italy and Japan agree to respect China's independence and territorial integrity and to maintain the principle of open and equal access for all nations to China's markets. The Washington treaty lays down a ratio of tonnage of warships as 5:5:3 between the fleets of the USA, Britain and Japan.

ECONOMY AND SOCIETY

22 Jan. Pope Benedict XV dies and is succeeded by Ambrogio Damiano Achille Ratti as Pope Pius XI (6 Feb.).

Feb. The US magazine *Reader's Digest* first appears, printing condensed articles from other publications.

14 Nov. The British Broadcasting Corporation, founded this year, makes its first broadcast.

– American publisher William Randolph Hearst develops the *New York Daily Mirror* as a major tabloid.

– In the USA Charles Atlas wins a competition for the World's Most Perfectly Developed Man and (from 1926) will develop Charles Atlas Ltd as a mail order course.

– US confectioner Frank C. Mars launches the Mar-O-Bar, a predecessor of the later, and more successful, Mars Bar (see 1933).

Ludwig Wittgenstein (1889–1951)

Wittgenstein was born in Vienna into a rich and well-connected family, then studied aeronautics at Manchester and logic at Cambridge. While serving with the Austrian artillery during World War I, he completed the work that transformed 20th-century philosophy, the *Tractatus Logico-Philosophicus* (1922).

Wittgenstein's life was marked by austerity and high seriousness. In 1920 he gave away most of his personal fortune and taught as a village schoolmaster in southern Austria. Appointed professor of philosophy at Cambridge in 1939, he spent the war years as a medical orderly. His seminars were dramas of anguished improvisation and exploration, and he resigned his chair in 1947. His later work was published posthumously as *Philosophical Investigations* (1953).

Wittgenstein preferred to use brief propositions and aphorisms rather than extended argument. His picture theory of meaning in the *Tractatus* states that words have sense only in so far as they are pictures of what they represent in the world. Ethical and aesthetic views are not genuine statements, therefore, since they are beyond the limits of what language can legitimately depict. Indeed, Wittgenstein argued, the whole of philosophy is really an impossibility. The natural sciences can give us genuine propositions, he believed, but beyond this 'What cannot be spoken must be passed over in silence.'

Wittgenstein later repudiated this view, having come to the conclusion that 'The meaning of a word is its use in language.' This second Wittgensteinian revolution extended the scope of the philosophy of language to include ethics, aesthetics and religion. There can be, he says, no such thing as a 'private language', for there is a multiplicity of rules (language games) governing the different contexts in which words are used. Most Western philosophy in the later 20th century was based on the application of this insight.

SCIENCE AND TECHNOLOGY

– Danish physicist Niels Bohr receives the Nobel Prize for Physics.

– Production of the Austin Seven motorcar starts in Cowley, near Oxford, England.

ARTS AND HUMANITIES

4 Nov. British archaeologists Howard Carter and the earl of Carnarvon discover King Tutankhamun's tomb at Luxor, Egypt.

– British archaeologist Leonard Woolley discovers the ancient Sumerian city of Ur on the River Euphrates, Iraq.

Literature

– T.S. Eliot's poem *The Waste Land* is published. A landmark of modernist literature, it expresses the sense of dislocation and disillusion that follow in the wake of the World War I.

– John Galsworthy's novels *The Man of Property* (1906), *In Chancery* (1920) and *To Let* (1921) are published together as *The Forsyte Saga*.

– James Joyce's modernist novel *Ulysses* is published in Paris (three US judges having banned further publication of chapters in the USA). It will be regarded by many as the 20th century's most important work of fiction in the English language.

Frank Harris, *My Life and Loves*, first of four volumes of sexually boastful memoirs (1922–7).

Sinclair Lewis, *Babbitt*, novel.

Walter Lippmann, *Public Opinion*, a study of the impact of political propaganda and mass advertising.

Osip Mandelstam, *Tristia*, poetry collection.

François Mauriac, *Le Baiser au lépreux* (The Kiss for the Leper), novel.

F(rancis) Scott Fitzgerald, *The Beautiful and the Damned*, novel, and *Tales of the Jazz Age*, short stories.

Oswald Spengler, *Der Untergang des Abendlandes* (The Decline of the West), historical critique of a civilization which the author deems to be in irreversible decline.

Ernst Toller, *Die Maschinenstürmer* (The Machine-Wreckers), Expressionist play.

Ludwig Wittgenstein (see p. 492), *Tractatus Logico-Philosophicus*, philosophy; the work, with its austere view of the function of language as a descriptor, revolutionizes philosophy.

Visual Arts and Architecture

30 May The Lincoln Memorial is dedicated in Washington, D.C.

– German-born American architect Mies van der Rohe develops ribbon windows: rows of windows divided only by concrete slabs.

Film

Alan Dwan, *Robin Hood*, starring Douglas Fairbanks.

Fritz Lang, *Dr Mabuse*.

F.W. Murnau, *Nosferatu, eine Symphonie des Grauens* (Nosferatu, a Symphony of Horror).

Fred Niblo, *Blood and Sand*, starring Rudolph Valentino.

1923

EUROPE

11 Jan. French and Belgian troops occupy the Ruhr valley with its associated coal-fields after Germany defaults on World War I reparations. German workers immediately strike, and France gains nothing materially. Internationally France is condemned and isolated, ensuring it will never again act unilaterally against Germany. The German government finances passive resistance by printing money, causing hyperinflation. This wipes out middle-class savings and undermines the Weimar regime still further. For Germany, the trauma of this experience will have a profound impact, and contribute greatly to the rise to power of Adolf Hitler (see 30 Jan. 1933).

20 May In Britain Andrew Bonar Law resigns as prime minister (he will die on 30 Oct.). A Midlands industrialist, Stanley Baldwin, becomes prime minister and forms a new Conservative cabinet (22 May).

24 May The Irish Civil War ends with the unconditional surrender of Republicans opposed to the Anglo-Irish treaty of 1921. Between Nov. 1922 and May 1923, 77 Republicans have been executed by the Irish Free State government, exacerbating the bitter legacy of the conflict.

9 June Alexander Stamboliski, prime minister of Bulgaria, is ejected in a pro-army coup. His pro-peasant reforms have disturbed the ruling order, and Stamboliski is assassinated (15 June).

6 July The Union of Soviet Socialist Republics (USSR), whose formation was agreed on 22 Dec. 1922, comes into existence.

10 July Fascist leader Benito Mussolini abolishes the democratic political parties in Italy. He forces through a law decreeing (14 Nov.) that two-thirds of the seats in parliament are allocated to the party that has the highest poll in an election, regardless of turnout.

12 Sept. Spanish general Miguel Primo de Rivera leads a military coup and becomes dictator, at the expense of King Alfonso XIII's authority. The general proclaims martial law throughout Spain, introduces press censorship, suspends trial by jury and crushes the liberal opposition.

8 Nov. With the German mark falling to one trillion to the dollar, as a result of the occupation of the Ruhr (see 11 Jan.), Adolf Hitler (see p. 509) mounts the Beer Hall Putsch in Munich. The National Socialist German Workers' Party (Nazi Party), which was founded in 1919, is the vehicle for Hitler's manipulation of German social unrest. With the support of Gen. Erich Ludendorff, Hitler plans to seize the city government in Munich as the first stage of a national revolution, a copy of Mussolini's 'March on Rome' (28 Oct. 1922). But his plans, already half-baked, are betrayed to the Bavarian government. Police open fire on the rebels, killing 16, and the rising ends in fiasco. Hitler will be tried for treason (see 1 April 1924).

Nov. By the end of this month the German mark has fallen to 4.2 trillion to the dollar. The Allied Reparations Commission appoints experts to investigate the German economy, including the US financier Charles G. Dawes (see 1 Sept. 1924).

6 Dec. In a UK general election fought on the issue of whether Stanley Baldwin's Conservative government should introduce protectionist policies to relieve unemployment, the Conservatives are returned as the largest party, but without a majority. Labour, as the second largest party, forms the official opposition to a government that is unlikely to survive long.

– Russian leader Lenin (see p. 480) approves the building of the first forced labour camp in the USSR, in the Solovetsky Islands (in the White Sea).

– In the USSR, a rich gold vein is found in the Aldan fields, Siberia. A Siberian gold rush follows, which helps the USSR to recover from the desperate famine of 1921–2.

MIDDLE EAST AND NORTH AFRICA

25 May Transjordan (modern Jordan), which occupies some 80% of the territory of Britain's Palestinian mandate, becomes an autonomous state under British supervision under Emir Abdullah ibn Hussein, son of King Hussein of the Hejaz (see 20 Oct. 1924). Transjordan will not achieve full independence until 1946.

Martin Buber (1878–1965)

The Austrian-born philosopher Martin Buber studied in Vienna, Munich and Berlin, and became active in the Zionist movement. The journal he founded, *Der Jude*, became central to the Jewish intellectual ferment in Central Europe, and Buber became the voice of Zionist socialism.

Buber was professor of religion at the University of Frankfurt from 1923 to 1933. In 1938 he left Germany for Palestine, where he taught at the Hebrew University of Jerusalem and became leader of the Ihud movement for Arab–Jewish understanding. He was an active advocate of a joint Arab–Jewish state in Palestine.

In his religious beliefs Buber was strongly personalist. He accepted Kant's position that an objective knowledge of the world is impossible. But he also developed the notion that personal relationships are essential to the human personality. Buber was the main channel through which the Jewish school of Hasidic thought made a decisive contribution to modern social and religious thought generally. These teachings are expounded in his work *I and Thou* (1923), which stresses the necessity of dialogue in relationships.

Through Buber the prophetic tradition of Judaism was revived to counter the Western philosophical tradition that viewed God as an 'It', an object of thought. Buber's God is the eternal Thou – known not through statements but through dialogue. He also thought that an I–Thou dialogue was possible with nature, so providing a philosophical basis for what was to become the environmental movement.

Buber's influence on socialist Zionism was deep and lasting, but he always emphasized that a personal transformation had to come first. He praised the early kibbutz movement as a realization of his communitarian thought, but he was highly critical of Zionism's policy towards the Arabs.

24 July The treaty of Lausanne between Greece, Turkey and the Allies overturns the treaty of Sèvres (1920). It returns E Thrace, Imbros and Tenedos to Turkey; Greece receives the other Aegean islands, while Italy receives the Dodecanese Islands. Turkey does not have to pay any reparations, and Britain retains Cyprus. No provisions are made for the Kurds. The treaty requires a massive population transfer of some 190,000 Greeks from Turkey to Greece and almost 400,000 Muslim Turks from Greece to Turkey.

23 Aug. Allied forces evacuate Constantinople, and Ankara becomes the capital of the new Turkish state (14 Oct.).

29 Oct. The Turkish Republic is proclaimed with Mustafa Kemal (Kemal Atatürk) as president. He promotes a policy of aggressive secularization: he abolishes the veil for women, introduces the Gregorian calendar and orders the wearing of Western dress and use of Roman letters instead of Arabic ones.

ASIA

1 Sept. An earthquake destroys both Tokyo and Yokohama; more than 140,000 people are thought dead.

THE AMERICAS

20 June The Mexican revolutionary Francisco 'Pancho' Villa is assassinated.

2 Aug. In the USA President Warren Harding dies of natural causes in San Francisco. He is succeeded by Vice-President Calvin Coolidge.

ECONOMY AND SOCIETY

3 Mar. In New York *Time* magazine is published for the first time.

28 April In England the FA Cup final is played at Wembley stadium in N London for the first time.

15 July Soviet airline Aeroflot starts its services.

– German aviation engineer Wilhelm Messerschmitt establishes his aircraft manufacturing firm.

ARTS AND HUMANITIES

Literature

– The Irish poet and dramatist W.B. Yeats wins the Nobel Prize for Literature.

Martin Buber (see box), *Ich und Du* (I and Thou), an account of the personal element in religious belief.

Robert Frost, *New Hampshire*, poetry collection.

Khalil Gibran, *The Prophet*, prose poems.

Jaroslav Hašek, *The Good Soldier Schweik*, satirical novel.

Sean O'Casey, *The Shadow of a Gunman*, play.

Charles Ogden and I(vor) A(rmstrong) Richards, *The Meaning of Meaning*, a work on the theory of language that lends a philosophical panache to modern linguistics.

José Ortega y Gasset, *El tema de nuestro tiempo* (The Theme of Our Time), philosophy.

Rainer Maria Rilke, *Duino Elegies* (begun in 1912) and *Sonnets to Orpheus*, poetry collections.

George Bernard Shaw, *St Joan*, play.

Italo Svevo (Ettore Schmitz), *La coscienza di Zeno* (Confessions of Zeno), novel.

Visual Arts and Architecture

– Le Corbusier publishes *Vers une architecture* (Towards a New Architecture), a manifesto of the modern movement in architecture.

– Mexican painter Diego Rivera paints a series of murals in Mexico City.

– Marcel Duchamp completes work on *The Bride Stripped Bare by her Bachelors, Even* (see 1915).

Max Beckmann, *Self-portrait with Cigarette*.

Constantin Brancusi, *Bird in Space*, sculpture.

Max Ernst, *Pietà, or Revolution by Night*, painting.

Music

12 June In *Façade*, performed at the Aeolian Hall, London, English writer Edith Sitwell recites her poems to William Walton's accompanying music.

14 June First performance in Paris of the ballet *Les Noces* (The

Wedding), danced by Diaghilev's Ballets Russes to words and music by Igor Stravinsky.

Béla Bartók, *Dance Suite*, orchestral work.

Arthur Honegger, *Pacific 231*, symphonic movement evoking a steam locomotive.

Jean Sibelius, Symphony No. 6 in D minor.

Film

– In the USA Cecil B. DeMille's film *The Ten Commandments* popularizes the biblical epic as a film genre.

1924

EUROPE

21 Jan. In the USSR Lenin (see p. 480) dies. Joseph Stalin, Grigori Zinoviev, Lev Kamenev and Leon Trotsky vie for power. Petrograd will be renamed Leningrad in Lenin's honour.

22 Jan. In Britain prime minister Stanley Baldwin's Conservative government loses office over the issue of protectionist policies (see 6 Dec. 1923). The first, minority, Labour government takes office with Ramsay MacDonald as prime minister. The government recognizes the Union of Soviet Socialist Republics (USSR) (1 Feb.) and in a commercial treaty Soviet Russia gives most favoured goods status to British exports. But MacDonald is not interested in radical policies; he simply wishes to show that the Labour Party can be trusted in government. Many of his supporters become impatient at the government's timidity.

1 April Adolf Hitler (see p. 509) is sentenced to five years in the Landsberg prison in Bavaria for his role in the abortive Munich Beer Hall Putsch (see 8 Nov. 1923). He will serve less than nine months. He spends the sentence writing *Mein Kampf* (My Struggle), but, more importantly, has learned to avoid the risks of an attempted *coup d'état* when power can be won by constitutional methods.

6 April In an undoubtedly fraudulent election in Italy 65% of those who vote back the *fascisti* (fascists). But the regime does enjoy a considerable degree of popular support, not least because of the stability it supplies.

4 May In German parliamentary elections the National Socialist German Workers' Party (Nazi Party) wins seats in the Reichstag for the first time.

10 June In Italy the socialist deputy Giacomo Matteotti is murdered by the *fascisti*. In his book, *The Fascisti Exposed*, Matteotti has detailed the movement's violent crimes. The non-fascist elements in the Italian parliament secede (15 June) and demand proof of the government's innocence of the murder. Mussolini dismisses those implicated, but press censorship is imposed (1 July). In short, under pressure from his own followers and faced with a scandal threatening his survival, Mussolini opts to abandon parliamentary forms of government and begins to establish a dictatorship. When *fascisti* members are tried for the murder they will only receive light sentences (1926).

11 June President Millerand of France resigns, accused by the radical Socialist Party leader Edouard Herriot of being too right-wing when a president should be neutral. Gaston Doumergue becomes president (13 June), and Herriot is prime minister (14 June).

1 Sept. In Germany the Dawes Plan is introduced. It results from a commission headed by the Chicago banker Charles G. Dawes, who advises Germany on its counter-inflation policy. A new Reichsmark is issued, which is worth one billion of the former marks, which cease to be legal tender. The Reichsbank is now administered under Allied control. Reparations to be paid by Germany are reorganized, and the Allies lend Germany 800 million gold marks. New taxes are introduced and inflation is reduced. Germany enters a period of economic stability and support for extremist politics, whether communist or National Socialist (Nazi), declines.

29 Oct. The Labour government in Britain is defeated in the general election and a new Conservative administration is formed (4 Nov.). Stanley Baldwin returns as prime minister. The Conservatives have benefited to some degree from the scare tactics associated with the release on the eve of the poll (25 Oct.) of the bogus Zinoviev Letter. The forgery, purporting to be written by the chief of the Comintern (see 2 Mar. 1919), calls on British communists to organize themselves into subversive cells within the British army. This suggests that Labour is either sympathetic to, or naïve in its dealings with, international communism. In fact, it proves to be a useful alibi for defeat for the party leadership and allows them to avoid addressing more important issues that have cost them the election, not least their lack of substantive policies.

20 Dec. In Germany Adolf Hitler is released from prison.

24 Dec. Albania becomes a republic.

MIDDLE EAST AND NORTH AFRICA

3 Mar. In Turkey Mustafa Kemal (Kemal Atatürk) abolishes the caliphate and exiles all members of the house of Osman; the Ottoman dynasty, founded by Osman in 1290, is thereby brought to an end.

20 Oct. In Arabia the sultan of Najd (an area of C Arabia), Abdul-Aziz ibn Saud, a Wahabi, enters Mecca. He has conquered the Hejaz (an area of W Arabia that contains the main centres of Islamic pilgrimage) and forced the abdication of the Hashemite king, Hussein ibn Ali. He will go on to establish the kingdom of Saudi Arabia (1932).

– During this year Reza Shah Pahlavi establishes his dominance in Persia at the expense of the Bakhtiari clans of the SW.

ASIA

– In China the Guomindang (Nationalist Party) welcomes Soviet advisers to its congress. The USSR returns to China the indemnity paid to Russia following the Boxer rising of 1900–1.

THE AMERICAS

3 Feb. Former US president Woodrow Wilson, incapacitated since 1919 by a stroke, dies.

4 Nov. President Calvin Coolidge, the Republican candidate, is re-elected president of the USA. He is the first president to campaign using newsreels.

1924

– Liberia rejects Jamaican-born African-American leader Marcus Garvey's resettlement plan for African-Americans.

ECONOMY AND SOCIETY

Jan.–Feb. The first Winter Olympic Games are held in Chamonix, SE France.

July The 8th Olympic Games are held in Paris.

– Trinity College, North Carolina, changes its name to Duke University when American tobacco mogul James Buchanan Duke endows it with $47 million on condition that the name is changed.

– French perfumier François Coty acquires French newspaper *Le Figaro*. He will make sure his conservative views are reflected in the paper.

– The Milky Way chocolate bar is launched by US confectioner Frank C. Mars.

SCIENCE AND TECHNOLOGY

– Chemical pesticides are introduced.

ARTS AND HUMANITIES

Literature

3 June The novelist Franz Kafka (see box) dies.

3 Aug. The novelist Joseph Conrad dies.

– Lowell Thomas, an American journalist, fuels the growing mythology surrounding T(homas) E(dward) Lawrence with his book *With Lawrence in Arabia*. Lawrence's own refusal of a knighthood and of a Victoria Cross has already developed his mystique.

E(dward) M(organ) Forster, *A Passage to India*, novel.

Thomas Mann, *Der Zauberberg* (The Magic Mountain), novel in which a sanatorium set high in the Swiss Alps is used as a metaphor for the ills afflicting European thought and society.

A(lan) A(lexander) Milne, *When We Were Very Young*, collection of verse for children.

Pablo Neruda, *Veinte poemas de amor y una cancion des esperada* (Twenty Love Poems and a Song of Despair), poetry collection.

Sean O'Casey, *Juno and the Paycock*, play.

Eugene O'Neill, *All God's Chillun Got Wings*, play. Paul Robeson plays the role of an African-American married to a white woman.

Saint-John Perse (Alexis Saint-Léger Léger), *Anabase*, French epic poem that becomes known in the English-speaking world via a translation by T.S. Eliot.

Mary Webb, *Precious Bane*, novel.

Visual Arts and Architecture

– French writer and critic André Breton publishes his *Manifeste de surréalisme* (Surrealist Manifesto).

– The Gran Hotel Bolivar opens in Lima and becomes the focus for political and social life in Peru.

Marc Chagall, *The Birthday*, painting.

Juan Gris, *Violin and Fruit Dish*, painting.

Oskar Kokoschka, *Venice*, painting.

Joan Miró, *Harlequin's Carnival*, painting.

Music

29 Nov. The opera composer Giacomo Puccini dies.

– Soviet ballet dancer Georgi Meilitonovitch leaves the Soviet state dancers when they visit Paris. He joins Diaghilev's Ballets Russes and changes his name to George Balanchine.

– First performance in Brno, Czechoslovakia, of Leoš Janáček's opera *The Cunning Little Vixen*.

– The US jazz cornettist Bix Beiderbecke starts his recording career.

George Gershwin, *Rhapsody in Blue*, symphonic jazz work, and *Lady be Good!*, musical starring Fred and Adele Astaire, with lyrics by Ira Gershwin.

Ottorino Respighi, *Pini di Roma* (The Pines of Rome), symphonic poem.

Jean Sibelius, Symphony No. 7 in C major.

Franz Kafka (1883–1924)

Kafka was born in Prague and educated at the town's German University. From 1907 until 1923 he worked for the Workers' Accident Insurance Institute and wrote his fiction at night, which contributed to his ill health. Tuberculosis was diagnosed in 1917 and he died in a sanatorium in Vienna, leaving instructions to his friend Max Brod that his unpublished writings should be burned. Brod disobeyed, and the novels *Amerika*, *The Trial* and *The Castle* were published posthumously.

Kafka is the prose poet of 20th-century bewilderment, and the word 'Kafka-esque' has become a catch-all description of any situation that involves a nightmarish lack of reason. His portrayals of an obdurate officialdom owe much to his experiences of office life and, perhaps, to his experience of chaotic bureaucracy in the declining years of the Austro-Hungarian Empire.

Judgement in Kafka's fiction is grotesquely disproportionate to any possible crime. In *The Trial* the protagonist is arrested for no given reason, but is strangely attracted to the power that eventually executes him. In *The Castle* the character known as K arrives as a land-surveyor in a village where he finds his expectations frustrated. No land-surveyor is needed, officials at the castle are elusive and K progresses from initial confidence to a kind of earned humility as the caretaker at the local school. The world strips him of his sense of selfhood and resists him at every point.

In Kafka's fiction human optimism and will is undermined by a mysterious and pervasive irrationality. His depiction of the divided and alienated being – a lost soul stumbling through a landscape that mingles the normal with the fantastic in a kind of symbolic hell – was prophetic of the alienation of the individual experienced in the 20th century in both totalitarian and capitalist-industrial societies.

Film
- The Metro-Goldwyn-Mayer film distribution company is founded in the USA.
- Columbia Pictures is founded in the USA by Harry Cohn.

Walt Disney, *Alice's Day at the Sea*, a film mixing cartoon and live action.

Erich Von Stroheim, *Greed*.

1925

EUROPE

1 Jan. The capital of Norway, Christiana, is renamed Oslo.

28 Feb. Friedrich Ebert, Social Democrat president of the German republic, dies. He has been hounded by the German extreme right and accused of treason since his appointment (1919). His death removes another force committed to German democracy and further undermines the Weimar republic. He is replaced by the war hero Field Marshal Paul von Hindenburg (elected on 25 April), who abides by the constitution but makes no secret of his contempt for republican government, democracy and politicians in general.

28 April In Britain Winston Churchill (see p. 523), recently returned to the Conservative party (he defected to the Liberals in 1904) and now the chancellor of the exchequer, returns Britain to the Gold Standard. In an attempt to rebuild a pre-1914 world dominated by sterling, the pound is fixed at a value of $4.86. This is, in fact, at least 10% too high. As a result unemployment rises as British goods become uncompetitively expensive for export purposes. The move will be one of the major causes of the outbreak of the General Strike (1926).

1 May Cyprus is made a colony of the British crown.

13 July French troops start to evacuate the Rhineland.

5–16 Oct. The Locarno Conference agrees on a treaty in which France, Germany, the UK and Italy guarantee the Franco-German and the German–Belgian frontiers. A freely negotiated treaty, seen as ending German isolation and freeing it from the humiliation of the treaty of Versailles (1919), it paves the way for German entry into the League of Nations and ensures an end (1930), ahead of the original schedule, of the Allied occupation of the Rhineland. Crucially, the treaty does not secure the German–Polish and German–Czech frontiers. No German government is willing to accept that these are permanent, and only France is willing to enter security agreements with Poland and Czechoslovakia. The British government is certainly not willing to commit itself to using force to guarantee frontiers that might need revision. The world powers, separately, have banned the use of poison gas in war (17 June) by protocol; the international arms trade is governed by the same protocol.

3 Dec. The prime ministers of Britain, the Irish Free State and Northern Ireland agree to shelve the report of the boundary commission and recognize the existing border between Northern Ireland and the Irish Free State.

8 Dec. The first part of Adolf Hitler's *Mein Kampf* (My Struggle) is published.
- The Welsh national party (later known as Plaid Cymru, 'Party of Wales') is founded.

MIDDLE EAST AND NORTH AFRICA

1 Jan. Syria is created by uniting Damascus and Aleppo. The French general Maurice Sarrail becomes high commissioner.

Feb. In Persia (Iran) Reza Shah Pahlavi is given dictatorial powers by the Majlis (parliament).

18 July The Druse (an unorthodox Muslim sect) start a general rebellion against French rule in the Lebanon.

Oct. The Druse uprising spreads to Damascus. French forces attack the city by land and air (18–19 Oct.). Henri de Jouvenal is appointed high commissioner (6 Nov.).

31 Oct. The shah of Persia (Iran), Ahmad Shah, is declared deposed. The Majlis proclaims Pahlavi to be shah (13 Dec.).

ASIA

15 Jan. In China strikes in Shanghai are suppressed by British and French troops. This leads to revolutionary upheavals and escalating violence. US troops land in Shanghai to intervene in a conflict that now threatens US nationals.

12 Mar. Sun Zhong Shan (Sun Yat-Sen), leader of the Guomindang (nationalist party) and de facto ruler of China, dies in Beijing. A wave of unrest at China's 'unequal treaties' with the Western powers sweeps the country. The Chinese boycott British trade and shipping.

Sept. In China Gen. Jiang Jieshi (Chiang Kai-shek) becomes commander-in-chief of the Guomindang. He brings Guangdong and Gwangxi provinces under Guomindang control. A campaign to reunify China, much of which is controlled by regional warlords, has become a more realistic proposition.
- In C Asia Turkmenistan and Uzbekistan become republics of the USSR (Soviet Union).

THE AMERICAS

17 Jan. President Coolidge defines the USA, and defends his policy of reducing taxes, especially on the middle class, in an address to the Society of American Newspaper Editors when he says: 'The business of America is business.' Coolidge opposes scaling down the extent of British and French war debt to the USA.

8 June In the USA leading socialist Benjamin Gitlow is convicted of subversion for his pamphlet 'The Left-Wing Manifesto', which calls for mass strikes and the dictatorship of the proletariat. The supreme court upholds his conviction but rules for the first time that freedom of speech and of the press and due process of law are fundamental rights and liberties. Gitlow goes on to become a leader of the US Communist Party, but in the 1940s turns against communism and denounces it.

10–12 July The Scopes Monkey Trial is held in the USA. John T. Scopes, a Tennessee schoolteacher, is tried under a state law banning the teaching of the theory of evolution. Clarence

Darrow defends Scopes while William Jennings Bryan, a former Democratic presidential candidate and fundamentalist Protestant, acts for the prosecution. Scopes is convicted and fined $100. The law will not be repealed until 1967.

- Johnny Torrio retires as a Chicago gangland boss after being shot. His assistant Al(phonse) Capone takes over and establishes dominance in the bootlegging, prostitution, gambling and light entertainment business in Chicago.
- Congress passes the Corrupt Practices Act, making it unlawful for a corporation to make a donation to a political campaign. Individual donors, however, can give up to $5000 to any individual political campaign and there are no limits on the number of committees that may receive such a donation from an individual donor.
- Marcus Garvey is convicted of fraud and receives a five-year prison sentence, which will be commuted by President Coolidge. Garvey will be then deported back to Jamaica (1927) as an undesirable alien.

ECONOMY AND SOCIETY

10 July The press agency Tass is founded in the USSR.
12 Dec. The first motel (hotel designed principally for motor vehicle users) opens at San Luis Obispo in California.
- In the UK the pensionable age is reduced from 70 to 65.
- American industrialist and philanthropist Simon Guggenheim and his wife establish the Guggenheim Foundation in memory of their son John, and endow the Guggenheim Fellowships, intended to aid US scholars studying abroad.
- At the age of 42 the English cricketer John Berry ('Jack') Hobbs scores 3024 runs in a season, with 16 centuries. Hobbs also breaks W.G. Grace's record of 126 centuries in a career.

SCIENCE AND TECHNOLOGY

- German inventor Oskar Barnack produces the Leica miniature camera.
- Scottish inventor John Logie Baird transmits television images.

ARTS AND HUMANITES

Literature

Feb. The *New Yorker* magazine starts publication.
- Franz Kafka's novel *Der Prozess* (The Trial) is published posthumously by Kafka's friend Max Brod. Kafka (see p. 496) had wished it to be destroyed after his death, but he will now become one of the most influental writers in European literature.
Noël Coward, *Hay Fever*, play.
John Dos Passos, *Manhattan Transfer*, novel.
Theodore Dreiser, *An American Tragedy*, novel.
T.S. Eliot, 'The Hollow Men', poem.
Sinclair Lewis, *Arrowsmith*, novel.
Anita Loos, *Gentlemen Prefer Blondes*, novel adapted for the stage in 1926.
Eugenio Montale, *Ossi di seppia* (Bones of the Cuttlefish), poetry collection.
Ezra Pound, *Cantos I–XVI*, epic poem published in sections; Pound will continue to publish further sections until 1968.

F. Scott Fitzgerald, *The Great Gatsby*, novel.
Virginia Woolf, *Mrs Dalloway*, novel.
Visual Arts and Architecture
15 April US painter John Singer Sargent dies.
28 Nov. The newly rebuilt Madison Square Garden opens in New York.
- Swiss architect Le Corbusier (Charles Jeanneret) exhibits a two-storey apartment (Le Pavilion de l'Esprit) at the Paris Exposition Internationale des Arts Décoratifs. The name of the exhibition will lead to the term 'Art Deco'.
- Walter Gropius's Bauhaus School of Design, Building and Crafts (see 1919) moves to Dessau from Weimar.
- The Hotel Bristol opens in Paris.
Otto Dix, *Three Prostitutes on the Street*, painting.
Pablo Picasso (see p. 467), *Three Dancers*, painting.
Chaim Soutine, *Carcass of Beef*, painting.
Music
14 Dec. First performance in Berlin of Alban Berg's opera *Wozzeck*.
Maurice Ravel, *L'Enfant et les sortilèges* (The Child and the Enchantment), opera with libretto by French novelist Colette.
Dmitri Shostakovich, Symphony No. 1 in F minor.
Jean Sibelius, *Tapiola*, tone poem.
Vincent Youmans, *No, No Nanette*, musical.
Film
Charlie Chaplin, *The Gold Rush*, starring Charlie Chaplin.
Sergei Eisenstein, *Battleship Potemkin*.
Fred Niblo, *Ben-Hur*, starring Ramón Novarro.
Sam Taylor, *The Freshman*, starring Harold Lloyd.
King Vidor, *The Big Parade*, starring John Gilbert.

1926

EUROPE

3–12 May Britain's greatest social crisis of the 20th century culminates in the General Strike called by the Trades Union Congress (TUC). The return to the Gold Standard (see April 1925) has overpriced sterling, made British coal uncompetitive against German and Polish coal and lowered mine-owners' profits. Mine-owners have responded with a lockout in an attempt to impose lower pay and longer hours. The miners strike with the rallying cry: 'Not a penny off the pay; not a minute on the day.' The TUC is reluctant to call a general strike, but fears pay cuts will follow for all their members. The strike is well supported but large numbers of volunteers maintain essential services, while the government has well-prepared plans to keep essential services running. The decisive factor, however, is that the TUC is terrified by the revolutionary implications of their actions and are only too willing to compromise. The coal miners, however, will strike until Nov.
16 May In Ireland Eamon de Valéra, who has resigned as leader of Sinn Féin (11 May), founds Fianna Fáil ('Soldiers of Destiny'), a new anti-treaty Republican party.
Aug. In an attempt to overcome increasing economic problems, the French franc is devalued to 20% of its pre-war levels.

These fragments I have shored against my ruins.

T.S. Eliot, *The Waste Land* (1922)

8 Sept. Germany joins the League of Nations.

2 Oct. Józef Pilsudski becomes Polish prime minister.

7 Oct. Fascist leader Benito Mussolini consolidates his dictatorship in Italy by making the party of the *fascisti* the official party of the state.

19 Oct. The Soviet Politburo expels Leon Trotsky and Grigori Zinoviev. They are subsequently expelled from Moscow. Nothing now stands between Joseph Stalin and dictatorial power. Trotsky will be expelled from the USSR (and assassinated in 1940). Zinoviev will be executed after a show trial (1936).

Oct.–Nov. The Imperial Conference in London defines Britain's white dominions as 'autonomous communities within the British Empire, equal in status and freely associated as members of the British Commonwealth of Nations'.

– German industrialist Fritz Thyssen founds Vereinigte Stahlwerke AG (United Steel Works Co.). It becomes the biggest steel concern in Germany. Thyssen goes on to provide valuable aid to Hitler in his rise to power until disagreements over Hitler's policies lead him to flee to Switzerland (1939).

MIDDLE EAST AND NORTH AFRICA

8 Jan. In Arabia Abdul-Aziz ibn Saud proclaims himself king of Hejaz.

8 May Damascus in Syria is bombed by the French air force as the Druse rebellion continues.

23 May The French government proclaims Lebanon to be a republic. The French grip on Lebanon remains strong until 1943.

ASIA

25 Dec. The Taisho emperor of Japan, Yoshihito, dies and is succeeded by his son, the Showa emperor, Hirohito.

– Jiang Jieshi (Chiang Kai-shek) is now leader of the Guomindang, China's nationalist party, and starts to unify the country from his power base in the S. Strongly supported by his allies in the Chinese Communist Party, he begins a campaign to tame the warlords in the N. His forces seize and occupy the city of Wuchang (Oct.).

THE AMERICAS

2 May US troops land in Nicaragua when a rebellion threatens US interests. Nicaraguan president Emiliano Chamorro will resign later in the year and go into exile.

ECONOMY AND SOCIETY

31 Oct. US magician and escapologist Harry Houdini dies after a punch to the stomach, delivered before he had tensed his muscles.

11 Nov. The American commercial broadcaster National Broadcasting Company (NBC) is founded.

– The British Broadcasting Company (BBC) is incorporated by royal charter.

SCIENCE AND TECHNOLOGY

16 Mar. US physicist Robert Goddard launches the first liquid fuel rocket in Massachusetts; it rises to 12.5m (41 feet).

– The Austrian theoretical physicist Erwin Schrödinger develops the wave mechanics theory that is at the heart of quantum mechanics. It becomes the basis of thinking about the science of the subatomic world.

ARTS AND HUMANITIES

Literature

Georges Bernanos, *Sous le soleil de Satan* (Under the Sun of Satan), novel.

Hart Crane, *White Buildings*, poetry collection.

Paul Eluard, *Capitale de la douleur* (Capital of Sorrow), poetry collection influenced by Surrealism.

André Gide, *Les Faux-monnayeurs* (The Counterfeiters), novel.

Henry Green (Henry Vincent Yorke), *Blindness*, novel.

Ernest Hemingway, *The Sun Also Rises*, novel (published in England as *Fiesta*, 1927).

Franz Kafka (see p. 496), *Das Schlosss* (The Castle), posthumously published novel.

D.H. Lawrence, *The Plumed Serpent*, novel.

T(homas) E(dward) Lawrence, *The Seven Pillars of Wisdom*, memoir describing his exploits in the Middle Eastern theatre of World War I.

Hugh MacDiarmid, *A Drunk Man Looks at the Thistle*, poem.

Sean O'Casey, *The Plough and the Stars*, play. Its realistic and unsentimental portrayal of the 1916 Easter Rising causes a riot at Dublin's Abbey Theatre.

R.H. Tawney, *Religion and the Rise of Capitalism*, history.

G(eorge) M(acaulay) Trevelyan, *History of England*, a narrative describing and justifying England's progressive evolution.

Visual Arts and Architecture

5 Dec. French painter Claude Monet dies.

Wassily Kandinsky, *Several Circles*, painting.

René Magritte, *The Last Jockey*, painting.

Henry Moore, *Draped Reclining Figure*, sculpture.

Edvard Munch, *The Red House*, painting.

Stanley Spencer, *The Resurrection*, painting.

Music

25 April First performance in Milan of Giacomo Puccini's opera *Turandot*.

– Josephine Baker becomes celebrated in Paris with her performances in La Revue Nègre and the Folies-Bergères.

Béla Bartók, *The Miraculous Mandarin*, ballet.

Ernest Bloch, *America*, epic rhapsody for orchestra, set to the words of Walt Whitman's poems.

Sergei Rachmaninov, Piano Concerto No. 4 in G minor.

William Walton, *Portsmouth Point*, concert overture.

Film

23 Aug. Italian-American actor Rudolph Valentino dies, aged 31, of a ruptured ulcer. The worldwide hysteria caused by the death of the screen's great lover shows that film has become an international art form.

Herbert Brenon, *Beau Geste*, starring Ronald Colman.

Sergei Eisenstein, *Oktober*.

Fritz Lang, *Metropolis*.

1927

EUROPE

24 May The British government breaks off diplomatic relations with the USSR, accusing the Russians of espionage.

23 June In Britain Parliament passes the repressive Trade Disputes Act. This declares illegal any repetition of the General Strike (1926), bans civil servants from membership of unions affiliated to the TUC, limits the right to picket and makes sympathy strikes illegal. It also requires that union members must 'contract in' to pay a levy to the Labour Party.

15 July Viennese workers set the Palace of Justice in Vienna alight after Austrian Nazis are acquitted of political murders.

21 July Ferdinand I, king of Romania, dies and is succeeded by his grandson Michael I, with his uncle Nicholas as regent. Michael's father, Carol, has been excluded from the succession by Ferdinand I as too much of a playboy.

12 Aug. In Ireland Eamon de Valéra and his anti-treaty Fianna Fáil deputies enter the Dáil (parliament). Hitherto Fianna Fáil has been an abstentionist party, but its members have now agreed to swear willingness to enter the Dáil.

14 Nov. Joseph Stalin expels Leon Trotsky from the Communist Party. Stalin is already moving to destroy any remaining potential rivals, such as Lev Kamenev, and indeed all surviving members of Lenin's politburo.

MIDDLE EAST AND NORTH AFRICA

20 May Britain recognizes Abdul-Aziz ibn Saud as king of Hejaz.

June The Druse rebellion in Syria ends, having been crushed by the French.

14 Oct. Oil is struck near Kirkuk, in N Iraq, at a well financed by the Iraq Petroleum Co. Ltd (formed by Iraqi, British and American businesses).

– Britain recognizes the independence of Iraq.

ASIA

Feb. In China Jiang Jieshi (Chiang Kai-shek), commanding united Guomindang and communist forces, takes Hangchow.

24 Mar. The Guomindang takes Nanjing.

April The Guomindang takes Shanghai. But the obvious strength and popularity of the communists alarms Jiang Jieshi (Chiang Kai-shek). In a reversal of his earlier anti-capitalism, he now enters into negotiations with Shanghai bankers and business-men. He turns against his erstwhile allies, and in a wave of terror attempts to exterminate communists wherever they can be found.

19 Sept. In China the communists launch an uprising in Guangdong (Canton) but are easily crushed. For the communists the future is bleak. Their urban organization has been destroyed along with many leaders. It does, however, allow for the emergence of a new leadership under Mao Zedong (Mao Tse-tung) (see p. 573), and the development of a new party based on the peasantry.

1 Dec. Having divorced his wife, Jiang Jieshi (Chiang Kai-shek) marries Song Meiling (Sung Mei-ling), a Christianized and US-educated member of one of China's richest families.

15 Dec. After an attempted communist uprising in Guangzhou, China breaks off diplomatic relations with the USSR.

THE AMERICAS

April In the USA spring floods wreak havoc in the lower Mississippi valley.

23 Aug. In the USA the Italian-born anarchists Nicolo Sacco and Bartolomeo Vanzetti are executed by electric chair for the murder in 1920 of two men during a robbery. Sacco and Vanzetti have been condemned on circumstantial evidence, and the trial judge has shown patent intolerance of the pair's radical politics.

– The US Supreme Court adjudicates that illegal income is taxable and inaugurates a new phase in the fight against mobsters. In 1931 Chicago gang boss Al Capone will fall foul of this ruling.

– In the USA the mechanical cotton picker invented by the Texan brothers John Daniel Rust and Mack Rust is now causing unemployment on the cotton fields of the S. A massive migration of African-Americans from the S states to the N starts.

ECONOMY AND SOCIETY

3–4 June The first Ryder Cup Golf match between the USA and Britain is held in Worcester, Massachusetts. The USA win.

– Expatriate Russian chess player Alexander Alekhine becomes the world chess champion and, with a gap in 1935–7, will hold the title until his death (1946).

– Stuart Chase and F.J. Schlink, *Your Money's Worth*, US consumer study that pioneers consumer testing and research.

SCIENCE AND TECHNOLOGY

7 Jan. Transatlantic telephone services begin between London and New York.

7 April Television is demonstrated for the first time in the USA.

20–21 May US pilot Charles Lindbergh achieves the first non-stop solo transatlantic flight and lands his aircraft, *Spirit of St Louis*, at Le Bourget airfield, Paris.

– The Volvo is developed by accountant Assar Gabrielsson and engineer Gustaf Larson as the first Swedish motorcar.

– German physicist Werner Heisenberg enunciates his Uncertainty Principle. It states that it is not possible to measure accurately the position and momentum of a particle at any one time, as the very act of observing alters the outcome. Although the principle is significant only at the level of subatomic physics, it serves to undermine Newton's mechanistic account of the universe. It has important philosophical implications, not least because it casts doubt on the concept of causation.

– US scientist Hermann Muller discovers that X-rays can cause mutations.

ARTS AND HUMANITIES
Literature
– US-born poet T.S. Eliot becomes a British subject and a member of the Anglican Church.
Hermann Hesse, *Steppenwolf*, novel.
Franz Kafka (see p. 496), *Amerika*, posthumously published novel.
Sinclair Lewis, *Elmer Gantry*, novel.
François Mauriac, *Thérèse Desqueyroux*, novel.
Marcel Proust, *Le Temps retrouvé* (Time Recaptured), posthumously published seventh and final novel of the novel-sequence *A la recherche du temps perdu* (Remembrance of Things Past) (see 1913).
Dorothy L(eigh) Sayers, *The Unpleasantness at the Bellona Club*, novel.
Thornton Wilder, *The Bridge of San Luis Rey*, novel.
Henry Williamson, *Tarka the Otter*, novel.
Virginia Woolf, *To the Lighthouse*, novel.
Visual Arts and Architecture
11 May Spanish artist Juan Gris dies.
Georges Braque, *Glass and Fruit*, painting.
George Grosz, *Ecce Homo*, collection of drawings viciously satirizing the perceived ills of contemporary society.
Edward Hopper, *Manhattan Bridge*, painting.
René Magritte, *Man with Newspaper*, painting.
Pablo Picasso (see p. 467), *Seated Woman*, painting
Music
14 Sept. American dancer Isadora Duncan is strangled to death in Nice, France, when her scarf is trapped in the wheels of car.
22 Nov. First performance in New York of George and Ira Gershwin's musical *Funny Face*.
27 Dec. First performance in New York of Jerome Kern and Oscar Hammerstein II's musical *Show Boat*.
– US jazz musician Edward Kennedy 'Duke' Ellington starts his five-year period performing at the Cotton Club, New York.
– The *Journal of American Folklore* publishes the traditional song 'He's Got the Whole World in His Hands'.
Leoš Janáček, *Glagolitic Mass*, for solo voices, chorus, organ and orchestra.
Film
11 May Louis B. Mayer of MGM founds the US Academy of Motion Picture Arts and Sciences.
Alan Crosland, *The Jazz Singer*, starring Al Jolson; it is the first full-length talking motion picture.
Sergei Eisenstein, *Ten Days that Shook the World*.
Victor Fleming, *The Way of All Flesh*, starring German actor Emil Jannings.
Abel Gance, *Napoleon*, starring Albert Dieudonné; many consider it to be the greatest masterpiece of the silent screen in the last year of that medium's dominance.
Hal Roach, *Putting Pants on Philip*, starring Stan Laurel and Oliver Hardy.

1928
EUROPE
12 May The Italian Fascist government restricts the vote to men who pay taxes of 100 lire or more. The vote is withdrawn from women, and the franchise is reduced from 10 million to 3 million. The remaining voters are restricted to approval or rejection en masse of the 400 candidates presented to them by the Fascist Party.
24 June The government of France, plagued by economic problems, devalues the franc against the US dollar.
2 July In Britain Parliament extends the franchise to women over 21, providing voting equality with men. This had not happened in 1918 because women outnumbered men, and it was feared that a specific women's party might emerge to dominate British politics. It is now clear that this will not happen.
27 Aug. At US prompting, the Kellogg–Briand Pact (named after US secretary of state Frank B. Kellogg and French foreign minister Aristide Briand) is signed by the representatives of 63 countries and renounces war as an arm of policy. As the USA has no intention of committing itself to enforcing the pact, it is generally seen as an empty gesture.
1 Sept. Albania, having been a republic since 1925, now becomes a kingdom. In Albania the former prime minister, Ahmed Bey Zogu, is crowned king as Zog I.
Oct. The Soviet government, faced with a shortage of grain, largely owing to its own pricing policies, decides that the independence of the peasantry is no longer tolerable. To crush opposition in the countryside, a policy of 'dekulakization' is adopted. The kulaks, moderately prosperous peasants, are denounced as class enemies: they are dispossessed of their property and deported to Siberia en masse. Not only is the death toll horrific, but the most productive farmers in the USSR are destroyed. The rest of the peasantry will face forced collectivization. This will end private ownership of land, which will be worked collectively, and theoretically more efficiently, by the community. Collectivization is an economic catastrophe that will lead to a famine of dreadful dimensions, killing millions. The Russian people are entering one of the most tragic episodes in their history.

MIDDLE EAST AND NORTH AFRICA
20 Feb. Transjordan becomes self-governing (while remaining within Britain's mandate).
9 April In Turkey, by constitutional amendment, Islam is no longer the state religion.
19 July In Egypt King Fuad suspends the constitution and begins to rule by decree.

ASIA
8 June Jiang Jieshi (Chiang Kai-shek) and his Guomindang nationalists capture Beijing.
6 Oct. Jiang Jieshi (Chiang Kai-shek) is elected president of China. China is unified, but in name only. Rather than destroy the N warlords, Jiang Jieshi has come to terms with them.

They maintain much of their former power and only nominally accept Jiang's authority.

THE AMERICAS

17 July Alvaro Obregón, president of Mexico, is assassinated. The former president Plutarco Calles, constitutionally barred from retaking office, is the de facto ruler of the country via the National Revolutionary Party.

6 Nov. The Republican candidate Herbert Hoover is elected president of the USA having made inroads into the previously Democratic strongholds of the S. In his election campaign he salutes 'the American system of rugged individualism' (22 Oct.). The election shows the strength of anti-Catholic prejudice directed against the Democratic candidate, the governor of New York, Alfred Smith (who is the first Catholic to be nominated presidential candidate by a major US party). This, and growing anti-Semitism, leads to the foundation of the National Conference of Christians and Jews.

6 Dec. Conflict over the Chaco territory leads to a series of frontier clashes between Bolivia and Paraguay. A Pan-American Conference attempts to mediate, but the conflict steadily escalates and will become a full-scale war in 1932.

ECONOMY AND SOCIETY

May–Aug. The 9th Olympic Games are held in Amsterdam, the Netherlands.

– Johnny Weissmuller, multiple Olympic gold medallist for Austria in swimming, retires from professional sport. Greater fame and fortune await him in the film industry where he will take on the role of Tarzan.

– The Australian cricketer Donald Bradman plays his first test match. In 52 test matches Bradman will average 99.94 runs per innings, the highest in test cricket history.

– Portugal outlaws the killing of bulls in bullfighting, though the sport's other rituals are allowed to continue.

– The US anthropologist Margaret Mead publishes *Coming of Age in Samoa*. Mead's work contributes to a developing cultural relativism by stressing the way in which social customs change and develop according to their natural surroundings and context.

– American broadcaster William S. Paley founds the Columbia Broadcasting System (CBS).

SCIENCE AND TECHNOLOGY

17 June US aviator Amelia Earhart becomes the first woman to fly across the Atlantic as she travels from Newfoundland to Burry Port, South Wales.

15 Oct. The airship *Graf Zeppelin* arrives in New Jersey on its first commercial flight and inaugurates the era of commercial transatlantic flight.

– The English physicist Paul Dirac publishes a paper in which he accounts for the behaviour of the electron by combining, for the first time, elements of relativity with elements of quantum mechanics. Dirac's paper predicts the existence of antiparticles.

– Scottish bacteriologist Alexander Fleming of St Mary's

Hospital, London, discovers by accident the anti-bacterial properties of penicillin.

– English physiologists Edgar Adrian and Charles Sherrington set out in their book *The Basis of Sensation* the means by which the nerves transmit messages to and from the brain.

ARTS AND HUMANITIES

Literature

– D.H. Lawrence's novel *Lady Chatterley's Lover* is privately published in Florence, Italy. Its graphic sexual descriptions ensure that it will not be published in Britain until 1960.

– The *Oxford English Dictionary*, the life work of James Murray (who died in 1915), is published in 12 volumes.

André Breton, *Nadja*, novel.

Ford Madox Ford, *Last Post*, last novel of a tetralogy entitled *Parade's End*.

John Galsworthy, *A Modern Comedy*, the second trilogy of *The Forsyte Saga*, consisting of the novels *The White Monkey*, *The Silver Spoon* and *Swan Song*.

(Marguerite) Radclyffe Hall, *The Well of Loneliness*, novel, a pioneering fiction of lesbian love.

Ben Hecht and Charles MacArthur, *The Front Page*, play.

Aldous Huxley, *Point Counter Point*, novel.

Eugene O'Neill, *Strange Interlude*, play.

Antoine de Saint-Exupéry, *Courrier-Sud* (Southern Mail), novel.

Evelyn Waugh, *Decline and Fall*, novel.

Virginia Woolf, *Orlando*, novel.

W.B. Yeats, *The Tower*, poetry collection.

Visual Arts and Architecture

Georges Braque, *Still Life with Jug*, painting.

Marc Chagall, *Wedding*, painting.

René Magritte, *Threatening Weather*, painting.

Henri Matisse, *Seated Odalisque*, painting.

Music

31 Aug. First performance in Berlin of *Die Dreigroschenoper* (The Threepenny Opera) with music by Kurt Weill and libretto by Bertolt Brecht, which adapts John Gay's *The Beggar's Opera* (1728) to the setting of early 20th-century Soho in London and stars Lotte Lenya (Weil's wife).

23 Oct. First performance of *Animal Crackers*, a musical comedy based on the book of Morrie Ryskind and George S. Kaufman; it is staged at the 44th Street Theatre, New York, and stars the four Marx Brothers with Margaret Dumont. Hereafter the Marx Brothers will perform almost exclusively as screen comics.

Nov. First performance in Paris of *Boléro*, a one-act ballet by Maurice Ravel featuring an orchestral crescendo utilizing the rhythm of the traditional Spanish dance of the same name.

Béla Bartók, *Rhapsody* No. 1.

Irving Berlin (Israel Baline), 'Puttin' on the Ritz', song.

Noël Coward, *This Year of Grace*, revue.

Cole Porter, *Paris*, musical including the song 'Let's Do It'.

Film

Luis Buñuel, *Un Chien andalou* (An Andalusian Dog), with collaboration by Salvador Dali.

Walt Disney and Ub Iwerks, *Steamboat Willie*; it introduces the character of Mickey Mouse in the first animated cartoon with a soundtrack.

Josef von Sternberg, *Docks of New York* and *The Last Command*.

1929

EUROPE

5 Jan. Alexander I, king of the Serbs, Croats and Slovenes, proclaims his country to be a dictatorship and political parties are dissolved (21 Jan.). The nation now becomes 'Yugoslavia' (meaning 'land of the southern Slavs'). Yugoslavia is dominated by a centralized 'Greater Serbia' during the interwar period, and is wracked by nationalist tensions.

Jan. Joseph Stalin tightens his grip on power by expelling Leon Trotsky from the USSR.

11 Feb. The Holy See arrives at an understanding with Mussolini in the Lateran treaty, which establishes the Vatican City State as a political entity independent of Italy and regulates the role of the Roman Catholic Church in Italy. The Italian government pays compensation for loss of papal property of 750 million lire and one billion lire in government bonds.

April–May In the USSR Joseph Stalin's five-year plan of economic development is launched. It is intended to make the Soviet economy catch up with, and surpass, the West in a single jump. Though its targets are unrealistic and constantly raised for political reasons, the plan catches the imagination of the Soviet people. A massive, if uneven, surge of industrialization follows.

30 May In the British general election (the first under universal adult suffrage) the Labour Party becomes the largest party, but does not enjoy a majority. Labour leader Ramsay MacDonald becomes prime minister and forms an administration (5 June). Much is expected of this government, but disillusion sets in when it proves to be as timid as its predecessor (1924). It has no answer to a steadily deepening economic crisis, in which Britain's unemployment figures soon top 12%.

7 June American lawyer and businessman Owen D. Young presents the Young Plan. It is intended to reschedule German reparations, already modified once under the Dawes Plan (1924). Now Germany will pay 121 billion marks over 59 years. Although the plan eases the burden on Germany, the Nazis (among others) bitterly denounce the German government for accepting again the terms of the treaty of Versailles, and for mortgaging unborn generations of Germans. Far from making the Weimar regime more secure, this plan undermines it further.

25 July Following the Lateran treaty of 11 Feb. Pope Pius XI becomes the first pope to leave the Vatican since 1870.

6 Aug. After Germany accepts the Young Plan (see above), the Allies agree to evacuate the Rhineland by June 1930.

17 Nov. Nikolai Bukharin, head of the Third International since 1926 and a potential rival of Joseph Stalin's, is expelled from the Soviet Communist Party.

MIDDLE EAST AND NORTH AFRICA

Aug. Violence erupts in Jerusalem with organized attacks by Arabs on Jews as a result of the Jewish use of the Wailing Wall for prayer.

ASIA

– Tajikistan is made a Soviet Socialist Republic within the USSR.

– Only some 20% of the Japanese population are eligible to vote in the country's general election, with the suffrage restricted to males who are over 25 years old. The rise of the military in politics means that this will be the last such election held in Japan before World War II.

THE AMERICAS

14 Feb. In the USA the Al Capone gang kill seven members of the George 'Bugs' Moran gang in the St Valentine's day massacre.

4 Mar. Herbert Hoover is inaugurated as 31st US president.

24–29 Oct. The Wall Street Crash marks the beginning of the Great Depression. Before the Crash speculation has increased to a point where prices paid for shares bear little relation to the economic strength of the companies concerned. As few shares have any real value, the US stock market crashes. On 'Black Thursday' (24 Oct.), nearly 13 million shares change hands. The panic continues on 28 and 29 Oct., when 16 million shares are traded. Soon over $30 billion of the paper value of stocks has been wiped out, a figure that will rise to £75 billion within three years. With loans to Europe, especially Germany, being recalled, only concerted and determined international action can prevent a depression developing. It is not forthcoming.

ECONOMY AND SOCIETY

31 Dec. Pope Pius XI opposes coeducation as 'false in theory and harmful to Christian training' in his encyclical *Divini Illius Magistri*.

– Unilever is created by the merger of Lever Brothers (established by English chemists William Hesketh and James Darcy Lever in 1895) with Anton Jürgens of the Netherlands.

SCIENCE AND TECHNOLOGY

9 Jan. Scottish bacteriologist Alexander Fleming applies penicillin in an operation at St Mary's Hospital, London.

– In Britain the Great West Aerodrome, which will become Heathrow airport, opens to the W of London.

– American scientist Edward Doisy and the German chemist Adolph Butenandt isolate the sex hormone oestrone. It is the first oestrogen identified.

ARTS AND HUMANITIES

Literature

– British linguist Charles Ogden proposes a fundamental vocabulary in his *Basic English* whose sanguine expectation is to promote world peace as a result of improved communication.

Jean Cocteau, *Les Enfants terribles* (The Incorrigible Children), novel.

Alfred Döblin, *Berlin Alexanderplatz*, novel.

William Faulkner, *The Sound and the Fury*, novel giving the American South an authentic literary voice.

Robert Graves, *Goodbye to All That*, memoir of World War I.

Henry Green (Henry Vincent Yorke), *Living*, novel.

Ernest Hemingway, *A Farewell to Arms*, novel.

Richard Hughes, *A High Wind in Jamaica*, novel.

Erich Kästner, *Emil und die Detektive* (Emil and the Detectives), children's novel.

Alberto Moravia, *Gli indifferenti* (A Time of Indifference), novel.

Sean O'Casey, *The Silver Tassie*, play.

J.B. Priestley, *The Good Companions*, play.

Erich Maria Remarque, *Im Westen Nichts neues* (All Quiet on the Western Front), novel. The Nazis will publicly condemn it as 'defeatist' in 1933 and will deprive Remarque of his citizenship.

R.C. Sherriff, *Journey's End*, play based on its author's experiences of life in the trenches of the Western Front in World War I.

Virginia Woolf, *A Room of One's Own*, essay that advances a feminist view of female independence.

Visual Arts and Architecture

8 Nov. The Museum of Modern Art, New York, opens.

– After 585 years of work, the Cathedral of St Vitus, Prague, Czechoslovakia, is completed.

– German-American architect Mies van der Rohe finishes the Tugendhat House, Brno, Czechoslovakia.

Salvador Dali, *The Good Masturbator*, painting.

Paul Klee, *Fool in a Trance*, painting.

Piet Mondrian, *Composition with Yellow and Blue*, painting.

Music

21 Mar. First performance in London of Ralph Vaughan Williams's opera *Sir John in Love*, based on Shakespeare's *The Merry Wives of Windsor*.

27 Nov. Cole Porter's musical comedy *Fifty Million Frenchmen* is performed for the first time at the Lyric Theatre, New York.

Noël Coward, *Bitter Sweet*, musical play.

Sergei Prokofiev, *The Prodigal Son*, ballet.

Heitor Villa-Lobos, *Amazonas*, symphonic poem.

William Walton, Viola Concerto.

Anton Webern, Five Movements for string quartet.

Film

16 May The US Academy of Motion Picture Arts and Sciences presents the first Academy Awards (known as 'Oscars' from 1935), covering films produced in 1927 and 1928. The first film to win the award for best picture is *Wings* (1927), directed by William Wellman.

Alfred Hitchcock, *Blackmail*, the first successful British all-talking film.

G(eorg) W(ilhelm) Pabst, *Pandora's Box*, starring Louise Brooks.

1930

EUROPE

21 Jan. The London Naval Conference opens.

23 Jan. In Thuringia, C Germany, William Frick becomes the first National Socialist (Nazi) minister (interior and education).

28 Jan. Miguel Primo de Rivera, dictator of Spain, resigns and dies in exile (16 Mar.). The Spanish king, Alfonso XIII, is in an

increasingly vulnerable position. By encouraging a dictatorship he has earned the enmity of the political left, while the political right no longer see him as the best protector of their interests.

23 Feb. In Germany Horst Wessel, a Nazi agitator, dies of blood poisoning in a Berlin hospital having been attacked on 14 Jan. He becomes a Nazi martyr, remembered in the Nazi song, 'Horst Wessel Lied', adapted from a traditional song by Wessel himself.

30 Mar. In Germany Heinrich Brüning becomes federal chancellor at the head of a minority right-of-centre government. With no majority in the Reichstag, he will be forced to rely increasingly on emergency powers.

22 April The London Naval treaty binds the USA, Britain, Japan, France and Italy to limit the tonnage of submarines and extends the moratorium on the building of new capital ships until 1936.

24 May Italian dictator Benito Mussolini states that the Versailles treaty should be revised. He has always denounced it as unjust to Italy, now he suggests it is unjust to Germany. He is toying with the vision of an equally powerful France and Germany, vying for expensive Italian favours, with himself playing the role of arbiter between them. It proves to be a delusion.

8 June Michael, the boy king of Romania, is removed from the throne and is succeeded by his father Carol II.

30 June The last Allied troops leave the Rhineland, four years earlier than the treaty of Versailles specified. Despite French concerns, the British are determined to conciliate Germany.

16 July In Germany federal chancellor Heinrich Brüning begins to govern by presidential decree.

Sept. As the Great Depression bites in Germany, unemployment reaches 3 million and is still rising (in 1932 it will reach over 6 million). For an electorate still remembering the trauma of hyperinflation (1923–4) it is a fearful blow. Support for political extremism spirals as voters abandon democratic parties incapable of meeting the crisis and embrace radical solutions on both the left and right. In elections to the German Reichstag (14 Sept.), the National Socialist (Nazi) party win 6,409,000 votes, second to the Social Democrats' 8,400,000. The improvement on the 1928 elections, when they won 800,000 votes and 12 seats is dramatic. They now have 107 seats. Nazi Party leader Adolf Hitler (see p. 509), as an Austrian citizen, cannot take his seat as a deputy but he is interested only in the highest office of government.

12 Dec. Allied troops leave the Saarland, German territory occupied since 1919. A plebiscite will be held (1935) to decide whether or not the territory will return to Germany.

MIDDLE EAST AND NORTH AFRICA

July A Kurdish revolt breaks out on Turkey's border with Persia (modern Iran). Combined Turkish and Soviet forces launch an attack on the Kurds (12 Aug.).

20 Oct. Sidney Webb (later Baron Passfield), British secretary of state for the colonies, produces his Passfield Paper on Palestine. A secularized Jew, Webb states that Jewish immigration to Palestine should stop while unemployment among the Arabs indigenous to the region remains so high.

– Turkish leader Mustafa Kemal (Kemal Atatürk), pursuing his secular campaign, renames Constantinople as Istanbul.

ASIA

12 Mar. Mohandas Karamchand Gandhi (see p. 476) starts his campaign of *satyagraha* (non-violent civil disobedience) against British rule in India. Supported by the All India Trade Congress, Gandhi leads his Salt March for 265km (165 miles) to the coast of the Arabian Sea at Gujarat. There he produces salt by the evaporation of salt water and so breaks the law, since the government enjoys a monopoly in salt production. Within a year over 60,000 will be arrested for following his example. In 1931 he will enter negotiations with viceroy Lord Irwin (later Lord Halifax). Constitutional reforms are already being considered and will follow (1935), but they will not satisfy Indian nationalists.

July In the Chinese Civil War, communist forces have established the Jiangxi Soviet, essentially a peasant-based communist state. They fail in their attempts to seize urban centres, but manage through guerrilla warfare to resist four Nationalist attempts to exterminate them. In 1934, however, they will be forced to abandon Jiangxi and embark on the Long March.

14 Nov. Hamaguchi Yuko, prime minister of Japan, is shot and wounded by a reactionary agitator following widespread domestic condemnation of his acceptance of Japanese naval reductions according to the terms of the London Naval Conference.

THE AMERICAS

31 Mar. The US Congress approves a Public Buildings Act and state road building programmes (4 April) in an attempt to create jobs.

May–June On Wall Street stock prices suffer further losses after a brief rally. More American banks are bankrupted.

17 June President Herbert Hoover approves an increase in tariffs as well as a Most Favoured Nation policy, which grants tariff reductions for certain nations. America's tariff increases lead to retaliatory increases worldwide, as other nations adopt 'beggar-my-neighbour' economic policies in the face of an increasingly catastrophic global economic crisis.

25 Aug. Augusto Leguía, president of Peru, resigns and flees following a coup launched by Col. Luis Sánchez Cerro.

5 Sept. In Argentina President Hipólito Irigoyen, who has been following a programme of liberal reform that has alienated business and land-owning interests, is ousted in a coup led by Gen. José Félix Uriburu. Uriburu becomes president.

3 Oct. A vast new oil field is discovered in Rusk County, Texas. The effect of the discovery is to depress world oil prices.

Oct. In Brazil Getúlio Dornelles Vargas leads a revolution that ousts President Luis Pereira de Sousa. Vargas becomes president (26 Oct.), dissolves congress (1 Nov.) and will be dictator until 1945.

20 Dec. In response to President Hoover's address to Congress, requesting up to $150 million to help ease unemployment (2 Dec.), the US Congress passes a further public works bill worth $116 million.

SUB-SAHARAN AFRICA

2 April Zauditu, empress of Ethiopia, dies and is succeeded by Ras Tafari, who has taken the name of Haile Selassie. He is crowned king of kings at Addis Ababa (2 Nov.). Rastafarians in Jamaica hail him as a living god. The cult of Rastafarianism, originating in Jamaica in the 1920s, is based on the ideas of Marcus Garvey and calls on black people to return to an African homeland.

19 May European women in South Africa are enfranchised; the vote is still denied to Africans of both sexes.

ECONOMY AND SOCIETY

31 Dec. Pope Pius XI's encyclical *Casti Connubii* condemns contraception and advocates the rhythm method of birth control.

– In Italy Mussolini's government makes abortion illegal for eugenic reasons, condemning it as an attack on racial health.

– Simon Kuznets, a Russian-born US economist, works on producing a Gross National Product index.

– In the USA American Airlines, United Airlines and Trans World Airlines are created during the year.

– The Institute for Advanced Study is established at Princeton University with an endowment from American businessman Louis Bamberger, who has made a fortune from his department store empire.

– US psychiatrist Karl Menninger's study *The Human Mind* popularizes psychiatry for a lay readership.

– Uruguay, the host nation, wins the first soccer World Cup, beating Argentina 4–2 in the final.

– Australian cricketer Donald Bradman scores a record 974 runs against England, in a series won 2–1 by Australia. England batsman Jack Hobbs plays his last test match during the series.

SCIENCE AND TECHNOLOGY

5–24 April English aviator Amy Johnson makes the first solo flight by a woman from Britain to Australia.

5 Oct. The British airship *R101* is consumed by flames near Beauvais, France, while flying from Cardington, Britain, to Karachi, India (now Pakistan). 44 travellers are killed.

18 Oct. The first S American subway opens in Buenos Aires, Argentina.

– American electrical engineer Vannevar Bush develops a 'differential analyser', the first analogue computer.

– The arrival of Dutch elm disease in the USA starts a long-term alteration in the country's landscape.

ARTS AND HUMANITIES

Literature

2 Mar. The novelist D.H. Lawrence dies of tuberculosis in the S of France.

14 April Russian Futurist poet and playwright Vladimir Mayakovsky commits suicide.

Noël Coward, *Private Lives*, play.

Hart Crane, *The Bridge*, poetry collection.

T.S. Eliot, 'Ash Wednesday', poem.

William Faulkner, *As I Lay Dying*, novel.

Dashiell Hammett, *The Maltese Falcon*, novel.

Hermann Hesse, *Narziss and Goldmund*, novel.

Vladimir Mayakovsky, *Banya* (The Bathhouse), play.

Robert Musil, *Der Mann ohne Eigenschaften* (The Man without Qualities), first volume of a three-part novel.

José Ortega y Gasset, *La rebelión de las masas* (The Revolt of the Masses), philosophy that analyses the new politics of fascism.

Arthur Ransome, *Swallows and Amazons*, family holiday adventure story for children, the first in a series of twelve such novels.

Joseph Roth, *Hiob* (Job), novel.

W.C. Sellar and R.J. Yeatman, *1066 and All That*, humorous survey of British history.

Evelyn Waugh, *Vile Bodies*, novel.

Visual Arts and Architecture

– In the USA the Chicago Board of Trade Building, the city's tallest so far, by American architects William Holabird and Martin Roche is completed. The Palmolive Building, also in Chicago, is completed.

– Swiss architect Le Corbusier finishes his Villa Savoye at Poissy sur Seine, France.

Edward Hopper, *Early Sunday Morning*, painting.

Grant Wood, *American Gothic*, painting.

Music

12 Jan. First performance in Leningrad of Dmitri Shostakovich's opera *The Nose,* based on Gogol's short story.

9 Mar. First performance in Leipzig of Kurt Weill's opera *Aufsteig und Fall der Stadt Mahagonny* (Rise and Fall of the City of Mahagonny), to a libretto by Bertolt Brecht. A one-act version, as *Singspiel*, had been performed at Baden-Baden in 1927.

12 April First performance in Brno of Leoš Janáček's opera *From the House of the Dead*.

8 June First performance in Berlin of Paul Hindemith's opera *Neues vom Tage* (The News of the Day).

– The BBC Symphony Orchestra is founded, with Adrian Boult as conductor.

Béla Bartók, *Cantata Profane*, concerto.

George Gershwin, *Girl Crazy*, musical.

Heitor Villa-Lobos, *Bachianas Brasileiras*, No. 1.

Film

Luis Buñuel, *L'Age d'or* (The Golden Age).

Mervyn LeRoy, *Little Caesar*, starring Edward G. Robinson.

Josef von Sternberg, *The Blue Angel* and *Morocco*, starring Marlene Dietrich.

1931

EUROPE

14 April King Alfonso XIII leaves Spain following a republican victory in the country's municipal election, widely treated as a plebiscite on the future of the monarchy, and is declared guilty of high treason (12 Nov.). A republic is proclaimed, but divisions are soon evident. Anarchist anti-clericalism and strikes are seen as a threat to property-owning, Catholic conservatives. Political violence is seen in the republic from its inception.

11 May The Austrian bank, Credit-Anstalt, goes into liquidation in Vienna, rocking Europe's financial system.

13 May Paul Doumer is elected to replace Gaston Doumergue as president of France.

13 July The Danatbank in Germany is declared insolvent. Successive German banks close by stages into the first week of August. The Bank of England, which has extended considerable credit to keep them solvent, is left alarmingly exposed. A run on sterling begins.

24 Aug. In a deepening economic crisis, Britain's Labour government resigns. The run on sterling has reached crisis proportions, and a substantial loan from French and US banks is deemed essential, but foreign bankers demand a balanced budget as a condition of the loan. This, in turn, requires reducing unemployment benefits, a step half the cabinet cannot bring themselves to contemplate. Alternatives, such as abandoning the Gold Standard, are treated with contempt by the chancellor of the exchequer, Philip Snowden. In what is seen by the Labour movement as an act of treachery, the Labour prime minister, Ramsay MacDonald, remains in office at the head of a new coalition: the National Government. The Labour Party expels MacDonald and Snowden. Arthur Henderson becomes Labour Party leader.

15 Sept. In the Invergordon mutiny elements of the Royal Navy mutiny in response to government-imposed pay cuts. There is panic within the government, as it seems that revolution is imminent.

21 Sept. As the run on sterling accelerates, beyond the ability of the foreign loans to cover Britain's liabilities, Britain abandons the Gold Standard, and sterling rapidly falls in value from $4.86 to $3.49. Riots against unemployed benefit reductions take place in Manchester and Glasgow (Oct.).

27 Oct. In the British general election the National Government wins an overwhelming majority. It is dominated by Conservatives (473 out of 554 seats), but is still led by the former Labour leader Ramsay MacDonald. Labour fares extremely badly in the election, winning just 52 seats.

Dec. The Statute of Westminster grants self-government and self-determination to all dominions within the British Commonwealth – Canada, Australia, New Zealand, the Union of South Africa and the Irish Free State.

– In Britain former Conservative politician Oswald Mosley quits the Labour Party to found the New Party. When this fails he will turn to fascism.

ASIA

17 June The Vietnamese communist leader Ho Chi Minh is arrested in Hong Kong, China, by the British authorities. The French government seek to extradite him, but friends help him escape to the USSR.

18 Sept. The Mukden Incident in Manchuria is engineered by right-wing Japanese army officers as an excuse for Japanese forces to occupy Manchuria, where the economic and strategic interests of Japan and China are in conflict. Since the end of the Russo-Japanese War in 1905, Japan has exercised certain rights in Manchuria, including the right to station troops to protect the South Manchurian Railway. When an explosion (caused by the Japanese) occurs on the railway near Mukden (now Shenyang), the Japanese military immediately blame the Chinese and, without reference to the civilian government in Japan, occupy Mukden, and then the rest of Manchuria. Chinese leader Jiang Jieshi (Chiang Kai-shek) believes that the West will sooner or later expel the Japanese, and he concentrates on the destruction of his communist enemies. The League of Nations denounces the invasion, which breaches Article 12 of the League's Covenant, but does little about it.

11 Dec. Japan abandons the Gold Standard.

THE AMERICAS

3 Mar. The US Congress votes in favour of making the 'Star Spangled Banner' the official US national anthem.

18 June Canada raises tariffs, reducing by two-thirds Canadian imports from the USA.

7 Dec. Hunger marchers protest outside the White House at a time when there are more than 8 million unemployed people in the USA.

8 Dec. President Hoover, in his message to Congress, urges a Reconstruction Finance Corporation and a programme of public works, aimed at easing unemployment.

– The Black Muslim movement is formed in Detroit: Elijah Poole becomes an assistant to the founder of the Nation of Islam sect, Walli Farad (Wallace D. Fard). Poole then changes his name to Elijah Muhammad and will establish the Temple of Islam No. 2 in Chicago (1934). When Farad disappears, Muhammad becomes the sect's leader.

– The Nevada State Legislature legalizes gambling.

– Brazil establishes a national coffee department, which destroys most of the country's product in order to boost its price. The world downturn in coffee prices has led to economic and political unrest in Brazil's S provinces.

– In the USA the abundant wheat harvest proves to be an economic disaster, depressing prices and driving farmers off the land.

SUB-SAHARAN AFRICA

1 July The trans-African Katanga–Benguela railway is completed.

ECONOMY AND SOCIETY

10 Sept. US gangster Charles 'Lucky' Luciano organizes the murder of fellow mobster Salvatore Maranzano. He restructures the whole of the US Mafia into a network of 'families'.

24 Oct. US gangster Al Capone is sentenced to 11 years imprisonment for evading taxation.

– In Britain Rolls Royce acquires Bentley Motors.

SCIENCE AND TECHNOLOGY

30 April The Empire State Building opens in New York, and will be the world's tallest building for over 40 years.

18 Oct. The US scientist and inventor Thomas Edison dies.

24 Oct. The world's largest suspension bridge, the George Washington Bridge, New York, opens, connecting Manhattan with New Jersey.

– The Chrysler Building opens in New York. The beauty of the steel and concrete building makes it into an immediate and enduring symbol of the city.

– Work begins on building the Rockefeller Center, New York.

ARTS AND HUMANITIES

Literature

Pearl S. Buck, *The Good Earth*, novel.

Noël Coward, *Cavalcade*, play.

William Faulkner, *Sanctuary*, novel.

Henry Miller, *Tropic of Cancer*, autobiographical novel; it is deemed obscene and banned in the USA until 1961.

Eugene O'Neill, *Mourning Becomes Electra*, play.

Wilfred Owen, *Collected Poems*, edited by Edmund Blunden.

Anthony Powell, *Afternoon Men*, novel.

Vita Sackville-West, *All Passion Spent*, novel.

Antoine de Saint-Exupéry, *Vol de nuit* (Night Flight), novel.

George Seferis, *I strofi* (The Turning Point), poetry collection.

Edmund Wilson, *Axel's Castle*, collection of critical essays.

Virginia Woolf, *The Waves*, novel.

Visual Arts and Architecture

– British rule of India achieves its architectural apotheosis with the creation of New Delhi, designed by Sir Edwin Lutyens and Sir Herbert Baker.

Salvador Dali, *The Persistence of Memory*, painting.

Edward Hopper, *Route 6, Eastham*, painting.

Eric Gill, *Prospero and Ariel*, sculpture for the wall of Broadcasting House, London.

Paul Klee, *The Ghost Vanishes*, painting.

Paul Landowski, *Christ the Redeemer*, sculpture in concrete, 38m (125 feet) high, dedicated on top of the Corcovado Mountain behind Rio de Janeiro.

Music

– Irish dancer Ninette de Valois founds the Sadler's Wells Ballet in London.

Duke Ellington, 'Mood Indigo', tune.

William Walton, *Belshazzar's Feast*, cantata.

Film

Tod Browning, *Dracula*, starring Bela Lugosi.

Charlie Chaplin, *City Lights*.

René Clair, *A nous la liberté* (Freedom for Us).

Fritz Lang, *M*, starring Peter Lorre.

Norman Z. McLeod, *Monkey Business*, starring the Marx Brothers.

James Whale, *Frankenstein*, starring Boris Karloff.

William Wellman, *Public Enemy*, starring James Cagney.

1932

EUROPE

Jan. In Berlin and Vienna Nazi students make violent attacks on Jewish students.

16 Feb. In the general election in the Irish Free State, Eamon de Valéra's Fianna Fáil becomes the largest party in the Dáil with 72 seats and de Valéra becomes president of the executive council (prime minister) of the Irish Free State. He is determined to win far greater separation from the UK than was accepted in the Anglo-Irish treaty (1921). His Fianna Fáil government abolishes the oath of allegiance to the British crown as well as the office of governor general. It will also withhold land purchase annuities owed to the British government, resulting in a damaging tariff war.

6 May Paul Doumer, president of France, is assassinated. He is succeeded by Albert Lebrun. The election for the national assembly (9 May) produces a left-wing majority, with Edouard Herriot as prime minister. He, however, has to resign (Dec.) since the assembly refuses to back his plan to repay by instalments the French war debt to the USA.

31 May President Hindenburg of Germany, who has withdrawn his support from chancellor Heinrich Brüning, asks Franz von Papen to form a new administration. Von Papen excludes National Socialist (Nazi) deputies from the new government.

June After a one-year moratorium on debts owed to the US government expires, Britain and France cease to pay debts owed from World War I. Germany has already ceased to pay reparations. American isolationism and hostility to Europe is strengthened.

5 July António Salazar is appointed prime minister of Portugal.

31 July In the German general election the National Socialist Party becomes the biggest single party in the Reichstag but with no overall majority. Adolf Hitler announces that he will not serve as vice-chancellor under Franz von Papen (13 Aug.).

24 Sept. In Sweden the socialist Per Albin Hansson becomes prime minister. He will retain office until 1946, and his Social Democratic Party will remain in power until 1976.

1 Oct. Sir Oswald Mosley, who has been both a Conservative and a Labour MP, founds the British Union of Fascists. He sees the economic crisis as an opportunity for his own personal ambition and develops a programme of economic action along broadly socialist lines to deal with the malady. The anti-Semitism of his followers, tolerated and supported by Mosley, will lead to riots in London's East End. Indeed, the violence associated with his movement will help ensure it never advances from the fringes of British politics.

6 Nov. A general election in Germany (the last genuinely free elections to the Reichstag before World War II) produces another deadlock. The National Socialists lose some seats to the Communists, but remain the biggest party in the Reichstag. Franz von Papen resigns as chancellor (17 Nov.).

4 Dec. Kurt von Schleicher becomes the last chancellor of the Weimar Republic. He hopes to bring the Nazis into a coalition administration but Hitler remains obdurate: he will accept nothing less than the office of chancellor.

– The tidal wave of protectionist policies across the world reaches the UK. Lacking any other answer to economic problems, the government imposes a 10% tariff on the bulk of imported goods. The exception is imports from Canada, Australia, New Zealand and some other parts of the British Commonwealth

under the Imperial Preference policy, negotiated through the Ottawa Agreements. This provides the UK with at least a limited market for its frequently uncompetitive goods. The net effect is to lower productivity and discourage investment.

MIDDLE EAST AND NORTH AFRICA

3 Oct. Britain's mandate over Iraq comes to an end. Independent Iraq joins the League of Nations.

ASIA

28 Jan. In the Sino-Japanese conflict Japanese forces attack and capture Shanghai, having used planes to bomb the city's civilian population. The US government declares its support for China and warns Japan that it will never recognize territorial changes imposed by force. The declaration has no impact on the Sino-Japanese conflict.

Feb. Japan proclaims Manchuria as the puppet-state of Manchukuo with former Chinese emperor Puyi (P'u-i) as nominal head of state.

15 May The prime minister of Japan, Inukai Tsuyoshi, is assassinated by a right-wing militant. Democratic politics in Japan come to an end with the rise of his successor, Saito Makoto.

24 June In a bloodless coup in Siam (Thailand) a group of radicals force King Rama VII to grant a constitution.

Sept. Though he is imprisoned and the Indian National Congress is banned, Mohandas Gandhi (see p. 476) starts a fast, which he says will continue 'unto death'. He aims to improve the treatment of the 'untouchables', India's lowest Hindu caste. The British authorities plan to provide them with separate electorates in a new constitution, but Gandhi also wants to force other Hindus to change their views of the untouchables. His six days of fasting, conducted with an unerring eye for publicity, cause great excitement, and new voting procedures are rapidly agreed between untouchables and other Hindu groups, endorsed by the British.

Oct. A League of Nations commission of inquiry into Manchuria proposes a special regime for the region that will recognize Chinese sovereignty and safeguard Japanese economic rights. Japan responds that it has only been acting in defence of its legitimate interests in the region and claims that in a China riven by internal conflict there was no central government with which to negotiate.

THE AMERICAS

22 Jan. In the USA a Reconstruction Finance Corporation is approved by Congress along the lines proposed by President Hoover. It will lend $1.8 billion to individual states to fund public works programmes.

Jan. Latin America has its first brief taste of communist rebellion: landowners, business interests and the army combine to launch a military coup, installing Gen. Maximiliano Hernandez Martinez as dictator of El Salvador. This in turn leads to a communist-led revolt, which is suppressed in two days and is followed by mass executions of thousands. Henceforth propertied interests in El Salvador will prefer the security of military dictatorships in the face of such a threat.

Adolf Hitler (1889–1945)

Born in Braunau, Austria, Hitler served as a corporal in the German army during World War I. In 1920 he joined the National Socialist German Workers' Party, and began to develop an irrational mix of ideas into the political doctrine of National Socialism or Nazism. There was the Social Darwinian concept of a struggle for survival (in which the 'superior' Germanic race would emerge triumphant over other 'inferior' races), the use of the Jews as a scapegoat for Germany's woes, a mystical, paganized and militaristic nationalism, a quasi-socialist belief in a centrally controlled economy, and above all the cult of the will and of the all-powerful leader.

Hitler made skilful use of mass communications – such as films, rousing speeches, posters and mass rallies – to convey his message. By the early 1930s the Nazi Party, with its platform of achieving full employment at a time of international economic depression, an end to class conflict, and the restoration of national self-respect after the defeat of World War I, was attracting considerable support, and in 1933 Hitler was voted into power. Once in office he set about destroying the democratic system, imprisoning or killing political opponents, and beginning the persecution of the Jews that was eventually to culminate in the murder of millions.

Internationally, Hitler's demands began to escalate in the late 1930s, ranging from the return of territories lost after World War I to claims to vast areas of eastern Europe that he saw as the destined homeland of the German race. But the ideal of strenuousness that had originally galvanized both Hitler and Nazism proved to be the undoing of both. Thus in World War II each conquest had to be surpassed by the next – leading Hitler to invade the USSR in 1941 before Britain had been defeated. This strategic error ultimately led to Hitler's defeat and the complete collapse of Nazi Germany.

1 Mar. In the USA the two-year-old son of pioneering aviator Charles Lindbergh is kidnapped. A ransom is paid but the child is found dead (12 May). Bruno Richard Hauptmann will be executed for the murder in 1936.

7 Mar. Congress votes to distribute to the American needy 40 million bushels of wheat held by the federal authorities.

29 May 'Hoovervilles', the shantytowns of the unemployed and dispossessed, are now a common sight around US cities, and the first contingents of the 'bonus army' arrive in Washington, D.C. Congress had voted (1924) for extra payments for World War I veterans, but these were not to be paid until 1945. Some 17,000 veterans, with their families, descend on Washington and found their own Hooverville, demanding immediate payment. Congress rejects their demands (17 June) and many disperse. The last 2000 are dispersed by troops using tanks (28 June), in an act that is politically damaging to President Hoover.

2 July Franklin D. Roosevelt, governor of New York, accepts the Democratic party nomination for the presidency of the US and declares: 'I pledge you, I pledge myself, to a new deal for the American people.'

8 Nov. Franklin D. Roosevelt wins the US presidential election by a landslide, with the outgoing Herbert Hoover winning only six states.

AUSTRALASIA AND OCEANIA
- The Sydney Harbor Bridge, linking North and South Sydney, is completed. It will take the city 56 years for the city to pay off the construction costs of $20 million.

ECONOMY AND SOCIETY
July–Aug. The 10th Olympic Games are held in Los Angeles, USA.
- There are now about 30 million unemployed in the world.
- Television production in Britain transfers from the Baird Company to the BBC (British Broadcasting Corporation).

SCIENCE AND TECHNOLOGY
- English physicists John Cockcroft and Ernest Walton split the atom and untap new sources of energy.
- English physicist James Chadwick discovers the neutron. The particle is without an electric charge and can therefore penetrate atoms.
- In the USA Route 66 opens, linking Chicago with Los Angeles.

ARTS AND HUMANITIES
Literature
- The Shakespeare Memorial Theatre opens in Stratford-on-Avon, Warwickshire, England.
Louis-Ferdinand Céline, *Voyage au bout de la nuit* (Journey to the End of the Night), novel.
William Faulkner, *Light in August*, novel.
Erle Stanley Gardner, *The Case of the Velvet Claws*, novel introducing the fictional detective Perry Mason.
Lewis Grassic Gibbon, *Sunset Song*, novel.
Stella Gibbons, *Cold Comfort Farm*, novel.
Ernest Hemingway, *Death in the Afternoon*, novel.
Aldous Huxley, *Brave New World*, novel.
John Cowper Powys, *A Glastonbury Romance*, novel.
Joseph Roth, *Radetzkymarsch* (The Radetzky March), novel.
Georges Simenon, *The Crime of Inspector Maigret*, novel.
James Thurber, 'The Secret Life of Walter Mitty', short story.
Evelyn Waugh, *Black Mischief*, novel.
Visual Arts and Architecture
Georges-Henri Rouault, *Christ Mocked by Soldiers*, painting.
Pablo Picasso (see p. 467), *Head of a Woman*, sculpture.
Maurice Utrillo, *Sacré Coeur*, painting.
Music
Duke Ellington, 'It Don't Mean a Thing if It Ain't Got that Swing', song.
Igor Stravinsky, *Duo Concertant*, chamber music.

Film

George Cukor, *A Bill of Divorcement*, starring John Barrymore and Katharine Hepburn.

Edmund Goulding, *Grand Hotel*, starring Greta Garbo and Joan Crawford.

Norman Z. McLeod, *Horse Feathers*, starring the Marx Brothers.

Josef von Sternberg, *Blonde Venus*, starring Marlene Dietrich, Herbert Marshall and Cary Grant.

W.S. Van Dyke, *Tarzan the Ape Man*, starring former Olympic swimmer Johnny Weissmuller.

1933

EUROPE

4 Jan. Adolf Hitler (see p. 509) and Franz von Papen meet and conspire to oust Kurt von Schleicher as German chancellor.

30 Jan. Adolf Hitler becomes German chancellor at the head of a minority right-wing coalition government largely composed of conservatives and nationalists who served in the previous administration; Franz von Papen becomes deputy chancellor. Papen and his conservative colleagues assume, since Hitler's National Socialists do not command a majority in the new cabinet, that they will be able to control him.

9 Feb. In Britain the Oxford University Union debates the motion 'that this house refuses in any circumstances to fight for King and Country'. The motion is carried by 275 votes to 153.

27 Feb. The Reichstag (German parliament) burns down; the Nazi regime uses the fire to justify its first repressive measures: the Decree of the Reich President for Protection of People and State suspends civil liberties in Germany. Hitler blames the German Communist Party (KPD) for the fire; Communist deputies are arrested and their offices and newspapers are closed.

5 Mar. In federal elections in Germany Hitler's National Socialists win 44% of the vote but fail to win an overall majority.

7 Mar. The conservative Austrian chancellor Engelbert Dollfuss suspends parliament but will soon be overwhelmed by events as pro-German sentiment sweeps Austria in the wake of the Nazis' rise to power in Germany. Austrian Nazis mount a mass demonstration which leads to rioting in Vienna (29 Mar.).

8 Mar. Nazi interior minister Wilhelm Frick announces the establishment of concentration camps. Dachau, near Munich, opens on 20 Mar. and will house communists and other opponents of the new regime.

13 Mar. Joseph Goebbels becomes Reich minister of public enlightenment and propaganda.

15 Mar. In Germany Hitler proclaims a Third Reich. An Enabling Act (23 Mar.) allows him to rule by decree until 1937. Hitler has quickly and easily established a personal dictatorship and now loses no time in imposing his racial policies: a racial hygiene department is established in the interior ministry (22 Mar.). The government offers cash rewards to families who produce Aryan children, while Jews are expelled from the civil service. Jewish shops and businesses are boycotted throughout Germany (1 April).

2 May Trade unions associated with the Social Democratic Party are banned by the Nazis.

14 July The National Socialist Party is declared the only legal political party in Germany.

15 July Italy, Germany, France and Britain sign a four-power pact. The pact will never be ratified, however.

Sept. In Ireland Cumann na nGaedheal, the pro-treaty party, which governed the Irish Free State from independence in 1921 until 1932, is subsumed into a new party, Fine Gael, comprising Cumann na nGaedheal and other, smaller, parties.

14 Oct. Hitler announces that Germany will withdraw from the League of Nations and the World Disarmament Conference (which has achieved nothing since it assembled in Feb. 1932).

12 Nov. In elections to the German Reichstag, 92% of voters vote for the Nazis.

30 Nov. In Nazi Germany Hermann Goering creates the Gestapo (*Geheime Staatspolizei* or secret state police) as an instrument of state terror.

– In Portugal prime minister António Salazar inaugurates what will be Europe's longest-lasting fascist state. The former university economics professor writes a new constitution for a 'unitary and corporative republic'. Salazar will rule personally until 1968 and the fascist regime will survive until 1974.

– In Spain José Antonio Primo de Rivera, son of former military ruler Miguel Primo de Rivera, founds the Falange Española (the Spanish Falange) Fascist Party. The Falange Party will be closely modelled on the Italian Fascists and the German Nazis.

ASIA

Feb.–Mar. Japan takes the N Chinese city of Jehol (now Chengde).

27 Mar. Japan declares that it will leave the League of Nations.

31 May An armistice is declared between China and Japan. Japanese forces withdraw to N of the Great Wall (Aug.).

8 Nov. Mohammed Nadir Shah, king of Afghanistan, is assassinated and is succeeded by his son, Zahir Shah.

THE AMERICAS

14 Feb. In the USA the city of Detroit defaults on its debts.

15 Feb. In the USA Anton Cermak, mayor of Chicago, is shot by a bullet intended for president-elect Franklin D. Roosevelt. Cermak dies on 6 Mar.

4 Mar. Franklin D. Roosevelt is inaugurated as 32nd president of the USA, declaring in the ceremony that 'the only thing we have to fear is fear itself'. He will serve in office for 12 years; in his first 100 days he will lay the foundation of the New Deal. This involves a dramatic extension of presidential and federal power: Roosevelt forbids the export of gold (5 Mar.), and by the Emergency Banking Act (6 Mar.) gains control over all banking transactions and foreign exchange. It also makes the hoarding or export of gold illegal. Banks begin to reopen (13 Mar.), and within three days three-quarters of the closed banks are open again. Roosevelt's presidential order (5 April) requires the surrender of all private gold holdings to the Federal Reserve in exchange for other coins or currency. By a presidential proclamation the USA abandons the Gold Standard (19 April). The Federal Emergency Relief Act (12 May) creates a $500 million fund to be distributed among the states. The Home Owners Loan Corporation established by Congress (13 June) grants loans to stop foreclosures on mortgages. The Glass–Steagall Act, signed into law by the president on 16 June, stops banks from speculating in stocks and shares. The National Industrial Recovery Act passed by Congress (16 June) encourages collective bargaining in the labour force. The president's regular 'fireside chats', a series of radio talks from the White House, boost morale.

30 April President Sanchez Cerro of Peru is assassinated and succeeded by Oscar Benavides.

9 Nov. The Civil Works Administration is established by US president Franklin D. Roosevelt to create jobs for the 4 million unemployed Americans.

16 Nov. The government of the USA establishes diplomatic relations with the USSR.

5 Dec. The 21st amendment to the US constitution is ratified. This repeals the 18th amendment, thus ending prohibition.

– Fiorello La Guardia is elected mayor of New York and embarks on a reform programme, tackling corruption, increasing slum clearances and improving social services.

ECONOMY AND SOCIETY

– French civil airline Air France is founded.

– In cricket England regains the Ashes from Australia, but England's use of 'bodyline' (short-pitched bowling directed at the batsman's body) to counter the threat posed by Australia's master batsman Don Bradman comes close to causing a diplomatic rift between Britain and Australia.

1–2 April In a cricket test match against New Zealand, English batsman Walter Hammond scores 336, a new record individual score for a batsman.

– Forrest Mars (son of Frank C. Mars, see 1922 and 1924) launches the Mars Bar in Slough, SE England.

SCIENCE AND TECHNOLOGY

– American physicist Carl David Anderson discovers positrons (positively charged electrons).

– British biochemist Ernest Kennaway isolates the first chemical carcinogens when he finds that the hydrocarbons present in cigarette smoke and air pollution can cause cancer.

ARTS AND HUMANITIES

Literature

31 Jan. The novelist John Galsworthy dies.

– The US district court at New York adjudicates that Irish writer James Joyce's *Ulysses* (see 1922) may be published in the USA.

Noël Coward, *Design for Living*, stage comedy.

André Malraux, *La Condition humaine* (The Human Lot), novel describing the anti-colonial struggle in French Indochina.

Pablo Neruda (Ricardo Reyes), *Residencia en la tierra* (Residence on Earth), poetry.

George Orwell (Eric Blair), *Down and Out in Paris and London*, social commentary.

Gertrude Stein, *The Autobiography of Alice B. Toklas*, memoir.

Visual Arts and Architecture

– The German Nazi government starts its campaign against artistic modernism and promotes a sterile representational style; many artists, including Kandinsky and Klee, leave Germany.

– Falling Water, a house near Pittsburgh, Pennsylvania, designed by Frank Lloyd Wright, is completed. It consists of cantilevered terraces straddling a waterfall.

Alberto Giacometti, *The Palace at four a.m.*, sculpture.

Music

1 July First performance in Dresden of Richard Strauss's opera *Arabella*.

Oct. Austrian composer Arnold Schoenberg (see box) leaves Germany for the USA. He is one of thousands of German cultural figures, Jewish and otherwise, fleeing the Nazi state.

Arnold Schoenberg (1874–1951)

The Austrian-born composer Arnold Schoenberg, who re-defined classical music for the 20th century, was a product of Vienna's intellectual and cultural flowering at the end of the 19th century. Along with his pupils Anton Webern and Alban Berg he formed what became known as the Second Viennese School (the First had included Haydn, Mozart, Beethoven and Schubert). He taught in Vienna and in Berlin, but left Germany when the rise of the Nazi Party made him unwelcome as a Jew. He emigrated to the USA, where he lived in California in straitened circumstances.

Schoenberg's early works, such as the programmatic chamber piece *Verklärte Nacht* (Transfigured Night, 1899), are characterized by a lush late Romanticism, influenced by Brahms and Wagner. But from 1907 Schoenberg began to abandon tonality, the principle that each piece should be dominated by a particle key. His works from this experimental period, such as the monodrama *Erwartung* (Expectation, 1909) for soprano and orchestra, are often described as 'expressionist', as they depict raw emotion and extreme states of mind.

But Schoenberg was concerned with the need to find a new organizing principle for music, now that tonality had been abandoned, and in about 1921 came up with his '12-note system'. The 12 notes concerned are all the semi-tones that make up the chromatic scale in an octave, and in any one piece a particular 'note row', using each of these notes in a particular order, becomes the organizing principle. Schoenberg saw this method as providing a 'higher and better order', and showed in such works as his opera *Moses und Aron* (1930–2) that it was far from limiting to creativity. The 12-note system was to dominate the avant-garde of Western music for much of the 20th century.

Béla Bartók, *Hungarian Peasant Songs*.

Dmitri Shostakovich, Concerto for Piano, Trumpet and String Orchestra.

Film

Merian C. Cooper and Ernest B. Schoedsack, *King Kong*, starring Fay Wray.

George Cukor, *Dinner at Eight*, starring Jean Harlow.

Alexander Korda, *The Private Life of Henry VIII*, starring Charles Laughton.

Fritz Lang, *The Testament of Dr Mabuse*.

Mervyn LeRoy, *Gold Diggers of 1933*, starring Ginger Rogers.

Rouben Mamoulian, *Queen Christina*, starring Greta Garbo.

Leo McCarey, *Duck Soup*, starring the Marx Brothers.

Lowell Sherman, *She Done Him Wrong*, in which Mae West delivers the line, 'Come up and see me sometime.'

Jean Vigo, *Zéro de conduite* (Zero for Conduct).

1934

EUROPE

3 Jan. In France the Stavisky affair reaches a climax. Serge Stavisky, a dealer in fraudulent bonds who has been protected by government officials, commits suicide. The royalist right and communist left both claim that he has been murdered as part of a cover-up protecting highly placed government figures. Demonstrators protesting against government corruption riot in Paris (6–7 Feb.) and a general strike takes place. The affair shows the shallow base of the Third Republic, but does at least lead to the establishing of a coalition government freed of the taint of corruption.

12 Feb. In Austria a workers' rising is suppressed by the regime of Engelbert Dollfuss. Dollfuss dissolves all political parties apart from his own Fatherland Front. The police raid the socialists' headquarters in Vienna.

19 May Fascism arrives in Bulgaria when a coup, actively aided by King Boris III, establishes a new government, which leads to a royal dictatorship.

30 June In Germany Hitler (see p. 509) brings the revolutionary elements in his movement to heel in the Night of the Long Knives. The violence of the *Sturm Abteilung* or SA (Stormtroopers) was essential in undermining the Weimar republic and gaining Hitler power, but now it is proving a liability. He accuses its leadership, under Ernst Röhm, of plotting a coup, and dozens are summarily executed, including Röhm. Hitler also uses the opportunity to rid himself of enemies from the past, such as former colleague Gregor Stresser, who turned against him, and former chancellor Kurt von Schleicher. A total of 170 leading Nazis are killed. Despite the absence of any evidence, most Germans are relieved to see the end of the SA's violence. The army is now much more willing to accept Hitler's leadership. His action paves the way for his assumption of the presidency of Germany.

20 July After the purging of the SA, the SS (*Schutzstaffel*, 'guard units') is founded as an organization independent of the SA, with Heinrich Himmler as its leader.

25 July In a move intended to lead to Austria's unification with Germany, Austrian Nazis occupy Vienna's radio station and broadcast that Chancellor Dollfuss has resigned. They then assassinate Dollfuss. Italian dictator Benito Mussolini, however, has no wish at this time to have a Greater Germany on his frontiers and sends troops to Italy's border with Austria. This deters any action by Hitler. Kurt von Schuschnigg succeeds Dollfuss (30 July) and suppresses the Austrian Nazis. Austrian independence has survived, at least temporarily.

2 Aug. German President Paul von Hindenburg dies and a plebiscite gives Adolf Hitler the presidency (19 Aug.). He declares himself *Führer* (Leader) and Reich chancellor. As both head of state and head of government, there is no constitutional way to remove him.

18 Sept. The USSR joins the League of Nations. Soviet leader Joseph Stalin is alarmed by the rise of Hitler and hopes the League will be able to curb his territorial ambitions.

9 Oct. Alexander I of Yugoslavia is assassinated in Marseilles. Croat separatists working from Hungary have participated in the murder. Yugoslavia and Hungary come close to war, but the League of Nations, for once, is effective and prevents war. Peter II, his son, succeeds Alexander.

1 Dec. In Leningrad, USSR, Sergei Kirov, a close associate of Joseph Stalin, is murdered (possibly with Stalin's connivance). More than 100 are executed following the murder, in response to what Stalin claims is a wide-ranging conspiracy. These events mark the beginning of the Great Purge (reaching its climax 1936–8), in which many Bolsheviks who took part in the revolution of 1917, along with anyone suspected of any form of dissent, will be killed in their thousands. Millions of others will end up in the *gulags* (labour camps).

– The Swiss parliament enacts its Bank Secrecy Law, and the Swiss banking system organizes its system of numbered bank accounts with the number written in script being the depositor's signature. The scheme originally helps German Jews.

– In Germany the *Erzeugungsschlacht* (battle for production) programme aims to revive and expand domestic agriculture. The Nazis have an idealized view of the German peasantry as the backbone of the nation, but despite their efforts the flight from the land accelerates as young people seek less onerous work in the expanding war industries.

– In Scotland the Scottish National Party is formed from the amalgamation of the National Party of Scotland and the Scottish Party.

MIDDLE EAST AND NORTH AFRICA

25 Nov. In Turkey Mustafa Kemal (Kemal Atatürk) states that all Turks must assume surnames as a westernizing measure. His own will be Atatürk or 'Father of the Turks'.

ASIA

21 Oct. In China communist leader Mao Zedong (Mao Tse-tung) (see p. 573) starts the Long March. Acting on the advice of agents of the Comintern, Chinese communists have abandoned their successful guerrilla tactics and attempt to defend their S China base at Jiangxi. This leads to their near extermination. The communist forces have no choice but to break out and flee to Yunnan in the far NW of China. The Long March will enter into the collective consciousness of the Chinese Communist Party. It will last a year, cross 18 mountain ranges and cover 9655km (6000 miles). Some 68,000 of the 90,000 men under Mao's command will be lost in action as they fight rearguard actions against the Guomindang.

THE AMERICAS

12 Feb. The Export-Import Bank of Washington is created. Its capital finances (mostly drawn from the Reconstruction Finance Corporation) finances the export and import of commodities.

21 Feb. Gen. Anastasio Somoza, of the Nicaraguan National Guard, invites Gen. Augusto César Sandino to a meeting. Sandino, a hero of the local resistance to the US occupation of 1927–33, is murdered when he arrives for the meeting. But his memory will live in the movement named after him, the Sandinistas. In 1936 Somoza will seize power in a military coup.

23 Feb. The Crop Loan Act is passed by the US Congress and grants loans to farmers to help them until the harvest arrives. The Farm Bankruptcy Act (28 June) postpones mortgage fore-closures for five years.

23 May US criminals Clyde Barrow and Bonnie Parker are killed in a police ambush near Gibsland, Louisiana, after a two-year career of robbery, violence and murder in Texas, Oklahoma, Missouri and Iowa.

May Dust storms devastate the topsoil in Kansas, N Texas, E Colorado and Oklahoma. With agricultural prices falling during the Great Depression, plains farmers have removed the hedges, trees and ditches that sheltered their land in a bid to increase the acreage under production, but these methods prove environmentally unsustainable. Between 1933 and 1937 some 300,000 'Okies' migrate to California in search of work.

12 June US Congress passes the Reciprocal Trade Agreement Act, which allows the President to negotiate tariff reductions: 18 such agreements follow in the next four years and, now that protectionism is seen to have contributed to – and not alleviated – the recession, world trade increases.

2 July Gen. Lázaro Cárdenas, minister of war, is elected president of Mexico and the constitution is amended to allow him to serve for six years. Despite being the nominee of the reactionary former president Plutarco Calles, Cárdenas wishes to 'revive the revolutionary activity of the masses'. He will resume the large-scale programme of land distribution to the pueblos (villages) and encourage trade union organization.

16 July The USA has its first general strike, in San Francisco, called to support the cause of the striking stevedores association led by union leader Harry Bridges.

22 July American bank robber John Dillinger, Public Enemy No. 1, is ambushed and killed by the FBI.

July The Brazilian assembly introduces a new constitution. Getúlio Vargas is elected president the same month.

Aug. US marines withdraw from Haiti after 19 years of military occupation.

– Roosevelt's New Deal meets its first organized resistance in the Liberty League, a group of industrialists (including the du Ponts), who see the extension of federal powers as a threat to their businesses.

– Drought throughout the USA will reduce the corn crop by one million bushels.

– Senator Huey Long of Louisiana, a populist and reactionary redistributist, presents his Share Our Wealth Program. He has already embarked on substantial public buildings programmes in Louisiana. His quick-fix solution attracts considerable attention in a depression-torn nation, but he is unable to unify the various radical movements in the USA. His appeal will wane before his assassination in 1935.

– Alcatraz Island, San Francisco Bay, is transferred from the US army to the Bureau of Prisons. The former army prison will house many of the USA's most notorious criminals.

SUB-SAHARAN AFRICA

– Ethiopian and Italian troops engage in hostilities at Ualula on the frontier between Italian Somaliland and Abyssinia (Ethiopia). The incident will be used by Mussolini to justify his decision to invade Abyssinia (1935).

ECONOMY AND SOCIETY

Mar. In Britain the Road Traffic Act introduces driving tests for the first time.

May–June Italy, the host nation, wins the 2nd soccer World Cup.

– The first US Masters golf tournament is held at the Augusta National Golf Club, Georgia.

– Shipping line Cunard merges with the White Star Line.

SCIENCE AND TECHNOLOGY

– Laurens Hammond of Chicago, USA, a clock maker, patents his invention, the Hammond Organ, the world's first pipeless organ.

– Monosodium glutamate becomes available commercially in the USA.

– About this time the Italian physicist Enrico Fermi discovers that energy can be got from the splitting of atomic nuclei into smaller pieces. In an uncontrolled form nuclear fission will be the principle behind the atomic weapons that the USA uses against Japan in 1945.

ARTS AND HUMANITIES

– The publication in Germany of *Macht und Erde* (Power and Earth), a geopolitical study by geographer Karl Haushofer, shows the extent of the infiltration of Nazi ideology in German aca-demic life. The book puts forward the claim that an expansionist Germany has a natural geopolitical right to dominate Eurasia.

Literature

– At the first Congress of Soviet Writers in the USSR, Socialist Realism is adopted as the official style for Soviet novelists.

Agatha Christie, *Murder on the Orient Express*, novel.

Jean Cocteau, *La Machine infernale* (The Infernal Machine), play.

F. Scott Fitzgerald, *Tender is the Night*, novel.

Federico García Lorca, *Yerma*, play.

Robert Graves, *I, Claudius* and *Claudius the God*, historical novels.

Dashiell Hammett, *The Thin Man*, novel.

James Hilton, *Goodbye, Mr Chips*, novel.

Henry de Montherlant, *Les Célibataires* (The Bachelors), novel.

George Orwell, *Burmese Days*, memoir.

John Cowper Powys, *Weymouth Sands*, novel.

Dorothy L(eigh) Sayers, *The Nine Tailors*, novel.

Mikhail Sholokhov, *And Quiet Flows the Don*, the first of the four-volume Russian epic is published in English for the first time.

Irving Stone, *Lust for Life*, novel fictionalizing the life of Vincent Van Gogh.

Evelyn Waugh, *A Handful of Dust*, novel.

Visual Arts and Architecture

– The Mexican muralists Diego Rivera, José Orozco and David Alfaro Siqueiros return to Mexico in triumph; they have, individually, made international reputations in their field and established the prestige of modern Mexican art.

René Magritte, *The Human Condition* and *The Rape*, paintings.

Pablo Picasso (see p. 467), *The Bullfight*, painting.

Music

22 Jan. First performance in Leningrad of Dmitri Shostakovich's opera *Ledi Makbet Mtsenskovo uyezda* (Lady Macbeth of the Mtsensk District). It is too radical for the Soviet authorities, who denounce it as 'un-Soviet, eccentric, tuneless and leftist'.

23 Feb. The English composer Edward Elgar dies in Worcester.

20 May First performance of Virgil Thomson's opera *Four Saints in Three Acts*, for which Gertrude Stein provides the libretto.

28 May The first Glyndebourne Festival begins in Sussex, S England with a production of Mozart's *Le nozze di Figaro*. John Christie, a music lover and husband of the soprano Audrey Mildmay, builds an opera house in the grounds of his Elizabethan country house at Glyndebourne.

– The Berkshire Music festival is held on the Tappan family estate near Lennox, Massachusetts. The Boston Symphony will take over the festival under the direction of Serge Koussevitsky (1936).

Ernest Bloch, *Avodath Hakodesh* (Sacred Service) for baritone, cantor, chorus and orchestra.

Noël Coward, *Conversation Piece*, musical starring George Sanders.

Duke Ellington, 'Solitude', tune.

Hugues Panassie, *Le Jazz Hot*, a book giving jazz its first serious work of analysis.

Cole Porter, *Anything Goes*, musical including the songs 'Anything Goes', 'I Get a Kick out of You' and 'You're the Top'.

Sergei Rachmaninov, *Rhapsody on a Theme of Paganini*, for piano and orchestra.

Film

– English film distributor J. Arthur Rank founds British National Films at Elstree, England. Studios will also be built in Denham and Iver (Pinewood Studios).

Frank Capra, *It Happened One Night*, starring Clark Gable and Claudette Colbert.

Jack Conway and Cedric Gibbons, *Tarzan and His Mate*, starring Johnny Weissmuller.

George Cukor, *David Copperfield*, starring W.C. Fields.

Rowland V. Lee, *The Count of Monte Cristo*, starring Robert Donat.

Hamilton McFadden, *Stand Up and Cheer*, film providing Shirley Temple with her debut.

W.S.Van Dyke, *The Thin Man*, starring William Powell and Myrna Loy.

Jean Vigo, *L'Atalante*, starring Jean Daste.

1935

EUROPE

13 Jan. The League of Nations organizes a referendum in the Saarland, which has been under League of Nations administration since 1920. The referendum shows that a 9 to 1 majority of the population prefer reunion with Germany to either of the other options: union with France or administration by the League. The region is reunited with Germany (1 Mar.).

April The prime ministers of Britain, France and Italy meet at Stresa in Italy. The resulting 'Stresa Front' is intended to counter German rearmament, but will soon fail in its purpose.

31 May The French government falls, a victim of the deteriorating position of the French franc. Pierre Laval becomes prime minister (4 June).

May As part of the reborn internationalism of the left, the Soviet Comintern urges communists to cooperate with others of the left in broad-based coalitions and in government in order to oppose fascism.

7 June In Britain the Conservative Stanley Baldwin replaces Ramsay MacDonald as leader of the National Government.

18 June Hitler signs an agreement with Britain promising not to expand the German fleet to more than 35% of that of the Royal Navy's surface fleet. The French are outraged that the British accept what is a violation of the treaty of Versailles. Hitler also secretly recreates the Luftwaffe (German air force, prohibited by the treaty of Versailles) with Hermann Goering as the air minister, and reintroduces conscription. German rearmament is now proceeding rapidly and ever more openly. Britain is beginning to pursue a policy of appeasement of Germany.

14 July Following a mass meeting in London, the antiwar Peace Pledge Union is founded.

30 Aug. Soviet miner Alexei Stakhanov and his team in a mine in the Donets basin are reported by the Soviet authorities to have shifted 14 times the average amount of coal in a single shift. The example of 'Stakhanovites' is used to attempt to increase the productivity of Soviet industry.

15 Sept. Meeting at its congress in Nuremberg, the Nazi Party approves the Nuremberg Laws, which deprive all Jews of German citizenship and forbid intermarriage between Aryan Germans and Jews. The definition of a Jew is extended (14 Nov.). It now includes the issue of marriages between Jews and gentiles, or *Mischlinge*; they are graded according to the generations of descent.

3 Nov. In France socialist groups merge into one united grouping under Léon Blum, and will later unite with other left-wing parties (including the communists) to form an anti-fascist Popular Front.

14 Nov. In Britain Stanley Baldwin's Conservatives resoundingly defeat the Labour Party, now led by Clement Attlee, who has replaced George Lansbury.

14 Dec. Tomáš Masaryk, the first president of Czechoslovakia and guiding spirit of the liberal Czech order, resigns from office. Eduard Beneš, the foreign minister, succeeds him.

– In Germany Heinrich Himmler, leader of the Nazi SS, has now started a eugenic breeding programme designed to produce an Aryan master race.

– As it enters the period of its greatest ineffectiveness, the League of Nations moves into a lavish new headquarters in Geneva.

– In Britain King George V celebrates his silver jubilee.

MIDDLE EAST AND NORTH AFRICA

– Persian ruler Reza Shah Pahlavi changes Persia's name to Iran.

ASIA

– The Government of India Act grants responsible government in domestic matters to provincial assemblies and attempts to create a new federal structure.

– Rama VII of Siam (Thailand) abdicates, and is succeeded by his 10-year-old nephew Rama VIII. Royal absolutism has now been abolished in Siam.

THE AMERICAS

27 May The US Supreme Court rules that the National Industrial Recovery Act is unconstitutional (see 1933). When it rules that the Railway Pensions Act (1934) is also unconstitutional (27 June), Congress passes a Railway Retirement Act to achieve the same effect, with the rail companies and their employees having to pay 3.5% of the first $300 earned each month in order to provide a pension.

12 June The three-year old Chaco dispute between Bolivia and Paraguay ends, but a peace treaty to resolve the disputed territory of Chaco will not be signed for another three years.

14 Aug. In the USA the Social Security Act becomes law, providing a programme of unemployment benefits and old age annuities.

23 Aug. In the USA the Banking Act increases the authority of the Federal Reserve system, created in 1913, and aims to establish the nation's money supply. Fort Knox is established in N Kentucky as the US Gold Bullion Depository.

30 Aug. The Revenue Act passed by the US Congress attempts some wealth redistribution and provides for taxation on inheritance and gifts. President Roosevelt has publicized a report from the Internal Revenue Service stating that 0.1% of US corporations own 52% of all corporate assets, and less than 5% own 87% of all corporate assets.

8 Sept. Huey Long, governor of Louisiana, is shot and killed by Dr Carl Austin Weiss. New Orleans has developed as a gambler's paradise during Long's governorship, and his unique brand of populism has alarmed many (see 1934).

18 Dec. Juan Vincente Gomez, president and dictator of Venezuela for 26 years, dies. He is succeeded by Gen. Eleázar López Contreras.

SUB-SAHARAN AFRICA

3 Oct. Italy invades Abyssinia from the Italian colony of Eritrea. Anglo-French attempts at appeasement have not satisfied Mussolini's craving for an Italian imperial role, seen grandiloquently as a revival of ancient Rome's imperium in *mare nostrum* (the Mediterranean). Italian troops occupy the Abyssinian city of Makale (8 Nov.), and in the first major international test of its authority the League of Nations imposes economic sanctions on Italy (18 Nov.). The British and French, however, have no desire to alienate a possible partner in containing German ambitions, and they ensure that the sanctions are limited. British foreign secretary Samuel Hoare and the French premier Pierre Laval suggest a secret deal (the Hoare–Laval Pact), which would surrender most of Abyssinia to the Italians, but when it leaks to the press, public outrage forces the resignation of Hoare (18 Dec.) and Laval (23 Jan. 1936). Mussolini is indeed alienated and seeks better relations with Hitler, while the League is seriously weakened.

ECONOMY AND SOCIETY

14 Jan. The Lower Zambezi railroad bridge opens and is (until Dec.) the world's longest such bridge.

May The Metropol underground system opens in Moscow.

10 June Reformed American alcoholics Bill Wilson and Robert Smith found Alcoholics Anonymous in New York.

10 Dec. The Huey Long Bridge is completed in Metairie, Louisiana.

– American statistician George Gallup of Iowa establishes the American Institute of Public Opinion, whose polls are designed to test readers' responses to newspaper articles.

– The Irish government outlaws the advertisement, importation and the sale of any artificial forms of birth control.

SCIENCE AND TECHNOLOGY

– During the year Scottish physicist Robert Watson-Watt starts to install radar warning systems along the coast of Britain.

– Charles Richter, a US seismologist, devises his scale for measuring earthquakes.

ARTS AND HUMANITIES
Literature

E.F. Benson, *Mapp and Lucia*, novel.

Elias Canetti, *Die Blendung* (The Blending), novel. It will be published in English as *Auto-da-Fé* in 1946.

T.S. Eliot, *Murder in the Cathedral*, play about the death of Thomas Becket, and 'Burnt Norton', the first poem of his *Four Quartets*.

William Empson, *Poems*.

Jean Giraudoux, *La Guerre de Troie n'aura pas lieu* (later translated by Christopher Fry (1955) as Tiger at the Gates), play.

Graham Greene, *England Made Me,* novel.

Christopher Isherwood, *Mr Norris Changes Trains*, novel.

Sinclair Lewis, *It Can't Happen Here*, novel warning against complacency about fascism.

P.G. Wodehouse, *Blandings Castle*, novel.

Visual Arts and Architecture

– The restoration of Williamsburg, Virginia, funded by US millionaire John D. Rockefeller, is completed.

Wallace Gilbert and Partners, Art Deco Hoover factory in W London.

Berthold Lubetkin, modernist Penguin Pool at London Zoo.

Ben Nicholson, *White Relief*, uncompromisingly abstract sculpture.

Music

10 Oct. First performance in New York of George Gershwin's opera *Porgy and Bess*.

12 Oct. The broadcasting of jazz music is banned in Germany.

24 Dec. Alban Berg, Austrian composer, dies in Vienna.

– US bandleader Benny (Benjamin David) Goodman evolves a new big band sound for jazz.

Film

28 Mar. Premiere of Leni Riefenstahl's *Triumph of the Will*, documentary of the Nuremberg rallies of 1934, one of the great propaganda films.

– The Academy Awards become the 'Oscars'.

Richard Boleslawski, *Les Misérables*, starring Charles Laughton.

Clarence Brown, *Anna Karenina*, starring Greta Garbo.

Alfred Hitchcock, *The Thirty-Nine Steps*, starring Robert Donat.

Mark Sandrich, *Top Hat*, musical starring Fred Astaire and Ginger Rogers.

James Whale, *The Bride of Frankenstein*, starring Elsa Lanchester and Boris Karloff.

1936

EUROPE

20 Jan. In Britain King George V dies. He is succeeded by his son Edward VIII who is in love with American divorcée Wallis Simpson.

23 Jan. Prime minister Pierre Laval of France resigns following criticism of the Hoare–Laval Pact (see 1935).

16 Feb. In Spain a Popular Front government, including socialist and communist elements, is elected. It introduces agrarian and other reforms that arouse the hostility of landlords and the Catholic Church. Interfactional violence explodes following the Popular Front victory.

7 Mar. The German army reoccupies the Rhineland while world powers are distracted by Italy's war in Abyssinia (see 1935). This is forbidden under the treaty of Versailles, but neither the British nor the French will risk war to eject German troops. This leaves Germany with secure frontiers and allows Hitler to attempt a more adventurous foreign policy. Hitler now denounces the Locarno Pact of 1925.

3 May In France the Popular Front (consisting of left-wing parties) gains a majority in the general election. Léon Blum, leader of the socialists, becomes prime minister and forms a government (5 June). Strikes give way to reforms, including a minimum wage and 40-hour week (12 June), reorganization of the Banque de France (30 June) and nationalization of the arms industry (17 July). But inflation returns with a vengeance as capital is sent abroad, production costs increase and rearmament needs dominate government spending. France abandons the Gold Standard (27 Sept.), and the franc is devalued (2 Oct.). Many working-class gains are subsequently lost, leaving the social and political divisions within France more bitter than ever.

17 July Right-wing nationalist army officers at Melilla, in Spanish Morocco, rebel against Spain's republican government. Rebellion soon spreads among the army garrison towns of Cadiz, Seville, Saragossa and Burgos. But the easy victory the rebels expect does not materialize as many troops and police remain loyal to the government. Civil war engulfs Spain when the government arms trade union militias. The leaders of the revolt, Gen. Francisco Franco and Gen. Emilio Mola (until his death on 3 June 1937), form a Junta of National Defence, in reality a form of provisional government (30 July). The rebels soon receive German and Italian men and matériel. The government looks to the USSR for aid, but Stalin will provide only limited, and expensive, help. Despite widespread sympathy for the government cause, which leads many individuals to volunteer to fight, the governments of the USA, Britain and France refuse to intervene.

Aug. In the USSR the first show trials of Stalin's purges are held. Former politburo members and colleagues of Lenin, Grigori Zinoviev and Lev Kamenev are sentenced to death for treason.

19 Oct. Germany embarks on its Four-year Plan for economic growth, designed to prepare the nation for war by late 1940.

25 Oct. An Axis or coalition is formed between Germany and Italy, which will become a full military alliance in 1939.

6 Nov. In Spain rebel forces lay siege to Madrid. Gen. Emilio Mola invents a new and potent phrase when asked which of his four columns will seize the city. A 'fifth column' will do it, says Mola, referring to nationalist sympathizers within the city ready to take up arms. This will be widely accepted as the explanation of rapid fascist victories anywhere and will lead to unreasonable fears of internal enemies in any country under threat.

25 Nov. Germany and Japan sign an Anti-Comintern Pact against the USSR. Italy will join the Pact in 1937.

Nov. During the siege of Madrid, republican defenders of the city are reinforced by members of the International Brigade of anti-fascist volunteers, formed by the Comintern to fight against the rebels in Spain.

Nov.–Dec. The abdication crisis in Britain: Edward VIII informs the prime minister Stanley Baldwin that he intends to marry Wallis Simpson, a twice-divorced US citizen (16 Nov.). Baldwin and others warn that the marriage would undermine the king's position as head of the Church of England and provoke a constitutional crisis. The British press breaks its self-imposed silence on the issue (3 Dec.). Faced with the decision to remain king or give up Mrs Simpson, Edward VIII chooses to abdicate, announcing his intention in a historic radio broadcast (11 Dec.).

– In Germany Heinrich Himmler, head of the Prussian police and the Gestapo (*Geheime Staatspolizei*, secret state police) is appointed chief of German police by Hitler. Himmler centralizes Germany's police force, bringing political police (Gestapo) and criminal police (Kripo) together in a security police force (Sipo).

– In Britain 200 men from the unemployment blackspot of Jarrow on the Tyne in NE England march to London in the Jarrow Crusade, led by the local MP, 'Red Ellen' Wilkinson.

– Armenia, Azerbaijan, Georgia and Kazakhstan become Soviet Socialist Republics within the USSR.

– The *Yezhovschina* or Great Purge starts in the USSR as Stalin exterminates his political opponents on a vast scale. Between 8 and 10 million people will be killed in the next two years, while the population of the gulags or prison camps becomes a slave labour force essential to the Soviet economy.

– The USSR restricts abortion to cases where the mother's life is threatened or the unborn child is likely to suffer from a disease.

MIDDLE EAST AND NORTH AFRICA

28 April King Fuad I of Egypt dies and is succeeded by his son Farouk, a playboy.

April Arab unrest erupts in Palestine.

26 Aug. Britain's protectorate over Egypt is ended by treaty. Britain agrees to grant full Egyptian independence and to maintain a military presence only in the Suez Canal zone.

– In Lebanon Pierre Gemayel, a Maronite Christian, founds the Phalanges Libanaises (Lebanese Phalange) to defend the interests of Maronite Christians in the Lebanon.

ASIA

26 Feb. Japanese politics is destabilized by an attempted military coup in Tokyo. A group of army officers kill the former prime minister, Saito Makoto, and the finance minister Takahashi Korekiyo. Seventeen of the officers are sentenced to death (7 July).

THE AMERICAS

2 June Gen. Anastasio Somoza deposes President Juan Sacasa of Nicaragua. He becomes president (1937) and his family will establish a personal regime of systematic corruption and brutality until the end of the dictatorship (see 1979).

29 June US Congress passes the Merchant Marine Act providing federal subsidies to offset the higher operating costs of US shipping lines and the lower ones of foreign lines.

3 Nov. F.D. Roosevelt is re-elected president of the USA, carrying every state except Maine and Vermont. New Deal propagandists now denounce their opponents as 'economic royalists', a term that reflects Roosevelt's anti-imperialism.

SUB-SAHARAN AFRICA

5 May The Italian army occupies Addis Ababa, and Italy formally annexes Ethiopia (9 May). The country is annexed to Eritrea and Italian Somaliland to create Italian East Africa. The conflict becomes emblematic of the battle between the military might of the developed world and the barefoot warriors of Africa,

---

John Maynard Keynes (1883–1946)

The English economist John Maynard Keynes had a profound practical impact on 20th-century life. His *General Theory of Employment, Interest and Money* (1936) changed the way Western governments organized public expenditure from 1945 until the 1970s, and was a reaction against the politics of mass unemployment. His work justified government intervention in the economy and argued that the state should itself be an investor in capital projects. By these means the 'Keynesianism' of the postwar world encouraged the goal of full employment.

In 1919 Keynes was appointed the British Treasury's representative at the Versailles Peace Conference. He resigned that post because of his disagreement with the reparations payments imposed on Germany and wrote *The Economic Consequences of the Peace*, a work that established the interwar liberal view that Germany had been unfairly treated.

The conventional economics of the time maintained that unemployment was caused by high wages or low productivity. Keynes argued that lower wages only reduced consumer demand. He believed the answer to unemployment was what he called 'the multiplier' – the effect that government stimulation of economic activity had on a whole economy. Keynes argued that excessive expansion could be controlled by cutting government expenditure and raising taxes. This 'Demand Management' theory maintained that demand creates its own supply.

Keynes supplied the theoretical framework for what many earlier governments had practised. The 1939–45 war produced its own economic boom as governments started to control economies and stimulate growth on an unprecedented scale. Keynes's theories ensured the rising living standards and social cohesion of postwar Europe. In time, however, this boom produced runaway inflation, and economists became disillusioned by the uncritical application of Keynesianism, dubbing it 'boom-and-bust economics'.

---

many of whom have been killed by bombs and mustard gas. Haile Selassie addresses the League of Nations (30 June) to demand 'the justice that is due to my people'. Despite widespread public sympathy, the governments of the great powers ignore his pleas.

ECONOMY AND SOCIETY

Aug. The 11th Olympic Games are held in Berlin. African-American sprinter Jesse Owens wins four gold medals. Hitler, however, leaves the stadium rather than present the medals to an African-American who has defeated Aryan competitors.

– English economist John Maynard Keynes (see box) achieves a Copernican revolution in economics with his *General Theory of Employment, Interest and Money*. Government investment in capital work projects and the encouragement of production by stimulating consumption can, he maintains, rescue the capitalist system, which he sees as the only practical way of increasing the wealth of nations. But the system does need to be rescued, says Keynes, from its periodic cycles of recession, and this can be managed by government action. As if to illustrate his immediate impact, France, Switzerland and the Netherlands abandon the Gold Standard (27 Sept.).

– American baseball player Joe DiMaggio signs with the New York Yankees at the start of a 15-year career.

SCIENCE AND TECHNOLOGY

May Gatwick Airport in Sussex, S England, begins a scheduled service to Paris.

Oct. The London–Paris night train service between Victoria Station and the Gare du Nord is introduced.

2 Nov. Transmitting from Crystal Palace in S London, the BBC (British Broadcasting Corporation) establishes the world's first high-definition television service.

– The British liner SS *Queen Mary* goes into service for the Cunard White Star line on the North Atlantic.

– In Britain the Spitfire fighter aircraft is designed by R.J. Mitchell.

– Tampax Inc. is founded in New Brunswick, New Jersey, USA, and commercial tampons become available for the first time.

ARTS AND HUMANITIES

Literature

18 Jan. The English writer Rudyard Kipling dies.

19 Aug. Spanish fascists murder the poet and playwright Federico García Lorca.

– In Britain Victor Gollancz founds the Left Book Club. Its aim is to oppose the rise of fascism and its most famous publication will be Orwell's *The Road to Wigan Pier* (see 1937).

– In Britain Penguin Books Ltd is established by Allen Lane and achieves a transformation in publishing with its paperback editions.

– Russian actor and theatre director Konstantin Stanislavsky publishes *An Actor Prepares*, a manual describing his ideas on acting.

Georges Bernanos, *Journal d'un curé de campagne* (Diary of a Country Priest), novel.

Dale Carnegie, *How to Win Friends and Influence People*, psychology; it becomes the ultimate guide to American know-how and can-do.

John Dos Passos, *The Big Money*, the final novel in his trilogy *USA*.

William Faulkner, *Absalom! Absalom!*, novel.

Federico García Lorca, *La casa de Bernarda Alba* (The House of Bernarda Alba), play.

Aldous Huxley, *Eyeless in Gaza*, novel.

Margaret Mitchell, *Gone with the Wind*, novel.

George Orwell, *Keep the Aspidistra Flying*, novel.

Dylan Thomas, *Twenty-Five Poems*, poetry collection.

Visual Arts and Architecture

Salvador Dali, *Premonition of Civil War*, painting.

René Magritte, *The Black Flag*, painting.

Piet Mondrian, *Composition in Red and Blue* and *Composition in Yellow and Black*, paintings.

Music

18 Dec. First performance in Brno, Czech Republic, of Leoš Janáček's opera *The Makropulos Case*.

Sergei Prokofiev, *Peter and the Wolf*, musical tale for children in which the narration is interspersed with orchestral interludes.

Sergei Rachmaninov, Symphony No. 3 in A minor.

Film

Frank Capra, *Mr Deeds Goes to Town*.

Charlie Chaplin, *Modern Times*, starring Paulette Goddard.

George Cukor, *Camille*, starring Greta Garbo.

Leni Riefenstahl, *Olympia*, a study of the Berlin Olympic Games.

George Stevens, *Swing Time*, starring Ginger Rogers and Fred Astaire.

James Whale, *Show Boat*, starring Paul Robeson.

1937

EUROPE

23 Jan. A second round of show trials start in Moscow with purported followers of Leon Trotsky as the main victims. More former prominent Bolsheviks and colleagues of Lenin are executed. Subsequently, after a secret trial, Marshal Mikhail Tukhachevski is convicted of treason and executed along with seven other generals (12 June). The destruction of the Red Army's officer corps has begun.

25 Mar. Italy signs a pact with Yugoslavia guaranteeing the status quo in the Adriatic.

26 April In Spain the Basque town of Guernica is destroyed by German bombers of the Condor legion, while German warships bombard Almeria (31 May). German intervention grows ever more blatant as British and French determination not to become involved in the Spanish Civil War becomes stronger.

28 May Stanley Baldwin retires as prime minister of Britain and is succeeded by the chancellor of the exchequer, Neville Chamberlain. Chamberlain, who has been a notably successful architect of social and economic policies to lift Britain from the recession, attempts the politics of appeasement in foreign relations and is supported in doing so by the new king, George VI, and by public opinion.

May Rebellion breaks out among the Muslims of Albania, who resent King Zog I's decree forbidding the veiling of women.

3 June In Spain Gen. Emilio Mola is killed in a plane crash, leaving Franco as undisputed head of rebel forces in the civil war. The outcome of the war is unclear: Malaga has fallen to Franco (8 May), but the republicans have defeated Italian forces at Brihuega (18 Mar.).

18 June In Spain rebel forces seize Bilbao, the Basque capital.

16 July In Germany the Buchenwald concentration camp opens near Weimar. Jews are now ordered to wear yellow badges showing the star of David.

July In Ireland a referendum endorses Eamon de Valéra's new constitution, which supersedes the constitution of the Irish Free State (1922). The new constitution makes Ireland a republic in all but name. Its provisions include a clause affirming the unity of the whole of Ireland (which displeases Ulster Unionists) and another recognizing the 'special position' of the Catholic Church in Ireland.

21 Oct. In Spain nationalist forces, which have moved to establish control of the Asturias in the N, capture the town of Gijon.

28 Oct. The Spanish government is forced to move from Valencia to Barcelona.

Oct. In Czechoslovakia there is unrest among ethnic Germans in the Sudeten region, where demands for unification with Germany attract considerable support.

6 Nov. Mussolini joins the Anti-Comintern Pact between Germany and Japan.

28 Nov. Franco announces a total naval blockade of the Spanish coastline, but the republicans launch a major counterattack in Aragon (5 Dec.).

29 Dec. By the terms of the new Irish constitution, the Irish Free State becomes Eire.

Dec. An anti-Semitic administration is formed in Romania under Octavian Goga. Jews are barred from the professions and from owning land.

– Britain begins a programme of rearmament.

MIDDLE EAST AND NORTH AFRICA

July A Non-Aggression Pact is agreed between Turkey, Iraq, Iran and Afghanistan.

11 Aug. Bakr Sidki, dictator of Iraq, is assassinated by a Kurd protestor.

– Unrest continues in the British mandate of Palestine. A British Royal Commission recommends the partitioning of Palestine into a British area, a Jewish state and an Arab area linked to Transjordan.

ASIA

7 July The Japanese, under the premiership of Konoe Fumimaro, launch a full-scale invasion of NE China. This marks the beginning of the second Sino-Japanese War, and the start of a conflict in E Asia that will last until 1945.

28 July Japanese forces take Beijing and then Tientsin (29 July).

5–13 Dec. The Japanese capture of Nanjing is followed by the 'Rape of Nanjing', an atrocity in which Japanese troops kill some 250,000 Chinese civilians. The Japanese go on to take Hangchow (24 Dec.).

THE AMERICAS

1 May US Congress passes a third Neutrality Act.

Nov. Fascism acquires a Brazilian dimension when, in a constitutional coup, President Getúlio Vargas annuls the liberal constitution set up in 1934, closes down congress and sets up the totalitarian Estado Novo (New State).

ECONOMY AND SOCIETY

27 May The Golden Gate Bridge opens in San Francisco Bay, USA.

22 June African-American boxer Joe Louis wins the world heavyweight championship in Chicago.

– The weekly news magazine *Newsweek* starts publication in New York.

SCIENCE AND TECHNOLOGY

– The *Graf Zeppelin*, the German airship, is withdrawn from ocean crossings and is replaced by the *Hindenburg*, which, however, explodes on arriving in New Jersey (6 May).

– Nylon, the first entirely artificial fibre, is patented to the ownership of the US chemicals company Du Pont.

ARTS AND HUMANITIES

Literature

W(ystan) H(ugh) Auden and writer Christopher Isherwood, *The Ascent of F6*, play.

Isak Dinesen (Karen Blixen), *Out of Africa*, novel.

C(ecil) S(cott) Forester, *The Happy Return*, novel introducing his naval hero Horatio Hornblower.

Ernest Hemingway, *To Have and Have Not*, novel.

George Orwell, *The Road to Wigan Pier*, an examination of working-class living conditions in N England.

John Steinbeck, *Of Mice and Men*, novel.

Wallace Stevens, *The Man with the Blue Guitar*, poetry collection.

J(ohn) R(onald) R(euel) Tolkien, *The Hobbit*, children's fantasy novel.

Visual Arts and Architecture

19 July In Munich the Nazis open an exhibition of 'degenerate art' (*entartete Kunst*) intended to show the decadence of modern art. Artists stigmatized as 'degenerate' include Klee, Kandinsky, Matisse and Picasso.

– German architect Walter Gropius, exiled from Nazi Germany since 1934, is appointed professor of architecture at Harvard.

Georges Braque, *Woman with a Mandolin*, painting.

René Magritte, *The Pleasure Principle*, painting.

Pablo Picasso (see p. 467), *Guernica*, mural study of the destruction of the Basque city (see 26 April) for the Spanish pavilion at the Paris World Fair.

Music

2 June First performance in Zurich of Acts 1 and 2 of Alban Berg's opera *Lulu*, which is based on *Erdgeist* (Earth Spirit) and *Die Büchse der Pandora* (Pandora's Box) by Frank Wedekind.

11 July The US composer George Gershwin dies.

28 Dec. The French composer Maurice Ravel dies.

Irving Berlin (Israel Baline), 'I've Got my Love to Keep Me Warm', song.

Benjamin Britten, *Variations on a Theme of Frank Bridge*, for string orchestra.

'Hoagy' (Hoagland) Carmichael, 'The Nearness of You', song.

Constant Lambert, *Horoscope*, ballet with Frederick Ashton's choreography.

Carl Orff, *Carmina Burana*, cantata based on medieval songs celebrating the pleasure of wine, women and song.

Dmitri Shostakovich, Symphony No. 5 in D minor, performed in Leningrad and, hailed by Soviet musicologists as ideologically correct, helps the composer to regain official approval; he has been out of favour since 1935.

'Fats' (Thomas Wright) Waller, 'The Joint is Jumpin'', song.

Film

Frank Capra, *Lost Horizon*, starring Ronald Colman.

John Cromwell, *The Prisoner of Zenda*, starring Ronald Colman.

Walt Disney, *Snow White and the Seven Dwarfs*. Disney's first full-length animated feature.

Julien Duvivier, *Pépé le Moko*, starring Jean Gabin.

Jean Renoir, *La Grande Illusion*, starring Erich von Stroheim and Jean Gabin.

Mark Sandrich, *Shall We Dance?*, musical starring Ginger Rogers and Fred Astaire. The music is by George Gershwin.

Sam Wood, *A Day at the Races*, starring the Marx Brothers.

1938

EUROPE

4 Feb. Joachim von Ribbentrop becomes German foreign minister.

12 Feb. Adolf Hitler threatens to invade Austria unless the Austrian chancellor Kurt von Schuschnigg includes Arthur Seyss-Inquart, a Nazi sympathizer, in his government and frees jailed Austrian Nazis. Schuschnigg complies with Hitler's demands.

20 Feb. Anthony Eden, the British foreign secretary, resigns over foreign-policy disagreements with prime minister Neville Chamberlain. He is succeeded by Lord Halifax on 25 Feb.

9 Mar. Austrian chancellor Kurt von Schuschnigg announces that a plebiscite on Austrian independence will be held on 12 Mar. Goering demands that Schuschnigg resign in favour of the Nazi sympathizer Arthur Seyss-Inquart.

10 Mar. The French government falls. Léon Blum tries to form a new Popular Front government but has to resign (10 April). Edouard Daladier forms a government that claims to be 'radical socialist' but in reality is of the right.

12 Mar. The *Wehrmacht* (German army) marches into Austria, supposedly to re-establish order. By the *Anschluss* (Union) of 13 Mar. Germany annexes Austria. A subsequent German-organized plebiscite (10 April) produces a vote of 99% in favour of the *Anschluss*.

14 Mar. In the USSR the former leading Bolshevik theorist Nikolai Bukharin is executed, on Stalin's orders, for treason.

Mar. In the Spanish Civil War the Italian air force bombs Barcelona, horrifying international opinion.

16 April An Anglo-Italian Pact is signed. Neville Chamberlain accepts Italy's annexation of Abyssinia in exchange for the withdrawal of some Italian troops from Spain. This further act of appeasement fails to wean Mussolini away from Hitler.

25 April Britain and Eire sign an agreement ending their economic war. Tariffs are withdrawn by both sides. Britain hands over to Eire three 'treaty ports' (retained for strategic reasons by the terms of the 1921 Anglo-Irish treaty).

25 July–Nov In the Spanish Civil War government forces launch their last major counter-offensive along the Ebro River.

29 Sept. British and French premiers Neville Chamberlain and Edouard Daladier meet Hitler (see p. 509) at Munich and allow him to occupy the Sudetenland, a part of N Czechoslovakia which contains a large number of ethnic Germans. The crisis has been developing for several months, and both the British and French governments are determined that this is not an issue worth fighting a war over. The Czechs, therefore, must give way. Chamberlain returns to London (30 Sept.), claiming to have brought with him 'peace with honour … peace for our time'. Both Chamberlain and Daladier (in France) are enthusiastically welcomed by cheering crowds on their return. In a break with constitutional precedent, George VI and Queen Elizabeth lend their support to the agreement and appear with Chamberlain on the balcony of Buckingham Palace. Chamberlain is convinced that any further outstanding grievances held by the Germans will now be settled peacefully. Hitler, however, has lost any respect he held for the British and does not share their revulsion against war. The Czechoslovak president Eduard Beneš resigns in disgust.

1 Oct. German troops march into the Sudetenland.

1 Oct. Czechoslovakia cedes Teschen (Cieszyn) in S Silesia to Poland. The area had been divided between Poland and Czechoslovakia in July 1920.

3 Oct. In Britain Alfred Duff Cooper, First Lord of the Admiralty, resigns over the Munich agreement. During a dramatic four-day House of Commons debate on the agreement, Winston Churchill (see p. 523) comments 'we have sustained a defeat without a war'.

6 Oct. The Italian fascist government introduces anti-Jewish legislation. Italian fascism has not persecuted Jews in its earlier phase, but the influence of Nazi Germany on Italy is now shaping policies.

7 Nov. Ernst Eduard von Rath of the German embassy in Paris is assassinated by the German-Polish Jew Herschel Grynzpan in protest at the treatment of Polish Jews deported from Germany.

9 Nov. *Kristallnacht* (the night of broken glass) in Germany. In an act of revenge for the murder of a German diplomat by a German-Polish Jew in Paris (see above), Jewish shops, homes and synagogues are looted and burned, and nearly 100 Jews are murdered. It marks a major escalation of Nazi persecution of the Jews and horrifies international opinion.

23 Dec. In the Spanish Civil War nationalist forces invade Catalonia and push government forces back to Barcelona.

Dec. Mussolini demands, without success, that France cede Corsica to Italy.

MIDDLE EAST AND NORTH AFRICA

4 Jan. Palestine erupts in violence when the British government announces the postponement of its partition. Jewish and Arab agitators bomb the markets in Haifa, Jerusalem and Jaffa.

23 Feb. Oil is discovered in SE Kuwait and transforms the economy of the British protectorate.

10 Oct. Arab activists seize Bethlehem and the old city quarter in Jerusalem (18 Oct.). The British government announces (9 Nov.) that partition of Palestine is impossible, and British troops stationed in the area are reinforced.

ASIA

10 Jan. In NE China the Japanese army takes Qingdao and, advancing through Shanxi province, reaches the Huang He (Yellow) River (6 Mar.).

11 July–10 Aug. Japanese and Soviet forces exchange fire in a series of engagements on the Chinese–Siberian border. The Japanese will henceforth avoid provoking the USSR.

Sept. The League of Nations condemns Japan as the aggressor in the Sino-Japanese War.

25 Oct. Guangzhou (Canton), capital of Guangdong province, falls to the Japanese, thereby cutting the railway link that supplies the Chinese army in the interior. The port of Hangzhou falls to the Japanese (24 Dec.).

– Britain opens a major base at Singapore.

THE AMERICAS

18 Mar. In Mexico the petroleum industry is nationalized by the government. President Lázaro Cárdenas proposes to barter oil for manufactured goods from foreign countries, but the most radical elements of his plans are soon shelved.

26 May In the USA a committee is established under Martin Dies to investigate 'un-American' activities attributed to American communists and Nazis.

15 June The Fair Labor Standards Act passed by Congress limits the working week to 40 hours by the third year after the Act's introduction, and a minimum wage is set at 60 cents per hour.

23 Sept. US aviator Charles Lindbergh writes to the US ambassador in London, Joseph P. Kennedy, that: 'It is wiser to permit Germany eastward expansion than to throw England and France, unprepared, into a war at this time.' Lindbergh has become a powerful advocate of American isolationism.

24 Dec. Fears that European fascist states may try to reclaim their S and C American possessions leads to the Declaration of Lima. The Pan-American Conference meeting in Peru pledges the states of the W hemisphere to consult if any one state is threatened. The sovereignty of the states is reaffirmed.

ECONOMY AND SOCIETY

20–24 Aug. In a cricket test match between England and Australia at the Kennington Oval, London, the English batsman Len Hutton scores 364, a new record individual score for a batsman.

– The BBC (British Broadcasting Corporation) begins foreign language broadcasts.

– Italy wins the 3rd soccer World Cup, held in France.

– Nestlé develop Nescafé, the company's first non-dairy product, in response to the Brazilian government's need to find an answer to the country's coffee surpluses.

SCIENCE AND TECHNOLOGY

4 Feb. Scottish physicist John Logie Baird demonstrates a colour television in the Dominion Theatre, London.

23 Oct. The US company Du Pont begins the commercial production of nylon.

18 Dec. German chemist Otto Hahn produces the first nuclear fission of uranium; he discovers that the nuclei of some uranium atoms can be split into two halves and release in the process energy as well as neutrons that can split more uranium atoms.

– The Spitfire fighter aircraft goes into service with the RAF.

– By now the Austrian engineer Ferdinand Porsche, commissioned by Hitler to produce a low-cost car, has designed the Volkswagen (people's car).

– The ballpoint pen, known as the biro, is patented by the Hungarian scientist Laszlo Bíró. He will emigrate to Argentina (1943) and get backing from the British businessman Henry Martin for the development of the product.

ARTS AND HUMANITIES

Literature

30 Oct. The power of mass communications is shown when H.G. Wells's *The War of the Worlds* is broadcast on CBS in a version by Orson Welles. Reports of Martian landings send some of the listening audience into a panic.

– American cartoonists Jerome Siegel and Joseph Shuster develop the character of Superman.

Eric Ambler, *Epitaph for a Spy*, novel.

Jean Anouilh, *Le Bal des voleurs* (Thieves' Carnival), play.

Antonin Artaud, *Le Théâtre et son double* (The Theatre and its Double), theatrical manifesto that puts forward the idea of a 'theatre of cruelty'.

Elizabeth Bowen, *The Death of the Heart*, novel.

Daphne du Maurier, *Rebecca*, novel.

Graham Greene, *Brighton Rock*, novel. Greene classes it as 'entertainment' but critics detect in it a strong Catholic message.

Nikos Kazantzakis, *I Odysseia* (The Odyssey), epic poem.

C(live) S(taples) Lewis, *Out of the Silent Planet*, novel.

Louis MacNeice, *Autumn Journal*, poetry collection.

George Orwell, *Homage to Catalonia*, memoir of his Spanish Civil War experiences.

Jean-Paul Sartre (see p. 533), *La Nausée* (Nausea), novel.

Evelyn Waugh, *Scoop*, novel based on Waugh's experiences of the Abyssinian war in 1936.

T.H. White, *The Sword in the Stone*, first novel in the Arthurian tetralogy *The Once and Future King*.

Visual Arts and Architecture

– Frank Lloyd Wright, the Welsh-American architect, finishes his new home Taliesin West near Phoenix, Arizona. Taliesin will also become a centre for architectural studies.

Music

8 May First performance of Igor Stravinsky's concerto *Dumbarton Oaks*, which is named after the private estate near Washington, D.C., of Mr and Mrs R.W. Bliss, who commissioned the work.

28 May First performance in Zurich of Paul Hindemith's opera *Mathis der Maler* (Matthias the Painter), which is based on the life of German painter Matthias Grünewald and which was banned by the Nazis (1934).

- US band leader Glenn Miller goes on tour with his own band for the first time. Miller will be lost flying over the English Channel in 1944.
- The samba and the conga become popular in US dance halls.

Samuel Barber, *Adagio for Strings*, orchestrated version of the slow movement of his string quartet Op. 11.

Benjamin Britten, Piano Concerto No. 1 in D major.

Film

Anthony Asquith, *Pygmalion*, starring Leslie Howard and Wendy Hiller.

Michael Curtiz, *The Adventures of Robin Hood*, starring Errol Flynn.

Sergei Eisenstein, *Alexander Nevsky*.

Howard Hawks, *Bringing up Baby*, starring Cary Grant and Katharine Hepburn.

Alfred Hitchcock, *The Lady Vanishes*, starring Michael Redgrave and Margaret Lockwood.

1939

EUROPE

26 Jan. In the Spanish Civil War nationalist forces take Barcelona.

14 Mar. At Hitler's insistence Slovakia declares its independence of Czechoslovakia. Slovakia will now become a puppet state under German domination until 1945.

15 Mar. German troops occupy the Czech heartlands of Bohemia and Moravia, which have become a German protectorate. Hitler, who has thereby broken the Munich agreement, enters Prague in triumph the same day. Czechoslovakia ceases to exist as an independent state.

16 Mar. Hungary annexes Ruthenia (previously part of Czechoslovakia).

21 Mar. Hitler demands that Poland relinquish the Free City of Danzig (modern Gdansk) and the 'Polish corridor' (a strip of territory allowing Poland access to the Baltic Sea).

28 Mar. Madrid falls to Franco and the Spanish Civil War ends. Gen. Francisco Franco's victorious Falange Party, closely modelled on the Italian *Fascisti* and the German Nazis, is now the only legal party in Spain. Franco will rule Spain until 1975.

31 Mar. The British government issues a guarantee that it will support Poland in the event of a German attack.

7 April Franco's Spain joins the Anti-Comintern Pact.

7 April Italy invades Albania.

11 April Hungary leaves the League of Nations.

22 May Hitler and Mussolini sign the Pact of Steel, a ten-year pact of friendship and alliance. The Pact holds each party to help the other unconditionally in the event of war.

May Military conscription is introduced in Britain.

23 Aug. Germany and the USSR sign a mutual non-aggression pact (the Nazi–Soviet Pact). The German foreign minister Joachim von Ribbentrop signs the agreement with V.M. Molotov, the Russian commissar for foreign affairs. The agreement includes a trade agreement heavily in Germany's favour and a secret protocol for the joint partition of Poland.

30 Aug. In France the authorities start to evacuate children from Paris. Women and children begin to be evacuated from London on 31 Aug.

1 Sept. After months of increasing tension and political agitation in the German-speaking areas of W Poland, Nazi activists in the German-speaking Free City of Danzig (modern Gdansk) begin an armed uprising, demanding that the city give up its independent status and return to the German Reich. Simultaneously, Nazis dressed as Polish soldiers carry out bogus 'Polish attacks' on German border posts on Poland's W frontier with Germany. Hitler declares his support for the Danzig Nazis and pledges to avenge the 'Polish invasion'. German forces invade Poland from the W.

3 Sept. The British government, having guaranteed the independence of Poland, declares war on Nazi Germany as does France. In Britain Winston Churchill (see p. 523) returns to office as First Lord of the Admiralty in Neville Chamberlain's war cabinet. Churchill held this same post on the outbreak of war in 1914. The Admiralty sends a message to all ships: 'Winston's back.'

10 Sept. In the battle of the Bzura, a river in W Poland, the main Polish field armies are defeated by the Germans. Using the new tactic of blitzkrieg (lightning war), the Germans send massed columns of heavy and light tanks supported by motorized infantry racing ahead of the main infantry forces to take strongpoints, destroy supply lines and capture strategic cities and transport hubs. The fast-moving columns are supported from the air by precision attacks carried out by Stuka dive-bombers that destroy centres of Polish resistance. The tactic is made possible by specially designed panzers (German armoured vehicles) and, crucially, by the fact that front-line officers and air units can talk to each other using secure radio transmissions. The tactics allow swift responses to enemy action and enable the Germans to gain and keep the initiative. The Germans will use blitzkrieg tactics repeatedly in the next two years.

17 Sept. Soviet troops invade Poland, claiming to be saving E Poland from German occupation.

21 Sept. Armand Calinescu, prime minister of Romania, is assassinated by the fascist Iron Guard.

27 Sept. Warsaw surrenders to the Germans and Poland is partitioned (28 Sept.) between Germany and the USSR.

Sept. A British Expeditionary Force (BEF) is sent to France, but no serious fighting occurs in the W of Europe. The period of military inactivity in the W of Europe between the outbreak of World War II and Hitler's assault on the W in April 1940 will be known as the 'Phoney War'.

5 Oct. The last organized resistance by Polish forces comes to an end. Ships of the Polish navy steam out of the Baltic to Britain, while thousands of Polish soldiers and airmen escape by way of Romania or Lithuania to reach France or Britain and so continue the fight against Nazi Germany. A Polish squadron will later fight with distinction in the battle of Britain.

14 Oct. The British battleship HMS *Royal Oak* is sunk by the Germans in Scapa Flow, off the N coast of Scotland.

Winston Churchill (1874–1965)

Churchill's career, first as soldier then as politician, journalist and popular historian, was based on the projection of his own mercurial personality, which came to be seen as the embodiment of England at its improvisational best. To his critics, however, 'Churchillianism' came to mean romantic egoism and the readiness to sacrifice others in order to maintain the protagonist's heroic stature.

As a historical writer Churchill celebrated – in a style regarded by some as somewhat rhetorical and affected – the achievements of the Whig aristocracy: constitutional government and English independence from Continental entrapment. As a military man, Churchill proved himself a brave soldier during the Boer War, but the Dardanelles disaster during World War I showed him to be a poor military strategist. As a politician, he showed a keen grasp of how a career among the political elite could be maintained by riding the tiger of democratic opinion. He therefore set out to court that fickle force through his writings, speeches and self-presentation. The notion of party loyalty was treated with contempt as he shifted from the Tories to the Liberals and then back to the Conservatives in the wake of the collapse of the Liberal Party in the 1920s.

The defence of the British Empire, and especially of British rule in India, was the sole consistent aim of Churchill's career. His recall to office as prime minister in 1940 yielded two years of personal glory – succeeded by three years in which he was sidelined both by his own generals and by American power. The concluding Churchillian irony was that the expense of the war bankrupted Britain, diminished its independence in matters of foreign policy and ensured the dismantling of the empire. But Churchill's role in holding up national morale during the darkest days of World War II secured him the continuing gratitude of the British people.

30 Nov. Following Finland's refusal to enter into a mutual assistance pact with the USSR, Soviet forces invade Finland but meet unexpectedly stubborn resistance in the 'Winter War'.

MIDDLE EAST AND NORTH AFRICA

4 April King Ghazi of Iraq is killed in a car accident. Anti-British riots follow when the rumour is spread that the British are responsible for the death. The British vice-consul is stoned to death. The three-year-old Faisal II succeeds to the throne.

17 May The British government, still administering Palestine under the League of Nations mandate, issues a white paper which limits the number of Jews who can be admitted to the region to 50,000 over the next five years. The independent Palestine envisaged by the British government now seems to be a mostly Arab country with a minority of Jewish immigrants. The Balfour Declaration of 1917 and its commitment to the establishment of a Jewish state appears to have been repudiated.

ASIA

May Renewed border clashes break out between Japanese and Soviet troops.

Nov. In the Sino-Japanese War, Japanese forces invade S China.

THE AMERICAS

3 Sept. In a 'fireside chat' (informal radio address from a White House fireside) President Roosevelt commits the USA to a policy of neutrality in World War II. He adds, however, that he cannot ask US citizens to remain neutral in thought as well as deed. Roosevelt will embark on a stealthy campaign to grant military aid to Britain without involving the USA in the war. He signs a bill (4 Nov.) that allows Britain and France to buy arms in the USA on a 'cash and carry' basis.

17 Sept. US aviator Charles Lindbergh claims in a radio broadcast that Stalin is as much of a threat as Hitler.

13 Dec. The German pocket battleship *Graf Spee* damages the British cruiser HMS *Exeter* in the battle of the River Plate, off Uruguay. The *Graf Spee* is driven into Montevideo harbour by British ships and is scuttled on Hitler's orders (17 Dec.).

– US industrialist Henry Ford and former President Herbert Hoover lead a movement to keep the USA out of the war.

AUSTRALASIA AND OCEANIA

24 April Robert Menzies, leader of the United Australia Party, becomes prime minister of Australia.

ECONOMY AND SOCIETY

Jan. The Trans-Iranian Railway, linking the Caspian Sea with the Persian Gulf, is completed.

10 Feb. Pope Pius XI dies and is succeeded by Eugenio Maria Giuseppe Giovani Pacelli, who becomes Pope Pius XII (2 Mar.).

28 June Pan American Airways starts the first commercial transatlantic passenger airway service.

9 Sept. In France, identity cards are made compulsory.

22 Sept. In Britain, petrol is rationed.

– In Britain the radio comedy series *ITMA*, devised by Tommy Handley, is broadcast for the first time.

SCIENCE AND TECHNOLOGY

25 Jan. The cyclotron of John Ray Dunning of Columbia University splits an atom for the first time in the USA. This confirms European research showing that the absorption of a neutron by a uranium nucleus can cause the nucleus to split with the release of vast amounts of energy. Enrico Fermi and Leo Szilard repeat the experiment (3 Mar.).

23 Sept. The Austrian psychologist Sigmund Freud dies.

– Albert Einstein (see p. 464) writes to President Roosevelt telling him that the splitting of the atom means that it would be possible to set up a nuclear chain reaction in a mass of uranium and that power and radium-like elements would then be generated: 'This new work would lead also to the construction of bombs.'

– On hearing that German scientists Otto Hahn and Fritz Strassmann have split uranium nuclei (see 18 Dec. 1938),

US president F.D. Roosevelt appoints an Advisory Committee on Uranium.

- In his book *The Nature of the Chemical Bond*, US chemist Linus Pauling develops a theory to explain how atoms and molecules combine with each other.
- US company Du Pont begins the production of nylon stockings, selling 64 million pairs in the first 12 months.

ARTS AND HUMANITIES

Literature

28 Jan. The Irish poet and dramatist W.B. Yeats dies. His *Last Poems and Two Plays* is published this year.

Raymond Chandler, *The Big Sleep*, novel introducing private detective Philip Marlowe.

Agatha Christie, *Ten Little Niggers*, detective novel (published in the USA as *Ten Little Indians*).

Rumer Godden, *Black Narcissus*, novel.

Henry Green (Henry Vincent Yorke), *Party Going*, novel.

Lillian Hellman, *The Little Foxes*, play starring Tallulah Bankhead.

Christopher Isherwood, *Goodbye to Berlin*, novel.

James Joyce, *Finnegans Wake*, novel.

Richard Llewellyn, *How Green was my Valley*, novel.

Henry Miller, *Tropic of Capricorn*, novel.

Eugenio Montale, *Le occasioni* (Occasions), poetry collection.

John Steinbeck, *The Grapes of Wrath*, novel describing the American Dustbowl and its migrants.

Visual Arts and Architecture

20 Mar. The Nazis burn 'degenerate' works of art in Berlin (see 1937).

Paul Klee, *Übermut,* painting.

Willem de Kooning, *Seated Man*, painting.

René Magritte, *Poison* and *Objective Stimulation*, paintings.

Music

- In Britain the pianist Myra Hess begins her morale-boosting lunchtime concerts at the National Gallery, London.
- US singer Frank Sinatra joins Harry James's band.

Samuel Barber, Violin Concerto.

Béla Bartók, *Divertimento* for strings.

Ross Parker and Hugh Charles, 'There'll Always be an England', song.

Dmitri Shostakovich, Symphony No. 6 in B minor.

Film

Frank Capra, *Mr Smith Goes to Washington*, starring James Stewart.

Marcel Carné, *Le Jour se lève* (Daybreak), starring Jean Gabin.

William Dieterle, *The Hunchback of Notre Dame*, starring Charles Laughton.

Victor Fleming, *Gone with the Wind*, starring Vivien Leigh and Clark Gable and *The Wizard of Oz*, starring Judy Garland.

John Ford, *Stagecoach*, starring John Wayne.

Sidney Lanfield, *The Hound of the Baskervilles*, starring Basil Rathbone and Nigel Bruce.

Jean Renoir, *La Règle du jeu* (The Rules of the Game).

1940

EUROPE

Jan. German SS troops surround the Jewish quarter in Czestochowa, Poland, torturing and killing the inhabitants.

12 Mar. The Soviet–Finnish 'Winter War' ends. The Finns are forced to accept peace on Stalin's terms and to cede their E territories.

20 Mar. In France Edouard Daladier resigns as prime minister and is succeeded by the finance minister Paul Reynaud.

Mar. In the Katyn Forest massacre, W of Smolensk, Soviet troops shoot 4143 Polish army officers captured after the German–Soviet partition of Poland.

9 April German forces occupy Denmark and Norway; a pro-Nazi government led by Vidkun Quisling is established in Oslo.

30 April A Jewish ghetto is established in the C Polish city of Lódz, SW of Warsaw.

7 May In Britain Neville Chamberlain resigns as prime minister. after being criticized for the failure of a British operation in Norway. A faction of Conservatives, as well as George VI and Queen Elizabeth, favour the foreign secretary Viscount Halifax to succeed him, but Winston Churchill (see p. 523) becomes prime minister at the head of a coalition government that includes Labour leader Clement Atlee as Lord Privy Seal and Ernest Bevin as minister of labour. He defines his premiership in a speech to the House of Commons (13 May): 'I have nothing to offer but blood, toil, tears and sweat.' The British war aim will be: 'Victory: victory at all costs … victory however long and hard the road may be; for without victory there is no survival.'

10 May The German tactic known as blitzkrieg ends the period of the Phoney War and signals the start of the major German offensive in W Europe. German divisions roll into Belgium and Holland; the German air force establishes an easy dominance in the skies. The German army crosses the Meuse at Sedan (12 May), and Rotterdam is destroyed by bombers (14 May). The Dutch army surrenders (14 May). German divisions then advance through Belgium and on to the Channel ports. The French army, led by Gen. Maxime Weygand, collapses under the onslaught; both the British and French armies are now cut off from their commanders at their base headquarters S of the German salient.

21 May Amiens and Arras in N France fall to the Germans.

26 May The evacuation of British and French troops starts from Dunkirk in NE France, codenamed Operation Dynamo.

28 May The Belgian army surrenders to the invading German forces.

May The Home Guard, a volunteer force trained for defence against the expected German invasion, is raised in Britain.

4 June In a speech to the House of Commons Churchill says that Britain 'shall not flag or fail … we shall defend our island, whatever the cost may be, we shall fight on the beaches, we shall fight on the landing grounds, we shall fight in the fields and in the streets, we shall fight in the hills, we shall never surrender.'

After days of ferrying across the channel by a flotilla of naval and civilian craft, both large and small (26 May–4 June), some 200,000 British troops and 140,000 French have been evacuated from Dunkirk, but some 30,000 are killed or taken prisoner by the steadily advancing German army.

9 June Norway surrenders to Germany.

10 June Italy declares war on France and Britain.

14 June German troops enter Paris. Reynaud resigns as prime minister (16 June) and is succeeded by Marshal Pétain, hero of World War I, who becomes head of the French state and asks for an armistice (17 June). Gen. Charles de Gaulle refuses to accept Pétain's truce with Germany and escapes to England the same day.

15–17 June The USSR invades Estonia, Latvia and Lithuania and assimilates all three countries into the Soviet Union.

18 June Gen. Charles de Gaulle makes a broadcast from London calling on the French to continue the war against Germany.

22 June The Franco-German armistice is signed at Compiègne. The armistice divides France into two zones: German forces occupy N France while a collaborationist French government administers the unoccupied S half of the country from the spa town of Vichy in C France.

24 June The Vichy French government signs an armistice with Italy.

27 June The USSR invades Romania. Germany has rejected an appeal for help from King Carol II after the USSR demands that Romania cede Bukovina and Bessarabia to the Soviet Union.

28 June Britain recognizes Gen. Charles de Gaulle as leader of the Free French.

30 June Germany occupies the Channel Islands.

3 July The British Royal Navy, afraid that the French fleet will fall into German hands, sinks the French fleet at Mers-el-Kébir, near Oran on the Mediterranean coast of Algeria. The French government at Vichy breaks off diplomatic relations with Britain (5 July).

10 July The battle of Britain begins. The Luftwaffe (German air force) attacks shipping convoys in British waters and bombs British ports. From Aug. until Oct. the Luftwaffe launches a prolonged attack on factories, installations and airfields in S England in preparation for an invasion of the British Isles. The Luftwaffe will be repulsed, however, by the Spitfires and Hurricanes of the RAF Fighter Command. In Aug. the RAF starts to bomb Berlin.

15 Aug. The RAF shoot down 76 German aircraft.

17 Aug. Germany announces a naval blockade of Britain.

5 Sept. Ion Antonescu becomes premier of Romania and assumes dictatorial powers. He forces the abdication of King Carol II, who flees the country (6 Sept.). Antonescu installs Carol's son Michael as monarch and allies with Germany against the USSR.

7 Sept. The Luftwaffe launches the systematic night-time bombing of British cities that will be known as the Blitz.

450 people are killed in a raid on London's East End. The raids, intended to bomb Britain into submission, inflict massive damage to Britain's cities, but public morale will not crack.

27 Sept. Germany, Italy and Japan agree a 10-year military and economic pact.

7 Oct. German forces take control of the Ploesti oil fields in Romania.

28 Oct. Italy invades Greece from Italian-held Albania. With British air support, the Greeks fight back.

Oct. Hitler abandons his plan to invade Britain (Operation Sea Lion).

3 Nov. British forces arrive in Crete.

11 Nov. British naval air forces attack and severely damage the Italian fleet anchored at Taranto, S Italy.

14–15 Nov. The centre of Coventry, a manufacturing and armaments centre in the English Midlands, is destroyed by Luftwaffe bombers. More than 1000 civilians are killed or injured, 50,000 houses destroyed or damaged and the medieval cathedral largely flattened.

20 Nov. Hungary joins the Axis powers, followed by Romania (23 Nov.).

MIDDLE EAST AND NORTH AFRICA

9 Dec. Gen. Sir Archibald Wavell, commanding the British 8th Army in Egypt, attacks Italian forces around Sidi Barrani, near the Libyan border. The Italians are forced to retreat across the border into Libya (15 Dec.).

ASIA

22 July Prince Fumimaro Konoe becomes Japanese prime minister.

9 Aug. Britain withdraws its garrisons from Shanghai and N China.

Sept. The Japanese army starts to occupy French Indochina after the Vichy government grants the Japanese the right to use some of the ports and airfields there.

THE AMERICAS

30 Jan. Social Security cheques are issued for the first time in the USA. But US unemployment after seven years of the New Deal remains high, with 14.6% (8 million people) of the workforce out of a job.

25 June The Revenue Act increases US income tax and a second Act (8 Oct.) levies an excess profits tax on corporation earnings. The US GNP, at $99 billion, is less than it was in 1929 ($103 billion), and government spending during the same period has increased from 10% of that total to 18%.

28 June Congress passes the Alien Registration Act, which makes it compulsory for non-US citizens to be fingerprinted and also makes it unlawful to work for the overthrow of the US government.

2 July Under the terms of the Export Control Act Congress gives the US president the power to curtail the export of any product that may be necessary for the defence of the country. In Oct. President Roosevelt embargoes the export – previously considerable – of scrap iron and steel to Japan.

21 Aug. In Mexico the Soviet agent Ramón Mercader, posing as a friend, kills the exiled former Soviet politician Leon Trotsky with an ice pick.

3 Sept. The US government gives 50 obsolete US Navy destroyers to Britain in return for the right to build naval and air bases in Newfoundland and in the Caribbean.

29 Oct. The first peace-time military draft in US history starts.

5 Nov. Franklin D. Roosevelt, who has broken with convention to seek a third term as president, is re-elected president of the USA. He defeats Wendell Wilkie, a New York Republican with liberal, internationalist views. Wilkie has opposed the isolationist views of Thomas Dewey within his party.

SUB-SAHARAN AFRICA

July Italian forces in E Africa invade British Somaliland from Italian-held Ethiopia.

27 Sept. British and Free French forces fail to take Dakar, in Senegal, which has been occupied by Vichy French forces.

– Serengeti National Park, the first such park in E Africa, is created in Tanganyika by the British colonial administration.

ECONOMY AND SOCIETY

Jan. Food rationing is introduced in Britain as a wartime measure.

Dec. The first Los Angeles freeway, the Arroyo Seco Parkway, is opened.

– Jacques Marsal, a French schoolboy, discovers the Lascaux caves near Périgueux in S France; the prehistoric wall paintings found in the caves are dated to about 17,000 BC.

– Eleanor Roosevelt, the US president's progressive wife, publicly endorses birth control.

SCIENCE AND TECHNOLOGY

– The MIG-1 fighter plane is developed in the USSR; it is named after the Soviet mathematician and aircraft designer Mikhail I. Gurevich.

– In the USA a four-wheel drive general purpose vehicle is launched for the US army. It will come to be known as the 'jeep' (i.e. GP or 'general purpose').

– In Oxford, England, the Australian pathologist Howard Florey prepares the antibiotic penicillin for medicinal use.

– Edwin Cohn of Harvard University separates the albumin, globulin and fibrin fractions of blood plasma. The discovery will have an immediate wartime application. Albumin will be used to treat shock, and globulin to treat infection. Serum gamma globulin will acquire a global role in mass immunization against measles, polio and other epidemic diseases.

ARTS AND HUMANITIES

Literature

1 Feb. The novelist John Buchan dies.

21 Dec. The novelist F. Scott Fitzgerald dies.

Louis Aragon, *Le Crève-coeur* (Heartbreak), poetry collection.

Graham Greene, *The Power and the Glory*, novel.

Ernest Hemingway, *For Whom the Bell Tolls*, novel.

Arthur Koestler, *Darkness at Noon*, a fictional account of Stalin's purges in the USSR.

Carson McCullers, *The Heart is a Lonely Hunter*, novel.

Michael Sadleir, *Fanny by Gaslight*, novel.

C.P. Snow, *Strangers and Brothers*, first novel in a sequence of 11 that explore power and bureaucracy in contemporary Britain.

Edmund Wilson, *To the Finland Station*, a classic account of the origins of the communist revolution in Russia that has transformed the 20th century.

Visual Arts and Architecture

21 June Edouard Vuillard, French painter and printmaker, dies.

29 June Paul Klee, Swiss painter and one of the masters of minimalist abstraction in modern art, dies in Switzerland.

17 Nov. The English sculptor and engraver Eric Gill dies.

– In Britain John Piper, Graham Sutherland and Paul Nash begin work as war artists. Henry Moore begins a series of drawings of Londoners sheltering in Underground stations during the Blitz.

Wassily Kandinsky, *Sky Blue*, painting.

Music

25 Dec. The musical *Pal Joey*, based on John O'Hara's short stories with music by Richard Rodgers and lyrics by Lorenz Hart, opens on Broadway.

– Joaquín Rodrigo's *Concierto de Aranjuez* for guitar and orchestra is performed for the first time in Barcelona, Spain.

– On BBC radio the singer Vera Lynn popularizes the song 'We'll Meet Again'.

– US singer Frank Sinatra leaves Harry James's band and joins the jazz-oriented Tommy Dorsey band.

Lewis Allan, 'Strange Fruit', song that becomes a classic indictment of racial lynchings in the US south.

Benjamin Britten, *Les Illuminations*, song cycle, based on poems by Arthur Rimbaud.

Jimmie Davis and Charles Mitchell, 'You are My Sunshine', song; Davis uses the song to campaign, successfully, for the governorship of Louisiana in 1944 and again in 1960.

Paul Hindemith, *The Four Temperaments*, subtitle of *Theme and Variations*, for piano and strings.

Jerome Kern, 'The Last Time I Saw Paris', song.

Dmitri Shostakovich, incidental music for Shakespeare's *King Lear*.

Film

Charlie Chaplin, *The Great Dictator*, comedy about a Jewish barber protesting against the persecution of the Jews in the fictional land of Tomania under its dictator Adenoid Hynkel.

George Cukor, *The Philadelphia Story*, starring Katherine Hepburn and Cary Grant.

Walt Disney, *Fantasia*, animated film with music by Bach, Beethoven and other classical composers.

John Ford, *The Grapes of Wrath*, starring Henry Fonda.

Howard Hawks, *His Girl Friday*, starring Cary Grant.

Alfred Hitchcock, *Rebecca*, starring Laurence Olivier, Joan Fontaine and George Sanders, based on Daphne du Maurier's 1938 novel.

Rouben Mamoulian, *The Mark of Zorro*, starring Tyrone Power.

1941

EUROPE

27 Mar. In Yugoslavia Prince Paul, regent to the young Peter II, is overthrown by pro-Allied groups opposed to Yugoslavia's alignment with the Axis powers (Yugoslavia having joined the Tripartite pact on 25 Mar.). This coup d'état will precipitate a German invasion.

28 Mar. In the battle of Cape Matapan (the southernmost cape of mainland Greece) a small British fleet destroys an Italian fleet sent to disrupt Allied shipping in the Mediterranean.

Mar. Britain sends 60,000 troops to Greece.

6 April German troops invade Yugoslavia and Greece.

10 April In Yugoslavia, Croatia declares itself independent. A pro-Nazi Croatian puppet regime is established under Ante Pavelic. This regime will adopt anti-Serb and anti-Semitic policies; some 100,000 Serbs and 55,000 Jews will be killed as Pavelic attempts to set up a Catholic Croatian republic.

12 April The Germans take Belgrade. Yugoslavia surrenders to German forces (17 April).

16 April Under US Lend-Lease legislation (see 11 Mar.), shipments of US food begin to arrive in Britain. Under Lend-Lease US-made weapons, used by the British army, enable the war to continue, but the price is a high one: Britain is not allowed by the USA to sell any articles abroad that contain Lend-Lease material or even similar goods. By 1944 Britain's exports will be down to a third of their level in 1938. Its economy will be almost entirely dependent on US business and financial interests. The management of Lend-Lease arrangements will also saddle Britain with a crushing postwar debt that will accelerate its withdrawal from empire.

21 April Greece surrenders to German forces. British troops withdraw from Greece (April–May).

April In Britain reserves of gold and dollars have sunk to $12 million, their lowest point so far in the country's history. The government's ability to pay for the war effort out of national resources is at an end, and payments currently due have been met only from a loan of gold from the Belgian government in exile.

10 May Rudolf Hess, one of Adolf Hitler's inner circle, lands by air in Scotland, apparently on a secret personal peace mission. He is interned. On the same day the chamber of the British House of Commons is destroyed in a German air raid.

20 May German forces invade Crete by air; Allied defenders fail to halt the invasion and are soon withdrawn by sea (1 June).

24 May The powerful German battleship *Bismarck* sinks the British battlecruiser *Hood* in the N Atlantic. The *Bismarck* is itself sunk by British air and naval forces (27 May). All but 110 of the *Bismarck*'s crew of 2192 are lost. The sinking of the *Bismarck* becomes a key event in raising British domestic morale.

4 June Former German Kaiser Wilhelm II dies.

22 June Germany invades the USSR, thereby breaking the Nazi–Soviet pact. In Operation Barbarossa, as the invasion is

called by German High Command, three German army groups will try to capture Leningrad, Moscow and the Ukraine. Deploying massive resources, including some 3350 tanks and four Luftwaffe air fleets, the Germans make rapid initial progress, overrunning Byelorussia (modern Belarus) and much of the Ukraine and laying siege to Leningrad by the end of 1941. The advance will stall by Christmas, however, and the needs of Hitler's war in the E will dominate Germany's wartime economy. Operation Barbarossa will come to be regarded as one of the most significant factors in Germany's eventual defeat.

2 July German SS troops murder 7000 in a massacre at Lviv in the Ukraine.

16 July The Germans take Smolensk in W Russia.

19 July Hitler diverts panzer units headed for Moscow N to Leningrad.

1 Sept. The Germans reach Leningrad and lay siege to the city. The siege of Leningrad reduces the population to terrible deprivation. By the time the siege is lifted in Jan. 1944 some 20–40% of the city's population of 3 million will have died. As a tribute to Leningrad's collective bravery the Soviet government awards the city with the Order of Lenin (1945) and names it (1965) Hero City of the Soviet Union.

3 Sept. The Germans use Zyklon B (hydrogen cyanide) for the first time to murder Jewish prisoners in Auschwitz concentration camp in S Poland.

19 Sept. The Germans take Kiev. On 29–30 Sept. SS squads machine-gun 33,771 Ukrainian Jews and Soviet prisoners at Babi Yar, a ravine on the outskirts of the city. The massacre takes place in the context of widespread mass murders of Jews by German *Einsatzgruppen* (task forces) who have followed the German armies into Poland and the USSR to eliminate those considered racially or politically undesirable by the Nazis. In Galicia, Lithuania, Latvia, Estonia, Poland, Czechoslovakia, the Ukraine and Russia the local Jewish populations are subjected to random killings or driven into ghettos or detention camps. Senior SS official Adolf Eichmann is now seeking a more effective method for a Final Solution, which he finds in Zyklon B (see 3 Sept.). It is decided to establish extermination camps in which Jews, gypsies and others will be murdered on an industrial scale. The first such camp opens at Chelmno, W Poland (Dec.).

16 Oct. The Soviet government leaves Moscow. The Germans are now just 100km (60 miles) from the city.

11 Dec. Germany and Italy declare war on the USA.

16 Dec. Following several failed assaults on Moscow, German forces on the Moscow front retreat.

MIDDLE EAST AND NORTH AFRICA

6 Feb. British forces advancing from Egypt occupy Benghazi in Libya.

12 Feb. German Lt-Gen. Erwin Rommel arrives in Libya with his Afrika Korps to reinforce the Italians against the British.

20 April German forces under Rommel attack Tobruk in NE Libya.

31 May Britain occupies Iraq because of fears that Axis sympathizers will seize control of the government.

June–July British and Free French troops occupy Syria and Lebanon as a pre-emptive move to stop German occupation.

Aug. British and Soviet troops in unison invade Iran. Reza Shah Pahlavi abdicates as shah of Iran and is succeeded by his son Muhammad Reza Shah Pahlavi, who is more accommodating towards the policies of the Allied powers in the region.

18 Nov. In Operation Crusader the British counterattack in N Africa. The besieged Libyan port of Tobruk is relieved (7 Dec.) and Rommel is pushed back. The British reoccupy Benghazi (24 Dec.).

– Jewish terrorist groups in Palestine, such as the Stern Gang, use violence to campaign for a Jewish state. Abraham Stern is eventually killed by the British (1942), but his group will continue its work.

ASIA

July Japanese forces occupy C and S Indochina.

16 Oct. Prince Fumimaro Konoe resigns as Japanese prime minister and is replaced by Hideki Tojo, who will turn Japan into a virtual military dictatorship.

8 Dec. Japanese forces invade Malaya and Siam (Thailand).

10 Dec. The battleship *Prince of Wales* and battlecruiser *Repulse*, the only significant British naval force in the Far East, are destroyed by Japanese bombers.

25 Dec. The British surrender Hong Kong to the Japanese.

THE AMERICAS

6 Jan. In a message to Congress US president Franklin D. Roosevelt recommends a Lend-Lease programme to help the Allied war effort. Roosevelt will steer Lend-Lease through Congress despite much isolationist sentiment in the USA.

11 Mar. Congress authorizes $7 billion in Lend-Lease aid and a further $1 billion to the USSR (7 Nov.). By the end of the war over $50 billion in Lend-Lease will be extended to the USA's allies.

April Roosevelt creates an Office of Production Management and an Office of Price Administration and Civilian Supply. Wartime demands will still drive US inflation up by 10% in the course of the year.

25 June Roosevelt appoints an Employment Practice Committee to ensure reasonable employment conditions. A march on Washington by African-Americans has been proposed in protest at the coercive employment practices of an economy now gearing itself for a world war.

9–12 Aug. Roosevelt and British prime minister Winston Churchill meet in secret off the coast of Newfoundland to establish the principles of the Atlantic Charter, which also contains a definition of joint aims. As the USA is still neutral, it appears to the Germans that Roosevelt is preparing his nation to enter the war.

20 Sept. The largest tax rise in US history is introduced to fund military spending.

Sept.–Oct. A series of incidents between US and Axis naval forces escalates tensions in the Atlantic. Roosevelt commands that German and Italian submarines are to be sunk on sight (11 Sept.). The US destroyer *Kearny* is torpedoed off the coast of Ireland (17 Oct.) and a German U-boat sinks the US destroyer *Reuben James* (31 Oct.). The US Navy is now effectively at war.

7 Dec. Without declaring war, the Japanese attack the US naval base of Pearl Harbor on the Hawaiian island of Oahu. The attack, executed by 360 Japanese planes launched from a carrier strike force, is a catastrophe for the US Pacific fleet. The USA loses 5 battleships, 13 other warships, 200 aircraft, 3400 men and much equipment. Wartime information restrictions mean that the US public are told that just one battleship has been sunk and one capsized. Speaking in Congress, Roosevelt declares that 7 Dec. is 'a date that will live in infamy'. The Senate votes for war, as does Congress, with Congresswoman Jeanette Rankin being the sole dissenting vote (as she had been in 1917). The US declaration of war on Japan follows (8 Dec.), and the Germans and Italians declare war on the USA (11 Dec.). Romania follows suit (12 Dec.), as does Bulgaria (13 Dec.). Winston Churchill arrives in Washington to discuss joint strategy (22 Dec.).

– Mexico's wheat harvest, a mainstay of the country's economy, is devastated by the fungal disease stem rust.

SUB-SAHARAN AFRICA

Feb. British forces invade Italian Somaliland.

7 Mar. British forces invade Italian-held Ethiopia. They take Addis Ababa on 5 April and go on to expel the Italian army of occupation.

AUSTRALIA AND OCEANIA

8 Dec. Japanese forces attack and then occupy the island of Guam, a US possession in the Mariana Islands in the W Pacific.

10 Dec. Japanese forces land on Luzon, the largest island in the Philippines.

ECONOMY AND SOCIETY

1 June In Britain clothes rationing is introduced, while utility clothing and furniture are officially encouraged.

SCIENCE AND TECHNOLOGY

May In Britain the Gloster Meteor, the first jet fighter (designed by Frank Whittle) has its test flight.

– General Motors builds the first US diesel freight locomotives.

– British chemist John Rex Whinfield invents terylene, a new polyester fibre (known as Dacron in the USA).

ARTS AND HUMANITIES

Literature

13 Jan. The Irish novelist James Joyce dies in Zürich, Switzerland.

28 Mar. The English novelist Virginia Woolf drowns herself.

April First performance in Zürich of Bertolt Brecht's play *Mutter Courage und ihre Kinder* (Mother Courage and her

Children), which reconstructs the horrors of the Thirty Years War (1618–48) in terms that resonate for the present generation.

31 May In Germany Gothic type is officially replaced by Roman type.

Noël Coward, *Blithe Spirit*, play.

F. Scott Fitzgerald, *The Last Tycoon*, posthumously published novel.

Erich Fromm, *The Fear of Freedom*, an examination of the philosophical and psychoanalytic roots of totalitarianism.

Ellen Anderson Gholson Glasgow, *In This Our Life*, novel.

François Mauriac, *La Pharisienne* (The Pharisean Woman), novel.

Alberto Moravia, *La Mascherata* (The Fancy Dress Party), novel offering a fictionalized portrayal of Benito Mussolini as a S American dictator. Moravia's work will be censored until the end of World War II.

Eugene O'Neill, *Long Day's Journey into Night*, play (it will not be produced and published until 1956).

Rebecca West, *Black Lamb and Grey Falcon*, a study of Yugoslavia.

Visual Arts and Architecture

– In South Dakota, USA, the Mount Rushmore Memorial to US presidents George Washington, Thomas Jefferson, Abraham Lincoln and Theodore Roosevelt is completed. Giant heads of the four presidents are carved on a rock face by the sculptor Gutzon Borglum.

– The National Gallery of Art, built with the bequest of US financier Andrew Mellon, opens in Washington, D.C.

Jackson Pollock, *Bird*, painting.

Music

– The opening of Beethoven's Symphony No. 5 is adopted as a theme to be whistled by the peoples of occupied Europe when in the presence of German soldiers. A message broadcast by the BBC (27 June) urges the adoption in occupied territories of the Morse code signal for the letter V (for Victory): three dots and a dash. The signal matches the rhythm of the first four notes of the symphony.

Richard Addinsell, *Warsaw Concerto*, score for the film *Dangerous Moonlight*.

Nat Burton and Walter Kent, 'There'll be Blue Birds Over the White Cliffs of Dover', song.

Olivier Messiaen, *Quartet for the End of Time*, written while the composer is a prisoner-of-war of the Germans in Silesia.

Sergei Rachmaninov, *Symphonic Dances for Orchestra*.

Don Raye and Hughie Prince, 'Boogie Woogie Bugle Boy', song.

Norbert Schultze and Hans Leip, 'Lile Marlene', song; the English lyricists Jimmy Phillips and Tommy Connor adapt the song with English lyrics.

Dmitri Shostakovitch, Symphony No. 7, a work dedicated to the besieged city of Leningrad (see 1 Sept.).

Film

Alfred Hitchcock, *Suspicion*, starring Cary Grant and Joan Fontaine.

John Huston, *The Maltese Falcon*, starring Humphrey Bogart and Peter Lorre.

Michael Powell and Emeric Pressburger, *One of Our Aircraft is Missing*.

Preston Sturges, *The Lady Eve*, starring Barbara Stanwyck.

Orson Welles, *Citizen Kane*, starring Welles and Joseph Cotten; based on the life of William Randolph Hearst, the film portrays the corruption of riches and power.

1942

EUROPE

2 Jan. The Allies agree not to make a separate peace with Germany.

5 Jan. The Red Army launches an offensive against the German invaders, retaking territory in the C and N between Jan. and early April.

20 Jan. At the Wannsee Conference in Berlin, high-ranking Nazis headed by Reinhard Heydrich discuss the Final Solution (the extermination of European Jewry). The Nazi leadership sets in motion the mass transportation of Jews to specially-built death camps where extermination will be carried out on an industrial scale using Zyklon B gas (see 3 Sept. 1941).

1 Feb. Nazi collaborator Vidkun Quisling becomes prime minister of Norway.

18 April On Hitler's orders, Marshal Philippe Pétain reinstates Pierre Laval as head of the Vichy government.

23–30 April German bombers launch 'Baedeker raids' on the historic British cities of Bath, Canterbury, Exeter and Norwich.

April On the E Front German forces launch a new offensive in the Ukraine.

27 May Czech forces parachuted in from Britain attempt to assassinate Reinhard Heydrich, 'protector' of Nazi-occupied Bohemia and Moravia and deputy leader of the SS. Heydrich dies of blood-poisoning eight days later.

30 May In the first of the '1000 bomber' RAF raids on Germany, Cologne is bombed.

10 June In retaliation for the assassination of Heydrich, German SS forces 'liquidate' the Czech village of Lidice. 172 men are shot and the women are transported to Ravensbrück concentration camp. 90 children are screened for racial purity, then dispersed throughout Germany to be renamed and brought up as Germans.

June The systematic mass murder of Jews begins in the gas chambers of Auschwitz and Treblinka (July).

16 July Some 30,000 Parisian Jews are rounded up to be sent to Nazi concentration camps and almost certain death.

July By the end of this month German forces, headed for the oilfields of the Caucasus, have reached the N Caucasus. Georgi Zhukov has now been given command of the Soviet armies of the S part of the front.

19 Aug. In a badly executed amphibious raid a combined force of British commandos and Canadian infantry and armoured units attempt to capture Dieppe in N France. The occupying German forces defeat the raiders, who suffer 3500 casualties.

22 Aug. On the E front the battle of Stalingrad (Volgograd) begins in SW Russia. The Germans see the city, of strategic value on the River Volga, as the key to breaking Soviet resistance. The assault marks the furthermost German advance into the USSR. The German 6th Army and 4th Panzer Army, supported by Romanian, Italian and Hungarian forces, batter at the defences of the Soviet 62nd Army, but fail to destroy them.

11 Nov. Following Allied landings in French N Africa (8 Nov.), the previously unoccupied parts of France are occupied by German troops. The crews manning the French fleet at Toulon scuttle their ships to prevent them being seized by the Axis (27 Nov.).

19 Nov. In a counter-offensive known as Operation Uranus, Soviet forces encircle the German army besieging Stalingrad. Refusing to accept defeat, Hitler orders Gen. Friedrich von Paulus and the German 6th Army to remain at Stalingrad until they can be relieved.

12–24 Dec. German forces under Field Marshal Erich von Manstein are repulsed by a Soviet counterattack as they attempt to relieve the German 6th Army trapped at Stalingrad.

Dec. Britain starts to plan for the postwar world with the publication of *Social Insurance and Allied Services* (usually called the Beveridge Report). William Beveridge, a Liberal economist, produces a report that recommends a combination of state provision and personal insurance schemes in developing a universal scheme of social security and health care. The report attracts great public interest in Britain, but the lack of enthusiasm for it shown by Conservative politicians will have serious consequences for them in the next general election (1945).

MIDDLE EAST AND NORTH AFRICA

May In N Africa the German Afrika Korps under Field Marshal Erwin Rommel start an offensive that will push British forces E into Egypt.

21 June German forces under Rommel seize Tobruk, NE Libya. Some 35,000 British soldiers are taken as prisoners of war. The Axis forces now head E towards Alexandria in Egypt.

July The British 8th Army holds off Rommel's advancing Afrika Korps in the first battle of El Alamein in Egypt. Rommel is repulsed again at Alam Halfa (30 Aug.–2 Sept.).

19 Aug. Gen. Bernard Montgomery is made commander of the British 8th Army.

23 Oct. The second battle of El Alamein begins with a massive British artillery bombardment. After prolonged fighting Rommel orders a general retreat (4 Nov.), from which the Axis forces in N Africa do not recover.

7–8 Nov. Allied troops under US general Dwight D. Eisenhower land in Morocco and Algeria in Operation Torch. The landings are facilitated by the former Vichy vice-premier Admiral François Darlan, who arranges a ceasefire that allows the landings to proceed. French garrisons in Casablanca, Oran and Algiers surrender to the Anglo-US forces. Eisenhower recognizes Darlan as French head of state in N Africa, enraging

the British and the Free French leader, Charles de Gaulle. Darlan is assassinated in Algiers (24 Dec.) by Fernand Bonnier de la Chapelle, a young royalist, operating as part of a group linked to de Gaulle's circle at the Comité Français de la Libération Nationale in London.

ASIA

10 Jan. The Japanese invade Burma.

11 Jan. Advancing through the Malay Peninsula, the Japanese take Kuala Lumpur. British forces in Malaya retreat to the British naval base of Singapore at the S tip of the Malay Peninsula.

15 Feb. Singapore falls to the Japanese. Some 130,000 British and imperial troops surrender. The British and their allies outnumber the Japanese forces of Gen. Yamashita Tomoyuki throughout the Malayan campaign, but they lack the equipment and skills in jungle warfare that might have made victory possible.

8 Mar. The Japanese take Rangoon (now Yangon) in Burma.

18 April A force of 16 specially adapted Mitchell bombers led by Lt-Col. James Doolittle take off from US carrier *Hornet* to bomb Tokyo. This raid does little material damage but is a huge shock to the Japanese, who shift resources away from planned attacks to air defence.

29 April In Burma the Japanese succeed in cutting the Burma Road, supply route to China. The Japanese conquest of Burma is completed with the fall of Mandalay (2 May).

8 Aug. The Indian National Congress passes the Quit India resolution, calling for immediate independence. British prime minister Winston Churchill (see p. 523) continues to resist the independence of India, just as he had done in the 1930s. Under pressure from the USA and the Labour Party, Churchill has sent cabinet member Stafford Cripps to negotiate a settlement to be implemented after the war. Gandhi (see p. 476), disregarding the war, refuses to wait. Following the resolution, Gandhi and the entire leadership of the Congress are imprisoned, and Churchill says (10 Nov.) in a speech delivered in London that: 'I have not become the king's first minister in order to preside over the liquidation of the British empire.'

THE AMERICAS

15 Jan. The world war acquires a pan-American dimension with the summoning of delegates to the Inter-American Conference held at Rio de Janeiro. Delegates pass a resolution calling for the severing of all relations with the Axis powers (21 Jan.).

19 Feb. President Roosevelt introduces internment for Japanese-Americans living on the W seaboard of the USA, although he has not done so for German-Americans or Italian-Americans. The wartime economic boom is now having a profound effect on unemployment, which at 3.6 million is just over a third of what it was in 1939 (9.5 million).

23 Feb. A Japanese submarine surfaces and shells an oil refinery at Golata, California.

13 June President Roosevelt establishes the Office of Strategic Services to undertake special operations.

AUSTRALIA AND OCEANIA

2 Jan. In the Philippines Manila is captured by the Japanese, who then invade the Dutch East Indies (10 Jan.).

22 Jan. Japanese forces take Rabaul, a port on the island of New Britain (now part of Papua New Guinea).

23 Jan. Japanese forces invade the Solomon Islands, E of New Guinea.

9 April Some 36,000 US troops stationed on the Bataan peninsula, Philippines, surrender to the Japanese. US commander Gen. Douglas MacArthur leaves, vowing 'I will return'. Some 70,000 US and Filipino prisoners are then forcibly marched to a Japanese prisoner-of-war camp in what will become known as the Bataan Death March. Only 54,000 prisoners reach the camp.

7 May The last US troops in the Philippines surrender on the island fortress of Corregidor.

3–6 June US forces defeat the Japanese at the naval-air battle of Midway. The Japanese lose 4 aircraft carriers and 12 other ships; the Americans lose one aircraft carrier and a destroyer. The military balance in the Pacific begins to turn against the Japanese.

7 Aug. US marines land on the island of Guadalcanal in the Solomon Islands. Six months of bitter fighting will follow before US forces force the Japanese to evacuate the island (Feb. 1943).

ECONOMY AND SOCIETY

Jan. In his crackdown on organized crime in New York, Mayor Fiorello La Guardia outlaws pinball machines.

– The Oxford Committee for Famine Relief (Oxfam) is founded in Oxford, England, to raise funds to feed hungry children in Greece.

– The *Negro Digest* begins publication in Chicago. The monthly circulation soars from 3000 to 100,000 when US first lady Eleanor Roosevelt writes a memorable piece for the journal, 'If I Were a Negro'.

SCIENCE AND TECHNOLOGY

24 Dec. Military technology is transformed when Wernher von Braun, a German rocket scientist, launches the first surface-to-surface guided missile at Peenemünde, N Germany.

– US scientists develop the first electronic computer.

– Harvard chemist Louis F. Fieser develops napalm, a jellied gasoline, which will increase the range of flame-throwers in combat.

– US corporation General Foods develops soluble coffee at its Maxwell House factory in New Jersey. The coffee forms part of the rations packaged for US troops.

ARTS AND HUMANITIES

Literature

– Modern French existentialism makes an appearance with the publication of Albert Camus's essay 'The Myth of Sisyphus', a work whose analysis of the nature of commitment reflects Camus's own service with the French Resistance. His novel *L'Etranger* (The Outsider) takes the analysis further.

Gerald Brenan, *The Spanish Labyrinth*, a history of the origins of the Spanish Civil War.

Joyce Cary, *To be a Pilgrim*, novel.

Lewis Namier, *Conflicts: Studies in Contemporary History*.

Antoine de Saint-Exupéry, *Pilote de Guerre* (Flight to Arras), auto-biographical work about the role of the pilot in World War II.

Upton Sinclair, *Dragon's Teeth*, novel.

Evelyn Waugh, *Put Out More Flags*, novel.

Visual Arts and Architecture

23 Jan. The British painter Walter Sickert dies.

Georges Braque, *Patience*, painting.

Edward Hopper, *Nighthawks*, painting.

Jackson Pollock, *Male and Female*, painting.

Music

– Irving Berlin writes the music and the lyrics for the film *Holiday Inn* (including the song 'White Christmas'), starring Bing Crosby and Fred Astaire.

– Glenn Miller becomes leader of the US Army Air Force Band in Europe.

John Cage, *Imaginary Landscape* No. 3.

Heitor Villa-Lobos, *Bachianas Brasileiras* No. 7 for orchestra.

Film

16 Jan. US actress Carole Lombard dies in a plane crash after finishing the filming of Ernst Lubitsch's *To Be or Not to Be*.

29 May US actor John Barrymore dies.

David Butler, *The Road to Morocco*, starring Bob Hope, Bing Crosby and Dorothy Lamour.

Michael Curtiz, *Casablanca*, starring Humphrey Bogart and Ingrid Bergman.

David Lean, *In Which We Serve*, starring Noël Coward.

Irving Rapper, *Now, Voyager*, starring Bette Davis.

Orson Welles, *The Magnificent Ambersons*.

William Wyler, *Mrs Miniver*, starring Greer Garson.

1943

EUROPE

14–23 Jan. Churchill and Roosevelt, meeting at the Casablanca Conference (see below), demand Germany's unconditional surrender.

Jan. Allied aircraft begin a sustained bombing campaign against the industrial towns and cities of Germany and occupied France.

2 Feb. At Stalingrad, the surviving Germans, some 91,000 men, surrender in defiance of Hitler's order to fight to the death. Losses on both sides are heavy: over one million Soviet and perhaps 800,000 Axis troops in the whole campaign. The German defeat is a turning-point of World War II.

15 Feb. The Red Army regains the Ukrainian city of Kharkov but loses it in a German counter-offensive (15 Mar.).

Feb. The Red Army succeeds in breaking through to Leningrad, which has now been besieged for 17 months. The Germans will continue to blockade the city, intermittently shutting off supplies, for another year.

1943

WARSAW GHETTO UPRISING □ RAF USES BOUNCING BOMBS TO DESTROY GERMAN DAMS □ ITALY SURRENDERS

19 April–16 May Survivors of the Jewish ghetto established in Warsaw by the occupying Germans stage an uprising against the Nazis. Some 60,000 Jews are murdered after the rising is suppressed.

17 May The RAF destroys dams in the Ruhr region of Germany using 'bouncing bombs' designed by Barnes Wallis.

5 July The battle of Kursk begins in W Russia. It proves to be the key battle of the war in E Europe. Some 2 million troops and 6000 tanks are involved. The massive and well-planned German attack falters on Soviet defence in depth. A Soviet counterattack leads to the recapture of Kharkov (23 Aug.).

9–10 July British and US forces invade Sicily from N Africa in Operation Husky.

19 July US aircraft bomb Rome for the first time.

25 July King Victor Emmanuel III of Italy demands the resignation of Mussolini, who is arrested. Marshal Pietro Badoglio succeeds as prime minister.

17 Aug. Allied forces occupy Messina, Sicily, then cross the Strait of Messina to invade S Italy. Badoglio's representatives meet Allied commanders in Algiers and agree to sign an armistice.

3 Sept. Italy surrenders unconditionally. German forces rush S to fill the breach.

9 Sept. The US 5th Army lands at Salerno, SE of Naples, Italy, but suffers serious casualties. US forces take Naples (1 Oct.), but German resistance makes further advance slow and costly.

25 Sept. The Red Army retakes Smolensk. The German collapse in the E begins.

4 Oct. In a key speech SS chief Heinrich Himmler tells Nazi officials that the plan for the total extermination of the Jewish race is now well established and that although the campaign will never be publicly proclaimed it will be 'an unwritten and never-to-be-written page of glory'.

13 Oct. Italy declares war on Germany.

Oct. The SS begins the arrest and deportation of Danish Jews, most of whom, however, escape to Sweden.

Oct. The Moscow Conference of Allied nations establishes the European Advisory Commission, which defines the terms for a German surrender, the separation of Austria from Germany and the dismantling of fascism in Italy.

6 Nov. The Red Army retakes Kiev.

24 Dec. In N France the Pas de Calais is attacked by combined formations of Allied bombers.

26 Dec. In the naval battle of the North Cape, fought in Arctic waters N of Norway, the Royal Navy sinks the German battle cruiser *Scharnhorst*.

MIDDLE EAST AND NORTH AFRICA

14–23 Jan. British prime minister Winston Churchill and US president Franklin D. Roosevelt meet at Casablanca, Morocco, to determine future Allied war strategy. Gen. Dwight D. Eisenhower is appointed commander of the Allied forces in N Africa. The Casablanca Conference also ends with the announcement that the Allies will seek nothing less than unconditional surrender by the Axis powers.

23 Jan. The British 8th Army takes Tripoli, robbing the Axis forces of a key supply port.

22 Feb. The Kasserine Pass in Tunisia is seized by a reinforced German army, inflicting heavy losses on US forces, but the Americans retake the pass (26 Feb.).

7 May Tunis and Bizerte fall, respectively, to the British and the Americans.

13 May German forces in Tunisia surrender to the Allies.

23–27 Nov. Roosevelt, Churchill and Chinese leader Jiang Jieshi (Chiang Kai-shek) meet at the Cairo Conference to discuss strategy against Germany and Japan and decide on a postwar policy for the Far East.

28 Nov.–1 Dec. Allied leaders Roosevelt, Churchill and Stalin attend the Tehran Conference, which discusses the planning of Allied military landings in France. In return for a definite date for an invasion of W Europe in 1944, Stalin promises to enter the war against Japan after Germany is defeated.

ASIA

– Beriberi, a disease caused by malnutrition, is now widespread in Japan. The government, ineffectually, urges the population to eat brown rice.

THE AMERICAS

15 Jan. The Pentagon, a building that houses the entire US military bureaucracy under one roof, is completed at Arlington, Virginia.

22 June Federal troops are sent in to suppress a two-day race riot in Detroit, which leaves 34 dead.

9 Nov. The United Nations Relief and Rehabilitation Administration (UNRRA) is established under the terms of an agreement signed in Washington, D.C. It has the task of providing humanitarian relief in newly liberated areas.

17 Dec. Roosevelt signs the Chinese Act, which repeals the Chinese Exclusion Acts of 1882 and 1902. Chinese who are resident in the USA are now eligible for naturalization. A regular quota of Chinese immigrants is established.

– Congressman J. William Fulbright drafts the resolution that will lead to the establishment of the United Nations.

AUSTRALASIA AND OCEANIA

22 Jan. US, Australian and New Zealand forces land in SE New Guinea and, in so doing, increase the security of Australia from a possible Japanese invasion.

Feb. Japanese forces evacuate the island of Guadalcanal.

Mar. US bombers sink 22 Japanese ships, including troopships bound for New Guinea, in an engagement known as the battle of the Bismarck Sea.

5 Aug. Allied forces occupy the Japanese air base of Munda in the Solomon Islands and proceed to destroy Japanese planes at the Wewak airfield in New Guinea (17–18 Aug).

18 Aug. Acting on military intelligence, US planes over Bougainville island shoot down the plane carrying Admiral Isoroku Yamamoto, who is killed. The event has symbolic importance since Yamamoto was the mastermind behind the attack on Pearl Harbor in 1941.

532 THE MODERN WORLD: 1900–2004

ECONOMY AND SOCIETY

- William Morris, Viscount Nuffield, British car manufacturer, creates the Nuffield Foundation to further research in the natural and social sciences.
- US psychologists Arnold L. Gesell and Frances Ilg herald a transformation in child rearing when they claim, in their work *The Infant and Child in the Culture of Today*, that children should be given more control over their lives.
- Forced by the US government to get rid of one of its two radio networks (for competition reasons), US corporation NBC sells the Blue Network to Edward Noble, who turns it into ABC (American Broadcasting Company).

SCIENCE AND TECHNOLOGY

- Russell Marker, a US chemist, heralds one of the 20th-century's most profound social changes with his discovery of the hormone progesterone in the barbasco plant, which grows wild in Mexico. Using an extract from the root, Marker produces 2000 grams of progesterone in two months. He will form Syntex, the drug firm that will became a major supplier of the raw materials for oral contraceptives.
- Albert Hofmann, a Swiss chemist, swallows by mistake some lysergic acid diethylamide (LSD) and discovers its psychedelic powers.

ARTS AND HUMANITIES

Literature

Nigel Balchin, *The Small Back Room*, novel.

Bertolt Brecht, *Der gute Mensch von Sezuan* (The Good Person of Szechwan) and *Leben des Galilei* (The Life of Galileo), plays.

Noël Coward, *Present Laughter* and *This Happy Breed*, plays.

T.S. Eliot, *Four Quartets*, poetry collection: 'Burnt Norton' (1935), 'East Coker' (1940), 'The Dry Salvages' (1941) and 'Little Gidding' (1942).

Hermann Hesse, *Das Glasperlenspiel* (The Glass Bead Game), novel.

Jacques Maritain, *Christianity and Democracy*, philosophy.

Robert Musil, *Der Mann ohne Eigenschaften* (The Man without Qualities), novel, is published posthumously after the author's death in exile in Switzerland (1942).

Ayn Rand, *The Fountainhead*, a novel based on the life of the Welsh-American architect Frank Lloyd Wright. Rand's work will become the centrepiece of US libertarian philosophy.

Antoine de Saint-Exupéry, *Le Petit Prince* (The Little Prince), a story for children. Saint-Exupéry is now serving with the Free French forces in N Africa.

Jean-Paul Sartre (see box), *L'Etre et le néant* (Being and Nothingness), work of existentialist philosophy.

Visual Arts and Architecture

- In New York the Dutch artist Piet Mondrian completes his painting *Broadway Boogie-Woogie* (begun in 1942).
- The Jefferson Memorial is dedicated in Washington, D.C.

Willem de Kooning, *Queen of Hearts*, painting.

Jackson Pollock, *The She-Wolf*, painting.

Music

28 Mar. Sergei Rachmaninov, Russian composer and pianist, dies in California.

Paul Hindemith, *Symphonic Metamorphosis of Themes by Carl Maria von Weber*.

Richard Rodgers and Oscar Hammerstein II, *Oklahoma!*, Broadway musical.

Arnold Schoenberg, *Theme and Variations* in G minor for orchestra.

Dmitri Shostakovich, Symphony No. 8 in C minor.

Film

Sergei Eisenstein, *Ivan the Terrible,* with a score by Sergei Prokofiev.

Edmund Goulding, *The Constant Nymph*, starring Alexis Smith, Charles Boyer and Joan Fontaine.

Michael Powell and Emeric Pressburger, *The Life and Death of Colonel Blimp*, satire of traditional British attitudes starring Roger Livesey and Deborah Kerr.

Jean-Paul Sartre (1905–80)

As a philosopher, novelist, playwright and essayist, Sartre maintained the French tradition of the public intellectual. He refused the Nobel prize for literature in 1964, saying that it made the writer an institution. He fought in the French army in 1940 and was captured by the Germans. On his release he joined the Communist Resistance in Paris, and although he later abandoned organized political parties, he never abandoned his support of left-wing causes. Sartre used contemporary events to illustrate and advance those fundamental ideas of commitment and authenticity that are the hallmarks of the existentialist school of philosophy.

Sartre's version of existentialism stated that the only moral action is one that arises out of a freely made choice to act. He argued that human existence comprises a series of active choices, and that choice is fundamental to humanity. Bad faith (*mauvaise foi*) means avoiding these truths and failing to acknowledge the need to choose, but referring instead to God, determinism or some other such 'higher' power. Humans who realize they are alone, and that their actions are entirely their own responsibility, suffer anguish or anxiety, but this is a badge of honour. Sartre outlined his philosophy in a number of works, most notably *Being and Nothingness* (1943), but he later attempted to reconcile existentialism with Marxism, especially in his *Critique of Dialectical Reason* (1960).

Sartre was a creative writer as well as a theorist, and viewed the artist as a privileged being who is able to find salvation through creativity. Commitment to political causes, however, implies an abandonment of this privileged spectator's position. The fruitful conflict between these two positions, notably embodied in his novel trilogy *The Roads to Freedom* (1947–50), makes Sartre a highly representative figure among 20th-century writers.

1944

EUROPE

20 Jan. The RAF bombs Berlin, dropping 2300 tons of bombs. George Bell, bishop of Chichester, becomes the leader of a campaign of domestic criticism at the savagery of the onslaught on the civilian population in Germany, which he claims is at odds with the morality of a war being waged on behalf of democratic values.

20 Jan. The Red Army regains Novgorod, S of Leningrad.

22 Jan. Allied troops land at Anzio beach, S of Rome. German defences are light, but the US commander Gen. John Lucas prefers to consolidate his bridgehead rather than advance. The Germans reinforce their defences, and the chance for a rapid conclusion to the Italian campaign is lost.

27 Jan. The Red Army breaks the siege of Leningrad. Soviet forces take Krivoi Rog in the Ukraine (22 Feb.), cross the Dniester (19 Mar.) and regain Odessa (10 April) and Sevastopol in the Crimea (9 May). Between 300,000 and 500,000 Crimean Tatars are rounded up by the Russians and sent into exile in C Asia as a punishment for having welcomed the German invaders.

15 Feb. In an attempt to break the stalemate in Italy, Allied bombers destroy the Benedictine monastery of Monte Cassino, but the ruins are fortified by the Germans.

19 Mar. SS units occupy Hungary. Following the German occupation, Hungarian Jews are rounded up and sent to the death camps.

24 Mar. Herbert Kappler of the SS orders the shooting of 335 Italian civilians in the Fosse Ardeatine caves on the Appian Way near Rome. The massacre is a reprisal for the killing by partisans of 35 German soldiers.

18 May Polish troops take Monte Cassino after three months of bitter fighting. Allied troops are now able to break out from the Anzio beachhead.

5 June Rome falls to the Allies.

6 June D-Day: Allied troops land on the Normandy beaches under the supreme command of US Gen. Dwight D. Eisenhower. The Germans have been tricked into believing that the Normandy landings are a diversion to draw their forces away from a real attack at Calais. Field Marshal Erwin Rommel tries to persuade Hitler that the Normandy landings are the heart of the campaign, but it is too late.

10 June The French village of Oradour-sur-Glane, NW of Limoges, is destroyed and 642 killed as a German reprisal against the French Resistance.

26 June Cherbourg is taken by Allied troops advancing from Normandy, and the road is open for the liberation of Paris.

June The first V-1 (*Vergeltungswaffe*, reprisal weapon) flying bombs fall on England.

3 July Soviet forces recapture Minsk, along with 100,000 Germans.

9 July The Allies take Caen.

17 July Iceland becomes an independent republic. Although enjoying sovereignty since 1918, the country has been a dependency of Denmark and has been occupied since 1940 by British and then by US forces in order to guard against a German invasion. US troops will remain stationed in Iceland until 1959.

20 July Adolf Hitler (see p. 509) survives an assassination attempt organized by some of his leading officers. Up to 200 conspirators are subsequently subjected to secret trial and execution.

23 July Soviet forces cross the Curzon Line in Poland and the Kremlin recognizes the Lublin Committee of Polish Liberation (meeting in Moscow) as the Polish government (26 July). The Polish government in exile in London, recognized by Britain and the USA, has proved unreceptive to Stalin's plans for frontier alterations.

1 Aug. Polish soldier Tadeusz Komorowski, assuming that he will receive Soviet support, leads the Warsaw rising against the Germans. Soviet forces, which had been approaching the city, halt until the Germans crush the rising after two months of fighting. Henceforth, there will be no effective opposition to Stalin's plans for Poland.

4 Aug. In Amsterdam Dutch Jew Otto Frank and his family are betrayed to the Gestapo after living in hiding for two years. The family, including their daughter Anne, are deported to extermination camps where they are killed. The diary Anne Frank has left behind in the family's place of refuge will become a classic of World War II literature.

11 Aug. In France Allied forces cross the River Loire.

14 Aug. The US 7th Army lands at Toulon, S France, and then moves N.

19 Aug. In Normandy the US 3rd Army under Gen. George Patton reaches the River Seine.

21 Aug. In Normandy Allied forces defeat the Germans in the Falaise Gap.

23 Aug. In the S of France French troops retake Marseilles.

24 Aug. Romania surrenders to the Russians, and Soviet forces enter Bucharest (5 Sept.).

25 Aug. Paris is liberated, and the leader of the Free French forces, Gen. Charles de Gaulle, enters the city. The French provisional government moves from Algiers to Paris (30 Aug.). The liberation of France is accompanied by a bloody settling of scores against those who have collaborated with the Germans.

4 Sept. The Allies take Antwerp and Brussels (5 Sept.).

5 Sept. The USSR declares war on Bulgaria, and Soviet troops enter Sofia (16 Sept.).

8 Sept. The Germans begin an assault on British cities with V-2 rockets, designed by Wernher von Braun. Some 1000 of the highly effective liquid-fuelled missiles will fall on Britain.

17–26 Sept. The battle of Arnhem: an attempt by the 1st British Airborne Division to secure a bridgehead over the River Rhine at Arnhem in Holland to facilitate the Allied advance into Germany fails when German units block the path of Allied divisions sent to reinforce the airborne troops.

5 Oct. The Poles in Warsaw surrender to the Germans, ending the Warsaw Rising in which more than 150,000 Poles have died.

6 Oct. The Red Army enters Hungary.

13 Oct. A combined force of British troops and Greek partisans retakes Athens.

16 Oct. Soviet forces enter E Prussia.

20 Oct. Belgrade falls to a combined force of Soviet troops and Yugoslav partisans. The political shape of postwar E Europe begins to be apparent as Soviet forces take control of nation after nation.

21 Oct. Aachen in the Netherlands is captured by the Allies.

12 Nov. The RAF sinks the German battleship *Tirpitz* near Tromso, Norway.

23 Nov. US forces liberate Strasbourg, E France.

16 Dec The battle of the Bulge (the Ardennes offensive): Hitler commits his final reserves and the bulk of his new tanks and other equipment to an ambitious plan to capture the Belgian cities of Antwerp and Brussels by splitting the Allied armies. The German attack begins well with sweeping advances in the Ardennes region but falters when US troops hold the key transport centre of Bastogne.

27 Dec. Soviet forces besiege Budapest, Hungary.

ASIA

Feb. Allied forces in the Pacific attack the main Japanese C Pacific base of Truk.

15 June US B-29 bombers based in China attack the Japanese island of Kyushu.

19–20 June US naval forces defeat the Japanese in the battle of the Philippine Sea, E of the Philippines.

9 July The battle for the island of Saipan in the Marianas marks a new stage in Allied supremacy in the Pacific. The Japanese lose some 400 planes, crippling their air power. US B-29 bombers can now reach Tokyo from Saipan. The Japanese government falls (18 July). Its replacement is no better equipped to counter the overwhelming US military superiority.

20 Oct. The Allied invasion of the Philippines begins.

Oct. Allied forces begin air raids on Taiwan, including one that destroys 300 Japanese planes (12 Oct.).

– In Vietnam the independence movement, the Viet Minh, declares Vietnamese independence.

THE AMERICAS

3 April The US Supreme Court rules that a citizen of the USA cannot be denied the right to vote because of colour.

22 June US Congress passes the GI Bill of Rights, which allows for 4% home loans to ex-servicemen and subsequently leads to a suburban housing boom in the USA. The development has major social implications for the USA: inner-city areas will be abandoned by residents and there will be a major shift from rural America to the developing suburbs.

1–22 July The United Nations Monetary and Financial Conference held at Bretton Woods, New Hampshire, leads to the establishment of the International Bank for Reconstruction and Development (World Bank) and the International Monetary Fund (IMF). Each participating country is to keep its currency to within a percentage or two of an agreed dollar value, with the IMF supplying the credit to keep the system solvent. The system will remain in force until 1973, when it becomes redundant after the USA separates the dollar from any gold value (1971).

23 Aug. The Dumbarton Oaks Conference opens: delegates from the USA, USSR, UK and China, meeting near Washington, D.C., draw up the framework for the United Nations.

7 Nov. Franklin D. Roosevelt is re-elected for a fourth term as US president, defeating Republican Thomas Dewey, who nonetheless receives 46% of the popular vote compared with Roosevelt's 53%. Senator Harry S Truman of Missouri becomes vice-president.

ECONOMY AND SOCIETY

– Swedish sociologist Gunnar Myrdal publishes *An American Dilemma*, examining the psychological effects of US hypocrisy in professing racial equality while practising inequality.

– Hungarian-born mathematician John von Neumann and German-born mathematician Oskar Morgenstern publish *Theory of Games and Economic Behaviour*. Their game theory is designed for application in any field of human decision-making where the agent cannot control all the variables. The book will prove influential in diplomatic and business circles.

– Austrian-born economist Friedrich von Hayek's *Road to Serfdom* attacks Keynesian theories of economic management.

– In Britain the Education Act (introduced by R.A. Butler, minister for education) raises the school-leaving age to 15 and provides for free, compulsory education. The Act divides education into primary, secondary and further stages and introduces the 'eleven plus' examination (to select children for education in grammar schools).

SCIENCE AND TECHNOLOGY

– A uranium pile is constructed at Clinton, Tennessee, a key step towards atomic power.

ARTS AND HUMANITIES

Literature

19 Dec. French daily newspaper *Le Monde* (The World) begins publication in Paris, edited by Hubert Beuve-Méry.

Jean Anouilh, *Antigone*, play.

Saul Bellow, *Dangling Man*, novel.

Jorge Luis Borges, *Ficciones* (Fictions), short stories.

Joyce Cary, *The Horse's Mouth*, novel, the third of a trilogy.

Charles Reginald Jackson, *The Lost Weekend*, novel studying alcoholism.

W. Somerset Maugham, *The Razor's Edge*, novel.

Jean-Paul Sartre (see p. 533), *Huis clos* (In Camera), play.

Visual Arts and Architecture

1 Feb. Dutch artist Piet Mondrian dies in New York.

17 Dec. Russian artist Wassily Kandinsky dies in Paris.

Francis Bacon, *Three Studies for Figures at the Base of a Crucifixion*, painting.

Max Ernst, *The King Playing with the Queen*, painting.

Pablo Picasso (see p. 467), *Death's Head*, painting.

Music

30 Oct. Aaron Copland's ballet *Appalachian Spring*, choreographed by Martha Graham, is performed at the Library of Congress, Washington, together with Paul Hindemith's ballet *Hérodiade*, also choreographed by Graham to the poem by French poet Stéphane Mallarmé.

16 Dec. An aircraft carrying the US band leader Glenn Miller disappears without trace over the English Channel.

– First performance of Michael Tippett's oratorio *A Child of Our Time*, inspired by the wartime persecution of the Jews.

Béla Bartók, *Rhapsody* No. 2.

Fred Heatherton, 'I've Got a Lovely Bunch of Coconuts', song.

Vincente Minnelli, *Meet Me in St Louis*, Broadway musical starring Judy Garland.

Cole Porter, 'Don't Fence Me In', song.

Sergei Prokofiev, Symphony No. 5 in B flat major.

Virgil Thomson, *Suite* (Portraits) Nos. 1 and 2.

Film

Frank Capra, *Arsenic and Old Lace*, starring Cary Grant.

Edward Dmytryk, *Farewell, My Lovely*.

Howard Hawks, *To Have and Have Not*.

David Lean, *This Happy Breed,* based on Noël Coward's play and starring John Mills and Celia Johnson.

Laurence Olivier, *Henry V.*

Billy Wilder, *Double Indemnity*.

1945

EUROPE

14 Jan. In the battle of the Bulge in Belgium US forces relieve US troops trapped in the key transport centre of Bastogne. The battle ends in defeat and massive casualties for Germany.

26 Jan. Soviet troops liberate Auschwitz, S Poland: fewer than 3000 inmates are still alive, about one million having been killed in the gas chambers.

30 Jan. Hitler's last radio speech is broadcast.

3 Feb. 1000 US bombers raid Berlin.

4–11 Feb. The Yalta Conference between Churchill, Roosevelt and Stalin takes place in the Crimea. In a rush to reach agreements on vital issues before the war ends, a number of fateful compromises are reached. Reparations and zones of occupation are agreed: the three leaders decide that postwar Germany will be divided into four separate zones of occupation, and Berlin will also have four zones. Stalin promises that the nations of E Europe will be democratic, while Churchill and Roosevelt assure him that the new governments of these countries will be friendly to the USSR.

13–14 Feb. The German city of Dresden, with a rich architectural and cultural heritage ('Florence on the Elbe'), is destroyed by Allied bombing raids. 135,000 Germans are killed.

7 Mar. The US 9th Armored Division seizes the Ludendorff Bridge at Remagen intact. By nightfall the US 1st Armored Division has established a bridgehead on the east bank of the Rhine.

19 Mar. Hitler orders the destruction of all industry useful to the Allies.

22 Mar. Troops of the US 5th Division cross the Rhine at Oppenheim (between Mannheim and Mainz) and establish bridgeheads on the east bank.

2 April The Red Army enters Austria.

11 April US Gen. George Patton's 3rd Army liberates Buchenwald concentration camp, NE of Weimar.

14 April The Red Army takes Vienna.

21 April The US 7th Army takes Nuremberg. By now Soviet forces are on the outskirts of Berlin, and many units lose discipline as soldiers commit atrocities against the civilian population.

24 April Dachau concentration camp, Bavaria, is liberated by Allied forces; most of the surviving inmates will soon die of the effects of hunger and insanitary conditions. The total number of 'racial inferiors' killed by the Nazi regime will amount to some 14 million, about 6 million of whom are Jews. Other victims include Slavs, Poles and gypsies.

25 April Allied and Soviet soldiers meet on the River Elbe, S of Berlin.

28 April Italian dictator Benito Mussolini, along with 12 of his former cabinet ministers, is executed at Lake Como, N Italy. German forces in Italy surrender unconditionally (29 April).

29 April In his bunker at the Reichs Chancellery, Berlin, Adolf Hitler marries his mistress, Eva Braun.

30 April Adolf Hitler (see p. 509) commits suicide with Eva Braun in his bunker at the Reichs Chancellery, Berlin. His propaganda chief, Joseph Goebbels, also commits suicide (1 May).

2 May Berlin capitulates to the Allies.

7 May Germany surrenders unconditionally. US president Truman proclaims 8 May to be VE (Victory in Europe) Day.

5 June The Allies take over the government of Germany.

9 June Soviet Military Occupation in Germany (SMAD) is established in Berlin.

1–4 July British and US forces withdraw from Saxony, Thuringia and Mecklenburg in E Germany.

17 July–2 Aug. The Potsdam Conference is attended by Allied leaders Truman, Stalin and Churchill, who is replaced by Labour Party leader Clement Attlee after the Conservative Party's defeat in the British general election (see below). The conference agrees on the demilitarization of Germany, the dissolution of all National Socialist institutions, the trial of its former leaders as war criminals and the systematic restoration of democratic life. But Truman, more suspicious of Stalin than Roosevelt has been, also tries to insist that US interpretations of agreements made shall be accepted. Stalin is unmoved.

26 July In the UK general election Labour wins by a landslide and Clement Atlee becomes prime minister.

6 Aug. The USA drops an atomic bomb on the Japanese city of Hiroshima, and three days later drops a second on Nagasaki. The Japanese government faces the certainty of annihilation and surrenders (14 Aug.). The world's second global conflict reaches its end. The count of the dead shows that among the military personnel who served during the war, the USSR lost

7.5 million, Germany nearly 2.9 million, China 2.2 million, Japan 1.5 million, the UK 398,000, Italy 300,000, the USA 290,000, France 211,000, Canada 39,139, India 36,092, Australia 29,395, New Zealand 12,262, South Africa 8681 and the remaining territories of the British empire 30,776. Total civilian deaths might amount to over 40 million, but precision proves to be impossible.

15 Aug. Marshal Philippe Pétain of France is condemned to death for treason, but the sentence passed on the 89-year-old hero of World War I is commuted to life imprisonment. Former Vichy French leader Pierre Laval, however, is executed (15 Oct.).

21 Oct. The elections for the French National Assembly are dominated by the successes of the French communists and socialists. The French Resistance begins to be portrayed as an inspiration of the left. The National Assembly, nonetheless, elects Charles de Gaulle, the representative of an alternative French ideal of conservative patriotism, as president of the provisional government (21 Nov.).

24 Oct. The United Nations comes into being. 29 nations ratify the UN Charter.

Nov. The trial of 22 Nazi leaders by an international military tribunal begins in Nuremberg, Bavaria.

MIDDLE EAST AND NORTH AFRICA

22 Mar. The League of Arab States is organized to include Egypt, Iraq, Jordan, Lebanon, Saudi Arabia, Syria and Yemen in a concerted move to achieve complete independence. Other Arab countries will later join the organization.

13 Aug. The World Zionist Congress issues a statement demanding the immediate admission of one million Jews to Palestine.

– Menachem Begin, a Polish immigrant and militant, leads the Irgun Zvai Leumi, a group of Jewish terrorists who bomb and murder British troops and officials who are trying to limit the number of Jewish immigrants entering Palestine.

ASIA

9 Jan. Gen. Douglas MacArthur leads US forces in an invasion of the Philippines; after a gruelling campaign he enters the capital, Manila (4 Feb.). MacArthur thus keeps his promise made on leaving in 1942, 'I will return'.

19 Feb. US forces land on the W Pacific Japanese island of Iwo Jima and secure it (26 Mar.). About 21,000 Japanese and nearly 7000 Americans die in the fighting. The island will serve as a base for US fighters escorting bombers to Japan.

9 Mar. A formation of US B-29 bombers destroys large parts of Tokyo in an aerial bombardment that kills perhaps 124,000 civilians.

21 June The Japanese island of Okinawa falls to US forces after three months of fighting that have cost nearly 50,000 Americans killed and wounded and about 100,000 Japanese dead.

5 July The US government formally announces the reconquest of the Philippines.

10 July US military strategists begin planning the invasion of the Japanese islands, starting with Honshu and Kyushu. Meanwhile, concerted aerial attacks start (17 July) to prepare for the invasion.

30 July After delivering components of an atomic bomb to Tinian in the Mariana Islands, the heavy cruiser USS *Indianapolis* is torpedoed in the Indian Ocean; about 600 men are eaten by sharks before 300 survivors are rescued.

30 July The Japanese government rejects the Potsdam Declaration, which has called for the immediate surrender of Japan.

6 Aug. An atomic bomb ('Little Boy') is dropped on the Japanese city of Hiroshima from the US B-29 bomber *Enola Gay*, piloted by Paul Tibbets Jr. The scale of the destruction awes even those who planned it: 100,000 Japanese die immediately and thousands more will die later from radiation sickness and burns.

8 Aug. The USSR declares war on Japan and sends its troops into Manchuria.

9 Aug. The B-29 bomber *Bock's Car* drops a second atomic bomb ('Fat Man') on the city of Nagasaki, the historic centre of Japanese Christianity on the island of Kyushu. About 75,000 people die immediately, leaving 75,000 survivors suffering from radiation sickness and varying degrees of burns.

10 Aug. Japan sues for peace. Truman declares 14 Aug. to be VJ (Victory over Japan) Day.

28 Aug. US forces land in Japan. Gen. Douglas MacArthur becomes supreme commander of Allied occupation forces.

2 Sept. The Japanese terms of surrender are signed aboard the battleship USS *Missouri* anchored in Tokyo Bay. Outer Mongolia, the Kuril Islands and S Sakhalin are ceded to the USSR. Inner Mongolia, Manchuria, Taiwan and Hainan are ceded to China. The USA and USSR occupy Korea pending the creation of democratic structures for the country. Emperor Hirohito is allowed to keep his throne but renounces his divinity (1 Jan. 1946). Japan is to be ruled by the US army of occupation run by MacArthur.

9 Sept. Japanese forces stationed in China, some one million men, surrender formally at Nanjing.

12 Sept. The 585,000 Japanese troops in SE Asia formally surrender to the British at Singapore.

– The British reoccupy Hong Kong despite the reservations of the US government, which favours ceding the colony to China.

THE AMERICAS

12 April US president Roosevelt dies two months after attending the Yalta Conference at which he, Stalin and Churchill pledged themselves to a postwar 'unity of purpose and action'. He is succeeded by the vice-president Harry S Truman, who becomes 33rd US president.

28 July A B-25 light bomber accidentally flies into the Empire State Building in New York City, tearing a hole between the 78th and 79th floors, killing 3 people on board and 10 bystanders.

25 Oct. President Getúlio Vargas of Brazil resigns, having been dictator for 15 years. The pro-democracy movement in Brazil ensures the election of Eurico Dutra as president (2 Dec.).

27 Dec. The International Bank for Reconstruction and Development starts operations with 21 countries, having clubbed together to subscribe some $7.2 billion, of which $3.2 billion comes from the USA. France will be the first country to receive a loan (May 1947).

– The Gross National Product of the USA stands at $211 billion, double that for 1929.

ECONOMY AND SOCIETY

– Japanese industrialist Nagano Shigeo founds Fuji Steel, which will become a major world steel producer.

– US entrepreneur Milton Reynolds sees Lazlo Biró (see 1938) ballpoint pens for sale in Buenos Aires in June. He develops a version that will avoid the problem of patents and biro pens go on sale in New York (29 Oct.).

SCIENCE AND TECHNOLOGY

18 July The world's first atomic bomb is tested successfully near Alamogordo, New Mexico.

– Soviet physicist Igor Kurchatov manages to engineer the first Russian atomic chain reaction using details obtained from the USA by Soviet spies.

– Grand Rapids, Michigan, becomes the scene of the first attempt at introducing fluoride into communal water supplies; the scheme arouses opposition and is dropped.

ARTS AND HUMANITIES

Literature

– Federico García Lorca's play *La casa de Bernarda Alba* (The House of Bernarda Alba) is performed for the first time (its author having been murdered in 1936).

Winston Graham, *Ross Poldark*, historical novel.

Henry Green (Henry Vincent Yorke), *Loving*, novel.

Arthur Koestler, *The Yogi and the Commissar*, collection of essays.

Carlo Levi, *Cristo si è fermato a Eboli* (Christ Stopped at Eboli), novel describing the impoverished lives of the Italian peasantry, among whom the author was exiled on account of his anti-fascism.

Nancy Mitford, *The Pursuit of Love*, novel.

George Orwell, *Animal Farm*, allegory of the corruptions of Soviet communism.

Bertrand Russell, *A History of Western Philosophy*.

Jean-Paul Sartre (see p. 533), *L'Age de raison* (The Age of Reason) and *Le Sursis* (The Reprieve), novels.

Evelyn Waugh, *Brideshead Revisited*, novel.

Tennessee Williams, *The Glass Menagerie*, play.

Visual Arts and Architecture

Diego Rivera, *Great Tenochtitlán* and *The Market in Tiangucio*, paintings for the Palacio Nacional in Mexico City.

Music

7 June First performance in London of Benjamin Britten's opera *Peter Grimes*, a tale of frustrated homosexuality based on the poem *The Borough* (1810) by George Crabbe.

15 Sept. Austrian composer Anton Webern dies near Salzburg, having been shot accidentally by a US military policeman.

26 Sept. Béla Bartók, Hungarian composer and collector of folk music, dies in New York.

– By now bebop, a variety of jazz music distinguished from the earlier jazz tradition by its harsher melodies, dissonant harmonies and faster tempos, is being developed in the USA by such musicians as Charlie Parker, Dizzy Gillespie and Thelonius Monk.

Mahalia Jackson, 'Move on up a Little Higher', song.

Dmitri Shostakovich, Symphony No. 9 in E flat.

Richard Strauss, *Metamorphosen*, study for 23 solo string instruments.

Charles Trenet, 'La Mer', song.

Film

Clarence Brown, *National Velvet*, starring the 14-year-old Elizabeth Taylor.

Marcel Carné, *Les Enfants du Paradis* (The Children of Paradise), starring Arletty and Jean-Louis Barrault. Although the film is set in 19th-century Paris, it reflects the conflicts in Nazi-occupied France.

Michael Curtiz, *Mildred Pierce*, starring Joan Crawford.

Alfred Hitchcock, *Spellbound*, starring Ingrid Bergman.

David Lean, *Blithe Spirit*, starring Rex Harrison and Margaret Rutherford.

Michael Powell and Emeric Pressburger, *I Know Where I'm Going*, starring Wendy Hiller.

Billy Wilder, *The Lost Weekend*, starring Ray Milland.

1946

EUROPE

7 Jan. The Western powers recognize the Austrian republic as a sovereign state within its 1937 borders.

10 Jan. The first session of the United Nations General Assembly is held in London, and the Norwegian politician Trygve Lie is elected secretary-general of the UN (1 Feb.).

11 Jan. Albanian communist leader Enver Hoxha declares his nation to be a People's Republic.

20 Jan. In France Charles de Gaulle resigns as president of the provisional government in the face of concerted opposition from parties of the left.

31 Jan. Yugoslavia adopts a Soviet-Socialist-type constitution.

1 Feb. Hungary is declared a republic.

13 Feb. In Britain Parliament repeals the Trade Disputes Act (1927), which had previously made sympathetic strikes illegal. Trade unions can now take industrial action to support each other's claims.

14 Feb. The British Labour government announces its intention of nationalizing the Bank of England.

18 April The League of Nations declares itself dissolved.

9 May Victor Emmanuel III, king of Italy, abdicates. His son proclaims himself king Umberto II, but a national Italian referendum (2 June) rejects monarchism and Umberto II goes into exile in Lisbon as Italy becomes a republic (3 June). The new Italian republic loses the Dodecanese islands to

Greece, and the small frontier tracts taken from France in 1940 are returned. Women are allowed to vote in Italy for the first time.

May The British government announces that it is to nationalize the coal industry with effect from 1 Jan 1947.

4 June The National School Lunch Act is passed in Britain, though bread rationing has to be introduced because of the worldwide shortage of wheat (1947).

14 July A massacre of Jews at Kielce kills some of the few surviving Jews in Poland, a country that before the war had one of the largest Jewish populations in the world.

15 Sept. After a referendum, Bulgaria rejects the monarchy and the country is declared to be a People's Republic. Georgi Dimitrov, the communist leader, returns from Moscow (21 Nov.) and becomes prime minister.

28 Sept. George II returns to Athens as king of the Hellenes after Greece votes to restore the monarchy. Communist partisans refuse to accept his restoration, and a brutal civil war breaks out. This conflict will end in 1949 with the defeat of the communists by government forces with British and US military support.

30 Sept. The Nuremberg Tribunal on war crimes delivers its verdicts. Leading Nazis Joachim von Ribbentrop and Hermann Goering are sentenced to death along with 10 others. Goering commits suicide by taking poison. Rudolf Hess and Walter Funk are sentenced to life imprisonment. Albert Speer is sentenced to 20 years imprisonment. Politician Franz von Papen and financier Hjalmar Schacht are acquitted. The convicted Nazis, including Speer and Hess, will be incarcerated in Berlin's Spandau prison.

– In Britain Parliament passes the National Health Service Act, based on the recommendations made by William Beveridge in his report of 1942. The Act is largely the work of Aneurin Bevan, Labour minister of health.

– The British government decides to develop the atom bomb.

– During the course of 1946, Hungary suffers the worst inflation in world history since records began. The gold pengo of 1931 falls in value to 130 trillion paper pengos (June). The government's response is to print 100 trillion pengo paper notes.

MIDDLE EAST AND NORTH AFRICA

10 Mar. British and French forces begin to evacuate Lebanon as the country gains its full independence after 26 years of French rule. A National Pact enshrines power-sharing between Maronite Christians and Muslims.

25 Mar. The government of the USSR declares that its forces will be withdrawn from Iran after severe pressure from the USA and UN.

25 Mar. Transjordan is proclaimed an independent kingdom following recognition by the British. Emir Abdullah reigns as King Abdullah. The Soviet government, however, vetoes Transjordan's admission to the UN.

– In Egypt serious anti-British riots take place in Cairo and Alexandria.

ASIA

6 Mar. The French recognize the independence of Vietnam, but only within the French empire. The nationalist rebellion continues under Ho Chi Minh, communist and Viet Minh leader.

10 April Elections are held for the Japanese diet (parliament). Women are allowed to vote under the terms of a Pax Americana, which is transforming the traditional Japanese hierarchies, and 34 are elected.

14 April The Chinese return to a state of civil war after a truce between the communists and Guomindang brokered by the USA breaks down. The return of the Guomindang government to Nanjing (1 May) is followed by another truce (12 May), and (10 Oct.) the Guomindang party elects Jiang Jieshi (Chiang Kai-shek) as president. The new Chinese government signs a Sino-US treaty of cooperation (4 Nov.), and a new Chinese constitution is adopted (25 Dec.). The paper agreements, however, ignore the fact that communist leader Mao Zedong (see p. 573) heads an armed movement of some 3 million people. The national assembly meets (15 Nov.) and excludes all communists. From Aug. onwards Mao begins organizing a military campaign to overthrow the Guomindang government and seize outright power for the communists.

9 June King Rama VIII of Siam (Thailand) is assassinated, ushering in a period of unstable government.

4 July The Philippines becomes independent of the USA: President Manuel Roxas has to confront a powerful communist party, which has seized and distributed land in Luzon.

13 Oct. The Siamese (Thai) government accepts the UN resolution, which decrees the return to Indochina of the provinces ceded to Siam when it was Japan's ally in 1941.

Oct. US lawyers draft a new Japanese constitution, which is now promulgated. Sovereignty is vested with the people rather than with the emperor, who becomes a figurehead ruler, having renounced his claims to divinity (1 Jan.). Article 9 of the constitution abrogates war, so Japan abandons high military expenditure in favour of a focus on business and economics. The Land Reform Act takes lands away from absentee landlords and limits the amount of land any single individual may cultivate. The changes in social attitudes and hierarchy in Japan are profound, as tenant farmers decline from 50% of the total population to just 10%.

15 Nov. By the terms of the Cheribon Agreement, the Netherlands agrees to recognize the independence of the Indonesian Republic, which includes Java, Sumatra, Madura, most of New Guinea and Borneo and nearly 14,000 smaller islands. The last British troops, who have been supporting the return of Dutch rule, leave (29 Nov.).

23 Nov. The French bombardment of Haiphong marks the start of the French Indochina War, which will last until 1954.

– Sir Charles Vyner Brooke, whose family have ruled the territory of Sarawak since 1841, cedes his lands to the British crown. Sarawak (NW Borneo) will become part of independent Malaysia in 1963.

THE AMERICAS

14 Feb. US president Harry S Truman announces a formula that grants US labour wage increases equal to the rise in the cost of living since Jan. 1941 (33%).

20 Feb. US Congress passes an employment act, which declares that the aim of the US government is maximum employment.

24 Feb. Right-wing populist Juan Perón is elected president of Argentina and starts his five-year rule aided by his manipulative second wife, Evita (Maria Eva de Duarte).

5 Mar. Former British prime minister Winston Churchill (see p. 523) delivers an address in Fulton, Missouri, announcing that: 'From Stettin in the Baltic to Trieste in the Adriatic an iron curtain has descended across the Continent.' Churchill's speech, made in the presence of President Truman, marks the beginning of a new awareness that the postwar world contains a totalitarian threat. The mutual hostility between communist East and capitalist West will lead to an armed stand-off known as the Cold War, which will last until 1989.

25 Mar. The UN Security Council meets in New York.

7 July Miguel Alemán Valdés becomes the first civilian president of Mexico and begins a programme of close links with the USA.

23 Oct. The UN General Assembly meets in New York and decides that New York is to be the permanent site of the UN (5 Dec.). The UN formally accepts a donation of $8.5 million from John D. Rockefeller to enable it to build a headquarters on the East River (14 Dec.).

14 Dec. President Truman has now removed price controls, and the US economy expands on the basis of a boom in credit and consumer spending. President Roosevelt's Office of Price Administration (created in April 1941) held down prices during the war, while wages rose. But Truman, haunted by memories of the 1930s, wants to prevent a postwar repetition of the Depression, and there seems little inflationary danger in a policy of economic expansionism. It will be 1971 before the US economy, for the first time since 1888, goes into deficit on its balance of trade.

ECONOMY AND SOCIETY

5 July The two-piece bikini, designed by French couturier Louis Réard, is modelled at a Paris fashion show, but it is soon banned at Biarritz.

– Marthe Ricard, newly elected to the French National Assembly as a deputy of the conservative and Catholic MRP (Mouvement Républicain Populaire), campaigns successfully for the closure of official brothels in Paris. Medical examinations for prostitutes are no longer required and street soliciting returns to Paris.

– New York paediatrician Benjamin Spock writes *The Common Sense Book of Baby and Child Care* (which will be republished as *Baby and Child Care*). The book advocates less rigid methods of rearing children.

SCIENCE AND TECHNOLOGY

– Italian helicopter designer Corradino d'Ascanio designs the Vespa (Wasp) motor scooter.

– The world's first automatic electronic digital computer, ENIAC (electronic numerical integrator and computer), is constructed at Harvard University, USA.

– The automatic assembly line becomes a postwar possibility when Delmar S. Harder, an engineer with the US Ford Motor Company, invents a system to assemble car engines by self-regulating means at the rate of one every 14 minutes.

ARTS AND HUMANITIES

Literature

8 June The German dramatist Gerhart Hauptmann dies.

13 Aug. The English writer H.G. Wells dies.

Sept. The Third Programme of the BBC starts broadcasting. It concentrates on the popularization of cultural and intellectual themes for a British audience.

– A committee of 22 biblical scholars, headed by Luther A. Weigle of Yale University, produces The Revised Version of the New Testament, revising the American Standard Version of 1901. It will be followed by the Old Testament Revised Version in 1952.

– German newspaper *Die Welt* (The World) starts publication in Hamburg, which is under the control of the occupying British forces. It will be acquired by German publisher Axel Springer in 1953.

– The Arts Council of Great Britain is established.

Jean Genet, *Miracle de la rose* (Miracle of the Rose), novel.

Christopher Isherwood, *Berlin Stories*, omnibus of novels.

Nikos Kazantzakis, *Zorba the Greek*, novel.

Philip Larkin, *Jill*, novel.

Eugene O'Neill, *The Iceman Cometh*, play.

Mervyn Peake, *Titus Groan*, first novel of the *Gormenghast* trilogy.

Terence Rattigan, *The Winslow Boy*, play.

Dylan Thomas, *Deaths and Entrances*, poetry collection.

Robert Penn Warren, *All the King's Men*, novel.

Visual Arts and Architecture

– The Australian painter Sidney Nolan starts a series of paintings of the bushranger Ned Kelly.

René Magritte, *Philosophy in the Boudoir*, painting.

Pablo Picasso (see p. 467), *The Joy of Living*, painting.

Music

12 July First performance at Glyndebourne of Benjamin Britten's opera *The Rape of Lucretia*. His *Young Person's Guide to the Orchestra* (*Variations and Fugue on a Theme of Purcell*) is written for the film *The Instruments of the Orchestra*.

Louis Guglielmi and singer Edith Piaf , 'La Vie en rose', song.

Paul Hindemith, *When Lilacs Last in the Dooryard Bloom'd* (Requiem for those we love), to texts by Walt Whitman.

Cole Porter, *Annie Get Your Gun*, Broadway musical starring Ethel Merman, including the songs, 'There's No Business Like Show Business' and 'Anything You Can Do'.

Film

Frank Capra, *It's a Wonderful Life*, starring James Stewart.

Jean Cocteau, *La Belle et la bête* (Beauty and the Beast), parable of gay love starring Cocteau's lover Jean Marais.

Howard Hawks, *The Big Sleep*, starring Humphrey Bogart and Lauren Bacall.

Alfred Hitchcock, *Notorious*, starring Cary Grant and Claude Rains.

David Lean, *Brief Encounter*, starring Trevor Howard and Celia Johnson, and *Great Expectations*, starring John Mills and Valerie Hobson.

Michael Powell and Emeric Pressburger, *A Matter of Life and Death* (*Stairway to Heaven*), starring David Niven.

Irving Rapper, *Deception*, starring Bette Davis.

Vittorio de Sica, *Sciucià* (Shoeshine), starring Rinaldo Smordoni.

1947

EUROPE

16 Jan. Vincent Auriol becomes president of France, beginning the Fourth Republic. Charles de Gaulle now heads a new party, the Rassemblement du Peuple Français (RPF), which will become informally known as the Gaullist party and will assert French national sovereignty.

25 Feb. The German state of Prussia is formally dissolved.

1 April King George II of Greece dies and is succeeded by his brother Paul I, but the civil war continues.

27 May In Germany the US and British zones of occupation merge to form the 'Bizone'.

30 May In Hungary the coalition government is overthrown by the Hungarian Communist Party, acting with Soviet backing.

July Under the leadership of British foreign secretary Ernest Bevin, 16 W European nations form the Committee for European Economic Cooperation. They are reacting to the invitation given by US secretary of state George C. Marshall (5 June) asking for a united European plan for recovery from the war, which the USA will support. Eventually, $13 billion in US aid will be donated and lay the foundations of future prosperity in W Europe.

Aug. In Britain the Labour government nationalizes railways, road transport and the electricity industry.

Oct. Charles de Gaulle's RPF becomes the dominant French political party in municipal elections, but the French communists become a strong second party. Robert Schuman becomes prime minister in the new French government, which takes office on 23 Nov. He will go on to help create (1952) the European Coal and Steel Community, a crucial step in the development of the European Union.

20 Nov. In Britain Princess Elizabeth marries Philip Mountbatten (who becomes Duke of Edinburgh).

– 23 nations sign the General Agreement on Tariffs and Trade (GATT), designed to boost world trade and avoid a world economic crisis by means of an agreement to keep tariffs to a minimum by regular international negotiations. It will become an agency of the United Nations, based in Geneva.

– Britain endures an economic crisis and a fuel crisis.

– In Britain the Town and Country Planning Act establishes 'green belts' and gives local authorities extensive powers.

MIDDLE EAST AND NORTH AFRICA

7 Feb. The British government tries to resolve the problem of Palestine by proposing a division into Arab and Jewish zones.

29 Nov. The UN General Assembly votes for the partition of Palestine. Although the proposal meets with Jewish approval, the Arab League declares that it will fight against partition (17 Dec.).

– In Egypt British troops are withdrawn from Cairo and Alexandria.

ASIA

15 Aug. 'At the stroke of the midnight hour' India becomes independent. The British viceroy, Lord Louis Mountbatten, has successfully proposed the partition of the subcontinent. Jawaharlal Nehru, leader of the Congress Party, becomes prime minister of India. Pakistan becomes an independent Muslim state, consisting of two territories, East and West Pakistan, to the E and W of India. Karachi is the new capital, and Muhammad Ali Jinnah, the formidably intransigent leader of the Muslim League, is the prime minister. Kashmir, however, which has been allocated to India, becomes the subject of tension between the two countries and millions die in the riots that follow the highly contentious partition. Discrimination against 'untouchables' (harijans) – members of the lowest caste – is outlawed in the new India, but prejudice against them remains an ineradicable feature of Indian life.

> *A moment comes … when the soul of a nation long suppressed finds utterance.*
>
> Jawaharlal Nehru, 14 Aug. 1947

THE AMERICAS

12 Mar. In the USA the Truman Doctrine, named after President Harry S Truman, is announced to Congress. The president proposes economic and military aid to countries supposedly threatened not just by the USSR but also by internal communism. The Doctrine is used to justify economic and military aid to Greece, which is threatened by a communist insurrection, and Turkey, under pressure from Soviet expansion in the Mediterranean.

5 June George C. Marshall, US secretary of state, proposes the Marshall Plan to give financial aid to European countries that are attempting to recover from the effects of the war; US influence in European domestic politics will be greatly increased by the Plan. Congress will authorize $540 million in immediate aid to France, Italy, Austria and China (23 Dec.).

23 June Despite President Truman's veto, the Taft–Hartley Act becomes law. The Act outlaws the closed shop and stops trade unions from using their money for 'political' purposes.

30 June Coal mining is denationalized in the USA.

26 July In the USA Congress passes the National Security Act, which allows the Central Intelligence Agency (CIA) to engage in counter-intelligence in Europe against Soviet expansionism and its system of satellite states.

Oct. Ten Hollywood producers, directors and screenwriters are summoned to appear before the House Un-American Activities Committee (HUAC) under suspicion of being communist sympathizers. They will be imprisoned (1948), and they and some 300 other artists in the film industry who are suspected of having communist sympathies will be blacklisted.

SUB-SAHARAN AFRICA

– The groundnut scheme, a British government-funded scheme to grow groundnuts on hitherto unprofitable land in Tanganyika, proves an expensive failure.

ECONOMY AND SOCIETY

16 Mar. A great gale in Britain uproots trees and causes massive floods and extensive agricultural damage. Britain has suffered its severest winter for 50 years.

28 Aug. The Spanish matador and national hero Manolete (Manuel Rodriguez) is gored to death at the bull ring in Linares, S Spain.

– The New Look, designed by French fashion designer Christian Dior, comes to dominate women's fashion.

SCIENCE AND TECHNOLOGY

– Britain starts to develop an atomic bomb. The first British nuclear reactor is built at Harwell, Oxfordshire.

– In the USA microwave ovens go on sale for the first time.

– Masaru Ibuka, a Tokyo engineer, starts Tokyo Tsushin Kogyo (the Tokyo Telecommunications Company), which will be renamed the Sony Corporation (1958).

ARTS AND HUMANITIES

Literature

– Francis Steele, an English archaeologist, deciphers the law code of Hammurabi of Babylon, dating from the 18th century BC.

– A Bedouin boy at Qumran, near the Dead Sea, Palestine, discovers scrolls of parchment containing most of the Old Testament Book of Isaiah. The Dead Sea Scrolls, scholars say, were written by members of an ascetic Jewish sect known as the Essenes in the 1st and 2nd centuries BC. Judaic scholarship is transformed by the discovery.

Albert Camus, *La Peste* (The Plague), novel.

Anne Frank, *The Diary of Anne Frank*.

L.P. Hartley, *Eustace and Hilda*, novel.

Malcolm Lowry, *Under the Volcano*, novel.

Compton Mackenzie, *Whisky Galore*, novel.

Thomas Mann, *Doktor Faustus*, novel.

James A. Michener, *Tales of the South Pacific*, novel that will later be adapted as the musical *South Pacific*.

Arthur Miller, *All My Sons*, play.

Alberto Moravia, *La Romana* (The Woman of Rome), novel.

Vladimir Nabokov, *Bend Sinister*, novel.

Stephen Potter, *Gamesmanship*, humorous study.

Hugh Trevor-Roper, *The Last Days of Hitler*, history.

Tennessee Williams, *A Streetcar Named Desire*, play starring Marlon Brando.

Visual Arts and Architecture

– Construction begins of Le Corbusier's Unité d'habitation, a multi-storey villa in Marseilles, S France.

Alberto Giacometti, *Pointing Man*, sculpture.

Oskar Kokoschka, *Das Matterhorn*, painting.

Henry Moore, *Three Standing Figures*, sculpture.

Pablo Picasso (see p. 467), *Ulysses with His Sirens*, painting.

Music

3 June First performance in Paris of Francis Poulenc's opera *Les Mamelles de Tirésias* (The Breasts of Tiresias), based on Guillaume Apollinaire's surrealist play.

20 June First performance at Glyndebourne of Benjamin Britten's opera *Albert Herring*.

– The Edinburgh Festival of Music and Drama is founded.

Darius Milhaud, Symphony No. 3 (*Hymnus ambrosianus*).

Sergei Prokofiev, Symphony No. 6 in E flat.

Film

John Boulting, *Brighton Rock*, starring Richard Attenborough.

Albert Lewin, *The Private Affairs of Bel Ami*, starring George Sanders.

Michael Powell and Emeric Pressburger, *Black Narcissus*, starring Deborah Kerr and Flora Robson.

Irving Rapper, *The Voice of the Turtle*, starring Ronald Reagan.

1948

EUROPE

25 Feb. With Soviet encouragement, the Czechoslovak Communist Party overthrows the coalition government. Now every state of E Europe is run by a communist government.

17 Mar. By the treaty of Brussels (signed by Britain, France and the Benelux countries) the Western Union (later the Western European Union) comes into being for collaboration in economic, social, cultural and defence matters.

20 Mar. In Germany Soviet delegates leave the Allied Control Council, unhappy at developments in the British, French and US zones of occupation.

20–21 June In Germany the Deutschmark is introduced in the British, French and US zones of occupation.

22 June The liner SS *Empire Windrush* docks at the English port of Tilbury carrying nearly 500 Caribbean immigrants to Britain.

24 June In response to the currency reform in the W zones of Germany, the occupying Soviet forces in E Germany blockade all road, rail and water links between Berlin and the W in an attempt to expel the Western powers from the city.

25 June The Deutschmark is introduced in the W part of Berlin.

28 June Yugoslavia is expelled from the Communist Information

Bureau (Cominform). The Yugoslav Communist Party, loyal to its leader, Marshal Josip Broz Tito, is following its own national path independent of Soviet influence. Much to Soviet fury, sanctions fail to bring Tito to heel.

5 July In Britain the National Health Service (NHS) begins to operate. It provides free and universal medical, dental and optical treatment.

25 July US and British aircraft start the Berlin Airlift to bring food and supplies to the populations of their occupation zones within the city. The Western Allies will airlift supplies of food, fuel and mail to Berlin until May 1949.

30 July In Britain Parliament passes the British Citizenship Act, which gives Commonwealth citizens the rights of British citizenship and the right to settle in Britain.

4 Sept. Wilhelmina, queen of the Netherlands, abdicates and is succeeded by her daughter Juliana (6 Sept.).

10 Dec. The UN General Assembly, meeting in Paris, adopts the Universal Declaration of Human Rights (mostly drafted by French jurist René Cassin). Eleanor Roosevelt, wife of the US president, has been the prime mover in working for the adoption of the declaration.

26 Dec. Cardinal József Mindszenty of Hungary is arrested for anti-communist agitation. He will be sentenced to death (1949), but the sentence will be commuted to one of life imprisonment.

– In Britain the gas industry is nationalized.

– In Britain non-means-tested old-age pensions are extended to the whole population.

– In Ireland Fine Gael (see 1933) forms a coalition government with a number of smaller parties. John A. Costello of Fine Gael is taoiseach (prime minister). Eamon de Valéra and his Fianna Fáil party are ousted from government for the first time since 1932.

MIDDLE EAST AND NORTH AFRICA

9 April 254 Palestinian Arab civilians are massacred in the village of Deir Yassin, between Tel Aviv and Jerusalem, by Jewish terrorists of the Irgun and Stern Gang. Many thousands of Palestinian Arabs flee the area in panic.

14 May The British mandate in Palestine ends and the Jewish National Council and general Zionist Council proclaim the state of Israel. Chaim Weizmann becomes the provisional president, and David Ben-Gurion is both prime minister and defence minister. The surrounding Arab states (Egypt, Transjordan, Lebanon and Syria) declare war on Israel in support of the Palestinian Arabs and invade Israel (15 May). The frontiers of the new state are decided by the ensuing war, in which the small and divided Arab armies prove no match for the Israelis. Four-fifths of the land of Palestine now becomes Israel. The Palestinian population flees the advancing Israelis, hoping for a rapid return behind Arab armies. Still more are forced to leave by Israeli militants bent on expelling them. Some 500,000 Palestinians leave the new country, while 200,000 remain. It is the beginning of a refugee problem that will become a permanent issue between Israelis and Arabs.

ASIA

4 Jan. Burma becomes a republic, independent of Britain.

30 Jan. Indian nationalist leader Mohandas Karamchand (Mahatma) Gandhi (see p. 476) is assassinated by an extremist Hindu, protesting against the partition of India and Pakistan.

1 Feb. The Federation of Malaya comes into being. Penang and Malacca remain British territory. Singapore becomes a separate British colony with its own government.

4 Feb. Ceylon (Sri Lanka) becomes independent of Britain.

16 June The Malayan Emergency begins: the Communist Party of Malaya demands immediate independence and launches an insurrection that will last until 1960.

15 Aug. The republic of Korea is proclaimed at Seoul, but in the N a communist-led Korean People's Democratic Republic is also proclaimed (9 Sept.). Both states claim sovereignty over the whole of the newly partitioned country.

23 Dec. After a lengthy trial conducted by the US occupying authorities, the wartime prime minister of Japan, Hideki Tojo, and six others are convicted of war crimes and executed.

– By the end of the year, communist forces have occupied Manchuria in the Chinese Civil War.

THE AMERICAS

3 April The Foreign Assistance Act passed by US Congress implements the Marshall Plan, under which $5.3 billion will be spent in the first year on economic aid for 16 W European countries.

3 May The US Supreme Court rules that private acts of discrimination (such as restrictive covenants in deeds forbidding the sale of a house to a member of a racial or ethnic minority) cannot be enforced in law.

10 May In order to frustrate a national rail strike, President Truman orders the US army to run the rail network. The railway system will remain under army control until 1952.

26 July By an executive order, President Harry S Truman ends racial segregation in the US armed forces.

3 Aug. Whittaker Chambers, senior editor of *Time* magazine, claims that Alger Hiss, president of the Carnegie Endowment for International Peace, was a Soviet agent while working for the State Department in the 1930s. Hiss sues for slander. The federal jury in New York indicts Hiss for perjury (15 Dec.), and his first trial ends in a hung jury. Californian congressman Richard Milhous Nixon campaigns for a congressional investigation and comes to national prominence for his outspoken anti-communism.

2 Nov. Harry S Truman defeats Thomas Dewey and is re-elected president of the USA.

SUB-SAHARAN AFRICA

26 May In elections in South Africa the Afrikaner National Party defeats the coalition headed by Jan Christiaan Smuts. In government the National Party adopts a policy of apartheid (separateness) to ensure the dominance of the White minority in South Africa. Apartheid laws define racial groups and enforce the strict separation of Blacks and Whites in work, housing, education, religion, marriage, sport and other areas of social life.

3 June D.F. Malan becomes South African prime minister.

ECONOMY AND SOCIETY

July–Aug. The 14th Olympic Games are held in London, the first such games since the Berlin Olympics of 1936.

26 Nov.–1 Dec. In Britain, London experiences a severe smog. Such smogs will continue throughout the early 1950s.

– Alfred Kinsey, a zoologist at Indiana University, writes *Sexual Behavior in the Human Male*. The Kinsey Report, based on interviews with 18,500 men and women, shocks many readers by its sexually explicit nature.

– The game of Scrabble is launched in the USA.

– The Australian cricketer Don Bradman plays his last innings in a test, scoring 0. He retires with a batting average of 99.94.

SCIENCE AND TECHNOLOGY

– At the Massachusetts Institute of Technology (MIT) in the USA mathematician Norbert Wiener writes *Cybernetics*, a work that founds the science of communications and control systems in both machines and animate beings.

– The hormone cortisone, synthesized by US biochemists Philip Showalter Hench and Edward Kendall, is used to treat victims of arthritis. By now all 13 vitamins essential to the body have been isolated and, in some cases, synthesized.

ARTS AND HUMANITIES

Literature

– The US poet Ezra Pound completes sections 72 to 84 of the *Pisan Cantos*.

Bertolt Brecht, *Der kaukasische Kreidekreis* (The Caucasian Chalk Circle), play.

Truman Capote, *Other Voices, Other Rooms*, novel.

Christopher Fry, *The Lady's Not for Burning*, play.

Jean Genet, *Les Bonnes* (The Maids), play.

Graham Greene, *The Heart of the Matter*, novel.

Norman Mailer, *The Naked and the Dead*, antiwar novel.

Yukio Mishima, *Confessions of a Mask*, an autobiographical novel of male homosexuality.

Alan Paton, *Cry the Beloved Country*, novel condemning the South African apartheid system.

Terence Rattigan, *The Browning Version*, play.

Nathalie Sarraute, *Portrait d'un inconnu* (Portrait of a Man Unknown), novel.

Gore Vidal, *The City and the Pillar*, novel.

Visual Arts and Architecture

Willem de Kooning, *Women*, painting.

Jackson Pollock, *Composition No. 1*, painting that pioneers abstract expressionism in visual art.

Music

11 Feb. Soviet composers Aram Khachaturian, Sergei Prokofiev and Dmitri Shostakovich are castigated by the Central Committee of the Communist Party for producing works of 'bourgeois decadence'.

24 May Benjamin Britten's version of John Gay's *The Beggar's Opera* and Britten's choral work *Saint Nicolas* are performed at the Aldeburgh Festival, Suffolk, England, which is founded by Britten and is celebrating its first season.

– The CBS engineer Peter Goldmark develops a 12-inch vinyl plastic phonograph record, which can turn at a rate of 33.3 revolutions per minute instead of the usual 78 rpm.

Frank Loesser, 'On a Slow Boat to China', song.

Richard Strauss, *Vier letzte Lieder* (Four Last Songs).

Film

Henry Cornelius, *Passport to Pimlico*.

John Huston, *The Treasure of the Sierra Madre* and *Key Largo*, both starring Humphrey Bogart.

David Lean, *Oliver Twist*, starring Alec Guinness and Robert Newton.

Laurence Olivier, *Hamlet*.

Michael Powell and Emeric Pressburger, *The Red Shoes*, starring ballerina Moira Shearer.

Vittorio de Sica, *Ladri di Biciclette* (Bicycle Thieves).

1949

EUROPE

18 Jan. The Council for Mutual Economic Assistance (COMECON) comes into being as an economic organization linking the USSR with Bulgaria, Czechoslovakia, Hungary, Poland and Romania.

8 April In Germany the French zone of occupation is added to the US and British zones to form the 'Trizone'.

18 April The Republic of Ireland is formally proclaimed in Dublin, and the British government recognizes the independence of Ireland (17 May) while preserving the political power of the Protestant majority in the six counties of Northern Ireland. Ireland leaves the Commonwealth.

5 May The Council of Europe is established. Its statute is signed in London by Belgium, Denmark, France, Britain, Ireland, Italy, Luxembourg, the Netherlands, Norway and Sweden.

12 May The Berlin blockade is lifted by the Soviets. The military governors approve the constitution of the Federal Republic of Germany.

23 May The Federal Republic of Germany (West Germany), consisting of the W zones of Allied occupation, is established with its capital in Bonn. West Berlin is not part of the new state but is associated with it.

16 June The Hungarian Communist Party embarks on a Stalinist purge with the arrest of the foreign minister Laszlo Rajk.

12 Sept. Theodor Heuss is elected first president of the Federal Republic of Germany.

15 Sept. Konrad Adenauer is elected first chancellor of the Federal Republic of Germany.

18 Sept. In Britain the government devalues the pound sterling from $4.03 to $2.80.

21 Sept. In the Federal Republic of Germany the statute of occupation comes into force, limiting the role of Allied occupation authorities.

7 Oct. The German Democratic Republic (East Germany) is established. It consists of the Soviet zone of occupation in Germany. The GDR will become a 'people's republic', like the other states in Soviet-dominated E Europe.

16 Oct. The Greek Civil War ends with the defeat of the communist rebels.

Nov. The Polish Communist Party purges its central committee of those thought to be anti-Soviet.

– In Britain Parliament passes an act nationalizing the iron and steel industries.

– Radio Free Europe, operating from Munich, S Germany, and run with Central Intelligence Agency (CIA) money, starts broadcasting to listeners behind the Iron Curtain.

MIDDLE EAST AND NORTH AFRICA

24 Feb. In the Arab–Israeli War, Israel and Egypt agree an armistice. Armistices follow between Israel and Lebanon (Mar.), Transjordan (3 April) and Syria (20 July).

2 June The former kingdom of Transjordan is renamed the Hashemite kingdom of Jordan.

ASIA

21 Jan. Jiang Jieshi (Chiang Kai-shek) resigns as president of China. The Guomindang armies have been defeated by the communists, who have taken Tianjin (Tientsin) (15 Jan.).

24 April In the Chinese Civil War the communists take the nationalist capital Nanjing (Nanking).

11 May Siam is renamed Thailand.

July In China Jiang Jieshi (Chiang Kai-shek) begins to move his Guomindang forces to the island of Formosa (Taiwan).

5 Aug. The USA stops giving aid to China.

1 Oct. The People's Republic of China is proclaimed, with Mao Zedong (see p. 573) as chairman of the party's central council. Zhou Enlai (Chou En-lai) is both premier and foreign minister. Famine in the course of the year devastates large areas of the new republic.

16 Dec. Achmed Sukarno is elected president of Indonesia and the Dutch recognize Indonesian independence (27 Dec.).

THE AMERICAS

7 Jan. Former under-secretary of state Dean Acheson becomes US secretary of state.

31 Mar. Newfoundland, a former dominion of the British Commonwealth, whose constitution had been suspended in 1931 because of bankruptcy, joins Canada as its tenth province.

4 April A treaty is signed in Washington, D.C., creating the North Atlantic Treaty Organization (NATO): the USA, Canada, Iceland, Britain, France, Denmark, Norway, Belgium, the Netherlands, Luxembourg, Italy and Portugal are signatories and pledge mutual assistance against aggression in what is fundamentally an anti-Soviet pact.

19 April US Congress approves a further $5.43 billion for European recovery. The US Import-Export Bank authorizes a $420 million loan to the Yugoslav government as an anti-Soviet measure (8 Sept.).

23 Sept. President Truman announces that the USA has evidence that the USSR has recently detonated a nuclear bomb. This has occurred several years earlier than US experts had expected, and espionage is blamed.

SUB-SAHARAN AFRICA

June The South African Citizenship Act becomes law: interracial marriage is now illegal.

AUSTRALASIA AND OCEANIA

27 June An Australian national coal strike begins and will last until Aug.; the government sends in troops to operate the mines.

17 Dec. In Australia Robert Menzies becomes prime minister of a Liberal Party–Country Party coalition government.

ECONOMY AND SOCIETY

– In Britain an act of Parliament creates National Parks and long-distance footpaths in England and Wales.

– Clothes rationing in Britain is ended.

ARTS AND HUMANITIES

Literature

– In East Germany the playwright Bertolt Brecht establishes the Berliner Ensemble theatre groups.

– The first of Enid Blyton's 'Noddy' books are published.

Simone de Beauvoir (see box), *Le Deuxième sexe* (The Second Sex), treatise beginning a new phase in the history of feminism.

Simone de Beauvoir (1908–86)

Like her life-long partner Jean-Paul Sartre, de Beauvoir was a professional teacher of philosophy who retired early to become a full-time writer, and with him she became something of a Parisian intellectual institution. Again, like Sartre, she came from a middle-class background but was supplied by existentialist philosophy with the conceptual tools to rebel against those origins, a process she describes in four fine volumes of autobiography.

De Beauvoir infused her novels with her existentialist philosophy and also with her own experiences. Her first novel, *She Came to Stay* (1943), is typical, examining how people prey on each other in relationships. Frustration is a typical de Beauvoir theme and reflects some of the tensions of her partnership with Sartre. She had a finer literary style but his was the dominant personality. Acclaim came with the novel *The Mandarins* (1954), which won her the distinguished Prix Goncourt. The work shows a group of women whose ambitions, whether in public or personal life, are frustrated by the force of circumstances.

De Beauvoir has been recognized as the founding mother of modern feminism. She supplied the terms of reference for the movement that was to change the way life was lived in the West in the later 20th century. Her most famous work, *The Second Sex* (1949), is a study of humanity's attitudes towards women, and in it she states that femininity is not an essential condition of being a woman, but rather a choice that women have made: 'One is not born a woman: one becomes one.' The equally distinguished *Old Age* (1970) is a similarly profound study of what de Beauvoir saw as another marginalized group.

Fernand Braudel, *The Mediterranean and the Mediterranean World in the Age of Philip II*, a landmark in historical scholarship with its emphasis on *la longue durée*, the long-term features of landscape, climate and mentality that predetermine the history of events.

Friedrich Dürrenmatt, *Romulus der Grosse* (Romulus the Great), play.

Naguib Mahfouz, *The Beginning and the End*, novel.

Arthur Miller, *Death of a Salesman*, play.

Nancy Mitford, *Love in a Cold Climate*, novel.

George Orwell, *Nineteen Eighty-four*, novel.

Nevil Shute, *A Town Like Alice*, novel.

Simone Weil, *L'Attente de Dieu* (Waiting for God), essay.

Visual Arts and Architecture

– Architect Philip Johnson of New York designs a glass house as his home in New Canaan, Connecticut, USA.

Francis Bacon, *The Screaming Popes*, painting.

Robert Motherwell, *Elegies to the Spanish Republic* and *At Five in the Afternoon*, abstract paintings.

Jackson Pollock, *Number 2*, painting.

Music

6 Sept. The German composer Richard Strauss dies.

– RCA releases the first 45 rpm 'single'.

Benjamin Britten, *Spring Symphony*.

John Cranko, choreography for French composer Maurice Ravel's ballet *Beauty and the Beast*.

Gerald Finzi, Clarinet concerto.

Francis Poulenc, Concerto for piano and orchestra.

Richard Rodgers and Oscar Hammerstein II, *South Pacific*, musical.

Jule Styne and Leo Robin, *Gentlemen Prefer Blondes*, musical.

Film

George Cukor, *Adam's Rib*, starring Spencer Tracy.

Cecil B. DeMille, *Samson and Delilah*.

Robert Hamer, *Kind Hearts and Coronets*, Ealing comedy.

Carol Reed, *The Third Man*, starring Orson Welles.

Jacques Tati, *Jour de fête* (The Big Day).

1950

EUROPE

23 Feb. In the British general election Labour's majority is much reduced (315 seats to the Conservatives' 298).

1 Mar. German-born physicist Klaus Fuchs is found guilty of passing British atomic secrets to Soviet agents. Sentenced to 14 years in prison, he will be released in 1959 for good behaviour.

8 Mar. Marshal of the Soviet Union Klimenti Voroshilov announces that the USSR now has an atomic bomb.

9 May French politician and economist Jean Monnet (see box) proposes a plan to the French foreign minister, Robert Schuman, for a common coal and steel policy for W Europe. The Schuman Plan will develop into the European Economic Community and then the European Union.

8 July The Federal Republic of Germany (West Germany) becomes an associate member of the Council of Europe.

11 Aug. Leopold III, king of the Belgians, abdicates in favour of his son, Baudouin.

1 Oct. The German Democratic Republic (East Germany) becomes a member of the COMECON alliance of Soviet-aligned states.

MIDDLE EAST AND NORTH AFRICA

3 Dec. Idris I is proclaimed king of Libya, which has now become independent.

ASIA

14 Feb. The People's Republic of China and the USSR sign a treaty of alliance.

1 Mar. In Formosa (now Taiwan) Jiang Jieshi (Chiang Kai-shek) becomes president of Nationalist China.

25 June War breaks out in Korea when the communist North invades the South. Seoul falls to the North (28 June). As the Soviet delegation is boycotting the UN Security Council and thus not able to use its veto, the USA can ensure the passing of a resolution calling on members of the UN to protect South Korea from aggression.

Jean Monnet (1888–1979)

Jean Monnet, the French businessman, economist and public official, was a founding father of the institutions that have become the European Union. The dissolution of trade barriers within Europe, the greater mobility of European peoples, the institutional details of Franco-German rapprochement as well as the Euro currency all flowed from his vision and personal drive.

Monnet was deputy secretary-general of the League of Nations from 1919 to 1923, then followed a career in business and banking until World War II, when he worked with the Free French. In 1945 he was placed in charge of French economic modernization and, as a result, became convinced that the future peace and economic prosperity of Europe depended on economic and political union. This was the basis of the *Monnet Note* (1950), which advocated a single authority to control the production of coal and steel in France and West Germany. Other countries joined this organization, which became the European Coal and Steel Community, with Monnet as its first president. It later developed into the European Economic Community, from which the EU has grown. In the early 1970s he started his campaign for European monetary union, but did not live long enough to see it come into being.

Monnet never ran for elected office, and worked exclusively among the financial, technocratic and political elites. But the fact that he steered clear of party politics was one reason for his success. His self-confidence reflected a belief in a grand historical scheme of European unity that dated back to Charlemagne's coronation in 800. Monnet's grandiose but detailed conception proved a counterpoint to Anglo-American free-market capitalism, and did much to consolidate the European peace.

29 June Gen. MacArthur arrives in Korea and takes charge of the combined UN forces to expel the communists (9 July).

26 Sept. UN forces retake Seoul and go on to occupy the North Korean capital Pyongyang (19 Oct.).

21 Oct. China invades Tibet after Tibet rejects an 'invitation' to join the communist system.

21 Nov. UN forces reach the Yalu River on Korea's N border with China, provoking the Chinese, who will not tolerate a US-led force on their frontier. In a massive joint counterattack (26 Nov.), Chinese and North Korean forces drive UN troops S and retake Pyongyang (8 Dec.).

28 Dec. Chinese forces cross the 38th parallel dividing North from South Korea.

THE AMERICAS

9 Jan. Senator Joseph McCarthy of Wisconsin alleges that there are 205 communists working in the US State Department and that there is an orchestrated communist campaign to infiltrate the US government at the highest level. McCarthy embarks on a campaign to root out 'un-American' activity in all walks of life.

25 Jan. US State Department official Alger Hiss (see 3 Aug. 1948) is found guilty of perjury. He is sentenced to five years' imprisonment.

31 Jan. US president Harry S Truman orders the Atomic Energy Commission to develop a thermonuclear, or hydrogen, bomb.

25 Aug. Because of a threat of strike action, federal troops are ordered by President Truman to operate the US railway system.

1 Nov. President Truman escapes an assassination attempt: White House guards shoot two Puerto Rican suspects.

− The USA resumes diplomatic relations with Gen. Franco's Spain.

SUB-SAHARAN AFRICA

29 Jan. In South Africa rioting breaks out in Johannesburg in protest against the new apartheid system.

2 Dec. The UN votes for the unification of Eritrea with Ethiopia.

ECONOMY AND SOCIETY

June–July Uruguay wins the 4th soccer World Cup, held in Brazil.

− There is now one passenger car for every 3.75 Americans, a figure that will double over the next 25 years.

− David Riesman publishes *The Lonely Crowd: a Study of the Changing American Character*, a work of sociology contrasting the 'outer-directed' mid-20th century Americans with their 'inner-directed' forebears.

SCIENCE AND TECHNOLOGY

− Ataraxic tranquillizer tablets are developed at the Wallace Laboratories in New Jersey, USA.

ARTS AND HUMANITIES

Literature

21 Jan. The English novelist and essayist George Orwell dies.

Isaac Asimov, *I, Robot*, novel.

Ray Bradbury, *The Martian Chronicles*, novel.

E.H. Carr, *A History of Soviet Russia: The Bolshevik Revolution,*

1917–23 (Vol. 1), history; Vols. 2 and 3 are published in 1952 and 1953 respectively.

T.S. Eliot, *The Cocktail Party*, play.

Graham Greene, *The Third Man*, novel from his own script for the film of the same name (see 1949).

Patricia Highsmith, *Strangers on a Train*, novel.

Eugène Ionesco, *La Cantatrice chauve* (The Bald Prima Donna), play exemplifying the 'theatre of the absurd'.

Doris Lessing, *The Grass is Singing*, novel.

C.S. Lewis, *The Lion, the Witch and the Wardrobe*, children's fantasy novel, the first in a sequence of seven novels about the mythical land of Narnia.

Pablo Neruda, *Canto General*, epic poem.

Mervyn Peake, *Gormenghast*, second novel in a trilogy.

Barbara Pym, *Some Tame Gazelle*, novel.

Visual Arts and Architecture

− The United Nations Secretariat building, New York, designed by Wallace K. Harrison, is completed.

− Ernst Gombrich publishes *The Story of Art*, a single-volume history of art.

Alberto Giacometti, *Seven Figures and a Head*, sculpture.

Willem de Kooning, *Excavation*, painting.

Music

Irving Berlin, *Call Me Madam*, musical starring Ethel Merman.

Frank Loesser, *Guys and Dolls*, musical.

Olivier Messiaen, *Turangalîla Symphony*.

Film

Robert Bresson, *Journal d'un curé de campagne* (Diary of a Country Priest), starring Claude Laydu.

John Huston, *The Asphalt Jungle*.

Joseph L. Mankiewicz, *All About Eve*, starring Bette Davis.

Max Ophüls, *La Ronde* (The Roundabout), starring Simone Signoret.

Billy Wilder, *Sunset Boulevard*, starring Gloria Swanson.

1951

EUROPE

18 April The founding treaty of the European Coal and Steel Community (ECSC) is signed, creating a single authority for the coal and steel industries of France, West Germany, Italy, Belgium, the Netherlands and Luxembourg.

22 April In Britain Aneurin Bevan and Harold Wilson resign from the Labour government over charges for NHS dentures and spectacles.

2 May West Germany joins the Council of Europe.

25 May British diplomats and Soviet spies Guy Burgess and Donald Maclean (the Cambridge Spies) are warned by a 'third man' (their fellow spy Kim Philby) that they are suspected of espionage. Burgess and Maclean flee Britain and will turn up in Moscow in Feb. 1956.

30 May General election in the Republic of Ireland: Eamon de Valéra returns to power as taoiseach (prime minister) at the head of a Fianna Fáil-dominated coalition government (13 June).

1951

IRANIAN REVOLUTION BEGINS □ KOREAN WAR REACHES STALEMATE □ USA TESTS FIRST HYDROGEN BOMB

May–Sept. The Festival of Britain, an artistic and cultural festival, is held in London. It commemorates the 100th anniversary of the Great Exhibition of 1851.

9 July Britain formally ends its state of war with Germany. France follows on 13 July, and the USA on 24 Oct.

26 Oct. In Britain the Labour government is narrowly defeated in the general election, even though the Labour Party wins more votes than the Conservatives. Winston Churchill (see p. 523) returns as prime minister.

MIDDLE EAST AND NORTH AFRICA

20 Mar. Iran nationalizes its oil industry, which includes British oil interests guaranteed by an Oil Convention of 1933.

28 April The shah of Iran appoints Muhammad Mossadeq prime minister.

5 July The International Court of Justice rules against Iran in its oil dispute with Britain.

20 July King Abdullah of Jordan is assassinated in Jerusalem. His son Talal succeeds him (6 Sept).

27 Sept. The Iranian military takes over the oil fields of Abadan. The Anglo-Iranian oil dispute marks the true beginning of the Iranian revolution and its populist rejection of Anglo-US intervention in Iranian politics and business.

– Egypt introduces restrictions in the Suez Canal on ships travelling to Israel. It ends its 1936 alliance with Britain as well as the condominium agreement of 1899 covering the Sudan.

ASIA

4 Jan. The communist Chinese and North Koreans retake Seoul, but UN forces reoccupy the devastated city (14 Mar).

29 Mar. China rejects Gen. Douglas MacArthur's call for a truce.

31 Mar. MacArthur publicly advocates air attacks on Chinese cities using atomic bombs. US president Harry S Truman, who is determined not to expand the war, duly relieves MacArthur of his command (11 April). He is replaced by Gen. Matthew B. Ridgway.

22–25 April UN forces hold the line against North Korean and Chinese forces in the battle of Imjin River. The Korean War now sinks into a stalemate as the line stabilizes along the 38th parallel.

3 May On Constitution Day Japan regains its sovereign independence: six years of military government imposed by the Western allies come to an end.

8 July Talks begin at Kaesong on a negotiated peace in the Korean War but end without agreement (23 Aug.). UN forces take Heartbreak Ridge (23 Sept.), and peace talks begin again at Panmunjom (25 Oct.). The trial armistice ends and fighting resumes (27 Dec.), but only with a view to influencing negotiations. Both sides have concluded that a total victory is unattainable.

8 Sept. Japan and the USA sign a treaty of mutual security; US troops are allowed to remain on Japanese soil in order to sustain UN operations in the Far East. US permission is needed before any other national force is allowed into a Japanese base.

– The French Indochina War is now characterized by guerrilla attacks by Vietminh fighters on French military targets.

THE AMERICAS

27 Feb. The 22nd Amendment to the US constitution is ratified and limits the president to two terms of office.

5 April In the USA Ethel and Julius Rosenberg are sentenced to death for having sold atomic secrets to the USSR.

13 April In Argentina Juan Perón acts to shut down *La Prensa* (The Press), a newspaper that has been critical of his personal dictatorship.

ECONOMY AND SOCIETY

11 Sept. Florence Chadwick becomes the first Englishwoman to swim across the English Channel.

– *The Goon Show* is broadcast on BBC radio for the first time. It will make stars of Spike Milligan, Peter Sellers, Harry Secombe and Michael Bentine.

SCIENCE AND TECHNOLOGY

6 Nov. The USA explodes the first thermo-nuclear (hydrogen) bomb on Enewetak Atoll in the Pacific Ocean.

– The US Atomic Energy Commission builds the first power-producing atomic reactor.

ARTS AND HUMANITIES

Literature

19 Feb. The French novelist André Gide dies.

29 April The philosopher Ludwig Wittgenstein dies.

William F. Buckley, *God and Man at Yale*, an account of his politically conservative views.

Albert Camus, *L'Homme révolté* (The Rebel), essay providing an existentialist rejection of Marxist communism.

Graham Greene, *The End of the Affair*, novel.

James Jones, *From Here to Eternity*, novel.

Carson McCullers, *The Ballad of the Sad Café and Other Stories*.

Nicholas Monsarrat, *The Cruel Sea*, novel.

Alberto Moravia, *Il conformista* (The Conformist), novel.

Anthony Powell, *A Question of Upbringing*, novel in which Powell embarks on his 12-volume sequence *A Dance to the Music of Time*, portraying the sequence of repetitions and recognitions in British life from World War I to the 1970s.

Steven Runciman, *A History of the Crusades* (Vol. 1), history; Vol. 2 is published in 1952 and Vol. 3 in 1954.

J.D. Salinger, *The Catcher in the Rye*, novel describing the adolescent rejection of the inauthentic and the search for genuine experience.

Herman Wouk, *The Caine Mutiny*, novel.

John Wyndham, *The Day of the Triffids*, novel.

Visual Arts and Architecture

– Leslie Martin, Peter Moro and Robert Matthew design the Royal Festival Hall on the South Bank of the River Thames in London for the Festival of Britain.

Lucian Freud, *Interior at Paddington*, painting.

Jackson Pollock, *Black and White*, painting.

548 THE MODERN WORLD: 1900–2004

Music

13 July The Austrian-born composer Arnold Schoenberg dies.

11 Sept. First performance in Venice of Igor Stravinsky's opera *The Rake's Progress*, which is based on William Hogarth's engravings (1732–5).

1 Dec. First performance in London of Benjamin Britten's opera *Billy Budd*.

Richard Rodgers and Oscar Hammerstein II, *The King and I*, musical.

Film

Anthony Asquith, *The Browning Version*, starring Michael Redgrave.

Charles Crichton, *The Lavender Hill Mob*, starring Alec Guinness and Stanley Holloway.

Alfred Hitchcock, *Strangers on a Train*, starring Farley Granger.

John Huston, *The Red Badge of Courage*, starring Audie Murphy and *The African Queen*, starring Humphrey Bogart.

Vincente Minnelli, *An American in Paris*, starring Gene Kelly.

1952

EUROPE

6 Feb. In Britain King George VI dies. His daughter succeeds to the throne as Queen Elizabeth II.

10 Sept. Israel and the Federal Republic of Germany sign a reconciliation treaty. A reparations plan is agreed.

2 Oct. The UK joins the USA and USSR as a nuclear power with the test of an atomic bomb at the Monte Bello Islands, off the Australian coast.

– In Britain the Conservative government reintroduces charges for NHS prescriptions.

MIDDLE EAST AND NORTH AFRICA

23 July Farouk I, king of Egypt, abdicates following a coup led by Gen. Mohammed Neguib. The new government signs an agreement with Sudan (13 Oct.) on the right to use water from the River Nile and abolishes the constitution of 1923 (10 Dec.).

11 Aug. The Jordanian parliament ends the rule of King Halal on grounds of mental illness. His English-educated son Hussein succeeds him.

22 Oct. Iran breaks off diplomatic relations with Britain over the Anglo-Iranian oil dispute (see 20 Mar. 1951).

7 Nov. Chaim Weizmann, president of Israel, dies. He is replaced by Itzhak Ben-Zvi.

– In SE Arabia the sheikdoms of Abu Dhabi, Ajman, Dubai, Fujairah, Ras al Khaimah, Sharjah and Umm al Qaiwain set up the Trucial Council with a view to establishing a federation. During the 1960s the so-called Trucial States will become extremely wealthy through the exploitation of their oil deposits.

THE AMERICAS

10 Mar. Gen. Fulgencio Batista, dictator of Cuba 1933–40, returns to power from exile after leading a military coup, which overthrows President Carlos Prió Socarrás.

29 Mar. US president Harry S Truman announces that he will not seek re-election.

28 April Gen. Dwight D. Eisenhower resigns as supreme Allied commander. The Republican Party will later nominate him as their candidate for the presidential elections. The Democrats will nominate Adlai Stevenson, governor of Illinois.

23 May The US railroads return to being run by private enterprise having been operated by federal troops for the past 21 months.

25 July Puerto Rico's new constitution makes it a commonwealth of the USA. The country's inhabitants become US citizens but without federal voting rights and without paying federal taxes.

26 July Evita Perón dies, soon achieving cult status in Argentina.

4 Nov. Despite accusations that his vice-presidential running mate, Richard Nixon, has taken money illegally from Californian businessmen, Dwight D. Eisenhower, the Republican candidate, wins a landslide victory in the US presidential elections.

– Future US black nationalist leader Malcolm Little changes his name to Malcolm X and, on release from prison for armed robbery, becomes a follower of the African-American Muslim leader Elijah Muhammad.

– Under the terms of the Declaration of Santiago, Chile, Ecuador and Peru extend their maritime jurisdiction (and fishing limits) to 320km (200 miles) from their coastlines. The maritime average for other countries is 20km (12 miles).

SUB-SAHARAN AFRICA

20 Mar. The supreme court of South Africa declares that the racist legislation passed by parliament is illegal. D.F. Malan, the prime minister, introduces legislation making parliament the supreme court (22 April).

11 Sept. Eritrea is federated to Ethiopia.

20 Oct. A state of emergency is declared in Kenya. The Mau Mau, a secret society centred on the Kikuyu tribe and led by Jomo Kenyatta, launches a rebellion aiming at the expulsion of white settlers by acts of terrorism and the withdrawal of the British from the colony. The Mau Mau insurgency will last until 1956 and will cost 13,000 lives, most of them Kikuyu killed by colonial government forces.

ECONOMY AND SOCIETY

July–Aug. The 15th Olympic Games are held in Helsinki, Finland.

5–9 Dec. London suffers a severe winter smog, caused by atmospheric pollutants. It will lead to some 4000 deaths.

– Austrian ethnologist Konrad Lorenz publishes *King Solomon's Ring: New Light on Animal Ways*. Lorenz, a former supporter of Nazi eugenics, seeks to show that the Darwinian 'survival of the fittest' is applicable to human behaviour, aggression and success.

SCIENCE AND TECHNOLOGY

– The British De Havilland Comet, the world's first jet airliner, enters service.

– The keel is laid for USS *Nautilus*, the world's first nuclear-powered submarine.

– The Baltic and the Black Seas are linked by the USSR's Volga–Don Ship Canal.

1952-3

ARTS AND HUMANITIES

Literature

25 Nov. Agatha Christie's murder mystery *The Mousetrap* opens at the Ambassador's Theatre, London. It will become the world's longest-running play.

Ernest Hemingway, *The Old Man and the Sea*, novel.

Eugène Ionesco, *Les Chaises* (The Chairs), play.

Terence Rattigan, *The Deep Blue Sea*, play.

John Steinbeck, *East of Eden*, novel.

Evelyn Waugh, *Men at Arms*, first novel of his *The Sword of Honour* trilogy.

Visual Arts and Architecture

Lucian Freud, *Portrait of Francis Bacon*, painting.

Music

14 Nov. In Britain the *New Musical Express* publishes Britain's first pop singles chart.

– First performance of John Cage's *4'33"*, for any instrument or any combination of instruments, in which no intentional sound is produced.

Film

Stanley Donen and Gene Kelly, *Singin' in the Rain*, musical starring Gene Kelly.

John Ford, *The Quiet Man*, starring John Wayne.

Akira Kurosawa, *Ikiru*.

Fred Zinnemann, *High Noon*, starring Gary Cooper.

1953

EUROPE

12 Jan. A new constitution is declared in Yugoslavia, and Marshal Josip Broz Tito becomes president of the new republic (14 Jan).

5 Mar. Soviet leader Joseph Stalin dies, and the succession is contested between three men: Georgi Malenkov, whose power base lies in the government posts he holds; Lavrenti Beria, who is in charge of the Soviet secret police (MVD); and Nikita Khrushchev, who is first secretary of the Communist Party. Beria is detested and feared, and Khrushchev and Malenkov plot to bring about his trial and execution for treason (23 Dec.). The contest between Khrushchev and Malenkov is less bloody and concentrates on domestic policy. On his defeat Malenkov is demoted rather than executed. Khrushchev will never exercise the power of Stalin, however, and a degree of collective decision-making returns to the Soviet hierarchy.

2 June In Britain Queen Elizabeth II is crowned in Westminster Abbey, London.

17 June In East Germany a construction workers' strike in East Berlin leads to a rising against the communist government. Soviet forces help crush the rising.

– French politician and economist Jean Monnet becomes the first president of the European Coal and Steel Community (ECSC), the forerunner of the European Economic Community.

– In Britain food rationing comes to an end.

– In Britain the Conservative government denationalizes the iron and steel industries.

MIDDLE EAST AND NORTH AFRICA

2 May King Hussein of Jordan reaches the age of majority.

19 Aug. The Central Intelligence Agency (with British collusion) is ordered by US president Dwight D. Eisenhower to topple the government of Muhammad Mossadeq in Iran. Mossadeq's nationalization of foreign oil holdings threatens the effectiveness of US foreign and commercial policy. Eisenhower sees covert CIA operations as an easy way to win Cold War victories. The shah of Iran Muhammad Reza Shah Pahlavi, who has been driven from the country, is restored to power and starts a reign in which he will operate as an agent of Western influences, both political and cultural.

9 Nov. Ibn Saud, king of Saudi Arabia and founder of the kingdom (1926), dies. He is succeeded by his son Saud ibn Abdul-Aziz.

ASIA

9 May France grants Cambodia its independence in military, judicial and economic affairs. But Norodom Sihanouk, the ruler of Cambodia, now presses for further measures to ensure complete independence. The French start to fortify Dien Bien Phu in North Vietnam as they try to retain control of Vietnam.

27 July An armistice is signed at Panmunjom near the 38th parallel, ending the Korean War. No permanent peace treaty will be signed, however. North Korean and Chinese casualties total 1,540,000. UN forces have lost about 54,000, mostly US soldiers. In addition, some 2 million Korean civilians have died.

THE AMERICAS

31 Mar. The Swedish statesman Dag Hammarskjöld is elected secretary-general of the UN.

April The US Justice Department files a civil complaint accusing Standard Oil, Gulf, the Texas Company, Socony-Mobil and Standard Oil of California of having organized an oil cartel, along with the foreign companies Anglo-Iranian and Royal Dutch-Shell.

19 June Convicted of being Soviet agents, Ethel and Julius Rosenberg are controversially executed for treason, a worldwide campaign for clemency having been rejected by US president Eisenhower. They are the first US civilians ever executed for espionage.

12 Sept. At Newport, Rhode Island, John Fitzgerald Kennedy marries Jacqueline Lee Bouvier.

22 Dec. US physicist and director of the atomic bomb project Robert Oppenheimer has his security clearance revoked. He is charged with communist affiliations because of his opposition to building a hydrogen bomb.

– President Getúlio Vargas of Brazil authorizes the creation of Petrobras, a company with a government monopoly in the oil business.

SUB-SAHARAN AFRICA

24 Feb. South Africa's prime minister, D.F. Malan, is given dictatorial powers by parliament to deal with anti-apartheid demonstrations.

8 April Jomo Kenyatta and five other Kikuyu tribal leaders are convicted of rebellion against the rule of British law in Kenya in relation to the Mau Mau rising. The Kenyan Supreme Court dismisses their convictions (15 July), but Kenyatta is banished.

– The Central African Federation is formed, consisting of Southern Rhodesia (Zimbabwe), Northern Rhodesia (Zambia) and Nyasaland (Malawi). It is designed as a counterweight to Afrikaner-dominated South Africa, but it will not last, Britain agreeing to separate independence for Zambia and Malawi.

ECONOMY AND SOCIETY

29 May Edmund Hillary of New Zealand and his Sherpa guide, Tensing Norgay, reach the summit of Mount Everest.

– L. Ron Hubbard, a US science fiction writer, establishes the Church of Scientology in Washington, D.C., and advocates therapeutic counselling to free individuals of the burden of their past experiences.

– In the USA *Playboy* magazine is published for the first time.

SCIENCE AND TECHNOLOGY

25 April In a paper published in *Nature*, English geneticists Francis Crick and James Watson (see box) of Cambridge University propose a structure for DNA (deoxyribonucleic acid). The basic structure is that of a double helix, which allows the duplication of genetic material in animal and human cells.

– US office equipment manufacturer IBM (International Business Machines Co.) produces its first computer.

ARTS AND HUMANITIES

Literature

9 Nov. The Welsh poet Dylan Thomas dies in New York.

27 Nov. The US playwright Eugene O'Neill dies.

– English cryptographer Michael Ventris deciphers ancient Minoan script dating from *c.*1500 BC and known as Linear B.

– *L'Express* is founded in Paris by French radical journalist and politician Jean-Jacques Servan-Schreiber as a news magazine of the left.

Jean Anouilh, *L'Alouette* (The Lark), play.

James Baldwin, *Go Tell It on the Mountain*, novel.

Samuel Beckett (see p. 558), *En attendant Godot* (Waiting for Godot), play typifying the 'theatre of the absurd'.

Saul Bellow, *The Adventures of Augie March*, novel.

Ray Bradbury, *Fahrenheit 451*, novel.

William S. Burroughs, *Junky: Confessions of an Unredeemed Drug Addict*, novel.

Ian Fleming, *Casino Royale*, novel introducing his hero, James Bond (British secret service agent 007).

L.P. Hartley, *The Go-Between*, novel.

Arthur Miller, *The Crucible*, play dramatizing the 17th-century witch trials in Salem, Massachusetts, and inspired by America's contemporary anti-communist witch hunt.

Alain Robbe-Grillet, *Les Gommes* (The Erasers), example of the anti-novel, rejecting conventional characterization and plot.

Dylan Thomas, *Under Milk Wood*, play for BBC radio.

John Wyndham, *The Kraken Wakes*, novel.

Francis Crick (1916–2004) and James Watson (1928–)
The science of genetics was transformed in the spring of 1953 when American scientist James Watson and his British colleague Francis Crick published their findings on the structure of DNA.

Scientists had concluded that the complex molecule DNA or deoxyribonucleic acid was the main constituent of chromosomes, the units in each living cell that contain genetic information. What they did not know was how DNA was structured to hold this information. Crick and Watson proposed that DNA was a long string constructed in the form of a double helix or spiral, in which sequences of various chemical units provide the genetic code. On the basis of this work they received the 1962 Nobel Prize for Medicine – along with their Cambridge colleague Maurice Wilkins.

The work of Crick and Watson was a true scientific revolution because it led to a transformed understanding of human personalities. Genetic mapping raises the controversial prospect that a human individual's character and propensity to diseases can be known at birth. Also controversial is the development of genetically modified crops. Advocates of this development see it as a green revolution that will increase yields and end hunger in the developing world. Others see it as an interference with nature that may lead to new forms of disease and the diminishment of species diversity. These critics see the genetic modification of plants – which often involves making a plant resistant to chemical herbicides, which can then be used extensively to get rid of unwanted weeds – as a regression from the trend toward organic farming methods.

Visual Arts and Architecture

23 Mar. French artist Raoul Dufy dies.

Francis Bacon, *Study after Velázquez: Pope Innocent X*, painting.

Georges Braque, *Apples*, painting.

Music

5 Mar. Sergei Prokofiev, Russian composer, dies in Moscow.

8 June First performance in London of Benjamin Britten's opera *Gloriana*, a portrayal of an aged and disillusioned queen, performed as part of Elizabeth II's coronation celebrations.

Michael Tippett, *Fantasia Concertante on a Theme of Corelli*, work for string orchestra.

Ralph Vaughan Williams, Symphony No. 7 (*Sinfonia Antartica*).

William Walton, *Te Deum* and *Orb and Sceptre*, marches performed to celebrate the coronation of Elizabeth II.

Film

Henry Cornelius, *Genevieve*.

Howard Hawks, *Gentlemen Prefer Blondes*, starring Jane Russell and Marilyn Monroe.

Fritz Lang, *The Big Heat*, starring Glenn Ford.

George Stevens, *Shane*, starring Alan Ladd.

Jacques Tati, *Les Vacances de M. Hulot* (Mr Hulot's Holiday).

Fred Zinnemann, *From Here to Eternity*, starring Burt Lancaster.

OLD EMPIRES AND NEW BEGINNINGS:
Decolonization and the Fall of Europe

Nationalism proved to be the most dynamic of all of Europe's exports: it was an ideology invented by Europeans, and, by a certain irony, it proved to be the nemesis of the their own empires. If the story of the later 19th century had been that of imperial expansion, the dominant theme in the mid-20th century was decolonization, as the colonized peoples gained the means and the confidence to rise against their rulers. Decolonization also changed Europe for good, as immigrants from the former colonies helped to create multicultural and multiethnic societies in the countries of the former colonial powers.

Some of the earliest examples of decolonization arose out of the weakness of the colonial power. For example, the Spanish colonies in Latin America embarked on their struggle for independence when the mother country was reeling from French invasion during the Napoleonic Wars. However, a century later European imperialism was still thriving. Indeed, following World War I the empires of Britain and France actually expanded, as these two powers were granted the right to run League of Nations protectorates in the former Ottoman- and German-ruled territories of the Middle East, Africa and Oceania (the islands of the Pacific Ocean). Their mandate was to prepare those countries for eventual independence – although the local people were not consulted.

Aggressive imperialism was still alive and well between the world wars. From 1931 Japan expanded into Chinese territory, while in 1935 fascist Italy invaded Abyssinia (Ethiopia) with the aim of turning it into an Italian colony. Less nakedly aggressive was the imposition of European-style laws and taxes in established colonies that had previously been allowed to follow traditional practices.

World War II provided the impetus for change. The victories of Japan, an Asian power, over the Europeans in 1941–2 showed that the white man was not invincible. The huge costs of waging war left Britain deeply in debt, and over the following two decades its empire was dismantled largely because it could not afford the expense. This process was generally peaceful, apart from the massacres that accompanied the partition of the Indian sub-continent and the guerrilla war waged by the Mau-Mau secret society in Kenya. Britain had largely prepared its colonies well for independence, but the same could not be said of the Belgian Congo, where the colonial power left hurriedly, abandoning the country to anarchy and civil war. Until 1975 Portugal fought a series of wars to resist demands for independence in its African colonies.

In some areas the French were unwilling to let go of their empire, fighting long and bitter wars in Indochina and Algeria. Even when they granted independence, in many former colonies in Africa they kept a measure of financial control and showed themselves willing to intervene militarily if the new rulers did not follow French wishes. The Algerian war (1954–62) not only dictated the course of domestic politics in France, but also contributed to a pan-Arab mood that fused nationalism with a radical political style.

In the Middle East this pan-Arab nationalism spread under the magnetic example of Gamal Abdel Nasser, who became president of Egypt in 1954 following a military coup d'état in July 1952. His nationalization of the Suez Canal led Britain to embark on its final colonial adventure. In 1956, in secret collusion with the Israelis and more open alliance with the French, the British invaded to retake control of the canal. The United States refused to support the venture – and Britain had to withdraw. Subsequently, the hostility between Israel and its Arab neighbours drew in the United States to support Israel, and the Soviet Union to support the Arab states. The Middle East became a theatre of war by proxy – part of the Cold War between the superpowers.

The end of the Cold War did nothing to halt the crisis in the Middle East, for left-leaning secular Arab nationalism lost ground to a radical, politicized and fundamentalist Islamic revival, which manifested itself in a hatred of Western culture, materialism and liberal democracy. This Islamist revival first took solid form in the Iranian revolution of 1979, in which the shah, regarded as a client of the USA, was overthrown and replaced by an Islamic theocracy. An even more extreme theocracy was established by the Taliban in Afghanistan in the 1990s.

Nationalism proved to be the most dynamic of all of Europe's exports.

The European powers who had started the colonial process were no longer the masters of foreign policy, either in the Middle East or in Africa. It was now the USA that had to decide how to deal with the anger of these post-colonial societies. But, since those European powers were partners in an alliance system dominated both militarily and politically by the USA, they were still regarded by their former colonies as sharing responsibility for all the perceived injustices suffered by the people of the Third World.

1954

EUROPE

8 April The Western Allies refuse to recognize East German sovereignty.

26 April The Geneva conference on Indochina opens.

18 May General election in the Republic of Ireland: Fine Gael forms a coalition government with a number of smaller parties. John A. Costello of Fine Gael returns as taoiseach (prime minister), replacing Eamon de Valéra (2 June).

18 June In France Pierre Mendès-France becomes prime minister, promising to end the war in Indochina after the French defeat at Dien Bien Phu (May, see below). He pursues a vigorous policy of decolonization in Tunisia, Morocco and Indochina.

− In Britain equal pay for men and women is introduced in the public sector.

MIDDLE EAST AND NORTH AFRICA

17 April Col. Gamal Abdel Nasser becomes leader of Egypt's military government. He signs a treaty with Britain ensuring Britain's withdrawal from the Suez Canal zone (19 Oct.) within 20 months. The British base at Suez can, however, be used by Britain if an outside power attacks Turkey or an Arab state.

31 Oct. War breaks out in Algeria as the Front de Libération Nationale (FLN) starts its campaign against French colonial rule.

ASIA

13 Mar. In North Vietnam the communist Vietminh (the Vietnam Independence League), led by Ho Chi Minh, begins its siege of French forces at Dien Bien Phu.

7 May French forces are defeated by Ho Chi Minh's communist Vietminh at Dien Bien Phu, North Vietnam, despite massive US aid. The defeat spells the end of French rule in Indochina. A Geneva conference of major world powers (26 April–21 July) resolves, at US insistence, that Vietnam be temporarily divided at the 17th parallel, between a communist North (led by Ho Chi Minh) and a non-communist South, pending elections. South Vietnam gains complete independence of France (4 Jun.). When it becomes clear that the Vietminh will win any election in the South, the US government moves to build a separate state and make Vietnamese partition permanent.

29 Dec. Laos becomes independent of France.

− Korean industrialist and evangelist Sun Myung Moon founds the anti-communist Unification Church (the Moonies) and will use it as his Korean power base.

THE AMERICAS

2 Mar. President López of Paraguay dies; Gen. Alfredo Stroessner is elected to succeed him in a one-party election. Stroessner will remain dictator of Paraguay until 1989.

Mar. France appeals to the USA for assistance in Indochina where its troops are now surrounded at Dien Bien Phu. President Eisenhower refuses to commit US forces to the region, though he subscribes to the 'domino' theory, which suggests that a communist victory in one state will allow the 'infection' to spread to its neighbours. He is determined, when the Geneva conference on Indochina opens (26 April), to limit communist gains in the region.

17 May The US Supreme Court rules that racial segregation in state schools is unconstitutional. The chief justice, Earl Warren, requires all states to integrate their educational systems.

Purity of race does not exist.

H.A.L. Fisher, *A History of Europe* (1935)

2 Dec. US senator Joseph McCarthy is formally condemned by the Senate for misconduct as chairman of the Senate's subcommittee investigating charges of communist subversion. During his anti-communist witch hunt, he has destroyed hundreds, if not thousands, of lives but has failed to prove a single case of subversion against the state.

− Canada agrees to the building of the DEW (Defence Early Warning) line, a system of early-warning stations across its N territory to warn the USA of an approaching missile or air attack.

ECONOMY AND SOCIETY

6 May At the Iffley Road Sports Ground, Oxford, the British athlete Roger Bannister becomes the first person to run a sub-four-minute mile (3 minutes 59.4 seconds).

− West Germany wins the 5th soccer World Cup, held in Switzerland.

− The US evangelist Billy Graham holds meetings in London, Berlin and New York.

SCIENCE AND TECHNOLOGY

− In the USA a kidney transplant operation is performed successfully for the first time by Harvard surgeons.

ARTS AND HUMANITIES

Literature

Kingsley Amis, *Lucky Jim*, novel.

William Golding, *Lord of the Flies*, novel.

Evan Hunter, *The Blackboard Jungle*, novel.

Thomas Mann, *Die Bekenntnisse des Hochstaplers Felix Krull* (The Confessions of Felix Krull, Confidence Man), novel.

Iris Murdoch, *Under the Net*, novel.

Terence Rattigan, *Separate Tables*, play.

Françoise Sagan, *Bonjour tristesse* (Good Morning, Sadness), novel.

Wallace Stevens, *Collected Poems*.

Visual Arts and Architecture

3 Nov. French artist Henri Matisse dies.

Jasper Johns, *Flag*, painting of the US flag regarded as marking the beginning of the Pop Art movement.

Graham Sutherland, *Winston Churchill*, portrait that is so disliked by its subject that it will eventually be burned by Lady Churchill.

Music

19 May The US composer Charles Ives dies.

– Herbert von Karajan succeeds Wilhelm Furtwängler as conductor of the Berlin Philharmonic Orchestra.

– US singer Elvis Presley makes his first commercial recording.

– First performance in Venice of Benjamin Britten's opera of childhood corruption and innocence *The Turn of the Screw*, which is based on Henry James's short story (1898).

William (Bill) Haley, 'Rock around the Clock', single.

Sandy Wilson, *The Boy Friend*, musical.

Film

Michael Anderson, *The Dam Busters*, starring Michael Redgrave and Richard Todd.

Edward Dmytryk, *The Caine Mutiny*.

Stanley Donen, *A Star is Born*, starring Judy Garland.

Federico Fellini, *La strada* (The Road).

Alfred Hitchcock, *Rear Window*, starring James Stewart.

Elia Kazan, *On the Waterfront*, starring Marlon Brando.

Akira Kurosawa, *The Seven Samurai*.

1955

EUROPE

15 Jan. The Soviet government recognizes the independence of West Germany. The prime minister, Georgi Malenkov, steadily losing power to Nikita Khrushchev, resigns and is succeeded by Nikolai Bulganin, who reaffirms the Sino-Soviet Pact.

25 Jan. The USSR ends its state of war with Germany.

5 Feb. The Algerian crisis causes the French government of Pierre Mendès-France to fall. Lawyer and former minister of finance and economic affairs Edgar Faure forms a new ministry (23 Feb).

5 April In Britain Winston Churchill (see p. 523) resigns as prime minister and is succeeded by foreign secretary Anthony Eden.

9 May West Germany is admitted into the North Atlantic Treaty Organization (NATO).

14 May The E European communist states sign the Warsaw Pact, a military alliance built as a response to NATO.

26 May In the British general election the Conservatives are returned to power, winning 345 seats to Labour's 277. The Liberals win just 6 seats.

27 July Austria becomes a sovereign state again by the signing of the treaty of Vienna; the army of occupation withdraws.

Sept. Diplomatic relations are established between West Germany and the USSR.

13 Dec. In Britain Hugh Gaitskell succeeds Clement Attlee as leader of the Labour Party.

– The Western European Union (formerly the Western Union) is established as a consultative forum on defence matters by Britain, France, Belgium, the Netherlands, Luxembourg, West Germany and Italy.

ASIA

28 April In South Vietnam, a power struggle between the prime minister Ngo Dinh Diem and the emperor Bao Dai results in a referendum (23 Oct.) ousting the monarchy and establishing the South Vietnamese Republic (26 Oct.), of which Diem will be president. He will enjoy vast US military and economic aid but will ignore the peasantry's desperate need for land reform, while his despotic ways and militant Catholicism will antagonize many. South Vietnam will find no stability, or even popular legitimacy, under Diem's rule.

– The US military occupation of Japan formally ends.

– In the People's Republic of China Mao Zedong's programme for the collectivization of agriculture gathers pace.

SUB-SAHARAN AFRICA

– In Sudan a civil war breaks out between the Muslim N and the Christian S.

THE AMERICAS

19 Sept. A military coup topples Juan Perón, president of Argentina. Perón has pursued a 'third way', which has nationalized the railways (previously owned by the British) and encouraged the development of a labour movement with trade unions. He has been an important figure in the evolution of third-world economies, encouraging their identity as a power block with their own agenda. But the death of his wife, Eva, (1952) has diminished his appeal among the Argentinian masses.

24 Sept. US president Dwight D. Eisenhower suffers a heart attack.

1 Dec. In the USA African-Americans led by Rev. Martin Luther King Jr in Montgomery, Alabama, begin a 381-day boycott of racially segregated local buses. The action marks the beginning of the modern US civil rights movement.

– Democrat Richard Daley becomes Mayor of Chicago. For 21 years he will rule the city and favour those who have supported him financially in his electoral campaigns.

ECONOMY AND SOCIETY

17 July Disneyland, an entertainment centre developed by Walt Disney, opens near Los Angeles, California.

– Britain's first programme of fluoridation of drinking water is introduced in Anglesey, Wales.

SCIENCE AND TECHNOLOGY

18 April The German-born US physicist Albert Einstein dies.

ARTS AND HUMANITIES

Literature

2 Aug. The US poet Wallace Stevens dies.

12 Aug. The German novelist Thomas Mann dies.

– In the USA William F. Buckley Jr founds and edits the *National Review*, a conservative magazine.

– US poet Allen Ginsberg's public reading in San Francisco of his poem 'Howl' makes him a cult figure among the now rapidly developing Californian youth movement.

J.P. Donleavy, *The Ginger Man*, novel.

Graham Greene, *The Quiet American*, novel.

Alistair Maclean, *HMS Ulysses*, novel.

Arthur Miller, *A View from the Bridge*, play.

Brian Moore, *The Lonely Passion of Judith Hearne*, novel.

Vladimir Nabokov, *Lolita*, novel.

J.R.R. Tolkien, *The Lord of the Rings*, trilogy consisting of *The Fellowship of the Ring*, *The Two Towers* and *The Return of the King*, a fantasy epic rooted in the values of pre-industrial England; it will acquire a cult following.

Evelyn Waugh, *Officers and Gentlemen*, second novel of *The Sword of Honour* trilogy.

Tennessee Williams, *Cat on a Hot Tin Roof*, play.

Visual Arts and Architecture

5 Nov. French artist Maurice Utrillo dies.

Giorgio de Chirico, *Italian Square*, painting.

Music

– First performance in London of Michael Tippett's opera *The Midsummer Marriage*.

Chuck Berry, 'Maybellene' and 'Roll Over Beethoven', singles.

Pierre Boulez, *Le Marteau sans maître* (The Hammer without a Master), fiercely modernist work for contralto and instruments.

Film

Elia Kazan, *East of Eden*, starring James Dean.

Alexander Mackendrick, *The Ladykillers*.

Nicholas Ray, *Rebel without a Cause*, starring James Dean.

Satyajit Ray, *Pather Panchali* (Song of the Road).

George Stevens, *Giant*, starring James Dean, who is killed in a car crash (30 Sept.).

Billy Wilder, *The Seven Year Itch*, starring Marilyn Monroe.

1956

EUROPE

24 Feb. Soviet leader Nikita Khrushchev denounces previous leader Joseph Stalin's crimes against the Communist Party but not against the Soviet people (crimes in which Khrushchev himself was implicated). The speech, made in secret to the Communist Party congress, soon becomes widely known, and will raise the hopes of dissidents and reformers throughout the USSR and E Europe. These hopes will be crushed.

April The Soviet leaders Nikita Khrushchev and Nikolai Bulganin visit Britain. A mystery emerges on 29 April when the British Admiralty announces that a Royal Navy frogman, Commander Crabb, has disappeared while diving in Portsmouth Harbour during a Soviet naval visit. Crabb's headless body will be discovered at sea on 26 June 1957.

28 June Workers in Poznań, Poland, riot against the communist government. Polish officers demand the removal of Soviet officers from the Polish army (16 Oct). Wladyslaw Gomulka, widely seen as a reformer, is freed after five years' imprisonment and rehabilitated. He becomes the first secretary of the Polish Communist Party (21 Oct.). But Soviet leader Khrushchev makes an uninvited appearance in Warsaw, demanding assurances of loyalty, while the Soviet army masses on the Polish–Soviet frontier. Gomulka ends some of the most objectionable features of communist rule in Poland – the collectivization of agriculture and persecution of the Roman Catholic Church – but does not grant intellectual, political or economic freedom.

23 Oct. Students protest in Budapest, Hungary, and are joined by workers in a march on parliament. They demand the return of Imre Nagy, widely seen as a radical reformer, to government, the release of Cardinal Mindszenty (see 26 Dec. 1948) and the withdrawal of Soviet troops. Nagy returns to office as prime minister (24 Oct), while in heavy street fighting Red Army tanks, unsupported by infantry, take heavy losses. Soviet forces withdraw from Budapest (30 Oct.), and Cardinal Mindszenty is released from prison. Red Army divisions, however, pour into Hungary to crush the rising. Nagy repudiates the Warsaw Pact and appeals to the West to guarantee Hungarian independence (1 Nov.). The West is not willing to risk a world war over Hungary, and 16 Soviet divisions quickly crush the revolt (4 Nov.). Nagy is replaced as prime minister by János Kádár and is seized and later executed. Cardinal Mindszenty takes refuge in the US embassy and will stay there for 15 years. The UN has condemned the invasion but neither it nor the USA intervene. Some 150,000 Hungarians leave the country.

Dec. In Northern Ireland the Irish Republican Army (IRA) begins a 'border campaign' against British rule with attacks on customs posts in Tyrone, Fermanagh and Armagh. The campaign will last until Feb. 1962.

– In Britain Jo Grimond becomes leader of the Liberal Party.

MIDDLE EAST AND NORTH AFRICA

1 Mar. Morocco becomes independent of France, and Spain yields its Moroccan territories to the new state (7 April). Spain retains Ceuta and Melilla as military bases, however.

20 Mar. Tunisia becomes independent from France. The bey of Tunis invites Paris-educated Tunisian nationalist Habib Ben Ali Bourguiba to form a government (10 April).

21 April Egypt, Saudi Arabia and Yemen agree to a military alliance, clearly aimed against Israel.

4 June The Egyptian government announces that the Suez Canal Company's concession will not be renewed once it expires in 1968. British troops leave the Suez Canal base (13 June). The US government, irritated at Nasser for accepting Soviet arms, refuses to finance Nasser's pet project, the Aswan high dam. Nasser, stung by the rebuff and needing an alternative source of money, orders the immediate seizure of the canal (26 July). The British and French decide, without informing the USA, to recover the canal by force and topple Nasser. They make a deal with Israel, and Israeli forces invade the Sinai peninsula (29 Oct). This gives the French and British a pretext to invade to 'protect' the canal, and deliver an ultimatum to both Egyptians and Israelis to withdraw from the canal zone. When Nasser refuses, Britain and France begin to bomb Egyptian air-fields (31 Oct). Their troops land at Port Said (5 Nov.) and make rapid progress inland. US President Dwight D. Eisenhower, however, refuses to support Britain and France. He arranges for a UN resolution calling for their immediate withdrawal and uses the USA's financial power to pressurize them into complying. This, combined with an Arab oil embargo, puts Britain under intense strain, and the government capitulates. A UN force arrives in the region (15 Nov.), and Anglo-French forces are humiliatingly withdrawn from Port Said (22 Dec). The episode has shown the limits and the illusions of British foreign policy; it is the effective end of Britain as a major power. Suez has also been a key event in British domestic politics. The prime minister, Anthony Eden, is broken by the crisis.

– In Libya King Idris I has granted an oil concession to the Libyan American Oil Co.; the first oil well now comes into production.

ASIA

29 Feb. Pakistan becomes an officially Islamic republic but stays within the British Commonwealth.

– Reliable reports in the West now indicate the full scale of the Chinese communist government's massacre of its opponents. Liquidation measures have accelerated since 1952, and by 1960 some 26.3 million Chinese will have been killed for opposing enforced communization.

– Louis St Laurent, prime minister of Canada, signs an agreement with Jawaharlal Nehru, prime minister of India, and pledges Canadian cooperation in helping India develop nuclear power for peaceful purposes.

THE AMERICAS

6 Nov. US president Dwight D. Eisenhower is re-elected, defeating Democrat candidate Adlai Stevenson.

13 Nov. The US Supreme Court rules that the segregation of bus passengers is unconstitutional. The Montgomery bus boycott (see 1 Dec. 1955) ends.

– A coup in Haiti results in the coming to power of François Duvalier, known as 'Papa Doc'. Duvalier's rule will degenerate into a brutal dictatorship, which he imposes by means of a notorious private militia, the Tontons Macoutes.

– A site in C Brazil is chosen as the location of the country's new capital city of Brasilia.

– The US Justice Department indicts General Motors for anti-competition measures, which enable it to get an 85% monopoly on the trade for new buses.

SUB-SAHARAN AFRICA

1 Jan. Sudan becomes an independent democratic republic and joins the Arab League (19 Jan.).

18 Sept. The Gold Coast becomes independent from Britain.

ECONOMY AND SOCIETY

27–31 July Jim Laker, an off-spin bowler, takes 19 Australian wickets in the fourth cricket test match between England and Australia at Old Trafford, Manchester.

Nov.–Dec. The 16th Olympic Games are held in Melbourne, Australia.

– In Britain the Clean Air Act begins to clear the air of smoke pollution.

– In Britain the government introduces premium bonds.

– US sociologist William H. Whyte Jr argues, in *The Organization Man*, that the bureaucratization of society has undermined the old ideals of American Protestantism. It has been replaced, he

thinks, by a debased creed, which emphasizes belonging rather than personal fulfilment, group activity rather than individualism.

– Edson Arantes do Nascimento (Pelé) joins the Santos association football team, Brazil. He will go on to be hailed as the world's greatest footballer.

SCIENCE AND TECHNOLOGY

– Henri Lhote, a French archaeologist, dates paintings discovered in the Tibetsi Mountains, in the Sahara Desert, to 3500 BC. The discovery, 1450km (900 miles) S of Algiers, shows that parts of the area now known as the Sahara were once fertile and that the desert has spread S.

ARTS AND HUMANITIES

Literature

8 May First performance at the Royal Court Theatre, London, of John Osborne's play *Look Back in Anger*. The play opens the attack of the 'Angry Young Men' on the British establishment.

14 Aug. Bertolt Brecht, German poet and playwright, dies at Brandenburg, near Berlin.

Nelson Algren, *A Walk on the Wild Side*, novel.

Albert Camus, *La Chute* (The Fall), novel.

Gerald Durrell, *My Family and Other Animals*, humorous memoir.

Friedrich Dürrenmatt, *Der Besuch der alten Dame* (The Visit), play.

William Golding, *Pincher Martin*, novel.

Patricia Highsmith, *The Talented Mr Ripley*, the first of five novels about the pathological Tom Ripley.

Rose Macaulay, *The Towers of Trebizond*, novel.

Eugene O'Neill, *A Long Day's Journey into Night*, play, performed posthumously.

Dodie Smith, *The Hundred and One Dalmatians*, children's story.

Patrick White, *The Tree of Man*, novel.

Angus Wilson, *Anglo-Saxon Attitudes*, novel.

Yevgeny Yevtushenko, *Stantsiya Zima* (Zima Junction), narrative poem. This same year Yevtushenko publishes, with Khrushchev's support, an anti-Stalinist poem entitled 'Stalin's Heirs'.

Visual Arts and Architecture

17 Aug. US artist Jackson Pollock is killed in a car accident.

– Finnish-born US architect Eero Saarinen starts work on what will be the TWA Kennedy terminal of New York's airport.

Richard Hamilton, *Just What is it that Makes Today's Homes So Different, So Appealing?*, collage seen as pioneering work of British Pop Art.

Music

– The US film *Rock Around the Clock* introduces rock 'n' roll to Britain and provokes right-wing hostility towards what is seen as a tide of juvenile delinquency. Teddy boys begin to emerge in Britain.

– In Britain skiffle music, a type of jazz folk, introduced by Lonnie Donegan, becomes widely popular.

– The soprano Maria Callas makes her New York debut, singing Bellini's *Norma*.

– The Eurovision Song Contest is held for the first time in Lugano, Switzerland.

Aram Khachaturian, *Spartacus*, music for ballet.

Frederick Loewe and Alan Jay Lerner, *My Fair Lady*, musical.

Olivier Messiaen, *Oiseaux exotiques* (Exotic Birds).

Carl Perkins, 'Blue Suede Shoes', single.

Elvis Presley, 'Love Me Tender', 'Hound Dog' and 'Heartbreak Hotel', singles.

Film

Ingmar Bergman, *Det Sjunde Inseglet* (The Seventh Seal).

Walter Lang, *The King and I*, starring Yul Brynner and Deborah Kerr.

Laurence Olivier, *Richard III*.

Satyajit Ray, *Aparajito*.

Roger Vadim, *Et Dieu créa la femme* (And God Created Woman), starring Brigitte Bardot.

1957

EUROPE

1 Jan. The Saarland, occupied by France in 1945, and part of the French customs union since 1948, is incorporated into West Germany as a federal state (*Land*).

9 Jan. In Britain Anthony Eden resigns as prime minister and is succeeded by Harold Macmillan. The former chancellor of the exchequer initially supported the Suez expedition but then, expeditiously, withdrew his support.

5 Feb. General election in the Republic of Ireland following the collapse of the Fine Gael-led coalition (28 Jan.). Fianna Fáil wins an absolute majority and the 75-year-old Eamon de Valéra returns as taoiseach (prime minister) (20 Mar.).

25 Mar. The treaties of Rome are signed and establish the European Economic Community (EEC). France, West Germany, Belgium, Italy, Luxembourg and the Netherlands agree to maximize trade by removing tariff barriers. The political dimension of the treaties is enshrined in a commitment to ever-greater union between the peoples of W Europe. The EEC's work will be dominated by the need to ensure Franco-German rapprochement. Britain, in the meantime, decides to stand apart from the enterprise.

18 July The French National Assembly votes to give the govern-ment special powers to combat the urban terrorism of the Algerian FLN (Front de Libération Nationale).

26 Oct. In the USSR Marshal Georgi Zhukov is sacked as defence minister, and former foreign minister Vyacheslav Molotov is sent as ambassador to Mongolia after an unsuccessful attempt to remove Khrushchev.

MIDDLE EAST AND NORTH AFRICA

18 Jan. The Chinese and Soviet governments announce their support of the Middle Eastern Arab states against Western 'aggression'.

22 Jan. Israeli forces withdraw from the Sinai Peninsula but remain in the Gaza Strip (within Egyptian territory).

6 Feb. Israel hands over the Gaza Strip to UN forces on the understanding that there will be free passage to navigate the Gulf of Aqaba. The closure of the Gulf of Aqaba, Israel repeatedly insists, will mean war.

11 July Aga Khan III (Sultan Sir Mohammed Shah), spiritual leader of the Ismaili Islamic sect, dies and is succeeded by his grandson, the Harvard-educated Aga Khan IV.

25 July Tunisia becomes a republic with the deposition of the bey of Tunis. Habib Ben Ali Bourguiba is elected president and asks the USA for military assistance (12 Sept.). This is duly promised (14 Nov.), and Bourguiba announces his rejection of a supposed Soviet offer of military aid (18 Nov.).

11 Aug. The Sherifian empire becomes officially the kingdom of Morocco. Sultan Sidi Mohammed ben Yusuf becomes King Mohammed V.

13 Aug. The Syrian government expels three US diplomats, charging them with attempting to subvert the government. The Americans retaliate by expelling Syrian diplomats in Washington. President Dwight D. Eisenhower claims that Moscow is bent on dominating Syria. Arab solidarity is strengthened by the episode, and Syria grows close to Nasser's Egypt. The USSR complains that Turkish troops are massing on the border with Syria (11 Sept.), and the Syrian government declares a state of emergency (16 Oct.).

– As part of increasing US involvement in the region, US aid is sent to Jordan. President Eisenhower asks Congress for the authority to intervene militarily in the Middle East if necessary.

ASIA

20 April Japan formally protests to the USSR about its nuclear tests.

31 Aug. Malaya becomes an independent state within the Commonwealth.

THE AMERICAS

5 Jan. US president Eisenhower announces the 'Eisenhower Doctrine', promising military or economic aid to any Middle Eastern country needing help in resisting communist aggression. The Doctrine is intended to check the increase of Soviet influence in the Middle East.

5 Sept. Little Rock, Arkansas, becomes the flashpoint of the struggle for US school integration when the governor, Orval Faubus, leads crowds who try to stop nine African-American children from entering the local high school. President Eisenhower sends in federal troops to suppress the disorder. The incident illustrates the depth of hostility among southern US Whites to civil rights reform.

9 Sept. US Congress passes a Civil Rights Bill, which authorizes the establishment of a Civil Rights Commission.

– Jimmy Hoffa of Detroit takes charge of the International Brotherhood of Teamsters and will develop it into the USA's most powerful trade union.

– US antiwar protestors found the National Committee for a Sane Nuclear Policy (Sane).

SUB-SAHARAN AFRICA

6 Feb. Ghana, the former Gold Coast, becomes the first colonial territory in Sub-Saharan Africa to gain independence. Western-educated Kwame Nkrumah becomes prime minister.

AUSTRALASIA AND OCEANIA

15 May The first British thermo-nuclear (hydrogen) bomb is tested on Christmas Island in the Pacific Ocean.

ECONOMY AND SOCIETY

Sept. In Britain Sir John Wolfenden has presided over a committee on homosexual offences and prostitution, and his report is now published. It proposes that homosexual acts 'between consenting adults in private' should no longer be illegal.

− In Britain the Homicide Act restricts the application of capital punishment.

SCIENCE AND TECHNOLOGY

4 Oct. The first artificial satellite, *Sputnik* 1, is launched by the USSR. It will orbit the earth once every 90 minutes and is followed by *Sputnik* 2, carrying the dog Laika (Nov.).

− Chinese irrigation increases vastly while the communist revolution in ownership and technology transforms both the Chinese economy and landscape. The Yellow (Huang He) River, which previously burst its banks regularly, is now controlled.

ARTS AND HUMANITIES

Literature

− Russian writer Boris Pasternak's novel *Dr Zhivago* is published in Italy. It is banned in the USSR, where the Soviet authorities declare it to be a 'hostile act'.

James Agee, *A Death in the Family*, novel.

Samuel Beckett (see box), *Endgame*, play.

John Braine, *Room at the Top*, novel.

Lawrence Durrell, *Justine*, first novel of his 'Alexandrian Quartet'.

Ted Hughes, *Hawk in the Rain*, poetry collection.

Jack Kerouac, *On the Road*, novel that becomes the manifesto of the 'Beat Generation'.

Bernard Malamud, *The Assistant*, novel.

John Osborne, *The Entertainer*, play.

Octavio Paz, *Piedra de sol* (Sun Stone), poetry collection.

Alain Robbe-Grillet, *La Jalousie* (Jealousy), novel.

Isaac Bashevis Singer, *Gimpel the Fool*, short story collection.

Stevie Smith, *Not Waving but Drowning*, poetry collection.

Wallace Stevens, *Opus Posthumous*, collection of poems, prose and plays.

Patrick White, *Voss*, novel.

Tennessee Williams, *Orpheus Descending*, play.

John Wyndham, *The Midwich Cuckoos*, novel.

Visual Arts and Architecture

16 Mar. Romanian sculptor Constantin Brancusi dies in Paris.

25 Nov. Mexican painter Diego Rivera dies in Mexico City.

Elisabeth Frink, *Wild Boar*, sculpture for Harlow New Town.

Alberto Giacometti, *Annette*, painting.

Robert Rauschenberg, *Painting with Red Letter 'S'*.

Diego Rivera, *Mujeres peinándose* (Women Combing), painting.

Music

6 June First performance in Zurich of Arnold Schoenberg's (see p. 511) opera *Moses und Aron*.

11 Aug. First performance in Munich of Paul Hindemith's opera *Die Harmonie der Welt* (The Harmony of the World). A symphony from the opera was premiered in 1951.

− First staging in New York of Leonard Bernstein's musical *West Side Story*, with lyrics by Stephen Sondheim. The story is an updated version of Shakespeare's *Romeo and Juliet* set in New York's West Side dockland area.

− Elvis Presley appears in the film *Jailhouse Rock* and sings its title song.

Samuel Beckett (1906–89)

The Irish writer Samuel Beckett was at the cutting edge of the modernist experiment with words and their meanings. He is the most significant successor of his fellow-countryman, the pioneering modernist James Joyce, and spent most of his life in Paris writing in both French and English. Beckett was a key figure in the movement known as the theatre of the absurd, in which the world is portrayed as God-less and meaningless, and all actions as random and motiveless. But Beckett is also important in the literature of existentialism, since he deals with questions of meaning and faith, hope and despair. This apparent high seriousness vies with a great comic sense, and Beckett's bleak vision is mitigated by moments of startling humour.

His most famous play is *Waiting for Godot* (1953), but earlier novels such as *Murphy* (1938), *Watt* (1953) and the trilogy written in 1946–9, *Molloy, Malone Dies* and *The Unnameable*, had already marked out the Beckett terrain of enclosed and seedy environments that trap the physically maimed and the mentally derelict. His subsequent aesthetic was determinedly minimalist, stripping down all action, location and speech to the bare human fundamentals. *Breath* (1969) lasts 15 seconds on stage and consists of a pile of rubbish accompanied by a single human breath.

Beckett is the most ascetic of writers and reflects with a perfect aesthetic poise what he saw as the mid-20th-century collapse of European civilization. His characters refuse easy solutions and Christian ideas of atonement and repentance – although their discourse is poignantly replete with theological terms. They are anti-pilgrims, increasingly immobile in a world that lacks meaning. Beckett avoids nihilism only because the vitality of language shows how existence can be understood and endured.

Pierre Boulez, *Improvisation sur Mallarmé*.

Duke Ellington, *Such Sweet Thunder,* jazz suite based on Shakespearean characters.

Dmitri Shostakovich, Symphony No. 11 in G minor (*The Year 1905*).

Karlheinz Stockhausen, *Gruppen* (Groups), for three orchestras, each playing different music.

William Walton, *Partita*.

Film

Ingmar Bergman, *Smultronstället* (Wild Strawberries).

Akira Kurosawa, *Throne of Blood*.

David Lean, *Bridge on the River Kwai*, starring Alec Guinness.

Sidney Lumet, *12 Angry Men*, starring Henry Fonda.

Billy Wilder, *Witness for the Prosecution*, starring Marlene Dietrich.

1958

EUROPE

1 Jan. The European Economic Community and the European Atomic Energy Community (Euratom), created by the treaties of Rome (see 25 Mar. 1957), come into force. Euratom consists of France, Belgium, Italy, Luxembourg, the Netherlands and West Germany. It receives an assurance from the US government that the USA will supply it with uranium for 20 years.

17 Feb. In Britain the Campaign for Nuclear Disarmament (CND) is founded. CND organizes a march from London to the nuclear research centre at Aldermaston, Berkshire (7 April).

27 Mar. In the USSR Nikita Khrushchev replaces Nikolai Bulganin as chairman of the Soviet council of ministers. Bulganin is allowed to retire.

1 June French politician Charles de Gaulle returns to French public life from self-imposed exile at Colombey-les-deux-Eglises to become prime minister at a time when France is threatened by civil war after the Algerian War has discredited the institutions and leaders of the Fourth Republic. France has imposed direct military rule on Algeria, but violence has escalated both in Algeria and in France. Under de Gaulle a new constitution is drawn up for the Fifth Republic.

8–9 Sept. In Britain race riots occur in Notting Hill, W London.

28 Sept. In France a referendum shows that a four to one majority approves the institutions of the proposed French Fifth Republic. In the Nov. elections de Gaulle's RPF (Rassemblement du Peuple Français) party gains a majority in the National Assembly.

4 Nov. The USA, Britain and USSR accept a voluntary moratorium on nuclear weapons testing.

27 Nov. A new crisis arises in Berlin: the USSR withdraws from the four-power agreement on the city, demanding the demilitarization of West Berlin and the establishment of Berlin's W sectors as a free city.

21 Dec. In France Charles de Gaulle is elected to serve as president for a seven-year term. The new government gives its colonies six months to decide whether to be incorporated into France as departments of the state or to become independent members of a French Community.

MIDDLE EAST AND NORTH AFRICA

1 Feb. Pan-Arab consciousness gains its first political expression in the post-colonial world when Egyptian leader Gamal Abdel Nasser declares the union of Egypt with Syria in a United Arab Republic.

14 Feb. Iraq is joined with Jordan in an Arab Federation headed by King Faisal II of Iraq. But the king is assassinated (14 July) in a military coup led by Gen. Abdul Karim Qassem, who declares a republic. King Hussein of Jordan succeeds Faisal as head of state, but he disbands the Arab Federation (1 Aug.).

17 June French forces are withdrawn from most of Tunisia, and Tunisia joins the Arab League (1 Oct.).

15 July US marines land in Beirut, and President Eisenhower pledges that the USA will defend Lebanese independence from a purported communist threat. When a new government is elected in Lebanon US troops are withdrawn (25 Oct.).

– Moroccan women are allowed the right to choose their husbands.

ASIA

3 Feb. President Sukarno of Indonesia seizes the assets of oil company Royal Dutch-Shell in his country.

23 Aug. Chinese communist forces begin intermittently shelling offshore islands still held by Guomindang forces. President Eisenhower pledges to support Taiwan.

Oct. In Pakistan Gen. Mohammed Ayub Khan takes power in a military coup. He suspends the constitution and all political parties, and declares martial law.

– Chairman Mao Zedong (Mao Tse-tung) (see p. 573) of China announces the Great Leap Forward. The collectivization of Chinese agriculture forces peasants to live together in communes and deprives them of private property. The Great Leap Forward also calls for a vast increase in steel production from small backyard furnaces. The resulting economic dislocation leads to a famine that will kill about 20 million people by 1962.

THE AMERICAS

3 Jan. The West Indies Federation is created by Britain. It includes Barbados, Grenada, Jamaica and Trinidad, but it does not survive beyond 1962. The islands will seek independence separately.

May During a goodwill tour of South America, US vice-president Richard Nixon encounters mob violence. In Caracas, Venezuela, an enraged mob threatens to drag him from his limousine and lynch him. President Eisenhower orders troops to stand by for a rescue, but Nixon is successfully smuggled out of Venezuela. A shocked president Eisenhower seeks to improve US relations with S American states.

SUB-SAHARAN AFRICA

– Under the terms set by the new French government, a series of referendums change the map of Africa. Guinea opts to become a completely independent republic, rejecting the idea of a French Community altogether (2 Oct). The other former French possessions opt for autonomy within a French Community.

These include Madagascar (the Malagasy Republic) (14 Oct.); Senegal (25 Nov.); Gabon, the Congo, Mauritania and the French Sudan (Mali) (28 Nov.). The Central African Republic (1 Dec.) and the Ivory Coast (4 Dec.) also opt for autonomy.

ECONOMY AND SOCIETY

6 Feb. Eight Manchester United footballers are killed in an air crash at Munich. The Manchester United manager, Matt Busby, is badly injured in the crash.

26 Feb.–4 Mar. During a cricket match in Kingston, Jamaica, the West Indies all-rounder Gary Sobers scores 365 not out, a new record individual score for a batsman (see 1938).

9 Oct. Pope Pius XII dies. He is succeeded (28 Oct.) by Angelo Giuseppe Roncalli, who becomes Pope John XXIII.

– The Preston bypass, the first stretch of motorway in Britain, is completed.

– The British government introduces life peerages.

– The Harvard economist John Kenneth Galbraith castigates consumerism in *The Affluent Society*. Advertising, he says, is creating unnecessary demand and consumption while public services are neglected. He also describes the necessary role of government in controlling the boom and bust effects of the market's cycles.

– Brazil wins the 6th soccer World Cup, held in Sweden.

SCIENCE AND TECHNOLOGY

– In the USA the National Aeronautics and Space Administration (NASA) is created to undertake research on space exploration.

– The first US-built commercial jet aircraft, the Boeing 707, starts to operate and will beat all other models for market dominance, including the British-built Comet (see 1952).

ARTS AND HUMANITIES

Literature

Chinua Achebe, *Things Fall Apart*, novel.

H.E. Bates, *The Darling Buds of May*, novel.

Samuel Beckett (see p. 558), *Krapp's Last Tape*, play.

Brendan Behan, *Borstal Boy*, autobiography.

Bertolt Brecht, *The Resistible Rise of Arturo Ui*, play.

Truman Capote, *Breakfast at Tiffany's*, novel.

Graham Greene, *Our Man in Havana*, novel.

Giuseppe Tomasi di Lampedusa, *Il gattopardo* (The Leopard), novel; an elegiac account of the passing of the old aristocratic order in 19th-century Sicily, which is published posthumously following the author's death in 1957.

Mario Vargas Llosa, *The City and the Dogs*, novel.

Cyril Northcote Parkinson, *Parkinson's Law*, a satirical treatment of modern bureaucracy and its management systems.

Harold Pinter, *The Birthday Party*, play.

Alan Sillitoe, *Saturday Night and Sunday Morning*, novel.

Leon Uris, *Exodus*, novel.

Evelyn Waugh, *The Ordeal of Gilbert Pinfold*, novel.

Arnold Wesker, *Chicken Soup with Barley*, play.

T.H. White, *The Once and Future King*, Arthurian tetralogy.

Tennessee Williams, *Suddenly Last Summer*, play.

William Carlos Williams, *Patterson*, epic five-book poem begun in 1946.

Visual Arts and Architecture

– The Pirelli Building, Milan, Italy, designed by Pier Luigi Nervi and Gio Ponti, is completed.

Jasper Johns, *Three Flags*, painting.

Mark Rothko, *Four Darks on Red*, painting that develops his monumental style.

Music

26 Aug. The English composer Ralph Vaughan Williams dies.

– The US National Academy of Recording Arts and Sciences introduces the Grammy awards.

Benjamin Britten, *Nocturne*, sequence of songs for tenor and orchestra.

Jerry Lee Lewis, 'Great Balls of Fire', single.

Film

Richard Brooks, *Cat on a Hot Tin Roof*, starring Elizabeth Taylor and Paul Newman.

Edward Dmytryk, *The Young Lions*, starring Marlon Brando and Montgomery Clift.

Alfred Hitchcock, *Vertigo*, starring James Stewart and Kim Novak.

Vincente Minnelli, *Gigi*, starring Maurice Chevalier.

Orson Welles, *A Touch of Evil*, starring Charlton Heston and Janet Leigh.

1959

EUROPE

19 Feb. The prime ministers of Britain, Greece and Turkey agree terms for the independence of Cyprus. Greek Cypriots have been campaigning for *enosis* (union with Greece), sometimes using terrorist methods, while Turkish Cypriots have been advocating partition of the island. A compromise is now agreed: the Cypriot president is to be Greek, the vice-president Turkish, and power is to be shared by the two communities.

21 April The Soviet government protests to the USA about the stationing of nuclear weapons in West Germany.

17 June In the Republic of Ireland Eamon de Valéra resigns as taoiseach (prime minister) and is succeeded by the tánaiste (deputy prime minister), Sean Lemass. De Valéra becomes Irish president.

24 July At a trade exhibition in Moscow US vice-president Richard Nixon and Soviet leader Nikita Khrushchev publicly debate the advantages of their respective political systems in a model American kitchen exhibit.

1 Oct. East Germany modifies its flag (hitherto the same as West Germany's) to include symbols of workers and peasants.

8 Oct. In the British general election the Conservatives, led by prime minister Harold Macmillan, are re-elected. Macmillan's slogan, 'You've never had it so good', reflects the growing affluence of the electorate. The Conservatives, wishing to escape their association with the economic hardships of the 1930s, have accepted the essential features of the British welfare state and pursue policies combining social security with economic growth. But Britain's nationalized industries are increasingly uncompetitive.

24 Dec. In Cologne, West Germany, racists deface a recently rebuilt Jewish synagogue.

ASIA

31 Mar. An anti-Chinese uprising breaks out in Tibet. The Dalai Lama, spiritual leader of Tibet, flees to India after the Chinese garrison in Lhasa is attacked. The Chinese-dominated government closes the border with India. Chinese and Indian forces on the border exchange fire.

27 April Mao Zedong (Mao Tse-tung) steps down as China's chief of state but remains chairman of the Communist Party.

3 June Britain grants Singapore self-government with the authoritarian Lee Kuan Yew as prime minister. Britain retains control of Singapore's defence and foreign affairs.

5 July President Sukarno of Indonesia dissolves the country's national assembly as the country moves towards a more authoritarian style of government run according to Sukarno's neo-Marxist ideology.

25 Sept. The prime minister of Ceylon, Solomon Bandaranaike, is killed by a Buddhist monk after concluding a trade deal with China.

THE AMERICAS

1 Jan. Fulgencio Batista, dictator of Cuba, flees into exile in Miami. Rebel leader Fidel Castro has conducted a two-year campaign against the dictator. Castro enters Havana in triumph (3 Jan.) and takes office as premier (16 Feb.). He promises moderate reform, to end corruption and to restore full civil and political liberties. Once securely in power, he proves far more radical, instituting wide-ranging land reforms and nationalizing industries but also persecuting political opponents. By confiscating US-owned businesses and estates he angers President Eisenhower, who concludes he is a communist and orders the CIA to prepare to overthrow him.

3 Jan. Alaska becomes the 49th state of the USA.

21 Jan. In the USA bus passengers are racially integrated in Atlanta, Georgia, but the state's segregationist governor asks citizens to continue with 'voluntary' segregation. Elsewhere in the S states buses mostly remain segregated.

21 Aug. Hawaii becomes the 50th state of the USA.

15 Sept. Soviet leader Nikita Khrushchev becomes the first head of state of the USSR to be received at the White House. Khrushchev goes on to tour the USA and receives a generally warm welcome.

SUB-SAHARAN AFRICA

17 Jan. Senegal and the French Sudan merge to form the Federal of Mali.

Jan. A total of 71 people are killed in anti-European riots at Leopoldville in the Belgian Congo.

Nov. In E Africa Rwanda, a UN trust territory, is rent by the rebellion of the majority Hutu people against the aristocratic Tutsi minority.

ECONOMY AND SOCIETY

– In Britain the Street Offences Act makes open soliciting on the street illegal but imposes no penalties on prostitutes' clients.

– The first section of the M1 motorway is completed in Britain.

– South Africa decides not to introduce television, a decision that will be upheld for the next 16 years.

SCIENCE AND TECHNOLOGY

– The first proper hovercraft successfully crosses the English Channel. Its inventor, the British engineer Christopher Cockerell, is on board.

– Jack Kilby and Robert Noyce, US engineers, patent the integrated circuit (or microchip), which, endowed eventually with logic and memory facilities, will lead to the personal computer.

ARTS AND HUMANITIES
Literature

– In Britain the Obscene Publications Act prohibits the publication of material that tends to deprave or corrupt, but the Act allows a defence of artistic or literary merit. This part of the Act is soon to be tested in the *Lady Chatterley* trial (see 1960).

John Arden, *Serjeant Musgrave's Dance*, play.

Saul Bellow, *Henderson the Rain King*, novel.

William Burroughs, *The Naked Lunch*, novel.

Jean Genet, *Les Nègres* (The Blacks), play.

Günter Grass, *Die Blechtrommel* (The Tin Drum), novel.

Geoffrey Hill, *For the Unfallen*, poetry collection.

Laurie Lee, *Cider with Rosie*, memoir of a Cotswold boyhood.

Colin MacInnes, *Absolute Beginners*, novel.

Raymond Queneau, *Zazie dans le Métro* (Zazie in the Metro), novel.

Alan Sillitoe, *The Loneliness of the Long-Distance Runner*, novella.

Muriel Spark, *Memento Mori*, novel.

Arnold Wesker, *Roots*, play.

Tennessee Williams, *Sweet Bird of Youth*, play.

Visual Arts and Architecture

9 April The US architect Frank Lloyd Wright dies.

– The Guggenheim Museum is completed: the New York building has been designed by US architect Frank Lloyd Wright with a circular inner ramp whose dramatic curve echoes the designs of medieval Celtic decoration.

– The Seagram Building in New York, designed by architects Mies van de Rohe and Philip Johnson, is completed.

Jasper Johns, *Numbers in Color*, painting.

Music

3 Feb. US popular singer Buddy Holly dies in an air crash along with Richie Valens and the Big Bopper.

– In Detroit, Michigan, Berry Gordy Jr founds Motown records, the first black-owned US record company. The 'Motown sound' (typified by such artists as the Supremes) will be a distinctive element in 1960s pop music.

Miles Davis, *Kind of Blue*, jazz album.

Francis Poulenc, *Gloria*, for soprano, chorus and orchestra.

Richard Rodgers and Oscar Hammerstein II, *The Sound of Music*, musical.

Film

21 Jan. Cecil B. DeMille dies.

John and Roy Boulting, *I'm All Right, Jack*, starring Peter Sellers.

Jean-Luc Godard, *A bout de souffle* (Breathless), starring Jean-Paul Belmondo.

Alfred Hitchcock, *North by Northwest*, starring Cary Grant and James Mason.

François Truffaut, *Les Quatre cents coups* (The 400 Blows), starring Jean-Pierre Léaud.

Billy Wilder, *Some Like It Hot*, starring Jack Lemmon, Tony Curtis and Marilyn Monroe.

William Wyler, *Ben-Hur*, starring Charlton Heston.

1960

EUROPE

1 May Soviet missiles shoot down a US U-2 espionage plane and capture the pilot, Gary Powers. After initial US denials that Powers was spying (5 May), President Eisenhower admits the truth (11 May) but refuses to apologize. The Paris summit meeting between Nikita Khrushchev, Eisenhower, Charles de Gaulle and Harold Macmillan breaks up acrimoniously (16 May). Powers is jailed in the USSR (19 Aug.) until he is exchanged in 1962 for Soviet spy Rudolf Abel.

3 May The European Free Trade Association (EFTA) comes into force. Its members are Austria, Britain, Denmark, Norway, Portugal, Sweden and Switzerland.

16 Aug. Cyprus becomes independent. Archbishop Makarios is president and Fazil Kütchüh (a Turkish Cypriot) is vice-president.

– In Britain the Anti-Apartheid Movement is formed to campaign for the abolition of the racist apartheid system in South Africa.

– Britain cancels a project begun in 1954 to develop a medium-range missile (Blue Streak).

– In Spain the Basque separatist organization Euskadi ta Askatasuna (Basque Nation and Liberty, or ETA) is founded.

MIDDLE EAST AND NORTH AFRICA

13 Feb. The first French atomic bomb is tested, in SW Algeria.

23 May Israel announces that it has arrested Adolf Eichmann after abducting him in Argentina (11 May).

Sept. The Organization of Petroleum Exporting Countries (OPEC) holds its first meeting in Baghdad. OPEC includes Saudi Arabia, Iran, Iraq, Kuwait and Qatar: it will later include Abu Dhabi, Algeria, Gabon, Libya, Nigeria, Indonesia, Ecuador and Venezuela. Its aim is to combat exploitation by Western oil companies and to encourage member-states to nationalize their oil production.

ASIA

19 Jan. A US–Japanese treaty of mutual security and cooperation is signed, but the treaty proves unpopular in Japan, causing weeks of street demonstrations against US influence. President Eisenhower is advised by the Japanese government to cancel a planned visit. Inajiro Asanuma, the leader of the Japanese socialist party, is assassinated by a Japanese nationalist, because of his support for the treaty (12 Oct.).

21 July In Ceylon (now Sri Lanka) Mrs Sirimavo Bandaranaike, widow of Solomon Bandaranaike (see 25 Sept. 1959), becomes the world's first woman prime minister.

31 July Britain ends its operations against communist insurgents in Malaya, and the 'Malayan Emergency' ends.

12 Nov. Ngo Dinh Diem regains power as president of South Vietnam after a military coup. Vietnamese communists start to organize themselves as an underground group and call themselves the National Front for the Liberation of South Vietnam, popularly known as the Vietcong (20 Dec.).

THE AMERICAS

13 Feb. Cuban leader Fidel Castro signs an agreement with the USSR, which undertakes to provide Cuba with $100 million of Soviet credit, and to buy five million tons of Cuban sugar. As US–Cuban relations deteriorate further, Castro threatens to seize all US-owned property and business interests in Cuba (23 June). President Eisenhower replies that the USA will never allow a communist state to operate in the western hemisphere (6 July). Khrushchev threatens to use missiles to defend Cuba (9 July), maintaining that the Monroe Doctrine (1823) is dead, but the US government re-affirms it (14 July). A confrontation between the two great powers becomes more likely as Castro's government nationalizes all banks and major commercial enterprises (14 Oct.). The US government retaliates by imposing an embargo on most exports to Cuba (except for foods and medical supplies) (19 Oct.). Castro's defiance of the power of the USA is becoming all the more repugnant to US public opinion because it is successful.

6 May Congress passes the Civil Rights Act despite prolonged obstruction by senators. The Act empowers federal authorities to act against the obstruction of African-American voting rights. The Department of Justice brings its first civil rights suit against such obstruction in the case of elections held in Tennessee (13 Sept.).

11 May In Buenos Aires, Argentina, Nazi war criminal Adolf Eichmann is kidnapped by Israeli agents. He will be smuggled out of the country and tried in Israel (see 11 April 1961).

8 Nov. John F. Kennedy, the Democratic Party candidate, defeats Richard Nixon, the Republican vice-president, in the US presidential election. It is the first presidential election to be decided by television. Although Nixon is the better debater, Kennedy's more telegenic appearance counts in his favour. Kennedy, the supposedly liberal Democrat (and the first Roman Catholic to be elected president of the USA), has campaigned on the issue of a 'missile gap' (the erroneous belief that the USSR enjoys a superiority over the USA in numbers of missiles) and proposes measures to increase defence spending. In a narrow victory, won by just 118,574 votes, the result in Cook County, Chicago, becomes crucial. Allegations are made that Mayor Richard Daley has rigged the Cook County count in favour of Kennedy.

– Grand juries in the USA indict 29 companies producing

electrical equipment, including General Electric, for acts in restraint of trade.
- Brasilia, a purpose-built city in the middle of the country, becomes the new capital of Brazil. Brazilian architect Oskar Niemeyer designs the buildings.

SUB-SAHARAN AFRICA

1 Jan. French Cameroon becomes an independent republic.

3 Feb. The British prime minister Harold Macmillan, speaking in Cape Town to the South African parliament, says: 'The wind of change is blowing through this continent.'

21 Mar. About 20,000 black protestors gather outside a police station in Sharpeville, a suburb of Johannesburg, South Africa, to protest against the law requiring them to carry identity papers. The police fire at the crowd: 56 are killed and a further 162 are wounded (of whom 16 die later). Although the Pass Law is suspended (26 Mar.), protests and violence continue as the anti-apartheid movement gains in influence both domestically and internationally.

27 April French Togoland becomes the independent republic of Togo.

26 June Madagascar becomes independent of France as the Malagasy Republic.

26 June British Somaliland becomes independent and joins with Italian Somaliland in the new state of Somalia.

30 June The Belgian Congo becomes independent as the Congo Republic with Joseph Kasavubu as president and Patrice Lumumba as prime minister. The new state descends into immediate anarchy when the Congolese army mutinies (5 July) and Belgian colonists flee.

8 July Belgian troops are sent to the Congo Republic. Prime minister Patrice Lumumba appeals to the UN for assistance.

11 July Moise Tshombe, prime minister of the mineral-rich Congolese province of Katanga, declares Katangan independence. Tshombe is backed by Belgian mining interests and white mercenaries.

15 July UN troops arrive in the Congo Republic. They will expel Belgian troops but will fail to deal with the Katangan secession.

Aug. The French colonies of Dahomey (1 Aug.), Upper Volta (5 Aug.), Ivory Coast (7 Aug.), Chad (11 Aug.), the Central African Republic (13 Aug.), Gabon (17 Aug.) and Mali (20 Aug.) become independent.

3 Sept. The French colony of Niger becomes independent.

5 Sept. The French colony of Senegal becomes independent.

5 Sept. President Kasavubu of the Congo Republic dismisses prime minister Patrice Lumumba.

14 Sept. The Congolese army commander Joseph-Désiré Mobutu seizes power in a military coup and arrests Patrice Lumumba.

1 Oct. The Nigerian Federation becomes independent of Britain.

28 Nov. The French colony of Mauritania becomes independent.

ECONOMY AND SOCIETY

Aug.–Sept. The 17th Olympic Games are held in Rome.
- In Britain the last conscripts begin National Service.

ARTS AND HUMANITIES

Literature

- In Britain Penguin Books are tried on a charge of obscenity for publishing D.H.Lawrence's novel *Lady Chatterley's Lover* (1928). The jury finds that the work is neither obscene nor corrupting (as had a US court in 1959) and Penguin Books go on to sell more than 3.5 million copies. The verdict opens the way to a much greater freedom in the treatment of sex in literature.

John Barth, *The Sot-Weed Factor*, novel.

Robert Bolt, *A Man for All Seasons*, play based on the life of the Tudor statesman Thomas More.

Eugène Ionesco, *Rhinoceros*, play.

Alan Garner, *The Weirdstone of Brisingamen*, children's novel.

Harper Lee, *To Kill a Mockingbird*, novel.

Sylvia Plath, *Colossus*, poetry collection.

William L. Shirer, *The Rise and Fall of the Third Reich*, popular history whose success marks the start of a new English-speaking interest in the rise of Nazism.

Isaac Bashevis Singer, *The Magician of Lublin*, novel.

David Storey, *This Sporting Life*, novel.

John Updike, *Rabbit, Run*, novel.

Visual Arts and Architecture

Joseph Beuys, *Bathtub* (a structure covered with felt and fat) in recognition of his rescue when shot down as a pilot over the Crimea during World War II: the Tatars who discovered him kept the injured Beuys warm with felt and fat.

Andy Warhol, *Soup Can* (*Tomato and Rice*), painting.

Music

11 June First performance in Aldeburgh of Benjamin Britten's opera *A Midsummer Night's Dream*.

Luciano Berio, *Circles*, for female singer, harp and percussion to texts by e e cummings.

Ray Charles, 'Georgia On My Mind', single.

Chubby Checker, 'The Twist', single giving rise to a new international dance craze.

Frederick Loewe and Alan Jay Lerner, *Camelot*, musical. President Kennedy attends a performance and so grows the myth of a 'Camelot' administration in a newly invigorated White House.

Luigi Nono, *Intolleranza*, opera.

Krzysztof Penderecki, String Quartet No. 1.

Elvis Presley, 'It's Now or Never', single.

William Walton, Symphony No. 2.

Film

Federico Fellini, *La dolce vita*, starring Marcello Mastroianni.

Alfred Hitchcock, *Psycho*, starring Anthony Perkins.

Stanley Kubrick, *Spartacus*, starring Kirk Douglas.

Karel Reisz, *Saturday Night and Sunday Morning*, starring Albert Finney.

Alain Resnais, *Hiroshima, mon amour*.

Tony Richardson, *The Entertainer*, starring Laurence Olivier.

John Sturges, *The Magnificent Seven*.

Billy Wilder, *The Apartment*, starring Jack Lemmon and Shirley MacLaine.

1961

EUROPE

4 June The Soviet government urges the demilitarization of Berlin. The USSR is concerned that joint occupation is providing an escape route through which so many young and skilled East Germans are passing that the very survival of East Germany is in doubt. The US government rejects the Soviet suggestion.

13 Aug. The East German government closes the border between East and West Berlin and begins to construct a barrier along it (the Berlin Wall), to stop any movement between East and West. This reduces the danger that tensions over the divided city will cause a general war. On the whole, the West is not dissatisfied with the solution, especially as it provides excellent Cold War propaganda: that communism is so unsuccessful that a wall has to be built to prevent its citizens from leaving *en masse*. The Western military garrison in Berlin is reinforced to reassure West Berliners of the continued commitment of the Western powers.

17 July Britain is now entering a period of prolonged economic crisis after the artificial economic boom of the first period of Harold Macmillan's premiership. The chancellor of the exchequer, Selwyn-Lloyd, proposes a wage freeze and a rise in the bank rate from 5% to 7% to deal with a persistent balance of trade problem.

31 July British prime minister Harold Macmillan announces that Britain is applying for membership of the European Economic Community (EEC).

30 Oct. A thermo-nuclear device is tested in the Novaya Zemlya archipelago in the USSR.

MIDDLE EAST AND NORTH AFRICA

11 April The trial of Nazi war criminal Adolf Eichmann begins in Jerusalem.

21 April Rebel French troops belonging to the Organisation de l'armée secrète (OAS) and led by Gen. Maurice Challe seize Algiers. Talks on Algerian independence are now proceeding, and many French settlers fear a sell-out. Forces loyal to the French government retake the city (26 April). The rebel leaders are tried and sentenced to death (11 July). The OAS, however, will embark on a terrorist campaign in both Algeria and France, including a number of attempts on the life of President de Gaulle, whom it considers has betrayed French settlers by countenancing Algerian independence.

28 Sept. The army revolts in Syria and establishes a new civilian government. Syria secedes from the United Arab Republic (29 Sept.).

ASIA

16 May The democratic government of South Korea is overthrown in a military coup. A military dictatorship is proclaimed (6 June), and Gen. Park Chung-Hee is named leader (3 July).

THE AMERICAS

3 Jan. The USA severs diplomatic relations with Cuba. Cuban groups in exile in New York urge a rebellion (Mar.) but meet with little response on the island.

20 Jan. J.F. Kennedy takes office as 35th US president.

Mar. President Kennedy announces an Alliance for Progress, whose aim is to modernize those S American countries prepared to be willing allies of the USA. The agreement that follows (Aug.) is signed by 19 S American states, which pledge themselves to agrarian and tax reform in return for US aid totalling $10 billion over a 10-year period.

17 April The CIA lands some 1600 Cuban exiles at the Bay of Pigs, Cuba, in an attempt to overthrow Fidel Castro. It is a complete failure. The insurgents assume their landing will provoke a general rebellion, but none occurs. Castro's troops fight well and enjoy popular support and most of the landing force is killed or captured by 20 April. Soviet leader Nikita Khrushchev demands that the invasion stop (18 April). President Kennedy asserts that the USA has the right of self-defence if threatened by communist expansion (20 April). Castro declares himself to be a Marxist-Leninist (2 Dec.). His aim now, he says, is to introduce a communist system to Cuba.

20 May White racists attack civil rights demonstrators in Birmingham, Alabama.

30 May Rafael Léonidas Trujillo, dictator of the Dominican Republic since 1961, is assassinated.

3–4 June US president Kennedy and Soviet president Khrushchev meet in Vienna; they affirm the neutrality of Laos and state that they are now discussing disarmament.

25 July President Kennedy proposes an increase of over 200,000 in US military personnel and a $3.4 billion increase in defence spending in order to respond to a 'worldwide Soviet threat'.

SUB-SAHARAN AFRICA

7 Jan. Representatives of Ghana, Guinea, Mali, Morocco and the United Arab Republic meet at Casablanca and sign an African Charter.

17 Jan. The former premier of the Congo Patrice Lumumba is murdered by Katangan secessionists. The government of Katanga, which announces his death (13 Feb.), claims that he is the victim of hostile tribesmen, but the CIA is widely suspected of having a hand in his murder. The UN Security Council demands an official inquiry into the murder.

28 Jan. Ruanda proclaims itself a republic. The monarchy of the dominant minority Tutsi people has been overthrown by the majority Hutu people.

27 April Sierra Leone becomes independent from Britain.

1 May Tanganyika becomes independent from Britain; Julius Nyerere, advocate of an African style of socialism, becomes premier.

31 May South Africa breaks away from the British Commonwealth and becomes a republic. South Africa's racial policies have been attacked at a recent Commonwealth conference.

18 Sept. UN secretary-general Dag Hammarskjöld is killed in a plane crash while travelling to mediate with the governor of Katanga. U Thant, a Burmese diplomat, is elected to succeed him. He orders UN troops to maintain their positions in the Katangan capital of Elisabethville (modern Lubumbashi), until a ceasefire is negotiated in the Congo (21 Dec.).

9 Dec. In Southern Rhodesia (modern Zimbabwe), nationalist leader Joshua Nkomo founds the Zimbabwe African People's Union (ZAPU).

– Angola embarks on a long insurrection against Portuguese rule; it will last until 1974.

ECONOMY AND SOCIETY

– The birth-control pill goes on sale in Britain (but only to married women).

– In Britain the new University of Sussex is founded NE of Brighton.

SCIENCE AND TECHNOLOGY

12 April The first manned space craft, *Vostok 1*, circles the earth. Soviet cosmonaut Yuri Gagarin completes the orbit in 89.1 minutes and provides Soviet science with a powerful demonstration of its effectiveness as the Cold War rivalry with the US reaches into space.

ARTS AND HUMANITIES

Literature

10 May In Britain the satirical revue *Beyond the Fringe* breaks new ground in British satire and expresses its scorn at what is now called the 'Establishment' (a term coined by the journalist Henry Fairlie in 1955 to describe those in power in Britain).

2 July The US novelist Ernest Hemingway commits suicide in Idaho.

Samuel Beckett (see p. 558), *Happy Days*, play.

Athol Fugard, *The Blood Knot*, play.

Graham Greene, *A Burnt-Out Case*, novel.

Joseph Heller, *Catch-22*, novel.

Richard Hughes, *The Fox in the Attic*, the first in a projected sequence of historical novels.

Iris Murdoch, *A Severed Head*, novel.

V(idiadhar) S(urajprasad) Naipaul, *A House for Mr Biswas*, novel.

Muriel Spark, *The Prime of Miss Jean Brodie*, novel.

Arnold Toynbee, *A Study of History*, in 12 volumes.

Evelyn Waugh, *Unconditional Surrender*, third novel of his *The Sword of Honour* trilogy.

Patrick White, *Riders in the Chariot*, novel.

Yevgeny Yevtushenko, 'Babi Yar', poem about the German SS massacre of Ukrainian Jews in 1941. It is denounced by the Soviet government, as it also critical of anti-Semitism in the USSR.

Visual Arts and Architecture

Richard Hamilton, *$he*, picture of a toaster and a fridge with a woman styled to match. It will have a major influence on Pop Art in Britain.

David Hockney, *We Two Boys Together Clinging*, painting.

Joan Miró, *Blue 11*, painting.

Tom Wesselmann, *Great American Nude No. 10*, painting.

Music

21 Mar. In Britain the Beatles perform for the first time at the Cavern Club in Liverpool.

6 Sept. Robert Zimmerman, who has changed his name to Bob Dylan in honour of the Welsh poet Dylan Thomas, makes his debut at the Gaslight Café, Greenwich Village, New York. Songs such as 'Blowin' in the Wind' and 'The Times They Are a-Changin'' will enter the popular consciousness of the youth movement of the 1960s and evoke the urgency of its rejection of their parents' world.

– US singing group the Supremes (Diana Ross, Mary Wilson and Florence Ballard) begin recording.

György Ligeti, *Atmosphères* (Atmosphere), work for orchestra.

Elvis Presley, 'Are You Lonesome Tonight?', single.

Dmitri Shostakovich, Symphony No. 12 in D minor (*1917*).

Film

Luis Buñuel, *Viridiana*, starring Fernando Rey.

Roger Corman, *The Little Shop of Horrors*.

Basil Dearden, *Victim*, starring Dirk Bogarde in a film that breaks the taboo on the portrayal of homosexuality.

Blake Edwards, *Breakfast at Tiffany's*, starring George Peppard and Audrey Hepburn.

John Huston, *The Misfits*, starring Marilyn Monroe and Montgomery Clift.

Alan Resnais, *Last Year in Marienbad*.

Robert Rossen, *The Hustler*, starring Paul Newman.

François Truffaut, *Jules et Jim*, starring Jeanne Moreau.

Robert Wise, *West Side Story*.

1962

EUROPE

Jan.–Mar. The OAS (Organisation de l'armée secrète) mounts a terrorist campaign in France.

26 Feb. In Northern Ireland the Irish Republican Army (IRA) declares a ceasefire in the 'border campaign' that it has waged since Dec. 1956.

Mar. Britain applies to join the European Coal and Steel Community (ECSC) and Euratom.

14 April Georges Pompidou becomes French prime minister.

12 July British prime minister Harold Macmillan sacks seven cabinet ministers in an attempt to salvage Conservative fortunes. The incident is dubbed 'The Night of the Long Knives'.

22 Aug. In France OAS terrorists try to assassinate President de Gaulle.

Dec. The Nassau agreement with the USA leads to Britain acquiring US Polaris nuclear missiles.

MIDDLE EAST AND NORTH AFRICA

18 Mar. The Evian agreements are signed, ending the Algerian War.

21 May After a public trial in Israel, Adolf Eichmann is executed for crimes committed as a concentration camp commander during World War II.

3 July The French government proclaims the independence of Algeria following a referendum in which Algerians have voted by almost 6 million to 16,534 for their own independent form of government. The provisional government is divided in its counsels until the national assembly asks (Sept.) Mohammed Ahmed Ben Bella to head a cabinet. Following Algerian independence, most French settlers (*pieds-noirs*) emigrate to France.

16 Aug. Britain signs an agreement whereby Aden, a British colony in SW Arabia, becomes part of the Federation of South Arabia.

ASIA

22 Mar. US money and arms help the South Vietnamese to launch Operation Sunrise against the Vietcong guerrillas. The International Control Commission on Indochina (composed of Canadian, Indian and Polish representatives) report that the North Vietnamese are aiding the Vietcong (2 June).

THE AMERICAS

3 Feb. President Kennedy embargoes US trade with Cuba.

8 May The US Department of Justice orders the racial desegregation of hospitals built with state money.

6 Aug. Jamaica becomes independent of Britain.

31 Aug. Trinidad and Tobago become independent of Britain.

30 Sept. Riots break out on the campus of the University of Mississippi when James Meredith, an African-American, is admitted as a student. Federal troops are sent to the campus to guard Meredith (1 Oct.) and continue to do so for the next 10 months.

14 Oct. The Cuban Missile Crisis begins. The US government discovers the presence of Soviet military installations in Cuba. President Kennedy orders an air and sea blockade of Cuba to prevent any further Soviet arms from reaching Cuba. The world appears on the brink of nuclear war as Soviet ships steam towards the blockade, threatening to defy it. But at the last moment they turn back. The USSR offers, in secret negotiations, to withdraw the nuclear missiles it has placed in Cuba. The offer is conditional on the USA withdrawing its nuclear missiles from Turkey and promising not to invade Cuba. Although Kennedy cannot publicly accept such a deal, he secretly indicates that it is an acceptable compromise. The Soviet government backs down and agrees to remove the Cuban missiles (28 Oct.). US missiles in Turkey are also subsequently removed. Frightened by how near to the brink they have come, both Khrushchev and Kennedy make urgent attempts to ease tensions and a 'hot line' will be agreed (20 June 1963) to allow direct communications between the White House and the Kremlin.

Nov. US politician Richard Nixon loses his campaign for the governorship of California and announces, at what is meant to be his last press conference: 'You won't have Dick Nixon to kick around any more.' He is convinced that he has been the victim of a press conspiracy.

SUB-SAHARAN AFRICA

13 Jan. Civil war breaks out again in the Congo as Katanga resumes its struggle for independence.

3 July The republic of Rwanda (formerly Ruanda) and the kingdom of Burundi (formerly Urundi, part of Ruanda-Urundi) become independent. In Rwanda Grégoire Kayibanda becomes president. Tribal violence between Hutu and Tutsi will continue.

9 Oct. Uganda becomes an independent state within the British Commonwealth. A federal form of government is adopted to satisfy the territory of Buganda, but tension grows within the new country.

9 Dec. Tanganyika becomes a republic with Julius Nyerere as its president.

− Eritrea is assimilated into Ethiopia after a 10-year period during which it has been a federated constituent of the state. Conflict continues between Eritrean Muslims and Ethiopian Christians.

AUSTRALASIA AND OCEANIA

1 Jan. Western Samoa, a UN trust territory administered by New Zealand, becomes the first independent Polynesian state.

ECONOMY AND SOCIETY

11 Oct. Pope John XXIII convenes the Second Vatican Council and, in so doing, inaugurates a period of self-critical renewal in the Roman Catholic Church.

− In Britain the last conscripts end their National Service.

− In Britain *That Was the Week That Was*, presented by David Frost, is broadcast by the BBC.

− In the USA the Philip Morris company begins the poster campaign that emphasizes the rugged virtues of 'Marlboro Country' in order to sell its cigarettes.

− Brazil wins the 7th soccer World Cup, held in Chile.

SCIENCE AND TECHNOLOGY

7 Feb. US astronaut John Glenn becomes the first American to orbit Earth in the Mercury spacecraft *Friendship* 7.

10 July The communications satellite *Telstar* 1 is launched and is used to transmit the first live transatlantic broadcasts between the USA and Britain.

29 Nov. Britain and France sign an agreement to develop Concorde, a supersonic airliner.

− The Lear jet, a private toy for the rich, is developed by William P. Lear.

− Alaskan Inuits are found to have high levels of caesium-137 in their bodies, as a result of eating the meat of caribou that, in turn, have eaten lichen contaminated by the dust of nuclear testing.

The white race is the cancer of human history.

Susan Sontag, *Partisan Review*, Winter 1967

– Thalidomide is withdrawn in Britain and France. The tranquillizer, widely used in early pregnancy, is now connected to birth defects.

ARTS AND HUMANITIES

Literature

6 July The US novelist William Faulkner dies.

3 Sept. The US poet e e cummings dies.

Edward Albee, *Who's Afraid of Virginia Woolf?*, play.

Helen Gurley Brown, *Sex and the Single Girl*, feminist study.

Anthony Burgess, *A Clockwork Orange*, novel.

William Faulkner, *The Reivers*, novel.

Eugène Ionesco, *Le Roi se meurt* (Exit the King), play.

Ken Kesey, *One Flew Over the Cuckoo's Nest*, novel.

Doris Lessing, *The Golden Notebook*, novel.

Marshall McLuhan, *The Gutenberg Galaxy*, social study of communications media.

Vladimir Nabokov, *Pale Fire*, novel.

Alexander Solzhenitsyn, *A Day in the Life of Ivan Denisovich*, novel.

William Carlos Williams, *Pictures from Brueghel*, poetry collection.

Visual Arts and Architecture

– In Britain Basil Spence's new Coventry Cathedral is completed. It contains Graham Sutherland's tapestry *Christ in Glory*, stained glass by John Piper and a statue by Jacob Epstein.

Bridget Riley, *Movements with Squares*, stencilled picture.

Andy Warhol, *100 Cans* (of Campbell's Soup), painting, a work that is, for some, an indictment of US commercialism.

Music

– Guy Carawan of Nashville, Tennessee, copyrights the song 'We Shall Overcome' (first sung by African-American tobacco workers in South Carolina in the 1940s). It will become the song of the US civil rights movement.

– Benjamin Britten's *War Requiem*, a sombre antiwar choral work combining nine poems by the World War I poet Wilfred Owen with the words of the Latin mass, is performed in the new Coventry Cathedral.

Bob Dylan, 'Blowin' in the Wind', single.

Elvis Presley, 'Return to Sender', single.

Cliff Richard, 'The Young Ones', single.

Dmitri Shostakovich, Symphony No. 13 in B flat minor (*Babi-Yar*).

Film

5 Aug. US actress Marilyn Monroe dies.

Robert Aldrich, *What Ever Happened to Baby Jane?*, starring Bette Davis and Joan Crawford.

Ingmar Bergman, *Winter Light*.

Luis Buñuel, *The Exterminating Angel*.

John Frankenheimer, *The Manchurian Candidate*.

David Lean, *Lawrence of Arabia*, starring Peter O'Toole.

Tony Richardson, *The Loneliness of the Long Distance Runner*.

Terence Young, *Dr No*, the first James Bond movie, starring Sean Connery as British secret service agent 007.

1963

EUROPE

14 Jan. The European Economic Community (EEC) vetoes British entry. President de Gaulle of France, fearing that Britain is a Trojan horse for US influence, has been the most influential figure among those who suspect Britain's late conversion to the movement for European integration.

18 Jan. Hugh Gaitskell, leader of the British Labour Party, dies suddenly. He is succeeded by Harold Wilson (14 Feb.).

26 June US president John F. Kennedy, in a speech in Berlin, declares 'Ich bin ein Berliner'. Although the phrase literally means 'I am a doughnut', his audience understands his intention to express solidarity with them and roars its approval. The speech continues Kennedy's theme of a global, US-led, war on communism and increases his popularity in Europe as a youthful and idealistic president of the 'new frontier'.

June In Britain John Profumo, minister for war, resigns after confessing to an affair with a prostitute, Christine Keeler. She is also sleeping with the Soviet naval attaché, Evgeny Ivanov. The association of sex with possible espionage excites the prurience of the British public and discredits the ruling Conservative Party.

30 July Soviet agent Kim Philby, while working as a journalist, has disappeared from Beirut and is now given asylum in the USSR. Although widely suspected of espionage, Philby has escaped the surveillance of the British security services, whose reputation for incompetence becomes part of a more general national malaise.

8 Aug. In Britain the Great Train Robbery takes place in Buckinghamshire, N of London. It is the biggest theft in British history (£2.6 million).

16 Oct. Konrad Adenauer resigns as chancellor of West Germany (an office he has held since 1963) and is succeeded by Ludwig Erhard.

18 Oct. In Britain premier Harold Macmillan, suffering from ill health, resigns. Internal Conservative Party manoeuvring leads to the emergence of the 13th earl of Home as the nominated prime minister. He renounces his peerage in order to sit in the House of Commons as Alec Douglas-Home, and searches for a possible constituency. The opposition Labour Party, led by Harold Wilson, ridicules the fustian nature of British Conservatism.

Dec. Power-sharing between the Greek and Turkish communities in Cyprus breaks down. Clashes occur between Greek and Turkish Cypriots.

– Crops fail in the harvest in Kazakhstan and Ukraine. Soviet leader Nikita Khrushchev has developed Kazakhstan as an area of intensive farming but now has to concede defeat. Two million tons of US wheat are sold to Russia in a move approved by President Kennedy and confirmed by his successor Lyndon B. Johnson.

ASIA

16 Sept. The federation of Malaysia comes into being, uniting Malaya, Singapore (until 1965), Sarawak and North Borneo: Tunku Abdul Rahman governs as prime minister.

1 Nov. The government of Ngo Dinh Diem in South Vietnam falls after a CIA-backed coup organized by Gen. Duong Van Minh. Diem is assassinated.

THE AMERICAS

1 Jan. African-American civil rights leader Martin Luther King Jr, declares 'I have a dream' as he addresses crowds gathered at the Lincoln Memorial, Washington, D.C. King's oratory will inspire those who work for the day when 'sons of former slaves and the sons of former slave-owners will be able to sit down together at the table of brotherhood'.

11 June President Kennedy puts the National Guard of Alabama under federal control. He orders Governor George Wallace to allow two African-American students to be admitted to the University of Alabama.

19 June President Kennedy asks Congress to pass legislation to bar prejudice in privately owned institutions used by the public.

28 Aug. Some 200,000 protestors march on Washington, D.C. in support of civil rights.

22 Nov. President John F. Kennedy is shot dead by Lee Harvey Oswald in Dallas, Texas. The vice-president, Lyndon B. Johnson, is sworn in as 36th US president. As police are moving the assassin to safer custody, Oswald is assassinated by Jack Ruby (24 Nov.).

SUB-SAHARAN AFRICA

12 Dec. Kenya becomes independent of Britain, and Jomo Kenyatta becomes president.

– The Central African Federation of Southern Rhodesia (Zimbabwe), Northern Rhodesia (Zambia) and Nyasaland (Malawi) is dissolved.

ECONOMY AND SOCIETY

3 June Pope John XXIII, who has released a wave of reform in the Roman Catholic Church, dies. He is succeeded by Giovanni Battista Montini, who becomes Pope Paul VI.

– In Britain the *Beeching Report* on the railway network leads to the closure of lines and thousands of stations.

SCIENCE AND TECHNOLOGY

June Valentina Tereshova, a Soviet cosmonaut, becomes the first woman to fly in space.

Dec. Valium is introduced as an anti-depressant drug.

ARTS AND HUMANITIES

Literature

29 Jan. US poet Robert Frost dies.

14 Feb. The US poet Sylvia Plath, wife of the English poet Ted Hughes, commits suicide in London.

3 Sept. The poet Louis MacNeice dies.

26 Sept. The *New York Review of Books* begins publication.

22 Nov. English writer Aldous Huxley dies.

– In Britain the National Theatre company is created.

– In Britain Joan Littlewood's Theatre Workshop produces *Oh, What a Lovely War!*

Hannah Arendt, *Eichmann in Jerusalem: A Report on the Banality of Evil*, history.

Heinrich Böll, *Ansichten eines Clowns* (The Clown), novel.

John Fowles, *The Collector*, novel.

Rolf Hochhuth, *Der Stellvertreter* (The Deputy), play.

Richard Hofstadter, *Anti-Intellectualism in American Life*, history.

John Le Carré (David Cornwell), *The Spy Who Came in from the Cold*, developing the spy novel in the Cold War age.

Yukio Mishima, *The Sailor Who Fell from Grace with the Sea*, novel.

Sylvia Plath, *The Bell Jar*, a novel that describes her own depression in fictional form.

Thomas Pynchon, *V*, novel.

Neil Simon, *Barefoot in the Park*, play.

C.P. Snow, *The Corridors of Power*, novel.

Visual Arts and Architecture

31 Aug. French painter Georges Braque dies.

Francis Bacon, *Man and Child*, painting.

Barbara Hepworth, *Single Form*, sculpture.

David Hockney, *I Saw in Louisiana a Live-Oak Growing*, painting.

Roy Lichtenstein, *Whaam!*, Pop-art painting of jet fighters.

Bridget Riley, *Fall*, painting.

Music

30 Jan. The French composer Francis Poulenc dies.

13 Oct. The Beatles (John Lennon, Paul McCartney, George Harrison and Ringo Starr) appear on British television on *Sunday Night at the London Palladium*. 15 million viewers watch them and Beatlemania is born.

30 Dec. The German-born composer Paul Hindemith dies.

The Beatles, 'Please Please Me', 'From Me To You', 'She Loves You' and 'I Want to Hold Your Hand', singles.

Gerry and the Pacemakers, 'How Do You Do It?' and 'You'll Never Walk Alone', singles.

Barry Mann and Cynthia Weil, 'Blame it on the Bossa Nova', song.

Cliff Richard and the Shadows, 'Summer Holiday', single.

The Searchers, 'Sweets for my Sweet', single.

Film

Lindsay Anderson, *This Sporting Life*.

Ingmar Bergman, *The Silence*.

Alfred Hitchcock, *The Birds*.

Joseph Losey, *The Servant*, starring Dirk Bogarde.

Tony Richardson, *Tom Jones*, starring Albert Finney.

John Sturges, *The Great Escape*, starring Steve McQueen.

Luchino Visconti, *Il gattopardo* (The Leopard), starring Burt Lancaster.

1964

EUROPE

15 Feb. Willy Brandt, mayor of West Berlin, becomes leader of the West German Social Democratic Party (SPD), which he will shape into a moderate socialist party.

6 Mar. Paul I, king of Greece, dies, and his son Constantine II succeeds.

4 April Archbishop Makarios, president of Cyprus, abrogates the 1960 treaty between Greece, Turkey and Cyprus. Fighting breaks out between the Greek and Turkish Cypriots on the island. In June Greece rejects talks with Turkey on the crisis.

8 Aug. The Turkish air force attacks Greek Cypriot settlements. The UN orders a ceasefire (9 Aug.). A UN peace-keeping force is set up to keep Greek and Turkish Cypriots apart.

13 Sept. In the USSR Nikita Khrushchev is toppled in an internal Communist Party coup. The failure of his economic reforms and foreign policy mistakes have undermined him. Leonid Brezhnev becomes party leader, and Alexei Kosygin becomes premier.

21 Sept. Malta becomes an independent state within the Commonwealth.

16 Oct. In Britain Harold Wilson becomes prime minister following the Labour Party's narrow victory in the general election. Wilson has fought a campaign emphasizing his own technocratic and classless credentials. He now forms a government intent on the technological modernization of Britain.

MIDDLE EAST AND NORTH AFRICA

May The Palestinian Liberation Organization (PLO) is founded. Its aim is to bring about an independent Arab state of Palestine.

2 Nov. Faisal ibn Abdul-Aziz is proclaimed king of Saudi Arabia after his brother Saud ibn Abdul-Aziz is deposed.

ASIA

27 May Jawaharlal Nehru, prime minister of India, dies and is succeeded by Lal Bahadur Shastri (2 June).

2 Aug. North Vietnamese naval forces fire torpedoes at US destroyer *Maddox* off the Vietnamese coast in the Gulf of Tonkin. For the past six months the US navy has been involved in covert action in the area. In response to what was presented in the USA as an unprovoked attack, US aircraft bomb North Vietnamese bases (5 Aug.). Congress passes the Tonkin Gulf Resolution (7 Aug.) authorizing the president to 'take all necessary measures to repel any armed attack against forces of the USA and to prevent further aggression'. The measure is passed by 88 to 2 votes in the Senate and by 416 to 0 in the House of Representatives. America's trial by fire has begun: the Vietnam War will transform and divide the USA, discredit its leaders' political judgement and lead to a generation's rejection of an American way of life that seems to promote death.

16 Oct. China tests its first nuclear weapon.

19 Dec. A military coup overthrows the high national council of South Vietnam.

THE AMERICAS

16 Mar. In the USA President Johnson calls for a 'total victory' in a 'national war on poverty'.

1 April A military coup in Brazil forces President Goulart to flee to Uruguay. Goulart's government has attempted to distribute federal land to landless peasants and has doubled the minimum wage. President Johnson orders a US naval force to sail S, but the Brazilian government orders an anti-communist purge. The US naval force is withdrawn. The Brazilian parliament elects Gen. Branco (11 April) to serve as president.

19 June Despite a 75-day filibuster by southern senators, the Civil Rights Act is passed by the US senate. President Johnson approves the Act (2 July), which now becomes law. The Act aims to outlaw all aspects of racial discrimination in the USA. Race riots break out in Harlem (18 July) and Philadelphia (28 Aug.).

30 July The Medicare Act is signed by US president Johnson. It provides a state health insurance programme for Americans aged 65 and over.

20 Aug. President Johnson signs the Economic Opportunity Act.

27 Sept. The report of the Warren Commission into the assassination of President John F. Kennedy (see 22 Nov. 1963) claims that there was no conspiracy. Scepticism about US institutions, however, is spreading, and the report's conclusion is widely questioned.

3 Nov. In the US presidential election President Johnson defeats decisively the Republican candidate, Senator Barry Goldwater of Arizona. Goldwater has appealed to the heart of the Republican Party with his attacks on federal spending programmes and has urged the escalation of hostilities in Vietnam. But his self-proclaimed extremism in the defence of 'liberty' alarms the US electorate. In a landslide victory, Johnson receives 61% of the popular vote and Goldwater only 38%: the biggest such majority to date in the history of US presidential elections.

11 Dec. President Johnson announces a huge increase in US aid to South Vietnam.

– Campus unrest has begun at the University of California at Berkeley. The student sit-in ends (3 Dec.) only when Governor Pat Brown orders police into the university. Some 730 demonstrators are arrested.

– In Haiti François 'Papa Doc' Duvalier (see 1956) makes himself president for life, with the power to nominate his son as his successor.

SUB-SAHARAN AFRICA

12 Jan. A nationalist coup topples the government of Zanzibar and a People's Republic is proclaimed, with Abeid Karume as president. Zanzibar merges with Tanganyika (26 April): the United Republic of Tanzania is proclaimed with Julius Nyerere as its president (29 Oct.).

13 April White supremacist Ian Smith becomes prime minister of Southern Rhodesia. After the independence of Northern Rhodesia as Zambia in Oct., Southern Rhodesia will simply be known as 'Rhodesia'.

12 June In South Africa the political activist Nelson Mandela is sentenced to life imprisonment for sabotage and subversion.

6 July Malawi (the former Nyasaland) becomes independent of Britain.

24 Oct. Zambia, a new state, is created out of the territory of Northern Rhodesia and Barotseland; Kenneth Kaunda is its president.

ECONOMY AND SOCIETY

25 Feb. US boxer Cassius Clay defeats Sonny Liston in Miami for the world heavyweight championship. Cassius Clay then converts to Islam, becoming Muhammad Ali.

30 April British television channel BBC 2 starts broadcasting and concentrates on cultural programming.

Oct. The 18th Olympic Games are held in Tokyo, Japan.

– In Britain violence breaks out between rival gangs of 'mods' and 'rockers' in seaside resorts.

SCIENCE AND TECHNOLOGY

– Leningrad (St Petersburg) on the Baltic is connected with the Caspian Sea when the USSR's Volga–Baltic Ship canal opens.

– In Japan bullet trains travelling at 164kph (102mph) start to operate between Tokyo and Osaka.

– In Scotland the Forth Road Bridge is opened.

ARTS AND HUMANITIES

Literature

18 Sept. The playwright Sean O'Casey dies.

– French writer Jean-Paul Sartre (see p. 533) refuses the Nobel prize for literature.

Chinua Achebe, *Arrow of God*, novel.

Saul Bellow, *Herzog*, novel.

William Golding, *The Spire*, novel.

Shirley Ann Grau, *The Keepers of the House*, novel.

Philip Larkin, *The Whitsun Weddings*, poetry collection.

Robert Lowell, *For the Union Dead*, poetry.

Herbert Marcuse, *One-Dimensional Man*, philosophy. Marcuse influences a generation of radical US university students with his view of the repressive nature of the country's institutions.

Arthur Miller, *After the Fall*, play.

Joe Orton, *Entertaining Mr Sloane*, play.

Hubert Selby Jr, *Last Exit to Brooklyn*, novel.

Peter Shaffer, *The Royal Hunt of the Sun*, play.

Peter Weiss, *The Persecution and Assassination of Jean-Paul Marat as Performed by the Inmates of the Asylum of Charenton under the Direction of the Marquis de Sade*, play.

Visual Arts and Architecture

Nov. Floods in Venice cause serious damage to the city's art treasures.

René Magritte, *La Grande Guerre*, painting.

Andy Warhol, *Shot Orange Marilyn*, painting.

Music

15 Oct. US composer and lyricist Cole Porter dies.

Louis Armstrong, 'Hello Dolly', single.

The Animals, 'House of the Rising Sun', single.

The Beatles, 'Can't Buy Me Love', 'A Hard Day's Night', 'I Feel Fine' and 'Eight Days a Week', singles.

Jerry Bock, *Fiddler on the Roof*, musical with lyrics by Sheldon Harnick.

Benjamin Britten, *Curlew River*, church parable inspired by Japanese Noh drama.

John Coltrane, *A Love Supreme*, jazz album.

Bob Dylan, *The Times They Are a-Changin'*, single and album.

Gerry and the Pacemakers, 'Ferry Across the Mersey', single.

Jerry Herman, *Hello, Dolly!*, musical starring Carol Channing.

Lulu, 'Shout', single.

Roy Orbison, 'Pretty Woman' and 'It's Over', singles.

The Rolling Stones, 'It's All Over Now', single.

The Supremes, 'Where Did Our Love Go?' and 'Baby Love', singles.

Film

George Cukor, *My Fair Lady*, starring Audrey Hepburn; derived ultimately from G.B. Shaw's play *Pygmalion* (1914).

Jacques Demy, *Les Parapluies de Cherbourg* (The Umbrellas of Cherbourg), starring Catherine Deneuve.

Cy Endfield, *Zulu*, starring Stanley Baker and Michael Caine.

Jean-Luc Godard, *Le Mépris* (Contempt), starring Brigitte Bardot.

Guy Hamilton, *Goldfinger*, starring Sean Connery.

Stanley Kubrick, *Dr Strangelove*, starring Peter Sellers.

Sergio Leone, *A Fistful of Dollars*, starring Clint Eastwood.

Pier Paolo Pasolini, *The Gospel According to St Matthew*.

Robert Stevenson, *Mary Poppins*, starring Julie Andrews.

1965

EUROPE

14 Jan. Sean Lemass, the Irish taoiseach (prime minister) meets Northern Ireland prime minister Terence O'Neill at Stormont in Belfast. It is the first de facto recognition of the state of Northern Ireland by a leader of the Irish Republic. Lemass's visit raises hopes of a rapprochement between Nationalists and Unionists in Ireland.

24 Jan. Sir Winston Churchill, former British prime minister, dies. He receives a state funeral (30 Jan.) and is buried at Bladon in Oxfordshire.

Mar. Nicolae Ceausescu becomes premier of Romania.

22 July Alec Douglas-Home resigns as leader of the British Conservative party. He is succeeded by Edward Heath (27 July).

19 Dec. President de Gaulle defeats François Mitterrand in the French presidential elections.

– Crop failure once again devastates the USSR harvest.

MIDDLE EAST AND NORTH AFRICA

– In Aden, SW Arabia, fighting breaks out between nationalists and British forces. It will continue until Britain withdraws in Nov. 1967.

ASIA

2 Jan. Indonesia withdraws from the UN, but an attempted communist takeover of the country is frustrated by the military. A massacre of communist supporters begins (8 Oct.) and as many as 400,000 are slaughtered. But the massacre is also an opportunity to kill the ethnic Chinese, who are powerful in the country's economy.

7–8 Feb. US bombers go into action in North Vietnam and the US government announces its policy of a bombing campaign against the North (11 Feb.). The campaign develops as 160 US planes bomb North Vietnamese targets (2 Mar. and 8–9 Mar.).

Some 3500 US marines land at Da Nang as US ground troops are committed for the first time in the war. The Vietcong response is rapid: a bomb explodes in the US embassy in Saigon (30 Mar.).

29 April The Australian government decides to commit troops to fight in Vietnam.

28 June US forces mount their first ground offensive in Vietnam.

8 Aug. Singapore secedes from the Federation of Malaysia.

19 Aug. US troops destroy a suspected Vietcong stronghold near Van Tuong.

Aug.–Sept. War breaks out between India and Pakistan in Kashmir. A ceasefire is agreed 22 Sept.

– Pakistan and India suffer widespread starvation because of crop failure as a result of drought.

– The Maldives (a group of 1196 islands SW of Sri Lanka) become an independent sultanate.

– Ferdinand Marcos becomes president of the Philippines. Backed by the USA for much of his increasingly dictatorial presidency, he will remain in power until 1986.

THE AMERICAS

4 Jan. US president Lyndon B. Johnson outlines his vision for a Great Society in his State of the Union address. The high-spending federal programmes will be undermined, however, by the spiralling costs of the Vietnam War.

21 Feb. Malcolm X (originally Malcolm Little), leader of the Organization of Afro-American Unity, is shot dead in Harlem, New York. He has broken from the African-American Muslim group the Nation of Islam, which helped bring him to prominence.

25 Mar. Viola Liuzzo, a civil rights leader, is shot dead by Ku Klux Klansmen near Montgomery, Alabama. Some 25,000 demonstrators arrive in Montgomery to protest against state regulations for voter registration.

17 April Students mount their first protests against US involvement in Vietnam and demonstrate in Washington, D.C.

28 April US marines land in the Dominican Republic, ostensibly to protect US lives in the face of a supposedly imminent communist takeover. President Johnson does not intend to allow a new Castro to gain power.

7 June The US Supreme Court rules that Connecticut's state law (1879) prohibiting the sale of birth control techniques is unconstitutional.

8 June Congress authorizes the use of US troops in ground combat in Vietnam. By the end of July 125,000 US troops are in Vietnam.

11–15 June More than 500 civil rights activists are arrested by the Chicago police. Martin Luther King Jr leads a march of 20,000 to City Hall, Chicago (26 July).

10 Aug. The Voting Rights Act becomes law, outlawing the discriminatory registration procedures that have effectively disenfranchised Southern Blacks. Registration of African-American voters starts in Alabama, Louisiana and Mississippi.

12 Aug. The Watts area of Los Angeles suffers looting and burning in a series of race riots. In six days of violence, 34 people are killed.

3 Oct. President Johnson signs an Immigration Act, which abolishes the quota system. Immigrants who are skilled and educated are now allowed to enter the USA regardless of origin, as long as their entry does not jeopardize the livelihood of a currently resident US citizen. Up to 120,000 visas may be issued annually for the W hemisphere countries and 170,000 for the rest of the world.

Nov. *Look* magazine reveals that the US government rejected secret peace talks (Sept. 1964) with the North Vietnamese organized by UN secretary general U Thant.

SUB-SAHARAN AFRICA

18 Feb. The Gambia becomes independent within the Commonwealth.

Oct. The British government refuses to grant independence to Rhodesia unless Ian Smith's government provides for eventual majority rule by the indigenous African population. In response, Smith unilaterally declares Rhodesia to be independent (11 Nov.). The British government imposes sanctions, but because Rhodesia enjoys economic support from South Africa these have little impact.

12 Nov. The UN calls for all nations to withhold recognition of Rhodesian independence.

24–25 Nov. Gen. Joseph Mobutu deposes President Kasavubu and proclaims himself president of the Congo Republic, which he now rules by presidential decree.

5 Dec. The Organization of African Unity demands that Britain use force to suppress the Rhodesian rebellion. This is rejected as being beyond British military capacity, unless Portuguese colonies or South Africa provide bases, which will not be forthcoming.

Dec. In the Central African Republic, President David Dacko is overthrown in a military coup by army commander Jean-Bédel Bokassa, who will prove to be a brutal despot.

ECONOMY AND SOCIETY

5 Mar. In Britain the Kray twins (Ron and Reggie) are sentenced to life imprisonment for the murder of George Cornell and Jack 'The Hat' McVitie.

– In Britain the Race Relations Act establishes the Race Relations Board.

– In Britain the Abolition of Capital Punishment suspends the death penalty for five years. Parliament will make the suspension permanent in 1969.

– In Britain Circular 10/65 requires local education authorities to reorganize secondary education along comprehensive lines.

– The Sanskrit scholar A.C. Bhaktivedanta founds the International Society for Krishna Consciousness in New York to popularize the Hindu religious teachings of Krishna. The Hare Krishna chant will henceforth become a familiar sound in Western cities.

– English fashion designer Mary Quant popularizes the mini-skirt.

SCIENCE AND TECHNOLOGY

– The Communication Satellite Corporation puts its *Early Bird* satellite into orbit. As the first commercial satellite, it will relay telephone calls and television programmes between Europe and the USA.

– Britain discovers significant deposits of oil in the North Sea.

ARTS AND HUMANITIES

Literature

4 Jan. The US-born poet T.S. Eliot dies.

– US consumer activist Ralph Nader publishes *Unsafe at Any Speed*, a consumer study of the US automobile industry. Nader, a former official with the US Department of Labor, is campaigning for greater consumer protection.

– *The Autobiography of Malcolm X* is published posthumously.

Edward Bond, *Saved*, play.

John Fowles, *The Magus*, novel.

Timothy Leary, *The Psychedelic Reader*, psychology; Leary's experiments with drugs lead him to advise: 'Turn on, tune in and drop out.'

Olivia Manning, *The Balkan Trilogy*, consisting of the novels *The Great Fortune* (1960), *The Spoilt City* (1962) and *Friends and Heroes* (1965).

Joe Orton, *Loot*, play.

Harold Pinter, *The Homecoming*, play.

Sylvia Plath, *Ariel*, posthumously published poetry collection.

Katherine Anne Porter, *The Collected Stories of Katherine Anne Porter*.

Neil Simon, *The Odd Couple*, play starring Walter Matthau.

Visual Arts and Architecture

27 Aug. The architect Le Corbusier dies.

David Hockney, *Rocky Mountains and Tired Indians*, painting.

Andy Warhol, *Campbell's Tomato Soup Can* and *'65 Liz*, paintings.

Music

– Robert Moog invents an electronic synthesizer. It will greatly broaden the range of sounds available in electronic music.

The Beach Boys, 'California Girls', single.

The Beatles, 'Ticket to Ride', 'Help!' and 'Day Tripper', singles, and *Rubber Soul*, album.

Leonard Bernstein, *Chichester Psalms*, for counter-tenor, chorus and orchestra.

Pierre Boulez, *Pli selon Pli* (Fold upon Fold), a work for soprano and orchestra.

The Byrds, 'Mr Tambourine Man', single.

Bob Dylan, 'Like a Rolling Stone', single.

Tom Jones, 'It's Not Unusual', single.

The Kinks, 'Tired of Waiting for You', single.

The Righteous Brothers, 'Unchained Melody', single.

Terry Riley, *In C*, minimalist orchestral work.

The Rolling Stones, '(I Can't Get No) Satisfaction', single bringing a sexually charged energy to British popular music.

Paul Simon and Art Garfunkel, 'Sounds of Silence', single.

Sonny and Cher, 'I Got You Babe', single.

Virgil Thomson, *Ode to the Wonders of Nature*, for brass and percussion.

The Who, 'My Generation', single.

The Yardbirds, 'For Your Love', single.

Film

Jean-Luc Godard, *Alphaville*.

David Lean, *Dr Zhivago*, starring Omar Sharif and Julie Christie.

Roman Polanski, *Repulsion*.

Gillo Pontecorvo, *La Battaglia di Algeri* (The Battle of Algiers).

Carol Reed, *The Agony and the Ecstasy*.

John Schlesinger, *Darling*, starring Julie Christie.

Robert Wise, *The Sound of Music*, starring Julie Andrews.

1966

EUROPE

11 Mar. French president Charles de Gaulle announces France's withdrawal from NATO's operational structures (but France remains a member of the alliance). He demands that all NATO bases be removed from France (by 1 April 1967). Subsequently (1 July), Supreme Headquarters Allied Powers Europe (SHAPE) moves from Paris to Casteau, near Brussels, Belgium.

31 Mar. Prime minister Harold Wilson leads the Labour Party to victory in the British general election with an increased majority of 98 seats.

4–6 July When the Warsaw Pact powers meet in Bucharest Romanian leader Nicolae Ceausescu proposes that both the Warsaw Pact and the NATO alliances be disbanded. The policy is a ploy aimed at securing a US withdrawal from Europe and is rejected by NATO.

1 Oct. Albert Speer, Hitler's architect, is released from West Berlin's Spandau prison.

21 Oct. A landslide of coal waste engulfs the local primary school at the village of Aberfan in S Wales: 116 children and 26 adults are killed in a disaster for which the nationalized coal industry bears direct responsibility. Waste from the Merthyr Vale mine has been heaped on the hillside above the village without thought for the consequences.

10 Nov. Sean Lemass resigns as Irish taoiseach (prime minister). He is succeeded by Jack Lynch, former Gaelic footballer and hurler.

– The Welsh National Party (Plaid Cymru) wins its first parliamentary seat in a by-election in Carmarthen.

MIDDLE EAST AND NORTH AFRICA

July Jordan breaks off diplomatic relations with the Palestine Liberation Organization (PLO). PLO raids on Israel, however, continue from Jordanian territory. Most of Jordan's population is now Palestinian, and King Hussein's position, although supported by the Saudis and the USA, is fragile.

July–Aug. Israeli–Syrian tensions escalate, with clashes between Israeli and Syrian forces near the Sea of Galilee.

ASIA

4 Jan. The Tashkent agreement ends the Indo-Pakistan War: both sides withdraw from Kashmir.

19 Jan. Indira Gandhi, daughter of Jawaharlal Nehru, is elected prime minister of India following the death of Lal Bahadur Shastri (11 Jan.). During this year India suffers from its worst famine in 20 years.

Mao Zedong (1893–1976)

Mao was the last great Marxist theoretician and one of the first great Asian leaders of the 20th century. He showed how the insights of Marxist-Leninism, evolved for a European and industrialized workforce, were also relevant to a peasant economy. His theories blended sophistication with empiricism and enabled him to govern a quarter of humanity for a quarter of a century.

A non-graduate schoolmaster, Mao was one of the founders of the Chinese Communist Party in 1921. During the civil wars of the 1930s and 1940s he rose to prominence as a military leader, teaching his guerrilla armies to blend with local peasants, gaining their support while hiding from enemy soldiers. As a political theorist, Mao simplified the Marxist doctrines and used his flair for ideological re-launch to make his theories comprehensible to a nation of 900 million people. Once in power, he successfully launched a number of mass-mobilization campaigns, such as the Great Leap Forward (1958) and the Cultural Revolution (1966–70), although these proved generally disastrous for the Chinese people.

Maoism built on existing Chinese intellectual concepts, such as the unity of opposites, in order to make them suited to Marxist-Leninism. The Confucian idea of the middle way and the need for compromise was basic to Maoist theory, even when Mao's government was torturing and murdering dissidents. Mao also elevated the idea of will as a force for change. Through the force of will, Mao taught, the bourgeoisie could transcend their socio-economic background and become part of the class struggle. Maoism became a factor in Third World nationalist struggles in the 1950s and 1960s, and still appeals to various guerrilla groups in the Third World. However, in China itself Mao's doctrines have long since been abandoned.

Aug. In China Mao Zedong (see box) launches the Cultural Revolution. Its aim is to recover the revolutionary spirit of the Communist Party, which Mao believes has been lost during its years in power. Mao wants to break the party and replace its members with revolutionary youths, the Red Guard, who are mobilized, causing violence and destruction. The party attempts to defend itself, claiming to act in Mao's name, and something akin to civil war grips China, which will not end until 1976.

27 Oct. China launches a nuclear warhead from a guided missile.

5 Dec. Jiang Qing, wife of Mao Zedong, is appointed cultural consultant to the general political department of the Chinese army. In the destruction wrought by the Cultural Revolution, the military are the only functioning tool of government, and Mao wants to throw them into the struggle. Despite the best efforts of Madame Mao, most units of the People's Liberation Army strive to maintain some measure of law and order.

THE AMERICAS

28 Jan. Senator J. William Fulbright, chairman of the Senate's Foreign Relations Committee, challenges the legality of the US intervention in Vietnam.

26 May Guyana (formerly British Guiana) becomes independent of Britain.

13 June The US Supreme Court, headed by Chief Justice Earl Warren, reinforces the protection against self-incrimination that is offered by the Fifth Amendment. US police officers, says the court, must remind prisoners that they have a right to counsel and a right to remain silent.

23 June African-Americans in Cleveland and on Chicago's West Side start to riot and loot. The violence continues intermittently for a month.

2 Sept. Governor George Wallace signs a bill forbidding Georgia's schools from complying with US federal desegregation requirements.

19 Oct–2 Nov. In order to bolster the anti-North Vietnamese alliance, President Johnson embarks on a round of diplomatic visits to New Zealand, Australia, the Philippines, South Vietnam, Thailand, Malaysia and South Korea. By the year's end some 390,000 US troops are committed in South Vietnam.

30 Nov. Barbados becomes independent within the Commonwealth.

– Joaquín Balaguer becomes, with US support, president of the Dominican Republic.

– Massachusetts elects Edward W. Brooke, the first African-American senator.

SUB-SAHARAN AFRICA

22 Feb. Milton Obote, premier of Uganda, assumes full executive powers after he orders troops, led by the young officer Idi Amin, to oust the Bugandan king Mutesa II.

24 Feb. President Kwame Nkrumah of Ghana is ousted in a military coup.

6 Sept. Hendrik Verwoerd, prime minister of South Africa and one of the principal promoters of apartheid as minister of native affairs (1950–8), is stabbed to death in parliament. Balthazar Johannes Vorster succeeds him.

30 Sept. Botswana becomes an independent republic within the Commonwealth. Sir Seretse Khama becomes prime minister of the former British Bechuanaland.

4 Oct. The former British colony Basutoland becomes the independent state of Lesotho within the Commonwealth.

5 Dec. Ian Smith's Rhodesian government rejects a provisional agreement arrived at in talks with the British government and opts for intransigent opposition to black majority rule.

6 Dec. The British government asks the UN to impose mandatory sanctions on Rhodesia; the UN complies.

– The UN ends South Africa's mandate to govern Namibia (South West Africa); South Africa's government rejects the decision.

AUSTRALASIA AND OCEANIA

20 Jan. In Australia Robert Menzies retires as prime minister after 16 years in the post (see 17 Dec. 1949). He is succeeded by Harold Holt (25 Jan.).

ECONOMY AND SOCIETY

July England, the host nation, wins the 8th soccer World Cup, defeating West Germany 4–2 in the final.

ARTS AND HUMANITIES

Literature

10 April The English novelist Evelyn Waugh dies.

3 Aug. US comedian Lenny Bruce dies of a drug overdose. Imprisoned for obscenity as a nightclub comedian in 1961, Bruce has become admired for his fearless tackling of taboo subjects.

Truman Capote, *In Cold Blood*, 'non-fiction novel'.

Seamus Heaney, *Death of a Naturalist*, poetry collection.

Mario Vargas Llosa, *The Green House*, novel.

Bernard Malamud, *The Fixer*, novel.

Mary Renault, *The Mask of Apollo*, novel.

Jean Rhys, *Wide Sargasso Sea*, novel.

Paul Scott, *The Jewel in the Crown*, first novel in his 'Raj Quartet'.

Peter Shaffer, *Black Comedy*, play.

Tom Stoppard, *Rosencrantz and Guildenstern are Dead*, play.

Visual Arts and Architecture

11 Jan. Swiss artist Alberto Giacometti dies.

Carl Andre, *Equivalent VIII*, installation of 120 firebricks. It will later become controversial as the 'Tate bricks' (see 1972 and 1976).

Bridget Riley, *Drift 2*, painting.

Music

29 Aug. In San Francisco the Beatles give their last public concert.

The Beach Boys, 'Good Vibrations' and 'God Only Knows', singles, and *Pet Sounds*, album.

The Beatles, 'Paperback Writer' and 'Yellow Submarine', singles, and *Revolver*, album including the song 'Eleanor Rigby'.

Bob Dylan, *Blonde on Blonde*, album.

John Kander and Fred Ebb, *Cabaret*, musical version of Christopher Isherwood's *Berlin Stories*.

The Kinks, 'Sunny Afternoon', single.

György Ligeti, *Lux aeterna*, choral work.

Manfred Mann, 'Pretty Flamingo', single.

Krzysztof Penderecki, *St Luke Passion*, oratorio.

The Rolling Stones, 'Nineteenth Nervous Breakdown', single.

Frank Sinatra, 'Strangers in the Night', single.

Ike and Tina Turner, 'River Deep, Mountain High', single.

Walker Brothers, 'The Sun Ain't Gonna Shine Anymore', single.

Film

Michelangelo Antonioni, *Blow-Up*, starring David Hemmings.

Lewis Gilbert, *Alfie*, starring Michael Caine.

Sergio Leone, *The Good, the Bad and the Ugly*.

Mike Nichols, *Who's Afraid of Virginia Woolf?*, starring Richard Burton and Elizabeth Taylor.

Alain Resnais, *La Guerre est finie* (The War is Over).

Andrei Tarkovsky, *Andrei Rublev*.

1967

EUROPE

18 Jan. In Britain Jeremy Thorpe succeeds Jo Grimmond as leader of the Liberal Party.

1 Feb. The Northern Ireland Civil Rights Association (NICRA) is founded in Belfast.

12 Mar. In France the Gaullist majority in the National Assembly is reduced to just one seat in the general election.

21 April George Papadopoulos leads a coup by right-wing colonels against the democratic government of Greece. King Constantine II flees to Rome.

10 Sept. In a referendum Gibraltar votes overwhelmingly to remain British rather than join with Spain (12,138 votes to 44).

18 Nov. In Britain the labour government of Harold Wilson devalues the pound from $2.80 to $2.40; inflation is undermining the economy, and the trade deficit remains a chronic problem.

18 Dec. France vetoes Britain's second application to join the European Economic community (EEC).

– The Scottish National party wins its first parliamentary seat in a by-election.

– The far-right National Front is formed in Britain.

– The steel industry is renationalized in Britain.

– In Britain Parliament passes the Welsh Language Act, granting equal status to Welsh on official documents and road signs.

– Civil discontent returns to France: strikers at Saint-Nazaire shipyard, Brittany, light the fuse, and the flame soon spreads to Paris and to other parts of France.

MIDDLE EAST AND NORTH AFRICA

5 June The Six Day War breaks out between Israel and its Arab neighbours. President Nasser of Egypt has precipitated hostilities by forming a military alliance with Syria and Jordan and blockading the Strait of Tiran, cutting off Israeli shipping. Israeli forces launch a pre-emptive strike to forestall an Arab invasion of Israel. The Egyptian and Syrian air forces are largely destroyed. The Israelis seize the Arab quarter of Jerusalem (7 June) and incorporate it with the rest of the city (27 June). The UN condemns the occupation and asks the Israelis to withdraw (4 July). The USSR, a major supplier of Syrian and Egyptian planes, breaks off diplomatic relations with Israel (10 June). Israel rejects the UN demands. It rains stunning blows on its Arab neighbours. Israeli forces capture, and keep, the seemingly impregnable Golan Heights in Syria and the previously Jordanian territory of the West Bank of the Jordan. Israeli tanks overwhelm Egyptian resistance, swarm across Sinai as far as the Suez Canal and hold on to that territory. The kingdom of Jordan has at a stroke lost half its population and a major source of its economy. Of the new Israeli population of 3.5 million, a million or so are Arab. There are new claims of Israelis forcibly ejecting Arabs from their homes to make the land permanently part of Israel. Egypt's authority has been badly damaged by the war, and

Nasser contemplates resignation. However, he starts to purge his army and air force, and also receives assurances of Soviet military aid. The Suez Canal has had to be closed because of the war and is badly affected by mines and scuttled ships: Egyptian revenues have suffered accordingly. For Arabs, the war has been a bitter blow; arguably for Israel the results are little better in the long term. With such confidence in their military prowess Israelis see little need to make concessions to win a permanent settlement.

Aug. Britain starts to withdraw its troops from Aden.

22 Nov. The UN Security Council approves, unanimously, resolution 242, calling for a withdrawal of the Israeli army of occupation from Gaza, East Jerusalem and the West Bank. It is ignored.

26 Nov. The People's Republic of South Yemen becomes independent. Aden joins the new state.

ASIA

2 Mar. The government of Thailand gives permission for US bombers to operate from Thai bases.

15 Mar. North Vietnamese President Ho Chi Minh demands that bombing of his country be halted and that US troops leave South Vietnam before he can respond to President Johnson's call for peace talks.

17 June The first Chinese hydrogen bomb is tested.

26 Dec. The government of South Vietnam threatens to pursue and attack communist troops in Cambodia. The Chinese government assures Cambodia's government of military support if this happens. Chinese workers have already been repairing bomb-damaged parts of the Ho Chi Minh trail in the north, a trail used to supply the communist guerrillas in South Vietnam.

– The USA exports some 6 million tons of wheat to famine-afflicted India.

THE AMERICAS

4 April US civil rights activist Martin Luther King's campaign broadens: he expresses what he sees as the need for the antiwar movement and the civil rights campaign to merge. In a speech he claims that the US government is 'the greatest purveyor of violence in the world'.

15 April 100,000 protestors in New York and 50,000 in San Francisco take to the streets to protest against the Vietnam War.

28 April US boxer Muhammad Ali (the former Cassius Clay) refuses to serve in the US army and is arrested. He will be stripped of his world heavyweight title and banned from boxing until 1970.

June–July Riots in Newark and Detroit are the worst of the explosions of African-American discontent that affect 127 cities in the USA. Those in Newark last five days (12–17 July) after an African-American is beaten by police for a traffic offence. The Detroit riots (23–30 July) have to be quelled by the use of federal troops.

26 July French president Charles de Gaulle, addressing crowds at Montreal, Canada, says: 'Vive le Québec, Vive le Québec libre.' French Québecois nationalism takes heart; the Canadian government is upset.

17 Aug. West Indian-born civil rights activist Stokely Carmichael rejects the non-violence of Martin Luther King Jr. In a famous Black Power speech he calls on African-Americans to arm for a revolution.

2 Oct. US jurist Thurgood Marshall is sworn in as the first African-American justice of the US Supreme Court.

9 Oct. The Argentinian revolutionary Ernesto 'Che' Guevara (see box) is killed by Bolivian troops. A key figure in Castro's Cuban revolution, he has been leading Bolivian guerrillas and attempting to replicate Castro's success. Guevara becomes a cult figure for radical youth in the late 1960s and 1970s.

21 Oct. A mass antiwar demonstration marches on the Pentagon in Washington.

– In an illiberal extension of US state power, the CIA has initiated Operation Chaos to survey antiwar groups it suspects of sympathizing with foreign powers.

Che Guevara (1928–67)

Guevara's face printed on millions of T-shirts became the universal symbol of left-wing revolution and student protest in the 1960s and 1970s, and showed the power of mass marketing in revolutionary struggle.

An Argentinian, Ernesto Guevara de la Serna – nicknamed Che – trained as a doctor at Buenos Aires University, but in 1955 abandoned his career to become a full-time revolutionary activist. In Mexico he joined the Cuban exiles who were plotting the overthrow of the corrupt, right-wing government of Fulgencio Batista. In 1956 he followed Fidel Castro to Cuba to begin a guerrilla war that lasted nearly three years. It was Guevara who led the revolutionaries into Havana on 2 January 1959.

Both in his *Reminiscences* and in *Guerrilla Warfare*, Guevara transformed the theory of revolutionary action by rejecting the classic Marxist-Leninist idea that a society needed to go through stages of economic development – from a predominantly agricultural peasant society to a capitalist-industrial one – before it could be ready for socialist revolution. He proposed, instead, that in under-developed countries an advance guard of violent guerrilla fighters, the foco, should create the conditions that would then be the catalyst for revolution. His goal was an integrated Latin-American revolution, itself an aspect of a wider Third World structure of mutual support and revolutionary exchange.

Guevara held a succession of governmental posts under Castro, but he was an activist, not an administrator. In 1965 he left Cuba to lead armed left-wing groups in the Congo and then in Bolivia, where he was killed by government forces.

SUB-SAHARAN AFRICA

27 Feb.–4 Mar. The Organization of African Unity urges the use of force to end the South African mandate in Namibia and to topple the Smith regime in Rhodesia.

Mar. By now Tutsi refugees are returning to Rwanda after Rwanda and Burundi arrive at a peace agreement.

30 May After massacres of Ibo people by Hausa in N Nigeria, Gen. Odumegwu Ojukwu leads his fellow Ibo out of the Nigerian Federation and a Republic of Biafra is proclaimed. France supplies Biafra with arms; Britain supplies the Lagos government with arms. In the resulting civil war, which causes famine and epidemics, at least 500,000 people die, possibly many more.

July The US government acts to support the rebels within the Congo who are supporting the former prime minister (and Katangan separatist) Moïse Tshombe.

4 Oct. Nigerian troops occupy the Biafran capital of Enugu, but conflict continues between the Ibo and the Yoruba in the W and the Muslim Hausa to the N.

ECONOMY AND SOCIETY

18 Mar. The oil tanker *Torrey Canyon* runs aground off Land's End in England. It discharges some 31 million gallons of oil, causing devastating pollution along the coast of Brittany.

28 May British yachtsman Francis Chichester, aboard *Gypsy Moth IV*, completes his one-man voyage round the world and sails into Plymouth harbour in SW England.

7 Nov. President Johnson signs the Public Broadcasting Act, which will give federal grants to National Public radio and to television's Public Broadcasting Service.

2 Dec. Colour television broadcasting begins in Britain.

– Birth control is legalized in France.

– The Sexual Offences Act becomes part of the law of England and Wales. It permits homosexual acts in private between consenting adults over the age of 21 and is an important element in the furtherance of what is now called 'the permissive society'. Nonetheless, prosecution rates for 'male indecency' almost double between 1967 and 1971.

– The Scottish football club Celtic becomes the first British team to win the European Cup.

SCIENCE AND TECHNOLOGY

3 Dec. In Cape Town South African surgeon Christiaan Barnard performs the first successful human heart transplant, on Louis Washkansky, who survives for 18 days.

– The L-dopa therapy developed by the US neurologist George C. Cotzias improves the treatment of Parkinson's disease sufferers.

ARTS AND HUMANITIES

Literature

15 Oct. The Berliner Ensemble performs for the first time in West Berlin.

Nov. *Rolling Stone* magazine, the organ of US rock culture, starts publication in New York.

Alan Ayckbourn, *Relatively Speaking*, play.

Richard Brautigan, *Trout Fishing in America*, novel.

Mikhail Bulgakov, *The Master and Margarita*, the Russian writer's posthumously published masterpiece (Bulgakov died in 1940).

Gabriel Garcia Márquez, *Cien años de soledad* (A Hundred Years of Solitude), novel.

Peter Nichols, *A Day in the Death of Joe Egg*, play.

William Styron, *The Confessions of Nat Turner*, novel.

Gore Vidal, *Washington, D.C.*, novel.

Visual Arts and Architecture

– Liverpool's Catholic Cathedral, designed by Frederick Gibberd, is completed.

Louise Bourgeois, *Homage to Bernini*, sculpture.

David Hockney, *A Bigger Splash*, painting.

Music

29 Oct. The rock musical *Hair* is performed for the first time in New York.

– The 'summer of love' marks the birth of the hippie movement. Peace, love and flowers are particularly on display in San Francisco, California.

– The Beatles release their groundbreaking album *Sergeant Pepper's Lonely Hearts Club Band*. Including the songs 'Lucy in the Sky with Diamonds', 'With a Little Help from My Friends', 'When I'm Sixty-four' and 'A Day in the Life', the album is the first to have a gatefold sleeve and to offer a set of printed lyrics.

Long John Baldry, 'Let the Heartaches Begin', single.

The Beatles, 'Penny Lane/Strawberry Fields Forever', single.

The Doors, 'Light My Fire', single.

The Jimi Hendrix Experience, *Are You Experienced*, album.

Engelbert Humperdinck, 'Release Me', single.

The Kinks, 'Waterloo Sunset', single.

Scott McKenzie, 'San Francisco (Be Sure to Wear Some Flowers in Your Hair)', single.

The Monkees, 'I'm a Believer', single.

Procol Harum, 'A Whiter Shade of Pale', single.

Sandie Shaw, 'Puppet on a String', single.

The Velvet Underground, *The Velvet Underground and Nico*, album.

Film

Robert Aldrich, *The Dirty Dozen*, starring Lee Marvin.

Luis Buñuel, *Belle de jour*, starring Catherine Deneuve.

Norman Jewison, *In the Heat of the Night*, starring Sidney Poitier.

Joseph Losey, *Accident*, starring Dirk Bogarde.

Mike Nichols, *The Graduate*, starring Dustin Hoffman.

Arthur Penn, *Bonnie and Clyde*, starring Faye Dunaway and Warren Beatty.

Stuart Rosenberg, *Cool Hand Luke*, starring Paul Newman.

John Schlesinger, *Far from the Madding Crowd*, starring Julie Christie and Alan Bates.

1968

EUROPE

2 April In West Germany two Frankfurt department stores are set alight by protestors: Andreas Baader and Gudrun Ennslin will later be found guilty of arson. The Baader-Meinhof gang will be active from now on against US and German capitalist targets.

1968

11 April The student leader Rudi Dutschke is shot in West Berlin.

20 April The British Conservative shadow minister Enoch Powell, a former professor of Greek and a vociferous opponent of non-White immigration, prophesies in an inflammatory speech: 'I see the River Tiber foaming with much blood.' He is sacked from the shadow cabinet by Edward Heath (21 April).

27 April In Britain the Abortion Act receives the royal assent and abortion becomes legal.

May An apparently revolutionary upheaval, *les événements,* marks a challenge to French bourgeois society and is part of an international chain of events. Students demonstrate at the University of Nanterre and then at the Sorbonne (Paris). The French universities have to close down. Industrial discontent spreads in a series of strikes. President de Gaulle appeals for order (24 May). Student leader Daniel Cohn-Bendit is exiled from France as a dangerous dissident. But, when the National Assembly is dissolved (30 May) and elections follow, de Gaulle's party wins the June elections comfortably. For all their revolutionary overtones, *les événements* are seen to have been an event in the consciousness of the children of the bourgeoisie, rather than a movement with genuine socio-economic bite. It is a pattern of events copied throughout the Western world.

20 Aug. In Czechoslovakia the Prague Spring comes to an end as 200,000 Soviet and Soviet-allied troops roll into the country. Alexander Dubček, the secretary of the Czechoslovak communist party, has attempted to liberalize communist rule, under the slogan 'socialism with a human face', but his liberal reforms, which include a degree of political plurality, alarm other communist leaders, especially in Moscow. The third national collapse of Czechoslovakia in its brief 20th-century history sees the Communist Party chiefs being summoned to Moscow. When they return the chastened leaders announce the banning of political clubs (6 Sept.), and the reintroduction of a censorship system (13 Sept.).

Sept. António Salazar, dictator of Portugal since 1933, suffers a stroke and is succeeded as prime minister by Marcello Caetano. Salazar had maintained Portugal's neutrality in both the Spanish Civil War and World War II.

27 Oct. Serious rioting takes place in Grosvenor Square, London, when anti-Vietnam War demonstrators led by Tariq Ali march from a rally in Hyde Park to the US embassy.

5 Nov. The British prime minister demands reform in Northern Ireland at a meeting with the Northern Ireland premier Terence O'Neill. Sectarian violence between Catholics and Protestants has broken out following civil rights demonstrations by the Catholic minority.

– In Britain concern about levels of immigration leads Parliament to pass an Immigration Act that excludes Kenyan Asians even though they have British nationality.

– In Britain the Race Relations Act makes racial discrimination illegal.

– Britain, France, the USSR and China sign the Nuclear Non-Proliferation treaty to limit the spread of nuclear weapons.

ASIA

23 Jan. North Korea seizes the spy ship USS *Pueblo,* claiming it was in their territorial waters. The US government denies this, begins a military build-up in the area and demands the release of ship and crew. Despite bellicose rhetoric, the incident is eventually settled by negotiation (23 Dec.).

30 Jan.–25 Feb. Vietcong and North Vietnamese troops launch the Tet offensive across South Vietnam, with attacks on Hué, Saigon and some 30 other South Vietnamese cities.

31 Jan.–24 Feb. In the Battle of Hué, C Vietnam, US forces attempt to retake the city from the Vietcong. US airstrikes inflict heavy civilian casualties. The campaign ends in a US military victory, with the Vietcong suffering crippling losses and failing in their primary aim of driving US forces out of Vietnam. But politically it is a major success for the Vietcong and North Vietnamese. The US public, bolstered by misleading 'body counts', has assumed the US is winning the war. The Tet offensive has come as a blow, showing that war promises to be a long, frustrating and bloody affair with no guarantee of victory. The antiwar movement in the USA is strengthened, while President Johnson is weakened and begins seriously to consider a negotiated settlement.

16 Mar. At My Lai village in South Vietnam, Lt William Calley leads a group of US soldiers who massacre 109 men, women and children.

31 Oct. President Johnson announces the end of air and naval bombardment N of the 20th parallel in North Vietnam.

THE AMERICAS

21 Feb. Hijacking becomes an arm of anti-US politics when a Delta Airlines jet flying over S Florida is forced to land in Cuba.

27 Feb. CBS anchorman Walter Cronkite suggests that the only way for the USA to 'escape the morass' of Vietnam is to negotiate directly with Hanoi.

31 Mar. President Johnson, disheartened by liberal Senator Eugene McCarthy's strong performance against him and broken by the Vietnam War, announces that he will not seek re-election. McCarthy's engaging and courageous campaign for the presidency has made a dramatic impact on US politics.

4 April Civil rights activist Martin Luther King Jr is shot dead on the balcony of a Memphis motel. James Earl Ray is arrested in London for the murder (8 June). Race riots follow across the USA in Baltimore, Boston, Chicago, Detroit, Kansas City, Newark and Washington, D.C. Mayor Richard Daley of Chicago tells his police officers to shoot to kill.

A riot is at bottom the language of the unheard.

Martin Luther King Jr, *Where Do We Go From Here* (1967)

21 April In Canada Pierre Trudeau, leader of the Liberal Party, becomes prime minister.

5 June Robert Kennedy, brother of assassinated president John F. Kennedy, is shot dead in Los Angeles by the Jordanian-American Sirhan Bishara Sirhan. Kennedy was campaigning for the Democratic presidential nomination.

26–29 Aug. The Democratic Party convention meets in Chicago for the most controversial and divisive meeting in its history. Peace candidate Eugene McCarthy has made a strong showing in primary elections, but Democratic Party bosses are determined to nominate Vice-President Hubert Humphrey, who is pledged to continue the Vietnam War, as Democratic presidential candidate. Thousands of antiwar protestors gather in Chicago to try to persuade Humphrey to change his policy on Vietnam. Brutal attacks on protestors, sanctioned by the mayor of Chicago, Richard Daley, are relayed on national television. The convention chooses Humphrey to be the presidential candidate.

31 Oct. President Johnson, attempting to help Humphrey's campaign, announces the end of US aerial, artillery and naval bombardment N of the 20th parallel in North Vietnam, but the campaign has been destroyed by the war. Richard Nixon has made a startling comeback to be the Republican candidate and is elected, by a narrow margin, to be US president (5 Nov.).

– In Canada René Lévesque founds the Parti Québecois, with the aim of achieving an independent French-speaking Quebec.

SUB-SAHARAN AFRICA

6 Sept. Swaziland becomes independent of Britain.

12 Oct. Equatorial Guinea in W Africa becomes independent of Spain.

– The island of Mauritius becomes independent within the Commonwealth.

– South Africa refuses to allow the England cricket team to tour South Africa if the South African-born 'Cape coloured' cricketer Basil D'Oliveira is included in the England touring party. The tour is cancelled.

– Mass starvation afflicts the Ibo people as they struggle to maintain Biafra's independence from Nigeria.

AUSTRALASIA AND OCEANIA

10 Jan. Harold Holt, prime minister of Australia, disappears while swimming and is succeeded by John Gorton.

31 Jan. Nauru, a UN trust territory in the SW Pacific, becomes independent within the Commonwealth.

ECONOMY AND SOCIETY

24 Mar. US boxer Joe Frazier becomes world heavyweight champion.

29 May Manchester United becomes the first English football team to win the European Cup.

Oct. The 19th Olympic Games are held in Mexico City.

– Jean-Jacques Servan-Schreiber's book *Le Défi américain* (The American Challenge) argues that European integration is a fundamentally pro-capitalist project. The author maintains that US multinationals have benefited from European economic integration. The book marks the emerging conviction in French intellectual and political circles that US 'Anglo-Saxon' economics is un-European.

– In the encyclical *Humanae Vitae* Pope Paul VI condemns all artificial methods of birth control. In so doing he raises a storm of controversy both within and beyond the Catholic world.

– Jacuzzi Bros. of California introduce their whirlpool bath.

SCIENCE AND TECHNOLOGY

– Oil is discovered in North Slope, Alaska, USA.

ARTS AND HUMANITIES

Literature

20 Dec. The US novelist John Steinbeck dies.

– In Britain the Theatres Act abolishes the power of the lord chamberlain to censor plays.

Alan Bennett, *Forty Years On*, play.

Arthur C. Clarke, *2001: A Space Odyssey*, novel.

Athol Fugard, *Boesman and Lena*, play.

Arthur Hailey, *Airport*, novel.

Ursula K. Le Guin, *A Wizard of Earthsea*, first in a series of fantasy novels.

Norman Mailer, *Armies of the Night*, novel.

N(avarre) Scott Momaday (Tsoai-talee), *House Made of Dawn*, novel.

Paul Scott, *The Day of the Scorpion*, second novel of the 'Raj Quartet'.

Alexander Solzhenitsyn, *The First Circle* and *Cancer Ward*, novels.

Tom Stoppard, *The Real Inspector Hound*, play.

John Updike, *Couples*, novel.

Gore Vidal, *Myra Breckinridge*, novel.

Tom Wolfe, *The Electric Kool-Aid Acid Test*, journalism.

Visual Arts and Architecture

2 Oct. French artist Marcel Duchamp dies.

– US pop artist Andy Warhol is shot and nearly killed by Valerie Solanas, a radical feminist.

Music

– First performance of Hans Werner Henze's oratorio *Das Floss der Medusa* (The Raft of the Medusa).

The Beatles, 'Lady Madonna,' and 'Hey Jude', singles and *The Beatles* (The White Album), including the song 'Back in the USSR'.

Harrison Birtwistle, *Punch and Judy*, opera.

Leonard Cohen, 'Suzanne', single.

Cream, *Wheels of Fire*, album.

Marvin Gaye, 'I Heard it Through the Grapevine', single.

The Jimi Hendrix Experience, 'All Along the Watchtower', single.

Manfred Mann, 'The Mighty Quinn', single.

The Rolling Stones, 'Jumpin' Jack Flash', single and *Beggar's Banquet*, album.

Van Morrison, *Astral Weeks*, album.

Film

Lindsay Anderson, *If…*, starring Malcolm McDowell.

Ingmar Bergman, *Shame*, starring Liv Ullmann.

Mel Brooks, *The Producers*, starring Zero Mostel.

Anthony Harvey, *The Lion in Winter*, starring Peter O'Toole.

George Roy Hill, *Butch Cassidy and the Sundance Kid*, starring Paul Newman and Robert Redford.

Stanley Kubrick, *2001: A Space Odyssey*.

Roman Polanski, *Rosemary's Baby*, starring Mia Farrow.

Carol Reed, *Oliver!*

Franco Zeffirelli, *Romeo and Juliet*.

1969

EUROPE

16 Jan. Czech student Jan Palach burns himself to death in Prague in protest at government repression. His suicide has little impact on the government. Alexander Dubček is forced to resign as communist leader and is replaced by more authoritarian Gustav Husák (17 April).

25 April 500 British troops arrive in Northern Ireland to help quell sectarian rioting.

27 April President de Gaulle of France attempts to reassert his authority through a referendum proposing constitutional reforms. Voters reject the reforms by a narrow margin and de Gaulle resigns (28 April).

28 April Terence O'Neill resigns as Northern Ireland prime minister and is succeeded by his cousin and fellow-Unionist James Chichester-Clark (1 May).

15 June Georges Pompidou becomes French president with Jacques Chaban-Delmas as prime minister.

1 July Prince Charles is invested as prince of Wales at Caernarfon Castle.

12–14 Aug. Serious sectarian rioting erupts in the Bogside area of Derry, Northern Ireland, after an inflammatory march by the Protestant Apprentice Boys. The 'battle of the Bogside' ends when British troops are deployed as peacekeepers on the streets of Derry. Rioting occurs in Belfast and several people are killed (15 Aug.). By the year's end a split has occured in the Irish Republican Army (IRA), and the Provisional IRA, a militant grouping determined to begin an armed struggle against British rule in Northern Ireland, has come into being. Northern Ireland's modern Troubles have begun.

21 Oct. In West Germany Social Democratic Party (SPD) leader Willy Brandt is elected chancellor at the head of the reforming social-liberal coalition.

– Italy starts a slide towards social and economic chaos: the country's trades unions embark on a policy of national strikes.

– In Britain the voting age is lowered to 18.

– The British government produces the white paper *In Place of Strife*, on industrial relations.

MIDDLE EAST AND NORTH AFRICA

3 Feb. Yasser Arafat, leader of al-Fatah, the dominant element within the Palestinian Liberation Organization (PLO), becomes chairman of the PLO.

1 Sept. In Libya Col. Moamar al-Qaddafi deposes King Idris in a military coup.

– Golda Meir of the Labour Party becomes prime minister of Israel.

ASIA

2 Mar. Soviet and Chinese forces clash along the River Issuri. Clashes will continue until Aug. The two states start to debate their differences in formal talks held in Beijing (19 Oct.).

25 Mar. In Pakistan Gen. Ayub Khan is overthrown and replaced as president by Gen. Muhammad Yahya Khan.

Mar. US bombers attack bases in Cambodia in a covert operation that escalates the Vietnam War and widens the theatre of war to include a neutral country. The US attacks succeed only in destabilizing the Cambodian government and pave the way for the communist Khmer Rouge to seize power and establish the murderous rule of Pol Pot (1975).

8 June President Nixon announces the start of a withdrawal of US troops from Vietnam; a new 'Vietnamization' policy will aim to establish a local solution to the regional conflict. It is a sign of Nixon's desperation to extricate the USA from an unwinnable war. His National Security adviser Henry Kissinger enters into secret talks with North Vietnamese negotiators in Paris (4 Aug.).

3 Sept. Ho Chi Minh, president of North Vietnam, dies.

12 Oct. President Nixon predicts that the Vietnam War will be over in three months.

THE AMERICAS

20 Jan. Richard Nixon takes office as 37th US president.

10 Mar. James Earl Ray is convicted of the murder of US civil rights leader Martin Luther King Jr (see 4 April 1968).

19 June President Nixon proposes the opening of Strategic Arms Limitation Talks (SALT), which were suspended with the Soviet invasion of Czechoslovakia (1968). The Soviet government agrees (10 July), and talks open in Helsinki, Finland (17 Nov.).

27 June The movement for gay (homosexual) rights becomes more vocal and self-confident after the Stonewall Inn riot in Greenwich Village, New York. Gay men have protested after the police raid a bar on Christopher Street.

18 July Intern (student on work experience) Mary Jo Kopechne dies when a car driven by US Senator Edward Kennedy (younger brother of John F. and Robert Kennedy) plunges into a river at Chappaquiddick Island, Massachusetts. The exact circumstances of her death are never clearly established, and the event ends any presidential ambitions Kennedy might have held.

Aug. The actress Sharon Tate and four others are murdered by followers of hippie psychopath Charles Manson at the California home of the film director Roman Polanski.

3 Nov. President Nixon makes a speech in which he appeals to 'the great silent majority of my fellow Americans'. The speech marks the beginning of Nixon's campaign against what he regards as the monopoly enjoyed by a liberal elite among the opinion formers and commentators of the USA.

SUB-SAHARAN AFRICA

15 Oct. Abdirashid Ali Shermarke, president of Somalia, is assassinated; Gen. Muhammad Siad Barre dissolves the national parliament and declares himself to be the ruler of the new Somali Democratic Republic. Barre's socialist Islamic Somalia will become an ally of the USSR.

ECONOMY AND SOCIETY

5 Oct. Comedy series *Monty Python's Flying Circus* is first broadcast on BBC television.

– In Britain the Open University, a distance-learning institution, is founded.

SCIENCE AND TECHNOLOGY

21 July The USA arrives on the moon: Neil Armstrong, commander of the *Apollo* 11 space module, walks on the lunar surface and is joined by Edwin 'Buzz' Aldrin.

1 Oct. Anglo-French supersonic passenger aircraft Concorde makes its first flight.

– The US Defense Department builds an experimental computer network designed to withstand a nuclear attack. This network will later provide the technical underpinning for the Internet.

ARTS AND HUMANITIES

Literature

21 Oct. The US novelist Jack Kerouac dies.

– In Britain the Booker Prize for Fiction is awarded for the first time (to P.H. Newby, for *Something to Answer For*).

– The nude revue *Oh, Calcutta!*, devised by Kenneth Tynan, is staged in New York.

Margaret Atwood, *The Edible Woman*, novel.

John Fowles, *The French Lieutenant's Woman*, novel.

Yukio Mishima, *Spring Snow*, novel.

Joe Orton, *What the Butler Saw*, play performed posthumously, after Orton's murder by his gay partner (1967).

Mario Puzo, *The Godfather*, novel.

Philip Roth, *Portnoy's Complaint*, novel.

Bernice Rubens, *The Elected Member*, novel.

Jean Stafford, *Collected Stories*.

Kurt Vonnegut, *Slaughterhouse-Five*, novel.

Visual Arts and Architecture

17 Aug. The architect Ludwig Mies van der Rohe dies.

– The Paris administration destroys the market area of Les Halles and embarks on the architectural redesign of the city.

Music

21–24 Aug. The four-day Woodstock Music and Art Fair in Bethel, New York state, a landmark event of 1960s youth culture, is attended by some 400,000 people.

The Beatles, 'Get Back', single and *Abbey Road*, album.

Jane Birkin and Serge Gainsbourg, 'Je t'aime … moi non plus', single banned by the BBC due to its sounds of sexual groaning.

David Bowie, *Space Oddity*, album.

Creedence Clearwater Revival, 'Bad Moon Rising', single.

Peter Maxwell Davies, *Eight Songs for a Mad King*, for male singer and chamber ensemble.

Fleetwood Mac, 'Albatross', single.

Olivier Messiaen, *La Transfiguration de Notre Seigneur Jésus-Christ*, for choir and orchestra.

Krzysztof Penderecki, *Diably z Loudun* (The Devils of Loudun), opera.

The Rolling Stones, 'Honky Tonk Women', single, and *Let it Bleed*, album.

Dmitri Shostakovich, Symphony No. 14 for soprano, strings, bass and percussion.

Frank Sinatra, 'My Way', single.

Dusty Springfield, 'Son of a Preacher Man', single.

The Who, *Tommy*, album.

Film

Richard Attenborough, *Oh! What A Lovely War*.

Federico Fellini, *Satyricon*.

Dennis Hopper, *Easy Rider*, starring Jack Nicholson and Peter Fonda.

Ken Loach, *Kes*.

Ronald Neame, *The Prime of Miss Jean Brodie*, starring Maggie Smith.

Sam Peckinpah, *The Wild Bunch*.

Ken Russell, *Women in Love*, starring Oliver Reed and Alan Bates.

John Schlesinger, *Midnight Cowboy*, starring Dustin Hoffman and Jon Voight.

1970

EUROPE

19 Mar. In the first ever meeting between the leaders of East and West Germany, Willi Stoph (East) meets Willy Brandt (West) at Erfurt, East Germany.

19 June In Britain the Conservatives, led by Edward Heath, return to office in the general election. Harold Wilson, the outgoing prime minister, remains leader of the Labour Party.

3–5 July Serious rioting in Belfast follows the British army's house-to-house search for arms in the 'Falls Road curfew'.

20 July In Britain the chancellor of the exchequer Iain MacLeod dies and is succeeded by Anthony Barber (25 July).

27 July Portuguese leader António Salazar, the last of Europe's fascist rulers, dies.

21 Aug. In Northern Ireland the Social Democratic and Labour Party (SDLP), a constitutional nationalist party, is founded by Gerry Fitt.

9 Nov. French statesman Charles de Gaulle dies.

14 Dec. Riots in Poland start in the Gdansk shipyards and spread across the country. The government has signed an agreement with East Germany recognizing the Oder–Neisse line as Poland's W frontier, but food shortages and price inflation have also contributed to the discontent. Polish communist leader Wladyslaw Gomulka is forced to resign, and Edward Gierek succeeds (20 Dec.).

– In the Republic of Ireland two government ministers, including the future taoiseach (prime minister) Charles J. Haughey, are sacked and charged with conspiring to use public funds to import guns for the IRA to defend Catholic communities in Belfast. The defendants are acquitted of conspiracy.

MIDDLE EAST AND NORTH AFRICA

16 Jan. Col. Moamar al-Qaddafi is formally named ruler of Libya following his coup four months earlier. France announces (21 Jan.) that it will support Libya with 100 military aircraft now that Libya has withdrawn its support of the rebels in Chad. Qaddafi sees the potential of Libyan oil as a diplomatic weapon and orders the scaling-down of oil production in his country as a way of increasing prices and harming Western economies.

16 Jan. Israeli jets attack the suburbs of Cairo, but this attempt to destabilize President Nasser's regime fails as Egyptians become increasingly defiant. Nasser accepts a US peace plan (24 July) and is followed by Syria (26 July) and then by Israel (31 July). The Palestinians, however, whose intransigence is becoming a major factor in the region's conflicts, reject the proposal. Israeli jets attack guerrilla bases in Lebanon (9 Aug.) but their actions have little effect on Palestinian militants.

6 Sept. Palestinian terrorist Leila Khaled helps to hijack an Israeli El Al flight from Tel Aviv to London. She is jailed in London after being overwhelmed by passengers. Palestinian terrorists hijack three further airliners (6–12 Sept) and force them to land near Amman, Jordan. The passengers are held hostage until Khaled and other activists are released by Western governments. The three airliners are blown up.

15–26 Sept. Jordan descends into civil war: King Hussein orders his army to eject the Palestinian Liberation Organization (PLO), which is carrying out raids on Israel from commando bases in Jordan. Syria dispatches Syrian-based PLO forces to challenge the Jordanian army but they are withdrawn because the Syrians fear US intervention. After fierce fighting the defeated PLO moves to Lebanon. Bitter Palestinian fighters refer to the month's events as 'Black September'.

28 Sept. President Nasser of Egypt dies and is succeeded by Anwar al-Sadat (14 Oct.).

13 Nov. Civilian government ends in Syria. Lt-Gen. Hafiz al-Assad, the defence minister, comes to power in a bloodless coup.

– From now until 1975, British troops will be involved in the suppression of a communist uprising in the sultanate of Oman, SE Arabia. Separatist guerrillas in the S Omani province of Dhofar are supported by South Yemen. Oman has a treaty of friendship with Britain dating from 1951, when it became independent.

ASIA

Feb. North Vietnam forces seize the Plaine des Jarres, a fortification in Laos. Criticism grows in the USA over the use of US troops in Laos.

18 Mar. Prince Norodom Sihanouk, ruler of Cambodia, is overthrown in a coup, which replaces him with the right-wing Lt-Gen. Lon Nol. The new ruler starts to persecute Vietnamese living in Cambodia and takes his country into the US sphere of influence. He asks for US assistance to stop a possible North Vietnamese invasion of Cambodia.

29 April South Vietnamese forces, with US air support, start to move into Cambodia. President Nixon announces that he has ordered US ground forces into Cambodia in order to destroy North Vietnamese bases in the country.

13 Nov. East Pakistan is devastated by a cyclone: some 300,000 people die as waves crash on to the coastline and engulf islands.

25 Nov. Wishing to rouse his country from the shame of US and Western influence, novelist Yukio Mishima attempts a military coup in Japan. Finding no support, he commits ritual suicide.

7 Dec. In elections in Pakistan (the first free elections since 1948), the Awami league, a Bengali nationalist party led by Sheikh Mujibur Rahman, wins a majority of the East Pakistan seats in the national assembly. Zulfiqar Ali Bhutto's Pakistan People's Party wins a majority of seats in West Pakistan. Tensions have been growing throughout the 1960s between heavily populated East Pakistan and West Pakistan, where political and miltary power is concentrated.

THE AMERICAS

8 Feb. Alabama's governor, George Wallace, urges further defiance of federal legislation to enforce racial integration in schools.

4 May At Kent State University, Ohio, students protest at the extension of the war in SE Asia. National Guardsmen fire at the crowd, killing four and wounding eight. The killings lead to the closure of many US universities. President Nixon responds by announcing that US troops will be out of Cambodia by the middle of June.

9 May In a massive antiwar rally, 75,000 to 100,000 demonstrators converge on Washington, D.C. A worried Nixon goes to the Lincoln Memorial before sunrise to talk to the protestors.

31 May An earthquake in Peru, originating in Mt Huascarán, kills some 70,000 people and injures 50,000.

17 June The USA's economic problems lead President Nixon to ask both unions and business leaders to deny themselves wage and price rises.

15 Oct. US President Nixon signs into law the Racketeer Influenced and Corrupt Organizations Act, which will be used to prosecute Wall Street insider dealing as well as the traditional mafiosi.

3 Nov. Salvador Allende becomes president of Chile. He is committed to the nationalization of the leading sectors of the economy and recognizes the Cuban government. Despite CIA activity in his country, Allende has become the first Marxist to be elected democratically as head of government of a Western hemisphere country.

2 Dec. Congress approves the creation of the Environmental Protection Agency, which will grow to become the largest regulatory agency in the history of US government.

29 Dec. President Nixon signs the Occupational Safety and Health Act and establishes an agency to regulate safety at work.

31 Dec. President Nixon signs the Clean Air Act, which forces car manufacturers to develop, within six months, engines that are 90% free of emission.

SUB-SAHARAN AFRICA

12 Jan. Biafran forces surrender and the Nigerian civil war ends.

2 Mar. Rhodesia (now Zimbabwe) declares itself a republic.

– In South Africa the Bantu Homelands Citzenship Act assigns Africans to 'homelands' or Bantustans (territories reserved for Bantu-speaking Africans), into which millions of Africans will be forcibly removed. Plans are made for the homelands to become 'independent' African republics within the borders of white-ruled South Africa.

AUSTRALASIA AND OCEANIA

10 Oct. Fiji becomes independent within the Commonwealth.

– Tonga becomes independent within the Commonwealth.

ECONOMY AND SOCIETY

May–June Brazil wins the 9th soccer World Cup, held in Mexico.

SCIENCE AND TECHNOLOGY

– The *Apollo* 13 moon landing is aborted after an explosion in the command module.

ARTS AND HUMANITIES

Literature

7 June The English novelist E.M. Forster dies.

25 Sept. Erich Maria Remarque, German author of antiwar novels, dies.

– Russian novelist Alexander Solzhenitsyn is awarded the Nobel prize for literature.

– Peter Brook's RSC production of *A Midsummer Night's Dream* applies an experimental approach to Shakespeare.

Saul Bellow, *Mr Sammler's Planet*, novel.

J.G. Farrell, *Troubles*, novel.

Dario Fo, *Accidental Death of an Anarchist*, play.

Germaine Greer, *The Female Eunuch*, feminist study which turns its author into a leading figure of the women's movement.

Christopher Hampton, *The Philanthropist*, play.

Ted Hughes, *Crow*, poetry collection.

Kate Millett, *Sexual Politics*, landmark feminist study.

Erich Segal, *Love Story*, novel.

Anthony Shaffer, *Sleuth*, play.

David Storey, *Home*, play, starring John Gielgud and Ralph Richardson.

Alvin Toffler, *Future Shock*, futurology.

Patrick White, *The Vivisector*, novel.

Visual Arts and Architecture

25 Feb. US artist Mark Rothko commits suicide.

Music

18 Sept. Jimi Hendrix dies of a drug overdose.

4 Oct. Janis Joplin dies of a drug overdose.

– The Beatles split up.

The Beatles, *Let It Be*, album and single.

The Carpenters, 'We've Only Just Begun', single.

Deep Purple, 'Black Night', single.

Sacha Distel, 'Raindrops Keep Falling on My Head', single.

Nick Drake, *Bryter Later*, album.

Free, 'All Right Now', single.

The Grateful Dead, *Workingman's Dead*, album.

The Jackson Five, 'I Want You Back', single.

The Kinks, 'Lola', single.

Led Zeppelin, *Led Zeppelin II* and *Led Zeppelin III*, albums.

Paul Simon and Art Garfunkel, *Bridge over Troubled Water*, album and single.

Film

Robert Altman, *M*A*S*H*, starring Donald Sutherland and Elliott Gould.

Bernardo Bertolucci, *The Conformist*.

Arthur Hiller, *Love Story*, starring Ryan O'Neal and Ali MacGraw.

Joseph Losey, *The Go-Between*.

Marcel Ophüls, *Le Chagrin et la pitié* (The Sorrow and the Pity), documentary film examining French collaboration in World War II. The controversy caused by its 1971 screening shows France's difficulty in confronting the recent past.

Bob Rafelson, *Five Easy Pieces*, starring Jack Nicholson.

Nicholas Roeg, *Performance*, starring Mick Jagger.

1971

EUROPE

4 Feb. The British company Rolls Royce Ltd is declared bankrupt; the Conservative government, reversing its previous economic policy, decides to support the company financially.

7 Feb. Female suffrage is introduced in Switzerland after a referendum.

Feb. In Northern Ireland Gunner Robert Curtis, shot by the Provisional IRA, becomes the first British soldier to die in the Northern Irish Troubles.

3 May Walter Ulbricht, the East German communist leader, resigns and is succeeded by Erich Honecker.

June In France a unified Socialist Party is founded by François Mitterrand.

9–10 Aug. In Northern Ireland internment without trial for suspected terrorists is introduced. The arrest of hundreds of Catholics alienates the Nationalist community and, rather than lowering the level of violence, triggers fresh rioting.

14 Sept. In Northern Ireland Rev. Ian Paisley founds the Democratic Unionist Party, a new hardline Unionist grouping.

28 Oct. In Britain Parliament votes to join the European Economic Community (EEC) by 356 votes to 244.

10 Dec. The West German chancellor Willy Brandt receives the Nobel peace prize for his policy of normalizing relations with East Germany (*Ostpolitik* or 'eastern policy').

– In Britain the Industrial Relations Act establishes an Industrial Relations Court with the power to require strike ballots, to compensate workers who have been unfairly sacked and to require employers to recognize trade unions. The Act ends the 'closed shop'.

MIDDLE EAST AND NORTH AFRICA

Jan. The Aswan High Dam is completed in Egypt, financed by the government of the USSR.

14 Aug. Bahrain, off the E coast of Arabia, becomes independent of Britain.

1 Sept. Qatar, in E Arabia, becomes independent of Britain.

1 Dec. Six of the Trucial States (see 1952), Abu Dhabi, Ajman, Dubai, Fujairah, Sharjah and Umm al-Qaiwan, federate as the United Arab Emirates (UAE). The seventh of the Trucial States,

Ras al Khaimah, will join the UAE in Feb. 1972. The British now withdraw their forces from the area.

ASIA

Jan. Sheikh Mujibur Rahman of the Awami League calls for full autonomy for East Pakistan. In response Pakistan president Yahya Khan suspends the constitution.

8 Feb. The South Vietnamese army invades Laos, with US support, in order to shut off supplies of arms to the Vietcong along the Ho Chi Minh trail. After six weeks of intense combat the South Vietnamese have to withdraw (24 Mar.).

1 Mar. A general strike begins in East Pakistan after Pakistan president Yahya Khan postpones the summoning of the new national assembly.

26 Mar. The Awami League declares the independence of East Pakistan as Bangladesh. Forces from West Pakistan invade East Pakistan to suppress the separatist movement, resulting in a flight of 10 million Bengali refugees into India, which expresses support for the Bengali nationalists.

31 Mar. Lt William Calley is convicted of murdering 20 civilians in the My Lai massacre (1968) but is later freed by President Nixon's executive order (6 April). Subsequently Capt. Ernest Medina is acquitted of responsibility for the massacre (22 Sept.).

9 Aug. India concludes a 20-year alliance of friendship with the USSR.

13 Sept. Chinese defence minister Lin Biao dies in a plane crash while fleeing to the USSR, possibly after leading a failed coup against Chairman Mao. Formerly Mao's designated successor, Lin Biao has recruited supporters among the armed forces and may have become too powerful for Mao's liking.

15 Nov. The People's Republic of China becomes a member of the UN and assumes Taiwan's permanent place on the Security Council. This step, hitherto resisted by the USA, is now acceptable to Nixon's government as a price to pay for Chinese assistance in concluding a settlement to the Vietnam War.

Dec. The Indian army invades East Pakistan to help the Bengali separatists. India recognizes the independence of Bangladesh (6 Dec.). West Pakistani forces in East Pakistan surrender to the Indian army (16 Dec.). A brief, bitter war fought on India's frontier with West Pakistan ends on the same day. East Pakistan becomes independent as Bangladesh (17 Dec.). Zulfikar Ali Bhutto replaces Gen. Yahya Khan as president of Pakistan (20 Dec.). The Awami League leader Sheikh Mujibur Rahman, who has been imprisoned in West Pakistan, is released (22 Dec.).

THE AMERICAS

8 Mar. The US Supreme Court rules that supposed 'objective criteria' for job recruitment (including written examinations) are in fact discriminatory towards minorities.

22 April President François 'Papa Doc' Duvalier of Haiti dies and is suceeded by his son, Jean-Claude 'Baby Doc' Duvalier. The president's brutal paramilitary forces, the Tontons Macoutes, continue to persecute the people of Haiti (see 1956).

13 June The *New York Times* starts to serialize the Pentagon Papers, a massive official study of the Vietnam War commissioned by the defense secretary Robert McNamara and leaked to the press by Daniel Ellsberg of the Defense Department. The study shows the extent of US government involvement in Vietnam from the immediate postwar years until 1968; it also shows the government has lied and concealed its true position in the region. The serialization is halted by a federal judge, but the Supreme Court overturns the ruling (30 June). Nonetheless, Ellsberg is indicted for espionage and conspiracy (29 Dec.). The revelation of the misdeeds of successive US administrations deeply embarrasses President Nixon, who is seeking re-election despite widespread and growing domestic opposition to the Vietnam War.

1 July The 26th Amendment to the US Constitution is ratified and lowers the US voting age from 21 to 18 years.

3 Aug. President Nixon orders that the bussing of schoolchildren to achieve racially desegregated schools be limited 'to the minimum required by law'.

15 Aug. The US economy is suffering high levels of inflation because of the costs of the Vietnam War, and President Nixon orders a New Economic Policy, which freezes wages and prices. He also temporarily suspends the conversion of dollars into gold, a move that heralds the breakdown of the Bretton Woods system (1944). The USA records its first trade deficit since 1888.

9 Sept. Attica prison in New York erupts in riots and protests against unfair sentencing policies, which discriminate against racial minorities: 39 prisoners are killed and more than 80 wounded when state police move in to restore order (13 Sept.).

SUB-SAHARAN AFRICA

25 Jan. Gen. Idi Amin leads a military coup that topples the government of President Milton Obote in Uganda: a murderous extermination of Amin's opponents will follow.

27 Oct. The Democratic Republic of Congo is renamed the Republic of Zaire under the continued dictatorial leadership of President Mobutu Sese Seko (formerly Joseph Mobutu).

ECONOMY AND SOCIETY

15 Feb. Decimal currency is introduced in Britain. The new pound consists of 100 pence. The introduction of decimal currency had been mooted in Britain as long ago as 1816, by the Tory MP John Croker.

– In Britain free milk for schoolchildren is abolished by Conservative minister of education Margaret Thatcher.

– US philosopher John Rawls publishes *A Theory of Justice*.

SCIENCE AND TECHNOLOGY

– Oil and natural gas are discovered in the North Sea, off Scotland. Much of its future production will be funded by US investment and technology. By 1981 North Sea oil production will exceed home demand.

– The first microprocessor, the Intel 4004, is designed by the Californian firm Intel, who will dominate the processor market.

– Greenpeace is founded as an anti-nuclear group in British Columbia, Canada, to oppose US nuclear tests in Alaska.

ARTS AND HUMANITIES

Literature

7 Mar. The poet Stevie Smith dies.

Heinrich Böll, *Gruppenbild mit Dame* (Group Portrait with Lady), novel.

Dee Brown, *Bury My Heart at Wounded Knee*, historical study of the destruction of Native American Peoples.

E.M. Forster, *Maurice*, novel written in 1914 but now published posthumously, describing a gay love affair across the English class boundaries.

Frederick Forsyth, *The Day of the Jackal*, thriller.

Geoffrey Hill, *Mercian Hymns*, collection of prose poems.

Yukio Mishima, *The Decay of the Angel* and *The Temple at Dawn*, posthumously published novels.

V.S. Naipaul, *In a Free State*, novel.

Paul Scott, *The Towers of Silence*, third novel of the 'Raj Quartet'.

Alexander Solzhenitsyn, *August 1914*, novel.

Wallace Stegner, *Angle of Repose*, novel.

David Storey, *The Changing Room*, play.

Francis Stuart, *Black List, Section H*, novel.

Keith Thomas, *Religion and the Decline of Magic*, history.

John Updike, *Rabbit Redux*, novel.

Herman Wouk, *The Winds of War*, novel.

Visual Arts and Architecture

David Hockney, *Mr and Mrs Clark and Percy*, painting.

Music

6 April Igor Stravinsky, Russian composer, dies in New York.

16 May First performance on BBC TV of Benjamin Britten's opera *Owen Wingrave*.

3 July Jim Morrison, lead singer of the Doors, dies in Paris.

8 Sept. The John F. Kennedy Centre for the Performing Arts opens in Washington, D.C.

George Harrison, 'My Sweet Lord', single.

Led Zeppelin, *Led Zeppelin IV*, album including the song 'Stairway to Heaven'.

John Lennon, *Imagine*, album.

Andrew Lloyd Webber and Tim Rice, *Jesus Christ Superstar*, musical.

Steve Reich, *Drumming*, minimalist work for drums, percussion and female voices.

The Rolling Stones, 'Brown Sugar', single, and *Sticky Fingers*, album.

Diana Ross, 'I'm Still Waiting', single.

Stephen Schwartz, *Godspell*, musical.

Dmitri Shostakovich, Symphony No. 15 in A major.

Rod Stewart, 'Maggie May', single.

T Rex, 'Hot Love' and 'Get it On', singles.

The Who, *Who's Next*, album.

Film

Peter Bogdanovich, *The Last Picture Show*.

William Friedkin, *The French Connection*, starring Gene Hackman.

Mike Hodges, *Get Carter*, starring Michael Caine.

Norman Jewison, *Fiddler on the Roof*, starring Chaim Topol.

Stanley Kubrick, *A Clockwork Orange*, starring Malcolm McDowell.

Sam Peckinpah, *Straw Dogs*.

Vittorio de Sica, *The Garden of the Finzi-Continis*.

John Schlesinger, *Sunday, Bloody Sunday*.

Don Siegel, *Dirty Harry*, starring Clint Eastwood.

Luchino Visconti, *Death in Venice*, starring Dirk Bogarde.

1972

EUROPE

9 Jan. In Britain a national coal strike begins. It continues for six weeks until the National Union of Mineworkers (NUM) accepts the government's wage offer. The strike leads to power rationing.

22 Jan. In Brussels Britain, Ireland, Denmark and Norway sign a treaty of accession to the European Economic Community (EEC). In Britain Parliament will vote in favour of British entry (14 July), but in Norway a referendum will reject EEC membership.

30 Jan. Ireland's second Bloody Sunday: British army paratroopers shoot dead 13 Catholic protestors during a banned civil rights march in Derry, Northern Ireland. The Irish Republican Army (IRA) calls for a general strike (31 Jan.), and when demonstrators protest in Dublin the British embassy is burnt down (2 Feb.). The British army will strenuously insist that they came under fire from the crowd, while republicans will call it a pre-planned massacre of peaceful demonstrators.

22 Feb. The Official IRA (a republican grouping that split with the Provisional IRA in 1969) bomb the headquarters of the Parachute Regiment in Aldershot, S England, killing seven people. The attack is assumed to be Irish republican revenge for Bloody Sunday.

30 Mar. The British government suspends the Stormont parliament and imposes direct rule over Northern Ireland. Rioting and violence between the Catholic and Protestant populations has worsened. The Conservative government in London is forced to admit that the constitutional expedient of a separate province ruled by the Protestant Unionist majority has failed, but they have left it too late. Catholics, who originally welcomed British troops to the province, now come to see them as upholders of Protestant oppression, a perception highlighted by Bloody Sunday. Support for the IRA and its brutal campaign grows.

19 April In Britain the Widgery Report into Bloody Sunday (see above) concludes that the IRA fired on the British army. Many regard the report as a whitewash.

April In Britain a rail strike damages the economy. A 14-day cooling off period is followed by a number of wildcat strikes.

22 May President Nixon, following a radical new policy of détente, arrives in Moscow for talks with Leonid Brezhnev, the Soviet Communist Party first secretary.

21 July Bloody Friday in Belfast. Provisional IRA bombs kill 11 people and injure 130.

5 Sept. During the Olympic Games in Munich, West Germany, members of the Palestinian terror group Black September (see 15–26 Sept. 1970) murder 11 members of the Israeli Olympic team in the Olympic village. West German police kill five terrorists.

Sept. In France Jean-Marie Le Pen, a former paratrooper with links to the Organisation de l'armée secrète (OAS), founds the extreme right-wing National Front.

21 Dec. West Germany and East Germany sign the *Grundvertrag* (Basic Treaty) by which the two states recognize each other's boundaries and independence and agree to establish a permanent reciprocal representation in both capital cities.

– A severe drought in the USSR forces Soviet grain buyers to look to the USA. They buy some 20 million tons of wheat in all, half of it being US wheat, a quarter of the entire US crop.

– In Britain the Local Government Act establishes a two-tier basis for the upper range of local government in England and Wales.

– From now until 1976 Britain is embroiled in a 'cod war' with Iceland, which has unilaterally extended its fishing limit from 12 to 50 miles.

MIDDLE EAST AND NORTH AFRICA

10 April An earthquake in Iraq kills some 5000 people over a 400km (250 mile) radius.

1 Jun. The Iraqi government nationalizes the Kirkuk oil field, previously owned by Iraq Petroleum.

ASIA

10 Jan. Sheikh Mujibur Rahman arrives back in newly independent Bangladesh (see Dec. 1971), of which he becomes prime minister (12 Jan.).

21–27 Feb. President Nixon establishes US relations with China when he arrives in Beijing for talks with communist leaders Mao Zedong and Zhou Enlai. Nixon is seeking Chinese assistance to gain acceptable terms with which to end the Vietnam War.

3 Mar. China formally lays claim to Hong Kong and Macao.

16 April In North Vietnam American planes attack Hanoi and Haiphong as the USA resumes its bombing policy.

1 May The South Vietnamese city of Quang Tri is taken by the North Vietnamese in a major offensive. The South Vietnamese 3rd Division withdraws to the S, while looting and arson spreads in the city of Hué. Vietcong forces surround the towns of Kontum and Pleiku. After the last US combat troops leave Vietnam (11 Aug.) South Vietnamese forces retake Quang Tri (15 Sept.).

19 May At a meeting in Beijing the Chinese, Soviet and North Vietnamese governments discuss how to aid North Vietnam, whose ports are now being mined by US forces.

Sept. President Ferdinand Marcos declares martial law in the Philippines and assumes absolute power.

20 Nov. North Vietnamese negotiators reject US peace proposals, as does South Vietnam's President Thieu (12 Dec.). USA forces launch a 'Christmas bombing' campaign against North Vietnam (18–30 Dec.) in a vain attempt to force the North Vietnamese to accept US terms.

– Under the terms of the Simla agreement Kashmir is divided into Pakistani Kashmir and the Indian state of Jammu and Kashmir.

THE AMERICAS

7 Feb. President Nixon signs the Federal Election Campaign Act, requiring that all electoral campaign contributions be declared and that spending on media campaigning be limited to 10 cents per person of voting age in the candidate's constituency.

22 Mar. The US Supreme Court rules that a Massachusetts state law forbidding the sale of contraceptives to unmarried people is unconstitutional.

15 May George Wallace, segregationist governor of Alabama, is shot while campaigning for the Democratic presidential nomination and is subsequently confined to a wheelchair.

May Oil is found at the Chiapas-Tabasco field in Mexico, which will become the Western hemisphere's largest oil reserve.

17 June Frank Wills, a security guard at the Watergate building in Washington, D.C., summons the police to the Democratic Party national headquarters inside the building. Five men are arrested with cameras and electronic surveillance equipment, three of whom are Cubans. John Mitchell, President Nixon's presidential campaign manager, denies any official involvement with the break-in (18 June), but the president's office admits (19 June) that one of the men, Bernard Barker, has met Howard Hunt, who (until 29 Mar.) had been a consultant to the presidential counsel Charles Colson. It is the start of one of the most infamous political scandals of the 20th century, as Nixon attempts to conceal his use of the CIA to spy on his political opponents.

29 June The US Supreme Court decides by a majority of five to four that the death penalty is unconstitutional since it is a 'cruel and unusual punishment'.

1 Aug. Journalists Bob Woodward and Carl Bernstein of the *Washington Post* start a series of reports on a link between the Watergate break-in and the Committee for the Re-Election of the President (CREEP).

30 Oct. In Canada the Liberal Party narrowly wins the general election. Pierre Trudeau remains prime minister.

7 Nov. Senator George McGovern of South Dakota, the Democratic candidate for the presidency, is defeated by Richard Nixon in the biggest US presidential landslide since 1936.

23 Dec. An earthquake destroys Managua, Nicaragua.

– In Chile President Salvador Allende nationalizes the country's major industries.

SUB-SAHARAN AFRICA

– In Sudan, the Addis Ababa accords end a civil war that has been fought since 1955 between forces of the Muslim Sudanese government and the mostly non-Muslim African population of the S of the country. President Nimeiri grants three S provinces a considerable degree of autonomy.

ECONOMY AND SOCIETY

Aug.–Sept. The 20th Olympic Games are held in Munich, West Germany.

Sept. Bobby Fischer defeats the Russian Boris Spassky to become the first US world chess champion.

SCIENCE AND TECHNOLOGY

22 July The Soviet space programme lands *Venus* 8 on Venus.

– *Apollo* 16 (April) and *Apollo* 17 (Dec.) are the last US-crewed missions to the moon.

– In N Kenya anthropologist Richard Leakey discovers a human skull that is datable to 2.5 million BC, the earliest sign of human life on earth.

ARTS AND HUMANITIES

Literature

1 Nov. The US poet Ezra Pound dies.

Richard Adams, *Watership Down*, novel.

John Berger, *G*, novel.

Anthony Burgess, *The Malayan Trilogy*, trilogy of novels comprising *Time for a Tiger* (1956), *The Enemy in the Blanket* (1958) and *Beds in the East* (1959).

Italo Calvino, *Le città invisibile* (Invisible Cities), novel.

Neil Simon, *The Sunshine Boys*, play.

Tom Stoppard, *Jumpers*, play.

Hunter S. Thompson, *Fear and Loathing in Las Vegas*, account of the Las Vegas drug scene.

Eudora Welty, *The Optimist's Daughter*, novel.

Visual Arts and Architecture

– The World Trade Center, New York, designed by Minoru Yamasaki, is completed and becomes the world's tallest building.

– The Tate Gallery in London purchases Carl Andre's installation *Equivalent VIII* (see 1966). It becomes known as the 'Tate bricks'.

Andy Warhol, *Mao*, painting on silkscreen and canvas.

Music

America, 'Horse with No Name', single.

Chuck Berry, 'My Ding-A-Ling', single.

David Bowie, *The Rise and Fall of Ziggy Stardust and the Spiders from Mars*, album.

Alice Cooper, 'School's Out', single.

Derek and the Dominoes, 'Layla', single.

Jim Jacobs and Warren Casey, *Grease*, musical.

Bob Marley, *Catch a Fire*, album that helps to popularize Jamaican reggae music in the wider world.

Don McLean 'American Pie', single.

Nilsson, 'Without You', single.

Donny Osmond, 'Puppy Love', single.

Lou Reed, 'Walk on the Wild Side', single.

The Rolling Stones, *Exile on Main Street*, album.

Roxy Music, *Roxy Music*, album.

T Rex, 'Metal Guru' and 'Children of the Revolution', singles.

Film

Woody Allen, *Play It Again, Sam*.

Ingmar Bergman, *Cries and Whispers*.

Bernardo Bertolucci, *Last Tango in Paris*, starring Marlon Brando.

Luis Buñuel, *The Discreet Charm of the Bourgeoisie*, starring Fernando Rey.

Francis Ford Coppola, *The Godfather*, starring Marlon Brando and Al Pacino.

Bob Fosse, *Cabaret*, starring Liza Minnelli, Joel Grey and Michael York.

Werner Herzog, *Aguirre, Wrath of God*.

Pier Paolo Passolini, *The Decameron* and *The Canterbury Tales*.

1973

EUROPE

1 Jan. Britain, Ireland and Denmark become members of the European Economic Community (EEC).

1 Mar. In the Republic of Ireland Fine Gael forms a coalition with the Labour Party. Liam Cosgrave of Fine Gael (son of William T. Cosgrave, prime minister of the Irish Free State 1922–32) becomes taoiseach (prime minister).

9 June Gen. Franco names Admiral Luis Carrero Blanco as prime minister but remains Spain's head of state; Carrero Blanco is assassinated (20 Dec.) and is replaced by Carlos Arias Navarro.

12 June In West Germany Helmut Kohl becomes leader of the right-of-centre Christian Democratic Union (CDU).

15 Sept. King Gustav VI of Sweden dies and is succeeded by his grandson, Charles XVI Gustav, who reduces the monarchy to a purely symbolic role.

18 Sept. East Germany and West Germany become members of the United Nations.

Nov. In Britain the Kilbrandon Report recommends separate assemblies (home rule) for Scotland and Wales.

Nov.–Dec. The British economy, already hit by a wave of strikes, is further damaged by the Middle Eastern 'Oil Shock' (see below). Faced with an energy crisis, the government cuts fuel and petrol supplies by 10% (Nov.). Prime minister Edward Heath orders British industry to work a three-day week from 31 Dec. in order to conserve energy. The likelihood of an all-out miners' strike in the near future completes a gloomy picture.

9 Dec. The Sunningdale Agreement between the British and Irish governments, together with representatives of Northern Ireland's political parties, creates a power-sharing executive in Northern Ireland.

– Britain raises the school-leaving age to 16.

– The Ecology Party is founded in Britain. It will change its name to the Green Party in 1985.

MIDDLE EAST AND NORTH AFRICA

3 Aug. The majlis (the Iranian parliament) ratifies the National Iranian Oil Company's plan to assume control of all oil field operations and to build a more equitable relationship with foreign buyers.

4 Sept. The Saudi Arabian government announces that it will not increase oil production since US policy in the Middle East is pro-Israeli.

6 Oct. A fourth Arab–Israeli War breaks out on the Jewish Day of Atonement (Yom Kippur). After the failure of diplomatic overtures aimed at recovering territory lost in the 1967 Six Day War, Egypt and Syria mount major attacks on Israel. Egyptian forces cross the Suez Canal and Syrian forces attack the Golan Heights. Israeli forces push the Syrians back to the 1967 cease-fire line (10 Oct.) and then strike out towards Damascus. A major tank battle starts in the Sinai Desert as Israeli forces cross the Suez Canal and trap the Egyptian 3rd Army (16 Oct.). Israel and Egypt agree on a ceasefire (24 Oct.). Although the war ends in another Israeli victory, it is achieved only after a bruising fight. An especially sinister aspect of this latest Arab–Israeli conflict has been the possibility that the war will escalate to involve both the USSR, which is supplying the Arabs with military equipment, and the USA, which is doing the same for Israel. The Israeli government is now prepared to consider a more conciliatory policy towards its most powerful enemy, Egypt.

Oct. In reprisal for US aid to Israel, the Arab-dominated Organization of Petroleum Exporting Countries (OPEC), restricts the supply and quadruples the price of their oil exports. The resulting 'Oil Shock' causes serious economic problems for the consumer nations of the West. An increase in the price of uranium follows, as nuclear fuel becomes a popular alternative to oil. The oil inflation, along with a major inflation in the price of grain, causes a world monetary crisis and a global economic recession on a scale not seen since the 1930s.

1 Dec. David Ben-Gurion, first prime minister of Israel, dies.

ASIA

28 Jan. A ceasefire takes effect in Vietnam and brings to a close a chapter of destructive futility in US and Indochinese history. US forces have suffered some 58,000 deaths; total Vietnamese losses are probably more than 1.5 million. The last US combat troops leave South Vietnam (29 Mar.), but the US bombing of Cambodia continues as part of US pressure for the repatriation of prisoners of war. The settlement, which leaves North Vietnamese and Vietcong forces occupying the ground they hold in South Vietnam, marks the first major US military defeat.

19 July A military coup in Afghanistan overthrows King Mohammed Zahir Shah. Gen. Mohammed Daoud Khan becomes president.

THE AMERICAS

2 Jan. The US Supreme Court rules that abortion during the first six months of pregnancy is a private matter between a woman and her doctor. The decision sparks a heated debate in the USA as 'right-to-life' groups turn to political campaigning against the ruling.

12 Feb. The dollar is devalued by 10% against the other major world currencies as the US administration tries to boost American exports.

17 April President Nixon announces the resignation of the White House chief of staff H.R. Haldeman and domestic adviser John Ehrlichman because of the charges made against them in relation to the Watergate break-in (see 17 June 1972).

1 June British Honduras changes its name to Belize.

20 June Juan Perón returns to Argentina from exile. The Perónist Héctor Cámpora, elected president on 11 Mar., resigns to make way for Perón, who is elected president for the second time in Oct. Isabel, Perón's third wife, becomes vice-president.

12 July The Bahamas become independent within the Commonwealth.

11 Sept. Following nationwide strikes, President Allende of Chile is ousted in a military coup sponsored by the CIA and,

allegedly, commits suicide. Gen. Augusto Pinochet becomes president and embarks on a 16-year period of dictatorial and repressive rule in Chile, which aims at exterminating Marxist and left-wing influences in the country's politics.

10 Oct. US vice-president Spiro Agnew resigns following a scandal about his evasion of income tax. He is replaced by Gerald Ford (3 Dec.).

20 Oct. Archibald Cox is dismissed as special prosecutor into the Watergate affair after demanding that the president hand over the tapes recording his conversations with officials about the break-in. The attorney general, Elliot Richardson, resigns in protest. Some tapes are released, but the ones relating to the crucial period are missing. These events trigger the introduction of 16 impeachment resolutions against Nixon in the House of Representatives. Preliminary impeachment hearings begin on 30 Oct. The scale of the Nixon administration's covert operations against its political enemies is becoming apparent.

7 Nov. The US Congress overturns President Nixon's veto and passes the War Powers Resolution, which limits the president's ability to send troops into battle in foreign theatres of war. The resolution affirms that Congressional approval is needed before such action is taken.

ARTS AND HUMANITIES

Literature

26 Mar. The English playwright Noël Coward dies.

2 Sept. The English novelist J.R.R. Tolkien dies.

23 Sept. The Chilean poet Pablo Neruda dies.

28 Sept. The English-born poet W.H. Auden dies.

Martin Amis, *The Rachel Papers*, novel.

Alan Ayckbourn, *Absurd Person Singular*, play.

Roland Barthes (see p. 588), *Le Plaisir du texte* (The Pleasure of the Text), an outline of the application of structuralist ideas to criticism.

Italo Calvino, *The Castle of Crossed Destinies*, novel.

J.G. Farrell, *The Siege of Krishnapur*, novel.

Erica Jong, *Fear of Flying*, novel.

Iris Murdoch, *The Black Prince*, novel.

Thomas Pynchon, *Gravity's Rainbow*, novel.

Peter Shaffer, *Equus*, play.

Gore Vidal, *Burr*, novel.

Patrick White, *The Eye of the Storm*, novel.

Visual Arts and Architecture

8 April Spanish painter Pablo Picasso (see p. 467) dies, aged 91.

– The Sears Tower, Chicago, designed by Skidmore, Owings and Merrill, is completed.

Music

16 June First performance of Benjamin Britten's opera *Death in Venice*, based on the novella by Thomas Mann.

David Bowie, 'Jean Genie', single, and *Aladdin Sane*, album.

Elton John, *Goodbye Yellow Brick Road*, album.

Richard O'Brien, *The Rocky Horror Show*, musical fusing rock 'n' roll and horror film clichés in a high-camp style. It soon attracts a cult following.

Roland Barthes (1915–80)

The French cultural critic Roland Barthes wrote on subjects as diverse as Racine, car design, female fashion and food. He developed the idea of cultural codes and showed how all the different phenomena of culture have systems of meaning that dictate what can and cannot be expressed within them. He was therefore at the heart of the structuralist movement that dominated European and Anglo-American intellectual life in the last third of the 20th century.

Structuralism maintains that language is to be understood as a means of communication in the present and that its history is irrelevant. The need is to understand how different components of language relate to each other, not how they came to have their present form. So, what matters in a system of meanings is the contrast between the different elements rather than the elements themselves. It is in this sense that 'structure' gives meaning. Barthes took this insight and related it to forms of culture other than language.

Barthes saw that culture involves the assertion of power and domination, even when this is not immediately apparent. He contrasted the language of culture with the language of science where the meanings are stable and all are agreed on what a sign means. Barthes believed that the language of culture aims to get away from the simple subject/object relationship, for it deals with a variety and dispersal of meanings. This is why his writings became increasingly fragmentary and why he abominated the didacticism of teaching, preferring the digressive to the rhetorical. He opposed the idea of a 'grand theory', a single over-arching system to explain how the world works, preferring instead to produce suggestive and witty works on individual subjects.

Mike Oldfield, *Tubular Bells*, album.
Pink Floyd, *The Dark Side of the Moon*, album.
Suzi Quatro, 'Can the Can', single.
The Rolling Stones, *Goat's Head Soup*, album.
10 cc, 'Rubber Bullets', single.
Stevie Wonder 'You are the Sunshine of My Life', single.

Film

Lindsay Anderson, *O Lucky Man!*, starring Malcolm McDowell.
Ingmar Bergman, *Scenes from a Marriage,* starring Liv Ullmann.
Rainer Werner Fassbinder, *Angst essen Seele auf* (Fear Eats the Soul).
William Friedkin, *The Exorcist*.
George Lucas, *American Graffiti*.
Nicholas Roeg, *Don't Look Now*, starring Julie Christie and Donald Sutherland.
Martin Scorsese, *Mean Streets*, starring Robert De Niro.
François Truffaut, *Day for Night*.
Fred Zinnemann, *The Day of the Jackal*, starring Edward Fox.

1974

EUROPE

1 Jan. In Northern Ireland the power-sharing executive takes office. The Ulster Unionist Party, however, repudiates the Sunningdale agreement (4 Jan.). Brian Faulkner, chief executive of the assembly, resigns the leadership of the Ulster Unionist Party (7 Jan.). Loyalists opposed to power-sharing disrupt the first meeting of the new assembly on 22 Jan. and all Unionist parties withdraw from the assembly the following day.

10 Feb. In Britain members of the National Union of Mineworkers (NUM) begin an all-out strike. They are seeking a wage rise of 30–40%.

28 Feb. In Britain the Conservative government loses a general election called by prime minister Edward Heath on the issue 'who governs Britain?' Union militancy has seriously undermined the government's credibility, and the electorate decide that the Conservatives have failed to govern. Britain is in the grip of widespread industrial unrest and energy shortages have forced industry to work a three-day week. After Heath has tried unsuccessfully to form a coalition with the Liberal Party, Harold Wilson forms a minority Labour administration without an overall majority (5 Mar.).

2 April In France President Pompidou dies in office and Valéry Giscard d'Estaing is elected to succeed him (19 May). Although continuing the Gaullist tradition, Giscard d'Estaing brings an edge of technocratic modernity to his party. He appoints Jacques Chirac as prime minister.

25 April A military coup of the left removes Marcello Caetano from power as prime minister of Portugal. Gen. Antonio de Spinola takes over as premier and promises to restore democracy and to end Portugal's colonial wars in S Africa.

6 May In West Germany Willy Brandt resigns as chancellor following the revelation that Günter Guillaume, a member of Brandt's staff, is an East German spy.

16 May Helmut Schmidt becomes West German chancellor.

28 May Northern Ireland's power-sharing executive collapses after just five months, brought down by a strike organized by the (Protestant) Ulster Workers Council with the connivance of hardline Unionists and Loyalist paramilitaries. Direct rule of Northern Ireland from Westminster resumes the next day.

15 July Greek Cypriot forces, favouring *enosis* (union with Greece), overthrow the government of Archbishop Makarios, who blames the Greek government for its complicity in the coup. Turkish troops invade Cyprus (20 July) and rapidly conquer the N part of the island, which they establish as an independent state. It fails, however, to gain international recognition.

23 July The Greek military government resigns – its attempt to mobilize in the face of the Turkish invasion of Cyprus has been a humiliating shambles. Constantine Karamanlis, former prime minister, returns to Greece to form a civilian government. He announces that Greece will not go to war over Cyprus.

13 Sept. West German terrorists Andreas Baader and Ulrike Meinhof start a hunger strike in their Düsseldorf and Cologne prisons. The Baader-Meinhof gang, also known as the Red Army Faction, has carried out a succession of terrorist attacks in West Germany.

5 Oct. In Britain the Provisional IRA bombs two public houses in Guildford, Surrey, killing five people.

10 Oct. In the second British general election of the year, the Labour Party gains an absolute majority of three seats.

21 Nov. In Britain the Provisional IRA bombs two public houses in Birmingham, killing 21 people and injuring 1200. In response, the British government pushes anti-terrorist legislation through Parliament. The Prevention of Terrorism Act allows police to hold suspects for five days without charge.

MIDDLE EAST AND NORTH AFRICA

18 Jan. Henry Kissinger, US secretary of state, negotiates an agreement between Israel and Egypt. Israel is to withdraw from the W bank of the Suez Canal, while Egypt will reoccupy the E bank. Israel subsequently agrees to withdraw from Syria and parts of the Golan Heights (June).

13 Nov. The Palestinian leader Yasser Arafat addresses the General Assembly of the United Nations.

ASIA

18 May India becomes a nuclear power when it announces a successful underground atomic test. Pakistan will obviously seek to counterbalance this development with its own nuclear weapons. The debate on how to stop the proliferation of nuclear weapons acquires a new urgency.

11 Nov. In Pakistan President Zulfikar Ali Bhutto's security forces kill his opponent Ahmad Raza Kasuri.

26 Nov. Kakuei Tanaka, prime minister of Japan, resigns because of financial corruption within his Liberal-Democratic Party and in his own business and political life. Miki Takeo becomes prime minister (9 Dec.).

THE AMERICAS

4 Feb. Californian heiress Patricia Hearst is kidnapped by the Symbionese Liberation Army, an urban guerrilla group who demand a $2 million ransom. She is later implicated in a bank robbery (15 April), having apparently been converted by her kidnappers to the SLA cause.

7 Feb. The Caribbean island of Grenada becomes independent within the Commonwealth.

1 July Argentinian president Juan Perón dies, and his wife, Isabel Perón, becomes Argentina's, and the Western hemisphere's, first female head of government.

9 Aug. US president Richard Nixon resigns from office, having admitted complicity in the Watergate cover-up (5 Aug.). Vice-president Gerald Ford is sworn in as 38th US president. The House Judiciary Committee has voted (30 July) to adopt three articles of impeachment: President Nixon has been charged with obstruction of justice, failure to uphold laws and refusal to produce material subpoenaed by the committee. The Supreme Court has ruled that the White House tapes must be handed over to a special prosecutor (24 July).

8 Sept. US president Gerald Ford pardons former president Nixon 'for all offenses against the US, he has committed or may have committed or taken part in'.

– In the USA the Electoral Reform Act (7 Aug.) tries to limit the effect of large individual donations to presidential campaigns, but the large sums that can still be raised by political action committees will circumvent the legislation.

SUB-SAHARAN AFRICA

– In Ethiopia famine has destroyed the country's institutions: the army seizes control and Haile Selassie is deposed (12 Sept.). The new regime announces its socialist character (20 Dec.) and leans towards the USSR.

– Nationalists in Angola, Mozambique and Portuguese Guinea press for their independence from Portugal now that the colonial power has been democratized. Portuguese Guinea becomes independent as Guinea-Bissau (10 Sept.).

ECONOMY AND SOCIETY

2 Jan. A nationwide 55mph (88kph) speed limit on US highways comes into effect.

July West Germany, the hosts, win the 10th soccer World Cup.

30 Oct. US boxer Muhammad Ali regains his world heavyweight championship title by defeating George Foreman in the so-called 'Rumble in the Jungle' in Kinshasa (Zaire).

– Jim Bakker of South Carolina establishes his television mass evangelization campaign Praise the Lord (PTL).

ARTS AND HUMANITIES
Literature

Alan Ayckbourn, *The Norman Conquests*, play.

Jacob Bronowski, *The Ascent of Man*, history based on his BBC TV series. He dies in a car accident in New York (22 Aug.).

Alex Comfort, *The Joy of Sex*, the first popular sex manual.

Nadine Gordimer, *The Conservationist*, novel.

Graham Greene, *The Honorary Consul*, novel.

Philip Larkin, *High Windows*, poetry collection.

John Le Carré, *Tinker, Tailor, Soldier, Spy*, novel.

Alison Lurie, *The War Between the Tates*, novel.

Stanley Middleton, *Holiday*, novel.

Iris Murdoch, *The Sacred and Profane Love Machine*, novel.

Robert M. Pirsig, *Zen and the Art of Motorcycle Maintenance*, philosophy.

Michael Joseph Shaara Jr, *The Killer Angels*, novel.

Alexander Solzhenitsyn, *The Gulag Archipelago*, history of the Soviet labour-camp network. Solzhenitsyn is arrested by the KGB and expelled from the USSR; he moves to the USA.

Tom Stoppard, *Travesties*, play.

Music

24 May The jazz pianist Duke Ellington dies.

– First performance of Michael Tippett's opera *The Knot Garden*.

Abba, 'Waterloo', single.

David Bowie, *Diamond Dogs*, album.

John Cale, *Fear*, album.

Eric Clapton, *461 Ocean Boulevard*, album.

Bob Marley and the Wailers, 'No Woman No Cry', single.

Mud, 'Tiger Feet', single.

Krzysztof Penderecki, *Magnificat*.

Leo Sayer, 'The Show Must Go On', single.

Steely Dan, *Pretzel Logic*, album.

Three Degrees, 'When Will I See You Again?', single.

Film

Ingmar Bergman, *The Magic Flute*.

Mel Brooks, *Blazing Saddles* and *Young Frankenstein*.

Francis Ford Coppola, *The Godfather Part II*, starring Al Pacino.

Federico Fellini, *Amarcord*.

Tobe Hooper, *The Texas Chainsaw Massacre*.

Louis Malle, *Lacombe Lucien*.

Roman Polanski, *Chinatown*, starring Jack Nicholson and Faye Dunaway.

1975

EUROPE

4 Feb. British Conservative Party leader Edward Heath resigns after being defeated in the first ballot of a leadership election. In the second ballot (11 Feb.) Margaret Thatcher defeats William Whitelaw and is elected leader. She is the first woman to lead a political party in Britain.

13 Feb. Turkish-held N Cyprus declares itself the Turkish Federated State of Cyprus.

5 June In Britain a referendum endorses British membership of the European Economic Community (EEC).

9 June In Britain the trial begins of the 'Birmingham Six' for the murder of 21 people in the Birmingham pub bombings (see 21 Nov. 1974). They will be sentenced to life imprisonment.

June In Britain the first oil from the North Sea is pumped ashore.

1 Aug. The Helsinki Accord is signed by 36 nations. In pursuit of détente the signatories recognize each other's boundaries and renounce the use of force. The Helsinki Final Act also includes a commitment to respect human rights. The Soviets do not take this seriously. The US government, however, does, and this will prove a major point of contention between the superpowers.

29 Aug. Eamon de Valéra, former Irish taoiseach and president, dies.

24 Oct. Rinka, a dog belonging to a former male model, Norman Scott, is shot dead on Exmoor in SW England. The shooting marks the beginning of a scandal that will end the career of British Liberal Party leader Jeremy Thorpe (see Jan. 1976).

20 Nov. Gen. Franco, dictator of Spain since 1939, dies. Prince Juan Carlos is proclaimed king (22 Nov.), marking the restoration of the Spanish house of Bourbon. He moves to restore democracy.

– In Britain inflation rises as trade unions continue to demand wage rises of up to 30%. Labour prime minister Harold Wilson proposes to negotiate a 'social contract' with trade union leaders.

– The British car manufacturer British Leyland is nationalized following a long decline in its share of the market.

MIDDLE EAST AND NORTH AFRICA

6 Mar. Iran and Iraq agree on their border: Iran now includes the Shatt-al-Arab estuary at the confluence of the Tigris and Euphrates rivers and, in return, promises Iraq not to support Kurdish rebels.

25 Mar. King Faisal of Saudi Arabia is assassinated by his nephew and is succeeded by his brother Khalid.

April Lebanon descends into civil war: struggles for power between Muslim and Christian groups are exacerbated by the presence in Lebanon of the forces of the Palestine Liberation Organization (PLO), which is using its bases in Lebanon to attack Israel. Lebanese Christian militias, armed by Israel, attack the PLO, which is in turn supported by left-wing Lebanese Muslim groups.

5 June The Suez Canal reopens for the first time since 1967.

10 Nov. The UN General Assembly approves, by 72 to 35 votes, a resolution defining Zionism as 'a form of racism and racial discrimination'. Some 32 nations abstain.

Nov. The International Court of Justice rules that the people of Spanish Sahara (a Spanish province since 1958, now Western Sahara) should be self-governing. Spain agrees to withdraw from the area by Feb. 1976.

ASIA

6 Mar. A wave of demonstrations undermine Indira Gandhi's rule in India. The high court finds her guilty of corruption in her electoral campaign of 1971 and rules that she must resign (11 June). Gandhi responds by arresting some 750 political opponents. She imposes press censorship, reduces peasant debts and announces a land-distribution programme.

30 Mar. North Vietnamese forces capture Da Nang in C Vietnam.

5 April Jiang Jieshi (Chiang Kai-shek) dies and is succeeded as premier and president of Taiwan by his son Jiang Jing Guo (Chiang Ching-kuo).

16 April The communist Khmer Rouge, led by Pol Pot, defeats Lon Nol's government in Cambodia and seizes Phnom Penh (17 April). Cambodia is renamed Kampuchea. The Khmer Rouge, seeking to create a self-sufficient workers' utopia, begins a mass extermination of peasants and dissidents, along with intellectuals and educated professionals. Everyone over the age of 10 is forced to work in the fields, and marriage is abolished.

30 April Communist North Vietnam wins the war for control of Vietnam when South Vietnamese Gen. Duong Van Minh surrenders Saigon. 1373 US personnel and 5595 Vietnamese refugees are evacuated by helicopter. It is a bitter humiliation for the US government, which lacked the public support to aid the South. President Thieu has been convinced such help would come if his state was near collapse, and his army has squandered mountains of military supplies in attempts to secure control over the countryside. US sanctions will, however, do much to strangle the economy of the newly reunified nation.

14 Aug. Sheikh Mujibur Rahman, first prime minister and now president of Bangladesh (see 1971), is assassinated. The army assumes control, and Gen. Zia ur-Rahman will rule until 1981.

2 Dec. The communist Pathet Lao leader, Souphanouvong,

abolishes the monarchy in Laos, which now becomes a people's democratic republic.

6 Dec. Indonesian troops invade East Timor, where nationalists have proclaimed independence (28 Nov.) following Portuguese withdrawal from the territory.

– In Sri Lanka the Liberation Tigers of Tamil Eelam (LTTE or Tamil Tigers) are founded to fight for a Tamil homeland in N Sri Lanka by political and military means. Sri Lanka's Tamils (like their fellow Tamils in S India) are predominantly Hindu, unlike Sri Lanka's majority Sinhalese, who are mainly Buddhist.

THE AMERICAS

3 Jan. President Ford signs the Trade Reform Act, designed to increase Soviet–American trade. Congress insists on attaching the Jackson–Vanik Amendment, making it conditional on greater freedom for Jewish emigration from the USSR. The Soviet government cannot tolerate such interference in internal affairs, and the trade agreement is cancelled (14 Jan.).

1 May The US Securities and Exchange Commission orders the abolition of the fixed commission rate on Wall Street. Lower rates increase the number of individual investors and the amount of money available for investment.

25 Nov. Suriname (formerly Dutch Guiana) becomes independent of the Netherlands.

SUB-SAHARAN AFRICA

25 June Mozambique becomes independent of Portugal, and Samora Machel forms a Marxist government.

5 July The Cape Verde Islands (off W Africa) become independent of Portugal.

6 July The Indian Ocean islands of Comoros become independent of France.

27 Aug. Former emperor of Ethiopia Haile Selassie dies under house arrest.

10 Nov. Angola becomes independent of Portugal. The new state descends into civil war, with three rival guerrilla groups vying for control. The Marxist-Leninist MPLA under Dr Agostinho Neto is opposed by the South-African aided UNITA in the S of the country, and by the FNLA. The MPLA, aided by Cuban troops, will gain the upper hand.

30 Nov. Dahomey is renamed Benin.

– Chinese technology has helped to complete the Great Uhuru railway, which links Zambia with Tanzania.

– In South Africa Chief Mangosuthu Gatsha Buthelezi founds the Inkatha organization to represent the nationalist aspirations of the Zulu, South Africa's largest ethnic group.

AUSTRALASIA AND OCEANIA

16 Sept. Papua and New Guinea, administered jointly by Australia since 1945, become independent within the Commonwealth.

11 Nov. The Australian Labor prime minister Gough Whitlam is dismissed by governor-general Sir John Kerr when Whitlam refuses to call a general election. Kerr installs a caretaker government under Liberal leader Malcolm Fraser, who wins the ensuing general election (Dec.).

29 Nov. In New Zealand Robert Muldoon becomes prime minister.

ECONOMY AND SOCIETY

1 Oct. In the Philippines Muhammad Ali defeats Joe Frazier in an epic heavyweight boxing bout dubbed the 'Thriller in Manila'.

– In Britain free birth control is made available to all women and men on the National Health Service.

– In Britain the Sex Discrimination Act introduces the Equal Opportunities Commission.

– In Seattle, USA, William Gates founds the Microsoft Corporation with his friend Paul Allen. It will become the dominant producer of computer software.

SCIENCE AND TECHNOLOGY

– The first personal computer, the Altair 8800, designed by Micro Instrumentation and Telemetry Systems, is launched.

ARTS AND HUMANITIES

Literature
14 Feb. The novelist P.G. Wodehouse dies.

Saul Bellow, *Humboldt's Gift*, novel.

Malcolm Bradbury, *The History Man*, novel.

Paul Fussell, *The Great War and Modern Memory*, history.

Eugene D. Genovese, *Roll, Jordan, Roll: The World the Slaves Made*, history.

Seamus Heaney, *North*, poetry collection.

Ruth Prawer Jhabvala, *Heat and Dust*, novel.

David Mamet, *American Buffalo*, play.

Gabriel García Márquez, *El otoño del patriarca* (The Autumn of the Patriarch), novel.

V.S. Naipaul, *Guerrillas*, novel.

Harold Pinter, *No Man's Land*, play.

Paul Scott, *A Division of the Spoils*, final novel in his 'Raj Quartet'.

Visual Arts and Architecture
David Hockney, stage set designs for a production at Glyndebourne of Igor Stravinsky's *The Rake's Progress*.

Roy Lichtenstein, *Cubist Still Life with Lemons*, painting.

Music
9 Aug. Dmitri Shostakovich, Russian composer, dies in Moscow.

Pierre Boulez, *Rituel in memoriam Bruno Maderna*, orchestral work dedicated to the Italian composer and conductor who died in 1973.

David Bowie, 'Space Oddity', single.

Bob Dylan, *Blood on the Tracks*, album.

Steve Harley and Cockney Rebel, 'Make Me Smile (Come Up and See Me)', single.

Led Zeppelin, *Physical Graffiti*, album.

Joni Mitchell, *The Hissing of Summer Lawns*, album.

Pink Floyd, *Wish You Were Here*, album.

Queen, 'Bohemian Rhapsody', single.

Patti Smith, *Horses*, album.

Bruce Springsteen, *Born to Run*, album.

Rod Stewart, 'Sailing', single.

10 cc 'I'm Not In Love', single.

Film

Milos Forman, *One Flew Over the Cuckoo's Nest*, starring Jack Nicholson.

John Huston, *The Man Who Would be King,* starring Sean Connery.

Stanley Kubrick, *Barry Lyndon*, starring Ryan O'Neal.

Sidney Lumet, *Dog Day Afternoon*, starring Al Pacino.

Jim Sharman, *The Rocky Horror Picture Show*.

Steven Spielberg, *Jaws*, starring Robert Shaw and Roy Scheider.

1976

EUROPE

Jan. In Britain Norman Scott, whose dog Rinka has been shot (see 24 Oct. 1975), alleges in court that he is the object of a murder conspiracy because of a supposed gay relationship between him and Jeremy Thorpe, leader of the Liberal Party.

16 Mar. In Britain Harold Wilson resigns as prime minister. He fears the onset of memory loss associated with Alzheimer's disease. James Callaghan, the foreign secretary, replaces him as Labour Party leader (3 April) and as prime minister (5 April).

9 May German terrorist Ulrike Meinhof commits suicide by hanging in a Stuttgart prison.

12 May In Britain Jeremy Thorpe is forced to resign as leader of the Liberal Party following the Norman Scott affair (see above). In 1978 Thorpe will be charged with conspiracy to murder Scott, but will be acquitted.

2 July In Britain David Steel becomes leader of the Liberal Party.

21 July The British ambassador to Ireland, Christopher Ewart-Biggs, is killed in a car bomb explosion engineered by the Irish Republican Army (IRA).

25 Aug. Jacques Chirac resigns as French prime minister and is succeeded by Raymond Barre.

26 Aug. Prince Bernhard, husband of Queen Juliana of the Netherlands, resigns all his public posts after being accused of corruption in his business dealings with the Lockheed Aircraft Corporation.

19 Sept. In Sweden 44 years of government by the Social Democrats ends when a new conservative coalition is elected.

Sept. The British government asks the International Monetary Fund (IMF) for a loan of $3.9 billion.

Dec. In France the Gaullist party becomes the Rassemblement pour la République (Rally for the Republic). Jacques Chirac becomes party president.

– An amendment to Britain's 1965 Race Relations Act establishes the Race Relations Commission to promote equal opportunities.

MIDDLE EAST AND NORTH AFRICA

27 Jan. The US delegate vetoes a UN Security Resolution calling for an independent Palestinian state and for the total withdrawal of all Israeli forces from territories occupied since 1967.

Feb. Spain withdraws from Spanish Sahara (now Western Sahara).

14 April Western Sahara (formerly Spanish Sahara, see Nov. 1975) is divided between Morocco and Mauretania. The pro-independence Polisario movement rejects partition and wages a guerrilla war with Algerian support.

31 May Syria intervenes in the Lebanese civil war, moving forces into the Bekaa Valley, E of Beirut, to oppose the Palestine Liberation Organization (PLO). Syria's President Assad, who has hitherto supported the PLO and their Lebanese Muslim allies, is now conniving with Lebanon's Phalangist Christian rulers to bring the PLO to heel. Assad has dreams of a Greater Syrian power-base, through which he aims to become the dominant Arab power in the region. Lebanon, beset by internal conflict and now by foreign intervention, will lapse into ungovernable chaos.

4 July Israeli commandos storm an Air France plane that has been hijacked by Palestinian activists and forced to land in Entebbe Airport, Uganda. They free 104 hostages.

10 Oct. The Israeli government promises Egypt that Israeli forces will withdraw from occupied territory in Sinai.

ASIA

8 Jan. Zhou Enlai, prime minister of China, dies: a public debate ensues about his legacy. Hardliners revile his memory. A mass protest occurs in Tiananmen Square, Beijing (5 April), when some 100,000 Chinese gather in support of the dead Zhou. Political prisoners begin to be released, and universities reopen for the first time since the Cultural Revolution (1966). Academic degrees, previously abolished as a sign of class distinction, will also return (1980).

2 April Prince Sihanouk of Kampuchea (Cambodia) is forced to resign by the Khmer Rouge and is replaced by a president, Khieu Samphan. A new constitution places the Khmer Rouge, led by Pol Pot, in control of the country.

29 April The supreme court of India rules that the government can imprison political opponents without legal hearings. Rumours are widespread that such prisoners are being tortured.

26 July The former prime minister of Japan, Kakuei Tanaka, is arrested on charges that he accepted bribes from the Lockheed Aircraft Corporation.

28 July The worst earthquake in modern history, at Tangshan, China, kills some 250,000 people.

July Indonesia declares East Timor (see 6 Dec. 1975) its 17th province. The United Nations does not recognize the annexation.

9 Sept. Chinese Communist Party chairman Mao Zedong (see p. 573) dies. Following a brief power struggle for the succession, Hua Guofeng becomes Mao's successor as chairman of the Chinese Communist Party (7 Oct.). Mao's widow, Jiang Qing, along with the other extreme radicals in her Gang of Four, is arrested on charges of subverting the state.

THE AMERICAS

15 Jan. Californian heiress Patricia Hearst goes on trial for bank robbery. Her claims that she was abused by her kidnappers (see 4 Feb. 1974) do not prevent her from being found guilty.

24 Mar. A military junta deposes Isabel Perón and her government; martial law is declared in Argentina.

2 July The US Supreme Court reverses its 1972 decision and rules that capital punishment is not a 'cruel and unusual punishment'.

4 July José López Portillo is elected president of Mexico. The Mexican peso is devalued (31 Aug.) and US imports quadruple in price. Inflation during the next year falls from 45% to 20%.

1 Aug. Trinidad and Tobago's new constitution creates a republic.

16 Sept. The Hyde Amendment (sponsored by the Republican Congressman Henry Hyde of Illinois) is approved by US Congress: it bars the use of federal money for abortions unless the mother's life is endangered.

21 Sept. Orlando Letelier, former Chilean ambassador to the USA and opponent of President Pinochet, is killed by a car bomb in Washington, D.C.

1 Oct. International banks meeting in New York agree a loan of 800 million eurodollars to aid Mexico's economic regeneration.

2 Nov. The Democratic candidate Jimmy Carter, former governor of Georgia, is elected president of the USA, defeating President Gerald Ford.

15 Nov. In Canada René Lévesque's Parti Québecois wins a resounding victory in provincial elections. Prime minister Lévesque promises a referendum on independence by 1980.

SUB-SAHARAN AFRICA

16 June Five days of rioting start at Soweto, a township of some one million people near Johannesburg, South Africa. School students start by protesting at the compulsory teaching of Afrikaans: 176 are killed and over a thousand injured. The language ruling is reversed (6 July).

25 June In Uganda Idi Amin is declared president for life.

29 June The Seychelles becomes an independent republic within the Commonwealth.

19 Sept. Rhodesian premier Ian Smith agrees to black majority rule by 1978.

26 Oct. The African homeland of Transkei (see 1970) becomes nominally independent within South Africa's borders. Some 1.3 million African Xhosa people who have been denied South African citizenship are thereby declared to be citizens of Transkei. No government recognizes Transkei as a state.

ECONOMY AND SOCIETY

July–Aug. The 21st Olympic Games are held in Montreal, Canada. 20 African nations boycott the Games in protest at New Zealand's rugby tour of South Africa.

24 Aug. In Britain Denis Howell is appointed minister for drought following a record hot summer. Rain falls in E England three days later.

SCIENCE AND TECHNOLOGY

21 Jan. Supersonic Concorde flights run by Air France and British Airways begin to operate between Paris and Rio, and London and Bahrain. Flights to Washington, D.C., start on 24 May.

26 July A cloud of poisonous dioxin gas escapes into the air after an explosion at the Icmesa chemical factory at Seveso near Milan, Italy.

13 Nov. The World Health Organization declares that Asia is free of smallpox for the first time in history.

– Legionnaires' disease, a form of pneumonia, is identified for the first time when it kills members of the American Legion meeting in Philadelphia.

– Apple Computers is founded in California by Steve Jobs and Stephen Wozniak.

ARTS AND HUMANITIES
Literature

12 Jan. Agatha Christie, English crime writer, dies.

– Rupert Murdoch, an Australian newspaper publisher, acquires the *New York Post*.

David Edgar, *Destiny*, play.

Alex Haley, *Roots*, chronicle of an African-American family.

Manuel Puig, *El beso de la mujer araña* (Kiss of the Spider Woman*)*, novel.

Muriel Spark, *The Takeover*, novel.

David Storey, *Saville*, novel.

Patrick White, *A Fringe of Leaves*, novel.

Visual Arts and Architecture

1 April German artist Max Ernst dies.

18 Nov. American artist Man Ray dies.

– The National Theatre on London's South Bank, designed by Denys Lasdun, is completed.

– In Britain a visitor to the Tate Gallery, London, throws dye over Carl Andre's *Equivalent VIII* (the 'Tate bricks') in protest at the perceived waste of public money they represent.

Music

21 July First performance in Avignon of Philip Glass's opera *Einstein on the Beach*, using new techniques of electronic music.

4 Dec. Benjamin Britten, English composer, pianist and conductor, dies at Aldeburgh, Suffolk.

– Punk Rock, a reaction against the commercialism and complacency of the pop music mainstream as well as the pretensions of progressive rock, develops in Britain, but soon becomes highly commercialized itself.

Abba, 'Mamma Mia', 'Fernando' and 'Dancing Queen', singles.

Chicago, 'If You Leave Me Now', single.

The Eagles, *Hotel California*, album.

Fleetwood Mac, *Fleetwood Mac*, album.

Henryk Górecki, Symphony No. 3 (*Symphony of Sorrowful Songs*).

Arvo Pärt, *Cantus in Memory of Benjamin Britten*, work for string orchestra.

The Ramones, *The Ramones*, album.

Steve Reich, *Music for 18 Musicians*.

Alfred Schnittke, *Piano Quintet*.

Sex Pistols, 'Anarchy in the UK', single.

Film

Derek Jarman, *Sebastiane*.

Alan Pakula, *All the President's Men*, starring Robert Redford and Dustin Hoffman.

Nicholas Roeg, *The Man Who Fell to Earth*, starring David Bowie.

John Schlesinger, *Marathon Man*, starring Dustin Hoffman and Laurence Olivier.

Martin Scorsese, *Taxi Driver*, starring Robert De Niro.

Wim Wenders, *Kings of the Road*.

1977

EUROPE

6 Jan. The former Labour home secretary Roy Jenkins becomes Britain's first president of the European Community (EC) Commission (a body that proposes EC legislation and is answerable to the European parliament).

26 Jan. The US State Department states that the Czech government is violating the Helsinki Accord (1 Aug. 1975) by persecuting the country's dissidents. Political opponents of the Czech government have signed Charter 77, a statement of human rights both in Czechoslovakia and in the wider world (7 Jan.). The US government warns the USSR not to persecute the Nobel scientist Andrei Sakharov (28 Jan.). Constant human rights criticism by President Carter angers the Soviet leadership, and a number of those associated with Charter 77 will be imprisoned. The Soviet Jewish dissident Anatoly Sharansky is arrested by the Soviet government, on charges of plotting with the CIA (15 Mar.).

23 Mar. British Labour prime minister James Callaghan and Liberal Party leader David Steel agree to a parliamentary pact (the 'Lib–Lab pact') to help Labour remain in power.

Mar. In France Jacques Chirac is elected mayor of Paris.

7 April Siegfried Buback, the West German chief prosecutor, is assassinated by Baader-Meinhof terrorists.

5–11 June In Britain celebrations are held to mark the Silver Jubilee of Queen Elizabeth II.

16 June In the Republic of Ireland Fianna Fáil defeats the Fine Gael–Labour coalition in a general election and returns to power with a rehabilitated Charles J. Haughey (see 1970) as taoiseach (prime minister).

5 Sept. Hanns Martin Schleyer, head of the West German Industries federation, is kidnapped by Baader-Meinhof terrorists.

21 Sept. Soviet and US delegates agree the terms of a Nuclear Non-Proliferation treaty, which is now signed; 13 other countries sign the treaty. Non-nuclear nations are invited to renounce nuclear weapons and accept the inspection of the nuclear facilities, but neither China nor aspiring nuclear powers such as Israel and South Africa will subscribe to it.

18 Oct. German terrorist Andreas Baader is found shot dead in his cell in Stuttgart prison. His death is recorded as a suicide. Hanns Martin Schleyer (see above) is murdered in reprisal.

– In Britain the shipbuilding and ship-repairing industries, and the aircraft-manufacturing industry, are nationalized.

MIDDLE EAST AND NORTH AFRICA

21 June In Israel Menachem Begin, a former member of the Irgun, a Jewish guerrilla group, and now leader of the right-wing Likud Party, becomes prime minister.

19–21 Nov. Egyptian leader Anwar al-Sadat visits Israel and enrages Arab sentiment by breaking ranks with other Arab states. Sadat calculates that the expression of such outrage is a price worth paying if he can negotiate the recovery of Sinai.

ASIA

20 Mar. Morarji Desai is elected prime minister of India. The 81-year-old replaces Indira Gandhi, whose Congress Party is defeated. Mrs Gandhi has been discredited by her imposition of an 18-month state of emergency, during which her son Sanjay has introduced a harsh compulsory birth-control programme.

2 July The Gang of Four are expelled from the Chinese Communist Party, and Deng Xiaoping, once purged by the party, returns to high office.

5 July Zulfikar Ali Bhutto is toppled as prime minister of Pakistan by a military coup led by Gen. Zia ul-Haq; martial law is imposed and political parties are banned. Bhutto is arrested on charges of having conspired to murder Ahmad Raza Kasuri in 1974 (3 Sept.).

19 Nov. Some 10,000 people are killed in Andhra Pradesh, India, after a cyclone hits the Bay of Bengal.

THE AMERICAS

17 Jan. Convicted murderer Gary Gilmore is shot by a firing squad in Utah. His execution ends a 10-year moratorium on capital punishment in the USA.

20 Jan. Jimmy Carter takes office as 39th US president. Carter pardons almost all those US citizens who evaded the military draft to serve in Vietnam but excludes deserters.

25 Jan. The US Supreme Court reverses a previous decision (1966) and rules that a suspect in a criminal inquiry who is not under arrest can be interrogated without being informed of their legal rights.

15 April In Argentina Jacobo Timerman, the publisher of the newspaper *La Opinión*, is arrested and tortured as part of a concerted move against dissidents by the ruling junta.

21 April President Carter proposes a national energy conservation plan to discourage waste and excessive consumption.

7 Sept. President Carter signs a treaty with the Panamanian government that returns the canal zone to Panama.

SUB-SAHARAN AFRICA

Feb. Tafari Benti, president of Ethiopia, is murdered in an army coup in Addis Ababa; Col. Haile Mariam Mengistu becomes head of state (23 April). He imports Cuban advisers and receives Soviet military backing, which has been diverted from Somalia. Mengistu institutes a reign of terror to stamp out opposition.

27 June Djibouti (formerly French Somaliland) becomes independent.

12 Sept. In South Africa Steve Biko, an African activist, dies in police custody six days after being arrested.

2 Dec. The South African judicial system decides that the security police were not responsible for the death of Steve Biko, despite evidence that he was savagely beaten.

4 Dec. In a ceremony that becomes emblematic of post-colonial vainglory, President Jean-Bédel Bokassa is crowned emperor of the Central African Republic, which has become the Central African Empire. France, the country's former colonial master, largely finances the ceremony.

ECONOMY AND SOCIETY

9 Mar. The US government bans the use of saccharin as an artificial sweetener because it is believed to be carcinogenic.

10 May Television is introduced in South Africa.

22 May The Orient Express train makes its last journey from Paris to Istanbul.

Sept. Laker Airways starts a low-fare service between London and New York in an attempt to break the international air fare cartel.

– J.K. Galbraith publishes *The Age of Uncertainty*.

ARTS AND HUMANITIES

Literature

2 July The Russian-born novelist Vladimir Nabokov dies.

Steven Berkoff, *East*, play.

Bruce Chatwin, *In Patagonia*, travel writing.

Patrick Leigh Fermor, *A Time of Gifts*, travel writing.

John Fowles, *Daniel Martin*, novel.

Colleen McCullough, *The Thorn Birds*, novel.

James Alan McPherson, *Elbow Room*, novel.

Paul Scott, *Staying On*, novel.

J.R.R. Tolkien, *The Silmarillion*, posthumously published collection of tales.

Visual Arts and Architecture

31 Jan. The Pompidou Centre, designed by Richard Rogers and Renzo Piano, opens.

David Hockney, *My Parents*, painting.

Music

16 Aug. US singer Elvis Presley dies in Memphis.

16 Sept. Greek-American soprano Maria Callas dies.

14 Oct. US singer Bing Crosby dies.

– First performance of Michael Tippett's opera *The Ice Break*.

The Clash, *The Clash*, album.

Elvis Costello, *My Aim is True*, album.

Julie Covington, 'Don't Cry For Me, Argentina', single.

Ian Dury, *New Boots and Panties!!*, album.

Fleetwood Mac, *Rumours*, album.

Bob Marley and the Wailers, *Exodus*, album.

Arvo Pärt, *Fratres*, work for chamber ensemble.

The Sex Pistols, *Never Mind the Bollocks, Here's the Sex Pistols*, album, including the punk band's contribution to Queen Elizabeth II's Silver Jubilee 'God Save the Queen'.

Weather Report, *Heavy Weather*, jazz-rock fusion album.

Wings, 'Mull of Kintyre', single.

Film

25 Dec. English-born actor and film director Charlie Chaplin dies.

Woody Allen, *Annie Hall*.

John Badham, *Saturday Night Fever*, starring John Travolta.

Luis Buñuel, *Cet obscur objet du désir* (That Obscure Object of Desire).

George Lucas, *Star Wars*.

Steven Spielberg, *Close Encounters of the Third Kind*.

Paolo and Vittorio Taviani, *Padre Padrone*.

Andrzej Wajda, *Man of Marble*.

Wim Wenders, *Der amerikanische Freund* (The American Friend).

1978

EUROPE

17 Feb. In Northern Ireland an IRA incendiary attack on the La Mon hotel in Belfast kills 16 people in a fireball.

16 Mar. Aldo Moro, former prime minister of Italy, is kidnapped by Red Brigades (*Brigate rosse*) terrorists. Moro is shot after the government rejects demands that imprisoned Red Brigades members be released. His body is discovered in Rome (9 May).

18 May Italians vote for the legalization of abortion within the first 90 days of pregnancy, and so reject the Catholic Church's teaching.

25 May In Britain the Lib–Lab pact (see 23 Mar. 1977) comes to an end.

14 July Soviet dissident Anatoly Sharansky is sentenced to 13 years' imprisonment and hard labour.

11 Sept. Georgi Markov, an exiled Bulgarian writer, is assassinated in London when he is stabbed with a poisoned umbrella.

30 Nov. In Britain *The Times* and *The Sunday Times* newspapers stop publication for 11 months as a result of disputes with the print unions on working practices. The unions see new technology as a threat to their traditional livelihoods, and the attempt to introduce computerized typesetting has already led to a series of slow-downs and strikes.

– Britain experiences the beginning of the 'Winter of Discontent' as industrial unrest continues and strikes proliferate in the public sector. The army assumes fire-fighting responsibilities and rubbish piles up on city streets.

MIDDLE EAST AND NORTH AFRICA

7 Jan. Riots break out in the holy city of Qom, Iran; the shah's land reform programme and his secular-minded promotion of female rights have angered Islamic religious leaders.

14 Mar. The Israeli army invades S Lebanon in search of Palestinian (PLO) guerrillas. The Israelis attack and force the withdrawal to the N of Palestinian forces, which have been attacking Israeli positions and soldiers. Having established a security zone in S Lebanon, the Israelis start a phased withdrawal (11 April), which is completed by 13 June. The Israelis hand over their posts to the Lebanese Christian militias. A United Nations peace-keeping force is set up in a buffer zone in S Lebanon.

9 June The head of the Iranian secret police, the Savak, is arrested on charges of corruption.

24 June The president of North Yemen is killed by a suitcase bomb carried by a South Yemen envoy. Two days later the president of South Yemen is deposed and executed.

17 Sept. President Carter brokers the Camp David Accord between president Anwar al-Sadat of Egypt and prime minister Menachem Begin of Israel. The Egyptians recognize Israel, and the Israelis agree to withdraw from Sinai, but a wider peace, settling the main issues of the region, especially the Palestinian question, is not in sight.

6 Nov. The shah of Iran imposes martial law in an attempt to contain escalating unrest. It has only limited effect. The shah, bowing to Islamic pressure, also closes casinos and dismisses from his employment members of the non-conforming Bahai sect. Islamic fundamentalism is not appeased.

17 Dec. The 13 member states of the Organization of Petroleum Exporting Countries (OPEC), meeting in Abu Dhabi, agree to raise oil prices by 14.5% in four stages by the end of 1979.

24 Dec. Demonstrators in Tehran try to storm the US embassy.

27 Dec. President Houari Boumédienne of Algeria dies and will be succeeded by Chadli Benjedid.

29 Dec. In Iran the shah asks Shahpur Bakhtiar to form a civilian administration. It is a last desperate attempt to prevent an Islamist fundamentalist revolution.

ASIA

3 Jan. In India the Congress Party suffers a schism: a faction led by Indira Gandhi splits off to become the Congress (I) Party.

18 Mar. In Pakistan the death sentence is passed on former prime minister Zulfikar Ali Bhutto.

27 April A left-wing coup ousts President Mohammad Daoud of Afghanistan (see 19 July 1973). Mur Mohammad Taraki heads the new Afghan government, which is backed by a 20-year economic and military treaty with the USSR. Daoud is executed. The coup is opposed by conservative Muslim groups. Many thousands of refugees flee to Iran and Pakistan.

12 Aug. The Chinese and Japanese governments sign a friendship treaty, which the Soviet leadership views as hostile to its interests.

15 Dec. The USA recognizes the People's Republic of China and will (from 1 Jan. 1979) break off diplomatic relations with Taiwan. The USA will put pressure on the Soviet leaders to improve their own relations with Washington and to make concessions in the current Strategic Arms Limitation Talks negotiations (SALT II).

25 Dec. Vietnamese forces invade Kampuchea (Cambodia).

– China adopts the Pinyin transcription system for transcribing Chinese characters in Roman letters, replacing the Wade-Giles system. Peking thus becomes Beijing and Mao Tse-tung becomes Mao Zedong.

THE AMERICAS

10 Jan. Pedro Joaquín Chamorro, publisher of *La Prensa* (The Press) newspaper, which is opposed to the Somoza regime in Nicaragua, is shot and killed in Managua.

16 Mar. and 18 April The two Panama Canal Treaties, between Panama and the USA, provide for the neutrality of the canal and its operation by the Panamanian authorities.

6 June The people of the US state of California vote for a 57% reduction in property taxes; tax revolts are now spreading to other states.

22 Aug. The Sandinista Liberation Front, named after the guerrilla leader Augusto César Sandino (killed in 1934), seizes the national palace in Managua, Nicaragua, and tries to eject the dictator, Anastasio Somoza.

24 Oct. Inflation in the USA is now running at 6% and President Carter proposes a voluntary prices and incomes policy.

3 Nov. The Caribbean island of Dominica becomes independent within the Commonwealth.

18 Nov. Followers of the San Francisco cult leader Jim Jones start to escape from the settlement he has founded in Jonestown, Guyana. Jones, however, orders his remaining acolytes to drink a punch laced with cyanide. 913 die, including 276 children. Jones shoots himself.

– In Guatemala Gen. Romeo Lucas García starts a four-year period of rule.

SUB-SAHARAN AFRICA

Mar. In Rhodesia, Ian Smith and three African nationalist leaders agree to form an interim power-sharing government that will work towards eventual black majority rule. The more radical nationalist leaders, Joshua Nkomo and Robert Mugabe of the Patriotic Front, are excluded from this government.

May–June French troops help crush a left-wing rising against President Mobutu of Zaire.

22 Aug. President Jomo Kenyatta of Kenya dies; he will be succeeded by Daniel arap Moi (10 Oct.).

20 Sept. In South Africa John Vorster resigns as prime minister and is replaced by P.W. Botha (29 Sept.). Vorster becomes president.

AUSTRALASIA AND OCEANIA

7 July The Solomon Islands become independent within the Commonwealth.

30 Sept. Tuvalu, a group of islands in the SW Pacific (formerly the Ellice Islands), becomes independent within the Commonwealth.

ECONOMY AND SOCIETY

2 April The US television series *Dallas* starts to be broadcast on CBS.

May–June Argentina, the host nation, wins the 11th soccer World Cup.

6 Aug. Pope Paul VI dies and is succeeded (26 Aug.) by Albino Luciani, archbishop of Venice, as John Paul I. However, he dies suddenly (28 Sept.). Cardinal Karol Wojtyla of Poland is elected as John Paul II (16 Oct.) and becomes the first non-Italian pope since 1523.

SCIENCE AND TECHNOLOGY

– The first test-tube baby is born in Britain. The technique of in vitro fertilization (IVF) allows eggs and sperm to unite to form an embryo under laboratory conditions. The embryo is then planted in the womb of an otherwise unfertile mother.

ARTS AND HUMANITIES

Literature

Beryl Bainbridge, *Young Adolf*, novel.
John Cheever, *The Stories of John Cheever*, short stories.
J.G. Farrell, *The Singapore Grip*, novel.
Graham Greene, *The Human Factor*, novel.
David Hare, *Plenty*, play.
John Irving, *The World According to Garp*, novel.

Emmanuel Le Roy Ladurie, *Montaillou: village occitan de 1294 à 1324* (Montaillou: Cathars and Catholics in a French Village, 1294–1324), history.

Ian McEwan, *The Cement Garden*, novel.

Armistead Maupin, *Tales of the City*, novel.

Iris Murdoch, *The Sea, the Sea*, novel.

Georges Perec, *Life, A User's Manual*, novel.

Harold Pinter, *Betrayal*, play.

Visual Arts and Architecture

10 July Italian artist Giorgio de Chirico dies.

13 Nov. American illustrator Norman Rockwell dies.

Andy Warhol, *Self-Portrait*.

Music

1 May Aram Khachaturian, Russian composer, dies in Moscow.

– First performance of György Ligeti's opera *Le grand macabre* (The Great Macabre).

– Disco music (exemplified by the Bee Gees' soundtrack of the film *Saturday Night Fever*) becomes popular.

John Adams, *Shaker Loops*, work for string quartet, later modified for septet.

Blondie, 'Denis', single, and *Parallel Lines*, album.

Kate Bush, 'Wuthering Heights', single.

Andrew Lloyd Webber and Tim Rice, *Evita*, musical depicting the life and death of María Eva de Péron, wife of Gen. Juan Péron, former ruler of Argentina.

Meat Loaf, *Bat out of Hell*, album.

10 cc, 'Dreadlock Holiday', single.

John Travolta and Olivia Newton-John, 'You're the One That I Want' and 'Summer Nights', singles (from the film *Grease*).

The Village People, 'YMCA' and 'In the Navy', singles.

Film

John Carpenter, *Halloween*, starring Donald Pleasence.

Michael Cimino, *The Deer Hunter*, starring Robert De Niro.

Richard Donner, *Superman*, starring Christopher Reeve.

Alan Parker, *Midnight Express*, starring Brad Davis.

1979

EUROPE

20 Feb. In a Belfast court, 11 members of a Loyalist gang known as the 'Shankill Butchers' are given life sentences for a series of brutal murders of Catholics in Northern Ireland.

1 Mar. Devolution referendums are held in Scotland and Wales. Scottish voters approve devolution but the required level of majority is not achieved. Welsh voters reject devolution.

13 Mar. The European Monetary System (EMS) comes into being. The EMS, an attempt to bring stability to Europe after the economic disruption of the 1973 'oil shock', is based on the Exchange Rate Mechanism (ERM), a voluntary system of controlling exchange rates.

28 Mar. In Britain, following a long period of industrial unrest, mostly by poorly paid public employees, the Labour government loses a vote of confidence in the House of Commons. The prime minister, James Callaghan, who decided against

calling a general election the previous autumn, is now forced into a general election.

30 Mar. Airey Neave, the Conservative shadow spokesman on Northern Ireland, is assassinated by a car bomb planted in the House of Commons car park by the Irish National Liberation Army (INLA), an offshoot of the IRA.

3 May The Conservatives win the British general election, winning 339 seats to Labour's 269. Margaret Thatcher becomes Britain's first woman prime minister. The Conservatives will remain in government for 18 years.

Let's face the music and dance.

Irving Berlin, *Follow the Fleet* (1936)

8 May In Britain the former Liberal Party leader Jeremy Thorpe goes on trial at the Old Bailey accused of conspiring to murder Norman Scott, who claims to have been Thorpe's lover. He is acquitted of all charges, but his career is ruined.

2 June In visiting his native Poland, Pope John Paul II becomes the first pope to visit a communist state.

27 Aug. The Irish Republican Army (IRA) kills Lord Mountbatten, last viceroy of India, by planting a bomb on his fishing boat off the coast of Co. Sligo, W Ireland. On the same day, 18 British soldiers are killed by an IRA bomb near Warrenpoint, Co. Down.

25 Oct. In Spain referendums approve devolved government for Catalonia and the Basque Country.

Oct. A scandal erupts in France when it is revealed that French president Valéry Giscard d'Estaing has accepted an undeclared gift of diamonds from Jean-Bédel Bokassa, emperor of the Central African Republic.

15 Nov. In Britain, in a statement to Parliament, Margaret Thatcher states that Sir Anthony Blunt, Keeper of the Queen's Pictures and art historian of international renown, has been known for many years to have been a Soviet spy during World War II. Having confessed (1964), he has been given immunity from prosecution. He is now stripped of his knighthood and other honours.

MIDDLE EAST AND NORTH AFRICA

16 Jan. The shah of Iran, Muhammad Reza Shah Pahlavi, leaves the country and arrives in Egypt. He is abandoning Iran to Islamic fundamentalists. Ayatollah Ruhollah Khomeini, a Shiite Muslim leader who has been living in exile in Paris for 15 years, returns to Tehran (1 Feb.). His supporters take to the streets and acclaim him as the country's leader. The prime minister, Shahpur Bakhtiar, flees Iran (12 Feb.). Thousands of Iranians are killed in rioting and in mass executions of the shah's supporters. The Iranian Revolution is a rebellion both cultural and political against the influence of the West and, specifically, that of the USA in domestic Iranian affairs. It abolishes co-educational schools and campaigns for women to veil their faces and bodies.

18 Jan. When a Palestinian bomb explodes in Jerusalem the Israelis retaliate (19 Jan.) by moving again into S Lebanon. The border conflict is stopped by a truce (24 Jan), but then continues when Israeli forces pursue into Lebanon the Palestinian guerrillas who have attacked an Israeli settlement (9 May).

17 Feb. Iran's new Islamic government announces that it will restart the export of oil (5 Mar.) but at a price 30% higher than that set by the OPEC agreement (see 17 Dec. 1978). There are renewed fears of recession in the West.

24 Feb. War breaks out between North and South Yemen over a border dispute. President Carter sends military advisers and arms to the North; Cuban and Soviet troops arrive in the South.

26 Mar. Egypt and Israel sign a peace treaty in Washington, D.C.; but Egypt's action is denounced by other Arab and Islamic powers in the region.

23 Oct. The shah of Iran is allowed entry to the USA for medical treatment. In reprisal, Iranian protestors seize the US embassy in Tehran (4 Nov.), take 66 hostages and demand the extradition of the shah from the USA to Iran. The shah leaves the USA for Panama (16 Dec.). Americans are shocked to discover that their successive governments' support for Israel and for other regimes in the region has made their country an object of such anger. The hostages' freedom is a major priority for President Carter. Their captors, however, care nothing for US power, and Carter's inability to bribe or browbeat them makes him look weak.

– In the first half of the year OPEC nations increase their oil prices by some 50%; the seven major oil-importing industrial democracies meet at Tokyo (29 June) and agree to set limits on their imports.

ASIA

7 Jan. Phnom Penh, capital of Cambodia, falls to the Vietnamese, who oust the Khmer Rouge. The true extent of the horrors of Pol Pot's rule begins to be revealed to the world.

14 Feb. Adolph Dubs, US ambassador to Afghanistan, is killed when Afghan police try to release him from the Islamic activists who have abducted him.

3 April The Chinese decide not to renew their 1950 treaty of friendship with the USSR.

4 April In Pakistan former premier Zulfikar Ali Bhutto is hanged for conspiracy to murder (see 3 July 1977).

7 July China is granted most-favoured nation status by the US government and is thereby granted lower tariff rates for exports to the USA.

16 Oct. Chinese journalist and pro-democracy activist Wei Jingsheng is imprisoned for criticizing the Chinese communist system; a brief Chinese experiment in liberalization ends.

26 Oct. Park Chung-Hee, president of South Korea, is assassinated by the director of his security agency and lifelong friend, Kim Jae Kyu. Park has become increasingly intolerant

while ruling a nation demanding change. Choi Kyu-ha, the new president, releases imprisoned political opponents.

24 Dec. Soviet troops invade Afghanistan. The president, Hafizullah Amin, is convicted by a revolutionary tribunal of crimes against the state and executed (27 Dec.). He is replaced by Barbrak Karmal. The Soviet invasion will lead to civil war in Afghanistan. For strategic and anti-Soviet reasons the US government supports, and the CIA trains, Islamic guerrilla fighters (mujahedin) who oppose the Soviet occupation. For the Soviet leadership, who assumed they were simply installing a new, more effective and more Soviet-friendly government before withdrawing after a few months, it is the beginning of a bitter, costly and protracted war.

THE AMERICAS

1 Jan. The US government breaks off diplomatic relations with Iran.

22 Feb. The Caribbean island of St Lucia becomes independent within the Commonwealth.

8 Mar. Panic about nuclear safety ensues after a serious accident at the Three Mile Island nuclear plant near Harrisburg, Pennsylvania.

13 Mar. Maurice Bishop, leader of the left-wing New Jewel Movement, leads a successful coup in Grenada.

5 April President Carter allows US domestic oil exporters to increase their prices to OPEC levels. He also proposes an Energy Security Fund to help US consumers meet increased fuel costs, to promote alternative energy and improve public transport.

22 May In Canada Pierre Trudeau's Liberal Party is ousted in a general election. The Progressive Conservatives form a minority government.

18 June The governments of the USSR and the USA sign, at Vienna, a Strategic Arms Limitation Treaty (SALT II). The US Senate blocks its ratification, suspicious that the Soviet delegates have won too much in the negotiations. Both governments, however, indicate their willingness to abide by the treaty.

27 June In its judgement on United Steel Workers vs. Weber, the US Supreme Court upholds American companies' policies of reverse discrimination.

17 July After a two-month civil war in Nicaragua, Anastasio Somoza flees to Miami. Left-wing Sandinista forces enter Managua in triumph (20 July). US President Carter at first welcomes the downfall of a repellent dictator, but there is uneasiness in Washington at the radical nature of the new regime.

Aug.–Sept. Hurricane David hits the E USA and the Caribbean, where the Dominican Republic is particularly badly affected.

15 Oct. Carlos Humberto Romero, military dictator and president of El Salvador, is overthrown. The new ruling junta embarks on a land-distribution programme to benefit the peasantry.

27 Oct. The Caribbean islands of St Vincent and the Grenadines become independent within the Commonwealth.

27 Dec. The US Congress approves a loan of $1.2 billion to save the car manufacturer Chrysler from bankruptcy.

SUB-SAHARAN AFRICA

30 Jan. In Rhodesia Ian Smith is forced to accept the extension of the franchise to the country's African majority. He introduces a new constitution which proves unacceptable to the Zimbabwe African People's Union (ZAPU) of Joshua Nkomo and the Zimbabwe African National Union (ZANU) of Robert Mugabe, who see it as an attempt to continue white domination.

10 April In Uganda Kampala is occupied by Tanzanian troops: after eight years of oppression, Idi Amin is forced into exile. His despotism has favoured his own Muslim Kakwa tribe at the expense of the majority Christians and other tribes.

1 June Bishop Abel Muzorewa, a compliant black nationalist leader who has accepted Ian Smith's new constitution (see above), becomes prime minister of Zimbabwe-Rhodesia (as Rhodesia is now renamed). The more radical nationalist leaders Joshua Nkomo and Robert Mugabe continue to oppose the new constitution.

4 June John Vorster, president of South Africa, is forced out of office because of abuse of government funds spent on propaganda attempts in the USA.

4 June Flight Lt Jerry Rawlings becomes head of state in Ghana after a military coup. He allows an elected president, Hilla Limann, to succeed him (July).

3 Aug. Francisco Macias Nguema, the pro-Soviet president of Equatorial Guinea, is ousted by his nephew Lt-Col. Teodoro Obiang Nguema Mbasogo. He is found guilty of genocide and corruption and is executed.

20 Sept. Jean-Bédel Bokassa, self-proclaimed emperor of the Central African Republic, is overthrown in a bloodless coup following reports that he has participated in the murder of 100 schoolchildren. This is too much for his French backers, and French paratroopers bring his reign to an end. He is given asylum in the Ivory Coast. David Dacko returns to power as president; Bokassa goes into exile.

Sept. A Constitutional conference on Rhodesia is held at Lancaster House, London, between Britain and the interested Zimbabwean-Rhodesian parties. Under the resulting Lancaster House agreement they agree to a brief resumption of British rule in order to achieve a settlement. A British governor-general will arrange a timetable for independence and Commonwealth monitors will supervise the disarming of guerrillas.

AUSTRALASIA AND OCEANIA

11 July Kiribati, a group of islands in the SW Pacific (formerly the Gilbert Islands), becomes independent within the Commonwealth.

SCIENCE AND TECHNOLOGY

24 Dec. The first *Ariane* European space rocket is launched.

ARTS AND HUMANITIES

Literature

14 May The novelist Jean Rhys dies.

J.G. Ballard, *The Unlimited Dream Company*, novel.

Fernand Braudel, *Civilization and Capitalism*, history.

André Brink, *A Dry White Season*, novel.

Italo Calvino, *Se una notte d'inverno un viaggiatore* (If on a Winter's Night a Traveller), novel.

Caryl Churchill, *Cloud Nine*, play.

Penelope Fitzgerald, *Offshore*, novel.

William Golding, *Darkness Visible*, novel.

Milan Kundera, *The Book of Laughter and Forgetting*, novel.

Norman Mailer, *The Executioner's Song*, fictionalized account of the execution of Gary Gilmore in 1977.

Mark Medoff, *Children of a Lesser God*, play.

V.S. Naipaul, *A Bend in the River*, novel.

Peter Shaffer, *Amadeus*, play.

Martin Sherman, *Bent*, play portraying the Nazi persecution of gays.

William Styron, *Sophie's Choice*, novel.

Visual Arts and Architecture

Howard Hodgkin, *Dinner at Smith Square*, painting.

Music

24 Feb. First complete performance in Paris of Alban Berg's opera *Lulu* (see 1935). Act 3 has been completed by Friedrich Cerha.

Boomtown Rats, 'I Don't Like Mondays', single.

The Clash, *London Calling*, album.

Elvis Costello, 'Oliver's Army', single.

Dire Straits, 'Sultans of Swing', single.

Joy Division, *Unknown Pleasures*, album.

Andrew Lloyd Webber and Tim Rice, *Joseph and the Amazing Technicolour Dreamcoat*, musical.

The Police, 'Walking on the Moon' and 'Message in a Bottle', singles.

Stephen Sondheim, *Sweeney Todd*, musical.

Rod Stewart, 'Do Ya Think I'm Sexy?', single.

Talking Heads, *More Songs About Buildings and Food*, album.

Film

11 June American actor John Wayne dies.

Woody Allen, *Manhattan*.

Robert Benton, *Kramer vs Kramer*.

Francis Ford Coppola, *Apocalypse Now*, starring Martin Sheen and Marlon Brando; a celebrated study of the consequences of the Vietnam War, it is loosely based on Joseph Conrad's novella *Heart of Darkness* (1902).

Rainer Werner Fassbinder, *Die Ehe von Maria Braun* (The Marriage of Maria Braun).

Volker Schlöndorff, *Die Blechtrommel* (The Tin Drum).

Ridley Scott, *Alien*, starring Sigourney Weaver.

1980

EUROPE

13 Jan. In West Germany The Greens (*Die Grünen*) are founded as a national party.

22 Jan. In the USSR physicist and human rights activist Andrei Sakharov is stripped of his honours and exiled to the city of Gorky (now Nizhniy-Novgorod) by the Soviet government.

31 Mar. In N Spain a devolved Basque parliament opens in Guernica.

2 April Black youths riot in the St Paul's area of Bristol, W England.

4 May Tito (Josip Broz), president of Yugoslavia, dies. It is widely feared that he was the one man capable of holding together the federation of S Slav states. He is succeeded by a collective leadership, but strains between the various national groups soon surface.

5 May In London the Special Air Service (SAS) storm the Iranian embassy, which has been seized (30 April) by terrorists demanding the release of political prisoners in Iran.

15 July The British government announces that Polaris missiles are to be replaced by the Trident system.

2 Aug. The bombing of Bologna railway station in N Italy by right-wing terrorists kills 82 people.

14 Aug. A strike starts at the Lenin Shipyard, Gdansk, Poland: the workers demand the right to strike and to form autonomous trades unions outside Communist Party control. Lech Walesa, an electrician at the works, becomes the leader of a national movement, Solidarity. The movement develops beyond the mere expression of workers' grievances, and Solidarity starts to make political demands, such as the release of political prisoners and an end to state censorship. Edward Gierek agrees to the demands and releases political prisoners (1 Sept.). Stanislaw Kania replaces Gierek as first secretary of the Polish Communist Party (5 Sept.). The Soviet government is disturbed by these developments and starts once again to jam Western radio broadcasts to the USSR (20 Aug.).

4 Oct. Four people are killed and 10 injured when a bomb explodes in a Paris synagogue.

15 Oct. James Callaghan resigns the leadership of Britain's Labour Party, having lost the general election in 1979.

27 Oct. In Northern Ireland seven republican paramilitary prisoners in the Maze prison begin a hunger strike. They are demanding 'political status' and the right to wear their own, rather than prison, clothing.

10 Nov. Michael Foot, a left-winger, becomes leader of the British Labour Party, defeating Denis Healey, the former chancellor of the exchequer.

18 Dec. Following the presentation by the British of a document that seems to offer concessions, the republican hunger strikers in Northern Ireland begin to take food again.

– In the course of the year unemployment figures in Britain reach 2.3 million (their highest level since the Depression of the 1930s). Industrial production falls by 5% and inflation stands at 21%. In the face of these challenges Mrs Thatcher will prove herself to be a vigorous advocate of the free-market philosophies of the New Right. She will espouse the anti-Keynesian doctrine of monetarism, limiting government intervention in economic policy to the management of the money supply. Critics in her cabinet (known as 'wets') attack her inflexible economic policies, but she tells them at the Conservative Party conference in Brighton (10 Oct.): 'You turn if you want to. The lady is not for turning.'

MIDDLE EAST AND NORTH AFRICA

23 Mar. The former shah of Iran leaves Panama and is invited to Cairo by President Sadat.

24 April The US attempt to free the hostages held in Tehran (see 1979) ends in humiliation. Eight helicopters are grounded by mechanical failure in the desert SE of Tehran, and in the confusion eight US servicemen are killed when one helicopter crashes into a refuelling tanker. The débâcle is a bitter blow to President Carter's authority.

June OPEC representatives meeting in Algiers set the price of oil at $32 a barrel.

27 July After an operation for lymphatic cancer the exiled shah of Iran, Muhammad Reza Shah Pahlavi, dies in Cairo, Egypt.

22 Sept. War breaks out between Iran and Iraq over the issue of control of the Shatt-al-Arab estuary (formed by the confluence of the Tigris and Euphrates rivers): Iraqi troops start to besiege the oil refinery at Abadan.

ASIA

6 Jan. Indira Gandhi returns to power as prime minister of India. Her son Sanjay, who attracts the same criticisms as his mother on account of his autocratic style, has also been accused of business fraud. As his mother's campaign manager, he is seen as her natural heir, but he dies in a plane crash (23 June).

THE AMERICAS

Jan. The vast riches of the Serra Pelada gold mine are discovered in Brazil.

2 Feb. The New Mexico State Penitentiary, Santa Fe, is engulfed by a 36-hour riot. The prisoners target informants within the prison; 36 prisoners are killed.

18 Feb. In Canada the Liberal Party defeats the Progressive Conservatives in a general election. Pierre Trudeau returns as prime minister, having campaigned on a platform of opposition to Quebec separatism.

24 Mar. Archbishop Oscar Romero of El Salvador, a leading critic of the country's despotic government, is shot while celebrating mass.

11 April New York City is hit by an 11-day public transport strike.

17 May Race riots return to the USA when African-Americans protest in Miami at the acquittal of four white ex-policemen accused of murdering an African-American man, Arthur McDuffie.

18 May Mount St Helens, a volcanic mountain in Washington state in the NW USA, erupts for the first time since 1857.

20 May A referendum in Quebec votes against independence from Canada.

2 July The US Supreme Court rules that the federal government may use racial quotas when awarding contracts and can thereby operate a policy of reverse discrimination.

17 Sept. Former Nicaraguan dictator Anastasio Somoza is assassinated in Asunción, Paraguay.

26 Sept. In Cuba the government closes down the port of Mariel and acts to prevent the mass emigration of Cubans.

4 Nov. The Republican candidate Ronald Reagan defeats Jimmy Carter and is elected 40th president of the USA. Against a background of inflation rising to 12.4% and a recession reducing overall output by some 10%, Reagan inflicts on the hapless Carter the heaviest-ever defeat of an incumbent president. The former governor of California and Hollywood actor proves to be a consummate television campaigner.

– Brazil attempts to develop its W territory of Rondônia with World Bank money, which helps to develop a road in the region. But the soil proves resistant to agriculturalization, and epidemics are introduced by the incomers to the indigenous population.

– In the USA a drought affects Ohio, Illinois, Indiana and Iowa; conditions not seen since the 1930s return to the 'Corn Belt'.

SUB-SAHARAN AFRICA

Feb. Elections are held in Zimbabwe-Rhodesia. Robert Mugabe's ZANU party emerges victorious (4 Mar.).

12 April William Tolbert, president of Liberia, is overthrown and assassinated in a military coup. Samuel K. Doe becomes president, and the former sergeant assumes the rank of general. His rule will prove despotic, brutal and ultimately disastrous for his nation.

17 April Zimbabwe becomes fully independent with Robert Mugabe as prime minister.

Dec. Milton Obote returns as president of Uganda after the first democratic elections in 18 years.

AUSTRALASIA AND OCEANIA

30 July The New Hebrides (an island group in the SW Pacific) becomes independent within the Commonwealth as Vanuatu.

ECONOMY AND SOCIETY

1 June In the USA Cable News Network (CNN), owned by Ted Turner, goes on air.

July–Aug. The 22nd Olympic Games are held in Moscow. The USA and 64 other countries (including West Germany and Japan) boycott the Games.

Nov. The Church of England replaces the old Book of Common Prayer with the updated language of the Alternative Service Book.

SCIENCE AND TECHNOLOGY

– The Japanese electronics company Sony launches the 'Walkman', a small portable tape recorder/player.

ARTS AND HUMANITIES

Literature

7 June Henry Miller, US novelist, dies.

15 April The French writer and philosopher Jean-Paul Sartre dies.

Howard Brenton, *The Romans in Britain*, play.

Anthony Burgess, *Earthly Powers*, novel.

Umberto Eco, *Il nome della rosa* (The Name of the Rose), novel.

David Edgar, *The Life and Adventures of Nicholas Nickleby*, play adapting Dickens's novel.

Brian Friel, *Translations*, play.

William Golding, *Rites of Passage*, novel.

Russell Hoban, *Riddley Walker*, novel.

David Lodge, *How Far Can You Go?*, novel.

Olivia Manning, *The Levant Trilogy*, consisting of the novels *The Danger Tree* (1977), *The Battle Lost and Won* (1978) and *The Sum of Things* (1980).

Iris Murdoch, *Nuns and Soldiers*, novel.

John Kennedy Toole, *A Confederacy of Dunces*, novel.

Visual Arts and Architecture

2 Feb. Austrian painter Oskar Kokoschka dies.

17 Feb. The British artist Graham Sutherland dies.

– Crystal Cathedral, Garden Grove, California, designed by Philip Johnson and John Henry Burgee, is completed.

Music

8 Dec. John Lennon is shot and killed by a crazed admirer in New York.

David Bowie, 'Ashes to Ashes', single.

Philip Glass, *Satyagraha*, opera inspired by Mahatma Gandhi's campaign of non-violent resistance to British authority.

The Jam, 'Going Underground', single.

John Lennon and Yoko Ono, *Double Fantasy*, album.

Pink Floyd, *The Wall*, album.

The Police, 'Don't Stand So Close To Me', single.

Kenny Rogers, 'Coward of the County', single.

Diana Ross, 'Upside Down', single.

Talking Heads, *Remain in Light,* album.

Film

29 April Film director Alfred Hitchcock dies.

Michael Cimino, *Heaven's Gate*.

Rainer Werner Fassbinder, *Berlin Alexanderplatz*.

Bill Forsyth, *Gregory's Girl*.

Stanley Kubrick, *The Shining*, starring Jack Nicholson.

Akira Kurosawa, *Kagemusha*.

George Lucas, *The Empire Strikes Back*.

David Lynch, *The Elephant Man*, starring John Hurt.

Louis Malle, *Atlantic City*, starring Burt Lancaster.

John Mackenzie, *The Long Good Friday*, starring Bob Hoskins.

Martin Scorsese, *Raging Bull*, starring Robert De Niro.

1981

EUROPE

1 Jan. Greece becomes the 10th member of the European Community (EC).

9 Feb. Gen. Wojciech Jaruzelski becomes prime minister of Poland.

1 Mar. Bobby Sands, leader of the Provisional IRA prisoners in Northern Ireland's Maze prison, begins a hunger strike, claiming that moves for a resolution of the prisoners' difficulties over special category status have broken down. Sands wins a by-election in Fermanagh and South Tyrone on 9 April, but by then he is approaching death.

26 Mar. The Social Democratic Party (SDP) is launched in Britain. It is founded by disaffected Labour MPs concerned at what they see as the leftward drift of the Labour Party, and its most prominent members are the so-called Gang of Four: former Labour home secretary Roy Jenkins (who will be the party's first leader), former foreign secretary Dr David Owen, former education secretary Shirley Williams and William Rodgers.

April Rioting breaks out in the Brixton district of S London. Similar disturbances will also occur in Toxteth (Liverpool), Manchester and elsewhere during the summer (July).

10 May François Mitterrand defeats Valéry Giscard d'Estaing to become France's first Socialist president.

13 May Mehmet Ali Agca, a Bulgarian-trained Turkish citizen, shoots and seriously wounds Pope John Paul II in Rome. It is widely believed that the attack, on one of the world's major anti-communist figureheads, has been organized by the KGB, the Soviet secret police.

26 May The Italian cabinet resigns after revelations of the influence of freemasons in the country's political and judicial system.

May–Aug. Ten republican prisoners (seven IRA, three INLA) die in the Maze prison as a result of hunger strikes (see 27 Oct. 1980). Among them is Bobby Sands, who dies on 5 May. The last to die is Michael Devine (20 Aug.). The British government of Margaret Thatcher has refused to yield to any of the hunger striker's demands in spite of intense local and international pressure. On 3 Oct. six republicans still on hunger strike begin to take food and three days later it is finally announced that paramilitary prisoners will be allowed to wear their own clothes. The entire episode galvanizes nationalist opinion in Northern Ireland against British government intransigence.

11 June In the Republic of Ireland Fianna Fáil is defeated in the general election. Fine Gael forms a coalition government with the Labour Party. Garret Fitzgerald becomes taoiseach (prime minister).

29 July Charles, Prince of Wales, marries Lady Diana Spencer.

18 Sept. France abolishes the death penalty.

Sept. In Poland the Solidarity trade union holds its first national congress. Gen. Jaruzelski orders a widespread crackdown on dissidents. Jaruzelski becomes first secretary of the Polish Communist Party (18 Oct.).

13 Dec. In the face of continuing agitation by the Solidarity trade union, Gen. Jaruzelski imposes martial law to forestall a Soviet invasion of Poland.

– In Britain the 1980 Employment Act, the first of a series of acts aimed at curbing the power of trade unions, comes into law. It outlaws secondary picketing in industrial disputes.

– In Britain the Conservative government of Margaret Thatcher separates British Telecommunications from the Post Office. Cable and Wireless and part of British Aerospace are privatized.

– France's Socialist government nationalizes banks as well as the arms, chemical, electronics and insurance industries.

– In Britain a women-only peace camp is set up outside the US cruise missile base at Greenham Common, Berkshire.

MIDDLE EAST AND NORTH AFRICA

20 Jan. Iran releases the US hostages held in Tehran after 444 days of captivity. The US government has agreed to release Iranian money held in the USA, and the Iranians will repay US loans. The announcement has been delayed until after Reagan is sworn in as US president.

7 June The Israeli air force attacks Iraq's nuclear reactor at Osirak. The Israeli government claims that it is acting in order to stop the Iraqis from producing weapons-grade plutonium.

22 June Iranian president Abolhassan Bani-Sadr is denounced by Ayatollah Khomeini and leaves for France (29 June). He has opposed the taking of US hostages.

17 July In Lebanon Israeli aircraft attack Palestinian positions in Beirut and S Lebanon. Fighting between Israeli and Palestinian forces continues until a ceasefire is brokered by Philip Habib, the US special envoy to the Middle East (29 July).

30 Aug. In Iran the president and prime minister are killed by a terrorist bomb attack in Tehran.

6 Oct. While watching a review of his own troops Anwar al-Sadat, president of Egypt, is assassinated by Muslim fundamentalists outraged by his dealings with Israel. His vice-president Hosni Mubarak succeeds him and reaffirms the peace treaty with Israel.

14 Dec. Israel annexes the Golan Heights (a plateau on the Syrian–Israeli border, occupied by Israel since 1967) following accusations that the Palestinians are moving artillery and ammunition within the supposed UN zone in Lebanon.

ASIA

17 Jan. Ferdinand Marcos ends martial law in the Philippines and is declared elected as president for another six years (16 June). The elections have, however, been rigged, Marcos having suppressed most forms of democratic opposition to his rule.

25 Jan. In a show trial in Beijing, China, the Gang of Four are convicted of treason. Mao's widow receives a suspended sentence of death.

30 May President Zia-ur Rahman of Bangladesh is assassinated by a group of army officers, but the wider coup fails.

THE AMERICAS

31 Mar. President Reagan is shot in an assassination attempt but survives.

7 July President Reagan appoints Sandra Day O'Connor to the Supreme Court. The first woman justice influences the Supreme Court in a conservative direction.

31 July Panamanian dictator Gen. Omar Torrijos Herrera is killed in a plane crash; Col. Manuel Antonio Noriega, a CIA operative in Panama, begins to develop his power base.

13 Aug. Ronald Reagan signs a bill authorizing the biggest tax and government expenditure cuts in US history. US economic policy is increasingly dominated by the school of theory known as supply-side economics (now dubbed Reaganomics) which rejects the theories of demand-led economic management associated with the legacy of British economist John Maynard Keynes (see p. 517). Britain's right-wing prime minister

Margaret Thatcher, who will form a close political relationship with Reagan, is pursuing similar economic policies.

20 Sept. In C America Belize becomes independent within the Commonwealth.

29 Sept. President Reagan states that he wishes to make a further $13 billion spending cuts.

1 Nov. The Caribbean islands of Antigua and Barbuda become an independent state within the Commonwealth.

22 Dec. Gen. Leopoldo Galtieri becomes president of Argentina.

SUB-SAHARAN AFRICA

31 Dec. Jerry Rawlings mounts his second successful coup in Ghana. This time he retains power.

ECONOMY AND SOCIETY

12 Jan. American television drama series *Dynasty* starts to be broadcast on ABC.

29 Mar. The London Marathon is held for the first time.

– A new disease is reported, first in San Francisco and New York. Gay men have started to die of a form of cancer known as Kaposi's sarcoma. Although the disease is common in Africa, it is rare elsewhere. In its new form, the disease is named Acquired Immune Deficiency Syndrome (AIDS). Drug addicts who have shared needles also suffer from the disease, which is acquired by an exchange of bodily fluids containing a retro-virus. The disease becomes a major epidemic in Africa where it affects both heterosexuals and homosexuals. In the USA and Europe, however, it is dubbed a 'gay disease', and at this stage of the disease's history it means certain death. Prejudice, fear and ignorance will surround the spread of AIDS.

– Australian press magnate Rupert Murdoch buys *The Times* newspaper in Britain.

– The Humber Bridge, Hull, N England is completed; it is the world's longest suspension bridge.

– Divorce is legalized in Spain.

– The English cricketer Ian Botham performs a series of astonishing batting and bowling feats to help England defeat Australia 3–1 in the summer's Ashes series.

SCIENCE AND TECHNOLOGY

12 April The US space shuttle *Columbia* makes its maiden flight.

22 Sept. The French high-speed train, the TGV (*train à grande vitesse*), starts to operate between Paris and Lyons. Its route will be extended to Marseilles (1983).

– IBM enters the personal computer (PC) market, introducing the PV-XT, which uses an 8-bit Intel 8088 processor. The new PC uses the Microsoft disk-operating system (MS-DOS), which becomes an industry standard.

ARTS AND HUMANITIES

Literature

Harvey Fierstein, *Torch Song Trilogy*, play.

Gabriel García Márquez, *Crónica de una muerte anunciada* (Chronicle of a Death Foretold), novel.

Alasdair Gray, *Lanark*, novel.

Simon Gray, *Quartermaine's Terms*, play.

Molly Keane, *Good Behaviour*, novel.

Salman Rushdie, *Midnight's Children*, novel.

Martin Cruz Smith, *Gorky Park*, novel.

Paul Theroux, *Mosquito Coast*, novel.

D.M. Thomas, *The White Hotel*, novel.

John Updike, *Rabbit is Rich*, novel.

Music

Luciano Berio, *Suite da 'La vera storia'* and *Accordo*.

Pierre Boulez, *Répons*, for chamber orchestra and digital equipment.

Human League, 'Don't You Want Me?', single.

Andrew Lloyd Webber, *Cats*, musical based on poems by T.S. Eliot.

Smokey Robinson, 'Being with You', single.

Soft Cell, 'Tainted Love', single.

Karlheinz Stockhausen, *Donnerstag aus Licht* (Thursday from Light), opera.

Ultravox, 'Vienna', single.

Stevie Wonder, 'Happy Birthday', single.

Film

Hugh Hudson, *Chariots of Fire*; the film communicates the competitive ethos and nostalgic view of the English past that are now becoming predominant in Margaret Thatcher's Britain.

Wolfgang Petersen, *Das Boot* (The Boat).

Karel Reisz, *The French Lieutenant's Woman*, starring Meryl Streep.

Steven Spielberg, *Raiders of the Lost Ark*, starring Harrison Ford.

Andrzej Wajda, *Man of Iron*.

Peter Weir, *Gallipoli*, providing a hostile view of the British leadership in the Gallipoli campaign of World War I, which led to major Australian and New Zealand casualties.

1982

EUROPE

Jan. In Britain unemployment reaches three million, its highest level since 1933.

18 Feb. In the Republic of Ireland Fianna Fáil defeats Garret Fitzgerald's Fine Gael-led coalition government in a general election. Failing to win an overall majority, Charles Haughey is elected taoiseach (prime minister) with the help of independent members (9 Mar.).

25 Mar. In Britain Roy Jenkins wins the parliamentary seat of Glasgow Hillhead for the Social Democratic Party (SDP) in a by-election.

4 April Following Argentina's invasion of the Falkland Islands (see below), the first ships of a Royal Navy task force set sail for the S Atlantic.

May Spain joins NATO.

14–15 June The Falklands War ends with the recapture of Port Stanley by British troops. Victory comes at a crucial stage in Margaret Thatcher's premiership. Criticism of her leadership has been increasing within the Conservative Party; her adherence to monetarist economic policies is perceived by many to have destabilized Britain's economy and led to social unrest.

The 'Falklands Factor', however, enhances her popularity and will give her premiership new impetus.

2 July In Britain Roy Jenkins is elected leader of the SDP.

9 Aug. A terrorist attack on a Jewish restaurant in the Marais area of Paris kills six people.

Aug. The French island of Corsica holds elections for its first regional assembly.

17 Sept. In West Germany the governing coalition of Social Democrats (SPD) and the Free Democrats (FDP) collapses when FDP ministers withdraw their support from the SDP and transfer it to the Christian Democratic Union (CDU). On 1 Oct. Helmut Kohl, leader of the CDU, replaces Helmut Schmidt as West German chancellor.

8 Oct. In Poland the trade union Solidarity is banned in a new law.

29 Oct. A socialist government led by Felipe Gonzalez is elected in Spain.

10 Nov. Soviet leader Leonid Brezhnev dies and is succeeded as first secretary of the Soviet Communist Party by former KGB head Yuri Andropov, who has reformist ideas but is an ageing and sick man.

24 Nov. In the second general election of the year in the Republic of Ireland Fianna Fáil, the governing party, again fails to achieve an overall majority. Fine Gael forms a coalition government with the Labour Party, with Garret Fitzgerald as taoiseach (prime minister) (14 Dec.).

6 Dec. In Northern Ireland 17 people (including 11 British soldiers) die in a bomb attack by the Irish National Liberation Army (INLA) on a pub in Ballykelly, Co. Derry.

31 Dec. In Poland martial law is suspended.

MIDDLE EAST AND NORTH AFRICA

21 April Menachem Begin, prime minister of Israel, orders the Israeli army to move against PLO bases in Lebanon. The PLO has repeatedly broken the terms of the ceasefire agreed previously (1981).

April The Israeli army, in accordance with the 1978 Camp David Agreement, withdraws from Sinai. UN peace-keeping troops will move into the area.

9 May Israeli aircraft attack the PLO bases S of Beirut.

24 May In the latest campaign of the Iran–Iraq War the Iranian army regains the city of Khorramshahr, close to the Shatt al-Arab waterway. Syria is now supplying Iran with Soviet weapons.

6 June Israeli forces invade the Lebanon with the aim of expelling the Palestinian guerrillas based there. The Israelis clash with Syrian forces in the S of the country. They reach the outskirts of Beirut on 10 June.

27 June Israel demands the surrender of PLO fighters in W Beirut. Israeli premier Menachem Begin gives the PLO 30 days to leave the city (17 July). Beirut is now under siege by the Israelis, who will destroy whole areas of the city to enforce the withdrawal of PLO forces. The Israeli air force bombs civilian areas of W Beirut, killing 120 people (27 July).

Aug. Palestinian fighters and Syrian troops are evacuated from Beirut under the terms of a US-brokered ceasefire agreement.

PLO leader Yasser Arafat leaves for Tunisia (30 Aug.). The Christian Phalangist leader Bashir Gemayel is elected president by the Lebanese parliament.

14 Sept. Bashir Gemayel, Maronite Christian Lebanese president-elect, is killed when a bomb explodes at the headquarters of his Phalangist party. His brother Amine Gemayel becomes president.

16 Sept. Israeli forces move into W Beirut. On 18 Sept., with alleged Israeli complicity, Christian Phalangist militias enter the Palestinian refugee camps of Sabra and Chatila where they kill hundreds of civilians left defenceless by the departure of the Palestinian guerrillas. The massacre causes international outrage. Israeli forces leave W Beirut on 26 Sept. to be replaced by a US-led peace-keeping force.

– President Assad of Syria suppresses an anti-government rising by Islamists in the town of Hama in the W of the country. 5000–10,000 people are killed.

THE AMERICAS

6 Feb. President Reagan asks for an increased military budget and for cuts in social expenditure. Congress approves a 6% increase in defence expenditure, but the Boland Amendment (8 Dec.) bans the use of defence expenditure to finance attempts at subverting the Sandinista government in Nicaragua.

23 Mar. Romeo Lucas García, dictator of Guatemala, is toppled by a military coup. Amnesty International will charge him with responsibility for some 5000 political assassinations. He is succeeded by General José Efraín Ríos Montt (June).

2 April Argentine forces invade the Falkland Islands in the S Atlantic. The islands, a British crown colony since 1833, have long been claimed by Argentina (for whom they are the Islas Malvinas). Britain has been negotiating a possible transfer of sovereignty with the Argentinians for some years. The British foreign office, however, has failed to react to reports of an Argentinian military build-up over the past few months, an oversight that the Argentinian junta, led by Gen. Leopoldo Galtieri, has mistaken for indifference.

3 April The United Nations Security Council passes a resolution calling for Argentina to withdraw its forces from the Falkland Islands. Argentinian forces seize the uninhabited S Atlantic island of South Georgia the same day.

4 April Britain sends a Royal Navy task force to recover the Falkland Islands. Britain imposes a 200 mile (320km) maritime exclusion zone around the islands (12 April).

17 April The North America Act (1867) is replaced by the Constitution Act which gives Canada its own constitution.

19 April The British government rejects a US plan to mediate in the Falklands conflict. After some internal debate the US government will declare its support for the British (30 April).

25 April British forces recapture South Georgia.

2 May The Argentinian cruiser *General Belgrano* is sunk by the British submarine HMS *Conqueror* with the loss of some 360 lives, ending any hope of a negotiated end to the Falklands conflict. Mrs Thatcher tells Parliament that the *Belgrano* was on course for the Falkland Islands at the time of the sinking, but it turns out that it was sailing in the opposite direction. Labour MP Tam Dalyell will campaign to expose the truth.

4 May The British destroyer HMS *Sheffield* is sunk by an Argentine missile.

14 May British forces land on East Falkland Island. They capture Port Darwin and Goose Green (28 May).

11 June The US government adopts a protectionist policy: since foreign steel companies receive state subsidies the US places tariffs on imported steel in order to protect its own steel industry.

14 June The Argentinians surrender at Port Stanley. The Falkland Islands return to British rule.The death toll in the Falklands War is 652 Argentinians and 255 Britons.

19 Aug. The US Congress approves a reversal of the tax-cutting measures previously adopted.

20 Aug. The Mexican government declares that it is defaulting on its $60 billion foreign debt. Brazil and Argentina will follow suit.

2 Oct. Paul Volcker, chairman of the US Federal Reserve System, states that the current anti-inflationary policy is damaging the US economy. Monetarism will be abandoned and, after peaking at 10.8% in Nov., unemployment will begin to decline. Lower inflation and interest rates lead to a Wall Street recovery.

13 Nov. The official Vietnam War memorial is dedicated in Washington, D.C.; the names of the 57,692 killed or missing members of the US forces are inscribed on black granite.

ECONOMY AND SOCIETY

2 Nov. Channel Four, Britain's fourth national TV channel, is launched.

– Italy wins the 12th soccer World Cup, held in Spain.

– In Britain *The Sloane Ranger Handbook* defines the Chelsea-dwelling archetype of the conservative upper-middle class Briton. (The term 'Sloane Ranger' was coined in 1975 by a sub-editor on *Harpers and Queen*.)

SCIENCE AND TECHNOLOGY

– CD (Compact Disc) players go on sale.

ARTS AND HUMANITIES

Literature
Isabel Allende, *La casa de los espíritus* (The House of the Spirits), novel.
Saul Bellow, *The Dean's December*, novel.
William Boyd, *An Ice-Cream War*, novel.
Bruce Chatwin, *On the Black Hill*, novel.
Caryl Churchill, *Top Girls*, play.
Michael Frayn, *Noises Off*, play.
Thomas Keneally, *Schindler's Ark*, novel.
Timothy Mo, *Sour Sweet*, novel.
Tom Stoppard, *The Real Thing*, play.
Alice Walker, *The Color Purple*, novel.
Edmund White, *A Boy's Own Story*, novel.

Music
17 Feb. The US jazz pianist Thelonious Monk dies.
Irene Cara, 'Fame', single.
Culture Club, 'Do You Really Want To Hurt Me', single.

Dexy's Midnight Runners, 'Come on Eileen', single.
Duran Duran, 'Rio', single.
Michael Jackson, *Thriller*, album and video.
Paul McCartney and Stevie Wonder, 'Ebony and Ivory', single.

Film
12 Aug. American actor Henry Fonda dies.
29 Aug. Swedish actress Ingrid Bergman dies.
14 Sept. Former US actress Grace Kelly (Princess Grace of Monaco) dies in a car crash.
Woody Allen, *A Midsummer Night's Sex Comedy*.
Richard Attenborough, *Gandhi*.
Peter Greenaway, *The Draughtsman's Contract*.
Taylor Hackford, *An Officer and a Gentleman*.
Werner Herzog, *Fitzcarraldo*.
Ridley Scott, *Blade Runner*, starring Harrison Ford.
Steven Spielberg, *E.T. the Extra-Terrestrial*.
Andrzej Wajda, *Danton*, starring Gérard Depardieu.

1983

EUROPE

Feb. The former Nazi SS commander Klaus Barbie (the 'Butcher of Lyon') is extradited from Bolivia to France to stand trial for crimes against humanity committed during the German occupation of France in World War II.

6 Mar. In West Germany the governing CDU-FDP coalition (see 17 Sept. 1982) wins a majority in the general election. Green Party candidates win parliamentary seats for the first time.

28 Mar. In Britain Ian MacGregor, who has little liking for public ownership or trade unions and has spent three years reducing the size of the nationalized British Steel Corporation, is appointed chairman of the National Coal Board (NCB) by prime minister Margaret Thatcher. MacGregor will introduce a programme of closures of pits deemed to be uneconomic. This puts the NCB on a collision course with the National Union of Mineworkers (NUM), led by Arthur Scargill, a fiery left-winger.

22 April The West German magazine *Stern* claims to have found Hitler's diaries. A first excerpt from the diaries is published in the British *Sunday Times* newspaper (24 April).

6 May The German Federal Archives declare the 'Hitler diaries' to be forgeries.

9 June In Britain the Conservative Party is re-elected to government in a landslide, gaining a majority of 144 seats over Labour, which now has a parliamentary representation of only 209 seats.

14 June In Britain Roy Jenkins resigns as leader of the Social Democratic Party (SDP). David Owen becomes leader (21 June).

2 Oct. In Britain Neil Kinnock is elected leader of the Labour Party, succeeding Michael Foot. Kinnock will reverse Labour's leftward shift of recent years, and will set about extirpating the far-left Militant Tendency from the party.

5 Oct. Polish Solidarity leader Lech Walesa receives the Nobel peace prize.

22 Oct. Massive public demonstrations take place across Europe in protest against plans to station US cruise missiles on the continent. Despite this, and long-term demonstrations at Greenham Common airbase, England, the first cruise missiles are deployed (15 Nov.).

23 Nov. Soviet leader Yuri Andropov leaves the arms limitations talks in Geneva following the deployment of US cruise missiles in Europe.

17 Dec. In Britain an IRA car bomb explodes outside Harrod's department store in Knightsbridge, London, killing six people.

– In Northern Ireland Gerry Adams, now MP for West Belfast, becomes president of Sinn Féin, the political wing of the Provisional IRA. While still adhering to its traditional policy of parliamentary abstentionism, the Irish republican movement is now pursuing an electoral strategy at the same time as continuing its anti-British guerrilla war.

MIDDLE EAST AND NORTH AFRICA

11 Feb. The Israeli defence minister Ariel Sharon resigns following an official investigation into the massacres of Palestinians at the Sabra and Chatila refugee camps in Beirut (see Sept. 1982).

18 April In Beirut, Lebanon, 63 people are killed when the US embassy is blown up. Fighting continues between the Lebanese army, Shiite Muslims and other factions in Lebanon's civil war.

May A US-brokered agreement requires all foreign forces to be withdrawn from Lebanon within three months. When Syria refuses to recognize the agreement, Israel keeps its forces in the S of Lebanon.

15 Sept. Menachem Begin resigns as prime minister of Israel; Yitzhak Shamir succeeds him.

Sept. Fighting breaks out between Phalangist and Druse militias in the Chouf mountains of Lebanon.

23 Oct. In Beirut, a suicide bomber of the militant Islamic Jihad faction blows up a military compound housing US and French peace-keeping troops. 242 American and 62 French soldiers are killed in the blast. US marines will soon be withdrawn from Lebanon.

4 Nov. A suicide mission blows up an Israeli military installation and kills 60 people, including 28 Israelis.

ASIA

21 Aug. Benigno Aquino, leader of the pro-democracy movement in the Philippines, is shot dead when he returns to Manila from the USA to organize the movement's campaign against the tyrannical president Ferdinand Marcos. Aquino's widow, Corazón, will take up his role, despite her lack of political experience.

Aug. In Pakistan Gen. Zia ul-Haq announces that elections will be held in 1985 and martial law lifted.

1 Sept. A Korean Air Lines Boeing 747, carrying 269 people on a flight from New York to Seoul, is shot down by a Soviet fighter jet. All on board are killed. The flight has violated Soviet air space, and the Soviet government insists it was on a spying mission. The US government has to concede that a 'reconnaissance' plane was in the same area earlier.

9 Oct. North Korean dissidents kill 19 people and wound 40 by

planting a bomb at the Martyrs' Mausoleum, Rangoon, Burma. Sixteen South Koreans are among the dead and South Korea's president Chun Doo Hwan, who is on a state visit, only narrowly escapes death.

12 Oct. Kakuei Tanaka, former prime minister of Japan, is sentenced to four years' imprisonment for bribery.

THE AMERICAS

8 Mar. President Reagan characterizes the USSR as 'an evil empire', which is 'the focus of evil in the modern world'. He goes on to announce (23 Mar.) a Strategic Defence Initiative (SDI), a system of satellites with laser technology that will destroy any incoming missiles attacking the USA. In the USA the idea is widely greeted with derision and is dubbed 'Star Wars', but the Soviets cannot ignore the possibility that it might work. Reagan's aggressive rhetoric has led the Soviets to fear that the US president may be preparing his people for war.

Extremism in the defence of liberty is no vice.

Barry Goldwater, 16 July, 1964

20 April President Reagan delays cost-of-living increases in welfare payments for six months, increases pay-roll deductions (from 1984) and raises the minimum retirement age to 67 (to take effect by 2027).

4 May President Reagan expresses support for the efforts of Nicaraguan Contra guerrillas to overthrow that country's left-wing Sandinista government.

19 Sept. The Caribbean islands of St Kitts-Nevis become independent within the Commonwealth.

12 Oct. Bernard Coard, a Soviet sympathizer, overthrows Maurice Bishop, prime minister of the Caribbean island of Grenada. The US government is concerned that Grenada will become an ally of Cuba and afford Soviet forces a convenient point of entry to C America. On the pretext of protecting American students studying on the island, US forces invade Grenada (25 Oct.) and disregard the international condemnation.

10 Dec. Raúl Alfonsín is elected president of Argentina.

– The reality of global climate change is revealed when the detrimental effects of El Niño, a warm ocean surge occurring cyclically in the E Pacific, are felt in Peru. El Niño, which may be linked to global warming, prevents the environmentally beneficial upwelling of colder waters along the coast of Ecuador and Peru, thereby disrupting the climate of the area with disastrous results. (El Niño is short for Spanish *El Niño de Navidad*, 'the Christmas Child', since it warms the water off the N Peruvian coast at Christmas.)

SUB-SAHARAN AFRICA

19 Jan. South Africa reimposes direct rule on South-West Africa (Namibia).

31 Dec. Gen. Mohammad Buhari leads a coup that returns Nigeria to military rule.

– In South Africa the United Democratic Front, led by Dr Allan Boesak, is founded as an anti-apartheid organization.

– Civil war breaks out in Sudan when President Nimeiri declares that strict Islamic (Sharia) law will be applied throughout the country, including the mainly Christian S. The Sudan People's Liberation Army (SPLA) of the S opposes the government.

AUSTRALASIA AND OCEANIA

5 Mar. Bob Hawke becomes prime minister of Australia following the Labor Party's victory in the general election.

ECONOMY AND SOCIETY

8 Feb. The racehorse Shergar, winner of the 1981 Epsom Derby, is kidnapped from a stud farm in Co. Kildare, Ireland. The horse will never be found.

Nov. Michael Milken, a Wall Street trader, advocates the use of 'junk bonds' to finance takeovers of companies. The assets of a target company are to be pledged to repay the junk bond principle. Junk bonds become popular among institutional investors.

– Crack, a form of crystallized cocaine, becomes a popular recreational drug in US cities.

SCIENCE AND TECHNOLOGY

– In France doctors at the Pasteur Institute identify the AIDS virus. It becomes known as the human immunodeficiency virus (HIV).

– The US space probe *Pioneer* 10 becomes the first spacecraft to leave the solar system.

ARTS AND HUMANITIES

Literature

25 Feb. The US playwright Tennessee Williams dies.

J.M. Coetzee, *The Life and Times of Michael K*, novel.

Geoffrey Hill, *The Mystery of the Charity of Charles Péguy*, extended religious verse.

William Joseph Kennedy, *Ironweed*, novel.

David Mamet, *Glengarry Glen Ross*, play.

Salman Rushdie, *Shame*, novel.

Graham Swift, *Waterland*, novel.

Visual Arts and Architecture

25 Dec. Spanish artist Joan Miró dies.

Music

8 Mar. The English composer William Walton dies.

Culture Club, 'Karma Chameleon', single.

Billy Joel, 'Uptown Girl', single.

Men At Work, 'Down Under', single.

Olivier Messiaen, *Saint François d'Assise* (St Francis of Assisi), opera.

The Police, 'Every Breath You Take', single.

Bonnie Tyler, 'Total Eclipse of the Heart', single.

UB40, 'Red Red Wine', single.

U2, *War*, album.

Tom Waits, *Swordfishtrombones*, album.

Film

Woody Allen, *Zelig*.

Ingmar Bergman, *Fanny and Alexander*.

Robert Bresson, *L'Argent*.

Bill Forsyth, *Local Hero*.

George Lucas, *Return of the Jedi*.

Andrei Tarkovsky, *Nostalghia* (Nostalgia).

Peter Yates, *The Dresser*, starring Albert Finney and Tom Courtenay.

1984

EUROPE

25 Jan. The British government outlaws union membership among the workforce at the General Communications Headquarters (GCHQ) at Cheltenham. Although presented as a security measure, the ban is widely seen as part of a general attack on trade union rights.

9 Feb. Soviet leader Yuri Andropov dies and is succeeded as first secretary of the Soviet Communist Party by Konstantin Chernenko. Unlike Andropov, Chernenko has no tolerance for reformers but, like his predecessor, he is an ageing and sick man.

Mar. In Britain the year-long miners' strike begins. NUM leaders support strikes in Yorkshire and Scotland (8 Mar.) and the strike spreads to 100 pits (12 Mar.). NUM president Arthur Scargill calls for a national strike on the same day. He does not, however, call for a national ballot (12 April), as is legally necessary. This loses the strike its potential legitimacy from the outset. Scargill has to rely on each district of the NUM to make the strike effective, but not all miners support it. In Nottinghamshire, where pit closures are few, miners continue to work and form a breakaway union, the Democratic Union of Mineworkers. The illegality of the strike will lead to the confiscation of NUM funds and allow the police to intervene to protect those miners who continue to work. This results in violence on the picket lines in Yorkshire and Nottinghamshire. The strike finds the Conservative government well prepared: learning from the crisis experienced by Edward Heath's government in 1973–4, it has built up stockpiles of coal in preparation for a long strike. The government regards the strike as a crucial battle in its campaign against what it regards as the outmoded working practices of the trade unions; the miners who are striking do not all share the far-left political opinions of Arthur Scargill – they are simply fighting for their jobs. The Conservative government will show little sympathy for the desperation of miners and their families.

17 April Gunmen inside the Libyan People's Bureau in London fire on demonstrators outside the building, killing WPC Yvonne Fletcher. Britain suspends its diplomatic relations with Libya (22 April).

29 May In Britain's miners' strike police use riot gear in violent clashes with pickets at Orgreave coking plant, near Sheffield. 64 people are injured.

12 Oct. In Britain an IRA bomb explodes at the Grand Hotel in Brighton during the Conservative Party conference, killing five and injuring 30. The IRA's intention is to eliminate the prime minister Margaret Thatcher, and her cabinet, but Mrs Thatcher has a narrow escape.

30 Oct. In Poland the body of missing pro-Solidarity priest, Father Jerzy Popieluszko, is found in a reservoir. He has been murdered by the security police.

22 Dec. Dom Mintoff, prime minister of Malta since 1971, resigns.

– In Britain a senior civil servant, Clive Ponting, passes documents to his MP suggesting there has been a cover-up over the sinking of the *General Belgrano* during the Falklands War (see 2 May 1982). Ponting is charged under the Official Secrets Act for 'leaking' the documents.

– Roman Catholicism ceases to be the state religion of Italy when the 1929 Concordat between the Vatican City State and the state of Italy is revised.

– The British government sells Jaguar Motors to the private sector and sells shares in British Telecom to the general public using mass-marketing techniques. In its second term the Thatcher government is now embarking on a wave of privatization measures that remove state-run industries from government control.

MIDDLE EAST AND NORTH AFRICA

18 Jan. Malcolm Kerr, president of the American University, Beirut, is assassinated by pro-Iranian guerrillas.

25–30 Jan. West German chancellor Helmut Kohl visits Israel. His visit is disrupted by demonstrations.

11 Feb. In the Iran–Iraq War, Iraq starts to bomb civilian targets in Iran.

Feb. US marines are withdrawn from Beirut. The brief US intervention in Lebanon's civil war has achieved little.

23 July Elections show the divided nature of Israeli society: Shimon Peres leads the Labour Party to victory with 44 seats in the Knesset. The right-wing Likud party led by Yitzhak Shamir gains 41 seats. With neither party having an overall majority, a coalition government is formed (14 Sept.), with Peres and Shamir following each other in 25-month periods of office as premier.

ASIA

1 Jan. The sultanate of Brunei, a British protectorate since 1888, becomes independent.

5–6 June Indian premier Indira Gandhi outrages Sikh opinion by sending in troops to end militant Sikh occupation of their sacred Golden Temple at Amritsar. 250 Sikhs are killed in the assault by the Indian army. Gandhi, devoted to the idea of India as a unitary state, is intolerant of calls for an independent Punjab. Now she has offended the most moderate Sikh opinion. She is assassinated (31 Oct.) by two Sikhs who are members of her private guard. She is succeeded, in dynastic fashion, by her son Rajiv. The Congress (I) Party wins a majority in a general election (24 Dec.).

Aug. Clashes takes place between Tamils and Sinhalese in Sri Lanka.

3 Dec. In C India a leak of toxic gas from the Union Carbide factory at Bhopal kills 2600. Some 300,000 people will suffer long-term health problems as a result of inhaling methyl isocyanate.

19 Dec. In Beijing Margaret Thatcher signs a treaty that will provide for the transfer of British sovereignty over Hong Kong to be completed by 1997, when the colony will revert to China.

– The Japanese government privatizes the country's telephone industry.

THE AMERICAS

17 Jan. The Reagan-nominated US Commission on Civil Rights declares that numerical quotas for the promotion of African-Americans and others 'may merely constitute another form of discrimination'.

12 April The US Senate votes to cut off money supplies used by the CIA to mine Nicaraguan harbours. The mining is presented as an attempt to stop arms being shipped to the rebels in El Salvador. Some see it as an attack on Nicaragua's economy.

May José Napoleon Duarte is elected president of El Salvador, and the country is voted further military and economic aid by the US Congress (July).

30 June Pierre Trudeau resigns as prime minister of Canada and is succeeded by Brian Mulroney when his Progressive Conservatives are elected to government (4 Sept.).

4 Nov. Daniel Ortega of the Sandinista Front is elected president of Nicaragua.

6 Nov. Ronald Reagan is re-elected president of the USA, defeating Democratic challenger Walter Mondale and gaining 59% of the popular vote.

22 Dec. In New York Bernhard Hugo Goetz achieves notoriety as a subway vigilante when he shoots four African-American youths who, he claims, have tried to rob him. One of the youths is paralysed as a result of the shooting. Goetz serves eight months for illegal weapon possession but is acquitted of attempted murder.

– The US economy is now growing at 6.6% and inflation is down to 3.7%, but the US budget deficit and trade deficit are out of control. The Continental Illinois Bank has to be saved from collapse by a $4.5 billion federal loan (10 May) and confidence in the US banking system falters.

– President Reagan's administration stops US funding of international birth-control programmes.

SUB-SAHARAN AFRICA

16 Mar. Mozambique and South Africa agree on a peace treaty.

3 Aug. Upper Volta is renamed Burkina Faso.

– Drought devastates large areas of sub-Saharan Africa. Conditions are desperate in Ethiopia, where some 300,000 people die of famine. The country's civil war stops relief from reaching the needy, and 800,000 Ethiopians will eventually die.

ECONOMY AND SOCIETY
- The 23rd Olympic Games, held in Los Angeles, are boycotted by the USSR and other nations.
- *The Yuppie Handbook* describes the young upwardly mobile professional, a go-getting archetype of Ronald Reagan's USA and Margaret Thatcher's Britain.

SCIENCE AND TECHNOLOGY
- The Internet comes into being when a communications network is introduced that allows US universities to share the resources of five regional supercomputing centres. Access is initially limited to scientists, academics and government employees.

ARTS AND HUMANITIES
Literature
14 Aug. The English writer J.B. Priestley dies.
Kathy Acker, *Blood and Guts in High School*, novel.
Martin Amis, *Money*, novel.
J.G. Ballard, *Empire of the Sun*, novel.
Iain Banks, *The Wasp Factory*, novel
Julian Barnes, *Flaubert's Parrot*, novel.
Anita Brookner, *Hôtel du Lac*, novel.
Angela Carter, *Nights at the Circus*, novel.
Marguerite Duras, *L'Amant* (The Lover), novel.
Michael Frayn, *Benefactors*, play.
Keri Hulme, *The Bone People*, novel.
Milan Kundera, *Nesnesitelná leykost bytí* (The Unbearable Lightness of Being), novel.
Alison Lurie, *Foreign Affairs*, novel.
Gore Vidal, *Lincoln*, novel.
Mary Wesley, *The Camomile Lawn*, novel.
Visual Arts and Architecture
- In Britain the Turner Prize, intended to encourage the collection of contemporary art, is awarded for the first time.
Andy Warhol, Jean-Michel Basquiat, and Francesco Clemente, *Polestar*, painting.
Music
24 Mar. First performance of Philip Glass's opera *Akhnaten*.
- The rock singer Bob Geldof organizes a series of charity projects after seeing a TV documentary about the famine in Ethiopia. He books an array of pop stars to record the single 'Do They Know it's Christmas?', released under the name Band Aid. Profits from the single, as well as T-shirts and videos, go to the famine victims.
Duran Duran, 'Reflex', single.
Frankie Goes to Hollywood, 'Relax', single.
Andrew Lloyd Webber, *Starlight Express*, musical.
Madonna, 'Like a Virgin', single.
Prince, *Purple Rain*, album.
Lionel Ritchie, 'Hello', single.
Stephen Sondheim, *Sunday in the Park with George*, musical.
Bruce Springsteen, *Born in the USA*, album.
Wham!, 'Freedom', single.
Film
21 Oct. The French film director François Truffaut dies.

James Cameron, *The Terminator*, starring Arnold Schwarzenegger.
Wes Craven, *Nightmare on Elm Street*.
Joe Dante, *Gremlins*.
Rob Epstein, *The Times of Harvey Milk*, documentary.
Milos Forman, *Amadeus*.
John Huston, *Under the Volcano*, starring Albert Finney and based on Malcolm Lowry's novel.
Roland Joffé, *The Killing Fields*.
David Lean, *A Passage to India*, based on E.M. Forster's 1924 novel.
Rob Reiner, *This is Spinal Tap*.
Bertrand Tavernier, *A Sunday in the Country*.
Wim Wenders, *Paris, Texas*.

1985

EUROPE
11 Feb. In Britain Clive Ponting, the civil servant charged under the Official Secrets Act over his leaking of documents relating to the sinking of the *General Belgrano* (see 1984), is acquitted by the jury against the direction of the judge, establishing the principle that the interests of the state are not necessarily identical with the interests of the government.
28 Feb. In Northern Ireland nine members of the Royal Ulster Constabulary (RUC) die when the IRA launches a mortar attack on Newry police station.
3 Mar. In Britain many miners have now returned to work. National Union of Mineworkers (NUM) delegates vote to return to work without a settlement of the year-long miners' strike.
11 Mar. In Moscow the first secretary of the Soviet Communist Party Konstantin Chernenko dies and is succeeded by Mikhail Sergeevich Gorbachev. The 54-year-old Gorbachev presents a comparatively youthful and reformist face for a Soviet government that has previously been run by a succession of elderly decrepits. Few of his colleagues realize how committed to reform he is, or they would have been unlikely to support him.
11 April Enver Hoxha, Marxist dictator of Albania, dies.
5 May West German chancellor Helmut Kohl and US president Ronald Reagan visit Bitberg military cemetery, thereby provoking a political furore since the cemetery contains the graves of SS men. Kohl and Reagan also visit the former Belsen concentration camp.
29 May English football's violence and criminality become a European problem: Liverpool fans attending the European Cup Final in Brussels, Belgium, attack supporters of the Juventus club of Turin. In all, 39 fans are killed when part of the Heysel stadium collapses. English football clubs are banned from all European competitions.
June In his first major statement, Soviet leader Mikhail Gorbachev talks of the need to make major structural reforms in the economy of the USSR.
2 July Eduard Shevardnadze, a Georgian, becomes foreign minister of the USSR.
6 Oct. During riots in Tottenham, N London, Keith Blakelock, a police constable, is murdered.

15 Nov. British prime minister Margaret Thatcher and Irish taoiseach (prime minister) Garret Fitzgerald sign the Anglo-Irish agreement at Hillsborough, Co. Down. The agreement provides for frequent consultation between the British and Irish governments about Northern Ireland and sets up a joint ministerial conference of British and Irish ministers; it also increases cooperation between police and security forces on both sides of the Irish border. Because the agreement gives the Irish Republic a greater voice in the affairs of Northern Ireland, it is opposed by most Unionists. All 15 Unionist MPs resign their seats in protest (17 Dec.).

21 Nov. Soviet leader Mikhail Gorbachev meets US President Ronald Reagan and they agree to resume arms control talks.

Dec. In Britain growing discontents within the Conservative Party over Margaret Thatcher's style of government come to a head in the Westland Affair, a political row centring on the Westland helicopter company. Defence minister Michael Heseltine favours a rescue bid by a European consortium, but is opposed by trade and industry secretary Leon Brittan, who, along with the Westland directors, prefers a deal with the US firm of Sikorski.

– In Britain the Local Government Act will lead to the abolition of the Greater London Council (GLC) in 1986.

MIDDLE EAST AND NORTH AFRICA

10 June Israel completes its withdrawal from Lebanon, leaving its troops only in a security zone in the S of the country.

14 June An American TWA jet is hijacked and flown to Beirut; passengers are held hostage for 17 days by Shiite Muslim gunmen.

17 Aug. In the ongoing war between the two countries, Iraqi jets attack Iran's oil terminal at Kharg Island.

13 Sept. The Saudi Arabian oil minister, Ahmad Zaki Yamani, announces the start of his country's pricing discount system in oil sales. The Saudi aim is to glut the market with oil and to force its competitors in the oil-producing countries of Norway, Canada, the USA, Mexico, Venezuela, Nigeria, Egypt, Britain and Algeria to shut down their comparatively higher cost oil wells. Over the next few months the world oil price will fall by 60%.

1 Oct. Israel attacks the PLO headquarters in Tunis in revenge for the killing of three Israelis in Cyprus.

7 Oct. Palestinian terrorists seize the Italian cruise ship *Achille Lauro* in the Mediterranean and kill Leon Klinghoffer, an elderly US Jewish passenger. The terrorists surrender to the Egyptian authorities on 9 Oct. Palestinian frustration at the hopelessness of their political situation is leading to an alarming surge in international terrorism.

23 Nov. An Egyptian airliner is hijacked by Palestinian terrorists and forced to land in Malta. 60 will be killed when Egyptian commandos storm the plane (24 Nov.).

20 Dec. Palestinian gunmen attack Vienna airport and then Rome airport (27 Dec.).

ASIA

Feb. In Kampuchea (Cambodia) the invading Vietnamese force the Khmer Rouge out of their last defensive positions.

Sept. Radical changes in the Politburo and Central Committee of the Chinese Communist Party see 74 older party members replaced by younger ones.

2 Dec. Corazón Aquino, widow of Benigno Aquino (see Aug. 1983), announces that she will challenge Ferdinand Marcos for the presidency of the Philippines.

30 Dec. In Pakistan Gen. Zia ul-Haq lifts martial law. During the course of the year direct elections have been held, on a non-party basis, to the national and provincial assemblies, as Gen. Zia gradually enlarges the civilian element in his government. Mohammad Khan Junejo heads an administration that is subservient to Gen. Zia.

THE AMERICAS

6 Feb. In the USA President Reagan returns to the theme of tax reform in his State of the Union message.

1 Mar. Uruguay's military dictatorship is toppled, and Uruguay returns to a civilian government led by President Julio María Sanguinetti. Following the restoration of democracy, thousands of Tupamaros guerrillas are released. The Tupamaros will reorganize as a legal political party.

1 Mar. Ronald Reagan states that the Nicaraguan Contras are 'the moral equal of our Founding Fathers'. He goes on to announce a trade embargo against Nicaragua (1 May).

15 Mar. Following the general elections (Jan.) that have returned Brazil to civilian government after 21 years of military dictatorship, President José Sarney takes office.

2 May The US banking firm of Merrill Lynch receives, at its New York offices, a fax that alleges insider dealing at the bank's branch in Caracas, Venezuela. It is a sign of things to come.

18 July Congress acts to control President Reagan's Nicaraguan policy, which aims to topple the Sandinista government; he is now only allowed to support the Contras with 'non-lethal aid'.

28 July Alan Garcia Perez replaces Fernando Belaúnde Terry as president of Peru, but the democratic succession takes place against a background of terrorism and militarism. The Marxist guerrillas of the Sendero Luminoso (Shining Path) movement control large areas of Peru.

16 Sept. A balance of payment deficit turns the USA into a debtor nation for the first time since 1914. The Department of Commerce announces that it has had to deal with the deficit by relying on the foreign buying of US treasury bonds and notes, instead of using money raised from general taxation.

19 Sept. About 5000 people are killed in an earthquake in Mexico City.

14 Nov. Some 25,000 people are killed when the Nevado del Ruiz volcano erupts in Colombia.

SUB-SAHARAN AFRICA

13 Jan. In Ethiopia a train travelling to Addis Ababa crashes: 392 people are killed and 370 injured.

6 April Gen. Abd al-Rahman Suwar al-Dahab, military chief of staff of Sudan, leads a successful military coup against President Nimeiri.

20 July The South African government declares a state of emergency: arrests are now possible without warrants and many are held indefinitely without trial. President Botha emphasizes his continuing commitment to the apartheid system (15 Aug.).

27 July President Milton Obote of Uganda is overthrown by a military coup and replaced by Gen. Tito Okello.

27 Aug. President Buhari of Nigeria is replaced by Maj. Gen. Ibrahim Babangida in a military coup.

27 Oct. Julius Nyerere resigns as president of Tanzania.

AUSTRALASIA AND OCEANIA

4 Feb. The New Zealand government bans a US warship from entering its territorial waters after the US government refuses to say whether it is carrying nuclear arms.

10 July A Greenpeace anti-nuclear ship, the *Rainbow Warrior*, is sunk in Auckland harbour, New Zealand. It was about to sail towards Moruroa Island in the Pacific to protest against the French government's nuclear weapons testing programme. French agents are responsible, and the sabotage causes an international scandal.

SCIENCE AND TECHNOLOGY

– The British Antarctic Survey finds a hole in the ozone layer above Antarctica.

ARTS AND HUMANITIES

Literature

7 Dec. The English writer Robert Graves dies.

Peter Ackroyd, *Hawksmoor*, novel.

Margaret Atwood, *The Handmaid's Tale*, novel.

Howard Brenton and David Hare, *Pravda*, play.

Peter Carey, *Illywhacker*, novel.

Robertson Davies, *What's Bred in the Bone*, novel.

Don DeLillo, *White Noise*, novel.

Douglas Dunne, *Elegies*, poetry collection.

Christopher Hampton, *Les Liaisons dangereuses* (Dangerous Liaisons), stage adaptation in English of Choderlos de Laclos's classic epistolary novel of moral corruption (1782).

William Hoffman, *As It Is*, the first of a crop of plays dealing with AIDS.

John Irving, *The Cider House Rules*, novel.

Garrison Keillor, *Lake Wobegon Days*, tales of the small-town US Midwest.

Gabriel García Márquez, *El amor en los tiempos del cólera* (Love in the Time of Cholera), novel.

Larry McMurtry, *Lonesome Dove*, novel.

Patrick Süskind, *Perfume*, novel

Anne Tyler, *The Accidental Tourist*, novel.

Jeanette Winterson, *Oranges Are Not the Only Fruit*, semi-autobiographical novel.

Visual Arts and Architecture

28 Mar. French painter Marc Chagall dies.

– In Britain Howard Hodgkin wins the Turner Prize with his painting *A Small Thing But My Own*.

Music

13 July Live Aid, a rock event organized by the Irish singer Bob Geldof and held in both Philadelphia and London, raises $70 million for African famine relief.

John Adams, *Harmonielehre*, orchestral work.

A-Ha, 'Take on Me', single.

The Cure, *The Head on the Door*, album.

Dire Straits, *Brothers in Arms*, album.

Madonna, 'Into the Groove', single.

The Pogues, *Rum, Sodomy and the Lash*, album.

Jennifer Rush, 'The Power of Love', single.

Claude-Michel Schonberg, *Les Miserables*, musical.

The Smiths, *Meat is Murder*, album.

Tears for Fears, 'Everybody Wants to Rule the World', single.

Tom Waits, *Rain Dogs*, album.

Film

2 Oct. American actor Rock Hudson dies of AIDS; he is the first public figure to die of the disease, and he does so in very public circumstances. His death heightens awareness of the disease.

Woody Allen, *The Purple Rose of Cairo*.

Hector Babenco, *Kiss of the Spider Woman*.

David Drury, *Defence of the Realm*, portraying the security services and surveillance techniques of Thatcher's Britain.

Stephen Frears, *My Beautiful Laundrette*.

Terry Gilliam, *Brazil*.

John Huston, *Prizzi's Honor*, starring Jack Nicholson.

Akira Kurosawa, *Ran*, adapting Shakespeare's *King Lear*.

Claude Lanzmann, *Shoah*, Holocaust documentary.

Sydney Pollack, *Out of Africa*.

Steven Spielberg, *The Color Purple*, starring Whoopi Goldberg.

Istvan Szabo, *Colonel Redl*.

Robert Zemeckis, *Back to the Future*.

1986

EUROPE

1 Jan. Spain and Portugal join the European Community (EC), bringing the number of EC members to 12.

9 Jan. Michael Heseltine, the British defence minister, resigns in the middle of a cabinet meeting when prime minister Margaret Thatcher insists that ministerial statements on the Westland Affair (see Dec. 1985) should be approved by the Cabinet Office. A letter critical of Heseltine is subsequently leaked from the solicitor general. The trade and industry secretary Leon Brittan resigns on 25 Jan., admitting that he has approved the leak. Untrammelled by cabinet loyalties, Heseltine is now free to pursue his ambition to oust Margaret Thatcher as leader of the Conservative Party.

23 Jan. By-elections are held in Northern Ireland following the resignations of Unionist MPs in protest at the Anglo-Irish agreement (see 15 Nov. 1985). 14 of the 15 MPs retain their seats.

11 Feb. Soviet physicist and dissident Anatoly Sharansky is allowed to leave the USSR as part of a liberalizing move by Mikhail Gorbachev's government.

12 Feb. Britain and France sign the treaty to build the Channel Tunnel.

28 Feb. Olof Palme, socialist prime minister of Sweden, is assassinated. Neither the assassin nor a motive is ever discovered.

16 Mar. In the French general election right-wing opposition parties narrowly defeat the Socialist Party. In a novel departure for the institutions of the French Fifth Republic, the Gaullist Jacques Chirac become prime minister of a right-of-centre government (20 Mar.), while socialist François Mitterrand continues as president. 'Cohabitation' was never envisaged under the original constitution as devised by Charles de Gaulle, but both the president and the new prime minister are suited to an opportunistic coupling.

31 Mar. In Britain the Greater London Council (GLC) is abolished. The Labour-controlled GLC, led by Ken Livingstone, has clashed repeatedly with the Conservative government over its proposals for economic regeneration, cheap public transport and aid to voluntary groups. Many of the GLC's powers will pass to central government, others to the boroughs and the City Corporation and yet others to new agencies such as the London Regional Transport Authority and the London Fire and Civil Defence Authority.

26 April The Chernobyl nuclear power plant, near Kiev in Ukraine, USSR, explodes. Radioactive clouds drift W across Europe. Huge areas of Soviet territory are turned into wasteland for the foreseeable future. The hesitation, denials and then admission of the disaster by Gorbachev's government raise doubts about its reformist rhetoric.

April Middle Eastern violence against the West continues unabated: four US citizens are killed when a bomb explodes on a TWA airliner flying over Athens, Greece (2 April); 2 people are killed and 230 injured when a bomb explodes in a West Berlin discothèque frequented by US servicemen (5 April). The hand of Libya is suspected in the latter.

11–12 Oct. US President Ronald Reagan and Soviet leader Mikhail Gorbachev meet for a summit in Reykjavik; the two leaders come close to an agreement to abandon all nuclear weapons, but the USA rejects any idea of decommissioning the Strategic Defence Initiative (SDI or 'Star Wars'). Nevertheless, a personal relationship has developed between the two, which bodes well for future disarmament negotiations.

– The British government privatizes British Gas and the British Airports Authority.

MIDDLE EAST AND NORTH AFRICA

7 Jan. The US government announces that it is imposing sanctions on Libya for involvement in international terrorism.

11 April Brian Keenan, an Irish teacher, is taken hostage by Muslim extremists in Beirut. John McCarthy, a British television journalist, is taken hostage on 17 April. The two men will endure four to five years in captivity.

15 April In response to recent Libyan terror attacks on US targets, US planes bomb the headquarters of Libyan leader

Moamar al-Qaddafi near Tripoli. Despite their efforts, the Americans fail to kill Qaddafi, but others are killed or injured.

28 Oct. Sheikh Yamani, architect of the policy of discounting oil, is removed from his post as minister for oil by King Fahd of Saudi Arabia. World oil prices have now collapsed.

– Iran is receiving secret military assistance from the USA. A deal has been struck in exchange for the release of US hostages held by the pro-Iranian Hezbollah (Party of God) guerrillas in Lebanon.

ASIA

7 Feb. Presidential elections are held in the Philippines. Corazón Aquino (see 2 Dec. 1985) stands against President Marcos, who has only agreed to hold the election as a last-ditch means of retaining US economic and diplomatic support. The national assembly declares Marcos the winner (15 Feb.), but it is clear that large-scale electoral fraud has taken place. With the backing of the Roman Catholic Church, Corazón Aquino instigates a non-violent protest, termed 'people's power', which gathers massive popular support for the ending of the dictatorial Marcos regime. Marcos also comes under strong pressure from the USA to step down.

24 Feb. Corazón Aquino becomes president of the Philippines. Ex-president Ferdinand Marcos flees to Hawaii, where he will die in 1989.

April Benazir Bhutto, leader of the Pakistan People's Party (PPP) and daughter of the executed former Pakistani leader Zulfikar Ali Bhutto (see 4 April 1979), returns to Pakistan from self-imposed exile in London to launch a campaign for open elections.

5 Sept. In another Muslim attack on a Western target, terrorists seize a PanAm jet at Karachi in Pakistan, killing 15 people and wounding 127.

2 Oct. Indian premier Rajiv Gandhi survives an assassination attempt in New Delhi.

– Mass demonstrations by Chinese students fail to convince the country's leaders of the need to reform.

THE AMERICAS

28 Jan. The US space shuttle *Challenger* explodes during take-off, killing the seven astronauts on board.

6 Feb. Jean-Claude 'Baby Doc' Duvalier, president of Haiti, resigns and flees to France. But the corrupt and cruel regime over which he has presided continues in power.

12 May US financier Denis B. Levine is accused by Wall Street's Securities and Exchange Commission of insider trading, which has earned him some $12.6 million. He pleads guilty and co-operates with the authorities in further investigations into the corruption that has spread in the US financial markets as a result of the wave of corporate takeovers and mergers.

26 June The US Congress approves $100 million in aid to the Contra rebels in Nicaragua.

22 Oct. In a radical act of tax simplification, Reagan approves legislation that reduces 15 tax brackets to just two (15% and

28%); tax breaks for the rich are removed, and the lowest paid are removed from the tax system. But higher taxation on businesses leads to higher prices.

7 Nov. The US government allows millions of illegal immigrants a legal right of residence under the Simpson–Mazzoli Act, which is now signed by President Reagan.

13 Nov. President Reagan admits to a secret arms deal with Iran (see above).

14 Nov. American financier Ivan Boesky pleads guilty to insider trading relating to merger bids and becomes one of the most celebrated of those accused in Wall Street's rash of insider dealing cases.

25 Nov. The Iran-Contra scandal breaks in the USA when National Security Adviser Vice-Admiral John Poindexter and his aide Lt-Col. Oliver North are sacked from their posts. Members of the Reagan administration have sanctioned arms sales to Iran in exchange for the release of US hostages in Lebanon, the proceeds being used (illegally) to fund the Contras' campaign of violence and terror against the elected Sandinista government of Nicaragua. President Reagan comes under much political pressure: he is accused of breaking the law, rewarding the taking of hostages and betraying the USA's allies. He will, however, survive the scandal.

– The US national debt is now $2 trillion dollars, having been $1 trillion in 1981. The dollar has weakened, but this makes no difference to the trade deficit, which, at over $170 billion, is running at record level.

SUB-SAHARAN AFRICA

7 Mar. In South Africa the state of emergency is lifted (see 20 July 1985).

18 April South African prime minister P.W. Botha announces the repeal of the pass laws which have restricted the movements of non-whites within South Africa since 1948.

1 May In a national strike to protest against apartheid 1.5 million South Africans stop work.

12 June Another state of emergency is declared in South Africa and critical press reporting is banned.

7 Sept. In South Africa Desmond Tutu becomes Anglican archbishop of Cape Town. He is the first African to be chosen for the post.

3 Oct. President Reagan has tried to veto economic sanctions against South Africa, but the US Senate now votes to override the presidential veto, as South Africa's international reputation continues to deteriorate.

19 Oct. President Samora Machel of Mozambique is killed in a plane crash on the South African border. He is succeeded by Joaquim Chissano (3 Nov.).

ECONOMY AND SOCIETY

May–June Argentina wins the 13th soccer World Cup, held in Mexico.

27 Oct. The City of London stock exchange is modernized in the 'Big Bang': the distinction between stockjobber and

stockbroker is abolished, and operations become fully computerized. The aim is to maintain London's position as a leading international financial centre.

– Cocaine is now widespread as a designer drug used by both the fashionable and the inner-city poor in the USA. The Cali and the Medellín gangs in Colombia control the trade, which sends some 75 metric tonnes of the drug to the USA every year.

– Nintendo video games are introduced in the USA.

SCIENCE AND TECHNOLOGY

– A vast engineering scheme is completed: the project to build a Danube–Black Sea canal from Cernavoda to Constanza has been pushed through by President Nicolae Ceausescu of Romania. The programme has used forced labour, including political prisoners.

– Halley's comet returns and is studied by space probes, including the European probe *Giotto*. The comet will next return in 2061.

ARTS AND HUMANITIES

Literature

4 Jan. The English writer Christopher Isherwood dies.

14 April The French writer and philosopher Simone de Beauvoir dies.

14 June The Argentinian novelist Jorge Luis Borges dies.

7 Oct. The *Independent*, which is intended to be a politically neutral newspaper, starts publication in London and aims at benefiting from the industrial unrest that disrupts publication of *The Times* and its associated titles.

Kingsley Amis, *The Old Devils*, novel.

Paul Auster, *The New York Trilogy*, trilogy of short novels.

John Banville, *Mefisto*, novel.

Wendy Cope, *Making Cocoa for Kingsley Amis*, poetry collection.

Richard Ford, *The Sportswriter*, novel.

John Le Carré, *A Perfect Spy*, novel.

Vikram Seth, *The Golden Gate*, verse novel.

Hugh Whitemore, *Breaking the Code*, play based on the life of Alan Turing, the gay Cambridge mathematician who pioneered computing and broke the German Enigma code in World War II.

Visual Arts and Architecture

23 Jan. German sculptor Joseph Beuys dies.

31 Aug. English sculptor Henry Moore dies.

– The Lloyd's of London building, designed by Richard Rogers, is completed in the City of London.

– The Musée d'Orsay, housed in a former railway station and displaying Impressionist and other paintings from the period 1848–1914, opens in Paris.

Lucian Freud, *Painter and Model*, painting.

Music

21 May First performance in London of Harrison Birtwistle's opera *The Mask of Orpheus* to a libretto by P. Zinoviev.

John Adams, *Short Ride in a Fast Machine*, orchestral work.

Berlin, 'Take My Breath Away', single.

Communards, 'Don't Leave Me This Way', single.

Andrew Lloyd Webber, *Phantom of the Opera*, musical.

Madonna, *True Blue*, album.

Pet Shop Boys, 'West End Girls', single.

Diana Ross, 'Chain Reaction', single.

Run-DMC, 'Walk This Way', single.

Paul Simon, *Graceland*, album.

The Smiths, *The Queen is Dead*, album.

Film

30 Nov. British-born Hollywood actor Cary Grant dies.

Woody Allen, *Hannah and her Sisters*.

Jean-Jacques Annaud, *The Name of the Rose*, starring Sean Connery.

Jean-Jacques Beineix, *Betty Blue*.

Claude Berri, *Jean de Florette*, starring Gérard Depardieu.

Derek Jarman, *Caravaggio*.

Spike Lee, *She's Gotta Have It*.

David Lynch, *Blue Velvet*.

Rob Reiner, *Stand By Me*.

Tony Scott, *Top Gun*, starring Tom Cruise.

Oliver Stone, *Platoon*.

Andrei Tarkovsky, *The Sacrifice*.

1987

EUROPE

25 Jan. In the West German parliamentary elections the governing CDU/FDP coalition wins a further term.

17 Feb. In the Republic of Ireland Fianna Fáil defeats Garret Fitzgerald's Fine Gael coalition government in the general election. Charles Haughey returns as taoiseach (prime minister) (10 Mar.).

6 Mar. The *Herald of Free Enterprise*, a British cross-Channel ferry, capsizes near Zeebrugge, Belgium: 192 people are killed.

11 May The trial of Klaus Barbie, the Gestapo chief in Lyons from 1941 to 1945, opens in Lyons, France (see Feb. 1983).

11 June In the British general election the Conservative Party win a third term under Margaret Thatcher, with a reduced, but still impressive, majority: the Conservatives win 375 seats to Labour's 229. The Liberals and Social Democrats, who, as in 1983, have contested seats in the Liberal–SDP Alliance, win 22 seats.

25 June Mikhail Gorbachev announces a new economic plan for the Soviet system. Perestroika (restructuring) means that Soviet factories will have greater local autonomy (from 1 Jan. 1988). The Soviet system of central economic planning is abandoned, but it remains uncertain whether renewal or complete collapse will follow the removal of the coercive structures that maintained the Soviet economy's creaking structures. Boris Yeltsin, mayor of Moscow and a prominent figure among the many critics of Gorbachev, is sacked after complaining about the slow pace of reform (10 Nov.) but is then brought back into government (18 Nov.).

1 July The Single European Act, signed and ratified by the member-states of the European Community (EC), comes into force. It begins a process intended to create a single European market by 1993.

4 July In France Klaus Barbie is sentenced to life imprisonment. His trial for war crimes heralds a new self-consciousness in France about the period of the occupation and the need to come to terms with that past.

6 Aug. In Britain Dr David Owen resigns as leader of the Social Democratic Party following a vote by party members to start merger negotiations with the Liberal Party.

17 Aug. Rudolf Hess dies in Spandau prison in Berlin.

7–11 Sept. East German leader Erich Honecker visits West Germany, the first such visit by an East German head of state.

16 Oct. The 'Great Storm' wreaks havoc across S Britain: 18 die and millions of trees are blown down.

19 Oct. 'Black Monday' on the London stock exchange: £50 billion is wiped off the value of publicly quoted companies. The crash follows panic on Wall Street the previous Friday and heavy selling on the Tokyo stock exchange.

1 Nov. French authorities board the trawler *Eksund* and discover arms intended for the Provisional IRA.

8 Nov. In Northern Ireland 11 people are killed when an IRA bomb explodes during a Remembrance Day service in Enniskillen, Co. Fermanagh. Given the particular reverence accorded by Northern Ireland's Protestants to their World War I dead, it is a deeply provocative act.

18 Nov. In a fire at King's Cross underground station, London, 32 people are killed.

29 Nov. A referendum is held on a new Polish constitution. The proposed changes need to be ratified by a poll in which at least 50% of the total electorate turn out to vote. Although still banned, Solidarity organizes a boycott and, as a result, elector absenteeism disqualifies the referendum results. It is clear that Polish dissent against the communist system is as strong as ever.

7 Dec. Mikhail Gorbachev flies to Washington for a three-day conference on security. The Soviet and US governments sign treaties that reduce the size of nuclear arsenals and agree to dismantle their medium and shorter range missile systems. A system of mutual weapons inspection is agreed.

17 Dec. Gustáv Husák resigns as leader of the Czechoslovak Communist Party. Milos Jakes takes over.

MIDDLE EAST AND NORTH AFRICA

20 Jan. Terry Waite, the archbishop of Canterbury's special envoy to the Middle East, disappears in Beirut. It emerges that he has been taken hostage (2 Feb.).

22 Feb. Syrian forces occupy West Beirut, Lebanon, to stop fighting between Shiite and Druse militias.

8 April In Beirut, Lebanon, Syrian troops relieve two Palestinian refugee camps that have been besieged for five months by Shiite Amal militiamen.

17 May The US frigate *Stark* is hit by Iraqi missiles and 37 US servicemen are killed. Saddam Hussein, president of Iraq, apologizes to the USA. It is eventually accepted that the incident was an accident.

1 June The Lebanese prime minister Rashid Karami is killed by a bomb attack on the helicopter in which he is travelling.

8 Dec. Four Palestinians are killed when they are hit by a truck driven by an Israeli in the occupied Gaza strip: the response leads to the *intifada* (uprising), which now spreads throughout the Israeli-occupied territories of Gaza and the West Bank.

– Gen. Zine al-Abidine Ben Ali overthrows President Bourguiba of Tunisia in a bloodless coup.

– The USA grants Kuwait's request that its tankers in the Persian Gulf be protected against Iranian attacks.

ASIA

17 April Tamil terrorists ambush a bus in Trincomalee, NE Sri Lanka, killing 129 people.

29 July President Jayawardene of Sri Lanka and Indian prime minister Rajiv Gandhi (who is attempting to mediate in Sri Lanka's ethnic conflict), sign a peace treaty with the aim of ending ethnic violence in Sri Lanka. Separatist Tamil guerrillas (the Tamil Tigers) are fighting for an independent Tamil home-land (Eelam) in the N of the country. Fighting between rival Tamil guerrilla groups, Sinhalese extremists and government forces has devastated the area. The peace agreement proposes to create a semi-autonomous Tamil homeland and to recognize the Tamil Tigers as representatives of the Tamil people once they have disarmed. An Indian peace-keeping force is sent to the Tamil-controlled Jaffna Peninsula to police the agreement.

1 Oct. Tibetans demonstrate against Chinese rule. The Chinese government is unmoved.

16 Dec. In democratic elections Roh Tae-woo, nominated successor to the military leader Chun Doo Hwan, is elected president of South Korea amid allegations of fraud.

– In China, Communist Party secretary general Hu Yaobang loses favour with Deng Xiaoping and is dismissed. He is replaced by the reform-inclined Zhao Ziyang.

THE AMERICAS

29 Jan. The Tower Report, commissioned by the US Senate, asserts that the Reagan administration has deceived Congress in the Iran-Contra affair (see 25 Nov. 1986). Oliver North appears before a congressional committee and states that the secret operations he conducted were authorized (July). John Poindexter testifies that he did use money made from Iran arms deals in order to finance the war against the Sandinistas. George Schultz, secretary of state, claims that he was deceived. President Reagan admits that US government policy was out of control (12 Aug.). The Congressional committee in its final report (18 Nov.) states that Ronald Reagan has failed to uphold the laws of the USA since, as president, he was responsible for his aides' actions. Some $48 million were distributed to the Contras by illegal means.

Feb. Brazil, the largest debtor nation in the third world, announces that it will suspend interest payments on loans from foreign banks.

19 Mar. Jim Bakker, the North Carolina evangelist, resigns from his ministry in a welter of financial and sexual scandal. He will be sentenced to 45 years in jail (1989), but will serve only five.

July The US trade deficit now stands at $16.5 billion. President Reagan has already announced a 100% tariff on some Japanese imports (17 April).

7 Aug. C American governments meet in Guatemala City: they agree to cooperate with Costa Rican president Oscar Arias Sánchez in implementing peace-keeping measures across the region. Arias is awarded the Nobel Peace Prize (13 Oct.), but the Nicaraguan tragedy continues.

Sept. Congress acts to enforce automatic budget reductions. President Reagan signs a measure to cut government spending rather than raise taxes (22 Dec.).

3 Oct. Canada and the USA sign a free-trade agreement.

19 Oct. The Dow Jones Index falls by 22.6% to close at 1738.74 (down by 508 points): the fall is the greatest since Oct. 1929.

Oct. A five-nation peace agreement begins to restore order in Nicaragua. The Sandinistas allow an anti-government news-paper, *La Prensa*, to resume publication.

8 Dec. The Soviet and US governments sign a treaty eliminating medium-range intermediate nuclear weapons in both countries.

18 Dec. US financier Ivan Boesky is sentenced to three years in jail for insider dealing and is fined $100 million.

SUB-SAHARAN AFRICA

22 Dec. In Zimbabwe Robert Mugabe and Joshua Nkomo agree to merge their ZANU and ZAPU parties.

ECONOMY AND SOCIETY

May–June The host country, New Zealand, wins the first rugby union World Cup.

SCIENCE AND TECHNOLOGY

16 Sept. An international conference held at Montreal, Canada, agrees to phase out, gradually, the chlorofluorocarbons (CFCs) that are damaging the Earth's ozone layer.

– Some relief for AIDS sufferers becomes available when AZT, a drug developed by Burroughs Welcome, becomes available.

– The world's population reaches 5 billion.

ARTS AND HUMANITIES

Literature

11 April The Italian writer Primo Levi commits suicide.

3 Oct. The French playwright Jean Anouilh dies.

30 Nov. The US writer James Baldwin dies.

– Boris Pasternak's novel *Doctor Zhivago* (1957) is published in the USSR for the first time.

Chinua Achebe, *Anthills of the Savannah*, novel.

Allan Bloom, *The Closing of the American Mind*, neo-conservative political philosophy and criticism.

Margaret Drabble, *The Radiant Way*, first novel of a trilogy.

William Golding, *Close Quarters*, novel.

Paul Kennedy, *The Rise and Fall of the Great Powers*, historical study.

Penelope Lively, *Moon Tiger*, novel.

Ian McEwan, *The Child in Time*, novel.

Toni Morrison, *Beloved*, novel.

Peter Hillsman Taylor, *A Summons to Memphis*, novel.

Tom Wolfe, *The Bonfire of the Vanities*, novel.

Visual Arts and Architecture

23 Feb. American artist Andy Warhol dies.

– *Irises*, a painting by Vincent Van Gogh, is sold by Christie's of London for a record £30 million.

Music

19 Oct. The cellist Jacqueline du Pré dies having suffered from multiple sclerosis for some years.

22 Oct. First performance in Houston, Texas, of John Adams's opera *Nixon in China*.

The Cure, *Kiss Me, Kiss Me, Kiss Me*, album.

Def Leppard, *Hysteria*, album.

Philip Glass, *Violin Concerto*.

Guns N' Roses, *Appetite for Destruction*, album.

Whitney Houston, 'I Wanna Dance With Somebody', single.

George Michael, *Faith*, album.

Prince, *Sign O' the Times*, album and single.

U2, *The Joshua Tree*, album.

Film

Gabriel Axel, *Babette's Feast*, starring Stéphane Audran.

Bernardo Bertolucci, *The Last Emperor*.

John Boorman, *Hope and Glory*.

Peter Greenaway, *The Belly of an Architect*.

John Huston, *The Dead*, starring Anjelica Huston and based on a short story from James Joyce's *Dubliners* (1914).

Stanley Kubrick, *Full Metal Jacket*.

Adrian Lyne, *Fatal Attraction*, starring Glenn Close and Michael Douglas.

Louis Malle, *Au revoir les enfants*.

Oliver Stone, *Wall Street*, starring Michael Douglas.

Paul Verhoeven, *Robocop*.

Wim Wenders, *Der Himmel über Berlin* (Wings of Desire).

1988

EUROPE

3 Jan. Margaret Thatcher becomes Britain's longest-serving 20th-century prime minister.

3 Mar. In Britain the Social and Liberal Democrats come in to being following a vote by members of the Liberal Party (23 Jan.) and the Social Democratic Party (31 Jan.) to merge and form a new political party of the centre. Liberal leader David Steel resigns and becomes the new party's foreign affairs spokesman, while Paddy Ashdown becomes its leader.

6 Mar. Three members of an IRA active service unit are shot dead by the SAS in Gibraltar. The circumstances of the shooting will provoke much controversy.

15 Mar. In Britain the chancellor of the exchequer Nigel Lawson reduces the standard rate of income tax to 25%.

16 Mar. In Northern Ireland three republican mourners are killed by Loyalist gunman Michael Stone in Milltown cemetery, Belfast.

19 Mar. In Northern Ireland two British soldiers are attacked and murdered by the IRA during a funeral procession in Belfast.

Mar. In Romania President Ceausescu announces a new programme to destroy 8000 villages and develop urban housing.

24 April–8 May François Mitterrand is re-elected as president of France to serve another seven-year term, defeating his Gaullist opponent Jacques Chirac. Mitterrand appoints the Socialist Michel Rocard as his prime minister (10 May).

22 May János Kádár is sacked as Hungary's communist leader and replaced by Karoly Grosz. This paves the way for major reform, including the legalization of political parties (10 Nov.).

1 June Soviet leader Mikhail Gorbachev and US president Reagan sign an Intermediate Nuclear Forces (INF) treaty in Moscow.

23 June In the Caucasus, following months of ethnic violence in the Soviet republics of Armenia, Azerbaijan and the disputed region of Nagorno-Karabakh (a Christian Armenian enclave within mainly Shiite Muslim Azerbaijan), Soviet forces move into the region. A state of emergency will be declared in Nagorno-Karabakh (Sept.).

28 June–1 July A special Communist Party conference convened by Soviet leader Mikhail Gorbachev approves far-reaching changes to the way the USSR is governed. A new legislature, the Congress of the USSR People's Deputies (CUPD) is to be created, from which a full-time working parliament will subsequently be elected, headed by a state president with increased powers.

6 July 169 people die in an explosion on the Piper Alpha oil platform in the North Sea.

20 Aug. In Northern Ireland eight British soldiers are killed by a landmine attack on a bus near Ballygawley, Co.Tyrone.

Aug. Polish workers strike for most of this month and demand that the trade union Solidarity be legalized. The first talks towards legalizing Solidarity open (31 Aug.), and the Polish strike ends (3 Sept.).

20 Sept. In a speech made to the Council of Europe in Bruges, Belgium, British prime minister Margaret Thatcher declares her opposition to closer European economic and political union, and her refusal to countenance any diminution of UK sovereignty. The Bruges Group of (mainly but not exclusively Conservative) anti-European MPs will take its name from her strongly worded speech.

30 Sept. Andrei Gromyko, former Soviet foreign minister (1957–85) and president of the USSR since 1985, retires.

1 Oct. Mikhail Gorbachev is named president of the USSR, and in an address to the UN he promises unilateral reductions in Soviet troops and arms along the old 'iron curtain' frontier dividing Europe (7 Dec.).

Oct. The British government forbids the broadcasting of interviews with members of 11 specified terrorist organizations, including Sinn Féin. The move is widely criticized, and British broadcasters sidestep the law by arranging for voice-overs spoken by actors to accompany the filmed interviews with people such as Gerry Adams and Martin McGuinness.

7 Dec. Some 25,000 people are killed in Armenia (a republic of the USSR) when an earthquake rocks the region.

12 Dec. In Britain 34 people die in a rail crash at Clapham Junction in S London.

21 Dec. PanAm flight PA 103, *en route* from London to New York, is blown up by a Libyan terrorist bomb as it passes over over Lockerbie, SW Scotland, killing all 259 people on board and 11 people on the ground.

– The British Steel Corporation is privatized.

– In Britain the Education Reform Act introduces a National Curriculum and testing at four Key Stages. The Act also allows state schools to opt out of the control of the local education authority.

– The pressure group Charter 88 publishes a document arguing that Britain needs, amongst other constitutional reforms, a written constitution, a bill of rights, devolution to a Scottish assembly, proportional representation and freedom of information.

MIDDLE EAST AND NORTH AFRICA

16 April Abu Jihad, the PLO official who is coordinating the *intifada*, is assassinated in Tunisia. The Israeli security service is held to be responsible.

18 April One of the great battles of the 20th century takes place in the course of the Iran–Iraq War when the Iraqi army retakes the city of Fao (an oil port at the mouth of the Shatt-al-Arab waterway): in a two-day struggle some 53,000 Iraqis and 120,000 Iranians die. Iran recovers its territorial positions, and in the stalemate that follows Ayatollah Khomeini agrees to a ceasefire (20 July). In subsequent negotiations Iran accepts the Iraqi peace proposal (8 Aug.). Khomeini abandons his earlier condition that Saddam Hussein must step down from office. Up to one million people have died in the war.

3 July By mistake the US warship *Vincennes* shoots down an Iran Air A300 Airbus in the Persian Gulf: 290 people are killed.

31 July King Hussein of Jordan announces that he is ceding the Israeli-occupied West Bank to the PLO.

Nov. The right-wing Likud party, led by Yitzhak Shamir, is elected to form a government in Israel amid scenes of violence in the occupied territories: the *intifada*, a coordinated mass protest of street rioters who use stones against Israeli weaponry, continues.

– Lebanon's civil war continues: President Amin Gemayel's term of office comes to an end but the Lebanese parliament fails to agree on a successor. Separate governments are formed under rival Christian and Muslim leaders: in East Beirut Gen. Michel Aoun is backed by Christian army units; in Muslim West Beirut Selim al-Hoss is backed by the Syrian army and Muslim militias.

ASIA

8 Feb. The USSR announces that it will withdraw its troops from Afghanistan. The occupation, since December 1979, has been opposed by Islamic *mujahedin* guerrilla fighters supplied, and in many cases trained, by the CIA.

April Aung San Suu Kyi, leader of the Burmese democratic opposition, returns to Burma from Britain. Pro-democracy protests and riots follow; more than 3000 unarmed demonstrators are killed when the government troops open fire on protestors in Rangoon (June).

May In Pakistan Gen. Zia ul-Haq dismisses the elected prime minister Mohammad Khan Junejo. He dissolves the National Assembly and decrees that strict Islamic (Sharia) law will be the country's law.

23 July Gen. Ne Win resigns as Burmese head of state. In the face of mass pro-democracy demonstrations a more moderate president, Maung Maung, takes office with a promise of multiparty elections within three months.

18 Aug. President Zia ul-Haq of Pakistan is killed in an air crash, along with the US ambassador to Pakistan.

Aug. Thousands are killed by floods on the E coast of China.

18 Sept. In Burma Gen. Saw Maung takes power in a military coup and imposes martial law.

Sept. Floods in Bangladesh kill more than 1000 and cause homelessness on a massive scale.

16 Nov. The Pakistan People's Party, led by Benazir Bhutto, wins the general election. Bhutto becomes prime minister of Pakistan on 2 Dec.

THE AMERICAS

5 Feb. US federal grand juries in Tampa and Miami indict Gen. Manuel Antonio Noriega, dictator of Panama, on charges of drug trafficking. A general strike is called in Panama in order to oust Noriega. The US government imposes sanctions on Panama in an attempt to force him from office.

April US unemployment falls to 5.4%.

31 Aug. In Canada parliament ratifies the free-trade agreement between the USA and Canada.

18 Sept. President Reagan vetoes an attempt by Congress to impose protectionist tariffs on the import of textiles.

8 Nov. George Bush, the vice-president, defeats Michael Dukakis, governor of Massachusetts and the Democratic candidate, to become 41st president of the USA. He has campaigned on a promise not to impose new taxes.

21 Nov. In Canada prime minister Brian Mulroney's Progressive Conservative Party wins the general election with a reduced majority. Mulroney has campaigned on a platform of free trade with the USA.

22 Dec. Francisco 'Chico' Mendes, leader of a Brazilian environmental group protesting against the clearing of the W Amazonian rainforest, is shot dead by Darci Alves, the son of a cattle rancher.

SUB-SAHARAN AFRICA

18 July On Nelson Mandela's 70th birthday, many voices around the world urge the South African government to release the leader of the African National Congress (ANC), imprisoned since 1964.

8 Aug. South Africa, Angola and Cuba sign a peace treaty. According to its terms South African troops will withdraw from Angola and Namibia and Cuban troops from Angola. The treaty includes acceptance by South Africa of Namibian independence.

AUSTRALASIA AND OCEANIA

April–May Kanak separatist guerrillas and French troops clash in the French dependency of New Caledonia in the SW Pacific.

ECONOMY AND SOCIETY

Sept.–Oct. The 24th Olympic Games are held in Seoul, South Korea. The Canadian sprinter Ben Johnson is stripped of his 100m gold medal after testing positive for a performance-enhancing anabolic steroid.

– American broadcaster Ted Turner founds Turner Network Television (TNT).

SCIENCE AND TECHNOLOGY

– The English physicist Stephen Hawking, confined to a wheelchair by motorneuron disease, publishes *A Brief History of Time*, an account of cosmology. It becomes an international bestseller.

ARTS AND HUMANITIES

Literature

12 April The South African writer Alan Paton dies.

– Salman Rushdie's novel *The Satanic Verses* enrages the Muslim world by its portrayal of the Prophet Muhammad.

Nicholson Baker, *The Mezzanine*, novel.

Peter Carey, *Oscar and Lucinda*, novel.

Bruce Chatwin, *Utz*, novel.

Umberto Eco, *Il pendolo di Foucault* (Foucault's Pendulum), novel.

Thomas Harris, *The Silence of the Lambs*, novel.

John Irving, *A Prayer for Owen Meany*, novel.

David Mamet, *Speed-the-Plow*, play.

Dennis Potter, *The Singing Detective*, BBC television series.

Anne Tyler, *Breathing Lessons*, novel.

Timberlake Wertenbaker, *Our Country's Good*, play.

A.N. Wilson, *Tolstoy*, biography.

Visual Arts and Architecture

12 Aug. American artist Jean-Michel Basquiat dies of a drug overdose at the age of 27.

Music

Phil Collins, 'A Groovy Kind of Love', single.

Guns N' Roses, *Lies*, album.

Kylie Minogue, 'I Should be So Lucky', single.

Steve Reich, *Different Trains*, for string quartet and sampled voices.

John Tavener, *Akathist of Thanksgiving*, choral work.

U2, *Rattle and Hum*, album.

Film

Pedro Almodóvar, *Women on the Verge of a Nervous Breakdown*.

Charles Crichton, *A Fish Called Wanda*.

Terence Davies, *Distant Voices, Still Lives*.

Stephen Frears, *Dangerous Liaisons*, starring John Malkovich and Glenn Close.

Peter Greenaway, *Drowning by Numbers*.

Barry Levinson, *Rain Man*, starring Dustin Hoffman and Tom Cruise.

John McTiernan, *Die Hard*, starring Bruce Willis.

Alan Parker, *Mississippi Burning*, starring Gene Hackman.

Martin Scorsese, *The Last Temptation of Christ*.

1989

EUROPE

14 Feb. Following the Ayatollah Khomeni's call for the novelist Salman Rushdie to be executed for blasphemy, the writer goes into hiding with police protection.

21 Feb. In Czechoslovakia the dissident playwright Václav Havel is imprisoned for inciting public disorder.

26 Mar. In the USSR, elections take place to the Congress of People's Deputies (CUPD), the new Soviet parliament. The radical politician Boris Yeltsin, who warns that Gorbachev's reforms are progressing too slowly, polls strongly in his Moscow constituency, defeating an official Communist Party candidate. The more conservative Communist Party apparatchiks fare less well in the elections.

17 April The trade union Solidarity is legalized in Poland. Lech Walesa has reached an agreement with the Polish government that political and economic reforms are to take place.

April The British government introduces the community charge, a form of poll tax, in Scotland.

May In the USSR, the Congress of People's Deputies (CUPD) elects Mikhail Gorbachev as state president. Gorbachev faces a number of crises: nationalist tensions are growing, especially in the Caucasus (see below); strikes are spreading in the USSR's coalfields; and popular discontent is mounting over the failure of *perestroika* to improve living standards.

4 June Elections to the Polish parliament are held. Solidarity candidates win all bar one of the parliamentary seats they contest, but many seats are reserved for candidates backed by the Polish Communist Party. The Polish parliament elects Gen. Jaruzelski to serve as the country's president (19 July).

15 June A general election in the Republic of Ireland produces a stalemate. Fianna Fáil, the largest party, enters into negotiations with other parties. Charles Haughey becomes acting taoiseach (prime minister) of a caretaker government (29 June).

12 July A Fianna Fáil–Progressive Democrat coalition government, headed by Charles Haughey, is formed in the Republic of Ireland.

19 Aug. The Polish Communist Party agrees to join a 'grand coalition' government led by Solidarity. Tadeusz Mazowiecki, editor of Solidarity's newspaper, is elected prime minister (24 Aug.).

19 Aug. 900 East Germans escape over the Austro-Hungarian border. Once in Austria they will travel on to West Germany.

23 Aug. Across the Baltic republics, the peoples of Latvia, Lithuania and Estonia form a human chain demanding the independence of their countries. The issue of Baltic independence highlights the fact of their absorption within the USSR according to the terms of the Nazi–Soviet Pact (see 1939).

4 Sept. In East Germany the first of a series of pro-democracy 'Monday demonstrations' are held in Leipzig. The Democracy Now movement is founded (12 Sept.).

10 Sept. Hungary opens its border with Austria.

12 Sept. The Solidarity-dominated coalition government takes office in Poland. It is the first non-Communist government in E Europe since the 1940s. The new government faces the problem of hyperinflation, which is running at 600%, and the zloty has to be devalued 12 times.

22 Sept. In Britain nine army bandsmen and one civilian are killed by an IRA bomb attack on the Royal Marines' barracks at Deal in Kent.

6–7 Oct. Soviet leader Mikhail Gorbachev visits East Berlin for the 40th anniversary of the German Democratic Republic (East Germany), on the eve of that state's dissolution.

17 Oct. In Britain the 'Guildford Four', imprisoned for life for the 1974 Guildford pub bombings, are released on appeal because of irregularities in police evidence.

18 Oct. East German Communist leader Erich Honecker resigns when his colleagues refuse to back a crackdown on dissent. Egon Krenz is elected general secretary of the SED (East German Communist Party).

18 Oct. Hungary adopts a more democratic constitution, and the country's Communist Party restyles itself as the Socialist Party. A democratic republic is proclaimed (23 Oct.).

23 Oct. Eduard Shevardnadze, the Soviet foreign minister, states that the country's invasion of Afghanistan was illegal.

26 Oct. In Britain Nigel Lawson resigns as chancellor of the exchequer. He is succeeded by the rapidly rising John Major, who has only recently succeeded Geoffrey Howe as foreign secretary.

31 Oct. East German leader Egon Krenz meets Mikhail Gorbachev in Moscow.

Oct. Thousands of East Germans who are 'visiting' Czechoslovakia leave E Europe for West Germany by train.

4 Nov. In East Berlin 500,000 East Germans demonstrate in Alexanderplatz. Three days later the entire East German government resigns (7 Nov.).

9 Nov. The border between East and West Germany is opened and exit from East Germany is allowed without visas.

10 Nov. Demolition of the Berlin Wall begins. Portions of this most potent of Cold War symbols will be sold off as souvenirs.

10 Nov. The biggest democratic rebellion in Europe since 1848 spreads to Bulgaria when Todor Zhivkov resigns as president. More than 50,000 people attend a pro-democracy rally in Sofia and demand an end to communist rule (10 Dec.).

13 Nov. Hans Modrow, a reformist Communist, is elected East German minister-president.

14 Nov. The Czech government announces freedom of travel to the West for its citizens. Vast pro-democracy rallies are held in Prague's Wenceslas Square and in other cities, forcing the resignation of Milos Jakes as Czechoslovak Communist Party leader (24 Nov.). The Communist monopoly on power ends (28 Nov.).

21 Nov. In Britain the proceedings of the House of Commons are televised for the first time.

5 Dec. The former East German Communist leader Erich Honecker is placed under house arrest.

7 Dec. Lithuania changes its constitution to end the legally enshrined dominance of the Communist Party.

10 Dec. Czechoslovakia's 'velvet revolution' gathers pace. President Gustáv Husák resigns and a new non-Communist government takes office. The Czechoslovak parliament votes to move towards a liberal democratic system (19 Dec.).

14 Dec. Former dissident Andrei Sakharov dies a few hours after warning the USSR's parliament, to which he has been elected, that the country faces a disaster.

16 Dec. The Romanian security force, the Securitate, shoots at protestors who have gathered in the town of Timisoara in order to support a Protestant clergyman, László Tökés, who has upheld the rights of ethnic Hungarians in Transylvania. Further loss of life occurs in street riots in Bucharest (21 Dec.). Communist leader Nicolae Ceausescu attempts to reassert his authority by addressing a mass rally of the presumed party faithful. Instead he is shouted down and has to flee his palace. After considerable confusion, the army joins the demonstrators and Ceausescu and his wife, Elena, are captured and executed by firing squad (25 Dec.), having been hastily tried by a military court. Ion Iliescu heads a provisional government of the National Salvation Front.

29 Dec. Playwright and former dissident Václav Havel is elected president of Czechoslovakia.

– Within the USSR itself the union is now faced with the threat of dissolution: Armenia, Azerbaijan, Georgia and Ukraine see the emergence of overt movements for political independence.

– In the Yugoslav republic of Slovenia opposition parties are legalized.

MIDDLE EAST AND NORTH AFRICA

14 Feb. In Iran Ayatollah Khomeini issues a *fatwa* (Islamic legal ruling) condemning British author Salman Rushdie to death for blasphemy in *The Satanic Verses*.

7 Mar. Iran severs diplomatic ties with Britain over the Rushdie affair.

4 June Ayatollah Khomeini, ruler of Iran, dies; Hashemi Rafsanjani succeeds as president.

Oct. Muslim and Christian militias in Lebanon arrive at a peace agreement, and the Lebanese parliament elects René Moawad, a Christian Maronite, as president (5 Nov.). But the assassination of the new president along with 23 others in Beirut heralds a return to conflict (22 Nov.). Elias Hrawi, another Maronite Christian, becomes president but he is opposed by a fellow Maronite Christian, the army commander Gen. Michel Aoun, who embarks on a military rebellion that will only be suppressed, with Syrian help, after a year.

ASIA

7 Jan. Emperor Hirohito of Japan dies; the Showa emperor has reigned for 62 years and is succeeded by his son Akihito, the Heisei emperor.

15 Feb. Soviet troops complete the withdrawal from Afghanistan. The Marxist regime of Ahmadzai Najibullah, however, survives as the various *mujahedin* groups are too divided to take Kabul.

7 Mar. China imposes martial law in Lhasa, Tibet.

17 April Chinese students, inspired by Gorbachev's reforms in the USSR, begin to gather in Tiananmen Square, Beijing, and demand political reform, including the resignation of the hardline Chinese premier Li Peng. The protests spread to other Chinese cities. Chinese Communist Party secretary general Zhao Ziyang, who favours a conciliatory approach to the student demonstrators, withdraws from office after disagreements with party colleagues.

19 May By now the pro-democracy demonstrators in Beijing's Tiananmen Square number many hundreds of thousands. Zhao Ziyang defies internal party discipline and apologizes to the demonstrators, assuring them that the government will talk to them about their grievances. For these actions Zhao Ziyang will be accused of committing serious political errors and dismissed from all his party posts. He will spend the rest of his life under house arrest in Beijing.

3–4 June Tanks and troops enter Tiananmen Square, killing hundreds of demonstrators. A period of harsh repression follows, in which the leaders of the pro-democracy movement are executed. Although the US Congress imposes sanctions on China, President Bush vetoes a bill that would extend the visas of some 40,000 Chinese students resident in the USA.

June Burma's name is changed to Myanmar.

26 Sept. Vietnamese troops leave Cambodia. The Khmer Rouge will continue to wage war on the Vietnamese-backed regime.

9 Nov. Chinese leader Deng Xiaoping retires from political life.

22 Nov. Rajiv Gandhi leads his Congress (I) Party to defeat in India's general election. Vishwanath Pratap Singh, an anti-corruption candidate, becomes prime minister at the head of a multiparty government (2 Dec.).

THE AMERICAS

20 Jan. George Bush is inaugurated as 41st US president.

2–3 Feb. Alfredo Stroessner, president of Paraguay, is overthrown after a 35-year dictatorship. He is succeeded by Gen. Andrés Rodríguez, who is elected president in May and promises to bring democracy to Paraguay.

19 Mar. In El Salvador Alfredo Cristiani of the right-wing alliance known as ARENA wins the presidential election amid accusations of ballot-rigging. The new government takes a hard line against left-wing rebels and other dissident elements.

Mar. The American financier and junk bond specialist Michael Milken is indicted, along with his brother Lowell, on 98 counts of conspiracy and fraud.

7 May In Panama Gen. Manuel Noriega is defeated in democratic elections, which he then proceeds to annul.

14 May Carlos Menem is elected president of Argentina. Although a declared Perónist, Menem undertakes to privatize the industries nationalized by Perón. He applies a drastic free-market solution to an economy ruined by hyperinflation. The country's foreign reserves have been depleted to less than $100 million, while its foreign debts amount to $60 billion.

18 Aug. Luis Carlos Galán is assassinated while campaigning for the presidency of Colombia. President Virgilio Barco Vargas

decides he must now wage a civil war against the Medellín and Cali drug gangs that control much of the country. Over 500 arrests are made on drug-related charges and leading members of drug cartels are extradited to the USA. The gang bosses launch a campaign of bombing and assassinations in retaliation.

30 Aug. Leona Helmsley, New York socialite and hotel owner, is convicted on 33 separate charges of income tax evasion and tax fraud. She is fined $7.1 million and imprisoned for four years. As she begins her sentence (12 Dec.), an unrepentant Helmsley opines that 'only the little people pay taxes'.

3 Oct. The Panamanian ruler Gen. Manuel Noriega suppresses a military coup directed against him.

17 Oct. An earthquake in San Francisco is N America's worst since 1906: 90 people are killed.

Oct. The US Congress votes to authorize Medicare payments for abortion in cases of rape and incest. President Bush vetoes the measure.

11 Nov. The dissident movement in El Salvador, known as the Farabundo Martí National Liberation Front, launches a military push against the US-backed government of President Alfredo Cristiani. Rebel guerrillas take over parts of the suburbs of San Salvador. On 16 Nov. six Jesuit priests, their housekeeper and her 15-year-old daughter are tortured and murdered by government forces. El Salvador's brutal civil war continues.

14 Dec. Patricio Aylwin is elected democratic president of Chile. Former dictator Augusto Pinochet, whose regime has used torture as an arm of repression, remains as military chief.

15 Dec. Colombian drug baron José Rodriguez Gacha is killed in a shoot-out with police.

17 Dec. Fernando Collor de Mello is elected president of Brazil.

19 Dec. US forces invade Panama to overthrow the regime of Gen. Manuel Noriega, an act condemned by the UN (20 Dec.). Noriega evades the US forces and receives political asylum at the Vatican embassy in Panama City (24 Dec.). US forces try to drive him out by playing rock music at a deafening volume.

– New York City elects its first African-American mayor, David Dinkins.

SUB-SAHARAN AFRICA

10 Jan. Cuban troops begin to withdraw from Angola.

18 Jan. P.W. Botha, president of South Africa, resigns and is succeeded by F(rederik) W(illem) de Klerk, who embarks on a liberalization of the country's regime.

July Gen. Ahmed el-Bashir leads a military coup in Sudan. He divides the country into nine provinces under a federal system. Fighting continues, however, between the Sudan People's Liberation Army (SPLA) and Islamic government forces in the S, where the mainly Christian Nuba people suffer persecution.

6 Sept. In South Africa's whites-only election the National Party prevails but with a reduced majority. F.W. de Klerk is elected president.

19 Sept. A bomb on board a French DC 10 flying from Chad to Paris explodes; the plane crashes in the Niger, killing all 171 people on board.

Oct. In South Africa President F.W. de Klerk releases the 77-year-old civil-rights and ANC activist Walter Sisulu.

ECONOMY AND SOCIETY

24 Mar. *Exxon Valdez*, an oil tanker, runs aground on Bligh Reef, Alaska, and releases 240,000 barrels of oil into Prince of Wales Sound: an ecological catastrophe.

15 April In Britain 96 Liverpool FC fans are crushed to death during the FA Cup semi-final at Hillsborough, Sheffield.

– Brazil is forced to react to the environmental scandal of the country's destruction of the Amazon rainforest: tax incentive schemes offered to developers are suspended and those who burn trees without first having permits are fined by the government. The new policy, however, is difficult to implement, and the illegal logging and forest burning continue.

– The Ford Motor Company buys Britain's Jaguar Motors.

– US motor group General Motors buys half of Saab of Sweden.

– The largest Christian church in the world is completed: the Basilica of Our Lady of Peace at Yamoussoukro, commissioned by President Félix Houphouët-Boigny of the Côte d'Ivoire.

SCIENCE AND TECHNOLOGY

17 July The USA's B2 'stealth' bomber makes its maiden flight.

Sept. The last technological achievement of the USSR is seen in the completion of the Baikal–Amur Mainline: the new trans-Siberian railroad is designed to advance the development of the region's mineral deposits.

ARTS AND HUMANITIES

Literature

14 Jan. Muslims in Bradford, N England, publicly burn Salman Rushdie's novel *The Satanic Verses*.

22 Dec. Irish playwright and novelist Samuel Beckett dies.

Julian Barnes, *A History of the World in 10½ Chapters*, novel.

William Golding, *Fire Down Below*, novel.

Allan Gurganus, *Oldest Living Confederate Widow Tells All*, novel.

Kazuo Ishiguro, *The Remains of the Day*, novel.

James Kelman, *A Disaffection*, novel.

Charles Palliser, *The Quincunx*, novel.

Terry Pratchett, *The Colour of Magic*, novel, the first in his long-running Discworld fantasy series.

Simon Schama, *Citizens: A Chronicle of the French Revolution*, history.

Rose Tremain, *Restoration*, novel.

Visual Arts and Architecture

12 Jan. A public controversy forces the Corcoran Gallery, Washington, D.C., to cancel a photographic exhibition by Robert Mapplethorpe. The show contains homoerotic images taken by the artist who has died of AIDS (1988).

23 Jan. Spanish painter Salvador Dali dies.

30 Mar. The new pyramid entrance to the Louvre, Paris, designed by I.M. Pei, opens.

– In Paris the Arche de la Défense, designed by Johan Otto van Spreckelsen and Paul Andreu, is completed. It commemorates the 200th anniversary of the French Revolution.

Music

30 Sep. Virgil Thomson, US composer, dies in New York.

– In Paris the new Bastille Opera opens.

Black Box, 'Ride On Time', single.

Jason Donovan, 'Too Many Broken Hearts', single.

Michael Jackson, 'Leave Me Alone', single.

Jive Bunny and the Mastermixers, 'Swing the Mood', single.

Madonna, 'Like a Prayer', single.

Simple Minds, 'Belfast Child', single.

The Stone Roses, *The Stone Roses*, album.

John Tavener, *The Protecting Veil*, for cello and strings.

Tone-Loc, 'Wild Thing', single.

Film

11 July The stage and screen actor Laurence Olivier dies.

Woody Allen, *Crimes and Misdemeanors*.

Bruce Beresford, *Driving Miss Daisy*.

Tim Burton, *Batman*, starring Michael Keaton.

Peter Greenaway, *The Cook, the Thief, His Wife & Her Lover*, starring Helen Mirren and Michael Gambon.

Spike Lee, *Do the Right Thing*.

Rob Reiner, *When Harry Met Sally*, starring Meg Ryan.

Jim Sheridan, *My Left Foot*, starring Daniel Day-Lewis.

Steven Soderbergh, *sex, lies and videotape*, starring James Spader.

Oliver Stone, *Born on the Fourth of July*, starring Tom Cruise.

Bertrand Tavernier, *Life and Nothing But*, starring Philippe Noiret.

Peter Weir, *Dead Poets Society*, starring Robin Williams.

1990

EUROPE

15 Jan. In Bulgaria the parliament votes to end the Communist Party's monopoly on power.

19 Jan. The congress of the Yugoslav Communist Party votes to end its monopoly on power.

7 Feb. In the USSR the Central Committee of the Communist Party surrenders its hold on power after a three-day summit with President Gorbachev. It endorses his campaign for a liberal political order.

Feb. In Yugoslavia a state of emergency is declared in Kosovo, an autonomous region of S Serbia, after fighting breaks out between ethnic Albanians and Kosovo Serbs. Kosovo's majority ethnic Albanian population aspires to join with Albania while the area's Serbs wish to merge fully with Serbia.

6 Mar. A property law is passed by the Soviet parliament allowing private individuals the right to own factories and businesses.

11 Mar. Lithuania declares itself independent of the USSR. Gorbachev denounces the move and sends Russian tanks into Vilnius (25 Mar.) and cuts off oil supplies in an effort to force Lithuania back into the USSR (April).

14 Mar. The Two-plus-Four treaty between East and West Germany and the four wartime Allies (Britain, France, the USSR and the USA), paves the way for the reunification of Germany.

18 Mar. Free elections to the East German parliament take place, the first of their kind in the region since 1932; conservative parties become the largest political force; Lothar de Maizière becomes minister-president of East Germany at the head of a coalition government (18 April). East Germany holds its first free local elections on 6 May.

31 Mar. In London a demonstration against the community charge (poll tax) turns into a riot. The community charge, implemented in England and Wales this year, replaces the existing property-based local taxation (the rates). Its unpopularity will contribute to the imminent political demise of prime minister Margaret Thatcher.

April A free, multiparty election is held in the Yugoslav republic of Slovenia. The Communists, renamed the Party of Democratic Reform, are convincingly defeated by a nationalist centre-right coalition campaigning for Slovenian independence.

April–May Croatia, one of the constituent republics of Yugoslavia, follows Slovenia's lead and holds a multiparty election. The Communists, who have renamed themselves the Party of Democratic Renewal, are defeated by the right-wing nationalist Croatian Democratic Union (CDU) led by Franjo Tudjman who becomes president of Croatia.

4 May Latvia declares its independence from the USSR.

8 May Estonia declares its independence from the USSR.

20 May Free elections are held in Romania, the first since 1937. Victory goes to the National Salvation Front, and Ion Iliescu becomes Romanian president. Iliescu's government will be dominated, however, by former Communists.

29 May Boris Yeltsin is elected president of the Russian Federation, defeating Gorbachev's candidate. Yeltsin will resign from the Soviet Communist Party in July.

May A Jewish cemetery is desecrated in Carpentras, S France, leading to nationwide demonstrations against anti-Semitism.

12 June The Russian parliament formally declares that the Russian Federation is a sovereign state whose laws take precedence over those of the USSR.

June The situation in Romania deteriorates when the new government of Ion Iliescu brings in armed miners to crack down on street protestors in Bucharest.

1 July Economic union between East and West Germany is announced. The East German Ostmark becomes convertible to West German Deutschmarks. The West German government has decided to use its own economic resources of postwar plenty to support the sickly economy of the East.

10 July In Britain the right-wing Conservative MP Ian Gow, a close ally of Margaret Thatcher, is murdered by an IRA car bomb.

14 July In France celebrations are held to mark the 200th anniversary of the French Revolution.

16 July The Ukrainian parliament votes for Ukraine to become an independent sovereign state.

July Soviet leader Mikhail Gorbachev agrees that the reunified Germany can be a member of NATO.

8–9 Sept. Britain dissents from the European Social Chapter on workers' rights, signed by other European Community member states at an EC summit in Strasbourg.

12 Sept. At a meeting in Moscow, Soviet, British, French, US and East and West German representatives agree to restore sovereignty to a reunified Germany.

20 Sept. The East and West German parliaments pass legislation for the political reunification of Germany.

26 Sept. Religious freedom of worship is introduced to the USSR: the government may no longer interfere in Church matters.

Sept. Kosovo is annexed by the Serbian parliament.

3 Oct. The German state is formally reunified. An all-German parliament meets in the Reichstag building in Berlin (4 Oct.).

5 Oct. The British government announces Britain's entry into the Exchange Rate Mechanism (ERM).

15 Oct. Mikhail Gorbachev is awarded the Nobel Peace Prize.

1 Nov. In Britain Sir Geoffrey Howe, the deputy prime minister and leader of the House of Commons, resigns in protest at prime minister Margaret Thatcher's opposition to the greater integration of Britain in Europe.

7 Nov. Mary Robinson becomes the first woman to be elected president of the Republic of Ireland.

17 Nov. With the Soviet economy now collapsing, Gorbachev asks for special powers to deal with the crisis. Although granted extensive powers to move quickly towards complete deregulation of the command economy, he moves slowly. The harvest has been good, but crops are rotting in the fields because of the country's political and economic crisis: bread is scarce in the towns and the threat of famine returns.

19 Nov. The Cold War ends and with it the era of confrontation that started in 1914 and then resumed in 1939: 22 leaders, convened in Paris, sign the Conventional Forces in Europe treaty. With the Red Army already withdrawing from E Europe, the Soviet government is forced to accept a numerical parity in conventional weapons in Europe. In terms of tanks, for example, there can now be no more than 20,000 held by each alliance and no more than 13,300 by any state. The Red Army is not allowed to evade the agreement by withdrawing weapons across the Urals into Asiatic Russia. The treaty marks a clear victory for NATO, which has always faced Soviet numerical superiority in conventional weapons.

20 Nov. In Britain the prime minister Margaret Thatcher is challenged by Michael Heseltine, her former defence secretary, in an election for the leadership of the Conservative Party. Mrs Thatcher's unbending style of government has isolated her from her cabinet colleagues, and the introduction of the community charge or 'poll tax', widely seen as unjust, has caused the Conservatives' standing to plummet in opinion polls. In the leadership election Thatcher gains a majority of votes cast (204 against Heseltine's 152) but the margin is not wide enough to ensure her authority. Although she decides to fight the next ballot, cabinet colleagues queue up to tell her that she has lost the confidence of the parliamentary party. Thatcher stands down from the second ballot (22 Nov.).

25 Nov. Solidarity leader Lech Walesa gains 40% of the vote for the presidency of Poland in the country's democratic elections.

He wins the second round (9 Dec.) against Stanislaw Tyminski, who has returned to Poland after 21 years of making money in Peru and Canada. The Polish economy has suffered from the abrupt introduction of free-market methods (1 Jan.), which have raised the prices of food and of consumer goods.

27 Nov. In Britain John Major, chancellor of the exchequer, wins the second ballot for the Conservative Party leadership. His challengers Michael Heseltine and Douglas Hurd withdraw from the third ballot and Major succeeds Margaret Thatcher as party leader and prime minister (28 Nov.). Suspicions about the manner of Mrs Thatcher's departure – and internal Tory guilt about the coup – mean that Major's authority is diminished from the very beginning of his premiership.

29 Nov. Andrei Lukanov, prime minister of Bulgaria, resigns: widespread anti-Communist street protests have undermined his authority.

2 Dec. In all-German elections the CDU/CSU becomes the largest party, but it is still dependent on its FDP coalition partner. Helmut Kohl becomes chancellor of the reunified Germany.

11 Dec. Talks on GATT (General Agreement on Tariffs and Trade) collapse in Brussels, Belgium, after a failure to agree on farm subsidies, a major point of contention between US and European Community (EC) negotiators.

20 Dec. The Soviet foreign minister Eduard Shevardnadze resigns and warns of 'reactionaries' who want to rein back on the reforms achieved so far.

23 Dec. A referendum in Slovenia votes for independence from Yugoslavia.

Dec. In multiparty elections in Serbia Slobodan Milosevic, leader of the the Serbian Socialist Party (as the Communists have renamed themselves), is elected president.

– The British Nationality (Hong Kong) Act prevents all but a small and wealthy minority of Hong Kong holders of British passports from settling in Britain.

– The Italian Communist Party abandons Marxist-Leninism and becomes the Democratic Party of the Left (PDS).

MIDDLE EAST AND NORTH AFRICA

22 May North and South Yemen merge to become the Republic of Yemen.

21 June Some 50,000 people are killed, 200,000 injured and 500,000 made homeless by earthquakes in N Iran.

June Following provisional and municipal elections in Algeria, the fundamentalist Islamic Salvation Front now controls most local assemblies.

2 July In Saudi Arabia 1426 pilgrims are crushed to death when a ventilation failure leads to a stampede by pilgrims at Mecca.

July Iraqi troops start to mass on the Iraq–Kuwait border. Iraqi leader Saddam Hussein has demanded that Kuwait pay compensation for drilling for oil on Iraqi soil, hand over disputed territories, raise oil prices and reduce oil output.

2 Aug. Iraq invades Kuwait and declares it to be a province of Iraq. The UN Security Council votes unanimously to impose economic sanctions on Iraq (6 Aug.). With Iraqi troops gathering on the borders of Saudi Arabia, the Saudis agree to the stationing of US troops, and President Bush sends the first US forces to Saudi Arabia (7 Aug.). Despite these developments, Saddam annexes Kuwait (8 Aug.). The governments of Egypt, Syria and Morocco call for Iraq to be opposed militarily (10 Aug.). Saddam holds some 10,000 foreigners hostage (18 Aug.), but then allows women and children to leave (29 Aug.) before releasing the remaining hostages (6 Dec.).

24 Aug. Brian Keenan, held hostage in Beirut since 11 April 1986, is released.

27 Sept. The emir of Kuwait, who has fled to Saudi Arabia, addresses the UN and urges the maintenance of sanctions against Iraq. Ali Abdullah Saleh, president of the newly created Republic of Yemen, decides to support Iraq and denounces Western sanctions. But he then stops Iraqi ships from unloading in his country.

8 Oct. Israeli forces open fire after Palestinians attack Jews who are worshipping at the Wailing Wall in Jerusalem: 17 Palestinians are killed and more than 140 wounded. The UN security council accepts a resolution condemning Israeli heavy-handedness (13 Oct.).

Oct. In Lebanon the rebel Christian leader Gen. Michel Aoun seeks political asylum in the French embassy. Following the imposition of economic sanctions on Iraq, the chief source of weaponry for his rebel forces, Aoun's arms supplies have dried up and he has been forced to surrender.

8 Nov. President Bush commits more forces to the Middle East. The UN Security Council votes to authorize its members to use all reasonable force necessary to expel the Iraqis from Kuwait (29 Nov.).

Nov. In Lebanon the government of Elias Hrawi regains control of Beirut.

– Hostilities in the Gulf causes oil prices to rise dramatically (Kuwait produces about one-fifth of the world's oil and Iraq is the world's second-biggest oil producer).

ASIA

20 June Uzbekistan declares itself an independent state.

6 Aug. In Pakistan charges of corruption are brought against Benazir Bhutto, and she is dismissed from office as prime minister by President Gulam Ishaq Khan. The president dissolves the national assembly and declares a state of emergency.

24 Oct. In a general election in Pakistan Benazir Bhutto's Pakistan People's Party (PPP) is heavily defeated by the Islamic Democratic Alliance. Nawaz Sharif becomes prime minister (6 Nov.).

26 Nov. Lee Kuan Yew, prime minister of Singapore, joins the increasingly long roll-call of retired authoritarian rulers. He resigns and is succeeded by his deputy Goh Chok Tong, who turns out to be a mere cipher for Lee's continued influence.

THE AMERICAS

3 Jan. In Panama Gen. Manuel Noriega surrenders to US forces. He is taken to Miami to face charges of drug-smuggling.

25 Feb. Daniel Ortega Saavedra, the leader of the Sandinistas, is rejected by the voters of Nicaragua when he stands for re-election. Though a ceasefire with the Contras is officially in place, their murderous campaign is continuing. The message from Washington is clear: a Sandinista victory will mean that the violence will continue. Violeta Barrios de Chamorro, leader of the National Opposition Union (UNO) and widow of an anti-Somoza activist who was murdered in 1978, is elected to the presidency.

26 June President Bush is forced to make the concession that will undermine his presidency. With a projected $160 billion budget deficit, he has to introduce tax rises as well as budget cuts. The legacy of the Reagan years has saddled the USA with an enormous national debt, and a compromise tax bill is eventually agreed to by Congress (Nov.) at which point the president repeats his 'no new taxes' pledge. From July the US economy goes into recession.

15 Nov. President Bush signs the Clean Air Act, which sets new standards in the regulation of car exhaust emissions.

21 Nov. US financier Michael Milken is sentenced to 10 years' imprisonment (subsequently reduced to 3 years) for insider trading (see 1989).

Nov. At an environmental conference in Geneva the USA and the USSR oppose demands that countries reduce their oil consumption.

18 Dec. Democratic elections are held in Haiti for the first time since 1957. Jean-Bertrand Aristide, a radical priest, is elected in a landslide after campaigning against the country's military rulers.

SUB-SAHARAN AFRICA

2 Feb. In South Africa F.W. de Klerk ends the 30-year ban on the African National Congress (ANC).

11 Feb. African National Congress (ANC) leader Nelson Mandela is released from Victor Verster Prison, near Cape Town, after 27 years of imprisonment. Mandela begins negotiations with the South African government about a multiracial future for his country.

16 Feb. Sam Nujoma, leader of the South West Africa People's Organization (SWAPO) is elected first president of independent Namibia.

21 Mar. Namibia formally becomes an independent sovereign state.

7 Aug. The ANC agrees to stop infiltrating its guerrillas and weaponry into South Africa. The South African government grants an amnesty to some 20,000 ANC exiles. However, violence is increasing between the ANC and supporters of Chief Mangosuthu Buthelezi's Inkatha organization. The potential exists for a Xhosa–Zulu tribal war in South Africa.

9 Sept. President Samuel Doe of Liberia is assassinated by rebels. 'Prince' Yormie Johnson states that he is the provisional head of state, but Charles Taylor, a former government official who fled to the USA when he was charged with corruption, opposes his claim. He has escaped from a Massachusetts jail (1985), is now backed by Libya and has landed with some 100 Libyan-trained troops in NE Liberia. As the country collapses in civil war, an international peace-keeping force tries to restore order.

Oct. South Africa's parliament repeals the Separate Amenities Act and so ends the legal basis to apartheid.

Dec. Oliver Tambo, president-in-exile of the ANC since 1977, returns to South Africa from London.

ECONOMY AND SOCIETY

4 Feb. In cricket the New Zealand fast bowler Richard Hadlee becomes the first bowler to take 400 test wickets.

May In the wake of concerns over 'mad cow disease' (bovine spongiform encephalopathy or BSE), home-produced beef is banned in British schools and hospitals.

June–July West Germany wins the 14th soccer World Cup, held in Italy.

SCIENCE AND TECHNOLOGY

– The crewless Hubble space telescope is placed in orbit by the space shuttle *Discovery*. Although it will not become fully operational until 1994 because of technical problems, it will take photographs of stars far superior to any that can be taken on Earth and will gather a wealth of scientific data.

– The first human gene experiment is carried out on a four-year-old girl with defective white blood cells.

ARTS AND HUMANITIES

Literature

26 Sept. The Italian novelist Alberto Moravia dies.

30 Sept. The Australian novelist Patrick White dies.

Martin Amis, *London Fields*, novel.

A.S. Byatt, *Possession*, novel.

Brian Friel, *Dancing at Lughnasa*, play.

John Guare, *Six Degrees of Separation*, play.

David Hare, *Racing Demon*, play.

Oscar Hijuelos, *The Mambo Kings Play Songs of Love*, novel.

Hanif Kureishi, *The Buddha of Suburbia*, novel.

Ian McEwan, *The Innocent*, novel.

John McGahern, *Amongst Women*, novel.

Thomas Pynchon, *Vineland*, novel.

Mordecai Richler, *Solomon Gursky Was Here*, novel.

John Updike, *Rabbit at Rest*, novel.

Derek Walcott, *Omeros*, extended poem.

Visual Arts and Architecture

– The Cathedral Church of St Peter and St Paul, Washington, D.C., designed by Philip Hubert Frohman, is completed after 80 years.

Jeff Koons, *Jeff and Ilona* ('Made in Heaven' series), sculpture.

Music

14 Oct. The US composer and conductor Leonard Bernstein dies.

2 Dec. The US composer Aaron Copland dies.

B52s, 'Love Shack', single.

Jon Bon Jovi, 'Blaze of Glory', single.

The Cure, *Mixed Up*, album.

Peter Maxwell Davies, *Strathclyde Concerto No. 4*.

Ice Cube, *Kill at Will*, album.

Elton John, 'Sacrifice', single.

James Macmillan, *The Confession of Isobel Gowdie*, orchestral work.

Madonna, 'Vogue', single.

New Kids on the Block, 'Hangin' Tough', single.

Sinead O'Connor, 'Nothing Compares 2U', single.

Primal Scream, 'Loaded', single.

The Righteous Brothers, 'Unchained Melody', single.

Film

Woody Allen, *Alice*, starring Mia Farrow.

Kevin Costner, *Dances with Wolves*.

Jonathan Demme, *The Silence of the Lambs*, starring Anthony Hopkins and Jodie Foster.

Stephen Frears, *The Grifters*, starring Anjelica Huston.

Jean-Paul Rappeneau, *Cyrano de Bergerac*, starring Gérard Depardieu.

Martin Scorsese, *Goodfellas*, starring Robert De Niro.

Giuseppe Tornatore, *Cinema Paradiso*.

1991

EUROPE

13 Jan. In a return to the old methods of repression, Soviet troops are sent into Vilnius, Lithuania, to seize the television station: 15 people are killed and hundreds injured. But neither here nor elsewhere in the Baltic states are calls for independence silenced. US pressure results in a reduction in the number of Soviet troops (29 Jan.) and Lithuanians vote overwhelmingly for independence in a referendum (9 Feb.).

7 Feb. In London the Provisional IRA fires mortar bombs at 10 Downing Street during a cabinet meeting but fails to harm members of the British government.

25 Feb. The remaining members of the Warsaw Pact decide to dissolve the organization.

Feb. The Croatian and Slovenian assemblies call for secession from Yugoslavia.

3 Mar. Referendums in Latvia and Estonia vote for independence from the USSR.

15 Mar. In Britain the 'Birmingham Six' (see 9 June 1975) are released following a lengthy campaign to demonstrate that they have been wrongly convicted.

Mar. In Yugoslavia, Serb militants in Krajina, an area of Croatia with 250,000 Serbs, announce that the 'Serbian Autonomous Region of Krajina' is seceding from Croatia.

9 April The parliament of the Soviet republic of Georgia votes for independence of the USSR.

15 May Edith Cresson becomes France's first woman prime minister following the resignation of Michel Rocard.

26 May Zviad Gamsakhurdia becomes president of Georgia.

13 June The Russian Republic holds the first democratic elections on a universal adult suffrage ever held on Russian soil: Boris Yeltsin is elected the republic's president.

20 June The German Bundestag (parliament) votes to move the country's capital from Bonn to Berlin.

25 June The governments of the Yugoslav republics of Croatia and Slovenia declare their independence from Yugoslavia. Fighting breaks out between the Serbs, adherents of the Orthodox Church, and the Catholic Croats. The Serb authorities in Belgrade use the history of World War II, during which Croatia, as a puppet state allied to the Nazis, massacred Serbs and Jews, as propaganda against the Croats. The Serb-dominated Yugoslav federal army moves in to crush separatists but is forced to agree to a ceasefire in Slovenia (3 July). Fighting continues in ethnically mixed Croatia, especially around the towns of Osijek and Vukovar.

28 June COMECON (the Communist bloc's equivalent of the European Community) is wound up.

7 Aug. Following a threat of sanctions by the European Community (EC) the Yugoslav federal president calls for a ceasefire in the fighting in Croatia. His call is not heeded for long.

19 Aug. In the USSR Communist hardliners led by Gennadi Yanayev, Gorbachev's vice-president, launch a reactionary coup. President Gorbachev is detained at his *dacha* (country house) in the Crimea. But the rebellion is led incompetently and the considerable forces available to the conspirators are not deployed. Boris Yeltsin, president of the Russian Republic, calls for a general strike to protest against the attempted takeover. The Moscow military commanders follow Yeltsin's lead and the coup collapses (21 Aug.). On his return to Moscow (22 Aug.) Gorbachev suspends the Communist Party (24 Aug.), which had largely supported the coup. The discredited Soviet Congress annuls itself, and the last vestiges of a common order disappear among the 15 constituent republics of the old USSR, several of which, including Ukraine, will now declare their independence. The Marxist-Leninist state will never recover from the blow, and its mechanisms of state power, along with the party structures and the security forces, have been utterly discredited.

27 Aug. In Croatia the town of Vukovar falls to the Serb-dominated Yugoslav federal army after an 86-day siege.

30 Aug. Azerbaijan declares its independence from the USSR.

6 Sept. The USSR formally recognizes the independence of Estonia, Latvia and Lithuania.

18 Sept. The Yugoslav republic of Macedonia declares its independence following a referendum on the issue. Albanian and Serb minorities within Macedonia have boycotted the referendum.

22 Sept. Armenia declares its independence from the USSR.

24 Sept. Leonid Kravchuk, president of Ukraine, declares provisional independence from the USSR, pending a referendum in Dec. (which will vote overwhelmingly in favour).

Sept. In the Yugoslav civil war, one-third of Croatia is now under Serbian control. The war is also spreading rapidly: areas of neighbouring Bosnia-Herzegovina, the most ethnically mixed of Yugoslavia's constituent republics (it has significant Muslim, Croatian and Serb populations), are being taken over by the

Serbs, who begin to form autonomous enclaves within Bosnia-Herzegovina.

Sept. In Germany neo-Nazi groups carry out violent attacks on guest workers, asylum seekers and other foreigners.

1 Oct. The Russian city of Leningrad officially becomes St Petersburg again.

1 Oct. The Serb-dominated Yugoslav federal army lays siege to the historic port city of Dubrovnik as part of its blockade of the Croatian coast.

15 Oct. The parliament of Bosnia-Herzegovina votes to secede from Yugoslavia as an independent sovereign state. Bosnia's Serbs, who wish to remain within the Yugoslav federation, reject the vote.

5 Nov. Czech-born British publisher Robert Maxwell (Jan Ludvik Hoch) falls off his yacht and drowns while sailing near the Canary Islands. The publisher and owner of the *Daily Mirror* newspaper is initially eulogized, but then reviled when the extent of his financial corruption is revealed. He has plundered the assets of the *Daily Mirror*'s pension fund to shore up his collapsing business empire and so deprived thousands of former employees of their future financial security.

Nov. In Chechnya, a strongly Muslim part of the Russian autonomous republic of Checheno-Ingush, Gen. Dzhokhar Dudayev seizes power. Chechenya declares its independence from the Russian Federation.

5 Dec. The federal Yugoslav president Stjepan Mesic resigns, remarking that the state of Yugoslavia no longer exists. The federal prime minister, Ante Markovic, resigns later this month.

21 Dec. Representatives of 11 of the republics of the USSR agree to form the Commonwealth of Independent States (CIS).

25 Dec. Mikhail Gorbachev resigns as president of the USSR, which formally ceases to exist.

– Britain's Conservative government privatizes the electricity industry.

– In Britain the National Economic Development Council, a forum established in 1961 for discussion between management, government and trade unions, is abolished.

MIDDLE EAST AND NORTH AFRICA

12 Jan. The US Congress authorizes President Bush to wage war on Iraq if it does not withdraw from Kuwait by 15 Jan. The Gulf War starts (17 Jan.); the campaign consists initially of aerial bombardment, and US pilots fly more than 1000 missions a day. The Americans use Turkish bases for their attacks. Iraq retaliates with Scud missile attacks on Tel Aviv and Haifa in Israel (18 Jan.), its intention being to detach the Islamic states from the anti-Iraq coalition by provoking an Israeli attack on Iraq. Israel, however, aware of the need to maintain the anti-Iraq coalition, does not retaliate. Two Kuwaiti oil refineries and an oil field are set on fire by Iraqi forces (22 Jan.) The destructive fires become an arm of Saddam's campaign and, during the next month, 732 Kuwaiti oil wells are set on fire. Iraq starts to pump Kuwaiti crude oil into the Persian Gulf (24 Jan.); extreme environmental pollution and dangers to human health ensue.

24 Feb. The culminating campaign of the Gulf War, Operation Desert Storm, starts. It lasts four days and ends in the defeat of Iraq. US Gen. Norman Schwarzkopf commands the combined air and ground attack. US, British and French forces attack Iraq from the W and aerial bombing severs the main road from Baghdad to Basra, which is the lifeline for Iraqi troops in the S. Some 100,000 Iraqi troops surrender and many are killed. Coalition forces liberate Kuwait City (27 Feb.) and US president Bush announces the end of hostilities (28 Feb.). The need to keep the allied coalition together, and the observance of the UN resolutions, means that the allied troops do not advance into Iraq itself. Saddam Hussein therefore remains in power. Rebel Kurdish and Shiite elements within Iraq attempt to strike against him while his authority is weakened (1 Mar.), but he suppresses the rebellions with characteristic ferocity by the end of Mar. The plight of the Kurds, who have been campaigning for their own state in N Iraq ever since their betrayal by the framers of the treaties that ended World War I in the Middle East, attracts worldwide sympathy. President Bush hesitates but then agrees to send material aid to them and to establish 'no-fly zones' in Iraq to support the Kurds in the N and the Shiite rebels in the S. When Iraqi troops launch attacks on Kurdish refugees (11 April), US, British and French forces enter N Iraq to set up and guard refugee camps for the Kurds (17 April). By the end of April Kurds are moving into these camps. The main purpose of the campaign has already been achieved: oil prices return to their previous levels as the security of Western supplies is once again assured.

4 June In Algeria the army fires on members of the Islamic Salvation Front. The prime minister Mouloud Hamrouche resigns, and national elections are promised.

8 Aug. John McCarthy, a British journalist held hostage in Beirut by Islamic militants since April 1986, is released.

18 Nov. Terry Waite, the archbishop of Canterbury's envoy, who has been held hostage in Beirut by Islamic militants since Jan. 1987, is the last British hostage in Lebanon to be released.

26 Dec. In the first round of Algeria's elections the ruling National Liberation Front is defeated by the fundamentalist Islamic Liberation Front.

ASIA

23 Feb. Chatichai Choonhavan, prime minister of Thailand, is overthrown in a military coup. Anand Panyarachun replaces him in a provisional government: a new constitution and democratic elections are promised.

30 April Bangladesh is hit by a cyclone: some 140,000 people and many livestock are killed.

21 May Rajiv Gandhi, the former prime minister of India, is killed by a Tamil suicide bomber while he is campaigning near Madras.

20 June P.V. Narasimha Rao, leader of the Congress Party, becomes prime minister of India and embarks on a policy of liberalization.

June Jiang Qing, widow of former Chinese leader Mao Zedong (Mao Tse-tung), is reported to have committed suicide.

23 Oct. A UN-brokered peace accord ending the Cambodian civil war is signed in Paris by the country's warring factions. Prince Sihanouk will head a coalition administration.

THE AMERICAS

Jan. A cholera epidemic strikes Peru. Some 100,000 people fall ill and more than 700 die. The outbreak then spreads to Brazil.

Feb. President Jean-Bertrand Aristide takes office in Haiti and dismisses the entire army high command.

23 May By a five to four majority the US Supreme Court upholds the decision of Congress (1970) preventing government-funded family planning clinics from providing information about abortion. President Bush opposes legislation to override the ban.

12 June Classified State Department information now made public shows that there are 250,000 names on a list of those prohibited from entering the USA. The Senate's foreign relations committee votes for almost all of the names to be removed and President Bush complies with its wishes.

19 June Colombian drug baron Pablo Escobar surrenders to the authorities on condition that he will not be extradited to the USA. The Cali group expands with the demise of the Medellín cartel.

30 Sept. In Haiti President Jean-Bertrand Aristide is overthrown in a military coup by Brig.-Gen. Raoul Cédras.

Oct. Clarence Thomas, a conservative anti-abortionist nominated by President Bush to the US Supreme Court, faces allegations of sexual harassment from former colleague Anita Hill, a professor at the University of Oklahoma Law School. The allegations, made by an African-American woman against an African-American man, prolong and complicate the process of his public scrutiny before his appointment can be confirmed. Eventually, the Senate votes by 52 to 48 to approve the president's nominee.

SUB-SAHARAN AFRICA

26 Jan. Mohammad Siad Barre, dictatorial ruler of Somalia, flees from the forces of the opposition United Somali Congress: Ali Mahdi Mohammad becomes interim president (29 Jan.).

21 May In Ethiopia communist president Haile Mariam Mengistu, now abandoned by his Soviet backers, flees to Zimbabwe as rebel forces close in on Addis Ababa.

31 May Angola's warring factions, the Cuban- and Soviet-backed MPLA and the US- and South African-backed UNITA, sign an agreement in Lisbon to end the country's long-running civil war. MPLA President José Eduardo dos Santos promises a return to multiparty politics.

17 June The Population Registration Act is repealed by the South African parliament. Children are no longer racially classified at birth. President Bush lifts US sanctions against South Africa (10 July).

Aug. Nigeria creates 9 new states, bringing the total in the federation to 30.

Oct. In Zambia the opposition Movement for Multiparty Democracy (MMD) wins multiparty elections, bringing to an end the 27-year presidency of Kenneth Kaunda. Frederick Chiluba becomes the new Zambian president (Nov.).

AUSTRALASIA AND OCEANIA

19 Dec. In Australia prime minister Bob Hawke is challenged by Paul Keating for the leadership of the Labor Party. Keating becomes party leader and prime minister.

ECONOMY AND SOCIETY

Oct.–Nov. Australia wins the 2nd rugby union World Cup, held in England (with some games played in Scotland, Wales, Ireland and France).

– South Africa is readmitted to the International Olympic Committee and to the International Cricket Conference.

SCIENCE AND TECHNOLOGY

– DDI, a cheaper anti-AIDS treatment than AZT, becomes available.

– By now domestic users are able to access the Internet using personal computers.

ARTS AND HUMANITIES

Literature

3 April The English novelist Graham Greene dies.

Martin Amis, *Time's Arrow*, novel.

Beryl Bainbridge, *The Birthday Boys*, novel.

Pat Barker, *Regeneration*, novel.

Alan Bennett, *The Madness of George III*, play.

Ariel Dorfman, *Death and the Maiden*, play.

Bret Easton Ellis, *American Psycho*, novel.

Jostein Gaarder, *Sophies verden* (Sophie's World: A Novel about the History of Philosophy), novel.

Milan Kundera, *Immortality*, novel.

Ben Okri, *The Famished Road*, novel.

Michael Ondaatje, *The English Patient*, novel.

Keith Waterhouse, *Jeffrey Bernard is Unwell*, play.

Visual Arts and Architecture

– English artist Damien Hirst presents the art world with a dead shark in a tank; it is called *The Physical Impossibility of Death in the Mind of Someone Living*.

Music

19 Mar. First performance in Brussels of John Adams's opera *The Death of Klinghoffer*, about the hijacking by Palestinian terrorists of the *Achille Lauro* (see 1985).

30 May First performance in London of Harrison Birtwistle's opera *Gawain*, based on the medieval poem *Sir Gawain and the Green Knight*.

24 Oct. The rock star Freddie Mercury of Queen dies of AIDS.

Bryan Adams, '(Everything I Do) I Do It for You', single.

The Clash, 'Should I Stay or Should I Go?', single.

Ice-T, *O.G.*, album.

Massive Attack, *Blue Lines*, album, including 'Unfinished Sympathy', single.

Nirvana, 'Smells Like Teen Spirit', single and *Nevermind*, album.

Primal Scream, *Screamadelica*, album.

R.E.M. *Out of Time*, album, including 'Losing My Religion', single.

Simply Red, *Stars*, album.

U2, *Achtung Baby*, album.

AMERICAN HEGEMONY:
The Victories, Dilemmas and Fears of a 21st-Century Colossus

During the 20th century, the American Way blazed its path through the history of the whole of the rest of the world. This became the century of the consumer, with the constant ebb and flow of consumer needs and desires dictating the direction of industrial and technological development, of mass communications and of popular culture – first in the cinema and radio and then in television. In all these areas the USA was the pioneer. And perhaps the most significant US triumph was in this area of 'soft' cultural influence, as many people around the world became American in tastes and views.

In the latter part of the century the USA showed how an economy based on heavy industry could move towards a new base of light industry and high technology. The revolution in information technology mostly began in California's Silicon Valley, and this revolution also demonstrated the importance of a flexible and educated work force. The oil crisis of 1973 ended the postwar economic boom in the West, and the associated social equilibrium, as governments cut back on expenditure and trade unions struggled to preserve their bargaining powers. At the same time, the new Asian economies started to compete with Western industry on the basis of their non-unionized, low-wage workforces. The USA's comparative lack of strong unions and its lightly regulated economy made it able to adapt to the challenge – but Europe faltered, embracing major, dislocating economic change only at the cost of social cohesion.

There were internal crises in the USA too. The 1960s saw race riots in the major cities and military intervention in the Vietnam War, a source of national grief and division. The USA was also nervous about its own backyard in Central America – and had been ever since the takeover of Cuba by the Marxist Fidel Castro. In the 1970s and 80s the USA supported a series of repressive military regimes in Central America purely on the basis that they claimed to be anti-communist. It did the same in South America, notoriously in Chile, where a coup sponsored by the CIA toppled a democratically elected government in 1973. American strategists thought they were fighting communism, when they were often confronting nationalist anti-imperialism, a creed that proved much more tenacious than Marxism.

In the Cold War, beginning in the late 1940s, the USA decided to face down what it saw as the global Soviet threat. The process started with the Marshall Plan, which helped the war-shattered western European economies to restructure themselves, so averting the threat of communist revolution. The 'Iron Curtain' and the Berlin Wall now became the eastern frontiers of the new American world order, facing the Soviet world. In the late 1960s détente on the basis of realpolitik opened the door to a new Chinese–American relationship. But there was no real détente with the Soviets. The Americans were prepared to outspend the Soviets on the arms race, the nuclear race and the space race. And they saw with satisfaction how the Soviet economy was first of all paralysed by the attempt to keep up, and then collapsed under the strain.

In the Middle East the USA had two major allies. The first was Saudi Arabia, which was a major guarantor of the oil supplies needed by the US economy. The second was the state of Israel, whose gross national deficit was converted to a surplus by a vast annual subsidy from the USA. After the collapse of the USSR, the USA came to regard the hostile Islamic states as the greatest threat to its security. But the alliance with the Saudis meant the arrival of US military bases in Saudi Arabia, the land of the holy Islamic places of Mecca and Medina – a fact that infuriated many Muslims. At the dawn of the 21st century it seemed – especially in the ruins of the World Trade Center in New York, destroyed by Islamic terrorists – that the USA now confronted a more implacable enemy than the USSR of old. After all, the

This became the century of the consumer ...

Soviets had been content to maintain a kind of uneasy co-existence. And the eventual victory over the Soviet system proved to be a largely peaceful one, since it was the individual citizens of eastern and central Europe who opted for the consumerism of the West. No such easy victory beckoned for the USA in the Middle East. Genuine and popular anti-American feeling pulsated up and down the streets of the Muslim world. And the anger was at two levels: first it was nationalist – especially among the Palestinians, uprooted since 1948 by the USA's ally, Israel – and second it was religious, as some elements of Islam turned militantly political. This was not a conflict that could be resolved by converting Islam to consumerism. All the nationalist fury of Vietnam, it seemed, had been reborn in a Middle Eastern context. But this time the nationalism was supplemented by religious zealotry as well.

1991 *continued*

Film

James Cameron, *Terminator 2: Judgment Day*, starring Arnold Schwarzenegger.

Joel and Ethan Coen, *Barton Fink*.

Jean-Pierre Jeunet and Marc Caro, *Delicatessen*.

Anthony Minghella, *Truly, Madly, Deeply*, starring Alan Rickman and Juliet Stevenson.

Ridley Scott, *Thelma and Louise*, starring Geena Davis and Susan Sarandon.

Oliver Stone, *JFK*, starring Kevin Costner.

Quentin Tarantino, *Reservoir Dogs*.

Paul Verhoeven, *Basic Instinct*, starring Sharon Stone and Michael Douglas.

1992

EUROPE

1 Jan. New free-market economic policies in the Russian Federation cause immediate, massive price increases. The speaker of the Russian duma (parliament), Ruslan Khasbulatov, calls on President Yeltsin to resign (13 Jan.), but Yeltsin manages to force a package of austerity measures through the duma (24 Jan.).

15 Jan. The European Community (EC) and the USA recognize Croatian and Slovenian independence.

30 Jan. In the Republic of Ireland Charles Haughey resigns as taoiseach (prime minister). Albert Reynolds, a former dance hall promoter and pet food manufacturer, is elected Fianna Fáil party leader and becomes taoiseach (6 Feb.).

Jan. In Croatia a UN-brokered peace agreement provides for a ceasefire, the withdrawal of the Yugoslav federal army from Croatia, and the deployment of 10,000 UN troops in the contested areas of Krajina and E and W Slavonia pending a political settlement.

Jan. Georgian president Zviad Gamsakhurdia, an extreme nationalist, is ousted by rebels and forced to flee to neighbouring Armenia.

Jan. Macedonia declares its independence from Yugoslavia.

7 Feb. Members of the European Community (EC) sign the treaty of European Union, otherwise known as the treaty of Maastricht. The treaty, which revises the treaty of Rome (1957) and the Single European Act (1986), aligns member-states towards greater union in political as well as economic matters; it also stipulates that a new currency, the Euro, issued by a central bank, will be in use by 1999. Britain's Conservative government refuses to accept some elements of the treaty, especially those relating to the new currency.

3 Mar. Following a referendum (boycotted by Bosnia's Serbs), Bosnia-Herzegovina declares itself independent of Yugoslavia. Violent clashes take place between Croats, Serbs and Muslims in the Bosnian capital of Sarajevo.

28 Mar. The government of Finland applies to join the European Union (EU).

Mar.–April In Croatia UN peace-keeping forces move into Krajina. The breakaway Serb leader in the area, Milan Babic, does not recognize the peace agreement.

2 April The French prime minister Edith Cresson resigns and is replaced by Pierre Bérégovoy.

7 April The European Community (EC) recognizes Bosnia-Herzegovina's independence. Yugoslav federal forces, aided by local Serb forces who wish to carve up the newly independent republic, start to bombard Sarajevo from high points overlooking the city. In pursuit of their aim of creating a Greater Serbia, the Bosnian Serbs – led by Radovan Karadzic – will carry out a policy of 'ethnic cleansing', creating ethnically homogenous Serb areas by forcibly moving entire populations of Bosnian Muslims and Croats from their homes and allowing Serbian families to occupy them. The Serbian siege of Sarajevo will last until 1994.

9 April In Britain's general election the Conservative Party wins a fourth consecutive term of government, contrary to the expectations of most political commentators. The Conservatives win 336 seats to Labour's 271. The Labour Party has now lost four successive general elections, and commentators begin to question its continued existence.

10 April In the City of London an IRA bomb explodes at the Baltic Exchange, killing three people.

13 April In Britain Neil Kinnock resigns as leader of the Labour Party.

27 April In Britain MPs elect Betty Boothroyd as the first woman speaker of the House of Commons.

April Serbia and Montenegro announce a new Federal Republic of Yugoslavia, consisting of the republics of Serbia and Montenegro.

May Bosnia-Herzegovina becomes a full member of the United Nations (UN).

May In Kosovo the area's majority Albanian population holds an election (regarded as illegal by Serbia), which chooses a president and a parliament.

May In Germany former East German leaders, including former Communist leader Erich Honecker (currently in exile in Moscow), are charged with manslaughter. The German government demands that Honecker return to face the charges (29 July).

2 June A referendum in Denmark rejects the treaty of Maastricht.

5–6 June In elections in Czechoslovakia, parties favouring independence prevail in Slovakia, while parties favouring a Czech–Slovak federation prevail in the Czech lands. Slovakian MPs deputies vote for Slovakia to become an independent state (17 July). The Czechoslovakian president Václav Havel resigns.

June British troops are sent to Bosnia as part of a UN mission.

June In South Ossetia, in the N part of Georgia, Ossetian secessionists – who wish to unite with their co-nationalists in the neighbouring autonomous Russian republic of Alania (formerly North Ossetia) – launch an offensive with the aim of unifying the two regions. Following a ceasefire (July) Russian and Georgian peace-keeping troops are deployed in the region.

18 July In Britain John Smith is elected leader of the Labour Party.

Aug. In Abkhazia, an autonomous republic in NW Georgia, fighting breaks out between invading Georgian forces and Muslim Abkhazi separatists, who have declared unilateral independence (July). Georgian troops seize the regional capital of Sukhumi and establish an interim government.

16 Sept. Britain experiences a sterling crisis on 'Black Wednesday': speculative selling of sterling forces chancellor of the exchequer Norman Lamont to devalue the pound and withdraw from the Exchange Rate Mechanism (the system for controlling exchange rates intended to prepare the way for the European single currency).

20 Sept. In France a referendum votes in favour of the Maastricht treaty by a narrow margin.

Sept. The United Nations suspends Yugoslavia's membership of the UN because of Serbia's alleged complicity in atrocities carried out by Bosnian Serbs against Muslims and Croats. By now Bosnian Serbs have taken control of two-thirds of Bosnia-Herzegovina and have declared this area an independent Serb state; in the Croatian-dominated W of the country an independent Croat state has been proclaimed. Bosnia's beleaguered Muslims struggle for control of their enclaves.

Oct. Eduard Shevardnadze, former Soviet foreign minister, is elected speaker of the Georgian parliament (effectively the country's president). More than 100 political parties are competing for power in Georgia, whose political instability is exacerbated by growing separatist tensions in South Ossetia and Abkhazia (where secessionist rebels have captured much of the territory lost to the Georgian army in Aug.).

25 Nov. Norway applies to join the European Union (EU).

Nov. A general election in the Republic of Ireland gives no party an overall majority. Fianna Fáil enters into negotiations with the Labour Party (which has made significant gains in the election).

9 Dec. In Britain the separation is announced of Charles, Prince of Wales, and the Princess of Wales. It is Britain's second royal separation of the year, the separation of the Duke and Duchess of York having been announced on 9 Mar.

20 Dec. Slobodan Milosevic, regarded by many as the instigator of Serbian 'ethnic cleansing' in Croatia and Bosnia, is re-elected president of Serbia.

– In Chechnya (see Nov. 1991), fighting breaks out between the forces of the separatist leader Gen. Dzhokhar Dudayev and anti-separatist forces, who have Russian backing.

MIDDLE EAST AND NORTH AFRICA

11 Jan. Algeria's armed forces cancel the second round of elections to prevent the victory of the fundamentalist Islamic Salvation Front (FIS). President Chadli Benjedid resigns. A ruling army junta is headed by Muhammad Boudiaf, who bans political activity in mosques and imprisons ISF leaders in an attempt to stem the rise of Islamic fundamentalism in Algeria. A state of emergency is declared (Feb.).

Feb. In Israel former Labour prime minister Yitzhak Rabin replaces Shimon Peres as leader of the Labour Party.

29 June President Boudiaf of Algeria is assassinated by the Islamic Salvation Front (FIS). He is replaced by Ali Kafi. A brutal cycle of tit-for-tat violence now starts: the FIS assassinates politicians, secular intellectuals and members of the police and army; while the government uses torture and judicial killing to suppress Islamic radicals. The FIS president and vice-president receive 12-year jail terms for conspiracy (July).

June An Iraqi health official, Abdul Abbas, claims that UN sanctions against his country have already killed over 40,000 people, many of whom are children.

June In Israel the Labour Party defeats Likud in a general election. Yitzhak Rabin becomes prime minister at the head of a Labour-dominated coalition government.

Aug. The UN Security Council imposes a 'no-fly zone' over S Iraq to protect Iraqi Shiites.

ASIA

16 April Islamic *mujahedin* fighters take Kabul. President Najibullah of Afghanistan is overthrown.

9 July The former Conservative cabinet minister Chris Patten becomes governor of Hong Kong.

8 Sept. The Japanese cabinet approves the dispatch of 1800 troops as UN peacekeepers in Cambodia. This is the first overseas deployment of Japanese forces since 1945.

6 Dec. In India Hindu extremists destroy the mosque of Ayodhya. The act triggers Hindu–Muslim violence throughout India in which some 1200 are killed.

Dec. Burhanuddin Rabbani, a guerrilla leader, becomes president of Afghanistan. Tensions between the Afghan government (now dominated by forces from the N of Afghanistan) and fundamentalist guerrillas (whose power base lies in the Pashtun lands of the S) have already led to fierce fighting between government forces and rebels (Aug.).

– Emperor Akihito makes the first-ever state visit by a Japanese emperor to China.

THE AMERICAS

29 Jan. President Bush announces a package of defence cuts amounting to $50 billion, a 'peace dividend' arising from the end of the Cold War.

29 April–4 May Serious rioting breaks out in San Francisco and other US cities. African-American motorist Rodney King has been savagely beaten by four police officers, who are acquitted despite the fact that the incident has been recorded on video-tape. In the resulting violence 58 die.

24 Aug. Florida is devastated by Hurricane Andrew.

12 Sept. In Peru Abimael Guzman, the leader of the Marxist revolutionary group Sendero Luminoso (Shining Path), is captured by security forces. He is sentenced to life imprisonment (Oct.).

Nov. William Jefferson Clinton defeats the incumbent Republican president, George Bush, to become 42nd president of the USA.

SUB-SAHARAN AFRICA

24 Jan. South African president F.W. de Klerk announces plans for a power-sharing administration that will include the African National Congress (ANC). In a whites-only referendum he wins a comfortable majority for ending apartheid (17 Mar.).

26 Jan. The European Community (EC) lifts sanctions against South Africa.

18 June In South Africa 40 people die in fighting between rival ANC and Inkatha supporters in the black township of Boipatong. Police have sided with Inkatha supporters in the violence. The ANC withdraws from negotiations on South Africa's new constitution in protest.

31 Aug. The UN announces that 2000 people are dying every day in Somalia. The state of anarchy that has followed the overthrow of the regime of Mohammad Barre (see 1991) is making the distribution of relief impossible.

Aug. The USA launches 'Operation Restore Hope' to relieve victims of famine and civil war in Somalia.

Aug. In Mozambique President Chissano signs a peace treaty with Afonso Dhlakama, leader of the Mozambique National Resistance (MNR or Renamo). Fighting between government forces and right-wing rebels continues, however.

Sept.–Oct. In Angola the governing MPLA wins the country's general election. UNITA leader Jonas Savimbi refuses to accept the election result and civil war breaks out again. UNITA takes over the S half of Angola (Nov.).

9 Dec. A force of US Marines lands in Mogadishu, Somalia, under UN auspices. The USA proposes to establish a significant military presence in Somalia as part of its relief operation.

AUSTRALASIA AND OCEANIA

3 June The Australian high court overturns the *terra nullius*, the ruling that Australia was an empty territory before the arrival of European settlers and that Aborigine nations have no title to land. As a result of the decision, Aborigines can now pursue land claims.

ECONOMY AND SOCIETY

April In France Euro Disney opens near Paris.

July–Aug. The 25th Olympic Games are held in Barcelona, Spain.

Aug. In England the first football matches are played in the Premier League, formed by 22 clubs that have broken away from the Football League.

SCIENCE AND TECHNOLOGY

3–14 June An International Conference on Environment and Development is convened by the UN in Rio de Janeiro, Brazil. Delegates agree to preserve biodiversity and to combat global warming. The USA, however, refuses to sign the agreement on biodiversity, seeing it as a threat to its economic growth.

10 July European Space Agency probe *Giotto* passes within 250km (155 miles) of comet Grigg–Skjellerup.

– There are now 1000 known computer viruses. In 1988 there were only five.

ARTS AND HUMANITIES

Literature

6 April American science fiction writer Isaac Asimov dies.

25 Nov. At St Martin's Theatre, London, Agatha Christie's murder mystery *The Mousetrap* gives its 16,648th performance.

Robert Olen Butler, *A Good Scent from a Strange Mountain*, novel.

Jung Chang, *Wild Swans*, family memoir of lives lived under Chinese communism.

Peter Høeg, *Frøken Smillas Fornemmelse for Sne* (Miss Smilla's Feeling for Snow), novel.

Nick Hornby, *Fever Pitch*, novel.

Patrick McCabe, *The Butcher Boy*, novel.

Cormac McCarthy, *All the Pretty Horses*, novel.

Ian McEwan, *Black Dogs*, novel.

Toni Morrison, *Jazz*, novel.

Donna Tartt, *The Secret History*, novel.

Jeff Torrington, *Swing Hammer Swing!*, novel.

Barry Unsworth, *Sacred Hunger*, novel.

Visual Arts and Architecture

28 April The English artist Francis Bacon dies.

Music

27 April Olivier Messiaen, French composer and organist, dies.

12 Aug. John Cage, US composer, dies in New York.

Mariah Carey 'I'll be There', single.

Whitney Houston, 'I Will Always Love You', single.

Michael Jackson, 'Heal the World', single.

kd lang, *Ingénue*, album.

Red Hot Chili Peppers, 'Under the Bridge', single.

R.E.M., *Automatic for the People,* album.

The Shamen, 'Ebeneezer Goode', single.

U2, 'One', single.

Film

Robert Altman, *The Player*.

Clint Eastwood, *Unforgiven*, starring Gene Hackman.

Spike Lee, *Malcolm X*.

Baz Luhrmann, *Strictly Ballroom*.

Ismail Merchant and James Ivory, *Howards End*, starring Anthony Hopkins and Emma Thompson.

Sally Potter, *Orlando*.

Penelope Spheeris, *Wayne's World*.

1993

EUROPE

1 Jan. Czechoslovakia becomes separate Czech and Slovak republics. The separation of the two states comes to be known as the 'velvet divorce'. In the Czech Republic Václav Klaus of the Civic Democratic Party (CDS) becomes prime minister and Václav Havel is elected president; in the Slovak Republic (or Slovakia) Vladimir Meciar becomes prime minister and Michal Kovac becomes president.

1 Jan. The European single market comes into force: all tariffs and restrictions on the movement of people and goods between EU member-states are abolished.

13 Jan. Former East German Communist leader Erich Honecker moves to Chile after the German courts rule that he is too sick to stand trial.

Jan. In the Republic of Ireland Albert Reynolds forms a Fianna Fáil–Labour coalition government and continues as taoiseach (prime minister).

Jan. Croatia attacks Serb-held areas of Krajina.

22 Feb. The UN Security Council votes to establish a war crimes tribunal to try cases relating to the civil war in the former Yugoslavia.

Feb. A major corruption scandal erupts in Italy. Judges accuse Bettino Craxi, leader of the Italian Socialist Party (PSI) since 1976 and former prime minister (1983–7), of involvement. Craxi resigns.

16 Mar. In Britain value added tax is imposed on domestic fuel. The decision undermines the credibility of John Major's Conservative government, which campaigned for re-election in 1992 on the promise of tax cuts.

20 Mar. The UN evacuates civilians from the besieged Bosnian town of Srebrenica.

20 Mar. An IRA bomb in Warrington, England, kills two children. Another IRA bomb in the City of London (24 Mar.) causes £1 billion in damage.

29 Mar. In French parliamentary elections held against a background of economic recession and high unemployment the Socialist Party is routed by the Gaullists. President François Mitterrand appoints Edouard Balladur of the Gaullist RPR as prime minister. Thus begins the second period of Gaullist–Socialist cohabitation of Mitterrand's presidency. The defeated Socialist prime minister Pierre Bérégovoy commits suicide (1 May) following his party's electoral débâcle.

April In Britain the black teenager Stephen Lawrence is murdered in a racially motivated attack.

6 May The UN Security Council creates six 'safe havens' in Bosnia-Herzegovina – Sarajevo, Tuzla, Zepa, Bihac, Gorazde and Srebrenica – to protect Bosnian Muslims who are fleeing Bosnian Serb aggression. Despite this move, Bosnian Serb forces attack Gorazde and Srebrenica on 30 May.

29 May In the Ruhr district of Germany, neo-Nazis murder five Turkish women and girls in an arson attack.

31 July Baudouin, king of the Belgians, dies. His brother Albert succeeds him.

2 Aug. The European Exchange Rate Mechanism (ERM) collapses as a result of currency speculation on the international financial markets. Currencies can now fluctuate within 15% either above or below the central rate.

21 Sept. A long-running confrontation between President Yeltsin and the Russian duma (parliament) comes to a head. Yeltsin orders the duma to be suspended pending new elections. The duma defies him, and members barricade themselves inside the duma building (the White House) and choose Alexander Rutskoi as president. The White House telephone lines, water and power are cut, and the building is surrounded by troops.

(27 Sept.). Yeltsin then orders the building to be shelled, and the members surrender (4 Oct.). It is a victory for Yeltsin but an ominous sign for Russia. Power politics, rather than the rule of law, have prevailed. A sign of growing disillusion with the democratic experiment follows on 12 Dec. when the neo-fascist Liberal Democratic party, led by Vladimir Zhirinovsky, gains the largest share of the vote for the new duma (22.8%).

Oct. In Abkhazia, an autonomous republic in NW Georgia, Muslim separatists capture the regional capital of Sukhumi. Most of Abkhazia is now in the hands of the rebels and many ethnic Georgians have fled the area. In Georgia itself nationalist forces loyal to former president Zviad Gamsakhurdia have rebelled in the W of the country. Eduard Shevardnadze (see Oct. 1992) calls for Russian military assistance to suppress the rebellion.

1 Nov. In accordance with the Maastricht treaty (Feb. 1992), the European Community becomes the European Union, as a sign of its commitment to further political integration.

15 Dec. The prime ministers of Britain, John Major, and Ireland, Albert Reynolds, make the Downing Street Declaration. They announce that talks to end the violence in Northern Ireland depend on constitutional changes in the province having the support of the majority of the electorate both there and in the Republic of Ireland.

– In Britain the Conservative government of John Major announces plans to privatize the railways.

– In Britain the controversial local tax known as the community charge (poll tax) is replaced by the council tax.

– The remains of the last Russian tsar, Nicholas I, and his family are identified using genetic fingerprinting. They receive a state funeral.

– In Italy proportional representation is changed to majority voting in the national senate.

MIDDLE EAST AND NORTH AFRICA

13 Jan. The US-led coalition in Iraq bombs targets in the S of the country to enforce the 'no-fly zone' protecting the Shiite population.

Mar. In Israel Binyamin ('Bibi') Netanyahu succeeds Yitzhak Shamir as leader of the right-wing Likud party.

April Peace talks mediated by Norwegian diplomats begin in Washington, D.C., between Palestinians and Israelis.

July Israel launches a heavy bombardment of Hezbollah targets in S Lebanon (Hezbollah guerrillas have been launching attacks on Israel from S Lebanon).

13 Sept. An Israeli–Palestinian peace accord is signed in Washington, D.C., by PLO leader Yasser Arafat and Israeli prime minister Yitzhak Rabin. The two men shake hands on the White House lawn. The accord provides for limited self-government for the Palestinians in the Gaza Strip and Jericho, and for eventual Palestinian self-government on the West Bank. Israel also agrees to a phased withdrawal of its troops from the occupied territories. The accord raises high hopes, but negotiations over its implementation will make slow progress and will be hampered by continuing violence between Palestinians and Jewish settlers in the occupied territories.

ASIA

Mar. Car bombs in Bombay, India, kill about 300 people.

18 July In elections in Japan the Liberal Democratic Party, which has ruled Japan since 1955 but which has been damaged by recent scandals, loses its overall majority in parliament. Morihiro Hosokawa, leader of the Japan New Party (JNP), becomes prime minister of a coalition government that does not include the LDP (Aug.).

July Pakistan's national assembly is dissolved; President Ghulam Ishaq Khan and premier Nawaz Sharif resign from office.

Sept. An earthquake in India kills 20,000 people.

Oct. In a general election in Pakistan Benazir Bhutto becomes prime minister for a second time after the Pakistan People's Party (PPP) wins a narrow victory over the Pakistan Muslim League (PML) led by Nawaz Sharif.

THE AMERICAS

3 Jan. Presidents Bush and Yeltsin sign START II, the second Strategic Arms Reduction Treaty, disposing of two-thirds of both US and Russian nuclear warheads.

20 Jan. Bill Clinton is inaugurated as 42nd president of the USA.

2 Feb. Colombian drug baron and racketeer Pablo Escobar is killed by police in Medellín, Colombia.

6 Feb. A bomb planted by terrorists explodes at the World Trade Center, New York: five people are killed and the building is badly damaged.

19 April In Waco, Texas, US cult leader David Koresh and 73 followers are killed when their compound burns down after a 51-day siege by federal agents.

13 May The US government decides to withdraw the Strategic Defence Initiative (SDI or 'Star Wars').

22 Sept. Hillary Clinton, wife of President Bill Clinton, unveils a plan for the radical reform of US health care.

25 Oct. The Progressive Conservative Party, which has held power since 1984, is crushed in the Canadian general election and reduced to just two seats; the Liberal Party returns to government. Jean Chrétien becomes prime minister. The Bloc Québecois is now Canada's second-largest party.

SUB-SAHARAN AFRICA

April Angola's MPLA government, led by President dos Santos, is formally recognized by the USA.

24 May After 30 years of civil war, Eritrea becomes independent from Ethiopia.

May In South Africa agreement is reached that non-racial multiparty elections will be held by April 1994.

June In Nigeria the first free presidential election is held but its result is annulled. Gen. Babangida resigns as Nigerian president (Aug.), having nominated Ernest Shonekan as his successor.

June US forces in Somalia launch an offensive against the warlord Gen. Aidid following an attack on UN peace-keeping troops.

Aug. A peace agreement is signed in Rwanda between President Habyarimana and the Rwandan Patriotic Front, an organization representing Rwanda's minority Tutsi population. A UN mission is sent to Rwanda to monitor the implementation of the agreement which is intended to establish power-sharing between the majority Hutu people and the Tutsis.

8 Oct. As South African negotiations prepare the way for democracy, the international community lifts sanctions in response to an appeal by the African National Congress (ANC) leader Nelson Mandela (24 Sept.).

15 Oct. South Africa's president F.W. de Klerk and ANC leader Nelson Mandela are joint winners of the Nobel Peace Prize.

Oct. Following a clash between US troops and Somali forces in Mogadishu, President Clinton announces that US troops will be withdrawn from Somalia.

Nov. Nigeria returns to military rule after a brief period of civilian government. President Ernest Shonekan is overthrown and replaced by Gen. Sani Abacha.

AUSTRALASIA AND OCEANIA

12 Mar. In Australia's general election Paul Keating leads the Labor Party to its fifth consecutive election victory.

ECONOMY AND SOCIETY

– In the Netherlands euthanasia is legalized.

– In Britain Parliament approves the ordination of women priests in the Church of England.

SCIENCE AND TECHNOLOGY

11 Feb. British explorers Sir Ranulph Fiennes and Dr Michael Stroud complete an unsupported crossing of Antarctica on foot.

– In Britain physicists at Lancaster University, UK, achieve a temperature lower than 0.3 millionths of a degree above absolute zero.

ARTS AND HUMANITIES

Literature

22 Nov. English writer Anthony Burgess dies.

Pat Barker, *The Eye in the Door*, novel.

Paul Coelho, *The Alchemist*, novel.

Roddy Doyle, *Paddy Clarke Ha Ha Ha*, novel.

Francis Fukuyama, *The End of History*, study of the supposed final victory of Western-style capitalism and liberal democracy.

Harold Pinter, *Moonlight*, play.

Annie Proulx, *The Shipping News*, novel.

Vikram Seth, *A Suitable Boy*, novel.

Carol Shields, *The Stone Diaries*, novel.

Robert James Waller, *The Bridges of Madison County*, novel.

Irvine Welsh, *Trainspotting*, novel.

Visual Arts and Architecture

– In Britain the Turner Prize is awarded to Rachel Whiteread for her work *Untitled (House)*, a concrete cast of the interior of a house in London's East End.

Music

6 Jan. Russian-born dancer Rudolph Nureyev dies.

Björk, *Debut*, album.

Elvis Costello, *The Juliet Letters*, album.

Jamiroquai, *Emergency on Planet Earth*, album.

Annie Lennox, *Diva*, album.

Radiohead, 'Creep', single.

R.E.M., 'Everybody Hurts', single.

Tina Turner, *What's Love Got to Do with It?*, album.

Film

20 Jan. American actress Audrey Hepburn dies.

31 Oct. Federico Fellini dies.

Andrew Davis, *The Fugitive*, starring Harrison Ford.

Lasse Hallström, *What's Eating Gilbert Grape?*, starring Johnny Depp.

Krzysztof Kieslowski, *Trois Couleurs: Bleu* (Three Colours Blue).

Adrian Lyne, *Indecent Proposal*.

Harold Ramis, *Groundhog Day*, starring Bill Murray.

Jim Sheridan, *In the Name of the Father*.

Steven Spielberg, *Jurassic Park*, starring Sam Neill and Laura Dern, and *Schindler's List*, starring Liam Neeson and Ralph Fiennes.

1994

EUROPE

13 Jan. In London the Conservative council in Westminster is officially criticized for gerrymandering election boundaries (1987–9). The Conservative government suffers guilt by association.

5 Feb. In the besieged city of Sarajevo, Bosnia-Herzegovina, a Serb mortar attack kills at least 68 civilians. The incident arouses international revulsion, and the clamour for intervention to end the civil war gets louder. NATO orders the Serbs to remove their artillery from Sarajevo or face airstrikes (9 Feb.). The Serbs largely comply, at least temporarily.

26 Feb. The Russian government announces an amnesty for political prisoners, including those involved in the coup of 1991 that brought down the USSR.

1 Mar. Terms are agreed for the entry of Sweden, Austria and Finland to the European Union. Terms are also agreed for Norway (16 Mar.), subject to their approval by a national referendum.

17 Mar. The trial begins in France of Paul Touvier, head of the Vichy militia in Lyons during World War II. He will be sentenced to life imprisonment (April).

18 Mar. In Bosnia-Herzegovina Croats and Muslims, who have ceased hostilities in the N of the country, sign an accord creating a federation of Bosnian Muslims and Croats. It is hoped that this new constitutional structure will eventually be linked to Croatia in a loose federal arrangement.

26–27 Mar. In Italy an alliance comprising Forza Italia (led by the right-wing entrepreneur Silvio Berlusconi), the federalist Northern League and the neo-fascist National Alliance wins the parliamentary elections. Berlusconi becomes prime minister of a coalition government. Concerns are immediately raised at a potential conflict between Berlusconi's responsibilities as premier and his business interests, which – alongside property development and wide-ranging media ownership – include

AC Milan football club and Italy's largest department store.

31 Mar. In Bosnia-Herzegovina Serb artillery bombards the UN 'safe havens' of Gorazde and Srebrenica. Following its earlier warning to the Serbs, NATO launches airstrikes on Serb positions near Gorazde (10 April), but the city falls to the Serbs on 17 April. Allegations of Serb massacres follow.

9 May In the former Soviet republic of Azerbaijan, a ceasefire is declared in the Armenian enclave of Nagorno-Karabakh. An international peace-keeping force monitors the agreement.

12 May In Britain the Labour Party leader John Smith dies suddenly following a heart attack.

May By now there are more than 20,000 UN troops in Bosnia-Herzegovina. Their job is to protect UN 'safe havens', to airlift relief supplies to the isolated Muslim enclaves of E Bosnia, and somehow to contain the fighting. In June a ceasefire is agreed between Bosnian Serbs and the Croat–Muslim federation, but it is soon violated.

21 July In Britain Tony Blair, shadow home secretary, is elected the youngest-ever leader of the Labour Party.

July The Bosnian Serbs reject an international peace plan that gives 49% of Bosnia to the Serbs and 51% to the Croat–Muslim federation (see above).

21 Aug. In Bosnia-Herzegovina the Muslim-dominated city of Bihac falls to the Serbs.

31 Aug. The IRA announces a cessation of violence, and the British government ends its ban on broadcasting by Sinn Féin representatives (16 Sept.). Negotiations between the British government and Sinn Féin are promised if the ceasefire holds.

Aug. Civil war breaks out in Chechnya between separatist and pro-Russian forces.

8 Sept. The last Russian troops leave Poland, and the last US, British and French forces leave Berlin.

17 Nov. The Republic of Ireland's coalition government collapses when the Labour Party abandons Fianna Fáil over a controversy centring on the extradition of a paedophile priest. Albert Reynolds resigns as taoiseach (prime minister).

21 Nov. NATO launches airstrikes against Serb positions around Bihac.

25 Nov. In Chechnya Russian-backed anti-separatist forces attack the rebel-held capital Grozny.

27 Nov. In Norway a national referendum rejects Norway's entry into the European Union (EU).

11 Dec. Russian forces invade Chechnya.

15 Dec. In the Republic of Ireland Fine Gael forms a coalition government with the Labour Party. John Bruton becomes taoiseach (prime minister).

22 Dec. In Italy prime minister Silvio Berlusconi resigns after allegations of corruption in his business empire.

31 Dec. In Chechnya Russian forces attack the capital Grozny.

31 Dec. In Bosnia-Herzegovina the warring factions sign a four-month ceasefire agreement.

– In Britain the Trident nuclear weapon system comes into use in the Royal Navy.

MIDDLE EAST AND NORTH AFRICA

Jan. In Algeria former minister of defence Gen. Liamine Zéroual replaces Ali Kafi as president.

25 Feb. An Israeli settler opens fire on a mosque in Hebron, killing over 50 Palestinians. The Israeli government responds by sealing off the West Bank and Gaza Strip to prevent retaliation.

13–18 May Israeli forces are withdrawn from Jericho and the Gaza Strip in accordance with the Israeli–Palestinian agreement of 13 Sept. 1993.

1 July PLO leader Yasser Arafat returns to Gaza to lead the new Palestinian authority: it is the first time he has set foot on Palestinian territory for 25 years.

15 Oct. The Nobel Peace Prize is awarded to PLO leader Yasser Arafat, Israeli foreign minister Shimon Peres and prime minister Yitzhak Rabin.

Nov. In Algeria talks between the government and Islamic fundamentalists collapse. Algeria's civil strife continues unabated.

ASIA

22 Mar. A full military alert is ordered in South Korea as talks with the North, including discussion of suspected attempts by the Pyongyang government to construct nuclear weapons, break down. The crisis is defused through the personal diplomacy of former US president Jimmy Carter, who visits Pyongyang (15 June).

8 July North Korean leader Kim Il Sung dies. His son, Kim Jong Il, succeeds him after a power struggle.

9 July The Chinese government announces its intention to abolish Hong Kong's legislative council once it regains sovereignty of the British colony in 1997.

21 Oct. The North Korean government agrees to international inspection of its nuclear facilities in return for political and economic benefits.

THE AMERICAS

1 Jan. The Zapatista National Liberation Army leads a revolt by native American peoples in the Mexican state of Chiapas.

1 Jan. NAFTA (North American Free Trade Agreement) comes into effect. Its signatories are the USA, Mexico and Canada.

21 Jan. In The USA Lorena Bobbitt is cleared of malicious wounding after cutting off her husband's penis.

24 Mar. Allegations are made in Congress that President Clinton and his wife behaved improperly in their dealings with the Whitewater Development Corporation. These allegations will prove politically damaging for the president.

11 Aug. President Fidel Castro lifts restrictions on emigration from Cuba, prompting a stampede as 20,000 leave for the USA. President Clinton ends automatic refugee status for Cubans and negotiates the return of travel restrictions (9 Sept.).

12 Sept. In Canada the Parti Québecois wins an overall majority in the provincial legislature.

19 Sept. US forces invade Haiti to overthrow the military junta led by Raoul Cédras. President Jean-Bertrand Aristide returns after a three-year exile (15 Oct.). He will be ousted in 2004.

26 Sept. US president Bill Clinton's planned health care reforms collapse.

Nov. George W. Bush Jr, son of former US president George Bush, is elected as Republican governor of Texas.

SUB-SAHARAN AFRICA

11 Mar. In South Africa government forces rout right-wing Afrikaaners attempting to maintain an independent white homeland in Bophuthatswana.

25 Mar. US forces withdraw from Somalia.

6 April The presidents of Rwanda and Burundi, Juvénal Habyarimana and Cyprien Ntaryamira, are killed when their aircraft crashes near the Rwandan capital Kigali. The plane appears to have been shot down by the Tutsi Rwandan Patriotic Front (FPR), which opposes the Rwandan president. In the weeks that follow, genocidal violence erupts in Rwanda: using guns and machetes, members of a Hutu militia known as the Interahamwe kill hundreds of thousands of Tutsis. Two million Rwandans, most of them Hutus fearing retribution at the hands of the Tutsi FPR which now invades Rwanda, flee into exile in neighbouring Zaire. The violence also spreads to the neighbouring state of Burundi, albeit on a lesser scale.

26 April The African National Congress (ANC) wins South Africa's first multiracial elections. Nelson Mandela becomes South African president (10 May). The new government includes representatives of all of South Africa's principal ethnic groups.

10 June South Africa rejoins the Commonwealth.

June French troops arrive in Rwanda as part of a humanitarian mission. The Rwandan Patriotic Front (FPR) has established control over most of Rwanda by the end of July.

14 Aug. In Khartoum, Sudan, international terrorist Carlos the Jackal (Ilich Ramírez Sánchez) is arrested and sent to France for trial.

Nov. A peace treaty between the MPLA and UNITA is signed in Lusaka. The signatories do not, however, include the UNITA leader Jonas Savimbi.

ECONOMY AND SOCIETY

16–18 April In a cricket test match between England and the West Indies in Antigua, West Indies batsman Brian Lara scores 375, a record individual score for a batsman. On 6 June, playing in England for Warwickshire at Edgbaston, Lara scores 501 not out, the highest-ever score in first-class cricket.

June–July Brazil wins the 15th soccer World Cup, held in the USA.

Nov. The British government launches a National Lottery to raise money for the arts, sports, charities and other good causes.

– In Britain the homosexual age of consent is lowered to 18.

– In N Russia, one of the worst oil spills in history occurs when a broken pipeline pollutes the Pechora River.

SCIENCE AND TECHNOLOGY

6 May The Channel Tunnel, linking Britain and France by rail, is opened.

– British mathematician Andrew Wiles proves Pierre de Fermat's last theorem, which has remained unproven since 1637.

– *Australopithicus ramidus*, the earliest known remains of a human ancestor, 4.4 million years old, is discovered in Ethiopia.
– The first trials of transfusions of artificial blood, containing genetically engineered haemoglobin, begin in the USA.
– The World Wide Web program, originally created in 1990 by Tim Berners-Lee and Robert Cailliau, is released on the Internet. It allows users to browse the Internet via hypertext.

ARTS AND HUMANITIES

Literature
28 Mar. Romanian-born French playwright Eugène Ionescu dies.
24 Dec. The British dramatist John Osborne dies.
John Berendt, *Midnight in the Garden of Good and Evil*, non-fiction novel.
Louis de Bernières, *Captain Corelli's Mandolin*, novel.
Amy Clampitt, *The Silence Opens*, poetry collection.
Joseph Heller, *Closing Time*, novel.
John Irving, *A Son of the Circus*, novel.
James Kelman, *How Late It Was, How Late*, novel.

Visual Arts and Architecture
– Bankside Power Station is chosen by the Tate Gallery to be the site of London's first Museum of Modern Art.

Music
8 April Kurt Cobain, lead singer of US grunge band Nirvana, is found dead. He is believed to have committed suicide on 5 April.
– In New York state, Woodstock 94, a rock concert celebrating the 25th anniversary of the original Woodstock concert, takes place.
Blur, *Parklife*, album.
Mariah Carey, *Music Box*, album.
D:Ream, 'Things Can Only Get Better', single.
Philip Glass, *La Belle et la Bête*, opera.
Oasis, *Definitely Maybe*, album.
Portishead, *Dummy*, album.
The Prodigy, *Music for the Jilted Generation*, album.
Snoop Doggy Dog, *Doggy Style*, album: rap music's rhythmic use of alliteration and rhyme has become an important US art form.
Steve Reich, *The Cave*, opera.

Film
19 Feb. English director Derek Jarman dies.
Woody Allen, *Bullets Over Broadway*.
Jan de Bont, *Speed*, starring Keanu Reeves and Sandra Bullock.
Tim Burton, *Ed Wood*, starring Johnny Depp.
Frank Darabont, *The Shawshank Redemption*, starring Tim Robbins and Morgan Freeman.
Neil Jordan, *Interview with the Vampire*, starring Tom Cruise and Brad Pitt.
Krzysztof Kieslowski, *Trois Couleurs: Blanc* (Three Colours White) and *Trois Couleurs: Rouge* (Three Colours Red).
Mike Newell, *Four Weddings and a Funeral*, starring Hugh Grant.
Michael Radford, *Il Postino* (The Postman).
Oliver Stone, *Natural Born Killers*.
Quentin Tarantino, *Pulp Fiction*, starring John Travolta.
Robert Zemeckis, *Forrest Gump*, starring Tom Hanks.

1995

EUROPE
1 Jan. Austria, Finland and Sweden join the European Union (EU), bringing the number of EU members to 15.
26 Jan. Britain's oldest merchant bank, Baring Brothers, goes into receivership after its futures trader in Singapore, Nick Leeson, accumulates losses of over £800 million.
Jan.–Feb. Bitter fighting takes place in Grozny as Russian forces grind down Chechen resistance. Forces loyal to Chechnya's separatist president Dzhokhar Dudayev leave Grozny (8 Feb.).
8 Feb. A 24-hour strike by 500,000 Russian miners warns president Boris Yeltsin of growing impatience over unpaid wages.
22 Feb. In Northern Ireland the British and Irish prime ministers present a 'framework document' preparing the ground for all-party peace talks.
2 Mar. Baring Brothers rogue trader Nick Leeson is arrested at Frankfurt airport. He will stand trial in Singapore (see below).
6 Mar. Russian forces announce that they have re-established control of the Chechen capital Grozny.
20 Mar. The ceasefire in Bosnia-Herzegovina (see 31 Dec. 1994) breaks down. Bosnian troops attack Serb positions. Serbs take UN peacekeepers hostage to deter renewed NATO airstrikes (28 Mar.).
26 Mar. The Schengen convention comes into force. It allows free movement among the populations of Europe.
23 April–7 May The Gaullist Jacques Chirac is elected French president, defeating the Socialist Party candidate Lionel Jospin. Alain Juppé becomes prime minister.
29 April In Britain the Labour Party abandons Clause Four of its constitution (a clause committing the party to public ownership). Party leader Tony Blair is steering the party away from the left and towards the centre in a bid to woo disaffected Conservative voters.
30 April The ceasefire in Bosnia-Herzegovina ends.
4 May In British local government elections, the Conservative Party has its worst results since 1945.
16 May In Bosnia-Herzegovina the Serbs resume their shelling of Sarajevo after Bosnian government forces launch a major anti-Serb offensive. NATO launches new airstrikes against the Serbs, but the Serbs attack the 'safe haven' of Tuzla, killing 67 civilians (25 May).
24 May Harold Wilson, former Labour prime minister of Britain (1964–70 and 1974–6), dies.
May In Northern Ireland Sinn Féin and British government officials engage in talks for the first time since 1973. Negotiations become deadlocked, however, on the issue of the decommissioning of IRA weapons. Sinn Féin refuses to accept the condition imposed by the British government and Ulster Unionists that the IRA must begin to decommission weapons before all-party talks can get under way.
9 June The Russian and Ukrainian governments agree to divide the former Soviet Black Sea fleet.

22 June In a desperate bid to bolster his authority, British prime minister John Major resigns as Conservative Party leader and insists on a leadership contest. Major will defeat the right-wing Eurosceptic John Redwood in the leadership ballot by 218 votes to 89, with 22 abstentions or spoilt ballot papers (4 July), but the episode does little to dissipate the aura of feuding and rancour that now hangs over the Conservative Party.

23 June Russians and Chechen rebels agree preliminary peace terms. The Chechens will disarm, most Russians will leave Chechnya, and new elections will be held in Sept. The peace agreement is signed on 30 July.

9 July In Portadown, Northern Ireland, the first of what will be a series of annual standoffs between Protestant Orange marchers and nationalist residents takes place as RUC officers prevent marchers from following their traditional route down the Garvaghy Road. The marchers refuse to disperse or take an alternative route. Eventually an uneasy compromise is reached and the marchers are allowed to walk silently down the road.

11 July In Bosnia-Herzegovina the Serbs storm the 'safe havens' of Srebrenica and Zepa (25 July). In Srebrenica there is an alleged massacre of 4000 Muslims by Bosnian Serbs.

July–Oct. France suffers a series of terrorist attacks by Algerian Islamic militants.

4–9 Aug. Croatian forces attack and overrun Serb-held areas of Croatia (Krajina and W Slavonia). Some 150,000 Croatian Serb refugees flee to Serbia and Serb-held areas of Bosnia-Herzegovina. Croatian forces also repel a Serb attack on the 'safe haven' of Bihac in E Bosnia.

30 Aug. Following a Serbian attack on Sarajevo market which kills 37 civilians, NATO launches airstrikes on Bosnian Serb positions.

Aug. In Northern Ireland David Trimble becomes leader of the Ulster Unionist Party, succeeding James Molyneaux.

8 Sept. In negotiations in Geneva Britain, France, Russia, Germany and the USA reach agreement with representatives of the warring groups in Bosnia-Herzegovina on basic principles for a peace settlement. A 60-day ceasefire is announced by US president Clinton (8 Oct.).

Sept. The trial begins in Italy of the former Italian prime minister Giulio Andreotti, who is charged with using his influence to protect Mafia leaders in exchange for political support.

1 Nov. Peace talks between delegations from Bosnia, Croatia and Serbia begin at an air force base near Dayton, Ohio, USA. A new constitution is agreed for Bosnia-Herzegovina (21 Nov.). By the terms of the Dayton peace accord the Bosnian Serbs keep 49% of Bosnian territory, while the Croat–Muslim federation receives 51%.

30 Nov. US president Bill Clinton visits Northern Ireland.

14 Dec. The Dayton peace settlement for Bosnia-Herzegovina is formally signed in Paris. A NATO-led Implementation Force (Ifor) will monitor the accord.

15 Dec. In Italy the trial of former prime minister Silvio Berlusconi on corruption charges begins.

MIDDLE EAST AND NORTH AFRICA

Sept. Israel and the PLO sign an agreement that Israeli troops will hand over the West Bank city of Hebron to Palestinian authority by Mar. 1996.

4 Nov. Israeli prime minister Yitzhak Rabin is assassinated at a peace rally in Tel Aviv. His killer is a student, Yigal Amir, angered by Rabin's concessions to the Palestinians. Shimon Peres, who succeeds Rabin as Israeli prime minister, pledges to continue the peace process.

Nov. A multiparty presidential election is held in Algeria but is boycotted by the main opposition parties. President Zeroual wins comfortably but can hardly be said to have a popular mandate for his continuing presidency.

ASIA

17 Jan. In Kobe, Japan, an earthquake kills more than 5000 people.

19 Mar. Members of the Aum Shinrikyo cult in Japan attack the Tokyo underground with the nerve gas sarin and kill 12 people. The sect's leader Shoko Asahara is arrested.

23 Mar. In Taiwan parliament approves the payment of compensation to relatives of native Taiwanese massacred by Guomindang troops after they were evacuated from mainland China in Feb. 1947.

10 July In Myanmar (Burma) the opposition leader Aung San Suu Kyi is released from house arrest.

4 Sept. The alleged rape of a 12-year-old girl by three US servicemen causes widespread protests against US presence in Japan.

29 Sept. The former Baring Brothers trader Nick Leeson agrees to return to Singapore to face trial for deception. He is sentenced to 6½ years in prison (2 Dec.).

– Because its population is growing at a faster rate than has been predicted by the authorities (it has now reached 1.2 billion), China begins to enforce more rigorously its policy of restricting each family to just one child.

– Separatist Muslim violence escalates in the Indian state of Jammu and Kashmir.

THE AMERICAS

1 Jan. Mercosur (Southern Common Market), consisting of Argentina, Brazil, Paraguay and Uruguay, comes into existence.

24 Jan. Former American football star O.J. Simpson goes on trial for the murder of his wife, Nicole. The trial becomes an international media circus.

26 Jan. Heavy fighting erupts along the disputed frontier between Peru and Ecuador. A peace treaty is signed (17 Feb.).

16 Mar. President Bill Clinton meets Sinn Féin leader Gerry Adams at the White House.

19 April In the worst terrorist attack in US history to date, a car bomb planted by Timothy McVeigh in Oklahoma City kills 166 people and injures 400.

11 Sept. After nine months of fighting, the Mexican government and the Zapatista National Liberation Army (EZNL) sign an accord to settle some of the rebels' grievances.

3 Oct. Former American football star O.J. Simpson is acquitted of the murder of his wife. Simpson's acquittal is ascribed by many observers to race-related causes.

16 Oct. In Washington, D.C., a 'million-man march' of African-Americans, organized by Nation of Islam leader Louis Farrakhan, asserts African-American pride and protests against white racism.

30 Oct. A referendum in the Canadian province of Quebec rejects by just 1% a proposal that Quebec should become an independent sovereign state.

SUB-SAHARAN AFRICA

28 Feb. UN peacekeepers leave Somalia after failing to end the civil war there.

9 Mar. Hutu leader Ernest Kabushemeye is assassinated in Burundi. There is immediate ethnic violence and a stampede of refugees, who fear a repeat of the 1994 genocide in Rwanda. Tutsi soldiers massacre 400 Hutu women and children (4 April).

May–Aug. Zaire suffers a outbreak of the deadly Ebola virus.

10 Nov. The Nigerian authorities execute author Ken Saro-Wiwa and eight other environmental activists. Nigeria is suspended from the British Commonwealth (11 Nov.).

13 Nov. Former Portuguese colony Mozambique becomes a member of the British Commonwealth.

Nov. South Africa sets up a Truth and Reconciliation Commission to investigate human-rights abuses during the apartheid era.

AUSTRALASIA AND OCEANIA

7 June Australian prime minister Paul Keating declares his aim that Australia should be a republic by 2001 and outlines the constitutional path towards that goal.

5 Sept. The French government defies worldwide condemnation and resumes nuclear weapons tests at Mururoa atoll in the S Pacific Ocean.

Oct. A deadly rabbit virus is deliberately spread throughout Australia, killing vast numbers of the animals, which pose a threat to cattle and sheep farming.

3 Nov. Queen Elizabeth II gives the royal assent to a law that restores land to the Tainui Maori people.

ECONOMY AND SOCIETY

1 Jan. The World Trade Organization (WTO) comes into being, aiming to ensure compliance among the countries that signed the General Agreement on Tariffs and Trade (GATT).

May–June The host country, South Africa, wins the 3rd rugby union World Cup.

16 June Greenpeace activists occupy the North Sea oil platform Brent Spa to prevent it being sunk in mid-Atlantic. After a boycott of Shell Oil in Europe, the company agrees not to dump the platform (20 June).

27 Aug. The International Rugby Football Board, the governing body of rugby union, votes to end the game's amateur status.

20 Nov. In Britain the Princess of Wales is interviewed on the BBC TV *Panorama* programme by Martin Bashir. A record 21.1 million viewers tune in.

25 Nov. In the Republic of Ireland the constitutional ban on divorce is abolished following a referendum.

– By now there are 1 million AIDS cases around the world.

SCIENCE AND TECHNOLOGY

June–July The US space shuttle *Atlantis* docks with the Russian space station *Mir*.

July US astronomers Alan Hale and Thomas Bopp independently discover what will be called the Hale–Bopp comet.

– In the USA trials begin in treating breast cancer through gene therapy.

– In a cave at Gran Dolina, Spain, the oldest human remains ever found in Europe are discovered. Over 780,000 years old, they far pre-date the earliest time (about 300,000 years ago) that humans were thought to have reached Europe.

ARTS AND HUMANITIES

Literature

4 Feb. US crime novelist Patricia Highsmith dies.

22 Oct. The English novelist Kingsley Amis dies.

2 Nov. Canadian novelist Robertson Davies dies.

Martin Amis, *The Information*, novel.

Pat Barker, *The Ghost Road*, novel.

James Ellroy, *American Tabloid*, novel.

Richard Ford, *Independence Day*, novel.

Nick Hornby, *High Fidelity*, novel.

Timothy Mo, *Brownout on Breadfruit Boulevard*, novel.

Philip Pullman, *Northern Lights*, first novel in his children's fantasy trilogy *His Dark Materials*.

Visual Arts and Architecture

Delmas Howe, *Liberty, Equality and Fraternity*, painting.

Music

– Britpop, a reaction against US grunge, and exemplified by bands such as Blur, Oasis and Supergrass, enjoys a brief heyday.

Blur, 'Country House', single.

Mariah Carey and Boyz II Men, 'One Sweet Day', single.

Coolio featuring LV, 'Gangsta's Paradise', single.

Michael Jackson, 'You Are Not Alone', single.

Alanis Morissette, *Jagged Little Pill*, album.

Oasis, 'Roll with It' and 'Wonderwall', singles, and *(What's the Story) Morning Glory?*, album.

Pulp, *Different Class*, album, and 'Common People', single.

Take That, 'Back for Good', single.

Film

25 April US actress and dancer Ginger Rogers dies.

23 Nov. French film director Louis Malle dies.

Mike Figgis, *Leaving Las Vegas*, starring Nicolas Cage.

Mel Gibson, *Braveheart*.

Ron Howard, *Apollo 13*, starring Tom Hanks.

Nicholas Hytner, *The Madness of King George*, starring Nigel Hawthorne.

Ang Lee, *Sense and Sensibility*, starring Emma Thompson.

Ken Loach, *Land and Freedom*.

Michael Mann, *Heat*, starring Robert De Niro and Al Pacino.

Kevin Reynolds, *Waterworld*, starring Kevin Costner.

Bryan Singer, *The Usual Suspects*, starring Kevin Spacey and Gabriel Byrne.

Oliver Stone, *Nixon*, starring Anthony Hopkins.

1996

EUROPE

8 Jan. François Mitterrand, president of France 1981–1995, dies.

9 Jan. Chechen separatists take 3000 people hostage in Kizlar, Russia, demanding that Russian forces evacuate Chechnya. Most are released the following day. The remainder are rescued by Russian security forces (24 Jan.).

18 Jan. Neo-Nazis petrol bomb a hostel for asylum seekers in Lübeck, N Germany, killing 10 people.

22 Jan. A mass grave containing the bodies of some 3000 Muslims and Croats – killed in 'ethnic cleansing' by Bosnian Serbs in 1992 – is discovered near Brcko in Bosnia-Herzegovina.

29 Jan. France's president Jacques Chirac bows to international pressure and ends French nuclear testing at Mururoa atoll in the S Pacific.

9 Feb. In London the IRA break their ceasefire (see 31 Aug. 1994) by detonating a bomb that kills two people in London's Docklands. A second IRA bomb explodes on a London bus on 18 Feb., killing an IRA member.

19 Feb. In Madrid, Spain, one million people demonstrate against the violence of Basque separatist group ETA (*Euskadi ta Askatasuna*).

25 Mar. The European Union (EU) bans the export of beef from Britain due to an outbreak of bovine spongiform encephalopathy (BSE or Mad Cow Disease). The British government responds by adopting a non-cooperation policy with the EU (21 May), disrupting its business, until a deal is made in which the ban is lifted while at-risk cattle are destroyed (21 June).

31 Mar. Boris Yeltsin announces a ceasefire and the withdrawal of Russian troops from Chechnya.

Mar. Spain's ruling Socialist Party loses its overall majority in parliament, ending 13 years of left-wing government in Spain. The ensuing elections are won by the conservative Popular Party (PP), led by José María Aznar, who forms a minority PP government (May).

21 April Chechen separatist leader Dzhokhar Dudayev is killed in a Russian rocket attack.

29 April In The Hague, the Netherlands, a UN war crimes tribunal opens to try cases relating to the civil war in former Yugoslavia.

2 May In Britain the governing Conservative Party continues its downward spiral when it gains only 28% of the poll in local-government elections.

10 June All-party talks on the future of Northern Ireland begin. Sinn Féin is not allowed to take part, however, because of the resumption of IRA violence.

11 June Russian troops begin to withdraw from Chechnya.

15 June In Britain a huge IRA bomb devastates Manchester city centre but claims no fatalities.

16 June The first round of presidential elections takes place in Russia. Boris Yeltsin beats Communist challenger Gennady Zyuganov into second place.

27 June In the Republic of Ireland the investigative journalist Veronica Guerin is murdered during her investigation into drug-dealing.

30 June The Bosnian Serb president Radovan Karadzic resigns.

7 July The German town of Konstanz elects a Green Party mayor.

9–11 July In Northern Ireland widespread civil disturbances break out after the RUC blocks the route of an Orange march through a nationalist area of Portadown (see 9 July 1995). Sir Hugh Annesley, chief constable of the RUC, decides to allow the march to proceed under RUC supervision. Nationalist violence erupts in Northern Ireland as a result (11–12 July).

11 July The war crimes tribunal in The Hague issues an international arrest warrant for the Bosnian Serb president Radovan Karadzic and the Bosnian Serb military commander Gen. Ratko Mladic.

6 Aug. Separatist rebels storm the capital Grozny and other towns in Chechnya.

9 Aug. President Boris Yeltsin becomes Russia's first democratically elected head of state.

28 Aug. In Britain the divorce of Charles, Prince of Wales and Diana, Princess of Wales is completed.

31 Aug. Russia and Chechnya sign a peace accord under whose terms the separatist Chechens agree to put aside their demands for independence for five years.

14 Sept. In Bosnia-Herzegovina President Izetbegovic, a Muslim, is elected chairman of the three-man collective presidency. A Bosnian Serb and a Bosnian Croat join him on the presidential panel.

5 Nov. Russian president Boris Yeltsin, who has a history of heart trouble, undergoes a heart-bypass operation in Moscow.

Nov.–Dec. After the Serbian government of President Slobodan Milosevic refuses to recognize opposition victories in municipal elections (17 Nov.), protestors in Belgrade hold daily demonstrations against government policy.

MIDDLE EAST AND NORTH AFRICA

15 Feb. In Israel Palestinian suicide bombers from the militant group Hamas attack Jerusalem and Ashkelon, killing 25 people. They wish to derail a peace process that will leave Palestinians with only a fraction of their former lands.

> *Those to whom evil is done*
> *Do evil in return.*
>
> W.H. Auden, '1 Sept. 1939' (1940)

25 Feb. In revenge for the alleged assassination of the bomb-maker Yahya Ayyash by the Israeli security services (6 Jan.), suicide bombers of the Palestinian militant group Hamas kill

26 people in Jerusalem and Ashkelon. When suicide bombers kill a further 32 people in Jerusalem and Tel Aviv (3–4 Mar.), Israel declares all-out war on Hamas. The bombings throw the Israeli–Palestinian peace process into crisis.

27 Mar. Yigal Amir, who assassinated Israeli prime minister Yitzhak Rabin in 1995, is sentenced to life imprisonment.

11 April Israeli helicopters attack Hezbollah bases in Beirut, Lebanon, in retaliation for Hezbollah rocket attacks on N Israel. A similar Israeli attack on a refugee camp at Qana in Lebanon kills 97 people (18 April).

29 May Binyamin Netanyahu, hardline leader of the right-wing Likud Party, becomes Israeli prime minister, narrowly defeating Labour's Shimon Peres. Netanyahu's election casts doubt on the future of the peace process, since Likud do not subscribe to Labour's policy of trading land for peace.

18 June In Israel Binyamin Netanyahu forms a Likud-dominated coalition government with the support of the smaller religious parties.

12 July Mass executions take place in Iraq after an attempted coup against Saddam Hussein.

28 Nov. In Algeria a new constitution recognizing the Islamic, Arabic and Berber cultures as the three main constituents of the Algerian nation is endorsed in a referendum. The constitution also effectively bans political parties with an Islamic basis: it thereby reignites Islamic fundamentalist anger, leading to a new cycle of violence in Algeria's civil war.

Nov. Under the terms of a Sept. 1995 Israeli–Palestinian agreement, Israel begins to withdraw troops from the West Bank city of Hebron, but renewed violence between local Palestinian Arab residents and Israeli settlers slows the withdrawal process.

ASIA

1 Feb. As famine threatens North Korea, the US government offers help to the UN food assistance programme to avert catastrophe.

8 Mar. Communist Chinese forces conduct military exercises in the Taiwan Strait. They are attempting to intimidate voters in forthcoming Taiwanese presidential elections, where a formal declaration of Taiwanese independence is being discussed. The pro-independence candidate, Lee Teng-hui, wins but no declaration ensues.

15 April The US military returns some bases to Japan and promises that US forces observe better discipline, in an attempt to dampen hostility to their presence after the rape of a child (1995).

April The former Pakistan cricket captain Imran Khan forms the Movement for Justice to fight against corruption and injustice in Pakistan.

April–May In Sri Lanka government forces launch a military offensive against Tamil separatists in the Jaffna Peninsula.

April–June In Indian national elections the Congress Party is beaten into third place. Congress leader P.V. Narasimha Rao resigns as prime minister. Following two weeks of minority

government by the Hindu-nationalist Bharatiya Janata Party (BJP) under Atal Vajpayee (16–28 May), a 13-party centre-left coalition government emerges with H.D. Deve Gowda as prime minister (1 June).

June–July The heaviest rainfall in China in 50 years causes landslides and floods that kill 800 people and devastate a vast area.

July Government forces and Tamil Tigers fight the biggest battle of Sri Lanka's civil war after Tamil Tigers attack an army base in NE Sri Lanka.

2 Sept. A peace accord is signed by President Ramos of the Philippines and the Moro National Liberation Front (MNLF), a Muslim separatist group; it brings to an end a 26-year rebellion by the Moro people of the S islands of the Philippines.

27 Sept. The Taliban, an army of Islamic fundamentalist students, take control of Kabul, Afghanistan, and execute communist president Ahmadzai Najibullah. They immediately impose Islamic *sharia* law.

5 Nov. The Pakistani president dismisses prime minister Benazir Bhutto after allegations of corruption and mismanagement are made against her and her government.

6 Nov. A cyclone devastates the S Indian state of Andhra Pradesh, killing 1000 people.

THE AMERICAS

3 April The US Defense Department denies the existence of Gulf War Syndrome, which, nonetheless, afflicts many veterans of the 1991 conflict.

3 April Theodore J. Kaczynski, suspected of being the shadowy 'Unabomber' who has waged a 16-year bombing campaign in the USA, is arrested in Montana. Between 1979 and 1995 his 16 bombs, mostly directed against people working in advanced technology, have killed three and forced the *New York Times* and *Washington Post* to print his 35,000-word manifesto, 'Industrial Society and its Future'. The police search for the 'Unabomber' has been the longest and costliest manhunt in US history.

17 April In Pará, Brazil, troops open fire during a demonstration by the Landless Workers Movement, killing 23 people.

11 June A damning US Senate report on the Whitewater affair accuses Hillary Clinton of complicity in a fraudulent land deal in Arkansas in the 1980s.

5 Nov. Bill Clinton is re-elected US president, defeating the Republican candidate Bob Dole.

5 Dec. President Clinton announces that Madeleine Albright will become the USA's first woman secretary of state (from 22 Jan 1997).

17 Dec. The Peruvian revolutionary group Túpac Amaru take over the Japanese embassy in Lima. They take 575 people hostage and demand the release of comrades from prison.

29 Dec. A peace agreement is signed between the Guatemalan government and the National Revolutionary Unity Movement, ending a civil war waged since 1960 and claiming more than 140,000 lives.

SUB-SAHARAN AFRICA

Mar. South African president Nelson Mandela and his wife, Winnie, are formally divorced. Winnie Mandela has been sacked from a ministerial post in the South African government for alleged corruption; she has also been linked with the murder of police informers during the apartheid era.

1 Aug. The Somalian warlord Gen. Muhammad Farah Aidid dies from wounds sustained during faction fighting. His son Hussein Muhammad Aidid is chosen as his successor.

Oct. In E Zaire fighting breaks out between government troops and Tutsi settlers who have been massacring Hutu refugees with Rwandan government support. Hundreds of thousands of Rwandan Hutus who flee the refugee camps are stranded without aid. Rwanda and Zaire come close to war.

15–18 Nov. Some 500,000 Hutu refugees return to Rwanda from E Zaire.

30 Nov. In the W African state of Sierra Leone the government and rebel forces sign a peace agreement to end a five-year-long civil war.

10 Dec. South Africa's new democratic and non-racial constitution is signed into law by President Mandela.

17 Dec. Kofi Annan, a Ghanaian, becomes the first black African UN secretary-general.

Dec. Some 450,000 refugees return to Rwanda from camps in Tanzania.

AUSTRALASIA AND OCEANIA

Mar. In Australia a right-wing coalition under John Howard, leader of the Liberal Party, wins the general election comfortably, ending 13 years of Labor government.

ECONOMY AND SOCIETY

12 Mar. In Barcelona, Spain, the World Health Authority launches a task force to tackle a worldwide rise in obesity.

July–Aug. The 26th Olympic Games are held in Atlanta, Georgia, USA. A bomb explodes in Atlanta during the Games, killing two people and injuring 110.

SCIENCE AND TECHNOLOGY

Jan. At Loch Fyne, Scotland, the first genetically modified salmon are hatched: they grow five times faster than ordinary salmon.

Jan. The American Astronomy Society announces the discovery of three new planets, orbiting other stars within 50 light years from Earth.

4 June The European Space Agency's £565-million *Ariane* 5 rocket explodes during liftoff.

ARTS AND HUMANITIES

Literature

Aug. The restored Globe Theatre opens on London's South Bank.

Margaret Atwood, *Alias Grace*, novel.

Seamus Deane, *Reading in the Dark*, memoir.

Daniel Jonah Goldhagen, *Hitler's Willing Executioners: Ordinary Germans and the Holocaust*, history.

Seamus Heaney, *The Spirit Level*, poetry collection.

Steven Millhauser, *Martin Dressler: Tale of an American Dreamer*, novel.

Rohinton Mistry, *A Fine Balance*, novel.

Graham Swift, *Last Orders*, novel.

Music

Boyzone, 'Words', single.

DJ Shadow, *Endtroducing*, album.

Manic Street Preachers, 'A Design for Life', single.

George Michael, 'Jesus to a Child', single.

Oasis, 'Don't Look Back in Anger', single.

Ocean Colour Scene, 'The Day We Caught the Train', single.

Orbital, *In Sides*, album.

The Prodigy, 'Firestarter', single.

Spice Girls, 'Wannabe', single, and *Spice*, album.

Film

Danny Boyle, *Trainspotting*, starring Ewan McGregor.

Joel and Ethan Coen, *Fargo*.

Roland Emmerich, *Independence Day*.

Milos Forman, *The People vs. Larry Flynt*.

Mark Herman, *Brassed Off*.

Scott Hicks, *Shine*, starring Geoffrey Rush.

Neil Jordan, *Michael Collins*, starring Liam Neeson.

Mike Leigh, *Secrets and Lies*.

Anthony Minghella, *The English Patient*, starring Ralph Fiennes.

Brian De Palma, *Mission: Impossible*, starring Tom Cruise.

Lars von Trier, *Breaking the Waves*.

1997

EUROPE

23 Jan. The Swiss government establishes a fund to compensate Holocaust victims after Nazi gold is found in Swiss banks (see 2000).

Jan. Massive demonstrations occur in the Serb capital Belgrade against the refusal of Slobodan Milosevic's government to recognize opposition successes in local elections.

Jan. Russian troops complete their withdrawal from Chechnya.

Jan–Mar. Albania lapses into chaos following the collapse of high-risk pyramid schemes in which most Albanians have invested. Protestors, who are convinced that the Democratic Party government of Sali Berisha is responsible for the collapse, take to the streets in the S Albanian towns of Fier and Vlorë (4–11 Feb.) and demand compensation. The government uses heavy-handed tactics to suppress the disturbances. The Albanian parliament decrees a nationwide state of emergency (1 Mar). In late Mar. some 13,000 Albanians will flee by boat to Italy.

4 Feb. President Milosevic of Serbia orders his government to recognize opposition victories in local elections held in Nov. 1996.

25 Feb. The prime minister of Estonia, Tiit Vahi, is forced to resign following a corruption scandal. Mart Siiman replaces him.

27 Feb. In Britain the discredited and divided Conservative government loses its parliamentary majority in a by-election defeat in Wirral South.

13 April An Italian-led UN multinational force arrives in Albania. Its task is to keep public order, to create a secure environment for international aid organizations and to help prepare elections due in June.

1 May The Labour Party wins the British general election by a landslide. Labour wins 418 seats, while the number of Conservative MPs is reduced from 336 to 165. Labour Party leader Tony Blair, who has rebranded his party as 'New Labour' and abandoned state socialism, becomes prime minister. Conservative leader John Major resigns after the worst electoral defeat in the modern history of his party (2 May).

6 May Gordon Brown, Britain's new chancellor of the exchequer, announces that the Bank of England is to be given the power to control the country's interest rates.

7 May The International War Crimes Tribunal in The Hague convicts Dusan Tadic, a Bosnian Serb reserve policeman, of war crimes committed during the Bosnian war. It is the first such conviction since World War II.

12 May Russian president Boris Yeltsin signs a peace treaty with President Aslan Maskhadov of Chechnya. Both leaders agree to renounce the use of force, but Chechnya's political status remains unresolved.

23 May The governments of Belarus and Russia agree a Union Charter, aimed at ultimately unifying the two nations.

25 May–1 June Victory for the Socialist Party in parliamentary elections in France ushers in yet another period of 'cohabitation' (in this case power-sharing between a left-wing parliament and a right-wing president). Socialist Party leader Lionel Jospin becomes prime minister.

27 May NATO and Russia sign the Founding Act on Mutual Relations, Cooperation and Security. A similar agreement between NATO and Ukraine is signed on 29 May.

6 June In a general election in the Republic of Ireland no party wins an overall majority. Bertie Ahern of Fianna Fáil forms a minority coalition with the Progressive Democrats and becomes taoiseach (prime minister) on 26 June, replacing John Bruton.

19 June In Britain the 36-year-old William Hague succeeds John Major as leader of the Conservative Party, defeating Kenneth Clarke in a leadership ballot of Conservative MPs.

20 July In Northern Ireland the IRA restores its ceasefire.

23 July Slobodan Milosevic becomes president of Yugoslavia (a federation consisting of Serbia and Montenegro).

July The European Commission agrees that Estonia, Poland, the Czech Republic, Hungary, Slovenia, and Cyprus, should start talks for their entry into the EU.

27 Aug. The Swedish and Norwegian governments admit that between 1934 and 1976 they sterilized thousands of people deemed 'substandard', including the disabled.

31 Aug. Diana, Princess of Wales, and Dodi Fayed, son of Harrods owner Mohamed Al-Fayed, are killed in a car crash in Paris.

6 Sept. The funeral takes place in Westminster Abbey of Diana, Princess of Wales. In Britain her death has triggered an extraordinary outpouring of grief, bordering on mass hysteria.

11 Sept. Scottish voters approve the creation of a Scottish parliament in a referendum. The creation of a Welsh assembly is also narrowly approved by referendum (18 Sept.).

Dec. Spain's Supreme Court jails 23 leaders of the Basque separatist party Herri Batasuna, which supports the terrorist group ETA.

MIDDLE EAST AND NORTH AFRICA

15 Jan. A new agreement for the much-deferred withdrawal of Israeli troops from the West Bank city of Hebron is signed by PLO chairman Yasser Arafat and Israeli prime minister Binyamin Netanyahu, but tensions in the city continue to run high.

22 Jan. In Iraq, Saddam Hussein's son Uday is crippled in an assassination attempt.

28 Feb. A powerful earthquake strikes NW Iran, close to the border with Azerbaijan.

7–18 Mar. Palestinian anger at the slow pace of Israeli withdrawal from the West Bank is exacerbated by the start of building work on a new Jewish settlement in Arab E Jerusalem (18 Mar.), which leads to renewed violence and a political crisis in Israel. The UN Security Council votes 14 to 1 against the building of the settlement (25 April), but the USA vetoes the resolution.

15 April Over 200 Muslim pilgrims die in a fire in a tent city near Mecca, Saudi Arabia.

April In Algeria Islamic rebels carry out a series of brutal massacres: 52 people are murdered in the village of Thalit, near Algiers (6 April) and 93 are killed in an attack on a farming community at Baouch Boukhelef-Khemisti (21 April).

10 May An earthquake in N Iran kills more than 1600 people.

May Turkey launches a major offensive against Kurdish guerrillas in SE Turkey and N Iraq.

30 July Hamas suicide bombers kill 13 in Jerusalem, jeopardizing peace talks that have recently resumed between Israel and the PLO. Israel declares economic war on Palestinians in the West Bank and Gaza.

17 Nov. In Egypt Islamic terrorists attack two tourist buses near Luxor, killing 68 people.

ASIA

Jan. Pakistan's interim government gives the military a formal role in the country's political power structure for the first time since 1988.

17 Feb. The Pakistan Muslim League wins the general election in Pakistan. Nawaz Sharif becomes prime minister.

19 Feb. Former Chinese leader Deng Xiaoping dies aged 92.

23–24 April In Moscow Chinese president Jiang Zemin and Russian president Boris Yeltsin issue a joint declaration calling for a pluralistic world order in which no nation plays a dominant role.

April In India the minority 13-party United Front government of H.D. Deve Gowda falls when the Congress Party withdraws its support. A new United Front government is formed, with Congress Party backing, led by the former foreign minister Inder Kumar Gujral (20 April).

June Indonesian landowners burning forests to clear land cause the worst forest fires in SE Asian history; much of the region is blanketed with smoke, which reaches life-threatening levels as far away as Malaysia. The fires continue into Oct.

1 July The British crown colony of Hong Kong reverts to Chinese control after 156 years of British rule. Hong Kong becomes a Special Administrative Area within China.

2 July A rapid fall in the value of the Thai baht is the first sign of a huge economic crisis across the region. The so-called Asian Tigers, such as South Korea and Taiwan, now experience recession after decades of post-World War II economic growth.

14 July K.R. Narayanan is elected Indian president; he is the first president of India to come from the 'untouchable' caste.

6 Sept. Mother Teresa (Agnes Gonxha Bojaxhiu), the Albanian-born nun who founded the Order of Missionaries of Charity in Calcutta, India, dies.

12 Sept. Jiang Zemin is confirmed as Chinese Communist Party general secretary by the Party's 15th Congress. It is also agreed that the liberal economic policies introduced by the late Deng Xiaoping will continue.

28 Nov. In India the Congress Party withdraws from the governing coalition, which collapses.

3 Dec. The International Monetary Fund (IMF) agrees a $57 billion package to rescue South Korea's shattered economy.

THE AMERICAS

20 Jan. Bill Clinton is sworn in for his second term as US president.

26 Mar. In the USA 39 members of a religious cult, Heaven's Gate, commit suicide in California, believing that they will be transported to a spaceship following the appearance of the Hale–Bopp comet.

31 Mar. In Denver, Colorado, the trial begins of Timothy McVeigh, accused of the Oklahoma bombing (see 19 April 1995). He will be found guilty and sentenced to death (13 June).

22 April Peruvian troops storm the Japanese embassy in Lima, where Marxist Tupac Amaru guerrillas have been holding hostages since 17 Dec. 1996. 14 guerrillas and one hostage die in the assault (most of the original 575 hostages having already been released).

2 June The Liberal Party of governing prime minister Jean Chrétien narrowly wins the Canadian general election.

19 June US fast-food chain McDonald's wins a two-year libel action against British environmental campaigners Helen Steel and Dave Morris, who have claimed that McDonald's exploited employees and polluted the environment. But the damages awarded are derisory, and the company is damaged by the bad publicity.

SUB-SAHARAN AFRICA

Jan. The Zairean government launches a counter-offensive against the Rwandan-backed rebels who have captured a large part of the E of the country.

9 April In Zaire Tutsi rebel forces led by Laurent Kabila take the key S town of Lubumbashi.

16–17 May In Zaire Tutsi rebel forces led by Laurent Kabila capture Kinshasa, the capital. Mobutu Sese Seko, president of Zaire since 1965, flees the country. Zaire is renamed the Democratic Republic of Congo. Kabila takes office as head of state (29 May).

25 May The civilian government of Sierra Leone, led by Ahmed Kebbah, is ousted in a coup. Major Johnny Paul Koroma replaces him. Other W African states warn that they may use force to reimpose civilian rule.

17 Dec. In South Africa Thabo Mbeki becomes president of the African National Congress (ANC), replacing Nelson Mandela who nonetheless remains the country's president.

29 Dec. Presidential and legislative elections in Kenya are disrupted by widespread violence.

AUSTRALASIA AND OCEANIA

May In Australia a political row erupts over a report that accuses previous governments of removing thousands of Aboriginal children from their families and placing them with white ones.

1 Oct. Fiji rejoins the Commonweath (discriminatory legislation against Indians caused it to be expelled in 1987).

ECONOMY AND SOCIETY

Jan. The World Health Organization estimates that 22.6 million people are now infected with HIV, the virus causing AIDS.

13 April 21-year-old US golfing prodigy Tiger Woods becomes the youngest-ever winner of the US Masters.

11 Dec. In Japan delegates at the Kyoto conference on global warming agree to reduce emissions of greenhouse gases by 5.2% of 1990 levels by 2012.

SCIENCE AND TECHNOLOGY

27 Feb. British geneticist Ian Wilmut announces the cloning of an adult sheep, Dolly.

23 Mar. Comet Hale–Bopp arrives at its nearest point to Earth, 196 million kilometres (122 million miles) away.

11 May Gary Kasparov, the world chess champion, is beaten by the IBM supercomputer Deep Blue.

– There are now up to 150 million pages on the World Wide Web.

ARTS AND HUMANITIES

Literature

2 Aug. US writer William Burroughs dies.

Don DeLillo, *Underworld*, novel.

Charles Frazier, *Cold Mountain*, novel.

Ted Hughes, *Tales from Ovid*, poetry.

Ian McEwan, *Enduring Love*, novel.

Philip Pullman, *The Subtle Knife,* children's novel.

Philip Roth, *American Pastoral*, novel.

J.K. Rowling, *Harry Potter and the Philospher's Stone*; first in the bestselling series of Harry Potter novels for children.

Arundhati Roy, *The God of Small Things*, novel.

Visual Arts and Architecture

29 Aug. Roy Lichtenstein, US artist, dies.

– In Greenwich, London, work starts on the Millennium Dome. Designed by Richard Rogers, it is a temporary structure intended to house a millennium exhibition.

Music

11 Jan. First performance in Munich of Hans Werner Henze's opera *Venus and Adonis*.

1 Aug. Sviatoslav Richter, Russian pianist and outstanding interpreter of Beethoven, dies.

– Wynton Marsalis becomes the first jazz musician to win a Pulitzer Prize, for his oratorio *Blood in the Fields*.

Blur, 'Song 2', single, and *Blur*, album.

Wyclef Jean, *The Carnival*, album.

Elton John, 'Candle in the Wind '97'; with the lyrics of his 1974 classic rewritten in memory of Diana, Princess of Wales, this rapidly becomes the bestselling single in the world, selling some 37 million copies.

Radiohead, *OK Computer*, album, including the single 'Paranoid Android'.

Spice Girls, 'Too Much' and 'Mama/Who Do You Think You Are?', singles, and *Spiceworld*, album.

The Verve, *Urban Hymns*, album, including the singles 'Bitter Sweet Symphony' and 'The Drugs Don't Work'.

Robbie Williams, 'Angels', single.

Film

Roberto Benigni, *La vita è bella* (Life is Beautiful).

James Cameron, *Titanic*, starring Leonardo DiCaprio and Kate Winslet.

Peter Cattaneo, *The Full Monty*, starring Robert Carlyle.

Curtis Hanson, *LA Confidential*, starring Kevin Spacey.

Ang Lee, *The Ice Storm*.

Barry Sonnenfeld, *Men in Black*, starring Will Smith and Tommy Lee Jones.

Steven Spielberg, *Amistad*.

Quentin Tarantino, *Jackie Brown*.

1998

EUROPE

27 Jan. The British government announces its intention to destroy its stocks of landmines in response to a worldwide campaign to abolish the weapons.

29 Jan. In Britain prime minister Tony Blair announces that there will be a new inquiry into the Bloody Sunday killings in Northern Ireland (1972).

14 Feb. In Northern Ireland police accuse the IRA of two murders. As a result, its political wing, Sinn Féin, is suspended from peace talks.

1 Mar. Serbia sends paramilitary forces into its S province of Kosovo to search for ethnic Albanian guerrillas. Serb forces

attack Albanian villages, killing men, women and children. In the Kosovan capital Pristina, 50,000 ethnic Albanians demonstrate against Serbia's methods (2 Mar.).

1 Mar. In London a 100,000-strong march, organized by the Countryside Alliance, takes place. Some marchers want to resist an increase in public access to privately owned land, some want to preserve fox hunting, while others simply feel the government is ignoring rural communities.

2 Mar. Gerhard Schröder, minister-president of Lower Saxony, becomes Social Democratic Party (SPD) candidate for the German chancellorship.

23 Mar. Russian president Boris Yeltsin dismisses his entire cabinet. He replaces prime minister Viktor Chernomyrdin with the 35-year-old Sergei Kiriyenko.

23 Mar. Sinn Féin is readmitted to the Northern Ireland peace talks.

31 Mar. The UN Security Council imposes an arms embargo on Yugoslavia in order to bring pressure to bear on Yugoslav President Milosevic to negotiate a peaceful settlement with Kosovo's ethnic Albanians. On 29 April the 'contact group' monitoring the Balkan conflict (Britain, France, Germany, the USA and Russia) freezes the Yugoslav government's foreign assets.

2 April In Bordeaux, France, Maurice Papon is found guilty of complicity in Nazi crimes against humanity committed under the Vichy regime. He is sentenced to 10 years' imprisonment.

10 April In Belfast the British and Irish governments and the main Northern Ireland political parties reach the Good Friday Agreement on the the province's political future. The main proposals of the agreement are for a cross-community assembly (the Northern Ireland Assembly) with a power-sharing executive elected by proportional representation; the setting up of a North–South ministerial council; a British–Irish intergovernmental conference; the right of all Northern Ireland citizens to be British or Irish or both; the decommissioning of paramilitary arms; reform of the police service; accelerated release of 'political' prisoners; and the removal of emergency powers and security installations. Most people welcome the Agreement, except militant Republicans (who see it as a sanitized version of the old Stormont parliament that ruled Northern Ireland 1920–72), and right-wing Unionists (who fear that it paves the way for a united Ireland).

30 April The US Senate votes to admit Hungary, Poland and the Czech Republic to NATO.

3 May The heads of European Union (EU) governments formalize the creation of the Euro (or EMU) zone; they confirm that 11 countries (all EU member-states except Britain, Denmark, Sweden, and Greece) will enter it on 1 Jan. 1999.

18 May Britain's Labour government announces that the minimum wage, coming into effect in April 1999, will be £3.60 per hour.

22 May Referendums in the Republic of Ireland and Northern Ireland endorse the Good Friday Agreement.

25 May Serbia launches a major offensive against the secessionist Kosovo Liberation Army (KLA), which holds some 40% of the region.

6 July A massive police and army operation in Northern Ireland prevents the annual Orange parade from marching down the mainly Catholic Garvaghy Road in Portadown. The ensuing standoff between Orangemen and the security forces generates a week of violence across Northern Ireland. The Orangemen are forcibly removed on 15 July.

7 July German car manufacturer Volkswagen AG agrees to pay compensation to those who were used as slave labour during World War II.

July By the end of the month Serbian forces have overrun the whole of Kosovo, displacing 100,000 ethnic Albanians.

15 Aug. Northern Ireland suffers the worst atrocity of the Troubles when a dissident Republican group known as the Real IRA explodes a car bomb in the centre of Omagh, Co. Tyrone, killing 29 people and wounding 310.

31 Aug. Following the collapse in value of the rouble, Boris Yeltsin tries to reinstate Viktor Chernomyrdin as prime minister, but the Russian duma (parliament) rejects him. Yeltsin eventually chooses Yevgeny Primakov as prime minister (Sept.).

Aug. The UN High Commission on Human Rights investigates allegations of torture by Serb forces in Kosovo.

27 Sept. In Germany's parliamentary elections the governing centre-right CDU/CSU-FDP coalition loses its absolute majority. Gerhard Schröder becomes chancellor at the head of a 'red-green' coalition of the Social Democratic Party (SPD) and the Greens (27 Oct.).

18 Oct. Gen. Augusto Pinochet, the former Chilean dictator, is arrested at a London hospital by police acting on an extradition request from Spain.

Oct. NATO threatens Serbia with renewed airstrikes unless Serbian forces are withdrawn from Kosovo.

– Britain's Labour prime minister Tony Blair sets in motion legislation to curtail the voting rights of hereditary peers in the House of Lords.

MIDDLE EAST AND NORTH AFRICA

Jan. Up to 2000 civilians are massacred in Algeria by Islamic fundamentalists.

Jan. The Israeli government rejects US appeals to evacuate troops from the West Bank for the sake of peace.

22 Feb. Iraq and the UN sign an agreement that affirms UN arms inspectors' right of immediate and unconditional access to suspected Iraqi weapons' sites.

17 May Binyamin Netanyahu loses Israel's prime ministerial elections to the Labour Party leader Ehud Barak.

24 Sept. The Iranian government agrees to lift the *fatwa* sentencing British novelist Salman Rushdie to death (see 14 Feb. 1989).

16–20 Dec. After months of wrangling and obstruction from Saddam Hussein's government over weapons inspection, British and US forces launch airstrikes on Iraq.

ASIA

Jan. The World Food Program makes an international appeal for help to avert famine in North Korea.

4 Feb. An earthquake in N Afghanistan kills over 4000 people.

23 Feb. Osama bin Laden, the exiled Saudi Arabian millionaire leader of the Islamic terrorist organization al-Qaeda, who is being sheltered by the fundamentalist Taliban regime in Afghanistan, releases a *fatwa* enjoining Muslims to '... kill the Americans and their allies – civilians and military ... in any country in which it is possible to do it, in order to liberate the al-Aqsa Mosque [in Jerusalem] and the holy mosque [in Mecca, Saudi Arabia] from their grip, and in order for their armies to move out of all lands of Islam, defeated and unable to threaten any Muslim'.

15 April Former Cambodian dictator Pol Pot dies, apparently of a heart attack, in his jungle hide-out.

11–13 May The Indian government orders the detonation of five nuclear warheads despite worldwide condemnation. The Pakistani government responds by detonating six warheads (28–30 May).

21 May After months of unrest and rioting, President Suharto of Indonesia resigns. Suharto has ruled Indonesia since 1967. Bacharuddin Habibie replaces him.

24 May In the first legislative elections in Hong King since it reverted to Chinese control, pro-democracy parties gain 60% of the poll.

12 June Japan confirms that its economy – the world's second-largest after the USA – is in recession.

16 June In Afghanistan the ruling Taliban close down the last private girls' schools in the territory they control. This territory steadily expands as they take Mazar-i-Sharif, the last city outside their control (3 Aug.).

31 Aug. North Korea test-fires a ballistic missile over Japan as a show of strength, increasing fears that it is covertly building nuclear weapons.

Aug. The Taliban refuse to surrender Osama bin Laden, who is sought by the US authorities following terrorist attacks on US embassies in E Africa by al-Qaeda (see below).

THE AMERICAS

7 Jan. In Canada the minister of Indian Affairs, Jane Stewart, officially apologizes to Native American and Inuit people for four centuries of mistreatment and injustice.

15 Jan. Five US cigarette manufacturers agree a settlement of $7.25 billion to the state of Texas as compensation for medical costs for cigarette-related diseases. It is the largest such payment in history. It is dwarfed (20 Nov.) when the four largest US tobacco firms offer a total of $206 billion to settle all such claims by all states.

21 Jan. An investigation is launched to establish whether US president Bill Clinton asked the 24-year-old intern Monica Lewinsky to lie under oath and deny that she had an affair with him. Clinton is forced to give testimony in a closed session, where he denies any misconduct. US first lady Hillary Clinton blames the sexual allegations against her husband on a right-wing conspiracy to destroy his presidency (27 Jan.).

3 Feb. The US state of Texas executes the murderess Karla Faye Tucker. It is the first time a woman has been executed in Texas since 1863.

Feb. Kenneth Starr is named special prosecutor to investigate the Monica Lewinsky affair.

10 Mar. Former dictator of Chile Augusto Pinochet steps down as chief of the armed forces and becomes a senator for life. This gives him immunity from prosecution for previous crimes. On a visit to London (16 Oct.) he is arrested after a Spanish magistrate issues an extradition warrant. Arguments over his case last for several months. He is released on grounds of ill health (18 Feb. 2000).

4 May Theodore Kaczynski, the 'Unabomber' (see 3 April 1996), receives four life sentences.

17 Aug. President Clinton testifies to special prosecutor Kenneth Starr via videolink. During his five-hour testimony he admits to 'inappropriate intimate physical contact' with Lewinsky. Clinton will later apologize in a public broadcast for having 'misled people, including my wife'.

11 Sept. The Starr report into the Monica Lewinsky affair concludes that President Clinton has committed 11 impeachable offences.

18 Dec. The US House of Representatives votes to impeach President Clinton.

SUB-SAHARAN AFRICA

5 Jan. Kenya's president Daniel arap Moi, who has held power since 1978, is sworn in for a further five-year term.

19 Jan. Food riots break out in Zimbabwe as the price of maize meal rises over 20%. Land confiscations and the misgovernment of President Robert Mugabe have brought economic chaos. A general strike is held (3–4 Mar.), despite the government's attempts at repression.

13 Feb. In Sierra Leone a Nigerian-led force of W African peacekeeping troops overthrows the military government of Maj. Johnny Paul Koroma and reinstates President Ahmad Tejan Kabbah.

1 May The former Rwandan prime minister, Jean Kambanda, pleads guilty to six counts of genocide before the UN International Criminal Tribunal for Rwanda.

May–June Ethiopia and Eritrea fight a border war that claims 2000 lives.

8 June The Nigerian dictator Gen. Abacha dies suddenly.

June In Sierra Leone heavy fighting takes place between W African peacekeepers and forces loyal to the instigators of the 1997 coup.

7 Aug. In coordinated bombings of US embassies in Nairobi, Kenya, and Dar es Salaam, Tanzania, about 330 people are killed. Al-Qaeda, an Islamic fundamentalist terrorist group led by exiled Saudi Arabian Osama bin Laden, is blamed. In retaliation, US cruise missiles attack purported al-Qaeda training camps in Afghanistan (20 Aug.). They also destroy a pharmaceuticals factory outside Khartoum, Sudan, claiming

that it is producing nerve gas. Subsequent investigations show the claims to be false, although the owner never receives either an apology or compensation and large numbers of Sudanese subsequently die for lack of affordable medicines.

21 Aug. In South Africa, former president P.W. Botha is convicted of contempt of court, fined and given a suspended prison sentence. He has refused to testify before the government's Truth and Reconciliation Commission, which is examining the misdeeds of the apartheid era.

AUSTRALASIA AND OCEANIA

13 Feb. In Australia delegates at a Constitutional Convention in Canberra vote 89 to 52 to replace the Queen as head of state with a president chosen by a bipartisan parliamentary majority. The Convention decides that a referendum will be held in 1999 on whether Australia should become a republic of this type.

31 Mar. The New Zealand government introduces a bill to compensate the Maori Ngai Tahu people for land thefts in the 19th century.

ECONOMY AND SOCIETY

June–July France, the host nation, wins the 16th soccer World Cup.

SCIENCE AND TECHNOLOGY

5 Mar. NASA satellite *Lunar Prospector* discovers ice beneath the lunar surface at the poles.

17 April A satellite detects that a 200 square km (77 sq miles) piece of the Larsen B Antarctic ice shelf has broken free. Global warming is blamed.

29 Sept. New Zealand scientists announce that the hole in the ozone layer has grown to 28 million square km (11 million sq miles).

ARTS AND HUMANITIES

Literature

25 June The new British Library opens in London.

28 Oct. Ted Hughes, Poet Laureate since 1984, dies.

Beryl Bainbridge, *Master Georgie*, novel.

Julian Barnes, *England, England*, novel.

Michael Cunningham, *The Hours*, novel.

Michael Frayn, *Copenhagen*, play.

Ian McEwan, *Amsterdam*, novel.

J.K. Rowling, *Harry Potter and the Chamber of Secrets*, children's novel.

Visual Arts and Architecture

– In Britain the Turner Prize is awarded to Chris Ofili for his work *The Adoration of Captain Shit and the Legend of the Black Star Part Two*, incorporating elephant dung.

Music

15 May Frank Sinatra, US singer, dies.

All Saints, 'Never Ever', single.

Cher, 'Believe', single.

Destiny's Child, 'No, No, No', single.

Celine Dion, 'My Heart Will Go On', single.
Fatboy Slim, 'Brimful of Asha', single.
Shania Twain, 'You're Still the One', single.

Film

Joel and Ethan Coen, *The Big Lebowski*, starring Jeff Bridges.
Daniel Myrick and Eduardo Sánchez, *The Blair Witch Project*.
Steven Spielberg, *Saving Private Ryan*, starring Tom Hanks.
Peter Weir, *The Truman Show*, starring Jim Carrey.

1999

EUROPE

1 Jan. The Euro is introduced for accounting purposes in 11 EU nations.

16 Mar. The entire EU Commission has to resign following an official audit's revelation of fraud and corruption in EU finances.

24 Mar. Airstrikes mark the start of the NATO military campaign against Serb forces in Kosovo. Serb leader Slobodan Milosevic remains defiant, and his forces succeed in shooting down a US F117-A stealth bomber. As ethnic Albanians flee from Kosovo, reports begin to circulate of Serb atrocities.

5 April The two Libyan suspects for the Lockerbie bombing (21 Dec. 1988), Abdel Baset al-Megrahi and Lamin Khalifa Fhime, arrive in the Netherlands to stand trial under Scottish law. The UN Security Council votes to end sanctions against Libya.

12 April Chancellor Gerhard Schröder becomes leader of the German Social Democratic Party (SPD).

19 April The German Bundestag (parliament) meets for its first regular session in Berlin.

April–May During the course of continuing airstrikes against Serbia, NATO accidentally kills 75 Albanian refugees in Kosovo (14 April) and then – also by accident – bombs the Chinese embassy in Belgrade (7 May). However, reports of low Serbian army morale and desertion by conscripts, together with the spread of antiwar demonstrations in Serbia, suggest that the NATO campaign will soon be over. Albania comes close to collapse under the pressure of some 250,000 Kosovan refugees.

6 May Electors in Scotland and Wales vote for their new assemblies. A large nationalist vote in both countries stops the Labour Party from gaining an overall majority, and coalition administrations are formed in Edinburgh and Cardiff.

12 May Russian president Boris Yeltsin dismisses premier Yevgeny Primakov. Primakov has done much to stabilize the economy and improve relations with the duma but is, perhaps, too popular for Yeltsin's liking. The duma (parliament) protests and debates impeaching Yeltsin, but the witnesses they call fail to appear, and the motion is voted down. Sergei Stepashin becomes the new prime minister. Yeltsin then changes his mind again and installs Vladimir Putin (9 Aug.). Yeltsin has now dismissed four prime ministers in 17 months.

3 June Yugoslav president Slobodan Milsosevic agrees to evacuate Kosovo. NATO troops enter the province on 11 June. Serb

forces complete their withdrawal and ethnic Albanian refugees start to return (20 June). Thousands of Serbs now flee Kosovo as vengeful ethnic Albanians begin their own programme of anti-Serb 'ethnic cleansing'. A NATO peace-keeping force is sent to Kosovo to contain the violence between Serbs and Albanians.

29 June Demonstrations against the rule of Slobodan Milsosevic begin to spread across Serbia.

Aug. In Britain Charles Kennedy succeeds Paddy Ashdown as leader of the Liberal Democrats.

9 Sept. The Patten Report on policing in Northern Ireland proposes changes that are intended to make the Royal Ulster Constabulary (RUC) a less sectarian and Protestant-dominated body.

Sept. A series of bomb explosions in Russia kills 293 people. Chechen separatists are blamed and, after airstrikes (23 Sept.), Russian troops invade Chechnya (30 Sept.). The chance to avenge the humiliation of the 1996 invasion makes premier Vladimir Putin popular in Russia.

31 Oct. In Britain 31 people die and more than 400 are injured in a train crash near London's Paddington station. Many blame the private companies that now run Britain's railway network for the safety failures that caused the crash.

17 Nov. In Northern Ireland an IRA statement effectively promising to decommission arms leads to further progress in the peace process.

20 Nov. A 'third way' conference of centre-left leaders is held in Florence; it is attended by US president Bill Clinton, British prime minister Tony Blair, German chancellor Gerhard Schröder and French premier Lionel Jospin.

28 Nov. A devolved power-sharing government takes office in Northern Ireland.

28 Nov. Russian forces in Chechnya start an intensive three-day bombardment of Grozny, leading to some 500 deaths.

31 Dec. Russian president Boris Yeltsin resigns because of ill health. He is succeeded as president by prime minister Vladimir Putin.

Dec. The French parliament approves a bill for a 35-hour working week.

– In Britain the number of hereditary peers allowed to participate in the work of the House of Lords is reduced to 92.

– In Britain the national minimum wage is introduced.

MIDDLE EAST AND NORTH AFRICA

3 Jan. Saudi Arabian-born terrorist Osama bin Laden gives an interview to *Time* magazine. He calls for *jihad* or holy war against the USA and Britain in response to their airstrikes against Iraq.

7 Feb. King Hussein of Jordan dies and is succeeded by his son Abdullah.

15 Feb. Turkish agents in Kenya capture Kurd separatist leader Abdullah Ocalan and take him back to Turkey to stand trial. Kurds respond by planting bombs in Turkey (Mar.). Ocalan is sentenced to death (29 June).

27 May In Israel former premier Binyamin Netanyahu resigns as leader of the opposition right-wing Likud party, and Ariel Sharon becomes its new leader.

7 July In Tehran, Iran, student demands for liberal reforms lead to rioting. Islamist vigilantes, the Ansar-e-Hizbollah, attack the university campus, killing eight people. Thousands of pro-democracy protestors take to the streets of Tehran (12 July).

23 July King Hassan II of Morocco dies; his son Mohammed VI succeeds him.

17 Aug. An earthquake in NW Turkey kills 14,000 people.

ASIA

9 Feb. The last Khmer Rouge troops in Cambodia surrender to government forces.

11 April Both India and Pakistan (14 April) carry out successful tests of their ballistic missiles.

May The dispute between India and Pakistan over Kashmir threatens to provoke war. Increasing incursions by Islamic guerrillas lead India to launch airstrikes against guerrilla bases, leading to border clashes with Pakistani troops. The two states agree to draw back from confrontation (4 July).

22 July The Chinese government bans the Falun Gong religious sect, which claims to have 70 million followers.

1 Aug. In China the Yangtze River bursts its banks and more than 5 million people are left homeless by the subsequent flooding.

30 Aug. In East Timor electors opt in a referendum for independence from Indonesia. Pro-Indonesian militias go on the rampage with the connivance of the Indonesian army until UN peacekeepers arrive (20 Sept.). Indonesian president Abdurrahman Wahid promises a referendum for independence in the province of Aceh in N Sumatra.

12 Oct. Gen. Pervez Musharraf overthrows the government of Nawaz Sharif in a military coup and names himself 'chief executive officer' of Pakistan.

14 Nov. The UN Security Council votes to impose sanctions against Afghanistan, in an attempt to force the ruling Taliban to surrender Osama bin Laden (see 1998).

19 Dec. The S Chinese peninsula of Macau is returned to Chinese sovereignty after 442 years of Portuguese rule.

THE AMERICAS

Jan. President Clinton is tried by the US Senate on impeachment charges relating to the Monica Lewinsky affair (1998). There is little likelihood of a conviction, because the necessary two-thirds majority would require several Democrats to vote against their own president. He is, therefore, acquitted (12 Feb.).

1 April The new Canadian territory of Nunavut is created for the Inuit people.

20 April Two US students, Eric Harris and Dylan Klebold, open fire in Columbine High School, Denver, Colorado, and kill 12 students and a teacher before killing themselves.

7 June Osama bin Laden is placed on the FBI's 'Ten Most Wanted List' and a $5 million reward is offered for his capture.

25 Dec. 11 Cubans die in an attempt to sail to America. Five-year old Elián González is rescued, however. By international law he should be returned to Cuba, but relatives in Florida begin a protracted custody battle.

31 Dec. The US government hands the Panama Canal over to Panamanian sovereignty.

SUB-SAHARAN AFRICA

6 Jan. Rebels seize control and loot Freetown, capital of Sierra Leone. A Nigerian-led coalition drives them out (10 Jan.).

6–10 Jan. Serious border clashes occur between Ethiopian and Eritrean forces.

10 Jan. In Zimbabwe the government of Robert Mugabe arrests 32 soldiers accused of plotting a coup, along with two journalists. The Zimbabwean press and judiciary criticize Mugabe's human-rights record, but Mugabe roundly denounces both.

18 Jan. Canaan Banana, the former president of Zimbabwe, is convicted on charges of 'sodomy' and sentenced to 10 years in prison, but Banana has already fled the country.

9 April President Ibrahim Baré Mainassara of Niger is assassinated by his own guards. His guard commander, Maj. Daouda Malam Wanke, takes power.

27 May Nelson Mandela retires as president of South Africa. Thabo Mbeki is elected his successor.

June Claims of human rights abuses by the government of Robert Mugabe resurface in Zimbabwe. Protests are also made at the rising price of food. A new political party, the Movement for Democratic Change, led by the trade unionist Morgan Tsvangirai, emerges.

23 Dec. Gen. Robert Guei leads a military coup in Côte d'Ivoire and suspends the constitution.

AUSTRALASIA AND OCEANIA

6 Nov. In a referendum on whether the country should become a republic, Australians choose to keep Britain's Queen Elizabeth II as their head of state.

ECONOMY AND SOCIETY

Oct.–Nov. Australia wins the 4th rugby union World Cup, held in Wales (with some games played in England, Ireland and France).

27 Oct. Brothels are legalized in the Netherlands.

– The world population reaches 6 billion.

SCIENCE AND TECHNOLOGY

23 Sept. NASA loses contact with the US Mars probe *Climate Orbiter*.

20 Nov. The Chinese launch a spacecraft capable of carrying a man.

ARTS AND HUMANITIES

Literature

J.M. Coetzee, *Disgrace*, novel.

Anita Desai, *Fasting, Feasting*, novel.

Jhumpa Lahiri, *Interpreter of Maladies*, short stories.

J.K. Rowling, *Harry Potter and the Prisoner of Azkaban*, children's novel.

Ahdaf Soueif, *The Map of Love*, novel.

Visual Arts and Architecture
– In Britain Tracey Emin's *My Bed*, featuring soiled sheets, empty vodka bottles and used condoms, fails to win the 1999 Turner Prize.

Music
Catatonia, 'Dead from the Waist Down', single.
Fatboy Slim, 'Praise You', single.
New Radicals, 'You Get What You Give', single.
Britney Spears, 'Baby One More Time', single.

Film
Spike Jonze, *Being John Malkovich*, starring John Malkovich.
Stanley Kubrick, *Eyes Wide Shut*, starring Nicole Kidman and Tom Cruise.
Sam Mendes, *American Beauty*, starring Kevin Spacey.
Andy and Larry Wachowski, *The Matrix*, starring Keanu Reeves.

2000

EUROPE

15 Jan. In Serbia the mobster and indicted war criminal Zeljko Raznatovic (Arkan), a supporter of Slobodan Milosevic, is assassinated.
16 Jan. In Serbia 16 opposition parties unite in demanding the removal of President Slobodan Milosevic.
5 Feb. Jörg Haider's extreme right-wing Freedom Party joins the Austrian coalition government. International condemnation follows.
6 Feb. Russian forces capture the Chechen capital of Grozny, a city now in ruins.
11 Feb. After no progress is made in decommissioning IRA weapons (see 1999), the Northern Ireland assembly is suspended, and direct rule from Westminster is reimposed on the province.
4 May Former GLC leader Ken Livingstone, a left-winger who is currently estranged from the Labour Party, becomes London's first elected mayor.
13 May Ex-premier and media magnate Silvio Berlusconi is elected prime minister of Italy.
29 May Devolved government is restored in Northern Ireland when the IRA undertake to put their arms 'completely and verifiably … beyond use'.
18 June In Dover, S England, 58 illegal Chinese immigrants are found dead from suffocation in a Dutch container lorry.
June In France the national assembly endorses a proposal to change the presidential term of office from seven to five years.
2–3 July In Chechnya, where fighting continues, Chechen suicide bombers kill 43 Russian soldiers.
July In Northern Ireland violence flares again after Orange marchers on their annual parade in Portadown are refused passage down the mainly Catholic Garvaghy Road.
12 Aug. The Russian nuclear submarine *Kursk* sinks in the Barents Sea off the coast of NW Russia. The entire crew of 118 die after the Russian government refuses international offers of assistance in their rescue.

17 Aug. Swiss banks approve a final settlement of $1.3 billion to compensate those Holocaust survivors and the surviving relatives of Holocaust victims whose assets have been seized and deposited in the banks since World War II.
7–14 Sept. Parts of Britain are brought to a standstill when protestors, mostly road hauliers and farmers protesting against high fuel costs, blockade refineries.
24 Sept. Presidential elections take place in Serbia. Slobodan Milosevic refuses to recognize Vojislav Kostunica, leader of the Democratic Party of Serbia, as the winner.
28 Sept. A national referendum in Denmark votes against the adoption of the Euro as the country's currency.
3 Oct. In Austrian parliamentary elections the radical right-wing Freedom Party (FPO) becomes the second largest party.
5 Oct. Slobodan Milosevic resigns as Serbian president and Vojislav Kostunica, who has the support of the Yugoslav army, becomes president (6 Oct.), with Zoran Djindjic as prime minister.
– The British government is strongly criticized in a report on its handling of the BSE crisis.

MIDDLE EAST AND NORTH AFRICA

4 Jan. As part of the peace process the Israeli government agrees to transfer to the Palestinians part of the occupied land on the West Bank.
8 Feb. In Turkey Kurdish separatist supporters of Abdullah Ocalan (see 15 Feb. 1999) announce a ceasefire. Ocalan is granted an indefinite stay of execution.
18 Feb. In elections to the majlis (parliament of Iran), reformers win a landslide victory. But power remains firmly in the hands of conservative clerics, who ignore calls for change.
24 May Israeli forces withdraw from S Lebanon.
28 Sept. In Israel the right-wing Likud party leader Ariel Sharon trespasses on an area of Muslim sanctuary in the Dome of the Rock, Jerusalem. Sharon's act is seen as highly provocative, since it takes place during a visit to the lost Jewish Temple of Jerusalem, which hardline Jews wish to recreate at the expense of the Muslim sanctuaries; it triggers a wave of violent attacks by Palestinians against Jews in Israel and the occupied territories.
Oct. Palestinian frustration at the lack of real progress towards statehood explodes into a new *intifada* (uprising) in the occupied territories.

ASIA

24 May The Russian government threatens airstrikes on the Taliban in Afghanistan in retaliation for supporting Chechen separatists.

THE AMERICAS

12 Jan. The US attorney general Janet Reno rules that the rescued Cuban child Elián González must be returned to his father in Cuba (see Dec. 1999). Armed agents of the Immigration and Naturalization Service seize the boy from his relatives, and he is returned to Cuba (28 June).

21 Jan. The president of Ecuador, Jamil Mahuad Witt, is overthrown in a coup. Vice-President Gustavo Noboa Bejarano replaces him.

6 Feb. The USA's former first lady Hillary Clinton announces that she will run for the US Senate in New York.

2 Mar. Former dictator Gen. Augusto Pinochet returns to Chile from Britain. The British government has refused, on grounds of his poor health, to approve extradition proceedings designed to ensure that the Chilean general is brought before European courts to face charges of torture and abuse of human rights (see 18 Oct. 1998).

7 Nov. In the most controversial presidential election in US history, the presidency hangs in the balance in Florida, where the governor, Jeb Bush, rules that about 4000 votes from poorer districts cannot be counted because holes have not been completely punched through the voting forms. This decision favours the Republican candidate, his brother George W. Bush. There is considerable confusion until the US Supreme Court decides to uphold the governor's decision (13 Dec.). It is later found that if the disputed votes had been included in the final count Democratic candidate Al Gore would have won the state and thus the presidency.

*Who controls the past
controls the future:
who controls the present
controls the past.*

George Orwell, *Nineteen Eighty-Four* (1949)

31 Dec. As one of his last acts in office, US president Bill Clinton signs a UN treaty to establish a permanent International Criminal Court, which will try cases of war crimes.

SUB-SAHARAN AFRICA

Feb. Land seizures in Zimbabwe continue after a new constitution is rejected in a referendum (12 Feb.).

1 May Britain sends 700 paratroopers to restore order in Sierra Leone after rebel forces attack UN peacekeepers.

11 Sept. In Zimbabwe the government is widely suspected of complicity in a hand-grenade attack on the offices of the Movement for Democratic Change (MDC). Renewed food riots take place on 16 Oct.

24 Oct. Laurent Gbagbo wins the presidential election held, under a new constitution, in the Côte d'Ivoire and Gen. Robert Guei has to flee from the country (26 Oct.).

ECONOMY AND SOCIETY

7 June A US court orders the breaking up of the Microsoft Corporation, because of its near monopoly in the computer software market.

Sept.–Oct. The 27th Olympic Games are held in Sydney, Australia.

SCIENCE AND TECHNOLOGY

1 Jan. Predictions of worldwide chaos through the 'millennium bug', a complete collapse of software unable to function when the year becomes '00, fail to materialize. Only a few minor problems are reported.

26 June US company Celera Genomics announces the complete mapping of the human genome.

25 July An Air France Concorde crashes outside Paris, killing all 109 passengers on board and signalling the approaching end of supersonic passenger flight.

ARTS AND HUMANITIES

Literature

10 Dec. Günter Grass is awarded the Nobel Prize for literature.

Margaret Atwood, *The Blind Assassin*, novel.

Kazuo Ishiguro, *When We were Orphans*, novel.

Matthew Kneale, *English Passengers*, novel.

Philip Pullman, *The Amber Spyglass*, children's novel.

J.K. Rowling, *Harry Potter and the Goblet of Fire*, children's novel.

Zadie Smith, *White Teeth*, novel.

Visual Arts and Architecture

12 May The Tate Modern art gallery, London, opens to the public.

Music

All Saints, 'Pure Shores', single.

Eminem, 'Stan', single.

Sonique, 'Feels So Good', single.

Britney Spears, 'Oops! … I Did It Again', single.

Film

Stephen Daldry, *Billy Elliot*, starring Julie Walters.

Ang Lee, *Crouching Tiger, Hidden Dragon*.

Ridley Scott, *Gladiator*, starring Russell Crowe.

Steven Soderbergh, *Traffic* and *Erin Brockovich*.

2001

EUROPE

21 Feb. In Sicily, Italy, one of the ten most wanted mafia bosses, Bernardo Provenza, is arrested after 38 years on the run.

23 Feb. In Britain the government bans the movement of all livestock in an attempt to contain an outbreak of foot and mouth disease.

1 April After losing an election the previous Dec., former Serbian president Slobodan Milosevic is arrested in Belgrade, Serbia, and is extradited to The Hague to stand trial for war crimes (28 June).

30 April In Macedonia ethnic violence breaks out in Skopje and Bitola between Macedonians and Albanians.

1 May On a day of worldwide anti-capitalist protest, the demonstration in London turns violent.

7 June In Britain the Labour Party is re-elected in a landslide general election victory virtually identical to that of 1997. Labour wins 413 seats, the Conservatives 166 and the Liberal Democrats 52. Turnout in the election, however, is significantly lower than in 1997. In Northern Ireland the election sees Sinn Féin overtake the Social Democratic and Labour Party (SDLP) as the largest nationalist party. William Hague announces that he will be resigning as Conservative Party leader (8 June).

June In Oldham and Bradford, N England, hundreds of Muslim Asian youths demonstrate against the racist British National Party (BNP).

13 Sept. In Britain, Iain Duncan Smith, a little-known Eurosceptic from the right wing of his party, becomes leader of the Conservative Party. He defeats Kenneth Clarke in the first-ever Conservative leadership contest decided by party members.

4 Oct. During a military exercise, Ukrainians accidentally launch a surface-to-air missile, which shoots down a Russian airliner, killing all on board.

23 Oct. The IRA announces the start of its process of decommissioning arms in Northern Ireland.

– Britain suffers an epidemic of foot-and-mouth disease.

MIDDLE EAST AND NORTH AFRICA

6 Feb. Israeli Labour Party leader Ehud Barak loses Israel's prime ministerial elections to the right-wing Likud Party leader Ariel Sharon, a controversial former general with a hard-line reputation. Sharon, who heads a coalition government, becomes Israel's fifth prime minister in six years. Barak refuses to serve as defence minister in the new government.

16 Feb. British and US forces launch airstrikes near Baghdad, Iraq. It is a signal from the new US president, George W. Bush, that he will tolerate no more prevarication from dictator Saddam Hussein over weapons inspections whose principle he accepted in 1991.

31 May 300,000 Berbers march in Algiers, Algeria, in support of their rights as the original, non-Arab inhabitants of the country.

May After a wave of Palestinian suicide bomb attacks, Israeli jets attack Palestinian targets. But the bombings continue. One bomber, Said Houtari, kills 20 Israelis in a Tel Aviv discotheque (1 June). The Israeli response (from 13 June) is to launch helicopter attacks intended to assassinate militants and to demolish Palestinian homes. Palestinian suicide bombings and guerrilla attacks on Israeli settlements increase.

27 Aug. In the West Bank town of Ramallah Israeli forces assassinate Abu Ali Mustafa, the deputy leader of the Popular Front for the Liberation of Palestine (PFLP).

ASIA

25 Jan. An earthquake in the state of Gujarat, W India, kills thousands and leaves more than 250,000 people homeless.

8 Mar. In Afghanistan, the ruling Taliban defy international outrage when they destroy the massive Buddhist statues of Bamiyan which they regard as idolatrous.

1 April After a mid-air collision with a Chinese fighter, a US spyplane makes an emergency landing on Chinese territory. In an attempt to pressurize the Chinese into releasing the aircraft and crew, President Bush authorizes the sale of advanced weaponry to Taiwan.

1 June The heir to the throne of Nepal, Crown Prince Dipendra, kills King Birendra, most of the royal family and, finally, himself.

15 Sept. Ahmed Shah Masud, leader of the United Islamic Front for the Salvation of Afghanistan and a major anti-Taliban figure, dies of wounds sustained in an assassination attempt.

7 Oct. A US-led coalition launches airstrikes against Afghanistan, with the aim of ending Taliban rule and of destroying the bases in Afghanistan of the terrorist network al-Qaeda, held responsible for the 11 Sept. attacks on the USA. The Taliban begin to collapse following the start of a ground war (Nov.). The last Taliban-held city, Kandahar, falls to coalition forces on 7 Dec. But there is no group within Afghanistan in a position to replace the Taliban, and chaos threatens to return. Al-Qaeda leader Osama bin Laden is not found.

13 Dec. In India 14 people die when Islamic terrorists attack the parliament. There is an immediate crisis between India and Pakistan, and war threatens.

THE AMERICAS

18 Jan. George W. Bush is sworn in as the 43rd president of the USA.

11 Mar. Subcommandante Marcos leads a march by the Zapatista National Liberation Army (EZNL) to Mexico City to lobby the Mexican congress on indigenous American rights. More than 175,000 people greet his arrival.

28 Mar. President George W. Bush withdraws the USA from the 1997 Kyoto protocol on climate change which committed its signatories to a reduction in 'greenhouse gas' emissions.

2 Aug. At the urging of US president Bush, the House of Representatives votes to authorize oil exploration in the Arctic National Wildlife Refuge in Alaska, ignoring Native American protests that this would mean their destruction as nations.

11 Sept. In the USA terrorists hijack four airliners and embark on a suicide mission that marks a new chapter in the history of relations between the Islamic states of the Middle East and the Anglo-American world. Two planes are crashed into the World Trade Center, New York, one into the Pentagon, Virginia, and one crashes in open country in Pennsylvania. Up to 3000 people are killed. US authorities quickly decide that the culprits are al-Qaeda, the Islamic fundamentalist group led by Osama bin Laden. President Bush declares a worldwide 'war on terror'. He issues an ultimatum to the Taliban rulers of Afghanistan, where bin Laden has sanctuary, to surrender him or face the 'full wrath of the United States'. His demands are rejected. US fears of terrorism are heightened when letters infected with anthrax are posted to government buildings in Washington (Oct.), although no evidence is found linking these to al-Qaeda.

2 Dec. In the USA the Enron Corporation collapses, with debts of $15 billion. It is the largest corporate collapse in US history. The scale of the concealed debt will leave employees and investors uncompensated. Fraud charges follow.

SUB-SAHARAN AFRICA

16 Jan. A dissident army officer assassinates the president of the Democratic Republic of the Congo, Laurent Kabila. Kabila's son Joseph succeeds as interim president.

16 April The government of Benin issues an arrest warrant for a Nigerian registered freighter, MV *Etireono*, and its crew, after receiving reports that it is carrying 250 children sold into slavery.

7 May The UN bans the export of Liberian diamonds because of the state's support for rebels in Sierra Leone.

SCIENCE AND TECHNOLOGY

9 Mar. Italian gynaecologist Severino Antinori announces his intention to clone a human being. This leads to calls for an international ban on such research.

23 Mar. The Russian space station *Mir* is destroyed in the Earth's atmosphere. First launched in 1986, it has long outlived its expected operational lifetime.

ARTS AND HUMANITIES

Literature

Peter Carey, *True History of the Kelly Gang*, novel.

Michael Chabon, *The Amazing Adventures of Kavalier and Clay*, novel.

Roger-Pol Droit, *101 Expériences de philosophie quotidienne*.

Jonathan Franzen, *The Corrections*, novel.

Jonathan I. Israel, *Radical Enlightenment: Philosophy and the Makings of Modernity, 1650–1750*.

Bruce Kuklick, *A History of Philosophy in America, 1720–2000*.

Margaret MacMillan, *Peacemakers: The Paris Conference of 1919 and Its Attempt to End War*.

Ian McEwan, *Atonement*, novel.

Orhan Pamuk, *My Name is Red*, novel

Visual Arts and Architecture

Martin Creed, *Work #227 The Lights Going On and Off*, an installation of lights in an otherwise empty room.

Music

Eva Cassidy, *Songbird*, album.

Dido, *No Angel*, album.

David Gray, *White Ladder*, album.

Kylie Minogue 'Can't Get You out of My Head', single.

Film

Robert Altman, *Gosford Park*, starring Helen Mirren and Alan Bates.

Mike Dibb, *Edward Said: The Last Interview*.

Ron Howard, *A Beautiful Mind*, starring Russell Crowe.

Peter Jackson, *The Lord of the Rings: The Fellowship of the Ring*, starring Elijah Wood and Ian McKellen; the first in Jackson's epic trilogy based on J.R.R. Tolkien's fantasy novel.

Baz Luhrman, *Moulin Rouge!*.

David Lynch, *Mulholland Drive*.

Simon West, *Lara Croft: Tomb Raider*, starring Angelina Jolie.

2002

EUROPE

1 Jan. The euro becomes legal tender in 12 member states of the European Union.

21 Jan. TV-6, the last independent broadcaster in Russia, is taken off the air when bailiffs move in. The move is widely seen as an attempt by the government to control the media.

7 Mar. In a national referendum in Ireland the legalization of abortion is narrowly rejected.

30 Mar. Death in Britain of Queen Elizabeth The Queen Mother.

21 April In a shock result in the first round of the presidential elections in France, the socialist candidate, Lionel Jospin, is defeated. Jean-Marie Le Pen, leader of the extreme right-wing National Front, goes through to the next round (5 May). Voters, however, rally to the incumbent president, centre-rightist Jacques Chirac, and re-elect him by a huge majority.

6 May In the Netherlands Pim Fortuyn, founder of an anti-immigration but pro-civil rights political party, is assassinated.

May Paddy Ashdown, former leader of the Liberal Democratic Party in Britain, is appointed as the international community's High Representative in Bosnia-Herzegovina.

14 Oct. Following allegations of an IRA spy ring in Northern Ireland government offices, the British government suspends the province's assembly and executive for the fourth time since devolution was attempted in 1999.

23 Oct. Some 40 Chechen separatists seize a theatre in Moscow. They take up to 850 hostages and demand that Russian troops withdraw from Chechnya. Russian special forces storm the theatre (26 Oct.), after deploying a paralysing nerve gas. All the Chechens die in what might have been a remarkable coup for the Russians, but over 100 hostages die from the effects of the gas, which Russian authorities initially refuse to identify to the hospitals treating them.

22 Nov. NATO members agree to invite Bulgaria, Estonia, Latvia, Lithuania, Romania, Slovakia and Slovenia to join in 2004.

MIDDLE EAST AND NORTH AFRICA

25 Jan. As the *intifada* gathers pace, 52 Israeli reservists refuse to serve on the West Bank on moral grounds. They object to the way the military treats Palestinians. The hard line taken by the Israeli government is proving divisive.

April As suicide bombings and guerrilla raids by Palestinians continue, the Israeli army reoccupies the whole of the Left Bank and starts (6 April) a six-day campaign to take charge of the refugee camp at Jenin, which is believed to harbour terrorists. Heavy fighting follows, and Palestinian leader Yasser Arafat is besieged in his compound at Ramallah. There is international outcry at the destruction of property by the Israelis, who protest that they are simply taking part in the international war on terrorism.

24 June President Bush supports Israeli calls on the Palestinians to find a new leader, but this merely rallies Palestinian support for Arafat, and the *intifada* continues.

ASIA

Jan. Following the terrorist attack on the Indian parliament (see 13 Dec. 2001), there is a major military standoff along the India–Pakistan frontier, involving about one million troops. War seems near. An attack by Muslims on a train carrying Hindu activists in Gujarat, W India, provokes a surge of brutal sectarian violence (27 Feb.).

16 Feb. In a continuation of the insurrection that started in 1996, Maoist guerrillas kill some 130 people in Nepal.

13 June The Loya Jirga, or Council of Elders, elects Hamid Karzai as interim president of Afghanistan.

12 Oct. In a major terrorist act 190 people are killed and more than 300 are injured on the island of Bali, Indonesia. Jemaah Islamiah, an Islamic group linked to al-Qaeda, is held responsible.

15 Nov. President Bush orders a US oil embargo against North Korea unless it halts its nuclear weapons programme.

12 Dec. Following state elections the Hindu nationalist Bharatiya Janata Party (BJP) consolidates its political control of Gujarat.

THE AMERICAS

29 Jan. In a major speech in the USA, President Bush describes an 'axis of evil', which includes North Korea, Iran and Iraq. The latter is presented as representing the gravest threat to the USA because of its obstruction of weapons inspection.

31 Jan. As part of President Bush's war on terrorism, 650 US special forces troops begin working with the Filipino army in counter-insurgency operations.

19 April The US Senate rejects President Bush's proposals to authorize oil exploration in the Arctic National Wildlife Refuge, Alaska (see 2 Aug. 2001).

12 Sept. Addressing the UN Security Council, US president Bush urges war against Iraq, claiming that Iraqi leader Saddam Hussein possesses weapons of mass destruction (WMD) and is actively supporting terrorism. The international response is lukewarm, but the US Congress authorizes Bush to use military action to deprive Iraq of WMD (9–10 Oct.). The UN Security Council passes resolution 1441, giving Saddam Hussein a last chance to comply with weapons inspection or face 'serious consequences' (8 Nov.). Most observers assume that this is not an authorization for war.

5 Nov. Following US Congressional elections, the Republicans have a majority in the Senate and the House of Representatives.

14 Nov. Argentina's government defaults on a loan repayment of $805 million to the World Bank.

SUB-SAHARAN AFRICA

9–11 Mar. In elections in Zimbabwe President Robert Mugabe is proclaimed to have been re-elected president, but the results are controversial, with allegations of vote rigging.

19 Mar. Zimbabwe is suspended from the Commonwealth.

20 Mar. Zimbabwean opposition leader Morgan Tsvangirai is charged with treason.

30 July Rwanda and the Democratic Republic of Congo arrive at a peace accord: Rwandan troops leave the Congo, while anti-Rwandan Hutu militias are disbanded.

19 Sept. Rebellion returns to Côte d'Ivoire as soldiers protest against their forced disbandment and turn against government forces. By the end of the month large areas of the country are controlled by the Patriotic Movement of Côte d'Ivoire. Following a ceasefire (17 Oct.) peace talks begin (30 Oct.).

– In Sudan peace talks begin between the government and southern-based rebels. Millions have died and been displaced in the ongoing civil war in the S of the country.

AUSTRALASIA AND OCEANIA

16 Jan. Asylum seekers in a camp at Woomera, S Australia, begin a hunger strike. They are protesting against living conditions and the Australian government's suspension of the procedure dealing with their cases.

ECONOMY AND SOCIETY

31 May–30 June Brazil wins the 17th soccer World Cup, held in South Korea.

ARTS AND HUMANITIES

Literature
Orlando Figes, *Natasha's Dance: A Cultural History of Russia*.
Yann Martel, *Life of Pi*, novel.
William Trevor, *The Story of Lucy Gault*, novel.
Carlos Ruiz Zafón, *The Shadow of the Wind*, novel.

Visual Arts and Architecture
Mario Testino, *Portraits* (a collection published for the photographer's exhibition at the National Portrait Gallery, London, 1 Feb.–4 June 2002).

Music
Coldplay, *A Rush of Blood to the Head*, album.
Norah Jones, *Come Away with Me*, album.
Jennifer Lopez, 'I'm Gonna be Alright', single.
Nelly, 'Hot in Here', single.

Film
Nuri Bilge Ceylan, *Uzak*, starring Mehmet Emin Toprak.
Stephen Daldry, *The Hours*, starring Meryl Streep.
Peter Jackson, *The Two Towers*.
Spike Jonze, *Adaptation*.
Roman Polanski, *The Pianist*.
Gabriele Salvatores, *I'm Not Scared*.
Martin Scorsese, *Gangs of New York*, starring Daniel Day-Lewis and Leonardo DiCaprio.

2003

EUROPE

20 Jan. The UK government announces that 30,000 British troops will go to the Persian Gulf. As preparations for war against Iraq gather momentum, the governments of both Germany and France make clear their opposition to military action (23 Jan.). In the British House of Commons 122 Labour MPs vote against the government in the debate (27 Feb.) on the imminent war.

4 Feb. The state of Yugoslavia formally comes to an end. A loose union, the Republic of Serbia and Montenegro, replaces it. In Kosovo ethnic Albanians demonstrate to make clear their opposition to inclusion within the state.

15 Feb. The biggest political demonstration in British history occurs when up to 2 million antiwar protestors march through London. Worldwide, some 30 million people demonstrate against the war.

9 Mar. In Ukraine mass demonstrations occur against President Leonid Kuchma's attempt to extend his term of office.

10 Mar. French president Jacques Chirac makes it known that he will veto any new UN Security Council resolution authorizing war as long as negotiations might settle the issue.

12 Mar. Zoran Djindjic, the prime minister of Serbia, is assassinated, and is temporarily replaced by deputy prime minister Nebojsa Covic. Serb nationalists, angered by the dissolution of Yugoslavia, are held responsible.

23 Mar. A referendum in Chechnya approves a new constitution for the breakaway republic. Few expect it will end the violence in the region. Indeed, Chechen suicide bombers will kill 77 Russians in May.

17 April Sergei Yushchenkov, co-chairman of the Liberal Russia Party and a critic of President Putin's policy in Chechnya, is shot dead, bringing to nine the number of deputies in the duma (parliament) who have been murdered since 1994.

29 April President Putin and British prime minister Tony Blair attend a one-day summit near Moscow: Putin openly mocks the US–British failure to discover weapons of mass destruction (WMD) in Iraq.

26 May The Convention on the Future of Europe issues a revised draft article for a European Constitution. The phrase 'United States of Europe' is dropped, but the right of national veto is abolished in 20 new areas (including asylum policy as well as social and environmental affairs), which will now be decided by qualified majority voting within the EU's Council of Ministers.

July Following the ending of Saddam Hussein's regime in Iraq, the failure to discover any weapons of mass destruction (WMD) arouses suspicions in Britain that the government misled the public and Parliament over the case for war. This becomes a major political scandal after the suicide of a British weapons inspector, Dr David Kelly (17 July), which threatens to undermine Tony Blair's premiership.

27–30 Oct. The Russian stock market falls by 16.5%, reflecting a loss of business confidence following the politically motivated arrest (25 Oct.) of Mikhail Khodorkovsky, chief executive of the Yukos oil company and a major supporter of the liberal political parties that oppose President Putin.

29 Oct. In Britain, the Conservative Party leader Iain Duncan Smith resigns after he narrowly fails to win the backing of his fellow MPs in a vote of confidence. Michael Howard, a former home secretary, replaces him as leader (6 Nov.).

25 Nov. Georgia's supreme court rules that the results of the country's legislative elections (2 Nov.) are invalid because of fraud. President Eduard Shevardnadze is forced to resign.

7 Dec. The Unified Russian Party, led by President Putin, gains 38% of the popular vote in the country's general election and a two-thirds majority of the 300 seats in the duma (parliament). Observers express concern over the lack of genuine democratic debate in the election.

MIDDLE EAST AND NORTH AFRICA

5 Jan. In Israel the Palestinian *intifada* continues as suicide bombers kill 22 in Tel Aviv.

1 Mar. The Turkish parliament rejects US use of Turkish territory to invade Iraq.

20 Mar. Despite worldwide condemnation, the US-led war on Iraq begins. Iraqi forces soon crumble under the firepower arrayed against them. Baghdad falls (7 April), as does Saddam Hussein's home city of Tikrit (14 April). The regime collapses in an orgy of looting, which coalition forces have made no preparations to prevent. No trace of Saddam Hussein or his weapons of mass destruction (WMD), used to justify the war, are found.

13 April President Bush accuses Syria of holding chemical weapons, and fears spread of a US attack on Syria until the president moderates his rhetoric (20 April).

29 April The Saudi and US governments announce the withdrawal of almost all US forces from the kingdom within a few months. The US use, for the past 10 years, of Saudi bases for its airborne forces in the Middle East has been a major cause of Islamist-fundamentalist hostility to US policy in the region.

30 April The so-called 'Road Map' to a permanent solution to the Israeli–Palestinian conflict, drawn up by the USA, the UN, the EU and Russia, is presented to Israeli prime minister Ariel Sharon.

1 May President Bush declares the Iraq war over, but casualties continue in attacks on coalition troops as Iraqi resentment against the occupation mounts.

21 May More than 2,000 people are killed and some 10,000 others are injured when an earthquake hits Algiers.

10 June In Iran student protests at Tehran University in favour of democratic reform become a mass movement involving many thousands. The protests spread to the rest of the city and to other Iranian cities by 16 June, but then fade away.

24 June Six members of the British Royal Military Police are killed in S Iraq and eight British soldiers are injured. The general security situation in Iraq is now deteriorating rapidly.

1 Sept. Israel has embarked on a policy of targeted killings of its Palestinian opponents and is calling for the Palestinian National Authority to disarm militant groups.

1 Sept. The composition of the governing council, a 25-member interim authority for the administration of Iraq, is announced: coalition-appointed advisers, mostly US personnel, supervise each ministry.

16–17 Oct. Rebellion against the US-led coalition forces in Iraq has now spread from Sunni areas to the predominantly Shiite S.

27 Oct. In suicide bombings in Baghdad 38 people are killed and more than 200 injured.

20 Nov. The first phase of operation Iron Hammer, launched by US troops in an attempt to regain the initiative in Iraq comes to an end: fighter jets, helicopter gunships and mortar attacks are deployed in and around Baghdad.

13 Dec. Saddam Hussein is captured by US-led forces near his home town of Tikrit, Iraq. Discovered in a hole in the ground, his dishevelled state disproves the idea that he has been master-minding an anti-coalition campaign. President Bush states that 'a hopeful day has arrived', but the movement against the US occupation of Iraq has now become a massive popular uprising, and a huge surge in violence consumes the country following Saddam's capture.

19 Dec. In what is seen as a victory for US foreign policy, the Libyan government agrees to disclose and dismantle its plans to develop nuclear and other weapons of mass destruction.

ASIA

10 Jan. The North Korean government announces its intention to withdraw from the 1970 Non-Proliferation treaty, which allows international inspection of nuclear facilities. It claims that the action is justified as a response to the 'hostile policy' of President Bush, who has named North Korea as part of an 'axis of evil'. Observers are uncertain whether the North Koreans are trying to develop nuclear weapons because of fear of US attack, or are repeating their nuclear blackmail of 1993 (using an artificially generated crisis to extract greater international aid).

Jan. After US forces operating in Afghanistan violate the Pakistani frontier while searching for Taliban fighters (29 Dec. 2002), there are widespread anti-USA demonstrations throughout Pakistan.

Mar. The pneumonia-like disease SARS (Severe Acute Respiratory Syndrome) breaks out in Hong Kong and S China. An international panic ensues but then fades.

2 April US forces launch air attacks on Taliban and al-Qaeda operatives based in the Tor Ghar mountains of S Afghanistan, near the Pakistan border.

23–24 April Talks on nuclear testing held in Beijing between the US and North Korea break up when the North Korean government states, provocatively, that it has almost finished the reprocessing of some 8000 spent fuel rods, which will provide it with the plutonium for eight more warheads.

2 May India and Pakistan decide to restore full diplomatic relations.

12 June In Ulan Bator, Mongolia, a mass grave is uncovered containing some 1000 bodies of Buddhist monks. In 1924–40 some 36,000 Buddhists were murdered in Mongolia, a puppet state of the USSR.

13–14 Dec. About 70 people are killed following attacks by Maoist communist rebels in Nepal.

THE AMERICAS

Jan. The US government announces the introduction of 'sky marshals' (armed agents) on airliners to prevent hijackings.

1 Feb. The US space shuttle *Columbia* is destroyed on re-entry into the atmosphere. Its seven astronauts are killed.

4 Mar. At Davao City international airport, on the island of Mindanao in the Philippines, 23 people are killed and 147 are injured when a bomb explodes. An Islamic organization, the Abu Sayyaf group, claims responsibility.

28 May US president Bush signs into law tax cuts of $350 billion over the next 10 years, having originally proposed $726 billion tax cuts during the same period.

26 June Christian Westermann, a senior US State Department expert on chemical and biological weapons, testifies in a closed hearing of the House of Representatives' Intelligence Committee and states that he was forced to modify his view of the Iraqi military threat to suit the purposes of the Bush administration.

7 July President Bush's spokesman says that the president relied on inaccurate information when he stated, in his State of the Union address (Jan.), that 'the British government has learned that Saddam Hussein recently sought significant quantities of uranium in Africa'.

7 Sept. President Bush announces that he will ask Congress for $87 billion to finance military operations and state reconstruction in Afghanistan and Iraq.

17 Sept. President Bush concedes that he has seen no evidence linking Saddam Hussein's regime with the terrorist attacks of 11 Sept. 2001.

SUB-SAHARAN AFRICA

Mar. A government of national unity is established in Côte d'Ivoire in an effort to end the country's civil war.

Mar.–April In Zimbabwe Robert Mugabe's government launches a sustained attack on opponents of his dictatorial rule, leading to the arrest, imprisonment and torture of many hundreds.

3 April In the Democratic Republic of Congo some 1000 people, mostly members of the minority Hema tribe, are killed. Civil war between forces loyal to Rwanda and Uganda, whose aim is eventual control of the vast mineral wealth of the Congo, has resumed. Ugandan-backed forces are widely believed to be responsible for the massacre.

15 May The British government suspends flights in and out of Kenya after Kenyan security claims of an imminent al-Qaeda attack.

11 Aug. Charles Taylor steps down as president of Liberia and flees to Nigeria. Taylor is accused of war crimes as well as backing rebel forces.

23 Sept. Rebel forces in Côte d'Ivoire withdraw from the government of national unity.

3 Dec. Two media executives and a journalist are convicted of genocide by the International Tribunal for Rwanda for their role in inciting the murder of ethnic Tutsis in 1994.

– A rebellion breaks out in the W Sudanese province of Darfur, where rebel groups accuse the government of continuing to oppress black Africans in favour of Arabs. Fighting breaks out between the Janjaweed, a government-sponsored Arab militia, and the non-Arab peoples of the region.

2003-4

AUSTRALASIA AND OCEANIA

18–19 Jan. Bush fires in the suburbs of the Australian capital Canberra kill four people and cause the evacuation of 2500.

ECONOMY AND SOCIETY

Oct.–Nov. England wins the 5th rugby union World Cup, held in Australia.

9–10 Oct. In a cricket test match between Australia and Zimbabwe in Perth, the Australian batsman Matthew Hayden scores 380, a new record individual score for a batsman.

SCIENCE AND TECHNOLOGY

2 July The World Meteorological Organization (WMO) warns that global warming will cause an increase in instances of extreme weather. In June the S of France records temperatures of 40°C (104°F), while in India the pre-monsoon heatwave hits 45–49°C (113–120°F). In the N hemisphere the temperature increases of the 20th century have been the largest recorded for 1000 years.

ARTS AND HUMANITIES

Literature

25 Sept. Edward Said, writer and critic, dies.

Monica Ali, *Brick Lane*, novel.

Anne Applebaum, *Gulag: A History of the Soviet Camps*.

Jeffrey Eugenides, *Middlesex*, novel.

DBC Pierre, *Vernon God Little*, novel.

Michèle Roberts, *The Mistressclass*, novel.

J.K. Rowling, *Harry Potter and the Order of the Phoenix*, children's novel.

Music

Christina Aguilera, 'Beautiful', single.

Daniel Bedingfield, 'Never Gonna Leave Your Side', single.

The Darkness, *Permission to Land*, album.

Katie Melua, *Call off the Search*, album.

Stereophonics, 'Maybe Tomorrow', single.

Justin Timberlake, *Justified*, album.

Film

Robert Altman, *The Company*, starring Malcolm McDowell.

Bruno Barreto, *View from the Top*, starring Gwyneth Paltrow and Mark Ruffalo.

Sofia Coppola, *Lost in Translation*, starring Bill Murray and Scarlett Johansson.

Clint Eastwood, *Mystic River*, starring Tim Robbins and Kevin Bacon.

Peter Jackson, *The Return of the King*.

Kim Ki-duk, *Spring, Summer, Autumn, Winter … and Spring*, starring Oh Yeong-su.

David Mackenzie, *Young Adam*, starring Ewan McGregor.

Michael Moore, *Fahrenheit 9/11*.

Gary Ross, *Seabiscuit*, starring Tobey Maguire.

Gus Van Sant, *Gerry*, starring Casey Affleck and Matt Damon.

Quentin Tarantino, *Kill Bill: Vol 1*, starring Uma Thurman.

Andy and Larry Wachowski, *The Matrix Reloaded* and *The Matrix Revolutions*, starring Keanu Reeves.

Peter Weir, *Master and Commander: The Far Side of the World*, starring Russell Crowe.

2004

EUROPE

28 Jan. The report by former Appeal Court judge Lord Hutton into the circumstances following the apparent suicide of the Ministry of Defence weapons expert David Kelly (17 July 2003) is published. Hutton clears the government of any serious wrongdoing and criticizes the BBC's handling of the claim that the government falsified intelligence relating to Iraq's weapon capability. Favourable press coverage for the government is secured by the leaking of the report's findings in advance of its publication.

3 Feb. Following President Bush's decision in relation to US security services (2 Feb.), British prime minister Tony Blair announces an official inquiry into the quality of the intelligence systems used by Britain to justify its war against Iraq.

10 Feb. The French National Assembly votes by 494 to 36 in favour of a government ban on the wearing of overt religious symbols, including Islamic headscarves and Christian crosses, in the country's state schools.

11 Mar. Ten bombs explode on commuter trains during Madrid's morning rush hour, killing 190 people and injuring more than 1400. Early speculation, fanned by the news manipulation of the ruling conservative Popular Party, blames the Basque separatist group ETA, but Islamist groups are eventually identified as the perpetrators of the atrocity. The Popular Party (PP) faces a general election and fears that the real cause for the tragedy will be deemed to be its strong support for the US-led invasion of Iraq, a policy that, according to recent opinion polls, is opposed by over 90% of Spain's population.

14 Mar. In a significant backlash the Popular Party is defeated in the general election by the Spanish Socialist Workers' Party, which has consistently opposed the war in Iraq. Its leader, José Luís Rodríguez, forms a minority government.

15 Mar. Spain's new government pledges the withdrawal of Spain's 1300 troops from Iraq if the UN does not take over all peace-keeping operations by 20 June.

21–28 Mar. In national elections a revived French Socialist Party gains control of 20 out of the country's 21 regional councils. The centre-right government of prime minister Jean-Pierre Raffarin is reconstituted in order to assert its authority.

19 April In a major policy change the British government trails a future decision to allow a national referendum on the proposed new European Constitution once Parliament has ratified the constitution at a future date.

1 May Ten new member-states join the European Union: Cyprus, the Czech Republic, Estonia, Hungary, Latvia, Lithuania, Malta, Poland, Slovakia and Slovenia. The EU is now the world's biggest trading bloc with a population of 455 million people in 25 states.

9 May Chechnya's pro-Russian president, Akhmad Kadyrov, is assassinated in Grozny, capital of the breakaway republic.

14 June Results for elections to the European Parliament reveal a turn-out across Europe of just 44.2% and a mere 28.7% in the EU's 10 new member states. In Britain the UK Independence Party (UKIP), which is campaigning for British withdrawal from the EU, doubles its previous share of the vote (7%). The Spanish Socialist Workers' Party consolidates its position after its recent election as the national government. More established governments do badly, especially in France and Germany.

14 July The official inquiry by Lord Butler into the intelligence used by the British government to justify its war on Iraq is published. The inquiry decides that the intelligence was defective and advances a doctrine of collective failure which avoids the attribution of particular and individual responsibility. The inquiry casts serious doubt on the claim, made in the government's dossier of Sept. 2002, that Iraq was capable of launching such weapons within 45 minutes.

29 Aug. In elections in Chechnya, the favoured candidate of the Russian government, Maj-Gen. Alu Alkhanov, becomes president despite considerable evidence of electoral irregularities.

1 Sept. In Beslan, a town in the republic of North Ossetia, S Russia, Chechen separatists force their way into the local school, shoot those who resist and detain the school's pupils as hostages in their campaign against the Russian government's military campaign in Chechnya. Russian troops storm the building after bombs start to explode inside the school (3 Sept). More than 200 lives are lost, including 27 of the hostage-takers; some 700 are injured, including 259 children. Foreign criticism of President Putin's policy of armed repression in Chechnya increases.

14 Sept. Britain's Labour government yields to parliamentary pressure and agrees to shorten the two-year period previously set by the government before the ban on hunting with hounds is implemented. It is now proposed that the ban will take effect in July rather than Nov. 2006.

19 Sept. In regional elections in the former East German states of Brandenburg and Saxony, neo-Nazi parties win 6% and 7% of the votes respectively. The party of Democratic Socialism (successor to the former East German Communist Party) wins 28% and 23.6% respectively. The results reflect the depth of the economic crisis in the former East Germany where unemployment has risen to more than 20%.

17 Oct. In Belarus, voters approve an amendment to the constitution allowing President Alexander Lukashenko to seek re-election for a third term in 2006.

29 Oct. In Rome, European heads of government sign a treaty introducing the European Constitution. But referendums on the constitution will have to be held in at least nine EU countries, including Britain.

21 Nov. In Ukraine, the Russian-backed prime minister Viktor Yanukovich claims victory in the country's presidential election. Viktor Yushchenko, the opposition candidate, refuses to accept the result and accuses the Ukrainian government of electoral fraud. Independent exit polls seem to confirm Yuschenko's claim and mass protests spread across Ukraine: the more Catholic and European-leaning W areas side with Yushchenko; while the more Orthodox, Russian-leaning and Russian-speaking areas of C and E Ukraine support Yanukovich. The Ukrainian Supreme Court rules that the election was rigged (3 Dec.) and orders that a new run-off between the two candidates should take place on 26 Dec.

8 Dec. The French national assembly passes a government bill which punishes sexist and homophobic insults with a maximum of six months' imprisonment and a €15,000 fine.

10 Dec. A court in Milan acquits the Italian prime minister Silvio Berlusconi of having bribed judges to protect his commercial interests in the 1980s.

13 Dec. In Romania, the reformist mayor of Bucharest, Traian Basescu, is elected president, defeating Adrian Nastase, candidate of the ruling Social Democrats whose 15 years in power since 1989 have seen the country mired ever deeper in poverty and official corruption.

28 Dec. Viktor Yushchenko wins the re-run Ukrainian presidential election. Yushchenko is sworn in as Ukrainian president on 23 Jan. 2005. Many observers see the result as marking the delayed arrival of full Ukrainian independence from Moscow.

MIDDLE EAST AND NORTH AFRICA

11 Jan. The Grand Ayatollah Ali Sistani, the leading Shiite religious leader, condemns the proposal for an appointed, rather than an elected, transitional national assembly in Iraq. About 100,000 Shiites march through Baghdad in support of Sistani (19 Jan.).

1 Feb. Internal Iraqi strife acquires a new twist with a suicide attack on the Kurdish political party's headquarters in the city of Arbil, N Iraq: more than 100 people are killed and about 250 others are injured.

20 Feb. Conservative candidates gain 149 seats in Iran's national election for membership of the country's parliament, the Majlis. Reformers gain only 65 seats following the decision by the senior constitutional body, the Council of Guardians, to ban most reformist candidates from standing.

22 Mar. Israeli forces assassinate Sheikh Ahmed Yassin, founder and spiritual leader of the Islamic Resistance Movement (Hamas) but also regarded as a terrorist who has plotted the killing of hundreds of Israelis.

31 Mar. In Fallujah, W of Baghdad, local civilians mutilate the corpses of four US civilian contractors.

6 April The uprising organized by the rebel Shiite Muslim cleric Hojatoleslam Moqtada al-Sadr is now spreading in Iraq, and more than 140 Iraqis and 30 US soldiers have been killed in the past three days. Al-Sadr's irregular army has occupied the Shiite holy city of Najaf, while in Fallujah fighting continues, led by Sunni forces loyal to Saddam Hussein.

16 April President Bush allows the UN to assume control of the shape of the interim Iraqi government, the writing of a constitution and the ensuing elections. He thereby abandons previous US plans for a transitional authority.

17 April Israeli security forces assassinate the new leader of Hamas, Abdul-Aziz al-Rantissi.

21 April Four co-ordinated suicide bombings kill 68 people and injure some 100 in the British-controlled city of Basra, Iraq.

29 April After 25 days of intense fighting US Marine battalions are ordered to withdraw from Fallujah and are replaced by an Iraqi force.

April By now the US government believes that Ahmad Chalabi, previously its favourite informant on the Iraqi situation and a prime candidate for high office in the new Iraq, has supplied it with false information and is suspiciously close to Iranian intelligence.

4 May US officials admit that two Iraqi prisoners have been murdered while in US custody and that an investigation by the US army has exposed 'sadistic, blatant and wanton criminal abuses' of Iraqi prisoners at the Abu Ghraib prison.

10 May A Gallup opinion poll shows that for the first time a majority of Americans polled (54%) oppose US policy in Iraq.

11 May A video is released showing the beheading of Nick Berg, a US contractor, by an al-Qaeda linked group in revenge for the 'Satanic degradation' of Iraqi prisoners at Abu Ghraib prison.

16 May The US and Britain draw up plans for a speedy withdrawal of coalition forces from Iraq and declare that coalition forces will leave the country if that is the expressed wish of the Iraqi interim government.

24 May The US and Britain table a draft UN Security Council resolution approving the handover of power to an Iraqi caretaker government on 30 June. Commanders of coalition forces will retain control of day-to-day security and counter-insurgency operations.

30 May At least 22 people are killed by Islamic terrorists who have kidnapped Westerners in Saudi Arabia.

1 June The US-appointed Iraqi governing council dissolves itself and is replaced by a 33 member UN-sponsored government.

8 June The UN Security Council approves unanimously the US–British plan to end the occupation of Iraq by 30 June: the coalition will therefore transfer power to the interim Iraqi administration on 30 June and a transitional government, to be elected in Jan. 2005, will draw up a constitution under which a constitutionally elected government will take office at the end of 2005. After 30 June military operations by the multinational force can happen only with the consent of the Iraqi interim government.

Aug. In the S Iraqi holy city of Najaf, supporters of the radical cleric Moqtada al-Sadr lead a fresh Shiite uprising, but the rebellion fails to spread to other S Shiite centres. Under the terms of a peace agreement (26 Aug.) Najaf and neighbouring Kufa are designated weapon-free zones and US troops are withdrawn from the two towns.

8 Sept. By now 1000 US soldiers have been killed in Iraq since the start of the invasion and some 7000 members of the American forces have been wounded. The Bush administration has ensured, however, that film crews are banned from filming the return of the coffins to US soil.

14 Sept. In Baghdad, a suicide car bomb kills 47 police volunteers and civilians; in the northern Iraqi town of Baquba 11 policemen are killed in an armed ambush. Responsibility for both attacks is claimed by the United and Holy War group of Abu Musab al-Zarqawi, a Jordanian linked to al-Qaeda, whose stronghold is the town of Fallujah.

30 Sept. After days of violence in Gaza, Israeli prime minister Ariel Sharon authorizes a military campaign to re-occupy the N part of the Gaza Strip.

7 Oct. Three bombs explode in the Egyptian Red Sea resorts of Taba, Nuwelba and Raas al Sultan killing 28 and injuring more than 100, most of them Israeli tourists. The timing of the attack is linked to Israel's military campaign in the Gaza Strip.

8 Oct. Kenneth Bigley, a British hostage held in Iraq, is beheaded by the Islamist terror group led by Abu Musab al-Zarqawi.

11 Oct. The European Union (EU) lifts its 18-year embargo on arms sales to Libya following the country's renunciation of weapons of mass destruction.

29 Oct. In a video statement released on the eve of the US presidential election, Osama bin Laden threatens more violence if the US does not change its policies in the Middle East.

11 Nov. The Palestinian national leader Yasser Arafat dies in a Paris hospital where he has been taken for medical treatment from the compound in Ramallah in which he has been effectively a detainee of the Israel forces for the past three years. Mahmoud Abbas, the secretary-general of the PLO, becomes the Fatah movement's official candidate to succeed Yasser Arafat as president of the Palestinian Authority in elections to be held on 9 Jan.

14 Nov. 20,000 US troops, assisted by 2000 Iraqi national guardsmen, retake Fallujah. The militant Abu Musab al-Zarqawi has, however, already escaped from the city.

21 Dec. In the deadliest single incident involving US troops in Iraq since the start of the war, insurgents attack a US army base near the northern city of Mosul, killing 19 US soldiers.

ASIA

2–3 Mar. Hundreds of rebels belonging to the underground Maoist Communist Party of Nepal launch a major attack on the Royal Nepalese Army in the Bhojpur district of Nepal.

8 Mar. The official newspaper of North Korea, a government mouthpiece, demands the withdrawal of all US forces from South Korea in return for the dismantling of North Korea's nuclear weapons programme.

16 Mar. In the mountainous area bordering Afghanistan the Pakistani army launches a major offensive against Islamic militants associated with al-Qaeda and the Taliban group. By the end of the campaign (30 Mar.) about 150 insurgents are reported killed, but most have escaped through a complex series of tunnels leading from the battlefields to the Afghan border.

13 May The Congress Party gains a surprise victory at the expense of the ruling Hindu-nationalist Bharatiya Janata Party (BJP) in India's general election. The result is seen as a victory for the traditional socialism of the Congress Party and its appeal to the Indian masses who have failed to benefit from the economic modernization presided over by the BJP.

July Floods in Bangladesh drive some 30 million people from their homes.

12 Sept. Pro-democracy parties fare badly in elections to the 60-seat legislative council in Hong Kong. Voters appear wary of offending China's Communist leaders: pro-Beijing factions win 34 seats and those favouring democracy 25 seats.

19 Oct. Khin Nyunt, reformist prime minister of Burma, is forced out of office by the country's ruling military junta. Aung San Suu Kyi, leader of the country's pro-democracy movement, has now been under house arrest for over 16 months, her third such period of detention since 1990.

Oct. Typhoons in Japan kill more than 150 people. A major earthquake hits NW Japan (22 Oct.).

7 Dec. In Kabul, Hamid Karzai, the former interim president, is sworn in as president of Afghanistan following his victory in the country's presidential elections (9 Oct.). 18,000 international troops remain stationed in the country where powerful warlords retain much of their influence.

26 Dec. A *tsunami* (tidal wave) caused by a massive earthquake devastates coastal areas of E and S Asia, making millions homeless, destroying homes and livelihoods and exacting a terrible death toll throughout the region. By the end of Jan. 2005 it is known to have claimed more than 225,000 victims: 166,000 in Indonesia's Aceh province in N Sumatra, 5300 in Thailand, 15,800 in mainland India, 5500 in India's Andaman and Nicobar Islands and 38,000 in Sri Lanka. The *tsunami* also claims the lives of thousands of holidaying Europeans. The exact number of victims will probably never be known. 20 of the 199 inhabited islands of the Maldives are totally destroyed. A huge global relief operation is launched for the disaster's traumatized and beleaguered survivors.

– By now the power to determine prices of raw materials has shifted decisively from the Atlantic to the Pacific region. Chinese economic demand, in particular, is setting the prices for raw materials and oil. In the past 12 years, 200 million people have moved in search of work and training from the W of China to the industrial areas concentrated along the country's Pacific coast. This, one of the great human migrations in history, has resulted in vastly increased levels of technological skill in China.

THE AMERICAS

2 Feb. An independent presidential commission is appointed by President Bush to examine failures by the US intelligence services in relation both to Iraq and other countries suspected

of holding weapons of mass destruction. Secretary of Defence Donald Rumsfeld concedes (4 Feb.) that the US and other Western powers may have been fooled by Iraqi propaganda about the country's military capability.

2 Mar. Senator John Kerry wins nine out of ten state primary and caucus elections and so effectively becomes the Democratic Party's candidate for the US presidency.

24 Mar. Richard Clarke, a former deputy national security adviser (until Oct. 2001), testifies before the National Commission on Terrorist Attacks upon the US, established by the US Congress to investigate the intelligence failures which led to the terrorist attacks of 11 Sept. He states that the government ignored the threat represented by al-Qaeda and concentrated instead on the issue of Iraq's supposed weapons of mass destruction.

5 June Ronald Reagan, US former president (1981–9), dies.

27 June In Mexico City, some 250,000 people take part in a mass demonstration against violent crime. Mexico now has the second highest rate of kidnapping in the world, after Colombia.

22 July In the US the National Commission on Terrorist Attacks publishes its final report on the terrorist attacks of 11 Sept. The Commission concludes that the US government failed to protect the country from the threat posed by al-Qaeda and that 'across the government there were failures of imagination, policy, capabilities and management'.

Aug. In Brazil, the chamber of deputies votes to allow the government to confiscate land from landowners who keep their workers in a state of virtual slavery.

Sept. Hurricane Ivan devastates Grenada, Jamaica, the Cayman Islands and Cuba.

1 Nov. In Uruguay the left-wing alliance Frente Amplio wins the general election, defeating the Colorados and the Blancos (the traditional parties that have ruled Uruguay for some 170 years). Left-wing governments now hold power in Venezuela, Brazil, Uruguay, Argentina, Chile, Peru and Ecuador.

2 Nov. George W. Bush is re-elected US president, defeating the Democratic challenger Senator John Kerry by a margin of 3.5 million votes. Bush becomes the first US president since 1936 to be re-elected at the same time as his party gains seats in both the Senate and the House of Representatives. Bush's victory owes much to the Republican party's targeted canvassing of evangelical Christians.

15 Nov. Gen. Colin Powell resigns as US secretary of state. national security adviser Condoleezza Rice is nominated by President Bush as Powell's successor (16 Nov.).

9 Dec. Representatives of the 12 countries of Latin America sign a new treaty establishing a South American Community of Nations whose aim is the eventual establishment of a common parliament and a single currency. The project builds on the two existing trade blocks of the region: Mercosur, composed of Brazil, Argentina, Uruguay, and Paraguay along with Chile as an associate member; and the Andean Community of Nations

(CAN) composed of Bolivia, Colombia, Ecuador, Peru and Venezuela.

SUB-SAHARAN AFRICA

29 Jan. The leaders of Somalia's 42 warring factions sign a peace agreement in Nairobi, Kenya, which leads to the creation of a transitional legislature whose 275 members are selected from within the country's different clans.

23 Feb. In the Democratic Republic of Congo Mai-Mai warriors are reported to have killed some 100 civilians and seven army officers in the SE province of Katanga.

29 Feb. President Jean-Bertrand Aristide of Haiti resigns suddenly and flees the country following an armed uprising and a series of strikes.

6 Aug. A UN report blaming the government of Sudan for crimes against humanity in the conflict in the W province of Darfur is released (see 2003). By now the Darfur conflict has turned into a major humanitarian crisis: more than a million people have been displaced by the fighting and 70,000 are reported dead from famine and disease. US secretary of state Colin Powell claims that the Sudanese government and the Janjaweed militia are pursuing a policy of genocide against non-Muslim Africans in Darfur (9 Sept.).

6 Nov. In Côte d'Ivoire nine French peacekeepers are killed when government war-planes bomb the rebel stronghold of Bouaké. A 4000-strong French force has been policing the peace deal signed between the government and the rebels (Jan. 2003). In retaliation the French government orders its forces to destroy the entire Côte d'Ivoire air force (9 Nov.). Anti-French rioters take to the streets of the capital, Abidjan.

26 Dec. In coastal areas of Somalia some 300 people are killed by the effects of the Asian *tsunami* (see above).

AUSTRALASIA AND OCEANIA

9 Oct. In a general election in Australia the governing Liberal Party–National Party coalition led by prime minister John Howard defeats the opposition Labour Party led by Mark Latham. Howard begins his fourth consecutive term in office.

Dec. Australia sends police officers and administrators to Papua New Guinea, which is on the verge of collapse. The country shares its problems of gang-warfare, economic collapse and a high incidence of disease in the native population with other Pacific states such as the Solomon Islands, Tonga, Fiji, Vanuatu and Tuvalu.

ECONOMY AND SOCIETY

10–12 April In a cricket test match between England and the West Indies in Antigua, the West Indies batsman Brian Lara scores 400, a new record individual score for a batsman.

Aug. The 28th Olympic Games are held in Athens, Greece.

21 Sept. The National Museum of the American Indian, devoted to the history and traditions of America's native peoples, opens in Washington, D.C.

SCIENCE AND TECHNOLOGY

14 Jan. President Bush relaunches the US space programme with a proposal to establish a permanent manned base on the moon by 2020 and a staging-post for expeditions to Mars by 2030. Total costs for the programme are estimated at between $300 billion and $500 billion.

11 June The Cassini–Huygens space mission, a joint US–European venture launched in 1997, starts its four-year tour of Saturn, its rings and satellites.

ARTS AND HUMANITIES

Literature

24 Sept. The French novelist Françoise Sagan dies.

8 Oct. The French philosopher Jacques Derrida dies.

Isabel Allende, *Kingdom of the Golden Dragon*, novel.

Dan Brown, *The Da Vinci Code*, novel.

Alan Hollinghurst, *The Line of Beauty*, novel.

Philip Roth, *The Plot Against America*, novel.

Colm Tóibín, *The Master*, novel.

Visual Arts and Architecture

– Japanese and Mongolian archaeologists announce that they believe they have discovered the tomb of Genghis Khan at Avraga in C Mongolia.

Anri Sala, *Làkkat*, video installation.

Music

10 June Ray Charles, singer, pianist and saxophonist, who pioneered a fusion of gospel, jazz, blues and country music, dies.

Norah Jones, *Feels Like Home*, album.

Scissor Sisters, *Scissor Sisters*, album.

The Streets, *A Grand Don't Come for Free*, album.

Film

1 July The actor Marlon Brando dies.

Pedro Almodóvar, *Bad Education*, starring Gael García Bernal.

Marc Evans, *Trauma*, starring Colin Firth.

Marc Forster, *Finding Neverland*, starring Johnny Depp and Kate Winslet.

Mel Gibson, *The Passion of the Christ*, starring Jim Caviezel.

Michael Goudry, *Eternal Sunshine of the Spotless Mind*, starring Kate Winslet and Jim Carrey.

Taylor Hackford, *Ray*, starring Jamie Foxx.

Agnès Jaoui, *Look at Me*, starring Marilou Berry and Agnes Jaoui.

Patrice Leconte, *Confidences trop intimes*, starring Sandrine Bonnaire.

Mike Leigh, *Vera Drake*, starring Imelda Staunton.

Govind Nihalani, *Dev*, starring Amitabh Bachchan.

Walter Salles, *Diarios de motocicleta* (The Motorcycle Diaries).

Martin Scorsese, *The Aviator*, starring Leonardo DiCaprio.

Conclusion: Towards One World

On 1 January 2000 people around the world celebrated the arrival of the third millennium. The day was marked and invented according to a Christian calendar – and to that extent it showed how the Christian civilization had permeated the rest of the world to create a neo-Christian cultural consensus. An originally Christian idea of providential purpose had, in its secular form of a belief in progress and human advance, influenced most of the rest of the world during the most recent quarter of the two millennia that had just elapsed. And so the birth of Christ seemed less of a particularly Christian event. The technology and communication systems invented by the West enabled one world to celebrate via television screens and satellite dishes, via mobile phones and radio and personal computers, in the course of 24 hours spread across the time zones. And yet, even as people celebrated together, the global nature of the event showed the cultural diversity of the world.

Many felt that the world was becoming more united, both culturally and economically. The collapse of the communist bloc had removed the doctrinal divisions between capitalism and communism that had fuelled the Cold War. A conflict that had daily held over humanity's collective head the possibility of extermination in nuclear war was over.

Others thought the world was becoming more divided. The growth of Islamic fundamentalism was driving a culture of hostility to the West. The establishment of theocratic states following strict Muslim law in both Iran and Afghanistan seemed to demonstrate that there was a viable and growing alternative to Western values. The horrors of the terrorist attacks on the World Trade Center, in Bali and elsewhere would soon appear to confirm the worst fears of those who felt that this alternative world order, like communism before it, would be incapable of achieving a stable co-existence with the West.

And yet the world was neither as united nor as divided as it might appear. It is true that a clear division existed between the West and the rest of the world. But neither area was homogeneous in cultural terms, nor saw itself as such.

There are many ways of describing the non-Western world. It could be called the Third World, after the Old World of Europe and the New World of the Americas. Developing and underdeveloped are alternative adjectives. Yet none of these terms was quite satisfactory. Latin America – that unique mixture of the European and the indigenous American – was populous and energetic but had been a victim of political and economic instability for most of the 20th century. Africa was not so much developing as

regressing, as country after country fell to dictatorship and tribal violence. Countries run by cruel and inefficient governments were more prone to famine and disease because these corrupt regimes failed to plan ahead, and so lacked reserves of foodstuffs as well as the infrastructure of transport, sanitation and healthcare that could improve the lot of their people.

South Asian civilization shared some of these tragedies. India was theoretically the world's largest democracy and also contained some powerful, regionalized, examples of economic expansion and commercial dynamism. But the sub-continent's power-structures remained vulnerable to local networks of privilege and bribery. China, meanwhile, was showing that economic growth based on abundant manpower was a possibility, as was the combination of political authoritarianism with capitalist economics. Elsewhere in Asia the so-called 'tiger economies' had adapted to the Western capitalist system with a competitive energy.

Some countries managed to cross the divide. Japan showed an interesting amalgam of styles: its technological and economic energies were prodigious and harnessed to Western-style economics; yet its traditional culture was not only preserved but grew and developed in its own way.

Within the West itself, political and economic fortunes were mixed. The triumphalism of the vaunted 'new world order' of 1989 had disappeared – and some very old forms of the European mind were proving resistant and powerful. In Russia and other formerly communist states, capitalism was sometimes no more than the rule of men armed with both guns and government contracts. This problem of legitimacy was not just a Russian one. As the European Union set its heart on enlargement in the first decade of the 21st century, many of the incoming member countries, such as Hungary, Poland and Lithuania, were deemed to be institutionally corrupt by some observers. But similar accusations have been made against the institutions of the European Union itself.

Rising above all these was the increasingly dominant and, some would say, dominating presence of the United States of America. Its language was the global one, and its culture was increasingly seen as the epitome of modernity and sophistication. Even those who rejected the USA and its ways expressed that rejection in American-English when they wished to be understood by a global community. Such rejection could come from within the West itself. In parts of Europe, especially in France, there was a deeply felt hostility to perceived Anglo-American domination. The new world order was seen to be brash and commercial, compared to the Eurocentricity, and particularly Francocentricity, of the 19th century.

The dominance of Western culture has been driven by the success of Western business practice, itself at least in part based on the selective application of a capitalist philosophy that denies trade opportunities to others while preaching open competition.

And the Western agenda of human rights continues to influence world politics, even in areas where communal welfare is seen as traditionally more important than individual rights. The search for human dignity and self-respect is, for many, the dominant theme of the early 21st century at a global level. It is a search for affirmation in the sight of others and by others because all world conflicts now carry with them the burden of a historical awareness of the past oppression that has helped to cause present suffering. The 20th century had been a secularizing century largely because that had been the experience of the West, and the language of anti-Western fury bears the imprint of that same process. Even those who claim to be working for religious goals are often in thrall to a politicized agenda that works its way through religious institutions and sacred language. Much of the new agitation was fundamentalist, the blind certainties of which are an answer of sorts to fear and unhappiness. It has affected not only the politically influential Christian and Islamic religions, but also other faiths, such as Hinduism and Judaism.

There has never been a time when there has been a greater consciousness of living in one world. Other, earlier, civilizations and empires established a dominant culture within their boundaries. Those boundaries seemed to them the limits of culture itself. But the capacity to see a single world with one pair of eyes – a moment that perhaps first arrived when humans first went into space in the 1960s – did have a deep emotional impact on such parochialism. At the same time, disease and suffering can no longer be regionalized – any more than economies can be. In the past, epidemics could affect some areas and be ignored by those who lived elsewhere. Now global travel by jet aircraft by masses of humans means that a newly discovered virus in Southeast Asia is of immediate concern in Europe, North America and elsewhere.

Governments are now finding it difficult to create a political order that expresses these new unities of the human condition. Indeed, the institutional competence and authority of government itself has come into question from the late 20th century onwards in a variety of fundamental ways. Not only Africa but also the Balkans and the Middle East showed the fragility of order. It seemed that the century of total war had yielded to a period of intermittent, smaller scale, conflicts waged within – as well as across – the precarious national boundaries. Even the long-established states are experiencing problems of authority. Economically, the global flows of capital have undermined the capacity of government to plan and control in the name of a national interest. European states, in particular, are struggling to maintain and reform the welfare systems that had helped guarantee social stability in the mid-20th century. The extent of guaranteed constitutional rights has been basic to the liberal state's moral authority and its popular appeal, but the governments of the US and Britain have proved themselves ready to abridge some of those liberties in order to prosecute the war against a stateless terror.

Along the world's north–south divide, mass communications are now conduits for mass empathy and charitable instinct as images of suffering are transmitted from wherever a capricious nature or human savagery has visited death and devastation on the local population. The persistence of such calamitous state-breakdown, as well as the self-interest of prosperous countries fearful of a contagious social disorder, is forcing some of those countries' leaders to consider ways of reducing the debt they are owed by third-world governments.

In both East and West, the loudest and most effective universal voices of the age are those of politicized religions, which reinforce dogmatism and tolerate violence. The emergent history of the 21st century shows that there can be no peace between the nations unless there is first understanding between the religions. Civilization started with a sense of the sacred. Sustaining it, against the odds, requires both the persistence of faith and the graft of good works.

Index

For ease of retrieval, index references specify the year entry or entries (4BC, 1066, 1945) in which the relevant person, event, institution, work of art etc. can be found, rather than the relevant page number. (A brief description of how information is arranged within the year entries will be found on page x at the front of the book.)

Notes for the reader

The Index to *Cassell's Chronology of World History* is arranged on a letter-by-letter basis up to the first comma.

As well as notable people and events in world history (Henry VIII; Gettysburg, battle of), the Index also lists historically significant places (Fashoda; Kosovo; Tiananmen Square), institutions (European Union; Hanseatic League; United Nations), scientific discoveries and technological breakthroughs (atom, splitting of the; telephone, invention of the) as well other key topics of historical interest (slavery; women's suffrage). The titles of significant works in the fields of literature, music, the visual arts and film are also listed.

For ease of retrieval, index references specify the year entry or entries (4BC, 1066, 1945) in which the relevant person, event, institution, work of art etc. can be found, rather than the relevant page number. (A brief description of how information is arranged within the year entries will be found on page x at the front of the book.)

References to historical individuals with the same forename are arranged in the order: saints, popes, rulers. Therefore the index reference to St Paul precedes the index reference to Pope Paul IV which precedes the index reference to Paul I, king of the Hellenes.

Monarchs and emperors with the same first name (Charles I, king of England; Charles VI, king of France; the Holy Roman emperor Charles V) are listed alphabetically according to country: thus French kings called Charles precede Holy Roman emperors called Charles as well as Spanish and Swedish kings of that name.

A

Accident 1967
Accidental Death of an Anarchist 1970
Accidental Tourist, The 1985
Accident Insurance Law (Germany) 1884
Accordionist, The 1911
Accordo 1981
Account of the Foxglove, An 1785
Account of the Sore Throat, Attended with Ulcers 1748
Accursius, Franciscus (Italian jurist) 1260
Acerba 1327
Achaean League 146BC
Achebe, Chinua (Albert Chinualumogo) (Nigerian writer) 1958, 1964, 1987
Achenwall, Gottfried (German historian) 1749
Acheson, Dean (Gooderham) (US statesman) 1949
Achille Lauro (cruise ship) 1985
Achtung Baby 1991
Acis and Galatea 1718
Acker, Kathy (US writer) 1984
Ackermann, Rudolph (German publisher) 1810
Ackroyd, Peter (English writer) 1985
Acosta, José de (Spanish missionary) 1584
Acre, siege of 1189
Actes and Monuments (Foxe's Book of Martyrs) 1563
Action Française movement 1899
Actium, battle of 31BC
Acton, John Emerich Edward Dalberg, 1st Baron (British historian and politician) 1887
Acton Burnell, Parliament at 1283
Acts of the Saints 1643
Adad-nirari III, king of Assyria 811BC
Adages 1500
Adalbert, St 997
Adam, Adolphe-Charles (French composer) 1841
Adam, Robert (Scottish architect) 1728, 1764
Adam Bede 1859
Adam de la Halle (French trouvère) 1262
Adams, Bryan (Canadian singer-songwriter) 1991
Adams, Gerry (Irish politician) 1983
Adams, Henry Brooks (US historian) 1880
Adams, James Hopkins (US politician) 1856
Adams, John (2nd US president) 1735, 1776, 1796, 1798, 1799, 1826, 1828
Adams, John (US composer) 1978, 1985, 1986, 1991
Adams, John Quincy (6th US president) 1825
Adams, Richard (George) (English writer) 1972
Adams, Samuel (US politician) 1775
Adams, Thomas (US inventor) 1872
Adam's Rib 1949
Adaptation 2002
Addington, Henry, 1st Viscount Sidmouth 1801
Addinsell, Richard (British composer) 1941
Addis Ababa, treaty of 1896
Addison, Joseph (English writer) 1672, 1711, 1713, 1719
Additional Petition and Advice 1657
Adelaide (Australia), foundation of 1836
Adelard of Bath (English philosopher) 1100, 1126
Adenauer, Konrad (German politician) 1949, 1963
Aden emergency 1965, 1966
Adiabene, annexation by Roman empire 116
Adid, al-, Fatimid caliph 1171
Admirable Crichton, The 1902

Adolf II, count of Holstein 1143
Adolf of Nassau, king of Germany 1291, 1298
Adolphe 1815
Adolph Frederick (Adolf Fredrik), king of Sweden 1770
Adoration of Captain Shit and the Legend of the Black Star Part Two, The 1998
Adoration of the Child 1435
Adoration of the Magi, The 1483
Adoration of the Shepherds, The 1630 (Champaigne); 1646 (Rembrandt)
Adornment of Spiritual Marriage, The 1350
Adowa, battle of 1896
Adrian, Edgar Douglas, 1st Baron (British physiologist) 1928
Adrianople, battle of 323
Adrianople, battle of 378
Adrianople, battle of 1878
Adrianople, treaty of 1829
Adrianople, truce of 1545
Adulteration of Food, Drink and Drugs Act (UK) 1872
Advancement of Learning, The 1605
Advancement of Science, British Association for the 1831
Adventures of Augie March, The 1953
Adventures of Huckleberry Finn, The 1884
Adventures of Peregrine Pickle, The 1751
Adventures of Robin Hood, The 1938
Adventures of Sherlock Holmes, The 1892
Adventures of the Ten Princes, The 700
Adventures of Tom Sawyer, The 1876
Advise and Consent 1959
Advocates' Library (Edinburgh), opening of 1689
Aegospotami, battle of 405BC
Aelle, king of Northumbria 867
Aemilianus (Marcus Aemilius Aemilianus), Roman emperor 253
Aeneas and Anchises 1618
Aeneas at Delos 1672
Aeneid 19BC, 1557
Aepinus, Franz 1759
Aerius Redivius 1670
Aeroflot begins service 1923
Aeschylus (Greek playwright) 472BC, 456BC
Aesthetic Movement 1894
Aetius, Flavius (Roman soldier) 451
Affleck, Casey (US actor) 2003
Affluent Society, The 1958
Afghanistan, independence of 1921
Afghanistan, Soviet invasion of 1979
Afghanistan, Soviet withdrawal from 1988
Afghanistan, US attacks on 2001, 2003
Afonso I (Afonso Henriques), king of Portugal 1128
Afonso II (the Fat), king of Portugal 1217
Afonso III, king of Portugal 1252
Afonso V, king of Portugal 1438, 1449, 1475
Afonso VI, king of Portugal 1656, 1662, 1667
Africa 1396
Africaine, L' (The African Woman) 1865
African Charter 1961
African Queen, The 1951
Afternoon Men 1931
After the Fall 1964
Agadir crisis 1911

Aga Khan I, Ismaili leader 1817
Aga Khan III (Aga Sultan Sir Mohammed Shah), Ismaili leader 1957
Aga Khan IV, Ismaili leader 1957
Agamemnon, king of Mycenae 1184BC
Agamemnon 456BC
Age (newspaper) 1854
Age de raison, L' (The Age of Reason) 1945
Age d'or, L' (The Golden Age) 1930
Agee, James (US writer) 1957
Age of Elizabeth, The 1950
Age of Innocence, The 1920
Age of Reason, The 1793
Age of Uncertainty, The 1977
Agesander (Greek sculptor) 38BC
Aggeson, Svend (Danish historian) 1187
Agha Mohammad Khan, Qajar shah of Persia 1794, 1797
Aghlabid dynasty, commencement of 800
Agilulf, king of the Lombards 590, 598
Agincourt, battle of 1415
Agis II, king of Sparta 419BC, 412BC
Agnadello, battle of 1509
Agnelli, Giovanni (Italian industrialist) 1899
Agnes Bernauer 1855
Agnese, Paolo (Italian pasta maker) 1824
Agnes Grey 1847
Agony and the Ecstasy, The 1965
Agricola, Georgius (Georg Bauer) (German metallurgist) 1544
Agricola, Gnaeus Julius (Roman soldier) 77, 83, 84
Agrippa, Marcus Vipsanius (Roman soldier) 36BC
Agrippina the Younger (wife of Emperor Claudius I) 50, 54, 59
Aguda (A-ku-ta, T'ai Tsu), emperor of China 1115
Aguilera, Christina (US singer) 2003
Aguirre, Wrath of God 1972
A-Ha (Norwegian group) 1985
Ahern, Patrick Bartholomew (Bertie) (Irish politician) 1997
Ahmad al-Mansur (the Golden), Sa'di sultan of Morocco 1590
Ahmad al-Nasawi (Arab mathematician) 1040
Ahmad ibn Buwayh Asud ad-Dawla, emperor of Persia 983
Ahmad ibn Hanbal (Arab theologian and jurist) 855
Ahmad ibn Tulun, ruler of Egypt 868, 872, 877
Ahmad Mirza, Qajar shah of Persia 1909, 1921, 1925
Ahmad Shah Durrani, emir of Afghanistan 1747
Ahmed I, Ottoman sultan 1603, 1608, 1617
Ahmed II, Ottoman sultan 1691, 1695
Ahmed III, Ottoman sultan 1713, 1730
Ahmose (Ahmosis, Nebpehtyra), 18th dynasty king of Egypt 1550BC
Aida 1871
Aidid, Hussein (Somali soldier and politician) 1996
Aidid, Muhammad Farah (Somali warlord) 1993, 1996
AIDS (Acquired Immune Deficiency Syndrome) 1981, 1983
Aigues-Mortes (France), building of 1241
Aimoin of Fleury (French chronicler) 1010
Ain al-Qudat al-Hamadhani (Sufi mystic) 1131
Ain Jalut, battle of 1260
air conditioning, invention of 1842

A

A

A

B

B

Batriq, al- (Arab scholar) 800
Battaglia di Algeri, La 1965
Battani, al- (Arab astronomer) 877
Batten, George (US advertiser) 1891
battery, invention of 1800
'Battle Hymn of the Republic' 1862
Battle of Maldon, The 993
Battle of San Romano, The 1450
Battle of the Books, The 1704
Battleship Potemkin 1925
Batu Khan, khan of the Golden Horde 1236, 1237, 1238, 1240, 1241, 1255
Baudelaire, Charles-Pierre (French poet) 1857
Baudouin, king of the Belgians 1950, 1992
Bauhaus (Weimar), foundation of 1919
Baum, Lyman Frank (US writer) 1900, 1903
Baumann, E. (German scientist) 1896
Bautista, Francisco (Spanish architect) 1563
Bautzen, battle of 1813
Bautzen, peace of 1018
Bavarian Academy of Science, foundation of 1759
Bavarian Succession, War of the 1778, 1779
Bax and Co. (London) 1851
Baxter, Richard (English churchman) 1651, 1657, 1691
Bayazid (Beyezid) I, Ottoman sultan 1389, 1402, 1403
Bayazid (Beyezid) II, Ottoman sultan 1481, 1512
Baybars (Baibars) I, Mamluk sultan of Egypt and Syria 1260, 1261, 1262, 1263, 1265, 1266, 1268, 1271, 1272, 1277
Bayeux Cathedral, building of 1049
Bayeux Tapestry, stitching of 1080
Bayle, Pierre (French philosopher) 1682, 1684, 1686, 1697, 1706, 1710
Bay of Pigs incident 1961
Bayrakdar Mustafa Pasa (Ottoman politician) 1808
Baytar, al- (Arab writer) 1248
Bazaine, Achille-François (French soldier) 1870
BBC (British Broadcasting Corporation), begins foreign-language broadcasts 1938
BBC (British Broadcasting Corporation), foundation of 1922
Beach Boys, the (US band) 1965, 1966
Beagle, HMS 1831, 1836
Beard, Charles (Austin) (US historian) 1913
Beardsley, Aubrey (English illustrator and writer) 1894, 1898
Beatles, the (British group) 1961, 1963, 1964, 1965, 1966, 1967, 1968, 1969, 1970
Beatles, The (The White Album) 1968
Béatrice et Bénédict 1862
Beatty, Warren (US actor) 1967
Beaufort, Louis de (French historian) 1738
Beau Geste 1926
Beauharnais, Eugène Rose de (French soldier) 1805
Beaumarchais, Pierre-Augustin Caron (French playwright) 1732, 1784, 1799
Beaumont, Francis (English playwright) 1619
Beauregard, Pierre Gustave Toutant (US soldier) 1861
'Beautiful' 2003
Beautiful and the Damned, The 1922
Beautiful Mind, A 2001
Beauty and the Beast 1949
Beauty of Angelica, The 1602

Beauvoir, Simone de (French philosopher) 1949, 1986
Beaux' Stratagem, The 1707
Beaverbrook, (William) Max(well) Aitken, 1st Baron (Canadian newspaper magnate) 1919
Bec Abbey Church (Normandy), building of 1066
Beccaria, Cesare Bonesana (Italian jurist) 1764
Becket, Thomas (English archbishop and politician) 1155, 1162, 1164, 1170
Beckett, Samuel (Irish writer) 1953, 1957, 1958, 1961, 1989
Beckford, William (English writer) 1786
Beckmann, Max (German painter) 1906, 1920, 1923
Becquerel, Antoine-Henri (French physicist) 1896
Bede (the Venerable) (English theologian and scholar) 731
Bedingfield, Daniel (New Zealand-British singer-songwriter) 2003
Bedriacum, battle of 69
Beeching Report (UK) 1963
Bee Gees, the (British-Australian group) 1978
Beerbohm, (Henry) Max(imilian) (English writer) 1911
Beer Hall Putsch (Munich) 1923, 1924
Beethoven, Ludwig van (German composer) 1770, 1795, 1798, 1799, 1800, 1801, 1803, 1804, 1805, 1807, 1808, 1809, 1813, 1814, 1819, 1824, 1826, 1827
Beeton, Isabella (Mrs Beeton) (English writer) 1861
Before and After 1730
Beggar's Banquet 1968
Beggar's Opera, The 1728 (Gay); 1948 (Britten)
Beghard order, foundation of 1200
Begin, Menachem (Israeli politician) 1945, 1977, 1978, 1982, 1983
Beginning and the End, The 1949
Beguine order, foundation of 1200
Behan, Brendan (Irish writer) 1958
Behanzin, king of Dahomey 1892
Behn, Aphra (Ayfara) (English writer) 1640, 1671, 1673, 1688, 1689
Beibl Cyssegr-lan, Y (The Sacred Bible) 1588
Beiderbecke, Bix (US jazz musician) 1924
Beijing, Japanese occupation of 1937
Beijing, peace of 1901
Beijing convention 1860
Beineix, Jean-Jacques (French film director) 1986
Being John Malkovich 1999
'Being with You' 1981
Beirut, Israeli bombing of 1982
Beisan, sack of 1217
Beissel, Johann Conrad (US clergyman) 1732
Beit, Alfred (South African financier) 1880
Bejarano, Gustavo Noboa (president of Ecuador) 2000
Bekenntnisse des Hochstaplers Felix Krull, Die (The Confessions of Felix Krull, Confidence Man) 1954
Bela I, king of Hungary 1060
Bela III, king of Hungary 1173
Bela IV, king of Hungary 1239, 1251
Bel-Ami 1885
'Belfast Child' 1989
Belfry of Bruges and Other Poems, The 1846
Belgium, German occupation of 1940
Belgium, independence of 1830
Belgrade, battle of 1717

Belgrade, treaty of 1739
'Believe' 1998
Believe As You List 1631
Belisarius (Byzantine soldier) 528, 530, 533, 534, 540, 543, 559
Belize, independence of 1981
Bell, Alexander Graham (Scottish-US scientist) 1875, 1876, 1880
Bell, Charles (Scottish surgeon) 1811
Bell, George (Kennedy Allen) (English prelate) 1944
Bellamy, Edward (US writer) 1888
Bellarmine, Roberto (St Francis) (Italian theologian) 1542, 1622
Bellay, Joachim du (French writer) 1549
Belleau Wood, battle of 1918
'Belle Dame Sans Merci, La' 1820
Belle de jour 1967
Belle et la bête, La (Beauty and the Beast) 1946 (film); 1994 (opera)
Belle Hélène, La (Fair Helen) 1864
Bell for Adano, A 1944
Bellini, Gentile (Venetian painter) 1507
Bellini, Giovanni (Venetian painter) 1505, 1516
Bellini, Vincenzo (Italian composer) 1830, 1831, 1835
Bell Jar, The 1963
Bellow, Saul (Canadian-US writer) 1944, 1953, 1959, 1964, 1970, 1975, 1982
Belly of an Architect, The 1987
Belmondo, Jean-Paul (French actor) 1959
Beloved 1987
Belshazzar, king of Babylon 546BC
Belshazzar's Feast 1931
Ben Ali, Zine al-Abidine (president of Tunisia) 1987
Benavides, Oscar Raimundo (president of Peru) 1933
Ben Bella, Mohammed Ahmed (president of Algeria) 1962
Bend in the River, A 1979
Bend Sinister 1947
Benedict IX (Theophylactus), pope 1045, 1046, 1047
Benedict VIII (Theophylactus), pope 1014, 1018
Benedict X (John Mincius), pope 1058
Benedict XI (Niccolò Boccasini), pope 1303, 1304
Benedict XII (Jacques Fournier) pope 1334, 1336, 1342
Benedict XIII (Pedro de Luna), antipope 1409, 1417
Benedict XIV (Lorenzo Lambertini), pope 1740, 1753, 1758
Benedict XV (Giacomo della Chiesa), pope 1914, 1922
Benedictine order, foundation of 529
Benedict of Nursia, St 529
Benefactors 1984
Benes, Eduard (president of Czechoslovakia) 1918, 1935, 1938
Benevento, battle of 1266
Benevento Cathedral (Italy), rebuilding of 1114
Bengal, Indian invasion of 1971
Ben-Gurion, David (Israeli politician) 1948, 1973
Ben-Hur 1925 (Niblo); 1959 (Wyler)
Ben-Hur, A Tale of the Christ 1880
Benigni, Roberto (Italian actor) 1997
Benington, battle of 1777
Benjedid, Chadli (president of Algeria) 1978, 1992
Bennett, Alan (English playwright and actor) 1968, 1991

B

Biruni, Aby Raihan al- (Persian scholar) 1048
Bishop, Maurice (Grenadian politician) 1979, 1983
Bishops' Wars: First 1639; Second 1640
Bismarck, Otto Eduard Leopold, Fürst von (Prussian
  politician) 1870, 1871, 1872, 1878, 1879, 1881,
  1884, 1887, 1888, 1890, 1891
Bismarck (German battleship) 1941
Bismarck Sea, battle of the 1943
Bitonto, battle of 1733
Bitter Sweet 1929
'Bitter Sweet Symphony' 1997
Bizet, Georges (French composer) 1863, 1875
Björk (Gundmundsdottir) (Icelandic singer) 1993
Black, James M(ilton) (US composer)
Black, Joseph (Scottish physicist) 1755
Black and Tans 1920
Black and White 1951
Black Beauty: The Autobiography of a Horse 1877
Blackboard Jungle, The 1954
Black Box (Italian group) 1989
Black Comedy 1966
Black Crook, The 1866 (musical)
Black Death reaches Europe 1346
Black Dogs 1992
Black Flag, The 1936
Blackfriars Theatre, London, opening of 1596
Black Friday on Wall Street 1869
Black Hand organization 1911, 1914
Black Hawk (chief of the Sauk and Fox) 1832
Black Lamb and Grey Falcon 1941
Black List, Section H 1971
Blackmail 1929
Black Mischief 1932
Black Monday on London Stock Exchange 1987
Blackmore, R(ichard) D(oddridge) (English writer)
  1869
Black Muslim movement, foundation of 1931
Black Narcissus 1939 (novel); 1947 (film)
'Black Night' 1970
Black Prince, The 1973
Black Robe, The 1881
Black September (Palestinian terror group) 1972
Blackstone, William (English jurist) 1769
Black Thursday on Wall Street 1929
Black Wednesday in UK 1992
Blade Runner 1982
Bladensburg, battle of 1814
Blair, Tony (Anthony Charles Lynton) (British politician)
  1994, 1997, 1998, 1999, 2003, 2004
Blake, Robert (English sailor) 1655, 1656, 1657
Blake, William (English writer and artist) 1783, 1789,
  1794, 1795, 1804, 1820
Blakelock, PC Keith, murder of (UK) 1985
'Blame it on the Bossa Nova' 1963
Blanc, (Jean-Joseph-) Louis (French politician) 1839
Blanchard, Jean-Pierre (-François) (French inventor)
  1785
Blanche of Castile, queen regent of France 1226
Blandings Castle 1935
Blasphemy Act (UK) 1648
Blast 1914
Blaue Reiter (Blue Rider) 1911
'Blaze of Glory' 1990
Blazing Saddles 1974

Bleak House 1853
Blechtrommel, Die (The Tin Drum) 1959 (novel);
  1979 (film)
Blendung, Die (The Blending) 1935
Blenheim, battle of 1704
Blenheim Palace, building of 1705
Blériot, Louis (French aviator) 1909
Blessings of Peace, The 1630
Bligh, William (English sailor) 1787
Blind Assassin, The 2000
Blindness 1926
Blithedale Romance, The 1852
Blithe Spirit 1941 (play); 1945 (film)
Blitz, the 1940
Blixen, Karen *see* Dinesen, Isak
Bloch, Ernest (US composer) 1916, 1926, 1934
Bloch, Marc-Ferdinand (French historian) 1916
Bloemfontein, convention of 1854
Bloemfontein conference 1899
Blois, treaty of 1504
Blonde on Blonde 1966
Blonde Venus 1932
Blondie (US band) 1978
Blondin, Charles (Jean-François Gravelet) (French
  acrobat) 1859
Blood and Guts in High School 1984
Blood and Sand 1922
Blood in the Fields 1997
Blood Knot, The 1961
Blood on the Tracks 1975
Blood River, battle of 1838
Bloody Assizes 1685
Bloody Friday (Belfast) 1972
Bloody Sunday (Dublin) 1920
Bloody Sunday (Londonderry/Derry) 1972, 1998
Bloody Sunday (St Petersburg) 1905
Bloom, Allan (US philosopher) 1987
Bloomer, Amelia Jenks (US reformer) 1851
Blount, Charles, 8th Baron Mountjoy (English soldier)
  1603
Blow, John (English composer) 1670, 1685, 1697,
  1708
'Blowin' in the Wind' 1961, 1962
Blow-Up 1966
Blücher, Gebhard Leberecht von (Prussian soldier)
  1742, 1813, 1814, 1815
Blue Angel, The 1930
Blue Boy 1779
Blue Danube, The 1867
Blue 11 1961
Blue Lines 1991
'Blue Moon' 1961
Blue Nude 1919
Blue Streak, cancellation of (UK) 1960
'Blue Suede Shoes' 1956
Blue Velvet 1986
Blue Window, The 1911
Blum, Léon (French politician) 1935, 1936, 1938
Blundell, James (British physician) 1818
Blunt, Anthony (British double agent) 1979
Blur (British band) 1994, 1995, 1997
Blur 1997
Blyton, Enid (English writer) 1949
Boating at Argenteuil 1875

Boccaccio, Giovanni (Italian writer) 1353
Boccanegra, Simon (Genovese politician) 1339,
  1363
Boccioni, Umberto (Italian artist) 1910
Bock, Jerry (US composer) 1964
Böcklin, Arnold (Swiss painter) 1880
Bock's Car 1945
Bocskay, István, prince of Transylvania 1606
Bodel, Jean (French poet) 1160, 1202
Bodin, Jean (French political writer) 1576, 1580
Bodleian Library (Oxford), opening of 1602
Bodley, Thomas (English scholar) 1598
Boehme, Jakob (German mystic) 1612
Boeing 707, introduction of 1958
Boekelszoon, Jan (John of Leyden) (Dutch religious
  leader) 1535
Boerhaave, Hermann (Dutch physician) 1708
Boer Wars: First 1881; Second 1899, 1900, 1902
Boesky, Ivan (US financier) 1986, 1987
Boesman and Lena 1968
Boethius, Anicius Manlius Severinus (Roman
  philosopher) 510, 522, 524
Boeuf sur le toit, Le 1919
Boffrand, Gabriel-Germain (French architect) 1712,
  1736
Bogarde, Dirk (British actor) 1961, 1967, 1971
Bogardus, James (US inventor) 1849, 1862
Bogart, Humphrey (US actor) 1941, 1942, 1946,
  1948, 1951
Bogdanovich, Peter (US film director) 1971
Bogomils 1022, 1110; *see also* Cathars
Bogside, battle of 1969
Bohème, La (The Bohemian Girl) 1896
'Bohemian Rhapsody' 1975
Bohemond II, prince of Antioch 1130
Bohemond III (the Stammerer), prince of Antioch 1164
Bohr, Niels Henrik David (Danish physicist) 1913,
  1922
Boileau-Despréaux, Nicolas (French writer) 1666,
  1674
Bokassa, Jean-Bedel (president of Central African
  Republic) 1965, 1977, 1979
Boke Named the Governor, The 1531
Boléro 1928
Boleslav I (the Cruel), prince of Bohemia 929
Boleslav II, prince of Bohemia 973
Boleslav I (Khrobry), king of Poland 992, 1000, 1002,
  1005, 1007, 1012, 1018, 1024, 1025
Boleslav II (the Bold), king of Poland 1076, 1081,
  1083
Boleslav III (the Wry-mouthed), king of Poland 1107,
  1109, 1138
Boleslawski, Richard (Polish film director) 1935
Bolívar, Simón (the Liberator) (S American
  revolutionary leader) 1811, 1813, 1815, 1819,
  1821, 1824, 1825, 1827, 1830
Bolivia, independence of 1825
Böll, Heinrich (German writer) 1963, 1971
Bolland, John (Jesuit scholar) 1643
Bologna, Concordat of 1516
Bologna, Giovanni de (Jean de Boulogne) (Flemish
  sculptor) 1590
Bologna, treaty of 1515
Bolshoi Ballet, foundation of 1776

B

B

Butt, Isaac (Irish nationalist) 1870
Butter, Nathaniel (English journalist) 1622
Buwayhid dynasty, commencement of 946
Buxar, battle of 1764
Buxtehude, Dietrich (Danish composer) 1673, 1705, 1707
Byatt, A(ntonia S(usan) (English writer) 1990
Bygmester Solnes (The Master Builder) 1893
Byng, George (English sailor) 1718
Byng, John (English sailor) 1757
Byrd, William (English composer) 1543, 1572, 1575, 1589, 1607, 1611, 1623
Byrd of Westover, William (American colonist) 1737
Byrds, the (US group) 1965
Byrhtnoth, ealdorman of East Anglia 991
Byrne, Gabriel (Irish actor) 1995
Byron, George Gordon, 6th Baron (Lord Byron) (English poet) 1812, 1814, 1818, 1819, 1823, 1824
Byzantium, foundation of c.659BC
Byzantium, sack of 196
Byzantium *see also* Constantinople *and* Istanbul
Bzura, battle of the 1939

C

Cabal (English ministry) 1667
Cabaret 1966 (musical); 1972 (film)
Cabinet of Dr Caligari, The 1919
Cabiz (Muslim theologian) 945
Cable, George Washington (US writer) 1879
Cabot, John (Giovanni Caboto) (Venetian explorer) 1496, 1497, 1498
Cabot, Sebastian (English explorer) 1496
Cabral, Gonçalo Velho (Portuguese explorer) 1432
Cabral, Pedro Alvarez (Portuguese explorer) 1500
Ca'da Mosto (Cadamosto), Alvise (Venetian explorer) 1455, 1507
Cadbury, John (Quaker businessman) 1824
Cadbury, William (British reformer) 1909
Cade, Jack (English rebel leader) 1450
Cadillac, Antoine Laumet de la Mothe, sieur de (French pioneer) 1701
Cadiz, sack of 1587, 1596
Cadmus and Hermione 1673
Cadwallon, king of Gwynedd 633
Caen, sack of 1346
Caesar and Cleopatra 1906
Caesarion (son of Cleopatra and Julius Caesar) 44BC, 30BC
Caetano, Marcello José das Neves Alves (Portuguese politician) 1968, 1974
Cage, John (US composer) 1942, 1952, 1992
Cage, Nicolas (US actor) 1995
Cagney, James (US actor) 1931
Cailler, François-Louis (Swiss confectioner) 1819
Cailletet, Louis-Paul (French physicist) 1877
Caine, Michael (British actor) 1964, 1966, 1971
Caine Mutiny, The 1951 (novel); 1954 (film)
Cairo, British occupation of 1882
Cairo Conference 1943
Caisse des Depots et Consignations (France), foundation of 1816
Caius, John (English physician) 1510, 1552
Cajetan (Tommaso de Vio), Cardinal 1518

Calais, retaken by France 1558
Calais, siege of 1346
Calais, taken by the English 1347
Calais Pier 1801
Calatafimi, battle of 1860
Calcutta, Black Hole of 1756
Calcutta University, foundation of 1857
Calderón, battle of 1811
Calderón de la Barca, Pedro (Spanish playwright) 1635, 1681
Cale, John (British singer-songwriter) 1974
Caledonian Canal, building of 1803
'California Girls' 1965
Caligula (Gaius Caesar), Roman emperor 37, 41
Calinescu, Armand (Romanian politician) 1939
Calixtus II (Guido di Borgogne), pope 1119
Calixtus III (Giovanni di Strumi), antipope 1168
Callaghan, James (British politician) 1976, 1977, 1979, 1980
Callas, Maria (Greek opera singer) 1956, 1977
Calles, Plutarco Elias (president of Mexico) 1928, 1934
Calley, William Laws (US soldier) 1968, 1971
Callinicium, battle of 530, 532
Call me Madam 1950
Call off the Search 2003
Call of the Wild, The 1903
Call to the Unconverted, A 1657
Calvin, John (Jean Cauvin) (French-Swiss religious reformer) 1509, 1519, 1532, 1536, 1553, 1554, 1564
Calvino, Italo (Italian writer) 1972, 1973, 1979
Camaldoli (Camaldolese Benedictine) order, foundation of 1012
Camargo, Marie-Anne de Cupis de (French dancer) 1726
Cambodia, US bombing of 1969
Cambodia, Vietnamese invasion of 1970, 1978, 1985
Cambrai, battle of 1917
Cambrai, League of 1508, 1509, 1510
Cambrai, treaty of 1529
Cambriae descriptio 1188
Cambridge University, foundation of 1209
Cambyses I, king of Persia 550BC
Cambyses II, king of Persia 546BC, 525BC
Camden, battle of 1780
Camden, William (English historian) 1551, 1586, 1615
Camelot 1960
Cameron, James (Canadian film director) 1984, 1991, 1997
Camilla, or a Picture of Youth 1796
Camille 1936
Camisards, rebellion of 1702
Camlan, battle of 537
Camões, Luis Vaz de 1580
Camomile Lawn, The 1984
Campaign for Nuclear Disarmament (CND) (UK) 1957
Campaign of Igor, The 1185
Campaldino, battle of 1289
Campanella, Tommaso (Italian philosopher) 1623, 1639
Campbell Soup Company 1869
Campbell, John (English sailor and inventor) 1757

Campbell, Joseph (US fruit merchant) 1869
Campbell's Tomato Soup Can 1965
Campbell-Bannerman, Henry (British politician) 1905, 1906, 1908
Camp David Accord 1978
Campion, Edmund (English martyr) 1580, 1581
Campion, Thomas (English writer and physician) 1567, 1620
Campi Raudii, battle of 101BC
Campo Formio, treaty of 1797
Cámpora, Héctor José (president of Argentina) 1973
Camus, Albert (French writer) 1942, 1947, 1951, 1956
Canabus, Nicholas, usurping Byzantine emperor 1204
Canada, formation of Dominion of 1867
Canada Act (UK) 1791
Canadian Pacific Railroad Co. 1887
Canal du Midi, building of 1681
Canaletto (Giovanni Antonio Canal) (Italian artist) 1725, 1740, 1746, 1768
Cancer Ward 1968
Cancioneiro geral 1516
Candia, siege of 1667
Candiano I, Pietro (doge of Venice) 887
Candide, ou l'optimisme (Candide, or Optimism) 1759
'Candle in the Wind '97' 1997
Canetti, Elias (Bulgarian writer) 1935
Cannae, battle of 216BC
Canning, George (British politician) 1809, 1822, 1827
Cano, Sebastien del (Juan Sebastián de Elcano) 1519
Canon of Medicine 1037
Canossa, submission at 1077
Canova, Antonio (Italian sculptor) 1801, 1822
Cantata Profane 1930
Cantatrice chauve, La (The Bald Prima Donna) 1950
'Can't Buy Me Love' 1964
Cantemir, Dimitrie (Dmitry Konstantinovich Kantemir) (Moldavian linguist and scholar) 1719
Canterbury Cathedral (Kent), building of 1070
Canterbury Tales, The 1387 (collection of tales); 1972 (film)
'Can't Get You out of My Head' 2001
'Can the Can' 1973
Canticle of Brother Sun, The 1225
Cantiones Sacrae
Canto General 1950
Canton, John (English physician) 1750
Canto Novo (New Poem) 1882
Cantos I–XVI 1925
Canute *see* Cnut
Can You Forgive Her? 1864
Canzoniere 1366
Cape Helles, battle of 1915
Capel, Arthur, 21st earl of Essex (English politician) 1679
Capeller, M.A. (French chemist) 1723
Cape Matapan, battle of 1941
Cape Passaro, battle of 1718
Capetian dynasty, commencement of 987
Cape Town (South Africa), foundation of 1652
Cape Verde Islands, discovery of 1455
Cape Verde Islands, independence of 1975
Capitale de la douleur (Capital of Sorrow) 1926
Capitulatio de partibus saxoniae 782

C

Cateau-Cambrésis, treaty of 1559
Catesby, Robert (English conspirator) 1605
Cathars (Albigensians) 1051, 1167, 1179, 1205, 1213, 1215, 1218, 1229; see also Bogomils
Catherine I, tsarita of Russia 1725
Catherine II (the Great), tsarita of Russia 1729, 1762, 1764, 1766, 1770, 1776, 1781, 1786, 1787, 1796
Catherine de Medici, queen of France (wife of Henry II) 1519, 1559, 1560, 1567, 1572
Catherine Howard, queen of England (5th wife of Henry VIII) 1540, 1542
Catherine of Aragon, queen of England (1st wife of Henry VIII) 1497, 1502, 1509, 1529, 1531, 1532
Catherine of Braganza, queen of England (wife of Charles II) 1661, 1662, 1705
Catherine of Siena, St 1377
Catherine Parr, queen of England (6th wife of Henry VIII) 1543, 1548
Cathleen ni Houlihan 1902
Catholic Emancipation Act (UK) 1829
Catholic League 1525, 1586, 1588, 1594, 1620, 1626, 1629, 1651
Catiline (Lucius Sergius Catilina) (Roman politician) 64BC, 63BC
Catiline, His Conspiracy 1611
Cato 1713
Cato the Elder (Marcus Porcius Cato) (Roman orator) 150BC, 149BC
Cats 1981
Cattaneo, Peter (British film director) 1997
Catullus, Gaius Valerius (Roman poet) 56BC
Catulus, Quintus Lutatius (Roman consul) 101BC, 78BC
Caucasian Chalk Circle, The 1948
Caudine Forks, battle of 321BC
Cavaignac, Louis-Eugène (French soldier) 1848
Cavalcade 1931
Cavalcanti, Guido (Florentine poet) 1300
Cavalleria rusticana (Rustic Chivalry) 1890
Cavalli, Francesco (Italian composer) 1654
Cave, The 1994
cave art in Europe 32,000–14,000 BP; 17,000 BP
Cavell, Edith (British nurse) 1915
Cavendish, Frederick Charles (British politician) 1882
Cavendish, Henry (English physicist) 1784
Cavendish, William, 4th earl and 1st duke of Devonshire 1688
Cavendish (Candish), Thomas (English navigator) 1586
Cavern Club (Liverpool, England) 1961
Caves du Vatican, Les (The Vatican Cellars) 1914
Caviana, treaty of 1441
Cavour, Camillo Benso, count of (Italian politician) 1852, 1855, 1858, 1861
Cawley, Thomas (English physician) 1783
Caxton, William (English printer) 1475, 1476, 1485, 1491
Cayley, George (English inventor) 1853
CBS (Columbia Broadcasting System), foundation of 1928
Ceausescu, Nicolae (president of Romania) 1965, 1966, 1986, 1988, 1989
Ceawlin, king of the West Saxons 577
Cecil, Robert, 1st earl of Salisbury (English politician) 1612

Cecil, Robert (Arthur Talbot Gascoyne), 3rd marquis of Salisbury (British politician) 1881, 1885, 1886, 1892, 1895, 1900, 1902
Cecil, William, 1st Baron Burghley (English politician) 1520, 1558, 1598
Cecilia 1782
Cédras, Raoul (military ruler of Haiti) 1991, 1994
Cefalu Cathedral (Sicily), building of 1131, 1148
celeripede (early bicycle), invention of 1816
Celestine III (Giacinto Bobo-Orsini), pope 1191, 1196, 1198
Celestine IV (Goffredo Castiglioni), pope 1241
Célibataires, Les (The Bachelors) 1934
Céline, Louis-Ferdinand (Louis-Ferdinand Destouches) (French writer) 1932
Cellini, Benvenuto (Italian writer) 1500, 1543, 1545, 1571
Celsius, Anders (Swedish scientist) 1736, 1742
Celsus, Aulus Cornelius (Roman physician) c.30
Celtic Twilight, The 1893
Cement Garden, The 1978
Cena de le Ceneri, La (The Ash Wednesday Supper) 1584
Cenerentola, La (Cinderella) 1817
Central America, Federation of 1823, 1838
Central America, SS 1857
Central Pacific Railroad, building of 1861, 1869
Central Park (New York), building of 1857
Cerha, Friederich (Austrian composer) 1979
Cermak, Anton Joseph (US politician) 1933
Cervantes (Saavedra), Miguel de (Spanish writer) 1547, 1571, 1585, 1605, 1615, 1616
Cetewayo (Zulu chief) 1879
Cet obscur objet du désir (That Obscure Object of Desire) 1977
Ceylan, Nuri Bilge (Turkish film director) 2002
Cézanne, Paul (French painter) 1873, 1874, 1882, 1892, 1900, 1902, 1906, 1907
Cien años de soledad (A Hundred Years of Solitude) 1967
Chabon, Michael (US writer) 2001
Chaban-Delmas, Jacques (French politician) 1969
Chabot, Anthony (US miner) 1852
Chacabuco, battle of 1817
Chaco War 1935
Chadwick, Edwin (British reformer) 1842
Chadwick, Florence (British swimmer) 1951
Chadwick, James (British physicist) 1932
Chaeronea, battle of 338BC
Chaeronea, battle of 86BC
Chagall, Marc (French artist) 1911, 1915, 1924, 1928, 1985
Chagrin et la pitié, La (The Sorrow and the Pity) 1970
'Chain Reaction' 1986
Chaises, Les (The Chairs) 1952
Chalabi, Ahmad (Iraqi informer) 2004
Chalcis, battle of 429BC
Chaldiran, battle of 1514
Challe, Maurice (French soldier) 1961
Challenger disaster 1986
Châlons, battle of 451
Chamberlain, (Arthur) Neville (British politician) 1937, 1938, 1939, 1940

Chamberlain, Joseph (Austen) (British politician) 1886, 1895, 1903
Chambers, Ephraim (English encyclopedist) 1728
Chambers, John (Graham) (British sportsman) 1867
Chambers, Robert (Scottish publisher) 1844
Chambers, Whittaker (US journalist) 1948
Chambers, William (English architect) 1786
Chambord, treaty of 1552
Chamorro, Pedro Joaquin (Nicaraguan publisher) 1978
Chamorro, Violeta Barrios de (president of Nicaragua) 1990
Chamorro Vargas, Emiliano (Nicaraguan politician) 1926
Champaigne, Philippe de (French artist) 1630, 1636, 1650
Champlain, Samuel de (French pioneer) 1608, 1613
Champollion, Jean-François (French historian) 1822
Chanak crisis 1922
Chancellor, Richard (English explorer) 1553
Chancellorsville, battle of 1863
Chandesvara (Indian writer) 1314
Chandler, Asa (US pharmacist) 1891
Chandler, Raymond (Thornton) (US writer) 1939
Chandragupta I, ruler of India 320
Chandragupta, Mauryan emperor 321BC, c.293BC
Chanel, Coco (Gabrielle) (French designer) 1913, 1921
Chang, Jung (Chinese writer) 1992
Changing Room, The 1971
Changsu, king of Korea 427
Channel Four (UK) 1982
Channel Tunnel (UK and France) 1986, 1994
Channing, William (Ellery) (US minister) 1819
Chanson d'Antioche 1225
Chanson de Roland, La (The Song of Roland) 778, 1095
Chapeau de paille d'Italie, Un 1851
Chaplin, Charlie (British-US actor) 1913, 1919, 1921, 1925, 1931, 1936, 1940, 1977
Chapman, George (English poet and dramatist) 1598, 1608, 1614, 1615
Chappaquiddick Island 1969
Character of a Trimmer, The 1688
Characterie: The Arte of Shorte, Swifte and Secrete Writing 1588
Chard, John (Rouse Merriott) (British soldier) 1879
Chardin, Jean-Baptiste (French artist) 1699, 1728, 1732, 1737, 1738, 1739, 1775, 1779
Chares of Lindos (Greek sculptor) 280BC
'Charge of the Light Brigade, The' 1854
Charitable Cookery, or the Poor Man's Regenerator 1847
Charlemagne (Charles the Great), king of the Franks and emperor of the W 768, 771, 772, 773, 774, 777, 780, 782, 783, 785, 796, 800, 801, 802, 804, 812, 813, 814
Charles I, emperor of Austria 1916, 1918
Charles I, king of Bohemia see Charles IV, Holy Roman Emperor
Charles I, king of England, Scotland and Ireland 1600, 1623, 1624, 1625, 1626, 1628, 1629, 1632, 1633, 1637, 1638, 1639, 1640, 1641, 1642, 1644, 1646, 1647, 1648, 1649

C

Constans II Pogonatus, Byzantine emperor 655, 663, 668

Constant Nymph, The 1943

Constant (de Rebecque), Benjamin (French politician) 1815

Constantine I (the Great, Flavius Valerius Aurelius Constantinus), Roman emperor 306, 311, 312, 313, 314, 321, 324, 325, 326, 330

Constantine II (Flavius Claudius Constantinus), Roman emperor 337, 340

Constantine III (Flavius Claudius Constantinius), usurping Roman emperor 407, 409, 411

Constantine IV Pogonatus, Byzantine emperor 668, 685

Constantine V Copronymus, Byzantine emperor 741, 742, 745, 746, 775

Constantine VI, Byzantine emperor 780, 790, 792, 797

Constantine VII (Porphyrogenitus), Byzantine emperor 920, 959

Constantine VIII, Byzantine emperor 976, 1025, 1028

Constantine IX Monomachus, Byzantine emperor 1042, 1045, 1055

Constantine X Ducas, Byzantine emperor 1059

Constantine XI Palaeologus, Byzantine emperor 1448, 1453

Constantine I, king of the Hellenes 1920, 1922

Constantine II, king of the Hellenes 1964, 1967

Constantine I, king of Scotland 862

Constantine Bodin, king of Zeta 1100

Constantine the African (Constantinus Africanus) (Latin scholar) 1087

Constantinople, crusaders riot in 1097

Constantinople, dedication of 330

Constantinople, destroyed by earthquake 1509

Constantinople, name changed to Istanbul 1930

Constantinople, sack of 1204

Constantinople, siege of 717

Constantinople, siege of 1422

Constantinople, siege of 1453

Constantinople, treaty of 1479

Constantinople, treaty of 1573

Constantinople, treaty of 1700

Constantinople, treaty of 1724

Constantinople, treaty of 1784

Constantinople *see also* Byzantium *and* Istanbul

Constantinople conference 1877

Constantius I Chlorus (Aurelius Valerius Constantius), Roman emperor 305, 306

Constantius II (Flavius Julius Constantius), Roman emperor 337, 350, 353, 356, 357, 361

Constantius III, Roman emperor 411, 421

Constitutio Domus Regis 1136

Constitution Act (Canada) 1982

Constitutio Romana 825

Constitution, US, amendments to 1791; 12th amendment 1804; 13th amendment 1865; 14th amendment 1868; 15th amendment 1870; 17th amendment 1913; 18th amendment 1919, 1920, 1933; 19th amendment 1919; 21st amendment 1933; 22nd amendment 1951; 26th amendment 1971

Constitution, US, came into effect 1788

Constitution, US, drawn up 1787

Constitution, USS 1812

Constitutional Convention 1787

Consulate in France 1799

contact lenses, invention of 1827

Contagious Diseases Act (UK) 1869

Contes d'Hoffmann, Les (The Tales of Hoffmann) 1881

Contes et nouvelles (Tales and Short Stories) 1664

Contes et nouvelles en vers (Tales and Short Stories Put into Verse) 1665

Continental Congress, First 1774

Continental Congress, Second 1775, 1777

Continental System, imposition of 1806

Contre les femmes (Against Women) 1666

Conventicle Act (UK) 1664

Conventional Forces in Europe treaty 1990

Conversation Piece 1934

Conversion of St Paul, The 1601

Conway, Jack (US film director) 1934

Conwy, treaty of 1277

Cook, James (English explorer) 1728, 1768, 1769, 1770, 1772, 1778, 1779

Cook, the Thief, His Wife and Her Lover, The 1989

Cook, Thomas (British travel agent) 1866

Cool Hand Luke 1967

Coolidge, Calvin (30th US president) 1923, 1924, 1925

Coolio (US rapper) 1995

Cooper, Alfred Duff, 1st Viscount Norwich of Aldwick (British politician) 1938

Cooper, Alice (US singer) 1972

Cooper, Anthony Ashley, 1st earl of Shaftesbury (English politician) 1621, 1667, 1676, 1679, 1682, 1683

Cooper, Anthony Ashley, 3rd earl of Shaftesbury (English politician) 1713

Cooper, Anthony Ashley, 7th earl of Shaftesbury (British politician) 1893

Cooper, Gary (US actor) 1952

Cooper, James Fenimore (US writer) 1823, 1826

Cooper, Merian C. (US film producer) 1933

Cooper, Peter (US inventor) 1830

'Cooper's Hill' 1642

Coote, Eyre (English soldier) 1760, 1761

Cope, Wendy (English writer) 1986

Copeland, William (US businessman) 1869

Copenhagen, battle of 1801

Copenhagen, peace of 1660

Copenhagen, treaty of 1776

Copenhagen 1998

Copernicus, Nicolaus (Polish astronomer) 1543

Copland, Aaron (US composer) 1944, 1990

copper mines in Sinai 2920BC

copper smelting at Çatal Hüyuk 6200BC; in China *c.*3000BC

Coppola, Francis Ford (US film director) 1972, 1974, 1979

Coppola, Sofia (US film director) 2003

Coptic Church 284, 341

Copyright Act (UK) 1709

Coram, Thomas (English philanthropist) 1739, 1751

Corday, Charlotte (French murderess) 1793

Cordoba University (Spain), founding of 961

Corelli, Arcangelo (Italian musician) 1653, 1682

Corelli, Marie (Mary Mackay) (English writer) 1886

Corenzini, Carlo (Carlo Collodi) (Italian writer) 1882

Corinthian League 338BC

Coriolanus 1608

Corman, Roger (US film director) 1961

Corneille, Pierre (French playwright) 1606, 1630, 1634, 1635, 1636, 1639, 1640, 1641, 1642, 1646, 1650, 1652, 1659, 1660, 1670, 1684

Cornelius, Henry (South African film director) 1948, 1953

Cornell University (New York), foundation of 1865

Cornish, Samuel (US newspaper editor) 1827

Cornish rising 1497

Corn Laws (UK), repeal of 1846

Cornwallis, Charles, 1st Marquis (English soldier) 1738, 1780, 1781, 1798

Coronation Ode 1902

Coronation of Napoleon, The 1807

Coronation of the Virgin, The 1483

Coronel, battle of 1914

Corot, Jean-Baptiste-Camille (French painter) 1836, 1850, 1875

Corporation Act (UK) 1661

Corrections, The 2001

Correggio (Antonio Allegri da) (Italian artist) 1494, 1515, 1530, 1534

Correggio, Ghiberto da (ruler of Parma) 1316

Corridors of Power, The 1963

Corriere della sera 1876

Corrupt Practices Act (US) 1925

Corsair, The 1814

Corsica, elections to first regional assembly 1982

Cort, Henry (English manufacturer) 1783

Corte Real, Gaspar de (Spanish navigator) 1500

Cortenuova, battle of 1237

Cortés, Hernán (Hernando) (Spanish conquistador) 1519, 1521, 1522

Corunna, battle of 1809

Corupedion, battle of 281BC

coscienza di Zeno, La (The Confessions of Zeno) 1923

Cosgrave, William Thomas (Irish politician) 1922

Cosgrave, Liam (Irish politician) 1973

Così fan tutte, ossia la scuola degli amanti (Women are All the Same, or The School for Lovers) 1790

Cosmas Indicopleustes 525

Cosmographie Introductio 1507

Costa Rica, independence of 1821, 1848

Costello, Elvis (British singer-songwriter) 1977, 1979, 1993

Costello, John Aloysius (Irish politician) 1948, 1954

Costner, Kevin (US actor) 1990, 1991, 1995

Côte d'Ivoire, anti-French riot in 2004

Cotten, Joseph (US actor) 1941

Cotton, John (English bibliophile) 1700

cotton gin, invention of 1792

Coty, François (French industrialist) 1924

Cotzias, George C. (US neurologist) 1967

Coubertin, Pierre de Fredi, baron de (French sportsman) 1896

'Coucher du Sol' 1753

Council for Mutual Economic Assistance (COMECON) 1949, 1991

Council of Europe 1949, 1950

C

Council of People's Commissars 1917
Council of Ten, founding of 1310
Counter-Remonstrants 1617
Count of Monte Cristo, The 1934
'Country House' 1995
Country Wife, The 1675
Counts' War 1533
Couperin, François (French composer) 1668, 1716, 1724, 1733
Couples 1968
Courbet, Gustave (French painter) 1850, 1855, 1877
Courland, James, duke of 1654, 1681
Courrier-Sud (Southern Mail) 1928
Cours de linguistique générale (Course in General Linguistics) 1916
Courteen, William (English pioneer) 1625
Courtenay, Tom (British actor) 1983
Courtenay, William (archbishop of Canterbury) 1382
Courtois, Bernard (French chemist) 1811
Courtrai, battle of 1302
Courtyard of a House in Delft 1658
Cousine Bette, La 1846
Coutances Cathedral (France), building of 1030
Covent Garden Church (London), building of 1625
Covent Garden Theatre (London), opening of 1732
Coventry, German bombing of 1940
Coventry Cathedral (England), completion of 1962
Coverdale, Miles (English scholar) 1537
Covic, Nebojsa (Serb politician) 2003
Covilhã, Pero da (Portuguese explorer) 1487
Covington, Julie (British singer) 1977
Coward, Noël (Pierce) (English actor and writer) 1925, 1928, 1929, 1930, 1931, 1933, 1934, 1941, 1942, 1943, 1944, 1973
'Coward of the County' 1980
Cowley, Abraham (English poet) 1633, 1647, 1656, 1663, 1667
Cowpens, battle of 1781
Cowper, William (English poet) 1779, 1800
Cox, Archibald (US prosecutor) 1973
Cox, James Middleton (US politician) 1920
Crabbe, George (English poet) 1783
Cracow Cathedral (Poland), building of 1080
Cranach, Lucas (the Elder) (German painter) 1553
Crane, (Harold) Hart (US poet) 1926, 1930
Crane, Stephen (US writer) 1895
Cranford 1853
Cranko, John (South African dancer and choreographer) 1949
Cranmer, Thomas (archbishop of Canterbury) 1533, 1556
Crashaw, Richard (English poet) 1646, 1649
Crassus, Marcus Licinius (Roman politician) 71BC, 70BC, 60BC, 56BC, 55BC, 54BC
Craven, Wes (US film director) 1984
Crawford, Joan (US actor) 1932, 1945, 1962
Crawford, William Harris (US lawyer) 1817
Craxi, Bettino (Italian politician) 1993
Crazy Horse (Sioux chief) 1876
Cream (British band) 1968
Creation (Nelson) Mass 1801
Crécy, battle of 1346
Credit-Anstalt, insolvency of 1931
Crédit Mobilier scandal 1873

Creed, Martin (English artist) 2001
Creedence Clearwater Revival (US band) 1969
Creek War 1813
'Creep' 1993
CREEP (Committee for the Re-Election of the President) 1972
Crefield (Krefeld), battle of 1758
Creighton, Mandell (English prelate) 1887
Crépy, treaty of 1544
Cresson, Edith (French politician) 1991, 1992
Crete, German invasion of 1941
Crete, union with Greece of 1897
Crève-coeur, Le (Heartbreak) 1940
Crichton, Charles (British film director) 1951, 1988
Crick, Francis Harry Compton (British biologist) 1953
cricket, banning of 1477
Cries and Whispers 1972
Crime and Punishment 1866
Crimean War 1853, 1854, 1855, 1856
Crime de Sylvestre Bonnard, Le 1881
Crime of Inspector Maigret, The 1932
Crimes and Misdemeanors 1989
Criminal Law Amendment Act (UK) 1885
Crippen, Hawley Harvey (US-born British murderer) 1910
Cripps, Stafford (British politician) 1942
Crispus, Flavius Julius (Roman soldier) 323, 326
Cristiani, Alfredo (president of El Salvador) 1989
Cristofori, Bartolomeo (Italian musical instrument maker) 1704
Cristo si è fermato a Eboli (Christ Stopped at Eboli) 1945
Critic, The 1779
Critique of Judgement (*Kritik der Urteilskraft*) 1790
Critique of Practical Reason (*Kritik der practischen Vernunft*) 1788
Critique of Pure Reason (*Kritik der reinen Vernunft*) 1781
Crivelli, Carlo (Italian artist) 1476, 1492
Croatia, secession from Yugoslavia of 1991
Crocyka, battle of 1739
Croesus, king of Lydia 550BC, 546BC
Cro-Magnon man, discovery of 1868
Crome Yellow 1921
Crompton, Samuel (English inventor) 1779
Cromwell, John (US film director) 1937
Cromwell, Oliver (soldier and Lord Protector of England, Scotland and Ireland) 1599, 1643, 1644, 1645, 1647, 1648, 1649, 1650, 1651, 1653, 1654, 1655, 1657, 1658
Cromwell, Richard (son of Oliver Cromwell and parliamentarian) 1658, 1659, 1712
Cromwell, Thomas (earl of Essex and chief minister to Henry VIII) 1529, 1532, 1535, 1538, 1540
Crónica de una muerte anunciada (Chronicle of a Death Foretold) 1981
Cronje, Piet Arnoldus (Boer leader) 1900
Cronkite, Walter (US TV anchorman) 1968
Cronstedt, Axel (Swedish mineralogist) 1751
Crop Loan Act (US) 1934
Crosby, Bing (US singer) 1942, 1977
Crosland, Alan (US film director) 1927
Cross in the Mountain, The 1808
Crouching Tiger, Hidden Dragon 2000

Crow 1970
Crowe, Russell (Australian actor) 2000, 2001, 2003
Crucible, The 1953
Crucifixion of St Peter, The 1600
Cruel Sea, The 1951
Cruise, Tom (US actor) 1988, 1989, 1994, 1996, 1999
cruise missiles, protests against 1981, 1983
Crum, George (US chef) 1853
Crusade, Albigensian 1208, 1209, 1215, 1218, 1226, 1229
Crusade, Children's 1212
Crusades: First 1095, 1099; Second 1145, 1146, 1149; Third 1187, 1189, 1191, 1192; Fourth 1198, 1199, 1202, 1204; Fifth 1215, 1217, 1218, 1219, 1221; Sixth 1227, 1229; Seventh 1248, 1254
Crystal Palace (London) 1851
Cry the Beloved Country 1948
Ctesiphon, battle of 1915
Cuba, annexation by Spain 1539
Cuba, independence of 1898, 1902
Cuban Missile Crisis 1962
Cuban revolution 1959
Cubist Still Life with Lemons 1975
Cugnot, Nicolas-Joseph (French engineer) 1769
Cukor, George (US film director) 1932, 1933, 1934, 1936, 1940, 1949, 1964
Culloden, battle of 1746
Culpeper, Nicholas (English herbalist) 1616
Cultural Revolution 1966
Culture Club (British group) 1982, 1983
Cumberland, William Augustus, 3rd duke of (Butcher Cumberland) 1721, 1745, 1746, 1747, 1757
cummings, e(dward) e(stlin) (US writer) 1962
Cunard, Samuel (British shipping magnate) 1840
Cunaxa, battle of 401–399BC
cuneiform script *c.*3000BC, 2900BC
cuneiform script, deciphering of 1872
Cunningham, Michael (US writer) 1998
Cunning Little Vixen, The 1924
Cupid and Death 1653
Cure, the (British band) 1985, 1987, 1990
Curie, Marie (Polish scientist) 1898, 1910
Curie, Pierre (French scientist) 1898
Curlew River 1964
Curl's Case (English law) 1727
Curragh mutiny 1914
Currency Act (UK) 1764
Curtis, Tony (US actor) 1959
Curtiz, Michael (Hungarian film director) 1938, 1942, 1945
Curzon, George Nathaniel, 1st Baron (British politician) 1901
Custer, George Armstrong (US soldier) 1876
Custine, Adam-Philippe de, Count (French soldier) 1792, 1793
Custozza, battle of 1848
Custozza, battle of 1866
Cuthwine (Saxon leader) 577
Cuvilliés, François de (French architect) 1750
Cuzco earthquake 1797
Cu zhi jing (*T'sun chih ching*) 1230
Cybernetics 1948
Cyclopedia, or Universal Dictionary of Arts and Sciences 1728

D

DDT (dichloridephenyl-trichlorothene), creation of 1873
Dead, The 1987
'Dead from the Waist Down' 1999
Dead Poets Society 1989
Dead Sea Scrolls, discovery of 1947
Dead Souls 1842
Deák, Ferencz (Hungarian politician) 1867
Dean, James (US actor) 1955
Deane, Seamus (Irish writer) 1996
Dean's December, The 1982
Dearden, Basil (British film director) 1961
De Architectura (On Architecture) 1486
De Arte cabbalistica 1517
De Arte Combinatoria (On the Art of Combination) 1666
De arte honeste amandi 1180
Death and the Maiden 1991
Death at the President's Lodging 1936
Death in the Afternoon 1932
Death in the Family, A 1957
Death in Venice 1912 (novella); 1971 (film); 1973 (opera)
Death of a Naturalist 1966
Death of a Salesman 1949
Death of General Wolfe 1770
Death of Ivan Ilyich, The 1886
Death of Klinghoffer, The 1991
Death of Marat, The 1793
Death of Pompey, The 1641
Death of Sardanapalus, The 1827
Death of Socrates, The 1787
Death of the Heart, The 1938
Death of Wolfe, The 1763
Death's Duell 1632
Death's Head 1944
Deaths and Entrances 1946
De Beers Mining Corp. 1880
De bellis (On the Wars) 550
De Bernières, Louis (English writer) 1994
Debierne, André-Louis (French chemist) 1910
de Bont, Jan (Dutch film director) 1994
Debrett, John (English publisher and biographer) 1769
Debrett's Peerage and Baronetage 1769
Debs, Eugene (Victor) (US socialist) 1893
Debussy, Claude (French composer) 1894, 1902, 1905, 1908, 1918
Debut 1993
Decades of the New World 1555
Decameron, The 1353 (collection of tales); 1972 (film)
Decatur, Stephen (US sailor) 1815
De Causis Errorum (The Causes of Error) 1645
Decay of the Angel, The 1971
Decebalus, king of Dacia 106
Decembrist uprising 1825
Deception 1946
decimal currency, introduction of (UK) 1971
Decius (Gaius Messius Quintus Trajanus), Roman emperor 249, 250, 251
Decken, Klaus von der (German explorer) 1860
Declaration of the People of Virginia 1676
Declaratory Act (UK) 1766
Decline and Fall 1928

Decretum 1139
Decretum Tripartium Juris 1514
De divina praedestinatione (On Divine Predestination) 851
De divisione naturae (On the Divisions of Nature) 865
De divortio Lotharii (On the Divorce of Lothair) 860
Deep Blue Sea, The 1952
Deep Purple (British band) 1970
Deerfield, massacre of 1704
Deer Hunter, The 1978
De excidio et conquestu Britanniae (The Ruin and Conquest of Britain) 542
Defence of Guenevere and Other Poems, The 1858
Defence of Poesie, The 1595
Defence of the Realm 1985
Defence of the Realm Act (UK) 1914
defenestration of Prague 1618
Défense et illustration de la langue française, La (The Defence and Illustration of the French Language) 1549
Defensio Catholicae Fidei contra Anglicanae Sectae Errores (Defence of the Catholic Faith against the Mistakes of the English Sect) 1613
Defensor pacis 1324, 1327
Défi américain, Le (The American Challenge) 1968
Definitely Maybe 1994
Def Leppard (British band) 1987
Defoe, Daniel (English writer) 1661, 1697, 1701, 1702, 1704, 1719, 1722, 1724, 1731
Degas, Edgar (French painter) 1874, 1878, 1894, 1917
de Gaulle, Charles (president of France) 1940, 1942, 1944, 1945, 1946, 1947, 1958, 1960, 1962, 1963, 1965, 1966, 1967, 1968, 1969, 1970
Degeyter, Pierre (Belgian woodcarver) 1888
De Hereticis (Concerning Heretics) 1554
De Humani Corporis Fabrica (On the Fabric of the Human Body) 1542
De Impressione Librorum (On the Printing of Books) 1515
Deiniol, St 560
Déjeuner sure l'herbe (Luncheon on the Grass) 1863
de Klerk, F(rederik) W(illem) (president of South Africa) 1989, 1990, 1992, 1993
de Kooning, Willem (Dutch-US painter) 1939, 1943, 1950
dekulakization in Soviet Union 1928
Delacroix, Eugène (French artist) 1824, 1826, 1827, 1828, 1830, 1831, 1832, 1834, 1838, 1863
De la démocratie en Amérique (Democracy in America) 1835
De la démonomanie des sorciers (On the Fiendishness of Sorcerers) 1580
De l'Allemagne 1810
de la Mare, Walter (English writer) 1902
De la recherche de la vérité (On the Search for Truth) 1674
De la sagesse 1601
Delaunay, Robert (French painter) 1910
Delaware and Hudson Canal, building of 1828
Della Robbia, Luca (Luca di Simone di Marco) (Italian sculptor) 1445, 1482
De Legibus ac Deo legislatore (On Law and God the Lawgiver) 1617

De l'esprit des lois (The Spirit of the Laws) 1748
Delessert, Benjamin (French financier) 1810
Delft after the Explosion 1654
Delibes, Leo (French composer) 1883
Delicatessen 1991
DeLillo, Don (US writer) 1985, 1997
De l'influence des passions (On the Influence of the Emotions) 1796
Delisle, Joseph-Nicolas (French astronomer) 1743
Delius, Frederick (English composer) 1907, 1908, 1913
Della scienza mechanica (On the Science of Mechanics) 1592
de l'Orme (Delorme), Philibert (French architect) 1564
Delphine 1802
De materia medica (On Medical Substances) 55
Demetrius I, king of Georgia 1125
Demetrius I Poliorcetes (the Besieger), king of Macedon 308BC, 301BC
Demetrius I Soter, Seleucid king of Syria 162BC, 150BC
Demetrius II Nicator, Seleucid king of Syria 145BC, 142BC
Demidoff Altarpiece, The 1476
DeMille, Cecil B(lount) (US film producer) 1923, 1949, 1959
Demme, Jonathan (US film director) 1990
Democracy, an American Novel 1880
Democracy Now movement (East Germany) 1989
Democratic Party of the Left (PDS) (Italy) 1990
Democratic Republic of Congo (Zaire), adoption of new name of 1997
Democratic Unionist Party (Northern Ireland) 1971
Democratic Union of Mineworkers (UK) 1984
Democritus (Greek philosopher) 330BC
Demoiselles d'Avignon, Les 1907
De monarchia 1312
Demosthenes (Athenian soldier) 426BC, 425BC, 414BC, 413BC
De Motibus Stellae Martis (On the Motion of the Star Mars) 1609
Demy, Jacques (French film director) 1964
De naturis rerum (On the Nature of Things) 1217
Deneuve, Catherine (French actor) 1964, 1967
Deng Xiaoping (Chinese politician) 1977, 1989, 1997
Denham, John (English poet) 1642, 1669
Denikin, Anton Ivanovich (Russian soldier) 1919
De Niro, Robert (US actor) 1973, 1976, 1978, 1980, 1990, 1995
'Denis' 1978
Denis Diderot 1770
Denmark, German occupation of 1940
Dennewitz, battle of 1813
De nugis curialium 1200
De Officio Principium (The Office of Princes) 1539
Deorham, battle of 577
De Origine Juris Germanici (On the Origins of Germanic Law) 1643
De Ortu et Causis Subterraneis (On Underground Origins and Causes) 1544
De Palma, Brian (US film director) 1996
Depardieu, Gérard (French actor) 1982, 1986, 1990
De Peste (On the Plague) 1649

D

Dior, Christian (French couturier) 1947

Dioscorides, Pedanius (Greek physician) 55

Dipendra, crown prince of Nepal 2001

Dirac, Paul (Adrien Maurice) (British physicist) 1928

Directory of Five (France) 1795, 1799

Dire Straits (British band) 1979, 1985

Dirty Dozen, The 1967

Dirty Harry 1971

Disaffection, A 1989

Disasters of War, The 1810

Discorsi e dimostrazioni matematiche intorno a due nuove scienze attenenti alla meccanica (Dialogues Concerning Two New Sciences) 1638

Discours, Les (The Discourses) 1560

Discours de la méthode (Discourse on Method) 1637

Discours sur l'économie politique (Discourse on Political Economy) 1755

Discours sur les lettres, sur les arts et les sciences (Discourse on the Sciences and the Arts) 1750

Discours sur le style (Discourse on Style) 1753

Discours sur l'histoire universelle (Discourse on Universal History) 1681

Discours sur l'origine de l'inégalité parmi les hommes (Discourse on the Origins of Inequality between Men) 1755

Discourse on Earthquakes 1668

Discourse Whether it be Lawful to Take Use for Money, A 1653

Discreet Charm of the Bourgeoisie, The 1972

Diseases of Children and their Remedies, The 1762

Disgrace 1999

Disney, Walt (US film producer) 1924, 1928, 1937, 1940

Disneyland (California), opening of 1955

Disputationes Anatomicae Selectiones (Selected Anatomical Disputes) 1746

Disquieting Muse, The 1917

Disraeli, Benjamin, 1st earl of Beaconsfield (British politician) 1831, 1844, 1845, 1846, 1852, 1868, 1870, 1874, 1875, 1876, 1878, 1880

Dissertation upon the Epistles of Phalaris 1699

Distant Voices, Still Lives 1988

Dit des jeux du monde, Le (The Tale of the World at Play) 1918

Diu, battle of 1509

Diurnall Occurences in Parliament 1641

Diva 1993

Divertimento 1939

Divina commedia (Divine Comedy) 1307

Divine Poem, The 1905

Divini Illius Magistri (encyclical) 1929

Division Act (US) 1800

Division of Labour, The 1893

Dix, Otto (German painter) 1925

Di-xin (Zhou Hsin, Chou Hsin), last Shang (Yin) emperor of China 1122BC

Djindjic, Zoran (Serbian politician) 2000, 2003

Djinns, Les 1884

Djoser (Netjerikhet), 3rd dynasty king of Egypt 2630BC

DJ Shadow (Josh Davis) (US musician) 1996

Dmitri, False (first) 1601, 1604, 1605, 1606

Dmitri, False (second) 1608

Dmitri, grand duke of Vladimir 1280, 1283

Dmitri, Russian prince (son of Ivan IV) 1591

Dmitri Donskoi, Russian prince 1380

Dmytryk, Edward (US film director) 1944, 1954, 1958

DNA (deoxyribonucleic acid) 1870, 1953

Döblin, Alfred (German writer) 1929

dock strike in London 1889

Docks of New York 1928

Dr Mabuse 1922

Dr No 1962

Doctor's Dilemma, The 1906

Dr Strangelove 1964

Dr Zhivago 1957, 1987 (novel); 1965 (film)

Doctrine and Discipline of Divorce, The 1643

Dodge City (Kansas), foundation of 1871

Dödsdansen (The Dance of Death) 1905

Doe, Samuel K(enyon) (president of Liberia) 1980, 1990

Doesburg, Theo van (Dutch painter) 1917

Dog Day Afternoon 1975

Dogen (Japanese Zen Buddhist teacher) 1227

Doge's Palace, San Giorgio Maggiore, The 1908

Dogger Bank Incident (North Sea) 1904

Doggy Style 1994

Doisy, Edward (Adelbert) (US biochemist) 1929

Doktor Faustus 1947

Dokyo (Japanese Buddhist priest) 761, 764

Dolce vita, La 1960

Dolci, Giovanni dei (Italian architect) 1473

Dole, Bob (Robert Joseph) (US politician) 1996

Dolet, Etienne (French humanist) 1546

D'Oliveira, Basil Lewis (South African-born English cricketer) 1968

dollar adopted as US currency 1785

Dollfuss, Engelbert (Austrian politician) 1933, 1934

Dolly the sheep (British cloning experiment) 1997

Dombey and Son 1848

Dome of Many-Colored Glass, A 1912

Dome of the Rock, Jerusalem 691

Domenichino (Domenico Zampieri) (Italian painter) 1608, 1641

Domesday Book 1085

Domestic Manners of the Americans 1832

Dominic, St 1205, 1221

Dominica, independence of 1978

Dominican order, constitution of 1220

Dominican Republic, independence of 1844

Dominican Republic, US occupation of 1916

Domitia (wife of Emperor Domitian) 96

Domitian (Titus Flavius Domitianus), Roman emperor 81, 84, 96

Donald I, king of Scotland 858

Donat, Robert (British actor) 1934, 1935

Donatello (Donato di Niccolò) (Florentine sculptor) 1409, 1415, 1466

Donation of Constantine 1236

Donation of Pepin 756, 774

Donauwörth, battle of 1704

Don Carlos of Bourbon *see* Charles III, king of Spain

Don Carlos 1787 (play); 1867 (opera)

Donegan, Lonnie (Scottish musician) 1956

Donen, Stanley (US film director) 1952, 1954

Don Giovanni 1787

Donizetti, Gaetano (Italian composer) 1832, 1833, 1835, 1843

Don Juan 1665 (play); 1823 (poem)

Donleavy, J(ames) P(atrick) (Irish writer) 1955

Don Manuel de Zuniga 1784

Donne, John (English poet) 1572, 1610, 1624, 1631, 1632, 1633, 1640, 1649, 1651, 1652

Donner, Richard (US film director) 1978

Donnerstag aus Licht (Thursday from Light) 1981

Donovan, Jason (Australian actor and singer) 1989

Don Pasquale 1843

'Don't Cry for me Argentina' 1977

'Don't Fence Me In' 1944

'Don't Leave Me This Way' 1986

'Don't Look Back in Anger' 1996

Don't Look Now 1973

'Don't Stand So Close To Me' 1980

'Don't You Want Me?' 1981

Doolittle, James (Harold) (US aviator) 1942

Doors, the (US band) 1967

Doré, Gustave (French illustrator) 1861, 1872, 1883

Dorfman, Ariel (Chilean writer) 1991

Doria, Andrea (Genoese sailor) 1535

Dornach, battle of 1499

Dorothea, Danish princess 1542

Dorrego, Manuel (president of Argentina) 1829

Dos Passos, John (US writer) 1925, 1936

dos Santos, José Eduardo (president of Angola) 1991, 1993

Dost Mohammad Khan, Barakzai emir of Afghanistan 1826, 1835, 1838, 1839, 1842

Dostoyevsky, Fyodor Mikhailovich (Russian writer) 1864, 1866, 1869, 1871, 1880

Do the Right Thing 1989

'Do They Know it's Christmas?' 1984

Douai–Reims Bible 1594

Double Fantasy 1980

Double Indemnity 1944

Doubleday, Abner (US soldier) 1839

Doubting Thomas 1600

Douglas, Kirk (US actor) 1960

Douglas, Michael (US actor) 1987, 1991

Douglas, Norman (English writer) 1917

Douglas, Stephen (US politician) 1856

Douglas and Mar, James, 2nd earl of 1388

Douglas-Home, Alec (Alexander Frederick), 14th earl of Home (British politician) 1963, 1965

Doumer, Paul (president of France) 1931, 1932

Doumergue, Gaston (president of France) 1924, 1931

'Dover Beach' 1867

Dover, treaty of 1670

Dowland, John (English musician and composer) 1563, 1597, 1605

Down and Out in Paris and London 1933

Downing Street Declaration (Britain and Ireland) 1993

'Down Under' 1983

'Do Ya Think I'm Sexy' 1979

Doyle, Arthur Conan (Scottish writer) 1887, 1890, 1891, 1892, 1894, 1902, 1912

Doyle, Roddy (Irish writer) 1993

'Do You Really Want To Hurt Me' 1982

Dózsa, George (Hungarian rebel leader) 1514

Drabble, Margaret (English writer) 1987

Draco (Greek lawmaker) 621BC

Dracula 1897 (novel); 1931 (film)

Dragasani, battle of 1821

E

Ebb, Fred (US lyricist) 1966
'Ebeneezer Goode' 1992
Ebers, Georg Moritz (German Egyptologist) 1872
Ebers papyrus 1872
Ebert, Friedrich (German politician) 1918, 1919, 1925
Eberth, Karl (Joseph) (German scientist) 1880
Ebola virus, outbreak in Zaire 1995
'Ebony and Ivory' 1982
Ecce Homo 1927
Ecclesiazusae (Parliament of Women) 392BC
Eck, Johann (German theologian) 1519
Eckhart, Meister (Johannes Eckhart) (German mystic)
  1327, 1337
Eclogues 41BC
Eco, Umberto (Italian writer) 1980, 1988
Ecole des femmes, L' (School for Wives) 1662
Ecology Party, foundation of (UK) 1973
Economic Consequences of the Peace, The 1919
Economic Interpretation of the Constitution 1913
Economic Opportunity Act (US) 1964
Economist, The 1843
Ecouen, edict of (France) 1559
Ecuador, independence of 1830
Eddas, The 1222
Eddy, Mary Baker (US religious leader) 1875, 1879
Eden, Anthony, 1st earl of Avon (British politician)
  1938, 1955, 1956, 1957
Eden, Richard (English scholar) 1555
Edessa, massacre at 1147
Edgar (Eadgar), king of England 959, 972, 973, 975
Edgar, king of Scotland 1097
Edgar (Eadgar) the Atheling (English prince) 1066,
  1097
Edgar, David (English playwright) 1976, 1980
Edgehill, battle of 1642
Edgeworth, Maria (Irish writer) 1798, 1800
Edible Woman, The 1969
Edictum Chlothacharii 614
Edinburgh, treaty of 1560
Edinburgh Festival of Music and Drama, foundation of
  1947
Edinburgh University, foundation of 1582
Edington, battle of 878
Edison, Thomas Alva (US inventor) 1876, 1877, 1878,
  1879, 1880, 1887, 1931
Edison Electric Light Co. 1878, 1879, 1882
Edison Illuminating Co. 1882
Edmund, St (Edmund Rich) 1240
Edmund I (the Deed-doer, the Magnificent), king of
  England 939, 940, 942, 944, 946
Edmund II (Ironside), king of England 1016
Edo (Japan), destruction by fire of 1772
Edred (Aedred), king of England 946, 948, 954, 955
Edrisi, al- (Arab geographer) 1154
Education Act (UK) 1870
Education Act (UK) 1902
Education Reform Act (UK) 1988
Education sentimentale, L' 1869
Edward I, king of England 1270, 1271, 1274, 1275,
  1277, 1279, 1282, 1284, 1286, 1287, 1290, 1292,
  1294, 1295, 1296, 1297, 1298, 1301, 1303, 1304,
  1305, 1307
Edward II, king of England 1307, 1308, 1311, 1314,
  1319, 1321, 1326, 1327

Edward III, king of England 1326, 1327, 1328, 1330,
  1333, 1337, 1338, 1340, 1343, 1344, 1346, 1348,
  1356, 1359, 1360, 1376, 1377
Edward IV, king of England 1442, 1460, 1461, 1465,
  1470, 1471, 1475, 1477, 1483
Edward V, king of England 1483
Edward VI, king of England 1537, 1547, 1552, 1553
Edward VII, king of Great Britain and Ireland 1841,
  1874, 1901, 1903, 1910
Edward VIII, king of Great Britain and Ireland 1936
Edward, king of Portugal 1433, 1435
Edward, Prince of Wales (Black Prince) 1355, 1356,
  1367, 1370, 1376
Edward Balliol, usurping king of Scotland 1332, 1333,
  1356
Edward Bruce, king of Ireland 1316, 1317, 1318
Edward (Eadward) the Confessor, king of England
  1042, 1043, 1045, 1051, 1056, 1065
Edward (Eadward) the Elder, king of Wessex 899, 910,
  914, 917, 918, 919, 924
Edward (Eadward) the Martyr, king of the English 975,
  978
Edward II 1594
Edward Said: The Last Interview 2001
Edwards, Blake (US film director) 1961
Edwin, king of Northumbria 626, 633
Egbert, archbishop of York 735
Egbert (Ecgberht), king of Wessex 815, 825, 839
Egil's Saga 1200
Egmont 1788
Egoist, The 1879
Ehe von Maria Braun, Die (The Marriage of Maria
  Braun) 1979
Ehrlichman, John (US presidential adviser) 1973
Eichmann, Adolf (German Nazi) 1941, 1960, 1961,
  1962
*Eichmann in Jerusalem: A Report on the Banality of
  Evil* 1963
Eiffel, Alexandre-Gustave (French engineer) 1889
Eiffel Tower, building of 1889
Eiffel Tower, The 1910
Eight Princes, rebellion of the (China) 291
Eight Songs for a Mad King 1969
1812 Overture 1880
LXXX Sermons 1640
Eighty Years War 1568, 1648
Eigtved, Nikolaj (Danish architect) 1754
Eikon Basilike 1649
Eikonoklastes 1649
Einhard (Frankish historian) 830
Einstein, Albert (German-US physicist) 1905, 1916,
  1921, 1939, 1955
Einstein on the Beach 1976
Eire, Irish Free State becomes 1937; proclamation of
  Republic of 1949
Eisai (Japanese Buddhist monk) 1191
Eisenhower, Dwight D(avid) (34th US president) 1943,
  1944, 1952, 1953, 1954, 1955, 1956, 1957, 1958,
  1959, 1960
Eisenstein, Sergei (Soviet film director) 1925, 1926,
  1927, 1938, 1943
Eissler, Fanny (Austrian dancer) 1840
Ekaterinburg, shooting of Russian royal family at 1918
Ekkehard of St Gall (Frankish monk) 937

Eksund (trawler) 1986
El Alamein, battle of 1942
El amor en los tiempos del cólera (Love in the Time
  of Cholera) 1985
El Arish, Convention of (NE Sinai) 1800
Elasa, battle of 160BC
Elbow Room 1977
El Dorado, search for 1595
Eleanor (sister of King Henry III) 1238
Eleanor of Aquitaine, queen of France and England
  (wife of King Louis VII and King Henry II) 1137,
  1152, 1204
Eleanor of Castile, queen of England (wife of King
  Edward I) 1291
Eleanor of Provence, queen of England (wife of King
  Henry III) 1236
'Eleanor Rigby' 1966
eleaticism 515BC
Eleazer, Rabbi (Jewish rebel leader) 132
Elected Member, The 1969
Election Campaign Act (US) 1972
Election, The 1754
Election of the Doge of Venice, The 1763
Electoral Reform Act (US) 1974
Electra c.420–413BC
Electric Kool-Aid Acid Test, The 1968
Electric Light Act (UK) 1882
Elegies 1985
Elégies, mascarades et bergeries (Elegies,
  Masquerades and Pastorals) 1565
Elegy Written in a Country Church-Yard 1751
Elektra 1909
Elementa Philosophica de Cive (Philosophical
  Elements Concerning Citizenship) 1647
Elementorum Philosophiae (Elements of Philosophy)
  1655, 1658
Elements c.300BC
Elephant Celebes, The 1921
Elephant Man, The 1980
Elgar, Edward (English composer) 1899, 1900, 1901,
  1902, 1904, 1905, 1908, 1911, 1919, 1934
Elgin, Thomas Bruce, 7th earl of (English diplomat)
  1803
Elgin Marbles 1803
Elhuyar y de Suvisa, Fausto d' (Spanish mineralogist)
  1783
Elhuyar y de Suvisa, Juan José d' (Spanish
  mineralogist) 1783
Elijah 1846
Eliot, George (Mary Ann Evans) (English writer) 1859,
  1860, 1861, 1863, 1866, 1872, 1876
Eliot, John (The Apostle to the Indians) (English-born
  US missionary) 1661
Eliot, T(homas) S(tearns) (US-British writer) 1917,
  1922, 1925, 1927, 1930, 1935, 1937, 1943, 1950,
  1965
Elisabeth-Charlotte, duchess of Orléans 1683
elisir d'amore, L' (The Elixir of Love) 1832
Elizabeth, empress of Austria (wife of Franz Josef I)
  1898
Elizabeth, queen of Bohemia (Winter Queen) 1611,
  1613, 1662
Elizabeth, queen of England (wife of George VI and
  queen mother) 1938, 1940, 2002

E

Essentials of Salvation 1017

Estaing, Valéry Giscard d' (French President) 1979, 1981

Este, Alfonso I d', duke of Ferrara 1497

Este, Cesare d', duke of Ferrara 1598

Este, Falco (Folco) d' (ruler of Ferrara) 1309

Esterhazy, (Marie-Charles-Ferdinand-) Walsin (French soldier) 1898

Esther 1689 (play); 1732 (oratorio)

Estienne, Robert (French printer) 1532

Estonia, independence of 1991

Estonia, Soviet invasion of 1940

ETA *see* Euskadi ta Askatasuna

Etampes, Anne de Pisseleu, duchess d' 1533

Etaples, peace of 1492, 1498

Et Dieu créa la femme (And God Created Woman) 1956

Eternal Sunshine of the Spotless Mind 2004

Ethelbald (Aethelbald), king of Mercia 716, 757

Ethelbert (Aethelberht), king of Kent 560, 597, 616

Ethelbert, king of Wessex 865

Ethelfrith, king of Northumbria 613

Ethelred (Aethelred) I, king of Wessex 865, 871

Ethelred (Aethelred) II (the Unready), king of England 978, 1002, 1011, 1013, 1014, 1016

Ethelward (Aethelweard) (Anglo-Saxon historian) 998

Ethelwulf (Aethelwulf), king of Wessex 839, 851

Etherege, George (English writer) 1676

Ethica ordine geometrico demonstrata (Ethics Demonstrated According to the Geometrical Order) 1677

Ethics 1547

Ethiopia, independence of 1941

Ethiopia, Italian annexation of 1936

Et in Arcadia Ego 1638

Etireono, MV 2001

Eton College (England), foundation of 1440

Etranger, L' (The Outsider) 1942

Etre et le néant, L' (Being and Nothingness) 1943

E.T. the Extra-Terrestrial 1982

Euclid (Greek mathematician) *c.*300BC

Eudes, king of France *see* Odo, count of Paris

Eugène, prince of Savoy (Austrian soldier) 1697, 1701, 1702, 1703, 1704, 1706, 1708, 1709, 1716, 1717

Eugene Onegin 1823 (Pushkin); 1879 (Tchaikovsky)

Eugenides, Jeffrey (US writer) 2003

Eugénie, empress of the French (wife of Napoleon III) 1853, 1862

Eugenie Grandet 1833

Eugenius III (Bernardo Pignatelli), pope 1145, 1146

Eugenius (Flavius Eugenius), Roman emperor 392, 394

Eulegius, archbishop of Toledo 859

Euler, Leonhard (Swiss mathematician) 1748

Eumenes (Macedonian general) 323BC, 316BC

Eumenides, The 456BC

Eunuch, The 161BC

Eunus (Syrian slave leader) 135BC, 132BC

Euphues, or the Anatomy of Wit 1578

Euratom (European Atomic Energy Community), 1958, 1962

Euric, king of the Visigoths 473

Euripedes (Greek playwright) 428BC, *c.*426BC, 412BC, 407–406BC

euro, adoption of as European currency 2002

European Coal and Steel and Community (ECSC) 1951, 1953, 1962

European Community (EC), single market of 1993

European Constitution 2004

European Economic Community (EEC), formation of 1957

European Economic Cooperation, Committee for 1947

European Free Trade Association (EFTA) 1960

European Monetary System (EMS), creation of 1979

European Union, naming of 1993

Europeans, The 1878

Eurovision Song Contest 1956

Euskadi ta Askatasuna (ETA) 1960

Eustace and Hilda 1947

Eustachio, Bartolommeo (Italian anatomist) 1552

'Evangeline' 1847

Evans, Arthur John (British archaeologist) 1900

Evans, Marc (British film director) 2004

Evelina, or the History of a Young Lady's Entry into the World 1778

'Eve of St Agnes, The' 1820

Evelyn, John (English diarist) 1620, 1641, 1706

Événements, les (France) 1968

Evening Post, The 1706

Evening Standard 1827

Eventyr, fortalte for børnl (Tales Told for Children) 1835

Everest, conquest of 1953

Everlasting Gospel, The 1202

'Every Breath You Take' 1983

Every Man in his Humour 1598

Every Man out of his Humour 1600

'Everybody Hurts' 1993

'Everybody Wants to Rule the World' 1985

'(Everything I Do) I Do it for You' 1991

Evian agreements (Algeria) 1962

Evil May Day riots (London) 1517

Evita 1978

Excavation 1950

Excellence de la langue française, L' 1683

Exclusion Bill (UK) 1679, 1680, 1681

Exclusion crisis (UK) 1679

Excursion, The 1814

Execution of Maximilian 1867

Executioner's Song 1979

Exercitatio Anatomica de Motu Cordis et Sanguinis (Anatomical Treatise on the Motion of the Heart and the Blood) 1628

Exercitationes de Generatione Animalium (Lectures Concerning the Generation of Animals) 1651

Exeter Cathedral (England), building of 1370

Exeter, HMS 1939

Exhibition (London), Great 1851

Exhibition, Paris International 1855

Exile on Main Street 1972

Exodus 1958 (novel); 1977 (album)

Exorcist, The 1973

ex parte Milligan (US) 1866

Expedition of Humphry Clinker, The 1771

Experiment on a Bird in an Air Pump, An 1767

Experiments on Vegetables 1779

Explications des maximes des saints sur la vie intérieure (An Explanation of the Sayings of the Saints on the Inner Life) 1697

Export Control Act (US) 1940

Export-Import Bank of Washington 1934

Exposition de la doctrine de l'église catholique sur les matières de controverse (Exposition of the Doctrine of the Catholic Church on Controversial Issues) 1671

Exposition du système du monde (Account of the System of the World) 1796

Exposition Internationale des Arts Décoratifs 1925

Express, L' 1953

Expugnatio Hibernica (The Campaign in Ireland) 1185

Exsurge (papal bull) 1520

Exterminating Angel 1962

extermination camps, German 1941

Exxon Valdez (oil tanker) 1989

Eyck, Hubert van (Netherlandish painter) 1432

Eyck, Jan van (Netherlandish painter) 1420, 1432, 1433, 1434, 1440

Eye in the Door, The 1993

Eyeless in Gaza 1936

Eye of the Storm, The 1973

Eyes Wide Shut 1999

Eylau, battle of 1806

Eyrbyggja Saga 1200

F

Fabian Society (Britain) 1884, 1900

Fables 1185

Fables choisies mises en vers (Selected Fables Put into Verse) 1668, 1678, 1693

Fabricius, Johannes (Dutch astronomer) 1610

Façade 1923

Factory Act (UK) 1833

Fadren (The Father) 1887

Faerie Queene, The 1590, 1596

Fahd ibn Abdul-Aziz, king of Saudi Arabia 1986

Fahrenheit 451 1953

Fahrenheit 9/11 2003

Fahrenheit, Gabriel Daniel (Polish-Dutch physicist) 1686, 1720, 1736

Fairbanks Sr, Douglas (Elton) (US actor) 1919, 1920, 1922

Fairfax, Thomas, 3rd Baron (Parliamentarian soldier) 1644, 1648, 1671

Fair Labor Standards Act (US) 1938

Fair Maid of Perth, The 1828

Fair Oaks, battle of 1862

Fairy Queen, The 1692

Faisal I, king of Syria and of Iraq 1916, 1920, 1921

Faisal II, king of Iraq 1939, 1958

Faisal II ibn Abdul-Aziz, king of Saudi Arabia 1964, 1975

Faith 1987

Falaise Gap, battle of 1944

Falange Party, Spanish 1933, 1939

Falconer, William (Scottish poet) 1762

Faliero, Marino (doge of Venice) 1355

Falkirk, battle of 1298

Falkirk, battle of 1746

F

Fiennes, Ranulph (British explorer) 1993
Fierstein, Harvey (US actor and playwright) 1981
Fieser, Louis Frederick (US chemist) 1942
FIFA (Fédération Internationale de Football Association) 1904
Fifth Monarchy sect (England) 1653
Fifty Million Frenchmen 1929
Fifty Sermons 1649
Figaro, Le 1854, 1924
Figes, Orlando (British historian) 2002
Figgis, Mike (British film director) 1995
Fighting Téméraire, The 1839
Figueroa, Leonardo de (Spanish architect) 1691, 1730
Fiji, independence of 1970
filioque controversy 867
Fillmore, Millard (13th US president) 1850, 1853
Filmer, Robert (English writer) 1653, 1680
Fils naturel, ou les épreuves de la vertu, Le (The Natural Son, or The Proofs of Virtue) 1771
Financial Times 1888
Financier, The 1912
Finding Neverland 2004
Fine Balance, A 1996
Fine Gael 1933, 1948, 1954, 1957, 1973, 1977, 1981, 1982, 1987, 1994
fingerprinting, invention of 1885
Finland, independence of 1917
Finland, Soviet invasion of 1939
Finlandia 1899
Finnegans Wake 1939
Finney, Albert (British actor) 1960, 1963, 1983, 1984
finta giardiniera, La (The Feigned Garden-girl) 1775
finta semplice, La (The Feigned Simpleton) 1769
Finzi, Gerald Raphael (English composer) 1949
Firdausi (Persian poet) 1020, 1336
Firebird, The 1910
Firebird Suite 1911
Fire Down Below 1989
'Firestarter' 1996
Firman, Leroy B. (US inventor) 1879
Firmian, Leopold von (archbishop of Salzburg) 1732
First Blast of the Trumpet Against the Monstrous Regiment of Women 1558
First Book of Selected Church Musik 1641
First Circle 1968
First Intermediate Period, commencement of 2134BC
Firth, Colin (British actor) 2004
Fischer, Bobby (US chess master) 1972
Fish, Hamilton (US politician) 1870
Fish Called Wanda, A 1988
Fisher, Irving (US economist) 1911
Fisher, John (British admiral) 1915
Fisher, St John (John of Rochester) (English prelate) 1535
Fistful of Dollars, A 1964
Fitch, John (US inventor) 1787
Fitt, Gerry (Irish politician) 1970
Fitzcarraldo 1982
FitzGerald, Edward (English poet) 1859
Fitzgerald, F(rancis) Scott (US writer) 1922, 1925, 1934, 1940, 1941
Fitzgerald, Garret (Irish politician) 1981, 1982, 1985, 1987
Fitzgerald, Penelope (English writer) 1979

Fitzralph, Richard (English religious writer) 1360
Five Articles of Religion 1617, 1618
five boroughs settled by Danes 877
Five Easy Pieces 1970
Five Hundred, Council of (Paris) 1796, 1798
Five Mile Act (UK) 1665
Five Thousand, Constitution of 412BC
Fixer, The 1966
Fizeau, Armand (-Hippolyte-Louis) (French physicist) 1849
Flag 1954
Flagellants 1349
Flaminius, Gaius (Roman soldier) 217BC
Flamsteed, John (English astronomer) 1675
Flatford Mill 1817
Flaubert, Gustave (French writer) 1857, 1869, 1877, 1880, 1881
Flaubert's Parrot 1984
Flavin, Martin (US writer) 1943
Fledermaus, Die (The Bat) 1874
Fleet, Thomas (Boston printer) 1765
Fleetwood Mac (British band) 1969, 1976, 1977
Fleetwood Mac 1976
Fleix, treaty of 1580
Fleming, Alexander (Scottish bacteriologist) 1928, 1929
Fleming, Ian (English writer) 1953
Fleming, Victor (US film director) 1927, 1939
Fletcher, John (English playwright) 1619
Fletcher, WPC Yvonne, shooting of 1984
Fleurs du mal, Les 1857
Fleury, André-Hercule de (French cardinal and minister) 1726, 1735
Fleury, Claude (French historian) 1691
fliegende Holländer, Der (The Flying Dutchman) 1843
Flight to Arras 1942
Flodden, battle of the 1513
Florence, battle of 406
Florence, foundation of c.62BC
Florey, Howard (Australian pathologist) 1940
Florianus (Marcus Annius Florianus), Roman emperor 276
Florida, cession to US 1819
Florio, John (English lexicographer) 1603
Floss der Medusa, Das (The Raft of the Medusa) 1968
Flower Vendors, The 1906
Flying Dutchman, The 1843
flying shuttle, invention of 1733
Flynn, Errol (US actor) 1938
Fo, Dario (Italian writer) 1970
Fokine, Michel (Russian-US choreographer) 1904, 1907, 1910
Foliot, Gilbert (Anglo-Norman cleric) 1187
Folkefiende, En (An Enemy of the People) 1883
Follies of 1907, The 1907
Fonda, Henry (US actor) 1940, 1957, 1982
Fonda, Peter (US actor) 1969
Fonesca, Manuel Deodora da (Brazilian politician) 1889, 1891
Fontaine, Joan (US actor) 1940, 1943
Fontainebleau, Alliance of 1743
Fontainebleau, treaty of 1631
Fontainebleau, treaty of 1785
Fontane, Theodor (German writer) 1878

Fontenoy, battle of 1745
Food and its Adulterations 1855
Fool in a Trance 1929
Foot, Michael Mackintosh (British politician) 1980, 1983
Football Association, foundation of 1863
Forced Marriage, The 1671
Force ennemie, La 1903
Ford, Ford Madox (English writer) 1915, 1928
Ford, Gerald Rudolph (38th US president) 1974, 1975
Ford, Glenn (US actor) 1953
Ford, Harrison (US actor) 1981, 1982, 1993
Ford, Henry (US manufacturer) 1913, 1939
Ford, John (English dramatist) 1633
Ford, John (US film director) 1940, 1952
Ford, Richard (US writer) 1986, 1995
Ford, Robert (US outlaw) 1882
Ford Motor Co. 1903, 1913
Foreign Affairs 1984
Foreign Assistance Act (US) 1948
Foreign Lands, A Book about 1349
Foreign Legion, creation of 1831
Foreign Plantations, Council for 1661
Foreman, George (US boxer) 1974
Forester, C(ecil) S(cott) (English writer) 1937
Forgotten Man, The 1883
'For He's a Jolly Good Fellow' 1709
Forman, Milos (Czech film director) 1975, 1984, 1996
Formigny, battle of 1450
Fornovo, battle of 1495
Forster, E(dward) M(organ) (English writer) 1905, 1907, 1908, 1910, 1924, 1970, 1971
Forster, Marc (German film director) 2004
Forster, William Edward (British politician) 1870
Forsyte Saga, The 1922
Forsyth, Bill (Scottish film director) 1980, 1983
Forsyth, Frederick (English writer) 1971
Fort Beauséjour, surrender of 1755
Fort Dearborn, sack of 1812
Fort Donelson, battle of 1862
Fort Duquesne, battle of 1755
Fort Duquesne, building of 1754
Fort Harrod, foundation of 1774
Fort Henry, battle of 1862
For the Unfallen 1959
For the Union Dead 1964
Fort Knox, foundation of 1935
Fort Royal, battle of 1779
Forth Railway Bridge, building of 1889
Forth Road Bridge, opening of 1964
Fort Stanwix, treaty of 1768
Fort Sumter, battle of 1861
Fort Ticonderoga, battle of 1758
Fortuyn, Pim (Dutch politician) 2002
Forty-Two-Line Bible 1455
Forty Years On 1968
For Whom the Bell Tolls 1940
'For Your Love' 1965
forza del destino, La (The Force of Destiny) 1862
Fosse, Bob (US film director) 1972
Fosse Ardeatine massacre 1944
Foster, Jodie (US actor) 1990
Fothergill, John (English physician) 1748
Foucault's Pendulum 1988

F

G

G

Gerry, Elbridge (US politician) 1812

Gerry 2003

Gerry and the Pacemakers (British group) 1963, 1964

Gershwin, George (Jacob Gersvin) (US composer) 1924, 1927, 1930, 1935, 1937

Gershwin, Ira (Israel) (US lyricist) 1924, 1927

Gertler, Mark (English painter) 1916

Gerusalemme Liberata (Jerusalem Liberated) 1581

Geschichte des dreissigjährigen Krieges, Die (The History of the Thirty Years War) 1793

Geschöpfe des Prometheus, Die (The Creatures of Prometheus) 1801

Gesel, Arnold Lucius (US psychologist) 1943

Gesner, Konrad von (Swiss naturalist) 1551

Gesta Danorum 1208

Gesta Dei per Francos (The Deeds of God through the Franks) 1111

Gestapo, formation of 1933

Gestetner, David (Hungarian-US inventor) 1888

Gestner, Abraham (US physician) 1855

'Get Back' 1969

Get Carter 1971

'Get It On' 1971

Gettysburg, battle of 1863

Geza I, king of Hungary 1075, 1077

Ghana (Gold Coast), independence of 1957

Ghazan, Mongol ruler of Persia 1295

Ghazi, Danishmend prince 1119

Ghazi, king of Iraq 1939

Ghazi Malik, sultan of Delhi 1320

Ghaznavid dynasty, commencement of 962

Ghazzali, al- (Algazel) (Persian theologian and mystic) 1111

Ghent, Pacification of 1576

Ghent, treaty of 1814

Ghent Altarpiece 1432

Ghiberti, Lorenzo (Florentine sculptor) 1424, 1455

Ghirlandaio, Domenico (Domenico di Tommaso Bigordi) (Florentine painter) 1494

Ghiyas-ud-Din Tughluq (Ghazi Malik), sultan of Delhi 1320, 1323, 1325

Ghost Road, The 1995

Ghost Vanishes, The 1931

Giacometti, Alberto (Swiss artist) 1933, 1947, 1950, 1957, 1966

Gianni Schicchi 1918

Giannoni, Pietro (Italian historian) 1723

Giant 1955

Gibb, James (English sportsman) 1880

Gibberd, Frederick (British architect) 1967

Gibbon, Edward (English historian) 1737, 1776, 1781

Gibbon, Lewis Grassic (James Leslie Mitchell) (Scottish writer) 1932

Gibbons, Cedric (US film director) 1934

Gibbons, Grinling (English sculptor) 1721

Gibbons, Orlando (English musician) 1583, 1609, 1611, 1612, 1625

Gibbons, Stella Dorothea (English writer) 1932

Gibbons, Thomas (US steamboat operator) 1824

Gibbons, William (English insurance policy owner) 1583

Gibbons vs. Ogden 1824

Gibbs, James (Scottish architect) 1714, 1722, 1724

GI Bill of Rights (US) 1944

Gibraltar, ceded to Britain 1713

Gibraltar, siege of 1727, 1728

Gibran, Khalil (Lebanese-US writer) 1923

Gibson, Edmund (English jurist) 1692

Gibson, Mel (Australian actor and film director) 1995

Gide, André (-Paul-Guillaume) (French writer) 1897, 1902, 1909, 1914, 1926, 1951

Gielgud, John (British actor) 1970

Gierek, Edward (Polish politician) 1970, 1980

Gifts to Observers Dealing with the Curiosities of Cities and Wonders of Journeys 1354

Gigi 1958

Gijon, battle of 1937

Gilbert, Bradford Lee (US architect) 1889

Gilbert, Humphrey (English explorer) 1572

Gilbert, John (US actor) 1925

Gilbert, Lewis (British film director) 1966

Gilbert, W(illiam) S(chwenck) (English writer) 1875, 1878, 1879, 1881, 1882, 1885, 1888, 1889

Gildas (British writer) 542

Gilded Age, The 1873

Gilgamesh, legendary king of Uruk 2000BC, 1872

Gill, (Arthur) Eric (Rowton) (English artist) 1931, 1940

Gillespie, Dizzy (US jazz musician) 1945

Gilliam, Terry (US film director) 1985

Gilmore, Gary (US murderer) 1977

Gimpel the Fool 1957

Ginger Man, The 1955

Gin Lane 1751

Ginsberg, Allen (US poet) 1955

Gioconda, La (The Joyful Girl) 1876

Giodarno, Umberto (Italian composer) 1896

Giorgione (Giorgio del Castelfranco) (Italian painter) 1508, 1510

Giotto di Bondone (Florentine painter) 1300, 1306, 1325, 1334

Giotto 1992

Giraudoux, (Hippolyte-) Jean (French writer) 1935

Girl Aged Five Holding a Red Carnation, A 1590

Girl Crazy 1930

Girl Guides 1910

Girls on the Bridge 1901

Girtin, Thomas (English painter) 1800, 1802

Girton College (Cambridge), foundation of 1869

Giscard d'Estaing, Valéry (president of France) 1974

Giselle 1841

Gish, Lillian (US actor) 1916

Gissing, George Robert (English writer) 1891

Gitangali: Song Offering 1912

Gitlow, Benjamin (US socialist) 1925

Giulio Cesare 1724

Giurgiu, battle of 1595

Giza, pyramids of 2551BC, 2520BC, 2490BC

Gladiator 2000

Gladstone, William Ewart (British politician) 1846, 1852, 1868, 1874, 1876, 1879, 1880, 1881, 1885, 1886, 1892, 1893, 1894, 1896

Glagolitic Mass 1927

Glasgow, Ellen Anderson Gholson (US writer) 1941

Glasgow University (Scotland), foundation of 1450

Glasperlenspiel, Das (The Glass Bead Game) 1943

Glass, Philip (US composer) 1976, 1980, 1984, 1987, 1994

Glass, Bottle and Newspaper 1914

Glass and Fruit 1927

Glass Menagerie, The 1945

Glass–Steagall Act (US) 1933

Glastonbury Cathedral (Somerset), rebuilding of 1182

Glastonbury Romance, A 1932

Glauber, Johnann Rudolf (German chemist) 1648

Glauca (Roman tribune) 100BC

Glencoe massacre 1692, 1695

Glengarry Glen Ross 1983

Glenn, John (US astronaut) 1962

Glenshiel, battle of 1719

Gli indifferenti (A Time of Indifference) 1929

Glinka, Mikhail Ivanovich (Russian composer) 1836, 1842

Glisson, Francis (English chemist) 1654

Gloag, Robert (Scottish cigarette manufacturer) 1856

global warming 1998, 2003

Globe Theatre (London), opening of 1599

Globe Theatre (restored) (London), opening of 1996

Gloria 1959

Gloriana 1953

Glorieta Pass, battle of 1862

Gloster Meteor (jet fighter) 1941

Gloucester, William duke of 1700

Gluck, Christoph Willibald (German composer) 1714, 1752, 1758, 1762, 1767, 1774, 1777, 1787

Glycerius, Roman emperor 473

Gniezno Cathedral (Poland), building of 1080

G N' R Lies 1989

Goat Amalthea, The 1615

Goat's Head Soup 1973

Go-Between, The 1953 (novel); 1970 (film)

Gobi Desert, exploration of 1692

Gobind Singh, 10th Sikh Guru 1675, 1699

God, Peace of (France) 1010

Godaigo (Daigo II), Japanese emperor 1331, 1333, 1336

God and Man at Yale 1951

Godard, Jean-Luc (French film director) 1959, 1964, 1965

Goddard, Paulette (US actor) 1936

Goddard, Robert (US scientist) 1926

Godden, Rumer (English writer) 1939

Goderich, Frederick John Robinson, Viscount (English politician) 1827

Godfather, The 1969 (novel); 1972 (film)

Godfather, The (Part II) 1974

Godfred (Gudfred), king of Denmark 808

Godfrey, Edmund Berry (English jurist) 1678

Godfrey of Bouillon, duke of Lower Lorraine 1099, 1100

God of Small Things, The 1997

Godolphin, Sidney, (English politician) 1st earl of 1679

Godomar, king of Burgundy 524

'God Only Knows' 1966

'God Save the King' 1745

'God Save the Queen' 1977

God's Dealings with George Whitefield 1747

Godspell 1971

Godunov, Boris, tsar of Russia 1584, 1598, 1601, 1604, 1605

Godwin, earl of Wessex 1045, 1051, 1052

Goebbels, (Paul) Joseph (German Nazi) 1933, 1945

G

Grande Illusion, La 1937
Grande Polonaise brillante 1831
Grand Hotel 1932
Grand Hotel (Brighton), bombing of 1984
grand macabre, Le (The Great Macabre) 1978
Grand Meaulnes, Le (The Lost Domain) 1913
Grand' Messe des Morts 1837
Grand Remonstrance (England) 1641
Grands Magasins du Louvre, opening of 1855
Grandson, battle of 1476
Grand Testament, Le (The Great Testament) 1461
Granger, Farley (US actor) 1951
Grant, Cary (British-US actor) 1932, 1938, 1940, 1941, 1944, 1946, 1959, 1986
Grant, Hugh (British actor) 1994
Grant, Ulysses S(impson) (18th US president) 1862, 1864, 1865, 1868, 1869, 1872, 1873
Grantham, battle of 1643
Grapes of Wrath, The 1939 (novel); 1940 (film)
Grass, Günter (German writer) 1959, 2000
Grasse, François-Joseph-Paul, count of (French sailor) 1781
Grass is Singing, The 1950
Grateful Dead, the (US band) 1970
Gratian (Flavius Gratianus), Roman emperor in the W 375, 378, 383
Gratian of Bologna (Italian theologian and jurist) 1139
Grattan, Henry (Irish politician) 1782
Grau, Shirley Ann (US writer) 1964
Graunt, John (English statistician) 1661
Gravelines, battle of 1588
Gravelotte, battle of 1870
Graves, Elisha (US inventor) 1852
Graves, Robert von Ranke (English writer) 1929, 1934, 1985
Graves, Thomas (English sailor) 1781
Gravity's Rainbow 1973
Gray, Alasdair (Scottish writer) 1981
Gray, David (British singer-songwriter) 2001
Gray, Henry (British anatomist) 1858
Gray, Simon (British playwright) 1981
Gray, Stephen (English scientist) 1729
Gray, Thomas (English writer) 1716, 1748, 1751, 1768
Grease 1972
Great (Gran) Colombia 1819, 1821, 1827, 1829, 1830
Great American Nude No. 10 1961
Great Awakening (US) 1738
'Great Balls of Fire' 1958
Great Book of Songs 967
Great Britain, SS 1843
Great Dictator, The 1940
Greater London Council (GLC), abolition of 1985, 1986
Great Escape, The 1963
Great Exhibition (London) 1851
Great Expectations 1861 (novel); 1946 (film)
Great Fire of London 1666
Great Game (India) 1855
Great Gatsby, The 1925
Great Leap Forward (China) 1958
Great Macabre, The 1978
Great Mosque (Mosul), building of 1145
Great Northern War 1700, 1701, 1702, 1703, 1712
Great Plague (London) 1665, 1666

Great Purge (USSR) 1934, 1936
Great Society (US) 1963, 1965
Great Standard of Administration, The 1331
Great Tenochtitlán 1945
Great Train Robbery (UK) 1963
Great Trek (South Africa) 1835
Great War and Modern Memory, The 1975
Great Western, SS 1838
Greco, El (Domenikos Theotokopoulos) (Greek-Spanish painter) 1541, 1577, 1586, 1597, 1598, 1608, 1612, 1614
Greece, German invasion of 1941
Greece, Italian invasion of 1940
Greece in the Ruins of Missolonghi 1826
Greed 1924
Greek Anthology 950
Greek War of Independence 1821, 1824, 1825
Greeley, Horace (US politician) 1872
Green, Henry (Henry Vincent Yorke) (English writer) 1926, 1929, 1939, 1945
Greenaway, Kate (English illustrator) 1879
Greenaway, Peter (Welsh film director) 1982, 1987, 1988, 1989
Greenback (US political party) 1874
Greene, (Henry) Graham (English writer) 1935, 1938, 1940, 1948, 1949, 1950, 1951, 1955, 1958, 1961, 1974, 1978, 1991
Greenham Common, protests at 1981, 1983
Green House, The 1966
Greenmantle 1916
Greenpeace, foundation of 1971
Greens, The (Die Grünen) founded (West German political party) 1980
Greenwich Hospital (London), building of 1694
Greenwich Observatory (London), foundation of 1675
Greer, Germaine (Australian writer) 1970
Gregor, William (English mineralogist) 1791
Gregoras, Nicephorus (Byzantine scholar) 1359
Gregorian Calendar 1582, 1584, 1752
Gregory I (the Great), pope 590, 597, 604
Gregory II, pope 730
Gregory III, pope 739
Gregory IX (Ugolino, count of Segni), pope 1227, 1228, 1231, 1234, 1236, 1239, 1240, 1241
Gregory V (Brunone di Carinzia), pope 996, 998
Gregory VI (Giovanni Graziano), pope 1045, 1046
Gregory VII (Hildebrand), pope 1073, 1075, 1076, 1077, 1078, 1080, 1083, 1084, 1085
Gregory VIII (Maurice Bourdin), antipope 1118
Gregory VIII (Alberto de Mora), pope 1187
Gregory X (Teobaldo Visconti), pope 1274, 1275, 1276
Gregory XI (Pierre-Roger de Beaufort), pope 1370, 1377, 1378
Gregory XII (Angelo Correr), pope 1406, 1409
Gregory XIII (Ugo Boncompagni), pope 1572
Gregory XIV (Niccolò Sfondrati), pope 1590, 1591
Gregory XV (Alessandro Ludovisi), pope 1621
Gregory XVI (Bartolomeo Alberto Cappellari), pope 1831, 1846
Gregory's Girl 1980
Gremlins 1984
Grenada, coup in 1979
Grenada, independence of 1974
Grenada, US invasion of 1983

Grenville, George (English politician) 1755, 1763, 1765
Grenville, Richard (English sailor) 1585, 1591
Grenville, Thomas (English politician) 1782
Grenville, William Wyndham, 1st Baron (British politician) 1806
Gresham, Thomas (English financier) 1518, 1566, 1579
Gresham College (London), foundation of 1596
Grettir's Saga 1200
Greuze, Jean-Baptiste (French painter) 1725, 1755, 1757, 1763, 1765
Greville, Fulke, 1st Baron Brooke (English writer) 1554
Grévy, (François-Paul-) Jules (French president) 1879, 1887
Grey, Charles, 2nd Earl (British politician) 1830
Grey, Edward, 1st Viscount Grey of Falloden (British politician) 1906
Grey, Joel (US actor) 1972
Grey, Lady Jane (great-granddaughter of Henry VII) 1553, 1554
Grief of Andromache, The 1783
Grieg, Edvard (Norwegian composer) 1864, 1868, 1876
Griffith, Arthur (Irish politician) 1905, 1921, 1922
Griffith, D(avid) W(ark) (US film director) 1915, 1916, 1919
Grifters, The 1990
Grillparzer, Franz (Austrian playwright) 1825, 1831, 1834, 1872
Grimaldi, Francis (Francesco Maria Grimaldi) (Italian physicist) 1665
Grimm, Jakob (German writer) 1812, 1854
Grimm, Wilhelm (German writer) 1812, 1854
Grimmelshausen, Hans Jakob Christoffel von (German writer) 1669
Grimond, Joseph (Jo) (British politician) 1956
Gris, Juan (José Victoriano Gonzalez) (Spanish painter) 1912, 1924, 1927
Griselda, La 1721
Gromyko, Andrei Andreyevitch (president of the USSR) 1988
'Grongar Hill' 1727
'Groovy Kind of Love, A' 1988
Gropius, Walter Adolph (German-US architect) 1911, 1919, 1925, 1937
Gros, Antoine (-Jean) (French painter) 1835
Grossbeeren, battle of 1813
Grosse Orgelmesse (Great Mass with Organ) 1766
Grosseteste, Robert (English scholar) 1253
Grossmith, George (English writer) 1892
Grossmith, Weedon (English writer) 1892
Grosz, George (German-US painter) 1916, 1927
Grosz, Karoly (Hungarian politician) 1988
Grotefend, Georg Friedrich (German scholar) 1837
Grotius, Hugo (Hugh de Groot) (Dutch scholar) 1583, 1619, 1625, 1645
Groundhog Day 1993
Grozny, Russian bombardment of 1999
Gruber, Franz Xaver (Austrian musician) 1818
Gruffudd ap Cynan, Welsh prince 1118, 1137
Gruffudd ap Llywelyn, Welsh prince 1039, 1055, 1056, 1063

H

H

Hakim, al-, Fatimid caliph 996, 1005, 1009, 1021
Hakkam II, al-, Umayyad caliph in Spain 961, 976
Hakluyt, Richard (English geographer) 1553, 1589, 1616
Haldemann, H(arry) R(obbins) (US government official) 1973
Hale, Alan (US astronomer) 1995
Hale–Bopp comet 1995, 1997
Haley, Alex (African-American writer) 1976
Haley, Bill (William John Clifton) (US singer) 1954
Halfdan II, king of York 910
Halidon Hill, battle of 1333
Halifax, Edward Frederick Lindley Wood, 1st earl of 1930, 1938, 1940
Halifax (Nova Scotia), destruction of 1917
Hall, Charles Martin (US chemist) 1886
Hall, Radclyffe (Marguerite) (English writer) 1928
Hallaj, al- (Sufi martyr) 922
Haller, Albert (Albrecht) von (Swiss scientist) 1746
Halle University (Germany), foundation of 1694
Halley, Edmond (English astronomer) 1656, 1679, 1682, 1693, 1700, 1705, 1718, 1742
Halley's comet 1705, 1986
Hallidie, Andrew Smith (US engineer) 1873
Halloween 1978
Hallström, Lasse (Swedish film director) 1993
Hals, Frans (Dutch painter) 1624, 1666
Halsted, William Stewart (US surgeon) 1884
Haly Abbas (Persian scholar) 994
Hamaguchi Yuko (Osachi) (Japanese politician) 1930
Hamburg, treaty of 1762
Hamdallah Mustawfi (Persian scholar) 1330
Hamer, Robert (British film director) 1949
Hamilcar Barca (Carthaginian soldier) 237BC
Hamilton, Alexander (US politician) 1790, 1793, 1800, 1804
Hamilton, Guy (British film director) 1964
Hamilton, James, 3rd marquis and 1st duke of Hamilton 1638
Hamilton, Richard (English artist) 1956, 1961
Hamlet 1948
Hamlet, Prince of Denmark 1601
Hammarskjöld, Dag (Swedish politician) 1953, 1960, 1961
Hammerstein II, Oscar (US lyricist) 1927, 1943, 1949, 1951, 1959
Hammett, (Samuel) Dashiell (US writer) 1930, 1934
Hammond, Laurens (US inventor) 1934
Hammond, Walter (English cricketer) 1933
Hammudid dynasty, commencement of 1025
Hammurabi, king of Assyria 1792BC, 1750BC
Hampden, John (English politician) 1637, 1642, 1643
Hampshire, HMS 1916
Hampton, Christopher (English writer and film director) 1970, 1985
'Hampton Court Beauties' 1694
Hampton Court Palace (London), building of 1515
Hamsun, Knut (Knut Pedersen) (Norwegian writer) 1890
Hamrouche, Mouloud (Algerian politician) 1991
Han dynasty, commencement of 209–202BC
Han (East) dynasty, commencement of 25
Hancock, John (US politician) 1775
Hancock, Winfield S(cott) (US politician) 1880

Handel, George Frideric (German-British composer) 1685, 1705, 1706 1710, 1711, 1712, 1717, 1718, 1720, 1723, 1724, 1727, 1732, 1733, 1735, 1739, 1741, 1742, 1743, 1746, 1749, 1752, 1759
Handful of Dust, A 1934
Handley, Tommy (British radio performer) 1939
Handmaid's Tale, The 1985
Handy, William (Christopher) (US composer) 1912
Hangchow, Japanese occupation of 1937
'Hangin' Tough' 1990
Hangzhou, Japanese occupation of 1938
Hanks, Tom (US actor) 1994, 1995, 1998
Hannah and her Sisters 1986
Hannibal (Carthaginian commander) 237BC, 218BC, 217BC, 216BC, 202BC, *c*.183BC
Hannudid dynasty, commencement of 1025
Hanoi, French occupation of 1882
Hanoi, US bombing of 1972
Hansard, Luke (English printer) 1774
Hanseatic League 1241, 1285, 1319, 1344, 1360, 1361, 1363, 1369, 1375
Hänsel und Gretel 1893
Hansen, Gerhard Henrik Armauer (Norwegian physician) 1869
Hansom, Joseph (Aloysius) (British inventor) 1834
Hanson, Curtis (US film director) 1997
Hansson, Per Albin (Swedish politician) 1932
Hanyu (Han Yu) (Chinese poet and philosopher) 823
Hanzala of Badghis (Persian poet) 875
'Happy Birthday' 1981
'Happy Birthday to You' 1893
Happy Days 1961
Happy Prince, The 1888
Happy Return, The 1937
Harappa, collapse of *c*.1800BC
Haraszthy de Mokcsa, Agoston (Hungarian count) 1857, 1861
Hara Takashi (Japanese politician) 1921
'Hard Day's Night, A' 1964
Hard Labour, treaty of 1768
Hard Times 1854
Harder, Delmar S. (US engineer) 1946
Hardie, (James) Keir (British politician) 1893
Harding, Warren Gamaliel (29th US president) 1920, 1921, 1923
Hardouin-Mansart, Jules (French architect) 1678, 1680, 1698, 1708
Hardy, Oliver (US actor) 1927
Hardy, Thomas (English writer) 1871, 1872, 1874, 1878, 1886, 1887, 1891, 1895
Hare, David (English playwright) 1978, 1985, 1990
Hare, William (Irish body-snatcher) 1829
Harel, Mari-Fontaine (French cheese maker) 1791
Hargreaves, Edward (Australian prospector) 1851
Hargreaves, James (English inventor) 1770
Harihara I, king of Vijayanagar 1336
Harington, John (English scholar) 1591
Harlequin 1915
Harlequin's Carnival 1924
Harley, Robert, 1st earl of Oxford (English politician) 1704, 1708, 1710, 1714, 1715, 1717, 1724
Harley, Steve (British singer) 1975
Harlot's Progress 1731
Harlow, Jean (US actor) 1933

Harmonice Musices Odhecaton 1501
Harmonie der Welt, Die (The Harmony of the World) 1957
Harmonielehre 1985
Harmony, Indiana, settlement of 1824
Harmony in Red 1908
Harmsworth, Alfred Charles William, 1st Viscount Northcliffe (British publisher) 1894, 1896, 1903
Harnick, Sheldon (US lyricist) 1964
Harold II (son of Svein I), king of Denmark 1014, 1018
Harold I (Harefoot), king of England 1035, 1037, 1040
Harold II, king of England 1045, 1053, 1063, 1066
Harold I (Fairhair), king of Norway 900, 930
Harold III (Hardrada), king of Norway 1066
Harold Bluetooth, king of Denmark 958, 965, 974, 987
Harold in Italy 1834
Harper's Ferry, raid on 1859
Harper's Monthly 1850
Harper's Weekly 1869
Harrington, James (English political philosopher) 1656, 1677
Harriott, Thomas (English astronomer) 1588, 1610
Harris, Joel Chandler (US writer) 1881, 1906
Harris, John (English editor) 1704
Harris, Thomas (US writer) 1988
Harrison, Benjamin (23rd US president) 1888, 1889, 1892
Harrison, George (British musician) 1971
Harrison, John (English horologist) 1726
Harrison, Peter (American architect) 1763
Harrison, Rex (British actor) 1945
Harrison, Wallace K(irkman) (US architect) 1950
Harrison, William Henry (9th US president) 1809, 1841
Harrod, James (US pioneer) 1774
Harrods, London, bombing of 1983
Harrods, London, opening of 1849
Harrowing of Hell, The 1295
Harrying of the North (England) 1069
Harry Potter and the Chamber of Secrets 1998
Harry Potter and the Goblet of Fire 2000
Harry Potter and the Order of the Phoenix 2003
Harry Potter and the Philosopher's Stone 1997
Harry Potter and the Prisoner of Azkaban 1999
Harsha, emperor of India 606, 612, 635
Hart, Lorenz (US lyricist) 1940
Harthacnut (Hardecanute), king of Denmark and England 1035, 1036, 1040, 1042
Hartley, David (English inventor and politician) 1776
Hartley, John (English tennis player) 1880
Hartley, L(esley) P(oles) (English writer) 1947, 1953
Harun al-Rashid, Abbasid caliph 786, 803, 806
Harvard College (Massachusetts), foundation of 1636
Harvey, Anthony (British film director) 1968
Harvey, William (English physician) 1578, 1619, 1628, 1651, 1657
Hasan, shah of Madura 1335
Hasan ibn al-Sabbah, al- (Persian founder of the Assassins) 1090, 1124
Hasdrubal (son-in-law of Hamilcar Barca) 237BC
Hasdrubal (son of Hamilcar Barca) 216BC
Hasek, Jaroslav (Czech writer) 1923
Hashemite dynasty, commencement of 1916

H

H

Hopper, Dennis (US actor) 1969
Hopper, Edward (US painter) 1927, 1930, 1931, 1942
Horace (Quintus Horatius Flaccus) (Roman poet) 35BC, 19BC, 17BC, 8BC
Horace 1639
Horemheb (Djeserkheperura), 18th dynasty king of Egypt 1319BC, 1307BC
Hormizd IV, Sassanian king of Persia 588
Hornby, Nick (English writer) 1992, 1995
Hornet, USS 1942
Horns of Hattin, battle of the 1187
Hornung, E(rnest) W(illiam) (English writer) 1899
Horoscope 1937
Horse Feathers 1932
Horses 1975
Horse's Mouth, The 1944
'Horse with No Name' 1972
Horthy de Nagybánya, Nikolaus Miklós (Hungarian politician) 1919
Horyu-ji Temple (Japan), building of 607
Hoskins, Bob (British actor) 1980
Hosokawa Yonyaki (Japanese shogun) 1368
Hotel Adlon (Berlin), opening of 1907
Hotel California 1976
Hôtel de Montmorency (Paris), building of 1712, 1772
Hôtel des Invalides (Paris), building of 1671
Hôtel-Dieu (Lyons, France), building of 1741
Hôtel du Lac 1984
'Hot in Here' 2002
'Hot Love' 1971
Hotman, François (French jurist) 1573
Houdini, Harry (Erich Weiss) (US magician) 1900, 1926
Houdon, Jean-Antoine (French sculptor) 1828
Houphouët-Boigny, Félix (president of Côte d'Ivoire) 1989
'Hound Dog' 1956
Hound of the Baskervilles, The 1902 (novel); 1939 (film)
Hours, The 2002
Housatonic, USS 1917
House, The 1998
House for Mr Biswas, A 1961
House of the Hanged Man, The 1873
'House of the Rising Sun' 1964
House Made of Dawn 1968
House of Mirth, The 1905
House of the Seven Gables, The 1851
House of the Spirits, The 1982
Housman, A(lfred) E(dward) (English writer) 1896
Houston, David Henderson (US inventor) 1881
Houston, Whitney (US singer) 1987, 1992
Houzou (Hou-Chu) dynasty, commencement of 951
hovercraft, invention of 1959
Howard, Charles, 2nd Baron Howard of Effingham 1596
Howard, Edward (English sailor) 1512
Howard, Henry, earl of Surrey 1517, 1547, 1557
Howard, John (Australian politician) 1996
Howard, Leslie (British actor) 1938
Howard, Michael (British politician) 2003
Howard, Ron (US film director) 1995, 2001
Howard, Thomas, 3rd duke of Norfolk (English politician) 1536, 1540

Howard, Thomas, 4th duke of Norfolk (English poet and soldier) 1572
Howard, Trevor (British actor) 1946
Howard University for Negroes (Washington, D.C.), foundation of 1867
Howards End 1910 (novel); 1992 (film)
Howe, Delmas (US artist) 1995
Howe, Elias (US inventor) 1846
Howe, Richard Edward Geoffrey (British politician) 1989, 1990
Howe, Julia Ward (US writer) 1862
Howe, Samuel Gridley (US reformer) 1862
Howe, William, 5th Viscount Howe (English soldier) 1776
Howell, James (Welsh scholar) 1660
How Far Can You Go? 1980
How Green was My Valley 1939
'Howl' 1955
How Late It Was, How Late 1994
How to Win Friends and Influence People 1936
Hoxha, Enver (Albanian politician) 1946, 1985
Hrawi, Elias (Lebanese president) 1989, 1990
Hsiao Yen (Liang Wu Ti), emperor of China 502, 517
Hsin (Xin) dynasty, commencement of 9
Hsu Wei (Chinese writer) 1560
Hua Guofeng (chairman of Chinese Communist Party) 1976
Huang Zhao (Huang Chao), usurping emperor of China 880, 883, 884
Huascarán, eruption of 1970
Hubbard, L(afayette) Ron(ald) (US writer and founder of scientology) 1953
Hubbarton, battle of 1777
Hubble space telescope, launch of 1990
Hubicka (The Kiss) 1876
Hudibras 1662, 1663, 1678
Hudson, Henry (English explorer) 1609, 1610
Hudson, Hugh (British film director) 1981
Hudson, Rock (US actor) 1985
Hué, treaty of 1883
Huerta, Victoriano (Mexican politician) 1913, 1914
Huey Long Bridge (Louisiana), building of 1935
Hugh Capet, king of France 987
Hughes, Charles Evans (US jurist) 1916
Hughes, David (British-US inventor) 1855
Hughes, Richard (English writer) 1929, 1961
Hughes, Ted (Edward James) (English poet) 1957, 1970, 1997, 1998
Hughes, Thomas (English writer) 1857
Hugo, Victor (French writer) 1830, 1831, 1838, 1862
Huguénots, Les 1836
Huis clos (In Camera) 1944
Huizinga, Johan (Dutch historian) 1919
Huizong (Hui Tsung), emperor of China 1125, 1127
Hülagü, Mongol khan 1253, 1256, 1258, 1260, 1262, 1265
Hulme, Keri (New Zealand writer) 1984
Human Condition, The 1934
Human Factor, The 1978
human genome, mapping of 2000
Human League (British group) 1981
Human Mind, The 1930
Human Nature, A Treatise on 1739
Humayun, Mughal emperor 1530, 1540, 1545, 1555

Humble Petition and Advice 1657
Humboldt, (Friedrich Wilhelm Heinrich) Alexander von (German geophysicist) 1800, 1802
Humboldt's Gift 1975
Hume, David (Scottish philosopher) 1711, 1739, 1748, 1751, 1753, 1754, 1757, 1758, 1762, 1776, 1779
Humperdinck, Engelbert (German composer) 1893
Humperdinck, Engelbert (British singer) 1967
Humphrey, duke of Gloucester 1422, 1426
Humphrey, Hubert Horatio (US politician) 1968
Humphrey de Hauteville (Norman soldier) 1053
Hunac Ceel (Maya leader) 1221
Hunayn ibn Ishaq al-Ibadi (Arab scholar) 873
Hunchback of Notre Dame, The 1939
Hundred and One Dalmations, The 1956
Hundred Years War 1337, 1453
Hungarian Peasant Songs 1933
Hungarian revolution 1848, 1849
Hungarian revolution 1956
Hungarian Rhapsodies 1851
Hungary, independence of 1918
Hunnenschlacht (Battle of the Huns) 1858
Hunt, Henry (Orator Hunt) (English politician) 1819
Hunt, Howard (US government consultant) 1972
Hunt, Richard Morris (US architect) 1892
Hunt, Thomas P. (US clergyman) 1836
Hunt, Walter (US inventor) 1833, 1849
Hunt, William Holman (English artist) 1848, 1849, 1853, 1854, 1856, 1910
Hunter, Evan (US writer, aka Ed McBain) 1954
Hunter, John (Scottish surgeon) 1771, 1773
hunter-gatherers, Jomon 14,000BP; Natufian 12,000BP; in Syria 11,000BP; in Zagros Mts 11,000BP
Hunting of the Snark, The 1870
Hunyadi, János (Hungarian nationalist) 1443, 1444, 1448, 1456
Hunyadi, Laszlo (Hungarian nationalist) 1457
Hurley Machine Corp. 1907
Hurricane Andrew 1992
Hurricane David 1979
Hurricane Ivan 2004
Hus, Jan (Bohemian religious reformer) 1408, 1414, 1415, 1420
Husák, Gustav (Czech politician) 1969, 1987, 1989
Huskisson, William (British train accident victim) 1830
Hussein (al-Husayn) (Fatimid ruler) 632, 661, 678, 680
Hussein I, bey of Tunis 1705
Hussein Hilmi Pasha, Ottoman grand vizier 1909
Hussein (Husain) ibn Ali, king of the Hejaz 1916, 1924
Hussein ibn Talal, king of Jordan 1952, 1953, 1958, 1966, 1970, 1988, 1999
Hussein, Saddam (president of Iraq) 1987, 1988, 1990, 1991, 2001, 2002, 2003
Hussein, Uday (son of Saddam Hussein) 1997
Hustler, The 1961
Huston, Anjelica (US actor) 1987
Huston, John (US film director) 1941, 1948, 1951, 1961, 1975, 1984, 1985, 1987
Hutcheson, Francis (Irish philosopher) 1725
Hutten, Ulrich von (German humanist) 1522, 1523, 1528

I

J

K

Kania, Stanislaw (Polish politician) 1980
Kansas City, foundation of 1838
Kansas–Nebraska Act (US) 1854
Kansu al-Guari, Mamluk sultan of Egypt 1516
Kant, Immanuel (German philosopher) 1724, 1755, 1781, 1785, 1788, 1790, 1797
Kanwanha, battle of 1527
Kapital, Das 1867, 1886
Kapodístrias, Avgoustinos (Greek politician) 1831
Kapodístrias, Ioánnes (Greek politician) 1829, 1831
Kapp, Wolfgang (German politician) 1920
Kappel, battle of 1531
Kappel, treaty of 1529
Kappler, Herbert (German Nazi) 1944
Kapp Putsch (Germany) 1920
Karadzic, Radovan (Bosnian-Serb war criminal) 1992, 1996
Karajan, Herbert von (Austrian conductor) 1954
Karamanlis, Constantine (Greek politician) 1974
Karami, Rashid Abdul Hamid (Lebanese politician) 1987
Kara Mustafa Pasa, Ottoman grand vizier 1676, 1683
Karbala, battle of 680
Kardis, peace of 1661
Karel, Elder of Zerotin (Czech leader) 1609
Karloff, Boris (William Henry Pratt) (British-US actor) 1931, 1935
Karlowitz, peace of 1699
'Karma Chameleon' 1983
Karnak, temple complex at 1391BC, 1307BC, 1306BC, 1270BC
Karrinmaru SS 1860
Karume, Abeid (president of Zanzibar) 1964
Karzai, Hamid (Afghan politician) 2002, 2004
Kasavubu, Joseph (president of Democratic Republic of Congo/Zaire) 1960, 1965
Kashani, al- (Persian writer) 1301
Kasparov, Gary (Soviet chess grandmaster) 1997
Kasserine Pass, battle of the 1943
Kästner, Erich (German writer) 1929
Kasuga Shrine (Nara), building of 768
Kasuri, Ahmad Raza (Pakistani politician) 1974
Káta Kabanová 1921
Kathio, battle of 1750
Katyn massacre (Russia) 1940
Katzbach, battle of 1813
Kauffmann, Angelica (Swiss painter) 1741
Kaufman, George S(imon) (US playwright) 1928
Kaukasische Kreiderkreis, Der (The Caucasian Chalk Circle) 1948
Kaunda, Kenneth David (president of Zambia) 1964
Kavadh II, Sassanian king of Persia 628
Kay, John (English inventor) 1733
Kay, battle of 1759
Kaye, Danny (US actor) 1941
Kayibanda, Grégoire (president of Rwanda) 1961
Kaykhusraw (Kaikorsu) II, Seljuk sultan of Rum 1241, 1243
Kazan, Elia (US film director) 1954, 1955
Kazantzakis, Nikos (Greek writer) 1938, 1946
Kean, Edmund (English actor) 1814
Keane, Molly (Irish writer) 1981
Kearny, USS 1941

Keating, Paul (Australian politician) 1991, 1993, 1995
Keaton, Michael (US actor) 1989
Keats, John (English poet) 1816, 1817, 1818, 1819, 1820, 1821
Kebbah, Ahmed (Sierra Leone politician) 1997
Keble, John (English clergyman) 1833
Keeler, Christine (British model) 1963
Keenan, Brian (British writer and hostage) 1986, 1990
Keepers of the House, The 1964
Keep the Aspidistra Flying 1936
'Keep the Home Fires Burning' 1914
Keiller, James (Scottish conserve maker) 1797
Keillor, Garrison (US writer) 1985
Keith, George Keith Elphinstone, Viscount (English sailor) 1800
Keith, Minor Cooper (US businessman) 1871
Kekulé von Stradonitz, Friedrich August (German chemist) 1858
Keller, Gottfried (German writer) 1855
Keller, Gottlob (German scientist) 1844
Keller, Helen (Adams) (US writer) 1887
Keller, Louis (US golf promoter) 1887
Kellogg, Frank B(illings) (US politician) 1928
Kellogg, John (Harvey) (US physician) 1876, 1898
Kellogg, W(ill) K(eith) (US businessman) 1898
Kellog–Briand Pact 1928
Kells, synod of 1152
Kelly, Charles (US labour leader) 1893
Kelly, David (British weapons inspector) 2003, 2004
Kelly, Gene (US actor and dancer) 1951, 1952
Kelly, Grace (US actor and wife of Prince Rainier of Monaco) 1982
Kelly, Ned (Edward) (Australian outlaw) 1880
Kelly's Industrial Army 1893
Kelman, James (Scottish writer) 1989, 1994
Kelmscott Press, foundation of 1890
Kelvin, William Thomson, 1st Baron (Irish physicist) 1824
Kendall, Edward (Calvin) (US biochemist) 1948
Keneally, Thomas (Australian writer) 1982
Kenesaw Mountain, battle of 1864
Kenilworth, Dictum of 1266
Kenilworth 1821
Kennaway, Ernest (British scientist) 1933
Kennedy, Arthur (Australian politician) 1877
Kennedy, Charles (British politician) 1999
Kennedy, Edward Moore (Teddy) (US politician) 1969
Kennedy, John F(itzgerald) (35th US president) 1953, 1960, 1961, 1962, 1963
Kennedy, Joseph P(atrick) (US diplomat) 1938
Kennedy, Paul (British writer) 1987
Kennedy, Robert F(rancis) (US politician) 1968
Kennedy, William Joseph (US writer) 1983
Kenneth I MacAlpin, king of Scotland 843, 858
Kensett, Thomas (US inventor) 1825
Kent, Walter (US songwriter) 1941
Kent, William (English artist) 1719, 1727, 1730, 1734, 1748, 1750
Kent State University, anti-Vietnam War protest at 1970
Kentucky Resolutions 1798
Kenya, independence of 1963
Kenyatta, Jomo (president of Kenya) 1952, 1953, 1963, 1978

Kepler, Johannes (German astronomer) 1571, 1604, 1609, 1615, 1630
Keppel, Christopher Guillaume (Swiss chemist) 1861
Kerensky, Alexander Fyodorovich (Russian revolutionary) 1917
Kern, Jerome David (US composer) 1927, 1940
Kerouac, Jack (US writer) 1957
Kerr, Deborah (Scottish actor) 1943, 1947, 1956
Kerr, Sir John Robert (Australian politician) 1975
Kerr, Malcolm (president of the American University, Beirut) 1984
Kerry, John (US politician) 2004
Kes 1969
Kesey, Ken (US writer) 1962
Ket kep (Two Pictures) 1910
Kett, Robert (English rebel) 1549
Kettler, Gotthard (master of Teutonic Knights) 1561
Key, Francis Scott (US writer) 1814
Key Largo 1948
Keynes, John Maynard (British economist) 1919, 1936
Key of the Sciences 976
Khachaturian, Aram (Armenian composer) 1948, 1956, 1978
Khafre (Chephren), 3rd dynasty king of Egypt 2520BC
Khaidu, Mongol leader 1268 1277
Khair ad-Din (Barbarossa) (Ottoman sailor and pirate) 1535, 1538
Khaki election in UK 1900
Khaled, Leila (Palestinian terrorist) 1970
Khalid II ibn Abdul-Aziz, king of Saudi Arabia 1975
Khalid ibn al-Walid (Arab general) 636
Khalji dynasty, commencement of 1290
Khalsa brotherhood, foundation of 1699
Khama, Seretse (president of Botswana) 1966
Khan, Agha Mohammed Yahya (president of Pakistan) 1969, 1971
Khan, Ayub Mohammed (president of Pakistan) 1958, 1969
Khan, Gulam Ishaq (president of Pakistan) 1990, 1993
Khan, Imran (Pakistani cricketer and politician) 1996
Kharkov, battle of 1943
Khartoum, siege of 1884, 1885
Khasbulatov, Ruslan (Russian politician) 1992
Khmelnitsky, Bogdan (Bohdan) (Cossack leader) 1648
Khmer Republic, declaration of 1970
Khmer Rouge 1969, 1975, 1985, 1999
Khodorkovsky, Mikhail (Russian businessman) 2003
Khomeini, Ruholla (Iranian ayatollah) 1979, 1981, 1988, 1989
Khrushchev, Nikita (Soviet politician) 1953, 1955, 1956, 1958, 1959, 1959, 1960, 1963, 1964
Khufu (Cheops), 4th dynasty king of Egypt 2551BC
Khusraw Khan, sultan of Delhi 1320
Khwarizmi, Muhammad ibn Musa al- (Persian mathematician) 850, 976
Kid, The 1921
Kidman, Nicole (Australian actor) 1999
Kidnapped 1886
Kiel, mutiny at 1918
Kiel, treaty of 1814
Kiel Canal, opening of 1895
Kielce massacre (Poland) 1946
Kierkegaard, Sören Aabye (Danish philosopher) 1843

K

L

L

Lehár, Franz (Hungarian composer) 1905

Leibniz, Gottfried Wilhelm (German mathematician) 1663, 1666, 1667, 1671, 1675, 1691, 1700, 1710, 1711, 1714, 1716

Leiden des Jungen Werther, Die (The Sorrows of Young Werther) 1774

Leif Ericsson (Icelandic explorer) 1003

Leigh, Janet (US actor) 1958

Leigh, Mike (British film director) 1996, 2004

Leigh, Vivien (British actor) 1939

Leip, Hans (German songwriter) 1941

Leipzig, battle of (battle of the Nations) 1813

Leiter, Joseph (US speculator) 1897

Lélia 1833

Lely, Peter (Pieter Van der Faes) (German painter) 1617, 1647, 1653, 1654, 1660, 1661, 1680

Le Mans Cathedral (France), building of 1150

Lemass, Sean Francis (Irish politician) 1959, 1965, 1966

Lemmon, Jack (US actor) 1959, 1960

Lemprière, John (English scholar) 1788

Lend-Lease Act (US) 1941

L'Enfant, Pierre Charles (French-born US architect) 1790

Lenin (Vladimir Ilyich Ulyanov) (Russian communist) 1895, 1900, 1903, 1907, 1916, 1917, 1921, 1922, 1923, 1924

Leningrad, name changed to St Petersburg 1991

Leningrad, siege of 1941, 1943, 1944

Le Nôtre, André (French architect) 1656, 1662

Lennon, John (British singer-songwriter and musician) 1971, 1980

Lennox, Annie (Scottish singer) 1993

Lenya, Lotte (Austrian singer) 1928

Leo III, pope 800, 816

Leo VIII, pope 963

Leo IX (Bruno), pope 1049, 1053, 1054

Leo X (Giovanni de' Medici), pope 1513, 1515, 1517, 1520, 1521

Leo XI (Alessandro Ottaviano de' Medici), pope 1605

Leo XII (Annibale Sermattei della Genga), pope 1823, 1829

Leo XIII (Gioacchino Vincenzo Pecci), pope 1878, 1891, 1903

Leo VI, king of Armenia 1375

Leo I, Byzantine emperor 457, 466, 467, 468, 473, 474

Leo III (the Isaurian), Byzantine emperor 717, 718, 726, 730, 741

Leo IV (the Khazar), Byzantine emperor 775, 780

Leo V (the Armenian), Byzantine emperor 813, 814, 815, 820

Leo VI (the Wise), Byzantine emperor 886, 896

Leo, prince of Ruthenia 1324

Leonardo da Vinci (Italian polymath) 1452, 1473, 1492, 1495, 1519

Leon Cathedral (Spain), building of 1160, 1255

Leoncavallo, Ruggiero (Italian composer) 1892

Leone, Sergio (Italian film director) 1964, 1966

Leonidas, king of Sparta 480BC

Leontius, Byzantine emperor 695, 698

Leopard, The 1958 (novel); 1963 (film)

Leopardi, Giacomo (Italian poet) 1818

Leopold IV, margrave of Austria 1138, 1140

Leopold V, duke of Austria 1192, 1193

Leopold I, duke of Austria 1315, 1318

Leopold V, archduke of Austria 1618

Leopold I, king of the Belgians 1831, 1865

Leopold II, king of the Belgians 1865, 1876, 1885, 1891, 1908, 1909

Leopold III, king of the Belgians 1950

Leopold I, Holy Roman Emperor 1658, 1660, 1663, 1668, 1672, 1673, 1681, 1683, 1684, 1688, 1700, 1705

Leopold II, Holy Roman Emperor 1765, 1790, 1791, 1792

Leopold I, grand duke of Tuscany *see* Leopold II, Holy Roman Emperor

Leopold, prince of Hohenzollern-Sigmaringen (candidate for Spanish throne) 1870

Léotard, Jules (French acrobat) 1859

Leo the Mathematician (Greek teacher and scholar) 863

Leovigild, Visigothic king of Spain 585, 589

Lepanto, battle of 1571

Le Peletier, Claude (French politician) 1683

Le Pen, Jean-Marie (French politician) 1972, 2002

Lepidus, Marcus Aemilius (Roman politician) 78BC, 77BC, 43BC, 40BC, 36BC

Lerdo de Tejada, Sebastián (Mexican politician) 1876

Lermontov, Mikhail Yurevich (Russian writer) 1837, 1840, 1841

Lerner, Alan Jay (US librettist) 1956, 1960

LeRoy, Mervyn (US film director) 1930, 1933

Lesage, Alain-René (French writer) 1715

Lescot, Pierre (French architect) 1546

Leslie, Alexander, 1st earl of Leven 1644

Lesotho (Basutoland), independence of 1966

Lesseps, Ferdinand (-Marie) de (French engineer) 1854, 1859, 1892

Lessing, Doris (English writer) 1950, 1962

Lessing, Gotthold Ephraim (German writer) 1729, 1767, 1772, 1783

L'Estrange, Roger (licenser of the English press) 1663

Leszek III (the Black), grand prince of Poland 1282, 1288

Letelier, Orlando (Chilean ambassador) 1976

Le Tellier, Michel, marquis of Louvois 1670

Le Thaito, Vietnamese emperor 1428

Let It Be 1970

Let It Bleed 1969

'Let's Do It' 1928

Letters on the Study and Uses of History 1752

'Let the Heartaches Begin' 1967

Lettow-Vorbeck, Paul von (German soldier) 1917

Lettres persanes (Persian Letters) 1721

Lettres philosophiques sur les Anglais (Philosophical Letters on the English) 1733

Lettres provinciales (Provincial Letters) 1656

Lettres sur le caractère et les écrits de Jean-Jacques Rousseau 1788

Lettre sur les aveugles à l'usage de ceux qui voient (Letter on the Blind for the Use of the Sighted) 1749

Leuthen, battle of 1757

Leutze, Emanuel (US painter) 1851

Levant Trilogy, The 1980

Le Vau, Louis (French architect) 1612, 1661, 1669, 1670

Leveller movement 1645, 1646, 1647

Lever, James Darcy (British industrialist) 1929

Lever, William Hesketh, 1st Viscount Leverhulme (British manufacturer) 1885, 1897

'Lever du Sol' 1753

Lévesque, René (Canadian politician) 1968, 1976

Levi, Carlo (Italian writer) 1945

Levi, Primo (Italian writer) 1987

Leviathan 1651

Levi ben Gerson (French Jewish mathematician and philosopher) 1321, 1323, 1329, 1343, 1344

Levine, Denis B. (US financier) 1986

Levinson, Barry (US film director) 1988

Lewin, Albert (US film director) 1947

Lewinsky, Monica (US White House intern) 1998

Lewis, C(live) S(taples) (English writer) 1938, 1950

Lewis, Jerry Lee (US singer) 1958

Lewis, Percy Wyndham (English writer) 1914, 1918

Lewis, Meriwether (US explorer) 1804, 1805, 1806

Lewis, (Harry) Sinclair (US writer) 1920, 1922, 1925, 1927, 1935

Lewis–Clark expedition (US) 1804, 1805, 1806

Lexicon Technicum, or, a Universal English Dictionary of Arts and Sciences 1704

Lexicon Tetraglotten (Four-way Dictionary) 1660

Lexicon Universale 1677

Lexington, battle of 1775

Leyden jar, invention of 1745

Leyland Motors, foundation of 1896

LHOOQ 1920

L'Hôpital, Michel de (French minister) 1560

Lhote, Henri (French archaeologist) 1956

Liaisons dangereux, Les (Dangerous Liaisons) 1782 (novel); 1985 (stage adaptation)

Liang dynasty, commencement of 502

Liao dynasty, commencement of 947

Liaoyang, battle of 1904

Libation Bearers, The 456BC

Liberia, foundation of 1820

Liberia, independence of 1847

Liber ludicorium 653

Liberty, Equality and Fraternity 1995

Liberty Bell, Philadelphia 1752

Liberty League in US 1934

Liberty on the Barricades 1830

Lib–Lab pact 1977, 1978

Library 891

Library of Congress, US, foundation of 1800

Libre de contemplacio en Deu (Book of Contemplation of God) 1271

Libre del orde de cavayleria (Book of the Order of Chivalry) 1275

Libro del cortegiano, Il (The Book of the Courtier) 1528

Libya, Italian annexation of 1911

Libya, US bombing of 1986

Licensing Act (UK) 1662

Licensing Act (UK) 1872

Licheng (Li Ch'eng) (Chinese painter) 967

Lichtenstein, Roy (US artist) 1963, 1975, 1997

Lichtenstein, independence of 1719

Licinius (Valerius Licinianus Licinius), Roman emperor 307, 313, 323, 324

Lidice massacre (Czechoslovakia) 1942

L

Lucretius (Titus Lucretius Carus) (Roman writer) 54BC
Lucrezia Borgia 1833
Lucullus, Lucius Licinius (Roman soldier) 71BC, 69BC, 68BC
'Lucy in the Sky With Diamonds' 1967
Luddite riots 1811, 1812, 1813, 1816
Ludendorff, Erich Friedrich Wilhelm (German soldier) 1914, 1918, 1923
Ludendorff Offensive 1918
Ludi Theatrales Sacri (Sacred Plays) 1666
Ludwig (Lajos) I (the Great), king of Hungary and of Poland 1342, 1347, 1350, 1351, 1358, 1362, 1367, 1370, 1374, 1382
Ludwig VI, Elector Palatine of the Rhine 1512, 1515
Ludwig of Bavaria *see* Louis IV, Holy Roman Emperor
Ludwig (Louis) of Brandenburg 1342
Ludwigslied (The Song of Louis) 881
Lugosi, Bela (Bela Ferenc Blasko) (Hungarian actor) 1931
Luis, king of Spain 1724
Luisa Miller 1849
Luis Pereira de Sousa, Washington (president of Brazil) 1930
Lukanov, Andrei (Bulgarian politician) 1990
Lukashenko, Alexander (president of Belarus) 2004
Lüleburgaz, battle of 1912
Lull, Rámon (Catalan scholar) 1271, 1273, 1275, 1276, 1315
Lully, Jean-Baptiste (Giovanni Battista Lulli) 1632, 1645, 1653, 1673, 1674, 1681, 1686, 1687
Lulu (British singer) 1964
Lulu 1937, 1979
Lumet, Sidney (US film director) 1957, 1975
Lumière, Auguste (-Marie-Louis-Nicolas) (French cinematographer) 1895
Lumière, Louis (-Jean) (French cinematographer) 1895
Lumley, Richard, 2nd Viscount (English politician) 1688
Lumumba, Patrice (Congolese politician) 1960, 1961
Lunar Prospector 1998
Luncheon of the Boating Party 1881
Lund, treaty of 1679
Lund University (Sweden), foundation of 1668
Lunéville, treaty of 1801, 1802
Luhrmann, Mark Anthony (Baz) (Australian film director) 1992, 2001
Lurie, Alison (US writer) 1974, 1984
Lusiads, The 1655
Lusitania, SS 1907, 1915
Lust for Life 1934
Lustige Witwe, Die 1905
Luther, Martin (German religious reformer) 1505, 1511, 1512, 1517, 1518, 1519, 1520, 1521, 1522, 1523, 1524, 1534, 1546
Lutter am Bamburg, battle of 1626
Lutyens, Edwin Landseer (British architect) 1931
Lützen, battle of 1632
Lützen, battle of 1813
Lux aeterna 1966
Luxe, calme et volupté 1905
Luxembourg, Francis Henry de Montmorency-Bouteville, duke of 1692
Luxembourg, siege of 1681

Luxemburg, Rosa (Polish-German socialist) 1899, 1919
Luxor, temple complex at 1391BC, 1270BC
Luxor, terrorist attack on 1997
Luzon, US seizure of 1899
Lviv, massacre at 1941
Lvov, Georgi Yevgenyevich (Russian politician) 1917
Lvov, battle of 1695
Lyceum, Athens 335BC
Lycidas 1638
Lycurgus 561BC
Ly dynasty, commencement of 1010
Lyly, John (English writer) 1554, 1578
Lynch, Charles (US planter) 1781
Lynch, David (US film director) 1980, 1986, 2001
Lynch, John Mary (Jack) (Irish politician) 1966
Lyne, Adrian (British film producer) 1987, 1993
Lynn, Vera (British singer) 1940
Lyons, treaty of 1504
Lyrical Ballads 1798, 1800
Lysander (Spartan soldier) 408BC, 407BC, 406BC
Lysias (regent of Syria) 163BC
Lysimachus (Macedonian general) 323BC, 301BC, 281BC
Lysistrata 411BC
Ly Thai-to, Vietnamese emperor 1010
Ly Thanh-ton, Vietnamese emperor 1068

M

M 1931
Maastricht, battle of 1747
Maastricht treaty 1992
Mabillon, Jean (French scholar) 1632, 1681, 1707
McAdam, John Loudon (Scottish engineer) 1815
MacArthur, Charles (US playwright) 1928
MacArthur, Douglas (US soldier) 1942, 1945, 1950, 1951
Macarthy, Charles (British soldier) 1824
Macassar Strait, battle of 1942
Macau, return to China of 1999
Macaulay, Catharine (Catharine Sawbridge) (English historian) 1763
Macaulay, (Emilie) Rose (English writer) 1956
Macaulay, Thomas Babington (British writer and politician) 1825, 1842, 1848, 1861
Macbeth, king of Scotland 1040, 1054, 1057
Macbeth 1606 (play); 1847 (opera)
McCabe, Patrick (Irish writer) 1992
McCarey, Leo (US film director) 1933
McCarthy, Cormac (US writer) 1992
McCarthy, Eugene (Joseph) (US politician) 1968
McCarthy, John (British journalist and hostage) 1986, 1991
McCarthy, Joseph (Raymond) (US politician) 1950, 1954
McCartney, Paul (British singer-songwriter) 1982
Macchu Pichu, discovery of 1911
MacClean, Shirley (US actor) 1960
McClellan, George Brinton (US soldier) 1861, 1862, 1864
McCormick, Cyrus Hall (US inventor) 1861
McCullers, Carson (US writer) 1940, 1951
McCullough, Colleen (Australian writer) 1977

MacDiarmid, Hugh (Christopher M. Grieve) (Scottish poet) 1926
Macdonald, Flora (Scottish Jacobite) 1746
MacDonald, Ramsay (British politician) 1924, 1929, 1931, 1935
McDowell, Malcolm (British actor) 1969, 1971, 1973, 2003
McDuffie, Arthur (US victim of police brutality) 1980
Macedonian War, Third 171-168BC
Macedonian, HMS 1812
McEwan, Ian (English writer) 1978, 1987, 1990, 1992, 1998, 2001
McFadden, Hamilton (US film director) 1934
McGahern, John (Irish writer) 1990
McGill University (Montreal), foundation of 1821
McGovern, George (US politician) 1972
MacGraw, Ali (US actor) 1970
McGregor, Ewan (Scottish actor) 1996, 2003
MacGregor, Ian (Scottish-British industrialist)
Machaut, Guillaume de (French composer) 1350, 1377
Machel, Samor Moïsés (president of Mozambique) 1975, 1986
Machiavelli, Niccolò (Italian philosopher) 1506, 1513, 1527, 1532
Machine infernale, La (The Infernal Machine) 1934
Macht und Erde (Power and Land) 1934
Macias Nguema, Francisco (president of Equatorial Guinea) 1979
McIlhenny, Edward (US businessman) 1868
MacInnes, Colin (English writer) 1959
Macke, August (German painter) 1911
McKellen, Ian (British actor) 2001
Mackendrick, Alexander (US film director) 1955
Mackenzie, Alexander (Scottish explorer) 1793
Mackenzie, Compton (Scottish writer) 1947
Mackenzie, David (British film director) 2003
Mackenzie, Henry (Scottish writer) 1771
Mackenzie, John (British film director) 1980
McKenzie, Scott (US singer) 1967
Mackenzie, William Lyon (Canadian insurgent) 1837
McKinley, William (25th US president) 1896, 1897, 1898, 1900, 1901
McKinley Tariff Act (US) 1890, 1892, 1894
Mackintosh, Charles (Scottish inventor) 1823
Mackintosh, Charles Rennie (Scottish architect) 1898, 1899
Maclean, Alistair (Scottish writer) 1955
McLean, Don (US singer-songwriter) 1972
Maclean, Donald (British traitor) 1951
McLeod, Iain (British politician) 1970
McLeod, Norman Z. (US film director) 1931, 1932
McLuhan, (Herbert) Marshall (Canadian writer) 1962
MacMahon, (Marie-Edmé-) Patrice-Maurice de (president of France) 1870, 1873, 1875, 1877, 1879
Macmillan, (Maurice) Harold, 1st earl of Stockton (British politician) 1957, 1959, 1960, 1962, 1963
MacMillan, James (Scottish composer) 1990
MacMillan, Kirkpatrick (Scottish inventor) 1839, 1861
McMurtry, Larry Jeff (US writer) 1985
McNamara, Robert Strange (US politician) 1971
MacNeice, Louis (Irish writer) 1938, 1963

M

Macpherson, James (Scottish poet) 1760
McPherson, James Alan (US writer) 1977
McQueen, (Terence) Steve (US actor) 1963
Macrinus (Marcus Opellius Macrinus), Roman
  emperor 218
McTiernan, John (US film director) 1988
McVeigh, Timothy (US extremist) 1995, 1997
mad cow disease *see* BSE
Madagascar, discovery of 1500
Madagascar becomes a French colony 1896
Madama Butterfly 1904
Madame Bovary 1857
Madame Charpentier and her Children 1878
Madame de Pompadour
Madame Récamier 1800
Maddox, Richard Leach (British photographer) 1871
Maddox, USS 1964
Mademoiselle de Maupin 1835
Madero, Francisco Indalécio (Mexican revolutionary)
  1910, 1911, 1913
Madikizela-Mandela, Winnie *see* Mandela, Winnie
Madison, James (4th US president) 1809, 1811
Madison Square Gardens, opening of 1874
Madness of George III, The 1991
Madness of King George, The 1995
Madonna (US singer) 1984, 1985, 1986, 1989, 1990
Madonna 1299
Madonna and Child Enthroned with Angels 1347
Madonna and Child with Angels 1355
Madonna Enthroned with Angels 1280
Madonna of St Francis 1515
Madonna of the Candle 1492
Madonna of the Harpies 1531
Madras University, foundation of 1857
Madrid, Franco takes 1939
Madrid, peace of 1617
Madrid, siege of 1936
Madrid, terrorist bombing in 2004
Madrid, treaty of 1526
Madrid convention 1880
Madrigals 1594
*Madrigals and Motets of Five Parts, Apt for Viols and
  Voices, First Set of* 1612
Madriz, José (Nicaraguan politician) 1909
Mad World, My Masters, A 1608
Maestà 1308
Maeterlinck, Maurice (Belgian writer) 1889, 1893,
  1908
Mafeking, relief of 1900
Mafeking, siege of 1899
Magdalene Church (Seville), building of 1691
Magdalene with the Lamp 1630
Magdeburg Cathedral, foundation of 967
Magdeburg Centuries, The 1588
Magellan, Ferdinand (Fernão de Magalhães)
  (Portuguese explorer) 1519, 1521
Magenta, battle of 1859
'Maggie May' 1971
Magic Flute, The 1974
Magica naturalis (Natural Magic) 1560
Magician of Lublin, The 1960
Magna Carta, reissue of 1225, 1297
Magna Carta, signing of 1215
Magnalia Christi Americana 1702

Magnentius (Flavius Popilius Magnentius), Roman
  emperor in the W 350, 353
Magnesia, battle of 190BC
magnet, invention of 1020
Magnificat 1974
Magnificat in E flat 1723
Magnificent Ambersons, The 1918 (novel); 1942 (film)
Magnificent Seven, The 1960
Magnum Opus Musicum 1604
Magnus I Olafsson (the Good), king of Denmark and
  Norway 1035, 1042
Magnus VI (the Lawmender), king of Norway 1263,
  1266, 1276, 1280
Magnus VII Erikson, king of Norway *see* Magnus II
  Eriksson, king of Sweden
Magnus I (Barn-Lock), king of Sweden 1290
Magnus II Eriksson, king of Sweden and Norway
  1319, 1363, 1374
Magritte, René (Belgian painter) 1926, 1927, 1928,
  1934, 1936, 1937, 1939, 1946, 1964
Maguire, Tobey (US actor) 2003
Magus, The 1965
Mahan, Alfred Thayer (US soldier and historian)
  1890
Mahaviri (Indian mathematician) 830
Mahdi *see* Muhammad Ahmed
Mahdi, al-, Abbasid caliph 775, 785
Mahfouz, Naguib (Egyptian writer) 1949
Mahler, Gustav (Austrian composer) 1888, 1894,
  1896, 1900, 1902, 1904, 1905, 1907, 1909, 1910
Mahmud I, Ottoman sultan 1730
Mahmud II (the Reformer), Ottoman sultan 1808,
  1826, 1827, 1839
Mahmud V, Ottoman sultan 1909
Mahmud, sultan of Ghazni 1001, 1009, 1018, 1025,
  1030
Maidens of Trachi, The c.430–c.420BC
Maid of Pskov, The (*Ivan the Terrible*) 1873
Maid Returning from Market, The 1739
Maidservant, The 1634
Maid's Tragedy, The 1619
Mailer, Norman (US writer) 1948, 1968, 1968, 1979
Maimonides, Moses *see* Moses ben Maimon
Mainassara, Ibrahim Baré (president of Niger) 1999
Maine, USS 1898
Main Street 1920
Maintenon, Mme de (Françoise d'Aubigné) (last wife
  of Louis XIV) 1684, 1686, 1719
Mainz Cathedral (Germany), building of 978
Mainz Cathedral (Germany), rebuilding of 1009, 1060
Mainz University (Germany), foundation of 1477
Maison de Saint-Cyr (near Versailles), foundation of
  1686
Maison tellier, La (The Tellier House) 1881
Maitland, John, 1st duke of Lauderdale (Scottish
  politician) 1667
Major, John (British politician) 1989, 1990, 1993,
  1995, 1997
Major Barbara 1905
Majuba Hill, battle of 1881
Makarios, Archbishop (Mikhalis Khristodoulou
  Mouskos) (president of Cyprus) 1960, 1964, 1974
'Make Me Smile (Come Up and See Me)' 1975
Making Cocoa for Kingsley Amis 1986

Makropulos Case, The 1936
Malachy II (Mael Sechnaill II of Meath), king of Tara
  980
Malade imaginaire, Le (The Imaginary Invalid) 1673
Malaga, battle of 1937
Malamud, Bernard (US writer) 1957, 1966
Malan, Daniël François (South African politician)
  1948, 1952, 1953
Malawi, independence of 1964
Malaya, independence of 1957
Malaya, Japanese invasion of 1941
Malayan Trilogy, The 1972
Malaysia, formation of federation of 1963
Malaysia, independence of 1946
Malcolm I MacDonald, king of Scotland 945
Malcolm II Mackenneth, king of Scotland 1031
Malcolm III Canmore, king of Scotland 1054, 1057,
  1058
Malcolm IV, king of Scotland 1157
Malcolm X (Malcolm Little) (US religious leader) 1952,
  1965
Malcolm X 1992
Maldives, independence of 1965
Maldon, battle of 991
Male and Female 1942
Malebranche, Nicolas de (French philosopher) 1674
Malenkov, Georgi Maksimilianovich (Soviet politician)
  1953, 1955
Malesherbes, Chrétien-Guillaume de Lamoignon de
  (French politician) 1776
Malherbe, François de (French poet) 1555, 1628, 1630
Malik al-Saleh, ruler of Samudra 1297
Malik Shah, Seljuk sultan of Iconium (Konya) 1117
Malik Shah, Seljuk sultan of Rum 1072, 1074, 1091,
  1092
Malkovich, John (US actor) 1988, 1999
Mallarmé, Stéphane (French poet) 1876, 1887, 1944
Malle, Louis (French film director) 1974, 1980, 1987,
  1995
Malmö, treaty of 1524
Malory, Thomas (English writer) 1485
Malplaquet, battle of 1709
Malraux, André (French writer) 1933
Malta, independence of 1964
Maltese Falcon, The 1930 (novel); 1941 (film)
Malthus, Thomas (Robert) (English economist) 1798,
  1832, 1834
'Mama/Who Do You Think You Are?' 1997
Mambo Kings Play Songs of Love, The 1990
Mamelles de Tiresias, Les (The Breasts of Tiresias)
  1947
Mamet, David (US writer) 1975, 1983, 1988
Mamluk dynasty, commencement of 1250
'Mamma Mia' 1976
Mamoulian, Rouben (US film director) 1933, 1940
Ma'mum, al-, Abbasid caliph 813, 819, 830, 833
Man Aged 27, A 1590
Man and Child 1963
Man and Superman 1905
Manasseh ben Israel (Manoel Dias Soeiro) (Dutch
  rabbi) 1656, 1657
Manchester Guardian 1821
Manchester Royal Infirmary, foundation of 1752
Manchester Ship Canal, opening of 1894

Manchester United, plane crash 1958; European Cup 1968
Manchester University, foundation of 1880
Manchuria, Japanese occupation of 1931, 1932
Manchuria, Russian annexation of 1900
Manchuria, Soviet invasion of 1945
Manchurian Candidate, The 1962
Man Clasping a Hand 1588
Manco Capac (Inca leader) 1200
Mandalay, foundation of 1853
Mandela, Nelson (South African statesman and president) 1964, 1988, 1990, 1993, 1994, 1996, 1997, 1999
Mandela, Winnie (South African politician) 1996
Mandelstam, Osip (Russian writer) 1913, 1922
mandragola, La (The Mandrake Root) 1513
Manet, Edouard (French painter) 1859, 1860, 1865, 1867, 1874, 1877, 1882, 1883
Man for All Seasons, A 1960 (play)
Manfred, king of Naples and Sicily 1254, 1265, 1266
Manfred Mann (British group) 1966, 1968
Manfred Overture 1849
Manfred Symphony 1885
Mangu-Temir, khan of the Golden Horde 1266, 1280
Manhattan 1979
Manhattan Bridge (New York), building of 1909
Manhattan Bridge 1927
Manhattan Transfer 1925
Mani (Manes, Manichaeus) (Persian religious leader) 276
Manichaeism 276, 867
Manic Street Preachers (Welsh band) 1996
Manifeste de surréalisme (Surrealist Manifesto) 1924
Manila, battle of 1898
Manila, Japanese occupation of 1942
Man in a Red Turban 1433
Mankiewicz, Joseph L(eo) (US film director) 1950
Mann, Barry (US songwriter) 1963
Mann, Heinrich (German writer) 1905, 1918
Mann, Michael (US film director) 1995
Mann, Thomas (German writer) 1901, 1912, 1924, 1947, 1954, 1955
Mannerheim, Carl (Gustaf Emil) von (Finnish soldier) 1918
Mannerism 1494
Manning, Olivia (English writer) 1965, 1980
Mann ohne Eigenschaften, Der (The Man without Qualities) 1930
Man of Feeling, The 1771
Man of Iron 1981
Man of Marble 1977
Man of Mode, The 1676
Man of Property, The 1906, 1922
Mann ohne Eigenschaften, Der (The Man without Qualities) 1943
Manolete (Manuel Laureano Rodriguez Sanchez) (Spanish bullfighter) 1947
Manon 1884
Manon Lescaut 1733 (novel); 1893 (opera)
Mansart, François (French architect) 1598, 1623
Mansfeld, (Peter) Ernst von (German soldier) 1618, 1624, 1626
Mansfield, William Murray, 1st earl of (Scottish jurist) 1772

Mansfield Park 1814
Mansion House (London), building of 1739
Manson, Charles (US cult leader) 1969
Manstein, Erich von (German soldier) 1942
Mansur, Abu Amir al- (Almanzor), Muslim regent of Cordoba 976, 988, 997
Mansur, Abu Yusuf Ya'qub al-, Mu'minid sultan 1199
Mansur, al-, 2nd Abbasid caliph 754, 757, 762, 775
Mansurah, battle of 1250
Mantegna, Andrea (Italian painter) 1459, 1506
Mantineia, battle of 419BC
Mantua, congress of 1512
Mantuan Succession, War of the 1631
Manual of Dutch Poetry 1650
Manuel I Comnenus, Byzantine emperor 1143, 1151
Manuel II Palaeologus, Byzantine emperor 1391, 1425
Manuel I (the Fortunate), king of Portugal 1495, 1521
Manuel II, king of Portugal 1908, 1910
Manuel lexique, ou dictionnaire portatif des mots français 1750
Manuel typographique 1764
Manufactures royales des meubles de la couronne 1667
Manuha temple (Burma), building of 1060
Manutius, Aldus (Italian printer) 1495
Man Who Fell to Earth, The 1976
Man Who Would be King, The 1975
Man with a Guitar 1913
Man with Newspaper 1927
Man with the Blue Guitar, The 1937
Man with Two Left Feet, The 1917
Manyoshu 759
Manzikert, battle of 1071
Manzoni, Alessandro (Italian writer) 1825, 1874
Mao 1972
Maori War 1843
Mao Zedong (Mao Tse-tung) (Chinese politician) 1927, 1934, 1946, 1949, 1955, 1958, 1959, 1966, 1966, 1971, 1972, 1976
Map, Walter (English ecclesiastic) 1200
Map of Love, The 1999
Mappa Mundi 1314
Mapp and Lucia 1935
Mapplethorpe, Robert (US photographer) 1989
Marais, Jean (French actor) 1946
Marais, Marin (French composer) 1728
Maranzano, Salvatore (US gangster) 1931
Marat, Jean-Paul (French politician) 1793
Maratha confederation 1818
Maratha War 1782
Marathon, battle of 490BC
Marathon Man 1976
Maravarman Kulasekhara (S Indian ruler) 1269
Marble House (Newport), building of 1892
Marble Palace (St Petersburg), building of 1772
Marbury vs. Madison 1803
Marc, Franz (German painter) 1911
Marcel, Etienne (French merchant) 1355, 1357, 1358
Marcellus II (Marcello Cervini), pope 1555
Marchand, Jean-Baptiste (French soldier and explorer) 1896, 1897, 1898
March Laws, adoption in Hungary 1848
March on Rome 1922

Marcian, Byzantine emperor 450, 457
Marconi, Guglielmo (Italian engineer) 1901
Marconi Wireless Telegraph Co. 1896
Marcos, Ferdinand Edralin (president of the Philippines) 1965, 1972, 1981, 1983, 1986
Marcos, Subcommandante (Mexican EZNL leader) 2001
Marcoussis, treaty of 1498
Marcus Aquillius (Roman consul) 99BC
Marcus Aurelius (Marcus Annius Verus), Roman emperor 161, 167, 168, 175, 176, 177, 180
Marcuse, Herbert (US philosopher) 1964
Mardonius (Persian general) 479BC
Mare Clausum 1632
Marengo, battle of 1800
Margaret, queen of Denmark, Norway and Sweden (wife of Haakon VI) 1387, 1389, 1397, 1412
Margaret II, countess of Flanders (Margaret of Constantinople) 1280
Margaret, queen of Scotland (Maid of Norway) 1286, 1289, 1290
Margaret, countess of Richmond and Derby 1509
Margaret, duchess of Parma (Margaret of Austria) 1522, 1566, 1567
Margaret of Anjou, queen of England (wife of Henry VI) 1445, 1460
Margaret of Austria, duchess of Savoy 1507, 1508, 1509
Margaret of Tyrol (wife of Ludwig of Brandenburg) 1342
Margaret of York, duchess of Burgundy (sister of Edward IV) 1468
Margaret Tudor, regent of Scotland (sister of Henry VIII) 1513
margarine, invention of 1867
Maria I, queen of Portugal 1777, 1816
Maria II (Maria de Glória), queen of Portugal 1826, 1828, 1833, 1853
Maria Anna, regent of Portugal (wife of Joseph I) 1774
María Cristina, regent of Spain 1885
María Cristina de Borbón, regent of Spain 1836
Maria of Anjou, queen of Hungary 1382
Maria Stuart 1800
Maria Theresa, archduchess of Austria and queen of Bohemia and Hungary 1717, 1722, 1737, 1740, 1741, 1742, 1743, 1744, 1745, 1746, 1749, 1780
Maria Theresa (Marie-Thérèse), queen of France (wife of Louis XIV) 1684
Mariage de Figaro, Le (The Marriage of Figaro) 1784, 1786
Mariana, Juan de (Spanish historian) 1599
Mariana de Austria, queen of Spain (wife of Philip IV) 1676, 1679
Marianus Scotus (Irish chronicler) 1083
Marie (Maria Leszczynska), queen of France (wife of Louis XV) 1703, 1725
Marie-Antoinette, queen of France (wife of Louis XVI) 1770, 1785, 1793
Marie de France (French poet) 1185
Marie de Medici, queen of France (wife of Henry IV) 1600, 1610, 1614, 1615, 1617, 1620, 1630
Marie Louise, Austrian princess (2nd wife of Napoleon I) 1810

M

M

Menninger, Karl (Augustus) (US psychiatrist) 1930
Mennonites *see* Anabaptists
Menshikov, Alexander Danilovich (Russian soldier) 1725, 1727
Menteur, Le (The Liar) 1642
Mentmore Towers (Buckinghamshire), building of 1857
Mentuhotep II (Nebhepetra), 11th dynasty king of Egypt 2040BC
Menzies, Robert (Australian politician) 1939, 1949, 1966
Mephisto Waltz 1861, 1881, 1883, 1885
Mépris, Le (Contempt) 1964
Mer, La (The Sea) 1905
'Mer, La' 1945
Mercader, Ramón (Soviet agent) 1940
Mercator, Gerardus (Flemish mapmaker) 1541, 1546, 1563, 1569
Merchant, Ismail (Indian film producer and director) 1992
Merchant Marine Act (US) 1936
Merchant of Venice, The 1600
Merchant Shipping Act (UK) 1876
Mercian Hymns 1971
Mercier, Jacques le (French architect) 1633
Mercoeur, Philippe-Emmanel of Lorraine, duke of (French politician) 1597
Mercosur (Southern Common Market) 1995, 2004
Mercurius Aulicus 1643
Mercurius Britannicus 1643
Mercury 1590
Meredith, George (English writer) 1859, 1879, 1885
Meredith, James (African-American student) 1962
Mérimée, Prosper (French writer) 1843
Merman, Ethel (US actor) 1946, 1950
Merneptah, 19th dynasty king of Egypt 1224BC
Merovingian dynasty, naming of 481
Merry-Go-Round 1916
Merry Wives of Windsor, The 1601
Mersen, treaty of 870
Merton, statute of 1236
Mesic, Stjepan (Croatian politician) 1991
Mesmer, Franz Anton (Austrian physician) 1778
Mesopotamia, annexation by Roman empire 115
Mesopotamia, British mandate over 1920
'Message in a Bottle' 1979
Messerschmitt, Wilhelm (German aircraft designer) 1923
Messiaen, Olivier (French composer) 1940, 1950, 1956, 1969, 1983, 1992
Messiah 1741
Messier, Charles (French astronomer) 1760
Metacomet (chief of the Wampanoags) 1675
metal coins, introduction of *c.*700BC, 625BC
'Metal Guru' 1972
Metamorphosen 1945
Metamorphoses AD7
Metaphysik der Sitten, Die (The Metaphysics of Morals) 1797
Metellus (Quintus Caecilius Metellus Celer) (Roman legate) 67BC
Metemma, battle of 1889
Méthode de traicter les playes, La (The Method of Treating Wounds) 1545

Methodist Association 1743
Methodius, St 862, 870, 874, 875, 885
Methodus medendo (Method for Physicians) 180
Methuen treaty 1703
Methven, battle of 1306
Métis, rebellion of 1885
metre, adoption of 1791
metric system, adoption in Europe of 1801
Metro-Goldwyn-Mayer 1924
Metro in Paris, opening of 1900
Metropolis 1916 (painting); 1926 (film)
Metropolitan Police, foundation in London of 1829
Metternich, Klemens Wenzel Nepomuk Lothar von (Austrian politician) 1809, 1810, 1816, 1819, 1832, 1848
Metz, siege of 1870
Meurthe, Boulay de la (French jurist) 1804
Mexican Revolution 1910
Mexican War 1846, 1847, 1848
Mexico, independence of 1821
Mey, Cornelius Jacobsen (explorer in N America) 1614
Meyerbeer, Giacomo (Jakob Liebmann Meyer Beer) (German composer) 1831, 1836, 1849, 1865
Mezzanine, The 1988
Mhlangana (Zulu chief) 1828
Michael Asen I, king of Bulgaria 1246, 1257
Michael Sisman, king of Bulgaria 1330
Michael I (Rhangabe), Byzantine emperor 811, 812, 813
Michael II, Byzantine emperor 820, 825
Michael III (the Amorian, the Drunkard), Byzantine emperor 855, 862, 866, 867
Michael IV Paphlagonian, Byzantine emperor 1034
Michael VI Stratioticus, Byzantine emperor 1056, 1057
Michael VII Ducas, Byzantine emperor 1071, 1075, 1078
Michael VIII Palaeologus, Byzantine emperor 1261, 1274, 1281, 1282
Michael (Wisniowiecki), king of Poland 1669, 1673
Michael I, king of Romania 1927, 1930, 1940
Michael I, Romanov tsar of Russia 1613, 1617, 1645
Michael III Obrenovic, king of Serbia 1839, 1842, 1860, 1868
Michael, grand duke of Vladimir 1319
Michael, George (British singer-songwriter) 1987, 1996
Michael Cerularius (patriarch of Constantinople) 1054
Michael Collins 1996
Michael the Brave, prince of Wallachia 1595, 1599
Michaux, Pierre (French inventor) 1861
Michelangelo (Michelangelo di Lodovico Buonarroti Simoni) (Italian artist) 1475, 1498, 1501, 1508, 1513, 1520, 1521, 1524, 1536, 1537, 1546, 1564
Michelet, Jules (French historian) 1846
Michelin, André (French industrialist) 1900
Michelin, Edouard (French industrialist) 1900
Michell, John (English geologist) 1760
Michelson, Albert Abraham (German-US physicist) 1881
Michener, James A(lbert) (US writer) 1947
Michigan University, foundation of 1817
Micrographia 1665

microscope, invention of 1608
Middle Kingdom Period, commencement of 2040BC
Middlemarch 1872
Middlesex 2003
Middleton, Stanley (English writer) 1974
Middleton, Thomas (English playwright) 1608, 1627, 1657
Midhat Pasha, Ottoman grand vizier 1876, 1877
Midlothian campaign 1879
Midnight Cowboy 1969
Midnight Express 1978
Midnight in the Garden of Good and Evil 1994
Midnight's Children 1981
Midsummer Night's Dream, A 1600 (play); 1960 (opera); 1970 (RSC production)
Midsummer Night's Sex Comedy, A 1982
Midway, battle of 1942
Midwich Cuckoos, The 1957
Miescher, Johann Friedrich (Swiss chemist) 1870
Mies van der Rohe, Ludwig (US architect) 1922, 1929, 1959, 1969
Mieszko I, king of Poland 963, 966, 979, 992
Mieszko II (Lambert), king of Poland 1031, 1033, 1034
'Mighty Quinn, The' 1968
Miguel, Dom (pretender to Portuguese throne) 1826, 1828, 1833, 1834
Mikado, or The Town of Titipu, The 1885
Miki Takeo (Japanese politician) 1974
Mikimoto Kokichi (Japanese pearl farmer) 1893
Milan, prince of Serbia 1839
Milan IV Obrenovic, prince and king of Serbia 1868, 1889
Milan, convention of 1707
Milan, edict of 313
Milan, sack of 1162
Milan, siege of 539
Mildmay, Walter (English ecclesiastic) 1584
Mildred Pierce 1945
Milhaud, Darius (French composer) 1919, 1947
Militz, Charles von (papal chamberlain) 1519
milk chocolate, invention of 1875
Milken, Michael (US Wall Street trader) 1983, 1989, 1990
Mill, John Stuart (British economist and philosopher) 1843, 1848, 1859, 1863
Millais, John Everett (English painter) 1848, 1850, 1852, 1886
Milland, Ray (US actor) 1945
Mill at Charenton, The 1758
Millennium Dome, construction of (UK) 1997
Miller, Arthur (US writer) 1947, 1949, 1953, 1955, 1964
Miller, Glenn (US bandleader) 1938, 1942, 1944
Miller, Henry (US writer) 1931, 1939, 1980
Miller, William (US religious leader) 1845
Millerand, Alexandre (president of France) 1920, 1924
Millesimo, battle of 1796
Millet, Jean-François (French painter) 1831, 1854, 1859, 1875
Millett, Kate Murray (US feminist writer) 1970
Millhauser, Steven (US writer) 1996
Milligan, Spike (Indian-born British comedian) 1951
Mill on the Floss, The 1860

M

Montaigne, Michel de (French writer) 1580, 1588, 1603
Montaillou: Village Occitan de 1294 à 1324 (Montaillou: Cathars and Catholics in a French Vilage, 1294–1324) 1978
Montale, Eugenio (Italian writer) 1925, 1939
Mont Blanc, first climbed 1786
Mont Blanc (French merchant ship) 1917
Montcalm-Gozon, Louis-Joseph, marquis of (French soldier) 1759
Monte Cassino, battle of 1944
Monte Cassino Abbey Church, dedication of 1071
Montecatini, battle of 1315
Montenegro, independence of 1878
Montenegro, rebellion in 1875
Montereau, battle of 1814
Monterrey, battle of 1846
Montes Claros, battle of 1665
Montesquieu, Charles Louis de Secondat, baron of (French philosopher) 1689, 1721, 1734, 1748, 1751, 1755
Montessori, Maria (Italian educator) 1912
Montessori Method, The 1912
Monteverdi, Claudio (Italian composer) 1567, 1607, 1608, 1610, 1613, 1642, 1643
Montezuma II, Aztec emperor 1519
Montfaucon, battle of 888
Montfort, Simon de (the Elder) (French soldier) 1209, 1213, 1215, 1218
Montfort, Simon de, earl of Leicester (English soldier) 1231, 1238, 1250, 1251, 1253, 1258, 1261, 1264, 1265
Montgisard, battle of 1177
Montgolfier, Jacques-Etienne (French inventor) 1783
Montgolfier, Joseph-Michel (French inventor) 1783
Montgomery, L(ucy) M(aud) (Canadian writer) 1908
Montgomery, treaty of 1267
Montherlant, Henry (-Marie-Joseph) Millon de (French writer) 1934
Montmorency, Anne, 1st duke of (marshal of France) 1536, 1541
Montpellier, treaty of 1622
Montrose, SS 1910
Montségur, French capture of 1244
Montt, José Efrain Rios 1982
Monty Python's Flying Circus 1969
'Mood Indigo' 1931
Moog, Robert (US engineer) 1965
Moon, Sun Myung (Korean evangelist) 1954
Moon and Sixpence, The 1919
Moonlight 1993
Moonlight: A Study at Millbank 1797
Moonstone, The 1868
Moon Tiger 1987
Moore, Brian (Irish-Canadian writer) 1955
Moore, Henry (English sculptor) 1926, 1940, 1947, 1986
Moore, John (Scottish soldier) 1809
Moore, Michael (US film director) 2003
Moore, Thomas (US inventor) 1803
Moore's Creek Bridge, battle of 1776
Moorish Couple on Their Terrace, A 1832
Moral Rearmament 1921
Moran, 'Bugs' (George) (US gangster) 1929

Moravia, Alberto (Italian writer) 1929, 1941, 1947, 1951, 1990
Moravian Brethren 1732
Moravian Church 1739
Moray, James Stuart, earl of Mar and of (regent of Scotland) 1567, 1568
Mordaunt, Charles, 3rd earl of Peterborough (English sailor) 1705
More, Thomas (English politician) 1510, 1516, 1523, 1529, 1532, 1535, 1543
Moreau, Gustave (French painter) 1898
Moreau, Jeanne (French actor) 1961
Moreau, Jean-Victor-Marie (French soldier) 1800
Morelos y Pavón, José María (Mexican revolutionary) 1813
More Songs About Buildings and Food 1979
Morgagni, Giovanni (Battista) (Italian physician) 1761
Morgan, Henry (Welsh pirate) 1671
Morgan, J(ohn) P(ierpont) (US financier) 1871, 1892, 1901, 1902, 1907
Morgan Jr, J(ohn) P(ierpont) (US financier) 1917
Morgan, Lewis Henry (US ethnologist) 1851
Morgan, William (Welsh prelate) 1588
Morgarten, battle of 1315
Morgenstern, Oskar (US economist) 1944
Morihiro Hosokawa (Japanese politician) 1993
Morissette, Alanis (Canadian singer-songwriter) 1995
Morley, Thomas (English composer) 1594
Morley–Minto reforms in India 1909
Mornay, Philippe de, seigneur du Plessis-Marly (French Huguenot) 1549, 1623
Morning, the Dance of the Nymphs 1850
Morning Toilette 1740
Morny, Charles-Auguste-Louis-Joseph, duke of (half-brother of Napoleon III) 1851
Moro, Aldo (Italian politician) 1978
Moroccan Crisis, First 1905
Morocco, independence of 1880, 1956
Morocco 1930
morphine, discovery of 1803
Morris, Dave (British environmental campaigner) 1997
Morris, Philip (British merchant) 1858
Morris, William (English writer and artist) 1858, 1866, 1890, 1891
Morrison, Jim (US rock singer) 1971
Morrison, Toni (US writer) 1987, 1992
Morrison, Van (Irish singer-songwriter) 1968
Morse, Samuel (Finley Breese) (US inventor) 1832, 1837, 1844
Morse code, adoption of 1912
Mort de quelqu'un (Death of a Nobody) 1911
'Morte d'Arthur' 1842
Morte d'Arthur, Le 1485
Mortemer, battle of 1054
Mortimer, Roger de, 1st earl of March (lover of Isabella, queen of England) 1326, 1327, 1330
Mortmain, statute of 1279
Morton, William Thomas Green (US dentist) 1846
Moscow, French retreat from 1812
Moscow Conference 1943
Moscow University, foundation of 1755
Moses (Jewish prophet) 620BC
Moses 1513

Moses ben Ezra (Ibn Ezra) (Jewis poet) 1139
Moses ben Maimon (Jewish philosopher) 1204
Moses de Leon (Spanish cabbalist) 1305
Moses und Aron 1957
Mosheim, Johann Lorenz von (German theologian) 1726, 1737
Mo shi (Mo Shih) 1329
Mosley, Oswald (British fascist politician) 1931, 1932
Mosquito Coast 1981
Moss, Moses (British shopkeeper) 1897
Mossadeq, Muhammad (Iranian politician) 1951, 1953
Mostel, Zero (US actor) 1968
Mosynopolis, battle of 1185
Mother Goose 1765
Mother-in-Law, The 165BC
Motherwell, Robert (US artist) 1949
Motorcycle Diaries, The 2004
Motown records 1959
Motte, Jeanne-Marie de la (Mme Guyon du Chesnoy) (French mystic) 1785, 1786
Moulin de La Galette, Le 1887 (Van Gogh); 1900 (Picasso)
Moulin Rouge! 2001
Mountain 1909
Mountain Interval 1916
Mount Badon, battle of 518
Mountbatten, Louis Alexander, 1st marquis of Milford Haven (British sailor and politician) 1947, 1979
Mountbatten, Philip, HRH Prince Philip, Duke of Edinburgh (consort of Queen Elizabeth II) 1946
Mount Gilboa, battle of c.1006BC
Mount of Olives, The 1652
Mount Rushmore Memorial 1941
Mount St Helens, eruption of 1980
Mourning Becomes Electra 1931
Mousetrap, The 1952, 1992
Movement for Democratic Change (Zimbabwe) 1999, 2000
Movements with Squares 1962
'Move on up a Little Higher' 1945
Mozambique, independence of 1975
Mozart, Wolfgang Amadeus (Austrian composer) 1756, 1762, 1763, 1764, 1765, 1766, 1769, 1770, 1772, 1773, 1775, 1776, 1778, 1779, 1780, 1781, 1782, 1783, 1784, 1785, 1786, 1787, 1788, 1790, 1791
Mr and Mrs Clark and Percy 1971
Mr and Mrs Robert Andrews 1749
Mr Deeds Goes to Town 1936
Mr Midshipman Easy 1836
Mr Norris Changes Trains 1935
Mr Sammler's Planet 1970
Mrs Dalloway 1925
Mrs Miniver 1942
Mr Smith Goes to Hollywood 1939
Mrs Philip Thicknesse 1760
Mrs Siddons as the Tragic Muse 1784
Mrs Warren's Profession 1902
'Mr Tambourine Man' 1965
Muawiyah I, Umayyad caliph 661, 678
Mu'azzam, al-, Ayubite king of Damascus 1227
Mubarak, Muhammad Hosni (president of Egypt) 1981

N

N

Naismith, James (US educator) 1891
Najaf (Iraq), US bombing of 2004
Nájera, battle of 1367
Najibullah, Ahmadzai (president of Afghanistan) 1989
Naked and the Dead, The 1948
Naked Lunch, The 1959
Name of the Rose, The 1980
Namibia, independence of 1990
Namier, Lewis (Polish-born British historian) 1942
Nana 1877 (painting); 1880 (novel)
Nanak (1st Sikh Guru) 1469
Nancy, battle of 1477
Nangis, battle of 1814
Nänie 1881
Nanjing, Japanese occupation of 1937
Nanjing, sack of 1864
Nanjing, treaty of 1842
Nan Paya temple (Burma), building of 1060
Nansen, Fridtjof (Norwegian scientist and explorer) 1893
Nantes, edict of 1598
Nantes, revocation of edict of 1685
Nantwich, battle of 1644
Napata, sack of 593BC
Napier, Charles (English soldier) 1840, 1843
Napier, John (Scottish mathematician) 1550, 1614, 1617
Napier, Robert (British soldier) 1868
Naples, siege of 1503
Naples University (Italy), foundation of 1225
Napoleon I, emperor of the French 1793, 1795, 1796, 1797, 1798, 1799, 1800, 1802, 1803, 1804, 1805, 1806, 1807, 1808, 1809, 1810, 1811, 1812, 1813, 1814, 1815, 1821
Napoleon III, emperor of the French 1848, 1850, 1851, 1852, 1853, 1858, 1859, 1862, 1863, 1864, 1867, 1870, 1871, 1873
Napoleon 1927
Napoleon Crossing the Alps 1801
Napoleon Distributing the Eagles 1810
Napoleon's 100 Days 1815
Narasimha Rao, P(amulaparti) V(enkata) (Indian politician) 1991, 1996
Narayanan, K(ocheril) R(aman) (president of India) 1997
Narmer, 1st dynasty king of Upper Egypt c.3100BC
Narrenschiff, Das (The Ship of Fools) 1494
Narses (Byzantine general and exarch of Italy) 550, 552, 553, 554
Narva, battle of 1700
Narváez, Ramón María, duke of Valencia (Spanish politician) 1868
Narziss und Goldmund 1930
NASA (National Aeronautics and Space Administration), formation of 1958
Naseby, battle of 1645
Nash, John (English architect) 1752, 1806, 1822, 1825
Nash, Paul (English painter) 1918, 1940
Nash, Richard 'Beau' (English social arbiter) 1762
Nashville, battle of 1864
Nashville (Tennessee), foundation of 1780
Nashville (US cruiser) 1903
Nasir Dawud, an-, prince of Kerak 1239

Nasir ud-Din, Qajar shah of Persia 1848, 1896
Nasir ud-Din Mahmud, sultan of Delhi 1246, 1266
Nasir ul-Mulk (Persian politician) 1907
Nasir Yusuf, an-, prince of Aleppo 1251, 1253, 1303
Nasrid dynasty, commencement of 1230
Nassau agreement 1962
Nasser, Gamal Abdel (president of Egypt) 1954, 1956, 1958, 1967, 1970
Nast, Condé Montrose (US publisher) 1909
Nast, Thomas (US illustrator) 1869, 1870
Natal (South Africa), declaration of British colony of 1856
Nastase, Adrian (Romanian politician) 2004
Natasha's Dance: A Cultural History of Russia 2002
Nathan the Wise 1783
National Assembly (France) 1789
National Association for the Advancement of Colored People (NAACP) 1909
National Coal Board (NCB) (UK) 1983
National Commission on Terrorist Attacks (US) 2004
National Covenant (Scotland) 1638, 1689
National Curriculum (UK) 1988
National Debt (England) 1692
National Defence, Junta of (Spain) 1936
National Economic Development Council, abolishment of (UK) 1991
National Front (UK), foundation of 1967
National Front (France), foundation of 1972
National Geographic 1888
National Government in Britain 1931, 1935
National Health Service Act (UK) 1946
National Industrial Recovery Act (US) 1933, 1935
National Labor Union (US) 1866
National Lottery, launch of (UK) 1994
National Museum of the American Indian, opening of 2004
National Review 1955
National Rifle Association (US) 1871
National School Lunch Act (UK) 1946
National Security Act (US) 1947
National Theatre (London) 1976
National Theatre Company, creation of (UK) 1963
National Trust, foundation of (UK) 1895
National Union of Mineworkers (NUM) (UK) 1972, 1974, 1983, 1984, 1985
National Velvet 1945
National Woman Suffrage Association (US) 1869
Nationalist Government, Spanish 1936
Nation of Islam 1931, 1965
NATO (North Atlantic Treaty Organisation), formation of 1949
NATO, French withdrawal from 1966
NATO, Spain joins 1982
NATO airstrikes against Serbs 1999
Natufian hunter-gatherers 12,000 BP
Natural and Experimental History 1622
Natural and Political Observations on the Bills of Mortality 1661
Natural Born Killers 1994
Natural History of the Human Teeth, The 1771
Naturalization Act (US) 1789
Nature 1836 (prose rhapsody)
Nature 1869, 1953 (magazine)
Nature of the Chemical Bond, The 1939

Nau, John-Antoine (Antoine Torquet) (French writer) 1903
Naupactus, battle of 429BC
Nauru, independence of 1968
Nausée, La (Nausea) 1938
Nautilus, USS 1952
Naval Academy (Annapolis), foundation of 1845
Naval Appropriations Act (US) 1916
Navarino, battle of 1827
Navarino Bay, battle of 425BC
Navarro, Pedro, count of Olivetto 1503, 1508
Navigation Acts (UK) 1381, 1660, 1849
Navy Discipline Act (UK) 1660
Nayler, James (English Quaker) 1653, 1656
Nazi–Soviet Pact 1939, 1941
NBC (National Broadcasting Co.), foundation of 1926
Neame, Ronald (British film director) 1969
Neanderthal man 40,000BP, 28,000BP, 1856
Nearchus, satrap of Lycia and Pamphylia 326BC, 325BC
'Nearness of You, The' 1937
Neave, Airey Middleton Sheffield (British politician) 1979
Nebuchadnezzar I, king of Babylon 1125BC
Nebuchadnezzar II, king of Babylon 605BC, 597BC, 562BC
Nechtansmere, battle of 685
Neckam, Alexander (English scholar) 1217
Necker, Jacques (Swiss-French politician) 1776, 1788, 1789
needle gun, invention of 1841
Neeson, Liam (Irish actor) 1993, 1996
Nefertiti, queen of Egypt (wife of Akhenaten) 1353BC
Nègres, Les (The Blacks) 1959
Negro Digest 1942
Neguib, Mohammed (Egyptian military ruler) 1952
Nehawand (Niharvand), battle of 642
Nehru, Jawaharlal (Indian politician) 1947, 1956, 1964
Neill, Sam (British actor) 1993
Neisser, Albert (Ludwig Sigesmund) (German physician) 1879
Nekau (Necho) II (Wehemibra), 25th king of Egypt 609BC, 605BC
Nelly (US rapper) 2002
Nelson, Horatio, 1st Viscount Nelson (British naval commander) 1798, 1801, 1805
Nemours, treaty of 1585
Nennius (Welsh chronicler) 830
Nepal, Maoist attacks in 2003, 2004
Nepal, unification of 1769
Nepos, Julius, Roman emperor 473, 475
Neptune and Triton 1620
Neri, St Philip (Italian mystic) 1515, 1533, 1564, 1595
Nernst, W(alter) H(ermann) (German chemist) 1908
Nero, Gaius Claudius (Roman consul) 216BC
Nero (Lucius Domitius Ahenobarbus), Roman emperor 54, 59, 64, 66, 68
Neruda, Pablo (Ricardo Eliecer Neftalí Reyes) (Chilean poet) 1924, 1933, 1950, 1973
Nerva (Marcus Cocceius Nerva), Roman emperor 96, 97
Nerval, Gérard de (Gérard Labrunie) (French poet and translator) 1854

N

Njal's Saga 1200
Nkomo, Joshua (Zimbabwean nationalist leader) 1961, 1978, 1979, 1987
Nkrumah, Kwame (president of Ghana) 1957, 1966
No Angel 2001
No, No Nanette 1925
'No, No, No' 1998
Nobel, Alfred Bernhard (Swedish chemist) 1866, 1901
Nobel, Ludwig (Swedish industrialist) 1873, 1901
Nobel, Robert (Swedish industrialist) 1873
Noble, L.C. (US businessman) 1869
Noble Order of the Knights of Labour 1869
Nobrega, Manoel de (Portuguese Jesuit leader) 1554
Noces, Les (The Wedding) 1923
Nocturne 1958
Nogaret de La Valette, Jean-Louis de, duke of Epernon (French politician) 1596
Nogay, Mongol khan 1280, 1283, 1291
Noh theatre 1383
Noiret, Philippe (French actor) 1989
Noises Off 1982
Nolan, Sidney (Australian artist) 1946
Nollekens, Joseph (English sculptor) 1737
No Man's Land 1975
Nomenoe (Breton chief) 826
Non-Aggression Pact (Turkey–Iraq–Iran–Afghanistan) 1937
Nono, Luigi (Italian composer) 1960
Nonsuch, treaty of 1585
Norbert of Xanten, St 1120
Nördlingen, battle of 1634
Nördlingen, battle of 1645
Noriega, Manuel Antonio (military leader of Panama) 1981, 1988, 1989, 1990
Norma 1831
Norman, Robert (English scientist) 1581
Norman Conquests, The 1974
Normandy landings 1944
Norman dynasty in England, commencement of 1066
Norryes, John (English sailor) 1589
North, Frederick, 2nd earl of Guilford (English politician) 1770, 1782, 1783
North, Oliver (US soldier) 1986, 1987
North 1975
North America Act (Canada) 1867, 1982
Northampton, Assize of 1176
Northampton, battle of 1460
North and South 1855
Northanger Abbey 1818
North Briton, The 1763
North by Northwest 1959
Northeastern University (Boston), foundation of 1898
Northern Earls, rising of 1569
Northern Ireland, British troops sent to 1969
Northern Ireland, formation of 1921
Northern Ireland Civil Rights Association 1967
Northern Lights 1995
Northern Pacific Railroad (US) 1883
Northern Song dynasty, commencement of 960
Northern War, First 1655, 1656, 1661
North German Confederation, formation of 1867
North of Boston 1914
North Sea oil (UK) 1965, 1971, 1975

Northwestern University (Chicago), foundation of 1851
Northwest Frontier Province, creation of 1901
Northwest Mounted Police see Royal Canadian Mounted Police
Norton, Thomas (English writer) 1565
Norway, German occupation of 1940
Nose, The 1930
Nosferatu, eine Symphonie des Grauens (Nosferatu, a Symphony of Horror) 1922
Nostalghia (Nostalgia) 1983
Nostradamus (Michel de Nôtredame) (French physician and astrologer) 1503, 1566
Nostromo 1904
Notables, Assembly of 1788
Notes from Underground 1864
Notes on Virginia 1782
'Nothing Compares 2U' 1990
Notium, battle of 407BC
Notorious 1946
Notre Dame Cathedral (Antwerp), building of 1518
Notre Dame Cathedral (Paris), building of 1163, 1345
Notre Dame de Paris (The Hunchback of Notre Dame) 1831
Notre Dame University (Indiana), foundation of 1842
Not Waving but Drowning 1957
Nourritures terrestres, Les (The Fruits of the Earth) 1897
Nouveau système de musique théorique (New System of the Theory of Music) 1726
Nouvelle Relation de l'Afrique occidentale (New Account of West Africa) 1728
Nouvelles de la république des lettres (News from the Republic of Letters) 1684
Novak, Kim (US actor) 1958
Novalis (Friedrich Leopold von Hardenberg) 1801
Nova Methodus Discendique Juris (A New Method for Teaching Jurisprudence) 1667
Novara, battle of 1849
Novarro, Ramón (Mexican actor) 1925
Nova Scientia (The New Science) 1537
Nova Stereometria Doliorum (New Stereometry of Wine Barrels) 1615
Novello, Ivor (David Ivor Davies) (Welsh composer) 1914
Novgorod Cathedral (Russia), rebuilding of 1045
Novi, battle of 1799
'No Woman No Cry' 1975
Now, Voyager 1942
Noyce, Robert (Norton) (US inventor) 1959
Noyon Cathedral (France), building of 1150
Noyon, treaty of 1516
nozze di Figaro, Le (The Marriage of Figaro) 1786
Ntaryamira, Cyprien (president of Burundi) 1994
Nuclear Non-Proliferation treaty 1968, 1977
Nude against the Light 1908
Nude Descending a Staircase, No. 2 1912
Nude in the Sun 1900
Nuffield, William Richard Morris, 1st Viscount (British car manufacturer) 1943
Nuit, La (Night) 1653
Nuits, Les (Nights) 1837
Nujoma, Samuel Daniel (president of Namibia) 1990

Numbers in Color 1959
Number 2 1949
Numerian (Marcus Aurelius Numerius Numerianus), Roman emperor 283, 284
Nunavut, Canada, creation of 1999
Nuns and Soldiers 1980
Nur ad-Din Ali, Mamluk sultan of Egypt 1257, 1259
Nur ad-Din, sultan of Syria and Egypt 1147, 1149, 1150, 1151, 1158, 1160, 1164, 1171
Nuremberg, League of 1538
Nuremberg Laws (Germany) 1935
Nuremberg Trials 1945, 1946
Nureyev, Rudolph (Russian ballet dancer) 1993
Nushirwan, shah of Persia 1349
Nutcracker, The 1892
Nyerere, Julius (Kambarage) (president of Tanzania) 1961, 1962, 1985
nylon, commercial production of 1938
nylon stockings, introduction of 1939
Nymphaeum, treaty of 1261
Nymphenburg, treaty of 1741
Nyunt, Khin (Burmese politician) 2004
Nzinga Mbemba, king of Kongo 1490

O

Oasis (British band) 1994, 1995, 1996
Oates, Titus (English conspirator) 1649, 1678, 1685, 1705
Oath of the Horatii, The 1784
Obedience of a Christian Man, The 1528
Oberammergau Passion Play 1634, 1662
Oberon 1826
Obian Nguema Mbasogo, Teodoro (president of Equatorial Guinea) 1979
Objective Stimulation 1939
Obote, (Apollo) Milton (president of Uganda) 1966, 1971, 1980, 1985
Obregón, Alvaro (Mexican soldier) 1920, 1928
O'Brien, Richard (British actor and theatrical producer) 1973
Obscene Publications Act (UK) 1959
Observationes Anatomicae (Anatomical Observations) 1561
Observations Concerning the Increase of Mankind 1755
Observer 1791
Ocalan, Abdullah (Turkish politician) 1999, 2000
O'Casey, Sean (Irish playwright) 1923, 1924, 1926, 1929, 1964
Occasioni, Le (Occasions) 1939
Occupational Safety and Health Act (US) 1970
Ocean Colour Scene (British band) 1996
Ochi, crown prince of Japan 770
O'Connor, Feargus (Irish politician) 1843
O'Connor, Sandra Day (US justice) 1981
O'Connor, Sinead (Irish singer) 1990
Octavia (wife of Mark Antony) 40BC, 38BC, 32BC
Octavian see Augustus Caesar
October Revolution (Russia) 1917
Odalisque in Red Trousers 1921
Oda Nobunaga (Japanese soldier) 1568, 1582
Odd Couple, The 1965
Odenaethus, prince of Palmyra 267

O

P

Piccolomini, Die 1799

Pichegru, Jean-Charles (French soldier) 1795

Pickford, Mary (Canadian actor) 1919

Pico della Mirandola, Giovanni (Italian philosopher) 1494, 1510

Picquigny, treaty of 1475

pictographic writing system c.3500BC, 2600BC, c.1600BC

Picture of Dorian Gray, The 1891

Pictures from an Exhibition 1874

Pictures from Brueghel 1962

Pièces de clavecin en concert (Concert Pieces for Harpsichord) 1741

Piedra del sol (Sun-stone) 1957

Pierce, Franklin (14th US president) 1852, 1853

Pieri, Joseph (Giuseppe) (Italian nationalist) 1858

Piero della Francesca (Italian painter) 1465

Pierre, DBC (Ausralian-Mexican writer) 2003

Pierrot lunaire (Moonstruck Pierrot) 1912

Pietà 1498

Pietà, or Revolution by Night 1923

Pilate, Pontius, procurator of Judaea 33

Pilgrim, bishop of Passau 942

Pilgrimage of Grace 1536, 1537

Pilgrim Fathers 1620

Pilgrim's Progress 1676, 1678, 1684

Pillnitz, Declaration of 1791

Pilote de Guerre (Flight to Arras) 1942

Pilsudski, Józef (Klemens) (Polish soldier and politician) 1916, 1918, 1919, 1920, 1926

Piltdown man, discovery of 1912

Pincher Martin 1956

Pinckney, Charles (US politician) 1809

Pindar (Greek poet) c.446BC

Pinero, Arthur Wing (English playwright) 1888, 1893, 1898

Pini di Roma (The Pines of Rome) 1924

Pinkerton, Allan (US detective) 1850, 1861

Pinkerton Detective Agency 1850

Pink Floyd (British band) 1973, 1975, 1980

Pinochet (Ugarte), Augusto (president of Chile) 1973, 1976, 1989, 1998, 2000

Pinter, Harold (English playwright) 1958, 1965, 1975, 1978, 1993

Pinzon, Vicente Yáñez (Spanish navigator) 1499

Pioneer 10 space probe 1983

Pioneers, The 1823

Piper, John (English artist) 1940, 1962

Piper Alpha oil platform (North Sea), explosion of 1988

Pippa Passes 1841

Piraeus, blockade of 1850

Pirandello, Luigi (Italian writer) 1904, 1921

Pirates of Penzance, or The Slave of Duty, The 1879

Pirelli, Giovanni Battista (Italian industrialist) 1872

Pirsig, Robert M. (US writer) 1974

Pisa, Council of 1409

Pisan Cantos 1948

Pisano, Andrea (Italian sculptor) 1330, 1336

Pisano, Giovanni (Italian artist) 1264, 1297, 1299, 1302

Pisano, Nicola (Italian sculptor) 1264

Pissarro, Camille (French painter) 1874, 1897, 1903

Pitman, Isaac (British educator) 1837

Pitt, Brad (US actor) 1994

Pitt, George Dibdin (English playwright) 1847

Pitt, William (the Elder, the Great Commoner), 1st earl of Chatham 1708, 1746, 1755, 1757, 1761, 1766, 1767

Pitt, William (the Younger) 1783, 1784, 1789, 1791, 1795, 1796, 1799, 1800, 1801, 1806

Pitts, Hiram (US inventor) 1837

Pitts, John (US inventor) 1837

Pius IV (Giovanni Angelo Medici), pope 1565

Pius V (Michele Ghislieri), pope 1566, 1570, 1572

Pius VI (Giovanni Angelo Braschi), pope 1775, 1797, 1798, 1799

Pius VII (Luigi Barnabà Chiaramonte), pope 1800, 1804, 1809, 1823

Pius VIII (Francesco Saverio Castiglione), pope 1829, 1830

Pius IX (Giovanni Maria Mastai-Ferretti), pope 1846, 1848, 1849, 1854, 1869, 1878

Pius X (Giuseppe Melchiorre Sarto), pope 1903, 1914

Pius XI (Ambrogio Damiano Achille Ratti), pope 1922, 1929, 1930, 1939

Pius XII (Eugenio Maria Giuseppe Giovanni Pacelli), pope 1939, 1958

Pizarro, Francisco (Spanish explorer) 1532, 1533, 1541

Pizarro, Gonzalo (Spanish explorer) 1548

Place, Francis (English reformer) 1822

Place Clichy 1888

Place de la Concorde (Paris), building of 1775

Place Vendôme (Paris), building of 1698

Plaid Cymru, Party of Wales 1925, 1966

Plaideurs, Les (The Litigants) 1668

Plains of Abraham, battle of the 1759

Plain Tales from the Hills 1888

Plain Truth, or Serious Considerations on the Present State of the City of Philadelphia 1747

Plaisir du texte, Le (The Pleasure of the Text) 1973

Planck, Max Karl Ernst Ludwig (German physicist) 1900

Planets, The 1916

Plan for Chicago 1909

Plantagenet dynasty, commencement of 1154

Plante, Gaston (French physicist) 1859

Plassey, battle of 1757

Plataea, battle of 479BC

Plath, Sylvia (US poet) 1960, 1963, 1965

Plato (Greek philosopher) c.387BC

Platoon 1986

Plautius, Aulus (Roman soldier) 43

Plautus (Roman playwright) c.205BC, 200BC, c.195BC, c.189BC, 184BC

Playboy 1953

Player, The 1992

Play It Again Sam 1972

Pleasence, Donald (British actor) 1978

'Please Please Me' 1963

Pleasure Principle, The 1937

Pleasures of the Town, The 1729

Plehve, Vyacheslav Konstantinovich (Russian government official) 1904

Pléiade group 1549

Plekhanov, Georgi Valentinovich (Russian philosopher) 1883, 1895

Plenty 1978

Plessey vs. Ferguson 1896

Pleven, Russian occupation of 1877

Plimsoll, Samuel (English reformer) 1876

Pliny the Elder (Gaius Plinius Secundus) (Roman historian) 79

Pli selon Pli (Fold upon Fold) 1965

Plot Against America, The 2004

plough, invention of 4500BC

Plough and the Stars, The 1926

Plowce, battle of 1331

Plumed Serpent, The 1926

Plum Street Temple (Cincinnati), building of 1866

Plutarch (Lucius Mestrius Plutarchus) (Greek biographer) 120

plutonium, discovery of 1940

Plymouth (Devon), Pilgrim Fathers leave 1620

Pocahontas (Matoaka) (American Indian princess) 1614, 1616, 1617

Poe, Edgar Allan (US writer) 1829, 1840, 1841, 1849

Poème sur le désastre de Lisbonne (Poem on the Disaster at Lisbon) 1756

Poèmes tragiques (Tragic Poems) 1884

Poem of Ecstasy, The 1908

Poems, Chiefly Lyrical 1830

Poems and Ballads 1866

Poems Chiefly in the Scottish Dialect 1786

Poems in Two Volumes 1807

Poems Lyric and Pastoral 1606

Poems of Affairs of State 1689

Poems of Emily Dickinson, The 1890

Poems on Several Occasions 1752

Poems upon Various Occasions 1673

Poésies (Poems) 1887

Poetical Blossoms 1633

Poetical Sketches 1783

Poetices Libri Septem (Seven Books of Poetry) 1561

Poggibonzi, Niccolo da (Italian scholar) 1349

pogroms in Russia 1881, 1903

Pogues, the (Irish band) 1985

Poincaré, Raymond (-Nicolas-Landry) (president of France) 1912, 1913

Poindexter, John F. (US sailor) 1986, 1987

Point Counter Point 1928

Pointing Man 1947

Point Pleasant, battle of 1774

Poison 1939

Poisson, Siméon (-Denis) (French mathematician) 1837

Poitier, Sidney (US actor) 1967

Poitiers, battle of 1356

Poitiers Cathedral, building of 1162

Pol Pot (Cambodian leader of the Khmer Rouge) 1969, 1975, 1976, 1978, 1979, 1998

Poland, partition of 1769, 1772, 1793, 1795, 1939

Poland, German invasion of 1939

Poland, independence of 1918

Poland, Soviet invasion of 1939

Polanski, Roman (Polish film director) 1965, 1968, 1969, 1974, 2002

Polaris missiles (UK) 1980

Pole, Edmund de la, earl of Suffolk 1501

Pole, William de la, 1st duke of Suffolk 1450

Polestar 1984

P

Prescott, William H(ickling) (US historian) 1837
Presentation at the Temple, The 1655
Present Laughter 1943
Presley, Elvis (US singer) 1954, 1956, 1960, 1961, 1962, 1977
Pressburg, diet of 1687
Pressburg, treaty of 1805
Pressburger, Emeric (Hungarian producer and scriptwriter) 1941, 1943, 1945, 1946, 1947, 1948
Prester John 1910
Preston, battle of 1648
Preston, battle of 1715
Prestonpans, battle of 1745
Pretenders, Wars of the 1155
Pretoria, treaty of 1881
Pretorius, Marthinus Wessel (Afrikaner soldier) 1856
'Pretty Flamingo' 1966
'Pretty Woman' 1964
Pretzel Logic 1974
Prevention of Terrorism Act (UK) 1974
Prévost d'Exiles, Antoine-François (Abbé Prévost) (French writer) 1733, 1750
Price Administration and Civilian Supply, Office of 1941, 1946
Prick of Conscience, The 1340
Pride, Thomas (English politician) 1648
Pride and Prejudice 1813
Pride's Purge 1648, 1659
Priestley, J(ohn) B(oynton) (English writer) 1929, 1984
Priestley, Joseph (English chemist) 1733, 1767, 1772, 1774, 1782
Primakov, Yevgeny (Russian politician) 1998, 1999
Primal Scream (British band) 1990
prima navigazione per l'oceano alle terre de'negri della Bassa Ethiopia, La 1507
Primary Chronicle, The 1110
Prime of Miss Jean Brodie, The 1961 (novel); 1969 (film)
Primo de Rivera, José Antonio (Spanish fascist) 1933
Primo de Rivera y Orbaneja, Miguel (Spanish soldier) 1921, 1923, 1930
Prim y Prats, Juan (Spanish politician) 1868
Prince (US singer) 1984, 1987
Prince, Hughie (US songwriter) 1941
Prince Baltasar Carlos as Hunter 1636
Prince Igor 1890 (Borodin); 1909 (Rimsky-Korsakov)
Prince of Wales, HMS 1941
Princes, League of 1785
Princes in the Tower 1483
Princeton, battle of 1777
Princeton University (New Jersey), foundation of 1746, 1896
Prince William of Orange 1641
Princip, Gavrilo (Serb nationalist) 1914
Principall Navigations, Traffiques and Discoveries of the English Nation, The 1589
principe, Il (The Prince) 1513, 1532
Principia Mathematica (Principles of Mathematics) 1729 (Newton); 1910 (Russell & Whitehead)
Principles of Action in Matter 1751
Principles of Chemistry, The 1870
Principles of Geometry 1830
Principles of Philosophy 1644

Principles of Political Economy 1848
Principles of Psychology 1855
Prior, Matthew (English writer) 1664
Prió Socarrás, Carlos (president of Cuba) 1952
Prisoner of Zenda, The 1894 (novel); 1937 (film)
Private Affairs of Bel Ami, The 1947
Private Life of Henry VIII, The 1933
Private Lives 1930
Prizzi's Honor 1985
Probus (Marcus Aurelius Probus), Roman emperor 276, 282
Procol Harum (British group) 1967
Procopius (Byzantine historian) 550, 553
Procter, Adelaide Anne (English poet) 1858
Procter and Gamble Co. 1878
Procuress, The 1656
Prodaná nevesta (The Bartered Bride) 1866
Prodigal Son, The 1929
Prodigy, the (British band) 1994, 1996
Prodromus Crystallographie (Introduction of Crystallography) 1723
Producers, The 1968
Production Management, Office of 1941
Professor Unrat 1905
Profumo, John (British politician) 1963
Progress and Poverty 1879
Prohibition in US 1919, 1933
Project pour la paix perpétuelle (Project for Perpetual Peace) 1713
Prokofiev, Sergei (Russian composer) 1918, 1921, 1929, 1936, 1943, 1944, 1947, 1948, 1953
Prokop, Andrew (Prokop Holy, Prokop the Bald) (Bohemian Hussite) 1434
promessi sposi, I (The Betrothed) 1825
Prometheus, the Poem of Fire 1911
Prometheus Unbound 1820
Propaganda Fide, founding of 1622
Propalladia 1517
Prophet, The 1923
Prophète, Le 1849
Proposal for Correcting the English Language, A 1712
Prosas profanas 1896
Prosopopeya 1601
Protecting Veil, The 1989
Protestant Ethic and the Spirit of Capitalism, The 1905
Protestant League 1651
Protogaea (The Primordial Earth) 1691
Proudhon, Pierre-Joseph (French socialist) 1840
Proulx, E. Annie (US writer) 1993
Proust, Marcel (French writer) 1913, 1919, 1927
Prout, William (English physician) 1824
Provenza, Bernardo (Sicilian mafia boss) 2001
Providence, Rhode Island, foundation of 1636
Provisional IRA, 1969, 1971, 1972, 1974, 1981, 1983, 1987, 1991
Provisors, statute of 1351
Provok'd Wife, The 1697
Prozess, Der (The Trial) 1925
Prufrock and Other Observations 1917
Prusias II (the Horseman), king of Bithynia *c.*183BC
Prussian Academy of Sciences, foundation of 1700
Prussian Chronicle, The 1338

Prynne, William (English pamphleteer) 1634, 1637, 1669
Psamtik III (Psammetichus, Ankhkaenra), 25th dynasty king of Egypt 525BC
Pseudodoxia Epidemica or Enquiries into Received Tenets and Commonly Presumed Truths (*Vulgar Errors*) 1646
Pseudo-martyr 1610
Psychedlic Reader, The 1965
Psycho 1960
Psychology of Dementia Praecox 1907
Ptolemy I (Soter), king of Egypt 323BC, 312BC, 308BC, *c.*300BC, 285BC
Ptolemy II (Philadelphus), king of Egypt 285BC, 281BC, 272BC, 246BC
Ptolemy III (Euergetes), king of Egypt 246BC, 245BC, 221BC
Ptolemy IV (Philopator), king of Egypt 221BC
Ptolemy XIII (Theos Philopator), king of Egypt 49BC, 44BC
Ptolemy Ceraunus, king of Macedon 281BC
Ptolemy (Claudius Ptolomaeus) (Egyptian geographer) 1410
Public Broadcasting Act (US) 1967
Public Buildings Act (US) 1930
Public Enemy 1931
Public Health Act (UK) 1848
Public Opinion 1922
Public Safety, Committee of 1642
Puccini, Giacomo (Italian composer) 1893, 1896, 1900, 1904, 1910, 1918, 1924, 1926
Puebla, battle of 1862
Pueblo, USS 1968
Puerto Rico, made into US territory 1917
Puerto Rico, US invasion of 1898
Puerto Rico becomes commonwealth of US 1952
Pufendorf, Samuel (German jurist) 1667, 1694
Pugin, Augustus (British architect) 1852
Puig, Manuel (Argentine writer) 1976
Pulcheria, Byzantine empress (sister of Theodosius II) 408, 412, 450
Pulcinella 1920
Pulitzer, Joseph (US newspaper publisher) 1878
Pullman, George (Mortimer) (US engineer) 1858
Pullman, Philip (English writer) 1995, 1997, 2000
Pullman (Illinois), building of 1881
Pulp (British band) 1995
Pultusk, battle of 1703
Punch 1841
Punch and Judy 1968
Punic Wars: First 264-241BC; Second 218BC, 202BC; Third 149BC, 146BC
'Puppet on a String' 1967
'Puppy Love' 1972
Purcell, Henry (English composer) 1659, 1680, 1683, 1689, 1691, 1692, 1695
Purchasing Power of Money, The 1911
Pure Land sect, foundation of 1175
Pure Land sect, persecution of 1207
'Pure Shores' 2000
puritani, I 1835
Purple Rain 1984
Purple Rose of Cairo, The 1985
Pursuit of Love, The 1945

R

Ramillies, battle of 1706
Ramiro I, king of Aragon 1063
Ramleh, battle of 1101, 1105
Ramones, the (US band) 1976
Ramos, Fidel Valdez (president of the Philippines) 1996
Ramsay, Allan (Scottish poet) 1726
Ran 1985
Ranavalona I, queen of Madagascar 1828
Rancé, Armand-Jean Le Bouthillier de (French monk) 1664
Rand, Ayn (Alisa Rosenbaum) (US writer) 1943
Rangoon (Yangon), foundation of 1755
Rangoon Oil Company *see* Burmah Oil Company
Ranjit Singh (the Lion of the Punjab), maharajah of Punjab 1834
Rank, J(oseph) Arthur, 1st Baron (British businessman) 1934
Rankin, Jeanette (US reformer) 1916, 1941
Ransome, Arthur Mitchell (English writer) 1930
Rantissi, Abdel-Aziz al- (Hamas leader) 2004
Rapallo, treaty of 1920, 1922
Rape, The 1934
Rape of Lucretia, The 1946
Rape of Proserpina 1621
Rape of the Lock, The 1712
Rape of the Sabine Women, The 1624
Raphael (Raffaello Santi) Italian painter) 1504, 1508, 1515, 1516, 1518, 1520
Raphia, battle of 219BC
Rappeneau, Jean-Paul (French film director) 1990
Rapper, Irving (US film director) 1942, 1946, 1947
Rappite sect 1803, 1824
Rapsodie espagnole 1907
Rashid ad-Din (Persian physician) 1314
Rasputin, Grigori (Russian monk) 1916
Rassemblement pour la République (Rally for the Republic) (France) 1976
Rastrelli, Bartolomeo Francesco (Italian architect) 1741, 1747, 1754, 1767
Rath, Ernst Eduard von (German diplomat) 1938
Rathbone, Basil (British actor) 1939
Rathenau, Walter (German politician) 1922
Ratio atque Institutio Studiorum (The Conduct and Institution of Studies) 1586
rationing, introduction in Britain 1918, 1941
Ratisbon, diet of 1613
Ratisbon, truce of 1684
Rattigan, Terence (English writer) 1946, 1948, 1952, 1954
Rattle and Hum 1988
Rauber, Die (The Robbers) 1782
Rauschenberg, Robert (US painter) 1957
Ravaillac, François (French assassin) 1610
Ravel, Maurice (French composer) 1899, 1907, 1911, 1912, 1917, 1919, 1925, 1928, 1937, 1949
Ravenna, battle of 1512
Ravenna, Ostrogothic siege of 488
Rawalpindi, battle of 1849
Rawalpindi, treaty of 1919
Rawlings, Jerry John (president of Ghana) 1979, 1981
Rawls, John (US philosopher) 1971
Ray, James Earl (US assassin) 1968, 1969

Ray, Man (Emanuel Rudnitsky) (US photographer) 1915, 1976
Ray, Nicholas (US film director) 1955
Ray, Satyajit (Indian film director) 1955
Ray 2004
Raye, Don (US songwriter) 1941
Raymond IV, count of Toulouse 1095, 1101, 1105
Raymond VI, count of Toulouse 1213, 1218
Raymond VII, count of Toulouse 1226, 1229
Raymond, archbishop of Toledo 1125
Raymond-Berengar, count of Barcelona 1064
Raymond-Berengar III, count of Barcelona 1112, 1113
Raymond of Poitiers, prince of Antioch 1149
Razi, al- (Persian philosopher) 925
Raznatovic, Zeljko (Arkan) (Serbian politician and war criminal) 2000
Razor's Edge, The 1944
rè pastore, Il 1775
Reade, Charles (English writer) 1861
Reader's Digest 1922
Readie and Easy Way to Establish a Free Commonwealth, The 1660
Reading in the Dark 1996
Reagan, Ronald Wilson (40th US president) 1947, 1980, 1981, 1981, 1982, 1983, 1984, 1985, 1986, 1987, 1988, 2004
Real Thing, The 1982
Reaper, The 1854
Réard, Louis (French couturier) 1946
Rear Window 1954
Reasonableness of Christianity, The 1695
Réaumur, René-Antoine Ferchault de (French scientist) 1722, 1731, 1737, 1752
Rebecca 1938 (novel); 1940 (film)
Rebecca of Sunnybrook Farm 1903
rebelión de las masas, La (The Revolt of the Masses) 1930
Rebel without a Cause 1955
Recared, Visigothic king of Spain 589
'Recessional' 1897
Recesswinth, Visigothic king of Spain 653
Recherches sur la probabilité des jugements (Researches on the Probability of Estimates) 1837
Reciprocal Trade Agreement Act (US) 1934
Reciprocity Act (US) 1828
Reclining Nude 1920
Reconquista begins in Spain 874
Reconstruction Finance Corp. (US) 1932
Record of the Legitimate Descent of Divine Emperors 1354
Recorde, Robert (Welsh mathematician) 1557
Recruiting Officer, The 1706
Recuyell of the Histories of Troye, The 1475
Red Army 1919
Red Badge of Courage, The 1895 (novel); 1951 (film)
Red Brigades 1974, 1978
Red Cross, International Federation of the 1863, 1864
Redentore, Il (Venice), building of 1576
Red Flag Act *see* Locomotives on Highways Act
Redford, Robert (US actor and director) 1968, 1976
Redgauntlet 1824
Redgrave, Michael (British actor) 1938, 1951, 1954
Red Hot Chili Peppers (US band) 1992
Red House, The 1926

Redon, Odilon (French painter) 1890
'Red Red Wine' 1983
Red River rebellion 1869
Redshirts 1849
Red Shoes, The 1948
Red Studio, The 1911
Redwood, John (British politician) 1995
Reed, Carol (British film director) 1949, 1965, 1968
Reed, John (US journalist) 1919
Reed, Lou (US singer-songwriter) 1972
Reed, Oliver (British actor) 1970
Reeve, Christopher (US actor) 1978
Reeves, Keanu (US actor) 1994, 1999, 2003
'Reflex' 1984
Réflexions, ou sentences et maximes morales (Reflections, or Axioms and Moral Maxims) 1665
Réflexions sur la cause générales des vents (Reflections on the General Cause of Winds) 1747
Reform Act (UK), First 1832
Reform Act (UK), Second 1867
Reform Act (UK), Third 1884
Réforme, La 1843
refrigerator, invention of 1858
Refutation of Machiavelli's Prince or Anti-Machiavel, The 1740
Regency Act (UK) 1811
Regency Bill (UK) 1789
Regeneration 1991
Regensburg, diet of 1541
Regensburg (Germany), foundation of 21BC
Regino of Prum (German chronicler) 906, 915
Règle du jeu, La (The Rules of the Game) 1939
Règles pour la direction de l'esprit (Rules for the Direction of the Mind) 1628
Regnans in Excelsis (papal bull) 1570
Regula monachorum (Rule of Monks) 529
Regulating Act (UK) 1773
Rehearsal on the Stage 1878
Rehoboam, king of Judaea 945BC
Reich, Steve (US composer) 1971, 1976, 1988, 1994
Reichenbach, treaty of 1790
Reichenbach, treaty of 1813
Reichsbank (Germany), foundation of 1876
Reichstag (Berlin), burning of 1933
Reiner, Rob (US film director) 1984, 1986, 1989
Reisz, Karel (Czech film director) 1960, 1981
Reivers, The 1962
Relatively Speaking 1967
'Relax' 1984
'Release Me' 1967
Religieuse, La (The Nun) 1760
Religio Laici, or a Layman's Faith 1682
Religio Medici (Religion of a Doctor) 1643
Religion and the Decline of Magic 1971
Religion and the Rise of Capitalism 1926
R.E.M. (US band) 1991, 1992, 1993
Remain in the Light 1980
Remains of the Day, The 1989
Remarque, Erich Maria (German writer) 1929, 1970
Rembrandt van Rijn (Dutch painter) 1606, 1631, 1635, 1640, 1642, 1644, 1646, 1652, 1655, 1656, 1661, 1665, 1666, 1669
Remembrance Day bombing (Northern Ireland) 1987
Remington Arms Co. 1878, 1879

R

Rio Salado, battle of 1340
Riot Act (UK) 1715
Ripley, George (US reformer) 1841
Riquet de Bonrepos, Pierre-Paul de (French engineer) 1681
Rise and Fall of the Great Powers, The 1987
Rise and Fall of the Third Reich, The 1960
Rise and Fall of Ziggy Stardust and the Spiders from Mars, The 1972
Ritchie, Lionel (US singer) 1984
Rites of Passage 1980
Rituel in memoriam Bruno Maderna 1975
Ritz, César (Swiss hotelier) 1883, 1889
Ritz Hotel (London), opening of 1902
Ritz Hotel (Paris), opening of 1898
Rivals, The 1775
Rivera, Diego (Mexican painter) 1923, 1934, 1945, 1957
'River Deep, Mountain High' 1966
Rivoli, battle of 1797
Rizzio, David (Italian favourite of Mary, Queen of Scots) 1566
Roach, Hal (US film producer) 1927
Road to Morocco, The 1942
Road to Serfdom 1944
Road to Wigan Pier, The 1937
Road Traffic Act (UK) 1934
Road with Cypress and Star 1890
Rob Roy 1817
Robbe-Grillet, Alain (French writer) 1953, 1957
Robbins, Tim (US actor) 1994, 2003
Robert II (the Pious), king of France 996, 1006, 1010, 1022, 1031
Robert (the Wise), king of Naples 1322
Robert II (Curthose), duke of Normandy 1079, 1087, 1106
Robert I (Robert Bruce), king of Scotland 1306, 1307, 1308, 1314, 1317, 1318, 1320, 1328, 1329
Robert II, king of Scotland 1371
Robert III, king of Scotland 1390, 1406
Robert, earl of Gloucester 1138, 1141
Robert, Louis 1798
Robert de Courtenay, emperor of Constantinople 1228
Robert de Sorbon (French theologian) 1258
Robert Guiscard (Robert de Hauteville), count of Sicily 1057, 1059, 1061, 1071, 1072, 1074, 1077, 1080, 1081, 1082, 1083, 1084, 1085
Robert le Bougre (French Inquisitor) 1235
Robert le Diable (Robert the Devil) 1831
Robert of Artois (French rebel) 1336
Robert of Chester (English scholar) 1143, 1144
Robert of Gloucester's Chronicle 1720
Roberts, Frederick Sleigh (British soldier) 1900
Roberts, Michèle (Anglo-French writer) 2003
Roberts, Richard (Welsh engineer) 1817
Robeson, Paul (US singer) 1936
Robespierre, Maximilien (French revolutionary) 1793, 1794
Robeval, François de (French soldier) 1541
Robie House (Chicago), building of 1909
Robin, Leo (US lyricist) 1949
Robin Hood 1922
Robins, Benjamin (English mathematician) 1747
Robinson, Edward G. (Romanian-US actor) 1930

Robinson, Henry Crabb (English writer) 1808
Robinson, James (US settler) 1780
Robinson, Mary (president of Ireland) 1990
Robinson, Smokey (US singer) 1981
Robocop 1987
Robson, Flora (British actor) 1947
Rocard, Michel (French politician) 1991
Rochambeau, Jean de Vimeur, count of (French soldier) 1780
Rochdale Society of Equitable Pioneers 1844
Roche, Martin (US architect) 1930
Rock Around the Clock (film) 1956
'Rock around the Clock' (song) 1954
Rock Drill, The 1914
Rockefeller Sr, John D(avison) (US industrialist and philanthropist) 1860, 1877, 1882, 1891, 1902, 1911
Rockefeller Jr, John (Davison) (US industrialist and philanthropist) 1935, 1946
Rockefeller Center (New York), building of 1931
'Rocket' (steam locomotive) 1829, 1830
Rockingham, Charles Watson-Wentworth, 2nd marquess of (English politician) 1765, 1782
'Rock of Ages' 1776
Rockwell, Norman (US painter) 1978
Rocky Horror Picture Show, The 1975
Rocky Horror Show, The 1973 (musical)
Rocky Mountains and Tired Indians 1965
Rocroi, battle of 1643
Roderick (Rodrigo), Visigothic king of Spain 711
Roderick Hudson 1876
Rodgers, Richard (US composer) 1940, 1943, 1949, 1951, 1959
Rodgers, William Thomas (British politician) 1981
Rodin, (François-) Auguste (-René) (French sculptor) 1886, 1888, 1895, 1917
Rodney, George (English sailor) 1781, 1782
Rodogune 1646
Rodrigo, Joaquín (Spanish composer) 1940
Rodríguez, José Luís (Spanish politician) 2004
Roe, Thomas (English diplomat) 1615
Roebling, John Augustus (US engineer) 1883
Roeg, Nicholas (British film director) 1970, 1973, 1976
Roger, archbishop of York 1170
Roger Borsa, duke of Apulia 1085
Roger I Guiscard, count of Sicily 1085, 1090, 1091, 1101
Roger II Guiscard, king of Sicily 1103, 1127, 1130, 1146, 1147, 1153, 1154
Roger of Salerno (Italian surgeon) 1170
Roger of Salerno, prince of Antioch 1119
Roger of Wendover (English chronicler) 1237
Roger's Book 1154
Rogers, Ginger (US actor) 1933, 1935, 1936, 1937, 1995
Rogers, Kenny (US singer) 1980
Rogers, Richard (British architect) 1977, 1986, 1997
Roget, Peter Mark (English scholar) 1852
Rohan, Benjamin of, seigneur de Soubise (French Huguenot) 1621
Rohan, Henry, duke of (French Huguenot) 1615, 1621, 1638
Rohan, Louis-René-Edouard de (French cardinal) 1785, 1786

Röhm, Ernst (German Nazi) 1934
Roh Tae Woo (president of South Korea) 1987
Roi David, Le 1921
Roi d'Ys, Le (The King of Ys) 1888
Roi se meurt, Le (Exit the King) 1962
Roland (nephew of Charlemagne) 778
Rolfe, Frederick (Baron Corvo) (English writer) 1904
Rolfe, John (English colonist) 1614, 1616
Roll, Jordan, Roll: The World the Slaves Made 1975
'Roll Over Beethoven' 1955
'Roll with It' 1995
Rolland, Romain (French writer) 1912
Rolle (of Hampole), Richard (English mystic) 1349
Rolle, Richard (English religious writer) 1496
Rolling Stone (magazine) 1967
Rolling Stones, the (British band) 1964, 1965, 1966, 1968, 1969, 1971, 1972, 1973
Rollo (Viking leader) 911, 925
Romagnosi, Gian Domenico (Italian scientist) 1802
Romains, Jules (Louis Farigoule) (French writer) 1911
Romana, La (The Woman of Rome) 1947
Romance of Two Worlds, A 1886
Roman comique, Le (The Comic Novel) 1651
Romances sans paroles (Songs without Words) 1874
Roman de la Rose, Le 1237
Romania, independence of 1878
Romania, Soviet invasion of 1940
Romanian Rhapsodies 1901
Romanov dynasty, commencement of 1613
Romans in Britain, The 1980
Romanus I Lecapenus, Byzantine emperor 920, 944
Romanus III Argyrus, Byzantine emperor 1028, 1034
Romanus IV Diogenes, Byzantine emperor 1071
Romartin, Edict of 1560
Rome, fire of 64
Rome, foundation of 753BC
Rome, sack of 390BC
Rome, sack of 410, 455
Rome, sack of 1084
Rome, sack of 1527
Rome, siege of 537
Rome, treaties of 1957
Romeo and Juliet 1594 (play); 1968 (film)
Roméo et Juliette 1839 (Berlioz); 1867 (Gounod)
Römer, Ole (Christensen) (Danish astronomer) 1706
Römerbrief, Der (The Epistle to the Romans) 1919
Romero, Carlos Humberto (military ruler of El Salvador) 1979
Romero, Oscar (El-Salvadorean priest) 1980
Rommel, Erwin (German soldier) 1941, 1942, 1944
Romney, George (English painter) 1763, 1782, 1802
Romola 1863
Romuald, St (Italian monastic reformer) 1012
Romulus (legendary co-founder of Rome) 753BC
Romulus Augustulus, Roman emperor 475, 476
Romulus der Grosse (Romulus the Great) 1949
Ronalds, Francis (British meteorologist and inventor) 1823
Roncesvalles, battle of 778
Ronde, La 1950
R101 (airship) 1930
Ronsard, Pierre de (French poet) 1550, 1552, 1560, 1565, 1578, 1585

R

Rutherford, Samuel (Scottish preacher) 1644
Rutskoi, Alexander (Russian politician) 1993
Ruy Blas 1838
Ruysbroeck, Jan van (Flemish theologian) 1350
Ruysdael, Jacob van (Dutch painter) 1682
Rwanda, genocidal violence in 1994
Ryan, Meg (US actor) 1989
Rye House Plot 1683
Rysbrack, John Michael (Belgian-English sculptor) 1727
Ryskind, Morrie (US writer) 1928
Rystad, treaty of 1721
Ryswick, treaty of 1697

S

Saarinen, Eero (Finnish-American architect) 1956
Sabines, Les (The Rape of the Sabine Women) 1799
Sacasa, Juan Bautista (president of Nicaragua) 1936
Sacco, Nicola (Italian-US radical) 1927
Sacheverell, Henry (English political preacher) 1710, 1724
Sachs, Hans (German writer) 1523
Sachsische Weltchronik 1237
Sackville, Thomas, 1st earl of Dorset and Baron Buckhurst (English playwright) 1565
Sackville-West, Vita (Victoria Mary) (English writer) 1931
Sacré Coeur 1932
Sacre du printemps, Le (The Rite of Spring) 1913
Sacred and Profane Love Machine, The 1974
Sacred Congregation for the Propagation of the Faith (Propaganda Fide) 1622
Sacred Hunger 1992
'Sacrifice' 1990
Sacrifice, The 1986
Sacrifice of Isaac, The 1715
Sadat, Mohammed Anwar al- (president of Egypt) 1970, 1977, 1978, 1981
Sade, marquis de (Dontatien-Alphonse-François, comte de Sade) (French writer) 1791
Sadleir, Michael (English writer) 1940
Sadowa, battle of 1866
Sadr, Hojatoleslam Moqtada al- (Iraqi cleric) 2004
Safavid dynasty, commencement of 1501
safety lamp, invention of 1815
Saffar, Yaqub bin Laith as- (Saffarid ruler of Persia) 872
Sagan, Françoise (French writer) 1954, 2004
Sagunto, siege of 218BC
Sahih, al- 870
Saicho (Dengyo Daishi) (Japanese monk) 805
Said, Edward Wadie (US writer) 2003
Sa'id al-Fayyumi (Saadia ben Joseph) (Arab scholar) 942
Sa'id Pasha, khedive of Egypt 1854, 1859, 1863
Saigon, blockade of 1861
sail, invention of 4500BC
'Sailing' 1975
Sailor Who Fell from Grace with the Sea, The 1963
Saimei *see* Kogyoku
St Agense (Rome), building of 1653
St Albans, battle of 1455
St Anastasia (Rome), building of 800

St Andrea (Rome), building of 1663
St Andrea della Fratte (Rome), building of 1653
St Andrew's Cathedral (St Petersburg), building of 1767
St Augustine's Abbey (Canterbury), building of 1073
St Bartholomew Day's massacre 1572
St Bartholomew's Priory (London), foundation of 1123
St Brieuc, battle of 937
St Carlo alle Quattro Fontane (Rome), building of 1638
St Clement Dane's Church (London), building of 1680
St Denis Cathedral (Paris), building of 1137, 1140
Sainte Chapelle (Paris), building of 1243
Saint-Exupéry, Antoine de (French writer) 1928, 1931, 1942, 1943
St Francis 1674
Saint François d'Assise (St Francis of Assisi) 1983
St George and the Dragon 1555
St George's Chapel (Windsor), building of 1519
St George's Church (London), building of 1720
Saint-Germain, treaty of 1919
St Germain-des-Pres (Abbey Church, Paris), building of 1005
St Germain-des-Pres (Abbey Church, Paris), consecration of 1163
St Germain-en-Laye, edict of 1594
St Germain-en-Laye, peace of 1679
St Germain-en-Laye, treaty of 1570
St Gothard pass, opening of 1140
St James's Church (London), building of 1683
St Jerome 1551
St Joan 1923
St John, Henry, 1st Viscount Bolingbroke (English writer and political philosopher) 1678, 1710, 1715, 1716, 1723, 1749, 1751, 1752
St John 1302
St John Lateran Church (Rome), building of 904
St John Passion 1724
St John the Divine (Episcopal Cathedral, New York), building of 1892
Saint-Just, Louis-Antoine-Léon de (French conspirator) 1794
St Kitts-Nevis, independence of 1983
St Laurent, Louis (Canadian politician) 1956
St Louis Dispatch 1878
St Louis of Toulouse 1317
St Louis Post 1878
St Lucia, independence of 1979
St Luke Passion 1966
St Maria dei Sette Dolori (Rome), building of 1655
St Marie de la Visitation (Paris), building of 1623
St Mark and St George 1415
St Mark Freeing a Christian Slave 1548
St Mark's Church (Venice), building of 1063
St Martin and the Beggar 1597
St Martin-in-the-Fields (London), building of 1722
St Mary-le-Strand (London), building of 1714
St Matthew 1597
St Matthew Passion 1727
St Mihiel, battle of 1918
St Miniato (Abbey Church, Florence), building of 1062
St Nicolas 1948
St Nicola's Church (Bari), building of 1089
St Patrick's Cathedral (New York), building of 1879
St Paul (Minnesota), foundation of 1838

St Paul 1836
St Paul's Cathedral (London), building of 1087
St Paul's Cathedral (London), rebuilding of 1675
St Paul's School (London), foundation of 1510
St Paul the Hermit 1647
St Peter's (Rome), rebuilding of 1505
St Petersburg Academy of Science, foundation of 1725
St Petersburg, Alliance of 1795
St Petersburg, Convention of 1747
St Petersburg, Convention of 1755
St Petersburg, name changed to Petrograd 1914
St Petersburg, treaty of 1762
St Petersburg, treaty of 1805
St Privat, battle of 1870
St Quentin, battle of 1557
Saints, battle of the 1782
Saint-Saëns, Camille (French composer) 1853, 1874, 1877, 1886
St Sernin Abbey (Toulouse), foundation of 1080
Saints' Everlasting Rest, The 1651
Saint-Simon, Louis de Rouvroy, duke of (French writer and courtier) 1675, 1740
St Stephen's Cathedral (Limoges), building of 1879
St Stephen's Walbrook (London), building of 1672
St Thomas's Hospital (London), foundation of 1215
St Valentine's Day massacre 1929
St Vincent and the Grenadines, independence of 1979
St Vitus's Cathedral (Prague), completion of 1929
Saint Zeno 1459
Saison en enfer, Une (A Season in Hell) 1873
Saito Makoto (Japanese politician) 1932, 1936
Sakharov, Andrei Dmitrievich (Soviet physicist) 1977, 1980, 1989
Saki *see* Munro, H.H.
Sala, Anri (Albanian artist) 2004
Saladin (Salah ad-Din), sultan of Egypt and Syria 1169, 1171, 1174, 1175, 1177, 1179, 1183, 1187, 1189, 1191, 1192, 1193
Salamanca, treaty of 1505
Salamanca Cathedral (Spain), building of 1152
Salamanca University (Spain), foundation of 1220
Salamis, battle of 480BC
Salazar, António de Oliveira (Portuguese politician) 1932, 1933, 1968, 1970
Salbai, treaty of 1782
Sale, George (English lawyer and scholar) 1734
Saleh, Ali Abdullah (president of Yemen) 1990
Salem Kamen, battle of 1691
Salian dynasty, commencement of 1024
Salih Ayyub, Ayyubid ruler of Egypt 1244
Salinator, Marcus Livius (Roman consul) 216BC
Salinger, J(erome) D(avid) (US writer) 1951
Salins, battle of 1493
Salisbury, earl and marquis of *see* Cecil, Robert
Salisbury (Rhodesia), foundation of 1890
Salisbury Cathedral (UK), building of 1220
Salisbury Cathedral 1831
Salles, Walter (Brazilian film director) 2004
Salomé 1896 (play), 1905 (opera)
Salonika, sack of 904
SALT (Strategic Arms Limitation Talks) 1969, 1978
Salt Lake City (Utah), foundation of 1847
Salt March (India) 1930

Sitwell, Edith (Louisa) (English writer) 1923
Sivaji (Grand Rebel), Maratha king 1674
Siva temple (Tanjore), building of 1004
Siward (the Strong), earl of Northumbria 1054
Six Acts (UK) 1819
Six Articles (German Confederation) 1832
Six Articles of Religion 1539, 1547
Six Day War 1967
Six Degrees of Separation 1990
Six livres de la république (The Six Books of the Republic) 1576
Six Pieces for Orchestra 1913
Sixteen, Council of the 1586
Sixtus IV (Francesco della Rovere), pope 1473, 1478, 1483, 1484
Sixtus V (Felice Peretti), pope 1587, 1590
'65 Liz 1965
Sjunde Inseglet, Det (The Seventh Seal) 1956
Skanderbeg (George Kastrioti), ruler of Albania 1443, 1468
Sketches by Boz 1836
Skidmore, Owings and Merrill (US architects) 1973
Skoda, Emil von (Czech engineer) 1866
Skurdo (Prussian leader) 1283
Sky Blue 1940
Slater, Samuel (British-US industrialist) 1793
Slaughterhouse Five 1969
Slave Kings of Delhi dynasty, commencement of 1206
slavery, abolition in Brazil 1888
slavery, abolition in British empire 1833
slavery, abolition in Denmark 1792
slavery, abolition in France 1794
slavery, abolition in Mexico 1829
slavery, abolition in US 1862
slavery, abolition in Zanzibar 1897
slavery, reintroduction to French colonies 1802
slave trade, abolition by the Netherlands 1814
slave trade, abolition in British empire 1807
Slave War, First 135BC, 132BC
Slave War, Second 104BC, 99BC
Slave War, Third 73BC
Slavonic Dances 1878
Slawata, Vilém (imperial regent in Prague) 1618
Sleeping Beauty 1890
Sleuth 1970
Slidell, John (US politician) 1861
Sloane, Hans (English physician) 1753
Sloane Ranger Handbook, The 1982
Sloat, John Drake (US commander) 1846
Slovakia, independence of 1939
Slovenia, secession from Yugoslavia of 1991
Sluys, battle of 1340
Small Back Room, The 1943
smallpox, inoculation against 1721
smallpox, vaccination against 1796
Small Thing But My Own, A 1985
Smart, Christopher (English poet) 1752, 1756, 1770
'Smells Like Teen Spirit' 1991
Smetana, Bedrich (Czech composer) 1861, 1866, 1876, 1879
Smith, Adam (Scottish economist) 1723, 1776, 1811
Smith, Alexis (Canadian actor) 1943
Smith, Alfred Emanuel (US politician) 1928
Smith, Dodie (English writer) 1956

Smith, George (British Assyriologist) 1872
Smith, Ian (Rhodesian politician) 1965, 1966, 1976, 1978, 1979
Smith, Iain Duncan (British politician) 2001, 2003
Smith, Jacob F. (US soldier) 1901
Smith, Jedediah Strong (US explorer) 1826, 1831
Smith, John (English colonist) 1607, 1612
Smith, John (British politician) 1992, 1994
Smith, Joseph (US Mormon leader) 1830
Smith, Maggie (British actor) 1969
Smith, Martin Cruz (US writer) 1981
Smith, Patti (US musician) 1975
Smith, Robert (US co-founder of Alcoholics Anonymous) 1935
Smith, Stevie (Florence Margaret) (English writer) 1957, 1971
Smith, Sydney (English clergyman) 1799
Smith, Will (US actor) 1997
Smith, Zadie (British writer) 2000
Smiths, the (British band) 1985, 1986
Smithson, James (British chemist) 1846
Smithsonian Institution, foundation of 1846
Smolensk, battle of 1812
Smollett, Tobias (Scottish writer) 1721, 1749, 1751, 1771
Smordoni, Rinaldo (Italian actor) 1946
Smultronstället (Wild Strawberries) 1957
Smuts, Jan Christiaan (South African politician) 1948
Smyrna, Greek occupation of 1919
Smyrna, Turkish occupation of 1922
Smyth, Ethel (English composer) 1906
Snefru (Sneferu), 4th dynasty king of Egypt 2575BC
Snoop Doggy Dog (US rapper) 1994
Snorri Sturluson (Icelandic writer) 1222, 1225
Snow, C(harles) P(ercy) (English writer) 1940, 1963
Snowden, Philip (British politician) 1931
Snow White and the Seven Dwarfs 1937
Sobers, Sir Garfield (West Indian cricketer) 1958
Sobrero, Ascanio (Italian chemist) 1847, 1866
Social and Liberal Democrats (UK), foundation of 1988
Social Contract, The 1762
Social Democratic and Labour Party (SDLP) (Northern Ireland) 1970
Social Democratic Party (Russian) 1903
Social Democratic Party (SDP) (UK) 1981, 1983
Social Security Act (US) 1935
Social War 91BC, 87BC
Society in America 1837
Society of Jesus (Jesuits), foundation of 1534
Socinian sect 1658
Socrates (Greek philosopher) 399BC
Soderbergh, Steven (US film director) 1989, 2000
Soft Cell (British group) 1981
Soga Iname (Japanese minister) 586, 587
Soga Umako (Japanese minister) 592, 593, 626
Sogno d'un mattino di primavera (The Dream of a Spring Morning) 1898
'Sohrab and Rustum' 1853
Soissons, council of 1092, 1121
Soissons Cathedral, building of 1200
Solemn League and Covenant 1643
Solferino, battle of 1859
Solidarity (Solidarnosc) 1980, 1981, 1982, 1987, 1988, 1989

Soliloquies 892
Solitary Brethren of the Community of Seventh-Day Baptists (Dunkards) 1732
'Solitude' 1934
Solomon, king of Judaea c.965BC, 945BC
Solomon, Isaac (US inventor) 1861
Solomon 1749
Solomon Gursky Was Here 1990
Solomonid dynasty, commencement of 1270
Solomon Islands, Japanese occupation of 1942
Solomon Islands, independence of 1978
Solon (Athenian politician) 594BC
Solvay, Alfred (Belgian chemist) 1863
Solvay, Ernest (Belgian chemist) 1863
Solzhenitsyn, Alexander (Russian writer) 1962, 1968, 1968, 1970, 1971, 1974
Somali Democratic Republic, declaration of 1969
sombrero de tres picos, El (The Three-Cornered Hat) 1919
Some Account of the Success of Inoculation for the Smallpox in England and America 1760
Some Like It Hot 1959
Somers, John, 1st Baron Somers of Evesham (English politician) 1694
Somerset House (London), building of 1786
Some Tame Gazelle 1950
Something to Answer For 1969
Somme, battle of the 1916
Somnath, sack of 1025
Somoza, Anastasio (president of Nicaragua) 1978, 1979, 1980
Somoza, Anastasio 'Tacho' (president of Nicaragua) 1934, 1936
Sonderbund War 1848
Sondheim, Stephen (US composer and lyricist) 1979, 1984
Songbird 2001
Songes of sundrie natures 1589
Song Meiling (Sung Mei-ling) (wife of Jiang Jieshi) 1927
Song of Hiawatha, The 1855
'Song of Myself' 1855
Song of the Cid, The 1140
Songs and Ayers, Book of 1597
Songs of Childhood 1902
Songs of Experience 1794
Songs of Innocence 1789
Songs of Innocence and of Experience: Shewing the Two Contrary States of the Human Soul 1795
'Song 2' 1997
Sonique (British singer) 2000
Sonnenfeld, Barry (US film director) 1997
Sonnetes pour Hélène 1578
Sonnets 1609 (Shakespeare)
Sonnets from the Portuguese 1850
Sonnets to Laura 1351
Sonnets to Orpheus 1923
Sonni Ali (Ali the Great), king of Songhai 1464
Sonny and Cher (US singing duo) 1965
'Son of a Preacher Man' 1969
Son of the Circus, A 1994
Sons and Lovers 1913
Sons of Liberty 1770
Sony Corporation 1947

S

S

T

U

U

V

V

W

W

X

Y